The Faber Book of Pop

by Jon Savage

THE KINKS
The Official Biography
ENGLAND'S DREAMING
Sex Pistols and Punk Rock

by Hanif Kureishi

Screenplays
MY BEAUTIFUL LAUNDRETTE with THE RAINBOW SIGN
SAMMY AND ROSIE GET LAID
LONDON KILLS ME
OUTSKIRTS AND OTHER PLAYS

Novels
THE BUDDHA OF SUBURBIA
THE BLACK ALBUM

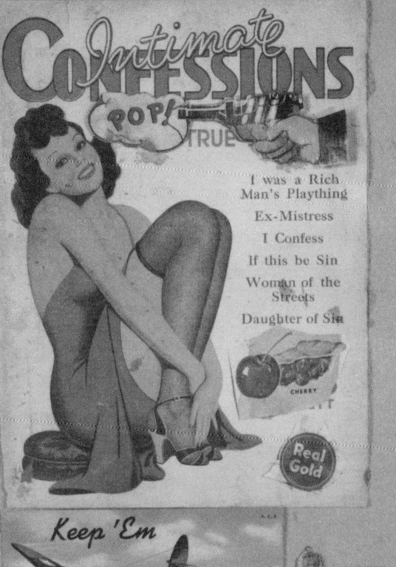

The Faber Book of
Pop

edited by

Hanif Kureishi and Jon Savage

faber and faber
LONDON · BOSTON

First published in 1995 by Faber and Faber
3 Queen Square London WC1N 3AU

Photoset by Parker Typesetting Service, Leicester
Printed in England by Clays Ltd, St Ives plc

Hanif Kureishi and Jon Savage are hereby identified as editors
of this work in accordance with Section 77 of the Copyright,
Designs and Patents Act 1988.

A CIP record for this book is available
from the British Library.

ISBN 0–571–16992–9

10 9 8 7 6 5 4 3 2 1

To Tracey Scoffield
for her help and
encouragement

Contents

List of Illustrations   xv
'That's how good it was' by Hanif Kureishi   xvii
'The simple things you see are all complicated' by Jon Savage   xxi

One: 1942–56 'Groovy, frantic scenes'
1942: Malcolm X, 'Laura'   7
1944: Bruce Bliven, 'The Voice and the Kids'   10
1945: Gordon Glover, 'Britain's Dance-band Leaders'   12
1947: John Ormond Thomas, 'Dark Harmony'   14
1949: Max Jones, 'A New Jazz Age'   15
1951: Ralph Ellison, 'Wild Jacks-in-the-Box'   17
1952: Raymond Thorp, 'Club Eleven'   21
1953: Don McCullin, 'Hunting Dogs'   23
1954: Robert Muller, 'Back to the Music Halls'   25
1955: Bernard McElwaine, 'Is Johnnie Ray a Mass Hypnotist?'   30
1956: Chuck Berry, 'The Creation of My Recordings'   32
1956: James Brown, 'Please Please Please'   35

Two: 1956–8 'A mass fit of screaming hysteria'
1956: Lionel Crane, 'Rock Age Idol: That's Elvis'   45
1956: Alfred Wertheimer, 'Studio One: Let's Try It Again'   47
1956: Charles White, 'Tutti-frutti'   51
1956: Nick Tosches, 'Great Balls of Fire'   57
1956: Gavin Lyall, 'Dean Worship in Britain'   60
1957: Trevor Philpott, 'Bermondsey Miracle'   63
1957: Bernard Kops, 'The Street Game'   67
1957: Richard Hoggart, 'Sex in Shiny Packets'   70
1957: Frank Cordell, 'Gold Pan Alley'   72
1957: Wolf Mankowitz, 'Bongo Scores at Tom-Tom'   77
1958: Colin MacInnes, 'Pop Songs and Teenagers'   81
1958: John Lambert and Peter Kinsley, 'Baby Snatcher'   91
1958: Alan Levy, 'You Didn't Put Beethoven in the Army'   92
1958: Colin MacInnes, 'In June'   95

Three: 1959–63 'Red, humming neon'

1959: Keith Waterhouse, 'The Roxy'   106
1959: Nik Cohn, 'Carnaby Street, Part One'   113
1960: Royston Ellis, 'The Big Beat Business'   115
1960: Penny Reel, 'Timin' is the Thing'   125
1961: Ray Gosling, 'Music That Spells Cash and Freedom'   127
1961: Joseph C. Smith, 'Chicago, January'   133
1961: Jeff Nuttall, 'Pop and Protest'   138
1961: John Lennon, 'The Dubious Origins of Beatles'   142
1961: Jack Good, 'The Same Fantastic Feeling for Beat'   143
1962: Anthony Burgess, 'Real Horrorshow'   144
1962: John Waters, 'The Nicest Kids in Town'   152
1962: Mary Wilson, 'Bigotry Head On'   159
1963: Andy Warhol, 'The Factory'   164
1963: Richard Barnes, 'Art School and Rhythm & Blues'   168

Four: 1962–6 'Shadows of boredom'

1962: Brian Epstein, 'Yes!'   179
1964: Michael Braun, 'York'   186
1964: Paul Johnson, 'The Menace of Beatlism'   195
1964: Derek Jarman, 'My Beatles Hat'   199
1964: Charles Hamblett and Jane Deverson, 'It was Like a Battlefield'   200
1964: Peter Burton, 'Clubland'   205
1964: George Melly, 'The Ad-Lib'   215
1964: Andrew Loog Oldham, 'Six Hip Malchicks'   216
1964: Peter Guralnick, 'The Soul Clan'   219
1965: Nik Cohn, 'The Rolling Stones'   225
1965: Barbara Hulanicki, 'A Uniform for an Era'   230
1965: Bob Dylan, 'Thru Dark Sunglasses'   236
1965: Noël Coward, 'Wednesday 23 June'   238
1965: Nick Jones, 'Well, What is Pop-Art?'   239
1965: Manthia Diawara, 'Afro-Kitsch'   240
1965: Jean Stein, 'Youthquaker People'   241
1965: Bob Feigal, ' "Real" Teen Revolt'   246
1965: Studs Terkel, 'The Gap'   248
1966: Richard Goldstein, 'Gear'   250
1966: Maureen Cleave, 'How Does a Beatle Live?'   254
1966: Robert Shelton, 'One Foot on the Highway . . .'   258

Five: 1966–71 'Blows the mind'
1966: Tom Wolfe, 'The Trips Festival' 269
1966: Richard Goldstein, 'A Quiet Evening at the Balloon Farm' 273
1966: Jon Wiener, 'First Steps toward Radical Politics: The 1966 Tour' 278
1966: Iggy Pop, 'Queering Out' 285
1967: Joe Orton, 'Monday 23 January' 287
1967: George Melly, 'Dedicated to Sensation' 289
1967: Hunter S. Thompson, 'The "Hashbury" is the Capital of the
     Hippies' 290
1967: Simon Napier-Bell, 'A Few Days in Germany' 302
1967: William Rees-Mogg, 'Who Breaks a Butterfly on a Wheel?' 307
1967: Jenny Fabian and Johnny Byrne, 'Satin Odyssey' 309
1967: Angela Carter, 'Notes for a Theory of Sixties Style' 316
1967: Stanley Booth, 'The Memphis Soul Sound' 320
1968: Dave Godin, 'R&B and the Long Hot Summer' 324
1968: Joan Didion, 'Missionaries of Apocalyptic Sex' 327
1968: Norman Mailer, 'The Yippies' 330
1969: Ed Sanders, 'Helter Skelter' 336
1969: Germaine Greer, 'Mozic and the Revolution' 339
1969: Sheila Weller, 'I Don't Want to Be a Clown Any More' 343
1969: Stanley Booth, 'Dance to the Death' 347
1970: Bob Christgau, 'Look at that Stupid Girl' 365
1971: Hunter S. Thompson, 'No Flowers in This Town' 369

Six: 1972–6 'The star ideal was reborn'
1972: Pete Fowler, 'The Emergence of the Skinheads' 378
1972: Andrew Holleran, 'The Twelfth Floor' 384
1972: Mick Watts, 'Oh You Pretty Thing' 391
1973: Richard Allen, 'Jolly Green Men' 396
1973: Dave Marsh, 'Iggy in Exile' 403
1974: Charles Shaar Murray, 'The View from Seat T39' 406
1974: Peter Burton, 'Music and Mayhem' 410
1974: Tom Wolfe, 'Funky Chic' 412
1975: Jean Peter, 'Doin' It Right' 418
1975: Sheryl Garratt, 'Teenage Dreams' 423
1975: Nik Cohn, 'Another Saturday Night' 425
1975: Idris Walters, 'Is Northern Soul Dying on Its Feet?' 443
1976: Fred and Judy Vermorel, 'Julie: He's Got a Lot to Answer for' 456

Seven: 1975–80 'My confusion, my faith'

1975: Penny Reel, 'Better Must Come' 471

1975: Lester Bangs, 'Kraftwerkfeature' 481

1975: Mary Harron, 'Ramones' 487

1976: Neil Spencer, 'Don't Look over Your Shoulder, but the Sex Pistols are Coming' 489

1976: Caroline Coon, 'Rock Revolution' 490

1976: Jonh Ingham, 'In Love with the Modern World' 493

1976: Mark Perry, 'Mark P. Pisses on the Lot of 'Em!' 497

1976: Stuart Greig, Michael McCarthy and John Peacock, 'The Filth and the Fury' 498

1977: Tony Parsons, 'Sten-guns in Knightsbridge??' 499

1977: Mark Kidel, 'Plymouth Punk' 506

1977: Jane Suck, 'New Musick' 508

1977: Angela Carter, 'Ups and Downs for the Babes in Bondage' 509

1978: Andy Warhol, 'Tuesday, January 3' 514

1978: Legs McNeil, 'Legs McNeil vrs. the Sex Pistols' 516

1979: Richard Dyer, 'In Defence of Disco' 518

1980: Dick Hebdige, 'Mistaken Identities' 527

Eight: 1980–85 'Baroque proportions'

1980: Rosetta Brooks, 'Blitz Culture' 537

1981: Dave Rimmer, 'The Birth of the New Pop' 539

1981: Vince Aletti, 'Golden Voices and Hearts of Steel' 542

1982: David Toop, 'Whiplash Snuffs the Candle Flame' 544

1982: Robert Elms, 'Hard Times' 547

1982: Paul Morley, 'A Salmon Screams' 551

1982: Judy Wade, 'Mister (or Is It Miss?) Weirdo' 559

1983: David Johnson, '69 Dean Street' 561

1983: Steve Dixon, 'Birth of the Wiseboys and Wisegirls' 566

1984: Peter Martin, 'Young, Bold and Aggressive' 570

1984: Simon Frith, 'Whistling in the Dark' 572

1984: Simon Garfield, 'Wham!: Young Guns Fall for It (Again)' 574

1985: Neil Tennant, 'Marilyn: Does Anyone Still Want Him?' 585

Nine: 1985–9 'A last cold cut'

1985: Simon Garfield, 'This Charming Man' 595

1985: Gordon Legge, 'Barely Conscious' 601

1985: Michael Ventura, 'The *Big Chill* Factor' 607

1986: Tama Janowitz, 'You and the Boss' 614
1986: Annette Stark, 'There's a Riot Going on' 618
1987: Mick Brown, 'Poor Boy, Rich Boy George' 627
1987: Donna Gaines, 'Children of Zoso' 635
1987: Greg Tate, 'I'm White!: What's Wrong with Michael Jackson?' 639
1987: Michael Bracewell, 'Sunday, 18th October' 643
1988: Barry Walters, 'Stayin' Alive' 644
1989: John Sweeny, 'The Sun and the Star' 653

Ten: 1988– 'The end of the century'
1988: The Timelords, 'The Golden Rules' 673
1988: Stuart Cosgrove, 'Seventh City Techno' 677
1988: Dave Rimmer, 'The Eastie Boys' 681
1989: Chris Heath, 'Friday, 30 June' 690
1989: Nelson George, 'Goin' off in Cali' 693
1990: Lou Reed, 'To Do the Right Thing' 696
1990: Norman Jay, 'I'm Going Overground (How the Soul was Sold)' 709
1990: Mike Noon, 'Freaky Dancing' 710
1990: Mike Soutar, 'Are Stock Aitken Waterman down the Dumper?!?' 716
1991: Gina Arnold, 'Did the Right Thing' 720
1992: Simon Reynolds, 'Rage to Live: 'Ardkore Techno' 730
1992: Kodwo Eshun, 'Outing the In-Crowd' 736
1992: Greil Marcus, 'Notes on the Life & Death and Incandescent Banality of Rock 'n' Roll' 739
1992: Ice-T and Heidi Siegmund, 'Fuck the Police' 753
1993: Kean Wong, 'Metallic Gleam' 761
1993: Barry Walters, 'Take It Like a Man' 767
1993: Mark Frith, 'We Love You!' 770
1993: Gavin Martin, 'Slayed in Fame' 775
1994: Ann Powers, 'Never More' 786
1994: 'Michael Jackson and Lisa Marie Presley' 795
1994: Joy Press, 'The Killing of Crusty' 797
1994: Andrew O'Hagan, 'Passing Poison' 806

Acknowledgements 814
Index 819

List of illustrations

Frontispiece 'I Was a Rich Man's Plaything' by Eduardo Paolozzi, 1947   iii
1   Frank Sinatra in concert, mid-1940s   2
2   Cover of *Fans' Star Magazine*, number 16, James Dean © Fleetway
    Publications Ltd, 1959   40
3   Cover of *Espresso Jungle*, © Fleetway Publications Ltd, 1959   102
4   Cover of ABC TV's *Thank Your Lucky Stars* annual, © TV
    Publications Ltd, 1965   174
5   Cover of *Teenset*, May 1968, courtesy of Capitol Records Distributing
    Corporation   264
6   Cover of *Glam*, © New English Library, 1973   374
7   *Anarchy in the UK*, © Glitterbest Ltd, 1976   466
8   Boy George from *i-D*, number 2, © Simon Brown, 1980   532
9   The Smiths, *Barbarism Begins at Home*, © 1985, Syndication
    International, courtesy of the *Sunday People*   590
10 Michael Jackson in Russia, © Rex Features, 1993   670

'That's how good it was'

In November 1989, not long after he'd published *The Bonfire of the Vanities*, Tom Wolfe wrote an essay for *Harpers* entitled 'Stalking the Billion-Footed Beast – a Literary Manifesto for the New Social Novel'. It stated that since the mid-1960s, Wolfe had been waiting for American writers to deliver versions of the novels of Balzac, Dickens and Zola, monsters of epic realism that would capture the tremendous social upheavals of the period. Hippies, the universities, feminism, political assassination, war, civil rights, black militancy in the boiling cities: what irresistible subjects they were for the novelist! The author only had to be able to write fast enough to get it all down. During this fervent period, Wolfe himself was working on *The Electric Kool-Aid Acid Test*; mere journalism, of course, but about this new subject, the psychedelic or hippie movement. Yet Wolfe was terrified. His book, which he was calling a 'non-fiction novel', would, he knew, be 'blown out of the water' by the real thing: great literary fiction. Wolfe waited and waited. It never happened.

Why not? Perhaps Philip Roth could help explain. In his essay 'Writing American Fiction', published in 1961, he wrote: 'The American writer in the middle of the twentieth century has his hands full in trying to understand, describe, and then make credible much of American reality. It stupefies, it sickens, it infuriates, and finally it is even a kind of embarrassment to one's own meagre imagination. The actuality is continually outdoing our talents, and the culture tosses up figures almost daily that are the envy of any novelist.' Roth then approvingly quotes Edmund Wilson's remark that after *Life* magazine, he feels he does not belong to the country depicted there, that he does not live in the country at all.

To Wolfe's annoyance and relief, most American novelists and intellectuals capable of taming the contemporary beast turned out, like Edmund Wilson, not to be living in the country. Reality was beyond them; it outdid their talents. They had allowed themselves to be cut adrift from the contemporary scene by the high introspection of modernism. Like Dylan's Mr Jones who, despite having read all 'F. Scott Fitzgerald's books' and being 'very well read, it's well known', they couldn't figure out what was happening. They would never know because they were snobs who imagined they were part of an intelligentsia, and 'the intelligentsia have always had contempt for the realistic novel'. What they wanted was to write French psychological novels. Poor Tom Wolfe, wanting Balzac when all he was getting was a lot of Robbe-Grillet. Later, during pop's greatest era between 1967 and 1970, although these writers might listen to pop music and even dance to it, or quote Dylan and the Stones at one another, they wouldn't dream of writing about it. The intelligentsia would prefer 'more refined forms' of fiction. This was doubly disappointing because Wolfe imagined that after the mid-century exhaustion of European culture, we could look to America for the new writing, for this was 'the American century'. And indeed it *was* America – South America – where it transpired that the freshest stories and most magical realisms of all were being penned.

Apart from the fact that it is absurd to think anyone today could write like Dickens, any more than we could have music like Beethoven's which wasn't pastiche, one wonders what exactly it was that Wolfe was thinking of in his yearning for the nineteenth century. How could he imagine in the middle of the twentieth century that 'reality' was something that could be agreed upon? Surely, the first lesson of LSD was that reality was more evanescent and fugitive than most of us imagined for much of the time. Also, whatever made him think that realism could be the most direct route to this reality, were it to be located?

However, this failure or refusal of modern Dickenses and Zolas was also, as Wolfe recognized, an opportunity. As the high-brow novelists moved away from ordinary people, leaving them to 'trash' – those pallid contemporary simulacra of the nineteenth-century novel – and thus opening the gap between 'high' and 'low' culture, outsiders of all sorts and young people in particular were finding other, quicker methods of communication.

This was pop. And making a virtue of its exclusion from the conventional world, pop wasn't interested in the kind of literature that Wolfe longed for. Literature had been too often used as a boot stamped on the face of the young to show them how little they knew and, by extension, how much the elite knew. It was rejected. The feeling was often mutual, as shown in Richard Hoggart's piece included here, which illustrates the Old Left's fear, condescension and implicit paternalism towards popular culture. For Hoggart, popular it might be, but culture it couldn't be. Worse, this 'myth-world compounded of a few simple elements which they take to be those of American life' would induce 'spiritual dry-rot'. This scepticism about the influence America might have on English life is interesting when compared to Bernard Kops's enthusiasm: 'the American civilisation had caught up with us. Everything was speeded and slicked up'. Looking back, it is interesting to compare Hoggart's hostility to pop to the place it had in the lives of the '68ers, as illustrated by Lou Reed's conversation with Václav Havel.

Of course, pop is a form crying out not to be written about. It is physical, sensual, of the body rather than the mind, and in some ways it is anti-intellectual; let yourself go, don't think – feel. Explaining 'My Generation' to someone turned pop into one of the subjects scorned at school, rendering it dry and part of the world it was rebelling against. But as this collection shows, pop may have rejected a certain notion of literature – the contrivances of plot, character, dramatic tension, setting; and the time it takes to construct them would have seemed unnecessary and extraneous in that speedy period – but its progress was accompanied from the beginning by literary comment. Pop's first literary attendant was journalism, which to this day remains its acolyte and accomplice. Music papers, style magazines and fanzines flourish; and all British newspapers, as Boy George and Elton John discovered, carry pop information, gossip and comment. But pop also stimulated auto-biography, the 'non-fiction novel', the fiction novel, personal journalism and many kinds of maverick forms. Pop, as Greil Marcus reminds us, is 'an argument where anyone can join in'.

Furthermore, pop provided writers with new areas to explore, as one can see particularly in the first part of this book, where writing about pop introduces us to the fringes of the respectable world, to marijuana, genera-tional conflict, clubs, parties, and to a certain kind of guiltless, casual sex that had never been written about before. Pop, too, has enlivened and altered the language, introducing a Jonsonian proliferation of idioms, slang and fresh locutions; once the semi-secret code of an excluded or reviled minority, these have become part of the mainstream. And as soon as that happens, newer secrets have to be created and new words minted with which to pass them on.

We have tried to give a sense of the range and variety of pop writing; and also, perhaps, to present – if sketchily – the alternative history of our time told from the standpoint of popular music, which is as good a position as any to look from, since pop, intersecting with issues of class, race and particularly gender, has been at the centre of post-war culture.

It may be that anthologies are the format of our time. Certainly the record shops are full of 'Greatest Hits' and dance collections. Everywhere people make up their own tapes. (I can listen to *Sgt Pepper* and never again have to hear 'When I'm Sixty Four'.) Of course, pop was made for the moment, to embody exhilaration; and it sprang from a momentary but powerful impulse: teenage sexual longing. Similarly, most of the pieces in this book were written for fun, for the moment, as ephemera, which gives it a certain lightness of touch. It would have been ridiculous to think that posterity – that airless room in which only the best books are available – would be interested in this stuff. But it's strange how long the disposable can last and how often it may return. Funny, too, how much it can tell us about a particular period, as if it's the easily forgotten things that we most need to recover.

The more commercial and accepted pop has become, the more fanciful and original it has been forced to make itself to order, to remain 'ours' rather than 'theirs'. This book celebrates the limitless and continuing invention of, mostly, young people in pop, those teenage dreamers and visionaries who guarantee pop's continuing vigour, relevance and liveliness in all areas, from clothes to language, from clubs to technology. This delirious extravagance of imagination is the wonder of post-war British and American culture and continues to live.

Hanif Kureishi, London, November 1994

The simple things you see are all complicated

In November 1985, I went on a pilgrimage: to meet an alchemist of image and fantasy. Five floors below the penthouse on the Cromwell Road, grid-locked traffic murmured in bright sunlight, but inside everything was still. It was decorated in high sixties-style – carpets up the wall, leather furniture; comfortable but dark, almost sepulchral. As its owner spoke, I began to sense a shadow with which I was unfamiliar, but which I now realize was death.

Larry Parnes's life was beginning to wind down. He looked nothing like his photos from the late fifties, when he was at the height of his powers, with his quiff and razor-sharp suiting. He was tanned, frizzy haired, somehow shrunken; enthusiastically garrulous about his past, morbid about the present. Fey rather than camp, he talked obsessively about two dearly loved, recently deceased dogs – Prince and Duke – who continued to watch over us from a framed photograph.

My excuse for being there was a Channel 4 documentary, broadcast that winter, called 'Parnes, Shillings and Pence'. It was OK, if full of what writer Dick Bradley calls the 'Hi-de-Hi-holiday-camp-like atmosphere of cheerful anti-intellectualism and vulgarity' in which British rock 'n' roll flourished. Parnes's story was presented as cosy, familiar, an end of the pier attraction. *The Face* had commissioned me to write 500 words about the programme but I stayed for hours, paying homage. For Parnes had done something very strange and very wonderful: he had invented British pop.

And he knew it. In typical showbiz style, it came out in chatty hyperbole. Talking about a 1959 interview in the *Daily Express*, he said: 'I believe that it was in that article that I was the first person ever to use the word "Pop". It was always called "popular music". For some reason or other, I said "This is pop music" and, from that day on, everything you read became pop music. If you could copyright a word . . .!' In fact, he was mistaken – this abbreviation was in the language by 1958 – but by then Parnes had already created an imaginative space that British pop could inhabit.

For Parnes, it had all begun in the early fifties: 'I loved the London Palladium, and I used to see all the big stars: Frankie Laine, Dean Martin, Billy Daniels, Johnny Ray. When I saw what was happening in the audience, the reaction, the screaming when Johnny Ray was there . . . Great Marl-borough Street was blocked off, cars couldn't get through because of the fans, he'd come out on to the roof at the back of the building and wave. People think that started with the Beatles but it didn't.

'If it was somebody who was dynamite, the moment they came out on stage, I used to get these funny, electrical shivers running through my body. I thought: 'here are all these middle-aged people coming over from America, surely there must be a load of talent over here, young people, who could do the same thing. Prior to that, you had excellent dance band singers like Dickie Valentine, Dennis Lotis, David Whitfield, who were stars, but they'd never really captured a teenage audience. Somebody should do something about it. The first time I saw Tommy, the moment he hit the stage in his jeans, it was electrifying.'

The worldwide success of 'Heartbreak Hotel' provided the key. Elvis Presley arrived in the UK, on record and in photographs, like an alien. The British music industry immediately looked for home-grown rockers, but were hampered by pop's Afro-American origins: what in the US was the result of a long musical process – the marriage of Country and R&B – was seen as a fad in a country where the popular traditions were music hall and balladeering. Like a tail-fin on a Buick, Elvis's gimmick was his hoodlum, androgynous sexuality; that's what entrepreneurs like Parnes sought to develop and promote, starting with Tommy Hicks.

Parnes immediately identified his problem. His raw material was working-class youth, who had decidedly non-technicolor names. 'Just imagine when I started to put on Sunday concerts and tours, a bill with rock stars Reginald Smith, Ronald Wycherley, John Askew, Clive Powell. Doesn't it look like an industrial firm advertising something? There's got to be some glamour and charisma. So Tommy Hicks became Tommy Steele, Reginald Smith became Marty Wilde, Ronald Wycherley became Billy Fury, John Askew became Johnny Gentle, Clive Powell became Georgie Fame.

Pseudonyms had long existed in Hollywood, where an ethnic or ugly name could be left behind, along with a previous life: so Frances Gumm became Judy Garland, Lucille Cassin Joan Crawford, Dino Paul Crocetti Dean Martin. Not so in pop music; although they sounded exotic to British ears, names like Elvis Presley and Jerry Lee Lewis were real. Parnes was the first to make up names that evoked emotional and sexual states that you couldn't find in a phone book.

Here they all are, once again, and some more: Steele, Wilde, Fury, Eager, Gentle, Power, Fame, Pride. Feasting with panthers, Parnes defined the plasticity of the first teenage British stars – that overt yet often passive sexuality – and made it clear that pop was about one thing: self-recreation.

You could be an inner-urban child with a boring circumstance, yet by one simple act – changing your name – you could be transformed for ever into an electronic deity.

The ramifications of this idea have been played out ever since in the naming of pop celebrities, whether Andy Warhol acolytes like Ondine, Ingrid Superstar, International Velvet; glam stars David Bowie and Marc Bolan; punks like Richard Hell, Johnny Rotten and Siouxsie Sioux; Prince and Madonna (first names which have a very different meaning when isolated); indeed every band member who keeps their name but submerges their individuality within a group name and look.

Parnes was much mocked at the time for this 'Stable of Stars' both by Peter Sellars, with a wicked cruelty, in *So Little Time*, and by Colin MacInnes, the earliest and most perceptive British observer of pop, in this memorable exchange from *Absolute Beginners*: 'Which of the boy slaves was it sung it? Strides Vandal? Limply Leslie? Rape Hunger?' 'No, no . . . Soft-Sox Granite, I think it was . . .' 'Oh that one. A Dagenham kiddy, He's very new.' Wolf Mankowitz made Parnes into the central character of his *Expresso Bongo* – the short story and film which both enforced the svengali archtype of the pop manager and made Soho Britain's central pop location.

Homosexuality was always hinted at in this new relationship between manager and artist, and the shade of Oscar Wilde hovered in this new dandyism. Parnes might have taken the satires in good humour, but any mention of the h-word, and the lawyers were called. As he asked me rhetorically: 'What is showbusiness without court cases?' Yet Parnes was gay, as some of his stars will now admit with a rueful smile; his death has unlocked that particular secret. His denial was his prerogative, understandable within a climate hostile to his sexuality.

Parnes was the first embodiment of the paradigm later described by Simon Napier-Bell in his catty memoir, *You Don't Have To Say You Love Me*: 'It was surprising that an industry generating so many millions of pounds was prepared to use little more than the managers's sexual tastes as its yardstick of talent. Most of the managers were men and most of them liked boys. A few of the managers were women and one or two of them liked girls.' In this exchange, gay desire = teenage female desire, an equation which has continued through the Beatles to today's *Smash Hits* pop groups.

The collective power of young women was another central factor: the very first teenage products – cosmetics, magazines (like the US *Seventeen*), singers like Sinatra – exclusively marketed at young women, and it was their extreme enthusiasm which, from 1943 on, was the most obvious manifestation of youth power. And to this day, pop music still requires the willing feminization of young men.

This emerges in the androgyny that has haunted pop since the late fifties and which has always been present in British popular entertainment, whether in music hall or pantomime or in phenomena such as J. M. Barrie's *Peter Pan*, one of this century's more prophetic documents. Here we face questions of gender, age and sexuality in a way that is both perplexing and resonant: Peter Pan is the boy who will never grow up in the text, who can never grow into a man, and on stage he is played by a young woman. Locked into a peculiar no man's land between childhood and adolescence, Peter Pan remains the archetype for pop icons as diverse as Cliff Richard and Michael Jackson, trapped in perpetual youth.

As David Dalton writes in his biography of James Dean, *The Mutant King*, 'Androgyny is the traditional sexuality of the classic performer.' Its constant appearance in pop reinforces the fact that music in itself has a power that transcends the usual discourse of marketing, fashion, process and nostalgia. In our literary culture, we barely have words for the physical, emotional and physiological impact of music on our bodies. Pop plays with verbal loss of meaning. It's like that Lou Reed one-liner, 'Electricity comes from other planets.'

Larry Parnes felt this electricity where it mattered, in the body, and became one of its first conductors. I wouldn't like to be too starry-eyed here. Parnes couldn't handle female performers; he was an often emotional and stubborn businessman; he had no sense of artistic development, unlike his acolyte Brian Epstein; although committed to youth at a time when the music industry was middle-aged, he moved, as Johnny Rogan notes in *Starmakers and Svengalis*, 'from rock 'n' roll into traditional showbusiness, and it was a logical development'. In this, he was a man of his time.

Nevertheless, Parnes stands, at that moment when pop was being created, at the crossroads between exploitation and shamanism, between overt sexuality and concealment, between dream and reality, between England and America. There are many pop laws, but one is enshrined in the Who's greatest lyric: 'The simple things you see are all complicated.' Larry Parnes first identified and then made practical a central pop fact: that it is not about the ordinary, but the extraordinary. Out of what many would have thought unpromising material, he turned base metal into gold. This is the beginning of British pop.

For such a small word, pop has a multitude of meanings. Part of that is due to its enclosed nature: as a palindrome it encourages circular, Ouroboros-like arguments. Yet, it is also indivisible, and retains a certain elemental purity. It is understood as an infinitely applicable abstract principle, yet functions as a specific description of market and musical style. Apotheosized in the title of Britain's most important music programme, *Top of the Pops*, it still provides the central narrative for the UK music industry.

Pop's multi-faceted nature begins with the word of which it is a diminuitive; popular, an adjective which has become a keyword in this century of mass production and mass culture. The *Shorter Oxford English Dictionary* gives many definitions, all deriving from the Latin populus, the people: 'adapted to the understanding, taste, or means of ordinary people. (1573); 'finding favour with the people, favourite, acceptable, pleasing' (1608); 'prevalent among, or accepted by, the people generally' (1603). Its first attachment to a noun is recorded in 1885: 'short for popular concert'.

Popular is an ambiguous term, however. Against its earlier uses are placed pejorative words like 'plebian', 'epidemic', while Bacon referred to a 'Nobleman of an ancient family, but unquiet and popular'. This meaning is amplified by the account given by Raymond Williams in *Keywords*: 'Popular culture was not identified by the people but by others, and it still carries two older senses: inferior kinds of work (cf. popular literature, popular press as distinguished from quality press); and work deliberately setting out to win favour (popular journalism as opposed to democratic journalism, or popular entertainment); as well as the more modern sense of being liked by many people.'

The mass is always seen as fickle, threatening, uncontrollable by the state. This has often translated into official disapproval and, worse, legislation against those products and events which openly manifest mass movements and preferences. You only have to think of contemporary 1920s descriptions of jazz as dangerous 'jungle music', the banning of *The Wild One* in 1954 and the 1994 UK ban on *Natural Born Killers*. There is an endless sequence of newspaper and government-derived 'moral panics' – horror comics, Edwardians, Mods, Punks, Rappers, right down to the recent legislation against raves. What is popular is often feared.

The march of the popular began in America, and has been unstoppable every since. It is in that country that we find the first use of pop in the post-war music industry. In 1949, a gossip item appeared in the *Melody Maker* describing Benny Goodman as the 'Consulting Director of Pop Music' on Russian language programmes; two year later, Mitch Miller – one of the most important figures in fifties music – was hired by Mercury as the 'A&R chief of their pop division'. By 1955, *Melody Maker* could talk about an American 'tune born of the hillbilly stables and turned into a pop'.

In Britain, an early sighting of the word comes in the autumn 1955 revamp of the well-established HMV label; POP as a new catalogue number. POP 101 was, aptly enough, Eddie Fisher's 'Song of the Dreamer'/'I'm Just a Vagabond Lover', a coupling that summarized the subjects that pop would make its own. HMV released Elvis Presley's first UK record in May 1956 – 'Heartbreak Hotel' (POP 182) – but even then it took a while to stick: at that time, Bill Haley and Elvis Presley were classified not as pop but rock 'n' roll.

The word was in general currency by February 1958, when Colin MacInnes published his groundbreaking essay, 'Pop Songs and Teenagers'. Even then, he found it necessary to issue an ironic preface: 'The Editor has warned me some readers may not know what pop discs are. So: pop=popular; disc=gramophone recording. In short, the elegantly boxed records of the high street music stores which, last year, sold 50 million of them. The music fodder of the juke-boxes, the radios and the radiograms. To the vast mysterious majority, the only kind of songs there are.'

By the early sixties, pop is a routine form of teenage product identification in annuals like *Top Pop Stars* or in BBC radio programmes like *Pick of the Pops*. There were many dissenting voices, however, exemplified by this line from 'Sex and Violence in Modern Media', a report published by the Educational Institute of Scotland, 'It should not be forgotten what while sales of "pop" music grow so do sales of records of good music.' Here, as Stuart Hall and Paddy Whannel note in their 1964 survey of this battleground, 'The Popular Arts', ' "Pop" music is seen here as universally the opposite of – implicitly the enemy of – "good" music.'

By 1964, however, this phase of the battle had been won. The Beatles made pop respectable, indeed they embodied the ascendancy of its values – youthful, androgynous, overtly sexual, breezily non-conformist, popular in the classic sense of a culture actually made by the people themselves – within mainstream society. The phrase 'pop star' entered popular currency and in November 1963 the BBC gave its imprimatur with the first prime-time broadcast of *Top of the Pops*.

By 1966, pop had officially become an abstract, as highlighted by Piri Halasz in his famous *Time* magazine fantasy about Swinging London: 'This spring, as never before in modern times, London is switched on. Ancient elegance and new opulence are all tangled up in a dazzling blur of op and pop.' Pop had become more than music, a perception that had come, not from the mass media nor the exploiters of pop themselves, but from the avant-garde, finally trickling down into pop culture through art school musicians. As Pete Townshend said in June 1965: 'We stand for pop art clothes, pop art music and pop art behaviour. We live pop art.'

As an abstract, pop became cast adrift from the parent ship popular and, like a message in a bottle, began its own voyage. One way of crossing these choppy waters is by word-surfing: the *Shorter Oxford English Dictionary* notes six new separate groups of allusions for pop that predate its mid-twentieth-century use. Most have to do with sound, whether noun or verb: 'a short abrupt explosion' (1591); 'a shot with a fire arm' or 'a pistol' (1728); 'a name for an effervescing beverage, esp. ginger beer' (1812); 'to burst or explode with a pop' (1576); 'to shoot, to fire a gun' (1725).

There are several associations of pop with quick movement: 'to pass, move, go or come promptly, suddenly or unexpectedly' (1530); 'with the action or sound of a pop: instantaneously, abruptly, unexpectedly' (1621). Pop can be a diminutive of father (US 1940s); it crops up in the proposal of marriage – 'to pop the question' (1593); it denotes the Eton college élite; it was used in connection with poverty and pawning – 'Pop Goes the Weasel'; it can be slang for the act of dying – 'to pop off' (1764).

This wide variety of meanings is contained in a founding pop art document: Eduardo Paolozzi's celebrated collage, *I Was a Rich Man's Plaything* (1947). The original has now faded with time, but it's possible to see its bright colours and American textures as having an extraordinary, aspirational force in austerity-hit Britain. Like others in the movement who would shortly cluster round this aesthetic, Paolozzi was fascinated by these images of consumer plenty, physical space and up-front sexuality: in the midst of rationing and restriction, America represented the dream future.

You could hardly get less British. Instead of stasis, there is movement – the Hudson bomber (bottom left); instead of Tizer, the real thing – Coca Cola (bottom right). In the main image, built on a *True Confessions* magazine cover, there is the conflation of sex with violence (the gun pointing at the women in red shoots with a 'POP' bubble) and food. The conveniently placed cherry is an obvious sexual pun, but it works the other way as well: in its sheer lusciousness, it epitomizes the allure that consumption – having things, buying things, seeing them stacked in supermarkets rather than cornershops – had for a people recovering from war.

Fizzy pop, cherry popping, a sex pistol: here was the future. In April 1952, Paolozzi gave an epidiascope lecture of mass media images at the ICA, which, according to David Robbins, in the MIT catalogue for the 1990 IG exhibition, many members now credit as 'the launching of the Independent Group'. For the next five years, an extraordinary group of painters, critics, musicians, architects, and academics would explore the possibilities of pop, mass media, technology, a people's art and architecture, half in love with America, half in reaction against 'the rearview-mirror mentality'. which dominated official British culture.

The IG went public in August 1956 with the highly popular exhibition, 'This is Tomorrow', not before members like Laurence Alloway and Frank Cordell had begun theoretical discussions about pop and the mass media: indeed, Alloway came up with the term 'pop art' during this period. Many of these are now reprinted – in the MIT catalogue and Cordell's 1955 lecture in this book – and remain required reading in a country still caught up in the old 'high culture, low culture' argument. In January 1957, fine artist Richard Hamilton coined the perfect modernist description of pop:

> 'Pop Art is:
> Popular (designed for a mass audience)
> Transient (short term solution)
> Expendable (easily forgotten)
> Low cost
> Mass produced
> Young (aimed at youth)
> Witty
> Sexy
> Gimmicky
> Glamorous
> Big Business.'

This is what the Beatles embodied in the mid sixties, before everyone realized that pop had done its job too well: it was too good to be simply transient and expendable. 1966 was the high point of British pop art and with top three hits like the Who's 'Substitute', the Yardbirds' 'Shapes of Things' and the Beatles' 'Paperback Writer' there was an incredible compression of ideas and emotions about the mass media, consumption, perception and gender, all poured into the three minute forty-five. These records and the black music being made that year – Tamla, Soul and Ska – remain touchstones for young musicians.

From 1967 on pop fragmented: the economic boom on which teenage consumption was predicted came to an end in 1966; America's involvement in the Vietnam war escalated; drugs arrived. The music industry discovered target marketing in selling records to post-teenagers (with balladeers like Englebert Humperdinck), pre-teenagers (with the Monkees), and those teens who wanted something more sophisticated. The new software medium was the long-playing record, needing a greater investment than the single, but potentially much more profitable. Around the time the notation 'File Under Pop' began to appear on EMI records, there were at least three quite separate pop economies.

By the early seventies, pop begins to enter what you could call its postmodern phase. By 1972, the year that Pete Fowler saw Marc Bolan's failure as a generational icon, and the year in which Simon Frith researched 'The Sociology of Rock', there was a clear division – commented on by both authors – between pop and rock. This division was conducted along gender lines (pop=girls and androgynes, or, as Frith recorded in his interviews, 'puffs'; rock=boys and real men) and revived the old polarities of working/middle-class, exploitation/expression, the mass/the élite.

At the same time, several books – notably Stanley Cohen's *Folk Devils and Moral Panics* – developed the theory and the critical history of pop. From 1972 on, we enter an age where today's pop climate – fragmented, selfconscious, reference-laden – becomes visible. As often happens, writers noted what was already occurring in pop as new stars like David Bowie and Bryan Ferry applied avant-garde ideas from British and American Pop Art to the mainstream; 'Virginia Plain' is a fifties Richard Hamilton painting come to life, while 'The Rise and Fall of Ziggy Stardust and the Spiders from Mars' is the first self-fulfilling prophecy in pop – writing himself into the character of a star, Bowie became one.

The next dozen years saw the further application of these ideas in the area of Britpop that bothered with theory. Punk had a moralistic, almost Maoist attitude which coexisted with the first generally accessible critique of the mass media and youth consumption. Programmed for failure, punk groups fell apart when they became successful. In this vacuum, pop, being successful, popular and pleasurable, became fashionable again in the early eighties, heralded by Paul Morley's influential phrase, 'New Pop'.

Theorizing about the nature of pop itself, rather than producing it, is a very British response, caused by the original distance which, in 1956, meant that teenage music in the UK had to start from scratch rather than evolve. One area which has suffered from this bias is black music – until the mid-seventies rarely written about in the UK. There is a good case for a separate anthology on Black Music which could include extracts from American magazines like *Ebony, Jet, Hue, Sepia* and *Hep* (1946–57).

With early mid-eighties stars like Culture Club, Madonna, Duran Duran and Wham!, the accepted version of pop history ends. There are several reasons for this. The first is pop's diaspora, borne around the world by the integrated circuit of the film, TV, publishing, advertising and music industries. Pop now infuses our everyday life to a degree unthinkable thirty years ago. At the same time, developments in commodity capitalism – from mass-access to exclusion – have increased the spread of niche-marketing (and thus, further fragmentation) and turned the thrust of consumption away from generational models along more traditional class lines. What teenagers were to the late fifties, yuppies were to the mid-eighties: this invariably affected content.

Digital technology, which came onstream in the mid-eighties, changed pop production for ever. Sampling and home recording enabled talented producers like Arthur Baker, Russel Simmons, June Atkins, M/A/R/R/S, Hank Shocklee, Frankie Knuckles, Marshall Jefferson and many many others to change the base of pop music from rock to dance. In Britain, today's ur-pop is dance music – whether House, Eurobeat, Techno, Rap, Jungle – a hyper-speed, electronic call and response.

Many of these records turn into form the qualities usually associated with the post-modernist style: self-consciousness, the fragmentation of perception and narrative, and constant sourcing. To take the simplest example, it is now routine for a new pop record to be either a cover of an old tune, or to actually contain an older performance as an integral part of its sound. The implications of this have been heavily contested in law yet remain creatively fascinating: they mark an entirely new perception, away from linear time (a progression) to circular time (a loop).

Critics here would point to this circulatory of form as indicating a loss of meaning: add this to pop's diaspora through the media industry and the shift away from youth consumption, and you get a perceived diminution in pop vigour. There has been a lot of talk, from the early nineties on, around the subject eloquently polemicized in May 1993 by Tony Parsons: 'The Death of Pop'.

The media definition of post-modernism presupposes a lack of political,. social or even narrative content. The fragment is all, and cannot refer to anything outside its closed loop. But a younger generation, many of whom aren't yet represented in the mainstream media, takes this loop-de-loop for granted to the extent that they quite naturally assemble new narratives out of the ruins of pop's past, narratives which resonate as powerfully to their audience as any record has done over the last forty years. Three recent examples of this are: Oasis, 'Shakermaker'; Shy F.X., 'Sound of the Beast'; and Whigfield, 'Saturday Night'.

Testimonies of this experience from within have yet to be written, such is the time-lag between music and journalism, let alone literature: as Jacqui Attali writes in *Noise*, 'Music is prophecy. It s styles and economic organization are ahead of the rest of society because it explores, much faster than material reality can, the entire range of possibilities in a given code.' Although they are placed in their contemporary time frame, some of our extracts were written several years after the events they describe: we don't yet have the luxury of choosing between twenty compulsive accounts of the present.

Pop hits the head, the heart, the soul and the feet. We've tried to select extracts which, throughout the book as a whole, capture that mixture of reportage, enthusiasm, attitude, analysis, scepticism, deep-level empathy, and visceral rhythm that the best writing about pop should contain in order to even think about matching its subject. Although much of the writing is and has been done by white males, we've tried to suggest that other humans can write about pop as well and, indeed, may have a more interesting viewpoint, one which reflects the diversity of pop itself.

This leads into our last circuit of the palindrome. There is another battle-ground of meaning, final but important, that harks right back to the original ambiguity contained in the word popular. Are the people, as a mass and individually, to be feared or celebrated? Is pop itself, to put the polarities crudely, the expression of the people or sheer exploitation? Is popularity to be desired or despised? Such contradictions are embedded in the way that we talk about pop, and the way in which it is produced – exemplified most starkly by the story of Kurt Cobain.

The current confusion sites itself around the words 'popular' and 'populist'. In musical terms, popular has no pejorative connotations. It can cover the extremes of Mr Blobby and Nirvana, which means that, yes, pop can be sheer exploitative novelty, yet can also do what it did in the much-disputed sixties – touch and guide people's lives in a way that politicians and media folk cannot. In this way, it still retains a power denied in many mainstream accounts, in the UK at least.

The word populism was first coined in the late nineteenth-century to describe what were essentially socialist political parties formed both in Russia and the US. In its course over the last hundred years, it has taken on a different meaning. Populism now is tied into right-wing economics, political systems and ideology. Although it proclaims itself to speak on behalf of the people, it cloaks a new dictatorship. Like any -ism, there is the persistent stain of simplification and dogma, the world reduced to a formula: in this case, the total, uncritical acceptance of market forces.

Pop would seem like a good arena for this populist approach. After all, the music industry is hyper-capitalistic. In the words of a musician friend, it has 'institutionalized the rip-off'. Indeed, during the last ten years, many main-stream accounts of pop have followed this agenda. Led by PR, market research, and the self-censorship of early middle age, many journalists have seen pop in terms of pure process: marketing, celebrity gossip, babyboomer nostalgia. (At the same time, cogent analyses of the industry are still few and far between.) Implicit in this, as often as not, is the sense that pop has no meaning, that it's all been done.

To the extent that this is heartfelt, it's a valid position. For much of the time, however, it is merely the expression of a trite cynicism – a cynicism which, along with the other 'end of' arguments stacking up in the media, marks the exhaustion of a twenty-year project. Since the mid-seventies, the New Right has launched a successful counter-attack against the sixties, and thus, by direct implication, pop. One result, in Britain at least, has been the renewal of an obsolete hierarchy of values – marked by that late fifties, high/low culture debate – which unquestionably states that the novel is the highest form of artistic endeavour, and that pop is, like the girl in '96 Tears'. put 'way down here'.

The great thing about pop is that it doesn't need the patronage of *The Sunday Times* or *The Late Show* for its own self-validation. It can be argued that the less it is in the mainsream, the better it can develop on its own terms. Yet, this is also to ignore another of pop's functions within Britain and America: it stands, by default, at the intersection between two quite separate perceptions – the public world of news, current affairs and media chat, and the private world of life as it is lived. In this, pop's perennial concentration on love is only the most obvious sign of its intention to make the private public. Hence also its flagrant concerns with sex and gender.

Tied to a PR agenda, determined never to be surprised, the populist approach can only ever tell part of the story. Pop begins in music and to be sure, the music industry is always exploitative, yet at the same time, it is less patrolled and even quicker moving than film, television, and publishing. The turnaround between the recording of a tune and its appearance on *Top of the Pops* can be under a month. Pop is a very effective parallel-communications system, transmitting messages about the present and the future which repre-sent a serious breach of etiquette within the vision of a fifties theme park Britain that cloaks the social Darwinism unleashed by unchecked market forces.

Unlike the New Right drive towards social and economic exclusion, pop is inclusive both in its form and its sociology. In the same way that its aesthetics ignore the high/low culture polarity, its Afro/America roots have given it a special place in the wider enfranchisement that occurred between the fifties and the eighties. Always inherent in pop is the drive, defined by Dave Marsh, 'to give a voice and a face to the dispossessed', and it continues to grant visibility and audibility to voices often excluded from the mainstream – Afro-Caribbeans, homosexuals, women, outsiders of all types.

In this way, the effectiveness of raves as a response to Britain's restrictive stasis – their concentration on community, and mental and physical space – can be seen in terms of the state apparatus that has been brought against them, with the punitive legislation contained in the Criminal Justice Bill. The continuing public struggles over this issue are a definitive rebuttal of cynical claims that pop has lost its politics, is simply about self-satisfied thirty-something consumption.

And this is where the last few extracts take us: into diversity, darkness, dissidence and death. This is partly a polemic against the populist approach to pop; it's also a recognition that pop is still tied up with youth, and that youth is a state which neither Britain or America seems able to handle. It is possible to abstract youth into that part of ourselves which, at whatever age, is still prepared to change: the fact that pop can embody the future makes it one of the few places in modern communications which transcends cynicism and populism to offer hope, joy and love.

Jon Savage, London, December 1994

one

1942–56

'Groovy, frantic scenes'

'*The young were living mostly in exile, but exile gave them possibilities of which they had seldom dreamed before. Everything around them became slightly abnormal, the new occupation, the environment, the dress they wore, the physical and emotional climate. The concrete things of the past, like postal addresses, time-tables, road-signs, became less probable and friendships became all-important because it was unlikely that they could last. Nearly all of them, willingly or unwillingly, became creatures of the moment, living in an everlasting present; the past had vanished, the future was uncertain.*'

Rodney Garland, The Heart in Exile (1953)

There is no precise origin of pop as we now understand it: as a culture, a way of perception and an industry, as well as a kind of music. With hindsight, though, it is possible to isolate a range of factors that conspired to create it: technological developments; a Fordist-style economy retained from wartime (quick turnover, mass production, instant obsolescence); the spread of American influence in the world; the democratizing thrust of the projected consumer society; a post-war, post-nuclear sensibility that could be best described as existential.

In the forties, the popular music of the day was much as it had been in the thirties – war is not a great promoter of popular aesthetics. It came from America and it was the big band jazz type usually called swing. Although other featured big band vocalists, such as Bing Crosby, had already made a considerable impact, the extraordinary success of Frank Sinatra – announced by his December 1942 engagement at the Paramount Theater, New York – marked a new era. This is one visible beginning of pop.

Sinatra's material was popular but it wasn't pop; however, the response of his fans and the media manipulation that went on behind the scenes were. Shrewdly promoted by press agent George Evans – who, at first, used plants in the audience – the hysteria of Sinatra's female fans (dubbed bobbysoxers) became an American media sensation in early 1943 and locates the origin of post-war pop in the purchasing and sexual power of young women. Bruce Bliven's account captures the wonder felt by contemporary observers when confronted with this new phenomenon.

1948 saw a series of technological breakthroughs which facilitated the worldwide spread of popular music: the slow supplanting of the shellac 78rpm record by vinyl (at 45 and 33); the coming onstream of the tape-recorder as a recording instrument and a domestic playback system; an extension of the frequency range of recordings, including the first stereo system. Recorded music became more important to the music industry, a shift ratified by the introduction of pop charts in America (1940) and England (1952).

British popular music had long been dominated by America. Contemporary articles by Gordon Glover (1945) and Robert Muller (1954) observe the phenomena of 'Britain's Dance-band Leaders' and post-Sinatra big band vocalists like Frankie Vaughan, David Whitfield and Dickie Valentine in typical *Picture Post*ese. These were sharply observed, readable accounts which simultaneously exploited and denigrated America's allure for its

5

readership in austerity-bound Britain.

To post-war Britain, America was the future, and people tend to fear the future as much as they celebrate it. To many adults, the products of the American entertainment industries were so bizarre that they might as well have come from Mars. Bernard McElwaine's report on Johnnie Ray, the Native American with a hearing aid whose frenzied stage act came directly from the black Gospel tradition, captures this attitude: enlisting a 'Bobby-Sox Doctor' who warns of 'the HIDDEN impulses in human beings', he sets the tone for the next forty years of tabloid pop coverage – titillatory censure.

Yet there is a germ of truth here: the slow emergence of pop brought what had been hidden to light. First off, this meant increased exposure for pop's Afro/American roots: the *Picture Post* story on the Ink Spots captures an early visit by black Americans to Britain. The decade after the war was a period of incredible creativity in black dance music, which moved away from big bands into small combo R&B, the style that would later be called rock'n'roll. There are few contemporary accounts of this and it was thirty years before Chuck Berry and James Brown – two of the most influential post-war musicians – could tell their stories of this time.

The lifestyle was as important as the music. Malcolm X's snapshots of life in forties Manhattan speak of a world which is now familiar but was then the preserve of a tiny urban, ghetto minority: sex, drugs, dancing, wild clothes. Across the Atlantic, Don McCullin's account of buying a navy-blue hopsack suit and spongy-soled crêpe shoes shows how this aspect of America had filtered through to metropolitan British whites, in the form of what is now recognized as the first youth subculture: the Edwardians or Teddy Boys.

This was one example of the inchoate existentialism which has marked pop ever since – an existentialism which has its roots in the peculiar tensions of the period. The war was over, its freedoms and anarchy now had to be contained. The ambition of the West, as advised by America, was to achieve ordered consumption within the binary Cold War system. Those who could not forget the freedoms of war were outcasts. As Greil Marcus writes in *Lipstick Traces*: 'Protests against the reorganization of social life appeared out of nowhere: refusals of ... a future whose promises were fixed in advance. "How can we live," [René] Char wrote in 1947, "without the unknown before us?" '

'This place is on the road to nowhere,' remarks a character in Jean Cocteau's existential recasting of the Orpheus myth. A nameless anomie flickered across the psychic landscape of the post-war decade, like distant lightning. This 'unknown' was as keenly felt by some teenagers as it was by

6

the more traditional outcasts of society. After Hiroshima and Nagasaki, Auschwitz and Belsen, they could not return to the pre-war world – to which many adults harked back wistfully – yet they had no recognizable language with which to express this difference.

In this period, things were acted out which didn't yet have a name. Ralph Ellison's extraordinary reverie, triggered by the appearance of Harlem zoot-suiters who look 'like African sculptures', shows how the public display of extravagant clothing can be as disruptive as any overtly political act. Because these 'remote, cryptic messages' are so new, so alien, they are all the more difficult to police.

These refusals spread across the British class system. In inner urban areas, Edwardians adapted the zooters' sartorial annexation of space from 1950 on. Clerk Raymond Thorp's insider account of the London drug underworld (published at the time of renewed public scares around the subject) shows how the everlasting present can be chemically, and illegally, prolonged. Max Jones's story on the art-student, trad jazz scene which developed around the New Orleans revival of the Humphrey Lyttleton Band and others describes the post-war bohemia where such an implicitly critical distance could flourish (and grow into the internationally exported Beat Boom of the mid-sixties).

It was here, on the margins, that the origins of the pop sensibility were to be found: in zoot-suiters, drug takers, blacks, homosexuals, Indians, criminals, the poor and the restless. Their appearance in mainstream society was a freak event, to be patrolled by medical men or by the police, but was also a harbinger of the future – as the psychic states that were once the province of outcasts moved to the heart of the Western consumer machine. 'They were men out of time,' Ralph Ellison wrote about the zooters. 'Who knew but that they were the saviours, the true leaders, the bearers of something precious?'

1942: Laura

Shorty would take me to groovy, frantic scenes in different chicks' and cats' pads, where with the lights and the juke down mellow, everybody blew gage and juiced back and jumped. I met chicks who were fine as May wine, and cats who were hip to all happenings.

That paragraph is deliberate, of course; it's just to display a bit more of the slang that was used by everyone I respected as 'hip' in those days. And in no time at all, I was talking the slang like a lifelong hipster.

7

Like hundreds of thousands of country-bred Negroes who had come to the Northern black ghetto before me, and have come since, I'd also acquired all the other fashionable ghetto adornments – the zoot suits and conk that I have described, liquor, cigarettes, then reefers – all to erase my embarrassing background. But I still harbored one secret humiliation: I couldn't dance.

I can't remember when it was that I actually learned how – that is to say, I can't recall the specific night or nights. But dancing was the chief action at those 'pad parties', so I've no doubt about how and why my initiation into lindy-hopping came about. With alcohol or marijuana lightening my head, and that wild music wailing away on those portable record players, it didn't take long to loosen up the dancing instincts in my African heritage. All I remember is that during some party around this time, when nearly everyone but me was up dancing, some girl grabbed me – they often would take the initiative and grab a partner, for no girl at those parties ever would dream that anyone present couldn't dance – and there I was out on the floor.

I was up in the jostling crowd – and suddenly, unexpectedly, I got the idea. It was as though somebody had clicked on a light. My long-suppressed African instincts broke through, and loose.

Having spent so much time in Mason's white environment, I had always believed and feared that dancing involved a certain order or pattern of specific steps – as dancing *is* done by whites. But here among my own less-inhibited people, I discovered it was simply letting your feet, hands and body spontaneously act out whatever impulses were stirred by the music.

From then on, hardly a party took place without me turning up – inviting myself, if I had to – and lindy-hopping my head off.

I'd always been fast at picking up new things. I made up for lost time now so fast that soon girls were asking me to dance with them. I worked my partners hard; that's why they liked me so much.

When I was at work, up in the Roseland men's room, I just couldn't keep still. My shine rag popped with the rhythm of those great bands rocking the ballroom. White customers on the shine stand, especially, would laugh to see my feet suddenly break loose on their own and cut a few steps. Whites are correct in thinking that black people are natural dancers. Even little kids are – except for those Negroes today who are so 'integrated', as I had been, that their instincts are inhibited. You know those 'dancing jigaboo' toys that you wind up? Well, I was like a live one – music just wound me up.

By the next dance for the Boston black folk – I remember that Lionel Hampton was coming in to play – I had given my notice to the Roseland's manager.

When I told Ella why I had quit, she laughed loud: I told her I couldn't find

8

time to shine shoes and dance, too. She was glad, because she had never liked the idea of my working at that no-prestige job. When I told Shorty, he said he'd known I'd soon outgrow it anyway.

Shorty could dance all right himself but, for his own reasons, he never cared about going to the big dances. He loved just the music-making end of it. He practiced his saxophone and listened to records. It astonished me that Shorty didn't care to go and hear the big bands play. He had his alto-sax idol, Johnny Hodges, with Duke Ellington's band, but he said he thought too many young musicians were only carbon-copying the big-band names on the same instrument. Anyway, Shorty was really serious about nothing except his music, and about working for the day when he could start his own little group to gig around Boston.

The morning after I quit Roseland, I was down at the men's clothing store bright and early. The salesman checked and found that I'd missed only one weekly payment; I had 'A-1' credit. I told him I'd just quit my job, but he said that didn't make any difference; I could miss paying them for a couple of weeks if I had to; he knew I'd get straight.

This time, I studied carefully everything in my size on the racks. And finally I picked out my second zoot. It was a sharkskin grey, with a big, long coat, and pants bellowing out at the knees and then tapering down to cuffs so narrow that I had to take off my shoes to get them on and off. With the salesman urging me on, I got another shirt, and a hat, and new shoes – the kind that were just coming into hipster style; dark orange colored, with paper-thin soles and knob-style toes. It all added up to seventy or eighty dollars.

It was such a red-letter day that I even went and got my first barbershop conk. This time it didn't hurt so much, just as Shorty had predicted.

That night, I timed myself to hit Roseland as the thick of the crowd was coming in. In the thronging lobby, I saw some of the real Roxbury hipsters eyeing my zoot, and some fine women were giving me that look. I sauntered up to the men's room for a short drink from the pint in my inside coat-pocket. My replacement was there – a scared, narrow-faced, hungry-looking little brown-skinned fellow just in town from Kansas City. And when he recognized me, he couldn't keep down his admiration and wonder. I told him to 'keep cool', that he'd soon catch on to the happenings. Everything felt right when I went into the ballroom.

Hamp's band was working, and that big, waxed floor was packed with people lindy-hopping like crazy. I grabbed some girl I'd never seen, and the next thing I knew we were out there lindying away and grinning at each other. It couldn't have been finer.

I'd been lindying previously only in cramped little apartment living-rooms, and now I had room to maneuver. Once I really got myself warmed and loosened up, I was snatching partners from among the hundreds of unattached, freelancing girls along the sidelines – almost every one of them could really dance – and I just about went wild! Hamp's band wailing. I was whirling girls so fast their skirts were snapping. Black girls, brownskins, high yellows, even a couple of the white girls there. Boosting them over my hips, my shoulders, into the air. Though I wasn't quite sixteen then, I was tall and rawboned and looked like twenty-one; I was also pretty strong for my age. Circling, tap-dancing, I was underneath them when they landed – doing the 'flapping eagle', 'the kangaroo' and the 'split'.

After that, I never missed a Roseland lindy-hop as long as I stayed in Boston.

The Autobiography of Malcolm X, with Alex Haley (1964)

1944: The Voice and the Kids

At nine o'clock in the morning, New York's Paramount Theater is full and already the line outside, waiting to buy tickets, goes around the corner. But this is nothing; you should have been here last Thursday, which was a holiday. There were 10,000 trying to get in, and 150 extra policemen totally failed to keep order. Shop windows were smashed; people were hurt and carried off in ambulances.

Because the average fan stayed for two or three performances, the trouble outside went on all day. Out of 3500 who were in their seats for the first show, only 250 came out when the second show started. Some people were in line before midnight of the previous day. One man said he had tried to buy an early place in line for his daughter for $8, but had been refused. A woman in line with her daughter long before the doors opened said the girl threatened to kill herself if kept home.

This, as you have guessed, is the magic spell of The Voice, a phenomenon of mass hysteria that is seen only two or three times in a century. You need to go back not merely to Lindbergh and Valentino to understand it, but to the dance madness that overtook some German villages in the Middle Ages, or to the Children's Crusade.

The Voice needs a hollow square of policemen to protect him anywhere he goes; his telephone calls swamp any switchboard; his mail runs into the thousands per day. So does his income; he averages more than $20,000 a week the year around. His admirers send him all sorts of presents, and when he advises them to put their money into war bonds, they try to give the war bonds to him, or one of his children.

One girl wore a bandage for three weeks on her arm at the spot where 'Frankie touched me.' Another went to 56 consecutive performances in a theater where he was playing. Merely to see him cross the sidewalk from an automobile to a broadcasting station, young idolators lined up five hours in advance. Two girls picked up by police in Pittsburgh had spent their whole savings and run away from their home in Brooklyn because The Voice was appearing in the Pennsylvania city. The Voice's home is invaded by young girls who make a pretext of asking for a drink of water, or to use the bathroom. Trained nurses have to be on the premises in any theater where he appears, to soothe the hysterical. (Some who faint have gone ten or 12 hours without food, to see successive performances.) It is something to think about.

At 9.10 a.m., inside the theater, the over-ornate red and gold decorations are almost submerged under a sea of youthful femininity. Almost all those present belong to the bobby-socks brigade, age perhaps 12 to 16. Hundreds of them are wearing the polka-dotted blue bow tie popularized by their idol. Although his appearance is still an hour away, they are in a mood to squeal, and squeal they do. The movie which grinds its way across the screen is a routine affair, but the bobby-socksers take it big, with wild bursts of applause in unexpected places.

The electric contagion of excitement steadily mounts as the film ends and the stage show begins. Then, at a familiar bar of music recognized by the devout, the crowd goes completely crazy. It is the entrance cue for The Voice. The shrieks rise to a crashing crescendo such as one hears but rarely in a lifetime. Through the portieres at the side of the stage comes a pleasant-appearing young man in an expensive brown tweed coat and brown doeskin trousers. With gawky long steps he moves awkwardly to the center of the stage, while the shrieking continues. The bobby-socksers are on their feet now, applauding frantically. A few of them slump into their seats, either fainting or catching their breath. Sinatra looks, under the spotlight, like a young Walter Huston. He has a head of tousled black curls and holds it awkwardly to one side as he gestures clumsily and bashfully with his long arms, trying to keep the crowd quiet enough for him to sing *Embraceable You*. Contrary to expectation, he appears in excellent health, with a face that seems tanned, not made up. A girl sitting by me says, 'Look, he has broad shoulders,' and her boy friend replies scornfully, 'Aw, nuts! Pads!' Obviously he is right.

Now, having with difficulty created a partial state of order, The Voice performs. Diffidently, almost bashfully, yet with sure showmanship and magnificent timing, he sings five or six songs, with intervals of patter between them. His voice seems a pleasant, untrained light baritone – a weak one, were it not boosted in power by the microphone. When he sings sadly 'I'll walk alone,' the child sitting next to me shouts in seemingly genuine anguish, 'I'll walk wid ya, Frankie,' and so, in various words, do several hundred others. When the song says that nobody loves him, a faithful protagonist on my right groans, 'Are you kiddin', Frankie?' Then the whole audience falls into an antiphony with him, Frankie shouting 'No!' and the audience 'Yes!' five or six times.

Bruce Bliven, *New Republic*, 6 November 1944

1945: Britain's Dance-band Leaders

In the early twenties a svelte and portly showman turned up in Britain from the United States. His name was Paul Whiteman. He brought with him a large company of his compatriots and about half a ton of instruments, brilliant with gold and silver plate. He decked out the company in – if the memory serves – purple velvet tuxedos, and set them, with their polished ironmongery, upon the West End stage. He then called for light, and, as the limes flooded down on musicians and their machinery, he raised his baton. He also came near to raising the roof, and with it the box-office receipts.

Until then, in Britain, not a note had been crooned, not a limelight shone (blue, green, silver or gold), not a quip cracked by a saxophonist bounding like a jack-in-the-box from his seat to crack it. Bing Crosby was selling pickles in Spokane, Ann Shelton was unborn, and that 'hep-cat' of a clarinet-tist Harry Parry, far from cutting the rug, was barely cutting his teeth. But as Whiteman and his men let loose the 'Rhapsody in Blue' upon the West End, the future careers of all such ladies and gentlemen became assured.

Band leaders were to become showmen. People were going to pay for looking as well as listening. Lancashire-born Jack Hylton became the best-known band magnate in Britain and beat Whiteman at his own game. The boy who used to sing and clog-dance for his supper around the bar-parlours of Lancashire, became the best-known back view from Aberdeen to Ankhara. The French awarded him the Legion d'Honneur. The Continent and his native acres heaped him with approbation, and the simple announce-ment 'Jack's Back' (coupled with rearward sketch of the famous dumpy torso) fetched the public in their thousands to the box-office tills. To-day the

'Singing Mill Boy' sits in Tree's famous room under the dome of His Majesty's Theatre, proud of his own shows and of the fact that, at the beginning of the war, he saved the London Philharmonic Orchestra from bankruptcy by turning the limes on its shirt-fronts in the music halls of the number-one towns.

Others stay where they are. Carrol Gibbons, darling of the Savoy supper tables, fingers the keys of his piano in the ballroom with the famous rising floor as he has done, off and on, for long enough to have become a tradition. He is part of an immaculate pattern and a history of musical excellence that reaches back to the days when wireless enthusiasts cat's-whiskered in Bert Ralston's famous Havana Band, when Debroy Somers and the Orpheans were sobbing 'What'll I do?' and Billy Mayerl was fooling with his piano like a hobgoblin inspired, to the joy of the not (now that one thinks of it) so wonderfully Bright Young People.

To the Savoy in those days – or just a little later – there came one evening a Mr Gerald Bright, twin brother to a Mr Sydney Bright, whose piano-playing had long been a pleasure to the epicures of rhythm. He had conceived something. He had conceived Geraldo, who was born shortly afterwards – a patent-leather dandy with a Gaucho orchestra, which he put back into dinner-jackets whenever he thought the public had had enough.

Geraldo exists with a formidable immaculacy and unlimited enterprises in an office not a crooner-call from Broadcasting House. He is efficient, diligent, and ambitious to conduct a great symphony orchestra. He did indeed offer to swop horses – or orchestras – with Dr Malcolm Sargent as the result of a remark deprecating dance music made by Sargent in a brains trust. The offer was not accepted, so Geraldo contents himself with his own 'Concert Orchestra'. Twin brother Sydney (plain Bright) continues as 'Gerry's' pianist.

The dance bands of Britain are for ever on the go. Long tenancies and traditions, such as those which for years kept the impeccable Ambrose at London's Mayfair, are unusual. Ambrose himself, patrician of his profession, has no orchestra of his own at present. But the soft-footed presence is there, and the slim fingers are in many pies.

Ever-articulate are *Monseigneurs* Payne and Hall, old tenants respectively of Savoy Hill and Broadcasting House, each at the same game of putting on dance-band shows of ever-increasing magnificence throughout the country. These are heavyweights who dish out their harmonies with the assistance of comics, crooners, dancers, and other accessories to the fact that they've got rhythm. They are here, there, everywhere, playing music from a labyrinth of contracts and sub-contracts.

Never – and don't the public and the 'pros' know it! – was there such a boom in bands. Ask Joe Loss, the very sleek ex-resident maestro of the London Astoria, about his receipts at Green's, in Glasgow, when he played there some little time ago. Ask Harry Leader with the red carnation (part, says his agent, of his personality) of the milling multitude at the Astoria where he plays to-day. If you can detach Oscar Rabin from the bass saxophone behind which he always sits in unobtrusively with his band, ask him about conditions on the provincial circuits.

Debroy Somers ('Bill' to all who know him) hits up a tremendously effective hullabaloo at the London Palladium in the new George Black show. Bill used to be an Army bandmaster and believes in discipline. He commands 44 players with the tough alertness of a master-welder. Contrast him as a leader with Ivy Benson, who, with her Girls' Band, has introduced a new decor to the appearance of dance music.

There are others, of course. There is only one, says a disdainful jazz-maniac, 'hep-cat' or what have you. It is Harry Parry, diffident, but vastly successful jazzman, composer of 'Parry Opus' and 'Paralytic', a cornerstone of the famous Radio Rhythm Club. No, no, says another, Vic Lewis and Jack Parnell, these are the jazzmen in the true tradition of the Dukes, Mugsys, Bix's, Hoagy's, Pee-Wees, and Dukes. 'Buddy Featherstonehaugh' exclaims a third. But jazzmen are best left, and welcome, to go to town and argue things out for themselves.

Gordon Glover, *Picture Post*, 3 February 1945

1947: Dark Harmony

A chord on the guitar and the Ink Spots are in key. The melodic drool and drawl begin, the sentimental song is being sung and swung, hummed with hymn-sincerity. Four voices nuzzle close around the theme and crane towards the microphone. Bill Kenny takes the solo, lingering on its notes and words with genuine, heart-felt feeling for the soft-jazz, saddened notes. He kisses his vowels as if he were taking leave of them for ever, and underlines his consonants with careful movements of his lips, teeth and tongue. The three mouths round him droon and crawl along their lines. A shake of the head, a flash of tooth or tie-pin, and his gently wandering voice is viced to a stricter tempo by the dusky bass beat of his brother Herbert.

The song slides down an octave, the four dark-dreamy, dark-skinned singers slightly rearrange themselves around the microphone. Brother

Herbert leans over it, as if he were going to tap it on the curly head, he so obviously sees over its gauze. 'Bless yoo, hunny,' he booms (his slight moustache hardly moves) 'for being an angel' (the guitar strings and the strummed accompaniment murmuringly move on) 'jest when it seemed (pause) that hevun was not for me!' The song continues, a mathematical two beats-and-a-half behind his benediction. Eight trouser-legs, creased and caught in time, flicker with the legs inside them, moved by melancholy mood. Eight hands gesticulate faintly but with an abundance of variation. Eight arms express restrained wild-rhythm. Eight lips savour every lyric-rhyme.

Wild-rhythm is let loose when Billy Bowen, short, expansive, round, 'Butterball' to his friends and publicity manager, trundles to town. The brown fingers stiffen in the spotlight, the trouser-creases begin to dance, the rings and tie-pins take on seven new colours, and the tragedy disappears. The wide grins take away the perfect articulation of the last number, and the plum richness of melody is lost in the cry of 'Drop a nickel in the pot, Joe,' or 'Oh slip me a slug from that wonderful mug!' Bill Kenny conjures with invisible eggs, the others wiggle thumbs.

The song is changed again and the ecstasy subsides and melancholy returns. Bill Kenny comes back to the meanderings of 'Whispering Grass'. There is indictment in his tone as with a whine, like that of a musical saw, but without the maddening tremolo, he sings 'Now dow'nt yoo tellit to the breeze ...' The quartet has its harmony in sentiment again, in the brown quavers of unwept stage-tears, in the still sorrows of the glib song-writers, the sorrows nobody ever felt.

John Ormond Thomas, *Picture Post*, 4 October 1947

1949: A New Jazz Age

When Humphrey Lyttelton stomps his foot to lead his seven musicians into 'Working Man Blues' or 'Panama Rag' he is not another bandleader selling hit songs and strict tempo. He is a cornettist in the classic jazz tradition, playing music he believes in. The music is New Orleans style, the original instrumental form of jazz. Humphrey Lyttelton, 28-years-old, a naturally creative musician, is a product of the English jazz revival.

To the Man-in-the-Street, jazz can mean anything from Gershwin to Nat Gonella. Properly, it is a generic name for the southern negro parade and dance music of the late nineteenth century and its immediate derivatives. In fifty years, jazz has been developed beyond recognition, its most aggressively modern outgrowths being 'progressive jazz' and 'bepop'. Feeling runs high between devotees of the two schools – the Traditionalists (New Orleans) and the Modernists (Bepop).

It was realisation of the blind alley into which jazz had got itself in the 'forties that caused young musicians to look to western art music for harmonic inspiration. These were the 'boppers'. Others, particularly those in Europe, examined jazz history (on gramophone records) to find out where it had taken the wrong direction. These were the revivalists for whom Lyttleton speaks. 'Ours was a long-term policy. To unearth the principles which distinguished the early jazz forms, which had become almost obscured beneath an accumulation of decadent influences, and to re-establish these as a basis for future development.'

Thus the revival began, several years ago; and it continues to gain momentum. It brought about the appearance in jazz of amateur music-making on a considerable scale. And this amateur approach is the revivalists' strength. The Lyttelton band earns good money out of jazz, as it happens. But it is the money the musicians make at their daytime jobs (Humphrey writes and draws for the *Daily Mail*, clarinettist Wally Fawkes is a cartoonist for the same paper, and so on) which enables them to play New Orleans jazz – tunes, old enough to be new, that no publisher is plugging, played in a spirited and spontaneous manner that gives pleasure to players and listeners alike.

Lyttelton has no pretensions about this music. 'Its origins were purely functional,' he says, 'and we are content to keep it that way. We don't believe that it should be dressed up in a starch shirt and hustled on to a concert platform. Jazz never was and never will be a highly intellectual music. But it can be a dance music which is worthier of the dancers' intelligence, and has more vitality, than the dreary products of Tin Pan Alley. We play for dancing as well as listening: and our music can only be fully appreciated if this is borne in mind.'

To appreciate it Londoners have only to go to 100 Oxford Street, any Monday or Saturday evening. There, at the London Jazz Club, Lyttelton and his band play to a full basement – 350 zealots who listen intently or dance with dangerous vigour.

It has been said that jazz 'glorifies the purely muscular level'. And there are dancers at the London Jazz Club who appear to confirm that view. But in good New Orleans style, the subtle instrumental interplay and disciplined sense of form make an appeal to the mind.

Detractors – and there are many – try to write off the New Orleans revival as an ephemeral cult. There are indications, though, that New Orleans-style clubs will be a lasting feature of our jazz landscape. And there is nothing cultist about the mass of these lusty dancers reacting naturally to the music's pulse. There is a student fringe, which expresses itself to a degree embarrassing to a stranger. But in the main, the members look like normal folk from shops and offices, turning to jazz as a release from the day's humdrum. And there is no doubt the music expresses something that most of them feel and think, and does it in a terse forthright way.

Basically, of course, the dancers like the bands they can dance to, and detest the others. Many had got bored with the polite shuffling that passes for dancing at the Palais, drifted into the Jazz Club one night, and stayed to become regulars. Freedom to wear what you like and to do almost what steps you like, were attractions. With these assets, the London Jazz Club has acquired a membership of 5,000 in its nineteen months' life.

So more and more young couples take up jazz dancing, and the revival movement grows. The dancers exert an influence on the band's music. And because they are concerned primarily with rhythmic urge and surface excitement, their demands – were they to over-ride Lyttelton's musical convictions – could prove disastrous to the quality of his jazz. Once again, the safeguard is the band's amateurism. 'Art for art's sake is no good if you can't afford it,' Humphrey says.

'Early jazz was full of interesting resources which have never been fully developed. We try to carry some of them a stage further. We are not concerned about being "progressive". The musician should be the pilot rather than the engine. Real progress can only be achieved by constant reference to first principles. The apostles of Bepop and Progressive Jazz are careering ahead at full throttle. But they've thrown the map out of the window.'

Max Jones, *Picture Post*, 12 November 1949

1951: Wild Jacks-in-the-Box

A body of people came down the platform, some of them Negroes. Yes, I thought, what about those of us who shoot up from the South into the busy city like wild jacks-in-the-box broken loose from our springs – so sudden that our gait becomes like that of deep-sea divers suffering from the bends? What about those fellows waiting still and silent there on the platform, so still and silent that they clash with the crowd in their very immobility;

standing noisy in their very silence; harsh as a cry of terror in their quietness? What about those three boys, coming now along the platform, tall and slender, walking stiffly with swinging shoulders in their well-pressed, too-hot-for-summer suits, their collars high and tight about their necks, their identical hats of black cheap felt set upon the crown of their heads with a severe formality above their hard conked hair? It was as though I'd never seen their like before: walking slowly, their shoulders swaying, their legs swinging from their hips in trousers that ballooned upward from cuffs fitting snug about their ankles; their coats long and hip-tight with shoulders far too broad to be those of natural western men. These fellows whose bodies seemed – what had one of my teachers said to me? – 'You're like one of these African sculptures, distorted in the interest of a design.' Well, what design and whose?

I stared as they seemed to move like dancers in some kind of funeral ceremony, swaying, going forward, their black faces secret, moving slowly down the subway platform, the heavy heel-plated shoes making a rhythmical tapping as they moved. Everyone must have seen them, or heard their muted laughter, or smelled the heavy pomade on their hair – or perhaps failed to see them at all. For they were men outside of historical time, they were untouched, they didn't believe in Brotherhood, no doubt had never heard of it; or perhaps like Clifton would mysteriously have rejected its mysteries; men of transition whose faces were immobile.

I got up and went behind them. Women shoppers with bundles and impatient men in straw hats and seersucker suits stood along the platform as they passed. And suddenly I found myself thinking, Do they come to bury the others or to be entombed, to give life or to receive it? Do the others see them, think about them, even those standing close enough to speak? And if they spoke back, would the impatient businessmen in conventional suits and tired housewives with their plunder, understand? What would they say? For the boys speak a jived-up transitional language full of country glamour, think transitional thoughts, though perhaps they dream the same old ancient dreams. They were men out of time – unless they found Brotherhood. Men out of time, who would soon be gone and forgotten . . . But who knew (and now I began to tremble so violently I had to lean against a refuse can) – who knew but that they were the saviours, the true leaders, the bearers of something precious? The stewards of something uncomfortable, burden-some, which they hated because, living outside the realm of history, there was no one to applaud their value and they themselves failed to understand it. What if Brother Jack were wrong? What if history was a gambler, instead of a force in a laboratory experiment, and the boys his ace in the hole? What if history was not a reasonable citizen, but a madman full of paranoid guile and these boys his agents, his big surprise! His own revenge? For they were outside, in the dark with Sambo, the dancing paper doll; taking it on the lambo with my fallen brother, Tod Clifton (Tod, Tod) running and dodging the forces of history instead of making a dominating stand.

A train came. I followed them inside. There were many seats and the three sat together. I stood, holding on to the centre pole, looking down the length of the car. On one side I saw a white nun in black telling her beads, and standing before the door across the aisle there was another dressed completely in white, the exact duplicate of the other except that she was black and her black feet bare. Neither of the nuns was looking at the other but at their crucifixes, and suddenly I laughed and a verse I'd heard long ago at the Golden Day paraphrased itself in my mind:

> Bread and Wine,
> Bread and Wine,
>   Your cross ain't nearly so
>   Heavy as mine . . .

And the nuns rode on with lowered heads.

I looked at the boys. They sat as formally as they walked. From time to time one of them would look at his reflection in the window and give his hat brim a snap, the others watching him silently, communicating ironically with their eyes, then looking straight ahead. I staggered with the lunging of the train, feeling the overhead fans driving the hot air down upon me. What was I in relation to the boys, I wondered. Perhaps an accident, like Douglass. Perhaps each hundred years or so men like them, like me, appeared in society, drifting through; and yet by all historical logic we, I, should have disappeared around the first part of the nineteenth century, rationalized out of existence. Perhaps, like them, I was a throwback, a small distant meteorite that died several hundred years ago and now lived only by virtue of the light that speeds through space at too great a pace to realize that its source has become a piece of lead . . . This was silly, such thoughts. I looked at the boys; one tapped another on the knee, and I saw him remove three rolled magazines from an inner pocket, passing two around and keeping one for himself. The others took theirs silently and began to read in complete absorption. One held his magazine high before his face and for an instant I saw a vivid scene: the shining rails, the fire hydrant, the fallen policeman, the diving birds and in the mid-ground, Clifton, crumpling. Then I saw the cover of a comic book and thought, Clifton would have known them better than I. He knew them all the time. I studied them closely until they left the train, their shoulders rocking, their heavy heel plates clicking remote, cryptic messages in the brief silence of the train's stop.

I came out of the subway, weak, moving through the heat as though I carried a heavy stone, the weight of a mountain on my shoulders. My new shoes hurt my feet. Now, moving through the crowds along 125th Street, I was painfully aware of other men dressed like the boys, and of girls in dark exotic-coloured stockings, their costumes surreal variations of downtown styles. They'd been there all along, but somehow I'd missed them. I'd missed them even when my work had been most successful. They were outside the groove of history, and it was my job to get them in, all of them. I looked into the design of their faces, hardly a one that was unlike someone I'd known down South. Forgotten names sang through my head like forgotten scenes in dreams. I moved with the crowd, the sweat pouring off me, listening to the grinding roar of traffic, the growing sound of a record shop loudspeaker blaring a languid blues. I stopped. Was this all that would be recorded? Was this the only true history of the times, a mood blared by trumpets, trombones, saxophones and drums, a song with turgid, inadequate words? My mind flowed. It was as though in this short block I was forced to walk past everyone I'd ever known and no one would smile or call my name. No one fixed me in his eyes. I walked in feverish isolation. Near the corner now a couple of boys darted out of the Five and Ten with handfuls of candy bars, dropping them along the walks as they ran with a man right behind. They came towards me, pumping past, and I killed an impulse to trip the man and was confused all the more when an old woman standing further along threw out her leg and swung a heavy bag. The man went down, sliding across the walk as she shook her head in triumph. A pressure of guilt came over me. I stood on the edge of the walk watching the crowd threatening to attack the man until a policeman appeared and dispersed them. And although I knew no one man could do much about it, I felt responsible. All our work had been very little, no great change had been made. And it was all my fault. I'd been so fascinated by the motion that I'd forgotten to measure what it was bringing forth. I'd been asleep, dreaming.

Ralph Ellison, *Invisible Man* (1952)

1952: Club Eleven

One evening at Feldmans I was talking to Johnny, a young Negro who worked at steaming saucepans in the kitchen of a Soho café and who was looked upon by our group as being someone really 'cool' – someone with all the answers. He wore a pair of blue jeans and a white sweat shirt that sparkled against his skin. Like most of us he was sweating slightly – partly from the atmosphere of the club, partly from the excitement of the music.

'Say, man,' he said excitedly. 'You heard about the Club Eleven? Was there last week. Man, but man it makes this 'ole town look like a model T Ford.' His eyes sparkled and soon he was telling us about a new jazz club that had opened in Great Windmill Street – a few yards from Piccadilly Circus. About the cool cats who were going there and the hot music that 'really gets the joint a'jumping'. Within weeks everyone was discussing the new club. At Feldmans people who had been to the Club Eleven were pointed out to you. Whispers went around that it had all the atmosphere of Basin Street and Dixieland days. But few among us seemed prepared to make the jump from Oxford Street to Soho. Because there were other whispers, ugly whispers . . .

But the more I heard about the Club Eleven the more determined I became to visit it. Pete was not so keen. 'I don't like getting mixed up with these Soho types,' he said doubtfully. But slowly I talked him into it and one Wednesday – the only night, at that time, that the new club opened – we made our way to Great Windmill Street.

We found the club behind some theatrical rehearsal rooms. They charged us five shillings membership fee and three shillings and sixpence to go in. The name of the club came from the fact that it was started by eleven musicians. They used to gather there to play the kind of music they liked for themselves and their friends. But its popularity and reputation grew so rapidly that very soon they took a manager into partnership to run it on commercial lines. If Feldmans had fitted me like a well-made off-the-peg suit, then the Eleven was made-to-measure. I drank in the basement atmosphere, the narrow passages and subdued lighting. I was at once at home with the relaxed feeling and 'gone' on the hot music. The musicians played what they liked as they liked – but it was mostly bebop and a lot more frantic than at Feldmans. There were no requests and there was no programme. If the music failed to please . . . well, you didn't have to stay. But there were hundreds like myself who liked the music. So we stayed while some left. And the more we stayed the more the Club Eleven crept into the marrow of our bones.

The clientele was crazy, really gone. From the Bohemian lunatic fringe to small-time crooks and Americans on furlough. From musicians dropping by for the fun of the ride to teenage girls following the pack. I began going regularly to the club and slowly my whole wardrobe went through a transformation.

I no longer bought my clothes from old-established suburban stores, but from the new, gaudily decorated, men's-wear shops springing up almost overnight in the Charing Cross Road district. As far as my meagre wages allowed I bought drape-style suits, *crêpe* shoes, bright ties and coloured shirts. I had my hair styled in a crew-cut and started to drink regularly for the first time. Slang was never absent from my speech. All coloured people had become spades; men were cats and girls chicks; dull people were square and smart people cool.

The popularity of the new club soared to fantastic heights. As they said in the theatre across the way, when business was extra good, it was a 'smasheroo'. The club was mentioned in the press. Its reputation as a centre for genuine jazz was second to none. And inevitably of course it began opening every night of the week. That was the moment for me to drop Feldmans completely. Already, in a few short months, I was finding it juvenile and something for the kids from the suburbs.

Night after night I left my work to go to a milk bar for a snack and then on to the Club Eleven. There, with a 'coke' in one hand and a cigarette in the other, feet tapping away, I felt like a king. I grew to be on nodding terms with a number of musicians and regular clients, and when the club closed for the night and I walked alone to the railway station, homewards bound, I walked in a cloud of contentment.

My parents could hardly fail to notice these changes – the new clothes, the strange speech and mannerisms, and the late hours. But my father was in bad health and my mother had more important things to worry about. Apart from the occasional warning, which I promptly forgot, nothing was ever said or done. One night, sitting alone eating when I had arrived home in the small hours, I heard my mother come down the stairs into the kitchen. She was wearing her old dressing-gown and she looked tired and aged. 'Be a good boy, Ray,' she said. And the way she said it I almost wanted to get up and hold her tight. But I laughed. I said I *was* a good boy. And I promised to get home a little earlier in future. Yet even as I said it I knew I had no intention of keeping my word. Poor mother. She didn't even shout too much when I showed her hire-purchase accounts that had fallen behind and asked her to pay for me. She paid, and that was that. Like I said, she was my mother – and mothers have the craziest way of doing things for the children they've borne.

22

And children have the craziest way of paying them back . . .

Pete had completely dropped away from the new club. He never quite managed to make it with the people who went there. My ego jumped. Now *Pete* was a drag and *I* was the cool cat. I told him so and he grew angry. After that we never talked much. I was nearly eighteen by now. My grammar school, dad's pet fish, his prize hens, the people I worked with and even the friends I had made at Feldmans – they belonged to another world.

Raymond Thorp, *Viper* (1956)

1953: Hunting Dogs

I spent my first savings on a suit for the Teddy Boy era. It was navy blue hopsack, and it cost £7-7s.6d. in Stoke Newington High Street. With it went the obligatory suedes with thick spongy soles, brothel-creepers, blue of course, and a black bootlace tie. I wore the outfit on my first date, with a girl in Hornsey, and it poured with rain. My hair hung down while the suit was shrinking on my back as we made our way to a dance in Highgate at a place called Holy Joe's, or St Joseph's Church, near where my father had died.

This was sophistication, though the kid in me was not buried far beneath the surface. On evenings when the old lady had to work late, I would be Michael's protector. Despite my age, we still shared the same bed, and we would lie there and listen to Valentine Dyall, 'The Man in Black', reading a series of radio horror stories with the blankets pulled over our heads to keep out the bogeyman.

At the same time, I was trying to train myself in all things that interested men. The bridge between boyhood and manhood for me was motorbikes. There was a boy down the road who kept his bike in the bedroom. He had trays for the oil laid out across the floor – so, he said, he could do an oil change and have his girl at the same time. To the rest of us in Finsbury Park this seemed to be the essence of cool. I swore that one day I too would own one of these machines. In the meantime I rode pillion.

I left the railway when I got a job at the cartoon animation studio W. M. Larkins, with a fashionable address in Mayfair. I had shown some of my art-school drawings to the boss, Peter Sachs, a Jew who had escaped from Nazi Germany, and he let me in on the ground floor as a messenger boy. If things turned out well, he said, he would allow me to mix colours.

Colour-mixing was not to last long, for it turned out that I was partially colour blind, and certainly not up to the subtlety of animation. I was all right when I stuck to blues, reds and yellows, but my browns, beiges and greens were less secure. I went back to running messages, too inexperienced in their eyes to be taken into the darkroom. The only photography I had ever encountered was sitting with my sister in Jerome's in the Holloway Road, having our portraits taken for the family.

Mayfair touched me in other ways. I became very conscious of my appearance. I was not conceited, but I fretted about not having enough money to buy clothes. Walking to work from the Underground at Piccadilly, I would catch sight of myself in the window of the Rolls-Royce showroom as I turned into Charles Street and go to work on the arrangement of my collar and cuffs. I also remember swinging round into Berkeley Square and smelling the scent of that wonderful shop Moyses Stevens, looking at the orchids in the window with water running down it. It made me aware of a different world, a world far removed from my biking mates and the boys from The Bunk, who were now emerging from their first confinements in corrective or penal institutions. Mayfair held out the promise of escape from Finsbury Park and all that.

But not yet. Biking was still in, and I bought a Valacetta 250, with a fish tail and girder forks, which would throb along at 50 miles per hour. I felt like an ace at Brooklands, with no such things as crash helmets in those days. We would drive out in formation on Sundays, down the A10 to Collier's End, where we would dive off an old survival dinghy from the war into the ice-cold river. We would eat some continental food at a café on the way home and then bomb the rest of the way up the arterial road to Finsbury Park. We were no Hell's Angels, and they were great days of freedom, with friendships quite different from the relationship I had with my old Bunk boys, the hunting dogs, who were now hanging out in packs looking for trouble.

Despite my biking friends, I still needed the mad dogs. Intimidation was always strong in Finsbury Park, and there was a force-field all the time trying to draw you into something mischievous. I avoided thieving, but gang warfare was a stronger temptation. There was suppressed aggression and a lot of resentment in me. I wanted the respect given to those serious street fighters – the swaggering élite of the neighbourhood – who wouldn't let you disown the tribe. At the pubs in the Seven Sisters Road the tribe had a name – The Guvnors. In a corralled car, the tribe would strut their stuff at the dance-halls or harry the whores in Shaftesbury Avenue. One or two did become ponces, but the sexual level then was little more than a flick through the carefully censored nudes in Health and Efficiency. On Saturday nights the tribe would turn up in force at the Royal dance-hall in Tottenham. A refusal to dance from a girl was hard to bear in front of this mob, and you'd hope for salvation in the rumbling sound at the start of a good punch-up. That would make the evening a winner and set up an electric air when you walked in next week.

With The Guvnors, though they were predators themselves, you felt safe from other predators, like the bigger, older criminals who lurked in the background of our neighbourhood, and the police. The police were our natural enemies. If you were caught in a cul-de-sac by the coppers, as I was on one occasion, you could be sure to be on light duties for the next week. All this, of course, was just before the first wave of coloured immigration in Britain. In some ways we were like white negroes, the out groups. Though we were a funny kind of negro, since most of us were as bigoted and racist as they come.

When it came to the time for national service, I was a pretty fractured personality. I had come to like my job in Mayfair, and the people there were kind to me, but I felt as if they could see 'Finsbury Park' indelibly written across my forehead and 'working class' on the other side of my head. I couldn't see how I was ever going to be much more than a messenger in the world. I was sure of one thing. I didn't want to go into the army and be pushed around. A few years of Bill Haley had taken all enthusiasm for the soldier's life out of me. So I smarmed my way into the air force.

Don McCullin, *Unreasonable Behaviour: An Autobiography*, with Lewis Chester (1990)

1954: Back to the Music Halls

When they first appear on the stage – any music-hall stage in England – a flashing smile visible above the inevitable midnight blue 'uniform', you must sit in the gallery to learn what popularity means in 1954.

They are mostly young girls up there, splashing in a crazy pool of adoration. Usually, they are 'unescorted', sitting hunched forward, eager little hands squashing shiny faces, half-open mouths emitting a strange, a continuous symphony of sound. The staple sound is an animal expression of joy – half shriek, half sigh. And the shrieks are bridged by a humming noise, accompanied by hugging movements, as if a running motor were waiting for the accelerator to be pressed down – by a remembered note of music, or a word, from the singer on the stage. And when the song is ended, the arms go into action, flapping and tearing the air. Hands are whipped together. And above the shrieks, and the moans, and the sighs, you hear the frenzied appeals: 'Oh, Frankie!'; 'Oh, Dickie!'; 'Oh—!'

Appeals for what? They cannot explain. After the show they run screeching down the gallery stairs to bunch in front of the stage door, giggling, chanting for the appearance of their favourite, the motor of agitation still running. And with the girls – the pale, bespectacled girls of 13 – the loud, shining-eyed girls of 16, whose lipstick invades the skin above the outline of their lips – the trim, well-dressed girls of 17 and 18, who already suspect the source of their emotion, and do not shout quite as much as the others – with them you see women who could be their mothers, and boys who could be their brothers, pretending to be aloof, but pushing for a place in front when nobody is looking.

The new singing idols are not – like their predecessors – Americans. They are British. But their records sell by the hundred thousands. And they draw packed houses wherever they appear. On Friday and Saturday nights, when Dickie Valentine, or Frankie Vaughan, or David Whitfield are appearing at the local Empire, policemen are assigned to the special job of controlling the crowds of youngsters, whose ambition is to get close to their idol, to speak to him, to see his dressing room, to get a signed autograph – ('To Joan with Love', 'Best regards to Jean', 'Good Luck, Doris!') – even to be kissed.

For the secret of Britain's new singing idols – who in the past year have moved alongside the Americans, the Johnnie Rays and Frankie Lanes, in popularity and provocation of juvenile frenzy – is that they are accessible. The other stars (like Marlene Dietrich) were inaccessible. They sang in the spotlight, and then the spotlight turned black and the apparition, glamorous and unattainable, disappeared.

What the new idols have in common, besides a voice that sells records, is a humbleness of background which appeals to the fans in the gallery. The new idols see everybody. They answer every letter personally, sign every proffered autograph book, kiss every offered cheek, listen to every problem – every confession. The girls write to them in lonely anguish by the thousand. From a two-minute meeting they concoct an elaborate fantasy. They turn to their Frankies and Dickies, as to the father who ignores them, the lover they have yet to meet.

The new idols know this. They know that the 'Common Touch' is an even greater asset than their voice. And they know the swollen head is their greatest enemy. 'If you're swollen-headed they know it,' says Dickie Valentine, whose record 'All the Time and Everywhere', has sold 100,000 copies.

'Be nice to people on the way up, I say. Without the kids, you are just nowhere. If the kids don't come, what's the good?'

Valentine, tousle-haired and shy, has the expressionless, one-dimensional, strip-cartoon type of face that is the bobbysoxers prevalent idea of male beauty, and a slightly hoarse speaking voice that adds to the attraction. He has made the difficult crossing from band singer (with Ted Heath) to top-of-the-bill variety artist in a few months.

Of the four singers discussed here (and there are others equally popular), Valentine probably has the most striking 'act'. He starts with a chain of songs, crooned in a mellow, contemplative, singing-only-to-you-style. Then he follows it with startlingly good impressions of Mario Lanza, Billy Daniels, Johnnie Ray and Edward G. Robinson.

Born in St Pancras 25 years ago, Valentine has worked as a packer in a Manchester dress shop, a page boy at the London Palladium (where he was fired for being cheeky to the head doorman), a call boy at Her Majesty's Theatre. There is an inhibited, withheld, quality in his stage personality when he sings his songs. 'I'm a Jekyll and Hyde, you see,' he explains in his hoarse, Cockney-tinged whisper. 'As Dickie Valentine, I feel shy, and handcuffed. What am I doing up here on this big stage, all by myself, I ask myself. Why me? It's when I'm imitating others, when I'm not myself, that I can throw myself about the stage.'

Where Valentine makes his impact by barely moving as he croons, Frankie Vaughan appears to be an unashamed extrovert. With his crisp, black, curly hair, and permanently toothy grin, he brings some of the old-time top-hat-and-cane atmosphere to his act. He makes the young shout by shouting louder than anybody else. With calculated bodily contortions, ecstatic bending of knees, undulating of shoulders (male versions of sexy feminine movements), he looks like Victor Mature giving an imitation of Al Jolson.

Passionately ambitious, and preoccupied with his career, Frankie Vaughan practises a jazzed-up neo-Mammyism – a marriage of old-time showmanship and modern bobby-sox appeal. Trying to escape from the Jolson–Cantor influence, he has searched for, and found, 'gimmicks' to give his act individuality.

He growls and howls and puts a 'yip' at the end of some of his notes. "I'm not a singer," he says. "I want to be an entertainer. I want to leave them happy, and excited. Because that's how I feel myself when I'm on the stage. They say I'm *hexy*."

The son of a Liverpool upholsterer, Vaughan was born 26 years ago, and discovered his voice while singing in a synagogue. As a youth, he won the

Lancashire Boxing Cup, and played centre-forward for the National Association of Boys' Clubs. He is still so interested in youth clubs that he makes money for them by selling his kisses (at a bob a time) to the feverish fans who invade his dressing room.

To everything Vaughan does he lends a sense of personal dedication. He won a scholarship at 19 to the Leeds College of Art. In the Army, he sang to the troops, and discovered that singing gave him more personal satisfaction than drawing. But it was as a £6 10s a week art teacher that he had his first professional audition.

Today, he can earn £1,000 a month. He has four secretaries, to answer the 150 letters he gets every day, and to run his 10,000-strong fan club. Yet, when touring the provinces as a bill-topper, he still stays at £4-a-week theatrical digs. He has no personal manager – no fast-talking publicity man. The former art teacher is the most communicative, the most articulate of the idols.

"It's like art, this business," he says. "Know your limitations. Never sing anything beyond your range. There's colour in presentation, composition in the continuity of the act, subtlety in leaving an act when it is ripe," he explains – more to reassure himself than to inform the interviewer. Then he goes on stage – gyrating, howling, yipping – a worried artist in a showman's loud disguise.

Another disguised intellectual (who, according to the record sellers, hasn't yet reached the same peak of popularity as the others) is Dennis Lotis. He sings with Ted Heath's band. However, like his former colleagues Lita Roza and Dickie Valentine, he hopes to "go out on his own" soon.

Dennis Lotis is a band singer. Nevertheless, when he sings few people dance. They crowd round the bandstand – the boys with their mouths open, the girls with their eyes closed, as he gives them the rhythmic numbers ("the Uh-Ah kind of number," he calls them), which Heath prefers him to sing. (Lotis himself would rather sing sentimental ballads.)

Rather slight, dark, sensitive, protecting himself with an armour of self-depreciation, 26-year-old Lotis comes from South Africa. He is the son of a Canterbury-born mother, and a Greek father, who "like most Greeks, owned a restaurant". In Johannesburg, he made his first broadcast at the age of nine, and felt himself attracted to films. ("I distinctly remember carrying a little picture of Jessie Matthews around with me as a kid.") At 13, when his voice broke, he ran away from school, to become a bus conductor.

In England, he made his début in a Henry Hall guest night, then joined Ted Heath's band in 1950. He hasn't a very strong voice. The girls go for the terse, jerky delivery – the suggestion of sex with a dose of humour, the Something that isn't quite there, which every girl thinks she could discover if she only knew him better.

One girl recently threatened to jump over a cliff if he didn't walk home with her. His wife, a coolly beautiful ex-model from South Africa, sorts out his letters, and acts as his personal manager. Unlike some of the new idols, he makes no secret of being married. Like most of them, he struggles to get away from American influences, from the danger of becoming a "British Johnnie Ray", or a "British Frank Sinatra" – labels which lift a singer to a brash, but very brief, prosperity.

Perhaps the most successful of the new idols is David Whitfield, the Golden Boy of Decca. He has sold a million records in the last 15 months – an achievement which even outstrips those of the most popular American singers. Whitfield is not a crooner. He is a tenor, who actually sounds as everybody thinks they sound in the echoing privacy of their own bathrooms.

A tall, well-built ex-sailor, with a blond mane of hair, Whitfield has embraced sincerity as his 'gimmick'. In many of his songs (such as 'I Believe' and 'The Book') he communicates directly with God, which tends to make him look a little like an overgrown choir-boy, and lends his act a vocal Billy Graham quality that endears it, not only to the young girls, but to their mothers as well.

Whitfield, who comes from a family of eight, started work in his native Hull at 13. He sang in the choir at school, and progressed to singing at vicarage parties. At 17, he joined the Navy, and stayed there for seven years. He sang so much, and so often, while on service, that his shipmates finally told him that he ought to go on the stage. "You've got to know somebody," the lad from Hull said, and forgot all about it. Now he takes lessons from Professor Cunelli, at Wigmore Hall, and fights the influence of the late Richard Tauber, whose voice resembles his own closely – except that the accent is Hull instead of Vienna.

Whitfeld is so unconscious of being a celebrity that interviewing him is impossible. He's just having a chat – like. "I've got a job at home, you know," he will tell you. "Cement loading. When I got this chance – singing you know – t'manager said, 'Have a go, lad!' Now I know t'job is always waiting for me if t'singing career doesn't go too well. But it goes all right. This Cunelli bloke took me to a doctor t'other day. 'You've got the biggest pair of vocal chords I've ever seen,' he says to me. 'You've got t'heart of a lion and a chest like a bull'."

And then Whitfeld squashes out his cigarette, downs his pint of bitter, roars with laughter, and goes on to sing 'The Book' with glimmering passion in his cornflower-blue eyes. And in the audience, mothers sigh with their daughters, overwhelmed by the fairheaded lad who makes religion so lovely, and so cosy.

"At home they used to tell me I was better than Tauber," he says, returning to his dressing room. "'Well,' I said, 'let them say so.' Now t'kids tear my clothes. I don't mind, really. It comes off Income Tax, for a start. I want to get a Cadillac – just black. Nothing fancy."

And then, in answer to my question, he echoes Dickie Valentine's sentiment. "It's no good getting a big head," he says. "It gets you a bad name, you see. They'd be saying, 'There goes that big-headed Whitfield.' Well – you see what I mean, don't you?"

The popularity of the new idols has had far-reaching effects in the entertainment world. Not only has it made gramophone records one of the boom industries. It has brought audiences back to the music halls which the nude revues had threatened to close down. Today, a theatre manager knows that it isn't only an American singer who can draw the crowds, topping the bill. The boys from Hull, St. Pancras, Johannesburg and Liverpool – groaning sentiments of love eternal to the young girlhood of the nation – do it just as well.

Picture Post, 7 August 1954

1955: Is Johnnie Ray a Mass Hypnotist?

Is Johnnie Ray – the singer who flays audiences of 2,000 at a time with an emotional hot live wire – a mass hypnotist?

How else does he rouse to a delighted, squealing frenzy the thousands of young girls who mob him when he appears, try to strip him of his clothing and pelt him with flowers?

How else could his voice get hundreds of youngsters jumping up and down like a jack-in-the-box?

Why else should normal girls who hear and see him break into uncontrollable body-twisting, sobs and gasps.

This slim, pallid singer has worked his musical mesmerism on girls in Scotland, the Provinces, Australia, America.

He worked it even in Mexico, where sobbing senoritas didn't understand a word of what he sang.

As he sings, Ray, a twitching bundle of nerves from every toothache in the world, stamps his feet, writhes, wriggles, pants and contorts like a pillow-case full of pythons.

He cries like a peeler in an onion-soup factory. His tears have the potency of pure nitro-glycerine.

Johnnie Ray's fans don't understand their actions. They just say, 'He SENDS us.'

Johnnie Ray himself doesn't really know why he prompts such a frenzy.

So the *Sunday Pictorial* asked its famous Bobby-Sox Doctor, a distinguished medical man, whose explanation of teenage behaviour opened the way to a new understanding.

The doctor last week attended Johnnie Ray performances at the Palladium.

At firsthand he watched the audience in the gallery, in the circle, in the stalls.

He met and talked with Johnnie Ray before the crooner went on.

He waited for him with more probing questions when the exhausted, limp, wringing-wet star managed to escape from his demanding fans.

The doctor's conclusions are startling. 'I waved my hand in front of a girl's face and she was completely unconscious of what I was doing,' he reported.

Is Johnnie Ray using a form of hypnotism? The doctor says: 'When a person uses a form of communication which is not directed to the intelligence – and when this communication produces uncontrolled physical effects – then that is hypnotism.'

Johnnie Ray certainly does that!

There is no doubt whatsoever in the doctor's mind that the effect of Ray on his fans is physical.

He carefully noted that Johnnie's fans were alternately rapt, flushed and entranced.

If any girl were to behave alone as she did in the mass audience, then a doctor would diagnose her condition as hysteria.

A stethoscope applied to the chest of any one of those deliriously carried-away girls would have recorded considerable changes.

Why? Because hypnosis short-circuits the intelligence and goes right to the control-room of all body functions.

Baffled parents – startled by the transformation Johnnie Ray induces in their daughters – can find relief in the doctor's assurance that: 'It is unlikely that Johnnie Ray does any harm. I think the girls feel better after a session with him.'

Yet this disturbing thought remains in the doctor's mind: 'Ray is a child playing with the key which can unlock, control, or divert the HIDDEN impulses in human beings.'

Johnnie is a sort of modern medicine man of music.

'His fans,' says the doctor, 'are mainly young people who feel they are tiny cogs in a huge machine, people who live from pay day to pay day.

'In the main, they are sufferers from the 20th-century complaint – Suburban Blues.

'Their employers think of them as "hands". They are growing up in a society which is failing to integrate the lives of us all.

'The unifying influence – which in other centuries was provided, say, by the Church – is less effective now.'

What Ray does is to break down self-consciousness, to make his fans feel that they are no longer mere cogs, no longer alone.

Bernard McElwaine, *Sunday Pictorial*, 1 May, 1955

1956: The Creation of My Recordings

I have been asked many times, 'Where did you get the idea to write that song, Chuck?' Offhand, I wouldn't know, but I always refer to the story within the song, which usually recalls my inspiration. Or sometimes the melodic lines bring me in sync with the time and place where the tune got its origin. The embarrassing thing is that sometimes when I have been asked about a song's origin I have made up a reason that is dramatic enough to get by the question. But the origins have varied under different circumstances or with different interviewers. In the pages that follow I'll recall whatever I can about a few of my songs' *true* origins. They appear in the order, according to my records and memory, that I recorded them.

Writing a song can be a peculiar task. So much time can pass during the intervals I would be putting a song together that each time I'd get back to it, the tune or story it was following would likely take an entirely different route.

The kind of music I liked then, thereafter, right now and forever, is the kind I heard when I was a teenager. So the guitar styles of Carl Hogen, T-Bone Walker, Charlie Christian and Elmore James, not to leave out many of my peers who I've heard on the road, must be the total of what is called Chuck Berry's style. So far as the Chuck Berry guitar intro that identifies many of my songs, it is only back to the future of what came in the past. As you know, and I believe it must be true, 'There is nothing new under the sun.' So don't blame me for being first, just let it last.

To quote the lyrics the genius Ray Charles sang, 'Sometimes I get sideways and stay up all night with a tune . . . I like what I am doing and sho' hope it don't end too soon.' The nature and backbone of my beat is boogie and the muscle of my music is melodies that are simple. Call it what you may: jive, jazz, jump, swing, soul, rhythm, rock, or even punk, it's still boogie so far as I'm connected with it. When I can't connect to it, I have no right to dispute its title. When it's boogie, but with an alien title, the connection is still boogie and my kind of music.

What about slow songs, love songs, or blues? I like! In fact, I love love songs when loving my love, just as I dig blues when I'm blue. The thing about a love song is that one is not likely to be able to compose a real good one if one is not endowed with that magnificent feeling during the process of writing it. So far in my career, I have felt or lived what I've written and have yet to mix dollars with desire – or better still, commerce with passion. I've been in love much more than twice, but in no period did I have the least desire to expose these beautiful intimacies in a song. Those artists that improvise or register their lovely feelings in lyrics may be blessed with the formula for expressing love, but I am cursed with only the fantasies and feelings thereof. I have composed so few songs about love, if any really were, but instead have had fairly good success with songs of novelties and feelings of fun and frolic in the lyrics of my compositions.

So here are the stories of how and why a few of my earlier compositions came about. The entire catalogue of all my songs will be in a *Chuck Berry Songbook* that will follow this one with much of when, where and who were involved in the recordings, plus information on every concert I ever played.

'Maybellene' was my effort to sing country-western, which I had always liked. The Cosmo clubgoers didn't know any of the words to those songs, which gave me a chance to improvise and add comical lines to the lyrics. 'Mountain Dew', 'Jambalaya' and 'Ida Red' were the favorites of the Cosmo audience, mainly because of the honky-tonk gestures I inserted while singing the songs.

'Maybellene' was written from the inspiration that grew out of the country song 'Ida Red'. I'd heard it sung long before when I was a teenager and thought it was rhythmic and amusing to hear. I'd sung it in the yard gatherings and parties around home when I was first learning to strum the guitar in my high-school days. Later in life, at the Cosmo Club, I added my bit to the song and still enjoyed a good response so I coined it a good one to sing.

Later when I learned, upon entering a recording contract, that original songs written by a person were copyrighted and had various rewards for the composer, I welcomed the legal arrangement of the music business. I enjoyed creating songs of my own and was pleased to learn I could have some return from the effort. When I wrote 'Maybellene' I had originally titled it 'Ida May', but when I took the song to Chess Records I was advised to change its title. That was simple because the rhythmic swing of the three syllables fit with many other names. The music progression itself is close to the feeling that I received when hearing the song 'Ida Red', but the story in 'Maybellene' is completely different.

The body of the story of 'Maybellene' was composed from memories of high school and trying to get girls to ride in my 1934 V-8 Ford. I even put seat-covers in it to accommodate the girls that the football players would take riding in it while I was in class. Just to somehow explain the origin of the lyrics of 'Maybellene', it could have been written from a true experience, recalling my high-school days thus:

> As I was watching from the windowsill,
> I saw pretty girls in my dream De Ville
> Riding with the guys, up and down the road
> Nothin' I wanted more'n be in that Ford
> Sittin' in class while they takin' rides
> Guys in the middle, girls on both sides.
>
> > Oh Pretty girl, why can't it be true
> > Oh Pretty girl, that it's me with you
> > You let football players do things I want to do.
>
> Girls in my dream car, door to door
> My Ford bogged down wouldn't hold no more
> Ring goes the last school bell of the day
> Hurrying outside, see 'em pullin' away
> Backseat full even sittin' on the hood
> I knew that was doing my motor good.
>
> > Oh Pretty girl, why can't it be true
> > Oh Pretty girl, that it's me with you
> > You let football players do things I want to do.
>
> The guys come back after all that fun
> Walking with the pretty girls, one by one
> My heart hangin' heavy like a ton a lead
> Feelin' so down I can't raise my head

> Just like swallowin' up a medicine pill
> Watching them girls from the windowsill.

These lines were written just to provide an example of the true depiction of an event. This differs from the improvised writing of a song, which does not necessarily, if ever, coincide with a true story but mostly goes along the pattern or close to the train of events. I have never, in my life, met or even known of any woman named 'Maybellene'. The name actually was first brought to my knowledge from a storybook, when I was in the third grade, of animals who bore names. Along with Tom the cat and Donald the duck, there was Maybellene the cow. Not offending anybody, I thought, I named my girl character after a cow. In fact, the girl was to be two-timing, so it would have been worse if I had used a popular name.

When I wrote 'Maybellene' I had never been in a funeral or parade which would have been the only opportunity I could have had to ride in a Cadillac, though I had sat in a new one on occasion.

Cadillacs don't like Fords rolling side by side because they hide half their beauty so I cause the Caddy to pull 'up to a hundred and four, my Ford got hot and wouldn't do no more/Created clouds detected rain/Elated motor to the passing lane/Heat gone down – highway sound/Caddy and the Ford bound dead downtown.' And so many times have guys' girls done unfavourable things that you wonder 'why can't 'cha be true . . . doin' the thing you used to do?'

The lyrics really explain the story. In fact, it was so popular that after five of the song's twenty-five years, I added another verse as I sing it on stage:

> I peeped in the mirror at the top of the hill
> 'Twas just like swallowing a medicine pill
> First thing I saw was that Cadillac grille
> Doing a hundred and ten dropping off that hill
> An uphill curve and downhill stretch,
> Me and that Cadillac was neck and neck.

Chuck Berry, *The Autobiography* (1987)

1956: Please Please Please

We were working down in Tampa when Clint called to tell us that King wanted us in Cincinnati to record right away. We hadn't heard from anyone there since Ralph Bass signed us the morning after he'd seen us at Sawyer's

35

Lake. Since then we'd been working clubs around Tampa and Jacksonville, and we were beginning to wonder if he'd really liked us.

The club work in Florida was all right, but the club owners had a meal ticket system that could wear you out. At the beginning of, say, a week-long engagement, they gave us a meal ticket to their place. With what we were making, that meal ticket could be our margin of profit on the gig, but there was a catch: if they served breakfast at six o'clock in the morning, you better be there at six o'clock in the morning if you want to eat, even if your show the night before had lasted until 2 a.m. I missed a lot of meals that way.

We drove the four hundred miles from Tampa to Macon, stopped and picked up some money there, and continued for another six hundred miles to Cincinnati in a station wagon that had *The Upsetters* painted on the side. Clint had let Little Richard use the car before, and now we were jammed into it with all our clothes and instruments. We rode all night, stopping only for gas. It was the first time out of the South for any of us, and when we got to the outskirts of Cincinnati somebody came out from King and led us to the hotel, a place called the Manse. It was a fleabag, but it was better than anything we'd stayed in before.

Instead of sleeping we went straight over to King Records, situated in an old icehouse at the end of a dead-end street. They did everything there, recording, mastering, pressing, shipping, even printing the album covers. At one end of the building, facing the street, there was a big opening where the ice used to come down; now the rollers that shot out the ice were shooting out the records, big boxes of albums and 78s rolling down the chute. An entrance on the other side led into the studio, consisting of some microphones and a plate-glass window separating this area from the control booth, and a little mixing room behind that.

We had never seen an operation like this before and walked around the place in a daze. From the studio you could go into the stockroom, where they pressed the records. We watched them lay small balls of soft vinyl on a sort of platter, and then the press would come down and mash them into records. They were just about to move entirely from the big, old 78s to 45s.

While we were being shown around, we were introduced to Earl Bostic. He was fixing to cut that day, and he invited us to watch. Back in the control room we met Syd Nathan, who had started the company back in 1945. Syd was Little Caesar – short, fat, and smoked a big cigar. He yelled all the time in a big, hoarse voice, and everybody was afraid of him. Even though Syd didn't know one note from another, King had been successful in all kinds of music. In the country field they had Moon Mullican, Cowboy Copas,

36

Grandpa Jones, Hawkshaw Hawkins, and a lot more. In R & B instrumentals they had, besides Earl Bostic, Lucky Millinder, Tiny Bradshaw, Bill Doggett, and Big Jay McNeely. They had singers like Bullmoose Jackson, Wynonie Harris, Cleanhead Vinson and Little Willie John, and groups like the Midnighters, the Five Royales and Otis Williams and the Charms. Mr Nathan also had several companies that published most of the songs King recorded.

We were supposed to record the next day, but when we showed up we found out Hank Ballard and the Midnighters had come in unexpectedly. Everybody at the studio was tied up in a big meeting with them, so our session was postponed until the following day. When we showed up, Little Willie John had come in to record, and our session was put off again. Little Willie John was just a shade over five feet tall, and he looked really sharp. Later on he came to mean a lot to me, but when I met him that day, I was thinking more about whether my own session would ever come to pass.

When it finally did, on February 4, 1956, I almost wished it hadn't. We were set up in the studio, with Mr Nathan and Gene Redd, the musical director, sitting in the control booth. Through the glass we could see Ralph Bass and the engineer, too. I didn't like the idea of a musical director because I felt I knew my music better than anyone else. Besides, our stuff wasn't put together in the conventional way. We used a lot of seventh chords. Fats played keyboards and voiced chords with the sevenths instead of the triad. And we used sevenths for passing chords, too. Playing in the key of G, for example, we might want to go from a G chord to a C chord, and to make the change we might play a G7 as the harmonic transition.

They rolled the tape, and we ripped into 'Please' in our style. When we were halfway through, Mr Nathan suddenly jumped up from the board.

'What's that? What the hell are they doing? Stop the tape,' he yelled. 'That doesn't sound right to my ears.' He was in a rage. 'What's going on here?' He turned on Gene Redd, who just shrugged because he didn't understand it, either. Then he turned to Ralph Bass. 'I sent you out to bring back some talent, and this is what I hear. The demo was awful, and this is worse. I don't know why I have you working here. Nobody wants to hear that noise.'

'It's a good song, Syd,' Ralph said. 'Give them a chance.'

'A good song?' He looked at Ralph like Ralph was crazy. 'It's a stupid song. It's got only one word in it. I've heard enough.' He stormed out of the room and up the stairs to his office.

We were frozen in the studio. We had made it through only half a track of our first professional recording session, and the owner of the company had

37

walked out in the middle saying we were so bad he couldn't use us. We were thinking, 'Oh, Lord, we're fixing to get sent away, and we just got here.' Gene came from behind the glass to talk to us.

'Can't you do it some other way?' he asked.

'That's the way we've always done it,' I said.

'But Mr Nathan doesn't like it,' he said.

'Mr Nathan doesn't understand it,' I said. He looked disturbed at that. 'Everybody's music can't be alike, Mr Redd. If everybody comes up here and goes to cutting alike, then nobody's going to do anything.'

I showed him the chord changes on the piano and explained to him what we were doing. Once he understood, and it made sense to him, he said he would go and tell Mr Nathan that they should try it, even if it sounded funny. He was gone a long time. While we were waiting, hanging out in the hall, we could hear them yelling upstairs behind closed doors. When Gene came back, all he said was, 'Okay, we're going to cut it.' When Mr Nathan never showed up again, we couldn't help feeling that the session wasn't legit, but we went ahead with it anyway. We cut 'Please', 'Why Do You Do Me Like You Do', 'I Feel That Old Feeling Coming On' and 'I Don't Know' – in spite of all the turmoil that day.

Usually, King pressed and shipped a record within days after it was recorded. Before we left Cincinnati we saw a handful of 78 rpm pressings of 'Please', but as soon as we got back to Macon we got worried. We heard that Ralph Bass had been fired and King wasn't going to release the record. Mr Nathan hated the master as much as he had hated the demo. Mr Brantly was on the phone to him every day for nearly a month. At the end of February, Mr Nathan told him that against his better judgement he was going to put the record out on his Federal label. So on March 3, 1956, 'Please Please Please' was released. Eventually, it sold a million copies.

James Brown: The Godfather of Soul, with Bruce Tucker (1986)

two

1956–8

'A mass fit of screaming hysteria'

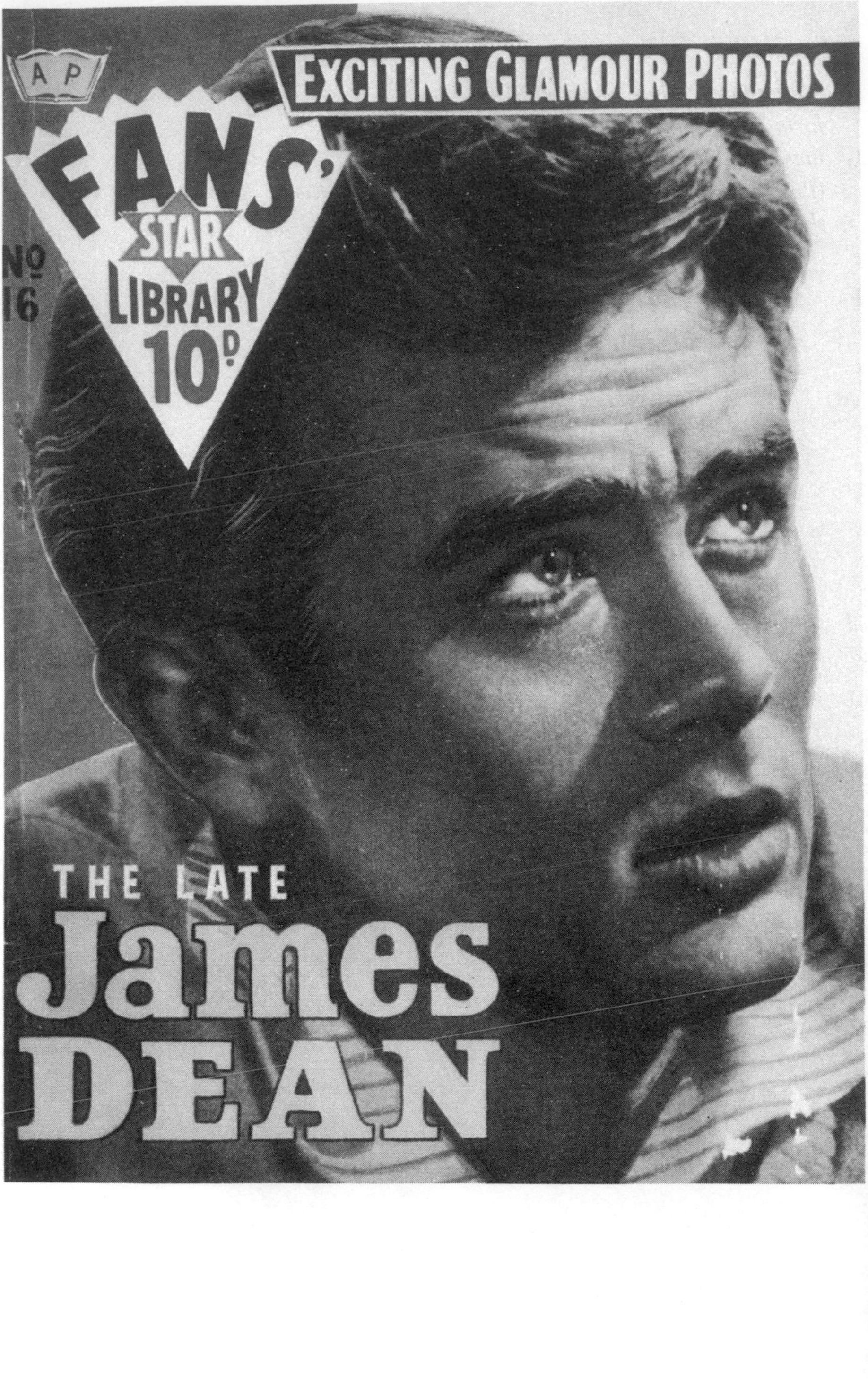
AP
EXCITING GLAMOUR PHOTOS
FANS'
STAR
LIBRARY
10D
No
16
THE LATE
James
DEAN

'*James Dean, Elvis, Jackson Pollock, Jack Kerouac. An idea was beginning to form in a few fitful heads that you could be famous, famous in the sense of mass popularity, and still make art. The equation of art + fame + Popness (Popness = fame now!) was a fantasy that many dreamed about so fiercely that it became true.*'

David Dalton, 'Mr Mojo Rising' (1991)

With the success of 'Heartbreak Hotel' during the first half of 1956 Elvis Presley arrived in both Britain and America – not just a pop star, but a harbinger of the new youth-inspired consumer age. As the *Daily Mirror* put it, in the first flush of breathy excitement, 'He's riding the crest of a teenage tidal wave.' Pop had become a mainstream event; by 1958, the idea of youth marketing – 'The Teenage Consumer', as it was called by market scientist Mark Abrams – was well established on both sides of the Atlantic.

This was an unprecedented phenomenon that left the young man at its centre breathless. As he said at the time, 'I can't believe all this has happened to me. I just hope it lasts.' By the end of 1956, manager Tom Parker had refused all access to Elvis. Alfred Wertheimer's eyewitness account of that first summer of success, snatched before the shutters came down, runs counter to the Elvis myths that proliferated in his absence. As far as his records were concerned, Presley knew exactly what he was doing.

What Elvis did was to fuse raw country with the Dionysia of black American music – sex, repetition and the big beat – and put both into the heart of white American culture. This combination was (and remains) so powerful that it was seen by hostile commentators at the time as the work of the devil. In the same way, Presley and the other musicians that came to prominence in his wake – wild men like Jerry Lee Lewis and Little Richard – struggled to reconcile the power of their performances with their religious backgrounds.

Little Richard, perhaps the greatest rocker ever, took a thinly disguised black, queer flamboyance into the heart of the American entertainment industry and the extract here from his autobiography is an unusually frank account of the sex in rock 'n' roll. In 1957, though, he gave up rock 'n' roll and all that came with it to become a preacher. This tension is also captured by Nick Tosches' transcription of the infamous conversation that occurred during the recording of 'Great Balls of Fire', as Lewis yells, 'Man, I've got the devil in me!'

1956 was the year not only of Elvis but also of James Dean – the twin spearheads of the American teenage. If Elvis epitomized sex, Dean embodied that existential post-war anomie, and reintroduced the Romantic ideal of early death into pop culture – an ideal which, like Dean's image, has remained in pop ever since. His contemporary impact in the UK can be gauged by the *Picture Post* feature from the last year of that magazine's life (a casualty of the pop era which it valiantly attempted to document).

43

'A great change suddenly came over London at that time,' Bernard Kops wrote. 'The American civilization had caught up with us. Everything was speeded and slicked up.' This Americanization was not without its critics. Kops himself wrote from within a generation of Sohoites – 'the gone poets' – who were displaced by the new pop culture, while Richard Hoggart put a sociological gloss on a more generally shared disapproval at the loss of pre-war certainties. However, the process was irreversible.

Britain had a domestic music industry, the pre-rock state of which is carefully explained by Alma Cogan's manager, Frank Cordell. After 1956, the 'Consumption Heroes' in Denmark Street decided to promote their own Elvis. 'The rise of Tommy Steele is the first British pop event,' writes George Melly in *Revolt into Style*; *Picture Post* was there. Steele's story was quickly fictionalized, most notably in *Expresso Bongo*, which, once filmed with Laurence Harvey and Cliff Richard, created some myths of its own: manager as Svengali; singer as barely articulate pop star; Denmark and Old Compton Streets as prime locations.

'Gold Pan Alley' is a rare example of writing from within the music industry. Apart from the Mass-Observation techniques of *Picture Post*, fifties pop was ill-served by contemporary commentators. Colin MacInnes's 'Pop Songs and Teenagers' (February 1958) is the first British article which attempts to take pop seriously on its own terms. An outsider himself, MacInnes was able to understand the codes that were so baffling to most adults. His conclusion remains as cogent now as it was then: 'England is, and always has been, a country infested with people who tell us what to do, but who very rarely seem to know what's going on.'

MacInnes converted his fascination with pop into that justly famous document of late fifties London, *Absolute Beginners*. The extract here plays with the very plasticity that was the hallmark of British pop. Written during 1958, the novel stands at that very moment when rock 'n' roll and its attendant subculture, the Edwardians, were over: Jerry Lee Lewis hounded out of England by Fleet Street papers like the *Daily Express*; Elvis in the army; third-generation Teds turning into racist thugs. Driving a Vespa, trying to make it as a photographer, MacInnes's hero looks forward to pop's modernist age.

1956: Rock Age Idol: That's Elvis

I have just escaped from a hurricane called Elvis Presley.

A few hints of what this tall, rangy singer is doing to young America with his rock-'n'-roll rhythm had already reached me.

* In Jacksonville, Florida, he had to be rescued from a crowd in a police wagon.
* In Wichita Falls, Texas, the fans broke every window in his car.
* In San Diego, California, a pack of teenage girls had covered his windscreen with phone numbers written in lipstick. . . .

But it was not until I went to the sun-baked desert town of Albuquerque, New Mexico, and saw what happened at two shows Elvis gave there that I realized what a frenzy this boy can stir up.

I've never seen anything like it.

When Elvis sings it isn't just a case of a few girls sighing and going swoony or stamping and shouting.

I saw him send 5,000 of them into a mass fit of screaming hysterics.

A few months ago Elvis was an unheard of youngster driving a lorry round his home town, Memphis, getting about £10 a week.

He made a few records: did one or two local TV shows. Routine, mildly successful sort of stuff.

He was spotted by showman Tom Parker who persuaded RCA, one of America's biggest recording companies, to sign him up.

Presley then cut his now famous 'Heartbreak Hotel' disc – and, bingo, the teenage tidal wave swept in.

'Heartbreak Hotel' was top of the hit parade seven weeks in a row and has sold the magical million.

And when Elvis goes to Las Vegas soon, a top hotel will pay him £8,000 for two weeks' work.

After that it's Hollywood with a contract for one film a year for seven years.

And all this for a lad of twenty-one who cannot read or write a note of music.

Why? Albuquerque gave me the answer.

It is a tough town. The people who live there are Westerners, Mexicans and Indians. They drag a living out of the hundreds of miles of desert around their back yards.

They are leathery and hard and their children are about as tough as they come.

So Parker, who is now Presley's manager, fixed up ten cops, ten ushers and two wrestlers to protect the singer. 'I hope that'll be enough,' he said.

A local helper chipped in to say: 'It had better be. If these kids run wild it will be like having 10,000 head of cattle coming at you.'

Hours before the show a queue of teenagers wound completely round the drill hall where it was to be held.

The girls wore suede-fringed jackets, check shirts, jeans held up by leather belts with silver buckles and moccasins.

The boys wore curly brimmed, flat-top, Western-style hats, jeans and high-heeled boots.

Directly the doors opened the girls rushed for the table where Presley pictures were being sold at 3s. 6d., 5s., and 7s. each.

'Gee, ain't he a living doll,' they sighed.

Then Elvis came in carrying his guitar and wearing a plum-coloured jacket and black trousers – with armed police guarding him on each side.

As he walked towards the stage the youngsters let out a scream that I thought would split the roof.

He has the build of a guardsman, an unbeatable DA haircut, sleepy eyes like Robert Mitchum and a handsome, olive-coloured face.

As he sings he stands with his legs wide apart. His whole body, from his shoulders to his feet, shakes in rhythm and every move draws a new deluge of howls from ecstatic fans.

A few seconds after he started sweat was dripping over his eyebrows and his hair was hanging down his forehead.

Every new number was greeted with screams; every rhythmic break got a howl. Girls with cameras rushed down to the stage to get a picture of their idol – and then just knelt there, forgetting to press the trigger.

When it was over and a wedge of police had brought Elvis back to the dressing room I asked him how he felt about this sort of reception.

He said: 'It makes me want to cry. How does all this happen to me?'

He showed me a gold horseshoe ring studded with eleven big diamonds he was wearing. 'Look at all these things I got,' he said. 'I got three Cadillacs. I got forty suits and twenty-seven pairs of shoes.'

I asked him how he knew it was exactly twenty-seven pairs and he said: 'When you ain't had nothing, like me, you keep count when you get things.'

What else is he doing with his money?

'I bought Mom and Pop a new house,' he said. 'I'm saving plenty, too. One day I aim to get married. No, there ain't no girl just now. But she'll come along.'

I wonder if it could be a fan like that little girl I saw when I was leaving.

She was blonde, about sixteen. She had found a broken string from Elvis's guitar.

When I left she was rolling it reverently round like a lock of hair and tucking it down inside her shirt.

Lionel Crane, *Daily Mirror*, 30 April 1956

1956: Studio One: 'Let's Try It Again'

At eleven on Monday morning, a Checker cab left me at 155 East Twenty-fourth Street, a six-story building that was headquarters for RCA Victor. The high-fashion glamour of noiseless carpeting, designer lighting and cosmopolitan receptionists had not yet glossed the lobbies of the recording industry. What distinguished this paneled, linoleum-floored room from any other industrial haven was the sculpted logo hanging behind the front desk – a big white mutt with his nose in an Edison phonograph.

Past a pair of swinging doors was a long hall lit by fluorescent lights with telephone booths and vending machines. To the right, a single door opened onto a small reception area with a coffee table, a few standing ashtrays, leather chairs and a small group of recording people. On the far side of this room was an exposed platform that supported the engineering console and the recording equipment.

A mono speaker was suspended over the door. Before the reception area and to the right of the engineering console, a wide, double-glass window looked onto Studio 1, where I could see Elvis, his musicians, the Jordanaires and, sitting in a corner, Junior Smith.

Of the several people in the reception area, I recognized only Anne Fulchino, the woman responsible for my being there, and Steve Sholes, head of the Country and Western Artist and Repertoire division. Neither the Colonel nor Tom Diskin were present.

I set down my lighting gear, greeted Anne, nodded to the engineer and his assistant and introduced myself to Mr Sholes. Steve was a big man with a gentle manner and a dedicated brow, a twenty-year veteran in the music business and a man whose ear had picked up on artists like Chet Atkins and Hank Snow. Steve had been instrumental in signing Elvis with RCA. My introduction was more than professional courtesy. In order for me to shoot freely I had to get people accustomed to my presence.

47

The studio looked like a set from a 1930s science fiction movie. It was a large rectangular space of acoustical tile walls ribbed with monolithic half cylinders. These ran vertically on the long sides of the rectangle and horizontally on the short sides. The high ceiling was rippled with more parallel cylinders and two pipes of fluorescent light. The floor was a series of short strips of wood scaled in a sawtooth pattern of right angles. In the centre of the room lay a patch of carpet on which the musicians had placed their instruments.

The assistant engineer placed mikes and said 'test' to the engineer. DJ 'Sticks' Fontana tightened his drumheads, tapping and booming. Bill Black plumbed his bass. Scotty Moore tuned his guitar. Shorty Long played the piano. Elvis joined the Jordanaires in a spiritual. I took a few pictures and, when they stopped for a break, I said good morning. Elvis, eyes bright and generous, asked me, 'How ya feel?'

'A little tired. It should be a good session today.'

I had no reason to believe it one way or the other. He just cocked his head like John Wayne surveying the cattle drive and said, 'Well, I hope so.'

Steve walked in and suggested they record 'Hound Dog' first. While Elvis and Steve conferred in a corner, the engineer set the levels.

Recording in those days did not enjoy the luxury of twenty-four-track tape recorders and post-recording mixes. Modern artists can add or subtract instruments, overdub, change levels and electronically alter the sound with so much range that the final product may barely resemble what was heard at the original session. Nineteen fifty-six was still in the era of monaural sound. The engineer ran single-track tape recorders and mixed the sounds as they were recorded. The entire process was restricted to the present: if it wasn't right from the beginning you had to stop and do it all over again. Patching separate takes together wouldn't do. The only way the musicians and singers knew what they sounded like was to perform a rehearsal take and listen to the playback. What the engineer heard at the moment of recording was what you got.

After a cold but punchy rendition in the studio (where the sound seemed so lopsided at times that I could barely hear Elvis over the drums), everyone sat on the floor around the one speaker in the room. Elvis held his forehead in his hand and concentrated on the sound. Steve Sholes stood by, shirt sleeves rolled up, his hands in his pockets, waiting for the reaction.

At the end of the playback, Elvis looked up, preoccupied and discontent. The engineer was concerned the drums were too loud. Elvis thought they were all right, he wanted more guitar and another run-through.

The second mix was satisfactory. Steve resumed his position in the control booth. The engineer cued, 'Hound Dog, take one.'

Elvis began, 'You ain't nothin' but aaah-oooh, let's try it again.'

'Okay, anytime you're ready, we're still rolling. Take two.'

A word stuck in his throat. 'Take three.'

Elvis opened, didn't like the way it sounded, and tried again. 'Take four.'

He got past the opening. As the rhythm overtook his body, he jerked and bounced, driving the beat into the music. Steve interrupted. 'Elvis, we're going to have to try it again.' Instead of cueing the engineer, Steve walked out of the booth and crossed over to Elvis. Calmly, he said, 'You went off-mike.' Elvis nodded. It looked as if they had had this problem before. 'Take five' . . .

His voice cracked, the drums were too loud, somebody hit a microphone, he went off-mike again. When the musicians blew it, they jokingly made it worse. Scotty fluffed a note and then slid into a completely different riff. DJ missed a beat and plummeted into a pirouetting drumroll. Elvis in reply mocked the lines, 'Ain't no friend of mi-ine?'

At around take fourteen, I stopped taking pictures. The humor that had started the session was fading and people began glancing at Elvis to check his mood. He wasn't happy. Out of seventeen takes, maybe four were complete. Not a very good record, considering the routine of a good cut after seven or eight takes which I had observed with other singers.

Elvis didn't lose his temper and he didn't look for a scapegoat. At other RCA recording sessions, sometimes I had become the excuse. 'I can't concentrate with the photographer here.' It didn't matter that I was crouched in some corner trying to look like a piece of furniture. It was still my fault.

Elvis was unique. In his own reserved manner he kept control, he made himself responsible. When somebody else made a mistake he sang off key. The offender picked up the cue. He never criticized anyone, never got mad at anybody but himself. He'd just say, 'Okay, fellas, I goofed.'

Elvis turned away from the mike to face the wall and shook the tension from his body, jerking his arms, twisting his torso, craning and bobbing his head. When he turned back to the microphone, he ran his hands through his hair and in a low, determined voice said, 'All right, let's try it.'

Take eighteen. Elvis closed his eyes, took a deep breath and grated into the microphone, grabbing the lyric and spiking it with a nastiness that made it bite. Scotty's guitar found its edge and Bill's bass surged with the momentum

49

they had been missing. By the end of the take, the Jordanaires thought they had it.

Elvis wanted to try it again. At take twenty-six, Steve thought they had it. Elvis still thought he could do it a little better. Four takes later, Steve called over the PA, 'Okay, Elvis. I think we got it.' They had engaged the law of diminishing returns. Mistakes were creeping in. Elvis rubbed his face, swept back his hair and resigned. 'I hope so, Mr Sholes.'

The working relationship at this session was a departure from what I had seen at other recording sessions. Other artists I had covered were directed by a producer. He was the man in charge, and often the atmosphere was formal and businesslike. With Elvis the mood was casual, relaxed, joking. Steve did not dictate, he managed. And though Elvis was not a forward, take-charge character, he was clearly the one who had to be pleased. When it concerned his music, no one was more serious.

The recording had taken over two hours and without the air conditioner turned on (the mikes would have picked up the noise) the air in the room hung low and close. The double doors were opened, admitting cool air, the noise of vending machines and visitors with glowing compliments. Elvis combed his hair, drank the Coke offered by Junior and shrugged in reply to comments about how good the music was. Steve trod lightly: 'Elvis, you ready to hear a playback?' As if bad news never had good timing, he said, 'Now's as good a time as any.'

Elvis sat cross-legged on the floor in front of the speaker. The engineer announced the take over the PA and let the tape roll. Elvis winced, chewed his fingernails and looked at the floor. At the end of the first playback, he looked like he didn't know whether it was a good take or not. Steve called for take eighteen.

Elvis pulled up a folding chair, draped his arms across its back and stared blankly at the floor. As his voice pierced the speaker grille, everyone waited for his reaction. Then, as if he had received a telegram bearing news that, yes, there's good rockin' tonight, he popped his head up and cracked a smile. Take eighteen was a contender.

The engineer racked take twenty-eight. Elvis left his chair and crouched on the floor, as if listening in a different position was like looking at a subject from a different angle. Again he went into deep concentration, absorbed and motionless. For someone who had to wring the music from his body, he sure took it back lying down. At the end of the song, he slowly rose from his crouch and turned to us with a wide grin, and said, 'This is the one.'

Alfred Wertheimer, *Elvis '56: In the Beginning* (1979)

1956: Tutti-frutti

LITTLE RICHARD: When people started admiring me and my songs went gold I decided to buy a home in Hollywood and bring my family there to live. Art Rupe gave me ten thousand dollars to put down on a house at 1710 Virginia Road, in West LA, the Sugar Hill district. The house cost twenty-five thousand dollars. It was next door to the world champion Joe Louis, who was raised in Macon, like me. Rupe wasn't giving me nothing that wasn't mine, you understand. He deducted it from my royalty checks. That's how it was.

But that was the happiest moment of my life, when I bought my mother that lovely home and moved her out of that little three-room house in Macon. Macon was country then, red mud everywhere, and my mother was a country woman. She didn't want to come at first and leave all her friends and neighbors. I had always wanted to do this for my mother and I also felt obligated to my sisters and brothers – through love. It was a great period in my life.

When Mother saw the house she couldn't believe it. She had never seen black people living in this type of house. It was the kind of house that white film stars lived in – big staircase, chandeliers, marble floors, plants, bedrooms upstairs and downstairs, and statues. Really lavish.

I tell you, until they saw the house and my 1956 gold Fleetwood Cadillac in the garage they never realized what a big hit record really meant. And I didn't either. None of us will ever forget that.

Richard was taking America by storm. The demand for personal appearances, even in the southern states, was eroding the taboos against black artists appearing in white clubs and dance halls. Everyone wanted to see the creator of this joyous new sound. America, however, was still a country where terrible things could happen to a black man who was seen as sexually attractive to white women, so Richard established a wild and bizarre image which was to stick throughout his career.

LITTLE RICHARD: We were breaking through the racial barrier. The white kids had to hide my records cos they daren't let their parents know they had them in the house. We decided that my image should be crazy and way-out so that the adults would think I was harmless. I'd appear in one show dressed as the Queen of England and in the next as the Pope.

His act was a whole new experience to audiences used to seeing groups like the Penguins or the Cadillacs, who were super-cool and concentrated on their singing, doing little rehearsed dance steps and hand gestures. He freed people from their inhibitions, unleashing their spirit, enabling them to do exactly what they felt like doing – to scream, shout, dance, jump up and down – or even more unusual things . . .

It was at a Little Richard show in the Royal Theater, Baltimore, Maryland, that US concert history was changed forever. The beat was charging the packed and fervid crowd with super-excitement as the Upsetters pumped out the music. People had to be restrained from jumping off the balcony. The show had been stopped twice while police drafted for the concert removed a dozen hysterical girls who were climbing on stage, trying to rip souvenirs from a wild-eyed and sweat-soaked Richard. Suddenly something flew through the air and landed on Chuck Connor's high-hat – a pair of panties. One of the frenzied girls in front had peeled off her briefs and thrown them at the band. Within seconds the air was filled with flying undergarments as the other girls followed suit.

CHUCK CONNOR: We didn't know what was happening. Grady and the rest of 'em were ducking and shouting 'Hey!' bumping heads trying to avoid all these flying panties. We cracked up. Stopped playing. We were laughing so much. I picked a pair up on my stick and waved them in the air. After that it happened lots of places we played. The girls would actually take their panties off and throw them at the bandstand. A shower of panties!

To watch the guys in the band playing on the stage was amazing. You couldn't miss a beat because those bodies were always moving in time. It was very exciting. Those guys were the first band to come out with dance steps. They would look like a well-drilled chorus line. And Richard, out there in front of them sweating, all that water and everything, and his hair falling all over his face – you'd get a natural high just by looking at him.

Some of the wildest theater dates we did were at the Howard Theater, Washington, DC. Wow! They used to have two or three shows a day. The kids wanted to see Richard so bad they would play hooky to come and see the show. For the kids just to *look* at Richard was really something. They had never seen a man like that, with long hair and all that makeup, and shaking his head and all that. And the band there, playing behind him, really exciting 'em.

In the intermission, you went to the bar to get a drink, people'd mob you. They'd recognize you – 'That's one of 'em right there . . .' You know. And the band was so close and warm. We used to walk down the street with our arms around Richard, and that made people love us, to see that the band was warm, good friends. We used to get respect out of black and white, like we were heroes. We never had a serious argument or anything like that, cos everything was going so well. Everyone was happy. It was a good experience to work in an environment like that, and I would like to live it again.

In those days, you didn't see many people with long hair. Well, they arrested Richard for that in Texas. We were playing El Paso, Texas, and the police came in and stopped the show, stopped the band and everything and put Richard in jail. He had this long hair, and he was shakin' about up on the stage, you know? Elvis Presley was due to be coming into that town a couple of weeks later, and the police told Richard, 'If you see that guy Elvis Presley tell him we're gonna lock *him* up, too, cos he has long hair.' Real rednecks.

Richard used to go to the beauty shop to get his hair done, and the band had to go too. I was wearing my hair curled in a process. We would go and get our hair curled, then the next week we had to go get a touchup. But what made us feel so great was that we had a whole lot of good-looking guys in the band, good builds and everything. We had different sets of colored suits and shirts and black and white gray tuxedos, uniform shirts and things. Everybody dressed alike.

Those teams were all wild. It was always a new experience. Really something. We had a beautiful time – wild parties, pretty girls, wild girls. A beautiful time.

H. B. BARNUM: When I first saw Richard, he was headlining a big package show – Etta James and the Peaches, the Five Chords, the Five Keys, the Robins and Bill Doggett. I was fourteen years old, playing saxophone with Chuck Liggins and Big Jay McNeely, making about ninety dollars a week. I'd come on with the show band and play the opening number. Then I'd run off stage and change clothes and come back on with the next group and then the next. I guess Richard took a fancy to me because he would let me play with his band, too.

You knew not, night to night, where he was going to come from. He'd just burst on to the stage from anywhere, and you wouldn't be able to hear anything but the roar of the audience. He might come out and walk on the piano. He might go out in the audience. His charisma was just a whole new thing to the business. Richard was totally out of this world, wild, and it gave people who wanted to scream a chance to go ahead and scream instead of trying to be cool.

We would go into the first number and we might vamp that first number for four to five minutes before he even got to the piano. He'd be on the stage, he'd be off the stage, he'd be jumping and yelling, screaming, whipping the audience on, whipping them on. Then when he finally hit the piano and just went into di-di-di-di-di-di-di-di, you know, well nobody can do that as fast as Richard. It just took everybody by surprise.

I'd been playing with Fats for a couple of years and I'd seen some pretty wild suits as far as colors go, but Richard with the diamonds, the different-colored stones and sequins, the capes, the blouse shirts, the way he used makeup, the way he did his eyes (Richard has eyes that would just look through you, but when he accentuated them with makeup – wow!), it was really very way out for the times. That's the first time I ever saw spotlights and flicker lights used at a concert show. It had all been used in show business, but he brought it into *our* world.

He pulled out all the stops. The audiences, they'd rush to touch him. Each night he could go to new heights. He could just come out and sing the same song and another dimension would happen. I've worked with some top artists, Presley, all those, and nobody's ever had that kind of magic. When Richard opened his mouth, man, everybody in the world could enjoy it. He's got a voice that would make 'em jump up and down.

Richard opened the door. He brought the races together. When I first went on the road there were many segregated audiences. With Richard, although they still had the audiences segregated in the building, they were *there* together. And most times, before the end of the night, they would all be mixed together. Up until then, the audiences were either all black or all white, and no one else could come in. His records weren't boy-meets-girl-girl-meets-boy things, they were *fun* records, all fun. And they had a lot to say sociologically in our country and the world. The shot was fired here and heard round the world.

LITTLE RICHARD: They were exciting times. The fans would go really wild. Nearly every place we went, the people got unruly. They'd want to get to me and tear my clothes off. It would be standing-room-only crowds and 90 percent of the audience would be white. I've always thought that Rock 'n' Roll brought the races together. Although I was black, the fans didn't care. I used to feel good about that. Especially being from the South, where you see the barriers, having all these people who we thought hated us, showing all this *love*.

We were doing one-nighters and we were doing one *every* night! We were working seven nights a week, two and sometimes three shows a night. The schedule was indescribable. You would get there and not even have time to unpack your bags. Whatever you were wearing that day, the valets would press with those little steam irons or send down to the hotel to be pressed. We'd barely have time to get ready and get to the show.

There we'd be, the band in all these pink-and-white suits, looking fine and feeling great. I was there with my hair long and beautiful. We used potato and lye and hot combing and curlers, because we had to have the new image. We knew we had it. We knew we could draw ten thousand people every night, and we were making more money than we had ever made before. We all had to change our clothes two or three times because of all the sweating. So, there I was doing this dancing. Chuck would call it my freaky-deaky dance. I used to have women coming up and throwing naked pictures of themselves on stage, with their phone numbers on 'em.

When we booked the hotel we might rent four or five different rooms. Probably the whole top floor. There would always be a lot of people come around. It was quite a show. Barnum and Bailey, you name it! There was never any problem getting girls. At the end of the show, they'd either come around to the dressing room or the hotel, and we'd sort them out – which ones we wanted. We had some parties!

There was one time we were in this hotel in Bloomsfield, West Virginia. They had a rule like you couldn't bring in any girl unless she's your wife. Well, this girl came over and she was really wild. She would take anything. All the band guys at once. We didn't know she was married. Her husband was downstairs trying to find out if his wife was up there with us. He was banging on the door, and we were trying to get her out. But she didn't want to go! She said, 'I don't wanna leave now, I'm enjoying myself.' The guys didn't care and I had to plead with them to let her go. Eventually we sneaked her down the fire escape, but it was close. The hotel was a wooden building and this guy was downstairs threatening to put a match to it and burn it down! That's the fun part, you see, when you're sneakin'. Makes it very much more exciting.

But it got difficult to have sex parties after a time, because we were so popular. People couldn't get to you. I wasn't used to that. It made me feel so important. So big, I felt unusual, you know, like I was a special person.

ETTA JAMES: I was so naïve in those days. Richard and the band were always having those parties and I'd knock on the door and try to get in. They'd say, 'Don't open the door, she's a minor!' Then one day, I climbed up and looked through the transom – and the things I *saw*!

LITTLE RICHARD: I used to like to watch these people having sex with my band men. I would pay a guy who had a big penis to come and have sex with these ladies so I could watch them. It was a big thrill to me. If the girls didn't think they could take it, I would watch him make them take it. As I was watching, I would masturbate while someone was eating my titties. They should have called me 'Richard the Watcher'.

My whole gay activities were really into masturbation. I used to do it six or seven times a day. In fact everybody used to tell me that I should get a trophy for it, I did it so much. I got to be a professional jack-offer. I would do it just to be doing something, seven, eight times a day. Feel bad after I did it though. I'd always be mad after I finished. Be mad at myself, don't want to talk about it, don't wanna answer any questions. I'd think, Why did you do it? You crazy? You could've . . . Most gay people fall in love with themselves.

Then I met Angel. We were in Savannah, Georgia. I was sitting in the hotel room with some of the band looking out of the window. I saw this beautiful young girl with this fantastic body, fifty-inch bust and eighteen-inch waist. It's true that nothing grows in the shade! She was with another girl walking towards the theater. I asked one of my band men to go across the street and ask her to come over to the hotel. She told me she was about to graduate from high school.

A few weeks later she turned up at a concert in Wilmington, Delaware. She had decided to come with me. When we left for Washington, DC, that night Angel traveled with us in my car. We checked into the Hotel Dunbar, in Washington, and we shared a room. She was a wonderful lover. She changed her name to Lee Angel and worked as a nude model, a dancer and a stripper. From the beginning she seemed to know exactly what I wanted in sex. She would do anything to excite me, including having sex with other guys while I watched. I loved Angel and Angel loved me, but in different ways. Marriage was a dream of hers, but I never wanted to marry her.

I loved Angel because she was pretty and the fellers enjoyed having sex with her. She could draw a lot of handsome guys for me. She was like a magnet. She drew everything to me. You ain't never seen a woman made like Angel. That fifty-inch bust. Natural, too. She was never a fat woman. She looked like a white girl, but she's black.

Angel would take in four guys at one time, and she wouldn't let 'em out. Most of 'em didn't want to get out, I noticed. I'd see some big guy and I'd say, 'Hey, c'mon by,' and Angel would say, 'Yeah, c'mon. I'd like to see what you got there.' She was some girl.

LEE ANGEL: Richard and I became very close friends to the point where we almost got married. He sent me to Tennessee to work with a piano player called Ray Charles. I was there about three weeks before Richard got there. He had planned to have his new record, 'Send Me Some Lovin'', released on that particular day all over the country. That night, at the show, Richard told me and about seven thousand other people that I was his fiancée and that we were getting married. That's how I found out. He dedicated 'Send Me Some Lovin'' specially to me.

We were so close that we could read each other's mind. I would be in a room with him and I'd start cursing him out because I'd know what he was thinking. Everybody in the room used to wonder what was going on between us. If he was away on the road and I wanted to talk to him, I would really concentrate on him and he'd call me within a few minutes.

I traveled with him when he was doing one-nighters. It was always fun. One time we were at the Civic Opera House, in Chicago. Richard introduced me to the audience. The place was packed with thousands of people. As we were leaving the auditorium his fans came up and ripped my dress off!

Charles White, The Life and Times of Little Richard (1984)

1956: Great Balls of Fire

During the third week of August, Jerry Lee recorded 'Great Balls of Fire', a song written by Jack Hammer, a New York session pianist, and Otis Blackwell, the eccentric black songwriter and singer who had supplied Elvis with his two biggest hits, 'Don't Be Cruel' and 'All Shook Up'. Blackwell brought 'Great Balls of Fire' to Jerry Lee after seeing him on *The Steve Allen Show*.

Sam Phillips and Jack Clement spent several days in the studio with Jerry Lee working on 'Great Balls of Fire'. At one of these sessions, everyone in the studio – Jerry Lee, Sam Phillips, Jack Clement, drummer James Van Eaton, bass player Billy Lee Riley – got to drinking. Jerry Lee became filled with the Holy Ghost, and he decided that the song 'Great Balls of Fire' was of the devil and that to sing it was to sin. Sam Phillips argued against Jerry Lee's stand. Jack Clement switched on the tape and recorded the argument.

'H-E-L-L!' Jerry Lee loudly spelled.

'I don't believe this,' Sam Phillips muttered.

'Great Godamighty, great balls of fire!' James Van Eaton proclaimed mockingly.

'That's right!' hollered Billy Lee Riley, right behind him.

'I don't believe it,' Sam repeated.

'It says make merry with the joy of God *only*,' Jerry Lee yelled. 'But when it comes to *worldly* music, rock 'n' roll . . .'

'Pluck it out!' Billy Lee Riley shouted.

'. . . anything like that,' Jerry Lee went on, fast, driven. 'You have done brought yourself into the world, and you're in the world, and you're still a sinner. You're a sinner and unless you be saved and borned again and be made as a little chile and walk before God and be holy – and, brother, I mean you got to be *so* pure. No sin shall enter there – *no sin*! For it says *no sin*. It don't say just a little bit; it says *no sin shall enter there*. Brother, not one little bit. You got to *walk* and *talk* with God to go to heaven. You got to be *so* good.'

'Hallelujah,' Riley said.

'All right,' Sam said. 'Now look, Jerry, religious conviction doesn't mean anything resembling extremism. All right. Do you mean to tell me that you're gonna take the Bible, that you're gonna take God's word, and that you're gonna revolutionize the whole universe? Now, listen. Jesus Christ was sent here by God Almighty – '

'Right!' said Jerry Lee.

'Did He convince, did He save all the people in the world?'

'Naw, but He tried to!'

'He sure did. Now, wait a minute. Jesus Christ came into this world. He tolerated man. He didn't preach from one pulpit. He went around and did good.'

'That's right! He preached everywhere!'

'Everywhere.'

'He preached on land!'

'Everywhere. That's right, that's right.'

'He preached on the water!'

'That's right, that's exactly right. Now –'

'Man, He done everything! He *healed*!'

'Now, now, here, here's the difference –'

'Are you followin' those that heal? Like Jesus Christ did? Well, it's happenin' every day!'

'What d'ya mean . . . you . . . what . . . I, I . . . what –'

'The *blind* had eyes opened. The *lame* were made to walk.'

'Jerry, Jesus Christ –'

'The crippled were made to walk.'

'Jesus Christ, in my opinion, is just as real today as he was when He came into this world.'

'Right! Right! You're so right you don't know what you're sayin'!'

'Now, I will say, more so –'

'Aw, let's cut it,' Riley interrupted disgustedly.

'It'll never sell, man,' Van Eaton said to him. 'It's not commercial.'

'Wait, wait, wait just a minute,' Sam said, throwing his arms up, 'we can't, we got to – now, look, listen, I'm tellin' you outa my heart, and I have studied the Bible a little bit –'

'Well, I have too,' said Jerry Lee. 'I studied it through and through and through and through, and I know what I'm talkin' about.'

'Jerry. Jerry. If you think that you can't, can't do good if you're a rock-'n'-roll exponent –'

'You can do good, Mr Phillips, don't get me wrong –'

'Now, wait, wait, listen. When I say *do good* –'

'You can have a kind heart!'

'I don't mean, I don't mean just –'

'You can help people!'

'You can save souls!'

'*No! No! No! No!*'

'*Yes!*'

'*How can the Devil save souls? What are you talkin' about?*'

'Listen, listen . . .'

'Man, I got *the Devil* in me! If I didn't have, I'd be a Christian!'

'Well, you may have him –'

'*Jesus!*' Jerry Lee yelled, pressing his fists to his breast. 'Heal this man! He cast the devil out. The devil says, Where can I go? He says, Can I go into this *swine*? He says, Yeah go into him. Didn't he go into him?'

'Jerry, the point I'm tryin' to make is, if you believe in what you're singin', you got no alternative whatsoever, out of – listen! – out of –'

'Mr Phillips! I don't care. It ain't what you believe, *it's what's written in the Bible!*'

'Well, wait a minute.'

'It's what's *there*, Mr Phillips.'

'No, no.'

'It ain't what you believe, it's just what's there.'

'No, by gosh, if it's not what you believe, then how do you *interpret* the Bible?'

'Man alive,' moaned Riley.

'Huh? How do you interpret the Bible if it's not what you believe?' repeated Sam.

'Well, it's just not what you believe, you just can't –'
'Let's *cut* it, man!' Riley screamed.
'No, you got to –' began Sam.
'You can talk . . .' Jerry Lee turned away from him, as from a fool.
'No, here's the thing –'
'You can talk, and you can talk . . .'

Between midnight and dawn they finally cut it, in violence, anger and weariness. It had been difficult, but in the end Sam Phillips knew that he had a hit, a record of unrelenting rhythm and mindless venereal splendor. Jack Clement made a comment about splitting the royalties with the Holy Ghost, but no one laughed.

Nick Tosches, *Hellfire: The Jerry Lee Lewis Story* (1982)

1956: Dean Worship in Britain

In Britain, as in every other Hollywood-film-going country in the world, Dean is still the most popular star, living or dead. Film magazine editors old enough to remember say that the craze is 'bigger than anything before. Even than Valentino'. Letters pour in to them, asking for the colour of Dean's eyes, the colour of his hair, his mother's maiden name. 'They want to know everything about him. They want to write to his father, or send flowers to his grave. One even wanted to build a Dean memorial in this country.'

At the *'Observer' Sixty Years of Cinema* exhibition in Trafalgar Square, more pictures of Dean were sold than of any other star. And once a week attendants had to wipe lipstick from the large Dean portrait on display.

Of the six thousand letters that arrive at Warner Brothers' Hollywood studios every month addressed to Jimmy Dean, nearly half come from abroad. In Sweden, 'Deanagers', dressed in the familiar jeans-and-jacket, have the police worried by their suicidal tactics on motor-scooters. In Paris, thirty schoolgirls wrote to the manager of their local cinema asking him to change the dates of *Rebel Without a Cause* so that they could see it before they went away on holiday. He agreed. It was the *fifteenth time* they had seen each of the two James Dean pictures so far released.

But such fervour is rare in England. Crazier things have been done in devotion to Liberace, who is far from dead and probably not much mixed-up-inside anyway. The most common reaction from a girl fan – and most Dean fans are girls – came from one nineteen-year-old: 'On the screen you felt he wasn't so much acting as being himself. He seemed lonely – and interesting. You felt you could be friends with him, but not swoon over him.'

By now the recording companies have a firm front seat on the Dean bandwagon. In America there are seven Dean records, ranging from the theme music from his films to *His Name Was Dean*. An eighth, *Jimmy Dean's Christmas in Heaven*, will be released shortly. Record shops in this country are being pestered for such recordings. But, as one salesgirl put it: 'They aren't the rock 'n' roll types, though. It's the more intelligent young-sters who want the records.'

And this is where Dean worship in England takes its most surprising and sinister twist. The simple fact that Dean managed – partly by the details of his own life, partly by his first-rate playing of teenage rôles – to touch some chord of sympathy in the average teenager of today needs no more proving. But as against the largely emotional reaction in America and elsewhere, Dean has also hit the British youngster on his intellectual funnybone. And most of this reaction is male, and comes from those who have never written a fan letter in their lives.

One significant facet of Dean worship is that there are no Dean fan clubs in Britain. A young man put it: 'He was an individual – look at the way he turned Hollywood upside down. And to appreciate him you have to be an individual, too. You've got to feel as lonely as he did.' One other reason, however, is that Warner Brothers refuse to risk charges of encouraging morbid interests by backing an official fan club. And there is no doubt that much of Dean's popularity stems from his being dead.

When *East of Eden* appeared, just three months before Dean's death, it 'hardly produced a flutter', the studios say. But from the moment Dean died it was packed out. *Rebel Without a Cause* was a hit from the start, despite its 'X' certificate. *Giant*, which, at the moment, is getting a nervous retouching from its makers, may break every record.

All of which is the more strange because the death of a film star usually makes his films box-office poison. But it is the very manner of Dean's death that makes it significant to his followers. 'He wouldn't conform to this world,' they say, 'his mad driving was part of his rebellion.'

And since the more intelligent a person is, the more aware of the world, the more likely is he to rebel against it. The belief that Dean founded a revolution against convention and was prepared to sacrifice his life to that cause is why so many intelligent youngsters have rallied to his standard. One such is Michael Hastings, aged eighteen, a tailor's apprentice from Brixton, who is determined to become a playwright.

Michael's first play, *Don't Destroy Me!*, put his disillusionment with the world on to the stage of the New Lindsey Theatre Club, London. The central character of the play, dedicated to James Dean, is fifteen-year-old Sammy Kirz, beset by such worldly problems as a drunken father, a philandering mother and neighbours in the same tenement who are either crazy, immoral or just deaf and dumb Italian spivs. This is Sammy, taken from the script:

His eyes are closed, his fists clenched, in a stiffness, shoulders loose, he zigzags up the stairs, slowly. His actions are grotesque, as if in a dream, barging from side to side like a straw-doll. '. . . Somebody wants me – Oh yes . . . but it's – not him, not her, somebody. A person . . . I'm wrong. Don't shut the door.' *He shakes the locked door.* 'Somebody please listen . . .'

Finally, whimpering 'they never done, they didn't try', he throws himself down the stairs. This, Michael claims, is a picture of a post-war boy being destroyed by his father and stepmother. 'You know, it is terrible to be born into my generation. Nobody wants new writers – they won't give us a chance. England is losing everything. If the Prime Minister could give up his seat to a seventeen-year-old boy then we'd get somewhere. And,' he added, 'Dean represented this – my generation – on the screen.'

A similar view of the world came from twenty-two-year-old Daniel Winter, of Shepherd's Bush. 'People just don't have any ideas any more,' he said. 'There's no philosophy, nothing new at all. Everybody's subconsciously waiting for the big bang that'll end it all. Dean knew this, I'm sure. He expressed it.'

Winter told me of a bond which he believed existed between himself and the dead actor. 'I'm shortsighted, the way Dean was. I like bullfights – so did he. And we had the same ideals, the same frustrations. And I believe in doing what I want to, too.'

Already Daniel – who bears a certain facial resemblance to Dean – wears the same clothes and speaks in the same manner. He hopes that somebody will believe in the resemblance sufficiently to try him out as Dean's successor. He has no acting experience, but believes that it was Dean's sincerity which was important.

'And now Dean's gone – who's going to express our frustration?' he asked. 'You need someone who's as frustrated as he was. I used to watch him on the screen and think "That's *my* frustration he's expressing." It was like,' and he said this quite sincerely, 'like looking on the face of God.'

Soon after I had spoken to him, he rang me up to say that he had been asked to give his views on Dean in ITV's *This Week*. He was worried about what he might say and wanted advice. 'Supposing I say what I really feel about this world?' he asked. 'People will think I've got no right to think that at my age. But it's true, all the same. The world isn't any good any longer.'

Finally I met a man who has seen the Dean 'rebellion' develop, Mr Michael Croft, a South London schoolmaster.

'The problem struck me very forcibly while I was teaching,' he said. 'It is as if this generation can find no moral code at all and is looking for a new one. But for them it must have a practical, not an ethical, basis. It is what you might call a "sensual journey".'

But not everybody who worships Dean is on this journey. Too many are apparently satisfied just knowing that their Great Man felt as frustrated as they do. Too many are just sitting complaining of the world left them by their elders without trying to do anything about it. In the long run, it might be better to have weepy fan-letters and a few hysterics. It would be better still to remember how hard Dean worked to be able to buy the car in which, like 38,300 other Americans last year, he killed himself.

Gavin Lyall, Picture Post, 22 October 1956

1957: Bermondsey Miracle

There were probably a thousand of them down there, nearly all girls, nearly all between fifteen and twenty-two. Across the provoking, gaudy front of their sweaters many of them had embroidered the name *Tommy* in proudly-proclaimed devotion.

They were standing, and had been for three hours, in the gardens of the De Montfort Hall at Leicester; chanting their adoration to a little square window on the second floor. Any movement behind the frosted glass set up a wave of squeals. Because *Tommy* was in there. That shadow *might* be his.

Somehow we wanted to get a few of them up to Tommy Steele's dressing-room for an interview. We went downstairs to the double doors and looked through the glass. They were pressed flat against it, clamouring, laughing, crying, loving, eager, anxious, desperate. Somehow we opened the doors and squeezed out without letting the flood in. 'We just want six – six who have come a long way.' The response was frightening. *Me! Me! Me! Take Me! Tell him it's Beryl from Sheffield. Tell him Barbara's here – the one he wrote to. Me. Please. Please. Please.* At last we got six of them inside, for the loss of a few buttons. They stood in a line and displayed the embroidered *Tommys* very proudly. Obviously fairy godmothers are getting younger.

For it is these teenage girls, in their thousands, very aware of becoming women, clamorous to become Tommy's girls, who have, in a few miraculous months, turned the Tommy Steele pumpkin into a sleek high-powered saloon and the Bermondsey white mice into trim-tailored, handsome agents to guard and enlarge what is fast becoming an entertainment empire.

Six months ago, this cheery-faced Cockney boy, his unruly fair hair forever reaching upwards like a feather duster, was an unknown officer's steward on a passenger ship – his name was Tommy Hicks. 'They used to pay me £30 a month as an ordinary cabin and dining-room bell boy. Then they made me an officer's steward and put the pay up to £60. No tips on that job.'

Tommy Hicks had been brought up in Frean Street, Bermondsey, which isn't likely to appear in any of the guide books on Beautiful Britain. At one end of the street, just behind Tommy's house, is the railway line to Greenwich, and at the other is a square patch of cinders surrounded by a high wire netting, which serves the local children (including Tommy's little brother and sister) as a recreation ground. It is a dock area, a district of big men and small houses.

Last September Tommy left the *Mauretania* on compassionate leave, because his mother was ill and his fifteen-year-old brother was about to go to sea. As he walked down the *Mauretania*'s gangway, he met his brother on the way up. 'So long,' Tommy said. 'You can have my bunk.'

That is how Colin Hicks, now in Bermuda, remembers Tommy. A ship steward stepping ashore on leave. When Colin gets home and finds the Rolls Royce outside the door and pushes his way through the almost permanent crowd of autograph hunters, he will wonder what the devil can have happened in the meantime.

This is roughly the size of it: Tommy Steele records have sold about three-quarters of a million, and Tommy gets threepence on each record. He gets a guinea every time a record is broadcast. His value as a top-of-the-bill variety act is about £1,000 a week. For a Sunday night concert he can ask around £600. A film of his life story is already under way. He has *turned down* an offer of £1,500 *a week for two years* – which is like saying 'no' to £150,000 – because 'we can do better elsewhere'.

His televised performance at the Café de Paris (and if he was going to get panned anywhere it was there, amongst the night-weary sophisticates) was good enough for them to ask for a month's extension at double the salary – which they didn't get.

There have been offers of tours in North America, South Africa and Europe.

Flooding on to the commercial market are Tommy Steele shoes, Tommy Steele shirts, blouses, panties, skirts, ear-rings, bracelets, pullovers and sweaters. Before long, we are likely to see Tommy Steele lipsticks, face powders and foundation creams. Nightdresses may be coming soon – one can imagine the publicity campaign – Bedtime With Tommy Steele. The soft drinks industry has caught him up in their war because the soft drink which Tommy Steele drinks is going to be really important to their profit margins.

How did it all happen? During that fortnight's leave Tommy was looking after his mother in the day time and going down to Soho to play his guitar in the coffee bars after his father had got home in the evening. It was towards the end of that fortnight that an astute New Zealand publicity agent, a young man of twenty-five who had stepped off a Swedish boat at Grimsby three years before with only the singlet and trousers that he stood up in, decided that Tommy was good for a bigger audience. John Kennedy, the agent, dragged Hugh Mendl, the Decca talent scout, to the 2 I's coffee bar to see Tommy. The next day he made a recording at the Decca studios and his rocket-like career had begun.

Kennedy played it tough. After getting Tommy a £20 a week engagement at the Stork Club he set out remorselessly after the real money. He approached one of the biggest theatrical booking agents in Britain and his first demand – for a boy who had never stepped on to a stage before – was £100 a week and top billing. 'You're mad,' the agent said. 'Stark raving mad.' But within a few days Harold Fielding had indeed booked him – not at £100 a week but at £150. And he has proved the best thing that variety theatres have had to bill for many years, certainly the best British product. Theatres accustomed to being half empty for most of the week are being sold out from the first performance, often with hundreds left disappointed outside.

The act itself is simple enough. It's ninety per cent youthful exuberance. There is not a trace of sex, real or implied. The Steele-men, bass, drums, saxophone and piano, all writhe around the stage with their instruments – even the pianist doesn't have a stool. All the antics they, as professionals, freely admit have nothing to do with music. As Tommy would put it: 'We do it for laughs.'

Let's get back to the De Montfort at Leicester. Beryl from Sheffield has talked her way into the dressing-room. *Y'see*, she says, *I know Tommy for a start, though I have never met him before. I ring him lots of times every week from Sheffield.*

How many times?

Well, it depends whether I am in the mood or not, never less than three times a week though. It costs about 3s. 4d. a call 'cause we always make it

personal. My friend, Eileen, stands with me in the box. We both work in a
solicitor's office, but the money's not very good – £2 5s. a week.

Well, what is it you like so much about Tommy?

Well, he's such a nice chap. I mean, that picture of him playing to the kids
in Bermondsey. When I saw that – 'ee I was right touched.

But you don't get that I'd-marry-him-if-I-could feeling?

I do, y'know. I would an' all.

But what would Mum and Dad say?

Well, it would be nothing to do with them, would it? It's just between me
and Tommy.

That is the way that most of the fans feel. The fan letters show the same
thing. In the front room of a little house in Charlton, south-east London, a
girl called Sylvia Stephen and her mother spend twelve hours a day answering
fan letters, now pouring in at the rate of 2,000 a week.

'You appeal to me as a nice quiet, unspoilt boy who still likes to spend an
evening with the family ... Your Friend, Pat. P.S. I enclose a photo of our
mum, Ivor, Gloria and myself and a letter from Gloria.'

'I hope you had a lot of nice Christmas presents. Please tell Sandra to write
back. If we lived near each other, she could come and play with my toys. I
love you Tommy, your girl friend, GLORIA.'

'Brackley is a small town, but nobody's allowed to forget Tommy Steele
... to me it is just one girl writing to one boy. Please don't let me have any
more sleepless nights. – ALICE.'

'I was shocked when I read you hadn't got a girl. Gosh, I'd jump at the
chance. I am 15. Am I too young? School is a bore, so *you* have to liven
things up a bit. – MARGARET. P.S. I have had my hair cut and waved, and my
measurements are 36-24-35.'

'The girls are saying that I don't stand a chance and you would never go
for the likes of me. I told them I didn't think you were the kind of person to
ignore people. – IVY.'

When Tommy Steele steps on to a theatre stage, it is like killing-day at
some fantastic piggery. There is little pretence of listening to the music. The
fans know the records by heart. They only want to see him in the flesh, to
thrust a little of their own personality out towards his. But in spite of the
feeling of mob hysteria in the auditorium, the swaying bodies, the stamping
feet, the girls hugging one another and crying in each other's arms, struggling
with the ushers to throw flowers upon the stage, in spite of all this, the feeling
comes over that, one by one, they know and love this boy with the guitar,
with the wide smile and the unconquerable tuft of hair, as one of themselves.

A nice boy. A boy who has a kid sister and two kid brothers. Who doesn't drink, who'd much rather spend a night at the Cat's Whisker coffee bar than at the Café de Paris. Who would as soon have a day at Southend than a month on the Costa Brava. They want him in the same way as they want the boy next door. For Tommy Steele is infinitely nearer the boy next door than any of the top American stars, like Presley, who come from places and home conditions that the ordinary English working girl can never understand. Tommy Steele's greatest talent is that he is an ordinary, likeable British kid who obviously gets a kick out of life.

Trevor Philpott, *Picture Post*, 25 February 1957

1957: The Street Game

A great change suddenly came over London at that time. The American civilization had caught up with us. Everything was speeded up and slicked up, and there was a great deal of violence in the streets. A wave of bitterness and cynicism broke out. The whole surface seemed to be cracking. Prostitutes were thronging the pavements of Old Compton Street and policemen were walking around with hands open behind their backs for their dropsy and the Pawnbrokers were raking it in. Cafés that we knew started closing, the leisurely ones where artists and anarchists argued all day. Coffee bars were opening in their place. The object was to get you in, make you feel uncomfortable under the harsh lighting, and then get you out as quickly as possible.

Skiffle swept through the streets. Groups of kids started twanging guitars under the arches near Charing Cross. Tommy Steele arrived.

Iris Orton was convinced that the millenium had also burst upon us, was sure that the great revolution of youth would break out at any moment.

In her wild cloak she went from cellar to cellar reading apocalyptical verse to the new crop of restless kids who had been spawned in war. And we, the old crop of the gone poets, sauntered the West End streets still thinking we would set the place alight and march on the citadels of the philistines.

We never went anywhere except the Coffee-House at Trafalgar Square, where there were bad paintings on the walls and good girls trying to look bad around the walls.

The age of the week-end Bohemian had arrived!

But the desperation hadn't departed. Most of the boys I knew, the would-be writers and the painters, had gone the way of all flesh, into the ground. The toll was endless. I thought of their once smiling faces now rotting.

Victims of the inner war. They were the unable, the unadjustable, the nothings, the unmighty fallen, the unsung, and I was waiting for my turn. I didn't see David Levine around, heard he was in a bad way, so I went to his room. He was completely gone, sat smothered in blankets saying over and over again, 'I'm so cold, I'm so cold.' He could no longer get high from drugs, but just needed them to stay alive. There was, however, still a tiny flickering of sensation when he stuck the needle in his veins. But he had no more conversation. Gone was his cry for compassion. He wasn't expecting anything except death. The once happy, mad, intelligent pianist sat with his teeth chattering, his glassy eyes fixed on nowhere. The little marijuana plant he had tried to grow in a little box of earth suspended from the electric light bulb was all dead and dried up.

He died quietly. When they opened him up they found the biggest tumour they'd ever seen in a brain.

For the old-timers of Soho things got desperate. Some tried to fit into the new coffee-bar society, became characters, dispensing old anti-social tales to the newly lost. They held court, were lionized but remained pathetic. Most of them died alone somewhere, at night in a lousy room, and they were forgotten within days.

I stayed at that time near Camden Town. I always heard a man moaning as I walked up the stairs to my room. He would just give one long-drawn-out sigh of boredom. He stopped moaning one day, put ten shillings in the gas meter and took the gas-ring under the bedclothes with him.

But the kids in the streets. They represented something. Some people said they were living for kicks. I could see they were kicking for life.

So I wandered through the scene, feeling that I belonged to another time and soon I started recalling the old blissful really gone bohemian days. I was already part of the past and still hadn't begun. So I continued killing time, having the sad girls, wanting to reach across the black wasteland, yearning for a kiss to ignite the world for just a moment. But girls gave themselves without much joy. Just lumps of dough with open legs yawning through the act.

London was floodlit and in the Coffee-House the hot air reached up and mixed with the hot air of Whitehall, creating a great nauseous wave of apathy.

I saw a picture of the H-bomb on television. It looked like a great monster crawling towards the world. I was obsessed with an ugly vision of the impending holocaust. An American from *Life* or *Time* went to Moscow, came back with photographs and said, 'Do you know, those Russians are human. Ordinary boys and girls walk down the street and what do you know, they even fall in love, in Moscow.' I wanted to be sick. To have to be told that people in another country shared human emotions showed to what extent we had descended.

I was thrown out of my room for the classical reason. Not having the wherewithal. So I wandered, slept around and jawed the night away, until another day came inevitably around.

Girls are attracted to homeless poets. I sat in the Coffee-House listening to all the shit about art and literature and the more withdrawn I became the more success I had. And I began exacting a sort of vengeance on them.

I began a novel. It started in the usual way. A boy and girl in bed.

One concave young friend had a tremendous facility for getting things done. 'Must get some money,' he suddenly said. Half an hour later he returned with fifty pounds. God knows what he did. He started a magazine there and then and paid me for poems. It was exciting for a few months, but my concave friend stopped being a publisher and decided to be a painter.

He paced in front of his easel, saying, 'I must find next year's trend now!' Suddenly his eyes lit up. He got a nail and a hammer and started knocking holes in to the canvas. 'That's it.' The age of the gimmick had arrived.

My concave friend got tired of painting. He said he wanted to marry an heiress. Later I saw him driving around with one. It cost him an awful lot of money in taxi fares; for she never had any money on her. But they married and are now living happily ever after. I liked him tremendously.

Meanwhile, St Martin's School of Arts and tarts were setting the fashion trends in faces. One year it was Little Girl Lost and the next year it was the East of Eden look. Then the Zombie stare. Lovely girls whose perfume was blown by the wind. Provocative, evocative, yet suburban, playing at art. Arty. Ultimately they would marry artists or designers and become ordinary housewives.

Peter Fisk said I could move in with him and Janice. So I did. When he wasn't in his Orgone box he was cooking or reading from Gertrude Stein or James Joyce.

We wrote poetry together, each an alternate line. Nothing made sense; it was wonderful. Then we wrote a play called *The Madhouse*. All about a house that went mad.

A friend of theirs came visiting. A pathologist. She looked sad one day. I asked her why. 'I'm homesick for the dead.' She explained she was on holiday.

I told her she needn't be homesick for the dead – they were all around us. There was such a deterioration in almost everyone, everything.

Bernard Kops, *The World is a Wedding* (1963)

69

1957: Sex in Shiny Packets

Perhaps even more symptomatic of the general trend is the reading of juke-box boys, of those who spend their evening listening in harshly lighted milk-bars to the 'nickelodeons'. There are, of course, others who read the books and magazines now to be discussed – some married men and women, perhaps in particular those who are finding married life a somewhat jaded affair, 'dirty old men', some schoolchildren – but one may reasonably take those who, night after night, visit these bars as typical or characteristic readers of these most developed new-style popular journals.

Like the cafés I described in an earlier chapter, the milk-bars indicate at once, in the nastiness of their modernistic knick-knacks, their glaring showiness, an aesthetic breakdown so complete that, in comparison with them, the layout of the living-rooms in some of the poor homes from which the customers come seems to speak of a tradition as balanced and civilized as an eighteenth-century town house. I am not thinking of those milk-bars which are really quick-service cafés where one may have a meal more quickly than in a café with table-service. I have in mind rather the kind of milk-bar – there is one in almost every northern town with more than, say, fifteen thousand inhabitants – which has become the regular evening rendezvous of some of the young men. Girls go to some, but most of the customers are boys aged between fifteen and twenty, with drape-suits, picture ties and an American slouch. Most of them cannot afford a succession of milk-shakes, and make cups of tea serve for an hour or two whilst – and this is their main reason for coming – they put copper after copper into the mechanical record-player. About a dozen records are available at any time; a numbered button is pressed for the one wanted, which is selected from a key of titles. The records seem to be changed about once a fortnight by the hiring firm; almost all are American; almost all are 'vocals' and the styles of singing much advanced beyond what is normally heard on the Light Programme of the BBC. Some of the tunes are catchy; all have been doctored for presentation so that they have the kind of beat which is currently popular; much use is made of the 'hollow-cosmos' effect which echo-chamber recording gives. They are delivered with great precision and competence, and the 'nickelodeon' is allowed to blare out so that the noise would be sufficient to fill a good-sized ballroom, rather than a converted shop in the main street. The young men waggle one shoulder or stare, as desperately as Humphrey Bogart, across the tubular chairs.

Compared even with the pub around the corner, this is all a peculiarly thin and pallid form of dissipation, a sort of spiritual dry-rot amid the odour of boiled milk. Many of the customers – their clothes, their hair-styles, their facial expressions all indicate – are living to a large extent in a myth-world compounded of a few simple elements which they take to be those of American life.

They form a depressing group and one by no means typical of working-class people; perhaps most of them are rather less intelligent than the average, and are therefore even more exposed than others to the debilitating mass-trends of the day. They have no aim, no ambition, no protection, no belief. They are the modern equivalents of Samuel Butler's mid-nineteenth-century ploughboys, and in as unhappy a position as theirs:

> The row of stolid, dull, vacant plough-boys, ungainly in build,
> uncomely in face, lifeless, apathetic, a race a good deal more like
> the pre-Revolution French peasant as described by Carlyle than is
> pleasant to reflect upon – a race now supplanted . . .

For some of them even the rough sex-life of many of their contemporaries is not yet possible; it requires more management of their own personalities and more meeting with other personalities than they can compass.

From their education at school they have taken little which connects with the realities of life as they experience it after fifteen. Most of them have jobs which require no personal outgoing, which are not intrinsically interesting, which encourage no sense of personal value, of being a maker. The job is to be done day by day, and after that the rest is amusement, is pleasure; there is time to spare and some money in the pocket. They are ground between the millstones of technocracy and democracy; society gives them an almost limitless freedom of the sensations, but makes few demands on them – the use of their hands and of a fraction of their brains for forty hours a week. For the rest they are open to the entertainers and their efficient mass-equipment. The youth clubs, the young people's institutes, the sports clubs, cannot attract them as they attract many of their generation; and the commercial people ensure, by the inevitable processes of development in commercial entertainment, that their peculiar grip is retained and strengthened. The responsibilities of marriage may gradually change them. Meanwhile, they have no responsibilities, and little sense of responsibilities, to themselves or to others. They are in one dreadful sense the new workers; if, by extra-polation simply from a reading of newer working-class entertainment litera-ture, one were to attempt to imagine the ideal readers for that literature, these would be the people. It is true, as I have said, that they are not typical.

But these are the figures some important contemporary forces are tending to create, the directionless and tamed helots of a machine-minding class. If they seem to consist so far chiefly of those of poorer intelligence or from homes subject to special strains, that is probably due to the strength of a moral fibre which most cultural providers for working-class people are helping to de-nature. The hedonistic but passive barbarian who rides in a fifty-horse-power bus for threepence, to see a five-million-dollar film for one-and-eightpence, is not simply a social oddity; he is a portent.

Richard Hoggart, *The Uses of Literacy* (1957)

1957: Gold Pan Alley

Amongst the arts that have emerged from the interaction of twentieth-century technology and mass communications, that of the popular song – the commercial product of Tin Pan Alley – has emerged as a prototype. Vast sums are spent annually in producing and selling the product, and no group or individual in the Western world can remain untouched by its manifest-ations. A study of the producer–consumer relationships involved can provide a revealing index to many cultural and sociological emphases in the contem-porary situation.

This vast continuum of production–consumption controls is controlled by those same factors of taste, fashion, behaviour, group approval, success goals, etcetera, expressed in ads, comic strips and movies, all of which possess autonomous values which are outside of, and indifferent to, the critical values of Western 'fine arts' and 'official culture'. Like other mass-produced products, the Pop song and its performers exhibit 'product dif-ferentiation' characteristics typical of competitive product design. As, say, cigarette manufacturers play their variations within rigorous limits of leaf, paper and packaging – so the pop song producer plays his within general limits of a thirty-two-bar chorus, a few basic harmonies and a specific tribal language. The consumers effect their delicate adjustments to these 'product differentiations' according to the 'right' preferences of their group, and their approval or non-approval exercises its 'feedback' control to the mass media itself.

The assembly line of music business, like other mass media, has its attend-ant co-operative of writers, artists, technicians and ad-men, wherein each individual may be supreme in his own field yet contributes to the whole without loss of personal status. The group is highly sensitive to all signals fed back from the consumer field and maintains a constant equilibrium between the fluctuations of group tastes and the styling of the product.

As with the movies, the mythology of pop songs and singers has its close producer–consumer relationships where myth and reality overlap. Chance elements may transform a garage-hand or waitress into a 'star' overnight – not within the relatively inflexible confines of Covent Garden Opera House – that would make them 'straight' singers, instead they become 'personalities', flexible and vernacular in a medium where approval is the only goal. The transition from 'unknown' to 'star' takes place in that vague area where the common myth is shared. Although our garage-hand is now a 'star', he is still an 'available' type identifiable with the mass and, as his press agent will underline, he still retains the tastes and allegiances of his group. His press stories generally portray him as a relatively static human being to whom a number of things *have happened*, and who is participating in a success which seems to be none of his doing. His personal affairs are recounted by the group and become part of contemporary folk-lore.

The Songwriters
There are, broadly speaking, two categories of songwriters: those with a background of traditional 'cultivated' European music, and those with a background of the medicine show or burlesque theatre and little or no formal musical orientation but rather a vernacular, empiric approach to an essentially expendable product. The former category includes writers such as Kern, Romberg, Rodgers and Hammerstein – all with strong ties to the nostalgic world of nineteenth-century operetta. Hammerstein, after completing a song said, 'What experiences of our own, what experiences of others, what a continuity of how many men's thoughts for how many generations, has resulted in this final assembly of words and music?' Here is the emphasis on the product – not the use of it made by the consumer. The terms are concerned with the manipulation of the material rather than people, an attitude recalling the period of the pre-World War I 'production hero' in its concern for the traditional virtues of craft and integrity.

The second category is of the 'consumption hero' type, who is more concerned with the market, i.e. people. The appearance of the 'consumption hero' is apparent from a study of popular biography. Before World War I attention was focused on political figures and captains of industry, but by the 1920s sportsmen and entertainers were admitted. Nowadays, the greater portion of popular biography concerns the private lives and relationships of 'consumption' and 'leisure' heroes from the worlds of sport and entertainment. This category also has roots in the minstrel show. The mechanization of communications and increasing mobility of population around the turn of the century enabled the travelling salesmen of the minstrel shows to hit the new railroad to the widening consumption frontiers and become dynamic links between songwriter and audience, their direct response to environment shaping the product in an organic rather than static form. This figure of songwriter as salesman emerged more clearly during the industrialization of urban centres. Nickelodeons, vaudeville and six-day bike races attracted audiences eager to participate in the conspicuous consumption of leisure. Writer and publisher soon learned that no matter how good a song was in their opinion, it needed that extra push to win public affection. Song slides on movie screens invited audience participation, and in one night an energetic song-plugger might sing in half a dozen movie houses, a couple of vaudeville theatres and a long route of dance halls and beergardens, finishing in the early hours.

The Songs

In the pioneering days of Tin Pan Alley, success was largely due to the energy and go-getting qualities of the individual; often as combination of songwriter, plugger and performer, he was totally involved in the cycle. With industrial specialization the group replaced this individual effort and powerful sales forces were geared to expose the product to the rapidly expanding audiences of the mass media. The musical arranger became an important styling factor, and the composer no longer had to 'hit the road' for plugs. The songs mirrored changes in behaviour, speech, dress and moral and ethical standards, and as mechanization took command so the songs ran – 'Wait for the Wagon', 'A Bicycle Made for Two', 'When the Midnight Choo-choo Leaves for Alabama', 'You've Got to Get Out and Get Under' (a document of the hazards of early motoring), 'Come Josephine in My Flying Machine', etc., etc. Gramophone recording helped to trigger off the dance crazes that swept the international scene and from the 'Turkey Trot' through to 'rock 'n' roll' follows the continuous pattern of changing fashions. Although arranger and performer shape stylings to varied group preferences, the lyrics of pop songs retain an autonomy irrespective of this package differentiation. A detailed evaluation of the lyric content of the pop song is the subject of an individual paper and must remain outside of this brief survey.

The Tech Men

Before the 'personalization' of the product by star performers and its sale in the open market of mass media, it is carefully processed by highly skilled technicians. Musical arrangers, musicians and engineers carefully steer the product to the final target of mass approval. The musical arranger emerged as an important styling factor around the time of Paul Whiteman and 'Symphonic' jazz in the early 1920s, with his inclusion of the 'jazz man's' technique of instrumental tone production and idiomatic procedures within a formalized musical structure. Academic instrumental requirements were extended, notably in the brass section, and mutes and other devices added a further range of tone colours. A new type of instrumentalist evolved who, besides having a thorough academic technique, had the idiomatic and stylistic nuances of jazz at his disposal, and the 'unschooled' jazz player was generally left to function outside of 'commercial' music. The new, and highly sophisticated, colours and rhythms were borrowed by the 'straight' men, and we find a continuous pattern of usage through to the present-day radio, recording and film studio orchestras.

Arrangers, performers and tech men are constantly interacting in the endless quest for 'product differentiation' gimmicks. The 'crooner' came with technology – the microphone providing an extension to performer so that both he and the audience could 'personalize' their relationship. The microphone created fresh problems for the musical arranger – it could reduce complex contrapuntal writing, satisfactory in the concert hall, to a one-dimensional monochrome – yet could reveal new colours and perspectives impossible in 'live' performance. A heavily loaded word in pop recording circles is 'presence', a term which describes technical procedures aimed at projecting the 'personality' and 'sincerity' factors of a performer on a scale rather larger than life. His voice is brought well 'forward' in the sound perspective, on a separate plane to the accompaniment. This effect of aural close-up, like its visual counterpart in movies, enables the audience the pleasure of participating within the aura of the performer's presence. The musical arranger assists by subjugating his musical role to that of 'background' and generally avoids the use of musical elements that might invoke prior claims of audience attention whilst singer is singing.

The vast consumption of gramophone recordings has brought about important changes in technical manufacture processes. The 'fine arts' attitude of making recordings 'to last' by imposing a fairly low volume level on the grooves has given way to the newer juke box attitude of maximum impact at the highest practical volume level, being equivalent in aural terms to the ad-man's 'attention-getting' factor.

The Singers
The contemporary type of pop singer appeared during the change from 'production' to 'consumption' heroes, when judgment criteria made the shift from 'content' to 'personality'. To him, group approval means success, and the most important quality demanded from him is 'sincerity' rather than aesthetic values or craft skills. He demonstrates his sincerity by placing both himself and his emotions at the disposal of his fans, and evokes a response in terms of 'personality' rather than 'content'. David Whitfield says: 'I recorded "The Book" – songs like these are in direct sympathy with my own beliefs, and that's a tremendous help to a singer who wants to be really sincere. I hope I shall always sound that way because, believe me, I'm a sincere sort of chap.'

Next in the performer's equipment comes the conspicuous display of the 'desire for approval'. Publicity stills generally show him leaning out of the frame, extending the glad hand and big smile to the consumers, or posed in an attitude that unambiguously invites adulation. Johnnie Ray says: 'I eat up affection. I can't get enough of it . . . when the fans *stop* mobbing me – that's the time to get worried.'

The sharing of the common myth, wherein producer may also be consumer, is also faithfully reported in the biographical stories. Johnnie Ray says: 'The best part of topping all those ritzy clubs was meeting the film stars that visit them. I had my picture taken with Ethel Merman at the Copa, and at Ciro's Joan Crawford came backstage and actually asked me for an autograph.'

The identification of the idol with the taste factors of his approval-group is exemplified by his urge to 'belong', no matter what changes have occurred now that he is a 'success'. Dickie Valentine says: 'I'm an ordinary sort of chap – my tastes are simple, but they are definite – just ask my wife. We are living with my parents at present, later we hope to have a house. The furniture will be modern in style – but not too bohemian. We haven't decided on a colour scheme – though Betty insists that the kitchen shall be in cream and white.'

There are other, slightly less characteristic, elements displayed – such as the insistence that success is not necessarily owed to craft skill. Johnnie Ray says: 'I can't read one note – I never had any training – all I know is what my ear tells me, and therefore I can put myself pretty much on the same level as the record-buying public.'

The accent is generally placed on 'the thing that is bigger than me', and a general insistence on the repudiation of craft skill in the materials of music.

Promotion

In the discussion of pop songs and singers there arises a factor which marks a fundamental difference between this and other forms of advertising. Ads about products usually concern themselves with statements, visual or otherwise, of the virtues of the 'thing' itself, the desirability of consumption or possession, but rarely *are* the 'thing' itself. The pop song *is* advertisement – advertisement contained within its own performance. It is uncommunicable to the mass audience until its own performance along a time-dimension, and only then can it assume a tangible existence. The act of performance is the act of advertisement – the union being indivisible.

Up to the period when the fireside story-teller moved over to make room for the domestic radio, music publishers often used 'ballyhoo' methods to attract public attention to their product. Jack Hylton's Band once flew over Blackpool and showered down thousands of copies of 'Me and Jane in a 'Plane', and elephants once rode down the Strand to publicize the song 'Baghdad'. The spread of mass communications made these stunts obsolete and now the product performs its own advertising, mainly at the hands of that omnipotent figure – the 'disc-jockey'.

Written and visual ads for the pop song are mainly confined to the circle of 'pro' trade papers, and the campaigns of record companies operate at a rather modest level, insignificant by comparison with other nationally consumed products. Radio, TV or movies can be the launching platform for the initial advertising performance of a new song or singer. If a 'positive' approval feed-back is registered from the consumers, the product embarks on its consumption continuum of 'requested' repeat performances, disc sales, further approval, more performances, more disc sales and an ephemeral life on the juke-boxes until its days are numbered, the consumers are satiated and their approval is being transferred to the newest marginally differentiated contender.

Frank Cordell, Ark 19, Spring 1957

1957: Bongo Scores at Tom-Tom

The picture in the fan-mag showed this gangly kid in jeans and a sweat shirt, his face contorted, mouth wide open, beating with both hands on a bongo set round his shoulder, over it the headline BONGO SCORES AT TOM-TOM. The same terrible stuff, but this time it was good, because it was me who dropped the dead-beat drunk columnist a fiver to run it. Because this new boy Bongo

Herbert, playing nightly for the past week at the Tom-Tom expresso back of Frith Street, is under contract to nobody but me. Half of the ten pounds he picks up this Friday comes to me. Half of everything he beats out of those little bongos for the next three years comes to me.

I checked my capital of twenty-three pounds and some shillings useful for unavoidable tips, the balance of a fifty-pound fee for publicizing the Wally Burn Flames tour. Free as a pimp or an artiste's manager, I walked over to the Tom-Tom to collect my first week's unearned income.

Not so unearned. For three weeks after I found my property beating and shouting himself into a frenzy on the corny 'Jazz Boat Stomp' which the Flames signed off with. I had wet-nursed that kid along, bought him cigarettes and coffee and sandwiches, a couple of sweat shirts with bongos painted on them, a pair of tailored black jeans, and a fancy haircut, turned him from Bert Rudge, snotty-nosed nobody, to Bongo Herbert, Britain's latest answer to America's latest solution of how to keep discs selling by the million. Not that Bongo was answering back yet. I wouldn't be in profit for another couple of weeks, and then only if Leon at the Tom-Tom kept him on that long.

'The boy's great, isn't he, Leon?' I said.

'I'm getting my Italian peasant-style cups and saucers broke,' Leon complained, 'from where these mad kids keep time bashing on the tables. Two tables also is already broke in the legs.'

'You're doing great business, Leon,' I told him, and showed him the fan-mag.

'It's a good publicity,' he said. 'How much costs a whole page in this paper?'

'More than the ten you're paying my boy,' I pointed out.

'I keep him another week maybe,' Leon said grudgingly as he handed over ten dirty but attractive notes.

'You take him for six weeks, Leon,' I replied, 'or we beat our tiny brains out in some other expresso.'

'Six weeks at ten,' he said.

'At fifteen,' I corrected.

So I sold Bongo to Leon for twelve a week for six weeks. At this rate Bongo would be a very old teen-ager before I could retire to the South of France. Kids with imitation American gimmicks were rocking their managers into comfort while I wasted my life on café expresso and doughnuts. It was humiliating.

Still, Bongo was a good boy – a good simple unspoiled boy. When I gave him his five, his first week's money, there were great oily tears in his eyes.

'That only leaves you five for yourself, guv,' he muttered. 'You should take more. I wouldn't get nothing without you.'

Such trust and honesty deserved my support.

'Take it, Bongo,' I told him with a he-man pulled-punch to his jaw. 'Half of everything you make is going to go to you, kid.'

I knew Bongo could be the answer. After all, Tommy Steele had been standing in for Elvis Presley (who was too busy counting his dollars to bother coming after softer currencies in person) for a year now. A year is a long time in the life of a teen-age idol. The seventeen-year-olds make the most capricious public in the world. They want someone new to get excited about every few months. It has to be someone who is (or can act) not much older than themselves, and since the mob is mostly female, the talent has to be male and sexy (or able to act it). It has to be someone with a nobody background – rags to riches in five yelping stages – from dirty sweaty shirt to gold lamé sweat shirt. It had to be Bongo.

That night at the Tom-Tom it was.

The place was stacked with sweating teen-agers (and a few who would like to be) wearing Vince Man's Shop jeans with heavy rollnecks, close-fitting Charing Cross Road teddy trousers and velvet-collared coats bought on the hire-purchase, string ties hanging in the cold coffee, suède Jeff Chandler lumber jackets, and bright strained cotton sweaters dashed with cigarette ash and crumbs from Leon's special pizza. There was smoke in the Tony Curtis hair-styles, and smoke around the pony-tails. Thick badly applied mascara ran down the face of a girl in a black jersey and ski pants crying in a corner, while a spade with big white teeth chipped one of Leon's valuable cups beating it out with Bongo.

Backed by a frantic skiffle group called the Beasts (hungry for pizza and applause), Bongo found rhythms which were crude enough for these simple-minded low-budget good-timers to believe in. He bashed the baby drums, twisted like an electric eel, and shouted a meaningless string of words we had thrown together.

The boy had something – a something which wasn't commodity in the days when talent with polish was expected. He was contemporary-style: elementary violent energy coupled to an inane but genuine gaiety (at this price what did he have to be gay about?) which hooked these yokels from Elephant and Castle and points south by the grubby scruffs of their immature emotions and flung them far away from the kitchen sink, the stale oilcloth, the nagging mothers, and the bellowing bewildered fathers, and dropped them writhing into a synthetic tropic confusion. Or, as Bongo, yelping and chi-yiking in his hoarse Hoxton voice, put it:

> Ex-presso – bongo
> Fla-menko – bongo
> Tooo-baygo – bongo
> Caa-lypso – bongo
> Bongo – bongo – calypso – bongo
> Olé

While Bongo broke off for a while to pour coffee down his gravel throat and let his bongos cool off, I turned to the thin, oily-eyed dyspeptic whose poker face had grown longer with every *bongo!*

'Another *cappuccino*, Mr Mayer?' For it was no other than the hard-to-get talent-spotter from Garrick Records himself whom I had caressed through an expensive dinner and dragged into this hellhole to hear my talented client. His eyes showed the glaze of six brandies and a genuine dislike for this kind of music.

'Have another, Mr Mayer?'

'Keeps me awake,' he complained.

I might as well get it over with, I thought. 'What's your feeling about the boy?' I asked him.

'Nausea,' he replied.

Well thank you and good-night, Mr Mayer, I thought.

'The kid's got a great gimmick, Mr Mayer,' I said, my eyes bursting with enthusiasm, my teeth bared in the full smile of the confident loser.

Mayer wiped coffee stains from the corners of his dry mouth on a grubby handkerchief monogrammed 'O' – must be for ostrich. He refused to see something great when it happened.

'You know,' he said, 'I am really by nature an opera man. I think *Aïda* is a work of beauty and excitement. All this' – he waved a thin, contracted claw in the direction of Bongo and the Beasts – 'all this kind of thing is deeply sickening to my temperament. It so happens, due to the irony of fate, in opera I lost my shirt . . .'

'You put on some great shows, Mr Mayer, show business doesn't forget,' I said, sycophantic as ever. I waved the fanmag with the Bongo headline under his nose like potpourri. 'This boy's not doing bad.'

Mayer sighed. 'I lost my shirt,' he repeated. 'Yet from this disc lunacy I make money.'

It was getting too late to sit listening to the reminiscences of an old O-for-ostrich has-been impresario.

'Well, thank you, Mr Mayer for being so frank,' I said (he should be this frank once more and drop stone dead).

'Like I say,' he continued sadly, 'for me personally this kind of thing is torture. I'll give thirty-five pounds for your client and the group, two sides, no royalty, one-way option to the company. Record next week. All right?'

'Mr Mayer,' I said, blinking, 'so you really think the boy has something?'

Mayer got up to go.

'I don't know – I don't care,' he said. 'These young idiots seem to want this kind of thing so let's sell them what they want. Maybe next week, with this Bongo boy, we lose a few pounds. So what? The week after we find a Tommy Steele and make a profit.'

The mob had gulped down the pizzas and expressos and was shouting for more Bongo.

'Listen to them, Mr Mayer,' I said with missionary fervour, 'they want him – they want him, Mr Mayer.'

'Don't get so excited,' he said, as he rose, a thin lost waif of an impresario. 'Here they don't have to pay for him. A record costs six shillings.'

As the kid, fresh again, began to beat on his little skin money-boxes, I worked out how many discs at six shillings Mayer had to sell before Bongo earned me my first thousand.

Assuming we got on to a royalty basis of 1½d a disc with our second recording, it came to almost half a million.

Meanwhile, take off a fiver for the skiffle Beasts and the evening's work showed me and my boy fifteen apiece cash. Not exactly the late Mike Todd's kind of money – but I was in profit.

In profit.

I love those words.

Wolf Mankowitz, *Expresso Bongo* (1960)

1958: Pop Songs and Teenagers

The Editor has warned me some readers may not know what pop discs are. So: pop=popular; disc=gramophone recording. In short, the elegantly boxed records of the High Street music stores which, last year, sold 50 millions of them. The music-fodder of the juke-boxes, the radios and radio-grams. To the vast mysterious majority, the only kind of songs there are.

I sense a shudder: 'Oh, he means jazz.' No, he doesn't. True jazz is, to pop music, what the austere harmonies of the Wigmore Hall are to the lush tremolos of the Palm Court and its gypsy violins. 'Then he means crooners.' That's a bit nearer, though the word's twenty years out of date and at once betrays the cultivated person who's never listened to a pop – or even, for that matter, most probably, to a crooner (unless perhaps to Crosby, *circa* 1932).

Warming to my theme, I'd like to say I think the abysmal ignorance of educated persons about the popular music of the millions, is deplorable. First, because pop music, on its own low level, can be so good; and I must declare that never have I met anyone who, condemning it completely, has turned out, on close enquiry, to know anything whatever about it. But worse, because the deaf ear that's turned, in pained disdain, away from pop music betrays a lamentable lack of curiosity about the culture of our country in 1958. For that music *is* our culture: at all events, the anthropologist from São Paulo or Peking would esteem it so, and rightly. Alfred Deller, yes; but what about Lonnie Donegan, he'd say? They're both of our world, and there's no doubt which of these siren voices penetrates and moulds more English hearts and brains.

But in England, pop art and fine art stand resolutely back to back. For all the interest educated persons take in the pop arts of their own people, they might be settlers among the tribesmen of darkest Ruanda-Urundi. No, no, not even! In that case, they'd certainly have collected a few native masks and ivories. But how many of my gentle readers possess, I wonder, a pop disc? The point isn't that you've got to like this music, if you can't. It is that, if you don't know it, you lose a clue to what lies behind those myriad faces in the bus and tube – particularly the young ones.

Let's open our *Melody Maker* and scan the list of the Top Twenty: of the recordings which have had the highest sales to our fellow-countrymen and women. What will it tell us of their tastes and dreams? In the week I write this, plenty. First, only three of the singers are over thirty, and a third of them are less than twenty-one (the youngest, Laurie London, is fourteen). The modern troubadours are teenagers, and the reason's not far to seek: the buyers are teenagers, too.

Gramophone recordings are one of the many industries that have come into being, in the past few years, to absorb the tremendous buying power of the young. We are in the presence, here, of an entirely new phenomenon in human history: that youth is rich. Once, the *jeunesse dorée* were a minute minority; now, all the young have gold. Earning good wages, and living for little, or even for free, like billeted troops on poor harassed Dad and Mum, the kids have more 'spending money' than any other age group of the population. Farewell the classic, century-old pattern of Youth the industrious apprentice, penniless, nose glued to grindstone, and Age, prosperous, authoritative, in fair round belly with good chump-chop lined. Today, age is needy and, as its powers decline, so does its income; but full-blooded youth has wealth as well as vigour. In this decade, we witness the second Children's Crusade, armed with strength and booty, against all 'squares', all adult nay-sayers. An international movement, be it noted, that blithely penetrates the political curtains draped by senile seniors, as yet unconscious of the rising might of this new classless class.

What are these teenage pop discs like to listen to? Let's look more closely at a typical best-seller in the Top Twenty, Mr Paul Anka's 'Diana'. Paul Anka is a Syrian-Canadian who was born in Ottawa sixteen years ago. He wrote the words and music of 'Diana' himself, it has sold over a million copies in England alone, and its world sales are said to have netted more than £100,000 to its young composer-singer. The tune has a slick, quick blare and beat, with crescendo passages of agonized ecstasy, and Paul puts it over with smack attack, total conviction, absolutely minimal subtlety, and a triumphal, unrestrained, juvenile animal vulgarity.

In this essay, alas, I cannot reproduce the voice and tune – only the lyric. This, on the whole, is undistinguished even by pop standards, with couplets like

> I love you with all my heart
> And I hope we will never part

yet there are some lines that hint at the reasons for its teenage appeal. It opens:

> I'm so young and you're so old . . .

And closes:

> Oh, please stay by me, Diana!
> Oh – please – DIANA!

Even the amateur psychologist can deduce, from this, the teenage triumph and the teenage yearning. It's wonderful to be 'so young' because it's *I* who am singing the song, I who am 'sending' my fellow teenagers by my singing, and yet . . . there is the underlying longing for the older woman (could it be the mother-figure?) whom the singer addresses, unequivocally, as

> Oh my darlin', oh *my lover*.

What's most striking of all about the whole tone of this song, and of young Mr Anka's delivery, is its overall mood of world-weary languor, as if it were a *cri du cœur* of a man saturated by an excess of experience. And it's startling (for anyone over twenty) to read, in the pop musical press, that the girl he originally had in mind when he wrote it was *eighteen years old*. Also, that he himself has announced that he proposes to retire when he reaches that same great age. No doubt about it: teenagers – in some senses, at any rate – ripen more quickly than they used to.

Continuing our examination of the weekly lists of the Top Twenty we shall find some other changes, during the past year or so, in the type of song and singer that's most liked. We've already seen that English kids no longer want to rip the drape suits off the backs of oldsters like Frankie Laine and Johnnie Ray; now they demand minstrels of their own age. But there's another reason why such singers are in decline: they are Americans. For what's sensational about the list I have before me is that no less than half the performers are British – something unthinkable a year ago.

Now, the pop song of the past decade is an American invention, and the best pop singers were (and still are) American. Moreover, practitioners like Elvis Presley (of whom more soon) are still dearly beloved of English fans. But there has been a shift of emphasis: English singers have gradually captured a place in the pop market. And they have done this by learning to sing the American pop style in a manner quite indistinguishable from the real thing, so that we have the paradox that teenagers like, increasingly, songs sung *by Englishmen in American*.

Let's make a comparison between two stars of the Top Twenty – trans-atlantic Elvis and our own Tommy Steele, both of whom swam to glory at the height of the rock 'n' roll craze, now mercifully in decline. With no less than four discs in the current list, Elvis must still be regarded, despite his relative antiquity (he is twenty-three), as the teenage *stupor mundi*. In contrast to the 1940s ideal of the crew-cutted, athletic, out-of-door American boy, Elvis represents something of a reversion to the Valentino era with his sleeked, slick locks and sideburns, and his baleful, full-lipped Neronic glare. His songs seem, melodically, absolutely identical, with words, where comprehensible, that are loaded with mildly smutty innuendo. You may not admire the frantic agitation of his hunched shoulders as he laces his electric guitar with loving arms, or the equivocal motion of his over-expressive shark-skin slacks, or even, for that matter, his ear-cracking, plexus-shaking voice. But there's no denying the punch, verve and gusto of his performance

– its utter certainty that what he gives, they need.

His act, in short, has all the frenzy of a jungle dance and war cry without their dignity. In complete contrast is England's Tommy Steele. If Elvis is the teenage witch-doctor, Tommy Steele is Pan. His tunes, originally derived from 'rock', but increasingly melodious and even, on occasions, tender, are an invitation to the forest, to the haywain, to the misty reaches of the Thames at Bermondsey from whence he comes. Not that Tommy cannot 'send' the kids with agitated, blue-jeaned leaps and caperings, and gollywog mop-shakes of his golden hair. But the whole effect, to use a silly word, is so much *nicer*. His voice and his cavortings are sensual, certainly, but in a strange way innocent, even pure. His speaking voice is that of a descendant of a long line of Cockney singers – Elen, Kate Carney, Chevalier – sardonic and sentimental. But when he sings, it's as if he spoke another language: for though the teenagers may accept a thoroughly English *singer*, they are indifferent to a contemporary English *song*. Indeed – except for old-style sentimental ballads – no such thing may yet be said to exist in early 1958.

At the risk of boring the reader with instances of this strange duality of the teenage mentality, I'd like to describe another American-style English singer – Lonnie Donegan. The reason I harp on this so is that I think a study of pop music may help to show in what ways young English boys and girls are 'Americanized', and in what ways they are not. Lonnie Donegan is a product of the skiffle cellars, and he has achieved a feat which is, in one sense, even more remarkable than that of Tommy Steele – that is, to become a top pop singer not only in his native English backwater, but in the transatlantic land of make-believe as well.

In case there's anyone who doesn't yet know about skiffle, let's recapitulate. Skiffle (onomatopoeic) music has existed in America certainly since the last century and, in its original form, it was played by groups of amateur musicians who sang traditional (and sometimes newly created) ballads accompanying themselves on home-made instruments – many of these, like the celebrated washboard, domestic utensils. It was thus, at first, a 'folk art' of sorts, and the reason why primitive instruments were used was simply that there was no money to buy real ones. A few years ago, for reasons that remain mysterious, and coinciding with the eruption of the coffee bars (and still more, their cellars) all over London, skiffle groups appeared and spread like mushrooms till there are today certainly many hundreds of them, several of which have won commercial fame. The movement is, of course, a 'mannerist' one – somewhat similar, in a way, to the revival of English folk-dancing some decades ago. That is to say, the teenagers in the groups are reviving, artificially, a musical style that was once spontaneous – though I'm not at all denying their enthusiasm (or, for that matter, the sincerity of the dactylographs and clerical workers who cavort in Morris dances at Cecil Sharp House).

But what's odd is that the ballads the skiffle musicians sing are American, and their singing accent even more so. Songs about transatlantic gals and jails and railroads, intoned in a nasal monotone, seem entirely convincing to Cockney kids from Camberwell and Wood Green, sitting huddled in the Soho basements – and their idol, Lonnie Donegan, has sold some of these back to the Americans with resounding success. And not only on records like his 'Rock Island Line', but even by himself in person, barnstorming triumphantly across the Limey-despising United States. What's odder still is that, as the process continues, some of these ballads will have crossed the Atlantic three times: from here to America in colonial days, from there back again to the London skiffle cellars, and now, with Mr Donegan and Miss Nancy Whiskey, over once more to the US.

I come now to two minor changes in pop disc fashions, and the first is the decline of the female singer: for in the list before me, only two of the Top Twenty songs are sung by women.

Now, I think there's no doubt that in the whole dreadful, wonderful pop song canon, among the top practitioners of the art women outnumber men by at least two to one: for every Sinatra there's a Clooney or a Lee, for every Eckstine, a Vaughan or a Horne. But not in the Top Twenty of the teenagers! May this suggest that, if the adult dream figure is a woman, among the kids it's the wolf-whistle of the adolescent male that 'sends' them most? And may we not see an analogy with the pop art of the films? Can anyone imagine, for example, that some female James Dean could have been, in the middle of our century, the emblematic figure that he had become? At all events, as the 'personal managers' and recording company talent-spotters prospect the jazz clubs and skiffle cellars for new adolescent gold mines, it's boys they almost invariably select. Even Tommy's younger brother, Colin Hicks, has been pressed into service, and it would seem that the unbroken voice of fourteen-year-old Laurie London is no bar to favour with the kids. Could it therefore be there's something *tribal* in the teenage ideology? Among adults, I think there's no doubt this is a woman's age; but perhaps the kids have reverted to a more primitive pattern. The sight of two London Teds, out with their girls, is perhaps in this connection of significance. The boys walked ahead, their expressionless faces, surmounted by Tony Curtis hair-dos, bent in exclusive masculine communion. Ten feet behind them, ignoring them completely but following on, come their twin Ted-esses. I've seen an identical sight among the Kikuyu.

The other minor change is the teenage aversion (or indifference) to 'coloured' pop singers. While 'coloured' artists certainly remain popular among adult fans, in the list of the Twenty there is only one – Belafonte. It's true, of course, that there are other 'coloured' singers, not in the list, whom teenagers admire – 'Fats' Domino, for instance, and the incredible, hypnotic, hysterical 'Little Richard'. But they're not generally esteemed, it seems: and I very much doubt if it's teenage purchases that have lifted Harry Belafonte's sentimental rendition of West Indian calypso to so high a place in the Top Twenty. At all events, I think the real reasons for his state of solitary splendour are twofold. First, that most 'coloured' artists simply cannot bring themselves to sing the sort of number the teenagers like. But even more, I think it is that young people wish, increasingly, to identify themselves *personally* with the singers they admire. It's not for nothing, after all, that Tommy Steele gets 2,000 letters a week, 150 of them proposing marriage.

The time's now come to draw – on, I admit, very slender evidence – some tentative conclusions about teenagers. But try to draw them I think we should, because the 'two nations' of our society may perhaps no longer be those of the 'rich' and 'poor' (or, to use old-fashioned terms, the 'upper' and 'working' classes), but those of the teenagers on the one hand and, on the other, all those who have assumed the burdens of adult responsibility. Indeed, the great social revolution of the past fifteen years may not be the one which redivided wealth among the adults in the Welfare State, but the one that's given teenagers economic power. This piece is about the pop disc industry – almost entirely their own creation; but what about the new clothing industry for making and selling teenage garments of both sexes? Or the motor-scooter industry they patronize so generously? Or the radiogram and television industries? Or the eating and soft-drinking places that cater so largely for them? Putting it at its lowest, there may well be

Kids of 15 to 23	Each with annual 'spending money' of	Making an annual teenage kitty of
2 millions	£3×52	£312,000,000

With this they can influence English economic – and therefore social – life. For let's not forget their 'spending money' does not go on traditional necessities, but on the kinds of luxuries that modify the social pattern.

And so, just as it's absurd for old Bournemouth belles to decry the Welfare State itself, as if what's done could ever be undone, it's equally vain to suppose that teenage *power* (for that is what it is) can suddenly be withdrawn. Short of a general economic collapse, the teenage 'spending money' is here to stay. And make no mistake of it, the kids are very well aware of this. They may not have the vote (or particularly want it), and they may be subject to certain legal restrictions. But as anyone who read the accounts of the recent law suit over Tommy Steele's earnings will have realized, though the eminent lawyers spoke of Tommy in somewhat disdainful terms (as lawyers, those naïve realists, love to) as being an 'infant', it was the twenty-year-old Bermondsey boy, with his colossal fortune, who held the key position in the wings (or rather, on the studio set where he was making, at the time, the second film about his life, *The Duke Wore Jeans*). The hostility of some adults to teenagers – which often takes the form of a quite unbalanced loathing of their idols, particularly of Tommy and poor Elvis – is as sterile as is that hatred educated people often seem to have for television: a morbid dislike of these symbols of popular culture which they feel are undermining not so much culture itself, as their hitherto exclusive possession of it.

And what are they like, the teenagers? What do they think and want? How much will they alter when they become wives and husbands? Here the anthropologists have a lot of work to do (very much neglected, it seems to me). Meanwhile, I offer these inexpert impressions.

1   They are much more *classless* than any of the older age groups are, or were. In the days when I was a teenager, it was impossible to step outside your class unless you joined the army, or went to jail; but now, the kids seem to do this quite effortlessly. An analysis of a jazz club membership would, I am sure, reveal the most varied social origins; and the point is, the kids just ignore this topic – they seem genuinely uninterested in it. In contrast with the earlier generation (say, now aged 23–35) that was emancipated by the Welfare State and who, in spite of economic gains, still seem almost ferociously obsessed by class, the kids don't seem to care about it at all.

2   They are not so much hostile to as blithely indifferent to the Establishment. In the two copies of *Fling*, the teenage weekly put out by the Mirror Group and, most unfortunately, suppressed, an extremely detailed poll was taken among the kids about Altrincham-and-all-that; and their answers suggested the boys and girls just weren't concerned by all that nonsense. In the same way, I have the impression that a play like *Look Back in Anger*,

with its cry of protest that so shook the old and staid, would seem quite meaningless to them. What is all this about outside lavatories and having to open sweet shops when you've got plenty of 'spending money'? What are the difficulties of meeting those who read 'posh' Sunday papers when you can dance with as many of them as you like at the local jazz club (with that splendid natural democrat, and old Etonian, Humphrey Lyttleton, presiding)? John Osborne's play exists within the context of the old order, and only takes on its meaning by being, in a sense, a part of it. To a teenager, it would seem thoroughly old-fashioned.

3   They are *not* 'Americanized'. I say this despite all the evidence I've adduced to the contrary. The paradox is that the bearded skiffle singers with their Yankee ballads, and Tommy Steele with his 'rock'-style songs, seem so resoundingly, so irreversibly, English. I don't at all deny an *influence* (which, incidentally, has been going on ever since ragtime hit this country before World War I). But the kids have transformed this influence into something of their own ... in a way that suggests, subtly, that they're almost *amused* by what has influenced them. Put an English teenager beside an American, and you'll see the difference: our version is less streamlined, less pattern-perfect, and more knobbly, homely, self-possessed. The last word on this was said by Tommy Steele himself. When asked, by an interviewer, if he was going to the States, he said (in characteristically transatlantic idiom): 'I don't dig America.' And whatever they may take from there, I think that goes for his admirers, too.

4   I think they are more internationally-minded than we were; and not, as we were, self-consciously ('Youth for Spain', and so on), but intuitively. They are as much at ease at the Moscow congress as at the jazz festival in the local Trocadero. Teenage songs, and even styles of clothing, are carried across Europe, it would seem, by a sort of international adolescent *maquis*; and it may be that this post-Hiroshima generation has realized, instinctively and surely, how idiotic are the lethal posturings and deadly infantile bluster of their elders, as they wave bombs and rockets and satellites at one another.

5   In their private lives, they don't like to be *told*. Because of their economic power, and perhaps because those born in the war years were forced towards independence at an early age, they're undoubtedly more mature than young-sters used to be. How profound, psychologically, this maturity may be, I do not know; but on the surface, at any rate, they face the adult world with an almost alarming aplomb, and a touch-me-if-you-dare look on their impassive faces.

They're undoubtedly *cleaner* than kids once were; and in them the English people, which loves to sneer at Continental filth, but is actually the dirtiest race in Europe, has at last had a collective wash-and-brush-up. And the improvement is not only on their persons. Dry-cleaners, rare twenty years ago except in bourgeois quarters, now abound. The bright, coloured jeans and sweaters worn by both sexes invite the laundry, and lend themselves more readily to it than did the drab 'men's wear' and 'frocks' of yesteryear. With their hair, they take immense pains – the boys as well as the girls; and though this excites the scorn and envy of prudes and sergeant-majors, I find it attractive – perhaps, of all the idiotic parallels that have been found between our own age and that of the first Elizabethans, the only real one.

They don't drink; and have thus created yet another industry, that of the non-alcoholic beverage.

As for their sex life, it's mysterious. Their gregarious sociability, their ease with one another, their interchange of clothing and the frank sensuality of their music and their dancing suggest promiscuity without pain. But whether this is so or not is hard to determine. My own guess is that while their social life is very uncomplicated as between boy and girl, it's not particularly 'immoral'.

In general, they're gayer than English people seem to have been for fifty years at least. Contemporary England is peculiar for being the most highly organized country, in the social sense, for ensuring the moral and material welfare of everybody – pullulating with decent laws, with high-minded committees, with societies for preventing or encouraging this or that – and yet it has produced, in consequence, the *dullest* society in western Europe: a society blighted by blankets of negative respectability, and of dogmatic domesticity. The teenagers don't seem to care for this, and have organized their underground of joy.

This is, on the whole, an optimistic view. But it would be equally possible to see, in the teenage neutralism and indifference to politics, and self-sufficiency, and instinct for enjoyment – in short, in their kind of happy mindlessness – the raw material for crypto-fascisms of the worst kind. I don't sense this myself at all, though I may very well be wrong. What I am certain of, though, is that adults who wish to remain aware of their own world must study the teenagers, and get to know them: for never before, I'm convinced, has the younger generation been so *different* from its elders. Therefore, let moralists – especially political moralists – take heed. England is, and always has been, a country infested with people who love to tell us what to do, but who very rarely seem to know what's going on.

Colin MacInnes, *The Twentieth Century*, February 1958

1958: 'Baby Snatcher'

Jerry Lee Lewis, the rock 'n' roll singer who married a 13-year-old girl, was booed and jeered at by teenagers in a 2,000 audience last night as he loped around the stage of the Granada Theatre, Tooting.

Twenty-two-year-old Lewis taunted his audience: 'Yo' all seem awful quiet out there. Ah'm alive. I sho' hope yo' all ain't half as dead as yo' sound.'

At once the teenagers in the theatre yelled back: 'Go home, baby snatcher.'

The pale face of Lewis – in a custard-coloured suit with black sequined braiding – became even paler when the shouts kept up: 'Get home, you crumb.'

Throughout the twenty-seven minutes of the act he was barracked non-stop.

At times he looked at his watch as if anxious to get the show finished.

The crowd shouted: 'We've had enough of you, too.'

Later a group gathered at the stage door. They squeaked insults through the keyhole, Lewis did not show his face.

Earlier, Mr Oscar Davis, Lewis's manager, sipped a cup of tea in Mayfair's Westbury Hotel and said that he was expecting cancellations in some 'unfavourable towns' during the tour, following disclosures about the marriages and divorces of Mr Lewis.

Mr Davis, a stocky Bostonian, speaking in the hotel lounge, said: 'There is every possibility of the tour ending abruptly. I heard Jerry's agent, Mr Harry Foster, discussing the possibility of cancellations in the West Country.'

Mr Lewis has bookings in Salisbury, Plymouth, Taunton and Southampton.

Grey-haired Mr Davis said American public opinion has been roused against Lewis. He fears the Parent-Teachers' Association may take some kind of action when he returns to the States.

He fears, too, that the £535,000 film *High School Confidential* – Lewis has a big part – which opens today in Atlantic City, New Jersey, could have a poor reception and poor bookings.

Record sales, he says, could drop, losing a great deal of money for £178,000-a-year Mr Lewis.

In Room 127 at the Westbury yesterday Jerry Lee Lewis had lunch of steak, strawberries and ice-cream, and a soft drink, heavily iced. It was 4 p.m. With him was his thirteen-year-old wife Myra.

He sat on the bed, his hair crumpled, and said: 'I was a bigamist at the age of 16. I have not told the full truth about my marriages before, but last night I had an abusive telephone call from my second 'wife' Jane Mitcham.

'I decided that if she wants to play it that way, so will I. Jane said on the phone, "You're giving me lots of good publicity over here, but you won't see your son when you come back."

'My second marriage – to Jane – was not legal. It was invalid under United States law.

'I married Dorothy Barton when I was 15. I was just a brat, and I didn't know what I was doing. She was a good girl, but I decided to leave her after a year because I realised I was too young for marriage.

'Then I met Jane. She was as wild as the wind. I married her one week before my divorce from Dorothy. So I married her bigamously. There it is. That's the truth. I hadn't wanted to tell it, but now it's all come out.

'Jane and I only saw each other about once every six months over four years.

'Why did I have a divorce last month? It was Jane who divorced me. I didn't defend it, to avoid publicity, and everyone thought I was married anyway. I am paying Jane 750 dollars a month to take care of my son.

'I was a young fool when I married at 15 and 16. My father should have put his foot on my neck and beaten a worm out of me.

'Everybody thinks I am a ladies' man and a bad boy, but I am not. I am a good boy and I want everyone to know that.

'Myra and I are very happy. I am buying her a wedding ring very soon in England – a diamond one.'

An American Embassy spokesman said yesterday: 'Mr Lewis cannot be deported unless he is described as an undesirable alien. His marriage and divorce are being investigated in America now.'

John Lambert and Peter Kinsley, *Daily Express*, 27 May 1958

1958: 'You Didn't Put Beethoven in the Army'

The deferment explosion and the early haircut skirmishes made it clear that Operation Elvis would never have the smoothness of a Guy Lombardo medley. It had already taken on an uncontrollable rock-'n'-roll frenzy. Navy recruiters – jumping in with appealing pitches to Elvis, the public, and anybody who'd listen – conducted themselves like blue-suited advertising agency men wondering too late how the boys over at Hup, Two, Three & Four, Inc., had snared the big account.

Newsmen tried to keep the controversy throbbing by exhuming the military histories of Joe Louis and several regiments of World War II celebrities, many of whom had earned their ribbons in Special Services, the Army's entertainment branch. The articles noted that draftees Vic Damone and Eddie Fisher had been assigned to entertain the troops during the Korean conflict. Damone, in fact, had been specifically entrusted with the mission of recruiting women for military service. One of his major Army duties was to popularize a song called 'The Girls are Marching'.

The hazards of making a musical hero stand reveille never were more incisively illustrated than in 1951, when accordionist Dick Contino received his 'Greeting'. Contino, a more wholesome-seeming type than Elvis Presley, was described by a Hollywood columnist as a youth who 'doesn't drink, doesn't smoke, takes his mother along on tours, turns over his pay-check to his father, doesn't swear or tell dirty jokes in front of ladies ... wishes he knew more girls like his sister ... and smiles as pretty as anyone since Valentino'.

Still smiling prettily, Contino took his mother and father along for his induction at Fort Ord, Cal. They arrived several days in advance. When Contino's name was called for the induction ceremony, his parents were still at Fort Ord but the 20-year-old accordionist was not. He had disappeared.

Five days later, Contino – accompanied by his mother, doctor, lawyer, priest, and press agent – turned himself in to federal authorities. He pleaded 'panic claustrophobia' and said, 'I just got confused and walked out ... I couldn't stand to be in an enclosure. Everything at Fort Ord was behind a fence and it just made me sick all over.'

Before Contino saw the fences of Fort Ord again, he spent four months contemplating the walls of a federal prison. He was redrafted in 1952 and sent to Korea, where he made sergeant in his two years – a difficult accomplishment for any draftee.

Army officers turned as green as their new uniforms whenever they anticipated another Contino crisis. Early in 1958, officers at Fort Chaffee abandoned their coffee breaks to plan Elvis Presley's initial processing and basic training. They drew up schedules to cover Zero-Hour-Minus and Zero-Hour-Plus. They relieved eight Public Information Office men of their extra military duties and alerted them to work on a 24-hour-a-day basis when

Presley arrived. The staff was bolstered temporarily by an extra information officer from the New Mexico Military District. The Pentagon, called upon for advice, simply urged caution: 'Make as few statements as possible and *keep them dignified.*'

Fort Chaffee's policy-makers, heeding the word from Washington, responded with a set of elaborate ground rules: 'No female partners allowed in photo coverage ... The possibility of fan clubs, local or otherwise, attempting to "crash in" should be considered. Public announcement should be made to the effect that such organizations and/or individuals are strictly off limits.'

In the Presley camp, too, there were long strategy meetings. The double objective was to give Elvis the best financial break during his two-year hiatus and to keep the Elvis Image fresh in the public mind.

The financial outlook boiled down to a $104,916.80 loss of income for each month Elvis was not a civilian. This was based on his minimum annual take from two movies and a dozen personal appearances.

Elvis's absence from the big-money market would also cost Uncle Sam more than $500,000 a year in taxes that would have been collected from Presley.

Despite this, Elvis Presley would remain a blue-chip corporation. In addition to his private's salary of $83.20 a month, he would receive a percentage of the gross from four earlier movies, a base salary of $1,000 a week from RCA-Victor, record royalties, plus receipts from his own music-publishing firm and various Elvis Presley novelties. If Elvis could make more recordings while on pass or furlough (30 days of leave time a year), his 1958 income would reach the six-figure bracket.

While his brain trust pondered his fiscal future, Elvis went about his business. On the set of *King Creole* a month before induction, Elvis was calm about his impending Army career. 'I'm looking forward to going in,' he confided to a syndicated Hollywood columnist. 'I think it'll be a great experience.'

He was asked if he thought a tough sergeant or two might try to give the famous Elvis Presley a hard time.

'Well, if they do, it won't be because of anything I do to provoke it. I'm goin' in to be a soldier and the Army can do anything it wants with me and send me any place.'

Here was a philosophical attitude that could be recommended to any youth of draft age and to the clamorous public.

Before returning to Memphis for a nine-day 'last fling', Elvis was given a pre-induction Hollywood send-off at which he received a Civil War musket and ate part of a cake topped by a figure of an Army private peeling potatoes.

In Memphis, Presley had to buy his civilian privacy. He rented a roller-skating rink for eight nights at $65 a night to indulge in his favorite recreation. He would show up some time after the rink officially closed at 10.30 p.m.

No fewer than twelve beautiful girls were in and out of his mansion as house guests that week. He also dated some Memphis belles. On his last Saturday night as a civilian, Elvis went rollerskating and remarked: 'I'd be crazy to get married now. I like to play the field.' This was a laundered reiteration of his famous earthy statement on the same subject: 'Why buy a cow when you can get milk through the fence?'

Alan Levi, *Operation Elvis* (1960)

1958: In June

'Aboriginal!' said Zesty-Boy Sift.

This Zesty, who had come up now beside me, was the only other teenage product present at the barbecue, and I hadn't spoken to him yet for two reasons: first, because I meant to borrow five pounds from him, and wanted to choose my moment, and second, because this Z.-B. Sift had come up very abruptly in the world since I first knew him, and I didn't want to show I was impressed.

But in actual fact, I was. In the far dawn of creation when the teenage thing was in its Eden epoch, young Zesty used to sing around the bars and caffs, and was notorious for being quite undoubtedly the crumbiest singer since – well, choose your own. *But* – here's the point – the songs he sang, their words as well as harmonies, were his invention, thought up by him in a garage in Peckham, where he used to toil by day and slumber in an old Bugatti. And though Zesty caught all the necessary US overtones to send the juveniles that he performed for, the words he thought up were actually *about* the London teenage kids – I mean not just 'Ah luv yew, Oh yess Ah du' that could be about anyone, but numbers like 'Ugly Usherette', and 'Chickory with my Chick', and 'Jean, your Jeans!', and 'Nasty Newington Narcissus' which all referred to places and to persons which the kids could actually identify round the purlieus of the city.

So far, so bad, because nobody was interested in Zesty-Boy's creative efforts – particularly the way *he* marketed them – until one of the teenage

95

yodellers who'd hit the big time remembered Zesty, and sold the whole idea of him (and of his songs) to his Personal Manager, and his A & R man, and his Publicity Consultant, and his Agency Booker, and I don't know who else, and behold! Zesty-Boy threw away his own guitar and saved his voice for gargling and normal speech, and started writing for the top pop canaries, and made piles – I mean literally piles – of coin from his sheet, and disc, and radio, and telly, and even filmic royalties. It was a real rags-to-riches fable: one moment Z.-B. Sift was picking up pennies among the dog-ends and spittle with a grateful grimace, the next he was installed in this same Knightsbridge area with a female secretary and a City accountant added to his list of adult staff.

'Those Aussies!' he said, 'have moved in for the slaughter. Did you know there's 60,000 of them in the country? And ever seen any of them on a building site?'

I didn't reply (except for a wise nod), because the matter of the five pounds was now uppermost in my mind, and about borrowing and lending, of which of both I have a wide experience, I could tell you several golden rules. The first is, come straight up smartly to the point: to lead up tactfully to the kill is fatal, because the candidate sniffs your sinister intention and has time to put up barricades. So I said, 'I want a fiver, Zesty.'

Zesty-Boy, I was glad to see, observed, on his side, the first golden rule of lending, which is to say yes or no *immediately* – if you don't, they'll hate you if you refuse, and never be grateful if you agree. He took out the note, said, 'Any time' and changed the subject. As a matter of fact, in this case we both knew it was actually a gift, because in his Cinderella days I've often enough handed Zesty-Boy the odd cigarette-machine money, and as a shilling then was worth what a pound is to him now, this really was only a repayment. And I could add – since we're on this topic – that if you're in a position, ever, to be a *lender*, the two kinds of people you should most watch out for are not, as you might expect, the dear old boyhood pals of Paradise Alley days, but any newcomer (because borrowers are attracted to fresh faces), or anyone you've just done a favour to (because borrowers think there where the corn grows, there's sugar-cane as well).

'Eh?' I said to Zesty-B, because, with these meditations, I hadn't been following attentively the trend his conversation had been taking.

'I said Dido's out for blood this evening. She's got the needle into Vendice, because he's not buying any more space in her fish-and-chip organ, and she's losing her cut on all the full-page spreads.'

'Bad,' I said, glancing over at the number he referred to, who was the one

I'd met earlier outside the door, and who was under the arcade that ringed the patio, strip-lit with lamps all hidden, so that you always got only a reflection, and couldn't read a book there, supposing that you'd wanted to.

'What does he do, this Vendice?' I asked Zesty-Boy. 'And is that his baptismal name?'

Zesty said yes, it was, and that Vendice Partners's job was well up somewhere in the scaffolding of one of those advertising agencies that have taken over Mayfair, making it into a rather expensive slum.

'And why has Partners's pimpery taken their custom away from Dido's toilet-paper daily?' I asked Zesty-Boy.

'It may be that Dido's slipping, or the paper's slipping, or just that everything these days is falling in the fat laps of the jungle kings.'

'I wonder why Dido doesn't do a quick change and crash-land in the telly casbah?'

'Well – could she? I mean, can a journalist really do anything *else*?'

'I see what you mean.'

The time had now come for me to flatter the young Mozart in him a little. 'I heard one of your arias on the steam, last evening,' I told him. '"Separate Separates", if I remember. Very nice.'

'Which of the boy slaves was it sung it? Strides Vandal? Limply Leslie? Rape Hunger?'

'No, no . . . Soft-Sox Granite, I think it was . . .'

'Oh, that one. A Dagenham kiddy. He's very new.'

'He sounded so. But I loved the lyric, and enjoyed the lilt.'

Zesty-Boy shot a pair of Peckham-trained eyes at me. 'Yeah?' he said. 'I tell you, man. I don't flatter.'

'Compliment accepted.' I could see the cat was pleased. 'You heard they gave me my first Golden?' he said cautiously.

'Boy, I was delighted. For "When I'm Dead, I'm Gone", wasn't it? A million platters, man – just fancy that!' How could the Sift kid fail to be delighted? 'How long will it all last, do you suppose?' I said to him.

'Companion, who knows? I gave it only a year, two years ago. And still they come – performers and, what's more, cash customers.'

'Still only boys for singers? No signs of any breasted thrushes?'

'We've tried one or two of them, but the kids just don't want to know. No, for the minors, it's still males.'

'And all those boys from Dagenham and Hoxton and wherever. You have to teach them how to sing American?'

'Oh no, they seem to pick it up – get the notes well up there in their noses

97

when they sing . . . Though when they *speak*, even in personal appearances, it's back to Dagenham again.'

'Weird spiel, isn't it.'

'Weird! Child, I'm telling you – it's eerie!'

You know the way that, when things start to go amiss at a function, everyone notices it long before they actually stop doing whatever it was they're doing – drinking, dancing, talking and etcetera – and this was what now occurred, because a battle was developing between our hostess and the Partners number. But soon, just as no one can resist listening to a bit of hot chat over the blower, we all turned ourselves into spectators at the gladiatorial show.

They started off with the mutes on, playing that English one-up game they teach you at Oxford, or is it Cambridge, anyway, one of those camp holiday camps, with Dido saying, at the point I managed to tune in, 'I didn't say barsted, I said bastard.'

'It's not your pronunciation, Dido, that I'm questioning,' the copy-writing cat was saying, 'but your definition.'

'Very well, I withdraw it,' Dido said, 'and say you're just a harlot.'

'Really, my dear, I don't think I'm a woman. Surely, I've given you proof positive of that . . .'

'Only just, Vendice, only just,' she said.

And so on and so forth, guest and hostess, both very cool and, what was really rather horrible, without any emotion in it I could see – and the friends looking on and listening with that kind of grin the mob wear at a prize fight in the municipal baths. I must be a prude at heart, because this thing really shocks me – not bawling-outs and even fights, of course, but this methodical, public blood-letting. And I must be a snob, because I really do think that when an educated English voice is turning bitchy, it's a quite specially unpleasant sound, besides being f—g silly, and an utter drag. So I was much relieved, and I think one or two others were, when into the middle of all this stepped wedding-bells Henley with my Suze.

As it happened, I was adjacent to the stereo, so I slipped on some Basie, turned on the juice well up, and, with a low bow to Henley, grabbed the girl. Now if there's one thing among many Suze has learned from her Spade connexions, it's how to dance like an angel, and enjoy it, and I myself, though perhaps a bit unpolished, have studied on hard floors around the clubs and palais and in all-night private sessions, and besides which, we know all each other's routines backwards – and sideways and front as well – so before long, there we were, weaving together like a pair of springs connected by invisible elastic wires, until we reached that most glorious moment of all in dancing, that doesn't come often, and usually, admittedly, only when you're whipping it up a bit to show the multitude – that is, the dance starts to do it for you, you don't bloody well know what you're up to any longer, except that you can't put a limb wrong anywhere, and your whole damn brain and sex and personality have actually become that dance, *are* it – it's heavenly!

When just a second we were in an electric clinch, I said 'Where you dine? He take you somewhere nice?' And she said, 'Oh, *him*!' Can you believe it? She said it just like that! So when we were close again a second, and the Count playing wonderfully in our ears, and the whole Lament lot standing round us thirty miles or so away, I cried out to her, 'Is he you? Is he really you?' And Suzette said, 'No, you are! But I'm going to marry him!' And at that moment the music stopped, because I'd jabbed the sapphire down too near the middle in the earlier excitement of the moment.

So I bid everyone goodnight, and do sleep well, and thanks for having me, and went out of the flat into the London dawn. It *was* dawn, as a matter of fact, already: or rather, to be exact, it was that moment when the day and night are fighting it out together, but you've no doubt whatever who will triumph. A cab was passing by, and slowed down politely for the wayfarer, but I didn't want to break into Zesty-Boy's fiver at the moment, and also wanted to remember what Suzie said about 10,000 times, so I set off to foot it back across the city to my home up the north in Napoli.

Colin MacInnes, *Absolute Beginners* (1959)

three

1959–63

'Red, humming neon'

ESPRESSO JUNGLE

W. Howard Baker

FP

SEXTON
BLAKE
LIBRARY Nº 435

INSIDE
SPECIAL
MAGAZINE
SECTION

1/-

Coffee

in an espresso
cellar-club in Soho
the Beat Generation
hoodlums planned
violence and terror

'I looked out of the window at the villages dwarfed by the mountains, at the road zooming past Switzerland, outpost of the West . . . gas station . . . Bibliotek . . . Gaststätter. Zipping by. It was too much. I leaned under the dash and switched on the radio. We picked up AFN.

"Super pop," said Marchmare.'

Derek Raymond, The Crust on Its Uppers (1962)

In *popism*, Andy Warhol and Pat Hackett recount a journey across America in the early sixties: 'The farther west we drove, the more Pop everything looked on the highways. Suddenly, we all felt like insiders because even though Pop was everywhere – that was the thing about it, most people still took it for granted, whereas we were dazzled by it – to us, it was the new Art. Once you "got" Pop, you could never see a sign the same way again. And once you thought Pop, you could never see America the same way again.'

Although there had been a dip in sales after the peaks of the late fifties, for the music industry and pop fans alike the early sixties were a golden age: the time of pop's pure innocence. Derek Raymond and Nik Cohn gave this fragile innocence a name, Superpop. It is celebrated here in extracts by Andy Warhol, that unsung chronicler of London low-life Penny Reel, and film director John Waters, who writes about the Baltimore TV show that provided the inspiration for *Hairspray*. Beat poet Royston Ellis gives a contemporary account of Britain's archetypal pop manager, Larry Parnes, while Jack Good, renowned for TV shows like *Oh Boy!*, offers a contemporary example of why he was thought by many to be the best pop columnist of his generation.

At the same time, there were powerful undercurrents. Although the black roots of rock'n'roll had been suppressed by the American music industry, black businessmen like Berry Gordy and teenage producers like Phil Spector were working towards positions of power within that industry. What their young artists had to deal with is recounted in Mary Wilson's memoir of her 'days as a Supreme', *Dreamgirl*. Reading her accounts of touring in the South, you can understand why the black American pop of the sixties, Tamla and soul, were so identified with the civil rights movement. The gaining of cultural power is brilliantly caught by Joseph C. Smith's forgotten novel *The Day The Music Died*, which features characters based on Gordy and Spector. In this extract, his black hero has his first, brief taste of autonomy.

In Britain, writers like Ray Gosling and Keith Waterhouse attempted to show how pop was integrating into everyday life. In the extract from *Sum Total*, Gosling lapses into reverie at a concert, pondering the vast distance between star and audience. Waterhouse relocates the existentialist hero to a northern city; here pop pervades the social, and offers limited space to dream. In both, pop is an American-accented form, distant from the realities of everyday British life, yet there are hints in *Billy Liar* of a time when the British would be able to produce their own.

This was to come from 'the lunatic fringe', slowly moving towards the mainstream. Nik Cohn charts how gay style came to dominate Carnaby Street, the centre of British fashion, as exported around the world in the sixties. Jeff Nuttall begins his essay on CND by isolating the class differences within English youth culture: pop (working class), protest and trad jazz (middle class). By the turn of the decade, however, pop was drawing in the bohemian middle classes, and the integration of art and pop dreamed of by the Independent Group in the early fifties was a step nearer. As Warhol noted, pop was becoming art.

An important location for this, as noted by Simon Frith and Howard Horne in *Art into Pop*, was the art school – that gap in the educational system so well exploited by misfits in the fifties, sixties and seventies. The stories of two such misfits are told here: John Lennon (Liverpool, Hamburg and *The Goon Show*) gives an absurdist account of his not yet successful group, while Richard Barnes, in his memoir of Pete Townshend's art-school days in Ealing, notes the minutiae of west London, suburban bohemia: another fertile breeding ground for English pop.

The extract from Anthony Burgess's *A Clockwork Orange* has a malignity that we have not yet encountered. In the casual, foppish brutality of its hero, Alex, the novel looks forward to later teen takeover novels like David Wallis's *Only Lovers Left Alive*, which the Rolling Stones were slated to film. *A Clockwork Orange* had a more direct impact on Stones' manager Andrew Loog Oldham, whose sleeve notes for *Rolling Stones 2* (see next section) were a direct crib of Burgess's vicious neologisms.

A Clockwork Orange was at least ten years ahead of its time. When filmed by Stanley Kubrick in 1971, it had such power that not only did it impact straight away on youth fashions but it was thought to incite copycat violence. Fearful of this, Kubrick refuses to show the film in the UK. Like a virus, phrases from the book have recurred in pop culture – the eighties pop group Heaven 17, the record label Korova – and there is no sign that we are free of it yet. Burgess's language, half British, half Russian, has a particular relevance in the brutalities of the free-market USSR.

1959: The Roxy

The Roxy was the last splash of light before Stradhoughton petered out and the moors took over. It was supposed to be a suburban amenity or something; at any rate its red, humming neon sign spluttered out the words 'Come

Dancing' six nights a week, and all the grownup daughters of the cold new houses round about converged on it in their satin frocks, carrying their dance shoes in paper bags advertising pork pies. Youths who had come from all over Stradhoughton for the catch sat around on the low brick banisters by the entrance, combing their hair and jeering at each other.

I approached the place warily, along the shadows, in case Rita was among the girls who promenaded up and down the cracked concrete forecourt, waiting for their escorts to come and pay for them in. I was still full of the evening's fiasco, with selected incidents from it swimming in and out of my head like shoals of bright fish, but as I stepped into the pool of light outside the Roxy I felt an overwhelming relief that another experience was finished with and not still to come. A girl I had once known was waiting by the entrance; I said, 'Hiya, Mavis!' boldly as I passed. I had once written a poem comparing her bosom with twin melons, and it was always fairly embarrassing to meet her nowadays. But it was something fresh to think about anyway. She said, 'Lo, Billy,' and I walked almost cheerfully up to the paybox.

Inside the Roxy it was hot and bright and, as Stamp had once put it, smelling like a ladies' bog. The foyer, separated from the dance floor by a certain amount of cream fretwork and a lot of big plants, was crowded with the same kind of youths I had seen in the X-L Disc Bar earlier; they were all pulling at their tight clean collars and working their heads round like tortoises. Their girl friends queued for the lavatory, and emerged with their zip-boots and their head-scarves discarded, each one making a sort of furtive entry like a butterfly that has turned into a caterpillar. I surveyed this scene with the usual distaste, hunching my shoulders and adopting the attitude of the visiting poet; I was not inclined at this moment towards the bit of No. 1 thinking, fairly standard in this quarter, where I took the floor to a cha-cha with one of the professional exhibition dancers who looked so much like wardresses. I could not see Liz anywhere. I wandered through the fretwork Moorish archway on to the fringe of the dance floor.

The floor was already crowded, with the revolving ball of mirrors overhead catching a hideous violet spotlight and dancing the colours over the pimpled face of, to name the first person I saw, Stamp. He was doing a smirking foxtrot with some girl in a tight, red-wool dress; when he turned her in my direction for a piece of cross-stepping that nearly had the pair of them flat on their backs, I saw that his partner was Rita. From her slightly dazed expression, open-mouthed and cloudy-eyed – a kind of facial rigor mortis that touched her whenever she got inside a dance hall – I guessed that

Rita had been here about half an hour. I was a little pained that she had not bothered to wait outside for me – she was, after all, still my fiancée, or thought she was – but I was glad to see that Stamp was taking care of her. He looked a little drunk; but that was his problem and not mine. They glided past without seeing me.

At the bandstand Arthur's friends, the Rockets, blew their muted instruments behind little plywood pulpits, the drummer brushing away and grinning round at everybody as though he knew them. Arthur himself, wearing a blue American-cut suit, was swaying about in front of the stick-shaped microphone, waiting to sing. He looked like Danny Kaye or somebody doing a relaxed season at the Palladium, and I could not help admiring his poise and the professional way he stood there doing nothing. I was glad that he had not seen my performance at the New House. I caught his eye and waved to him, a half-wave arrested before it began. Arthur gave me the same mock bow that, in his situation, I had given to the old man; but he did it with a casual dash that made it part of the act.

The people on the dance floor hung around holding hands limply as one tune finished and the Rockets started on the next. Arthur, splaying his hands out, began to sing. '*Yooo're – my – ev'rthring, ev'ry li'l thing I know-oo.*' He always affected an American accent when he sang. I disliked it, but I had to admit it was good. Then swaying couples brushed past me and, as Stamp and Rita came round for the second time, I began to pick my way upstairs to the balcony.

Liz was sitting by herself at one of the wickerwork tables, gazing down over the dance floor with her chin resting on her plump arms, and smiling happily to herself. I sat down without saying anything to her. She reached out her hand across the table and I took it.

'Late,' said Liz reprovingly as the song finished.

'Yes,' I said. 'I've had an exciting day.'

'I bet you have. Where've you been?'

'Oh, here and there –'

'– round and about.' This was a common exchange between us. We used it most when I brushed, without actually asking, on the subject of where Liz kept disappearing to for weeks at a time. I took her hand again. She was still wearing her old black skirt, but with a fresh white blouse. Her green suède jacket hung on the back of the basket chair. I was happy to be with her; it was like being in a refuge, her beaming, comfortable presence protecting me from the others.

'Tell me some plans,' said Liz luxuriously.

'What plans?'

'Any plans. *Your* plans. You *always* have plans. What are you going to do next?'

'I'm thinking of going to London,' I said.

'Only thinking?'

'Well, *going*. Soon, anyway.'

'When's soon?' Liz and I could talk like this for hours, batting the same moonbeams backwards and forwards across the table, enjoying ourselves enormously.

'Well, *soon*.'

'That sounds remote. Why not now?'

'Difficult,' I said.

'No, it's easy. You just get on a train and, four hours later, there you are in London.'

'Easy for you,' I said. 'You've had the practice. Liz –?' We were both leaning over the balcony, our hands dove-tailed together. On the packed dance floor, near the bandstand, there was a small arena of space where Stamp and Rita, gyrating dangerously, were working out a dance of their own invention. They were both looking down at the floor to see what their feet were doing.

'Yes?' said Liz.

'Stamp calls you Woodbine Lizzie,' I said.

'You should hear what I call Stamp,' said Liz.

I scanned the dance floor idly, and then sat up with a jolt. I had once read about Shepheard's Hotel in Cairo that if you sat there long enough everyone you knew would pass your table. The Roxy was this sort of establishment too and why someone didn't blow *that* up I could never understand, because the next person I picked out, bouncing along the pine-sprung floor with fresh chalk on his uppers was Shadrack himself, doing the quickstep as it might be performed by a kangaroo. The girl he was with, just to complete the wild pattern of coincidence, was Mavis, the one with the twin-melon bosom I had spoken to outside the Roxy. They were no doubt talking about me. Stamp and Rita were still milling around near the bandstand, and I suddenly knew for certain that somewhere on the premises the Witch, too, was waiting, breathing through her nose and swinging her skirt and looking in general as though she had come to dance the Gay Gordons over a couple of swords.

'Let's go for a walk,' I said.

'Soon,' said Liz, mocking me.

Downstairs the drums rolled and Arthur came to the microphone, lifting his hands to quell the faint suggestion of applause. He put his face close to the mike and, in his half-American accent, began the smooth talk that went down so well.

'*Lazengenelmen, are we all happy? Thank* you, *madam. Next week at the Roxy we have another all-pop night, feat'ring the Rockets, that golden songstress Jeannie Lewis — Jeannie Lewis, I'm not saying she's fat but she's the only girl I know who when she has a chest complaint, she gets her treatment wholesale — and by popular request, yours truly.* Success! *Lazengenelmen, when I came to Stradhoughton I only had one clog. Now I ride around in taxis. I have to take a taxi I've only got one clog.*'

There were waves of relaxed laughter for Arthur, a cabaret sort of atmosphere that suited him perfectly. Jeannie Lewis, the singer, was sitting on a cane chair by the band, heaving her sequined bosom. Arthur waited for silence, clicking his fingers and smiling confidently.

'*And now a special treat for us all. I want to continue the dance with a little number which I wrote in conjunction with my very good friend Billy Fisher. Where are you, Billy?*' The spotlight played hopefully about the floor, while the Rockets' drummer made a facetious clacking on the kettle-drum.

'That's *you!*' said Liz excitedly.

'I'm all right,' I muttered, hiding my face.

'*Well I know he's out there somewhere,*' said Arthur. '*Maybe he's celebrating the big news, because I know you'll all be glad to know that Billy has just landed himself a big job in London, writing scripts for that verywellknown comedian Danny Boon! I'm sure we wish him all the best in the world.*'

'You stupid *cow!*' I hissed. There was a bit of desultory applause, and one or two of the people on the balcony who knew me slightly looked at me curiously. In spite of it all, I tried to look reasonably famous.

'*Now on with the dance with the little number by Billy Fisher and yours truly — "Can't get along without you"!*' He said it in the coy way that television disc jockeys have, putting the eye on a random girl when he pronounced this soft word 'you'.

'I wish he'd stop calling himself yours truly,' I said through my teeth.

'Shush,' said Liz. 'I want to hear your song.'

The band struck up far too slowly for the number and Arthur, the wry creases in his forehead, began to sing.

> '*Soon you will be saying good-bye,*
> *Just let me mention that I*
> *Can't get along without you.*

You seem to have changed with the moon,
Now my heart beats out of tune,
Can't get along without you.'

I squinted craftily at Liz, hoping she would think the song was dedicated to her. Then I looked down over the balcony at the people dancing below. Nobody seemed to be taking much notice of the song, and in fact Arthur's American accent had become so pronounced that it was difficult to understand what he was singing about. Shadrack and the girl Mavis had vanished, and so had Rita. Stamp was loitering on the brass-rimmed edge of the dance floor, obviously trying to find some way of sabotaging the number. I thought Arthur was doing that effectively himself.

'I want to discover
If I'm to blame,
Because as a lover
You're not the same so tell me why.'

'He's singing it all wrong,' I muttered, getting up. 'Anyway, I suppose I'd better go and congratulate him.' Liz wrinkled her nose at me, and I ran self-consciously down the stairs, keeping my eyes peeled for people who might want to see me.

'Please tell me why we must part,
Darling it's breaking my heart,
Can't get along without you.'

I reached the bandstand as Arthur, his arms outstretched, touched the last note. The Rockets went straight into 'American Patrol' and he jumped down, flexing his shoulders and waving to his friends.

'And then I wrote –' I began, striking a dramatic pose for the beginning of our song-writing routine.

'Ah yes, and do you remember the little tune that went something like this,' said Arthur, clutching his heart with one hand and cupping the other to his ear.

'*You made me love you, I didn't want to do it, I didn't want to do it,*' I sang dutifully in the cracked phonograph voice.

'To think I wrote that song on the back of a menu in a fish restaurant –'

'– and today that menu is worth hundreds of pounds.'

'Yes, the price of fish rose steeply between the wars,' said Arthur, finishing the routine. But it was not the usual thing between me and him; this time he was talking loudly, addressing an audience, the admiring girls who stood around the band giggling and doing little solo jigs.

'And then I wrote —' he said, looking round. I drew him on one side.

'Bloody good, man,' I said. 'How did you manage to persuade them to let you sing it?'

'In your honour,' said Arthur, and now that we had dropped the routine I thought that he was talking in a curiously formal sort of voice.

'Bloody good. Wish you hadn't announced that bit about Danny Boon, though.'

'Why not. It's all fixed up, isn't it?' For the first time, I noticed the slight glint of malice in his eye and the corner of his lower lip twitching.

'Yes, course it is. Only I just didn't want anyone to know just yet, that's all. We ought to get that song recorded and send it up to a publisher.'

'We're going to do it,' said Arthur, meaning him and the Rockets, and also meaning without any help from me.

'Only one thing,' I said in the light voice. 'You want to sing it with a bit less of an American accent.'

Arthur turned to me full-face, and I got the whole effect of the studied, indifferent approach.

'I'll sing it with a *Yorkshire* accent if you like.'

I flared up. 'I don't want you to sing it with *any* flaming accent. Just sing it as it's flaming well written, that's all.'

'Listen, boy, if I sing that song the way you wrote it it'd clear the bleeding hall. You've still got a lot to learn, cocker.'

'Oh, for Christ sake —'

Arthur nodded his chin. 'Yes, I can see them taking *you* down a peg or two when you get to London. *If* you get to London, I should say. Anyway, don't tell *me* how to sing, matey. Anyone'd think you were going to work for bleeding Glenn Miller.'

'Oh, it's like that, is it?' I said.

'Yes, it's like that. And another thing. I don't know what bloody crap you've been telling my mother about the Witch being this bloody sister of yours, but she's been doing her nut all afternoon. So bloody lay off, for Christ sake.'

He strode back to the bandstand, grabbing the microphone and switching on the American voice. '*And now folks,* by *request — the Hokey-Cokey!*' I turned away, miserable and depressed.

Keith Waterhouse, *Billy Liar* (1959)

1959: Carnaby Street, Part One

In the beginning, Bill Green was a photographer, specializing in stage portraiture. Then, during the war, he got involved in weight-lifting and, after he'd been demobbed, he began to photograph muscle boys and wrestlers, doing figure studies for the male magazines. For this he called himself Vince.

At first, he had problems: 'In those days, it was all very perilous, shooting the male nude. Several photographers had got into serious trouble that way. So I reached a compromise – I made my models wear briefs, and I had them specially made up from cut-down Marks & Spencer roll-ons. They were skimpy but ever so comfy and they caused a terrific reaction among my models and my readers. Everyone was thrilled.

'After a time, I began to make the briefs myself and I thought perhaps I should sell them commercially. So, in 1950, I took out an advert in the *Daily Mirror*. It came out on Saturday and, on the Monday morning, I took £200 worth of orders.'

Very quickly, selling briefs was taking so much of his time that his photography was swamped. In 1951, he started a mail-order business working from a studio in Manchester Street, then he went to France: 'This was during the existential phase. All the boys were wearing black sweaters and black jeans, which were unheard of in England. Over here, everyone still dreamed of imported Levi's, so I could see a potential and I brought out a catalogue of sweaters and pants.'

These were also successful and, in 1954, Green opened a shop in Newburgh Street, which was just round the corner from Carnaby Street, which in turn was just behind Regent Street. He called the shop Vince.

It was a pretty shabby district. Technically, it may have belonged in Soho but it had nothing colourful or sinful, nothing remotely exotic. It was full of attics and small workshops, scuffling tailors and locksmiths.

From Bill Green's angle, its attractions were simple: the rents were cheap and Newburgh Street was just next to Marshall Street baths, where all the muscle boys and butch trade trained. As they came out, they were confronted by a dazzle of hipster pants, expensive tight sweaters (about £7), briefs and shirts in bright reds, yellows and purples.

This was the start of Drag, not in the transvestite sense, but as used by the menswear trade, to mean fashionable fancy dress. For the period, it was all quite outrageous and, straightaway, Vince became the butt of much music-hall hilarity: 'The only shop where they measure your inside leg each time you buy a tie', said George Melly and, ten years later, David Frost was saying it still.

113

The camp element was undeniable, but Vince had other qualities. At a time when men's shops were almost all pompous, it was fun, and so were its clothes: lurid and sometimes badly made but, at least, never boring. 'I always put the emphasis on impact, not make,' says Green. 'I used materials that had never been used before – lots of velvets and silks, trousers made of bed-ticking, and I was the first with pre-faded denims – and I made everything as colourful and bold as I could.

'You'd be surprised by our customers, too. Everyone thought we only sold to Chelsea homosexuals but, in actual fact, we catered to a very wide public, within an age range of about twenty-five to forty. They weren't teenagers, because teenagers couldn't meet our prices, but artists and theatricals, muscle boys, and celebrities of every kind.

'I don't like to name-drop but my customers included Peter Sellers, John Gielgud and Lionel Bart. The King of Denmark bought swimming trunks from me; Picasso ordered a pair of suede trousers; Lord Snowdon used me for most of his trousseau.'

Green is quite right – not all his custom was homosexual. But if he'd been in business before the war, it would have been, and that's what made Vince new and important; it sold stuff that could once have been worn by no one but queers, and extremely blatant ones at that; now the same things were bought by heteros as well.

Behind this, obviously, there was a major shift in male identity. 'One of the things about us,' says Simon Hodgson, speaking of Chelsea, 'nobody gave a damn what sex you were. Everyone realized that we're all a bit of everything.'

In other words, men were coming to terms with the feminine sides of themselves. They were beginning not to be afraid. Narcissism and flirtation and cattiness – all these things had become acceptable as male components, in a way that the Victorian age would have found horrific, and skin-tight pants expressed the change.

This was yet another facet in the same central break-up, the crumbling of the English structure. Nothing seemed fixed any more – all the roles were blurring, and there was an evolving of the whole concept of what makes men attractive. It seemed much less important, suddenly, to look like a he-man, to have biceps like grapefruit and hairs on your chest; if you were good in bed that was all that counted and there, clearly, a certain ambiguity was no bad thing.

Of course, as yet, this was on a very small scale. Soho and Chelsea, and Vince's celebrities 'of every kind', were hardly typical of the country as a whole and the new expansiveness was unthought of outside London.

Still, once the first breach has been made, the cracks are bound to get wider and, within a few years, the same sexual relaxation was to form the basis for Carnaby Street and all its triumphs. Drag was worn by teenagers, suburban swingers, middle-aged tourists from Idaho.

To an extent, in fact, all male fashion of the sixties was homosexual-derived. In that, the retired Indian Army majors and lorry drivers were quite correct, yelling 'Fairies' and 'Poufs'. They remembered the signals of their youth and, now that the message had altered and complexified, it was natural that they should be confused.

In that sense, Bill Green was a seminal figure. He was not a great designer, aesthetically, nor a great theorist and he probably had no clear idea of what he represented. Nevertheless, his was a vital breakthrough: 'I invented a long-felt need,' he says and, despite the non sequitur, it's true.

Vince was also a major force towards informality, as well as ambivalence. For the first time, leisure wear became high fashion. Sweaters and jeans began to be chic, not yet worn for business, perhaps, but quite all right for evenings out or parties. 'Male costume evolves by adopting a sports costume for ordinary wear,' as James Laver has written [in *Dandies*], and that's exactly what was happening in Newburgh Street.

On paper, Bill Green should have made his fortune. Apart from his shop, his mail-order business was flourishing, too, and he started a wholesale business, with contracts at Marshall & Snelgrove and Macys in New York. When the Carnaby Street boom came in, one would have thought, he should have been made.

It didn't happen like that. 'I understand promotion,' he says. 'I could photograph something dull and make it look glamorous and sell it. But I never learned business. I didn't know how to set things up so that I'd receive the proper benefit. I needed some tough Jewish pusher behind me, to cash in, but I never found him.'

Nik Cohn, *Today There are No Gentlemen* (1971)

1960: The Big Beat Business

As an off-shoot of show business, the big beat is very much a profitable concern to a few people behind the scene. The main brain is undoubtedly Larry Parnes. Under his aegis a remarkable crowd of boys, with stage names based on their peculiar talents – Power, Keene and Gentle are examples – have been hurtled on to the scene.

Larry Parnes' 'stable' as it is known, consists of a group of rocksters all under contract to Parnes. Whereas other singers have managers and agents who take a percentage of their earnings, Parnes employs his singers instead of them employing him. Discovering them in various towns around the country (a surprising number come from Liverpool), he then grooms what talent they have and puts them under contract to him.

This contract (usually a five-year one) provides the boys with a regular weekly wage whether they are working or not. At first the wage is low (sometimes as low as £20 per week) but the contract promises a regular pay increase until the fifth year when his stable boys are assured of astronomical earnings. As yet none of the current crop have been working for Parnes for five years, and so they are not yet earning as much as, say, one of the self-employed singers who may collect £500 per week after only three months in the business.

However, the Parnes beatsters consider the way they are working infinitely better than being entirely dependent on a fickle public for their personal fortune and fame. Working with a five-year contract, the boys do have some security with Larry Parnes behind them. Bearing in mind the way that singers can shoot overnight to oblivion as well as to stardom, some form of security is highly desirable.

The Parnes stable includes, Joe Brown, Dickie Pride, Tommy Bruce, Johnny Gentle, Duffy Power, Nelson Keene, Peter Wynne, Georgie Fame, Davy Jones, Johnny Goode and Vince Eager. One boy Parnes has under contract is one of the most artistically creative and sincere singers involved with the teenage side of show business. Lumbered with a stage name which seems to mock his true character, this boy still stands out in the beat scene as an individual in his own right. He is known as Billy Fury.

These words may seem ridiculous when used to describe a singer so often slated for his near-obscene performances. One paper referring to his appearance at a theatre stated that Billy Fury turns into a 'sex symbol of deformed contortions and suggestive songs the minute he walks on to the stage'. Critics have claimed that 'the simple act of lighting a cigarette takes on a deeper meaning when performed by one of these masters of the suggestive'. Billy Fury, say critics, is one of 'the rock 'n' roll entertainers who purveys badly disguised sex' to his audience. Those reports are quoted from a 1960 newspaper. They were saying the same thing about Presley years ago.

So Billy Fury's show business reputation snowballs. The result of press reports stressing supposed lewdness in his performance is that Billy as his friends know him has never been seen by the public eye. This is the way he would like it. He does not make friends easily, and he genuinely hates the blown up publicity of being a teenagers' idol.

Born, Ronald Wycherley, in Liverpool in 1940, Billy's early life was a tumultuous affair. He loved his parents, and still is extremely fond of them, but he was a mischievous child. For him, the unhappiest period of his life was whilst at his secondary modern school. Resenting the petty authority wielded by his teachers, he was always in trouble. To young Billy, his teachers' attitude towards him amounted to persecution. He longed for the day when he would be free and leave school for good.

In 1955 at the end of summer term ('Summer season' Billy called it when telling his story) his last day of school came round. Billy recalled it like this: 'There were about five minutes to go before the final bell. I couldn't stand it. I put my feet up on the desk and lit a cigarette. The teacher told me to put it out – said school wasn't over yet. I just laughed; "Go on teach, make me!" I said.

'With only a minute to go before the end of school he caned me. He thrashed me six times on my hand. With each stroke I laughed louder, until the bell rang as he brought down the cane for the sixth time. Then I was free. I hated school: it was like being in jail. Now I was being released, a free man. I went wild, running out of school shouting "I'm free, I'm free, I'm free!"'

As Billy remembered those days he seemed to relive each moment, each emotion, in his mind. His eyes were troubled until a rare smile broke up the sadness of his features and he laughed at his own schoolday rebelliousness. ' "You'll achieve nothing; you'll come to a bad end," they told me at school,' he said. 'So I went back there in my car just to show them.' Billy's eyes glinted at the memory of this. 'They seemed different somehow. More human than I thought. But I showed them the car.'

When he left school, Billy started as an engineering apprentice in a job fixed for him by his father. All might have gone well for him, but he soon discovered he was only allowed to help the experienced workers; no one would give him a chance to do it himself. So one day Billy took up a few plates and welded them together for his own amusement. Unfortunately, the plates had been cleaned down for a precision engineering job, and no one appreciated his handiwork. He was sacked.

Then came what Billy has described as some of the happiest days he has ever known. His father got him a job as a deck hand on the tug boats operating around Merseyside. This job was to change not only Billy's whole life, but his whole outlook as well. For a few days each job, the boats would be away from Liverpool, Billy living and mixing happily with the crew. One of the seamen, a fellow called Jack, used to spend his free moments strumming country and western numbers on a battered guitar.

Billy would watch fascinated. A moody boy, even then, he liked to sit in silence listening to the river and Jack's guitar playing. Flattered by the youngster's interest, Jack offered to teach young Billy how to play. He was an eager and attentive pupil, picking up chords and tunes without too many snags.

On the tug boats Billy's closest friend was a young man who, from the very first day that Billy came aboard, took him under his wing. They worked together, Billy learning all he could from his new mate; a firm trust and friendship grew up between them. The end of this happy phase came with the tragic death of his friend. Billy transferred to another boat and although he was a conscientious worker (he was promoted to Ordinary Seaman) he was eventually fired.

At the time this was a terrible blow to Billy. For ten weeks he was out of work. He began to think that his teacher's prophecy was coming true. In desperation he turned out some of the songs which he had jotted down in odd moments. Marty Wilde was appearing in a Larry Parnes show at Birkenhead just across the water. Billy decided to take his songs along to see if he could get them published.

He got to the theatre and pushed through the crowd of girls at the stage door. Feeling very nervous, he walked straight in whilst the doorman was busy somewhere else. Going along a corridor, a man stopped him and asked him what he wanted. 'I'm looking for Mr Parnes,' said Billy. 'I'm Larry Parnes,' the man replied. Whereupon Billy told the man about his songs.

Instead of turning him out, Parnes took him to Marty Wilde's dressing room. There Billy sang a few of his numbers in the hope that Parnes could use them. Larry Parnes not only liked the songs, he liked the singer as well, asking Billy to go on stage and sing something for the audience.

In the wings there was a terrible argument. Billy did not want to do it. 'No, no; there's been a mistake,' he kept on saying. 'I don't want to sing. I just want you to publish my songs.' The compere announced him, the curtain went up. Parnes pushed, and Billy was on stage. For a few seconds he just stood there, stricken with nerves and anger. He looked furious, glaring at Parnes and really hating him for making him look a fool. But the girls in the audience loved him, squealing with delight at his singing. There and then Parnes renamed him: Billy Fury was born.

He joined the show permanently the next day. At first his parents could not believe it when their son told them he was leaving home to join a rock 'n' roll show. When he started packing they knew he was serious. For Billy Fury this was the beginning of a career that has already brought him into the charts with 'Maybe Tomorrow', 'Margo', 'Colette', 'That's Love', etc., as well as fame and a certain amount of fortune. But, unlike every other beatster, these are not the things that make him happy.

'I don't feel a happy person,' Billy has said. 'I'm easily affected by sorrow or sadness. I went to a hospital once, sick people everywhere. Some of them had no arms even. I could talk to them. I stayed with them for hours. I felt something for them.

'And I like to sit by myself without anyone talking to me, just thinking. I don't make friends easily because of that. Most people are loud mouthed, all talk; they don't see what's going on.'

Billy seems to live on his emotions; fright being the one emotion he is most conscious of. Billy would never be a coward in any dangerous situation. This is not because he considers himself particularly heroic, he just likes the feeling of being scared.

As a young kid, he and his pals would take part in a form of chicken run. They would walk along the railway tracks towards an oncoming train. 'We used to jump clear in plenty of time,' said Billy, 'there was no real danger.' They stopped that when one of the kids, paralysed by the train bearing down on him, caught his leg and was killed.

Now Billy is a car driver and a speed fan. 'I never want to be passed in a car,' he has said, 'and neither do a lot of other drivers. They seem to dare me to overtake them when I try to pass. I get a kick out of that sometimes. I might catch up with a car on a bend. My sense tells me to slow down, but my foot won't come off the accelerator. The tension builds up – will I be able to make it? That's when I capture that scared feeling.'

Frequently Billy is plunged into bouts of depression. Sometimes these phases are the prelude to a spurt of songwriting. Many of his hit songs have been written this way. If he was a better educated person, Billy Fury might well produce poems to enrich the heritage of English literature. But because he was born in a Dingle backstreet and brought up as a yob in a rock 'n' roll era, he has become a teenagers' idol, writing poetry in the only medium he knows about – blues-style songs. He is in effect a modern day equivalent of the great tragic poets of the seventeenth and eighteenth centuries.

In appearance Billy Fury is casual. When he first came to London he had the authentic Liverpool look of a few years back, drape jacket and drainpipe trousers. Now he favours jeans, sweater, and cowboy boots. Suits bore him for being too much of the same colour. At the time of writing he has just started to learn how to tie a tie properly. Formal occasions are certainly not for him.

He also shows his individuality as a beat star by really detesting recognition. He cannot abide being recognized, pointed at, and spoken to by complete strangers. His efforts to avoid being recognized and treated as a freak lead him to slink past people, keeping entirely to himself. But when he is called 'scruffy' by fans, it hurts.

Of all the singers connected with the business, Fury is probably the one who has changed least since the day he started. Unchanged in personal valuation by the 'big time' treatment, that is. He has, however, become considerably dazed during his months as an idol. He genuinely never has any ideas of what date, month, even year, it is. He takes absolutely no interest in the so-called importance of world news and affairs. His preoccupation with his own thoughts makes it difficult for him to remember anyone other than his closest acquaintances.

When he sings, he means whatever he is singing. Admittedly, when he first started in the business he did imitate Presley, but that was because he liked it and thought it felt natural singing that way on stage. Now, as he learns to understand himself more, his act becomes completely genuine and original.

Occasionally at night he dreams. Some of these dreams have been of death, his death; death in flames with smoke and bits flying everywhere. Convinced he was going to die before he was twenty-one, Billy went to his mother on the day he was twenty and asked for the key she had promised would be his on his twenty-first birthday. She gave it to him; he wears it on a chain round his neck as a talisman.

In the Parnes' stable there is a remarkable collection of talent and tousled haired contortionists. A lad who now has the most professional outlook of the stable crowd is someone known as Dickie Pride. Originally dubbed, perhaps unfortunately, as the 'Sheikh of Shake' because of his novel stage routine, he is fast becoming an accomplished and versatile young singer.

Dickie Pride is a slight, dark-haired lad with a strong individual appearance. His entry into the business must have been achieved solely through his singing talent, for he lacks the sex appeal of most teenage idols. In fact he does not regard himself as a teenage idol, nor does he think it likely that he will ever become one. His main interest is singing, and his kicks come from that rather than from any adulation from screaming fans.

His chance to enter show business came when he was spotted singing by that piano-playing family entertainer Russ Conway in the Union Tavern in London's Old Kent Road. Russ Conway then tipped off Larry Parnes and, after a trial appearance at the Gaumont State, Kilburn, Dickie Pride was away. But this step was not achieved overnight. His school days had been spent at the Royal College of Church Music and singing as a choir boy at Canterbury Cathedral.

Although Dickie has appeared many times on television and has a recording contract, he has not yet had a disc in the hit parade.

'When I first came into the business I thought it was great. I did a lot of silly things because I could not really believe it at first. Now I've settled down to serious singing. Singing is my life – a hit record would mean I might become a flash-in-the-pan.'

Dickie Pride broke into the beat business in 1959 with his shaking gimmick. Since then he believes he has learned a lot, although he would be the first to admit that he still has plenty more to learn.

Having settled down in the business, Dickie Pride has grown used to the differences in his life. 'I've become quite scatterbrained during the past few months,' he has said. 'It's the pace I suppose. Normal life seems so unusual now. And I've got so used to late nights that I can't possibly sleep before one o'clock. Old friends come up to me and say I've got it cushy. But I haven't. It's much harder work in this business than anything else I've done.'

As a singer, he favours jazz numbers, not way-out jazz but strictly commercial tunes. He much prefers big beat numbers to beat ballads. His main aim is to be able to work with and gain experience from real artistes. Rather than have a hit single record, Dickie Pride's ambition is to be a successful album seller. For such a conscientious young man, his ambitions should not be impossible to achieve.

Joe Brown is the self-confessed 'scruffy nit' of the Parnes stable. He is also a happy-go-lucky beatster who has the makings of a comedy entertainer. A product of London's Cockney East End, his background includes a variety of jobs from barrow boy to British Railways' fireman. His first break came as a guitarist when Jack Good signed him for his television show *Boy Meets Girls*. Straight away his vivacious personality and lively guitar playing endeared him to viewers.

Now Joe Brown has ventured into singing. He has a charming way of under-estimating his own abilities, saying quite definitely that if he were a producer he would sack himself. He does not consider his talents at all exceptional and, bearing in mind the resilient natural humour of the Cockneys, he is quite possibly right. However, he is dedicated to guitar playing, although his approach to the beat business may seem casual – 'The mere fact that I am playing my guitar is good enough for me,' he has said.

Joe Brown does not have any strong ambition in show business. He finds it laughable to trot out the hackneyed phrase about wanting to become an 'all round entertainer'. The songs he would like to sing, he believes, are way beyond his capabilities. Listening to him talking it is easy to get the impression that the future does not worry him very much. Providing he can see that he will still be playing his guitar and making people happy in the immediate future, he is quite content.

For Tommy Bruce who made a smash hit recording of 'Aint Misbehaving' in 1960, giving the number yet another lease of life with his raucous, untutored voice, the future does present some problems. His entry into the beat business was a complete surprise to him, and his success as a singer a surprise to everyone else. Spotted by actor Barry Mason who, thinking he at least looked like a singer, persuaded him to sing for the first time in his life and make a test recording, Bruce was snapped up by the record buying public as a refreshing novelty. His rasping voice which, even when he speaks, grates uneasily on the ear, has won him for a time, a place in the fans' hearts.

Having sampled life as a beatster, he would like the present spate of prosperity to last, although he has found it much harder mentally than he imagined. He has said hopefully that he will stay in the business as long as the public want him. His attitude is to have a go at anything, for he feels he has nothing to lose and certainly everything to gain. For him, remembering his accidental discovery, the beat business is a big laugh – 'I like a nice lark about,' he has said.

Of the other beatsters on the Parnes' books, it is difficult to choose any who stand out as potential top names in the teenage world. A big name could well be Peter Wynne, a handsome six-footer with musical associations through a relative being a Covent Garden principal tenor. Or the lucky break could come to a good-looking Parnes' favourite who has been trying for a long time to get ahead, Duffy Power.

The really big time might hit Vince Eager, dubbed the dandy of the beatsters, who has appeared many time on the teenage television shows. Or it might be the turn of that Liverpudlian ex-merchant sailor, Johnny Gentle. Then there is Nelson Keene whose 'Image of a Girl' vied with Mark Wynter's for hit-parade honours in 1960. These boys, and others bearing equally bizarre stage names, represent Larry Parnes' investments in the big beat business.

Although Larry Parnes is the only impresario of any consequence who employs his own chain of big beat names, there are other shrewd managers adopting the same methods. In Southampton, for instance, there is Reg Calvert. In 1960 he had under contract to him a character going under the name of Eddie Sex. This nineteen-year-old, once known as Eddie Thunder whose real name is Edward Bennett, was employed by Calvert at £16 per week to perform at dance halls throughout the South and Midlands.

Taking a feather out of Larry Parnes' cap, Reg Calvert has christened his boys with odd – and at times crazy – stage names. He has created Ricky Fever, Babby Bubbly, Buddy Britten, Colin Angel and Danny Storm. It will probably not be long before we have a Norman Passion or an Elmer Twitch. Another of Calvert's gimmicks is to have singers appearing as other singers' doubles. Vince Taylor, when he worked for Calvert, was employed to imitate Elvis Presley. Eddie Sex himself looks remarkably like Vince Taylor!

For each beat singer launched on stage touring the country, a backing group is needed. Normally, one would expect a worthwhile promoter to pay a fair wage to the backing group for a week's work. This should be around £25 each with travelling and maybe hotel expenses provided. The backing groups would either be paid by the show's promoter or, if they are a singer's regular group, by the singer himself.

During the early years of rock, certain unscrupulous promoters in the business, in an effort to spend as little money as possible and reap the largest profits, decided to get their backing groups as cheaply as they could. Using the glory of being in show business as bait, they would pick up a guitarist or drummer of suitable ability in a coffee bar and offer him work at, say, £12 10s a week. The youngster, probably an apprentice by day and a musician in his spare time, would naturally jump at the offer.

At first all would seem well under this system. A group ('the Blanks') would find they had only three nights a week to play at local dance halls. Their £12 10s would be easy money. Then comes the step when the promoter puts the Blanks on tour with a stage show. Their job would then be to back all the artistes on the bill for two shows a night, six nights a week.

Not until the tour has started do the Blanks realize just what it is they have let themselves in for. Out of their £12 10s they find they are expected to pay their hotel bills and contribute towards their fares to each show. They also have to stamp their own insurance cards. This means that for a week's work they receive only between five and six pounds. Being famous and signing autographs, the Blanks realize, is no compensation for poor wages. But if they don't like it, the promoter tells them, they can get out. There is always another group only too eager to break into show business.

From the musicians' point of view the trouble is this. Once caught in the clutches of a shrewd promoter it is not easy to escape. There is nowhere to run to. To leave would mean that the musician would be out of work with little prospect of finding another job. For what well-paid jobs there are available, there are dozens of talented guitarists and drummers to fill them. Because of this situation, there are many rock musicians who receive no more than meagre wages even today.

Those boys who once had steady jobs in the humdrum life of ordinary people would say to aspiring beatsters, 'Don't come into the beat business!' The beat is like a drug. Once a boy has sampled life in the rock 'n' roll world, he is hooked. Even though he can earn more and not work so hard as a builder's labourer, he is loath to quit the beat business. Addicted to the world of big beat he still believes some day he will make the big time and knock up a thousand quid a week.

This is the situation which prevents really talented groups from earning the money that they deserve. If they were to ask a theatre owner for £500 a week, they would be laughed at. That owner knows that he can get groups for £50 per week. Although they may not have the drawing power of a star group, the profit margin should be greater.

Fortunately, the cheeseparing ways of these promoters are turning against them. A man's reputation soon spreads, even on the fringe of the scene. More and more musicians are refusing to work for promoters with bad reputations. At the same time, the fans have been expressing their disgust at the quality of some of the shows they have been offered by staying away.

In the early days all that was needed to pack in audiences was a single star name. He would stroll on stage, sing a few numbers, and then wander off. Fans, having more taste than the rock tycoons credited them with, have grown tired of sloppy routines like that. The result is that a new form of stage show has taken to the roads. Lavishly produced, these shows are comparable to first class West End revues.

The production of any show is in itself a new idea. Until recently these package shows, providing the road manager had assembled the artistes in the right theatre at the right time, just happened. Larry Parnes made some attempt at showmanship by, amongst other gimmicks, getting Billy Fury's backing group to bleach their hair. The result was not too successful; whenever they appeared the group became known as 'Fury's Fairies'.

Realizing the need for skilled streamlined presentation to win back to the theatres the audiences who had been driven away by shoddy productions, impresario Larry Parnes sponsored his Rock 'n' Trade Show in 1960. This was a completely new innovation on which no expense was spared. Parnes engaged Jack Good to produce it, together with famed choreographer Leslie Cooper. The success of this is a superb example of what enterprising promoters can do when they try. Larry Parnes' efforts suggest that the gloomy reign of the cut-throat promoters is on the verge of being overthrown.

Under the old conditions when groups were expected to pay for their own lodgings out of small wage packets, many used to take the easy way out. Signing autographs for the crowd round the stage door, they would mention that they could not afford to stay at a hotel because their pay had not arrived. Could anyone, they would ask casually, put them up for the night?

Someone in the crowd would be only too glad to have a 'star' staying with them, and so the beatsters would get free board and lodging for the night. One group managed on a complete four-week tour like that in early 1960. 'But we were careful,' their leader explained, 'to go with the monsters. The pretty chicks usually expected something in return.'

The seamy side of life, the swindles, the hard work, and the failures; the Big Beat Scene has an exaggerated share of them all.

Royston Ellis, *The Big Beat Scene* (1960)

1960: Timin' is the Thing

What would have happened if you and I
Hadn't just happened to meet?
We might have spent the rest of our lives
Walking down misery street.

Chatsworth Road, in the heart of Homerton, is a singularly dismal arcade of Victorian terrace houses, shop fronts, fifties-style high rise flats and the forbidding wall of the Eastern Hospital; dribbling, at one end, into Marsh Hill as it descends towards Hackney Marshes; negotiating, at the other, a particularly infecundite market of cheap drapery and vegetables, before emerging finally into Lea Bridge Road. Its only claim to fame is that the 22 bus, having trundled the sights of Chelsea, Piccadilly, Holborn and Dalston, finally comes to rest there.

In 1960, however, its significance was something else. Then, it meant the dreaded route to our school's woodwork annexe and a small transport café, a twice-weekly retreat from school dinners, where egg and chips and a cup of tea cost one and three pence (8p); it meant a dusty, delightful pin table and, most spectacular of all, it meant the best juke box in the mighty whole of Hackney. It meant Hank Ballard and the Midnighters' 'Finger Poppin' Time', Conway Twitty's 'Is a Buebird Blue', the Coasters' 'Run Red Run' and Gene Vincent's 'Pistol Packin' Mama'.

Mare Street and Stamford Hill could boast every new Elvis and Fats

Domino goodie, but it was Chatsworth Road-consciousness alone that demanded Bobby Vee's 'Devil Or Angel', long before 'Rubber Ball' had escalated the teen pixie to public favour, via Marty Wilde; and it was Chatsworth Road-consciousness alone that dictated no less than *eight* rebel-rousing Duane Eddy instrumentals in play, servicing a grateful greedy custom.

More than this, it was Chatsworth Road-consciousness that had me first swooning over Brenda Lee as she whispered in my ear 'Sweet Nothin's'; had me munching the lyrics of Dee Clark's 'Just Keep It Up'; shaking tomato ketchup to Johnny and the Hurricanes' 'Red River Rock'; lasciviously spending sixpences (two plays for . . .) to hear once again Eddie Cochran climb his 'Three Steps to Heaven' and, great double-sider, Miss Lucy yelling 'Cut Across Shorty' as 5' 6" Cochran beat out those incredible riffs; a small consolation to midgets everywhere. To bask in the café's crowning glory: Jimmy Jones and 'Handy Man', the most endearing falsetto this side of Maurice Williams.

'Handy Man' was an especial favourite of the café's choice clientele. Strong men, who drank beer and ate pork sausages, spun it as regularly as they did Marty Robbins' 'El Paso' and Johnny Mathis's 'Misty'; huge rockers gave it the treatment normally reserved for Gene Vincent and Norton motorbikes, while their teddy-boy cousins accorded it the Berry and Presley over-kill. Schoolgirls from nearby Clapton Park, Helen Shapiro among them, would include it in their selection of Cliff, Billy, Craig and Adam hits; heel-high secretaries adored it, and so did the café's small spill of married women, arms overflowing with both shopping and children; Jimmy Jones nibbling at the loose change in their half-empty purses. In deprived Homerton, handy men were more the exception than the other, but both sexes indulged their fantasies to the full; and the erstwhile, mechanically adept, greasers really took it to heart.

It was also my own favourite disc at the time, slightly diminishing a fascination with Bobby Darin; and in the second week of March the rest of the nation approved Chatsworth's good taste as it entered the British Top Twenty. It was a good-sized hit, peaking at number four, and staying in the charts, for a total of eighteen weeks.

Wherever you went that spring, the voice of Jimmy Jones yelling 'well if your broken heart needs repair/I yiii yam the man to see/I fix broken hearts/you tell all your friends/and they'll come running to me yee yee yee' was to be heard. If it didn't quite outshine Lonnie Donegan's old man, who spoke in cockney rhyming slang and was an insult to everybody born east of

Liverpool Street Station, it at least helped to make the latter a bit more bearable. Eventually 'Cathy's Clown' was released, and the MGM label came once more to mean Conway Twitty (hooray) and Connie Francis (boo).

Chatsworth Road was a little slow off the mark with Jimmy's follow-up 'Good Timin'', and it took them more than a week after its release to include it on their juke box. In the meantime *Record Mirror* had published details of the disc's incredible chart ascent in the US, courtesy of *Cashbox*, and MGM had rush-released it. Radio Luxembourg was the first airing it received; and hearing 'Good Timin'', through a fog of poor reception and weak transistors, I died slowly.

Few records have that instant impact, that purely subjective *élan* of half-hysterical, stomach-constricting, sublimated sex ecstasy. The description suffers; it cannot be described, only felt. US Bonds' joyous 'Quarter to Three' was one, so was the Doors' 'Love Me Two Times', also Lorna and Scotty's 'Skank in Bed', Jessie Hill's 'Ooh Poo Pah Doo', and maybe half-a-dozen others. 'Good Timin'', with its catchy horn intro, swirling fairground sound; with Jimmy's warm black vocal, goofy tick-a-tick-a-tick-a gimmick, and chilling falsetto was also in this league.

Two weeks after entering the charts, in June, it had repeated its American success and bestrode the nation, a position it was to covet for four weeks, until Cliff Richard and 'Please Don't Tease' toppled it. My dislike for Richard dates from that day. 'Good Timin'' descended as rapidly as it had risen, and four weeks later it was out of the chart. A ten week wonder, pure Superpop flash!

Jimmy Jones was never to score again, although he had a few minor hits, Stateside, with 'Ready for Love', 'I Just Go for You', and 'I Told You So'. The sole album was a collection of these, plus 'Handy Man' and 'Good Timin''; and their flips, love songs in pseudo doo-wop style. It was remaindered for a quid, three months after release.

Penny Reel, *Let it Rock*, May 1975

1961: Music That Spells Cash and Freedom

I find the music, find the words. I put them together and get them just as I want them. But it takes a long while, and a lot of moving about. All this moving about, it's like waiting for some outer direction to set the words to the music, music that spells cash and freedom and all that.

It's like being a pop star. You stand up there on the stage. You move your finger, to the right – a simple action – and you're terribly conscious of it; conscious of a sort of inner audience that is watching, not critically but just watching like an echo that will come back to make yourself into the critic. You're alone in a great white spot, and hearing the band start up, and the backing group going aah, aah, and you take the mike into your hands. I have got to sing, and you think of the words, and then you look out towards where the people are and you swing in, and make noise, and go just wild – and you see people watching you, some of them just staring, taking it all in, and some of them being very clinical; only you can't see them for the white light blinds you. You can only feel them, and they're watching, watching hard because they don't know your next move, and they think that you ought to; that even if they don't know which way you're going to move next, then you will. I mean, everybody thinks that you know what you're doing, only they're so wrong. But then I tell you what I'm going to do next and you don't believe me. You keep on looking. I keep thinking, now you want a surprise, and the band starts up and I keep trying to think. I must get the words straight, compose, work out what I want to say – but you keep looking. I know you're looking and I don't want to disappoint, or fail to surprise or hold you, so I go on bash, bash, all wild – take this while you're waiting, take this and like it.

There's something so very wonderful and vital about a singer, be it Yves Montand, Cliff Richard, Judy Garland, Sinatra, Elvis, Ella. The pop concert, so different from a straight music concert like a symphony or a jazz; the whole thing gets personalized. The message that comes across and through is that of the star of the show, not an idea or a theme, or a general feeling, or a collection of sounds. A link has to be forged between the star and the individuals of the audience. If the link isn't made; if the thing doesn't get across then the results are immediate. It's not a rejection slip from an agent, or a no-sale ticket from a publisher but a knife thrown at the stage to hit not an idea, or a sound but a person. The reaction and the response are made clear there and then, at once. There is an immediacy there isn't with the TV, or the film or a book.

Maybe 2,000 people go to the Hall for the one-night stand of the star show. Assume 50 per cent of these have come to look, to clinically analyse, to take the mick; that is, there are in the audience 1,000 sociologists at work, cranks, statisticians, amateur and professional talent scouts, et cetera et cetera. That still leaves 1,000 people who have come to take in person the message, the rhythm, the beat of the star whose image they have cottoned on to; the legend they've picked up in the TV magazine, movie; the gossip wise.

They know some part of the legend. They have an image of you, what you will do, what you will be like.

Paul Robeson – Old Man River – Keep the Red Flag Flying – big black man.
Judy Garland – A Star is Born – Somewhere Over the Rainbow – tragedy, female.
Creature X – male – teen – lean.

So, there are about 1,000 people who have come for the message, to get uplifted, to be reconverted, to take a night off, to see the live show. There are 1,000 people who are going, up to a point, to take in wholesale the show and the star of the show, or just the star.

I'm not interested now with the funny ha ha show, or the satirical shows, or the Tommy Steele, Tom Lehrer; or even the plain variety shows like the Perry Como thing which are better on TV and let's hope they stay for ever as unlive as that.

I am concerned with the great religious shows, the romantic, the heroic, the ones where you can forget; immerse yourself with another person; the union with you shows.

Ella, Edith, Nat, Cliff, I have come to cry with you because you get across to me just how I feel when I'm not able quite to put into words or actions how I feel; when I can find no form to put what I feel into. You see I'm ordinary brown card 797 in the crowd. I am married to XY. I am married because I didn't want to feel and to be alone, and reading those poems about the pee stains on the underwear frightened me; and also let's face it, please, getting married is the most respectable and the most permanent way known to man of getting his oats. I am ordinary working chap X leading the life any man in the street, any brown card on the shop floor would lead. Ella, show me show me what life could have been, up and down, happy and sad; a life with a spontaneity and a movement and a generosity, and a living pitch and depth of feeling, show me this. Show me life through coloured spectacles, because that is how I wanted it, how I still want it, and how I only find it one day, even if that, in the 365. Take me away from my daylight and fluorescent white light life, and show me the spectrum; take my functional spectacles away from me. Just for tonight let me dare to leave my functions and my self-inflicted tasks at home. Do not let me for one moment see life as it is for me; but throw in the drama, the punch, the goodness, the fun, the glory, the greatness, the bad, the moment of passion, the moment of despair. Tell me all about them deep blues, and tell me like Judy Garland that somewhere over

... Yes, I wanted to go there. When I was a child I wanted to go there. I saw *Peter Pan* at Christmas time in a provincial theatre that is now a super-market, and I wanted to be like Peter Pan; to never grow up; never have to see straight; never have my blinkers put on. I want to go there, be like Peter Pan. Even now I want this. But I couldn't. I was afraid, and now I can't. It's too late. I'm young only in heart. I am just X in the crowd at seat No. J 17 Circle of the show on tour calling at this place for one night, two shows, and then on.

I cannot book the whole front row for the Floyd Patterson fight. I could not even fill the front row with my supporters, or even loyal friends, or even enemies. I don't know anybody. I am no Sinatra. I sit at Hall K, Town Z, seat No. J 17 Circle, and I wish and dream. I want to go to that beautiful land where the lemonade springs from the soda water fountain, and the cigarette trees ... Let me fly round the earth like the first cosmonaut, and leave this world to the sounds of this world, and then with the greatest of ease in a red velvet chair recline to the heavenly music of love, relayed from Cairo or Moscow or Rome, it wouldn't matter. It would seem as if it came from the heavens themselves, and being out in a cosmos like Peter Pan: one moment of ecstasy, of timelessness, of weightlessness, love infinity. But then, you get up there, go round one, two, three, and then down, and they change the music, and come down to 'The Northern Lights of Old Aberdeen'; 'Motherland, Motherland I Can Hear You Calling'; 'Keep the Red Flag'. You know if I was up there all timeless and weightless and enjoying it all and they started playing 'The Yellow Rose of Texas', or 'God Bless the Prince of Wales' or something like that, I'd want a button to press to burn me and the whole thing up. You couldn't come down to that.

It's strange, that for all the efforts of the Elders of our tribes to provide the younger generation with fitting and suitable heroes, we've got heroes in a set of unzipping the banana young men, and women of maturity to cuddle and comfort the poor banana once it's bin unzipped, and young girls who look like boys. But let's be honest, all the Soviet achievements, they're a little unsatisfying, emotionally. The moralists have tried to provide the world with honest, happily married two kids, secondary modern to tec at night and skilled technocrat to Party member and Government commission sitter; provincial ordinary suburban ever so nice and normal, fit and healthy and the heroes are still a long list of Ishmaels. The figure is on the stage, the banana, the Boy-god, the Ishmael. The backing starts up. He moves into a solitary blue spot. He cannot sing, talk, express; but the youth and the beauty he has are worth more than all the other qualities he does not have. The other cerebral and emotional qualities we can have all through life, but the youth and the beauty are over before you have the chance to put them across. He moves alone across the desert of the stage. It is the face, the look, the loneliness, the uncommunicable, unclubable – the figure we would all like to be or be in physical contact with – tall, dark, slim. Letting in a little light, bringing in a little life. With our 7/6's we must buy him and kill him and then love the image and read the magazines and start all over again.

For every sale there is a price, and this price is the desert. He stands like Billy Budd and we cry out as he sits on his stool to say 'I wanna be loved by you, by you'. Yes, me, me, we are gone. We are round the bent bend. He won't come down. He can't. He must wait for us, for us the judge and the jury and the god to crucify him, and his only hope can be through a resurrection in the magazines; an eternal and indivisible and twice nightly sacrifice. He looks all lonesome and blue and we cry out to him to come down from the cross. There's a flicker of a smile across his face. After all, he's paid to be crucified twice nightly, and the mood changes and he annoys us. Like Dorian Gray he is conscious of his looks and his body and soul (the mind and the emotions are not important); of his everything and our feelings, our emotion. It is we who are all alone, and we are not paid professional martyrs. We do not have the riches, the little compensations his public loneliness has brought him. Save us, save us – and others and our own other halves, say come down from your perch. You say you send them, send yourself. Oh Boy call the tune for us and make us happy, and we shall give ourselves to you. We fall prostrate on the edge of the stage, and he smiles and throws us a flower some disciple threw him some hours ago, and then the spotlight dies and the curtain comes down, and the band plays 'God Save the Queen' and we are helped to stand straight by the impartial police, and that is the end of the show.

The lonely boy is physical. It is we and not the artist who have to supply the emotion, the thoughts, the feelings. All he does is give us the body and the soul, the centre of an idea. As we grow older we can't hope for anything that perfect. We can't hope anything like that will come our way, and in any case even if it did we wouldn't have the price we would need to pay. We know that there are no oases in the desert, no desert islands in the sea; only oil wells that spurt out a black liquid and twist tall Texans and cover the earth with a blackness and a part of it with money, to become a part of the jungle man prepares to give back to his god. There is no heaven on earth, no dream to come true. But still we turn to the lonely boy; in the city but not of the city. We can only hope that out of our dull ordinary lives there may come not only the one-night stand, and the movie and the magazine and the art, but the real, one little compensation to make up for the rest, one knife thrust deep enough to hurt, one tense moment to remember. Your wife is dead. You mourn. You cry. But there are the bills to pay, the solicitors to see, and funeral directors and the arrangements to attend to, the notice to put in the paper, and there is no sick pay.

Love – you wait for the turn of the key in the door, that never comes. You wait for the steps in the hall, for the bell to ring. You have gotten the blues and you wanna cry. There is the train to catch, the office – no time to mourn. I cried a river over you. I waited ten, eleven, twelve o'clock scanning every train, bus, car, taxi, and motor-cycle, waiting for you but you didn't turn up. There was no message and no arrival.

You don't really wait that long. You're very upset. You're moody, annoyed; but you take the coach back all the miles you came, mourning the unnecessary expense, and the things like weeding those rows of peas, or reading that novel that you might have done if you had known in advance that the journey would be fruitless. You turn up at the office after a restless night dreaming of the things you might have done if there had been an arrival. You go back home and ask: any post, any post, anyone call, anyone call, any message, a telegram? but life goes on. We are the crowd. We are brand X. The nearest we can get is the banana. We give up the waiting and the no arrivals. We give up the great hopes of a real, and marry and settle down and moan. One night we went to bed, and I did not take the usual precautions and we made such love and all the time I was dreaming of a banana and there was a child. This child will never know that he had three parents – me and you and the banana, and perhaps your banana too. It has three, and maybe it has four. If only we knew who the banana was. Illegitimate births have nothing, nothing on banana babies – there's the tragedy, not in the bastard.

We have come here tonight, Ella, Nat, Edith, Judy, Frankie, Boy, for you to tell us how we felt or could have felt when she didn't turn up. We who have often wanted, but never dared to sit up all night over the whisky bottle. We who have not physically cried over a broken heart, have come to hear you put the words to the music, the expression to the feeling, the lines of definition to our vague sensations, to our half-sensed and unexplored desires. We did not cry through the wee small hours. We went to bed and slept; but we would have cried if we hadn't duties, responsibilities, and the 7.55. The factory, the office, they dictate every day of our lives, bar Saturday nights, Sunday mornings and the Bank and Big Holidays.

Ray Gosling, *Sum Total* (1962)

1961: Chicago, January

It was late afternoon. The building was quiet, the office staff already gone for the day.

Monroe and Willie were huddled over Monroe's desk, tightening up the year's album-production schedule, so engrossed in what they were doing that neither of them heard the man enter the room.

''Scuse me, y'all . . .'

They looked up, startled.

He was about thirty-five, wearing a baggy, one-button-roll suit and a shirt with a frayed Mr. B collar. He had a home haircut – chopped unevenly all over his scalp, the sides shaved – and the muscular, stocky look of a black man who has dragged a lot of sixteen-foot cotton sacks through a lot of furrows.

'How'd you get in here?' Monroe asked sharply, angry at the interruption.

'The front door was open. There wasn't nobody out front, so I just kept walking around till I found somebody.' He smiled, showing a gap where his two front teeth should have been, and stuck out a callused hand. 'My name's Rydell Mercer. I come to audition for y'all.'

'You got to make an appointment,' Monroe said, dismissing him.

'I can't make no appointment . . .'

'What you mean, you can't make no appointment?'

'I don't live here, I lives in Indiana.'

'Well, what you doing here, then?'

'I told you, I come up here to audition for y'all.'

Monroe dropped his pen on the desk, sighed, and leaned back in his chair, resigned to spending a few minutes getting rid of him.

'Okay, what do you do? Sing, write, what?'

'We sings and plays.'

'We? What you mean, "we"? What you got, a frog in your pocket?'

'I got my band outside. We all come up here together.'

'From Indiana?'

'Yeah, Evansville.'

'Damn! You brought your band all the way up here on the chance somebody might listen to you?' Monroe made a face. 'You sure got a lot of nerve, man. How many cats in your band?'

'They's usually seven of us, but one couldn't come – one of his children is sick.'

'Where you all parked?'

'Out front, down the street a little ways.'

'Okay, as long as you came this far, I might as well hear what you niggers sound like. Pull your car around back and start unloading your stuff.'

Monroe talked to Willie a few minutes longer, then walked down the hall and opened the back door to a burst of cold air just as a muddy brown DeSoto was pulling into the parking lot, dragging a dirty U-Haul trailer with an Indiana license plate hanging by one screw.

The six blacks who climbed out of the car ranged in age from eighteen or nineteen to a bald man who looked old enough to be Mercer's father.

Monroe shook his head. These were some of the most soulful blacks he had ever seen. He didn't know men like this were still around.

Mercer grabbed a ragged blue imitation-alligator saxophone case from the floor of the trailer and stood off to the side, giving orders. It took almost no time for the men to get their instruments inside. The last piece of equipment was an old Hammond B-3 organ with most of the shellac worn off. They set it on a splintered dolly with wobbly wheels and made a lot of noise pushing it over the hump in the doorway.

Monroe closed the door quickly, trying to keep some of the heat inside, and followed the musicians down the hall.

'What you niggers call yourselves, man?' he asked Mercer.

'Rydell Mercer and the Indiana Blues Boys,' Mercer answered, making it obvious that Monroe should have heard of them before now.

Monroe shook his head disgustedly.

He went inside the control booth and watched through the window as Willie placed the microphones where the sound could be picked up and played inside.

Willie joined him a few minutes later, taking his customary seat behind the console. 'You want me to tape them, Mr Wilcox?'

'Hell, no! Man, if these niggers sound anything like they look, we about to hear some sad shit!'

He gave the band a few more minutes to finish tuning up, then pushed the button on the studio mike. 'Lemme know when you guys are ready,' he said to Mercer.

'We's ready now.'

'You ready?' Monroe asked Willie.

'Umm-hmmm,' Willie said, fooling with the knobs, already sounding bored.

'Okay,' Monroe said into the mike, 'lemme hear what you got.'

He took his hand off the button and heard Mercer issuing some last-minute instructions, followed by four clicking noises as the drummer banged his sticks together to set the tempo.

Mercer had the introduction – a honking, preaching four-bar saxophone solo. It didn't take him long to set the groove. After the first couple of notes, he had his eyes rolled back in his head, the gap where his two front teeth should have been firmly clamped around the mouthpiece of his dented, silver-plated old saxophone.

Monroe was surprised: the nigger could play.

On the downbeat of the fifth bar, when the other instruments joined in, Monroe sat up straight in his seat.

God damn! Those raggedy-looking characters were cooking!

Monroe turned to Willie. Willie was moving back and forth in his seat in time to the music, slapping the console with his palm, a wide grin on his face.

Monroe knew the sound blaring from the two speakers above his head was *exactly* what he had been waiting for. It was genuine, it was telling the true story:

> *Saturday night in the neighborhood ... scraping up the rent money ... hanging out on the corners ... trying to jive some foxy little mama out of her phone number ... or her drawers ... chewing on a rib ... drinking red soda pop ... squeezing bedbugs ... sitting on the back porch in your undershirt ... sticky hot ... swatting flies with a rolled-up Pittsburgh* Courier *... shooting rats with a .22 ...*

He had their asses now!

There wasn't a white musician in the world who could 'cover' the music that was coming out of that studio. Not yet. Not unless he had spent the last ten years of his life on the back of an Evansville, Indiana, dump truck, picking up trash in subzero weather, with the handles on the cans so cold that they stripped the flesh off his fingers when he set them back down.

The fix wasn't quite in. A year, maybe two, and it would be. But right now, today, there wasn't enough money or leverage in the music business to keep Rydell Mercer off the pop charts – not if he was promoted right.

The song ended. Mercer was getting ready to go right into another tune when Monroe pushed the mike button down. 'C'mon in, man. I don't need to hear no more,' he said. He was already on his feet when Mercer came through the studio door. 'Let's go in my office, we gotta talk.'

Mercer followed him down the hall. When he had sat down across the desk from Monroe, he lit a cigarette, showing nervousness for the first time.

'That your tune?' Monroe asked.

'Yeah, how you like it?'

'What you call it?'

'We calls it "The Up-and-Down Boogie".'

'Umm-hmmm,' Monroe said. 'I might have to change that title. You write it?'

'Yeah, me and the organ player.'

'Dig, you cats ain't signed with nobody, are you?'

'No, that's why we's here.'

'Anybody ever publish any of your tunes before?'

'No, we ain't never played them for nobody before.'

Monroe reached into the top drawer. 'Here, read this,' he said, thrusting a contract at Mercer.

Mercer took it, looked through it with a puzzled expression.

'It ain't nothing but a standard recording contract,' Monroe said. 'You can take it to a lawyer if you want.'

'I don't need no lawyer, man,' Mercer said defensively. 'I can read it myself.' He squinted at it for a few seconds, making it obvious that he couldn't. 'I ain't got my glasses with me,' he concluded. 'What do it say?'

'All it says is, if you sign with me, you can't sign with nobody else. And that I'll pay you five percent of ninety percent of every record I sell on you.'

Mercer thumbed through the contract. 'It take eight pages just to say that?'

'No, it's got a lot of lawyer talk in it, too,' Monroe explained. ' "The party of the first part", "henceforth and to wit", that kind of bullshit, you know what I mean?'

Mercer looked a little dubious.

'Lemme tell you something,' Monroe said firmly, looking Rydell Mercer straight in the eye. 'I got one rule at this company: I don't fuck over nobody and I don't let nobody fuck me over. Can you dig that?'

Mercer nodded.

'So if you want to take it to a lawyer, that's cool. I ain't gonna try to con you into doing nothing you ain't sure about. But if you want to sign it now, I'll cut you as soon as I can, and get a record out on you cats immediately.'

Mercer looked down at the contract in his hand, back up at Monroe, back down at the contract, back up at Monroe, trying to resolve his indecision.

'Okay,' he finally said. 'This is what we come up here for. If you wants to mess over us, this piece of paper ain't gonna make a damn bit of difference. Where do I sign?'

'You don't have to sign right this minute,' Monroe said. 'It ain't filled in yet.'

'That's okay, you done give me your word. If I'm gonna trust you, I might as well start trusting you now. Where do I sign?'

Monroe showed him.

Mercer signed three blank recording contracts and four blank publishing contracts, his scrawly 'Rydell D. Mercer' so cramped and illegible that Monroe could hardly make it out.

'Okay,' Monroe said, sticking the contracts back in his desk, 'I got a girl coming in in the morning. I'll have her fill everything in. Then I'll sign them and make sure you get a copy, okay?'

Mercer nodded. 'When we gonna make a record?' he asked.

'The sooner the better.'

'The band's here, the stuff's already set up, the contracts is already signed. How come we can't go 'head and do it now?'

'The studio ain't set up yet for making a record. It'll take about a half-hour. You guys wanna go eat or something?'

Mercer's dark eyes shone with determination. 'Man, we can eat anytime, but this might be the only chance we ever gets to make a record. Go on and get your studio ready while I rehearse my band. I got five babies to feed. I got to make some money!'

Monroe had the record pressed and shipped within ten days.

By the middle of February it was number one on the rhythm-and-blues charts.

That same week, it jumped on to the pop charts: number thirty-nine and with a bullet next to the number, which meant it was coming up fast.

The next week, it was number thirteen with a bullet.

The week after that, it was number three with a bullet.

The week after that, it was number one.

He had done it.

It had taken him the better part of five years to get another number-one record, but this one was all his. He owned the tune, the group, the company, the whole damned thing.

For the first time since he had formed his company, he had some leverage with his distributors.

It was what he had been waiting for.

He stopped shipment.

Before he would send out more records, they had to pay him every penny they owed for delinquent accounts.

They paid.

The second week the record was number one, he had two pressing plants going around the clock. His publishing company already had five cover records on the song, including one country and western version in the top ten on the country-music charts. He had shipped out 1,750,000 singles. He had actually received payment for more than a million of them.

To date, including the squaring up of delinquent accounts, the song had earned him more than a half-million dollars.

It was the wildest, most exhilarating month of his life, like nothing he could have imagined. His whole catalog came alive. His label was suddenly the hottest line in the business. Young buyers, previously unaware of its existence, were now flocking to the stores to grab every Big City record they could get their hands on.

Friday morning, *Ebony* magazine phoned. They wanted to do a cover story on him.

He worked straight through the weekend, filling orders.

Monday after, two white men came to see him.

They were gangsters.

Joseph C. Smith, *The Day the Music Died* (1981)

1961: Pop and Protest

Up to the point of the failure of CND it would be broadly true to say that pop was the prerogative of working-class teenagers, protest was the prerogative of middle-class students, and art was the prerogative of the lunatic fringe. The pop fans despised protest as being naïve and art as being posh, the protesting students despised pop as being commercial and art as being pretentious, and the artists despised pop for being tasteless and protest for being drab.

There had, however, been occasional bridges. The hood, the rocker, the ted, had long been idolized by artists who saw him as the champion of the oppressed class (Sillitoe), the incarnate will (Gunn), the noble savage (Brando), the free libido (Kerouac) or a good lay (Ginsberg). When trad jazz became widely popular it was enjoyed, in one form or another, by all three groups. Skiffle, an offshoot of trad jazz, was folksy enough for the protesters, creative enough for the artists and twangy enough for the pop fans. When the West Coast Beats and Horovitz and Brown in England started to perform poetry informally, with jazz, that was a further bridge. When they did it under the auspices of CND that was yet another.

Ray Gosling sensed that something was changing in 1961. He wrote in an open letter to an old friend: 'You finish off your letter by saying, "Don't change. I know I won't." Well, Howard, my old duck, I think I have. The way I look at it is that the whole world's changing out here, and I'm moving with it because I like the way it's changing all the way. Oh, you don't see it in the papers, but you wait five, ten, fifteen years' time when you come back. You won't know this little old island. Perhaps I won't either. But I know I'm loving every minute of this changing, seeing a whole way of life come through, seeing a world change right in front of my eyes and knowing, I'm part of it, caught right in the middle, helping to change it all and being changed by it all at the same time.

'Remember when we were at school. Oh, don't worry, the school hasn't changed one little bit. The change hasn't gone that far. But remember the old crowd. Mo (he's in New York now) with that face and the haircut – all straight and floppy and unstyled. And Jerry (he's got this play coming off in Coventry some time next year) with those black unused jeans, tight in all the wrong places, and that curly black hair all over the place. Remember the talk all about Tennessee Williams and James Dean and "I wanna go to America", and Music with a capital M, and bringing Culture to the People and all that. The way we all took the rise out of the Pops and the People and Politics.

'Well, Howard, now there's a new crowd. The new arty-crafties are different. They're still the same terribly conscious lot, getting all worked up over what's happening. They're still the all brain and no sport, still looking and listening and talking and laughing in all the right places, but you want to see the way they dress. They've got all tight in the right places and their hair's all sharp and well razored and they're as much involved in things as the secondary modern kids. It's not just looking and listening and talking and laughing any more. They have got mixed up in things, all involved. I tell you if you lined this new generation up with the same age lot from the sec. modern, you'd have a job to tell one from tother. The superior air has got left behind. They've got their feet on the ground. The capital letters for art and music and culture have been missed out. You remember the fifth-formers, the old teddy boy lot when we were in our last year in the Sixth. Well, this new lot have taken over from there. They're all keyed up and with it all and in. For them things have become a whole way of life. It's De Beat generation all Europeanized, with Banning the Bomb and Jazz and De popular arts. And the point is that down in the beer and piana bars and in the jazz rooms they really are mixing. Howard, they're all right.'

Perhaps the most important bridge, though, was *The Goon Show*, a radio comedy programme that ran throughout the late fifties and went a long way towards preparing the ground for the current hybrid sub-culture. The origin of *The Goon Show* and its curious humour lay, I believe, in British National Service. National Service in the time of the H-Bomb, when all defence was geared to massive nuclear retaliation anyway, was an imposed absurdity which English teenage conscripts sustained by forming their own sense of humour, a combination of corny music-hall comedy, the humour of English comic papers like *Dandy* and *Beano*, hatred of war and the officer classes – the army is one place where class distinction is imposed by law – and a wild nihilistic surrealist element which derived from the absurdity of the army itself. Polishing boot-studs and painting coal black were, after all, master-pieces of Dada. The International Christmas Pudding rolled along inevitably. We all heard our Barrack Room fantasies articulated and performed per-fectly by *The Goon Show* team of Spike Milligan (also a trad trumpeter), Michael Bentine, Harry Secombe, Peter Sellers and the bop drummer Ray Ellington. *The Goon Show* catchphrases and *The Goon Show* caricature voices spread into everybody's conversation and provided us all with schizoid subterfuges, vocal disguises. Our attitudes became inflected with Bentine's manic hatred of war and governments (he had been among the troops who released the Belsen prisoners), with Spike Milligan's socialism (a founder member of the Committee of 100 and the Direct Action Committee) and his public conduct (a radio discussion on the nature of humour when he suddenly dried up and refused to speak – another radio interview when he claimed that *The Goon Show* farces were an accurate representation of the world – a fabled public reception where he sat on the steps outside and peppered the arriving guests with inane remarks – the time he sent his wife a telegram asking her to please pass the marmalade). *The Goon Show* was protest. *The Goon Show* was surrealist and therefore art, and *The Goon Show* was every National Serviceman's defence mechanism, and therefore pop.

Two alien traditions had tentatively come together. The influence was widespread.

The chaotic paintings and novels of John Bratby give a graphic picture of the world of the London art schools at this time. Throughout this world the prevailing mood was pure 'Goon' and the prevailing sentiment was anti-bomb. The crowning expression of both mood and sentiment was the comedy-trad of two bands, the Temperance Seven and the Alberts. The Temps, who started off with a brilliant freak-clarinettist called Joey, finished up in the Top Twenty.

The Alberts, far wilder than the Temps, with disturbing elements of genuine lunacy in their make-up, consisted of the Grey Brothers and Bruce Lacey. The Grey Brothers owned an extensive collection of Edwardian clothes and redundant wind instruments, all of which Dougie and Tony could play with disarming skill. They appeared on all anti-bomb demonstrations and most Communist rallies, Dougie in Norfolk jacket and plus-fours, or white ducks and yachting cap, his cornet and his lecherous greyhound both on golden chains. When they performed at Colyer's, ravers staggered back from the blinding explosives flashing from the bells of the instruments and the sight of Dougie's magnificent genitals hanging in splendour as he sat in kilt and tam-o'-shanter with pheasant plume, blowing the guts out of 'Dollie Grey', while Professor Lacey accompanied on the amplified penny-farthing bicycle. Before their legendary San Francisco engagement (where they flopped miserably – 'Now listen, Mac, what the act needs is a little polish' – and escorted a stuffed camel back through the lost motels of the Western Desert) they performed their riotous 'Evening of British Rubbish' in London and sank a boat in which they were being interviewed by the BBC, or so the story goes. Bruce Lacey made his magnificent hominoids, sick, urinating, stuttering machines constructed of the debris of the century, always with pointed socialist/pacifist overtones but with a profound sense of anger, disgust and gaiety that goes far beyond any simple political standpoint. The hominoids, radio-controlled, began to appear in the act.

Screaming Lord Sutch, with his pop-adaptation of sadistic melodrama, Jack-the-Rippering up his volunteer victim to the thunder of steel guitars, took some of the Alberts' lunacy into the rock-'n'-roll clubs. With his bid for Parliament he took the same spirit into the General Election.

Dick Lester, the director of the Beatles films in which Lacey played, also the producer of films with Spike Milligan, the Bonzo Dog Doodah Band, and Arthur Brown, swinging down to the stand with a flaming hat, the face of Queequeg and the voice of Michael Bentine, all owe a good deal to this privately run looneybin of *Goon Show* humour. Other corners of the same madhouse contain the 'Wham' cartoons of Leo Baxendale (simultaneously Secretary of Scottish CND) and the anarchic plays of John Antrobus, whose *You'll Come to Love Your Sperm Test* worked nicely on the guardians of Edinburgh morality. His *Bed-Sitting Room*, co-written with Milligan, is possibly the most moving and uncompromising of works about the Bomb. Like Milligan, Secombe and Lacey, Antrobus lives and works in a state of near-manic deadlock with society.

Jeff Nuttall, *Bomb Culture* (1968)

1961: The Dubious Origins of Beatles

Translated from the John Lennon

Once upon a time there were three little boys called John, George and Paul, by name christened. They decided to get together because they were the getting together type. When they were together they wondered what for after all, what for? So all of a sudden they all grew guitars and formed a noise. Funnily enough, no one was interested, least of all the three little men. So-o-o-o on discovering a fourth little even littler man called Stuart Sutcliffe running about them they said, quote 'Sonny get a bass guitar and you will be alright' and he did – but he wasn't alright because he couldn't play it. So they sat on him with comfort 'til he could play. Still there was no beat, and a kindly old aged man said, quote 'Thou hast not drums!' We had no drums! they coffed. So a series of drums came and went and came.

Suddenly, in Scotland, touring with Johnny Gentle, the group (called the Beatles called) discovered they had not a very nice sound – because they had no amplifiers. They got some. Many people ask what are Beatles? Why Beatles? Ugh, Beatles, how did the name arrive? So we will tell you. It came in a vision – a man appeared on a flaming pie and said unto them 'From this day on you are Beatles with an A.' Thank you, Mister Man, they said, thanking him.

And then a man with a beard cut off said – will you go to Germany (Hamburg) and play mighty rock for the peasants for money? And we said we would play mighty anything for money.

But before we could go we had to grow a drummer, so we grew one in West Derby in a club called Some Casbah and his trouble was Pete Best. We called 'Hello, Pete, come off to Germany!' 'Yes!' Zooooom. After a few months, Peter and Paul (who is called McArtrey, son of Jim McArtrey, his father) lit a Kino (cinema) and the German police said 'Bad Beatles, you must go home and light your English cinemas.' Zooooom, half a group. But even before this, the Gestapo had taken my friend little George Harrison (of Speke) away because he was only twelve and too young to vote in Germany; but after two months in England he grew eighteen, and the Gestapoes said 'you can come.' So suddenly all back in Liverpool Village were many groups playing in grey suits and Jim said 'Why have you no grey suits?' 'We don't like them, Jim' we said speaking to Jim. After playing in the clubs a bit, everyone said 'Go to Germany!' So we are. Zooooom. Stuart gone. Zoom zoom John (of Woolton), George (of Speke) Peter and Paul zoom zoom. All of them gone.

Thank you club members, from John and George (what are friends).

Mersey Beat, 6–20 July 1961

1961: The Same Fantastic Feeling for Beat

I have always thought of Brenda Lee as the female counterpart to Eddie Cochran when she is singing rock 'n' roll. The same roughness, the same attack, the same fantastic sense of beat is there. Eddie used to flip over Brenda's work. He and Gene would discuss the new releases of sixteen-year-old Miss Dynamite with great enthusiasm.

It gives me a kick to see Eddie's record and Brenda's so close together in the charts . . . particularly as they are linked by the strange hand of coincidence. You see, 'Dum Dum' is written by Sharon Sheeley – who was Eddie's girlfriend. Sharon also wrote the flipside of 'Weekend' – which again by a strange coincidence, is called 'Cherished Memories'.

But quite apart from that Sharon has been responsible for composing some of the all-time rock 'n' roll classics – like 'Poor Little Fool' and 'Somethin' Else'.

Songwriting is not Sharon's full-time occupation, however. She is primarily a film actress and her work in Hollywood is keeping her from making a return visit to this country – something which in her letters she repeatedly tells me she wants dearly to do.

She feels Britain is almost Eddie's homeland by adoption. So do I.

Kip at Apollo

Walking down Shaftesbury Avenue the other day I was suddenly overtaken by an irresistible urge to have a kip. I could hardly remain on two feet and my eyelids dropped as if lead-weighted.

Then it occurred to me that I was near the new offices of Lionel Bart's publishing company, Apollo Music.

I staggered into the shiny reception. The smart secretary looked up from her typewriter. 'Can I help you?' she enquired. 'Yes,' I mumbled uneasily. 'My name is Jack Good and I wondered if I might sleep here for an hour.'

She batted not a mascara'd eye-lid and went to fetch Lionel's personal assistant, a very charming young lady, and his able manager, Leslie Paul.

They were kindness itself. You'd think that they were quite used to people dropping in to have a doss.

Ronnie Carroll in fact was there and he confessed that he had only just woken up – such is the seductive luxury of the place. I was ushered into a lovely unoccupied room, drew up a beautiful turquoise armchair and dropped off easily to the land of Nod.

Some hours later I awoke with the sound of a very familiar voice warbling outside the room – Billy Fury's.

Now in the course of duty I've listened to Bill's voice for some hours on end, so I know it pretty well. Imagine my surprise when I shambled out to the reception hall and there was no Billy, but another boy of about the same age doing an impersonation for the benefit of the smart secretary, and the voice was identical – quite uncanny. I rolled away bemused.

If I had had any sense I'd have taken the boy's name and address, but I was much too dozy.

The moral to all this is, I suppose, that if you're scouting for talent, you can do worse than to drop in on Apollo Music for a nap . . . but you have to keep your eyes wide open.

Worst yet?

I often hear a disc – not infrequently one I have produced myself – with the deep-rooted conviction that this really must be the worst record ever made and that it is inconceivable that I should ever hear a worse one. But I always do.

Folks, a new all-time low has been fearlessly plumbed by a current Warner Bros. release. The song is called 'The Boy I Left Behind' and is rendered unmercifully by someone called Little Suzie.

An unnamed callow youth has a soul-searing recitative mid-way through the side. In the context of any other record this spoken passage would be agony. Here, however, it is an oasis.

Actually if you are in the right frame of mind, this is the most hilariously funny record imaginable. It is worth almost anything to hear it – short of buying it, of course.

Jack Good, *Disc Magazine*, 5 August 1961

1962: Real Horrorshow

The next morning I woke up at oh eight oh oh hours, my brothers, and as I still felt shagged and fagged and fashed and bashed and my glazzies were stuck together real horrorshow with sleepglue, I thought I would not go to school. I thought how I would have a malenky bit longer in the bed, an hour or two say, and then get dressed nice and easy, perhaps even having a splosh about in the bath, make toast for myself and slooshy the radio or read the gazetta, all on my oddy knocky. And then in the afterlunch I might perhaps, if I still felt like it, itty off to the old skolliwoll and see what was vareeting in that great seat of gloopy useless learning. O my brothers. I heard my papapa grumbling and trampling and then ittying off to the dyeworks where he rabbited, and then my mum called in in a very respectful goloss as she did now I was growing up big and strong:

'It's gone eight, son. You don't want to be late again.'

So I called back: 'A bit of a pain in my gulliver. Leave us be and I'll try to sleep it off and then I'll be right as dodgers for this after.' I slooshied her give a sort of a sigh and she said:

'I'll put your breakfast in the oven then, son. I've got to be off myself now.' Which was true, there being this law for everybody not a child nor with child nor ill to go out rabbiting. My mum worked at one of the Statemarts, as they called them, filling up the shelves with tinned soup and beans and all that cal. So I slooshied her clank a plate in the gas-oven like and then she was putting her shoes on and then getting her coat from behind the door and then sighing again, then she said: 'I'm off now, son.' But I let on to be back in sleepland and then I did doze off real horrorshow, and I had a queer and very real like sneety, dreaming for some reason of my droog Georgie. In this sneety he'd got like very much older and very sharp and hard and was govoreeting about discipline and obedience and how all the malchicks under his control had to jump hard at it and throw up the old salute like being in the army, and there was me in line like the rest saying yes sir and no sir, and then I viddied clear that Georgie had these stars on his pletchoes and he was like a general. And then he brought in old Dim with a whip, and Dim was a lot more starry and grey and had a few zoobies missing as you could see when he let out a smeck, viddying me, and then my droog Georgie said, pointing like at me: 'That man has filth and cal all over his platties,' and it was true. Then I creeched: 'Don't hit, please don't, brothers,' and started to run. And I was running in like circles and Dim was after me, smecking his gulliver off, cracking with the old whip, and each time I got a real horrorshow tolchock with this whip there was like a very loud electric bell ringringringing, and this bell was like a sort of a pain too.

Then I woke up real skorry, my heart going bap bap bap, and of course there was really a bell going brrrrr, and it was our front-door bell. I let on that nobody was at home, but this brrrrr still ittied on, and then I heard a goloss shouting through the door: 'Come on then, get out of it, I know you're in bed.' I recognized the goloss right away. It was the goloss of P. R. Deltoid (a real gloopy nazz, that one) what they called my Post-Corrective Adviser, an overworked veck with hundreds on his books. I shouted right right right, in a goloss of like pain, and I got out of bed and attired myself, O my brothers, in a very lovely over-gown of like silk, with designs of like great

145

cities all over this over-gown. Then I put my nogas into very comfy woolly toofles, combed my luscious glory, and was ready for P. R. Deltoid. When I opened up he came shambling in looking shagged, a battered old shlapa on his gulliver, his raincoat filthy. 'Ah, Alex boy,' he said to me. 'I met your mother, yes. She said something about a pain somewhere. Hence not at school, yes.'

'A rather intolerable pain in the head, brother, sir,' I said in my gentle-man's goloss. 'I think it should clear by this afternoon.'

'Or certainly by this evening, yes,' said P. R. Deltoid. 'The evening is the great time, isn't it, Alex boy? Sit,' he said, 'sit, sit,' as though this was his domy and me his guest. And he sat in this starry rocking-chair of my dad's and began rocking, as if that was all he had come for. I said:

'A cup of the old chai, sir? Tea, I mean.'

'No time,' he said. And he rocked, giving me the old glint under frowning brows, as if with all the time in the world. 'No time, yes,' he said, gloopy. So I put the kettle on. Then I said:

'To what do I owe the extreme pleasure? Is anything wrong, sir?'

'Wrong?' he said, very skorry and sly, sort of hunched looking at me but still rocking away. Then he caught sight of an advert in the gazetta, which was on the table – a lovely smecking young ptitsa with her groodies hanging out to advertise, my brothers, the Glories of the Jugoslav Beaches. Then, after sort of eating her up in two swallows, he said: 'Why should you think in terms of there being anything wrong? Have you been doing something you shouldn't, yes?'

'Just a manner of speech,' I said, 'sir.'

'Well,' said P. R. Deltoid, 'it's just a manner of speech from me to you that you watch out, little Alex, because next time, as you very well know, it's not going to be the corrective school any more. Next time it's going to be the barry place and all my work ruined. If you have no consideration for your horrible self you at least might have some for me, who have sweated over you. A big black mark, I tell you in confidence, for every one we don't reclaim, a confession of failure for every one of you that ends up in the stripy hole.'

'I've been doing nothing I shouldn't, sir,' I said. 'The millicents have nothing on me, brother, sir I mean.'

'Cut out this clever talk about millicents,' said P. R. Deltoid very weary, but still rocking. 'Just because the police have not picked you up lately doesn't, as you very well know, mean you've not been up to some nastiness. There was a bit of a fight last night, wasn't there? There was a bit of shuffling with nozhes and bike-chains and the like. One of a certain fat boy's friends was ambulanced off late from near the Power Plant and hospitalized, cut about very unpleasantly, yes. Your name was mentioned. The word has got through to me by the usual channels. Certain friends of yours were named also. There seems to have been a fair amount of assorted nastiness last night. Oh, nobody can prove anything about anybody, as usual. But I'm warning you, little Alex, being a good friend to you as always, the one man in this sore and sick community who wants to save you from yourself.'

'I appreciate all that, sir,' I said, 'very sincerely.'

'Yes, you do, don't you?' he sort of sneered. 'Just watch it, that's all, yes. We know more than you think, little Alex.' Then he said, in a goloss of great suffering, but still rocking away: 'What gets into you all? We study the problem and we've been studying it for damn well near a century, yes, but we get no further with our studies. You've got a good home here, good loving parents, you've got not too bad of a brain. Is it some devil that crawls inside you?'

'Nobody's got anything on me, sir,' I said. 'I've been out of the rookers of the millicents for a long time now.'

'That's just what worries me,' sighed P. R. Deltoid. 'A bit too long of a time to be healthy. You're about due now by my reckoning. That's why I'm warning you, little Alex, to keep your handsome young proboscis out of the dirt, yes. Do I make myself clear?'

'As an unmuddied lake, sir,' I said. 'Clear as an azure sky of deepest summer. You can rely on me, sir.' And I gave him a nice zooby smile.

But when he'd ookadeeted and I was making this very strong pot of chai, I grinned to myself over this veshch that P. R. Deltoid and his droogs worried about. All right, I do bad, what with crasting and tolchocks and carves with the britva and the old in-out-in-out, and if I get loveted, well, too bad for me, O my little brothers, and you can't run a country with every chelloveck comporting himself in my manner of the night. So if I get loveted and it's three months in this mesto and another six in that, and then as P. R. Deltoid so kindly warns, next time, in spite of the great tenderness of my summers, brothers, it's the great unearthly zoo itself, well, I say: 'Fair, but a pity, my lords, because I just cannot bear to be shut in. My endeavour shall be, in such future as stretches out its snowy and lilywhite arms to me before the nozh overtakes or the blood spatters its final chorus in twisted metal and smashed glass on the highroad, to not get loveted again.' Which is fair speeching. But, brothers, this biting of their toe-nails over what is the *cause* of badness is what turns me into a fine laughing malchick. They don't go into the cause of

147

goodness, so why the other shop? If lewdies are good that's because they like it, and I wouldn't ever interfere with their pleasures, and so of the other shop. And I was patronizing the other shop. More, badness is of the self, the one, the you or me or our oddy knockies, and that self is made by old Bog or God and is his great pride and radosty. But the not-self cannot have the bad, meaning they of the government and the judges and the schools cannot allow the bad because they cannot allow the self. And is not our modern history, my brothers, the story of brave malenky selves fighting these big machines? I am serious with you, brothers, over this. But what I do I do because I like to do.

So now, this smiling winter morning, I drink this very strong chai with moloko and spoon after spoon after spoon of sugar, me having a sladky tooth, and I dragged out of the oven the breakfast my poor old mum had cooked for me. It was an egg fried, that and no more, but I made toast and ate egg and toast and jam, smacking away at it while I read the gazetta. The gazetta was the usual about ultra-violence and bank robberies and strikes and footballers making everybody paralytic with fright by threatening to not play next Saturday if they did not get higher wages, naughty malchickiwicks as they were. Also there were more space-trips and bigger stereo TV screens and offers of free packets of soapflakes in exchange for the labels on soup-tins, amazing offer for one week only, which made me smeck. And there was a bolshy big article on Modern Youth (meaning me, so I gave the old bow, grinning like bezoomny) by some very clever bald chelloveck. I read this with care, my brothers, slurping away at the old chai, cup after tass after chasha, crunching my lomticks of black toast dipped in jammiwam and eggiweg. This learned veck said the usual veshches, about no parental discipline, as he called it, and the shortage of real horrorshow teachers who would lambast bloody beggary out of their innocent poops and make them go boohoohoo for mercy. All this was gloopy and made me smeck, but it was like nice to go on knowing one was making the news all the time, O my brothers. Every day there was something about Modern Youth, but the best veshch they ever had in the old gazetta was by some starry pop in a doggy collar who said that in his considered opinion and he was govoreeting as a man of Bog IT WAS THE DEVIL THAT WAS ABROAD and was like ferreting his way into like young innocent flesh, and it was the adult world that could take the responsibility for this with their wars and bombs and nonsense. So that was all right. So he knew what he talked of, being a Godman. So we young innocent malchicks could take no blame. Right right right.

When I'd gone erk erk a couple of razzes on my full innocent stomach, I started to get out day platties from my wardrobe, turning the radio on. There was music playing, a very nice malenky string quartet, my brothers, by Claudius Birdman, one that I knew well. I had to have a smeck, though, thinking of what I'd viddied once in one of these like articles on Modern Youth, about how Modern Youth would be better off if A Lively Appreciation Of The Arts could be like encouraged. Great Music, it said, and Great Poetry would like quieten Modern Youth down and make Modern Youth more Civilized. Civilized my syphilised yarbles. Music always sort of sharpened me up, O my brothers, and made me like feel like old Bog himself, ready to make with the old donner and blitzen and have vecks and ptitsas creeching away in my ha ha power. And when I'd cheested up my litso and rookers a bit and done dressing (my day platties were like student-wear: the old blue pantalonies with sweater with A for Alex) I thought here at least was time to itty off to the disc-bootick (and cutter too, my pockets being full of pretty polly) to see about this long-promised and long-ordered stereo Beethoven Number Nine (the Choral Symphony, that is), recorded on Masterstroke by the Esh Sham Sinfonia under L. Muhaiwir. So out I went, brothers.

The day was very different from the night. The night belonged to me and my droogs and all the rest of the nadsats, and the starry bourgeois lurked indoors drinking in the gloopy worldcasts, but the day was for the starry ones, and there always seemed to be more rozzes or millicents about during the day, too. I got the autobus from the corner and rode to Center, and then I walked back to Taylor Place, and there was the disc-bootick I favoured with my inestimable custom, O my brothers. It had the gloopy name of MELODIA, but it was a real horrorshow mesto and skorry, most times, at getting the new recordings. I walked in and the only other customers were two young ptitsas sucking away at ice-sticks (and this, mark, was dead cold winter and sort of shuffling through the new pop-discs – Johnny Burnaway, Stash Kroh, The Mixers, Lay Quiet Awhile With Ed And Id Molotov, and all the rest of that cal). These two ptitsas couldn't have been more than ten, and they too, like me, it seemed, evidently, had decided to take the morning off from the old skolliwoll. They saw themselves, you could see, as real grown-up devotchkas already, what with the old hip-swing when they saw your Faithful Narrator, brothers, and padded groodies and red all ploshed on their goobers. I went up to the counter, making with the polite zooby smile at old Andy behind it (always polite himself, always helpful, a real horrorshow type of a veck, though bald and very very thin). He said:

'Aha, I know what you want, I think. Good news, good news. It has arrived.' And with like big conductor's rookers beating time he went to get it. The two young ptitsas started giggling, as they will at that age, and I gave them a like cold glazzy. Andy was back real skorry, waving the great shiny white sleeve of the Ninth, which had on it, brothers, the frowning beetled like thunderbolted litso of Ludwig van himself. 'Here,' said Andy. 'Shall we give it the trial spin?' But I wanted it back home on my stereo to slooshy on my oddy knocky, greedy as hell. I fumbled out the deng to pay and one of the little ptitsas said:

'Who you getten, bratty? What biggy, what only?' These young devotchkas had their own like way of govoreeting. 'The Heaven Seventeen? Luke Sterne? Goggly Gogol?' And both giggled, rocking and hippy. Then an idea hit me and made me near fall over with the anguish and ecstasy of it, O my brothers, so I could not breathe for near ten seconds. I recovered and made with my new-clean zoobies and said:

'What you got back home, little sisters, to play your fuzzy warbles on?' Because I could viddy the discs they were buying were these teeny pop veshches. 'I bet you got little save tiny portable like picnic spinners.' And they sort of pushed their lower lips out at that. 'Come with uncle,' I said, 'and hear all proper. Hear angel trumpets and devil trombones. You are invited.' And I like bowed. They giggled again and one said:

'Oh, but we're so hungry. Oh, but we could so eat.' The other said: 'Yah, she can say that, can't she just.' So I said:

'Eat with uncle. Name your place.'

Then they viddied themselves as real sophistoes, which was like pathetic, and started talking in big-lady golosses about the Ritz and the Bristol and the Hilton and Il Ristorante Granturco. But I stopped that with 'Follow uncle,' and I led them to Pasta Parlour just round the corner and let them fill their innocent young litsos on spaghetti and sausages and cream-puffs and banana-splits and hot choc-sauce, till I near sicked with the sight of it. I, brothers, lunching but frugally off a cold ham-slice and a growling dollop of chilli. These two young ptitsas were much alike, though not sisters. They had the same ideas or lack of, and the same colour hair – a like dyed strawy. Well, they would grow up real today. Today I would make a day of it. No school the afterlunch, but education certain, Alex as teacher. Their names, they said, were Marty and Sonietta, bezoomy enough and in the heighth of their childish fashion, so I said:

'Righty right, Marty and Sonietta. Time for the big spin. Come.' When we were outside on the cold street they thought they would not go by autobus, oh no, but by taxi, so I gave them the humour, though with a real horrorshow in-grin, and I called a taxi from the rank near Center. The driver, a starry whiskery veck in very stained platties, said:

'No tearing up, now. No nonsense with them seats. Just reupholstered they are.' I quieted his gloopy fears and off we spun to Municipal Flatblock 18A, these two bold little ptitsas giggling and whispering. So, to cut all short, we arrived. O my brothers, and I led the way up to 10–8, and they panted and smecked away the way up, and then they were thirsty, they said, so I unlocked the treasure-chest in my room and gave these ten-year-young devotchkas a real horrorshow Scotchman apiece, though well filled with sneezy pins-and-needles soda. They sat on my bed (yet unmade) and leg-swung, smecking and peeting their highballs, while I spun their like pathetic malenky discs through my stereo. Like peeting some sweet-scented kid's drink, that was, in like very beautiful and lovely and costly gold goblets. But they went oh oh oh and said, 'Swoony' and 'Hilly' and other weird slovos that were the heighth of fashion in that youth group. While I spun this cal for them I encouraged them to drink and have another, and they were nothing loath, O my brothers. So by the time their pathetic pop-discs had been twice spun each (there were two: 'Honey Nose', sung by Ike Yard, and 'Night After Day After Night', moaned by two horrible yarbleless like eunuchs whose names I forget) they were getting near the pitch of like young ptitsa's hysterics, what with jumping all over my bed and me in the room with them.

What was actually done that afternoon there is no need to describe, brothers, as you may easily guess all. Those two were unplattied and smecking fit to crack in no time at all, and they thought it the bolshiest fun to viddy old Uncle Alex standing there all nagoy and pan-handled, squirting the hypodermic like some bare doctor, then giving myself the old jab of growling jungle-cat secretion in the rooker. Then I pulled the lovely Ninth out of its sleeve, so that Ludwig van was now nagoy too, and I set the needle hissing on to the last movement, which was all bliss. There it was then, the bass strings like govoreeting away from under my bed at the rest of the orchestra, and then the male human goloss coming in and telling them all to be joyful, and then the lovely blissful tune all about Joy being a glorious spark like of heaven, and then I felt the old tigers leap in me and then I leapt on these two young ptitsas. This time they thought nothing fun and stopped creeching with high mirth, and had to submit to the strange and weird desires of Alexander the Large which, what with the Ninth and the hypo jab, were choodessny and zammechat and very demanding, O my brothers. But they were both very very drunken and could hardly feel very much.

When the last movement had gone round for the second time with all the banging and creeching about Joy Joy Joy Joy, then these two young ptitsas were not acting the big lady sophisto no more. They were like waking up to what was being done to their malenky persons and saying that they wanted to go home and like I was a wild beast. They looked like they had been in some big bitva, as indeed they had, and were all bruised and pouty. Well, if they would not go to school they must still have their education. And education they had had. They were creeching and going ow ow ow as they put their platties on, and they were like punchipunching me with their teeny fists as I lay there dirty and nagoy and fair shagged and fagged on the bed. This young Sonietta was creeching: 'Beast and hateful animal. Filthy horror.' So I let them get their things together and get out, which they did, talking about how the rozzers should be got on to me and all that cal. Then they were going down the stairs and I dropped off to sleep, still with the old Joy Joy Joy Joy crashing and howling away.

Anthony Burgess, *A Clockwork Orange* (1962)

1962: 'The Nicest Kids in Town'

The Buddy Deane Show was a teenage dance party, on the air from 1957 to 1964. It was the top-rated local TV show in Baltimore and, for several years, the highest-rated local TV program in the country. While the rest of the nation grew up on Dick Clark's *American Bandstand* (which was not even shown here because Channel 13 already had *Buddy Deane*), Baltimoreans, true to form, had their own eccentric version. Every rock 'n' roll star of the day (except Elvis) came to town to lip-sync and plug their records on the show: Buddy Holly, Bill Haley, Fats Domino, the Supremes, the Marvelettes, Annette Funicello, Frankie Avalon and Fabian, to name just a few.

You learned how to be a teenager from the show. Every day after school kids would run home, tune in and dance with the bedpost or refrigerator door as they watched. If you couldn't do the Buddy Deane Jitterbug (always identifiable by the girl's ever-so-subtle dip of her head each time she was twirled around), you were a social outcast. And because a new dance was introduced practically every week, you had to watch every day to keep up. It was maddening: the Mashed Potato, the Stroll, the Pony, the Waddle, the Locomotion, the Bug, the Handjive, the New Continental and, most important, the Madison, a complicated line dance that started here and later swept the country.

*

In the beginning there was Arlene. Arlene Kozak, Buddy's assistant and den mother to the Committee. Now a receptionist living in suburbia with her husband and two grown children, Arlene remains fiercely loyal, organizing the reunions and keeping notebooks filled with the updated addresses, married names and phone numbers of all 'my kids'.

She met Winston J. 'Buddy' Deane in the fifties when she worked for a record wholesaler and he was the top-rated disc jockey on WITH – the only DJ in town who played rock 'n' roll for the kids. Joel Chaseman, also a DJ at WITH, became program manager of WJZ-TV when Westinghouse bought it in the mid-fifties. Chaseman had this idea for a dance party show, with Buddy as the disc jockey, and Buddy asked Arlene to go to work for him. On the air *before* Dick Clark debuted', the show 'was a hit from the beginning,' says Arlene today.

The Committee, initially recruited from local teen centers, was to act as hosts and dance with the guests. To be selected you had to bring a 'character reference' letter from your pastor, priest or rabbi, qualify in a dance audition and show in an interview ('the Spotlight') that you had 'personality'. At first the Committee had a revolving membership, with no one serving longer than three months.

But something unforeseen happened: the home audience soon grew attached to some of these kids. So the rules were bent a little; the 'big' ones, the ones with the fan mail, were allowed to stay. And the whole concept of the Committee changed. The star system was born.

If you were a Buddy Deane Committee member, you were on TV six days a week for as many as three hours a day – enough media exposure to make Marshall McLuhan's head spin. The first big stars were Bobbi Burns and Freddy Oswinkle, according to Arlene, but 'no matter how big anyone got, someone came along who was even bigger'.

Joe Cash and Joan Teves became the show's first royalty. Joanie, whose mother 'wanted me to be a child star', hit the show in early 1957 at age thirteen (you had to be fourteen to be eligible, but many lied about their ages to qualify), followed a few months later by Joe, seventeen. Like many couples, Joe and Joan met through the show and became 'an item' for their fans. Many years later they married.

'I saw the show as a vehicle to make something of myself,' remembers Joe. 'I was aggressive. I wanted to get into the record business' – and years later he did.

Joe started working for Buddy as 'teen assistant' and, along with Arlene, oversaw the Committee and enforced the strict rules. You received demerits for almost anything: chewing gum; eating the refreshments (Ameche's Powerhouses, the premiere teenage hangout's forerunner of the Big Mac), which were for guests *only*; or dancing with other Committee members when you were supposed to be dancing with the guests (a very unpopular rule allowed this only every fourth dance). And if you dared to dance the obscene Bodie Green (the Dirty Boogie), you were immediately a goner.

'I got a little power-crazed,' admits Joe. 'I thought I was running the world, so they developed a Board, and the Committee began governing itself.' Being elected to the Board became the ultimate status symbol. This Committee's committee, under the watchful eye of Arlene, chose new members, taught the dance steps and enforced the demerit system, which could result in suspension or explusion.

Another royal Deaner couple who met on the air and later married was Gene Snyder and Linda Warehime. They are still referred to, good-naturedly by some, as 'the Ken and Barbie of the show'. Gene, a member of 'the *first* Committee, and I underline *first*', later became president of the Board. Linda reverently describes her Committee membership as 'the best experience I ever had in my life'. They later became members of the 'Permanent Committee', the hall of fame that could come back to dance even after retiring. 'That was our whole social life, being a Buddy Deaner,' says Gene. 'It was a family: Buddy was the father, Arlene was the mother.'

Even today Gene and Linda are the quintessential Deaner couple, still socializing with many Committee members, very protective of the memory, and among the first to 'lead a dance' at the emotion-packed reunions. 'Once a Deaner, always a Deaner,' as another so succinctly puts it.

The early 'look' of the Committee was typically fifties. And although few will now admit to having been drapes, the hairstyles at first were DAs, Detroits and Waterfalls for the guys and ponytails and DAs for the girls, who wore full skirts with crinolines and three or four pairs of bobby socks. Joe remembers 'a sport coat I bought for $5 from somebody who got it when he got out of prison. I was able after a while to afford some clothes from Lee's of Broadway' (whose selection of belted coats and pegged pants made it the Saks Fifth Avenue of Deaners).

One of the first ponytail princesses was 'Peanuts' (Sharon Goldman, debuting at fourteen in 1958, Forest Park High School Chicken Hop), who went on the show because Deaners were 'folk heroes'. She remembers Paul Anka singing 'Put Your Head on My Shoulder' to her on camera as she did just that. She became so popular that she was written up in the nationwide *Sixteen* magazine.

'On the show you were either a drape or a square,' explains Sharon. 'I was a square. I guess Helen Crist was the first drapette: the DA, the ballet shoes, oogies [tulle scarves], eye-shadow – eye-liner was *big* then – and pink lipstick.'

Helen Crist. The best little jitterbugger in Baltimore. The first and maybe the biggest Buddy Deane queen of all. Debuting at a mere eleven years of age, taking three buses every day to get to the show, wearing that wonderful white DA (created by her hairdresser father) and causing the first real sensation. She was one of the chosen few who went to New York to learn how to demonstrate the Madison and was selected for the 'exchange committee' that represented Baltimore's best on *American Bandstand*. She was the only one of the biggies who refused to be on the Board ('They had power; a lot were disliked because of it.').

Helen's fans flocked to see her at the Buddy Deane Record Hops (Committee members had to make such personal appearances and sign autographs). 'I got all these letters from the Naval Academy,' Helen remembers, 'so I went there one day, and all the midshipmen were hanging out the windows. It was a real kick!' Her fame even brought an offer to join the circus. 'This man approached me, telegrammed me, showed up at the show. He wanted me to go to a summer training session to be a trapeze artist. I wanted to go, but my parents wouldn't let me. I was really mad. I wanted to join the circus.'

Two other ponytail princesses who went on to the Buddy Deane hall of fame were Evanne Robinson, the Committee member on the show the longest, and Kathy Schmink. Today they seem opposites. Over lunch at the Thunderball Lounge, in East Baltimore, Kathy remembers, 'I could never get used to signing autographs. "Why?" I'd wonder.' She wasn't even a fan of the show. 'It was a fluke. My mother wanted me to go; she took me down to the tryouts. At first I was so shy I hid behind the Coke machines.'

But Evanne 'used to come right home and head for the TV. I had always studied dance, and I wanted to go on [the show]. I'm the biggest ham.' Although she denies being conscious of the camera, she admits, 'I did try to dance up front. I wasn't going to go on and not be seen.' But even Evanne turned bashful on one show, when Buddy made a surprise announcement. 'I was voted prettiest girl by this whole army base. I was so embarrassed. Buddy called me up before the cameras, and I wasn't dressed my best. The whole day on the show was devoted to me.'

Being a teenage star in Baltimore had its drawbacks. 'It was difficult with your peers,' recalls Peanuts. 'You weren't one of them anymore.' Outsiders envied the fame, especially if they lost their steadies to Deaners, and many were put off by boys who loved to dance. 'Everybody wanted to kick a Buddy Deaner's ass,' says Gene, recalling thugs waiting to jump Deaners outside the studio.

'It was so painful. It was horrible,' says Joe. 'I used to get death threats on the show. I'd get letters saying, "If you show up at this particular hop, you're gonna get your face pushed in."' And Evanne still shudders as she recalls, 'Once I was in the cafeteria. One girl yelled "Buddy Deaners" and then threw her plate at me. My mother used to pick me up after school to make sure nobody hassled me.'

The adoring fans could also be a hassle. 'I must have had ten different phone numbers,' says Helen, 'and somehow it would get out. There were a lot of obscene phone calls.'

And the rumors, God, the rumors. 'They all thought all the girls were pregnant by Buddy Deane,' remember several. 'Once I was off the show for a while, and they said I had joined the nunnery,' says Helen, laughing. 'It was even in the papers. It was hilarious.'

Some of the rumors were fanned on purpose. Because *Buddy Deane's* competition was soap operas, the budding teenage romances were sometimes played up for the camera. 'One time I was going with this guy, and he was dancing with this guest I didn't like,' says Evanne. 'Buddy noticed my eyes staring and said, "Do the same eyes." And the camera got it.' Kathy went even further. 'I was with this guy named Jeff. We faked a feud. I took off my steady ring and threw it down. We got more mail: "Oh, please don't break up!" Somebody even sent us a miniature pair of boxing gloves. Then we made up on camera.'

Romance was one thing; sex was another. Most Deaner girls wouldn't even 'tongue-kiss', claims Arlene, remembering the ruckus caused by a Catholic priest when the Committee modeled strapless Etta gowns on TV. From then on, all bare shoulders were covered with a piece of net.

Other vices were likewise eschewed. If a guy had one beer, it was a big deal. Some do remember a handful of kids getting high on cough medicine. 'Yeah, it was Cosenel,' says Joe. 'They would drive me nuts when they'd come in the door, and I'd say, "Man, you're gone. You are out of here. You are history."'

Although many parents and WJZ insisted that Committee members had to keep up their grades to stay on the show, the reality could be quite different. With the show beginning at 2.30 in some years, cutting out of school early was common.

'I'd hook and have to dance in the back so the teachers couldn't see me,' says Helen. 'I *had* to get up there on time. My heart would have broken in two if I couldn't have gone on.' Finally Helen quit Mergenthaler (Mervo) trade school, at the height of her fame. 'The school tried to throw me out before. I couldn't be bothered with education. I wanted to *dance*.'

'We had a saying: "The show either makes you or breaks you," ' says Kathy. 'Some kids on the show went a little nuts, with stars in their eyes; they thought they were going to go to Hollywood and be movie stars.'

Yet Joe was a dropout when he went on the show and then, once famous, went *back* to finish. And according to Arlene, Buddy encouraged one popular Committee member (Buzzy Bennet) to teach himself to read so he could realize his dream of being a disc jockey. He eventually became one of the most respected programmers in the country and was even written up in *Time* magazine.

With the 1960s came a whole new set of stars, some with names that seemed like gimmicks, but weren't: Concetta Comi, the popular sister team of Yetta and Gretta Kotik. And then there was teased hair, replacing the fifties drape with a Buddy Deane look that so pervaded Baltimore culture (especially in East and South Baltimore) that its effect is still seen in certain neighbourhoods.

Some of the old Committee kept up with the times and made the transition with ease. Kathy switched to a great beehive that resembled a trash can sitting on top of her head ('I looked like I was taking off.'). And Helen, Linda and Joanie all got out the rat-tail teasing combs.

Fran Nedeloff (debuting at fourteen in 1961, Mervo High School cha-cha) remembers the look: 'Straight skirt to the knee, cardigan sweater buttoned up the back, cha-cha heels, lots of heavy black eyeliner, definitely Clearasil on the lips, white nail polish. We used to go stand in front of Read's Drugstore, and people would ask for our autograph.'

Perhaps the highest bouffants of all belonged to the Committee member who was my personal favorite: Pixie (who died several years later from a drug overdose). 'You could throw her down on the ground and her hair would crack,' recalls Gene. Pixie was barely five feet tall, but her hair sometimes added a good six to eight inches to her height.

But by far the most popular hairdo queen on *Buddy Deane* was a fourteen-year-old Pimlico Junior High School student named Mary Lou Raines. Mary Lou, the Annette Funicello of the show, was the talk of teenage Baltimore. Every week she had a different 'do' – the Double Bubble, the Artichoke, the

157

Airlift – each topped off by her special trademark, suggested by her mother, the bow. 'We really sprayed it,' remembers Mary Lou today from her home in Pennsylvania. 'The more hair spray, the better. After you sprayed it, you'd get toilet paper and blot it. Sometimes you'd wrap your hair at night. If you leaned on one side, the next day you'd just pick it out into shape.'

Mary Lou was the last of the Buddy Deane superstars, true hair-hopper royalty, the ultimate Committee member. 'We have a telegram,' Buddy would shout almost daily, 'for Mary Lou to lead a dance', and the camera-man seemed to love her. 'When that little red light came on, so did my smile,' she says, laughing. At her appearances at the record hops, 'kids would actually scream when you'd get out of the car: "There's Mary Lou! Oh, my God, it's Evanne!" Autograph books, cameras, this is what they lived for. They sent cakes on my birthday. They'd stand outside my home. They just wanted to know if you were real. I was honored, touched by it all.'

Mary Lou was aware that in some neighborhoods it was *not* cool to be a Buddy Deaner. 'Oh sure, if you were Joe College [pre-preppie], you just didn't do *The Deane Show*.' 'Did you ever turn into a Joe College?' I ask innocently. 'No!' she answers, with a conviction that gives me the chills.

But as more and more kids (even *Deane* fans) *did* turn Joe College, many of the Committee made the mistake of not keeping up with the times. Marie Fischer was the first 'Joe' to become a Committee member – chosen simply because she was such a good dancer. As with the drapes and squares of the previous decade, she explains, 'there were two classes of people then – Deaners and Joe College. The main thing was your hair was *flat*, the anti-thesis of Buddy Deane,' she says, chuckling. 'I was a misfit. Every day I'd come to the studio in knee-highs, and I'd have to take them off. You *had* to wear nylons. Before long I started getting lots of fan mail: "I think you're neat. I'm Joe, too." There was a change in the works.'

Part of that change was the racial integration movement. 'I had a lot of black friends at the time, so for me this was an awkward thing,' says Marie. 'To this day, I'm reluctant to tell some of my black friends I was on *Buddy Deane* because they look at it as a terrible time.'

Integration ended *The Buddy Deane Show*. When the subject comes up today, most loyalists want to go off the record. But it went something like this: *Buddy Deane* was an exclusively white show. Once a month the show was all black; there was no black Committee. So the NAACP targeted the show for protests. Ironically, *The Buddy Deane Show* introduced black music and artists into the lives of white Baltimore teenagers, many of whom learned to dance from black friends and listened to black radio. Buddy offered to have three or even four days a week all black, but that wasn't it. The protesters wanted the races to mix.

At frantic meetings of the Committee, many said, 'My parents simply won't let me come if it's integrated,' and WJZ realized it just couldn't be done. 'It was the times,' most remember. 'This town just wasn't ready for that.' There were threats and bomb scares, integrationists smuggled whites into the all-black shows to dance cheek to cheek on camera with blacks, and that was it. *The Buddy Deane Show* was over. Buddy wanted it to end happily, but WJZ angered Deaners when it tried to blame the ratings.

On the last day of the show, January 4, 1964, all the most popular Committee members through the years came back for one last appearance. 'I remember it well,' recalls Evanne. 'Buddy said to me, "Well, here's my little girl who's been with me the longest." I hardly ever cried, but I just broke down on camera. I didn't mean to because I *never* would have messed up the makeup.'

John Waters, Crackpot (1989)

1962: Bigotry Head On

As we pulled into Savannah, Georgia, we were surprised to see the Staples Singers going into a motel. A number of the other artists with us had worked with them before, so we all jumped off the bus and were introduced to Pops Staples and his daughters Mavis, Cleo, Yvonne, and his son Pervis. Though the Staples weren't as well known as they would be after signing to the Stax label in the late sixties, their gospel style had been popular with blacks since the forties.

'Oh, I love your music,' I told Mavis.

'Well, thanks. What is your group called?'

'The Supremes,' I answered proudly.

'Well, if you girls sing as good as you look, you will really go places,' she said, smiling.

'Thank you!' I was so thrilled. After that they talked with us a while, giving us encouragement and tips on how to deal with life on the road.

As we continued through the South, we ran into bigotry head on. These were the years when blacks were openly challenging the white supremacists, and with civil-rights legislation right around the corner, some racists seemed more determined than ever to keep what they considered 'uppity niggers' in their place. Of course, I was no stranger to racism, but somehow I'd come to think that a troupe of artists like ourselves might escape confrontations.

I learned quite differently in Macon, Georgia, when a big barrel-bellied white sheriff stopped our bus. He introduced himself, then said, 'I am the peace officer in this here town, and if you folks have any trouble, you just let me know. I'll take care of you.'

As it happened, we'd just come from a local service station where the workers had refused to do some work on our bus. 'Y'all go right on back down to that same fillin' station,' he said. 'I'll make sure they do the repairs y'all need.'

We turned around and headed back. As we pulled in, we could hear the attendants loudly 'muttering' about 'them damn niggers'. Even if they had never said a word, we would have known what they thought from the looks of disgust and hatred on their faces. They stood around, just shuffling their feet and refusing to help us until the sheriff arrived.

'Hey, service that bus!' he yelled. 'Don't y'all know a new integration law has passed?'

The attendants reluctantly gave in and did some minor repairs and filled the tank. A satisfied sheriff boarded our bus just as we were about to leave. At this point, we were all convinced that we'd found a champion.

'As y'all can see, the local folks down here are not adjusting too rapidly to the new laws and the change in customs. But never you mind. If you run into any problems, you just let me know. In this county, you are under my jurisdiction, and I will not fall short of my duty to uphold the law just because y'all are black and I'm white.'

Once he learned our destination, he told us that the theater we were going to play had a 'colored'-folks night where blacks were allowed to sit down-stairs and the whites were relegated to the balcony. Since this was the opposite of the usual blacks-in-the-balcony arrangement down South, this was considered pretty progressive.

'Take the intermission time to let the people get settled before you start. Because if niggers and white folks get to fighting, I'll put the lights on so bright, it'll all be over. Do you hear me? The dance will be over.' Then he added, 'I don't want them blacks and whites together anyway.'

At first we were shocked, but we were impressed that he put the law before his own personal prejudices, and not the other way around, as so many people did.

A few days later, as we headed out of town, we had many a laugh imitating the sheriff. He was the perfect prototype of the Southern lawman. Unfortunately, however, we didn't have too many more encounters with bigots that we would be able to laugh about. People like the sheriff were few and far between down there. Our biggest problems were always with restaurants. The bus driver would stop and check out the atmosphere, but most times he'd be told, 'Yeah, sure y'all can eat here. Tell 'em to come around to the back.'

Hearing this, we would all scream indignantly, 'We're *not* going around to the back!'

Once, after being told to come in through the back door, Bobby Rogers of the Miracles jumped off the bus and told the owner, who was standing out in the parking lot, that he wanted to enter the place like everybody else – through the front door. 'Hey,' he informed the owner, 'I'm Bobby Rogers of the Miracles!'

Unimpressed, the owner replied, 'If you want to eat, you're going to use the back.'

By this time, some of the other guys started shouting insults at the owner. A few had gotten off the bus and were practically up in the guy's face.

'Don't you know there's been a law passed against this kind of stuff?'

'Who do you think you are, anyway, honky?'

'I don't want to eat in your funky old restaurant –'

'You need your ass kicked by us niggers. That will show you –'

'Well,' the owner said after a few minutes of this, 'I'm gonna get my pistol and . . .'

With that he ran inside and the fellows ran for the bus. The man was serious and we expected shots to be fired any second. We tore out and after a few minutes all breathed a sigh of relief. As usual, though, the musicians found something to laugh about.

'What did that man say, Bobby?' a voice from the back of the bus teased. ' "You're going to need a Miracle to get your behind out of this"?'

Although our itinerary followed the chitlin' circuit and we performed in the larger black theaters, we also played other gigs, some in open-air arenas and smaller clubs. In Birmingham, Alabama, we were scheduled to perform at a ballpark – picture the bandstand set up over the pitcher's mound and you get the idea of how small-time and tacky it was. What made this particular show special was that it was the first time in the community that an integrated audience got to see a show.

I saw more blacks and whites mingling and certainly more integrated couples than I'd ever seen in Detroit. During the show I heard there had been some trouble in the crowd and that the police had shot someone, but that may have been only a rumor. The show itself went along quite smoothly.

James Jamerson passed a guard backstage and asked if he could use the rest room. As James was coming out, another guard was called, and he said to James, 'Hey, nigger, what are you doing here?' James was understandably upset; after all, the promoter should have seen to it that there were accommodations. We seemed to have been put in the middle of a conflict between the townspeople and the promoter, but nothing was said. No one wanted trouble. We just wanted the show to be over so that we could get out.

We were pleased that the shows were a success and the crowd begged for encores, but it had been a long, tense day, and we had to go. We were slowly boarding the bus when we heard several sharp, loud cracks.

'Someone's throwing rocks,' one of the Vandellas said as we all looked around to see where they were coming from.

'Them's bullets!' Choker shouted, and at that we ran for the bus. In her panic to board the bus, Mary Wells had fallen down on the bus steps and refused to get up, barring the entrance to the rest of us. Everyone tried to push her out of the way, but she was so big it was impossible.

'Get out of the way, girl!' we all shouted, but she just screamed back, 'I am not getting up!'

Finally she moved, and we all got on board as fast as we could. Once the bus was loaded, we flew out of Birmingham. Only after we'd traveled quite a distance did the driver stop to examine the bus. Sure enough, there were bullet holes in some of the windows. None of us – not even the musicians – could find anything to laugh about this time.

The big problem with touring the South was that even when you weren't being shot at or called 'nigger', you could never forget where you were. Bigots who were too smart to get violent used intimidation and insults to put you in your place.

One day we stopped at a motel in Miami Beach, where we were scheduled to play that evening. Beans Bowles went into the front office to book our rooms. Suddenly, from out of nowhere, there appeared fifteen police cruisers with dogs. They didn't make a move toward us; they just sat outside and watched us.

At first the owner didn't want any blacks staying at his motel, but once Beans explained our situation to him, he became a total businessman. 'I'm not supposed to rent you any rooms,' he said, 'but this is my motel and I need the money. Come on and check in.'

This motel wasn't the Ritz, but it was clean and comfortable. After days on the road, just being able to bathe and rest a few hours before the rehearsal and show was a luxury. It was also a relief to know that we would get a good night's sleep after the show.

But things could never be that simple down South. When we returned after the show, the same cruisers and dogs were waiting.

'You would think we're Martin Luther King on a freedom march,' Choker remarked.

Beans decided that enough was enough and approached the police. As road manager, he was responsible for our safety and well-being. Always articulate and personable, Beans was invaluable in this kind of situation. He told the police who we were, what we were doing and so on. After he'd finished talking with them, they took their dogs and left.

The other interesting thing about people in general is that they have two different standards: one for common blacks and another for entertainers and other famous blacks. I saw this clearly demonstrated once in South Carolina. We pulled up in front of a motel called the Heart of the South, and the whole time we were unloading our stuff and checking in, two rednecks stood outside making offensive remarks, which they made sure we could hear very clearly. It was hard to believe that they wanted to provoke a fight, especially since there were so many strong young men in our group, and one of them was old enough to be a grandfather, but they kept it up, ending their little tirade with this gem:

'By gosh, that's a shame. We gotta get rid of that President Kennedy 'cause he ain't doin' the right thing letting them niggers go and do whatever they want.'

Of course, we were all insulted, but we regarded them as just a couple of backwoods fools and ignored them. As I entered the hotel, I saw Choker sitting on his horn case with his back to the two fools, cracking up. I could see that he didn't want them to see that he was laughing and I can't blame him. But one look at Choker and I almost started laughing myself. After we'd checked in, Choker was still sitting there, wiping tears of laughter from his eyes. Here they were acting like they were so superior, yet talking like idiots. We couldn't help but laugh at them.

As soon as we were settled, we jumped into our swimsuits and headed for the pool. The minute we dived in, the white people started climbing out. They sat on the lounge chairs and stared at us for a while, but when they saw what good divers and swimmers some of us were, they eased themselves back in. A few minutes later, they started getting out again. It took us a while to figure out what was going on. Unbeknownst to us the local radio stations had been playing all of our records over the past few weeks. Once word had spread that they were sharing the pool with the Miracles, Little Stevie Wonder, the Marvelettes and so-and-so, they ran to get paper and pens for our autographs and asked how they could get tickets for the show.

Our tours made breakthroughs and helped weaken racial barriers. When it came to the music, segregation didn't mean a thing in some of those towns, and if it did, black and white fans would ignore the local customs to attend the shows. To see crowds that were integrated – sometimes for the first time in a community – made me realize that Motown truly was the sound of young America.

Mary Wilson, *Dreamgirl: My Life as a Supreme* (1987)

1963: The Factory

A few months before, I'd gotten the word that the hook and ladder company building would have to be vacated soon, and in November I found another loft, at 231 East 47th Street. Gerard and I moved all my painting equipment – stretchers, canvases, staple guns, paints, brushes, silkscreens, workbenches, radio, rags, everything – over to the space that would soon turn into the Factory.

The neighborhood wasn't one that most artists would want to have a studio in – right in midtown, not far from Grand Central Station, down the street from the United Nations. My loft was in a dirty brick industrial building – you walked into a gunmetal-gray lobby and to your right was a freight elevator that was just a rising floor with a grate. We were on the next-to-the-top floor; there was an antiques place called the Connoisseur's Corner on the floor above us. We were right across the street from the YMCA, so there were always guys around with those little bus depot-type valises that probably have socks and shaving cream in them. And there was a modelling agency nearby, so there were plenty of girls with portfolios around, and lots of photography labs in the area.

The Factory was about 50 feet by 100, and it had windows all along 47th Street looking south. It was basically crumbling – the walls especially were in bad shape. I set up my painting area with the workbench near the front by the windows, but I kept most of the light blocked out – that's the way I liked it.

At the same time that we were making the move to 47th Street, Billy Name and Freddy Herko were leaving their apartment downtown. Freddy went to stay somewhere else in the Village and Billy came up to live in the Factory.

The back of the loft space gradually became Billy's area. Right from the beginning it had an aura about it that was sort of secret; you never really knew what was going on there – strange characters would walk in and say, 'Is Billy around?' and I'd point them toward the back.

A lot of them were people I recognized from the San Remo, and after a while I got to know the regulars – Rotten Rita, the Mayor, Binghamton Birdie, the Duchess, Silver George, Stanley the Turtle, and, of course, Pope Ondine. They were always discreet about what they did back there. No one so much as took a pill in front of me, and I definitely never saw anyone shoot up. I never had to spell anything out, either; there was sort of a silent understanding that I didn't want to know about anything like that, and Billy was always able to keep everything cool. There were a couple of toilets in Billy's area and a slop sink and a refrigerator that was always stocked with grapefruit juice and orange juice – people on speed crave vitamin C.

The Factory A-men were mostly fags (they knew each other originally from Riis Park in Brooklyn), except for the Duchess, who was a notorious dyke. They were all incredibly skinny, except for the Duchess, who was incredibly fat. And they all mainlined, except for the Duchess, who skin-popped. All this I only found out later, because at the time I was very naive – I mean, if you don't actually see a person shooting up, you don't believe they could really be doing it. Oh, I'd hear them call someone on the wall pay phone and say, 'Can I come over?' and then they'd leave and I'd just assume they were going to pick up some amphetamine. But where they went I never knew. Years later I asked somebody who'd been around a lot then where exactly all the speed had been coming from, and he said, 'At first, they got all their speed from Rotten, but then his speed got so bad he wouldn't even touch it himself, and from then on, everybody got it from Won-Ton.' That was a name I'd heard a lot, but I'd never laid eyes on him. 'Won-Ton was really short and barrel-chested and he never left his apartment – he always answered the door in the same shiny satin latex royal blue Jantzen bathing suit. That was all he ever wore.' Was he a fag? I asked. 'Well' – this person laughed – 'he was living with a woman, but you got the idea he'd do anything with just about anybody. He worked in construction – he had something to do with the Verrazano Bridge.' But where did Won-Ton get the speed? 'That was something you just didn't ask.'

Billy was different from all the other people on speed because he had a manner that inspired confidence: he was quiet, things were always very proper with him, and you felt like you could trust him to keep everything in line, including all his strange friends. He had this way of getting rid of people immediately if they didn't belong. If Billy said, 'Can I help you?' in a certain way, people would start to actually back out. He was a perfect custodian, literally.

For a while Gerard also lived at the Factory, but that didn't last too long. Billy and his crowd took over the scene there. The big social thrust behind the Factory from '64 through '67 was amphetamine, and Gerard didn't take it. Gerard was a different type – he was more apt to take a down like Placidyl when he took anything, which he usually didn't – a few downs, a little acid, some marijuana, but nothing regularly.

Amphetamine doesn't give you peace of mind, but it makes not having it very amusing. Billy used to say that amphetamine had been invented by Hitler to keep his Nazis awake and happy in the trenches, but then Silver George would look up from the intricate geometric patterns he was drawing with his Magic Markers – another classic speed compulsion – and insist that it had been invented by the Japanese so they would export more felt-tip pens. Anyway, they both agreed that it hadn't been invented by any Allies.

All I knew about Billy was that he had done some lighting at Judson Church and that he'd been a waiter at Serendipity. He gave the impression of being generally creative – he dabbled in lights and papers and artists' materials. In the beginning he just fussed around like the other A-heads, doing all the busy stuff, fooling with mirrors and feathers and beads, taking hours to paint some little thing like the door to a cabinet – he could only concentrate on a little area at a time – and sometimes he was so high he wouldn't even realize that he'd just painted it. He wasn't into astrology and charts and occult things yet.

I picked up a lot from Billy, actually – just studying him. He didn't say much, and when he did, it was either very practical and mundane or very enigmatic – like if he was ordering from the Bickford's coffee shop downstairs, he'd be completely lucid, but if you asked him what he thought of something, he'd quietly say things like 'You cannot be yes without also being no.'

Billy was a good trasher; he furnished the whole Factory from things he found out on the street. The huge curved couch that would be photographed so much in the next few years – the hairy red one that we used in so many of our movies – Billy found right out in front of the 'Y'.

In the sixties good trashing was a skill. Knowing how to use what somebody else didn't, was a knack you could really be proud of. In other decades people had sneaked into Salvation Armies and Goodwills, embarrassed that somebody might see them, but in the sixties people weren't embarrassed at all, they bragged about what they could scavenge here and there. And nobody seemed to mind when a thing was dirty – I'd see people, kids especially, drinking right out of a cup they'd just found in the trash.

One day Billy brought in a phonograph from somewhere. He had a big collection of opera records – I think it was Ondine who started him on that. They both knew every obscure opera singer – I mean, singers no one had ever heard of – and they haunted the record stores for all the out-of-prints and private recordings. They loved Maria Callas best of all, though. They always said how great they thought it was that she was killing her voice and not holding anything back, not saving anything for tomorrow. They could really identify with that. When they'd go on and on about her, I'd think of Freddy Herko, the way he would just dance and dance until he dropped. The amphetamine people believed in throwing themselves into every extreme – sing until you choke, dance until you drop, brush your hair till you sprain your arm.

The opera records at the Factory were all mixed in with the 45s I did my painting to, and most times I'd have the radio on while the opera was going, and so songs like 'Sugar Shack' or 'Blue Velvet' or 'Louie, Louie' – whatever was around then – were blended in with the arias.

Billy was responsible for the silver at the Factory. He covered the crumbling walls and the pipes in different grades of silver foil – regular tinfoil in some areas, and a higher grade of Mylar in others. He bought cans of silver paint and sprayed everything with it, right down to the toilet bowl.

Why he loved silver so much I don't know. It must have been an amphetamine thing – everything always went back to that. But it was great, it was the perfect time to think silver. Silver was the future, it was spacy – the astronauts wore silver suits – Shepard, Grissom and Glenn had already been up in them, and their equipment was silver, too. And silver was also the past – the Silver Screen – Hollywood actresses photographed in silver sets.

And maybe more than anything, silver was narcissism – mirrors were backed with silver.

Billy loved reflecting surfaces – he'd prop broken bits of mirror here and there and paste little sections of them onto everything. This was all amphetamine busywork, but the interesting thing was that Billy could communicate the atmosphere to people who weren't even taking drugs: usually people on speed created things that only looked good to them. But what Billy did went past the drugs. The only things that ever came even close to conveying the look and feel of the Factory then, aside from the movies we shot there, were the still photographs Billy took.

The mirrors weren't just decoration. They got used a lot by everybody primping for parties. Billy especially spent a lot of time looking at himself. He positioned the mirrors so he could see his face and body from every angle. He had a dancer's strut that he liked to check in motion.

Andy Warhol and Pat Hackett, *Popism: The Warhol '60s* (1980)

1963: Art School and Rhythm & Blues

I first met Pete at Ealing Art School and we soon became friends. Pete also struck up a friendship with an American student in the photography section of the college, Tom Wright. One day Pete had asked if he could play a guitar belonging to a student called Tim Bartlett in the student's common room. The following day this guy told his friend Tom Wright how well this new student could play and Tom approached Pete the next day to ask if he could teach him some of the 'fancy guitar licks' he'd played. Pete told Tom years later that Tom had been the first person to come up and speak to him at art college. In return for Pete teaching Tom some guitar licks at Tom's flat in Sunnyside Road opposite the college, Tom introduced Pete to two things that were probably more crucial to his life than the rest of art school put together. Tom had an absolutely amazing collection of blues, R & B and jazz albums that he'd brought over from the States. Tom also had a stash of pot which was in 1962 relatively unknown in Britain outside of the West Indian community and merchant seamen.

Tom recalls, 'We put in a lot of research into rhythm 'n' blues in that small flat in Sunnyside Road – most of it flat on our backs.'

The main focal point of the college life was the café 'over the road'. Tom had secured half the spaces on the juke box for the student's use, the rest were for the lorry drivers that used the café too. So on this juke box Frank Ifield's 'I Remember You', Pat Boone's 'Speedy Gonzales' and Cliff Richard's 'Bachelor Boy' would exist alongside Jimmy Reed's 'Shame, Shame, Shame', Booker T's 'Green Onions' and Slim Harpo's 'King Bee'.

Art schools produced many British rock musicians in the sixties, such as John Lennon and Keith Richard, and Ealing Art School at that time also had Ronnie Wood, Roger Ruskin Spear and Freddie Mercury as students.

By some fluke, Tom was busted for possessing pot and ordered to be deported. He asked Pete and myself, who were in the process of trying to find a flat to rent near the college, whether we would take over his place and look after the contents. We, of course, jumped at the chance.

Pete could now immerse himself in Tom's 150 or so high-calibre album collection and Sunnyside Road became a focal point for him for a couple of important years. The albums in Tom's collection included all of Jimmy Reed's albums, all of Chuck Berry's, all of James Brown's, Bo Diddley, John Lee Hooker, Snooks Eaglin, Mose Allison, all of Jimmy Smith's, Muddy Waters, Lightnin' Hopkins, Howling Wolf, Slim Harpo, Buddy Guy, Big Bill Broonzy, Sonny Terry and Brownie McGhee, Joe Turner, Nina Simone, Booker T, Little Richard, Jerry Lee Lewis, Carl Perkins, The Isley Brothers, Fats Domino, The Coasters, Ray Charles, Jimmy McGriff, Brother Jack McDuff, John Patton, Bobby Bland, The Drifters, The Miracles, The Shirelles, The Impressions, and many jazz albums including Charlie Parker, Mingus, Coltrane, Miles Davis, Milt Jackson, Wes Montgomery, Jimmy Guiffre, Dave Brubeck, plus albums by Jonathon Winters, Mort Sahl, Shelly Burman and particularly Lord Buckley. There were also about thirty classical albums.

Pete told *Zig-Zag* magazine some years later, 'When I first got into pot I was involved in the environment more; there was a newness about art college, having beautiful girls around for the first time in my life, having all that music around me for the first time, and it was such a great period – with the Beatles exploding and all that all over the place. So it was very exciting, but although pot was important to me, it wasn't the biggest thing: the biggest thing was the fact that pot helped to make incredible things even more incredible.'

None of the other members of the band were interested in smoking marijuana and they rarely came back to his flat. Pete's life revolved around art school, playing four or five nights a week, getting stoned and absorbing his new treasure trove of American blues and jazz. He went to sleep to music and woke up to music, usually the slow lazy rhythm of Jimmy Reed. Art school also gave a sense of self-confidence to go with his new musical inspiration.

Ealing Art School was a very unusual art school. This normally staid and conservative institution had, in the same year that Pete enrolled, acquired a new head tutor, Roy Ascot. He had replaced most of the staff with young fresh sixties designers and artists and was to begin a revolutionary experiment in art tuition based on the science of cybernetics. Cybernetics is the study of systems of control and communication in such things as diverse as animals, calculating machines and economics. Just what such an obscure science had to do with art and design was a bit of a mystery. Roy Ascot maintained that 'Art is more than just "old apples on tables".' This truism might have been an effective dig at the 'old guard' of the Art School but it was never really helpful to the excited but fairly confused students. However, Pete got caught up in this daring experiment. Cybernetics, the 'science of sciences', the theory of computer thinking, became the watchword. Printmaking, basic design, sculpture and colour theory were all intermingled with feedback, noise-interference and automation principles. There is no doubt that, confusing as the course appeared and, to a certain extent, was, it was the most exciting and aware and radical at that time. Nevertheless, unless involved with the day-to-day evolution of the project, any comprehension of what was happening was practically impossible.

For instance, one day a visiting group of educationalists from Sierra Leone or Canada or somewhere were looking in bewilderment at the polythene and perspex 'artificial environments' that the students had built into the college classrooms. They were further perplexed to see Pete push himself along the corridor on a kids trolley-cart made out of old orange boxes and pram wheels. The other students didn't give him a second glance as they had become quite used to seeing him like that. Pete had been using his trolley-cart for several weeks as part of a serious college project where students were given different characteristics to the ones they had. It was part of a process of breaking down their preconceived ideas about art, design, life and themselves. Pete had been given as one of his characteristics, the physical disability of having no legs. So as a way round this particular problem he and his group of students had made him the trolley-cart to get around on. 'Not only did I have to push myself about on this cart, but I also had to communicate in a phonetic alphabet that my group had to think up,' remembers Pete. 'In a way it was like fucking acting school. The lecturers always expected something incredible to happen. I think I started to confuse them because I found that by acting impulsively you could come up with some good creative ideas but that you couldn't always explain them. And they wanted explanations for everything. They were very academic.'

Apart from the actual daily courses at Art School, there were a number of lunchtime lectures and concerts that were particularly significant to Pete. The Jewish radical playwright David Mercer gave a devastating speech which epitomised the early sixties British working-class cultural explosion and cleverly exposed the 'Ford Anglia outside – but expecting a Ford Consul' mentality of the narrow-minded suburban middle classes.

Both Larry Rivers, the American pop art painter, and Robert Brownjohn, an American London-based graphic designer (who designed the credits for the early James Bond films and did the sleeve for the Stones *Let it Bleed*), impressed the students by their 'hipness' and casual but outrageous manner, to the disgust of the 'old guard' ladies from the plant-drawing and pen-lettering departments.

Pete, of course, was to have no idea how valuable to him in later years would be the lecture and slide show given by Gustav Metzke on autodestructive art. He showed slides of paintings done in acid on sheets of metal showing the stages of 'beauty' as the acid slowly destroyed the metal and was later publicly acknowledged by Pete for his inspiration on autodestruction. 'Metzke turned up at some of our shows when we were smashing stuff up. He really got into it,' said Pete.

A student friend of Pete's called Dick Seamen used to go on about this mysterious person that he knew who was a post office engineer by day and some sort of lonely undiscovered genius musician at night. Dick arranged for him to play at the Art School in the lecture theatre one lunchtime. The resulting concert by Thunderclap Newman (real name Andy Newman) on piano and kazoo was an incredible experience. He was a very strange and mysterious person who had never played to an audience before and he played and sung mostly his own weird compositions. He set a metronome going on top of the grand piano and just played for over an hour until he was stopped. He never looked at the audience once. The students went wild at the end.

Pete became slightly obsessed with him and regarded him as a sort of undiscovered genius. He got from Dick an album by Thunderclap Newman and Richard Cardboard called *Ice and Essence*. There were only two copies of this album which were cut from a tape recording of some of Thunderclap's numbers performed by himself and Dick (Richard Cardboard) in a church hall and it was an amazingly inventive album with all sorts of convoluted time changes. It had an eerie, delicate, echoey quality about it and Pete played it constantly.

Richard Barnes *The Who: Maximum Rhythm & Blues* (1982)

four

1962–6

'Shadows of boredom'

'*Pop is now so basic to the way we live, and the world we live in, that to be with it, to dig the Pop scene, does not commit anyone to Left or Right, nor to protest or acceptance of the society we live in. It has become the common language, musical, visual and (increasingly literary), by which members of the mechanized urban culture of the Westernized countries can communicate with one another in the most direct, lively and meaningful manner.*'

Reyner Banham, The Atavism of the Short Distance Mini-Cyclist *(1963)*

The arrival of the Beatles marks the moment when the post-war babyboomers claim their time. As the group said at the time, 'Youth is on our side, and it's youth that matters right now.' The Beatles have attracted more words than perhaps any entertainers before or since, many of these occurring in the formerly dismissive media. Both the youth market and the media were expanding rapidly in England ₊the early sixties saw a boom in glossy magazines and newspaper colour supplements; 1964 saw the highest level of singles sales ever). The relationship was fruitful for both parties.

Instead of reproducing American styles, the Beatles and the groups that followed them added their own twist. Britain was now a major pop producer, as signalled by the Beatles' unprecedented American success in early 1964. Many people, including the Beatles themselves, couldn't believe it. As they said at the time, 'There's been nothing so fantastic in science fiction as the monster impact this group has made.' Pop became respectable – indeed desirable – across all social barriers. Youth became a national obsession and all classes, including prime ministers, queued at the altar of these new, north-western gods.

Brian Epstein tells the story of how he sold the group in an extract from his book *A Cellarful of Noise*, in itself proof of the Beatles' impact: who had ever heard of a pop manager's autobiography before then? Michael Braun's *Love Me Do* remains one of the best Beatles' books: fly-on-the-wall reportage of the group in the first flush of success. 'York' captures the four off-duty, bickering and commenting on the world with the sharp intelligence that had most of the media captivated – for a while. And Derek Jarman illustrates how a Beatles cap could improve your sex life.

The Beatles' success made Britain, and London in particular (later called 'Swinging London'), the centre of pop – music, fashion, clubs, a whole way of life. It was a seemingly self-contained teenage world. Barbara Hulanicki shows how clothes could be designed, produced, featured on television and sold to customers from around the world. Peter Burton traces the links between the gay world and the new, highly visible youth subculture – the Mods – while George Melly penetrates the inner fastnesses of what was quickly becoming the pop aristocracy.

This 'Youthquake' was not without dissenting voices: a characteristically incensed Paul Johnson in an infamous *New Statesman* article, 'The Menace of Beatlism'; the spring 1964 media scare about 'Mods and Rockers' after small disturbances at seaside resorts. This scare – later used as a textbook example of a 'moral panic' by sociologist Stanley Cohen – prompted the first Vox Pop teenage paperback, *Generation X*. The extract here was later used by the Clash for a manifesto; the title was appropriated by a punk group and US author Douglas Coupland for his best-selling 1991 novel.

These understandable concerns were exploited by Rolling Stones' manager Andrew Loog Oldham, whose notes for the group's second album sought to bring *A Clockwork Orange* to life (the section which exhorted violence was edited on subsequent editions). The Rolling Stones were successfully set up as a rebellious anti-system to the Beatles' cross-age appeal. As Nik Cohn noted in 1965, they were 'like creatures off another planet, impossible to reach or understand, but most exotic, most beautiful in their ugliness'.

Time sped up. As the Who said in *Melody Maker* that summer, pop had become art. Andy Warhol found his own pop star, Edie Sedgwick. She didn't play music, but with her androgynous, fleeting grace – frozen here by Jean Stein's oral history – she embodied the moment. This relentless, surging energy was captured by Bob Dylan's sleeve notes for *Bringing It All Back Home.* Dylan himself was an exemplar of these possibilities: the committed, political folk star who found electricity and became the oddest, most psychotropic pop star yet. Studs Terkel's equivocal, speedy notes on a late 1965 concert describe 'this metamorphosis out of Kafka'.

British and American pop culture were closer than they had ever been before or would be after. The Beatles had opened up the American market to English acts – for which they were made Members of the British Empire in late 1965 (an award tartly commented on by Noël Coward in his diaries), while Richard Goldstein's lightly fictional portrait of a suburban fourteen-year-old itemizes the impact the British groups had on teenage America.

Dazzled by the sheer hysteria that surrounded the British groups, the mainstream media glossed over a golden era of black music – soul and Motown – where confidence was replaced by a new assertiveness. Peter Guralnick captures the power of soul in the mid-sixties from a white perspective: 'There was clearly a sense of entering into an alien environment, of stepping out of my world into a land uncharted and inviolable.' Manthia Diawara's account of James Brown's impact on Mali is an extract from a history that has still to be fully written.

By mid-decade, then, it seemed as if the outcasts of the fifties were moving into the mainstream. With this realization came a new insistence on, as the Byrds put it in late 1965, a teen 'revolution', an insistence which began to alienate adults who had embraced the idea of youth. 'At times it gets very black,' Bob Dylan says in Robert Shelton's March 1966 interview. Maureen Cleave's interview with John Lennon that same month was a turning point. Published in the UK, it passed without comment; reproduced in the US, it initiated a religious backlash, death threats and hostile publicity. The spell cast by the Beatles was over and, with it, the spell of youth.

1962: Yes!

'One day they will be greater than Presley.' Shadows of boredom flickered over the bland faces of the Decca executives. Hadn't every manager with something to sell offered them 'Britain's answer to Presley', or 'Decca's reply to Columbia's Cliff Richard'.

I have long since forgiven all the record companies their disbelief of my wilder claims. What I cannot understand or forget is their indifference to the *sound* of the Beatles on tape.

Mr Rowe and Mr Stevens pursued their point. 'The boys won't go, Mr Epstein. We know these things. You have a good record business in Liverpool. Stick to that.'

I was deeply disappointed but I was determined they wouldn't know and as they piled pessimism on pessimism, I fought through the gloom to keep a calm front and I spoke quietly and at length about these Beatles who were the rage of Liverpool, who had ousted the Shadows as group heroes, four lads who played in a warehouse cellar by the Mersey.

The men of Decca took me to a luncheon in another room in the company headquarters. Whether it was the well-being of a good meal or my ceaseless talk of the Beatles' potential I don't know, but by the coffee stage there was a tiny crack in their determination not to record the boys.

I had paused in a long and probably overstated piece of sales-talk and the two men stared at each other. Dick Rowe drummed his fingers on the table and nodded knowingly. He turned to me and said, 'I have an idea that something might be done. You know who might help you? Tony Meehan.'

Meehan, one of the original 'Shadows', later to form a successful – though brief – partnership with Jet Harris, was then A and R man with Decca and it was explained that I would be given the benefit of his experience and the use of a studio on payment of something approaching £100.

This annoyed me because I couldn't see why I should have to pay £100 to make one recording of a group who were going to conquer the entire record world. But it was stupid (I argued to myself in a frantic inward tussle between enthusiasm and anxiety about money) to turn down the first real concession I had won from Decca.

So, the following day I arrived at the Decca studios to meet Meehan. Dick Rowe was with him in the control room listening to a recording session and he nodded to me. After thirty minutes he introduced me to Meehan and said, 'Tony, take Mr Epstein out and explain the position.'

We left the room and went into another where there were two chairs facing each other. The A and R man who, two years later I was to book as a drummer on one of my Prince of Wales bills, looked me straight between the eyes without enthusiasm and said, 'Mr Epstein, Mr Rowe and I are very busy men. We know roughly what you require so will you fix a date for tapes to be made of these Beatles, phone my secretary and make sure that when you want the session, I am available.'

For the third time in three months I walked out of Decca with only the slightest whisper of hope. I was very upset and, I believed, almost at the end of my extended tether.

The date was arranged, but later abandoned because I felt that no useful purpose was served. I realized that there was nothing doing with Decca.

I hailed a taxi to Euston station on the start of a glum cold journey to Lime Street Station where I telephoned Paul McCartney to ask the Beatles to meet me 'for a little talk'.

They arrived in the city centre and I took them to Joe's Cafe in Duke Street – a warm friendly haunt of night-workers, drivers, young Beatles and anyone else with not a lot of money – anyone, in fact, who wants a cup of tea and a plate of chicken and chips and somewhere to go until 4 a.m.

We had a lot of tea and we smoked a little and I said this and that about the future and asked them about the beat scene in Liverpool. Then George, blowing a cloud of smoke in the air as if he couldn't care less about anything, suddenly turned to me and said, 'What about Decca, Brian?'

'I'm afraid it's no use,' I said. 'I've had a flat "No".'

None of the Beatles spoke. So I went on: 'And Pye have turned us down,' for I had also taken our beloved tapes to this other major company only to be rejected by their executives.

John picked up a tea-spoon, flicked it high into the air and said, 'Right. Try Embassy.'

Embassy – the Woolworth's label where you can get low-priced copies of the pops on the counter next to the cold-cream and curling-pins and the ice-cream. This was not the grand break through we had planned and dreamed about.

Embassy. John had broken the spell and the gloom vanished and we all talked at once about 'these rotten companies', and 'that lousy A and R man', and I decided with totally unjustifiable confidence that after a few days catching up on business affairs back in the Liverpool store, I would return to London with our tapes. Once again something in the Beatles was giving me strength and buoyancy.

On the local scene they were progressing well. The Beatles were booked on both sides of the Mersey, earning, when they played, £15 a night. I had finally secured their signatures on a contract on January 24th, 1962, but, curiously, I had not, as I say, signed it myself. It provided them with safe-guards against unemployment, protected them and me against any breach of faith and made the terms of my percentages quite clear.

Why had I not signed it? I believe it was because even though I knew I would keep the contract in every clause, I had not 100 per cent faith in myself to help the Beatles adequately. In other words, I wanted to free the Beatles of their obligations if I felt they would be better off.

I feel the same about them even now. I would not hold the Beatles or any artiste to contractual formalities if I learned that they didn't want to stay. There is no room in our relationships for contract-slavery.

In 1962, however, neither the Beatles or I thought very much about our own contract. We were after the signature of a major recording executive on a stiff sheet of parchment. For the 1950s had made it clear that no artiste could succeed without records – and good records. The way to stardom lay in the charts.

During the lag between Decca's first session and the final refusal, we had played our first engagement as contracted artistes and manager at the Thistle Cafe, a genteel little spot on the sea-front at West Kirby, an exclusive dormitory town on the estuary of the River Dee 10 miles from Liverpool. Their success there as at the Cavern was an early sign that there was more than one-audience appeal in this group.

Our fee in West Kirby, by the way, was £18 out of which I took 36/- which just about covered petrol, oil, and wear and tear on tyres.

After the night in Joe's, I tackled a substantial backlog of work in Whitechapel, and told my father I wanted to take my tapes to London for an all-out, all-or-failure attack on the remaining record outlets. He agreed, provided it was only for a day or two and I made, this time, for the HMV record-centre in Oxford Street, London.

There I met Kenneth Boast, an exceedingly pleasant and interested execu-tive with the HMV Retail Store within the mighty EMI company. Rather

pompously, I told him I had tapes which were going to become very significant in British pop music, and he, being a nice chap, listened patiently to me,
and to the tapes.

A technician making a record of my tapes – because I realized a record was
handier to carry about and more convenient for people who might want to
listen to Beatle music with a view to buying it – said to me, 'I don't think
these are at all bad.' He told Boast who had a word with Syd Coleman, a
music publisher who had an office upstairs. Coleman became quite excited
and said 'I like these. I would be quite willing to publish them.'

So ignorant was I at that time that I thought this meant an immediate £50
on a publishing advance, because I really had no idea what publishing meant.
Coleman also said he would speak to a friend of his at Parlophone a man
named George Martin. Said Coleman, 'I would like George to hear these. I
think he might be very interested indeed.'

The acetones were made and Syd Coleman made his call. George Martin,
an A and R man with Parlophone – a less fashionable label in those days –
was away but Coleman arranged for me to meet George's delightful and
gracious secretary and assistant Judy Lockhart-Smith. She arranged for me to
come to EMI the following day.

I was becoming very unpopular at home, for my father, quite rightly,
wanted to know whether I was employed by four leather-jacketed teenagers
or by him. And if by him, when was I going to do some work?

Every day I spent in London increased his irritation. But I was adamant
because I was determined not to give up the hunt for a record contract until I
had been refused by every label in England. Even by Embassy.

So I allowed myself a final 24 hours to exhaust the remaining disc companies and I booked into the Green Park Hotel and tried, in vain, to sleep. I
was worried about everything – the future of the Beatles who had shown
such faith in my ability to make them stars, my own future with Nems – and
the limits of my parents' patience.

In the morning I took a cab to the EMI offices in Manchester Square – part
of a handsome building – to meet the man who would, within less than two
years produce 16 Number One discs by my artistes.

George Martin was very helpful and discussed the difficulties of the record
business, and the problems I would meet if I was going to be persistent, and
said, 'I like your discs and I would like to see your artistes.' Wonderful news
and we fixed a provisional date there and then. Martin I liked immensely. He
is a painstaking man with a magnificent ear for music and a great sense of
style. I do not think he could produce a bad disc.

Also at the offices I established an instant friendship with Judy Lockhart-Smith and there was an atmosphere about the place which gave me tremendous hope. George, a tall, thin elegant man with the air of a stern but fair-minded housemaster had up to that time been doing good work with Peter Sellers on the famous and extremely successful LPs, but not very much with the new hard-driving beat music which was to sweep the world. He had a fine reputation, however, as a dedicated arranger, composer and oboist.

I liked the way he listened to the discs, his long legs crossed, leaning on his elbow, he rocked gently to and fro and nodded and smiled encouragingly. Judy also smiled her delicious smile and I sat with a face like stone as if my very life was at stake. In a way it was.

George had commented, 'I know very little about groups, Brian, but I believe you have something very good here,' and this to me had been the highest praise.

George also took the trouble to discuss the quality in this voice and that. He liked very much 'Hello Little Girl' recorded many months later and many hits later by the Fourmost – one of my Liverpool groups – but at that time it was merely one of many Beatles samples.

George also liked George Harrison on guitar and was excited by Paul's voice. 'He has the most commercial voice of the lot,' he commented and this is probably still true, though each Beatle has an equal amount to contribute to the total disc content.

We shook hands on the coming session and though there was still no contract, I left EMI as the happiest Liverpudlian in London and I hurtled North with the wonderful news. I had phoned the Beatles to say I was arriving with news and when my train arrived at Lime Street the four of them were waiting on the platform – an unusual event for they are not sentimental people given to waving people off or to welcoming them back.

'Well,' said George. And eight eyes looked at me with scarcely suppressed excitement.

'You have a recording session at EMI as soon as you like,' I said and to celebrate we sped to the National Milk Bar in Liverpool where we got intoxicated with power and Coca-Cola and four packets of biscuits.

The Beatles were beside themselves with delight and relief. We planned a wild future of hit records and world tours and ticker-tape welcomes in every foreign capital. Kings, we dreamed, would want to meet us and Dukes would seek autographs. Impossible fantasies were weaved until the milk-bar closed. 'The evening's not going to stop now,' said John so we adjourned to a club and got pretty drunk and I lost a girl friend called Rita Harris who worked for me and who said: 'I'm not going to compete with four kids who think they're entering the big time.'

Two years later the Beatles were the greatest entertainers in the world; they had met the Queen Mother and the Duke of Edinburgh and their pictures were on the walls of all the noble bedrooms of the young aristocracy. Prince Charles had all their records and San Francisco had the ticker-tape ready. They played the Hollywood Bowl, had the freedom of Liverpool. Ringo Starr was asked to be President of London University and John Lennon was the world's best-selling writer.

Back to June 1962 – the month of their first meeting with George Martin, and their introduction to Parlophone whose profits they were to 'up' by some millions before they were through.

George liked them immensely and thought they were very polite and amusing. John Lennon was keen on George as a man to work with because he worshipped the Goons, and in particular, Sellers. George himself was anxious to make complete contact with these off-beat provincial lads and sought to establish it by asking: 'Let me know if there is anything you don't like.'

'Well, for a start,' said George Harrison, deadpan from under his fringe, 'I don't like your tie,' which Martin thought was as good a basis for friendship as anything. From that moment on they have been a dream of a team.

At the first EMI session the Beatles taped 'Love Me Do', a haunting piece by Paul and John which employed a harmonica, then a very original novelty which, like many Beatle innovations, has been overworked and debased since.

They also taped 'P.S. I Love You' and George Martin and his technicians liked them both. But there was still no contract and the Beatles and I left EMI full of hope but without money or security. They flew again to Hamburg for a further stint behind the vulgar neon of the Reeperbahn and I returned to Liverpool and the record store to wait for further news.

It came in July. I signed a recording contract with Parlophone Records. The Beatles were on the way and the £ sign which Parlophone use as a trade mark was to become a symbol of unbelievable wealth.

I sent cables to all the boys in Germany. 'EMI contract signed, sealed. Tremendous importance to all of us. Wonderful.' They sent back postcards. From Paul: 'Please wire £10,000 advance royalties.' From John: 'When are we going to be millionaires.' 'Please order four new guitars,' – from George.

They came back from Germany to a wild welcome in Liverpool and on September 11th, 1962, the Beatles made their first British disc . . . 'Love Me

Do' on the A-side, 'P.S. I Love You' on the B-side. It was released on October 4th and it came into the record charts forty-eight hours later at number 49. Finally it reached Number 17 and the Beatles from Liverpool were in Britain's Top Twenty.

Their home city was thrilled beyond description. I had told everyone I knew that it was a magnificent disc, asked *Merseybeat* – the local music paper – to plug it and the kids of Liverpool bought it in thousands.

But there was a rumour – which lingered until it became acceptable currency – that I had bought the disc in bulk to get it into the charts. Possible though this would have been – had I the money, which I hadn't – I did no such thing, nor ever have. The Beatles, then as now, progressed and succeeded on natural impetus, without benefit of stunt or back-door tricks and I would like to make this quite clear.

'Love Me Do' was enough to convince all of us concerned with the Beatles – and by now I was no longer alone, since we had George Martin and a very nice and well-respected music publisher called Dick James on our side – that another disc must follow very quickly. Mitch Murray sent us a tune called 'How Do You Do It?' which the Beatles attempted and didn't like. (It eventually went to a lad named Gerry Marsden . . . but that is another story.) Paul and John submitted one of their own, appealingly called 'Please, Please Me', and it was made on November 26th 1962, and so pleased everyone that by early Spring in 1963 it was clear leader of every disc chart in the country.

Inch by inch, the Beatles were creeping into the newspapers. Prophets, one knows, have a thin time in their own locality and though Tony Barrow – now one of my press officers, then a record reviewer – had been kind to 'Love Me Do', I had difficulty in 'selling' the importance of the Beatles to News Editors and general-news columnnists. I arranged a meeting with a writer on the *Liverpool Echo*, the namesake of Beatle George Harrison – though much older – and he met them for a drink in a Liverpool city-centre pub called The Dive.

But I don't think he liked them very much. He thought they lacked conventional manners and also they didn't buy drinks and they didn't make George Harrison's column 'Over the Mersey Wall' until he had a day off and another man, Bill Rogers, took it over. George Harrison was to become a friend and loyal supporter of the Beatles and a constant companion on our foreign trips.

Merseybeat, under the energetic editorship of Bill Harry, a self-taught expert on the Beat-Scene, was pushing the Beatles very hard and I was grateful for this because I still had to make them a respected proposition for bookings in Northern halls. On one occasion I recall being paid in coins – £15 in sixpences and florins and even half-pennies and I kicked up an awful fuss, not because £15 isn't £15 in any currency, but because I thought it was disrespectful to the Beatles. I felt that if one was to be a manager then one should fight for absolute courtesy towards one's artistes.

I didn't get the £15 in notes, by the way, but I had made my point and I and the Beatles felt better for it.

We entered 1963 full of confidence, our earnings up from that nightly £15 to £50; with new suits and one new Beatle. For Peter Best, drummer Beatle, had been replaced to his disappointment and to the dismay of many savage fans, by a little bearded chap from the Dingle ... His name was Richard Starkey but he called himself Ringo Starr.

Brian Epstein, A Cellarful of Noise (1964)

1964: York

The Beatles are in their hotel bedrooms finishing their dinners. George feels tired and goes to sleep. John, wearing a T-shirt and an old pair of trousers, wanders down the hallway past the guard into the room shared by Paul and Ringo. The table filled with the empty dinner dishes is at the foot of Ringo's bed. Ringo, dressed in pyjamas, is sitting up in bed. Paul, also in pyjamas, is talking about a film, *The Trial*, which he has just seen in London, He is describing a scene in which there is a misunderstanding about a word, when the telephone rings.

'Hello, helloho,' says Paul in a falsetto and then, realizing it is a friend, says Hello seriously. The radio on the bedside night table is playing 'Our Love is Here to Stay'. Paul asks what days they have off the following week. Ringo starts to tell him, and John tries to confuse them by mentioning other days. The radio plays 'Old Devil Moon'. Paul continues to talk on the phone. 'That was "That Old Devil Moon" in a magnificent interpretation by the Mac-Guire Sisters,' says the radio, 'Now straight from the moon to the stars.' The radio plays 'Swinging on a star'.

They start talking about their forthcoming appearance in America and decide they will not be successful. 'After all,' says John, 'Cliff went there and he died. He was fourteenth on a bill with Frankie Avalon, and George said that "Summer Holiday" was second feature at a drive-in in St Louis.'

The radio played 'You'll Always Be Mine', and Paul returned from the telephone to announce, 'We've been invited to a masque, what's that?' John tells him it means a masked ball. 'It sounds like a rave,' says Paul, and returns to the phone.

'Wonderful singing by Mark Wynter,' says the radio. 'Only you would say that,' says Paul. 'Sure Trader Vic's is great . . . first the friends come, then the relatives of the friends . . . I mean the friends are bad enough.'

Paul finishes his telephone conversation and resumes talking about films. 'What I liked best in *The Trial*,' he says, 'was when they walked quietly through the concentration camp. It was so dead quiet, just like another world and Elsa Martinelli in the background just necking like mad.'

'Now the Shadows sing to you,' said the radio and I asked Paul whether he had seen *8½*. 'Oh, Peter told me to see that,' he said. 'But I don't know. I have this friend and every time he tells me to see something it turns out to be a drag for an evening's entertainment. He told me to go see *Next Time I'll Sing to You* and it was a dead bore. Then he suggested *A Severed Head* – it was the crappiest thing I'd seen for years. It's all this bit outside, "Well worth crossing the Atlantic for". Eccch, you can have it – crap.'

He turned to John. 'Stupid things like getting up in bed – no clothes on – fucking soft – they could have just had her herself without him getting into bed. I was getting bored and I spent most of the time watching this woman putting this scarf on and off and thinking that's not with it, tying it that way.'

He starts to joke with John and Ringo over just what is the right way to tie a scarf. After this he says, 'When I see an ordinary film – you know, one made without tricks – I know it sounds crap calling them tricks, but anyway, you get the idea . . . and then it cuts into a whole new action. When you're used to that it's hard to get used to the new kind like *The Trial* and *8½* I suppose. It sort of foxes me. I'm used to when they cut it's always a new thing happening.'

During the discussion about *A Severed Head* Ringo has turned the radio off. Now he turns it back on. 'Du-ah-du-ah . . .'

'Uh, I need another drink, baby,' says John.

Paul goes to the phone. 'Hello? Yeah, send us six single Scotches – No, make it doubles, yeah, doubles.'

'Du-ah-du-ah . . . And now a number from Xavier Cugat,' says the radio.

'Uh, no, thank you,' says John, 'I always thought he was a kind of saint until I saw a photograph of his wife Abbie Lane. You know, St Francis Xavier with the cows.'

'No, he was somebody else,' says Paul. 'Assisi, with the cows or birds or something.'

The radio plays 'I'm in Love'.

John: 'Nothing better than British country and western.'

Paul: 'Ringo likes this.'

Ringo: 'What? I can't hear.'

Paul: 'Ringo has trouble with his ears.' (To Ringo) '*I say you love this song.*'

Ringo: 'I love the words.'

Paul (in heavy Liverpool accent): 'He loves the words. Have they brought your grapes then?'

Ringo: 'No, they didn't bother today.'

Paul: 'We brought you a couple of eggs.'

Ringo: 'Put them in here and the nurse will take them and do them for me.'

Paul: 'Have you got your potty?'

Ringo: 'It's in there in the bath-tub. You've changed your hair since you last came to see me.'

Paul: 'Well, keep a fresh mind about all things.'

There is a moment of silence. Then Paul says that people from the Dingle in Liverpool have a basic fear of hospitals and always seem to bring people eggs.

'You see,' says John, 'psychologically they still regard the egg as something precious from the harder years. The egg is a sort of symbol of fertility and wealth.'

John notices that the radio has been turned off and asks who did it. Both Ringo and Paul deny it and John says he saw Ringo do it.

Paul: 'Tension is mounting.'

John: 'Tension all shipping.'

Paul: 'I once knew a fellow on the Dingle who had two dads. He used to call them number one dad and number two dad. Now apparently number one dad wasn't nice. He used to throw the boy on the fire – which can develop a lot of complexes in a young lad.'

Ringo: 'I remember my uncle putting the red-hot poker on me, and that's no lie. He was trying to frighten me.'

Paul: 'Tell me, Ringo, do all your relatives go around applying red-hot pokers to you?'

John: 'It's the only way they can identify them.'

Paul: 'You see, Ringo comes from a depressed area.'

John: 'Some people call it the slums.'

Ringo: 'No, the slums are farther.'

The drinks arrive and they begin discussing the derivation of American names like Melvin, Clyde and Dusty. They say that most of the slang that they have picked up is American Negro slang.

'Except that we get it late,' says John. 'For instance, we say "with it", which went out in America two years ago. And also, we sing "Yeah, yeah", that went out a couple of years ago although it's still featured by American coloured groups.'

They start to talk about fads and how they get started. 'For instance,' says Paul, 'it's taken a long time for the papers to realize that we've caught on. We knew a year ago that we were catching on. But it's taken until this Command performance for the papers to say, "What is this thing?" I mean when Maureen Cleave wrote her first thing in the *Evening Standard* we thought it was just a piece of old hat.'

'The thing is,' says John, 'British journalists refused to accept that we were nothing more than ordinary in the pop world and they just weren't interested, you see.'

'A fella called Dick Fontaine from Granada TV in Manchester came to the Cavern to see us,' said Paul. 'He was raving. He kept saying, "I must do a film with you fellas." Nobody wanted to know. They actually made the film and of course they show it now.'

Another thing they say hurt them was being from Liverpool. Paul recalls that their manager Brian Epstein was told, 'You'll never make it, from the provinces. Move down to London and you'll really get moving.' 'Our publicity man had trouble getting things in the paper because as soon as people heard Liverpool they thought we were all from the docks with sideboards. And the name. Practically everybody who knew told us to change it. "Beatles?" they'd say. "What does that mean?" '

They talked about Dick Rowe, an A and R man at Decca Records who had turned them down when they first sent in demonstration tapes.

'He must be kicking himself now,' says Paul.

'I hope he kicks himself to death,' says John.

'I don't blame him for turning us down,' says Paul.

They started discussing the feelings of adults towards pop music. 'We're definitely fighting a prejudice,' says John.

'That's why I'm interested in John getting his book out,' says Paul. 'I mean, I haven't got a cut or anything. It's just that one of us would be doing something to make people notice. I mean, it's the same as if one of us wrote a musical. People would get rid of their prejudice and stop thinking that pop people can only sing or go into a dance routine.'

'Which is what the normal pop artist does,' says John. 'He learns to tap-dance. We don't want to learn to dance or take elocution lessons.'

'People keep asking us whether we're going to broaden our scope,' says Paul. 'I don't know whether we will or not. One of the things about us is that we intrigue people. We seem a little bit different. If you read about Cliff Richard you know the things that he says; you've read about them before. But us . . . it's like when Maureen Cleave interviewed us – she asked us what we were doing culturally. I had read about *The Representative* and said I wanted to see it. She was reading *The Naked Lunch* and I said I was reading *The Packed Lunch* by Greedy Blighter. It's also like when people ask why they like the Beatles. Quite a few people mention the word genuine . . .'

'Which we're not,' interrupted John.

'. . . because they feel that's the impression we give. I remember thinking, about two years ago, "What have the people who have made it – I mean really made it – got?" It seems it's a sort of awareness of what's going on. I mean, I can imagine Sinatra to be, you know, not thick. I also thought, "What about the people who made it and then just sort of went?" I mean, look at Marty Wilde. I remember seeing him and being very impressed. Then when he started falling off I wondered what happened? Then we met him; and then we understood.'

They started to talk about idols and whether they have to have sex appeal. John said that Bill Hayley was the first person to sing rock 'n' roll but that he was too old to appeal to the girls that Elvis appealed to. 'After all,' said Paul, 'a young girl just couldn't see herself married to Bill Hayley.'

John said that they have been told that girls masturbate when they are on stage.

'We're still at the masturbating stage ourselves,' interrupted Paul. 'You just can't get any on stage. I'm joking, of course. Seriously, anybody that gets as much publicity as we are and who are idols, I hate saying that because we don't feel like idols particularly but obviously we must be by now . . .'

John starts to laugh and Paul protests.

'No, I really don't feel like one . . . I really don't . . . that is I don't feel like I imagine an idol is supposed to feel; however, anybody who gets this amount of publicity is in ordinary people's eyes a fantastic being; he always was in my eyes, anyway – y'know, Presley . . . Well, anyway, today this woman came up to the car; she'd never go up to just anybody in the street and kiss them; I mean, she was about forty; she was just sort of talking to me and she suddenly grabbed hold of me and kissed me. I mean, I was definitely embarrassed. What is it that with anybody who has had this amount of publicity . . .? It creates some sort of reaction which doesn't have to do with sex or anything. They just say, "Look, there's that person we've been reading about in our good-as-the-Bible *Daily Express* every day." It's like the royal family. You have to like them because you've read so much about them.'

'Why?' says John. 'I didn't like *them* even when I was little. I disliked having to stand, which sometimes I didn't.'

'Another thing,' says Paul, 'we get letters saying, "You probably won't get this letter; it probably will never reach you", and before they have started out on the letter they're sure it will never reach you anyway. Letters that start out, "If you read this letter please read it to the end." I mean, there's no hope of us reading it as far as they're concerned.'

'Then there's people like my cousin Stanley,' says John, 'who I admired as a boy because he had a car and a Meccano set; and, uh, now that I have, uh, made it he treats me as if I was royalty or something. It unnerves me; I mean, he's thirty and I'm young and it's, uh, rather embarrassing from my boyhood hero.'

'But maybe it's only human,' says Paul. 'I mean, I know that if one of us had gone up and shaken Cliff's hand only two years ago we would have leapt home to the fellas – "I've met him! I've met him, there you go!" – and we would have been like that . . .'

John: 'Even though we never bought any of his records.'

Paul says, 'I remember the first time we did meet him. We were in the business and Cliff and the Shadows invited us to this great kind of party. I mean all I could say was "Oh, wait till I tell the girls back home." Mind you, I knew it was a soft thing to say . . .'

'Yeah, you're supposed to make up things like, uh, "What a great job you're doing in the industry,"' said John.

Paul: 'Because we've never been fans of Cliff's.'

John: 'We've always *hated* him. He was everything we hated in pop. But when we met him we didn't mind him at all. He was very nice. Now when people ask us if he's a bit soft we say no. We still hate his records but he's really very nice.'

'I really don't think there is anything sad about idol-worshipping,' says Paul. 'I mean it's the same as when you haven't got religion, you can say, "Isn't it sad that all the Catholics believe that there's a God and they go to mass every morning and get up early and those poor buggers have the priest as their god. I used to think they're having a rough time, until you think about it again and think they're the blokes who're having a great time, 'cause in actual fact they believe.

'I mean, we think a lot of people lead dull lives but they don't really. Like the woman who comes to clean our house and make meals. If I actually analysed it, all she does is get up in the morning, see her sons off to work, comes to our house, does the meals for us, goes home, watches telly and goes to bed and the same next day. Compared to us it's dull but for her it's not dull. She comes to our house, y'know, the great stars' house . . .'

John: 'You're a great star, eh?'

Paul: 'Huh? Oh, yeah, yeah . . . this is all purely fictional . . .'

John: 'What it is is that people will go to see the original instead of a copy. Like I took a look at the original mouldy Mona Lisa in Paris – eccch, crap!'

Paul: 'I mean, it's like the Eddie Cochrane show. We all used to think he was fantastic. I remember thinking before the show that I was actually there. I mean, it's the same thing as when you go to people's houses, mates, or people you used to know, sort of thing . . .'

John: 'Notice he said *used* to?'

Paul: 'And they have all your records – there's always one of them who will say "Give us a song." They want to see you, even though it will sound terrible. It's like why people want to see the film of Picasso drawing . . .'

John: 'Uh, he saw it at school. Uh, we all did.'

Paul (laughing): 'You see the film of Picasso actually creating . . .'

We started to talk about the reaction of fans. Paul said he thought that a lot of the reaction now came from what people believed they ought to do. I mentioned reading about the violent reception in Liverpool of *Rock Around the Clock*.

'I went to see it,' said John, 'and I was most surprised. Nobody was screaming and nobody was dancing. I mean, I had read that everybody danced in the aisles. It must have all been done before I went. I was all set to tear up the seats too but nobody joined in.'

'I know if I went to see our show,' said Paul, 'I wouldn't scream no matter how great I thought it was. I remember seeing the Eddie Cochrane show and there was this coloured fellow. Well, he walked to the front of the stage and did one of those great big actions, y'know, and everyone just laughed at him.'

We got on to the subject of the importance of fans and the press. Paul said there were so many people who claimed to have 'made' the Beatles in a short year that 'I sometimes wonder just who actually did make us.'

'You remember after that big spate of publicity we got in the national papers,' says John, 'which was uncalled for by our office. We were news at the time, and it only just happened we clicked in fourteen editors' minds at the same time. One day Paul was ill and I believe one of the papers wanted a picture of him. Nell told them they couldn't have it, and the photographer said: "You mean, after all the publicity we gave them – we *made* them." I'd like to meet this fella who said it.'

Paul explained that they never talk to the teenage magazines. 'They just make it up. I think they prefer it that way. Also photographers ... We work much harder with someone like Robert Freeman or Parkinson than with the nationals, who only want a cheesy grin. Of course, you have to start somewhere. What happens is that you get magazines like *Boyfriend* or *Valentine* first, then the *New Record* and *Show Mirror*. They will do an article even if you're not known. Then you get to the *New Musical Express*, and *Melody Maker*, which, though it's not the top-selling one, has a jazz influence, and you can talk sense to them. Then you really have to be very well known to be in *Time* or the *Observer* or the *Sunday Times*. I mean, the *Sunday Times* – a lot of the old codgers who read that just never know what's happening.

'But really your tastes change in everything. I remember when we first got a photographer in Britain. We got this fella Dezo Hoffmann. It sounded good – Dezo Hoffmann – when he came to the studio we did all our good poses. He's all right for a pop photographer. But I remember at the beginning of this year we thought Dezo was the greatest photographer in the world.'

I mentioned Avedon and Cartier-Bresson. They had never heard of either. 'What makes Cartier-Bresson so great?' asked Paul.

We talked about him for a moment and then Paul said that Parkinson was doing a book on the Beatles. 'As far as photos are concerned and techniques of photography it may all be very good. Some of the things looked a bit contrived. For instance he had over-exposed film and film that was so obviously wrong that they *had* to be great.'

'Uh, Robert Freeman thinks it's old, out-dated,' says John, 'but I suppose some think a lot of the things Robert Freeman does are out-dated also.'

'Parkinson's big thing with us,' said Paul, 'was, "Where did you get those eyes?" and he kept lining us up and instead of pulling faces we had to pull eyes. Uh, John and George didn't oblige. Listen, do you think this boy Avedon will do things for us? Because we'll hire him.'

'Right now we're using Freeman. He's sort of in-betweensville,' said John.

We talked about Liverpool. Paul said, 'There is a certain awareness about some people in Liverpool. Like Ringo; he's never been to school except two days. Three times they told his mum he was going to die.'

'Anyway,' said John, looking at Ringo, 'to be so aware with so little education is rather unnerving to someone who's been to school since he was fucking two onwards.'

Ringo looked up and said, 'My grandad used to ask whether my hair was too long for butting because he'd do it if I gave him any cheek.'

'Butting is a Liverpool term for hitting with your head,' said Paul. 'I remember a little hooligan boy saying to my brother, "If you don't watch out I'll butt you", which he did.'

'Butting,' said John, 'is the first move used by the Liverpool lout. I only tried it once but my opponent moved and I nearly cracked my head open.'

I said that sometimes a poor childhood was fortunate, that it could be a real handicap to have a famous father.

'Uh, I don't agree,' said John. 'I could have stood a famous father rather more than the ignoble Alf, actually.'

Paul said, 'I think it would have been a drag if my father was famous.'

'I would have enjoyed the money,' said John. 'Never mind the fame. I think it is a working-class fallacy that you have to fight your way up. I think there must be people who have enjoyed a happy and fruitful life without having to fight for it. People who are made great are only made great by people of the class they leave. Let's say there are five people from the working class and one makes it. He's only great in the eyes of the other four.'

Paul said, 'Frank Sinatra didn't have wealthy parents but he's recognized by rich people.'

On the subject of children they agreed that they would probably make the same mistakes with theirs as their parents did with them. 'I know when my kid is about sixteen,' said John, 'and I say, "Come in at such and such a time" and he does, I'll be saying, "At my age when I was told to come in I didn't." I'll say, "When they told me not to have sex I did; when they told me not to smoke I smoked." If he turns out to be one of them who does everything he's told, I'll be dead choked.'

'I mean, what's wrong with us?' says Paul. 'Our parents used all the old clichés and look how we turned out.'

John asked Ringo, 'Why don't you ever say anything except "I'm the drummer"?'

'I don't like talking,' says Ringo. 'It's how I'm built. Some people gab all day and some people play it smogo. I don't mind talking or smiling, it's just I don't do it very much. I haven't got a smiling face or a talking mouth.'

Paul (whispering): 'Shakespeare's songs – you like Shakespeare's songs – go on' (to me) 'ask him what kind of music he likes.'

I asked him what kind of music he liked.

'I like real blues.' (They laugh.)

'And what kind of poetry?'

'Mozart's poetry.'

'One more ciggy,' says John, 'and I'm gonna hit the sack; "hit the sack" being an American thing we got off Gary Coople as he struggled along with a clock in *Hi, Goons*. But I really never liked "sack", it's, uh, something you put potatoes in over here.'

'The whole thought of hitting the sack,' says Paul, 'it's so – so dirty, and it can mean a lot of things.'

'You can sack Rome,' says John, 'or you can sack cloth – or you can sacrilege, or saxophone, if you like, or saccharine.'

'Or sacrifice,' says Ringo.

Michael Braun, *'Love me Do': The Beatles' Progress* (1964)

1964: The Menace of Beatlism

Mr William Deedes is an Old Harrovian, a member of the cabinet and the minister in charge of the government's information services. Mr Deedes, it will be remembered, was one of those five ministers who interviewed Mr Profumo on that fateful night and were convinced by him that he had not slept with Miss Keeler. Now any public relations man, even a grand one who sits in the cabinet, can use a touch of credulity; but even so I remember thinking at the time: 'If Deedes can believe that, he'll believe anything.' And indeed he does! Listen to him on the subject of The Beatles:

> They herald a cultural movement among the young which may become part of the history of our time ... For those with eyes to see it, something important and heartening is happening here. The young are rejecting some of the sloppy standards of their elders, by which far too much of our output has been governed in recent years ... they have discerned dimly that in a world of automation, declining craftsmanship and increased leisure, something of this kind is essential to restore the human instinct to excel at something and the human faculty of discrimination.

Incredible as it may seem, this was not an elaborate attempt at whimsy, but a serious address, delivered to a meeting of the City of London Young Conservatives, and heard in respectful silence. Not a voice was raised to point out that the Emperor wasn't wearing a stitch. The Beatles phenomenon, in fact, illustrates one of my favourite maxims: that if something becomes big enough and popular enough – and especially commercially profitable enough – solemn men will not be lacking to invest it with virtues. So long as The Beatles were just another successful showbiz team the pillars of society could afford to ignore them, beyond bestowing the indulgent accolade of a slot in the Royal Variety Performance. But then came the shock announcement that they were earning £6,250,000 a year – and, almost simultaneously, they got the stamp of approval from America.

This was quite a different matter: at once they became not only part of the export trade but an electorally valuable property. Sir Alec Home promptly claimed credit for them, and was as promptly accused by Mr Wilson of political clothes-stealing. Conservative candidates have been officially advised to mention them whenever possible in their speeches. The Queen expressed concern about the length of Ringo's hair. Young diplomats at our Washington embassy fought for their autographs. A reporter described them as 'superb ambassadors for Britain'. It is true that the Bishop of Woolwich has not yet asked them to participate in one of his services, but the invitation cannot be long delayed. And, while waiting for the definitive analysis of their cultural significance by Messrs Raymond Williams and Richard Hoggart we have Mr Deedes' contribution on behalf of the cabinet.

Of course, our society has long been brainwashed in preparation for this apotheosis of inanity. For more than two decades now, more and more intellectuals have turned their backs on their trade and begun to worship at the shrine of 'pop culture'. Nowadays, if you confess that you don't know the difference between Dizzy Gillespie and Fats Waller (and, what is more, don't care) you are liable to be accused of being a fascist.

To buttress their intellectual self-esteem, these treasonable clerks have evolved an elaborate cultural mythology about jazz, which purports to distinguish between various periods, tendencies and schools. The subject has been smeared with a respectable veneer of academic scholarship, so that now you can overhear grown men, who have been expensively educated, engage in heated arguments on the respective techniques of Charlie Parker and Duke Ellington. You can see writers of distinction, whose grey hairs testify to years spent in the cultural vineyard, squatting on the bare boards of malodorous caverns, while through the haze of smoke, sweat and cheap cosmetics comes the monotonous braying of savage instruments.

One might, I suppose, attribute such intellectual treachery to the fact that, in jazz circles, morals are easy, sex is cheap and there is a permissive attitude to the horrors of narcotics. Men are, alas, sometimes willing to debauch their intellects for such rewards. But I doubt if this is the real reason. The growing public approval of anti-culture is itself, I think, a reflection of the new cult of youth. Bewildered by a rapidly changing society, excessively fearful of becoming out of date, our leaders are increasingly turning to young people as guides and mentors –or, to vary the metaphor, as geiger-counters to guard them against the perils of mental obsolescence. If youth likes jazz, then it must be good, and clever men must rationalise this preference in intellectually respectable language. Indeed, whatever youth likes must be good: the supreme crime, in politics and culture alike, is not to be 'with it'. Even the most unlikely mascots of the Establishment are now drifting with the current: Mr Henry Brooke, for instance, finds himself appointing to the latest Home Office committee the indispensable teenager, who has, what is more, the additional merit of being a delinquent.

Before I am denounced as a reactionary fuddy-duddy, let us pause an instant and see exactly what we mean by this 'youth'. Both TV channels now run weekly programmes in which popular records are played to teenagers and judged. While the music is performed, the cameras linger savagely over the faces of the audience. What a bottomless chasm of vacuity they reveal! The huge faces, bloated with cheap confectionery and smeared with chain-store makeup, the open, sagging mouths and glazed eyes, the hands mindlessly drumming in time to the music, the broken stiletto heels, the shoddy, stereotyped, 'with-it' clothes: here, apparently, is a collective portrait of a generation enslaved by a commercial machine. Leaving a TV studio recently, I stumbled into the exodus from one of these sessions. How pathetic and listless they seemed: young girls, hardly any more than 16, dressed as adults and already lined up as fodder for exploitation. Their eyes came to life only when one of their grotesque idols – scarcely older than they – made a brief appearance, before a man in a camel-hair coat hustled him into a car. Behind this image of 'youth', there are, evidently, some shrewd older folk at work.

And what of the 'culture' which is served up to these pitiable victims? According to Mr Deedes, 'the aim of The Beatles and their rivals is first class of its kind. Failure to attain it is spotted and criticised ruthlessly by their many highly-discriminating critics.' I wonder if Mr Deedes has ever taken the trouble to listen to any of this music? On the Saturday TV shows, the merits of the new records are discussed by panels of 'experts', many of whom seem barely more literate or articulate than the moronic ranks facing them. They are asked to judge each record a 'hit' or a 'miss', but seem incapable of explaining why they have reached their verdict. Occasionally one of the 'experts' betrays some slight acquaintance with the elementals of music and makes what is awesomely described as a 'technical' point; but when such merit is identified in a record, this is usually found to be a reason for its certain commercial failure.

In any case, merit has nothing to do with it. The teenager comes not to

197

hear but to participate in a ritual, a collective grovelling to gods who are themselves blind and empty. 'Throughout the performance,' wrote one observer, 'it was impossible to hear anything above the squealing except the beat of Ringo's drums.' Here, indeed, is 'a new cultural movement': music which not only cannot be heard but does not *need* to be heard. As such I have no doubt that it is, in truth, 'first class of its kind'.

If the Beatles and their like were in fact what the youth of Britain wanted, one might well despair. I refuse to believe it – and so, I think, will any other intelligent person who casts his or her mind back far enough. What were we doing at 16? I remember the drudgery of Greek prose and the calculus, but I can also remember reading the whole of Shakespeare and Marlowe, writing poems and plays and stories. It is a marvellous age, an age of intense mental energy and discovery. Almost every week one found a fresh idol – Milton, Wagner, Debussy, Matisse, El Greco, Proust – some, indeed, to be subsequently toppled from the pantheon, but all springing from the mainstream of European culture. At 16, I and my friends heard our first performance of Beethoven's Ninth Symphony; I can remember the excitement even today. We would not have wasted 30 seconds of our precious time on The Beatles and their ilk.

Are teenagers different today? Of course not. Those who flock round The Beatles, who scream themselves into hysteria, whose vacant faces flicker over the TV screen, are the least fortunate of their generation, the dull, the idle, the failures: their existence, in such large numbers, far from being a cause for ministerial congratulation, is a fearful indictment of our education system, which in 10 years of schooling can scarcely raise them to literacy. What Mr Deedes fails to perceive is that the core of the teenage group – the boys and girls who will be the real leaders and creators of society tomorrow – never go near a pop concert. They are, to put it simply, too busy. They are educating themselves. They are in the process of inheriting the culture which, despite Beatlism or any other mass-produced mental opiate, will continue to shape our civilisation. To use Mr Deedes' own phrase, though not in the sense he meant it, they are indeed 'rejecting some of the sloppy standards of their elders'. Of course, if many of these elders in responsible positions surrender to the Gadarene Complex and seek to elevate the worst things in our society into the best, their task will be made more difficult. But I believe that, despite the antics of cabinet ministers with election nerves, they will succeed.

Paul Johnson, *New Statesman*, 28 February 1964

1964: My Beatles Hat

August 1964: My Beatles hat which cost me a fortune – £8 – in Herbert Johnson's has paid dividends, as everywhere I've travelled it's made me instantly recognizable as the most desirable of foreigners – an inhabitant of swinging London. Hitching up the coast from San Simeon to San Francisco, with the hat, has been easy, the people extraordinarily friendly. Some girls asked me if we had chocolate in England, offering me a Hershey bar! When I told them that in my childhood I lived in a house, parts of which were seven hundred years old they looked sad. 'You must be very poor,' they said. This puzzled me, until I remembered everything has to be brand-new in California.

I picked up a stoned boy on a bike called Michael, and we drove for a couple of hours up the coast. We booked into a cabin at the motel at Big Sur!! It was set in the Redwoods alongside a stream, and here we carried on smoking his grass. The oranges of Hieronymous Bosch. Tomorrow we're off to Monterey, where Joan Baez and Dylan sing.

September 1964, NYC: When I got into the Greyhound terminal I was exhausted after the non-stop ride from San Francisco. I tossed a coin for which of the Reverends I'd ring – the least obnoxious, as Ron would say – and decided on Tom, who without hesitating invited me round. When I got to his place, he told me there was no time to unpack as we were going to a party. All I wanted to do was to go to sleep, but he wouldn't leave me behind. So we arrived at a small flat which was so packed that people were hanging out of the windows. In the centre of the room a gang of black drag queens were swishing around announcing they were the most 'glamorous', and when some weedy-looking white drag queen took them on in the beauty stakes the room divided, and it nearly started a fight in which someone pulled a knife. I took refuge in a bedroom with a black boy, Marshall Hill, who was at art college – painting. We curled up on the floor and made love.

Afterwards, I was so drunk and exhausted, deprived of food and sleep, he offered to drive me back as Tom had disappeared, leaving me stranded. Tom hadn't arrived home, so we lay on the carpet outside the front door and fell asleep in each other's arms. When Tom arrived back at 4.30 I asked him if Marshall could come in and stay. He began shouting, telling us we were a disgrace and threw me and my luggage into the hallway and slammed the door. So much for Christian charity – Marshall and I spent the rest of the day sightseeing, then he took me out to the airport in the evening more dead than alive.

Derek Jarman, *Dancing Ledge* (1984)

1964: It was Like a Battlefield

'I'd marry anyone to spite my parents'

'VERMIN,' SAYS MARGATE JP

Sending a Whitsun rowdy to a detention centre today, Dr George Simpson, chairman of Margate magistrates, said: 'It would appear that you did not benefit from yesterday's proceedings. You were part of the dregs of those vermin which infested this town. As such you will go to a detention centre for three months. Take him away.'

London Evening Standard, 19 May (1964)

MEAT PRICE AT HIGHEST EVER

Ibid, same front page

Shortly after we read these headlines we talked to John Braden, 18, a London mechanic. He had this to say:

'Yes, I am a Mod and I was at Margate. I'm not ashamed of it – I wasn't the only one. I joined in a few of the fights. It was a laugh, I haven't enjoyed myself so much in a long time. It was great – the beach was like a battlefield. It was like we were taking over the country.

You want to hit back at all the old geezers who try to tell us what to do. We just want to show them we're not going to take it. It was like a battlefield. I felt great, part of something important instead of just being something they look down on because you haven't passed GCE.

I know some old men were knocked down but none of them were hurt. They might've got a bit of a shock but they deserve it – they don't think about us, how we might feel.

It was great being in the newspapers – sure, we love reading about ourselves. Who doesn't. Blinkin' film stars and debs delights and social climbers hire publicity men to get their bleedin' names in the papers. We punch our way in, cost-free.

Reading the linens afterwards is part of the kicks. Makes you feel you've done something, made people sit up and take notice. What these old squares don't realize is we've got far more guts than they ever had, and don't talk to me about the bleedin' war. War is for ginks. That magistrate was protecting his own kind, you can't blame him for that, but why take it out on us? They're jealous of us, that's why they make all that fuss.

Bashing rockers is something to do, isn't it? The funniest thing was seeing the cops getting tough. If they want a fight we'll give it to them.

It's something that gets into you. You don't know what it is. I can't explain it – you just go wild. There's a lot of hate in me, I accept that. Why be a hypocrite? Okay, sometimes I get worried about it. But what can you do? The thing I hate most is people in authority – they're idiots – they deserve all they get. I could kill them.

I suppose it's because I don't have a chance. I don't talk right and I haven't been to the right schools – I haven't had the education. That makes you sick – to see them preaching at you.'

An extreme case, admittedly. We sought him out because his special involvement gave him a certain journalistic interest. We doubt the complete honesty of his plea because we declared ourselves and thus made his reaction artificial, studied. Television has made even the most retrograde citizen an instant pundit, ready to give his half-baked views on any conceivable topic an immediate airing. But this has been one of the occupational hazards we decided, at an early stage of our task, to accept at its face value rather than attempt to shade in subtleties beyond the range and comprehension of our subjects. In this case we asked for a snap reaction and got it.

We now propose to take the subject further on the basis of an impressionistic documentary . . .

> 'After sending a second youth to detention, he said: 'Measures will be employed to stamp out this hooliganism. What happened to these two sentenced this morning may add to the deterrent we used yesterday. If I may use a misquotation, "The hooligans and thugs depart, and the tumult and shouting dies." That concludes the business of this court.'

'Why the hell do grown-up men and women run down today's teenagers so much? Calling them street corner layabouts, dressed in weird clothes, with a mouthful of chewing gum, a cigarette drooping from the mouth and carrying a noisy transistor radio. It's true to say there's a minor section of us who do dress like this, but this is mainly because they feel the need to look big and look hard among the other boys – and the tougher they look the more girls they get hanging around them. Can you blame a bloke for trying to get birds?'

THE BLACKEST WHITSUN EVER ON THE ROADS. 100 MILES OF
JAMS ON BIG TREK HOME.

Daily Mirror, 19 May (1964)

'We wear leather jackets studded with polished brass buttons because tighter
than tight striped trousers and strange-shaped shoes make us look bigger and
feel tougher.

Some of the boys want to follow in big brother's footsteps. He's been
nicked at the law shop more than once and made a big name for hisself in the
district. Or it may be the old man's who's an ex-con and been a bit of a
bastard in his time, who comes home drunk every night and starts lashing out
at the old woman. Good for him, this is the life many of us have been brought
into.

Me, I failed the 11-plus, and I felt bitter, my parents were disappointed in
me and instead of getting the bike I was promised, I was bagged for the next
six weeks. On the other hand the boy who sat next to me in class passed with
flying colours, got a bike and became a snob, and who wants to be one of
those?

From then on it was if you can't beat them with your brains, beat them
with your fists. With a gang you feel you belong somewhere, have a place in
society. Among a gang you can be somebody. You soon learn the tricks. The
country is short of police and robbery and violence are dead easy. The
excitement makes you feel important.

But not all of us are that bad. Most of us get steady jobs after a while and
can earn good money. Although we try to look hard and act big we're often
soft-hearted inside. Take the youth club where I live in one of the rough areas
of London. Some of the teenage members have been run into the law station
a few times for minor offences, but as the warden of the club says to all and
sundry: "I let them join whether they have been in trouble or not, because I
know that down under they are different persons, kind and always willing to
help people in need." '

'Immature, Irresponsible . . . No Regard For Law'
The 'wild ones' of Clacton's fateful week-end were fined up to
£75 at Clacton magistrates' court today. A parade of 25 youths –
five of them 16-year-olds – and a man of 30 appeared before Mr
J. W. Boardman, Deputy Lieutenant of Essex. They faced charges
including theft, assault, using threatening behaviour, having
offensive weapons and loitering with intent.
And they heard prosecutor Mr Thomas Holdcroft say of them

and those others in the 'battle of Clacton': 'As a whole they are immature and irresponsible and lacking in any regard for the law, for the officers of the law, for the comfort and safety of other persons and lacking in regard for the property of others. Large numbers have been identified with groups such as Mods and Rockers. If they choose fancy dress it is their own concern. I am concerned with their behaviour.'

'We help people in our youth club . Every member does his part whether it's saving silver paper for our "Operation Guide Dog" or helping out at the spastic children's outings and parties, and the girl members on their Sunday monthly rota help the nurses at Queen Mary's Hospital in the East End. For some time we have been collecting silver paper to buy a guide dog for a blind person. I overheard one of the boys saying one night: "I've got other things to do than collect silver paper, they can get enough without me helping," then taking his last cigarette from the packet he went over to the collection box and dropped in the silver paper thinking nobody had seen him. You can't afford to seem soft in this life, can you?'

Teenagers, go home!
We hear teenagers complain – 'What can we do?' 'Where can we go?'
The answer is – go home – clean the windows, paint the woodwork, rake the leaves, mow the lawns, shovel the walk, wash the car, scrub some floors, help the minister, rabbi or priest, the Red Cross, or the Salvation Army.
Your parents do not owe you entertainment. The world does not owe you a living. You owe it to your time and energy and your talent so that no one will be at war or in poverty – or sick or lonely again. In Heaven's name – Grow up and go home!
Letter in late *Daily Herald*

'Both Mods and Rockers like pop music, but Mods are more way out in what they listen to. The same applies to the clothes they wear, the Mods design their own fashions and have them made – and, really, you have to have something new every week if you want to keep up with them.
At the moment they're wearing blue beat hats (small brims, in dark blue with pale blue ribbon), Ivy League-style suits with three buttons on the jacket and narrow lapels and two vents at the back. Trousers have seventeen inch bottoms, boots have round toes and are in imitation crocodile or python. Blue

suits and blue shirts with peg collar – giraffe collar three inches high – they're very uncomfortable and crease up.

The shirts are about 39s. 6d. and a Mod will pay thirty guineas for a suit and up to £5 for a shirt. Most popular is John Michael, the Mod Shop in Carnaby Street, Soho. The Dunn's shops are fab for hats. We pay up to £5 for shoes and £2 10s. for a hat.

Hair styles are high for men, parted in the middle with a puffed up top-and-back which you do by back-combing – the girl friend will do it for you if you can't do it yourself, and it has to be lacquered well to stay in place. Mod girls have a short back-and-sides hair-cut like men used to, wear shift-style dresses with round collars. No lipstick and hardly any make-up. Stacked heeled shoes, white stockings. They go dancing in stretch slacks, black and white tweed coats with leather collar and cuffs. Two-colour combinations, e.g., pink and blue. Fitted '1930s' shoulders.

Mods go to dance halls, Hammersmith Palais, the Marquee and the various 'discotheques' – clubs where they play gramophone records; there's a very popular one in Wardour Street. They think the Rockers are prehistoric with the boys in leather gear and wearing their hair long with Elvis-type sideboards. As for the Rocker girls, phui! They too wear leather gear, flat shoes, hair bouffant-style with loads of lacquer, lots of dirty, thick make-up, Elvis pendants, brooches and rings. Elvis is very old-fashioned now – only the Rockers keep him up. And they're still faithful to the jive and twist. Rockers are any age up to twenty-five, but you've got to be young to be a Mod.

The Mod boys are the smartest dressed every time. They might look a bit effeminate but they're not really. People talk about them taking Purple Hearts, but not many of them do. The Mod holiday resort is Jersey – no passport and you can get drunk on ten bob. You go in groups; one hotel there with adjoining bedrooms is booked a year in advance. The Mods don't watch TV except teenage programmes – *Ready, Steady, Go* and *Thank Your Lucky Stars*. They read James Bond because they fancy themselves with women like the ones he has. Oh, and Micky Spillane. Girls read love stories and women's magazines and pop mags – they read more on the average than Rocker girls.

Mods don't like films, they prefer dancing, unless it's a really good film like *The Servant*. The Mods say the Beatles must go out now.* They all dance the Blue Beat – stiff at knees, throw arms everywhere and make like a gospel

* June 1964

204

singer, all emotional. Hips to the side four beats at a time and the rhythm is like a locomotive thumping along a track, sound like a drum and the words are really mad.

The music's been around about five years. It came in with the Jamaicans but was caught on by Mods. It's played in the Marquee, Oxford Street. Ziggy Jackson, head of Blue Beat label records, made it popular. There's a coloured singer they're catching on to called Prince Buster, who sings 'Madness', a silly song but the rhythm gets the kids. It's sold 15,000 records and is top of the Blue Beat Top Twenty. Most shops sell Blue Beat records now – they're catching on.

A lot of Mods used to be CND, but that's gone out now. It was just a craze and if you wore a CND badge you were in at one time, but if you asked half of them why they were wearing it they wouldn't know. It was just a bit of a laugh. I think most of the people in CND now are really sincere about it.

Advanced Mods are only found in London and Manchester, though. The Mod scene changes so fast that the provinces couldn't possibly stay up to date with it.'

Charles Hamblett and Jane Deverson, *Generation X* (1964)

1964: Clubland

Clubs in the early sixties were nothing like those which these days seem to beckon from every street corner. For a start, all of them were small – intimate might be a more appropriate adjective. Most of them hidden away in obscure streets and in the nether reaches of unobtrusive buildings.

These clubs were really clubs in the proper sense of the word. Membership was necessary – and anyone wishing to join usually went through the formalities of being 'introduced' and seconded. Once a fully-fledged member of a gay club you were part of a select fraternity, and though within each venue there operated cliques, generally most members were on nodding acquaintance with each other. There was at least a certain level of human contact.

With varying degrees of affection, I remember clubs like the Calabash, the Festival, the A & B, the Apollo, as well as coffee bars like the Coffee House and the As You Like It.

I was taken to the Calabash by a bookshop assistant whom I rather fancied. The club was in Drayton Gardens in Kensington, up a flight of rickety stairs directly behind the Paris-Pullman cinema. Run by a highly theatrical photographer called Laon Maybanke, the decor was decidedly flock wallpaper and red plush. The walls were decorated with framed photographs of stars – there was a stunning shot of Vivien Leigh – all taken by the owner. The entrance and the cloakrooms were guarded by a squat old woman – Spanish, I think – dressed in black bombazine. Though way off my usual beaten track, the Calabash entranced me for a while. I became a regular visitor – and for a brief time pot-boy and sweeper-up. This was my first experience of working in a club.

The Festival, in Brydges Place (a narrow alley which runs down the side of the London Coliseum), was run on very different lines. At this club all the members had keys to the street-level front door. Open at lunchtime (pub hours) and in the evenings, the Festival was run by a charming – slightly rapacious – Canadian called Ted Rogers-Bennett. Because of the club's nearness to the bookshop, it became a regular stopping-off place and often the focal point for an evening.

By this time I had a small gaggle of gay friends. We'd meet in the Festival after work and have a few drinks. We might progress along St Martin's Lane to the Salisbury, which in those days was very much a theatrical pub in both the professional and the gay sense of the word. I have seen Elizabeth Taylor in the Salisbury – also Clint Eastwood and Edward Albee (probably around the time that *Who's Afraid of Virginia Woolf* was first staged in London).

From the Salisbury we might go on to the Carousel or the Apollo or the A & B. We'd almost certainly find ourselves later in the evening in the Huntsman. And, invariably, we'd end up at the As You Like It in Monmouth Street.

The As You Like It represented true High Bohemia. A slightly seedy coffee-cum-snack-bar, it seemed to be open all hours. During the day it catered to the office trade – lunchtimes were busy, with typists and clerks munching their way through salads and sandwiches. The early evenings were quieter from a customer point of view – though the staff were busy preparing snacks and beverages for the workers at the nearby theatres. But it wasn't until late at night that the As You Like It really came to life.

Barrie Stacey, now a successful entrepreneur, ran the place and ruled it with a benign rod of iron. At a level which allowed for conversation, records played. Barrie's choice of music was somewhat restricted – most usually songs by the legendary movie queens who even then had become a part of history.

So devoted was Barrie to the queens of the silver screen that he organised early evening Sunday showings of selected classics such as *Sunset Boulevard* and *Queen Christina*. We'd all meet up at the café beforehand, swill down coffee and then troop off to the nearby screening-room that had been hired. After the film – tear-stained or giggly hysterical – we'd return in a camp gaggle for more coffee and sandwiches, discussions about the film just seen and impersonations of the female stars.

The denizens of the As You Like It were an extraordinary – and often talented – bunch. Amongst the eccentric regulars were the Countess Irene, a big lady; Ernest, a white-bearded astrologer; Quentin Crisp – who went on to achieve international fame late in life; Lindsay Kemp, then a struggling dancer/mime artist; and Long John Baldry, who *always* seemed to be just back from Hamburg. We would all sit at our separate tables with our own special cohorts – screaming and chattering like monkeys on speed, or else sedately regal, exchanging sophisticated banter and polished witticisms. I used to drink strong black coffee laced with salt – God knows why. I'm sure it must have been disgusting.

I sometimes wonder if any of us then realised that at least a few of us would make reputations of one kind or another for ourselves. We were certainly a curious crowd – all poor, mostly over-the-top camp, generally friendly and not at all like anyone you'd meet today.

The best discovery of all was the Lounge in Whitehall, a coffee-bar which lurked in the shadow of Scotland Yard. Run by an attractive and gay ex-policeman, the Lounge was the first venue in London for predominantly gay teenagers with an eye to style and an ear for music. Sadly, it didn't last long. Yet the Lounge deserves a niche in gay history simply because it was the forerunner of and the inspiration for one of the most fondly remembered clubs of that era: Le Duce.

By the mid-Sixties, everything was changing. Those of us from the immediate post-war generation were developing our own tastes and inventing our own styles. We were evolving our own look and we had adopted our own music. We had found the drug we wanted to take and we had a language of our own – albeit a language that some gay men had been using for years.

Though those of us who used the Lounge and later Le Duce were gay, we shared many things in common with the other youth group who'd sprung up at about the same time: the Mods. In fact, the premiere Mod club – the Scene in Ham Yard behind Shaftesbury Avenue – was basically a straight version of Le Duce.

Economically, those who frequented the Scene and Le Duce both came from the same working-class – South and East London – backgrounds. Both groups paid the same attention to clothes; both groups looked much alike.

Not surprising, really, as their clothes came from the same shops – initially Vince in Carnaby Street (whose catalogue of swim- and underwear could *almost* be classified as an early gay magazine) and eventually from the John Stephen shops in the same street. Both groups took the same drug – basically 'speed', alternatively known as 'purple hearts', 'blues', 'doobs' or 'uppers'. Blues was the name we used most, with uppers the most common second choice.

Part of the ritual of the weekend was waiting for the blues to arrive or trekking off to someone's flat to collect them. Blues gave you energy, they kept you awake for the all-night sessions – if straight at the Scene; if gay at Le Duce. They gave you confidence. You felt you could talk to anyone; you could dance all night.

And dancing was important. As was the music that was popular with the Mods and the young gays who frequented Le Duce.

The two groups shared the same music. The mid-Sixties saw the slow beginnings of acceptance of black music – soul, blue beat, ska (which subsequently transmuted into reggae) and Tamla Motown. Except for isolated instances, none of these records were chart hits – certainly not on first release.

Records by performers like Prince Buster or Desmond Dekker and the Aces had to be searched for – and were most commonly found in specialist shops. They certainly weren't the kind of thing you'd hear on the radio – the BBC would have rather packed up shop than play the blatantly sexual, patently 'rude' songs by the likes of Prince Buster. Nor were the performers to be seen on the television music programmes of the day. It was all a bit too raw, and the media were really interested only in the clean-cut (the naughty but nice Beatles) or the acceptably watered down (the Rolling Stones).

Early Motown was 'gay music' every bit as much as Hi-Energy is now. Today, listening to songs like the Marvelettes' 'When You're Young and in Love', Martha Reeves and the Vandellas' 'Third Finger, Left Hand' (the wonderful 'B' side to 'Jimmy Mack'), Jimmy Ruffin's 'What Becomes of the Broken Hearted?' and 'I've Passed This Way Before', the Supremes' 'Stop in the Name of Love', Marvin Gaye's 'I Heard It Through the Grapevine', the Isley Brothers' 'This Old Heart of Mine (Been Broke a Thousand Times)', the Four Tops' 'Reach Out, I'll Be There' and 'Standing in the Shadows of Love', the Temptations' 'My Girl' and 'Ain't Too Proud to Beg', Mary Wells' 'My Guy' or Smokey Robinson and the Miracles' 'You've Really Got a Hold on Me' and 'I Gotta Dance (to Keep from Crying)' – I realise how romantic and deeply sentimental they were. But they spoke directly to *us*.

This wasn't mass-produced music accepted by all and sundry. It seemed – to us – to be our exclusive preserve. Speeding out of our minds, generally filled with a sense of well-being and affection towards our fellows, we *were* sentimental and romantic. Whilst speed might have encouraged aggression in the Mods, it seemed to heighten our emotional feelings.

As we danced along to Motown's idealistic songs, we fell in love. We fell in love every weekend. Often affairs were brief – started on Sunday morning, over by Monday night. But the high obtained from the speed, the music and the companionship meant that these transitory flings were passionate and intense. And who is to say they were any less valid than romances which last for weeks, months, years?

We didn't listen to much 'white' music. Most of what was around seemed unutterably bland and wet. Almost the only white music we listened to was that performed by singers who had been influenced by black American soul music – who themselves had soul. The Righteous Brothers' 'You've Lost That Lovin' Feeling' – with a blockbuster Phil Spector production – hit the right emotional button. Dusty Springfield's 'You Don't Have to Say You Love Me' was another firm favourite. But then we all agreed – Dusty, with her panda-eye make-up and stiffly lacquered beehive hair-do, was always guaranteed to crank out a good heart-rending number sung with as much soul as any white singer could decently manage.

We were generally fairly promiscuous, though I don't suppose we thought of our behaviour as particularly sexually abandoned. And though we might have a love affair a week, these still had about them something of the ritual quality of old-fashioned romance.

I remember a pattern – Saturday night, Le Duce. Standing against a wall. Looking around. Seeing someone. Thinking: he's cute. But that might be as far as it would go on that occasion. However, the following weekend you'd maybe nod to each other, dance together a few times. Maybe make a date to meet later in the week – for a drink, a movie. As Le Duce was very much a 'youth' club, a lot of the members still lived at home with mum and dad – which added complications to the process of getting someone into bed. Of course, it happened. But the very difficulties of the situation added to the romantic aura. Sex was led up to – rather than an instant inevitability.

Of course, I may simply be looking back down the time tunnel with distorting glasses. That's certainly the way *I* remember it. Yet Ian McGee – whom I first became friendly with at that time and whom I've lived with, in one way or another, for the past twenty years – recollects things very differently. Always more sexually active then me, he remembers the pulling of those days in a far more prosaic way.

We certainly agree, however, that Le Duce was a Saturday night ritual.

In the days when the club was in decline, I wrote an article for John Stamford's original *Spartacus* magazine which tried to capture some of the magic of those Soho nights. What I wrote then still stands and the following is a revised version of that account of a soul sound, Soho, Saturday night.

It's any Saturday night. The setting is Soho, the pubs are just turning out. From each of these watering places rises an incredible motley din and from the areas fast around rises an awful stink. The din is made by those drinking up, slurping their beer in last frenzied moments; singing, shouting, brawling.

The stink shivering in the air, hovering over all, comes from the vegetables rotting underfoot – the debris of the daytime market which is plied in Berwick Street – from the pools of vomit and the walls running with piss from those already out of the pubs and lurching about the streets in search of further pleasures.

High, perched in tiny windows, sit the weary whores, beckoning, calling down to prospective punters – and withdrawing sharply at the sight of 'Old Bill', the police. Low, in the gutters, are the cabbage leaves and fish-heads discarded from the market stalls. Fallen amongst this vegetable matter are the men who are too drunk to move.

By day Berwick Street is a market for one kind of essential; by night a market for every other kind of essential in a man's life. And mixed with all this is a heap of muck awaiting the sweep of the big corporation broom which can never – however hard it tries – get this area clean.

This is Saturday night.

The crowd. Late night theatre parties, lost in the noise, scream shrill Saturday night sounds, lost off Shaftesbury Avenue. Bold explorers quickly made timid by the drunks – raucous, reeling, jovial at the moment, but ever ready to turn and push fist into flesh and then, a little after midnight, find their way home.

The body of the crowd – the flesh to the spine of drunkenness – the teenagers, the three-quarters reason for this mid-Sixties Soho life. The young, fifteen to early twenties, come into the West End from, most especially, the south and east of London, only within the last hour or so. Boys and girls together. Boys so often seeming small, pretty, peacock-preened; girls often appearing tougher – with hair sometimes boyishly cropped and wearing less exotic garb. The boys rainbow-arrayed, with elaborate coils of hair, clothes in different colours and fabrics. Boys and girls together – who can tell them apart, who wants to be apart, who plays which role now?

Some of them may have come into town after hours dancing at their local palais, but most will have arrived, slightly bleary-eyed, from hours – six 'til ten – preening and peering before a mirror. The West End crowd is almost completely different from those who stick to local clubs and haunts. And as they step aboard the underground trains – in John Stephen, Take 6, Lord John, Girl or Fifth Avenue clothes; at outer London stations, Leytonstone, Tooting, Clapham or Mile End – the ritual of Saturday night is beginning.

The young. Compass-pointed towards their all-night clubs. The point for which the rest of the week is all too often lived through. What else do those who must struggle all their lives have to do? What expectations have they? Too soon even this small pleasure will be gone and they who see life clearly, clearly don't want to. They know that ambition's for a select few and that few even of those are capable of fulfilling it.

All-night clubs. Clubs which cater to all tastes, which, astonishingly, show very little of the prejudices and discriminations fed down from older generations – parents, newspapers, television, radio. Clubs whose brief but busy life extends from Friday night to Sunday morning – but which are always there, mostly empty during the week, sad with a hungry juke-box and a bar-boy eager to talk to relieve the boredom.

Hurrying up through unseen sordidness, no more than five foot six, with dark unruly hair which flops about as he speeds along, large dark eyes and a mischievous mouth ever ready to break into a warm and friendly grin. This is Johnnie and he comes from the East End.

He is the youngest of a family of eleven, he is under-educated; he is vital and alive, full of fun. It is extremely unlikely that he will ever go far in the world. He has too much against him. Johnnie is fifteen and gay, has been for a couple of years. Already he drifts from job to job – looking for something that will suit him, something that will hold his interest, something which will pay a decent wage. Not much chance of that.

Though he moves quickly, there is no sense of haste. The dirt and violence do not touch him – he is part of it and it is part of him. This is Soho, this is Saturday night. This is part of what he lives and works the dreary week for.

He turns the corner into Darblay Street and is momentarily knocked back by the smell of fish from the kosher fishmongers. Ignoring this, he continues walking. With a few more strides he has attained his goal. 'The club.'

It's always called *the club* – though it does have a rarely used name: Le Duce. To all who go there, *the club* is sufficient designation. Le Duce is situated in a far from comfortable basement – pine-panelled, with upholstered benches around the walls and a fish-tank embedded in the central partition. It's always crowded in the club on Saturday nights, some-times hellishly so. Steaming hot. Membership is ten shillings a year, admission five shillings per night.

Johnnie considers that five shillings is money well spent, for he will be on the premises for the next eight hours – crammed, not knowingly uncomfortable, dancing, talking, never standing still. Never with time to be unhappy. Without time to face the cold reality of his life. He will be *happy*.

Down the stairs, money slipped through the little hatch, a ticket pushed into his hand. The pugilistic-looking boy at the cash-desk presses a buzzer and the door into the club swings open.

The until now soft Motown sounds blast out, fly up the stairs as if in an attempt to escape. Then they are once again trapped as Johnnie slips into the club and the door slams shut behind him. Inside the club his ticket is taken from him, torn in half and a half returned to him with the warning that he should hang on to it. If he goes out of the club for any reason he will need this stub to regain entrance once more. This is business – and without the ticket stub he could be made to pay admission a second time.

Inside the lighting is dim, cigarette smoke hangs heavy in the air. By now the club has been in action for over two hours. The heat is intolerable, the noise is deafening. The jukebox won't stop grinding out its selection of Tamla and soul favourites until the last staff member has left. The coffee machine won't stop hissing and groaning – and breaking down – until that same moment. Above this din, the members shout to make themselves heard. Shout, whisper confidentially and sing along with favourite records.

The club is famous for its jukebox, which houses a massive selection of Motown favourites, soul sounds and a mixture of old and new favourites dating back over the past five years.

'This old heart of mine's been broke a thousand times . . .' sing the Isley Brothers, and a hundred or so voices are raised to echo the sentiment. Eyes lock for a brief moment as all those on the dance floor sing the words and a feeling of togetherness, of belonging – though few would admit that's what it is – surges through the place.

All these hearts have been broken a thousand times – or that's what it feels like. At each comedown party, on each Sunday, these hearts break a little. Suddenly everyone is slightly, shockingly linked.

Little Johnnie wanders around the club, greeting people, stopping here to talk, nodding, grinning, excited, executing a rapid dance to a song which strikes into his consciousness.

By now the eyes of most people in the place are slightly glassy. The jaws chew, chew, chew on the gum which is a necessary accompaniment to the speed.

The litany begins.

'Got any doobs, mate? Got any gear? I want some sweeties to crunch on. Gotta get high. It's Saturday night. Gotta get blocked out me mind. A handful of blues? Got any doobs, mate? Got any gear?'

Round, round. Easily found. Into the loo with a handful or two. Standing in line with the boys and the girls with the pills, the phials, methedrine, heroin, waiting to fix, he, Johnnie, waiting for the chance to get to the sink and fill his tumbler with the water which will wash the chemical handful into his bloodstream.

Somewhere in the club Maria, from Liverpool, who fixes H, is better off by a pound. She gets doobs on scrip and pushes them so that she can afford to buy her fix. Soon she'll have to register for H and a source of pills will disappear, but no matter. Someone else will sign on with a bent doctor, complaining they're overweight, and the fast-flowing river of speed will continue to run.

He's happier, bouncier, more irrepressible now. He can't keep still. Each new record sets his body afire with the urge to thrust and gyrate in an orgy of movement at once erotic yet curiously sexless. All around the dancers, boys with boys, girls with girls, boys with girls and boys and girls alone – pill happy, dancing, forgetting the awful drabness of their everyday living. They can welcome eight hours without sleep; remain active and – only slightly tired – complain as, at seven o'clock, the call goes up: Last record! This is your last record!

Fifteen-year-old Johnnie, who's been hopping in and out of bed with other men since he was thirteen, looks around at the men with the anglepoise bodies – the slightly older gays who are ever ready to twist and bend and turn to catch sight of a bit of bona trade. They belong to a different world. Le Duce is predominantly a club for teenagers, it is almost incidental that they are gay or bisexual. *They* come here for the music, to dance, for the speed. Sex is a part of their pleasure, but a minor part. Something that happens *afterwards*. The older club members are different. The new attitudes confuse them and though they try hard to fit into this unisexual world, they feel a little incongruous.

They leave early – long before the club closes. But if they go home alone they feel no sense of self-pity, they leave with the hope that next week they'll pull, next week things will be easier.

The elated hours wind around. Hours of movement broken up by trickles of talk and rumination, glasses of milk and coca-cola (the club is not licensed), cigarettes. Then the hands of their watches are pointing near to seven o'clock. The strains of the long night begin to tell. The walls sweat. The floor is a slippery mess. Heat and dryness choke all speech into silence. The music is everything, the sounds reverberate on and like some primitive, automatic ritual, the dancing continues. Eyes glaze and sight is at half power. Palms are sticky and oozing sweat. Crotches are shrunken and prickly-heat uncomfortable. Hair is wet and matted, noses foggy with smoke, clogged; heads aching, feet trodden on and sore.

The last record. Everyone still awake – and many have by now fallen asleep on the seats – gets up to dance. The record is slow, romantic. People cling onto each other and shuffle numbly around the floor. The song surges and bursts and the dancers fling into a final moment of abandon. Then . . . a moment of utter silence.

Noise begins again with a buzz of disappointment. The weekend's over. There is a mounting chatter as a mob of bodies struggle for coats and bags from the tiny cloakroom. Up the stairs and out into the seamy Soho sunless early Sunday morning.

Little knots of people stand around shivering and planning their day. Some will stay together in an attempt to keep alive – to extend for a few more exhausted hours – the euphoria of Saturday night. Others drift off along the narrow street. 'See you next weekend, girl,' one calls as he trudges away from his friends. 'Bona night!'

One group link arms and in a last defiant burst of energy skip away down the street and out of sight.

Johnnie joins a crowd off to a flat in nearby Greek Street where they'll come down off speed together, bitch about those no longer present, argue, make love, maybe take some more blues and talk, talk, talk. But the weekend is over. This is just another way of parting. The weekend has had its triumphant ten hours or more; the week looms large ahead – gaunt, lacking in pleasure – and this spectre brings descending depression. Yet the thought that another soul sound, Soho, Saturday night is only six days away causes the cloud of gloom to lift. Who cares? It will soon be here.

Peter Burton, *Parallel Lives* (1985)

1964: The Ad-Lib

The Ad-Lib opened in February 1964 on the Soho penthouse premises of an unsuccessful night club called Wips. Nick Luard of the Establishment and the late Lord Willoughby had founded Wips and aimed it at the jet set. It was very expensive, projected a mild flavour of perversity, fur walls and carnivorous fish, and meant nothing. It was bought by Bob and Alf Barnett, who already owned several trad night clubs, and they put in John Kennedy, who had been Tommy Steele's first manager, to run it for them. He too suspected that the time for the discothèque had arrived. He installed amplification, cut down the tables to knee-height, replaced the chairs by stools and banquettes, got rid of the fish. Above all he hung large mirrors everywhere. 'A club needs movement,' is how he puts it, but I feel he realized, whether consciously or not, that the whole hippy world is obsessively narcissistic. They don't dance for each other's benefit but for their own. Kennedy told me he never got over his amazement at the indifference of the men. 'The girls at the Ad-Lib,' he said, 'they're such little dollies, but where do they come from? You don't see them anywhere else. And they dance so sexily, but for all the reaction they get they might as well not be there. Now when I was that age, they'd have driven me mad!' Being extremely bright he has drawn profit out of these observations. The club discourages older members because of their tendency to leer. It bars girls on their own and, although less rigidly, boys too. The physical set-up helps avoid arguments. The only way up to the club is in a small lift which is less conducive to aggression than being able to blunder in out of the street. The club itself has a low ceiling with inset coloured lights. Its great asset is a huge window looking down on London. For the pop stars, fashion photographers and young actors this must suggest a conquered world. The music is very loud: a constant feud with a nearby Catholic priest is the club's one headache; the clothes reflect Carnaby Street at its most extreme; the dancing is really breathtaking in its expertise. It's not very expensive, you can eat steak or chicken in a basket for about a pound, and drinks, after twenty-five shillings for the first one which includes cover, are about ten shillings a miniature with ice and coke thrown in. The mid-Atlantic bias of the pop world is carried over into its drinking habits. It is, however, extremely difficult to become a member nowadays without some special distinction. Admittedly the eminence involved is unlikely to carry much weight in the Corridors of Power, but this club is the celebration of a certain breakthrough. It is dedicated to the triumph of style. It may be chic, non-committed and a-moral, but it's also cool, tolerant and physically beautiful.

215

It's essentially to do with being young, and those who attack it are in many cases motivated by envy at the sight of young people, many of them of working-class origin, with the means and poise to enjoy themselves. These critics remind me of women who oppose painless childbirth because *they* suffered. There's a lot of snobbery involved, and the idea that this club and what it represents is somehow undermining serious art is to turn the whole thing upside down. It's not the young who are to blame, but those older people, whether artists or not, who ape them.

The Ad-Lib was lucky in that it opened just after the beat groups had begun to make it, and provided an atmosphere in which they felt at ease. John Lennon was the first Beatle to go there. Then Ringo came and, to quote Kennedy, 'made it his home'. Within seven weeks the club had it made.

George Melly, *Revolt into Style* (1970)

1964: Six hip malchicks

It is the summer of the night
London's eyes be tight shut
all but twelve peepers and
six hip malchicks who prance
the street. Newspaper strewn
and grey which waits another day
to hide its dirgy countenance
the six have been sound ball
journey made to another sphere
which pays royalties in eight months
or a year.
Sound is over back eight visions
clear and dear. Friends, here
are your new groovies so please
a-bound to the sound of THE ROLL-
ING STONES. We walk past flat-
blocks 'There's a femme in a frock'.
'Come on luv', says Bill, 'Give us
a kiss of Christmas', 'for why I
should,' says she, 'You bods ain't
Mistahs, with hair like that
you should wear skirts, not shirts!'

What about Charles I? says Mick,
'I am Charles I' says she – 'ah
dear' foiled again said Keith, whose
quite a wit, 'she'd have kissed you in
Richmond'.
Well, my groobies, what about Richmond?
With its grass green and hippy scene
from which the Stones untaned. The cry
in those days of May was have you heard
of STONES, a new groupie who look wild
and good. Their music is Berry-
chuck and all the Chicago hippies.
Travel to Chicago and ask the malchek
plebbies where is Howlin' Wolf?
Be he be not the one with Cheyanie
Bodie. Oh my groogie back to your window
box. Meanwhile back in Richmond, THE
STONES have grown and people come from
far and wide to hear the STONES
'Somewhat like the Pied Piper',
one mal observed. 'What a wit',
said Keith. A day in May at
Richmond came to the treen, two
showbiz genties with ideas plenty
for THE STONES, Easton and Oldham
named they were. The rest is not
history so I'll tell you bout it.
Records followed so did
fame, Beatles wrote a song for them
that got to number ten. Tours
of the country and fame at large THE
STONES were here, and we'll be back
with you when break commercial is
over. (This is THE STONES new disc
within. Cast deep in your
pockets for loot to buy this disc
of groovies and fancy words. If
you don't have bread, see that blind man
knock him on the head, steal his

wallet and low and behold you have
the loot, if you put in the boot, good,
another one sold!)
Back to the show, all was on the go,
fame was having its toll of sweat and
grime of a million dimes, ah! What a
lovely war, Man, Easton called a
meet one day; Stones arrived. 'Columbus
went to America, so shall we!', so we
went, naturally. They want you in France,
in Germany you can dance. No, Brian,
no need to grow a moustache. That's all over.
It's different now –
come on, just you see.
So see we did, all over the globe, here
and there. I remember when we arrived
one day at a town called Knokke-le-Zoute.
Imagine my surprise and of the plane we got
that Charlie had on the same suit. 'Never
mind', said Mick, 'go to your analyist,
he'll sort you out'.
So off we went, Charlie and me.
The doctor knew the score. 'Change
your tailor', said he, as he handed
us a bill for 50 gins. 'Ah', said
Keith, who is quite a wit, 'such is
fame'. So now it's time to ponder
as my penmind can write no longer.
What to say on the back of this bag
of groovies. I could tell, tale of
talent, fame and fortune and stories
untold of how these teen peepers
(eyes, that is, to you) have taken
groupdom by storm, slur you with
well-worn cliches, compare them
to Wagner, Stravinsky and Paramour.
I could say more about talent that
grows in many directions. To
their glory and their story, let the

trumpets play. Hold on there, what
I say is from the core of this
malchik. To this groupie that I have
grown with and lived with . . . Dear
Mick, Keith, Brian, Bill and Charlie –
please autograph this leg I send you
'cause man, that's the sign
of a real fan!

Andrew Loog Oldham, sleeve note: Rolling Stones No. 2 (1964)

1964: The Soul Clan

This is where I came in – with the pre-revolutionary rise and legend of James
Brown. Not that I had any idea about Muscle Shoals or Macon or even James
at the time. Stax was just a name on a record label to me, and while the
red-and-black Atlantic logo may have been just as hallowed in my mind as it
was in Jim Stewart's or Rick Hall's, my only connection to soul music in
1964–1965 was as a star-struck, uninformed, but dedicated fan. I want to
describe my introduction to soul music a little bit, though, not because it is
significant in itself but because it is to some degree emblematic. And because
if what I have written so far suggests a logical, or reasoned, historical
progression, it is important to emphasize that the pattern which linked such
structural anarchists as Dan Penn and Chips Moman, such sui generis
performers as Solomon Burke and James Brown, was decidedly less discern-
ible at the time.

The first soul show I went to see came to town in June of 1964 and was
booked into the long-since-demolished Donnelly Theatre on the edge of
Roxbury, Boston's black community. Sam Cooke was still alive, Ray Charles
(whom my friends and I had gone to see at Jordan Hall while still in high
school) was already a legend, and the Summer Shower of Stars had been
hyped for weeks with lung-bursting fervor on WILD, Boston's only all-black
radio station. Headlining the bill was Solomon Burke, whose current hit was
'Good-bye Baby'. Garnet Mimms and a virtually unknown Otis Redding got
second billing, while underneath them on the poster were Joe Tex (yet to
have his breakthrough hit), the Tams, and a very sexy Sugar Pie DeSanto. My
memories of the occasion are clear; my recollections of Solomon's apocalyptic message and Otis's rather blocky presence, as well, of course, as Sugar
Pie DeSanto's torrid dance, remain vivid. The revue was just coming off a

Southern tour, I have since learned, on which James Brown served as cohead-liner, and if my image of the show that I saw is mind-boggling, the fantasy projection of James and Solomon competing each night on the same stage almost defies imagination. And yet the reality was at the same time both more prosaic and more exotic.

More prosaic in that this was only one of thirty or forty-five days out on the road for each of the headliners, all of them crammed on to a single tour bus (Solomon was very likely the lone exception) which might travel no farther than Hartford, Connecticut, for the next night's show or then again might continue on nonstop to Raleigh, North Carolina. I don't think Rufus Thomas or Joe Tex even showed up for that evening's performance, but that, I soon came to realize, was par for the course, and, so far as I can recall, their absence was never even announced from the stage or remarked upon by the cheerful, well-dressed, and enthusiastic audience which seemed to saunter in and out of the theater in waves, with many missing the opening act, some leaving before the closing act was done. It was the *occasion*, I came to understand very quickly, that was of consequence as much as the show itself. There was a spirit of community in that packed theater, encouraged, cer-tainly, by the performers but springing from a common experience, an openly shared perception of reality, that was both palpable and infectious. *New York Times* reporter Clayton Riley has described his childhood mem-ories of the Apollo in a somewhat earlier, more decorous era, how 'folks just showed out, as the saying went, came gliding through the Apollo lobby with proud, confident grace, wearing the best clothes and finest manners, women in delicate veils, big hats, men wearing fabulous overcoats and sculptured mustaches, the air around everybody turning into a mixed breeze of perfume and lotion ... We could hear from every space in the Apollo that good old rich laughter of recognition ... We thought it was magic.'

I certainly did, and I wished with every fiber of my being that the recogni-tion could include me, or at least my good intentions, that I, who was so visibly not part of the community, could somehow be absorbed within it. Everyone has their stories of being the lone white face in the crowd, and I don't think mine or anyone else's are particularly significant, but there was clearly a sense – both then and now – of entering into an alien environment, of stepping out of my world into a land uncharted and inviolable. Perhaps this added to the romance of the occasion, perhaps it added to the suspense, knowing that at any moment all this *oneness* could turn on you – but I don't think so. I think I was merely envious and scared; my exclusion was only one more impetus to make me wish I was black and free of all the encumbrances of a bourgeois world, the same duality that Donnie Fritts must have come face to face with in Florence, Alabama, or Mick Jagger in Dartford, England.

The next time I saw Otis Redding, it was a couple of years later, and he was at the height of his fame, but he was playing at a club called Louie's Showcase Lounge in Roxbury, which couldn't have seated more than 500 people. In the daylight I'm sure Louie's must have appeared drab enough, little more than a seedy joint stuck on the corner of Northampton and Washington streets in the shadow of the El, but at night it took on the dimensions of an enchanted palace, with its stage set windows of cheap colored glass, its crowded dance floor filled with all manner of the most explosively languid and graceful dancers, and its air of convivial expectation, the easygoing, good-hearted assumption that everyone was going to have a good time. The MC was Jimmy 'Early' Byrd, who was never loath to let on that he might be the cousin of Famous Flame Bobby Byrd and who was then the reigning DJ on WILD (which meant that he broadcast in the afternoon, since WILD went off the air at sunset). The band would strike up an introduction, Byrd, a big good-looking man, would come ditty-bopping on with a grin a mile wide, and it was Showtime, Ladies and Gentlemen, the man who brought you 'These Arms of Mine', 'That's How Strong My Love Is', 'I've Been Loving You Too Long', 'Mr Pitiful' himself – pregnant pause – Otis . . . Redding . . .

Speedo Simms, Otis's road manager, still remembers Louie's fondly. So do Alan Walden and Otis's brother, Rodgers. I don't know why this should have surprised me, but somehow I think it must have seemed to me that Louie's was an aberration; the memory of the occasion is so invested with significance, so full of consequence that the tawdry surroundings seem in retrospect as if they must have represented an indignity best forgotten. But, of course, they did not. Louie's *was* the r&b world, and Boston, for some inexplicable reason, welcomed the Southern soulsters (Otis, Solomon, Joe Tex, and even James Carr were regular visitors) with a warmth that, I understand from hometown chauvinist Joe McEwen, a more geographically logical city like Philadelphia did not. On the corner a couple of blocks up from Louie's sat Skippy White's Mass. Records: Home of the Blues, a little bandbox of a record store run by a white man named Fred LeBlanc (Skipp was an invention, White a translation), who, with his own show on WILD and local distribution of many of the independent r&b labels, had his own dreams of empire at the same time that we constructed mythologies about *him*. Probably there was a Skippy White in every city. Very likely every Skippy White had a speaker out on the sidewalk broadcasting the latest sides and inviting passersby to try out the latest, smoothest, slickest steps with all the signifying that public performance entailed. To me and my friends, I know, it was the outpost of a new world to which we eagerly, humbly, and, as anonymously as our skin color would permit, sought entrance.

After that first Summer Shower of Stars I never missed a show. At some point a girl I knew started living with a guy who had something to do with bringing in the revues to the Donnelly, by now the Back Bay, and I got a chance to be an 'usher'. Not much of an usher, I must confess, since, though the seats were reserved, the idea of approaching a rather large gentleman and telling him he was occupying the wrong space was not within my sense of civic responsibility, and when the balcony fire-escape doors flew open and a bunch of kids came bursting in, I always managed to be occupied in some other part of the building. I was twenty, twenty-one, twenty-two, in love with the blues, writing even then for fledgling magazines like *Crawdaddy!* and the *Boston Phoenix* strictly out of devotion to the music and surprise that anyone else could be interested enough in it to provide a forum for what I had to say. What really startled me, though, was to find that the music was still alive, to discover in soul a contemporary analogue to the blues – with a somewhat different musical base perhaps, but with the same direct message, the same generous outpouring of spirit, the same warmth, unpredictability, and prizing of naked truth.

This may well have been a somewhat romantic distortion of reality, and it may also have been what closed off the world of Motown to me. Perhaps I simply rejected Motown out of ideological considerations, for the very reason that it was so much more popular, so much more socially acceptable, so much more arranged and predictable, so much more white – but I felt like what *I* was listening to was the harbinger of a new day. In these terms I would no more have judged the shows that we attended than I would have judged the Civil Rights Movement, the French New Wave, my own vocation as a writer, or anything else to which I gave my wholehearted assent. The shows were spectacle, an existential process (not mere entertainment) which followed its own logic, its own time frame, and offered the pace, contrasts, and variety of vaudeville and life. If a performer was not to your taste, there was always the audience. If I didn't especially like the sound of Little Anthony and the Imperials (frequent visitors to Boston), I could certainly appreciate the group's acrobatics. The comedians – Pigmeat Markham and Slappy White, George Kirby and Boston's own Wildman Steve – were uniformly vulgar, and uniformly predictable, but reassuringly so, lending further credence to the notion that everyone could let their hair down because they were at home and among friends. As commonplace as any aspect of the show might be, it was always met with a sense of appreciation and good-natured tolerance that I observed in no other area of the world in which I lived.

Surprisingly I never considered approaching any of the performers directly. Taking my heart in my hand, I was already interviewing blues singers like Skip James and Buddy Guy and Howlin' Wolf. Overcoming the gravest reservations of self-consciousness and self-doubt, I had addressed serious, respectful, blushing questions to these earlier heroes of mine. Why not Jackie Wilson or Otis Redding, then? Why not Solomon Burke or James Brown, whose performance and records I was enthusiastically recommending in print? I'm not altogether sure. Looking back on it, it has come to seem to me that the magazines I was writing for were more interested in interviews with the legendary blues figures precisely *because* the blues form in effect had been abandoned by its original partisans (black) and was ripe for the taking by a new breed of audience and enthusiast (white), which could establish its own terms of appreciation. Maybe this is overly cynical or simplistic, but there *weren't* any interviews with Otis Redding, all that remains of Sam Cooke's on-the-record observations are the usual fan club trivia, and I know that the idea of approaching Joe Tex would no more have occurred to me than the notion of seeking a presidential audience. The closest I came to a backstage insight was one time when Jackie Wilson came offstage after a typically vigorous performance, and I happened to be standing in the wings. He marched off, shoulders back, chest outthrust, seemingly impervious to the blood that was trickling down his shirt from the clutchings of an overzealous fan. The band kept vamping as Jackie stood beside me and seemed almost to shrivel, his chest slumped, his chin fallen; then, as the applause kept up, he strutted out on stage again, and I felt as if I had gained a first-hand glimpse into the oldest conundrum in show business. The idea of asking Jackie himself his thoughts on the subject would simply never have entered my mind.

I listened to the radio. I hung out at Skippy White's, cashed my paycheck in his store in exchange for 45s, and picked up his soul charts, designed perhaps to push the product that he was distributing and the music that he unqualifiedly loved as much as to reflect true sales figures in the Boston area. It didn't matter. This was romance, not life. Where in my devotion to the blues I pored over matrix numbers, drew elaborate connections, subscribed to a magazine called *Blues Unlimited*, which originated in England, and considered myself a bona fide pursuer of the truth, in soul, although I soon became aware of the existence of a number of English fanzines, neither their earnest scholarship nor the fellowship of a faraway coterie of true believers seemed as significant. On the radio it was the *sounds* that mattered, not the names, it was the DJ rapping and my parents' cleaning man (Woodrow Wilson Moon, who had introduced me to WILD in the first place) chuckling and singing along with song after song by artists like Jesse James, Phil Flowers and Freddie Scott, who in many cases had never been heard from before and very likely would never be heard of again. It wasn't the *stars* primarily, it was the seamless sound of soul, the brotherhood and sisterhood and common aspirations of man. For me the experience suggested that there was a community out there speaking in a single voice, the rhetoric was all of unity and freedom – in politics and literature as well as music. That I was not of that community, that I could not even *presume* to seek inclusion, was not of real consequence – it was heartening simply that this unified feeling could exist at a time when I saw society fragmenting all around me, not least on the issue of race. I could introduce quotes from my writing at this point that would mortify me for their assumption of liberal guilt; I could unearth passages from this period that refer unabashedly, I'm sure, to the 'nobility of suffering', the 'cry of an anguished people'. But my firmest memories are of the music.

James Brown we still hadn't seen, but the legends about him grew and grew, even as 'Papa's Got a Brand New Bag' and 'I Got You (I Feel Good)' careened to the top of the charts, and his 1963 album, *Live at the Apollo*, remained the standard by which we measured all live performance. James Brown, we heard, had performed at some unlikely venue in Worcester. He had made an unannounced appearance at the Masonic Lodge in Roxbury. James Brown was so hot he was banned in Boston. The rumors were endless, the reputation almost mythic, but the focus was on a performer so galvanizing in person, so charismatic that, just as at the gospel shows, strong men fainted and women wept. The first that we actually saw of James Brown was in the movie, the *T.A.M.I. Show*, with a string of pop stars (the Beach Boys, Petula Clark, Chuck Berry, and the Miracles among them) and a performance by James that was nothing less than revelatory. He screamed, he stood stock-still, he exploded with lightning precision, he skated on one leg – and he completely stole the show from the Rolling Stones, whom my friends and I were initially almost as interested in seeing. Not six months after that, in December 1965, we saw James Brown in person. A friend got married, and we drove directly from the wedding reception to the Providence Arena (further confirming our suspicion that Boston was simply not prepared for

James, though hindsight tells me it was probably only a promoter's injunction that prevented him from appearing there), where we entered into yet another world.

'The show is ritual,' I wrote of it sagely about a year later, in preview of James Brown's first subsequent Boston-area appearance. 'The Famous Flames hypnotically sway and harmonize as a background to his performance, the audience cries out, and James's voice rises above theirs. He dances with wonderful grace and agility, he slides across the floor on one leg, he pushes the mike out into the audience and catches it bouncing back, his feet move with such speed as to make him appear suspended in air. As he goes into "Please, Please, Please", he lets go of the mike and catches it, falling to his knees. He screams and then his voice sinks to a low moan ... The Flames wrap a cape around his shoulders, help him to his feet and lead him off. In frustration he shakes off the cloak, stamps his feet, grabs the mike, and screams as he falls to the floor once again. It happened last night, and it's going to happen again tomorrow night; it may all be carefully calculated, but he's into it now, he loses himself in it each time. It happens in front of our eyes.'

I didn't go far enough. This was the greatest theater I had ever seen, or most likely ever would see. This was what all the 'happenings' and 'be-ins' that we attended looking for a new form of participatory drama could only grope for, this was a kind of magic that no theory or academic study could even envision, let alone conjure up. James Brown, a tiny figure on a large stage, moving like a marionette without strings, driven to perform in a manner that invited comparison with no one but a compulsive entertainer like Al Jolson – James Brown was a figure whose legend only suggested his reality.

Peter Guralnick, *Sweet Soul Music* (1986)

1965: The Rolling Stones

In Liverpool one time, early in 1965, I was sitting in some pub, just next to the Odeon cinema, and I heard a noise like thunder.

I went outside and looked around but I couldn't see a thing. Just this noise of thunder, slowly getting closer, and also, more faint, another noise like a wailing siren. So I waited but nothing happened. The street stayed empty.

Finally, after maybe five full minutes, a car came round the corner, a big flash limousine, and it was followed by police cars, by police on foot and police on motorbikes, and they were followed by several hundred teenage girls. And these girls made a continuous high-pitched keening sound and their shoes banged down against the stone. They ran like hell, their hair down in their eyes, and they stretched their arms out pleadingly as they went. They were desperate.

The limousine came up the street towards me and stopped directly outside the Odeon stage door. The police formed cordons. Then the car door opened and the Rolling Stones got out, all five of them and Andrew Loog Oldham, their manager, and they weren't real. They had hair down past their shoulders and they wore clothes of every colour imaginable and they looked mean, they looked just impossibly evil.

In this grey street, they shone like sun gods. They didn't seem human, they were like creatures of another planet, impossible to reach or understand but most exotic, most beautiful in their ugliness.

They crossed towards the stage door and this was what the girls had been waiting for, this was their chance, so they began to surge and scream and clutch. But then they stopped, they just froze. The Stones stared straight ahead, didn't twitch once, and the girls only gaped. Almost as if the Stones weren't touchable, as if they were protected by some invisible metal ring. So they moved on and disappeared. And the girls went limp behind them and were quiet. After a few seconds, some of them began to cry.

In this way, whatever else, the Stones had style and presence and real control. They are my favourite group. They always have been.

To begin with, they used to play the Crawdaddy Club in Richmond and they laid down something very violent in the line of rhythm 'n' blues. They were enthusiasts then, they cared a lot about their music. Really, that was the only thing that linked them because they'd come from different backgrounds, very different situations, but they'd all grown up to the blues and, for a time, they got along.

At this point, they were only archetypal drop-outs. I mean, they weren't art students but they should have been, they had all the symptoms, that aggression, that scruffiness and calculated cool, that post-beat bohemianism. And in these very early 60s, before the age of T-shirts and baseball boots, the heavy art school cults were Ray Charles and Chuck Berry and Bo Diddley, Muddy Waters, Charlie Mingus and Monk, Allen Ginsberg and Jack Kerouac, Robert Johnson. If you were pretentious about it, you might stretch to a paperback translation of Rimbaud or Dostoyevsky, strictly for display. But the Stones weren't pretentious – they were mean and nasty, full-blooded, very tasty, and they beat out the toughest, crudest, most offensive noise any English band had ever made.

[Up to this, the British R&B scene had been desperately thin: Chris Barber,

226

the trad trombonist, had started a few sessions in the late 50s but, by 1960, the obvious boss was a harmonica-blower called Cyril Davies, who died just as the blues boom was finally lifting off the ground.

Davies was an earnest man and a good musician but he mostly rehashed the Americans, he made almost no attempt to translate things into English terms and that limited him. Still, he laid foundations.)

At any rate, the Stones were at the Crawdaddy, peddling stuff about midway between the bedrock Chicago blues of Muddy Waters and the pop-blues of Chuck Berry, and they built themselves a following. Naughty but nice, they were liked by Aldermaston marchers and hitch-hikers, beards and freaks and pre-Neanderthal Mods everywhere. Simply, they were turning into the voice of hooliganism.

As groups go, they were definitely motley: Mick Jagger, who sang, came out of a solid middle-class background and had been to the London School of Economics; Keith Richards came from Tottenham and was quite tough; Brian Jones wasn't tough at all – he was from Cheltenham, very safe, but he was insecure, neurotic, highly intelligent.

Charlie Watts had worked in an ad agency and, being a drummer, never talked; Bill Wyman was older, was married – he didn't quite belong.

Anyhow, the thing about them was that, unlike the Beatles, they didn't balance out but niggled, jarred and hardly ever relaxed. At all time, there was tension to them – you always felt there was a background chance of a public holocaust. That was partly what made them exciting.

In 1963, Andrew Loog Oldham became their manager.

Oldham, without doubt, was the most flash personality that British pop has ever had, the most anarchic and obsessive and imaginative hustler of all. Whenever he was good, he was quite magnificent.

His father having been killed in the war, he'd grown up with his mother, quite rich, and he was sent to public school. By the time he was sixteen, he was doing window displays for Mary Quant, the clothes designer, and then he spent a year bumming round the South of France before he came back to work in the cloakroom at the Ronnie Scott Club and be a publicist with Brian Epstein's NEMS. And that was the whole sum of his achievement at the time he first met the Stones. He was then nineteen years old.

What he had going for him was mostly a frantic yen to get up and out: he loathed slowness and drabness, age and caution and incompetence, mediocrity of all kinds, and he could not stand to work his way up steady like anyone else.

Instead, he barnstormed, he came on quite outrageous. He slabbed his face with make-up and wore amazing clothes and hid his eyes behind eternal shades. He was all camp and, when he was batting off nothing at all, he still shot fat lines and always played everything as ultimate big-time.

The great thing was, the way he pushed himself, he could either clean up or bomb completely. He couldn't possibly get caught by compromise.

Anyhow, the Stones were obviously just his meat. He caught them at Richmond and got hooked by their truculence, their built-in offensiveness. Also, he struck up immediate contact with Mick Jagger, who was greatly impressed by him and became almost his disciple, his dedicated follower in the ways of outrage.

So Oldham brought in Eric Easton, who was his partner and had capital. Easton, a stock businessman who handled such showbiz stuff as Bert Weedon and Julie Grant, wasn't unimpressed. 'But the singer'll have to go,' he said. 'The BBC won't like him.'

As manager, what Oldham did was to take everything implicit in the Stones and blow it up one hundred times. Long-haired and ugly and anarchic as they were, Oldham made them more so and he turned them into every-thing that parents would most hate, be most frightened by. All the time, he goaded them to be wilder, nastier, fouler in every way and they were – they swore, sneered, snarled and, deliberately, they came on cretinous.

It was good basic psychology: kids might see them the first time and not be sure about them, but then they'd hear their parents whining about those animals, those filthy long-haired morons, and suddenly they'd be converted, they'd identify like mad.

(This, of course, is bedrock pop formula: find yourself something that truly makes adults squirm and, straight away, you have a guaranteed smash on your hands. Johnnie Ray, Elvis, P. J. Proby, Jimi Hendrix – it never fails.)

So their first single, 'Come On', got to the edge of the twenty, and then 'I Wanna Be Your Man' was number ten, and 'Not Fade Away' was number three and, finally, 'It's All Over Now' was number one. Their initial album did a hundred thousand in a week and, by this time, they were running hot second to the Beatles and they kept it like that for two years solid. Later on, in America, they even temporarily went ahead.

All this time, Oldham hustled them strong: he was hectic, inventive and he pulled strokes daily. Less obviously, he was also thorough, he worked everything out to the smallest spontaneous detail. Well, the Stones were really his fantasy, his private dream-child and, healthy narcissist as he was, he needed them to be entirely perfect.

The bit I liked best, about both Oldham and the Stones themselves, was the stage act. In every way, both individually and collectively, it expressed them just right.

Charlie Watts played the all-time bombhead drummer, mouth open and jaw sagging, moronic beyond belief, and Bill Wyman stood way out to one side, virtually in the wings, completely isolated, his bass held up vertically in front of his face for protection, and he chewed gum endlessly and his eyes were glazed and he looked just impossibly bored.

Keith Richards wore T-shirts and, all the time, he kept winding and unwinding his legs, moving uglily like a crab, and was shut in, shuffling, the classic fourth-form drop-out. Simply, he spelled Borstal.

Brian Jones had beautiful silky yellow hair to his shoulders, exactly like a Silvrikin ad, and he wasn't queer, very much the opposite, but he camped it up like mad, he did the whole feminine thing and, for climax, he'd rush the front of the stage and make to jump off, flouncing and flitting like a gymslip schoolgirl.

And then Mick Jagger: he had lips like bumpers, red and fat and shiny, and they covered his face. He looked like an updated Elvis Presley, in fact, skinny legs and all, and he moved like him, so fast and flash he flickered. When he came on out, he went bang. He'd shake his hair all down in his eyes and he danced like a whitewash James Brown, he flapped those tarpaulin lips and, grotesque, he was all sex.

He sang but you couldn't hear him for screams, you only got some background blur, the beat, and all you knew was his lips. His lips and his moving legs, bound up in sausage-skin pants. And he was outrageous: he spun himself blind, he smashed himself and he'd turn his back on the audience, jack-knife from the waist, so that his arse stuck straight up in the air, and then he'd shake himself, he'd vibrate like a motor, and he'd reach the hand mike through his legs at you, he'd push it right in you face. Well, he was obscene, he was excessive. Of course, he was beautiful.

The weird thing was, Jagger on-stage wasn't like Jagger off-stage but he was very much like Andrew Oldham. Andrew Loog Oldham. I mean, he was more a projection of Oldham than of himself. (This happens often. For various obvious physical reasons, most managers aren't capable of getting out and being stars themselves. So they use the singers they handle as transmitters, as dream machines. Possibly, that's the way it was with Jagger and Oldham.)

Anyhow, what I was saying, the Stones had a wild stage act and, that time in Liverpool, the night I mentioned before, they put on maybe the best pop show I ever saw: final bonanza, hysterical and violent and sick but always stylized, always full of hype, and Jagger shaped up genuinely as a second Elvis, as heroic and impossible as that.

After the show, I hung around in the dressing-rooms. The Stones were being ritually vicious to everyone, fans and journalists and hangers-on regardless, and I got bored. So I went down into the auditorium and it was empty, quite deserted, but there was this weird smell. Piss: the small girls had screamed too hard and wet themselves. Not just one or two of them but many, so that the floor was sodden and the stench was overwhelming. Well, it was disgusting. No, it wasn't disgusting but it was strange, the empty cinema (chocolate boxes, cigarette packs, ice-lolly sticks) and this sad sour smell.

Nik Cohn, *Pop from the Beginning* (1969)

1965: A Uniform for an Era

It took me a while to learn what impact the colours I had ordered would make when they were delivered from the factory. When I saw our opening stock it looked like a funeral. The blackish brown and dark prune looked awful. I could only save it by stitching gold braid on the necks and sleeves. Poor Mother was commandeered with her needle. Biba and she sewed braid all night. The dresses still looked awful to me but we opened the shop the next day.

We had been looking for a manageress and Liz Dickson suggested a girl called Sarah Plunkett who worked at Belinda Bellville's. We immediately loved her. She was so calm and dignified and ladylike. But was she too aristocratic for us? We took the chance and she turned out to be marvellous. Sarah could control a crowd without upsetting anybody.

After a couple of weeks Sarah could hardly stand up for exhaustion. She needed help. She pointed out that there were two little girls who came in every evening after work. They were so pretty, with long blonde hair, and couldn't she ask them if one of them wanted a job? An interview was arranged one evening after the shop closed. After we had flushed out the last customer, two beautiful blonde girls came in. Irene and Eleanor: Eleanor Powell, pure Saxon and a very formal Virgo; Irene, of Polish-Russian extraction – a dreamer with her head in the clouds. They looked like fresh little foals with long legs, bright faces and round dolly eyes. They worked in Harrod's export department, but they wanted to work at Biba. The only problem was we had only reckoned on one assistant. We felt we couldn't run to two, but the girls were adamant. No division. We took on the pair of them.

The combination of the three girls was great. Sarah was twenty and Irene and Elly sixteen. We were the first shop to stay open until 8 p.m. every night but even we had not realized how busy we would be after 6 o'clock. The girls became exhausted. While Irene and Elly's social life flourished by their being in the shop, Sarah's suffered. Her private life was outside the shop hours, and by the time she got home it was 9 p.m. Liz Dickson again came to our rescue. In the street one day she had met a friend who had been working in Capri. Liz Smith came for an interview, which was conducted outside on the corner of Abingdon Road. Now we had another glamorous twenty-year-old to take over whenever one of the others flaked out after a heavy day. They were a powerful band of lovely girls, and completely involved in the work.

Fitz and I now had no other life than Biba. When the shop opened we had both given up our jobs. Every morning we would feel great anxiety. We were never sure if our customers would come back again. One Tuesday morning the weather was awful. The sky was grey, there was a feel of a thunderstorm coming. The shop was empty. By noon the shop was still empty. I was feeling really depressed – it had all been a flash in the pan, the bonanza was over. We dashed up the road to Kensington High Street. It was empty, too. Not a soul, not one old lady with a shopping basket on two little wheels. We soon realized that the shopping public reacts identically to the weather and the political situation. When they are depressed, they are *all* depressed at the same time. When the sun comes out they are *all* happy and go out shopping. When the sun is hot they go to the park to sunbathe and you've lost them. When it rains, if you're a little shop they don't come, if you are a big store they stay with you all day. But it was this neurosis that we found so exciting. For Fitz it was like fishing, and for me it was like junking. You never knew when you would catch a big one.

Our Saturdays were always spectacular, whatever the weather. If it was raining the shop stank of wet wool and the floor would be awash. If it was sunny the groups of newly found friends would congregate outside the shop. It became a meeting place. Years later I had letters from people who met at Biba, spent their courtship in Biba on Saturdays, married, had babies and wrapped them in Biba purple nappies. Our neighbour called her dog Biba, and recently I heard a beautiful girl at the airport calling, 'Biba, Biba' to a little girl of six in a straw hat and smock. Her mother told me that she had named her after our shop. We had become a big part of many people's lives.

At twenty-six Fitz and I felt much older than the others, like Mum, and

Dad. We worried about the girls and their fast life. Some could cope, but many fell by the wayside by nineteen. The fashion for LSD terrified me. My real life had become a sort of trip so I couldn't see why others needed this dangerous stimulation. But I know when I was eighteen I used to take a Preludin in the mornings to feel I was jumping from the moment I opened my eyes, and I suppose it was the same. Sometimes I pinched one of my mother's purple hearts, which the doctor prescribed for her to lift her spirits when she was feeling low. It's quite funny to think how many middle-aged women in the sixties were unknowingly reliant on amphetamines.

I don't think our girls were promiscuous; they picked and chose. If they fancied someone they went right out and got what they were after instead of weaving webs and hypocritical traps, as we had to in the fifties. In their flats and bedsits they had no mother waiting for them to see if they came home with a crumpled dress. In the buoyant mid-sixties they all had jobs and they were not used to eating massive meals. They were the postwar babies who had been deprived of nourishing protein in childhood and grew up into beautiful skinny people. A designer's dream. It didn't take much for them to look outstanding. The simpler the better, the shorter the better. Their legs seemed to be never-ending. Suddenly London was filled with long-legged girls and boys who became envied all over the world.

The girls and boys started to travel on new all-in cheap holidays, and to pick up continental elegance, too. There were masses of them and they all seemed to flock to Abingdon Road. With Cathy McGowan endorsing our clothes by wearing them nearly every week on TV, there was a sort of underground grapevine which was growing daily. As soon as there was a new style the tom-toms would beat out a message throughout the clubs and offices and the shop would be full again. Every girl could buy a new dress for her evening date. They might all turn up wearing the same uncomfortable Biba smock that itched and stopped their arms from bending, but it was a uniform for an era.

The girls aped Cathy's long hair and eye-covering fringe. Soon their little white faces were growing heavier with stage make-up, lids weighed down with doll-like fake lashes. Their matchstick legs were encased in pale tights and low-cut patent pumps. Miniskirts led to the adoption of tights. They seldom needed to wear roll-ons or bras. Their bosoms and tummies were so tiny there was no need for the heavy upholstery. The natural form was beginning to show.

All classes mingled under the creaking roof of Mr O'Grady's wobbly house. There was no social distinction. Their common denominator was youth and rebellion against the establishment. Sarah was the red light for the beat offspring of aristocratic families, while Irene and Elly knew the young working girls. Stars and would-be stars also flocked to the shop. One night as we were closing a tiny blonde girl came in and began taking the clothes off the hatstands. Instead of trying them on behind the dangerously wobbly screens she stripped off in the shop and proceeded to try on smocks and trouser suits. Fitz was told to stay in the back office as the tiny, uninhibited girl was prancing around dressed only in her knickers. She was magnetic – her skin was like marble and her features larger than life. It was Julie Christie, getting her wardrobe together for the film *Darling*.

One day a huge black limousine parked by the spiky railings outside the shop. A very strange group got out and sauntered in. All, female and male, were wearing the most exaggerated flared trousers. Ours were flared but not as much as these. For once I felt upstaged! The tops of those pants were so tight and so low on the hip they looked as if they might slip off. The boy who seemed to be the leader of the pack wore a sheepskin waistcoat. Excitement mounted in the shop. It was Sonny and Cher. Fitz and I had never heard of them. After their visit, during which they bought the entire shop out, Elly became very friendly with them and they visited her and she them for many years after. She would always send their daughter Chastity our newest baby clothes.

Another prominent American visitor was Richard Avedon. The young ones didn't know who the hell he was and I had to explain to them he was the top photographer in the world, and the one who had taken the pictures of Audrey Hepburn in *Funny Face*. This didn't impress our girls, who had their own heroes. These were Cilla Black, Sandie Shaw, the Beatles. Jane Ormsby Gore came to the shop wearing jeans she had cut off at the ankles and fringed at the hems. We were all ushered out from the back office to see this spectacle. It was odd at the time to see a society belle like this. She was tall and angular with short jet-black hair and a striking, angular face. She and her boyfriend Michael Rainey had opened a clothes shop in Chelsea for male pop stars, called Hung On You. Sometimes Mick Jagger would come in with his girlfriend Chrissie, who was Jean Shrimpton's sister. As he waited for her he would sit on the table by the till, chatting to Fitz. So many famous people were seen in the shop that our girls became very blasé about it, though they would usually buzz us upstairs to tell us who was in. I could never resist the opportunity to have a peep at a star.

There was a lovely skinny girl who visited Abingdon Road very frequently. She was even thinner than the rest of the crowd. Her thoughtful face was really beautiful, with big grey eyes, a very high forehead and small, slightly turned-up nose. Her name was Lesley Hornby, and she became Twiggy. Our clothes were minute, but we were once asked by Justin de Villeneuve, her manager, to take them in. Fitz and I didn't really get to know Twiggy until, many years later, she and her husband Michael became our closest friends.

In early 1965 we acquired a new member of the family, Kim, who was barely sixteen. Liz Smith had left us to become fashion editor on *Petticoat* magazine, and later of the *Observer* Colour Magazine, a meteoric rise! I know Liz now says she was the only smiling assistant, but I was quite adamant that the girls should not impose themselves on the customers. We were not going to become another 'Can I help you, madam?' shop. I wanted the customers to feel at home, not hounded by sales assistants. More to the point, our customers would have fled if they had been accosted. Irene, Elly and Kim became their friends. There was one very serious little girl who used to come to the shop and scrutinize every garment with a beady eye. Fitz would watch her face to see what had made a reaction. If *she* ever bought anything it *had* to be good. At our next round-up for more staff, the girl with the deadpan expression had applied for a job, and Eva was with us right up to the end in Big Biba. All our girls wore Biba clothes at work and, later, to go dancing.

On Friday nights we would go to the TV studio to watch *Ready, Steady, Go*. Would Cathy wear a Biba dress or a Tuffin and Foale? Cathy was professional: she would wear the best clothes she had been shown that week. I was green with envy when she chose 'Tuffy Fluffies', as Fitz called them. Sometimes Cathy wore Laura dresses, imported by Top Gear in the Kings Road. Laura was a shop in the suburbs of Paris; the designer there was Sonia Rykiel. The shop I was most envious of was Top Gear. It was run by James Wedge and Pat Booth. They imported the most beautiful of the French clothes, the sort that appeared in *Elle*. John Stephen's Carnaby Street was growing from strength to strength. Tourists from all over Europe were pouring into London for cheap weekends. They could buy suitcasefuls of clothes for virtually nothing as the exchange rate was so good. London was vibrating with French, Italians, Germans and Swedes coming to listen to the music, see the shops and gawp at the beautiful girls. We were selling mounds of T-shirts, accessories and still those one-size smocks and Winnie-the-Pooh hats.

I had given up the hope of getting the hats made outside because they were so difficult to sew. But one day a very strange lady came into the shop. She seemed very old to me, almost thirty, and she looked like a French existentialist. She wore violet stockings, black stiletto pointed shoes, a black and white dogtooth check pencil skirt and a ribbed skinny polo-neck jumper. On her Juliette Greco-like head she wore a black squashy felt hat. Round her beatnik legs hovered two pretty little blonde girls. That day Molly Parkin took over the manufacturing of our hat, which immediately became the Molly hat. Fitz was terrified of her because whenever Mol appeared she came to chase him for money. Our lookout would warn Fitz that Molly was marching down Abingdon Road with her two little girls in tow. Fitz would leap out of the back window and speed towards the Earls Court Road to hide in the nearest pub.

In the sixties the girls were prepared to suffer to look good. Our long skinny sleeves were so tight that they hindered the circulation. We used most extraordinary fabrics. We discovered that our local big store, Ponting's in Kensington High Street, had a large fabric hall. It was a knock-down-price department store which bought up old stocks from bankrupt factories. Some rolls of fabric were so old that the edges were faded yellow cotton. We became very friendly with the fabric buyer, who would let us into the pitch-dark stock rooms to buy them. Not until we got the stuff back to Abingdon Road did we sometimes discover many more yellow stains when the fabric was unrolled.

Our big breakthrough was the first fashion T-shirt. I went to Admiral, the sportswear people, and asked them to elongate their classic rugger shirt. This became a dress when dyed in sludgy colours. We found some fuddy-duddy firms who produced old ladies' underwear, and I adapted a vest with very high armholes and a skinny body. It had a little rayon ribbon running through the neckline. We then dyed it at least twenty different colours. At first our orders were quite modest, but for the opening of the season in the Big Biba they reached one hundred thousand. Fitz would call in some funny old reps and ask them to make a sample of their old lady shape in a Minnie Mouse size. You could see their faces thinking in disbelief, 'They're mad.' Then they would go away and after weeks of telephone calls and chasing they would come back with a sample. Two days after their delivery we would be reordering twice as many T-shirts. This would tickle them pink, but little did they know that in the future we would in many cases take over their whole production.

We recoloured football scarves, hats and socks in Auntie colours: mulberries, blueberries, rusts and plums. Sometimes there were disasters with dyes. The paint just washed out, as the printer had forgotten to give it the final bake that fixes the pigment to the fabric. People were walking round in

235

faded grey op art print dresses. It never occurred to them to return them. A few irate mothers brought back dresses with faded geometric impressions. They got their 3 guineas back and stormed off vowing not to allow their daughters to cross our threshold again. To some mothers Biba represented 'filthy culture', what Auntie would have called 'vulgar'. Auntie and I were no longer on speaking terms.

Barbara Hulanicki, *From A to Biba and Back Again* (1983)

1965: Thru Dark Sunglasses

i'm standing there watching the parade/
feeling combination of sleepy john estes.
jayne mansfield. humphrey bogart/morti-
mer snurd, murph the surf and so forth/
erotic hitchhiker wearing japanese
blanket. gets my attention by asking didn't
he see me at this hootenanny down in
puerto vallarta, mexico/i say no you must
be mistaken. i happen to be one of the
Supremes/then he rips off his blanket
an suddenly becomes a middle-aged druggist.
up for district attorney. he starts screaming at me you're the one. you're the one
that's been causing all them riots over in
vietnam. immediately turns t a bunch of
people an says if elected, he'll have me
electrocuted publicly on the next fourth
of july. i look around an all these people
he's talking to are carrying blowtorches/
needless t say, i split fast go back t the
nice quiet country. am standing there writing
WHAAAT? on my favorite wall when who should
pass by in a jet plane but my recording
engineer 'i'm here t pick up you and your
latest works of art. do you need any help
with anything?'

(pause)

my songs're written with the kettledrum

in mind/a touch of any anxious color. un-
mentionable, obvious. an people perhaps
like a soft brazilian singer . . . i have
given up at making any attempt at perfection/
the fact that the white house is filled with
leaders that've never been t the apollo
theater amazes me. why allen ginsberg was
not chosen t read poetry at the inauguration
boggles my mind/if someone thinks norman
mailer is more important than hank williams,
that's fine. i have no arguments an i
never drink milk. i would rather model harmonica holders than discuss aztec anthropology/
english literature. or history of the united
nations. i accept chaos. i am not sure whether
it accepts me. i know there're some people terrified
of the bomb. but there are other people terrified
t be seen carrying a modern screen magazine.
experience teaches that silence terrifies people
the most . . . i am convinced that all souls have
some superior t deal with/like the school
system, an invisible circle of which no one
can think without consulting someone/in the
face of this, responsibility/security. success
mean absolutely nothing . . . i would not want
t be bach. mozart. tolstoy. joe hill. gertrude
stein or james dean/they are all dead. the
Great books've been written. the Great sayings
have all been said/I am about t sketch You
a picture of what goes on around here sometimes. tho I don't understand too well
myself what's really happening. i do know
that we're all gonna die someday an that no
death has ever stopped the world. my poems
are written in a rhythm of unpoetic distortion/
divided by pierced ears. false eyelashes/sub-
tracted by people constantly torturing each
other. with a melodic purring line of descriptive
hollowness – seen at times thru dark sunglasses

an other forms of psychic explosion. a song is
anything that can walk by itself/i am called
a songwriter. a poem is a naked person . . . some
people say that i am a poet
(end of pause)
an so i answer my recording engineer
'yes. well i could use some help in getting
this wall in the plane'

Bob Dylan, sleeve note: Bringing It All Back Home (1965)

1965: Wednesday 23 June

. . . The Beatles have all been awarded MBEs, which has caused a considerable outcry. Furious war heroes are sending back their bravely-won medals
by the bushel. It is, of course, a tactless and major blunder on the part of the
Prime Minister, and also I don't think the Queen should have agreed. Some
other decoration should have been selected to reward them for their talentless but considerable contributions to the Exchequer.

Sunday 4 July
. . . On the Sunday night, I went to see the Beatles. I had never seen them in
the flesh before. The noise was deafening throughout and I couldn't hear a
word they sang or a note they played, just one long, ear-splitting din.
Apparently they were not a success. The notices were bad the next day. I
went backstage to see them and, after being met by Brian Epstein and Wendy
Hanson and given a drink, I was told that the Beatles refused to see me
because that ass David Lewin had quoted me saying unflattering things about
them months ago. I thought this graceless in the extreme, but decided to play
it with firmness and dignity. I asked Wendy to go and fetch one of them and
she finally reappeared with Paul McCartney and I explained gently but firmly
that one did *not* pay much attention to the statements of newspaper reporters. The poor boy was quite amiable and I sent messages of congratulation
to his colleagues, although the message I would have liked to send them was
that they were bad-mannered little shits. In any case, it is still impossible to
judge from their public performance whether they have talent or not. They
were professional, had a certain guileless charm, and stayed on mercifully for
not too long.

I was truly horrified and shocked by the audience. It was like a mass masturbation orgy, although apparently mild compared with what it usually is. The whole thing is to me an unpleasant phenomenon. Mob hysteria when commercially promoted, or in whatever way promoted, always sickens me. To realize that the majority of the modern adolescent world goes ritualistically mad over those four innocuous, rather silly-looking young men is a disturbing thought. Perhaps we are whirling more swiftly into extinction than we know. Personally I should have liked to take some of those squealing young maniacs and cracked their heads together. I am all for audiences going mad with enthusiasm after a performance, but *not* incessantly *during* the performance so that there ceases to be a performance.

The Noël Coward Diaries (1982)

1965: Well, What is Pop-Art?

What is pop-art? For weeks the hit-parading London group, The Who, have been at the centre of a big storm.

Some say it is a lot of bunk. Others defend pop-art as the most exciting musical development since the electric guitar boom started.

Who guitarist Pete Townshend defined pop-art for the MM this week.

'It is re-presenting something the public is familiar with, in a different form.

'Like clothes. Union Jacks are supposed to be flown. We have a jacket made of one. Keith Moon, our drummer has a jersey with the RAF insignia on it. I have a white jacket, covered in medals.

'We stand for pop-art clothes, pop-art music and pop-art behaviour. This is what everybody seems to forget – we don't change off stage. We live pop-art.'

Trowel-nosed Townshend, aged 20, was sitting in a high-class restaurant wearing a loud check jacket, and an open-necked shirt.

The Who are frequently ridiculed for smashing pounds worth of equipment. Why do they do it? Pop-art?

Pete, the culprit wrecker, answered: 'I bang my guitar on my speaker because of the visual effect. It is very artistic. One gets a tremendous sound, and the effect is great.

'What annoys me, is the person who comes up after a show, and says: 'Why didn't you smash your guitar tonight?' In fact it's split right down the middle of the neck, but the audience don't realise.

'If guitars exploded and went up in a puff of smoke, I'd be happy. The visual effect would be complete.

'Roger Daltrey, our singer, smashes his microphone on Keith's cymbal.

239

'He does this every night, because it's a sound. I use feedback every night. That's a sound.

'But, if the audience isn't right I don't smash guitars. They wouldn't appreciate the full visual effect.'

What is pop-art about The Who's music?

'Well, our next single is really pop-art. I wrote it with that intention. Not only is the number pop-art, the lyrics are 'young and rebellious'. It's anti-middle-age, anti boss-class and anti-young marrieds!

'I've nothing against these people really – just making a positive statement.

'The big social revolution that has taken place in the last five years is that youth, and not age, has become important.

'Their message is: "I'm important now I'm young, but I won't be when I'm over 21."

'Even London's streets are making a massive anti-establishment statement, every Saturday night.

'This is what we are trying to do in our music, protest against "showbiz" stuff, clear the hit-parade of stodge!

'We play,' continued Townshend, 'pop-art with standard group equipment. I get jet-plane sounds, morse-code signals, howling wind effects. Mind you near pop-art discs have been produced before.

'The Shangri-Las, with seagulls and motorbikes, and Twinkle's "Terry".

'Hey! We should have done "Trains and Boats and Planes".'

Nick Jones, Melody Maker, 3 July 1965

1965: Afro-Kitsch

In 1965, Radio Mali advertised a concert by Junior Wells and his All-Star Band at the Omnisport in Bamako. The ads promised the Chicago group would electrify the audience with tunes from such stars as Otis Redding, Wilson Pickett and James Brown. I was very excited because I had records by Junior Walker, and to me, at that time, with my limited English, Junior Wells and Junior Walker were one and the same. (That still happens to me, by the way.) It was a little disappointing that we couldn't have James Brown in person. I had heard that Anglophone countries like Ghana, Liberia and Nigeria were luckier. They could see James Brown on television, and they even had concerts with Tyrone Davis, Aretha Franklin and Wilson Pickett.

Sure enough, the concert was electrifying. Junior Wells and his All-Star Band played 'My Girl', 'I've Been Loving You Too Long', 'It's a Man's

World', 'There Was a Time', 'I Can't Stand Myself', 'Papa's Got a Brand New Bag', 'Respect', 'Midnight Hour' and, of course, 'Say It Loud (I'm Black and I'm Proud)'. During the break, some of us were allowed to talk with the musicians and to ask for autographs. The translator for us was a white guy from the United States Information Services. I remember distinguishing myself by going past the translator and asking one of the musicians the following question: 'What is your name?' His eyes lit up, and he told me his name and asked for mine. I said, 'My name is Manthia, but my friends call me JB.' He said something about James Brown, and I said something else. By that time, everybody else was quiet, watching us. I had only two years of junior high school English and the three-month summer vacations I had spent in Liberia to assist me. I got the nickname JB from my James Brown records.

The next day the news traveled all over Bamako that I spoke English like an American. This was tremendous in a Francophone country where one acquired subjecthood through recourse to *Francité* (thinking through French grammar and logic). Our master thinker was Jean-Paul Sartre. We were also living in awe, a form of silence, thinking that to be Francophone subjects, we had to master *Francité* like Léopold Senghor, who spoke French better than French people. Considered as one who spoke English like Americans and who had a fluent conversation with star musicians, I was acquiring a new type of subjecthood that put me perhaps above my comrades who knew by heart their *Les Chemins de la Liberté* by Sartre. I was on the cutting edge – the front line of the revolution.

You see, for me, then, and for many of my friends, to be liberated was to be exposed to more R & B songs and to be *au courant* of the latest exploits of Muhammad Ali, George Jackson, Angela Davis, Malcolm X and Martin Luther King, Jr. These were becoming an alternative cultural capital for the African youth – imparting to us new structures of feeling and enabling us to subvert the hegemony of *Francité* after independence.

Manthia Diawara, in *Black Popular Culture* (1992)

1965: Youthquaker People

RENÉ RICARD: It was the high point in Edie's career. She was the girl on fire with the silver hair close to her head, the eyes, the Viceroy in her fingers, the sleeves rolled up, those legs, yoicks! . . . all you saw was her!

PATTI SMITH: The first time I saw Edie was in *Vogue* magazine in 1965. I was seventeen or eighteen then. You have to understand where I came from. Living in south Jersey, you get connected with the pulse beat of what's going on through what you read in magazines. Not even through records. *Vogue* magazine was my whole consciousness. I never saw people. I never went to a concert. It was all image. In one issue of *Vogue* it was Youthquaker people they were talking about. It had a picture of Edie on a bed in a ballet pose. She was like a thin man in black leotards and a sort of boat-necked sweater, white hair, and behind her a little white horse drawn on the wall. She was such a strong image that I thought, 'That's it.' It represented everything to me . . . radiating intelligence, speed, being connected with the moment.

Vogue, August 1965

People Are Talking About . . . YOUTHQUAKERS

. . . Edith Sedgwick, twenty-two, white-haired with anthracite-black eyes and legs to swoon over, who stars in Andy Warhol's underground movies. 'It's like watching a Henry Moore sculpture out of focus,' said Edith Sedgwick, who toyed with the movie name Mazda Isphahan for *Poor Little Rich Girl*. With Pop artist Andy Warhol on camera, undergrounds roll out like crepes: *Vinyl* is in the can; *Vacuum* about to turn 'when we find a pure white kitchen'. *Rich Girl* was made in Miss Sedgwick's apartment, where she is shown here arabesquing on her leather rhino to a record of The Kinks. . . . In Paris Warhol's gang startled the dancers at Chez Castel by appearing with fifteen rabbits and Edie Sedgwick in a black leotard and a white mink coat. In her deep, campy voice, strained through smoke and Boston, she said: 'It's all I have to wear.'

PATTI SMITH: I would read about these discotheques. I would come all the way up to New York to loiter in front of a discotheque, watch people go into Arthur's or Steve Paul's The Scene. For me it was like seeing Hollywood. I saw Edie dance once. It was the big moment of my life. I think I said I had to use the bathroom, and some weak guy at the discotheque door let me through. I remember I had on a green wool mini-skirt. For New Jersey I looked pretty hot, but I didn't look so hot there. What I remember most of all were their earrings. I thought they were really neat dancers but unusual. We didn't dance like that in New Jersey. I was brought up in a really black area and we were really great dancers. I thought they danced like weird chickens. They just didn't have that fluid nigger grace that my friends and I possessed.

Everything was angles. Everybody was skinny, and it was elbows and angles and knees and earrings. It wasn't a question of my wanting to be them. I just liked that they existed so I could look at them.

ROY LICHTENSTEIN: My wife, Dorothy, and I went to a Halloween costume party given by the painter Adele Weber, dressed as Andy Warhol and Edie. Andy looked somewhat different then – leather jacket, blue jeans, funny sunglasses, and funny shoes that were all broken up . . . silver paint on them. Easy to imitate. I sprayed my hair with silver paint and I powdered my face to look very pale. When people said anything to me at the party, I said, 'Oh, wow!' or 'How glamorous!' Even though Andy can be unusually articulate, I reduced his repertoire to those two expressions. Dorothy wore hot pants and very high heels and put on a lot of silver glitter. She had short hair like Edie's. Andy does exactly what I don't do. *He* was his art. His studio was his art. Edie was part of his art, and a lot of other people. I was an old-fashioned artist compared with him. When I looked at Andy, I looked at him as a tourist would, I guess . . . with wonderment. How glamorous. How strange.

VICTOR NAVASKY: I was on a David Susskind panel on his television show. 'Who's In and Who's Out' was the topic for the night, and Edie as Girl of the Year was on it, along with Gloria Steinem, Russell Baker and I forget who else. Susskind began the show by making fun of Edie. 'Why do you dress like that? Why do you . . .?' And she was answering half defensively and half in a Warhol way. Her whole life was a media event.

New York *World-Telegram*, August 18, 1965
Gotham-Go-Round, Joseph X. Dever, Society Editor
EDIE SEDGWICK AND ANDY WARHOL,
ROYAL MEMBERS OF UNDERGROUND MOVIES

Chez Catharsis: At a low decibel point amid the deafening sound of the Executives trio last night at the Scene, we shouted into the ear of Edie Sedgwick, silver-topped queen of the underground movies: 'Where is the *real* Edie Sedgwick – home with a book?' The bob-haired, 20-year-old heiress from California looked to see if we were serious, then shouted back: 'The real Edie is where the action is. Fast cars, fast horses, and people doing things!' With that, she watusied away, her trademark leotards lost in a swirl of hip-huggers, tight blue jeans, Pucci slacks, and little-girl mod dresses. That swinging catacomb on W. 46th St., the Scene definitely was where the action was last night.

243

ANDY WARHOL: She was always making fun of the kind of clothes she wore – saying that not wearing underwear, and things like that, was her way of showing that her family didn't give her any money. Actually, she invented all those new clothes and stuff. She always looked so good. Edie was a beauty, gee!

WENDY VANDEN HEUVEL: She came to a party at my mother's. The maid said, 'Can I take your coat?' She said, 'No, I don't think so. I'm a little cold.' Later Edie told me the real reason she didn't want to take her coat off was that she wasn't wearing any clothes under it. I was about five years old at the time. I thought it was funny that she would come to a party with no clothes on, just a coat. We had funny conversations. I would say 'Hi', and she would say 'Hi', and then I would say 'Hi', and we'd just keep on saying 'Hi', 'Hi', 'Hi', to each other. It seemed like she had so many friends, but when you really looked at her face, it was like she never had *any* friends.

ANDY WARHOL: She always wanted to leave. Even if a party was good, she wanted to leave. It's the way they work now in St Moritz: I mean, people who spend fortunes to have parties can't wait until they're over so they can go somewhere else. I don't understand that. Can't wait to go . . . and there's no place to go. These people in big, expensive cars can't wait to get to the next party . . . and there's no next party. They just get up and leave. It's really funny. But Edie was like that. She just couldn't wait to get to the next place.

One night, when the parties were over, I guess she didn't want to sleep with somebody, so she asked me to share a room with her. She always had to have her glass of hot milk and a cigarette in one hand. In her sleep her hands kept crawling: they couldn't sleep. I couldn't keep my eyes off them. She kept scratching with them. Perhaps she just had bad dreams . . . I don't know, it was really sad.

New York *World-Telegram*
September 14, 1965
Gotham-Go-Round, Joseph X. Dever

. . . Clip-coiffed Edie Sedgwick upstaged *The Vampires* on screen at the Lincoln Center film festival last night as she swept in on the arm of pop artist Andy Warhol. Edie's outfit included her usual black leotard plus a trailing black ostrich-plumed cape like a camp version of Mme Dracula . . .

Life, November 26, 1965

FASHION:

The Girl with the Black Tights

This cropped-mop girl with the eloquent legs is doing more for black tights than anybody since Hamlet.

RENÉ RICARD: I was one of Edie's escorts the night the limousines pulled up to The Scene, where she met Mick Jagger. I was there, and you don't know how I felt, seventeen years old. It was an extraordinary moment! Edie Sedgwick, the most famous girl in New York, and Mick Jagger, the most famous singer and the one everybody wanted to fuck! And there he was.

We were at least two hours late at The Scene. Edie was always brilliantly late: Andy would wait for her; he'd never say a word. He trusted her aristocratic instincts. He always said, 'She knows what she's doing.' When she'd arrive, it would always be when the tension was at its greatest. Everyone at The Scene was saying, 'Edie's going to meet Mick. It's Mick and Edie . . . New York's big girl and England's big boy, and they're going to be together.'

Edie was wearing the Gernreich dress she had modeled somewhere – breathtaking and in such great style – made of a cinnamon-colored, satiny football jersey. Her sleeves were pushed up and she wore a million bangle bracelets and very high, high heels. Earrings. We went down the stairs. Edie never, never carried anything when she went out on these evenings; I don't even remember a coat.

It was in front of the coat-check place that it happened. Mick Jagger was there and Edie was there, facing each other. She said, 'How do you do? I just love your records.' Well, what *do* you say? And he said, 'Oh, thank you.' Then, all of a sudden, there was an explosion of people and every corner of The Scene emptied into the tiny vestibule where we were standing. People were pushing and banging up against each other. The flashbulbs were blinding. Edie was able to get to the ladies' room. The poor thing! She was appalled by the crush. I don't remember what happened the rest of the night. All I know is that the picture of the two of them standing together in The Scene, the dingiest and most disgusting place in the world, is imprinted on my retina because it was so glamorous!

Jean Stein, *Edie: The Life and Times of Andy Warhol's Superstar*,
edited with George Plimpton (1982)

1965: 'Real' Teen Revolt

The Byrds' sound is uniquely beautiful and their success is evident not only in the sale of their records but also in the rapidity with which their 'sound' is being copied.

And, although the Byrds dislike the label 'folk-rock', they are considered by many in the music field to be the founders of the folk-rock trend and one of contemporary music's most important influences!

There have been countless articles written about the Byrds, so many in fact that the average fan could probably tell you more about them than they could themselves. Yet, an air of mystery surrounds these five young musicians.

In keeping with *The BEAT's* policy to bring its readers fact rather than fiction and real-life situations rather than make-believe, we asked the Byrds to answer some of our questions and give us their concept of the so-called 'Teenage Revolution'. A subject in which we are all very interested and, in some way, involved.

Q: What is your concept of the 'Teenage Revolution'?

JIM MCGUINN: I think the natural evolution of man has stages, like each generation does a thing – a growing thing.

A generation will span into consciousness – another level – everybody will catch up to it. And then another generation will emerge and one generation gets on top and then another comes from underneath and goes ahead of the last. And the last generation resents it.

I think the label "Teenage Revolution" is given by people who resent the fact that another generation is here.

Q: Do you think teenagers understand these 'message' songs?

JIM: If they listen to a song that has a message they're bound to pick up what the words are saying because they're hip to what words say in songs. They know.

Q: Do you think the teenagers are actually interested in the problems these songs talk about?

JIM: I don't know what the whole feeling about that is. But I think the kids today are hip to it. They're sensitive, alert human beings, intelligent and well educated. And, as a mass, they have a feeling that everything should be harmonious.

Q: What is your concept of the 'Teenage Revolution'?

DAVID CROSBY: It definitely is a revolution and it definitely involves the teenagers and a great many more people than the teenagers.

Over half of the people in the country are under 25. The country isn't being run as they know and feel it should be. The discrepancies are too obvious. The wrongness and the corruption disturbs and upsets them.

And the uncertainty of the nuclear thing, which is something we've lived with since we were born. They definitely want to change this and a lot of other things.

Q: And what are they interested in changing?

DAVID: They're interested, as far as I've been able to discern, in the possibility of love as opposed to war. They're interested in trying to learn, trying to grow and they're resentful of the situation they've been handed as their lot.

Q: Do you think that the vast majority of young people know what the problems are?

DAVID: I think that, naturally, only a small percentage of them are intellectually aware of that. However, they are emotionally disturbed with the feeling of the times.

Q: Do you think that message songs help to make them more aware?

DAVID: Message songs imply an area which I doubt adds very much. I think people get a great deal of truth out of Dylan's word collages but I doubt if they get much truth at all out of the 'surface' or very shallow copies of Dylan and Dylan's work.

Q: Chris, what do you think about the 'Teenage Revolution'?

CHRIS HILLMAN: It's really happening. We run across a lot of very bright kids these days. For example, not as many kids watch TV anymore – that's good.

Q: When does this start?

CHRIS: As young as 11 or 10. They're asking more questions. They're much sharper.

Q: And is music the main source of communication?

CHRIS: Well, not just music but everything that goes on around them. Their eyes are much more open to things.

Q: Do you think the 'protest' songs are an important factor?

CHRIS: I don't know if it would take a song to do it. There are some good protest songs and there are some which are not very subtle. They come right out and say, 'this is bad' without saying 'how' or 'why'.

Q: Are there too many 'protest' songs?

CHRIS Yes, there are. It's becoming very commercial. They're just writing songs to attack something without any reasons.

Q: With the variety in popular music, do you think people are becoming more sensitive to sound?

GENE CLARK: Yes, I think so – I really do. I think that people are becoming much more sensitive to music because music in the pop field is much more sensitive.

Q: With this increased sensitivity do you think the 'Teenage Revolution' is an extention of this?

GENE: 'It's a reality instead of a fad. It's real and it counts.

Q: And when do they find this out?

GENE: Whenever they are capable of comprehending what it could possibly mean.

Q: What do you think about Herman's statement that 'the Byrds are second hand Rolling Stones'?

MIKE CLARK: I don't know any Herman. Who's he?

Bob Feigal, *The Beat*, 27 November 1965

1965: The Gap

Let me tell you about Rose. She's sixteen and has a black heart tattooed on her pale arm. When I asked her why she dug protest songs, she said: 'It just get t'rough to ya. 'At's all I can say.' That's plenty. She's terribly excited about attending Dylan's concert in Chicago. (I'm not interested at all in the controversy, real or manufactured, raging about him. I don't give a damn whether his guitar is electric or acoustic. I'm a little hard of hearing on one ear, anyway.) What's important is that he gets through to Rose. The tattooed girl has been trying to get through to her mother, a lost soul, by sending her love poems. (It's beautiful poetry by an untutored bard, who has been to hell, purgatory and back.) To no avail. She did not get through.

Short-hand thoughts, neither merry nor mournful, on attending Dylan performance. November 26, 1965.

First half. Boy Alone. All business. Serious of mien. I, here; Thou, there. Edwardian uniform, expensive cut. Where have you been, my blue-eyed boy? Pucci your tailor? Small matter. Half-dozen fairly strong searching songs. 'Desolation Blues' awfully good. Suddenly, intermission. Rose overwhelmed: 'I'm going back to recover my mind. He stole it.'

Conclusion: Dylan controversy missed point by a Minnesota mile. Question of best of broadside balladeers becoming probing introspective poet wholly irrelevant. Excellent subject for high school debate, but irrelevant.

Wry truth: original become show biz wind-up doll. It sings, plays (doesn't talk), walks on, walks off. Have seen toy before. Called Sinatra at one time; Ella, at another. (Unlike, say, Billie Holiday or Woody Guthrie, for that matter. They were nobody's toys. Always, they revealed themselves in all their human vulnerability. This is the hallmark of an artist, Paul Nelson's dreary nonsense to the contrary. This was the Boy in the beginning – the one I had met two, three years ago; he had moved me profoundly. It was before the alchemy of commerce transmuted him into a Golden Boy Toy. The rich juices are still in him; witness 'Desolation Row'. Perhaps, there's still a chance, the Boy Poet will disenthrall himself from the grossness that has encircled him.) Goes over big, can't miss. Secret is in packaging.

Second half. Metamorphosis out of Kafka. Boy no longer alone. Four colleagues (La Dolce Vita paparazzi?), plugged into wall sockets. Organ glows fluorescently, all orange and green. A good night for Commonwealth Edison. Verse comes to mind, Woody – whom Boy is said to have visited about 553 year ago:

> I'm going to tell papa, I am, mama
> I'm going to tell papa, I am, haha
> He might not like it but I don't care
> 'Cause we'll have electricity and all.

Boy heads toward piano, ala Bix of another time. 'Mr Jones', a fine piece. Good bite. Lyrics audible. Returns to wall socket. Word or two occasionally heard way out there in wilds of third row. What's happening here, Mr Jones? Who is putting on whom? Not only is the executioner's face always well hidden. Perhaps Rimbaud is on stage or the other Dylan, he of south Wales. One never knows, do one? as Fats did say. And one never will. 'Cause we have electricity and all. Content is overwhelmed. Suddenly it's over. Boy nods ever so slightly. Minces off. No encores. House lights. Andy Frain ushers en garde. Look past you, as did Boy: cool; no nonsense.

Rose, highly impressed: 'Man, he's home. He zooms right at ya.' I stare at mirror, across bar. The Gap is twin-level. Rose and I versus the Establishment and one, equally as deep, between the tattooed girl and me. The flaw, Medea to the contrary, may be not in the stars but in me. Still, I ask: Where have you been, my blue-eyed boy? Comes the answer, blowing in the wind: Who said I was ever yours?

Studs Terkel, *Sing Out!*, February 1966

1966: Gear

Too early to get up, especially on Saturday. The sun peeks over his windowsill. Isolated footsteps from the street. Guys who have to work on Saturday. Boy! That's what they'll call you all your life if you don't stay in school. Forty-five definitions, two chapters in *Silas Marner* and three chem labs. On Sunday night, he will sit in his room with the radio on, bobbing back and forth on his bed, opening the window wide and then closing it, taking a break to eat, to comb his hair, to dance, to hear the Stones – anything. Finally, cursing wildly and making ugly faces at himself in the mirror, he will throw *Silas Marner* under the bed and spend an hour watching his tortoise eat lettuce.

In the bathroom he breaks three screaming pimples. With a toothpick he removes four specks of food from his braces, skirting barbed wires and week-old rubber bands. Brooklyn Bridge, railroad tracks, they call him. Metal mouth. They said he smiled like someone was forcing him to. Bent fingers with filthy nails. Caved-in chest with eight dangling hairs. A face that looks like the end of a watermelon, and curly hair – not like the Stones, not at all like Brian Jones – but muddy curls running down his forehead and over his ears. A bump. Smashed by a bat thrown wildly. When he was eight. Hunchback Quasimodo – Igor – Rodan on his head. A bump. Nobody hip has a bump or braces. Or hair like a fucking Frankenstein movie. He licks his braces clean and practices smiling.

Hair straight and heavy. Nose full. Lips bulging like boiling frankfurters. Hung. Bell bottoms and boss black boots. He practices his Brian Jones expressions. Fist held close to the jaw. Ready to spring, ready to spit. Evil. His upper brace catches on a lip.

He walks past his parents' room, where his mother sleeps in a gauzy hairnet, the covers pulled over her chin, her baby feet swathed in yellow calluses. Her hand reaches over to the night table where her eyedrops and glasses lie. He mutters silently at her. The night before there had been a fight – the usual fight, with Mommy shouting 'I'll give you money! Sure, you rotten kid! I'll give you clothing so you can throw it all over the floor – that's blood money in those pants of yours!' And him answering the usual 'geh-awf-mah-bak' and her: 'Don't you yell at me, don't you – did you hear that (to no one). Did you hear how that kid . . .?' and him slamming the door – the gray barrier – and above the muffled '. . . disrespects his mother . . . He treats me like dirt under his feet! . . . and he wants me to buy him . . . he'll spit on my grave' . . . and finally dad's groaning shuffle and a murmured 'Ronnie, you better shut your mouth to your mother', and him whispering silently, the climactic, the utter: 'Fucking bitch. Cunt. Cunt.'

Now she smiles. So do crocodiles. He loves her. He doesn't know why he cursed, except that she hates it. It was easy to make her cry and though he shivers at the thought of her lying across the bed sobbing into a pillow, her housedress pulled slightly over a varicose thigh, he had to admit doing it was easy.

On the table he sees the pants she bought him yesterday. Her money lining his pocket, he had taken the bus to Fordham Road and in Alexander's he had cased out the Mod rack. Hands shaking, dying for a cigarette, he found the pants – a size small but still a fit. He bought them, carried them home clutched in his armpit, and deposited them before her during prime *Star Trek* TV time.

'Get away. I can't see. Whatsamaddah, your father a glazier or something?' and when he unveiled the pants and asked for the usual cuff-making ritual (when he would stand on the ladder and she, holding a barrage of pins in her mouth, would run the tailor's chalk along his shoeline and make him drag out the old black sewing machine), the fight began – and ended within the hour. The pants, hemmed during *The Merv Griffin Show* as the last labor of the night, now lay exposed and sunlit on the table. $8.95 pants.

They shimmer. The houndstooth design glows against the formica. Brown and green squares are suddenly visible within the gray design. He brushes the fabric carefully so the wool bristles. He tries them on, zipping up the two-inch fly, thinking at first that he has broken the zipper until he realizes that hip-huggers have no fly to speak of. They buckle tightly around his hips, hug his thighs, and flare suddenly at his knees. He races to the mirror and grins.

His hips are suddenly tight and muscular. His waist is sleek and his ass round and bulging. Most important, the pants make him look hung. Like the kids in the park. The odor of stale cigarettes over their clothing, medallions dangling out of their shirts. Their belt buckles ajar. They are hip. They say 'Check out that bike.' Get bent on Gypsy. Write the numbers of cruising police cars all over the walls. R O T, they call themselves. Reign of Terror. In the park they buzz out on glue, filling paper bags and breathing deeply, then sitting on the grass slopes, watching the cars. Giggling. Grooving. High.

Sometimes they let him keep the models that come with the glue. Or he grubs around their spot until, among the torn bags and oozing tubes, he finds a Messerschmitt or Convair spread across the grass ruins as though it had crashed there.

He unzips his pants and lets them hang on the door where he can watch them from the living room. He takes a box of Oreos from the kitchen, stacking the cookies in loose columns on the rug. He pours a cup of milk and turns on the TV. Farmer Gray runs nervously up and down the screen while a pig squats at ease by his side. His pants are filled with hornets. He runs in a cloud of dust toward a pond which appears and disappears teasingly, leaving Farmer Gray grubbing in the sand. Outasight!

He fills his mouth with three Oreos and wraps his feet around the screen so he can watch Farmer Gray between his legs. Baby habit. Eating cookies on the floor and watching cartoons on Saturday morning. Like thumbsucking. They teased him about it until he threw imaginary furniture into their faces. A soft bulge on his left thumb from years of sucking – cost them a fortune in braces. Always busting his bump.

He kills the TV picture and puts the radio on softly, because he doesn't want to wake Daddy, who is asleep on his cot in the middle of the living room, bunched up around the blanket, his face creased in a dream, hands gripping his stomach in mock tension. Daddy snores in soft growls.

He brushes a flock of Oreo crumbs under the TV and rubs a milk stain into the rug. Thrown out of your own bed for snoring. You feel cheap, like Little Bo Peep; beep beep beep beep.

There is nothing to stop him from going downstairs. The guys are out already, slung over cars and around lampposts. The girls are trickling out of the project. It's cloudy, but until it actually rains he knows they will be around the lamppost, spitting out into the street, horsing around, grubbing for hooks, singing. He finishes four more cookies and stuffs half an apple onto his chocolate-lined tongue.

Marie Giovanni put him down bad for his braces. When she laughs her tits shake. Her face is pink; her hair rises in a billowing bouffant. In the hallway, she let Tony get his fingers wet. Yesterday she cut on him; called him metal mouth.

He flicks the radio off, grabs the pants from the hanger, and slides into them. He digs out a grown turtleneck from under a rubble of twisted clothing (they dress him like a ragpicker) and shines his boots with spit. They are chipping and the heels are worn on one side, but they make him look an inch taller, so he wears them whenever he can.

He combs his hair in the mirror. Back on the sides, over the ears, so the curl doesn't show. Over the eyes in the front to cover up his bump. Straight down the back of his neck, so it rests on his collar. He checks his bald spot for progress and counts the hairs that come out in his brush. In two years he knows he will be bald in front and his bump will look like a boulder on his forehead.

He sits on his bed and turns the radio on. From under the phonograph he lifts a worn fan magazine – *Pop* in bright fuchsia lettering – with Zal Yanovsky hunched over one P, Paul McCartney contorted over the other, and Nancy Sinatra touching her toes around the O. He turns to the spread on the Stones and flips the pages until he sees The Picture. Mick Jagger and Marianne Faithfull. Mick scowling, waving his fingers in the air. Marianne watching the camera. Marianne, waiting for the photographer to shoot. Marianne. Marianne, eyes fading brown circles, lips slightly parted in flash-bulb surprise, miniskirt spread apart, tits like two perfect cones under her sweater. He had to stop looking at Marianne Faithfull a week ago.

He turns the page and glances at the shots of Brian Jones and then his eyes open wide because a picture in the corner shows Brian in Ronnie's pants. The same check. The same rise and flare. Brian leaning against a wall, his hands on the top of his magic hiphuggers. Wick-ked!

He flips the magazine away and stands in a curved profile against the mirror. He watches the pants move as he does. From a nearby flowerpot he gathers a fingerful of dirt and rubs it over his upper lip. He checks hair, nose, braces, nails and pants. He likes the pants. They make him look hung. He reaches into his top drawer and pulls out a white handkerchief. He opens his fly and inserts the rolled cloth, patting it in place, and closing the zipper over it. He looks boss. Unfuckinbelievable.

In the elevator Ronnie takes a cigarette from his three-day-old pack and keeps it unlit in his mouth. Marie Giovanni will look at his pants and giggle. Tony will bellow 'check out them pants', and everyone will groove on them. In the afternoon, they will take him down to the park and turn him on, and he will feel the buzz they are always talking about and the cars will speed by like sparks.

Brian Jones thoughts in his head. Tuff thoughts. He will slouch low over the car and smoke with his thumb over the cigarette – the hip way. And when he comes back upstairs they will finally get off his back. Even on Fordham Road, where the Irish kids crack up when he walks by, even in chemistry and gym, they will know who he is and nod a soft 'hey' when he comes by. He'll get laid.

Because clothing IS important. Especially if you've got braces and bony fingers and a bump the size of a goddam coconut on your head.

And especially if you're fourteen. Because – ask anyone. Fourteen is shit.

Richard Goldstein, *The Village Voice*, July 1966

1966: How Does a Beatle Live?

It was this time three years ago that The Beatles first grew famous. Ever since then, observers have anxiously tried to gauge whether their fame was on the wax or on the wane; they foretold the fall of the old Beatles, they searched diligently for the new Beatles (which was as pointless as looking for the new Big Ben).

At last they have given up: The Beatles' fame is beyond question. It has nothing to do with whether they are rude or polite, married or unmarried, 25 or 45; whether they appear on *Top of the Pops* or do not appear on *Top of the Pops*. They are well above any position even a Rolling Stone might jostle for. They are famous in the way the Queen is famous. When John Lennon's Rolls-Royce, with its black wheels and its black windows, goes past, people say: 'It's the Queen', or, 'It's The Beatles.' With her they share the security of a stable life at the top. They all tick over in the public esteem – she in Buckingham Palace, they in the Weybridge–Esher area. Only Paul remains in London.

The Weybridge community consists of the three married Beatles; they live there among the wooded hills and the stockbrokers. They have not worked since Christmas and their existence is secluded and curiously timeless. 'What day is it?' John Lennon asks with interest when you ring up with news from outside. The fans are still at the gates but The Beatles see only each other. They are better friends than ever before.

Ringo and his wife, Maureen, may drop in on John and Cyn; John may drop in on Ringo; George and Pattie may drop in on John and Cyn and they might all go round to Ringo's, by car of course. Outdoors is for holidays.

They watch films, they play rowdy games of Buccaneer; they watch television till it goes off, often playing records at the same time. They while away the small hours of the morning making mad tapes. Bedtimes and mealtimes have no meaning as such. 'We've never had time before to do anything but just be Beatles,' John Lennon said.

He is much the same as he was before. He still peers down his nose, arrogant as an eagle, although contact lenses have righted the short sight that originally caused the expression. He looks more like Henry VIII than ever now that his face has filled out – he is just as imperious, just as unpredictable, indolent, disorganised, childish, vague, charming and quick-witted. He is still easy-going, still tough as hell. 'You never asked after Fred Lennon,' he said, disappointed. (Fred is his father; he emerged after they got famous.) 'He was here a few weeks ago. It was only the second time in my life I'd seen him – I showed him the door.' He went on cheerfully: 'I wasn't having *him* in the house.'

His enthusiasm is undiminished and he insists on its being shared. George has put him on to this Indian music. 'You're not listening, are you?' he shouts after 20 minutes of the record. 'It's amazing this – so cool. Don't the Indians appear cool to you? Are you listening? This music is thousands of years old; it makes me laugh, the British going over there and telling them what to do. Quite amazing.' And he switched on the television set.

Experience has sown few seeds of doubt in him: not that his mind is closed, but it's closed round whatever he believes at the time. 'Christianity will go,' he said. 'It will vanish and shrink. I needn't argue about that; I'm right and I will be proved right. We're more popular than Jesus now; I don't know which will go first – rock 'n' roll or Christianity. Jesus was all right but his disciples were thick and ordinary. It's them twisting it that ruins it for me.' He is reading extensively about religion.

He shops in lightning swoops on Asprey's these days and there is some fine wine in his cellar, but he is still quite unselfconscious. He is far too lazy to keep up appearances, even if he had worked out what the appearances should be – which he has not.

He is now 25. He lives in a large, heavily panelled, heavily carpeted, mock Tudor house set on a hill with his wife, Cynthia, and his son, Julian. There is a cat called after his aunt Mimi, and a purple dining room. Julian is three; he may be sent to the Lycée in London. 'Seems the only place for him in his position,' said his father, surveying him dispassionately. 'I feel sorry for him, though. I couldn't stand ugly people even when I was five. Lots of the ugly ones are foreign, aren't they?'

We did a speedy tour of the house, Julian panting along behind, clutching a large porcelain Siamese cat. John swept past the objects in which he had lost interest: 'That's Sidney' (a suit of armour); 'That's a hobby I had for a week' (a room full of model racing cars); 'Cyn won't let me get rid of that' (a fruit machine). In the sitting room are eight little green boxes with winking red lights; he bought them as Christmas presents but never got round to giving them away. They wink for a year; one imagines him sitting there till next Christmas, surrounded by the little winking boxes.

He paused over objects he still fancies; a huge altar crucifix of a Roman Catholic nature with IHS on it; a pair of crutches, a present from George; an enormous Bible he bought in Chester; his gorilla suit.

'I thought I might need a gorilla suit,' he said; he seemed sad about it. 'I've only worn it twice. I thought I might pop it on in the summer and drive round in the Ferrari. We were all going to get them and drive round in them but I was the only one who did. I've been thinking about it and if I didn't wear the head it would make an amazing fur coat – with legs, you see. I would like a fur coat but I've never run into any.'

One feels that his possessions – to which he adds daily – have got the upper hand; all the tape recorders, the five television sets, the cars, the telephones of which he knows not a single number. The moment he approaches a switch it fuses; six of the winking boxes, guaranteed to last till next Christmas, have gone funny already. His cars – the Rolls, the mini-Cooper (black wheels, black windows), the Ferrari (being painted black) – puzzle him. Then there's the swimming pool, the trees sloping away beneath it. 'Nothing like what I ordered,' he said resignedly. He wanted the bottom to be a mirror. 'It's an amazing household,' he said. 'None of my gadgets really work except the gorilla suit – that's the only suit that fits me.'

He is very keen on books, will always ask what is good to read. He buys quantities of books and these arc kept tidily in a special room. He has Swift, Tennyson, Huxley, Orwell, costly leather-bound editions of Tolstoy, Oscar Wilde. Then there's *Little Women*, all the *William* books from his childhood; and some unexpected volumes such as *Forty-One Years in India*, by Field Marshal Lord Roberts, and *Curiosities of Natural History*, by Francis T. Buckland. This last – with its chapter headings 'Ear-less Cats', 'Wooden-Legged People', 'The Immortal Harvey's Mother' – is right up his street.

He approaches reading with a lively interest untempered by too much formal education. 'I've read millions of books,' he said, 'that's why I seem to know things.' He is obsessed by Celts. 'I have decided I am a Celt,' he said. 'I am on Boadicea's side – all those bloody blue-eyed blondes chopping people up. I have an awful feeling wishing I was there – not there with scabs and sores but there through *reading* about it. The books don't give you more than a paragraph about how they *lived*; I have to imagine that.'

He can sleep almost indefinitely, is probably the laziest person in England. '*Physically* lazy,' he said. 'I don't mind writing or reading or watching or speaking, but sex is the only physical thing I can be bothered with any more.' Occasionally he is driven to London in the Rolls by an ex-Welsh Guardsman called Anthony; Anthony has a moustache that intrigues him.

The day I visited him he had been invited to lunch in London, about which he was rather excited. 'Do you know how long lunch lasts?' he asked. 'I've never been to lunch before. I went to a Lyons the other day and had egg and chips and a cup of tea. The waiters kept looking and saying: "No, it *isn't* him, it *can't* be him."'

He settled himself into the car and demonstrated the television, the folding bed, the refrigerator, the writing desk, the telephone. He has spent many fruitless hours on that telephone. 'I only once got through to a person,' he said, 'and they were out.'

Anthony had spent the weekend in Wales. John asked if they'd kept a welcome for him in the hillside and Anthony said they had. They discussed the possibility of an extension for the telephone. We had to call at the doctor's because John had a bit of sea urchin in his toe. 'Don't want to be like Dorothy Dandridge,' he said, 'dying of a splinter 50 years later.' He added reassuringly that he had washed the foot in question.

We bowled along in a costly fashion through the countryside. 'Famous and loaded' is how he describes himself now. 'They keep telling me I'm all right for money but then I think I may have spent it all by the time I'm 40 so I keep going. That's why I started selling my cars; then I changed my mind and got them all back and a new one too.

'I want the money just to *be* rich. The only other way of getting it is to be born rich. If you have money, that's power without having to be powerful. I often think that it's all a big conspiracy, that the winners are the Government and people like us who've got the money. That joke about keeping the workers ignorant is still true; that's what they said about the Tories and the landowners and that; then Labour were meant to educate the workers but they don't seem to be doing that any more.'

He has a morbid horror of stupid people: 'Famous and loaded as I am, I still have to meet soft people. It often comes into my mind that I'm not really rich. There are *really* rich people but I don't know where they are.'

He finds being famous quite easy, confirming one's suspicion that The Beatles had been leading up to this all their lives. 'Everybody thinks they *would* have been famous if only they'd had the Latin and that. So when it happens it comes naturally. You remember your old grannie saying soft things like: "You'll make it with that voice."' Not, he added, that he had any old grannies.

He got to the doctor 2¾ hours early and to lunch on time but in the wrong place. He bought a giant compendium of games from Asprey's but having opened it he could not, of course, shut it again. He wondered what else he should buy. He went to Brian Epstein's office. 'Any presents?' he asked eagerly; he observed that there was nothing like getting things free. He tried on the attractive Miss Hanson's spectacles.

The rumour came through that a Beatle had been sighted walking down Oxford Street! He brightened. 'One of the others must be out,' he said, as though speaking of an escaped bear. 'We only let them out one at a time,' said the attractive Miss Hanson firmly.

He said that to live and have a laugh were the things to do; but was that enough for the restless spirit?

'Weybridge,' he said, 'won't do at all. I'm just stopping at it, like a bus stop. Bankers and stockbrokers live there; they can add figures and Weybridge is what they live in and they think it's the end, they really do. I think of it every day – me in my Hansel and Gretel house. I'll take my time: I'll get my *real* house when I know what I want.

'You see, there's something else I'm going to do, something I must do – only I don't know what it is. That's why I go round painting and taping and drawing and writing and that, because it may be one of them. All I know is, this isn't *it* for me.'

Anthony got him and the compendium into the car and drove him home with the television flickering in the soothing darkness while the Londoners outside rushed home from work.

Maureen Cleave, Evening Standard, 4 March 1966

1966: One Foot on the Highway . . .

In the dark, Lincoln Municipal Airport blended into the surrounding farmland. It was just past the break of midnight on a Saturday in mid-March 1966. As Dylan, The Band, two roadies and I arrived, runway lights flashed on, tower controllers stirred and mechanics busied themselves around Dylan's private plane, the two-engine Lockheed Lodestar jet.

Denver was next, then back to New York, then up to the Pacific Northwest, Hawaii, Australia, Scandinavia, Ireland, England, France, then back home. This was the beginning of the end of one of Dylan's many careers. As he walked into the lunch-canteen room, a mechanic in white overalls peered into the night. 'It must get lonely out here,' Bob said. Both looked at the field. 'It does,' the mechanic replied, 'but it's a job. I just take the hours they give me.' 'I know how that feels, I really do,' Dylan said, as they stared across prairie land.

He had just evaded fifty fans at his hotel, but a half dozen clustered around the plane. He scribbled his autograph a few times. A shy youth, about seventeen, approached. 'Mr Dylan,' he said nervously, 'I'm interested in poetry too.' 'Yeah, is that so?' Dylan replied. 'Yes, sir,' the boy answered. 'I was wondering if you could spare a few minutes, sometime, to read some poems I've written.' 'Sure,' Bob responded. The young man handed Dylan a large envelope that bulged like a football. 'Are all these poems?' Dylan asked. 'Yes ... I've been writing more since I began to study your songs.' 'Well,' Dylan said, 'thank you. I'll try to read some tonight. Is your address on the envelope? I'll let you know what I think of them.' The boy glowed: 'That's wonderful. I hope you like them.'

Inside the plane, The Band members were dozing off, a pile of slumping bodies. Road managers Bill Avis and Victor Maimudes checked everyone's seat belt. Dylan and I sat face to face. On one knee rested a packet of proofs of his book *Tarantula*. On his other knee was the fan's envelope. I fussed with my tape recorder, cursing the engine noise. His eyes were nearly slits, but he told me he wouldn't have slept even if I hadn't been there. He just had too much to do.

'It takes a lot of medicine to keep up this pace,' Dylan said. 'It's very hard, man. A concert tour like this has almost killed me. It's been like this since October ... It really drove me out of my mind ... I'm really going to cut down. Next year, the concert tour is only going to last a month ... or two. I'm only doing it like this because I want everyone to know what we're doing.' Dylan sent a cloud of cigarette smoke over his head, tugged his shirt collar and continued: 'It's just absurd for people to sit around being offended by their own meaninglessness, so that they have to force everything else to come into the hole with them, and die trying. That's the hang-up here. But I'm not involved with that anymore. I've told you that many times. I don't know if you think I'm kidding, or if you think it's a front. I really just don't *care* – honestly just don't *care* – what people say about me. I don't care what people think about me. I don't care what people know about me.

'Playing on the stage is a kick for me, now. It wasn't before, because I knew what I was doing then was just too empty. ... It was just dead ambassadors who would come and see me and clap and say: "Oh, groovy, I would like to meet him and have a cocktail. Perhaps I'll bring my son, Joseph, with me." And the first thing you know you've got about five or six little boys and girls hanging around with coke bottles and ginger-ale bottles ... and you're confronted by some ambassador who's got his hand in your pocket trying to shake your spine and give you compliments. I won't let *anybody* backstage anymore. Even to give me a compliment. I just don't care. . . .'

His eyes cleared: 'You can't ask me about how I sleep. You can't ask me about how I make it, and you cannot ask me what I think I am doing here. Other than that, we'll just get along fine. You just ask me anything and I will shoot right back ... Now, we have one thing straight about the book. I'm going to tell Albert we have come to an understanding about the book. I'll give you as much time as I can. I'll come very quickly to the point in all the things that I want done, but you can easily go back on me ... But I won't forgive you for doing that, man. It's not going to be a biography, because I'm not dead yet. It's going to be a timeless thing, right?

'Nobody knows about me. What do people really know? That my father's name is Zimmerman and my mother's family is middle class? I'm not about to go around telling people that this is false ... I'm not covering up anything I did before. I'm not going back on anything, any statement or anything I've ever done ... I've given up trying to tell anybody that they are wrong in their thinking about anything, about the world, or me, or whatever ... Now, you are not going to say "authorized by Bob Dylan". I'll write that on the cover. I'll write four sentences on the cover and sign my name, to something like "Bob Shelton wrote me up in *The New York Times* five years ago. And he's a nice guy and I like him. And he wrote this book and for that, it is not" – just to make sure it sells in Nebraska and Wyoming – "it's not chintzy".' Dylan laughed.

'There is nothing anybody can expose about me. Everybody thinks that there is such an exposé, on millions of little tiny things, like name change. It doesn't really matter to me. Obviously, there are people who like to read that shit. And people might say, "Oh, I don't believe it", or, "That doesn't matter to me." But it tickled them, you know.' Twisting restlessly, Dylan was getting angry at the hungers of his audience. He seemed to want to *explain* himself. He tried a new beginning: 'I think of all that I do as my *writing*. It cheapens it to call it anything else but writing. But there is not a person on the earth who takes it less seriously than I do. I know that it's not gong to help me into heaven one little bit. It's not going to keep me out of the fiery furnace. It's not going to extend my life any and it's not going to make me happy.'

What did he think would make him happy? I asked. 'I'm happy, you know,' he said. 'I'm happy to just be able to come across things. I don't need to be happy. Happiness is a kind of cheap word. Let's face it, I'm not the kind of cat that's going to cut off an ear if I can't do something. I would commit suicide. I would shoot myself in the brain if things got bad. I would jump from a window ... You know, I can think about death openly. It's nothing to fear. It's nothing sacred. I've seen so many people die.' I asked: Is life sacred? 'Life's not sacred either,' Dylan replied. 'Look at all the spirits that actually control the atmosphere, which are not living and yet which attract you, as ideas, or like games with the solar system. Or look at the farce of politics, economy and war.'

Another variation on an old theme: inner despair battling outer hope. 'It's become so easy for me to do everything, you have no idea, man, everything at my command. I can make money now doing absolutely anything. But I don't want that kind of money. I'm not a millionaire now, in terms of everything I have. But it is really close ... This next year, I'm going to be a millionaire, but that means nothing. To be a millionaire means that next year you can lose it all. You must realize that I have not copped out on one thing. I mean, I love what I do. I also make money off it ... Hey, I sing honest stuff, man, and it's consistent. It's *all* I do. I don't give a damn what anybody says. Nobody can criticize what I do that's going to have any effect on me. I never really read what people say about me. I'm just not interested.

'When I first really knew that I had money that I couldn't see, I looked around to see what a few of my agents were doing with it. First of all, I like chauffeurs. When I came back from England last time, I didn't buy a chauffeur, but I sure rented one. I make no bones about it ... I *need* the money to *employ* people. It all works hand in hand. If I had no money, I could walk *invisible*. But it costs me money now to be able to walk invisible. That's the *only* reason I need the money. I don't need the money to buy clothes or nothing ...' Again his anger mounted. 'I'm sick of giving creeps money off my soul. When I lose my teeth tomorrow, they are not going to buy me a new pair of teeth. I don't like little short people who smoke Tiparillo cigarettes and have their pockets turned inside out all the time and wear glasses and who once wanted to be Groucho Marx making all the money off me. And there are a lot of them ... All in the music business.

'Oh, if it's not the promoter cheating you, it's the box office cheating you. Somebody is always giving you a hard time ... Even the record company figures won't be right. Nobody's going to be straight with you because nobody wants the information out. Do you know that up to a certain point I made more money on a song I wrote if it were on an album by Carolyn Hester, or anybody, than if I did it myself. That's the contract they gave me. Horrible! Horrible! ...

'I'm not going to be accepted, but I would like to be accepted ... by *The Hogtown Dispatch* literary crowd, who wear violets in their crotch and make sure that they get on all the movie and TV reviews and also write about the ladies' auxiliary meetings and the PTA gatherings, you know, all in the same column. I would like to be accepted by them people. But I don't think I'm ever going to be. Whereas The Beatles have been.' Did he want The Beatles' sort of acceptance? 'No, no, no ... I'm not saying that. I'm just saying The Beatles have arrived, right? In all music forms, whether Stravinsky or

261

Leopold Jake the Second, who plays in the Five Spot, The Black Muslim Twins, or whatever. The Beatles are accepted, and you've got to accept them for what they do. They play songs like "Michelle" and "Yesterday". A lot of smoothness there.'

When I told him Joan Baez planned to record 'Yesterday' on her next album, Bob responded: 'Yeah, it's the thing to do, to tell all the teeny-boppers, "I dig The Beatles", and you sing a song like "Yesterday" or "Michelle". Hey, God knows, it's such a cop-out, man, both of those songs. If you go into the Library of Congress, you can find a lot better than that. There are millions of songs like "Michelle" and "Yesterday" written in Tin Pan Alley.' There aren't millions of songs like *his* being written by anyone, I suggested. 'I don't know if I fully appreciate that because it's going to get to the point where nobody else is going to be able to sing my songs but me. Like, I'm going to drive myself right out of business. I'll have to put out ten thousand records a year, for God's sake, because nobody will record the songs I write.' Did he influence young people because he broke the rules? 'It's not a question of breaking the rules, don't you understand? I don't break the rules, because I don't see any rules to break. As far as I'm concerned, there aren't any rules . . .'

Like Lenny Bruce, he was riffing, in and out of communication, like a jazzman going in and out of a melody line. It was word music, chin music, symbol music. 'My thing is with colors. It's not black and white. It's always been with colors, whether with clothes or anything. Color. Now, with something like that driving you, sometimes it gets very fiery red, you under-stand? And at times it gets very jet black.'

Robert Shelton, No Direction Home (1986)

five

1966–71

'Blows the mind'

TEENSET ®

THE MAGAZINE FOR TODAY'S MUSIC SCENE • MAY, 1968   50c

BARRY GIBB   GRACE SLICK   PAUL McCARTNEY

MUSIC SPECIAL 1968: SAN FRANCISCO AND BOSTON FLY A KITE WITH TEENSET! THE BEE GEES! HOW TO INTERVIEW PAUL McCARTNEY! BE A TEENSET CAMPUS REPORTER! SEE PAGE 43

'. . . for the adolescent with potential pop talent in any field, pop culture offers the only key to the instant golden life, the passport to the country of "Now" where everyone is beautiful and nobody grows old.'

George Melly, Introduction, Revolt into Style (1970)

The unprecedented expansion of the youth and music industries encouraged a new, generational politics which was broadly libertarian (sex, drugs), oppositional (on a wide variety of issues, most obviously the Vietnam War), Utopian. This naïve but electrifying conflation of purchasing with political power was concentrated in America but coincided with the social liberalization then occurring in the UK, where in 1967/8 the laws on divorce, abortion and homosexuality were relaxed. This was the period of pop's greatest outreach.

For a brief moment, there seemed to be no limits. This was the 'everlasting present' that pop had always promised, and which was now compounded by new chemicals like LSD. As Cherry Vanilla says in Jean Stein's *Edie*: 'You really believed that you were going to travel in this bubble right out to the end of the stratosphere.' Richard Goldstein and Tom Wolfe record here the beginnings of the acid subculture – the light (Ken Kesey, San Francisco) and the dark (Andy Warhol, New York). In Britain, LSD culture was far more of a fashion: both George Melly and Joe Orton note the drug's arrival with a sharp eye for social nuance.

Pop became messianic, the harbinger of a new society. During this period, its coverage was often marked by high seriousness, as literary writers queued to record this new phenomenon: Joan Didion's eyewitness account of a Doors' recording session is a good example. This was the heyday of the New Journalism, as writers like Tom Wolfe, Hunter S. Thompson and Norman Mailer found stories that they could get their teeth into, stories that suited a style which many thought excessive but in fact merely matched the tempo of the times.

New media opened up to pop writing. In America, the success story from this period was the magazine *Rolling Stone*, founded in 1967 by Jann Wenner and freely available in England soon after: Sheila Weller's article on Jimi Hendrix is a good example of the magazine's early style. In England, the underground magazine *OZ* provided a platform for writers like Germaine Greer – whose 'Mozic and Revolution' is a bulletin from within the underground which attests to the power of music itself.

One upside of the 'sexual revolution' was the slow progress of feminism: charted here by Robert Christgau in an article that is part apology, part call-to-arms. The potential downside is highlighted by Jenny Fabian and Johnny Byrne's infamous *roman-à-clef*, *Groupie*, which, based on real-life pop groups like Pink Floyd (Satin Odyssey) and Family (Relation),

267

introduced the figure that was an object of media fascination in the late sixties: the ever-available woman, the Groupie.

The mainstream media also opened up. The New Journalism could be found in *Esquire*, *New York Magazine* and the *New York Times*. There were fewer outlets in England: the colour supplements of the broadsheets and magazines like *New Society*. Angela Carter's ruminations on 'Sixties Style' is in the *NS* tradition of social observation (MacInnes and Gosling), but with an entirely fresh slant: fusing analysis and mythology with gender politics. And William Rees-Mogg's July 1967 *Times* editorial is still seen as a benchmark in the English establishment's acceptance of pop culture.

'Who Breaks a Butterfly on a Wheel?' was published at the point when hysteria about youth and drugs was at its height, and the Rolling Stones were the scapegoats. In May 1966, guitarist Brian Jones had talked to a *News of the World* reporter about his use of drugs – marijuana, LSD. The paper ran the story but attributed the quotes to Mick Jagger. Jagger started legal proceedings, which were overtaken by his arrest on 12 February, along with Keith Richard, Marianne Faithfull and art dealer Robert Fraser.

On 29 June 1967, Jagger and Richard were sentenced by Judge Leslie Block to custodial sentences of three months and one year respectively. After a day in jail, they were released on bail pending an appeal. The *Times* editorial appeared the next day. On 31 July, Lord Chief Justice Parker quashed Richard's conviction and substituted a one-year conditional discharge for Jagger's prison sentence. Jagger was flown by helicopter to one of the more surreal media events of the decade: a televised summit meeting with four embodiments of the establishment – former Home Secretary Lord Stow Hill, the Bishop of Woolwich, leading British Jesuit Father Corbishley, and Rees-Mogg himself. This *World in Action* special for Granada TV was produced by John Birt.

The scandal highlighted an essential fact: the more confident youth became, the more many adults were resistant to youth's perceived (and actual) excesses. In *Come Together*, John Wiener spotlights the radicalization of John Lennon, whose opposition to the Vietnam War was echoed on the ground by teens like Iggy Pop, who did anything they could to escape the draft – in this case, 'queering out'. Simon Napier-Bell's acid memoir shows how the bacchanalia of managers like the Who's Kit Lambert was matched by the anarchic behaviour of groups like John's Children.

In America, the dream of black/white integration that had been the project of the Civil Rights Movement began to fade with the summer 1967 riots in Detroit and Newark. There was a sudden polarization, captured in the gap between Stanley Booth's description of Otis Redding recording his break-through hit 'The Dock of the Bay' and soul doyen Dave Godin's warnings about integration only a few months later – 'the inevitable confrontation'. Redding himself, the embodiment of integration after his appearance at the Monterey Pop Festival, died in a plane crash in December 1967.

The American struggle between youth and adulthood reached its height in July 1968, when demonstrations at the Chicago Democratic Convention spilled over into open warfare between acid-politicos the Yippies and Mayor Daley's police. Norman Mailer was there, and his description of the group MC5 – 'the sound of mountains crashing' – freezes pop at the height of its sixties curve. Together with the assassinations of Martin Luther King and Robert Kennedy, the Chicago riots marked the end of hope in American pop – and, by implication, in America itself.

Three extracts record just how grim things had got by the turn of the decade: poet turned sleaze chronicler Ed Sanders details how false messiah Charles Manson wilfully appropriated the Beatles' lyrics to his own homicidal ends; Stanley Booth takes you right into the collective irresponsibility, false consciousness and failure of will which resulted in the blood-bath of Altamont – the collapse of the 'Woodstock Nation' festival fantasy; and Hunter S. Thompson records how what had promised liberation – drugs, sex, rock music – had become the means of obliteration, 'a powerful continuous hiss to drown out everything strange'.

1966: The Trips Festival

This was a beautiful mess and no two ways about it. A second offense for possession of marijuana carried an automatic five-year sentence with no possibility of parole. At the very least he stood to get the full three-year sentence in San Mateo County now, as one of the judge's conditions had been that he no longer associate with the Pranksters. Mountain Girl was ready to take the whole rap herself. 'We were just tying it off,' she told the press. 'He wasn't supposed to hang around with any of us wild, giddy people any more. This was the last time we were gonna see him.' Well . . . she tried. Kesey's probation officer in San Mateo County advised him for godsake stay away from the Trips Festival or he was in for it, but the whole thing was miles beyond in-for-it, out towards old Edge City, in fact.

Kesey left Municipal Court in San Francisco on January 20 with Mountain Girl and Stewart Brand and onto the whole bus full of Pranksters to roll through San Francisco advertising the Trips Festival. They got out at Union Square. Kesey wore a pair of white Levi's with the backsides emblazoned with HOT on the left side and COLD on the right and TIBET in the middle – and a pair of sky-blue boots. They all played Ron Boisie's Thunder Machine for loon vibrations in Union Square in the fibrillating heart of San Francisco.

If nothing else, Kesey's second arrest was great publicity for the Trips Festival. It was all over San Francisco newspapers. In the hip, intellectual and even social worlds of San Francisco, the Trips Festival notion was spreading like a fever. *The dread drug LSD.* Acid heads. An LSD experience without the LSD, it was being billed as – moreover, people actually believed it. But mainly the idea of a new life style was making itself felt. Do you suppose this is the *new wave . . .?*

And you buy y'r ticket, f'r chrissake – an absurd thought to Norman Hartweg – *and we've got a promoter* – all absurd, but the thousands pour into the Longshoremen's Hall for the Trips Festival, thousands even the first night, which was mostly Indian night, a weird thing put on by Brand's America Needs Indians, but now on Saturday evening the huge crush hits for the Acid Test. Norman is absolutely zonked on acid – and look at the freaks running in here. Norman is not the only one. 'An LSD experience without LSD' – that was a laugh. In fact, the heads are pouring in by the hundreds, bombed out of their gourds, hundreds of heads coming out into the absolute open for the first time. It is like the time the Pranksters went to the Beatles concert in full costume, looking so bizarre and so totally *smashed* that no one could believe they were. Nobody would *risk* it in public like this. Well, the kids are just having an LSD experience without LSD, that's all, and this is what it looks like. A hulking crazed whirlpool. That's nice. Lights and movies sweeping around the hall; five movie projectors going and God knows how many light machines, interferrometrics, the intergalactic science-fiction seas all over the walls, loudspeakers studding the hall all the way around like flaming chandeliers, strobes exploding, black lights with Day-Glo objects under them and Day-Glo paint to play with, street lights at every entrance flashing red and yellow, two bands, the Grateful Dead and Big Brother and the Holding Company and a troop of weird girls in leotards leaping around the edges blowing dog whistles – and the Pranksters. Paul Foster has wrapped black friction tape all around his shoes and up over his ankles and swaddled his legs and hips and torso in it up to his rib cage, where begins a white shirt and then white bandaging all over his face and skull and just a slit for his eyes, over which he wears dark glasses. He also wears a crutch and a sign saying, 'You're in the Pepsi Generation and I'm a pimply freak!' Rotor! Also heads from all over, in serapes and mandala beads and Indian headbands and Indian beads, the great era for all that, and one in a leather jerkin with 'Under Ass Wizard Mojo Indian Fighter' stenciled on the back. Mojo! Oh the freaking strobes turning every brain stem into a cauliflower erupting into corrugated ping-pong balls – *can't stand it* – and a girl rips off her shirt and dances bare-breasted with her great mihs breaking up into an endless stream of ruby-red erect nipples streaming out of the great milk-and-honey under the strobe lights. The dancing is ecstatic, a nice macaroni of braless breasts jiggling and cupcake bottoms wiggling and multiple arms writhing and leaping about. Thousands of straight intellectuals and culturati and square hippies, North Beach style, gawking and learning. Dr Francis Rigney, Psychiatrist to the beat Generation, looking on, and all the Big Daddies left over from the beat period, Eric 'Big Daddy' Nord and Tom 'Big Daddy' Donahue, and the press, vibrating under Ron Boise's thunder machine. A great rout in progress, you understand.

And in the center of the hall – the Pranksters' tower of Control. It had come to that, and it was perfect. Babbs had supervised the building of a great scaffolding of pipes and platforms in the center of the hall. It rose and rose, this tower, as the Pranksters added equipment, all the mikes and amplifiers and spots and projectors and all the rest of it, the very architecture of Control, finally. Babbs at the controls, Hagen up there taking movies; the Movie goes on. Kesey, meanwhile, was up on an even higher plateau of control, up on a balcony in a silver space suit complete with a big bubble space helmet. He conceived of it first as a disguise, so he could be there without the various courts being raggy and outraged, but everyone recognized the Space Man immediately, of course, and he perched up above the maelstrom with a projection machine with which you could write messages on acetate and project them in mammoth size on the walls.

Zonker dancing in a spin of pure unadulterated bliss, higher than he had ever been in his life, which for Zonker was getting up there. Norman, smashed, but with a mission. Norman to circulate among the multitudes with movie camera. Only he has no power pack, so he has to plug the camera in a wall socket and go out with a great long cord. His eye pressed against the sighting lens and gradually the whole whirlpool coming into his one eye, unity, *I*, the vessel, receiving all. Atman and Brahman, letting it all flow in until – *satori* – the perfect state is reached and he realizes he is God. He has traveled miles through this writhing macaroni ecstasy mass and could the camera still possibly be plugged in? – or could that possibly matter? *deus ex machina*, with the world flowing into one eye. Becomes essential that he

271

reach the Central Node, the Tower of Control, the great electric boom of the directional mike picking up the band sticking out from atop the scaffolding tower – *and there it is* – it is all there in this moment. Starts clambering up the scaffolding with the huge camera still over his shoulder and up to his eye, all funneling in, and the wire and plug snaking behind him, through the multitudes. And who might *these* irate forms be? – in truth, Babbs and Hagen, Babbs gesturing for Norman to get off the platform, he's in the way, *there's no room, get the hell off of here* – a cosmic laugh, since obviously they don't know who he is, viz., God. Norman, the meek, the mild, the retiring, the sideliner, laughs a cosmic laugh at them and keeps on coming. At any moment, he fully realizes, he can make them disappear down . . . his eye, just two curds in the world flow, Babbs and Hagen.

'Norman, if you don't get the hell off of here, I'm going to *throw* you off!' – Babbs looking huge and untamable in the same stance he gave the San Francisco cops at the Fillmore, and Norman's mind split just slightly along the chiasma, like a San Andreas fault, one part some durable hard-core fear of getting thrown off and breaking his ass, him, Norman, but the other, the Cosmic laugh of God at how useless Babbs' stance is now, vibrating slightly between God and not-God, but then the laugh comes in a wave, just the cosmic fact that he, Norman, now dares do this, *defiance*, the new *I* and there is not one thing, really, they can do about it – Babbs staring at this grinning, zonked figure with the huge camera climbing up the scaffolding. Babbs just throws his hands up, gives up, Norman ascends. *God!* in the very Tower of Control. *Well, if I'm God, I can control this thing.* Gazing down into the whirlpool. He gestures – and it comes to pass! – there is a ripple in the crowd *there* and again and there is a ripple in the crowd *here* – also so clear what is *going* to happen, he can predict it, a great eruption of ecstatic dancing in *that* clump, under the strobes, it will *break out now*, and it does, of course – a vibration along the crack, the fault, *synchronicity* spoken here, and we are at play, but they **do** it – *start the music!* – and it starts – *satori*, in the Central Node, as it was written – but I say unto you – and at that very moment, a huge message in red is written on the walls.

ANYBODY WHO KNOWS HE IS GOD GO UP ON STAGE

Anybody? – The chiasmic halves vibrate, the God and the not-God, and then he realizes: Kesey wrote that. Kesey up on the balcony in his space suit wrote that with his projection machine and flashed it on the wall, in that very moment. What to do, Archangel of mine, Norman stares unbelieving – unbelieving in what? – up on stage climbs a spade with a wild head of natural spade hair with a headband wrapped around the hairline so that the hair puffs up like a great gray dandelion, a huge shirt swimming under the lights, and it is Gaylord, one of the few spades in the whole thing, gleaming the glistening grin of acid zonk and going into a lovely godly little dance, this Gaylord God . . . What the hell. Norman gestures toward the crowd, and it does not ripple. Not here and not there. He predicts *that* clump will rise up in ecstatic levitation, and it does not rise up. In fact, it just sinks to the floor like it was spat there, sad moon eyes glomming up in the acid stare. Sayonara, God. And yet . . . And yet . . .

Three nights the huge wild carnival went on. It was a big thing on every level. For one thing, the Trips Festival grossed $12,500 in three days, with almost no overhead, and a new nightclub and dance-hall genre was born. Two weeks later Bill Graham was in business at the Fillmore auditorium with a Trips Festival going every weekend and packing them in. For the acid heads themselves, the Trips Festival was like the first national convention of an underground movement that had existed on a hush-hush cell-by-cell basis. The heads were amazed at how big their own ranks had become – and euphoric over the fact that they could come out in the open, high as baboons, and the sky, and the law, wouldn't fall down on them. The press went along with the notion that this had been an LSD experience without the LSD. Nobody in the hip world of San Francisco had any such delusion, and the Haight-Ashbury era began that weekend.

Tom Wolfe, *The Electric Kool-Aid Acid Test* (1968)

1966: A Quiet Evening at the Balloon Farm

Mixed media. Lots of light. Noise enough to make your ears sing back. Blows the mind.

Okay; a psychedelic discotheque. But what's with this balloon farm thing?

Bob Dylan named it. You're supposed to figure out what it means to you.

Inside, there's this couple. Dancing. The girl, in a paisley shift and tree-bark stockings, seems to be moving to some internal rhythm. Her partner is bathed in light: electric blue. He swings low, encircling her waist without touching. His tongue darts snakelike toward her hips, retreating as she grinds forward. The girl takes off her glasses and hands them to her partner. She swoops as the walls play a strobe-lit threnody. Wow – you don't see that stuff on 'Hullabaloo'.

The dance is called 'The Gobble'. It started on the Lower East Side, with the Fugs. Now, they're grinding out that kind of hip ritual in Forest Hills (where a spade is something you garden with). But the Gobble can be done anywhere. Which is fortunate, because the Balloon Farm is not your average rock-'n'-ravage joint. The place has atmosphere. Originally called the Dom (which is Polish for 'home'), it's a huge, mirrored ballroom where generations of immigrants came to dance, drink and maybe find a little affection. The men's rooms still retain that compelling stench of wine and sausage. The dance floor is still scuffed from the pounding of a million stomping polkas. Even though the hippies have made St Mark's Place their drag, the old gestalt lingers on, haunting the Balloon Farm with the irony of a Straight tradition.

Which brings us to Andy Warhol. This is Andy's club so it shows his movies. On one screen, a lady who is possibly a man munches away on a ripe banana. ('I don't give a damn; either way, it's suggestive,' says a timid soul to my right.) On another screen, someone is eating peanuts, cracking the shells, gnawing the insides, spitting out the husks. And on the center screen, they have tied someone to a chair and are putting cigarettes out in his nose, winding belts around his neck and fitting a tight leather mask over his face. Just like in the movies!

That's called *Vinyl*. Its creator (call him 'A-a-ah-ndy', and smile a lot when you say that) is sitting quietly in the balcony. He is working the projector, pensive and subdued in his black-chino-polo-shirt-leather-jacket-uniform. Close-up, his face is leathery as well. Mirror sunglasses make his eyes totally inaccessible. His hair is straight, bright silver.

'Hi,' he says.

'Who's the peanut man?' you ask, to return the greeting.

'Henry.'

'Uh-huh.'

'Geldzahler.'

('Isn't he with the Jordanaires,' you long to ask, but you content yourself with a soft, knowing, 'Beautiful.')

He turns back to the projector, his fingers busily shuffling tins of film. Lights crackle like horsewhips around him. ('When it looks like they're enjoying it, he makes it all go faster,' someone near me offers.) Onstage, Gerard Malanga grabs a roll of phosphorescent tape and wraps it around his partner and himself. Handed a whip, he snaps it in time to the strobes. As a finale, he smothers his body in yellow paint and grabs a purple spotlight, which makes him glow and deepens the shadow around his eyes and teeth. Speed zone. He untangles two blinking strobe lights and swings them around his hips, sending violent, stabbing rays into the audience. ('At least he didn't piss on us,' I heard a teeniebopper whisper; her friend grumbled back, 'They said he would, too.')

Definitely light. For the next ten minutes, electricity becomes a weapon of frontal assault. Bulbs blink patterns onto the ceiling and the mirrored walls. Colored sparks twinkle ominously and those two portable strobes make your entire line of vision sway. It's all very much like sitting stoned in the middle of a tinseled Christmas tree.

'Okay,' says the girl in the tree-bark stockings. 'It's a little confusing at first, I'll admit. My shrink could probably give out calling cards at the exit. But ... see ... it's like one of those connect the dots pictures, where everything is jumbled until you take a pencil and put it all together. Then it becomes a picture – it makes sense.'

Which brings us to the Velvet Underground, not a first class car on the London transit system, but Andy's rock group. Sometimes they sing, sometimes they just stroke their instruments into a single, hour-long jam. Their sound is a savage series of atonal thrusts and electronic feedback. Their lyrics combine sado-masochistic frenzy with free-association imagery. The whole thing seems to be the product of a secret marriage between Bob Dylan and the Marquis De Sade. It takes a lot to laugh; it takes a train to cry.

Andy says he is through with phosphorescent flowers and cryptic soup-cans. Now it's rock. He may finally conquer the world through its soft, teenage underbelly.

'It's ugly,' he admits. 'It's a very ugly effect when you put it all together. But it's beautiful. You know, you just look at the whole thing – the Velvets playing and Gerard dancing and all the film and light, and it's a beautiful thing. Very Vinyl. Beautiful.'

'Yeah, beautiful. There are beautiful sounds in rock. Very lazy, dreamlike noises. You can forget about the lyrics in most songs. Just dig the noise, and you've got our sound. We're putting everything together – lights and film and music – and we're reducing it to its lowest common denominator. We're musical primitives.'

That's John Cale, composer, guitarist and resident Welshman for the Velvet Underground. He plays a mean, slashing viola. And piano, when he has to. He and Lou Reed once shared a three-room flat on Ludlow Street and a group called the Primitives. Their place was cold (broken crates in a wood-burning fireplace looked very chic but also kept the blood circulating). The group was cold too, bassman Sterling Morrison recalls: 'Sometimes we'd do more jumping around in a night than the goddam waitresses. Before Andy saw us at the Cafe Bizarre (which isn't exactly the Copa of McDougal Street) we were busting our balls in work. Up to here. And you can't do anything creative when you're struggling to keep the basic stuff coming. Now it seems we have time to catch our breath. We have more direction – that's where Andy comes in. We eat better, we work less and we've found a new medium for our music. It's one thing to hustle around for odd jobs. But now we're not just another band; we're an act. See – when a band becomes an act, you get billing. You get days off. You don't just work nights – you're, like, Engaged.'

Nightly at the Balloon Farm the Velvets demonstrate what distinguishes an act from a band. They are special. They even have a chanteuse – Nico, who is half goddess, half icicle. If you say bad things about her singing, she doesn't talk to you. If you say nice things, she doesn't talk to you either. If you say that she sounds like a bellowing moose, she might smile if she digs the sound of that in French. Onstage, she is somewhat less communicative. But she sings in perfect mellow ovals. It sounds something like a cello getting up in the morning. All traces of melody depart early in her solo. The music courses into staccato heats, then slows into syrupy feedback. All this goes on until everyone is satisfied that the point has gotten across.

Oh yeah; the point! John Cale sits dreamily eyeing a Coke, pushes his hair back from his face to expose a bony nose, and observes: 'You can't pin it down.' (Granted.) 'It's a conglomeration of the senses. What we try to get here is a sense of total involvement.' (You mean acid, scoobie-doobie-doo?)

'Coming here on a trip is bound to make a tremendous difference. But we're here to stimulate a different kind of intoxication. The sounds, the visual stuff – all this bombarding of the senses – it can be very heady in itself, if you're geared to it.'

John Cale is a classicist. His first composition was 'written on a rather large piece of plywood'. He studied viola and piano at the London Conservatory of Music and came to the United States as a Leonard Bernstein fellow. His sponsor was Aaron Copland, 'We didn't get on very well,' John says, 'Copland said I couldn't play my work at Tanglewood. It was too destructive, he said. He didn't want his piano wrecked.'

Cale pursued his vision with John Cage. On the viola, he would play a single note for as long as two hours. Then he met Lou Reed, and the sound that John calls 'controlled distortion' was born.

The Velvets, with Nico and Andy and all that light, began to construct a scene around the title 'Exploding Plastic Inevitable'. They've done quite a bit of traveling since, and their reviews reflect the ambivalence a quiet evening at the Balloon Farm can produce. Said the *Chicago Daily News*: 'The flowers of evil are in full bloom.' *Los Angeles* magazine compared the sound to 'Berlin in the decadent thirties.' Even Cher (of Sonny and Cher) was heard to mutter: 'It will replace nothing except suicide.'

Dauntless, the troupe returned home. Now they are popping eardrums and brandishing horsewhips on a nightly basis. Their first album sounds a bit restrained (though a long, harrowing cut called 'Heroin' isn't exactly calculated to make the radio as a 'good-guy sure-shot'). But it's still The Sound. And the group is brimming with innovation.

'We want to try an electronic drum,' says John. 'It would produce subsonic sounds, so you could feel it even when you couldn't hear it. We'd then be able to add it to a piece of music, and it would be like underlining the beat' (in cement).

Onstage, Gerard Malanga motions wildly. They have run out of records, and that means it's time for another set. John puts down his Coke and wraps a black corduroy jacket over his turtleneck. He slides his hair over his face, covering his nose again. Lou tucks his shirt in.

'Young people know where everything is at,' he says. 'Let 'em sing about going steady on the radio. Let 'em run their hootenannies. But it's in holes like this that the real stuff is being born. The university and the radio kill everything, but around here, it's alive. The kids know that.'

The girl in the bark stockings is leaning against the stage, watching them warm up. 'You can tell this is going to be a very atonal set,' she says. 'It's something about the way they handle their instruments when they first come on stage.'

'Beautiful,' sighs her partner, rolling his larynx and his eyes. With a single humming chord, which seems to hang in the air, the Velvet Underground launches into another set. John squints against a purple spotlight. Lou shouts against a groaning amplifier. Gerard writhes languidly to one side. Sterling turns his head to sneeze. And Nico stands there, looking haunted. The noise, the lights, the flickering images – all happen. Everybody grooves.

From the balcony, Andy Warhol watches from behind his glasses. 'Beautiful,' he whispers. Sterling sneezes audibly but it seems to fit. 'Beautiful.' Gerard hands his partner a bullwhip and the girl in bark begins to sway. 'Just beautiful.'

Richard Goldstein, *New York Magazine*, 1967

1966: First Steps toward Radical Politics: The 1966 Tour

When the Beatles arrived in Memphis on their 1966 summer tour, they discovered that a massive Christian rally, organized by a hundred fundamentalist ministers, had been scheduled to protest their appearance. The problem was John. He had recently said the Beatles were 'more popular than Jesus'. The English, in their matter-of-fact way, had concluded he was correct. But in the God-fearing United States, the religious right accused him of 'blasphemy' and took after him like a pack of wolves while the media watched and chuckled. The 'more popular than Jesus' controversy pushed John to take his first steps away from the Beatles and toward the antiwar activism that would become central to his life and work.

The leader of the Memphis ministers had a name that could have come out of a B movie: the Reverend Jimmy Stroad. He issued a grim challenge, declaring that the Christian rally would 'give the youth of the mid-South an opportunity to show Jesus Christ is more popular than the Beatles'. And he offered as competition against the Beatles not only Jesus but also Jay North, the child actor who had played Dennis the Menace on TV.

Until John's 'Jesus' comment the Beatles had been the good boys of rock, in contrast to the nasty and sexually aggressive Rolling Stones. Parents considered the Beatles playful and harmless. Ed Sullivan liked them. But America's fundamentalist ministers saw them in a completely different light. 'What have the Beatles said or done to so ingratiate themselves with those who eat, drink and think revolution?' asked David Noebel, author of a series of anti-Beatle tracts beginning in 1965. 'The major value of the Beatles to the left in general ... has been their usefulness in destroying youth's faith in God.' He carefully combed through all of John's work and came up with strong evidence that the 'Jesus' remark was part of a larger and more sinister pattern. In John's book *A Spaniard in the Works* he had written about 'Father, Sock and Mickey Most'. (Mickey Most produced records by Herman's Hermits.) That phrase, Noebel felt, did a lot to destroy youth's faith in God and his only begotten sock.

In Memphis the city commission agreed with the fundamentalists. An official statement declared, 'The Beatles are not welcome in Memphis.' Memphis, where Elvis Presley had recorded his first songs, awakening John Lennon from his teenage torpor; Memphis, the subject of a Chuck Berry classic the Beatles had played over and over in their early days; Memphis, where Jerry Lee Lewis had sung about the shaking that was going on; Memphis, a center of black music, where that very summer of 1966 Carla

Thomas recorded the rocking 'Let Me Be Good to You' and Sam and Dave recorded the stirring 'Hold On, I'm Comin'' – how could the Beatles not be welcome in Memphis?

The day after the city fathers issued their statement, Beatles manager Brian Epstein revealed his strategy: apologize for everything. He released a telegram to the press declaring that he 'wished to assure the people of Memphis and the mid-South that the Beatles will not, by word, action or otherwise, in any way offend or ridicule the religious beliefs of anyone throughout their forthcoming concert tour . . . Furthermore, John Lennon deeply and sincerely regrets any offence that he might have caused.'

The week before the concert, the local newspaper was filled with debate, including statements from several ministers attacking the fundamentalist counterrally. The rector of Holy Trinity Episcopal Church wrote, 'I do not care for the Beatles. I would not go to their concert. I do not even think that the noise which they produce falls in the category of what we call music. Nevertheless, the truth of John Lennon's statement cannot be denied.'

A Methodist pastor quoted part of John's statement and declared that it contained a correct description of the anti-Beatle ministers in Memphis: 'Jesus was all right but his disciples are thick and ordinary. It's them twisting it that ruins it for me.' A Memphis youth attending Louisiana State University wrote that the city fathers should 'for once in their lives overcome the idea that everything that enters Memphis not carrying a cross is evil . . . Is your religion so weak that four rock-and-roll players can shake it?'

The Beatles and their entourage had been frightened as the Memphis date approached. When they left London, fans had screamed, 'John, please don't go; they'll kill you!' John had the same fear. Later he explained, 'I didn't want to tour because I thought they'd kill me – 'cause they take things so seriously there. They shoot you, and then they realize it wasn't that important. So I didn't want to go. But Brian, and Paul, and the other Beatles persuaded me to come. I was scared stiff.' He wasn't the only one. Paul McCartney had 'a horror of being shot on stage', according to Peter Brown, the Beatles' personal assistant. As the Beatles got off their plane in Memphis, Paul remarked ironically, 'We should be wearing targets here.' Because of the fear of a sniper in the audience, police at the concert were asked to 'keep a lookout for firearms'.

Subsequent accounts of what actually happened at the Beatles concert and the counterrally were confused. A best-selling history of the Beatles reported that while the Beatles were getting ready to go onstage, 'outside the Ku Klux Klan were holding an 8,000-strong counter demonstration'. In fact, the number of demonstrators outside the concert hall was closer to eight than eight thousand, but they were indeed Klansmen, wearing full white-sheet regalia. That never happened to Mick Jagger, despite his efforts to be outrageous. It was an honor of sorts for John to be the only white rock-and-roller to provoke a Klan picket line.

In the middle of their performance a sound like a gunshot rang out. A wave of fear crossed the Beatles' faces. 'Every one of us looked at each other,' John later explained, ''cause each thought it was the other that had been shot. It was that bad. I don't know how I did it.' Each quickly saw the others were okay, and they continued playing without missing a beat. Later they learned that what they had heard was only a cherry bomb.

While twenty thousand heard the Beatles, only eight thousand showed up across town for the counterrally, half of whom were adults. They didn't really count in the battle for the hearts of the mid-South's youth. Reverend Stroad implicitly conceded that Christ did not seem to be as popular as the Beatles, even in Memphis. He issued a new statement: the rally had 'shown the whole world that Christianity will not vanish', so at least John had been disproven on that point.

Poor attendance was not the counterrally's only problem. Dennis the Menace did not appear. Some of the fundamentalists objected to the program, and a group of thirty walked out of the rally in protest. Their spokesman declared that young people had been 'decoyed' by promises of a 'Christian testimonial service', but instead they had been given music inspired by Satan. They objected in particular to a vocal group that sang Christian songs 'to a modified "twist" while an accompanying combo maintained a throbbing beat,' the newspaper reported. It quoted the protesters: 'We might as well have gone to the Beatles.'

From the beginning of rock and roll, fundamentalist churches and white racists had organized against it. In 1956 the New York *Times* had reported that Southern white church groups were attempting to suppress 'Negro style' rock music because it corrupted white youth. The Alabama White Citizens Council, which had been organized to combat the civil rights movement, also took a stand on rock and roll, calling it 'a means of pulling the white man down to the level of the Negro. It is part of a plot to undermine the morals of the youth of our nation.' Members of the White Citizens Council attacked and beat Nat 'King' Cole during a concert in Birmingham in 1956. Ten years later John's 'Jesus' remark brought the same social forces back into the limelight.

Memphis was not the first American city to witness right-wing protests against Lennon's remark. The first demonstrations had been organized in Birmingham, the city which in 1966 symbolized the violent repression of civil rights. Three years earlier the Birmingham police had attacked civil rights demonstrators with high-pressure fire hoses and arrested 2,543 of them in a single week. Later the same year a black church in Birmingham was bombed, killing four girls. Now, at the end of July 1966, two weeks before the Beatles were to begin their fourth American tour, Birmingham was back in the news, as a local disc jockey named Tommy Charles organized a rally at which 'protesters' tossed their Beatles albums into a giant tree-grinding machine, turning them into dust. Mr Charles told visiting reporters that he was thirty-six years old 'but I think like a teenager'.

Within a few days, thirty other radio stations announced that they were banning Beatles records. Most were in the South, but stations in Boston and New York joined the ban. They included the one that had first promoted Beatlemania, calling itself 'W-A-Beatle-C'. Newspapers across the country published striking photos of kids in crew cuts grinning at Beatles record-burnings. The TV news showed a girl gleefully ripping the pages out of John's book *In His Own Write* and tossing them into the flames. The Grand Dragon of the South Carolina Ku Klux Klan held a ceremony in which he attached a Beatles record to a large wooden cross and set the cross on fire. The symbolism of the Beatles' music on the cross apparently escaped his notice.

The most striking event took place in Longview, Texas, where a record-burning was held on Friday the thirteenth of August, organized by radio station KLUE. The next day its transmitter was hit by lightning, knocking its news director unconscious and blasting the station off the air. The anti-Beatle organizers failed to draw the obvious conclusion.

The American demonstrations gained international support as the right-wing governments of Franco Spain and South Africa banned all Beatles music. South Africa lifted its ban on the Beatles when the group split in 1970, but continued to prohibit the broadcast of John's records. The Vatican's official newspaper *L'Osservatore Romano* announced that 'some subjects must not be dealt with profanely, not even in the world of beatniks'. Beatniks?

John's 'Jesus' remark had been at the top of the agenda at the first press conference when the Beatles began their tour on August 12 in Chicago. That city had just been the site of organized attacks on black people. The previous month Martin Luther King, Jr., had led a demonstration of forty thousand

281

people in Chicago, seeking to end discrimination in jobs and housing there. The campaign was his first attempt to confront institutional racism in the North. A week before the Beatles arrived in the city, a mob of four thousand whites, led by members of the American Nazi Party and the Ku Klux Klan, attacked and beat seven hundred black marchers, including King. He stated afterward, 'I have seen many demonstrations in the South, but I have never seen anything so hostile and so hateful as I've seen here today.'

For the media, however, the big news in Chicago on August 12 was not racist violence, but rather John's apology to Christians: 'If I said television was more popular than Jesus, I might have gotten away with it – I just said what I said and it was wrong, or it was taken wrong, and now there's all this.'

The reporters were unsatisfied. The next question was, 'But are you prepared to apologize?'

John tried again. 'I'm not anti-God, anti-Christ or antireligion. I am not saying we are greater or better. I believe in God, but not as one thing, not as an old man in the sky. I believe that what people call God is something in all of us. I believe that what Jesus and Mohammed and Buddha and all the rest said was right. It's just that the translations have gone wrong. I wasn't saying that Beatles are better than God or Jesus. I used "Beatles" because it's easy for me to talk about Beatles.'

Reporters continued to press him: 'Are you sorry about your statement concerning Christ?'

'I wasn't saying whatever they're saying I was saying . . . I'm sorry I said it, really. I never meant it to be a lousy antireligious thing . . . I apologize, if that will make you happy. I still don't know quite what I've done. I've tried to tell you what I did do, but if you want me to apologize, if that will make you happy, then okay, I'm sorry.'

'Would you say you are being crucified?'

. . . Although the Jesus remark captured the public's attention that summer, the Beatles involved themselves in another political controversy that would become much more important for John: the war in Vietnam. Two months before the 'Jesus' controversy, American disc jockeys had received the new Beatles album, '*Yesterday*' . . . *and Today*. Its cover showed the Beatles surrounded by slabs of raw, red meat and decapitated dolls. *Time* announced that the cover was 'a serious lapse in taste', and frightened Capitol Records executives issued an apology for what they called an 'attempt at pop satire'.

John, asked to explain, told reporters the butcher cover was 'as relevant as Vietnam'. He intended to be neither witty nor irreverent. He spoke seriously.

The Beatles may not have intended the butcher cover to be a comment on American butchery in Vietnam, but once it was suppressed, John cast it in that light. His statement showed for the first time that John perceived the 'relevance' of Vietnam – that the war was on his mind.

During the Beatles' American tour that summer of 1966, the Johnson administration escalated its war. In June the United States bombed Hanoi for the first time and announced a policy of systematic bombing of North Vietnam. The antiwar movement was growing. The previous year Students for a Democratic Society had sponsored the first march on Washington protesting the war, and twenty-five thousand people came. Shortly afterward students at Berkeley held a thirty-six hour teach-in against the war, and twelve thousand came to listen. In 1966 antiwar activity was spreading to campuses not usually considered centers of radicalism. When Johnson went to Princeton that spring to defend his Vietnam escalation, he was met with a large demonstration. LBJ questioned the manhood of opponents of the war: he called them 'nervous Nellies'.

John followed the news closely. Maureen Cleave wrote during that summer that he 'recalls all the daily newspapers ... He watches all TV news coverage.' The air war filled the front pages. As the Beatles left Memphis, the local newspaper reported, 'Reds gun down US' hottest pilot as Communist gunners score their heaviest toll of the war in bringing down US planes. US warplanes struck back, smashing North Vietnam with a record 139 bombing missions. US fliers streaking from Guam bagged their 18th MiG and hammered Communist targets in the South.'

When the Beatles held their ritual New York press conference later in the same week, the first questioner asked them to comment on any aspect of the Vietnam conflict. They answered in unison, 'We don't like war, war is wrong,' several times in a row. John later gave his own brief and trenchant answer to the question, what did they think about the war? 'We think of it every day. We don't like it. We don't agree with it. We think it's wrong.'

It was a bold and risky move, which Brian Epstein had urged them to avoid. John was aligning himself with antiwar students. He knew that only 10 percent of the public agreed with them at this time, according to opinion polls. And it was unprecedented for a leading rock group to take a political stand of any kind. That was only for Bob Dylan and Phil Ochs. John's 1966 statement deserves scrutiny. British historian Eric Hobsbawm commented, 'Most British people at the time would have said they thought the war in Vietnam was wrong, but very few would have said, "We think about it every day." That's remarkable.'

The contrast with their earlier New York press conferences was striking: no more playful banter, no more smiling faces. The Fab Four looked 'tired and pale', the New York *Times* reported. They were becoming part of the growing political conflict in America. On August 24, the same day the Beatles played their second Shea Stadium concert, newspapers reported that the House Un-American Activities Committee (HUAC) had proposed legislation to set criminal penalties for 'obstruction of the Vietnam war effort'. HUAC had investigated a Berkeley plan, led by Jerry Rubin, among others, to send medical supplies to North Vietnam and block troop trains.

That same day Stokely Carmichael announced a new political strategy for the Student Nonviolent Coordinating Committee, 'Black Power'. 'We must form our own institutions, credit unions, co-ops, political parties, write our own histories,' he declared, calling on white radicals in SNCC to leave the organization and instead work among whites to fight racism. Newspapers that day also reported that Mao's 'Red Guards for the cultural revolution' held their first major demonstration in Peking.

The antiwar movement, black power, Maoism – each of these would become increasingly important in John's life and music over the next few years, first when he denounced radicals 'carrying pictures of Chairman Mao' in his 1968 song 'Revolution' and then when he returned to New York in 1971 wearing a Mao badge, joining Jerry Rubin and sharing the stage with Black Power spokesmen.

John expected the mass media to trumpet the news that the Beatles had joined the antiwar camp. Everything about the Beatles sold newspapers. In fact, Epstein shouldn't have worried. The antiwar statement was published only in local New York newspapers, and even they did not feature it. The *Daily News* devoted six pages to Beatles coverage but only one sentence to the antiwar declaration. *Time* and *Newsweek* ran long stories on the Beatles' tour, focusing on the storm over John's 'Jesus' remark and ignoring the antiwar statement completely. John was portrayed as an arrogant egomaniac who had finally been slapped down by an outraged public. 'Lennon forgiven,' *Newsweek* chuckled, failing to see a crucial event in his life: his first step out of the role of the 'lad from Liverpool' toward radical politics. In the future, John would make sure that his political statements could not be ignored.

Jon Wiener, *Come Together: John Lennon in His Time* (1984)

1966: Queering Out

When I was first supposed to go up for the draft, it was the biggest quarterly callup, and hopefully would be the last, in modern American history in the absence of a DECLARED war. It was late 1966. They needed 650,000 guys to sign the dotted line within three months; each was to serve for two years. The authorities were accepting any and all, regardless of physical deformations. Such disregard of cost efficiency was blowing your mom and dad's bucks, dear reader. They were taking anybody: guys 'wid' ten teeth. Now Bill Figg, a drummer and friend of mine in a group called the Rationals, his knee had been held together with a steel rod since he was a kid. Bill must have been scared of the draft, but, unlike me, he was more scared of the disapproval of his peer group. It is army policy to induct all draftees, not by residence, but by school. Therefore, if you want to rebel you gotta do it right in front of all your fucking friends. Are they your friends? Fuck no! So why are they in the army? To be accepted and get killed. Bill Figg didn't come back.

I didn't want to go up for the draft for several reasons. One, I couldn't stand the idea of being a pawn of the sick society of America, dominated by men. Two, there was my musical career – the odds are so great anyway that, hey, you can't have an interruption. Anyway, no way José am I going to sleep in a bunkhouse with a bunch of crewcut machos: I hate guys – at least ones who call themselves guys – they are full of shit-shit-shit. I'm glad they are all dead, in one sense or another.

But mainly what kept me out of the army was the utter terror of two more years of even more closely enforced society, confined with the goddamn weasely little things – the sons of World War II vets – those cruel bottleneck-ers who comprised my peer group in America.

So I was still in the Prime Movers band at this time. They were older guys, a blues band. I was waiting, smelling out the right move: waiting for the Stooges to appear.

So what did I do? My strategy to get out was this. First, I said to my mom: 'Mom, you know I've really been looking like a ragamuffin.' So she bought me the kind of clothes that a mother buys, right? A pair of nice gray slacks that fit really absurdly, you know, and a funny crew neck, mauve sweaterish sort of polo shirt. I had my hair cut very short. I looked great as a mamma's boy, my disguise was impeccable.

My idea was to queer out. It was very difficult at that time. So I went down to the station, down to Fort Wayne, with my peer group. We all went down on a special bus line. They don't just say come to the fort. You can't do that, you have to go by way of the local designated private bus line. This is whatever firm that has secured the army contract for transport of inductees to God's cafeteria for food processing.

We all did a mental test, and then we took physicals, starting at station one. Station one is where you take off your clothes down to your skivvies, and then you're supposed to get in line for the next bullshit test. So, in my part of the room, I stripped off and didn't have any underwear, just bare naked – pretty clever plan, eh? I just whacked it a little bit and walked out with just the most enormous hard-on (11″ x 1¾″ at approximately a 94 degree angle), straight toward my place in line. I'd not gone four steps when a shout rang out: 'Halt!' A sergeant approached me. 'Where's your UNDERWEAR!!!'

So I got noticed right away. 'Help me out, man,' I said. So they sent me to a rest station to collect myself. I then hyperventilated and ran down the hall, stopping just before I saw a medic – so I was really shaking – and he said, 'What's wrong?' And I said, 'I'm gay, man, I'm scared to be here with my clothes off around other men.' So I went to the shrink, and he asked me questions like, 'What does gay mean? What's a queen?' things like that. By this time I was really into it, and he bought it and took me downstairs to the captain. I was almost in tears, I was so wrapped up in my role – lots of convulsions and tears. I started disgusting him and undermining his professional attitude, and he asked me to leave. It only took me an hour and a half to evade the draft: all in a good day's work.

Now that was one method. Rock Action had a whole different method. Rock's a few years younger than me, so he went in a couple of years later. First of all – I don't know how he did it – he refused to take the bus. He just showed up: he had a van. I was still in the Prime Movers at the time, and he was my protégé – a drummer. He went with an ATTITUDE, baby. He's been up for about two and a half days, drunk and crazy, right? And just before he left he painted a huge two-color lightning bolt with lipstick on the front of his head. This was a BAD looking dude, right? With rolled up sleeves and a motorcycle jacket, he just walks up to the front gate, drops a 16 ounce can of beer, and strides in there like Bulldog Drummond. You know, just a mess, and this was before leather fashion. He went through a whole different trip. They immediately put him in detention barracks. But he got out, and that was the name of the game.

The army is such a deterrent to young artists!

Iggy Pop, I Need More, I Need More: The Stooges and Other Stories,
with Anne Wehrer (1982)

Monday 23 January

Brian Epstein's adviser rang while I was eating a meal of mashed potatoes, tinned salmon and beetroot. He asked if I could meet 'the boys' on Wednesday. Said I'd ring him back tomorrow to confirm.

I got to Brian Epstein's office at 4.45. I looked through *The New Yorker*. How dead and professional it all is. Calculated. Not an unexpected line. Unfunny and dead. The epitaph of America. After about five minutes or so a youngish man with a hair-style which was way out in 1958, short, college-boy, came up and said, 'I'm Peter Brown, Brian Epstein's personal assistant. I'm afraid there's been a most awful mix-up. And all the boys' appointments have been put on an hour and a half.' I was a bit chilly in my manner after that. 'Do you want me to come back at six?' I said. 'Well, no. Couldn't we make another appointment?' 'What guarantee is there that you won't break that?' I said. 'I think you'd better find yourself a different writer.' This said with indifferent success, though the effect was startling. He asked me to wait a minute and went away to return with Brian Epstein himself. Somehow I'd expected something like Michael Codron. I'd imagined Epstein to be florid, Jewish, dark-haired and over-bearing. Instead I was face to face with a mousey-haired, slight young man. Washed-out in a way. He had a suburban accent. I went into his office. 'Could you meet Paul and me for dinner tonight?' he said. 'We do want to have the pleasure of talking to you.' 'I've a theatre engagement tonight,' I replied, by now sulky and unhelpful. 'Could I send the car to fetch you after the show?' I didn't much relish the idea but agreed and, after a lot of polite flim-flammery, left almost tripping over the carpet and crashing into the secretary who gave a squeal of surprise as I hurtled past her. This I never mention when re-telling the story. I always end on a note of hurt dignity.

When I got back home, Kenneth, all dressed up to go, announced that Peter Willes had rung up to say he wasn't coming to the theatre. 'I've a high funeral Mass tomorrow and I really can't,' he'd said. Kenneth said he was a fucking pest. 'Well, Kenneth,' Willes replied, mournfully, 'I'm afraid I can't help my relatives passing away.' Kenneth suggested that I rang Brian Epstein and agreed to meet him and Paul McCartney for dinner after all. So I did. And said I'd meet them at eight at Epstein's house in Belgravia. Chapel Street. I told P. Willes about this. He seemed as relieved as I was not to be going to the Royal Court to see that wretched Otway.

Arrived in Belgravia at ten minutes to eight having caught a 19 bus which dropped me at Hyde Park Corner. I found Chapel Street easily. I didn't want to get there too early so I walked around for a while and came back through a nearby mews. When I got back to the house it was nearly eight o'clock. I rang the bell and an old man opened the door. He seemed surprised to see me. 'Is this Brian Epstein's house?' I said. 'Yes, sir,' he said, and led the way into the hall. I suddenly realised that the man was the butler. I've never seen one before. He took my coat and I went to the lavatory. When I came out he'd gone. There was nobody about. I wandered around a large dining-room which was laid for dinner. And then I got to feel strange. The house appeared to be empty. So I went upstairs to the first floor. I heard music, only I couldn't decide where it came from. So I went up a further flight of stairs. I found myself in a bedroom. I came down again and found the butler. He took me into a room and said in a loud voice, 'Mr Orton'. Everybody looked up and stood to their feet. I was introduced to one or two people. And Paul McCartney. He was just as the photographs. Only he'd grown a moustache. His hair was shorter too. He was playing the latest Beatles recording, 'Penny Lane'. I liked it very much. Then he played the other side – Strawberry something. I didn't like this as much. We talked intermittently. Before we went out to dinner we'd agreed to throw out the idea of setting the film in the thirties. We went down to dinner. The crusted old retainer – looking too much like a butler to be good casting – busied himself in the corner. 'The only thing I get from the theatre,' Paul M. said, 'is a sore arse.' He said *Loot* was the only play he hadn't wanted to leave before the end. 'I'd've liked a bit more,' he said. We talked of the theatre. I said that compared with the pop scene the theatre was square. 'The theatre started going downhill when Queen Victoria knighted Henry Irving,' I said. 'Too fucking respectable.' We talked of drugs, of mushrooms which give hallucinations – like LSD. 'The drug not the money,' I said. We talked of tattoos. And, after one or two veiled references, marijuana. I said I'd smoked it in Morocco. The atmosphere relaxed a little. Dinner ended and we went upstairs again. We watched a programme on TV. It had phrases in it like 'the in-crowd', and 'swinging London'. There was a little scratching at the door. I thought it was the old retainer, but someone got up to open the door and about five very young and pretty boys trooped in. I rather hoped this was the evening's entertainments. It wasn't, though. It was a pop group called The Easybeats. I'd seen them on TV. I liked them very much then. In a way they were better (or prettier) offstage than on. After a while Paul McCartner said 'Let's go upstairs.' So he and I and Peter Brown went upstairs to a room also fitted with a TV ... A French photographer arrived with two beautiful youths and a girl. He'd taken a set of new photographs of The Beatles. They wanted one to use on the record sleeve. Excellent photograph. And the four Beatles look different with their moustaches. Like anarchists in the early years of the century. After a while we went downstairs. The Easybeats still there. The girl went away. I talked to the leading Easybeat. Feeling slightly like an Edwardian masher with a Gaiety Girl. And then I came over tired and decided to go home. I had a last word with Paul M. 'Well,' I said, 'I'd like to do the film. There's only one thing we've got to fix up.' 'You mean the bread?' 'Yes.' We smiled and parted. I got a cab home. It was pissing down.

Told Kenneth all about it. We talked for an hour or so. Then he got up to make a cup of tea. And we talked a little more. And went to sleep.

The Orton Diaries, ed. John Lahr (1987)

1967: Dedicated to Sensation

Just about the time 'Strawberry Fields' was released my wife and I went to dinner with a friend of ours whose whole life is dedicated to sensation.

The actual dinner party was staid enough although the conversation tended to roam over some pretty recherché sexual territory involving rubber, sado-masochism and baths full of machine oil, but while we were sipping our brandy – 'and there's no need to meet anymore. I can tell him what I want him to do over the telephone' – the door bell rang. In came a Comus-like rout of exotic creatures, the first time I'd laid eyes on the beautiful people as it happens, although I'd known several of them in the days when they'd worn ordinary if fashionable suits and floral ties. There was a girl in the shortest mini I'd ever seen, who lit up a joint and blew the smoke into our mouths. There were other girls hung with as-then esoteric beads and bells, and there were several young men in kaftans or matador pants and floral shirts or shepherds' smocks, and they all giggled a great deal, or went suddenly totally silent, or touched each other in a curiously non-sexual way, and there was Dylan whining away on the hi-fi.

Wandering into the bedroom I discovered our host in conversation with one of these bizarre figures and I heard him ask him if he'd brought the LSD and I thought what an old-fashioned expression for money.

George Melly, *Revolt into Style* (1970)

1967: The 'Hashbury' is the Capital of the Hippies

In 1965 Berkeley was the axis of what was just beginning to be called the 'new left'. Its leaders were radical, but they were also deeply committed to the society they wanted to change. A prestigious faculty committee said the Berkeley activists were the vanguard of 'a moral revolution among the young', and many professors approved.

Now, in 1967, there is not much doubt that Berkeley has gone through a revolution of some kind, but the end result is not exactly what the original leaders had in mind. Many one-time activists have forsaken politics entirely and turned to drugs. Others have even forsaken Berkeley. During 1966, the hot centre of revolutionary action on the coast began moving across the bay to San Francisco's Haight-Ashbury district, a run-down Victorian neighbourhood of about forty square blocks between the Negro/Fillmore district and Golden Gate Park.

The 'Hashbury' is the new capital of what is rapidly becoming a drug culture. Its denizens are not called radicals or beatniks, but 'hippies' – and perhaps as many as half are refugees from Berkeley and the old North beach scene, the cradle and the casket of the so-called beat generation.

The other half of the hippy population is too young to identify with Jack Kerouac, or even with Mario Savio. Their average age is about twenty, and most are native Californians. The North beach types of the late nineteen-fifties were not nearly as provincial as the Haight-Ashbury types are today. The majority of beatniks who flocked into San Francisco ten years ago were transients from the East and Midwest. The literary artistic nucleus – Kerouac, Ginsberg, et al. – was a package deal from New York. San Francisco was only a stop on the big circuit: Tangier, Paris, Greenwich Village, Tokyo and India. The senior beats had a pretty good idea what was going on in the world; they read newspapers, travelled constantly and had friends all over the globe.

The word 'hip' translates roughly as 'wise' or 'tuned-in'. A hippy is somebody who 'knows' what's really happening, and who adjusts or grooves with it. Hippies despise phoniness; they want to be open, honest, loving, free. They reject the plastic pretence of twentieth-century America, preferring to go back to the 'natural life', like Adam and Eve. They reject any kinship with the Beat Generation on the ground that 'those cats were negative, but our thing is positive'. They also reject politics, which is 'just another game'. They don't like money, either, or any kind of aggressiveness.

A serious problem in writing about the Haight-Ashbury is that most of the people you have to talk to are involved, one way or another, in the drug traffic. They have good reason to be leery of strangers who ask questions. A twenty-two-year-old student was recently sentenced to two years in prison for telling an undercover narcotics agent where to buy some marijuana. 'Love' is the password in the Haight-Ashbury, but paranoia is the style. Nobody wants to go to jail.

At the same time, marijuana is everywhere. People smoke it on the sidewalks, in doughnut shops, sitting in parked cars or lounging on the grass in Golden Gate Park. Nearly everyone on the streets between twenty and thirty is a 'head', a user, either of marijuana, LSD, or both. To refuse a proffered 'joint' is to risk being labelled a 'nark' – narcotics agent – a threat and a menace to almost everybody.

With a few loud exceptions, it is only the younger hippies who see themselves as a new breed. 'A completely new thing in this world, man.' The ex-beatniks among them, many of whom are now making money off the new scene, incline to the view that hippies are, in fact, second-generation beatniks and that everything genuine in the Haight-Ashbury is about to be swallowed – like North Beach and the Village – in a wave of publicity and commercialism.

Haight Street, the great white way of what the local papers call 'hippieland', is already dotted with stores catering mainly to the tourist trade. Few hippies can afford a pair of $20 sandals or 'mod outfit' for $67.50. Nor can they afford the $3.50 door charge at the Fillmore Auditorium and the Avalon Ballroom, the twin wombs of the 'psychedelic, San Francisco, acid-rock sound'. Both the Fillmore and the Avalon are jammed every weekend with borderline hippies who don't mind paying for the music and the light shows. There is always a sprinkling of genuine, barefoot, freaked-out types on the dance floor, but few of them pay to get in. They arrive with the musicians or have other good connections.

Neither of the dance palaces is within walking distance of the Hashbury, especially if you're stoned, and since only a few of the hippies have contacts in the psychedelic power structure, most of them spend their weekend nights either drifting around on Haight Street or loading up on acid – LSD – in somebody's pad. Some of the rock bands play free concerts in Golden Park for the benefit of those brethren who can't afford the dances. But beyond an occasional Happening in the park, the Haight-Ashbury scene is almost devoid of anything 'to do' – at least by conventional standards. An at-home entertainment is nude parties at which celebrants paint designs on each other.

There are no hippy bars, for instance, and only one restaurant above the level of a diner or a lunch counter. This is a reflection of the drug culture, which has no use for booze and regards food as a necessity to be acquired at the least possible expense. A 'family' of hippies will work for hours over an exotic stew or curry in a communal kitchen, but the idea of paying $3 for a meal in a restaurant is out of the question.

Some hippies work, others live on money from home and many are full-time beggars. The post office is a major source of hippy income. Jobs like sorting mail don't require much thought or effort. A hippy named Admiral Love of the Psychedelic Rangers delivers special-delivery letters at night. The admiral is in his mid-twenties and makes enough money to support an apartmentful of younger hippies who depend on him for their daily bread.

There is also a hippy-run employment agency on Haight Street and anyone needing part-time labour or some kind of specialized work can call and order as many freaks as he needs; they might look a bit weird, but many are far more capable than most 'temporary help', and vastly more interesting to have around.

Those hippies who don't work can easily pick up a few dollars a day panhandling along Haight Street. The fresh influx of curiosity-seekers has proved a great boon to the legion of psychedelic beggars. During several days of roaming around the area, I was touched so often that I began to keep a supply of quarters in my pocket so I wouldn't have to haggle over change. The panhandlers are usually barefoot, always young and never apologetic. They'll share what they collect anyway, so it seems entirely reasonable that strangers should share with them.

The best show on Haight Street is usually on the sidewalk in front of the Drog Store, a new coffee bar at the corner of Masonic Street. The Drog Store features an all-hippy revue that runs day and night. The acts change sporadically, but nobody cares. There will always be at least one man with long hair and sunglasses playing a wooden pipe of some kind. He will be wearing either a Dracula cape, a long Buddhist robe, or a Sioux Indian costume. There will also be a hairy blond fellow wearing a Black Bart cowboy hat and a spangled jacket that originally belonged to a drum major in the 1949 Rose Bowl parade. He will be playing the bongo drums. Next to the drummer will be a dazed-looking girl wearing a blouse (but no bra) and a plastic mini-skirt, slapping her thighs to the rhythm of it all.

These three will be the nucleus of the show. Backing them up will be an all-star cast of freaks, every one of them stoned. They will be stretched out on the sidewalk, twitching and babbling in time to the music. Now and then somebody will fall out of the audience and join the revue; perhaps a Hell's Angel or some grubby, chain-draped impostor who never owned a motorcycle in his life. Or maybe a girl wrapped in gauze or a thin man with wild eyes who took an overdose of acid nine days ago and changed himself into a raven. For those on a quick tour of the Hashbury, the Drog Store revue is a must.

Most of the local action is beyond the reach of anyone without access to drugs. There are four or five bars a nervous square might relax in, but one is a Lesbian place, another is a hangout for brutal-looking leather fetishists and the others are old neighbourhood taverns full of brooding middle-aged drunks. Prior to the hippy era there were three good Negro-run jazz bars on Haight Street, but they soon went out of style. Who needs jazz, or even beer, when you can sit down on a public kerbstone, drop a pill on your mouth, and hear fantastic music for hours at a time in your own head? A cap of good acid costs $5, and for that you can hear the Universal Symphony, with God singing solo and the Holy Ghost on drums.

Drugs have made formal entertainment obsolete in the Hashbury, but only until somebody comes up with something appropriate to the new style of the neighbourhood. This summer will see the opening of the new Straight Theater, formerly the Haight Theater, featuring homosexual movies for the trade, meetings, concerts, dances. 'It's going to be a kind of hippy community centre,' said Brent Dangerfield, a young radio engineer from Salt Lake City who stopped off in San Francisco on his way to a job in Hawaii and now is a partner in the Straight. When I asked Dangerfield how old he was he had to think for a minute. 'I'm twenty-two,' he said finally, 'but I used to be much older.'

Another new divertissement, maybe, will be a hippy bus line running up and down Haight Street, housed in a 1930 Fagol bus – a huge, lumbering vehicle that might have been the world's first house trailer. I rode in it one afternoon with the driver, a young hippy named Tim Thibeau who proudly displayed a bathtub under one of the rear seats. The bus was a spectacle even on Haight Street: people stopped, stared and cheered as we rumbled by, going nowhere at all. Thibeau honked the horn and waved. He was from Chicago, he said, but when he got out of the Army he stopped in San Francisco and decided to stay. He was living, for the moment, on unemployment insurance, and his plans for the future were hazy. 'I'm in no hurry,' he said. 'Right now I'm just taking it easy, just floating along.' He smiled and reached for a beer can in the Fagol's icebox.

Dangerfield and Thibeau reflect the blind optimism of the younger hippy element. They see themselves as the vanguard of a new way of life in America – the psychedelic way – where love abounds and work is fun and people help each other. The young hippies are confident that things are going their way.

The older hippies are not so sure. They've been waiting a long time for the world to go their way, and those most involved in the hip scene are hedging their bets this time. 'That back to nature scene is okay when you're twenty,' said one. 'But when you're looking at thirty-five you want to know something's happening to you.'

Ed Denson, at twenty-seven, is an ex-beatnik, ex-Goldwaterite, ex-Berkeley radical and currently the manager of a successful rock band called Country Joe and the Fish. His home and headquarters is a complex of rooms above a liquor store in Berkeley. One room is an art studio, another is an office; there is also a kitchen, a bedroom and several sparsely furnished areas without definition.

Denson is deeply involved in the hippy music scene, but insists he's not a hippy. 'I'm very pessimistic about where this thing is going,' he said. 'Right now it's good for a lot of people. It's still very open. But I have to look back at the Berkeley scene. There was a tremendous optimism there, too, but look where all that went. The beat generation? Where are they now? What about hula-hoops? Maybe this hippy thing is more than a fad; maybe the whole world is turning on but I'm not optimistic. Most of the hippies I know don't really understand what kind of a world they're living in. I get tired of hearing about what beautiful people we all are. If the hippies were more realistic they'd stand a better chance of surviving.'

Most hippies take the question of survival for granted, but it's becoming increasingly obvious as the neighbourhood fills with penniless heads, that there is simply not enough food and lodging to go around. A partial solution may come from a group called the Diggers, who have been called the 'worker-priests' of the hippy movement and the 'invisible government' of the Hashbury. The Diggers are young and aggressively pragmatic; they have set up free lodging centres, free soup kitchens and free clothing distribution centres. They comb the neighbourhood soliciting donations of everything from money to stale bread to camping equipment. Diggers' signs are posted in local stores, asking for donations of hammers, saws, shovels, shoes and anything else that vagrant hippies might use to make themselves at least partially self-supporting.

The name and spirit derive from small groups of seventeenth-century

English rural revolutionaries, called both Diggers and the True Levellers, who had socialist ideas. Money should be abolished, communal farms could support all those willing to work them, and individual ownership of land would be outlawed. The Diggers were severely harassed and the movement eventually caved in under the weight of public opprobrium.

The Hashbury Diggers have fared a bit better, but the demand for food and lodging is beginning to exceed the supply. For a while, the Diggers were able to serve three meals, however meagre, each afternoon in Golden Gate Park. But as the word got around, more and more hippies showed up to eat, and the Diggers were forced to roam far afield to get food. Occasionally there were problems, as when Digger chieftain Emmett Grogan, twenty-three, called a local butcher a 'fascist pig and a coward' when he refused to donate meat scraps. The butcher whacked Grogan with the flat side of his meat cleaver.

The Digger ethic of mass sharing goes along with the American Indian motif that is basic to the Hashbury scene. The cult of 'tribalism' is regarded by many of the older hippies as the key to survival. Poet Gary Snyder, a hippy guru, sees a 'back to the land' movement as the answer to the food and lodging problem. He urges hippies to move out of the cities, form tribes, purchase land and live communally in remote areas. He cites a hippy 'clan' calling itself the Mama-Lila as a model (though the clan still dwells in the Hashbury).

'Well, now,' Snyder says, 'like, you are asking how it's going to work. Well, the Maha-Lila is a group of about three different families who have sort of pooled their resources, which are not very great. But they have decided to pay together and to work together and to take care of each other and that means all of them have ways of getting a small amount of bread, which they share. And other people contribute a little money when it comes in. And then they work together on creative projects, like they're working together on a light-show right now for a poetry reading that we're going to give. And they consider themselves a kind of extended family or clan.

'That's the model. They relate it to a larger sense of the tribe, which is loose, but for the time being everybody has to be able – from time to time – to do some little job. The thing that makes it different is that you don't have a very tight monogamous family unit, but a slightly larger unit where the sharing is greater.'

The tribal concept makes a lot better sense than simply depending on the Diggers. There are indications, however, that the youthful provincialism of the Haight-Ashbury is due for a forced consciousness-expansion. For the past few months, the scene has been filling up with would-be hippies from other parts of the country, primarily Los Angeles and New York. The real influx is expected this summer. The city is rife with rumours, reliable and otherwise, that anywhere from 50,000 to 200,000 'indigent young people' will descend on San Francisco as soon as the school year ends.

The Diggers are appalled at the prospect. 'Where are they going to stay?' says one. 'What are they going to do?' A girl who works in one of the Digger kitchens shrugs and says: 'The Diggers will continue to receive the casualties of the love generation.' Local officials, from the Mayor down, are beginning to panic. Civic leaders in the Haight-Ashbury have suggested that sleeping facilities be provided in Golden Gate Park or in nearby Kezar Stadium but Police Chief Tom Cahill said no.

'Law and order will prevail,' he insisted. 'There will be no sleeping in the park. There are no sanitation facilities and if we let them camp there we would have a tremendous health problem. Hippies are no asset to the community. These people do not have the courage to face the reality of life. They are trying to escape. Nobody should let their young children take part in this hippy thing.'

In March, the city's health director, Dr Ellis Sox, sent a task force of inspectors on a door-to-door sweep of the Haight-Ashbury. Reports of as many as 200 people living in one house or fifty in one apartment had stirred rumours of impending epidemics in the neighbourhood. In a two-day blitz, eight teams of inspectors checked roughly 1400 buildings and issued a total of sixty-five deadline notices to repair sanitation faults. But only sixteen of the sixty-five notices, according to the *San Francisco Chronicle*, were issued to occupants 'whose bizarre dress and communal living habits could class them as hippies'.

Dr Sox had no choice but to back off. 'The situation is not as bad as we thought,' he said. 'There has been a deterioration [of sanitation] in the Haight-Ashbury, but the hippies did not contribute much more to it than other members of the neighbourhood.' Dr Sox went on to deny that his mass inspection was part of a general campaign against weirdos, but nobody seemed to believe him.

The Haight-Ashbury Neighbourhood Council, a nonhippy group of permanent residents, denounced Dr Sox for his 'gratuitous criticism of our community'. The council accused city officials of 'creating an artificial problem' and harassing the hippies out of 'personal and official' prejudice.

As recently as 1962, the Haight-Ashbury was a drab, working-class district, slowly filling with Negroes and so plagued by crime and violence that residents formed vigilante patrols. Housewives were mugged on the way to the grocery store, teenagers were slashed and stomped in gang rumbles, and every drunk on Haight Street was fair game for local jack-rollers.

Now, with the coming of the drug culture, even the squarest of the neighbourhood old-timers say the streets are safer than they have been for years. Burglaries are still a problem but violence is increasingly rare. It is hard to find anyone outside the hippy community who will say that psychedelic drugs have made the neighbourhood a better place to live. But it's even harder to find a person who wouldn't rather step over a giggling freak on the sidewalk than worry about hoodlums with switchblades. The fact that the hippies and the squares have worked out such a peaceful coexistence seems to baffle the powers at City Hall.

A lot of cheap labels describe what is happening in the Hashbury, but none of them make much sense: the love generation, the happening generation, the combine generation and even the LSD generation. The last is the best of the lot, but in the interest of accuracy it should probably be amended to the head generation.

'A head', in the language of hip, is a user of psychedelic drugs: LSD, marijuana ('grass'), mescaline, peyote, methedrine, benzedrine, and a half-dozen others that are classified in the trade as mind-stimulating, consciousness-expanding, or 'head' drugs. At the other end of the spectrum are 'body' drugs: opium, heroin, barbiturates and even alcohol. These are basically depressants, while head drugs are stimulants. But neither type comes with a manufacturer's guarantee, and the Hashbury is full of people whose minds have been jerked around savagely by drugs that were supposed to induce peaceful euphoria.

Another hazard is the widespread tendency to mix two or three drugs at one time. Acid and alcohol can be a lethal combination, causing fits of violence, suicidal depression and a general freak-out that ends in jail or a hospital.

There is widespread concern, at least in San Francisco, about the dangers of so many people using so much LSD. A doctor at San Francisco General Hospital says there are at least 10,000 hippes in the Haight-Ashbury, and that about four of them a day wind up in a psychiatric ward on bad trips. He estimates that acidheads make up only one-and-a-half per cent of the city's population, but that the figure for the Haight-Ashbury is more like 100 per cent.

The estimate is absurd; if every hippie in the Hashbury took acid every day, the percentage of users in the neighbourhood would still be less than fifty per cent. Many of the local squares try grass from time to time, but few have worked up an appetite for LSD; the difference in potency is roughly the same as the difference between beer and grain alcohol. Even among hippies, anything more than one dose of acid a week is considered excessive.

Most heads are relatively careful about their drug diets, but in recent months the area has attracted so many young, inexperienced hippies that public freak-outs are a fairly routine thing. Neighbourhood cops complain that acidheads throw themselves in front of moving cars, strip naked in grocery stores and run through plate-glass windows. On weekdays, the action is about on a par with Macdougal Street in Greenwich Village, but weekend hippies and nervous *voyeurs* from the suburbs make Saturdays and Sundays a nightmarish traffic jam. The sidewalks are so crowded that even a mild freak-out is likely to cause a riot.

Municipal buses no longer use Haight Street on weekends; they were rerouted after mobs of hippies staged sit-down strikes in the street, called mill-ins, which brought all traffic to a standstill. The only buses still running regularly along Haight Street are those from the Gray Line, which recently added 'hippieland' to its daytime sightseeing tour of San Francisco. It was billed as 'the only foreign tour within the continental limits of the United States' and was an immediate hit with tourists who thought the Haight-Ashbury was a human zoo. The only sour note on the tour was struck by the occasional hippy who would run alongside the bus, holding up a mirror.

Last year in Berkeley, hard-core political radicals who had always viewed hippies as spiritual allies began to worry about the long-range implications of the Haight-Ashbury scene. Students who once were angry activists were content to lie back in their pads and smile at the world through a fog of marijuana smoke – or, worse, to dress like clowns or American Indians and stay zonked for days at a time on LSD.

Even in Berkeley, political rallies during 1966 had overtones of music; madness and absurdity. Instead of picket signs and revolutionary slogans, more and more demonstrators carried flowers, balloons and colourful posters featuring slogans from Dr Timothy Leary, the high priest of acid. The drug culture was spreading faster than political activists realized. Unlike the dedicated radicals who emerged from the Free Speech Movement, the hippies were more interested in dropping out of society than they were in changing it. They were generally younger than the political types, and the press dismissed them as the 'pot left', a frivolous gang of druggies and sex kooks who were only along for the ride.

Then Ronald Reagan was elected Governor by almost a million-vote plurality. Shortly afterwards, Clark Kerr was fired as president of the University of California – a direct result of Reagan's victory. In that same November, the GOP gained fifty seats in Congress and served a clear warning on the Johnson Administration that despite all the headlines about Berkeley and the new left, most of the electorate was a lot more hawkish, hard-nosed and conservative than the White House antennae had indicated.

The lesson was not lost on the hippies, many of whom still considered themselves at least part-time political activists. One of the most obvious casualties of the 1966 elections was the new left's illusion of its own leverage. The radical-hippy alliance had been counting on the voters to repudiate the 'right-wing, warmonger' elements in congress, but instead it was the 'liberal' Democrats who got stomped.

So it is no coincidence that the Haight-Ashbury scene developed very suddenly in the winter of 1966–7 from the quiet, neo-Bohemian enclave that it had been for four or five years to the crowded, defiant dope fortress that it is today. The hippies, who had never really believed they were the wave of the future anyway, saw the election returns as brutal confirmation of the futility of fighting the establishment on its own terms.

There had to be a whole new scene, they said, and the only way to do it was to make the big move – either figuratively or literally – from Berkeley to the Haight-Ashbury, from pragmatism to mysticism, from politics to dope, from the hang-ups of protest to the peaceful disengagement of love, nature and spontaneity.

The credo of the Haight-Ashbury was expressed, about as well as it can be, by Joyce Francisco, twenty-three-year-old advertising manager of the new hippy newspaper, the *San Francisco Oracle*. She was talking a few months ago to a columnist from the establishment press, trying to explain what the hippy phenomenon meant: 'I love the whole world,' she said. 'I am the divine mother, part of Buddha, part of God, part of everything.'

'How do you live?' the columnist asked.

'From meal to meal. I have no money, no possessions. Money is beautiful only when it's flowing; when it piles up it's a hang-up. We take care of each other. There's always something to buy beans and rice for the group, and someone always sees that I get grass or acid. I was in a mental hospital once because I tried to conform and play the game. But now I'm free and happy.'

Next question: 'Do you use drugs often?'

'Fairly. When I find myself becoming confused I drop out and take a dose of acid. It's a short cut to reality; it throws you right into it. Everyone should

299

take it, even children. Why shouldn't they be enlightened early, instead of waiting till they're old? Human beings need total freedom. That's where God is at. We need to shed hypocrisy, dishonesty, phoniness and go back to the purity of our childhood values.'

The columnist then asked if Miss Francisco ever prayed.

'Oh, yes,' she said. 'I pray in the morning sun. It nourishes me with its energy so I can spread my love and beauty and nourish others. I never pray *for* anything; I don't need anything. Whatever turns me on is a sacrament: LSD, sex, my bells, my colours . . . that is the holy communion, you dig?'

The columnist wasn't sure if she did or not, but she passed on the interview for the benefit of those readers who might. Many did. Anyone who thinks all the hippies in the Bay Area are living in the Hashbury might just as well leave his head in the sand.

In normal circumstances, the mushrooming popularity of psychedelics would be a main factor in any article on hippies. But the vicious excesses of our drug laws make it impossible, or at least inhuman, to document the larger story. A journalist dealing with heads is caught in a strange dilemma. The only way to write honestly about the scene is to be part of it. If there is one quick truism about psychedelic drugs, it is that anyone who tries to write about them without firsthand experience is a fool and a fraud.

Yet to write from experience is an admission of felonious guilt; it is also a potential betrayal of people whose only 'crime' is the smoking of weed that grows wild all over the world but the possession of which, in California, carries a minimum sentence of two years in prison for a second offence and a minimum of five years for a third. So, despite the fact that the whole journalism industry is full of unregenerate heads – just as many journalists were hard drinkers during Prohibition – it is not very likely that the frank, documented truth about the psychedelic underworld, for good or ill, will be illuminated at any time soon in the public prints.

If I were to write, for instance, that I recently spent ten days in San Francisco and was stoned almost constantly . . . that in fact I was stoned for nine nights out of ten and that nearly everyone I dealt with smoked marijuana as casually as they drank beer . . . and if I said many of the people I talked to were not freaks and dropouts, but competent professionals with bank accounts and spotless reputations . . . and that I was amazed to find psychedelic drugs in homes where I would never have mentioned them two years ago – if all this were true, I could write an ominous screed to the effect that the hippy phenomenon in the Haight-Ashbury is little more than a freak show and a soft-sell advertisement for what is happening all around them . . . that drugs, orgies and freak-outs are almost as common to a much larger and more discreet cross section of the Bay Area's respectable, upward-mobile society as they are to the colourful drop-outs of San Francisco's new Bohemia.

There is no shortage of documentation for the thesis that the current Haight-Ashbury scene is only the orgiastic tip of a great psychedelic iceberg that is already drifting in the sea lanes of the great society. Submerged and uncountable is the mass of intelligent, capable heads who want nothing so much as peaceful anonymity. In a nervous society where a man's image is frequently more important than his reality, the only people who can afford to advertise their drug menus are those with nothing to lose.

And these – for the moment, at least – are the young lotus-eaters, the barefoot mystics and hairy freaks of the Haight-Ashbury – all the primitive Christians, peaceful nay-sayers and half-deluded 'flower children' who refuse to participate in a society which looks to them like a mean, calculated and soul-destroying hoax.

As recently as two years ago, many of the best and brightest of them were passionately involved in the realities of political, social and economic life in America. But the scene has changed since then and political activism is going out of style. The thrust is no longer for 'change' or 'progress' or 'revolution', but merely to escape, to live on the far perimeter of a world that might have been – perhaps should have been – and strike a bargain for survival on purely personal terms.

The flourishing hippy scene is a matter of desperate concern to the political activists. They see a whole generation of rebels drifting off to a drugged limbo, ready to accept almost anything as long as it comes with enough 'soma'.

Steve DeCanio, an ex-Berkeley activist now doing graduate work at MIT, is a good example of a legion of young radicals who know they have lost their influence but have no clear idea how to get it back again. 'This alliance between hippies and political radicals is bound to break up,' he said in a recent letter. 'There's just too big a jump from the slogan of "flower power" to the deadly realm of politics. Something has to give, and drugs are too ready-made as opiates of the people for the bastards (the police) to fail to take advantage of it.'

DeCanio spent three months in various Bay Area jails as a result of his civil rights activities and now he is lying low for a while, waiting for an opening.

'I'm spending an amazing amount of time studying,' he wrote. 'It's mainly because I'm scared; three months on the bottom of humanity's trash heap got to me worse than it's healthy to admit. The country is going to hell, the left is going to pot, but not me, I still want to figure out a way to win.'

Meanwhile, like most other disappointed radicals, he is grimly amused at the impact the hippies are having on the establishment. The panic among San Francisco officialdom at the prospect of 200,000 hippies flocking into the Hashbury this summer is one of the few things that ex-Berkeley radicals can still laugh at. DeCanio's vision of the crisis was not written as prophecy, but considering the hidden reality of the situation, it may turn out that way: 'I can see Mayor Shelley standing on the steps of the Civic Center and shouting into TV microphones, "The people cry bread! Bread! Let them turn on!"'

Hunter S. Thompson, New York Times Magazine, 14 May 1967

1967: A Few Days in Germany

The Dusseldorf venue was a huge flat indoor sports arena, with wooden seats laid out in enormous rows and criss-crossed with wide aisles. The stage was unusually high; about ten feet. I had an idea and I told Andy, 'Marc and the other two should come on first and start playing a real heavy riff, get the audience excited with the rhythm, and then, suddenly, you appear from the side of the stage running like a demon. You run right across the stage towards the audience as if you can't stop, and then you do a great ten-foot leap down into the aisles and keep on going, running like fuck the whole time. They'll all try to grab you. It'll be a stunning "winder-upper" to get the show off to a good start. You'll have to keep running like crazy all the way. Right to the back of the hall, across to the other aisle and then back to the stage. I'll arrange for two guys to be there to give you a flying leg-up just in time to grab the mike and plunge into the first number.'

The group thought it was a great idea, but having said it I realised how dangerous it might be if the audience grabbed Andy. I wouldn't be sure exactly where he was and he might be needing urgent rescue. So I tried to think of a way of pinpointing his whereabouts. I thought of a water-pistol full of dye, or a couple of Christmas streamers he could throw through the air. But as we were walking round Dusseldorf we passed an ironmonger's shop that had something I'd never seen before – feathers sold by the kilo. There were all sorts and sizes, stacked along one side of the shop in great barrels. That was the answer. Andy could take a little sack with him, and as he ran he could throw feathers in the air. Then I could see exactly where he'd got to.

I went in and bought a couple of kilos of best ducks' fluff. I'd never bought feathers before and it turned out that two kilos filled the boot of the car, the back seats and most of the front seats too. But at least it would keep us going for the rest of the tour. Then, just as we were leaving the ironmonger's we saw some marvellous chains. Not the average factory-made iron links. These were hand-forged rings of power. They were irresistible and I bought ten metres of them. I didn't know quite what they were going to be used for, but eventually I figured out something for a finale. John and Andy would strip off their shirts and get into a fight. A real fight. 'None of this tame acting stuff,' I told them. 'Once you start fighting you must hate each other totally. I don't want any stage punches. I want real decadent violence.'

Meanwhile Marc would stride over to his amplifier and lay his guitar across it, so that it fed back with unmusical screeches of abuse; pick up the length of the chain I'd bought, wrap it round his shoulders, walk across to where John and Andy lay writhing on the floor and start beating them across their backs. On the drum rostrum Chris could smash his kit to bits, out-Mooning Keith Moon, and finish off by throwing the wreckage into the audience.

All in all it seemed like it could be quite a jolly pantomime, and we looked forward to it expectantly.

Our hopes were well fulfilled. It turned into a total riot. When Andy leapt off the stage at the beginning of the first number, the audience reacted in perfect German style. They tried to grab him and kick him to death. But he streaked through them like an electric hare, and created a Siberian blizzard with fistfuls of feathers. Then, before the audience knew it, he was back down the other aisle and up on the stage with the mike in his hand.

In the auditorium there was chaos. Yelling. Fighting. And a snowstorm which wouldn't stop.

When the finale came John and Andy stripped off and fought to the death. And just in case one of them might survive, Marc attempted to brand them for life with slashes from his black iron chain. At the same time, Chris smashed up his drum kit. But he couldn't bring himself to throw the pieces to the riot-crazed crowd who were now leaping wildly at the front of the stage, being beaten back by a team of heavy German bouncers who hadn't been so happy since the SS days.

After John's Children had gone off, The Who still made a good impact with their performance. But the reaction was quieter than usual, more

303

subdued, and Roger Daltry kept coughing on the feathers that were still floating around. As a result, he didn't sing too well.

I felt we were getting somewhere at last. But the next day Kit Lambert came to my hotel room and suggested we had lunch together. He wasn't happy about our stage act. 'You'll have to leave out the feathers,' he told me, 'otherwise Roger can't sing.'

I said I didn't want to change anything.

'In that case,' Kit said, 'you'll have to leave the tour.' He said it in his most pompous and authoritative voice, but underneath I guessed he rather enjoyed what we were doing. He loved mayhem and anarchy, but on the other hand he was The Who's manager and had to look after their interests. And why should they allow an upstart support group to wreck a million dollar German tour?

I didn't intend to alter anything for the next night's show, but I told Kit I would. So he got more friendly and said, 'I've got to get some things for the group. You want to come with me?'

I knew he was talking about getting drugs, and I asked, 'Where d'you have to go?'

'There's a very good man in this town who can get anything you want. I'm not sure what his real name is, but everyone calls him Bumburger, Hans Bumburger. We'll go to his house. He keeps a lot of pretty young men there who can entertain us while he sends out for the stuff we want.'

We jumped in a taxi and Kit shouted complex instructions to the driver in forceful and arrogant German. 'Bloody Germans,' he told me, 'it's bad enough having to learn a disgusting language like theirs, but worse still that in order to make them do anything for you, you have to talk to them like a Nazi general. It's no good just asking them politely. If you want something done you have to become as German as they are. Mind you, I'm not a racialist. I don't object to someone *being* German, only to his *behaving* like one.' Having said that, he then did a passable imitation of the German High Command to get us to his drug-contact's house. It was in a neat modern terrace of middle-class respectability.

The door was answered by a delicate-looking teenager with a fluffy Angora jumper and a gap in his front teeth. Behind him was another boy, rather tall, and with juicy spots on both cheeks.

Kit stopped the military approach and put his arm round Angora's neck. The boy whispered something in his ear and Kit turned to me and said, 'This place is marvellous. It's so decadent you won't believe it. Do you fancy a boy?'

Judging by the selection so far I couldn't say that I did. I shook my head and said, 'Not really. But you have one if you want.'

'Oh I shall,' Kit said haughtily. 'In fact, I think I might have two.' And he preceded me up the stairs with his arms tightly round Angora and Spots.

At the top of the stairs we were met by Hans Bumburger, oily and obsequious. He shook my hand limply and asked if I was going to join Kit with a boy. I told him no, I'd just like somewhere to wait please; and he showed me into a small room with a couple of armchairs and a television. Kit popped in to see if he could change my mind and seemed rather annoyed when he couldn't. Then he went off to another room to make his choice of partner and I heard Bumburger tell him the 'stuff' would be there in half an hour.

There was nothing to do in the room and I was about to turn on the television when Bumburger came in and pulled a curtain back from along the wall. Behind, there wasn't the window one might have expected. Instead there was a sheet of dark glass that looked into the next room. And there was Kit, sitting on a sofa with a boy, their arms round each other's necks.

I said, 'I don't want to watch that. It's dreadful. Kit's a friend of mine. It'd be embarrassing.'

Bumburger said, 'My dear chap, I thought that's what you meant when you said you wanted somewhere to wait. But if you don't want to watch, just pull the curtains back.' And he left the room in a huff.

I pulled the curtain over the window and turned on the TV. After about ten minutes there was loud shouting from the next room, so I pulled back the curtain and looked in. Kit was hopping round the room pulling his trousers up angrily. I couldn't hear exactly what he was yelling, but after a few seconds he disappeared from view and the door into the passage was flung open with a crash. Kit's voice was suddenly loud and clear. He was yelling in German and I went into the passage and saw him shaking Bumburger violently. Then two tough-looking youths came charging up the stairs and restrained him. Kit struggled to get free but they had him firmly in their grip.

When he'd quietened down slightly they let him go and put him in an armchair, and Bumburger said, 'Really, Kit, you are very rude sometimes. You don't have to shout at me. If you have any complaints about the boys you can tell me quietly.'

'That boy's a disgusting little thief,' Kit yelled vehemently. 'And you know it.'

'But Kit,' Bumburger purred smoothly, 'that boy is one of our best. All the top pop people come here from England, and many of them have enjoyed themselves very much with this boy. I think he is an excellent boy.'

'He's a dirty little thief,' Kit hissed, 'and I'm not paying.'

'But he's not stolen anything from you,' Bumburger insisted.

'Not now,' Kit admitted, 'but he did. Before.'

I was in the dark as to what they were talking about so I just waited for the thing to get resolved. But it didn't. The talking fizzled out. Kit insisted he wasn't paying. Bumburger insisted he wasn't letting Kit leave. Then, to top it all, another boy arrived back at the house with the drugs Kit had asked for. Not knowing what had been going on he came upstairs and put them right into Kit's hands, and Kit, on a sudden impulse, leapt from his chair and yelled, 'Come on, Simon.'

He ran like crazy down the stairs and I followed sort of half-heartedly — which was just as well, because at the bottom Kit met the two heavy youths who'd restrained him before. Only this time they started thumping him.

Then Keith Moon arrived.

I don't know how, or where from, or why, but he arrived. The doorbell rang. One of the thugs opened it, and there on the doorstep was Keith and someone I didn't know.

They just rushed straight in. Kicked, yelled and thumped blindly. Shouted at me to run out the door with Kit. And then we were in a Mercedes driving off at great speed with Kit giggling wildly. It was like a commando rescue operation.

When Kit recovered from his fit of giggles, he didn't try to thank Keith, he just scolded him, 'You were late!'

Keith ignored the reprimand and asked, 'What happened to that bastard who stole the money? Did you find him?'

'Find him?' Kit shouted gleefully. 'I fucked the little bugger. And I didn't even know it was him till I'd finished.'

Keith asked, 'You got the stuff didn't you?' And he anxiously took the packet of drugs out of Kit's hands.

I asked Kit, 'What the hell's this all about? What are you up to? Why did you get me mixed up in all this madness?'

But it sent Kit off into another hysterical fit of giggles, and when he'd controlled them he turned on his arrogant voice again and said, 'None of your business. You're only the support group manager. It absolutely does not concern you.'

Keith was more forthcoming. He said, 'We had a bit of a barney with some bloke who nicked money from us for drugs. So we thought we'd get our own back.'

Kit told him to shut up, that it was none of my business. So Keith changed the subject somewhat and told me, 'Rescuing people from brothels seems to be one of my specialities.'

It must have been a private joke between them because this time both Keith and Kit went off into fits of hysteria. Then when they'd quietened down they set to work stuffing themselves with pills from out of the packet. Kit shoved two pills into my hand and said, 'If I get too noisy give me the pink one, and if I fall asleep give me the blue one.' Then he started taking great sniffs of white powder.

Simon Napier-Bell, *You Don't Have to Say You Love Me* (1982)

1967: Who Breaks a Butterfly on a Wheel?

Mr Jagger has been sentenced to imprisonment for three months. He is appealing against conviction and sentence, and has been granted bail until the hearing of the appeal later in the year. In the meantime, the sentence of imprisonment is bound to be widely discussed by the public. And the circumstances are sufficiently unusual to warrant such discussion in the public interest.

Mr Jagger was charged with being in possession of four tablets containing amphetamine sulphate and methyl amphetamine hydrochloride; these tablets had been bought, perfectly legally, in Italy, and brought back to this country. They are not a highly dangerous drug, or in proper dosage a dangerous drug at all. They are of the benzedrine type and the Italian manufacturers recommend them both as a stimulant and as a remedy for travel sickness.

In Britain it is an offence to possess these drugs without a doctor's prescription. Mr Jagger's doctor says that he knew and had authorized their use, but he did not give a prescription for them as indeed they had already been purchased. His evidence was not challenged. This was therefore an offence of a technical character, which before this case drew the point to public attention any honest man might have been liable to commit. If after his visit to the Pope the Archbishop of Canterbury had bought proprietary airsickness pills on Rome airport, and imported the unused tablets into Britain on his return, he would have risked committing precisely the same offence. No one who has ever travelled and bought proprietary drugs abroad can be sure that he has not broken the law.

Judge Block directed the jury that the approval of a doctor was not a defence in law to the charge of possessing drugs without a prescription, and the jury convicted. Mr Jagger was not charged with complicity in any other drug offence that occurred in the same house. They were separate cases, and no evidence was produced to suggest that he knew that Mr Fraser had heroin tablets or that the vanishing Mr Sneidermann had cannabis resin. It is indeed no offence to be in the same building or the same company as people possessing or even using drugs, nor could it reasonably be made an offence. The drugs which Mr Jagger had in his possession must therefore be treated on their own, as a separate issue from the other drugs that other people may have had in their possession at the same time. It may be difficult for lay opinion to make this distinction clearly, but obviously justice cannot be done if one man is to be punished for a purely contingent association with someone else's offence.

We have, therefore, a conviction against Mr Jagger purely on the ground that he possessed four Italian pep pills, quite legally bought but not legally imported without a prescription. Four is not a large number. This is not the quantity which a pusher of drugs would have on him, nor even the quantity one would expect in an addict. In any case Mr Jagger's career is obviously one that does involve great personal strain and exhaustion; his doctor says that he approved the occasional use of these drugs, and it seems likely that similar drugs would have been prescribed if there was a need for them. Millions of similar drugs are prescribed in Britain every year, and for a variety of conditions.

One has to ask, therefore, how it is that this technical offence, divorced as it must be from other people's offences, was thought to deserve the penalty of imprisonment. In the courts at large it is most uncommon for imprisonment to be imposed on first offenders where the drugs are not major drugs of addiction and there is no question of drug traffic. The normal penalty is probation, and the purpose of probation is to encourage the offender to develop his career and to avoid the drug risks in the future. It is surprising therefore that Judge Block should have decided to sentence Mr Jagger to imprisonment, and particularly surprising as Mr Jagger's is about as mild a drug case as can ever have been brought before the Courts.

It would be wrong to speculate on the Judge's reasons, which we do not know. It is, however, possible to consider the public reaction. There are many people who take a primitive view of the matter, what one might call a pre-legal view of the matter. They consider that Mr Jagger has 'got what was coming to him'. They resent the anarchic quality of the Rolling Stones' performances, dislike their songs, dislike their influence on teenagers and broadly suspect them of decadence, a word used by Miss Monica Furlong in the *Daily Mail*.

As a sociological concern this may be reasonable enough, and at an emotional level it is very understandable, but it has nothing at all to do with the case. One has to ask a different question: has Mr Jagger received the same treatment as he would have received if he had not been a famous figure, with all the criticism and resentment his celebrity has aroused? If a promising undergraduate had come back from a summer visit to Italy with four pep pills in his pocket would it have been thought right to ruin his career by sending him to prison for three months? Would it also have been thought necessary to display him handcuffed to the public?

There are cases in which a single figure becomes the focus for public concern about some aspect of public morality. The Stephen Ward case, with its dubious evidence and questionable verdict, was one of them, and that verdict killed Stephen Ward. There are elements of the same emotions in the reactions to this case. If we are going to make any case a symbol of the conflict between the sound traditional values of Britain and the new hedonism, then we must be sure that the sound traditional values include those of tolerance and equity. It should be the particular quality of British justice to ensure that Mr Jagger is treated exactly the same as anyone else, no better and no worse. There must remain a suspicion in this case that Mr Jagger received a more severe sentence than would have been thought proper for any purely anonymous young man.

William Rees-Mogg, *The Times*, 1 July 1967

1967: Satin Odyssey

I realized soon after pulling Nigel Bishop that I'd done something very clever. It was a much better scene to turn up at clubs with the group than being one of many in the audience. It wasn't that I had minded being part of an audience, I just hadn't known any better. Now I had the privilege of the dressing rooms I also seemed to have a new identity. I *knew* the Satin Odyssey, and that was a pretty cool thing to be able to say. The Satin Odyssey are the first underground group to get anywhere. They started down at UFO, which is an underground club for people on that scene, like me. In fact, it was the only club where you could hear the really original groups like the Satin play. They were the first group to open people up to sound and colour, and I took my first trip down there when the Satin were playing, and the experience took my mind right out and I don't think it came back the same.

Nigel was their manager, and I hadn't really felt like being pulled by him until I found out who he was. I had been impressed, and thought what a groove to get back-stage and meet the Satin. Ben in particular, everybody was talking about him and saying how weird he was. He wrote for the group, and his mind, through his words and music, came over in fragments, like signals from a freaked-out fairyland, where nothing made sense and everything held meaning. And I used to watch his shadowy figure on stage, and wonder about him. It had been difficult to see his face with all those colours flashing and swirling over him, but what I saw I liked. And when I saw it in the bare light of the dressing room I liked it even more. He had this thin nose which separated the sunken circles under his very dark eyes, and a pale skin that was stretched almost unbearably tight over the bones of his face. He was tall and thin, and his eyes had the polished look I'd seen in other people who had taken too many trips in too short a time. I found him completely removed from the other three in the group; he was very withdrawn and smiled a lot to himself. As I got to know them all better I realized that the others and Nigel were worried about him. They muttered that he might freak right out soon if he didn't watch it. They complained that it was impossible to get new group things together with him when he was in this state. They weren't the only ones failing to get through to Ben. I was trying to let him know I fancied him, but it seemed hopeless, so I didn't push it.

Anyway, I was enjoying this new scene. The Satin had started making real bread now, and their shows were always packed. Underground groups were suddenly commercial, and straight industry people were moving into our scene and exploiting it. Imitators changed their equipment, got light shows, and followed where the Satin led. And the Satin were important, and there I was, being seen around with them. With Nigel, that is. I didn't know many of the faces yet, so I kept myself in the background, or stuck with Nigel and listened to him talking business. Everyone seemed to talk business, and I wished I knew more about it all. But I gradually started sussing things out, fitting names to faces and picking up little bits of knowledge here and there. And it made me feel one-up that I knew about these things.

Some of the group's image and importance rubbed off on to me, and my friends and people like that were always asking me questions about the Satin. I had a sort of status, because now they could say they knew someone who knew the Satin. And when Nigel took me on gigs I could feel the stage-door groupies' envy, and I found I liked to be envied. I was different to them, because I was with the group and they weren't and they wanted to be. Though I was well aware that without Nigel I would be back in the audience again, for, on my own, what was I – a 19-year-old groover who had just happened to pull a face. I'd sussed out the competition from the senior groupies, the type of chicks I saw at places like The Joint. The Joint is a nightclub for the popelite where nearly everybody is somebody. Ben didn't seem to notice all the pretty chicks that managed to find some excuse to talk to the group, but I watched the others getting it together, and I noticed that the girls had got classier now the group was bigger. One or two of these chicks lasted, but more came and went, and I wondered what happened to them. Maybe they ended up like Roxanna, a very obviously senior groupie I met at The Joint one night when the Satin were playing down there.

She came over to our table and said Hello, great to see you all. She obviously knew them, though I didn't know her. She sat down, and I watched. She had long dark hair and a fantastic figure, though her face wasn't all that special. She spoke fast in a very decisive way, as though she really knew what she was talking about, in a rather obvious educated accent. I was a bit knocked out by her, by her confidence, and by the way she seemed to know everyone down there.

'Hello, Tony,' she would call out to some shadowy figure sitting at another table, 'I want to talk to you in a minute.' Then she would dash off and sit at this table and that, engrossed in conversation with these different faces. I could never have done that. It made me realize there was a long way to go before I could be like her, and when I realized that, I also realized that I envied her just like the stage-door groupies envied me. I wanted to leap about saying hi to everyone too, I wanted to call these famous people by their first names and speak to them in their own language. She seemed pretty flash, and I wondered if she was for real. I asked Nigel what her scene was and he said she pulled pop musicians, the best and grooviest around. Did she have a job, I asked. No, chicks like Roxanna didn't have jobs. Unless it was something in the pop business, their's was a full-time occupation, he told me.

I wondered if she got hung up on the guys she pulled, and if so, what happened then. I mean, I get hung up on guys, and if I had to dash about pulling groovy musicians I'd probably get hung up on someone somewhere along the way, because I'm gullible, I believe things people say to me. I mean I even believe telly ads and things like that. Anyway, I was impressed and I envied her scene, and wondered how I would do if I tried.

During all the gigs Nigel took me to I made as much contact as I could with Ben. Nigel often left me alone in the dressing rooms while he hustled with promoters and stage managers, and Ben would sometimes talk to me. He showed me how to roll spliffs – as he called them – so that I could roll for him. Though I was still Nigel's chick I tried very hard to let Ben know how I felt about him. But he was so stoned all the time that without being completely uncool, I doubt if my message got across. He may well have interpreted my longing eyes as transitory hallucinations or something. And I really did want him, to me he was the actual *thing* that Nigel only represented. Although I dug the status I got from being Nigel's chick there was even more prestige in being Ben's. But only an incident of some kind could make this happen, and I just had to wait for my opportunity.

At the Oxford Summer Ball it happened. All in all it was a pretty busy day. Our flat got busted in the afternoon. I live in a large pad with two guys and another chick. One of the guys does light shows at UFO and the other is a recently dropped out encyclopaedia salesman who now manages a bad, nowhere group. The chick is called Wendy, and she does nothing in particular except loon about. But she's very intelligent, and I get on well with her.

I suppose we looked pretty suspect, the guys with their long hair and acid clothes, me with my Jimi Hendrix head and all the people going in and out late at night. It was a nuisance getting busted, it meant wasting time and bread on solicitors and appearing in court, and the nagging thought at the back of my mind that I might be treated as an example and put away. Although it was quite fashionable to be busted, everyone groovy seemed to be having the same trouble. And ours was a dramatic bust – nine fuzz, two women fuzz, and two hash hounds. It took them ages to search the place and I was the only one who had anything, the others were just lucky not to have had anything around that day. After I'd been through all the bad scenes at the police station and I had been bailed, I found that I'd missed my lift to the gig. But Nigel rang up from Oxford and told me to come up by train, and he would send Bat, the second roadie, to meet me at the station.

It was quite late when Bat took me to the college where it was all happening. There were all these students and deb chicks in long dresses looning about with guys in DJs, all getting stoned on strawberries and cream and champers. Nigel was grooving around with some people he had been to college with, so I got Bat to take me to where the group was. They said the whole thing was too much for them, and as they had plenty of time before they were due to play, we decided to split down to the river and turn on. I managed to sit with Ben on a punt somewhere apart from the others and rolled some spliffs for him. There was this warm mist creeping along the river, and the sounds of the water lapping against the sides of the boat made us both feel relaxed and peaceful. I told Ben how groovy it was to be here with him, and quite suddenly he put his arm round me and started talking about Japanese temples. I sat leaning against him, and wondered if I was getting anywhere. I was afraid to speak, I didn't want to interrupt his voice or spoil the almost transcendental mood I was in. Though maybe I felt more on the edge of victory than transcendental. I didn't really understand what Ben was talking about, but it didn't matter. We stayed there until it was time for them to go back and play.

Nigel was a bit uptight when I got back, and wanted to know what was going on between me and Ben. I handed him a flower that someone had given me, and that seemed to do instead of an explanation. Then I escaped to watch the show from the light tower. The Satin were pretty good, and had quite an effect on the students, who probably hadn't seen anything like them before. Being a bit stoned, the strobes seemed especially effective tonight; from where I watched it was like the entire concert platform lifted into the air and jerked sideways in movements of sudden frenzy. The contrast of the quiet electronic pluckings of Ben's guitar and the sheer volume they worked up to as they all gradually joined in to form a tune, left me breathless. But I managed to get it together to go over and stand by the stage just before they finished. But I had to fight my way through a mob of long dressed chicks who had gathered there, saying how super, and trying to attract the group's attention. I was sure there was very little holding them back from grabbing at the group like out-of-town groupies.

When it was time to go, the distribution of the passengers between car and van had to be decided. Normally I travelled in the car with Nigel, but I knew Ben would be in the van, so I hid behind a hot dog stand outside and watched Nigel drive furiously away without me. Then I emerged and said.

'Oh, has the car gone?'

'You're in the van with us,' Ben said.

The back of the van was full, so I sat in the front with Ben, and Boris, the roadie. I could feel the curious eyes of the others on us from the back. This was my first ride in a group van, but I was so hung up on wanting Ben that I forgot to savour it. Side by side we sat, with a silent Boris driving very fast. The night was finishing now and we were into the early morning, with a huge red sun climbing its way up in front of us.

'Lean on my shoulder if you're tired,' Ben said, and incredibly wide awake I leant, and closed my eyes. It stayed like that for a long time. Then, as we neared London, I realized that I would have to get something more positive together, for nothing was settled yet, except that I was blowing my scene with Nigel. I sat up and felt a little panicky. I alternated between looking grimly ahead and then questioningly at Ben. He didn't even seem to notice me and I just didn't know what to do. Then, blowing my cool completely, I leaned over and asked him straight out if he was going to stay at my place, but he just gave a sort of superior smile and stayed dumb.

Boris knew where I lived and made for my place first. The van drew up, and I slid the door open and climbed reluctantly out. Ben moved over into my place and then casually swung his legs out on to the ground. 'Too much,' my mind flashed. 'He's coming with me.' With the others staring at us out of the van windows we waved our good-byes and went into the house. We went upstairs and into the flat, then down the passage and into my room. And now, having wanted him for such a long time, here he was, alone with me in my room.

We wasted time exchanging vague remarks and smoking a couple of joints. Finally Ben reached down and untied his gymshoes. He always wore gymshoes, as a sort of protest about all the money they were making.

'Let's go to bed,' he said.

We undressed silently and got in beside each other. At first we just lay there, he on his back, me on my side looking at him. I pulled back the covers and ran my hand over his body. In the half light of the room his long thin body looked longer and thinner, and his paleness was emphasized by the absence of hair. I kissed his nipples and after that I ran my tongue gently round his navel. He liked it. I felt his body stiffen and his erection came rising up hard. He shoved his hands into my hair and held my head steady. I wondered whether I should plate him. I hadn't done much of that, but I knew guys on the scene liked it because Nigel had told me so. So I covered him with my mouth, and started doing things with my lips and tongue. His hands still in my hair seemed to lose their strength. He never spoke or made a sound and hardly moved; he just lay flat on his back with his eyes wide open, and kind of blank. It took a long time and I enjoyed every minute of it. Not like with Nigel, who used to go berserk every time he got into bed and fucked me so hard I'd sometimes end up on the floor. This was cool and somehow much sexier, and I really worked at controlling it for him. I'd take him to the edge and, feeling the tension rising in his body, I'd bring him right back and circle him around and then up again and back again and so on for a long, long time. Then it happened and I thought his body would crack under the strain, the way it buckled. He tasted sweet, and when it finished I found there were tears in my eyes. He lay in exactly the same position he had started in and still he hadn't spoken. It didn't matter. I didn't know where Ben's mind was at; it was enough to be lying there beside him. When I woke up early in the afternoon he had gone.

It was just as well it happened when it did with Ben, because soon after our night together, he freaked out completely. He turned up at my place without any warning to take me on a gig, and looked really ill. He wasn't speaking to anyone and his face was deathly white and beaded with sweat. He went on to play and I noticed half-way through the first set he wasn't singing and hardly playing a note. The bass player was covering up for him well, so not many people noticed. I just had to ask someone about him, so I cornered Nigel. Nigel had accepted the new situation with me rather sourly, but he didn't mind telling me.

'Nobody's talking about it,' Nigel said. 'We've been expecting something like this to happen. His mind is blown to pieces by all the acid he's dropped this summer. You won't be able to help him,' he added, 'though I wish somebody could.'

After the first set Ben said he wanted to get away from the club and sit somewhere quiet. So we took a taxi back to my flat, promising to return in time for the second set. He sat down and suddenly started talking about all the people who were now putting down the group because they had made it. I told him there would always be people like that. But he believed the group had sold out, and he couldn't reconcile what he wanted to do with what he was actually doing. Commercialism had nothing to do with being a religious artist, he said. I wanted to help, but didn't really understand what was wrong. They were the best and grooviest musicians around. They could play where they liked and what they liked, and still make more bread than they needed. They were in a position to experiment with new musical ideas, and there was nothing Ben couldn't do if he had just half a mind to get it together. I just didn't understand. It was like his mind was burning up right in front of my eyes. I'd tripped and turned on, perhaps not enough to realize what he was going through, but certainly enough to know what acid did to minds. But this beautiful pop musician, shivering and pouring out his torture and miseries, was something else. He seemed to have lost touch with reality, and there's no convincing someone like that. So I kept silent and just listened. When it was time to go he rose without argument and we went back for the second set.

This time he made no bones about his problem, nor the effect it was having on him. He went on stage, silent, pale and sweaty again, and just sat on the floor with his guitar in his lap. He stayed like that for the whole set. It was the last time he played for the Satin, and the last time I saw him. He left for some Spanish monastery to find himself. The Satin got themselves a new lead guitarist. They were established and could do without Ben. For me, the Satin's magic went with him.

Jenny Fabian and Johnny Byrne, *Groupie* (1970)

315

1967: Notes for a Theory of Sixties Style

Velvet is back, skin anti-skin, mimic nakedness. Like leather and suede, only more subtly, velvet simulates the flesh it conceals, a profoundly tactile fabric. Last winter's satin invited the stroke, a slithering touch, this winter's velvet invites a more sinuous caress. But the women who buy little brown velvet dresses will probably do so in a state of unknowing, unaware they're dressing up for parts in our daily theatre of fact; unaware, too, how mysterious that theatre is.

For the nature of apparel is very complex. Clothes are so many things at once. Our social shells; the system of signals with which we broadcast our intentions; often the projections of our fantasy selves (a fat old woman in a bikini); the formal uniform of our life roles (the businessman's suit, the teacher's tweed jackets with leather patches and ritual accessory of pipe in breast pocket); sometimes simple economic announcements of income or wealth (real jewellery – especially inherited real jewellery, which throws in a bonus of class as well – or mink). Clothes are our weapons, our challenges, our visible insults.

And more. For we think our dress expresses ourselves but in fact it expresses our environment and, like advertising, pop music, pulp fiction and second-feature films, it does so almost at a subliminal, emotionally charged, instinctual, non-intellectual level. The businessmen, the fashion writers, the designers and models, the shopkeepers, the buyers, the window dressers live in the same cloud of unknowing as us all; they think they mould the public taste but really they're blind puppets of a capricious goddess, goddess of mirrors, weather-cocks and barometers, whom the Elizabethans called Mutability. She is inscrutable but logical.

The inscrutable but imperative logic of change has forced fashion in the sixties through the barriers of space and time. Clothes today sometimes seem arbitrary and bizarre; nevertheless, the startling dandyism of the newly emancipated young reveals a kind of logic of whizzing entropy. Mutability is having a field day.

Let us take the following example. A young girl, invited to a party, left to herself (no mother to guide her), might well select the following ensemble: a Mexican cotton wedding dress (though she's not a bride, probably no virgin, either – thus at one swoop turning a garment which in its original environ-ment is an infinitely potent symbol into a piece of decoration); her grand-mother's button boots (once designed to show off the small feet and moneyed leisure of an Edwardian middle class who didn't need to work and rarely had

316

to walk); her mother's fox fur (bought to demonstrate her father's status); and her old school beret dug out of the loft because she saw Faye Dunaway in *Bonnie and Clyde* (and a typical role-definition garment changes gear).

All these eclectic fragments, robbed of their symbolic content, fall together to form a new whole, a dramatisation of the individual, a personal style. And fashion today (real fashion, what real people wear) is a question of style, no longer a question of items in harmony. 'What to wear with what' is no longer a burning question; in the 1960s, everything is worn all at once.

Style means the presentation of the self as a three-dimensional art object, to be wondered at and handled. And this involves a new attitude to the self which is thus adorned. The gaudy rags of the flower children, the element of fancy dress even in 'serious' clothes (the military look, the thirties revival), extravagant and stylised face-painting, wigs, hairpieces, amongst men the extraordinary recrudescence of the decorative moustache (and, indeed, the concept of the decorative man), fake tattooing – all these are in the nature of disguises.

Disguise entails duplicity. One passes oneself off as another, who may or may not exist – as Jean Harlow or Lucy in the Sky with Diamonds or Al Capone or Sergeant Pepper. Though the disguise is worn as play and not intended to deceive, it does nevertheless give a relaxation from one's own personality and the discovery of maybe unsuspected new selves. One feels free to behave more freely. This holiday from the persistent self is the perpetual lure of fancy dress. Rosalind in disguise in the Forest of Arden could pretend to be a boy pretending to be a seductress, satisfying innumerable atavistic desires in the audience of the play. And we are beginning to realise once again what everybody always used to know, that all human contact is profoundly ambiguous. And the style of the sixties expresses this knowledge.

The *Bonnie and Clyde* clothes and the guru robes certainly don't indicate a cult of violence or a massive swing to transcendental meditation (although *Rave* magazine did feature a 'Raver's Guide' to the latter subject in the November issue); rather, this rainbow proliferation of all kinds of fancy dress shows a new freedom many people fear, especially those with something to lose when the frozen, repressive, role-playing world properly starts to melt.

Consider a typical hippy, consider a typical Chinese Red Guard. One is a beautiful explosion of sexually ambiguous silks and beads, the other a sternly-garbed piece of masculine aggression, proclaiming by his clothes the gift of his individual self to the puritan ethic of his group. The first sports the crazy patchwork uniform of a society where social and sexual groupings are willy-nilly disintegrating, the second is part of a dynamically happening society where all the individuals are clenched together like a fist. One is a fragment of a kaleidoscope, the other a body blow. One is opening out like a rose, the other forging straight ahead.

Of course, one does not have to go so far afield as China to see this dichotomy of aim. If you put the boy in the djellibah next to a middle-aged police constable, each will think of the other: 'The enemies are amongst us.' For the boy in the djellibah will be a very young boy, and the class battle in Britain (once sartorially symbolised by Keir Hardie's cloth cap) is redefining itself as the battle of the generations.

The Rolling Stones' drugs case was an elegant confrontation of sartorial symbolism in generation warfare: the judge, in ritually potent robes and wig, invoking the doom of his age and class upon the beautiful children in frills and sunset colours, who dared to question the infallibility he represents as icon of the law and father figure.

The Rolling Stones' audience appeal has always been anti-parent, anti-authority, and they have always used sartorial weapons – from relatively staid beginnings (long hair and grime) to the famous *Daily Mirror* centre spread in superdrag. They are masters of the style of calculated affront. And it never fails to work. The clothing of pure affront, sported to bug the squares (as the Hell's Angels say), will always succeed in bugging the squares no matter how often they are warned, 'He only does it to annoy.'

The Hell's Angels and the other Californian motor-cycle gangs deck themselves with iron crosses, Nazi helmets, necklets and earrings, they grow their hair to their shoulders and dye their beards green, red and purple, they cultivate halitosis and body odour. Perfect dandies of beastliness, they incarnate the American nightmare. Better your sister marry a Negro than have the Oakland chapter of Hell's Angels drop in on her for coffee.

But this outlaw dress represents a real dissociation from society. It is a very serious joke and, in their Neanderthal way, the Hell's Angels are obeying Camus' law – that the dandy is always a rebel, that he challenges society because he challenges mortality. The motor-cycle gangs challenge mortality face to face, doing 100 mph on a California freeway in Levi's and swastikas, no crash helmet but a wideawake hat, only a veneer of denim between the man and his death. 'The human being who is condemned to die is, at least, magnificent before he disappears and his magnificence is his justification.'

In the decade of Vietnam, in the century of Hiroshima and Buchenwald, we are as perpetually aware of mortality as any generation ever was. It is small wonder that so many people are taking the dandy's way of asking unanswerable questions. The pursuit of magnificence starts as play and ends as nihilism or metaphysics or a new examination of the nature of goals.

In the pursuit of magnificence, nothing is sacred. Hitherto sacrosanct imagery is desecrated. When Pete Townshend of The Who first put on his jacket carved out of the Union Jack, he turned our national symbol into an abstraction far more effectively than did Jasper Johns when he copied the Old Glory out in paint and hung it on his wall. Whether or not Pete Townshend fully realised the nature of his abstraction is not the question; he was impelled to it by the pressures of the times.

Similarly, fabrics and objects hitherto possessing strong malignant fetishistic qualities have either been cleansed of their deviational overtones and used for their intrinsic textural charm, or else worn in the camp style with a humorous acknowledgement of those overtones. Rubber, leather, fur, objects such as fish-net stockings and tall boots are fetishes which the purity of style has rendered innocent, as sex becomes more relaxed and the norm more subtle.

Iconic clothing has been secularised, too. Witness the cult of the military uniform. A guardsman in a dress uniform is ostensibly an icon of aggression; his coat is red as the blood he hopes to shed. Seen on a coat-hanger, with no man inside it, the uniform loses all its blustering significance and, to the innocent eye seduced by decorative colour and tactile braid, it is as abstract in symbolic information as a parasol to an Eskimo. It becomes simply magnificent. However, once on the back of the innocent, it reverts to an aggressive role: to old soldiers (that is, most men in this country over forty) the secularised military uniform gives far too much information, all of it painful. He sees a rape of his ideals, is threatened by a terrible weapon of affront.

A good deal of iconic clothing has become secularised simply through disuse. It no longer has any symbolic content for the stylists and is not decorative enough to be used in play. Mutability has rendered it obsolescent. The cabaret singer in her sequin sheath which shrieks 'Look at me but don't touch me, I'm armour-plated' survives as an image of passive female sexuality, the *princesse lointaine* (or, rather, the *putain lointaine*) only in the womb-like unreality of the nightclub or on the fantasy projection of the television screen. The tulle and taffeta bride in her crackling virginal carapace, clasping numinous lilies, the supreme icon of woman as a sexual thing and nothing else whatever, survives as part of the potlatch culture at either end of the social scale – where the pressures to make weddings of their daughters displays of conspicuous consumption are fiercest.

On the whole, though, girls have been emancipated from the stiff forms of iconic sexuality. Thanks to social change, to contraception, to equal pay for equal work, there is no need for this iconography any more; both men and women's clothes today say, 'Look at me and touch me if I want you.' Velvet is back, skin anti-skin, mimic nakedness.

Angela Carter, *New Society*, 1967

1967: The Memphis Soul Sound

Two weeks before, Otis Redding and Steve Cropper had been sitting on folding chairs, facing each other, in the dark cavern-like grey-and-pink studio at the Stax/Volt recording company. Stax is located in a converted movie theater in McLemore Street in Memphis, next to a housing project. The marquee is still there, with red plastic letters that spell 'Soulsville, USA'. The sign was changed once to read 'Stay in School', but the kids from the project threw rocks at it, so it was changed back again.

Otis Redding grew up in a housing project and left school at fifteen, but now when he came to the studio he was in a chauffeured Continental. Still, he had not forgotten who he was, where he had come from. The boys from the project knew this, and called Otis their main man. When he got out of the long white car and started across the sidewalk, he took the time to say, 'What's happening?' to the boys in bright pants, standing at the curb.

'I was born in Terrell County, Georgia, in a town called Dawson. After I was one year old we moved to Macon. I've stayed in Macon all my life. First we lived in a project house. We lived there for about fourteen years. Then we had to move out to the outskirts of the city. I was going to Ballard Hudson High School, and I kind of got unlucky. My old man got sick, so I had to come out of school and try to find some kind of gig to help my mother. I got a job drilling water wells in Macon. It's a pretty easy job, it sounds hard but it's pretty easy. The hardest thing about it is when you have to change bits. They have big iron bits that weigh 250 pounds, and we'd have to change them, put them on the stem so we could drill – that was the hardest thing about it.

'I was almost sixteen at this time, just getting started singing. I used to play gigs and not make any money. I wasn't looking for money out of it then. I just wanted to be a singer.

'I listened to Little Richard and Chuck Berry a lot. Little Richard is actually the guy that inspired me to start singing. He was from Macon, too. My favorite song of his was "Heebie Jeebies". I remember it went, "My bad luck baby put the jinx on me." That song really inspired me to start singing, because I won a talent show with it. This was at the Hillview Springs Social Club – it's not there any more – I won the talent show for fifteen Sunday nights straight with that song, and then they wouldn't let me sing no more, wouldn't let me win that five dollars any more. So that . . . really inspired me.

'Later on I started singing with a band called Johnnie Jenkins and the Pinetoppers. We played little night-club and college dates, played at the University of Georgia and Georgia Tech. Then in 1960 I went to California to cut a record, "She's All Right". It was with Lute Records, the label the Hollywood Argyles were on. It didn't do anything. I came back to Macon and recorded a song I wrote called "Shout-bama-lama". A fellow named Mickey Murray had a hit off the song recently, but it didn't sell when I did it. It kind of got me off to a start, though, and then I came to Memphis in November 1961.

'Johnnie Jenkins was going to record, and I came with him. I had this song, "These Arms of Mine", and I asked if I could record it. The musicians had been working with Johnnie all day, and they didn't have but twenty minutes before they went home. But they let me record "These Arms of Mine". I give John Richbourg at WLAC in Nashville a lot of credit for breaking that record, because he played it and kept playing it after everybody else had forgot about it. It took nine months to sell, but it sold real good, and – and I've just been going ever since.'

Otis is playing a bright red dime-store guitar, strumming simple bar chords as he sings:

> 'Sittin' in the mornin' sun,
> I'll be sittin' when the evenin' comes –'

The front of the guitar is cracked, as if someone has stepped on it. As he sings, Otis watches Steve, who nods and nods, bending almost double over his guitar, following Otis's chords with a shimmering electric response.

> 'Sittin' in the mornin' sun –'

'But I don't know why he's sittin',' Otis says, rocking back and forth as if he were still singing. 'He's just sittin'. Got to be more to it than that.' He pauses for a moment, shaking his head. Then he says, 'Wait. Wait a minute,' to Steve, who has been waiting patiently.

'I left my home in Georgia,
Headed for the Frisco bay –'

He pauses again, runs through the changes on his fractured guitar, then sings:

'I had nothing to live for,
Look like nothing's gonna come my way –'

'I write music everywhere, in motels, dressing rooms – I'll just play a song on the guitar and remember it. Then, usually, I come in the studio and Steve and I work it out. Sometimes I'll have just an idea, maybe for a bass line or some chord changes – maybe just a feeling – and we see what we can make out of it. We try to get everybody to groove together to the way a song feels.'

When Steve and Otis have the outlines of a song, they are joined by the rest of the MGs. Booker and Duck come in first, followed by drummer Al Jackson. Duck is telling Booker about his new stereo record player. 'I got me a nice one, man, with components. You can turn down one of the speakers and hear the words real clear. I been listening to the Beatles. Last night I played *Revolver*, and on "Yellow Submarine", you know what one of 'em says? I think it's Ringo, he says, "Paul is a queer." He really does, man. "Paul-is-a-queer", bigger'n shit.'

Booker sits at the piano, Duck gets his bass, which has been lying in its case on the worn red rug, and they begin to pick up the chord patterns from Steve and Otis. Al stands by, listening, his head tilted to one side. Duck asks him a question about counting the rhythm, and Steve looks up to say, 'In a minute he'll want to know what key we're in.' Duck sticks out his lower lip. He plays bass as fluently as if it were guitar, plucking the stout steel strings with his first two fingers, holding a cigarette between the other two. Booker sits erect, his right hand playing short punctuating notes, his left hand resting on his left knee. Otis is standing now, moving around the room, waving his arms as he conducts these men, his friends, who are there to serve him. He looks like a swimmer, moving effortlessly underwater. Then something happens, a connection is made in Al Jackson's mind, and he goes to the drums, baffled on two sides with wallboard. 'One, two,' he announces. 'One-two-three-four.' And for the first time they are all together, everyone has found the groove.

The Mar-Keys drift into the studio and sit on folding chairs behind another baffle, one wall of which has a small window. They listen, sucking on reeds, blowing into mouthpieces, as Otis and the rhythm section rehearse the song. When Steve calls, 'Hey, horns! Ready to record?' they are thrown into confusion, like a man waked in the middle of the night. They have nothing to record; there are, as yet, no horn parts. Steve and Otis develop them by singing to each other. 'De-de-da-dee,' Steve says. 'De-de-da-*daaah*,' says Otis, as if he were making a point in an argument. When they have the lines they want, they sing them to the Mar-Keys, starting with the verse part, which the Mar-Keys will forget while learning the parts for the chorus. After a few tries, however, they know both parts, and are ready to record. 'That feels good, man, let's cut it.'

During the rehearsal, one of the neighborhood kid, wearing blue jeans, an old cloth cap, and Congress basketball sneakers with one green and one yellow lace, has slipped into the studio. He sits behind a cluster of microphones, unnoticed by Otis, who passes directly by him on his way to the far corner of the room, where he strikes a wide, flat-footed stance facing a wallboard partition. Otis can hear but cannot see Al Jackson, holding one stick high as if it were a baton, counting four, then rolling his eyes toward the ceiling and starting to play.

After 'Dock of the Bay' was recorded, Steve and Booker added guitar and piano fills. The song boomed into the studio from a speaker high on the rear wall, and Booker played precise little bop, bop-bop figures, while Steve followed the vocal with an almost quivering blues line. The speaker went dead, then the engineer's voice came: 'Steve, one note's clashing.'

'Sure it is,' Steve tells him. 'It was written to clash.' Which, in point of fact, is not true, since nothing has been written down so far. 'Let's do it once more,' Steve says. 'We can do that bridge better. I can. First part's a groove.'

Inside the control room, Otis and Duck are talking. 'I wish you all *could* go with me to the Fillmore on Christmas,' Otis says.

'Man, so do I. I got some *good* fren's in San Francisco. We could rent one of them yachts.'

'I *got* one already. Three bedrooms, two baths, sumbitch is nice, man.'

'My ole lady's kill me,' Duck says.

When the recording is finished, Steve and Booker come into the control room, followed after a moment by the little boy in Congress sneakers. The tape is played back at a painful volume level. Steve and Otis stare deep into each other's eyes, carrying a kind of telepathic communication. The little boy, looking up at the speaker the music is coming from, says, 'I like that. That's good singin'. I'd like to be a singer myself.'

'If you got the feelin', you can sing soul. You just sing from the heart, and – there's no difference between nobody's heart.'

'That's it,' Otis says when the record ends.
'That's a mother,' says Booker.

Stanley Booth, *Rythm Oil* (1991)

1968: R&B and the Long Hot Summer

One of the reasons why we in Britain have developed R&B and Soul records into such an objective cult is, I think, due to the fact that we are 3,000 miles from the place where it is all happening. We are 3,000 miles from the radio stations which play R&B 24 hours a day (a diet that would probably tire even the most dedicated of us), and we are 3,000 miles from the Negro* ghetto and the racial tensions that are always making the world newspaper headlines each and every summer. In many ways we in Britain lead shockingly sheltered lives (and if you don't believe this then see films like 'Africa Addio' or 'The Pawnbroker', both of which show the thin crust of civilization cracking under pressure), and so often it is perhaps too easy to assume a 'holier-than-thou' attitude simply because these problems and racial confrontations do not affect us personally. It is easier to place the blame than it is to suggest a cure, and yet I feel that everyone who buys and enjoys R&B records should be fervently concerned with race relations, and should be engaged in action that will prevent the American tragedy from ever repeating itself in this country.

In 'Billboard's' supplement 'The World of Soul', Otis Redding's manager Phil Walden was quoted as saying: 'Otis Redding ... has done more to improve the racial situation in the South than a hundred sit-ins.' This to my mind is a particularly naïve statement, and is sadly typical of the Southern attitude towards the handful of Negro citizens who have increased their personal wealth and thus their personal prestige and power. Apart, too, from a tacit disapproval of 'sit-ins' (which I am sure are easier to verbally dismiss than actively take part in), such a statement makes little sense, particularly in a context that must include freedom marchers being beaten to death with chains, and Negro Sunday Schools being bombed by Caucasian hoodlums. Even to use the word 'hoodlum' is probably wrong of me, since experience has shown that often the perpetrators of such outrages are in most other respects quite ordinary citizens – it is on this one issue of race that the devil within breaks out with virulence and savagery. However, it is the psychology

*The author wishes to make clear that 'in 1968 the term "Negro" was politically correct, whereas the term "black" was derogatory'.

of British fans in relation to the American Negro performer that I wish to examine. Artists (with a few militant exceptions) are often reluctant to be drawn on the racial issue, and one can perhaps sympathize, since they have found so often to their disappointment that it is the white person who needs to get his position and attitude sorted out and defined.

When a truth is so self-evident as that of the equality of the races, there is no virtue to be gained in acknowledging it or following its irresistible impulses, and yet so often a fan will imply with his (or her) attitude – 'Look at me – I'm free of prejudice – aren't I good?' Well, big deal! And yet this patronizing attitude which has plagued the American Negro for so many decades *must* be seen for the arrogant stupidity it is before the races can meet on equal terms. Now in music itself this same feeling will manifest itself in subtle (but none the less repulsive) terms. The fans who are only interested in artists, who have never seen the inside of the Hot Hundred, are (without realizing it) throwing crumbs to an artist (since the royalties from the sales of records in Britain by those esoteric artists wouldn't keep them in cigarettes or lipsticks for a month), and then to drop them and almost sneer at them just because they make the top ten and make a commercial hit shows a childish petulance that is again showing a patronizing (and therefore prejudiced) 'admiration'. On her visit to Britain Miss Maxine Brown was asked by a 'fan' – 'is your hair straight or frizzy under your wig?' One can draw your own conclusions about this by the simple trick of putting yourself in Miss Brown's place and imagining how you would feel to be the recipient of such a gauche remark.

British fans do their own intelligence and the cause of equality for all people of colour no service by assuming that all American Negroes are just like the artists they admire and perhaps occasionally have met. I've met R&B fans who are avid followers of American Negro artists and yet intensely dislike West Indians. What is so particularly unfortunate in this is that they cannot see the dichotomy of their thoughts and (not wishing to mince words) the immorality of their attitude. But, immorality and hypocrisy are not prerogatives of any one race or people and wealthy Negroes often prefer to overlook the very real struggle for equality that is an everyday facet of American life just because it no longer affects them, since money can often break down barriers which in the past were stony-faced in their resistance to the voice of reason and simple justice.

Many Negroes have so despaired of the Mr Charlies (their nick-name for white folk who pose as liberals and yet seethe with subconscious bigotry) that they want as little as possible to do with them, and shun and avoid as much contact and intercourse as they can. Whilst one can perhaps sympathize by understanding the cause of this, it is in no way to say that this is right or desirable, and such attitudes are as mistaken in their false assumptions as those of their white counterparts who boost their fearful prejudice by repeating myths which everyone has heard and knows about. No doubt in time the Negro subculture of these prejudiced people will produce their own repertoire about white people. Both are wrong, and both will propel their propagandists towards the inevitable confrontation in which only the innocent will suffer and get caught up in.

To get back to Phil Walden's remark, however (which sparked this article off anyway), it has long been acceptable for the white Southerner to accept the Negro (and one might significantly add the Jew) on certain clearly defined terms. While Southerners do buy many records by Negro artists; they do employ them about the house (if they can afford it); and they even employ a Negro lady to act as a wet-nurse when they have to (the pestilence of racism in the South has never quite reached the loony stature it is given in South Africa), and yet that is about as far as it can go. Mention miscegenation (that spectre that festers in every racist's mind) and they'll jump up like a shot and invoke biblical 'justification' to assuage their guilt-ridden minds.

R&B music must have done a lot for integration, it must have made a lot of people think about problems which, before their interest, would not perhaps have entered their minds, and all this is to the good, but is it enough? It must also have moved some people in the other direction and towards an opposite extreme of thinking that only a Negro can artistically give expression to suffering and sorrow. Whilst I will acknowledge that only the wearer knows where the shoe pinches, it is wrong to insist that the Negro must continue in his previous role of troubadour to jaded white whims and frustrations. Many times I have been asked whether I think that the progress of integration will also bring in its wake a demise of R&B, Soul and Negro culture in general, and it is a question that no one can really answer – we must wait and see. Other ethnic groups with their distinctive subcultures have been absorbed into the mainstreams of the environments into which they were thrust without having to abandon their individuality, and I hope this will be the case with the American Negro. But, were I faced with having to choose between the demise of R&B and Soul and the advance and surge upwards of full integration then I'd choose the latter every time. If R&B and Soul were removed from the world tomorrow (and what a bleak, unimaginable prospect that'd be!) it still wouldn't be the *end* of the world, but how much more joyous would be the removal of hatred, bigotry and prejudice! If the passing of R&B were to be the price that we have to pay for true race equality then I'd gladly pay it – over and over. Would you?

Dave Godin, *Soul Music Magazine*, March 1968

1968: Missionaries of Apocalyptic Sex

It was six, seven o'clock of an early spring evening in 1968 and I was sitting on the cold vinyl floor of a sound studio on Sunset Boulevard, watching a band called The Doors record a rhythm track. On the whole my attention was only minimally engaged by the preoccupations of rock-and-roll bands (I had already heard about acid as a transitional stage and also about the Maharishi and even about Universal Love, and after a while it all sounded like marmalade skies to me), but The Doors were different, The Doors interested me. The Doors seemed unconvinced that love was brotherhood and the Kama Sutra. The Doors' music insisted that love was sex and sex was death and therein lay salvation. The Doors were the Norman Mailers of the Top Forty, missionaries of apocalyptic sex. *Break on through*, their lyrics urged, and *Light my fire*, and:

> Come on baby, gonna take a little ride
> Goin' down by the ocean side
> Gonna get real close
> Get real tight
> Baby gonna drown tonight –
> Goin' down, down, down.

On this evening in 1968 they were gathered together in uneasy symbiosis to make their third album, and the studio was too cold and the lights were too bright and there were masses of wires and banks of the ominous blinking electronic circuitry with which musicians live so easily. There were three of the four Doors. There was a bass player borrowed from a band called Clear Light. There were the producer and the engineer and the road manager and a couple of girls and a Siberian husky named Nikki with one gray eye and one gold. There were paper bags half filled with hard-boiled eggs and chicken livers and cheeseburgers and empty bottles of apple juice and California rosé. There was everything and everybody The Doors needed to cut the rest of this third album except one thing, the fourth Door, the lead singer, Jim Morrison, a 24-year-old graduate of UCLA who wore black vinyl pants and no underwear and tended to suggest some range of the possible just beyond a suicide pact. It was Morrison who had described The Doors as 'erotic politicians'. It was Morrison who had defined the group's interests as 'anything about revolt, disorder, chaos, about activity that appears to have no meaning'. It was Morrison who got arrested in Miami in December of 1967 for giving an 'indecent' performance. It was Morrison who wrote most of The Doors' lyrics, the peculiar character of which was to reflect either an ambiguous paranoia or a quite unambiguous insistence upon the love-death as the ultimate high. And it was Morrison who was missing. It was Ray Manzarek and Robby Krieger and John Densmore who made The Doors sound the way they sounded, and maybe it was Manzarek and Krieger and Densmore who made seventeen out of twenty interviewees on *American Bandstand* prefer The Doors over all other bands, but it was Morrison who got up there in his black vinyl pants with no underwear and projected the idea, and it was Morrison they were waiting for now.

'Hey, listen,' the engineer said. 'I was listening to an FM station on the way over here, they played three Doors songs, first they played "Back Door Man" and then "Love Me Two Times" and "Light My Fire".'

'I heard it,' Densmore muttered. 'I heard it.'

'So what's wrong with somebody playing three of your songs?'

'This cat dedicates it to his family.'

'Yeah? To his family?'

'To his family. Really crass.'

Ray Manzarek was hunched over a Gibson keyboard. 'You think *Morrison*'s going to come back?' he asked to no one in particular.

No one answered.

'So we can do some *vocals*?' Manzarek said.

The producer was working with the tape of the rhythm track they had just recorded. 'I hope so,' he said without looking up.

'Yeah,' Manzarek said. 'So do I.'

My leg had gone to sleep, but I did not stand up; unspecific tensions seemed to be rendering everyone in the room catatonic. The producer played back the rhythm track. The engineer said that he wanted to do his deep-breathing exercise. Manzarek ate a hard-boiled egg. 'Tennyson made a mantra out of his own name,' he said to the engineer. 'I don't know if he said "Tennyson Tennyson Tennyson" or "Alfred Alfred Alfred" or "Alfred Lord Tennyson", but anyway, he did it. Maybe he just said "Lord Lord Lord".'

'Groovy,' the Clear Light bass player said. He was an amiable enthusiast, not at all a Door in spirit.

328

'I wonder what Blake said,' Manzarek mused. 'Too bad *Morrison*'s not here. *Morrison* would know.'

It was a long while later. Morrison arrived. He had on his black vinyl pants and he sat down on a leather couch in front of the four big blank speakers and he closed his eyes. The curious aspect of Morrison's arrival was this: no one acknowledged it. Robby Krieger continued working out a guitar passage. John Densmore tuned his drums. Manzarek sat at the control console and twirled a corkscrew and let a girl rub his shoulders. The girl did not look at Morrison, although he was in her direct line of sight. An hour or so passed, and still no one had spoken to Morrison. Then Morrison spoke to Manzarek. He spoke almost in a whisper, as if he were wresting the words from behind some disabling aphasia.

'It's an hour to West Covina,' he said. 'I was thinking maybe we should spend the night out there after we play.'

Manzarek put down the corkscrew. 'Why?' he said.

'Instead of coming back.'

Manzarek shrugged. 'We were planning to come back.'

'Well, I was thinking, we could rehearse out there.'

Manzarek said nothing.

'We could get in a rehearsal, there's a Holiday Inn next door.'

'We could do that,' Manzarek said. 'Or we could rehearse Sunday, in town.'

'I guess so.' Morrison paused. 'Will the place be ready to rehearse Sunday?'

Manzarek looked at him for a while. 'No,' he said then.

I counted the control knobs on the electronic console. There were seventy-six. I was unsure in whose favor the dialogue had been resolved, or if it had been at all. Robby Krieger picked at his guitar, and said that he needed a fuzz box. The producer suggested that he borrow one from the Buffalo Springfield, who were recording in the next studio. Krieger shrugged. Morrison sat down again on the leather couch and leaned back. He lit a match. He studied the flame awhile and then slowly, deliberately, lowered it to the fly of his black vinyl pants. Manzarek watched him. The girl who was rubbing Manzarek's shoulders did not look at anyone. There was a sense that no one was going to leave the room, ever. It would be some weeks before The Doors finished recording this album. I did not see it through.

Joan Didion, *The White Album* (1979)

1968: The Yippies

The Yippies like the Hippies were famous for their optimism. The permit was not granted by Stahl or Daley. In turn, an offer by Daley on August 21 to allow a march from 1 p.m. to 4 p.m. in a part of Chicago miles away from the convention was rejected by the Mobilization. Hayden said that marchers coming to Chicago 'by the tens of thousands' preferred to be at the Amphitheatre. So the city got ready for a week of disorders its newspapers had advised it to avoid. One can only divine the expression on Daley's face when he read literature like the following – it comes from a throwaway in Lincoln Park, given out on Sunday afternoon August 25:

YIPPEE!

Lincoln Park

VOTE PIG IN 68

Free Motel
'come sleep with us'

REVOLUTION TOWARDS A FREE SOCIETY: YIPPIE!

By A. Yippie

1. An immediate end to the War in Vietnam . . .
2. Immediate freedom for Huey Newton of the Black Panthers and all other black people. Adoption of the community control concept in our ghetto areas . . .
3. Legalization of marihuana and all other psychedelic drugs . . .
4. A prison system based on the concept of rehabilitation rather than punishment.
5. . . . . abolition of all laws related to crimes without victims. That is, retention only of laws relating to crimes in which there is an unwilling injured party, i.e. murder, rape, assault.
6. The total disarmament of all the people beginning with the police. This includes not only guns, but such brutal devices as tear gas, MACE, electric

prods, blackjacks, billy clubs, and the like.

7. The Abolition of Money. The abolition of pay housing, pay media, pay transportation, pay food, pay education, pay clothing, pay medical help, and pay toilets.

8. A society which works toward and actively promotes the concept of 'full employment'. A society in which people are free from the drudgery of work. Adoption of the concept 'Let the Machines do it.'

9. . . . elimination of pollution from our air and water.

10. . . . incentives for the decentralization of our crowded cities . . . encourage rural living.

11. . . . free birth control information . . . abortions when desired.

12. A restructured educational system which provides the student power to determine his course of study and allows for student participation in over-all planning . . .

13. Open and free use of media . . . cable television as a method of increasing the selection of channels available to the viewer.

14. An end to all censorship. We are sick of a society which has no hesitation about showing people committing violence and refuses to show a couple fucking.

15. We believe that people should fuck all the time, anytime, whomever they wish. This is not a program to demand but a simple recognition of the reality around us.

16. . . . a national referendum system conducted via television or a telephone voting system . . . a decentralization of power and authority with many varied tribal groups. Groups in which people exist in a state of basic trust and are free to choose their tribe.

17. A program that encourages and promotes the arts. However, we feel that if the Free Society we envision were to be fought for and achieved, all of us would actualize the creativity within us. In a very real sense we would have a society in which every man would be an artist.

. . . Political Pigs, your days are numbered. We are the Second American Revolution. We shall win. Yippie!

But let us go to Lincoln Park on this Sunday afternoon.

A moment:

The following is a remark by Dino Valente, an electric guitarist. It ran as the headline in an advertisement in the *East Village Other* for an album of his records.

> You shall take this electrical power out of the wall and you send
> it through the guitar and you bend it and shape it and make it
> into something like songs for people and that power is a
> wonderful thing.

Yes, the Yippies were the militant wing of the Hippies, Youth International Party, and the movement was built on juice, not alcoholic juice
which comes out of the mystery of fermentation – why, dear God, as fruits
and grains begin to rot, does some distillate of this art of the earth now in
decomposition have the power to inflame consciousness and give us purchase
on visions of Heaven and hell? – no, rather, we are speaking of the juice
which comes from another mystery, the passage of a metallic wire across a
field of magnetism. That serves to birth the beast of all modern technology,
electricity itself. The Hippies founded their temple in that junction where
LSD crosses the throb of an electric guitar at full volume in the ear, solar
plexus, belly, and loins. A tribal unity had passed through the youth of
America (and half the nations of the world) a far-out vision of orgiastic revels
stripped of violence or even the differentiation of sex. In the oceanic stew of a
non-violent, tribal ball on drugs, nipples, arms, phalluses, mouths, wombs,
armpits, short-hairs, navels, breasts and cheeks, incense of odor, flower and
funk were humping into Breakthrough Freak-out Road together, and children on acid saw Valhalla, Nepenthe, and the Taj Mahal. Some went out
forever, some went screaming down the alleys of the mad where cockroaches
drive like Volkswagen on the oilcloth of the moon, gluttons found vertigo in
centrifuges of consciousness, vomitoriums of ingestion; others found love,
some manifest of love in light, in shards of Nirvana, sparks of satori – they
came back to the world a twentieth-century tribe wearing celebration bells
and filthy garments. Used-up livers gave their complexion a sickly pale, and
hair grew on their faces like weeds. Yet they had seen some incontestable
vision of the good – the universe was not absurd to them; like pilgrims they
looked at society with the eyes of children: society was absurd. Every
emperor who went down the path was naked, and they handed flowers to
policemen.

It could hardly last. The slum in which they chose to live – for they were
refugees in the main from the suburbs of the middle class – fretted against
them, fretted against their filth, their easy casual cohabiting, their selflessness
(which is always the greatest insult to the ghetto, for selflessness is a luxury to
the poor, it beckons to the spineless, the undifferentiated, the inept, the
derelict, the drowning – a poor man is nothing without the fierce thorns of

his ego). So the Hippies collided with the slums, and were beaten and robbed, fleeced and lashed and buried and imprisoned, and here and there murdered, and here and there successful, for there was scattered liaison with bikers and Panthers and Puerto Ricans on the East Coast and Mexicans on the West. There came a point when, like most tribes, they divided. Some of the weakest and some of the least attached went back to the suburbs or moved up into commerce or communications; others sought gentler homes where the sun was kind and the flowers plentiful; others hardened, and like all pilgrims with their own vision of a promised land, began to learn how to work for it and finally, how to fight for it. So the Yippies came out of the Hippies, ex-Hippies, diggers, bikers, drop-outs from college, hipsters up from the South. They made a community of sorts, for their principles were simple – everybody, obviously, must be allowed to do (no way around the next three words) his own thing, provided he hurt no one doing it – they were yet to learn that society is built on many people hurting many people, it is just who does the hurting which is forever in dispute. They did nt necessarily under-stand how much their simple presence hurt many good citizens in the secret velvet of the heart – the Hippies and probably the Yippies did not quite recognize the depth of that schizophrenia on which society is built. We call it hypocrisy, but it is schizophrenia, a modest ranch-house life with Draconian military adventures; a land of equal opportunity where a white culture sits upon a Black; a horizontal community of Christian love and a vertical hierarchy of churches – the cross was well designed! a land of family a land of illicit heat; a politics of principle, a politics of property; nation of mental hygiene with movies and TV reminiscent of a mental pigpen; patriots with a detestation of obscenity who pollute their rivers; citizens with a detestation of government control who cannot bear any situation not controlled. The list must be endless, the comic profits are finally small – the society was able to stagger on like a 400-lb policeman walking uphill because living in such unappreciated and obese state it did not at least have to explode in schizo-phrenia – life went on. Boys could go patiently to church at home and wait their turn to burn villages in Vietnam. What the Yippies did not recognize is that their demand for all-accelerated entrance into twentieth-century Utopia (where modern mass man would have all opportunities before him at once and could thus create and despoil with equal conscience – up against the wall mother-fucker, let me kiss your feet) whether a vision to be desired or abhorred, was nonetheless equal to straight madness for the Average Good American, since his liberated expression might not be an outpouring of love, but the burning of his neighbor's barn. Or, since we are in Chicago, smashing

333

good neighbor's skull with a brick from his own back yard. Yippies, even McCarthyites, represented nothing less by their presence than the destruction of every saving hypocrisy with consequent collision for oneself – it is not so easy to live every day of your life holding up the wall of your own sanity. Small wonder the neighbourhood whites of Chicago, like many small-town whites in other places, loved Georgie Wallace – he came in like cavalry, a restorer of every last breech in the fort.

Somber thoughts for a stroll through Lincoln Park on a Sunday afternoon in summer, but the traffic of the tourists and the curious was great; one had to leave the car six blocks away. Curiosity was contained, however, in the family automobile: the burghers did not come to the park. Young tourists and cruisers were there in number, tough kids, Polish and Irish (not all plainclothesmen) circulating around the edges of the crowd, and in the center of the southern part of Lincoln Park where the Yippies had chosen to assemble on an innocuous greensward undistinguished from similar meadows in many another park, a folk-rock group was playing. It was an orderly crowd. Somewhere between one and two thousand kids and young adults sat on the grass and listened, and another thousand or two thousand, just arrived, or too restless to sit, milled through an outer ring, or worked forward to get a better look. There was no stage – the entrance of a flatbed truck from which the entertainers could have played had not been permitted, so the musicians were half-hidden, the public address system – could it work off batteries? – was not particularly clear. For one of the next acts it hardly mattered – a young white singer with a cherubic face, perhaps eighteen, maybe twenty-eight, his hair in one huge puff ball teased out six to nine inches from his head, was taking off on an interplanetary, then galactic, flight of song, halfway between the space music of Sun Ra and 'The Flight of the Bumblebee', the singer's head shaking at the climb like the blur of a buzzing fly, his sound an electric caterwauling of power come out of the wall (or the line in the grass, or the wet plates in the batteries) and the singer not bending it, but whirling it, burning it, flashing it down some arc of consciousness, the sound screaming up to a climax of vibrations like one rocket blasting out of itself, the force of the noise a vertigo in the cauldrons of inner space – it was the roar of the beast in all nihilism, electric bass and drum driving behind out of their own non-stop to the end of mind. And the reporter, caught in the din – had the horns of the Huns ever had noise to compare? – knew this was some variety of true song for the Hippies and adolescents in the house, in this enclave of grass and open air (luxury apartments of Lake Shore Drive not five football fields away) crescendos of sound as harsh on his ear, ear of a generation which had danced to 'Star Dust', as to drive him completely out of the sound, these painted dirty under-twenties were monsters, and yet, still clinging to recognition in the experience, he knew they were a generation which lived in the sound of destruction of all order as he had known it, and worlds of other decomposition as well; there was the sound of mountains crashing in this holocaust of the decibels, hearts bursting, literally bursting, as if this were the sound of death by explosion within, the drums of physiological climax when the mind was blown, and forces of the future, powerful, characterless, as insane and scalding as waves of lava, came flushing through the urn of all acquired culture and sent the brain like a foundered carcass smashing down a rapids, revolving through a whirl of demons, pool of uproar, discords vibrating, electric crescendo screaming as if at the electro-mechanical climax of the age, and these children like filthy Christians sitting quietly in the grass, applauding politely, whistles and cries of mild approval when the song was done, and the reporter as affected by the sound (as affected by the recognition of what nihilisms were calmly encountered in such musical storm) as if he had heard it in a room at midnight with painted bodies and kaleidoscopic sights, had a certainty which went through gangs and groups and rabble, tourists and consecrated saints, vestal virgins with finger bells, through the sight of Negroes calmly digging Honkie soul, sullen Negroes showing not impressed, but digging, cool on their fringe (reports to the South Side might later be made) through even the hint of menace in the bikers, some beaks alien to this music, come to scoff, now watching, half turned on by noise so near to the transcendencies of some of their own noise when the whine of the gears cohabited with the pot to hang them out there on the highway singing with steel and gasoline, yeah, steel and gasoline exactly equal to flesh plus hate, and blood plus hate; equations were pure while riding the balance of a machine, yes, even the tourists and the college boys who would not necessarily be back contributed nonetheless to the certainty of his mood. There was a mock charade going on, a continuation of that celebration of the Yippie Convention yet to come, when Pigasus, a literal pig, would be put in nomination. Vote Pig in 68, said the Yippie placards, and now up at the stage, music done, they announced another candidate to a ripple of mild gone laughter across the grass, Humphrey Dumpty was the name, and a Yippie clown marched through the crowd, a painted egg with legs, 'the next President of the United States', and in suite came a march of the delegates through an impromptu aisle from the stage to the rear of the crowd. A clown dressed like a Colorado miner in a fun house came first; followed Miss America with hideous lipsticked plastic tits, stars of rouge on

335

her cheeks; Mayor Daley's political machine – a clown with a big box horizontal to his torso, big infant's spoon at the trough on top of the box, and a green light which went on and off was next; then the featured delegate, the Green Beret, a clown with a toy machine gun, soot and red grease on his face, an Australian bush hat on his head. Some sort of wax vomit pop-art work crowned the crown. Yes, the certainty was doubled. Just as he had known for one instant at the Republican Gala in Miami Beach that Nelson Rockefeller had no chance of getting the nomination, so he knew now on this cool gray Sunday afternoon in August, chill in the air like the chill of the pale and the bird of fear beginning to nest in the throat, that trouble was coming, serious trouble. The air of Lincoln Park came into the nose with that tender concern which air seemed always ready to offer when danger announced its presence. The reporter took an unhappy look around. Were these odd unkempt children the sort of troops with whom one wished to enter battle?

Norman Mailer, *Miami and the Siege of Chicago* (1968)

1969: Helter Skelter

By the middle of January 1969, the new Beatles' white double album had already grossed twenty-two million dollars in the United States alone. The white double album was the first cultural instruction from the Beatles since the album *Magical Mystery Tour* a year previous. Even its all white cover was symbolic to the family – all white, dig it?

Something freaked Manson out in early 1961 enough for him to prepare for the end of Western civilization. He had already talked about an impending Armageddon of some sort but he had always preached 'submission is a gift, give it to your brother'. This is, walk humble beneath the violence.

Along oozed Helter Skelter.

Manson had a hypnotic rap about how the modern blacks were arming themselves, how he, Manson, had talked to blacks in prison and he had learned of heavy arms caches here and there.

He had a way of stirring up paranoia that was legendary. Goose bumps shivered the back of the arms during his whispered superstitious lectures on karma and imminent doom. With language as flawed as a president's announcing an invasion of a South Asian country, he announced that the blacks would rise up, kill a few million whites, take over the reins of government.

Then, the story continues, after forty or fifty years the blacks would turn the government over to Manson when they supposedly found themselves unfit to run the world. Oo-ee-oo.

It was the pig Christian wealthy Americans that were going to get cut. He, Christ, he, Devil, was going to pull off the Second Coming. 'Now it's the pigs' turn to go up on the cross,' he would say.

On a metaphysical plane, Manson linked the impending Helter Skelter with the concept of The Hole. For inside this mystic Hole in Death Valley, Manson and his family would live and dwell while the blacks and the whites in the cities would fight to a bloody end and then the blacks would take over.

From The City in The Hole, Manson would make forays to sack cities with his hairy locusts of the Abyss. And the blacks, through their 'super aware-ness' – in the words of the family – would know that Charlie was where it was at, and nod him into the power.

On a higher level, if *higher* is any word to be used, Manson taught that the family bringing the seven holes on the seven planes into alignment would be the ones to squirt through to the other side of the universe. And The Hole was to be the magic paradise – magic, because where else can you find subterranean chocolate fountains?

He even over-dubbed a weirdo exegesis atop the chapters and verses of the Book of Revelation, to back up his claims.

The dune buggies were the horses of Helter Skelter with those 'breastplates of fire', described in the Book of Revelation of St John the Divine, Chapter 9. And the Beatles, unknown to them, were the 'four angels' who would wreak death upon a third part of mankind. And Manson found a scriptural basis for announcing that the Beatles were destined to have a fifth member or 'angel' – the angel of the bottomless pit, otherwise known as guess who.

One of Manson's favorite passages from Revelation 9 was: 'Neither repented they of their murders, nor of their sorceries, nor of their fornication, nor of their thefts' – words he would quote over and over again, preparing his worshippers to kill. And did not the family have 'hair as the hair of women, and their teeth were as the teeth of lions'?

And was not Manson the king of the pit?

'And they had a king over them, which is the angel of the bottomless pit, whose name in the Hebrew tongue is Abaddon, but in the Greek tongue hath his name Apollyon.' When they translated the Bible from Latin to English, the translators left out another name in the text besides Abaddon and Apollyon, for the angel of the bottomless pit. The name in Latin is Exter-minans.

Exterminans – what a word to sum up Charles Manson.

The correlations that Manson found between the Book of Revelation and the Beatles and his own crazies could be continued in moonfire profusion but the reader will be spared.

Manson began to listen to the song 'Helter Skelter' off the new Beatles' album with earphones and somehow, as of a miracle, he began to hear the Beatles whispering to him urging him to call them in London. It is unfortunate that Manson evidently did not know that a helter skelter is a slide in an English amusement park.

The girls say that at one point Manson placed a long-distance phone call to London to try to talk to the Beatles. There is no doubt that the song 'Helter Skelter' on the white Beatles double album is a masterful, insistent, rock and roll number – and it is very weird-sounding, especially the long final section which fades out twice at the end, sounding like a universal march of wrecked maniacs.

'Charlie, Charlie, send us a telegram' was what he thought lay beneath the noise plexus of the composition 'Revolution 9'. It was felt that if one were to listen closely on headphones, one could hear the Beatles softly whispering just that. As it is, so be it.

'Rise! Rise! Rise!' Charlie would scream during the playing of 'Revolution 9' (which Manson associated with Revelation, Chapter 9). Later they wrote *Rise* in blood on the LaBiancas' wall.

It is necessary to listen to the Beatles white double album to understand what Manson was hearing and seeking to hear. The album, as a whole, is of confusing quality. It has flashes of the usual Beatle brilliance but it was produced at a time that the Beatles were locked in bitter quarrels and it is reflected in the album.

The album has the song 'Piggies', of course, and, more creepily, a song called 'Happiness Is a Warm Gun'. Other songs like 'Blackbird', 'Rocky Racoon', etc., were interpreted strictly as racist doom-songs.

The song 'Sexie Sadie' must have sent Susan Atkins, aka Sadie Mae Glutz, into spasms of happiness. 'Sexy Sadie, you came along to turn everybody on,' the song croons, and 'Sexy Sadie, you broke the rules, you laid it down for all to see.'

Ed Sanders, *The Family* (1971)

1969: Mozic and the Revolution

When Joshua fit the Battle of Jericho the walls came tumbling down. That's revelation. The holy Ghost talking. So it can be done. The way to crack a mirror or shiver a wineglass is to find the right frequency and pound it. Like those strobe lights that picked up the B-rhythms of some kids dancing around in Ealing or somewhere, and threw them into epileptic fits. T.C. knows a cat in Australia who used to make strange music sitting between two huge columns and singing into them and feeding and feeding it back and back. Finally, he burst a blood vessel in his head and now he's crazy. If you sit a man with a bucket on his head and let a water-tap drip onto it, he'll be crazy within hours. The Japanese taught some Australians that. Music hath charms to tame the savage beast, as Shakespeare noticed. Music hath alarums to wild the civil breast, as well, as Tuli Kupferberg pointed out. It is partly a matter of the mode of the music, but then as well something to do with the ears the music exists in. He that has ears to hear, let him hear. The bell tolling in the desert makes no sound.

What then is the mode of revolutionary music in October 1969? And who's it for? Mick Farren is right to agonise over the superficiality of the rock revolution. The underground is falsely complacent, living on an exaggerated notion of its own importance and effectiveness, which Mick Farren tirelessly deflates and derides. He looks back with furious nostalgia at the time when ugly, desperate, grinding songs were million sellers. When shop-girls, mechanics, storemen, packers, gasfitters, wharf labourers and their girls, found dignity, lust and anger in the music of rock. It is painful to hear the skinheads saying as they look over the crowds, past the enclosure where the beautiful people bask in a cloud of Mick Jagger's spittle, 'Well, the Stones are one of us, arnay?' Expensive drugs, more expensive butterflies, dead mates, Baby Jane Holzer's dildo, no, baby, the Stones are not one of you. By Marianne Faithfull's sacred Mars bar they are not one of you. They are being protected from you by the underground's favourite scapegoats, the poor old phoney Hell's Angels. In the official souvenir of that concert there is a photograph of the groupies' enclosures backstage, which features, in filthy yellow plush trousers, Ibiza vest, chain, and dilly-bag, the underground impresario himself. The expression on his face sums up the whole blind alley of revolutionary music. 'Why isn't it working' those hot eyes are saying. 'What the fuck happened?'

Why did Mick Jagger not tell those quarter of a million people to take over the city? Why did they behave so well and pick up all their garbage? They

339

were celebrating their togetherness, boasted the underground. They showed the parent-generation how they were gentle and loving and co-operative. Mick Farren knew that that was not how it was. The phenomenon had been contained. No one need be afraid of the Rolling Stones any more. They couldn't change a thing. They didn't want to change a thing. They arrived at the head of the pop wave expressing the vague discontent of their generation. They were rewarded with money and initiated into the fancy vices of the upper class, drugs, buggery, cruelty and vicarious violence. Home video of the Aberfan disaster with 'Yes sir, that's my baby' for a backing. Loving, gentle, co-operative, my arse. Still it was genuine. The greasers, the rockers, the mods, the skinheads, the hippies, the yippies, all of your genuine working-class youth would have been corrupted in the same way. Only the bourgeois revolutionary can spurn the insidious rewards this society offers to successful subversion. Only the middle-class rebel yearns for the proletariat.

> Someone told me times are
> changing
> But looking all around it seems the
> same
> Buying selling running hiding
> Wondering if the world has any
> shame
> Looking from my window
> Blank faces queue for something
> new to come
> But nothing ever changes
> And their dreams all wither in the
> sun.

[The Deviants. Transatlantic.]

The rock revolution failed because it was corrupted. It was incorporated in the capitalist system which has power to absorb and exploit all tendencies including the tendencies towards its own overthrow. The Rolling Stones have been absorbed, and their music has been corrupted too. 'Honky-Tonk Woman' like 'Salt of the Earth' is merely a new perversion, a kind of self-conscious slumming. It stinks. And yet, even if Frank Zappa has had to throw Mick and Marianne out of his house in Laurel Canyon, Mick Jagger is still a better man than he, because the deficiencies in his revolutionary theory do not matter, because the corruption and faggotisation of his own character are irrelevant. What is only important, is that the Rolling Stones found the frequency, they sounded the chime, they dripped the tap on to the bucket, they cracked the mirror and busted the glass. 'Satisfaction' can never be unwritten. It has been heard, for there were ears to hear.

Frank Zappa is more intelligent and a better musician than any of the Stones, and that is probably why he would never risk immolation as a pop hero. For Mick Jagger is a victim, after all, and it makes little difference whether he is aware of the fact. Though, when he chooses to dance in a studded dog collar and his white clown suit, perhaps we may assume that he has an inkling. Zappa may enjoy his artistic and other sorts of integrity, but he will never make a contribution to the revolution of sensibility which is the pre-requisite of political revolution. The converted seek out Zappa and learn more about their attitudes from him, but the Stones helped thousands of kids to bust out. What pains Mick Farren, and it pains him terribly all of the time, is that the bust out was so trivial in its immediate effects. So his music dashes itself against the horns of a polylemma – every proposition has its *but*. Music must reach an audience, *but* it will then become commercial. Music must please those who hear it, *but* it must not make the unbearable bearable. Music must be violent and exciting *but* it must not provide harmless expression for violence and frustration. In such a conflict Mick Farren's Deviants could only use music as a weapon. Tune, harmony, rhythm were a bunch of Uncle Tomisms. The Deviants were offensive. Mick screamed. Russ battered. When the equipment collapsed, or silence ensued for any reasons, Mick bawled at his audience, pleading with them to tear the hall down, to fuck, or shit. Telling them the home truths about the management, libelling, protesting, complaining, cursing. But the audience remained an audience. They listened. They stood still, patient under barrages of feedback and Mick's incomprehensible yelling. They wanted to have a good time and there was this wheezing Jeremiah begging them to hate something. They were too good mannered even to hate him. Mick ended up hating nearly all his audiences. He meant to yell at their parents, but he ended up yelling at them,

We are the people who pervert your
children
Who lead them astray from the
lessons you taught them,
We are endangering civilisation,
We are beyond rehabilitation.
[The Deviants. Transatlantic.]

But they aren't endangering civilisation. It's all fantasy. The Stones could claim this, they still could, but they never would. Mick Farren is convinced, passionate, sincere and unsparing of himself in his service of the revolution, and that's just what's wrong with him. Electronic music was a glimpse into the possibility of liberation, not expounded but demonstrated on the nerves; kids began to dance, to leap, and their want was born. Mick Farren understood the phenomenon politically, intelligently. He is still the best critic the English Underground has, and like Jeremiah he ought to be heeded. But he cannot sing. He cannot sing because, although he has a freaky throat, he cannot *hear*. And he never did hear what rock music really was, in terms of guts and glory. He is an impresario, but he does not understand exactly what it is that he's peddling, any more than any Denmark Street wheel-and-dealer. The most significant part of the rock revolution, because it did happen, was that kids got into their bodies. Music is a curious medium. Utterly abstract in its construction, but completely sensuous in its apperception. Tunes, rhythms can only be conveyed by exact mimicry. They are not ideas. Mick Farren writes lovely prose, he has good, tough, sharp, ideas, but he is not and never will be into his body. He is a victim of one of the meanest tricks that our sick civilisation plays upon the body–soul hook-up, chronic asthma. As a result of it, he is addicted to a particularly brutal form of stimulant. This tyrannical dance with death has too much to do with the kind of music he makes; and with the deadly if microscopic efficiency of the Pink Fairies' operations in fucking up other people's music. King Crimson are still apologising for the gig they did at the Speakeasy, which is the only regime the Pink Fairies will ever upheave because they were put off and harassed by a more than usually drunken and drugged Twink, Steve Tooke and Mick Farren.

But something has happened. The Deviants are no longer Mick Farren's Deviants. Under all the bullshit flummery of the Pink Fairies something was really happening. A leather giant with a deformed arm, and a natural Charles II mane, leans into the mike and says with a maniacal smile, 'Let's have some fun' before he drives off on deranged lead guitar. That's it. That's the pulse. He has it. The bass player can find it from him and Russ boxes out the frenzy on drums. The words are inaudible. The band practises these days. They dig it. They are into it. Soon their audiences will fuck without being told. The Deviants have discovered music. They used to be frail and pious. Mick's yelling was still preaching after all. Now Paul Rudolf's 'Let's have some fun' could set up a sympathetic vibration in the foundations of the Home Office. Mick has responded to the pressure, which looks these days like bouncing him clean off the stage, with a change in the group's public image. He is no longer *il Duce*. Russ and Sandy and Paul talk to the papers too. Mick has swapped 'The Pink Fairies are organising a musical attack on authority, like the MC5 in Chicago [sic] a strategic, organised and effective attack on the straights' type bullshit for the 'If Nat Joseph thinks you're sincere he just lets you get on with it your way' type bullshit.

Factory has yet to publish its deal on the Pink Fairies, with its special record and all that. If it does it really ought to change its name to Fantasy. The basic weapon of the Pink Fairy conspiracy is conservative. The machine gun that will rip open a policeman's chest and furnish Mick Farren with a satisfactory orgasm at last is the weapon of the straights: to kill a man is simply murder; it is revolution to turn him on.

It is not the groups who call themselves Underground who will provide the music that will shake the walls of the city. It is not the polemicists who choose a microphone and electronic backing to continue an argument who will enlighten the straights who continue to be born. It is not the best musicians, and it is not the worst. But it will be done with music.

Beware a man who is not moved by
sound.
He'll drag you to the ground
Come dance with me, come dance
with me in [Wilson's] land
Come dance with me, we'll beat
that hoary band.
[Tulig Kupferberg]

Germaine Greer, *Oz*, November 1969

1969: 'I Don't Want to Be a Clown Any More . . .'

LIBERTY, NEW YORK – Records, film, press and gossip are collectively ambitious in creating the image of a rock superstar. With Jimi Hendrix – as with Janis Joplin, Mick Jagger and Jim Morrison – mythology is particularly lavish.

Unfortunately, it is also often irreversible – even when it's ill-founded or after the performer himself has gone through changes.

Several weeks ago, *Life* magazine described Jimi as 'a sick demigod' and devoted several color pages to kaleidoscopic projections of his face. Well, why not? The fisheye lens shot on his first album cover shows him in arrogant distortion; on the second album, he becomes Buddha. Lest anyone forget, Leacock-Pennebaker's *Monterey Pop* has immortalized his pyromaniacal affair with the guitar. Rock media bedroom talk makes him King Stud of the groupies. Stories circulate that he is rude to audiences, stands up writers, hangs up photographers, that he doesn't talk.

What Jimi's really all about – and where his music is going – is an altogether different thing.

For most of the summer and early fall, Jimi rented a big Georgian-style house in Liberty, New York – one of Woodstock's verdant 'suburbs' – for the purpose of housing an eclectic family of musicians: Black Memphis blues guitarists; 'new music' and jazz avantgardists; 'Experience' member Mitch Mitchell; and – closest to Jimi and most influential – Juma Lewis, a multi-talented, ex-progressive jazzman who is now leader of the Woodstock's Aboriginal Music Society.

The hilltop compound – replete with wooded acreage and two horses – was intended for a peaceful, productive musical growth period. But hassles did come, sometimes sending Jimi off on sanity-preserving vacations in Algeria and Morocco; local police were anxious to nab 'big-time hippies' on anything from dope to speeding; the house was often hectic with hangers-on; pressure mounted from Jimi's commercial reps to stay within the well-hyped image and not go too far afield experimentally.

But with it all, growth, exchange and – finally – unity was achieved among Jimi and the musicians, whose work-in-progress was evidenced in occasional public appearances in the New York area (at the Woodstock/Bethel Festival, Harlem's Apollo Theater, Greenwich Village's Salvation discotheque, and ABC's Dick Cavett show) and has been recorded for Reprise on an LP which will be released in January.

With close friends of Jimi, I drove up to Liberty on a quiet September weekend. The melange of musicians and girls had departed. In a few weeks, Jimi himself was to give up the house, woods and horses for less idyllic prospects: a Manhattan loft and a November hearing on the narcotics possession charge he was slapped with in Toronto, May 3rd.

Photographs have a funny way of betraying his essentially fragile face and body. He is lean. Almost slight. Eating chocolate chip cookies on the living room couch in his big house – furnished straight and comfortable – he seems boyish and vulnerable.

He offers questions with an unjustified fear of his own articulateness that is charming – but occasionally painful, 'Do you, uh – where do you live in the city?' 'What kind of music do you li— would you care to listen to?' He is self-effacing almost to a fault: 'Do you ever go to the Fillimore? No? – that was a silly question, sorry.' 'I'm sorry, am I mumbling? Tell me when I'm mumbling. Damn . . . I always mumble.'

It becomes uncomfortable, so one says: 'Jimi, don't keep putting yourself down. There's everybody else to do that for you.' He attaches to that statement, repeats it slowly, whips out the embossed Moroccan notebook in which he jots lyrics at all hours of day and night, and scribbles something down.

Fingering through his record collection (extensive and catholic; e.g., Marlene Dietrich, David Peel and the Lower East Side, Schoenberg, Wes Montgomery), he pulls out *Blind Faith*; *Crosby, Stills and Nash*; and *John Wesley Harding*. The Dylan plays first. Jimi's face lights: 'I love Dylan. I only met him once, about three years ago, back at the Kettle of Fish [a folk-rock era hangout] on MacDougal Street. That was before I went to England. I think both of us were pretty drunk at the time, so he probably doesn't remember it.'

In the middle of a track, Jimi gets up, plugs in his guitar, and – with eyes closed and his supple body curved gently over the instrument – picks up on 'Frankie Lee and Judas Priest', riding the rest of the song home with a near-religious intensity.

He talks intently to Juma and his girl. He cherishes real friends and will do anything for them. They, in turn, feel protective toward him. 'Poor Jimi,' one says. 'Everyone's trying to hold him up for something. Those busts . . . Even the highway patrol exploits him. They know his car: they stop him on the road between New York and Woodstock and harass him. Then they have something to gloat about for the rest of the day. Once a cop stopped *me* on the highway and started bragging: "Hey, I just stopped Jimi Hendrix for the second time today." '

On the bookcase is a photograph of a Fifties Coasters-type R&B group: processed hair, metallic-threaded silk-lapel suits, shiny shoes. The thin kid on the far left in a high-conked pompadour, grinning over an electric guitar: is it? – 'That's okay,' Jimi smiles at the impending laughter. 'I don't try to cover up the past; I'm not ashamed of it.' But he is genuinely humble about the present. For example, he'd been wanting for some time to jam with jazz and 'new music' avantgardists, but worried that such musicians didn't take him seriously enough to ever consider playing with him. 'Tell me, honestly,' he asked a friend, 'what do those guys think of me? Do they think I'm jiving?'

We are listening now to the tape of such a session, the previous night's jam: Jimi on electric guitar, avantgarde pianist Michael Ephron on clavichord, Juma on congas and flute. A beautiful fusion of disparate elements, disjunct and unified at alternating seconds. Now chaotic, now coming together. 'Cosmic music' they call it. Ego-free music. Not the sort of stuff the waxlords make many bucks off. Not the kind of sound guaranteed to extend the popularity of a rock superstar.

345

'I don't want to be a clown any more. I don't want to be a "rock and roll star",' Jimi says, emphatically. The forces of contention are never addressed but their pervasiveness has taken its toll on Jimi's stamina and peace of mind. Trying to remain a growing artist when a business empire has nuzzled you to its bosom takes a toughness, a shrewdness. For those who have a hardness of conviction, but not of temperament it isn't a question of selling out but of dying, artistically and spiritually. Refusing to die yet ill-equipped to fight dirty, many sensitive but commercially-lionized artists withdrew. I watch Jimi quietly digging the pictures of faraway people and places in a book, *The Epic of Man* ('South America . . . wow, that's a whole different world. Have you ever been there?') and I wonder just where he will be and what he will be doing five years from now.

We crowd into Jimi's metal-fleck silver Stingray ('I want to paint it over – maybe black') for a sunrise drive to the waterfalls. ('I wish I could bring my guitar – and plug it in down there.') The talk is of puppies, daybreak, other innocentia. We climb down the rocks to the icy brook, then suddenly discover the car keys are missing. Everyone shuffles through shoulder pouches and wallets. 'Hey, don't worry,' Jimi says. 'They'll turn up. No use being hassled about it now.' Jimi's taking pictures and writing poetry. 'I want to write songs about tranquility, about beautiful things,' he says.

Back at the house, he pads around, emptying ashtrays, putting things in order. 'I'm like a clucking old grandmother,' he smiles. 'I've just gotta straighten things out a little.' It's 7 a.m. and he has to be at the recording studio in Manhattan at 4 in the afternoon. Everyone's exhausted.

After a few hours of sleep, Jimi floats into the kitchen looking like a fuzzy lamb unmercifully awakened and underfed. He passes up the spread of eggs, pork chops, crescent rolls and tea; breakfast, instead, is a Theragram and a swig of tequila in milk. 'Jimi, you never eat . . .' Juma's girl worries aloud.

We pile into the car for the two-hour drive into Manhattan. Passing two Afro-haired guys in an Aston-Martin, Jimi turns and flashes a broad grin, extending his fingers in a peace salute. We turn up the radio on Stevie Wonder's 'My Cherie Amour'; groove on Neil Diamond, Jackie DeShannon, the Turtles. Everything is everything: We're playing with a puppy, grateful for clear skies, clear road, clear AM station. What more could a carload of travelers in an inconspicuous blus Avis ask?

We pull into a roadside stop. No giggly bell-bottomed young girls in sight, Jimi gets out and brings back chocolate milk and ice cream for everyone. Truckers pay no attention. Middle-aged couples glare disdainfully.

The talk is of the session. They'll record at a studio on West 44th Street, then go somewhere else to mix it – maybe the Bell Sound of A&R – because Jimi says the recording studio they're going to 'has bad equipment . . . likes to take advantage of so-called longhair musicians.'

Downtown traffic on the West Side highway is light at rush hour. The fortresses of upper Riverside Drive are handsome in the sun, but the air has lost its freshness. Getting off the highway at 45th Street, it's 4:45. The session costing $200 an hour, was booked to begin at 4:00. But delay couldn't be helped; no hassle. A carful of teenagers alongside us has the radio turned up loud on 'If Six Was Nine' – the cut being used as part of an advertisement for *Easy Rider*.

I ask Jimi if he's seen the film; he doesn't answer.

Turning around, I find him stretched out on the back seat, legs curled up embryonically, hands clasped under his cheek. Sleeping soundly.

Sheila Weller, Rolling Stone, 15 November 1969

1969: Dance to the Death

The Stones were coming up the four steps between the trucks onto the stage, a brightly lit center in the black fold of hills. The crowd, estimated by the news media at between two and five hundred thousand, had been tightly packed when we struggled through them about five hours ago. Now they were one solid mass jammed against the stage. There were eager-eyed boys and girls down front, Angels all around, tour guards trying to maintain positions between the Angels and the Stones. A New York City detective at Altamont was a long way off his beat. The expressions on the cops' faces said they didn't like this scene at all, but they're not scared; just sorrowful-eyed like men who know trouble and know that they are in the midst of a lot of people who are asking for it. Against the stage, in the center of the crowd, a black cop with a mustache watched, his expression mournful, his white canvas golf-hat brim pulled down as if he were in a downpour.

Sam came to the singer's mike and in an infinitely weary voice said, 'One two testing,' then with a glimmer of enthusiasm, 'I'd like to introduce to everybody – from Britain – the Rolling Stones.'

There was a small cheer from the crowd – they seemed numb, not vibrant like the audiences in the basketball gyms after Tina Turner – whoops and yells and shrieks but not one great roar. Bass-thumps, guitars tuning, drum diddles, Mick: 'All right! Whooooh!' – rising note – 'Oww babe! Aw yeah!

347

Aww, so good to see ya *all*! Whooo!' Last tuning notes, then the opening chords of 'Jumpin' Jack Flash'.

> But it's all right, it's all right
> In fact it's a gas

Some people were dancing, Angels dancing with their dirty bouffant women. A pall of wariness and fear seemed to be upon the people who were not too stoned to be aware, but the music was pounding on and though the drums were not properly miked and the guitars seemed to separate and disappear in places and you couldn't really hear Wyman's bass, it was hanging together.

'Ooh, yah,' Mick said as the song ended. He stopped dancing, looked into the distance, and his voice, which had been subdued, now began to sound pacific, as he glimpsed for the first time the enormity of what he had created. One surge forward and people would be crushed. Half a million people together, with neither rules nor regulations as to how they must conduct themselves, can through sheer physical weight create terrible destruction. 'Oooh, babies –' low motherly tone '– there are so many of you – just be cool down front now, don't push around – just keep still.' He laughed as if he were talking to a child, looking down at the pretty stoned faces before him. 'Keep together – oh yah.'

Keith tested the first three notes of 'Carol', unleashed the riff, and Mick leaned back to sing

> Oh, Carol! Don't ever steal your heart away
> I'm gonna learn to dance if it takes me all night and day

The sound was better, drums and bass clearer, guitars stronger. At the end Mick said, 'Whoo! Whoo! Aw, yes!' He hoisted a bottle of Jack Daniel's that was sitting in front of the drums. 'I'd like to drink, ah, drink one to you all.'

Keith set out on 'Sympathy for the Devil'. As Mick sang, 'I was around when Jesus Christ had his moment of doubt and pain', there was a low explosive *thump!* in the crowd to the right of the stage, and oily blue-white smoke swirled up as if someone had thrown a toad into a witches' cauldron. People were pushing, falling, a great hole opening as they moved instantly away from the center of the trouble. I had no idea people in a crowd could move so fast. Mick stopped singing but the music chugged on, four bars, eight, then Mick shouted: 'Hey! Heeey! Hey! Keith – Keith – *Keith*!' By now only Keith was playing, but he was playing as loud and hard as ever, the way the band is supposed to do until the audience tears down the chicken wire and comes onstage with chairs and broken bottles. 'Will you cool it and I'll try and stop it,' Mick said, so Keith stopped.

'Hey – hey, peo-ple,' Mick said. 'Sisters – brothers and sisters – *brothers* and *sisters* – come *on* now.' He was offering the social contract to a twister of flailing dark shapes. 'That means everybody just cool *out* – will ya cool out, everybody –'

'Somebody's bike blew up, man,' Keith said.

'I know,' Mick said. 'I'm hip. Everybody be cool now, come on – all right? Can we still make it down in the front? Can we still collect ourselves, everybody? Can everybody just – I don't know what happened, I couldn't see, but I hope ya all right – are ya all right?' The trouble spot seemed still. Charlie was making eager drum flutters, Keith playing stray notes.

'Okay,' Mick said. 'Let's just give ourselves – we'll give ourselves another half a minute before we get our breath back, everyone just cool down and easy – is there anyone there who's hurt – huh? – everyone all right – okay – all right.' The music was starting again. 'Good, we can groove – summink very funny happens when we start that numbah – ah, ha!'

Keith and Charlie had the rhythm pattern going, tight and expert, and Mick asked again to be allowed to introduce himself, a man of wealth and taste, but not about to lay anybody's soul to waste. Keith's solo cut like a scream into the brain, as Mick chanted, 'Everybody got to cool out – everybody has got to cool right out – yeah! Aw right!'

Sounding like one instrument, a wild whirling bagpipe, the Stones chugged to a halt. But the crowd didn't stop, we could see Hell's Angels spinning like madmen, swinging at people. By stage right a tall white boy with a black cloud of electric hair was dancing, shaking, infuriating the Angels by having too good a time. He was beside an Angel when I first saw him, and I wondered how he could be so loose, nearly touching one of those monsters. He went on dancing and the Angel pushed him and another Angel started laying into the crowd with a pool cue and then a number of Angels were grabbing people, hitting and kicking, the crowd falling back from the fury with fantastic speed, the dancer running away from the stage, the crowd parting before him like the Red Sea, the Angels catching him from behind, the heavy end of a pool cue in one long arc crashing into the side of his head, felling him like a sapling so that he lay straight and didn't move and I thought, My God, they've killed him. But they weren't through. When he went down they were all over him, pounding with fists and cues, and when he was just lying there they stood for a while kicking him like kicking the dead carcass of an animal, the meat shaking on the bones.

The song was over and Mick was saying, 'Who – who – I mean like people, who's fighting and what for? Hey, peo-ple – I mean, who's fighting and what for? Why are we fighting? Why are we fighting?' His voice was strong, emphasizing each word. 'We don't want to fight. Come on – do we want, who wants to fight? Hey – I – you know, I mean like – every other scene has been cool. Like we've gotta stop right now. We've gotta stop them right now. You know, we can't, there's no point.'

Sam took the microphone. 'Could I suggest a compromise, please.' He was a bit more awake now and the soul of peace and reason. 'Can I ask please to speak to the –' He stopped then because the logical conclusion was '– to the Hell's Angels and ask them please to stop performing mayhem on people.'

'Either those cats cool it,' Keith said, 'or we don't play. I mean, there's not that many of 'em.'

It was a fine brave thing to say, but I had made up my mind about fighting the Hell's Angels while one of them had me in the air, and probably the rest of the people present had concluded some time ago that the first man who touched an Angel would surely die. Even as Keith spoke an Angel was ripping into someone in front of stage left.

'That guy there,' Keith said, 'if he doesn't stop it –'

There was a pause while another Angel did slowly stop him. Still another Angel yelled to ask Keith what he wanted. 'I just want him to stop pushin' people around,' Keith said.

An Angel came to the mike and bellowed into it. 'Hey, if you don't cool it you ain't gonna hear no more music! Now, you wanta all go home, or what?' It was like blaming the pigs in a slaughterhouse for bleeding on the floor.

Horowitz was leading some of the women in our group back to the trailer. Michael Lydon asked me, 'Can I use your notes later? My old lady's had a bad acid trip and she cut her foot and I need to get her out of here.' Later Michael wrote of the Angels, 'Their absolute solidarity mocks our fearful hope of community, their open appetite for violence our unfocused love of peace.' At the time I thought, Notes? He thinks I'm taking notes?

Stu, in his blue windbreaker, was at the mike, saying in a cool but unhappy voice, 'We need doctors down here *now*, please. Can we have a doctor down here now to the front?'

You felt that in the next seconds or minutes you could die, and there was nothing you could do to prevent it, to improve the odds for survival. A bad dream, but we were all in it.

I looked around, checking my position, which if not the worst was not good, and saw David Maysles on top of a truck behind the stage. Ethan

Russell and Al Maysles were up there with their cameras, and more people, including a couple of Hell's Angels sitting in front dangling their legs over the side like little boys fishing at a creek in the nineteenth century.

'Hey! David!' I said.

'You want to get up here?'

'Sure.' I stuck my notebook behind my belt and swung aboard, being careful not to jostle the Angels. At least now I would be behind them, instead of having it the other way round, which had given me worse chills than the wind did up here. It was cold away from the warm amps but this was, I hoped, a safer place and better to see from.

Hunkered behind the Angels, I noticed that only one wore colors, the other one in his cowboy hat and motor cycle boots was just a sympathizer. Sam was saying, 'The doctor is going through in a green jumper and he's just here –' pointing in front 'wavin' his hand in the air, look.' The mass, like a dumb aquatic beast, had closed up again except for a little space around the body. (The boy didn't die, to my – and probably his – surprise.) 'Can you let the doctor go through please and let him get to the person who's hurt?' Someone in front spoke to Sam, who added wearily, 'We have also – lost in the front here – a little girl who's five years old.'

Charlie was playing soft rolls, Keith was playing a slow blues riff. 'Let's play cool-out music,' Keith said to Mick.

They played a repeating twelve-bar pattern that stopped in half a minute. 'Keep going,' Mick said, and it started again, a meditative walking-bass line, the Stones trying to orient themselves by playing an Elmore James/Jimmy Reed song they had played in damp London caverns. 'The sun is shining on both sides of the street,' Mick sang. 'I got a smile on my face for every little girl I meet.' The slow blues did seem to help things a little. A huge Angel with long blond hair, brown suede vest, no shirt, blue jeans, was standing behind gentle Charlie, patting his foot, one giant hand resting on Charlie's white pullover. The song ended without event and Mick said, 'We all dressed up, we got no place to go,' which was all too true.

'Stray Cat,' Keith said, but there was another flurry of fighting stage right, partly hidden from us by the PA scaffold, a tower of speakers.

'Hey – heyheyhey look,' Mick said. Then to Keith or to no one he said, 'Those *scenes* down there.'

I leaned forward and spoke to the cowboy hat. 'What's happening, man?' I asked. 'Why are they fighting?'

Over his shoulder, out of the corner of his mouth, he said, 'Some smart asshole, man, some wise guy wants to start trouble – and these guys are tired,

351

man, they been here all night, some wise guy starts something they don't like it – arhh, I can't tell you what happened.' Taking a jug of acid-apple juice from his Angel friend, he drank till his eyes looked, as Wynonie Harris used to say, like two cherries in a glass of buttermilk. Me, I lay low.

'Stray Cat' started, Mick sounding perfunctory, forgetting the words here and there, Keith playing madly.

A girl down front was shaking with the music and crying as if her dream of life had ended. In the backstage aisle between the trucks, the Angels and their women were doing their stiff jerking dance. Most of the women were hard-looking tattooed types with shellacked hairdos, but one of them, no more than fourteen, with a dirty, pretty-baby face, wearing a black leather jacket, was moving the seat of her greasy jeans wildly, and I thought of the little guerrilla in Fort Collins and was glad she wasn't in this crowd.

The Angel standing with his hand on Charlie's shoulder was being asked to step down off the stage by one of the New York heavies, a red-faced, red-haired, beefy man dressed in the light golf-jacket uniform. You could follow what they were saying by their gestures. The cop told the Angel to step down, the Angel shook his head, the cop told him again and pushed him a little. The cop had a cigarette in his mouth and the Angel took it out, just plucked it from between the cop's lips like taking a rose from the mouth of the fair Carmen, causing the cop to regard the Angel with a sorrowful countenance. It was only when two more men in golf jackets turned around and faced the Angel with expressions equally dolorous that he went down the steps. He came back a minute later but stayed at the rear of the stage, dancing, twitching like a frog attached to electrodes.

As 'Stray Cat' ended, Mick said 'Ooh baby', looking up as if for deliverance and finding a shapeless human mass reaching into the darkness as far as he could see. 'Baby – all along a hillside – hey, everybody, ah – we gone do, we gone do, ah – what are we gonna do?'

'Love in Vain,' Keith said. The slow, elegant Robert Johnson line began, building slowly. 'I followed her to the station with my suitcase in my hand – oh, it's hard to tell, when all your love's in vain.' The Stones had not forgotten how to play, but nobody seemed to be enjoying the music, at least nobody who could be seen in the lights that made the stage the glowing center of a world of night. Too many people were still too close together and the Angels were still surly. At stage right an Angel with a skinful of acid was writhing and wringing his hands in a pantomime of twisting Mick's neck. At stage left Timothy Leary huddled with his wife and daughter, looking as if he'd taken better trips. The stage skirts were so crowded that Mick had only a limited area to work. He looked cramped, smaller than ever and cowed, frightened, but he kept on singing.

Things were quiet during 'Love in Vain' except for some heavy jostling down front, the prevailing mood of impending death, and the fear and anguish you could see in the faces. 'Aw yeah,' Mick said as the song ended. 'Hey, I think – I think, I think, that there was one good idea came out of that number, which was, that I really think the only way you're gonna keep yourselves cool is to *sit down*. If you can make it I think you'll find it's better. So when you're sitting comfortably – now, boys and girls –' withdrawing the social contract – 'Are you sitting comfortably? When, when we get to really like the end and we all want to go absolutely crazy and like jump on each other then we'll stand up again, d'you know what I mean – but we can't seem to keep it together, standing up – okay?'

In the background Keith was tooling up the opening chords of 'Under My Thumb'. A few people in front of the stage were sitting, going along with Mick, who for the first time in his life had asked an audience to sit down. The anarchist was telling people what to do. Then, just before he began to sing, he said, 'But it ain't a rule.'

'Under My Thumb' started – 'Hey! Hey! Under my thumb is a girl who once had me down –' and Mick had sung only the first line of the song when there was a sudden movement in the crowd at stage left. I looked away from Mick and saw, with the now-familiar instant space around him, bordered with falling bodies, a Beale Street nigger in a black hat, black shirt, iridescent blue-green suit, arms and legs stuck out at crazy angles, a nickel-plated revolver in his hand. The gun waved in the lights for a second, two, then he was hit, so hard, by so many Angels, that I didn't see the first one – short, Mexican-looking, the one who led me onstage? – as he jumped. I saw him as he came down, burying a long knife in the black man's back. Angels covered the black man like flies on a stinking carcass. The attack carried the victim behind the stack of speakers, and I never saw him again.

The black man, Meredith Hunter, nicknamed Murdock, was eighteen years old. He had come to Altamont with his girlfriend, Patty Bredehoft, a blond Berkeley High School student, and another couple. They had arrived in Hunter's car at about two o'clock in the afternoon, parked on the highway and walked over to hear the bands. Near the end of the day Patty Bredehoft and the other couple were back at the car when Hunter, who had been hanging around the stage area, came to get her to go hear the Rolling Stones. Later she told the Alameda County Grand Jury, 'When we finally worked our way up to the front of the crowd and the Rolling Stones started playing, there was a lot of pushing and there were Angels on the stage. And Murdock kept trying to go farther up toward the front. I couldn't keep up with him because I wasn't strong so I sort of waited back, didn't try to get as far as he did. He was as close as he could get, where there was about five people in between me and him, estimating, because the crowd was moving around, but I could see the upper part of his body.

'I was getting pushed around, and as I glanced up there, I saw either he had hit Murdock or pushed him or something, but this Hell's Angel who was standing, pushed him or knocked him back. It didn't knock him down, but knocked him back over the stage, and as he started to come back forward towards the Hell's Angel, another Hell's Angel who was on the stage grabbed him around the neck. They were scuffling around. I'm not sure which Hell's Angel it was, but I just remember he was scuffling around and there was a couple of people blocking my view of him because he was down on the ground. I couldn't really see him. As the people backed away, Murdock came around by my side and pulled a gun out. Then they came toward – well, a group of Hell's Angels – I'm not sure they were all Hell's Angels, but I know most of them were – they came toward him and they reached for his arm and then they were all kicking and fighting and stuff, Murdock and the Hell's Angels, and the fight more or less moved around towards where the scaffold was on the edge of the stage.

'I followed them around and then I was standing there watching them fight, or watching whatever – I couldn't really tell what was going on underneath the scaffold, and the Hell's Angel – I thought he was, was a Hell's Angel, but I wasn't quite sure because he had the jeans jacket on, but I couldn't see the back to see if it had colors on. He was holding the gun in his hand, laying in the palm of his hand, to show it to me, and he said something like, "This is what we took from him. He was going to kill innocent people, so he deserved to be dead." '

A young man named Paul Cox, who had been standing beside Meredith Hunter before the violence started, talked to the grand jury and to *Rolling Stone*. 'An Angel kept looking over at me and I tried to keep ignoring him and I didn't want to look at him at all, because I was very scared of them and seeing what they were doing all day and because he kept trying to cause a fight or something and kept staring at us. He kept on looking over, and the next thing I know he's hassling this Negro boy on the side of me. And I was trying not to look at him, and then he reached over and shook this boy by the side of the head, thinking it was fun, laughing, and I noticed something was going to happen so I kind of backed off.

354

'The boy yanked away, and when he yanked away, next thing I know he was flying in the air, right on the ground, just like all the other people it happened to. He scrambled to his feet, and he's backing up and he's trying to run from the Angels, and all these Angels are – a couple jumped off the stage and a couple was running alongside the stage, and his girlfriend was screaming to him not to shoot, because he pulled out his gun. And when he pulled it out, he held it in the air and his girlfriend is like climbing on him and pushing him back and he's trying to get away and these Angels are coming at him and he turns around and starts running. And then some Angel snuck up from right out of the crowd and leaped up and brought this knife down in his back. And then I saw him stab him again, and while he's stabbing him, he's running. This Negro boy is running into the crowd, and you could see him stiffen up when he's being stabbed.

'He came running toward me. I grabbed onto the scaffold, and he came running kind of toward me and fell down on his knees, and the Hell's Angel grabbed onto both his shoulders and started kicking him in the face about five times or so and then he fell down on his face. He let go and he fell down on his face. And then one of them kicked him on the side and he rolled over, and he muttered some words. He said, "I wasn't going to shoot you." That was the last words he muttered.

'If some other people would have jumped in I would have jumped in. But nobody jumped in and after he said, "I wasn't going to shoot you," one of the Hell's Angel said, "Why did you have a gun?" He didn't give him time to say anything. He grabbed one of those garbage cans, the cardboard ones with the metal rimming, and smashed him over the head with it, and then he kicked the garbage can out of the way and started kicking his head in. Five of them started kicking his head in. Kicked him all over the place. And then the guy that started the whole thing stood on his head for a minute or so and then walked off. And then the one I was talking about, he wouldn't let us touch him for about two or three minutes. Like, "Don't touch him, he's going to die anyway, let him die, he's going to die."

'Chicks were just screaming. It was all confusion. I jumped down anyway to grab him and some other dude jumped down and grabbed him, and then the Hell's Angel just stood over him for a little bit and then walked away. We turned him over and ripped off his shirt. We rubbed his back up and down to get the blood off so we could see, and there was a big hole in his spine and a big hole on the side and there was a big hole in his temple. A big open slice. You could see all the way in. You could see inside. You could see at least an inch down. And then there was a big hole right where there's no ribs on his

355

back – and then the side of his head was just sliced open – you couldn't see so far in – it was bleeding quite heavily – but his back wasn't bleeding too heavy after that – there – all of us were drenched in blood.

'I picked up his legs and someone else . . . this guy said he was a doctor or something . . . I don't know who he was . . . he picked up his arms and he said, "Got to get him some help because he's going to die. We've got fifteen or twenty minutes, if we can get him some help . . ." And so we tried to carry him on the stage. Tell Mick Jagger to stop playing so we could get him on the stage and get some attention for him. No one told Jagger that, but someone was trying to tell him to stop and he kept leaning over and looking out at the crowd like he was paying attention and trying to figure out what was happening. He kept leaning over with his ear trying to hear what somebody was telling him, but he couldn't hear. So they kept on playing and the Hell's Angel wouldn't let us through . . . get on the stage. They kept blocking us, saying go round, go through some other way. They knew he was going to die in a matter of minutes. They wanted him to die probably so he couldn't talk. And so we carried . . . we turned around and went the other way. It took about fifteen minutes to get him behind the stage. We went around that whole thing and got behind where there was a Red Cross truck, something like that. And someone brought out a metal stretcher and laid him on that. Well, first we laid him on the ground. And then we felt his pulse and it was just barely doing it . . . real slow and real weak. His whole mouth and stuff is bashed up into his nose and stuff and he couldn't breathe out of his nose. He was trying to breathe out of his mouth. There really wasn't anything you could do. We carried him over to some station wagon and then whoever owned the car hopped in and some other people hopped in and I stayed there. I went over and they had this thing of coffee and I had it . . . poured it all over to wipe off all the blood.'

The doctor who helped to carry Hunter backstage was Robert Hiatt, a medical resident at the Public Health Hospital in San Francisco. 'He was limp in my hands and unconscious,' Hiatt said. 'He was still breathing then, though quite shallowly, and he had a very weak pulse. It was obvious he wasn't going to make it, but if anything could be done, he would have to get to hospital quickly. He had very serious wounds.'

Dr Richard Baldwin, a general practitioner from Point Reyes who saw Hunter backstage, said, 'He got a bad injury in that they got him in the back and it went in between the ribs and the side of the spine, and there's nothing but big arteries in there, the aorta, the main artery in the body, and a couple kidney arteries. And if you hit one of those you're dead. You're dead in less than a minute and there's nothing anyone can do. In other words, if you're standing in front of the hospital or even if he was stabbed in an operating room, there's nothing they could have done to save him. That's one of those injuries that's just irreparable.'

When the trouble with the boy in the green suit started, the Stones had stopped playing. 'Okay, man,' Keith said, 'look, we're splitting, if those cats, if you can't – we're splitting, if those people don't stop beating everybody up in sight – I want 'em *out of the way.*'

An Angel in front of the stage was trying to tell Keith something, but Keith wouldn't listen. 'I don't like *you* to tell me –' he went on, but another Angel, onstage, stopped him. 'Look, man,' the Angel said, 'a guy's got a gun out there, and he's shootin' at the stage –'

'Got a gun,' someone else yelled.

Mike Lang, one of the organizers of Woodstock, who had been helping with this concert, took the microphone. 'People – hey people – c'mon let's be cool – people, please – there's no reason to hassle anybody, please don't be mad at anybody – please relax and sit down . . .'

Sam, who'd been standing by with his hands jammed in his pockets, took over. 'If you move back and sit down,' he said, 'we can continue and we will continue. We need a doctor under the left-hand scaffold as soon as possible please.' He was listening to shouts from the front of the crowd. He listened to a girl for a few seconds and went on: 'There's a Red Cross building at the top of the stage and there's been lots of lost childing, children, under the scaffold – if you've lost a child go and collect him or her there please – it's a Red Cross van . . .'

After another pause during which no one onstage did anything but look anxiously around, Mick said, 'It seems to be stuck down to me – will you listen to me for a minute – please listen to me just for one second a'right? First of all, everyone is gonna get to the side of the stage who's on it now except for the Stones who are playing. Please, everyone – everyone, please, can you get to the side of the stage who's not playing. Right? That's a start. Now, the thing is, I can't see what's going on, who is doing wot, it's just a scuffle. All I can ask you, San Francisco, is like the whole thing – this could be the most beautiful evening we've had this winter. We really – y'know, why, why – don't let's fuck it up, man, come on – let's get it together – everyone – come *on* now – I can't see you up on the hillsides, you're probably very cool. Down here we're not so cool, we've got a lot of hassles goin' on. I just – every cat . . .'

There were shouts from the darkness. Mick peered out blindly past the stage lights and answered, 'Yeah, I know, we can't even see you but I know you're where – you're cool. We're just trying to keep it together. I can't do any more than ask you – beg you, just to keep it together. You can do it, it's within your power – everyone – Hell's Angels, everybody. Let's just keep ourselves together.

'You know,' Mick said with a sudden burst of passion, 'if we *are* all one, let's fucking well *show* we're all one. Now there's one thing we need – Sam, we need an ambulance – we need a doctor by that scaffold there, if there's a doctor can he get to there. Okay, we're gonna, we gonna do – I don't know what the fuck we gonna do. Everyone just sit down. Keep cool. Let's just *relax*, let's get into a groove. Come on, we can get it together. Come on.'

'Under My Thumb' was starting to churn again. The band sounded amazingly sharp. The crowd was more still. Without knowing exactly what, we all felt that something bad had happened. I assumed, and I was not given to flights of horrible imaginings, that the Angels had killed several people. Gram told me later that he saw Meredith Hunter lifted up, with a great spreading ketchup-colored stain on the back of his suit. Ronnie was running to the First Aid tent, outdistancing the Hell's Angel who had been leading him. Hunter was there when Ronnie came up, calling for a doctor. A cop said, 'You don't have to scream for a doctor for this guy, he's dead.'

Over the last notes of 'Under My Thumb,' Mick sang, 'It's all right – I pray that it's all right – I pray that it's – it's all right –'

'Let's do "Brown Sugar",' Mick Taylor said.

'"*Brown Sugah*"?' Keith said.

'"Brown Sugar"?' Bill said.

'What?' Charlie said.

'He wants to do "Brown Sugar",' Mick said.

'Wait, let me change guitars,' Keith said.

'Thank you,' Mick said to the crowd. Charlie was playing rolls. 'Thank you. Are we all, yeah, we're gettin' it together – we gonna do one for you which we just ah –' pausing, remembering that making the record was breaking the law '– we just ah – you've never heard it before because we just written it – we've just written it for you –' as Keith was tuning – 'I dunno how good this is gonna be, baby – ah, this is the first time we've played it – the very first time we've played it.' Keith finished tuning and played the song's first chords. Mick shouted, '*We gonna do one f'you now which we did for you, which we haven't ever played ever before, we gonna play it for you for the very first time, it's called "Brown Sugah".*'

Stacked like cordwood at the sides of the stage were bouquets of red and yellow long-stemmed roses. As the Stones played, Angels threw the bouquets into the crowd as if pitching babies out of airplane windows.

> Scarred old slaver knows he's doin' all right
> Hear him whip the women, just around midnight
>
> Oh – brown sugar – how come you taste so good
> Oh – brown sugar – just like a black girl should

It was a song of sadism, savagery, race hate/love, a song of redemption, a song that accepted the fear of night, blackness, chaos, the unknown – the fear that the mad-eyed Norsemen, transplanted from Odin-drunk mead halls to California desert, were still seeking mad-eyed to escape.

'Ahhh, one mo' time – whoo, baby. Yeah – 'ang you – awww –' Taking a harp from Stu, Mick played a few menacing riffs of 'Midnight Rambler'. Keith had changed guitars and was tuning again. Mick played soft harp notes that trailed off as, head bent over the mike, he began singing lullaby phrases, trying to soothe and gentle the great beast. 'Aw now, baby baby – hush now, don't cry.' His voice was tender, a tone of voice that Mick Jagger had never before used in public and maybe never in his life. 'Hush now, don't you cry –' A few more notes on the harp, and then, as if he were coming out of a reverie, gaining strength with each word, Mick said, 'We gonna do you one which we hope you'll *dig* – which is called "The Midnight Rambler". Wshoo!' (expostulation of a field hand stripping the sweat off his forehead with a dusty forefinger)

> Sighing down the wind so sadly –
> Listen and you'll hear him moan

The song had scared me when I first heard it, because it was true, as nobody at Altamont could deny, the dark is filled with terror, murder and evil ride the night air. 'I'll stick my knife right down your throat, honey, and it hurts!'

Things seemed to be settling down, as if the killer-lover lament had worked some psychic release on the crowd.

'Aw yah! Aw yah! Stand up if you can stand up,' Mick said. 'Stand up if you can keep it cool.' He raised the Jack Daniel's bottle. 'One more drink to you all.' He drank and spoke again in his lullaby tone, 'Awww, babies'. Then, as if he were coming to again, he said, 'It's so – sssweet! It's really sssweet! Would you like to live with – each other? I mean, you're really close to each other.' He stared into the crowd and seemed to drift away again. 'Wow,' he said.

'You ready?' Keith asked.

'Yeah, I'm ready,' Mick said.

'One two three faw,' Keith snarled, and they started 'Live with Me'.

Around the stage people were dancing, but in front of the stage, staring at Mick, one curly-haired boy in a watch cap was saying, Mick, Mick, no – I could read his lips. Behind the boy a fat black-haired girl, naked to the waist, was dancing, squeezing her enormous breasts, mouth open, eyes focused on a point somewhere north of her forehead. As the song ended, the girl, her skin rose-florid, blinking off and on like a pinball machine in orgasmic acid flashes, tried to take the stage like Grant took Richmond. Completely naked now, she was trying to climb over the crowd to get a foot onstage, where five Angels were at once between her and the Stones, kicking her back, her smothering weight falling on the people behind her.

'Hold it,' Mick said.

'Stop that one,' Keith said.

'Hey – heyheyheyheyheyheyheyhey*hey*! One cat can control that chick, y'know wot oi mean. Hey, fellows. Hey, fellows. One of you can control her, man,' Mick said, speaking the last sentence to the Angel nearest him onstage.

'Yeah, we're gonna do it,' the Angel said, in a world of his own, as were all the Angels looking down into the crowd, trying to reach the girl with fists or boots, wanting to get down there and smash her face, stomp on her throat, kick her tits off and send them sailing over the heads of this dumb sheeplike crowd, and kick her in the pussy till she bleeds to death.

'Hey, come on, fellows,' Mick was saying, getting a bit frantic, 'like one of you can control one little girl – come on now, like – like – like – just sit down, honey,' he said to the girl, who was still on her back, flashing her black-pelted pelvis, her eyes black whirlpools staring at the sky as if she were trying to get above the stage, above the lights. If she could come up to there and keep coming into the night, above the world, she would shed her grossness like a chrysalis and be reborn, airborne, an angel of God. The Hell's Angels leaned out over the stage to stop her, to grab her, to slap her teeth out and smash her goddam gums, thumb her crazy eyes out, pop her eardrums, snatch her bald-headed, scalp the cheap cunt.

'Fellows,' Mick said, trying gently to move the Angels away, 'can you clear – uh – and she'll – let – let – let them deal with her – they can deal with her.' The people down front were managing to crawl out from under the girl, the Angels wanting to stay and get their hands on her. 'Fellows, come on, fellows,' Mick said, 'they're all right.'

Keith started playing and Wyman and Charlie and Mick Taylor joined in, as the Angels slunk bloodlusty to the side. Mick was singing:

Yeah, I see the storm is threatening
My very life today
If I don't get some shelter
I'm gonna fade away
War, children, it's just a shot away

The Angels were cracking their knuckles, looking around red-eyed for flesh to rip. How are we gonna get out of here? I wondered. *Will* we get out, or will we die here, is it going to snap and the Angels like dinosaurs kill themselves and all of us in a savage rage of nihilism, the plain to be found in the morning a bloody soup littered with teeth and bones, one last mad Angel, blinded by a comrade's boots and brass knuckles, gut sliced asunder by his partner's frogsticker, growling, tearing at the yawning slit under his filthy T-shirt, chomping on his own bloody blue-white entrails?

'Rape – murder – it's just a shot away,' Mick sang over and over. In the crowd by stage left, where the trouble with the black boy in the green suit had taken place, an Angel was punching someone, but the victim went down fast and it was over. Standing close by, looking on, was a girl with phosphorescent white hair, a chemical miracle. It was impossible to tell whether she was with the Angel or the victim. 'Love, sister, it's just a kiss away,' Mick sang as the song thundered to a stop.

'Yuhh,' Mick said, very low, then 'Yuhhh,' again, lower, like a man making a terrible discovery. 'Okay . . . are we okay, I know we are.' He was looking into the crowd. As if he had waked up once again, he shouted, 'Are y'havin' a good ti-i-ime? OOH-yeah!'

'Little Queenie' was starting; it was the moment in the show when the lights went on to reveal rapt fresh faces. But not tonight. Even the people who were dancing in spite of the danger looked unhappy. At times Mick's voice sounded light, as if he had lost the bottom part of it, but Keith was playing like a man ready to dance on his own grave.

The song ended to cheers from the crowd, some people perking up. 'I – I – I thank you very much,' Mick said. 'Thank you very much.' The opening notes of 'Satisfaction' turned on like a current of electricity. It would probably never be played better. Charlie kept a straight boogaloo like the Otis Redding version and it went on and on, Mick chanting, 'We got to find it – *got* to find it – got to *find* it – early in the mornin' – late in the evenin' –' He shouted the song to an end, gave three Indian-style war whoops, and as his voice died to a whisper, looked out at the multitude, hundreds of thousands of people who had come because he had asked them, and he could give them nothing better than this, mayhem and terror.

'Justliketosaaaayyy,' Mick said, then paused and seemed to lose himself once more, wondering what it was he'd like to say. After a moment he went on briskly: 'Well there's been a few hangups you know but I mean generally I mean ah you've been beau-ti-ful –' in a lower tone – 'you have been so groovy – aw!' (brisk again) 'All the loose women may stand and put their hands up – all the loose women put their hands up!' But the loose women were tired like everybody else. A few girls stood up, a few hands were raised into the murk. On this night no one would think of playing 'I'm Free', though that had been the whole idea of the concert, to give some free glimmer to Ralph Gleason's rock-and-roll-starved proletariat and to get away from the violence of the system, the cops' clubs, Klein's mop handle. The biggest group of playmates in history was having recess, with no teachers to protect them from the bad boys, the bullies, who may have been mistreated children and worthy of understanding but would nevertheless kill you. The Stones' music was strong but it could not stop the terror. There was a look of disbelief on the people's faces, wondering how the Stones could go on playing and singing in the bowels of madness and violent death. Not many hands were in the air, and Mick said, 'That's not enough, we haven't got many loose women, what're ya gonna do?'

The band started 'Honky Tonk Women', playing as well as if they were in a studio, Keith's lovely horrible harmonies sailing out into the cool night air. Nobody, not even the guardians of public morality at *Rolling Stone* who pronounced that 'Altamont was the product of diabolical egotism, hype, ineptitude, money manipulation, and, at base, a fundamental lack of concern for humanity', could say that the Rolling Stones couldn't play like the devil when the chips were down.

When 'Honky Tonk Women' was over, the sound system stopped working, then started again. 'Hello – I got it back,' Mick said. 'Yahh – come back to – ah – we gonna, ah, we gonna, ah – we gonna kiss you goodbye – and we leave you to kiss each other goodbye – and – you – we're gonna see ya, we're gonna see ya, we're gonna see ya – again . . .' And with that sudden softness he asked 'All right?' in a voice as small as a kitten's. 'Kiss each other goodbye – sleep – good night –'

The last song, 'Street Fighting Man', started. '. . . the time is right for fighting in the street,' Mick sang, a leader with an international constituency, unable to save anyone.

> Ah, but what can a poor boy do
> But to sing with a rock 'n' roll band

The music pounded hard enough to drive even the naked fat girl to Heaven. 'Bye bye bye bye,' Mick sang. 'Bye bye bye bye.' Stu handed me Keith's twelve-string guitar and told me the station wagons to take us to the helicopters would be at the top of the hill, straight back and up to the left. I slipped off the truck, taking the guitar by the neck, and struck out into the night, trying to get the people in the passageway between the backstage trucks to move and let me out. '*Please let me through,*' I shouted.

A boy about seventeen walked backwards ahead of me, saying, 'We're gonna build a superhighway, man, never built one before but we're gonna build one on our own to show we can do it without grown-ups –'

Behind me Mick was saying, 'Bye – by-y-y y-e – bye', as I plunged on among shouts from unknown voices, trying not to run into people. I heard the Stones coming and Gram and Michelle's voices and called to them, all of us stumbling through the fucking blackness. At last, with our lives, we were off the stage, struggling through the dark, trying not to lose anyone. 'Regroup!' Ronnie's voice rasped, and then we had reached the hillside, a steep slope that we were scrambling up through dusty clay and dead grass, me on one hand, elbow, and knees, holding the guitar. At the top of the hill was a cyclone fence, but we passed through a hole in it, still running, to a car and an ambulance. I got into the back of the ambulance, followed by a half-dozen or so New York heavies. Blowing the horns, we drove through the crowd that swarmed around us, moving as fast as we could. When we stopped near a helicopter and got out, I gave the guitar to Sam. The Stones, Astrid, Jo, Ronnie, Sam, Tony, David Horowitz, Jon Jaymes, Mike Scotty, Ethan Russell, among others, boarded the small aircraft. Gram, Michelle and I stood just outside the spinning blades wondering what would happen if we were left, lost in the blackness in this crowd, but Sam called, 'Come on!' Gram helped Michelle on and got on himself and I got on. The little bulbous capsule was packed with heads and knees and I gladly hopped onto the only place where there was room to sit, the lap of David Horowitz, silly ass or not. The helicopter was shaking and lifting like an ostrich waking up, its hums and rattles drowning out everything except shouts. Mick and I exchanged glances, his eyes wide, lowering, lips pursed to whistle. I looked up and away, indicating how I wasn't even ready for glances.

In a few minutes the overloaded helicopter descended at the Tracy or Livermore airport, dropping too fast, the ground rushing up at us, instead of settling down gently like a hummingbird we came in on the skids at an angle like an airplane. We hit sharply but kept upright and bounced flat. We climbed out and Keith, walking under the blades, headed for the airport building; he was denouncing the Angels: 'They're sick, man, they're worse than the cops. They're just not ready. I'm never going to have anything to do with them again.' He sounded like an English public school boy whose fundamental decency and sense of fair play had been offended by the unsportsmanlike conduct at soccer of certain of his peers.

Mick sat on a wooden bench in the little airport, eyes still hurt and angry, bewildered and scared, not understanding who the Hell's Angels were or why they were killing people at his free peace-and-love show. 'How could any-body think those people are good, think they're people you should have around?' he said.

'Nobody in his right mind could,' I said, 'that's why –' I started to say, That's why I said last night that you believe too much of the hype, but I didn't. He had paid for his beliefs and nobody had the right to condemn him.

'Some people are just not ready,' Keith was saying, but how ready was any of us to live in the real world, a world that would each year become more like Altamont?

'I'd rather have had the cops,' Mick said.

'The Angels are worse than cops,' Gram said. 'They're bozos, just a bunch of bozos. They're so dumb. Michelle and I were standing by the right-hand side of the stage not bothering anybody, just standing as far away as we could be and still see, and one Angel kept trying to push us back, every two minutes. Every two minutes I'd have to explain to him all over again just like the first time that we were supposed to be there.'

'Some people are just not ready,' Keith said again. He had taken off the red Nudie shirt he'd worn onstage and slung it over his shoulder, and he was starting to shiver. 'Hey, where are my jackets? Hey, Sam! Sam! Did you get my jackets outa the caravan?'

'They're on the helicopter,' Horowitz said, without any idea where in hell the jackets were.

'Don't let it take off,' Keith said, 'a black velvet jacket and a Hungarian sort of gypsy jacket,' forgetting the moldy Nazi greatcoat. 'They both cost a fortune, don't let the copter take off with them.'

Horowitz looked in the helicopter and came back with an old sheepskin jacket, saying, 'They weren't there, they must be in the trailer, we'll get them, don't worry, please, we'll get them but for now will you just put this on just for the moment, please?'

Keith did finally deign to toss the jacket over his shoulders, whereupon Horowitz, ever desperate to do the wrong thing, said to Gram and Michelle, 'There's limited seating on the plane' – which had just landed – 'but there's already another one on the way. You won't mind staying, will you, it'll only be about ten minutes.'

Hearing this, I said, 'Just a minute,' to Gram and walked over to Keith. 'There's room for Gram and Michelle on the plane, isn't there?'

'Sure,' Keith said.

We went out to the plane, a fifteen-seater. After so many, the names all blend together and it doesn't matter if they're red and white or white and gold or if the seats are brown or two-tone green. It was a short ride to San Francisco and a not so short ride in limousines back to the Huntington, safe and more or less sound. Gram was kissing Michelle, trying to make out with her, and she seemed to be enduring it like a high school senior making do with a sophomore boy on the way home from a church hayride. 'We wouldn't even be here if it wasn't for you,' Gram said to me. 'Thanks a lot.'

'It was nothing,' I said. We grew quiet as we approached the hotel. It was beginning to dawn on us that we had survived.

By the elevators was an *Examiner* with the headline, 300,000 SAY IT WITH MUSIC. Say what?

Stanley Booth, The True Adventures of the Rolling Stones (1985)

1970: Look at that Stupid Girl

I have not made an exhaustive study, but I have been struck by how little writing has appeared on the subject of rock and women. A woman should be writing this. But no woman has written it yet, and I've felt for at least a year that somebody had better. Because I believe women's oppression demands the most far-reaching analysis of social structures ever attempted, I feel obliged to ignore the certain ridicule of the satisfied oppressors and the inevitable resentment of the conscious oppressed and try to analyse the problem myself.

I received my own sexism sensitivity training from a militant feminist who is almost as fervent about rock as I am, and I know that to a lesser extent such enthusiasm is shared by many active women's liberationists, so I don't believe indifference causes the silence. On the contrary, many women are explicitly perplexed by the paradox of their attraction to a music that is not only male chauvinist – almost everything is – but even, to call upon a useful distinction, male supremacist. I think a similar paradox plagues the women's movement as a whole.

To charge that the typical feminist wants to 'be like a man' is a canard. She wants only the freedom to explore what it is to be a woman. But in order to gain such freedom she is obliged to gather power, and in the process of gathering power she accrues 'masculine' characteristics. Without some minimal share of 'male' autonomy/activism/energy (these may seem like perfectly unexceptionable qualities, but they aren't when, as is so often the case, they block their equally unexceptionable opposites: communality/responsiveness/equanimity), she would never be able to assert herself in the first place. And it is with self-assertiveness, counted so 'unfeminine' by many men (and women), that her struggle must begin. Of course, that is not where it's supposed to end. In the most productive pattern of self-liberation the new feminist both declares her independence – from her man, her job, her life training – and discovers her solidarity – with other women.

A like pattern of release and new community emerges from a political analysis of rock and roll. Musically, rock has always been an affirmation of energy – aggressive where pop was acquiescent and folk reflective – and it has always instilled in its audience a penchant for activity, beginning, I suppose, with foot-tapping and ending, I suppose, with state-smashing. The independence this activity implies and reifies has also led to solidarity, mostly generational, with music the great adhesive. In fact, insofar as the new feminism results from a certain style of heightened political awareness that began with the civil-rights movement, it can be said to have some of its roots in the adolescent rebellion symbolized by rock and roll. This is a far-fetched rationalization and there is no need to take it as more than a curiosity, but it does help resolve the paradox. Women like rock not only because it has human value but also because some of that human value is, or has been, good for them *as women*.

I assume that by now I have lost most of those who begin this column every time in the hope that I will be writing about rock and roll. I have lost them, dudes and chicks both. After all, they're in it for the sex in the first place. The metaphor around which rock's liberating energy collects itself – the content of that energy – is sexual. Since we grew up in an antisexual society, we have tended to embrace that giant breakthrough with the total passion we think it deserves. But because rock draws upon traditional folk attitudes dating back (at least) to African tribal dances and Scottish ballads – or, more directly, blues and country music – its sexual energy, like all formalized sexual energy I know about, is also sexist energy. It posits the classic pattern of man the pursuer/actor and woman the pursued/acted-upon. The subculture that is identified with rock – and the more precise the identification, the more this is true – has instituted this pattern with a vengeance that is almost liberal, sloughing off all the genteel post-Victorian camouflage so many of us grew up with and getting back to basics. For the hard-core rock freak, a chick's place is not only in the home but between the sheets, and a feminist is more fucked up than fucked over and better off just plain fucked.

The sexist message can be discerned in one form or another in just about every rock song that concerns men and women, but lyrics, except when they are clearly audible and blatant, are the least of it. It is in the theater of rock, both in the media and in live performance, that sexism really prevails. Don't even think about groupies – just name female rock musicians. The idea, of course, is ridiculous. Among concert-calibre groups, the total is two drummers – Maureen Tucker, of the Velvet Underground, and Ruth Underwood, of the Hamilton Face Band – and the two women who perform with Sly Stone. There are also a few singer-pianists and many folkies who accompany themselves on (low-energy) acoustic guitar. No electric guitarists at all.

It is possible to argue that women – as a function of cultural deprivation, of course, not innate disadvantage – have little bent for instrumental improvisation. As rock exists now, that may be true, although if so, it is even more true of jazz. But the deeper truth, I think, is more unpleasant than any cant about cultural deprivation. First, women cannot play rock guitar because men won't listen to them, and there is no need to belabor phallic analogies to explain why. Second, women cannot play rock because they cannot and/or do not want to create in blues-based male styles.

Granted, this is speculation, and granted too that there have to be a lot more men with guitar chops than women. The nicest thing about such speculations is that anyone is free to make them because they're never fairly tested. I know by name of three female rock groups: Joy of Cooking (wonderful pun), the Enchanted Forest (who according to a recent *Rat* were put through the ringer by a male manager), and the Ace of Cups. I saw the Ace of Cups two years ago. They were strong vocally but didn't have much instrumental kineticism. They were, however, much more than professional, and I think it is significant that the group, despite its professionalism and gimmick appeal, never got a recording contract. I hope for my sake and for the sake of the music that women see fit to defy the odds and enter rock in capacities other than Resident Female Principle.

You see, I have felt over the past year and a half a steadily increasing disaffection with rock's male chauvinism. I am acutely uncomfortable with songs of cock-pride (Led Zeppelin's 'Whole Lotta Love', for instance), even though I still dig them as artifacts. I perceive all too well the other side of the born-to-be-wild theme – sorry to break your heart, babe, but the road is calling me. I am so far gone that I am offended by the Guess Who's 'No Time' and uplifted by Janis's 'Turtle Blues'. I listen to 'Do Right Woman', purportedly a hymn to the equality of the sexes, and hear its message: A well-fucked woman has nothing to complain about. I can't even take the good-hearted condescension of John Sebastian without wincing a little. So far, of course, I have managed to overcome my distress. Music is one of my great pleasures, and I'm not able to give it up. But there are times when I wonder how acutely conscious women continue to stand for it.

The carrot-and-stick of sexism is subtle and pervasive. Sexism predates any political or economic system, and it is carried by the entire culture. Just because it can be so far-reaching, feminist analysis fascinates the kamikaze left. A woman in a properly destructive frame of mind can justifiably reject almost all the art that has ever existed in the world. I can't, and I won't. My love for popular culture has always been nourished by one overriding assumption – that there is a human spirit strong enough to break through the distortions of any structure imposed upon it.

Whether we admit it or not, we always perceive art through a built-in set of compensations; we judge it and respond to it not only in terms of what we feel about the limitations of its creator. No civil-liberation atheist blames John Locke for having been a deist in 1690. Unless a woman wants to contend that it was only masochism that induced her to dig on 'Heart of Stone' in 1965, then she has to admit that there was something there – some energy, as my rhetoric would have it – that was good for her. Even if the energy of rock is nothing more than sublimated (or not so sublimated) machismo, such machismo can be a step on the way out, a naïve reaction against apparent sources of oppression, and in that way it is beautiful.

There is another false trap here. Aesthetic reactions ought to come from the whole person. When a woman is turned off by some cocksure chauvinist on the stage of the Fillmore East, she is not 'judging art politically'. On the contrary, she is responding naturally to what she has come to feel as her own experience, just like the black man who doesn't want to be called boy, even by D. W. Griffith. The quality of a man's response to such implied insult has a lot in common with the quality of a white's response – secondhand, perhaps, but also gut-level if he's conscious enough. Nevertheless, I think hypersensitivity ought to be avoided. There is a sense, for instance, in which 'Back Street Girl' is a sexist song, but there is also a sense in which it is a biting, accurate indictment of sexism – not to mention class oppression – at its most humiliating. In this and other, vaguer cases I tend toward the kinder interpretation and reaction. When you love something as much as I love rock, that's probably a good rule and instinct.

I am rarely sanguine about politics these days. I believe the women's movement is going to make a lot of people, male and female, excruciatingly unhappy before it starts doing a whole lot of unequivocal good, but for all that it must continue, and it will. The prospects for a sexually integrated music in the near future are nonexistent, but it's nice to think that the next time music is revitalized, women may do the revitalizing. Maybe the sensibilities of all of us will be extended in ways difficult to imagine and trying to undergo, but deeply pleasurable when we get there. Whenever that is.

Robert Christgau, Esquire, June 1970

1971: No Flowers in This Town

My attorney was in the bathtub when I returned. Submerged in green water – the oily product of some Japanese bath salts he'd picked up in the hotel gift shop, along with a new AM/FM radio plugged into the electric razor socket. Top volume. Some gibberish by a thing called 'Three Dog Night', about a frog named Jeremiah who wanted 'Joy to the World'.

First Lennon, now this, I thought. Next we'll have Glenn Campbell screaming 'Where Have All the Flowers Gone?'

Where indeed? No flowers in this town. Only carnivorous plants. I turned the volume down and noticed a hunk of chewed-up white paper beside the radio. My attorney seemed not to notice the sound-change. He was lost in a fog of green steam; only half his head was visible above the water line.

'You ate this?' I asked, holding up the white pad.

He ignored me. But I knew. He would be very difficult to reach for the next six hours. The whole blotter was chewed up.

'You evil son of a bitch,' I said. 'You better hope there's some thorazine in that bag, because if there's not you're in bad trouble tomorrow.'

'Music!' he snarled. 'Turn it up. Put that tape on.'

'What tape?'

'The new one. It's right there.'

I picked up the radio and noticed that it was also a tape recorder – one of those things with a cassette-unit built in. And the tape, *Surrealistic Pillow*, needed only to be flipped over. He had already gone through side one – at a volume that must have been audible in every room within a radius of one hundred yards, walls and all.

' "White Rabbit",' he said. 'I want a *rising* sound.'

'You're doomed,' I said. 'I'm leaving here in two hours – and then they're going to come up here and beat the mortal shit out of you with big saps. Right there in the tub.'

'I dig my own graves,' he said. 'Green water and the White Rabbit . . . put it on; don't make me use this.' His arm lashed out of the water, the hunting knife gripped in his fist.

'Jesus,' I muttered. And at that point I figured he was beyond help – lying there in the tub with a head full of acid and the sharpest knife I've ever seen, totally incapable of reason, demanding the White Rabbit. This is it, I thought. I've gone as far as I can with this waterhead. This time it's a suicide trip. This time he wants it. He's ready . . .

'OK,' I said, turning the tape over and pushing the 'play' button. 'But do me one last favor, will you? Can you give me two hours? That's all I ask – just two hours to sleep before tomorrow. I suspect it's going to be a very difficult day.'

'Of course,' he said. 'I'm your *attorney*. I'll give you all the time you need, at my normal rates: $45 an hour – but you'll be wanting a cushion, so why don't you just lay one of those $100 bills down there beside the radio, and fuck off?'

'How about a check?' I said. 'On the Sawtooth National Bank. You won't need any ID to cash it there. They know me.'

'Whatever's right,' he said, beginning to jerk with the music. The bathroom was like the inside of a huge defective woofer. Heinous vibrations, overwhelming sound. The floor was full of water. I moved the radio as far from the tub as it would go, then I left and closed the door behind me.

Within seconds he was shouting at me. 'Help! You bastard! I need help!'

I rushed back inside, thinking he'd sliced off an ear by accident.

But no . . . he was reaching across the bathroom toward the white formica shelf where the radio sat. 'I want that fuckin radio,' he snarled.

I grabbed it away from his hand. 'You fool!' I said. 'Get back in that tub! Get away from that goddam radio!' I shoved it back from his hand. The volume was so far up that it was hard to know what was playing unless you knew *Surrealistic Pillow* almost note for note . . . which I did, at the time, so I knew that 'White Rabbit' had finished; the peak had come and gone.

But my attorney, it seemed, had not made it. He wanted more. 'Back the tape up!' he yelled. 'I need it again!' His eyes were full of craziness now, unable to focus. He seemed on the verge of some awful psychic orgasm . . .

'Let it roll!' he screamed. 'Just as high as the fucker can go! And when it comes to that fantastic note where the rabbit bites its own head off, I want you to throw that fuckin radio into the tub with me.'

I stared at him, keeping a firm grip on the radio. 'Not me,' I said finally. 'I'd be happy to ram a goddam 440-volt cattle prod into that tub with you right now, but *not* this radio. It would blast you right through the wall – stone-dead in ten seconds.' I laughed. 'Shit, they'd make me *explain* it – drag me down to some rotten coroner's inquest and grill me about . . . yes . . . the *exact details*. I don't need that.'

'Bullshit!' he screamed. 'Just tell them I wanted to get *Higher*!'

I thought for a moment. 'Okay,' I said finally. 'You're right. This is probably the only solution.' I picked up the tape/radio – which was still plugged in – and held it over the tub. 'Just let me make sure I have it all lined up,' I said. 'You want me to throw this thing into the tub when "White Rabbit" peaks – is that it?'

He fell back in the water and smiled gratefully. 'Fuck yes,' he said. 'I was beginning to think I was going to have to go out and get one of the goddam *maids* to do it.'

'Don't worry,' I said. 'Are you ready?' I hit the 'play' button and 'White Rabbit' started building again. Almost immediately he began to howl and moan . . . another fast run up that mountain, and thinking, this time, that he would finally get over the top. His eyes were gripped shut and only his head and both kneecaps poked up through the oily green water.

I let the song build while I sorted through the pile of fat ripe grapefruit next to the basin. The biggest one of the lot weighed almost two pounds. I got a good Vida Blue fastball grip on the fucker – and just as 'White Rabbit' peaked I lashed it into the tub like a cannonball.

My attorney screamed crazily, thrashing around in the tub like a shark after meat, churning water all over the floor as he struggled to get hold of something.

I jerked the AC cord out of the tape/radio and moved out of the bathroom very quickly . . . the machine kept on playing, but now it was back on its own harmless battery power. I could hear the beat cooling down as I moved across the room to my kit-bag and fetched up the Mace can . . . just as my attorney ripped the bathroom door open and started out. His eyes were still unfocused but he was waving the blade out in front of him like a man who meant to cut something.

'Mace!' I shouted. 'You want *this*?' I waved the Mace bomb in front of his watery eyes.

He stopped, 'You bastard!' he hissed. 'You'd *do* that, wouldn't you?'

I laughed, still waving the bomb at him. 'Why worry? You'll *like* it. Shit, there's nothing in the world like a Mace high – forty-five minutes on your knees with the dry leaves, gasping for breath. It'll calm you right down.'

He stared in my general direction, trying to focus. 'You cheap honky sonofabitch,' he muttered. 'You'd *do* it, wouldn't you?'

'Why not? I said. 'Hell, just a minute ago you were asking me to *kill* you! And now you want to kill *me*! What I should do, goddamnit, is call the *police*!'

He sagged. 'The cops?'

I nodded. 'Yeah, there's no choice. I wouldn't dare go to sleep with you wandering around in this condition – with a head full of acid and wanting to slice me up with that goddamn knife.'

He rolled his eyes for a moment, then tried to smile. 'Who said anything about slicing you up?' he mumbled. 'I just wanted to carve a little Z on your forehead – nothing serious.' He shrugged and reached for a cigarette on top of the TV set.

I menaced him again with the Mace can. 'Get back in that tub,' I said. 'Eat some reds and try to calm down. Smoke some grass, shoot some smack – shit, do whatever you *have* to do, but let me get some rest.'

He shrugged and smiled distractedly, as if everything I'd said made perfect sense. 'Hell yes,' he said very earnestly. 'You really *need* some sleep. You have to *work* tomorrow.' He shook his head sadly and turned back toward the bathroom. 'God damn! What a bummer.' He waved me off. 'Try to rest,' he said. 'Don't let me keep you up.'

I nodded, and watched him shuffle back into the bathroom – still holding the blade, but now he seemed unaware of it. The acid had shifted gears on him; the next phase would probably be one of those hellishly intense introspection nightmares. Four hours or so of catatonic despair; but nothing physical, nothing dangerous. I watched the door close behind him, then I quietly slid a heavy sharp-angled chair in front of the bathroom knob and put the Mace can beside the alarm clock.

The room was very quiet. I walked over to the TV set and turned it on to a dead channel – white noise at maximum decibels, a fine sound for sleeping, a powerful continuous hiss to drown out everything strange.

Hunter S. Thompson, *Fear and Loathing in Las Vegas* (1972)

six

1972–6

'The star ideal was reborn'

NEW ENGLISH LIBRARY

GLAM

Johnny Holland fights to stay idol of a million fans.
By Richard Allen

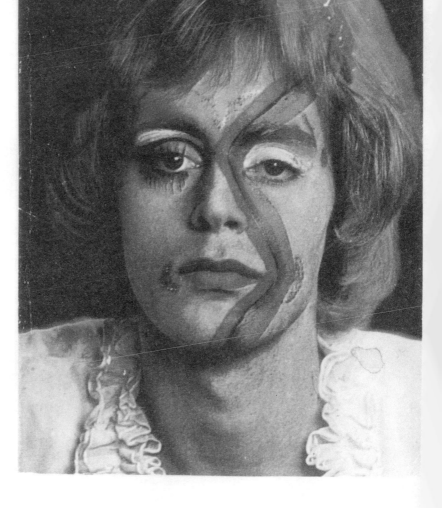

'In 1972, *the year I did my research, the rock/pop division seemed absolute, and the division of musical tastes seemed to reflect class differences: on the one hand, there was the culture of middle-class rock – pretentious and genteel, obsessed with bourgeois notions of art and the accumulation of expertise and equipment; on the other hand, there was the culture of working-class pop – banal, simple-minded, based on the formulas of a tightly knit body of business.*'

Simon Frith, Sound Affects *(1978)*

You could be forgiven for thinking that, in the previous section, we'd strayed away from the classic definition of pop music and, if you did, you'd be reflecting what a large section of the audience felt then. The early seventies were a time of retrenchment. The Utopia that had seemed possible in 1966–7 had soured into excess and cynicism; pop music had polarized into teenypop and rock, which, it could be argued, was not usually pop. In this recessionary era, youth was no longer in the vanguard: far from being a desirable state, it was seen as a problem.

In England, this retrenchment was embodied in the figure of the skinhead: the austere, delinquent, working-class style which, as Pete Fowler noted in 1972, also marked the split in the once unified pop market. The twists and turns of early seventies street style were monitored by Richard Allen in a sequence of brutal, mediated novels which had an extraordinary success: *Skinhead, Sorts, Suedehead*. This extract from *Teenybopper Idol*, where ex-skinheads gatecrash a televised concert, is uncannily prescient of the Sex Pistols' early days.

Teenybopper Idol reflected tabloid obsessions: pop stars like David Cassidy and the Bay City Rollers attracted fanatical reactions, huge sales and screaming headlines – but failed to reach the cross-generational impact of sixties pop stars. Charles Shaar Murray's wry observations on an Osmonds concert captures the hermetic frenzy of audiences at the time; while in one of the first attempts to tell the fan's side of the story, Sheryl Garratt remembers an adolescence dominated by the Bay City Rollers.

There were strong currents beneath the surface. A new generation of English pop stars – who were not as successful in America – freely took from fine art (UK and US pop) and literature (Burroughs). With David Bowie and Roxy Music, pop became self-conscious. Both pop star and cultural hero, Bowie had an enormous influence in the UK, crystallizing a new pop generation marked by an extreme, theatrical androgyny – 'Glam'. Mick Watts's January 1972 interview was a milestone in pop journalism: the first time that any performer had admitted in public to being homosexual.

Much as feminism had created a space for women writers (although comparatively few performers at this stage), so the drive towards what was then called gay liberation impacted on popular culture. In his novel *Dancer from the Dance*, Andrew Holleran re-creates the very beginning of the musical style that would sweep the world in the late seventies: disco.

Recalling his time as Rod Stewart's PA, Peter Burton shows how homosexuality could be freely expressed as the freedoms of the sixties – sex
and drugs and pop – became industrialized for the mass market.

With the failure of rock to capture the imagination, dance music took
centre stage. These were the early years of disco, the final years of black
self-confidence – epitomized by the 'blaxploitation' movies of the early
decade and the spread of funky chic throughout Britain and America, as
the hedonism that had been promised in the late sixties finally became
available to the mass market a few years later. Tom Wolfe tracks this with
the attention to detail which would become a staple of style journalism a
decade later.

From a perspective still rarely heard in popular culture, Jean Peter gives
a West Indian woman's point of view on the dance culture of the day and
attempts to answer that age-old question: why can't white people dance?
Nik Cohn charts the spread of disco from the gay clubs into the suburbs.
Another Saturday Night used the sixties Mod experience as a framework
through which to discuss this new, headlong hedonism – all too successfully: the article formed the basis for *Saturday Night Fever*, the film which
on release in late 1977 made disco into an industry.

The shadow side of the period was to be found in androgynous, self-
destructive rock acts like Iggy and the Stooges captured here by a great
rock writer in his prime, Dave Marsh. The limits of the early seventies
dreams – pure pop fandom and dancing as a way of life – are explored by
the final articles in this section. Fred and Judy Vermorel chart a Bowie
fan's gradual disillusion, love turning to hostility, while Idris Walters
freezes the disintegration of a genuine subculture, Northern Soul: 'It used
to be We Hate Pompey or We Hate Derby. Now it's just We Hate.'

1972: The Emergence of the Skinheads

In 1969, the backlash started. It had to happen sometime: once the star idea
was reborn, once the gaps arose between artist and performer, once the focal
point of the new culture became rooted in the States, the time was ripe for
change. The Skinheads came from the same areas that had witnessed the rise
of the Mods – the East End of London and the outer ring of suburbs. But
whereas the Mod had seen his 'enemy' as the rocker, and had rationalized his
life style accordingly (Cleanliness vs. Grease; Scooter vs. Motor Bike; Pills vs.
Booze), the new Skinheads reacted against the Hippies. Their hair was short

to the point of absurdity, they were tough and went around in their 'bovver boots' for the express purpose of beating hell out of any deviants, and they wore braces. Braces! For God's sake, some sort of weird throwback to the Thirties.

At Hyde Park in July 1969, they showed their strength. According to Geoffrey Cannon's report on the event, a free concert given by the Stones, it was 'A Nice Day in the Park'. It was things 'nice' that the Skins objected to. John Peel and the other beautiful people saw everything as being 'really nice' – the Skins wanted others to see them as really horrible.

The concert was odd. Here were the Rolling Stones, the old Mod idols, being defended by the Hells Angels, the descendants of the old Rockers, and the whole scene was laughed at by the new Skinheads, who were the true descendants of the old Mods. After all, it seems likely that most of their elder brothers and sisters had spent their teens down Soho getting blocked on a Saturday night. The wheel had come full circle.

Since that concert, we've learnt to live with Skinheads. They have the same austerity of style as the early Mods, and they hunt in packs like the Mods tracked down the Rockers on the beaches of Margate and Clacton.

Though their style has been determined to a large extent by their opposition to the Hippies, other factors have played a crucial role and, in particular, the impact of the West Indian community. Many of the Skin gangs have West Indians not only in the group but actually leading them, the short hair style having been, without doubt, lifted from the old Blue Beat days in the London clubs.

In Birmingham, a city with a large immigrant community, the pattern is especially evident. The Skins will still profess to hate the niggers, but by 'niggers' they generally mean the Pakistanis. Their hatred of the Pakkis might appear crazily illogical in the light of their friendship with the West Indians, but there is a certain, cruel logic about it. Take the story of Des, a garage worker and a Skin of three years standing.

'I'll tell you why I hate the bloody Paks. I'll tell you a story. A week or so ago I was walking down the street with a couple of mates. I wanted a light for my fag, so I walk up to this Pakki git and ask him, "You got a light, mate?" And what do you think the fucker did? I'll tell you. He walks – no, runs – into this shop and buys me a box of matches! Now, I ask you! What the fuck could I do with a bleeder like that but hit him? And another thing. Have you ever been in their restaurants? Have you seen the way they *grovel* round you, the way they're always trying to please you? I hate them, that's all.'

The next time you go in an Indian restaurant, think of Des's story – and look around at the clientele. You'll find an almost straight *middle-class* content. Des and his mates just go in there for the occasional giggle – all pissed and raring for trouble.

The logic of their hatred is this: the West Indian kids are mixing, and their influence is taking hold. They are beginning to see this country as their home. The Indians and the Pakistanis keep themselves to themselves and in Birmingham interaction between white *working class* and Asian is non-existent. To put it another way, the Indians and the Pakistanis are aspiring (if they are aspiring towards anything whilst they're living here) towards a middle-class set of values. They dress in carefully tailored suits, they are polite, they are *nice*. The West Indian kids on the other hand are more 'normal' in the Skins' eyes. They get drunk, they like dancing, they like dressing up in Skingear. They are willing to join forces.

There's nothing nice about the Skins. And likewise there's nothing nice about their taste in music. They completely reject the music of the counterculture. Nothing is more loathsome to them than the junk of Progressive Rock. Music is for dancing to, Music is for getting off with birds to. And the best music for that, they have decided, is Reggae and Tamla Motown. Their love of this twin spearhead is, of course, a direct legacy of the impact of the West Indians in the late 60s. But their idolization of this music should not be mixed up with the Mods' relationship to their Faces – it's something quite different. For the new relationship is essentially *impersonal*, whereas the Mods related to a set of individual Faces, like Steve Marriot or Rod the Mod Stewart. The Skins relate to *types* of music, like Motown. The Four Tops, to take an example, are not revered for being the Four Tops; they are simply one aspect of the Motown machine. If T Rex has any appeal with this audience, it's on this same impersonal level, a brand name for formula-produced dance records.

Moreover, there's the question of distancing. A group like the Kinks could be seen 'live' every week somewhere round the country because the central factor of the Mod-music scene was the live club appearance. The Skins tend more towards discos, mainly because there are so few British groups they like.

The result of this has been important. Music is still important to the Skins, but it's not of such overriding importance as it was for the Mods. Music, it has been argued, was central to the Mod experience. It dictated style. For the Skinheads, music has become *peripheral*: style is in no way determined by it. If the Skins do have Faces, they are elsewhere and, usually, they are out there playing on the football field.

Disliked in certain quarters for his virtues as much as his faults, George Best has become a cult for youth, a new folk hero, a living James Dean who has become a rebel with no real cause to rebel.

Geoffrey Green, *The Times*, 22 May 1972

Only a few weeks ago, Charlie George scored an important goal at Derby, and then ruined the goal and dragged Arsenal's mighty name through the mud by facing the County crowd and jolting them with a double V-sign. . . . At Ipswich, again just a few weeks ago, he was involved in another unsavoury incident when he refused to retreat the statutory 10 yards from the ball when a Town player took a free kick. . . .

His problems have been likened to those of the other George, Best of Manchester United and Ireland, and his hair is even longer. But there is one essential difference. Best creates headlines almost as much *off* the field. So far at least Charlie George has confined himself to foolishness only during games.

Iain Mackenzie, *Observer*, March 1972

Two views on contemporary soccer idols. Best and George are both relevant to this essay, but for different reasons. George Best is 26 years old, Charlie George 21. They might both be idols (though I doubt whether Best is any more) but they are very different kinds of idols.

George Best's life-style was determined in the Mod's era. His clothes, his hair, his mode of living were decided by Pop. Though he lives in Manchester, he was, and still remains, a swinging Londoner. Indeed, much of his dilemma vis-à-vis soccer probably stems from this: had he been playing this past five years for Arsenal or Spurs he might have managed all right. But, as he's said so often, Manchester's too small for him. Best sees himself as made for the trendy world of boutiques, night clubs, and dolly birds. He's become, though he might not yet realize it, a living anachronism.

Charlie George, on the other hand, fits into none of these patterns. George is, despite the length of his hair, a Skinhead's dream. His focal point, as Iain Mackenzie implies, is on the soccer field. George Best's focal point is in Carnaby Street. The two players are poles apart.

Charlie George is a Skinhead who's made it: George Best is a Face who's lost his public. This being the case, Charlie George's position in Soccer is far more secure than Best's will ever be.

Yoko Ono . . . said that Pop 'Should not alienate the audience with its

381

professionalism, but should communicate to the audience the fact that they can be just as creative as those on stage.'

When the Skins root for Charlie George at Highbury – they are rooting for *themselves*. For Charlie is simply one of them who's happened to make it out there on the stage. They hate the opposition, and so does Charlie. They adore him for his V-signs and his tantrums, just as they adore kicking in the teeth of an enemy fan.

Linking this with Pop is interesting, for analogies suggest themselves with ease. Watching Charlie George at Highbury is, for the Skins, much the same experience as watching the Who at the Railway Hotel in Wealdstone was for the Mods. Or, to cross the Atlantic, the same experience as watching Johnny Cash at San Quentin was for the prison inmates. They are all watching their *equals* acting out their *fantasies*. And they can all hold on to these fantasies because those 'stars' on the stage are just the same as they are.

And this, for the Skinheads, is the great difference between them and the Mods. Their point of reference is different. The Mods were inextricably tied up with Pop. The Skins are inextricably linked with Soccer.

Before we ever heard of Skinheads, we all knew about football hooligans – but it's only in the last three or four years that the problem has come through with any force. And this is simply because the area of 'play' for deviant teenyboppers has changed.

The Skins have changed a lot since that first major public appearance at Hyde Park in 1969. The braces and the cropped hair gave way to the two-tone Trevira suits, and these in turn have given way to crombies, and – for the girls – Oxford bags and check jackets. But their attitude to music hasn't changed that much, nor has their attitude to football. On most crombie jackets, there is the obligatory football club badge, as central to the Skin's uniform as a pocket handkerchief. But on none of their clothes is there any sign of Pop worship.

This, really, is why Marc Bolan isn't as popular as he likes to make out. He's made no positive impression on the Skins at all. Bolan is popular and it would be silly to completely write him off – after all, he has had four No. 1's on the trot – but the basis for his support is very narrowly confined. To be accurate, Marc Bolan is idolized by Grammar School girls between the ages of 11 and 14. (The Skins, who might buy T Rex records to dance to, don't idolize or identify with *Bolan* at all.)

Other groups win support from this 'teenybopper' area and Slade are the best example. Slade, it might be remembered, were, at one time, a Skinhead group though if they ever were really Skins I don't know. But it is a fact that they no longer enjoy much support from that area, if they ever did.

Meanwhile, although previous generation groups like the Stones and the Who can still fill a hall wherever they play, their support is not growing. It's a constant factor; those who have stayed with them through their changes over the past five years aren't giving them up, and they could still fill any of their old haunts if they so desired. But they're winning no new fans, and probably haven't for the last three or four years.

If this analysis is correct, then the Rock perspective that exists is hopelessly out of balance, and has been for some time.

Take, as an example, the Pop Press. Each of the musical papers have latched on to the wrong equation that Rock = Underground, or, when they are feeling patronisingly liberal, Rock = Underground + Teenyboppers. The last couple of years has witnessed the sad spectacle of most of the Pop Press trying desperately to halt their fall in sales by becoming fashionable. The Underground, they have decided, is *where it's at*. So, we have an increasingly one-sided 'too much' 'far out' 'got it together' Pop Press, ever more channelled into the one area where support certainly isn't getting any stronger.

The same, really, with television. *Top of the Pops* clings to the Teenyboppers, and the only alternatives are either 'family entertainment' with Lulu or Cilla, or the Progressive *Old Grey Whistle Test* (served up, it's true, with a good helping of old Rock).

Together, these factors have helped perpetuate the Skins' alienation from Pop.

There have been signs, becoming increasingly evident these past few months, of a change of direction by some of the Skinhead girls – two stars in particular have catapulted to superstar/idol status. At the moment of writing, Donny Osmond is at No. 1 in the charts with *Puppy Love*, and David Cassidy at No. 3 (with the Partridge Family) with *Breaking up is Hard to Do*.

It's appropriate that both of these songs are old 50s material and that the 'new' treatments given them are in essence no different than the original treatment given in the 50s by Paul Anka and Neil Sedaka: appropriate because the relationship between the fans and their idols is very close to that of parallel 50s relationships. When some of the Skinhead girls have finally latched on to Pop idols, they have done it in such a way as to completely invalidate the British 60s experience – there is no greater proof of the ephemeral success of the Beatles era than the idolisation of pretty boys like Cassidy and Osmond.

But the boys that these girls go around with – rather than the images they idolize – remain outside the Pop experience, and it's this that strikes at the heart of Rock. The bovver boys look like becoming the first major sub-cultural group not to produce any major rock stars! They, for Rock, are the lost generation.

The survival of Rock has depended on its position as the core of *Male* Teen Culture. But the bovver boys have rejected Rock's traditional status which explains the lack of vitality in British rock in the early 70s.

Rock File, edited by Charlie Gillett (1972)

1972: The Twelfth Floor

Long before journalists discovered the discotheques of Manhattan, long before they became another possession of the middle class, in the beginning, that particular autumn, two gentlemen whose names I forget opened up a little club on the twelfth floor of a factory building in the West Thirties. The West Thirties, after dark, form a lunar landscape: the streets that are crowded with men running racks of clothes down the sidewalk during the day, and trucks honking at each other to get through the narrow passage-ways of factory exits, are completely deserted at night. The place is as still as the oceans of the moon. The buildings are all dark. There isn't a soul in sight – not a bum, a mugger, or a cop. But late on Friday and Saturday nights, around one a.m., flotillas of taxis would pull up to a certain dim doorway and deliver their passengers who, on showing a numbered card, would go up in a freight elevator to the twelfth floor. Everyone who went there that first year agrees: there was never anything before or since so wonderful.

In a town where clubs open and close in a week, no one expected it to last more than one winter. The second year it was too famous, and too many people wished to go. Film stars and rock stars, and photographers, and rich Parisians, and women from Dallas came to look, and it was finished. There were arguments in the lobby about who was whose guest, and there were too many drugs; and toward the end of it, I used to just sit on the sofa in the back and watch the crowd.

The first year contained the thrill of newness, and the thrill of exclusivity – that all these people who might not even know each other, but who knew who each other were, had been brought together in the winter, in this little room, without having done a single thing to bring it about. They all knew each other without ever having been introduced. They found a group of people who had danced with each other over the years, gone to the same parties, the same beaches on the same trains, yet, in some cases, never even nodded at each other. They were bound together by a common love of a certain kind of music, physical beauty, and style – all the things one shouldn't throw away an ounce of energy pursuing, and sometimes throw away a life pursuing.

Within this larger group – for some of them came but once a month, or twice all season – was a core of people who seemed to have no existence at all outside this room. They were never home, it seemed, but lived only in the ceaseless flow of this tiny society's movements. They seldom looked happy. They passed one another without word in the elevator, like silent shades in hell, hell-bent on their next look from a handsome stranger. Their next rush from a popper. The next song that turned their bones to jelly and left them all on the dance floor with heads back, eyes nearly closed, in the ecstasy of saints receiving the stigmata. They pursued these things with such devotion that they acquired, after a few seasons, a haggard look, a look of deadly seriousness. Some wiped everything they could off their faces and reduced themselves to blanks. Yet even these, when you entered the hallway where they stood waiting to go in, would turn toward you all at once in that one unpremeditated moment (as when we see ourselves in a mirror we didn't know was there), the same look on all their faces: take me away from this. Or, Love me. If there had been a prison for such desperadoes, you would have called the police and had them all arrested – just to get them out of these redundant places and give them a rest.

There was a moment when their faces blossomed into the sweetest happiness, however – when everyone came together in a single lovely communion that was the reason they did all they did; and that occurred around six-thirty in the morning, when they took off their sweat-soaked T-shirts and screamed because Patty Jo had begun to sing: 'Make me believe in you, show me that love can be true.' By then the air was half-nauseating with the stale stench of poppers, broken and dropped on the floor after their fumes had been sucked into the heart, and the odor of sweat, and ethyl chloride from the rags they clamped between their teeth, holding their friends' arms to keep from falling. The people on downs were hardly able to move, and the others rising from the couches where they had been sprawled like martyrs who have given up their souls to Christ pushed onto the floor and united in the cries of animal joy because Patty Jo had begun to sing in her metallic, unreal voice those signal words: 'Make me believe in you, show me that love can be true.'

(Or because the discaire had gone from Barrabas's 'Woman' to Zulema's

'Giving Up', or the Temptations' 'Law of the Land'. Any memory of those days is nothing but a string of songs.)

When the people finally left, the blood-red sun was perched in the fire escape of a factory building silhouetted on the corner, and the cornices of the buildings were all gold-edged, and they would strip off their T-shirts, in the cold fall morning, and wring them out over the gutter. And the sweat would fall into the gutter like water dripping from a pail, the sweat of athletes after a long and sweaty game of soccer on some playing field to the north, on a fall day as pure as this one; and they would walk up Broadway together, exhausted, ecstatic, their bones light as a bird's, a flotilla of doomed queens on their way to the Everard Baths because they could not come down from the joy and happiness.

They looked, these young men gazing up toward the sky with T-shirts hanging from their belts, like athletes coming from a game, like youths coming home from school, their dark eyes glowing with light, their faces radiant and no one passing them would have gathered the reason for this happy band.

Toward the end, I used to sit on the sofa in the back of the Twelfth Floor and wonder. Many of them were very attractive, these young men whose cryptic disappearance in New York City their families (unaware they were homosexual) understood less than if they had been killed in a car wreck. They were tall and broad-shouldered, with handsome, open faces and strong white teeth, and they were all dead. They lived only to bathe in the music, and each other's desire, in a strange democracy whose only ticket of admission was physical beauty – and not even that sometimes. All else was strictly classless: the boy passed out on the sofa from an overdose of Tuinols was a Puerto Rican who washed dishes in the employees' cafeteria at CBS, but the doctor bending over him had treated presidents. It was a democracy such as the world – with its rewards and penalties, its competition, its snobbery – never permits, but which flourished in this little room on the twelfth floor of a factory building on west Thirty-third Street, because its central principle was the most anarchic of all; erotic love.

What a carnival of people. One fellow came directly from his tour of duty in the Emergency Room at Bellevue on Saturday nights, and danced in his white coat sprinkled with blood. A handsome blond man whom the nation saw on its television sets almost every day eating a nutritious cereal, came to stand by the doorway to the bathroom, waiting for someone to go in whose piss he could drink. Chatting with him was a famous drug dealer from the Upper East Side who was sending his son through Choate and his daughter through Foxcroft, and who always dressed like a gangster from the forties. They were talking to a rich art collector, who one day had resolved to leave all this, had cursed it and gone to the Orient the next day to live there; within a year he had reappeared standing beside the dance floor, because, as he told his friends, Angkor Wat was not nearly so beautiful as the sight of Luis Sanchez dancing to 'Law of the Land' with his chest glistening with sweat and a friend stuffing a rag soaked with ethyl chloride into his mouth.

The art collector walked up to talk to a handsome architect who had also tried to escape this room and the life, and society, which flowed out from it, as a river does from a spring. He had decided one night he was dissipating himself, he had looked in the mirror and decided he was going to waste physically. And so he bought a car and drove west till he found a little shack high in a mountain pass with not a single mirror in the house. Four months of snow, and two of flowers, in the pure mountain air, however, did not arrest the progress of these physical flaws. They were age itself. And so one morning in May, with flowers on the meadows and the valley beneath him, he decided to go back to Manhattan and rot with all the beauties in this artificial hothouse of music and light. For what was this room but a place to forget we are dying? There were people so blessed with beauty there they did not know what to do with it. And so the doctor who came direct from the Emergency Room (whose dark, bearded face was that of a fifteenth-century Spanish saint), the archangelic son of a famous actress, the man who had driven west to leave time behind, breathed now the air of Olympus: everyone was a god, and no one grew old in a single night. No, it took years for that to happen . . .

For what does one do with Beauty – that oddest, most irrational of careers? There were boys in that room, bank tellers, shoe salesmen, clerks, who had been given faces and forms so extraordinary that they constituted a vocation of their own. They rushed out each night to simply stand in rooms about the city, exhibiting themselves to view much as the priest on Holy Saturday throws open the doors of the Tabernacle to expose the chalice within.

Nevertheless Malone, the night Frankie nearly beat him up on the sidewalk outside the Twelfth Floor (a commotion I was unaware of long after it had occurred, since I had arrived early that night to watch the place fill up with dancers and hear the music that began the whole night, as an overture begins an opera, and that the dancers never heard) and had to be taken off by the police, had by that time come to loathe being looked at; could not bear the gaze of amorous strangers; and the only reason he came out at all, during that period after he left Frankie, when he wanted to go away and hide forever, was the crazy compulsion with which we resolved all the tangled impulses of our lives – the need to dance.

Everyone there, in fact, like Malone, was a serious dancer and they were by no means beautiful: Archer Prentiss, who had no chin or hair; Spanish Lily, a tiny, wizened octoroon who lived with his blind mother in The Bronx and sold shoes in a local store – but who by night resembled Salome dancing for the head of John the Baptist in peach-colored veils; Lavalava, a Haitian boy who modeled for *Vogue* till an editor saw him in the dressing room with an enormous penis where a vagina should have been; another man famous for a film he had produced and who had no wish to do anything else with his life – all of them mixed together on that square of blond wood and danced, without looking at anyone else, for one another.

They were the most romantic creatures in the city in that room. If their days were spent in banks and office buildings, no matter: their true lives began when they walked through this door – and were baptized into a deeper faith, as if brought to life by miraculous immersion. They lived only for the night. The most beautiful Oriental was in fact chaste, as the handmaidens of Dionysius were: he came each night to avoid the eyes of everyone who wanted him (though for different reasons than Malone ignored their gaze), and after dancing for hours in a band of half-naked men, went home alone each night refusing to tinge the exhilaration in his heart with the actuality of carnal kisses. The gossips said he refused to sleep with people because he had a small penis – the leprosy of homosexuals – but this explanation was mundane: he wanted to keep this life in the realm of the perfect, the ideal. He wanted to be desired, not possessed, for in remaining desired he remained, like the figure on the Grecian urn, forever pursued. He knew quite well that once possessed he would no longer be enchanted – so sex itself became secondary to the spectacle: that single moment of walking in that door. And even as he danced now he was aware of whose heart he was breaking; everyone there was utterly aware of one another.

For example: I sat on the sofa watching Archer Prentiss dance with two other men in plaid shirts and moustaches, who looked as if they had just come down from the Maine woods – two people I had seen for years and years, yet never said a word to, as was the case with Archer Prentiss. This technical distance did not keep us from knowing a great deal about each other, however. Although I had no idea who the two strangers on my left were, nor had ever been introduced to Archer Prentiss, I knew, to the quarter inch, the length and diameter of each one's penis, and exactly what they liked to do in bed.

But then so did everyone else in that room.

If one of the figures in this tapestry of gossip woven at the Twelfth Floor vanished – like the man who fled to Cambodia, or the one who drove west – such a disappearance was, in that crowd, less mysterious than most vanishing acts. If a face in that crowd vanished, it was usually for one of three reasons: (1) he was dead, (2) he had moved to another city whose inhabitants he had not all slept with, or (3) he had found a lover and settled down, spending his Saturday nights at home with his mate, going over the plans of the house they hoped to build in Teaneck, New Jersey.

The two strangers in plaid shirts who had sat down on the sofa to my left were discussing at that moment such a move. The big, blond fellow (whose face decorated a dozen billboards on the Long Island Expressway, smiling at a Winston cigarette) said to the dark one: 'He wants me to move in with him, after he comes back from Portugal.'

'Oh, God, he lives on Beekman Place, doesn't he?'

'Yes, but Howard lives off Sutton, and he wants me to move in, too. Damn, I don't know what to do.'

'Marry John! Sutton Place is all Jewish dentists.'

And they burst into laughter over their solution to this problem: while at the next instant, the creature who, for a reason I could not put my finger on, fascinated me more than any of the habitués of that place came in the door: Sutherland. He swept in trailing a strange coterie of Egyptian cotton heiresses, the most popular male model to come over from Paris in a decade, a Puerto Rican drug dealer, and an Italian prince. Sutherland was dressed in a black Norell, turban, black pumps, rhinestones, and veil. He held a long cigarette holder to his lips and vanished among the crowd. The dark man began to debate idly whether he should go to bed with Archer Prentiss, who was (a) very ugly, but (b) had a big dick.

In the midst of their deliberations, Zulema's 'Giving Up' suddenly burst out of the recapitulations of Deodato, and the two woodsmen got up to dance; at their rising, two other boys in black with tired, beautiful eyes, sat down immediately and began discussing the men who had just left: 'I call him the Pancake Man,' said one. '*He* doesn't use makeup!' said the other. 'Oh, no,' the first replied. 'The opposite! Because he's the kind of man you imagine waking up with on Saturday morning, and he makes pancakes for you, and then you take the dog out for a walk in the park. And he always has a moustache, and he always wears plaid shirts!'

'I agree he's gorgeous,' said his friend, 'but someone told me he has the smallest wee-wee in New York.'

And with that, as if the boy had snapped his fingers, the big, blond woodsman standing by the dance floor in all his radiant masculinity, crumbled into dust.

'Oh please,' said the one, 'I don't need that.' He covered his face with his hands. 'I'm already on downs, why did you say that?'

'Because it's true,' said the other.

'Oh, God,' the first moaned, in the nasal wail of Brooklyn, 'oh, God, I can't believe that. No, he's my Pancake Man.'

'They *all* wear plaid shirts, and they all have moustaches,' said his friend. 'You might as well pick one with a big dick. None of them will look at you, anyway.'

He looked out between his fingers at the woodsman, who was now talking animatedly to Sutherland in his black Norell and turban and long cigarette holder, and said, 'Who is that woman he's talking to?' And the other side: 'Her name is Andrew Sutherland, and she lives on Madison Avenue. She's a speed freak. She hasn't long to live.' At that moment, 'Needing You' began, buried still in the diminishing chords of 'You've Got Me Waiting for the Rain to Fall', and the two boys on the sofa – with hearing sharper than a coyote's, and without even needing to ask each other – bounded up off the sofa and headed for the dance floor. Instantly their seats were taken by an older, gray-haired man and his friend, an even older fellow who because of his hearing aid, toupee, and back brace was known among the younger queens as Spare Parts. 'I find him so beautiful,' said the man of the boy who had just left, 'like a Kabuki, that long neck, those heavy-lidded eyes. He never looks at me, do you think because he's afraid?' They began to discuss a friend on the dance floor who had recently learned he had cancer of the lungs. 'No, no,' said Spare Parts, 'he has cancer of the colon, I think, his mother has cancer of the lungs.' 'Yes,' said the friend, 'he used to scream at his mother for smoking too much, and she used to scream at him for eating too fast. And now look.' 'He flies out to the clinic tomorrow,' said Spare Parts. 'Do you suppose he wants to go home with someone?' 'You know,' said the friend, 'I would think the fact that he's dying would give him the courage to walk up to all these boys he's been in love with all these years but never had the nerve to say hello to.' 'Well, he has a look about him,' said Spare Parts. 'He looks . . . ethereal.' At that moment two Puerto Rican boys, oblivious to everything but their own heated discussion, stopped to snuff out their cigarettes in the ashtray beside the sofa.

'And the reason you don't know any English,' the one said suddenly in English to his friend, 'is because you waste too much time chasing dick!'

And they hurried off into the crowd, the accused defending himself excitedly in rapid Spanish to his friend.

The gray-haired man on the sofa rolled his eyes, sighed a long sigh as he snuffed out his own cigarette in the ashtray, and said: 'My dear, whole *lives* have been wasted chasing dick.' He sat up suddenly. 'Oh!' he said. 'There's that song!'

At that moment, 'One Night Affair' was beginning to rise from the ruins of 'Needing You', and they both put down their plastic cups of apple juice and started towards the dance floor.

Andrew Holleran, Dancer from the Dance (1978)

1972: Oh You Pretty Thing

Even though he wasn't wearing silken gowns right out of Liberty's, and his long blond hair no longer fell wavily past his shoulders David Bowie was looking yummy.

He'd slipped into an elegant-patterned type of combat suit, very tight around the legs, with the shirt unbuttoned to reveal a full expanse of white torso. The trousers were turned up at the calves to allow a better glimpse of a huge pair of red plastic boots with at least three-inch rubber soles; and the hair was Vidal Sassooned into such impeccable shape that one held one's breath in case the slight breeze from the open window dared to ruffle it. I wish you could have been there to varda him; he was so super.

David uses words like 'varda' and 'super' quite a lot. He's gay, he says. Mmmmmm. A few months back, when he played Hampstead's Country Club, a small greasy club in north London which has seen all sorts of exciting occasions, about half the gay population of the city turned up to see him in his massive floppy velvet hat, which he twirled around at the end of each number.

According to Stuart Lyon, the club's manager, a little gay brother sat right up close to the stage throughout the whole evening, absolutely spellbound with admiration.

As it happens, David doesn't have much time for Gay Liberation, however. That's a particular movement he doesn't want to lead. He despises all these tribal qualifications. Flower power he employed, but it's individuality that he's really trying to preserve. The paradox is that he still has what he describes as 'a good relationship' with his wife. And his baby son, Zowie. He supposes he's what people call bisexual.

They call David a lot of things. In the States he's been referred to as the English Bob Dylan and an avant-garde outrage all rolled up together. The *New York Times* talks of his 'coherent and brilliant vision'. They like him a lot there. Back home, in the very stiff upper lip UK, where people are outraged by Alice Cooper even, there ain't too many who have picked up on him. His last but one album, *The Man Who Sold the World*, cleared 50,000 copies in the States; here it sold about five copies, and Bowie bought them.

Yes, but before this year is out all those of you who puked up on Alice are going to be focusing your passions on Mr Bowie and those who know where it's at will be thrilling to a voice that seemingly undergoes brilliant metamorphosis from song to song, a songwriting ability that will enslave the heart, and a sense of theatrics that will make the ablest thespians gnaw on their sticks of eyeliner in envy. All this and an amazingly accomplished band, featuring super-lead guitarist Mick Ronson, that can smack you round the skull with their heaviness and soothe the savage breast with their delicacy. Oh, to be young again.

The reason is Bowie's new album, *Hunky Dory*, which combines a gift for irresistible melody lines with lyrics that work on several levels – as straight-forward narrative, philosophy or allegory, depending how deep you wish to plumb the depths. He has a knack of suffusing strong, simple pop melodies with words and arrangements full of mystery and darkling hints.

Thus 'Oh! You Pretty Things', the Peter Noone hit, is on one strata, particularly the chorus, about the feelings of a father-to-be; on a deeper level it concerns Bowie's belief in a superhuman race – homo superior – to which he refers obliquely: 'I think about a world to come/where the books were found by The Golden Ones/Written in pain, written in awe/by a puzzled man who questioned what we were here for/Oh, The Strangers Came Today, and it looks as though they're here to stay.' The idea of Peter Noone singing such a heavy number fills me with considerable amusement. That's truly outrageous, as David says himself.

But then Bowie has an instinct for incongruities: On *The Man* album there's a bit at the end of 'Black Country Rock' where he superbly parodies his friend Marc Bolan's vibrato warblings. On *Hunky Dory* he devotes a track called 'Queen Bitch' to the Velvets, wherein he takes off to a tee the Lou Reed vocal and arrangement, as well as parodying, with a storyline about the singer's boyfriend being seduced by another queen, the whole Velvet Underground genre.

Then again, at various times on his albums he resorts to a very broad Cockney accent, as on 'Savior Machine' (*The Man*) and here with 'The Bewley Brothers'. He says he copped it off Tony Newley, because he was mad about 'Stop the World' and 'Gurney Slade': 'He used to make his points with this broad Cockney accent and I decided that I'd use that now and again to drive a point home.'

The fact that Bowie has an acute ear for parody doubtless stems from an innate sense of theatre. He says he's more an actor and entertainer than a musician; that he may, in fact, only be an actor and nothing else: 'Inside this invincible frame there might be an invisible man.' You kidding? 'Not at all. I'm not particularly taken with life. I'd probably be very good as just an astral spirit.'

Bowie is talking in an office at Gem Music, from where his management operates. A tape machine is playing his next album, *The Rise and Fall of Ziggy Stardust and the Spiders from Mars*, which is about this fictitious pop group. The music has got a very hard-edged sound like *The Man Who Sold the World*. They're releasing it shortly, even though *Hunky Dory* has only just come out.

Everyone just knows that David is going to be a lollapalooza of a superstar throughout the entire world this year, David more than most. His songs are always ten years ahead of their time, he says, but this year he has anticipated the trends: 'I'm going to be huge and it's quite frightening in a way,' he says, his big red boots stabbing the air in time to the music. 'Because I know that when I reach my peak and it's time for me to be brought down it will be with a bump.'

The man who's sold the world this prediction has had a winner before, of course. Remember 'Space Oddity', which chronicled Major Tom's dilemma, aside from boosting the sales of the stylophone? That was a top ten hit in '68, but since then Bowie has hardly performed at all in public. He appeared for a while at an arts lab. he co-founded in Beckenham, Kent, where he lives, but when he realized that people were going there on a Friday night to see Bowie the hit singer working out, rather than for any idea of experimental art, he seems to have become disillusioned. That project foundered, and he wasn't up to going out on one-nighters throughout the country at that particular time.

So in the past three years he has devoted his time to the production of three albums, *David Bowie* (which contains *Space Oddity*) and *The Man* for Philips, and *Hunky Dory* for RCA. His first album, *Love You Till Tuesday*, was released in 1968 on the new Deram label but it didn't sell outstandingly, and Decca, it seems, lost interest in him.

It all began for him, though, when he was 15 and his brother gave him a copy of Gerry Mulligan's autobiography. Wanting to play an instrument he took up sax because that was the main instrument featured in the book (Gerry Mulligan, right?). So in '63 he was playing tenor in a London R and B band before going on to found a semi-pro progressive blues group, called David Jones and The Lower Third (later changing his name in '66 when Davy Jones of The Monkees became famous). He left this band in 1967 and became a performer in the folk clubs.

Since he was 14, however, he had been interested in Buddhism and Tibet, and after the failure of his first LP he dropped out of music completely and devoted his time to the Tibet Society, whose aim was to help the lamas driven out of that country in the Tibetan/Chinese war. He was instrumental in setting up the Scottish monastery in Dumfries in this period. He says, in fact, that he would have liked to have been a Tibetan monk, and would have done if he hadn't met Lindsay Kemp, who ran a mime company in London: 'It was as magical as Buddhism, and I completely sold out and became a city creature. I suppose that's when my interest in image really blossomed.'

David's present image is to come on like a swishy queen, a gorgeously effeminate boy. He's as camp as a row of tents, with his limp hand and trolling vocabulary. 'I'm gay,' he says, 'and always have been; even when I was David Jones.' But there's a sly jollity about how he says it, a secret smile at the corners of his mouth. He knows that in these times it's permissible to act like a male tart, and that to shock and outrage, which pop has always striven to do throughout its history, is a balls-breaking process.

And if he's not an outrage, he is, at the least, an amusement. The expression of his sexual ambivalence establishes a fascinating game: is he, or isn't he? In a period of conflicting sexual identity he shrewdly exploits the confusion surrounding the male and female roles. 'Why aren't you wearing your girl's dress today?' I said to him (he has no monopoly on tongue-in-cheek humour). 'Oh dear,' he replied, 'you must understand that it's not a woman's. It's a man's dress.'

He began wearing dresses, of whatever gender, two years ago, but he says he had done outrageous things before that were just not accepted by society. It's just so happened, he remarks, that in the past two years people have loosened up to the fact that there are bisexuals in the world – 'and – horrible fact – homosexuals'. He smiles, enjoying his piece of addenda. '

'The important fact is that I don't have to drag up. I want to go on like this for long after the fashion has finished. I'm just a cosmic yob, I suppose. I've always worn my own style of clothes. I design them. I designed this.' He broke off to indicate with his arm what he was wearing. 'I just don't like the clothes that you buy in shops. I don't wear dresses all the time, either. I change every day. I'm not outrageous. I'm David Bowie.'

How does dear Alice go down with him, I asked, and he shook his head disdainfully: 'Not at all. I bought his first album, but it didn't excite me or shock me. I think he's trying to be outrageous. You can see him, poor dear, with his red eyes sticking out and his temples straining. He tries so hard. That bit he does with the boa constrictor, a friend of mine, Rudy Valentino, was doing ages before. The next thing I see is Miss C. with her boa. I find him very demeaning. It's very premeditated, but quite fitting with our era. He's probably more successful than I am at present, but I've invented a new category of artist, with my chiffon and taff. They call it pantomime rock in the States.'

Despite his flouncing, however, it would be sadly amiss to think of David merely as a kind of glorious drag act. An image, once strained and stretched unnaturally, will ultimately diminish an artist. And Bowie is just that. He foresees this potential dilemma, too, when he says he doesn't want to emphasize his external self much more. He has enough image. This year he is devoting most of his time to stage work and records. As he says, that's what counts at the death. He will stand or fall on his music.

As a songwriter he doesn't strike me as an intellectual, as he does some. Rather, his ability to express a theme from all aspects seems intuitive. His songs are less carefully structured thoughts than the outpourings of the unconscious. He says he rarely tries to communicate to himself, to think an idea out.

'If I see a star and it's red I wouldn't try to say why it's red. I would think how shall I best describe to X that that star is such a colour. I don't question much; I just relate. I see my answers in other people's writings. My own work can be compared to talking to a psychoanalyst. My act is my couch.'

It's because his music is rooted in this lack of consciousness that he admires Syd Barrett so much. He believes that Syd's freewheeling approach to lyrics opened the gates for him; both of them, he thinks, are the creation of their own songs. And if Barrett made that initial breakthrough, it's Lou Reed and Iggy Pop who have since kept him going and helped him to expand his unconsciousness. He and Lou and Iggy, he says, are going to take over the whole world. They're the songwriters he admires.

His other great inspiration is mythology. He has a great need to believe in the legends of the past, particularly those of Atlantis; and for the same need he has created a myth of the future, a belief in an imminent race of supermen called homo superior. It's his only glimpse of hope, he says – 'all the things that we can't do they will'.

It's a belief created out of resignation with the way society in general has moved. He's not very hopeful about the future of the world. A year ago he was saying that he gave mankind another 40 years. A track on his next album, outlining his conviction, is called 'Five Years'. He's a fatalist, a confirmed pessimist, as you can see.

'Pretty Things', that breezy Herman song, links this fatalistic attitude with the glimmer of hope that he sees in the birth of his son, a sort of poetic equation of homo superior. 'I think,' he says, 'that we have created a new kind of person in a way. We have created a child who will be so exposed to the media that he will be lost to his parents by the time he is 12.'

That's exactly the sort of technological vision that Stanley Kubrick foresees for the near future in *A Clockwork Orange*. Strong stuff. And a long, long way away from camp carry-ons.

Don't dismiss David Bowie as a serious musician just because he likes to put us all on a little.

Michael Watts, *Melody Maker*, 22 January 1972

1973: 'Jolly Green Men'

Johnny Holland nudged Peter Acroyd in the ribs. 'Pass the word along. Get ready!' His gaze never left the stage. Never seemed to wander from Scrambled doing their act.

Down their row the 'Jolly Green Men' and spare Roundheads bent forward expectantly. They'd all been waiting for an order. For some upper-echelon remark relating to the forthcoming assault, not just a comment about this or that performance.

Gloria Derrick sighed, shifted until her thigh was plastered against Johnny's. 'Can't I . . .?' she started to ask.

'No! Bleedin' hell, must I go through this again!' Johnny tore his eyes from Scrambled's energetic number. 'I've told you – this is for the blokes. Just the blokes!' He glanced down at her thigh. 'And quit that, too! I'm not interested.'

Peter whispered against the sound bursting from the walls: 'They're set, Johnny. Say when . . . and how!'

Johnny viewed the front facing security men. They appeared to have the stage effectively blocked off from the screaming, jumping, hand clapping teeny boppers. Other guards along the Discodrome's curved walls carried whistles – warning devices to alert a stand-by force, no doubt.

He had paid attention to how the guards worked back and forth along the stage forecourt. Watched how they moved in groups to head off sections of the audience showing signs of erupting into unmanageable mobs.

'When Bobby Sharp starts singing there's gonna be some movement,' he said over the music's blare. He paused waiting for those nearest to get their heads closer. 'I want us to move with the girls. Right down front. To the left of centre . . .'

Bruce Barnes studied the situation. 'Christ, Johnny – that's the spot they're really guarding!'

Johnny nodded eagerly. 'Yeah – and that's their weakest link. Look . . .' His finger jabbed air. 'See the way those girls have a wedge in there?'

A group of schoolgirls all wearing the same uniform formed an arrowhead near the place. They didn't seem bent on rushing the performers. Just swooning every time one of the group gyrated his hips or tossed long hair in their direction.

'Well,' Johnny continued as if this was a military operation and he the general in command. Which, in a sense, he was! 'Well,' again, 'those blokes ain't going to be worried. They've got their lot in hand. But when the bloody Discodrome explodes they'll spread.'

Bruce grinned. 'Yeah, they will – won't they!'

'I want you guys to cover us,' Johnny told his Roundheads. 'Give 'em the boot! Start an aggro . . .' He rubbed his palms down his trousers. 'They're big but big balls make a lovely target!'

The Roundheads laughed.

The Jolly Green Men laughed.

Only Gloria Derrick didn't laugh.

She didn't want to knock Johnny's plan but she wondered if the security heavy mob would let a bunch of kids wearing boots get near enough to inflict damage.

Steve Morash fondled Carole Latham's bottom and whispered, 'We'll leave here right after the show.'

'I've promised Bobby I'll go back with him!'

Steve glared, dropped his hand from her flesh. 'You what?'

'Jasmyn doesn't want a repeat,' Carole murmured. 'I volunteere

'You crazy bitch! Didn't we have it off good?'

'Yeah, sure – but it's Bobby I really want.'

'There's no understanding taste,' Steve growled and left the girl
the wings. Any respect he had for Carole vanished in a twinkling
rate Bobby as an equal in the love-making department. In fact, he
Bobby for more than a temporary meal-ticket.

Already, Steve was wrestling with the deployment of his 'arouse
next tour stop. Becky deserved a prime territory for her efforts. Ja
Carole always did an excellent job but his current mood gave Ja
advantage of 'soft' regions.

He halted, caught sight of Bobby emerging from his three-star
room. The teeny bopper idol's gaudy costume brought back men
triumph. And tribulation. Triumph in the States. Tribulation w
goddamned fan had spotted the outfit showing from under Bobby's
on his stage door arrival.

God, he could kill the little bastard for that!

Bobby strutted towards Steve, cocky to the last. Sequins glistene
gear, the mauves and purples royally declaring this was the king
boppers.

'You're next,' Steve grated.

'Man, ain't you late tellin' me?'

Steve's fist formed, unclenched. 'Wipe that smug smile off your face
I smash you!'

'You know,' and Bobby's stiffened finger jabbed relentlessly at
chest, 'when we get back home I'm gonna hire Murder Incorporated to
you, man.'

'They'd like you for free,' Steve shot back. His arm brushed Bobby's
'What's this I hear about you and Carole? Wasn't Jasmyn enough?'

'That bitch!' Bobby spat. 'She hates me. She's gotta get her ass kicked
my scene!'

Steve smiled mysteriously. 'Didn't she wear your kookie tricks?'

A stagehand came rushing up. 'You're call, Mister Sharp ...' His
fastened worshipfully on Bobby's face. A face that changed from undisg
hate for his agent to charm for the man.

'I'll be there directly ...'

The stagehand darted away.

Steve mimicked Bobby's personality role. From normal to assur
'Christ, ain't we wonderful,' he lisped.

'Get offa my back, man,' the idol yelled.

'Is that what Jasmyn said?'

Bobby glared. He detested his deviationist tactics spoken aloud where sympathetic souls could overhear. He wanted the image of a typical, decent young American to remain inviolate.

'You bastard!' Steve hissed.

'It takes one to know one,' Bobby said after a pause. Striding off, he wondered if his comeback had been original. When he decided it wasn't his temper rose. Enough to slam past his backing group without the customary smile, the encouraging word, the star's willingness to admit, in privacy, that he owed them a debt of gratitude.

'Christ, who the hell . . .'

Josh Getz, drummer, placed a hand on Carl Tucson's shoulder. 'Let the bastard rot in hell,' he growled. 'We get paid.'

Carl shrugged off the smooth hand. 'One day . . .' he threatened.

'One day,' Josh grinned, 'we'll be tops of the pops. On the "Lucky Strike Hit Parade" . . .'

'I smoke Camels,' Carl replied and, smiling away his ire, followed Bobby on stage.

The scream ripped through Discodrome.

'*BOBBY . . . BOBBY . . . BOBBY . . .*'

'Ohhhh!'

'Aroooo!'

'Bobby – don't ever leave me!'

'Kiss me, Bobby . . .'

'My darling . . .'

Johnny Holland witnessed the scene as one who wanted the adoration for himself. The last girl had almost fainted when she cried 'My darling . . .'

His gaze centered on Bobby Sharp. On the uniform . . . *The uniform* . . .

'Jesus – I got it!'

Peter and Bruce danced out of Johnny's way.

'I got the bloody bloke's number!' Johnny shouted.

Peter shrugged as Bruce tried to figure out what was wrong. They were supposed to rush the stage. Now . . .

'Look at his gear,' Johnny yelled above the deafening roar for the star of this and any other show. 'Look at it!'

Peter looked.

Bruce looked.

Gloria, Mike, Bill, Walter, Ted, George, Frank, Ian, Sam, Jim, Victor, Larry, Bob all looked.

'A bleedin' load of sparklers,' Peter said.

Gloria squinted, tried to catch what Johnny had caught. She knew enough to recognize the signs. There had to be something about that outfit . . .

'I see it!' Gloria screamed. She did a little jig. 'I bloody see it!'

Johnny grinned triumphantly.

'The name,' Gloria chanted. 'Bobby Sharp . . . and . . .' She shielded her eyes from the fifteen spots focusing on the star. 'And . . . *I got it!*'

'L-O-V-E!' Johnny said.

'LOVE,' Gloria repeated.

Johnny grunted, drew Peter and Bruce into his tight circle of confidants. 'He's got bleedin' L-O-V-E stitched in fuckin' sequins onto his gear!'

The Roundheads squinted, narrowed their eyes, tried to see what their leader had seen. Some did. Some didn't. The Sharp regalia had been designed by experts. By men paid a fantastic sum to transmit a message that registered in the subconscious. Not the conscious. Men determined to circumvent government decrees. Men beyond the fringe of commercialism's decency. Men recruited by an astute Steve Morash to *implant* a LOVE relationship even if the by-product of that same commercialism happened to be a detestable little bastard!

'Now what?' Bruce asked, shattered by Johnny's discovery.

'We wait,' Johnny snapped. 'We wait for the last number. OUR NUMBER . . .' He chuckled.

Gloria looked down at the wedge which had broken under security pressure. 'They've beat us, Johnny,' she wailed.

'Like shit,' Johnny hollered. He pointed at the right of stage area which now supported screaming teeny boppers doing their nut for Bobby. 'You stir 'em up. Get 'em ravin' like hell.'

Gloria welcomed a chance to show her worth. She kicked, battered, clawed her way past bouncing, happy fans. She understood. A strain here. A strain there. And the security boys would be hard put to offer solidified resistance to Johnny's determined attack . . .

Alan Foxx still did not feel in any way, shape or form that the reception for Bobby Sharp had progressed beyond live television's capabilities to handle. In the obviously hysterical reaction to Bobby's appearance on stage he found a new dimension. A new format. His guest at that crucial moment was none other than fandoms greatest exponent of the publicity barb. The ever-effervescent and ever controversial Arthur Kyle. He of the frock coat, the opera-topper, the cape and cane.

'You have been linked with many causes and many changes in the pop scene. You're an exponent of self-expression. Can you honestly state that this . . .' and Alan generously covered the background shots with a magnanimous wave, 'is typical of today's youth. That this is a teeny bopper world gone stark, raving crazy?'

Kyle adjusted his monacle, presented his silver-headed cane for viewing dissention and tilted his topper. A shock of golden hair tumbled forth. 'I say this is what young people want,' he pontificated. 'Bobby Sharp is just an example of liberation. Sexual liberation. Parliament talks about free contraceptives for the poor, the deprived. Who is more deprived than today's younger girls? They need a legislation aimed to encourage adolescent awareness . . .'

Alan Foxx's face showed where he stood on Kyle's issue. 'You misunderstood my question, Arther . . .'

'I didn't, you know,' the man replied. 'I'm taking this golden opportunity to bring home to every parent the need for daughters to have The Pill, to have . . .'

Foxx rebelled. Drastically. 'I'm a parent, sir . . .' he interrupted sharply. 'I wouldn't want my daughter to be on The Pill at age fourteen. Or fifteen. Not even at sixteen.'

'Why not?' Kyle cut in quickly. 'She would be subhuman if she didn't have an awakening of sexual desire. Like those girls out there. They're opting for Bobby Sharp because he represents the best choice for the release of masturbatory . . .'

Alan Foxx coughed, erased the final innuendo. His voice, when it rose above Kyle's, sounded strained. 'Thanks, Arthur. You've been an invaluable help in understanding this phenomenon . . . or should that be phenomena?'

The phenomenon exploded in Alan Foxx's eyes. In Wilf Russell's eyes. In Charles Treffry's eyes. In some four million viewers' eyes.

Suddenly, as if catapulted from top-secret rocket installations, Johnny and his men charged. Broke through the security veneer. Gained the stage.

A frantic signal reached Alan Foxx and he swung to catch the spreading disease . . .

Johnny sensed the magic of being in front of an audience. On stage. He charged forward, sent Bobby Sharp flying as he grabbed the mike. He swung, saw his 'Jolly Green Men' take care of their instrumental opposites. He glowed. This was it . . .

Alan Foxx wanted to cut his throat. All their careful planning. All their taking into account of the endless probabilities. All Gerstein's self-praising security precautions. All blown. Gone for a burton.

Phyllis Shankley almost threw a fit. Her eyes popped and she forgot that the monitor carried the scene. She wheeled on her chair, stared through the plate-glass window separating the television discussion from the Disco-drome's continuous activities. 'My God,' she gasped. 'It's a happening . . . A real honest-to-goodness happening!'

And, for once, the ever-cool, ever-right columnist whose judgements on topics ranging from what-shall-I-do-with-my-too-sexy-boyfriend-now-he's-got-another-girl to the sublime have-I-the-right-to-demand-a-three-night-week suddenly found herself exposed for the inconsequential twit she always had been. When she pointed, panted and said: 'Jesus, Murphy, they can't do this to me!' she covered the subject admirably.

Johnny Holland clutched his hard-won mike. He ignored Bobby Sharp screaming at him from the stage forecourt. He didn't count the bodies strewn across the raised dais. All he saw were his men – the Jolly Green Men – giving him the high-sign.

'Go, Johnny!'

A wave.

A nod.

And the music blasted . . .

'This is JOHNNY HOLLAND AND THE JOLLY GREEN MEN,' he told the frenzied audience, his voice strong – getting to them over the shouts and roars of the security heavies. 'And now – *Virginia's Love!*' Grinning, he swung on his 'men'. 'Let's go, gang . . .'

Wilf Russell's hand moved to terminate the transmission. Hesitated. *This kid's got something*, he thought as the 'new' sound rose sweepingly to fill the Discodrome. His eyes tore away from the frightening spectacle of Bobby Sharp struggling to climb back on-stage as a pair of youths clung to him, doing their best to prevent him reaching his goal.

'Kill it, Wilf! For God's sake – kill it!'

Reluctantly, Wilf's hand moved again. As producer he could prolong the moment of Johnny Holland's triumph. But . . .

The monitor screen blanked out . . .

'Christ, now what?'

Wilf flicked fingers across his control console. The voice belonged to Ed Cronin. But the urgency belonged to the network. To Charles Treffry. To those various boards responsible for the codes of broadcasting standards.

'Wilf . . . can you hear me?'

Wilf thought about Johnny Holland. If he ever got another opportunity to produce a television show he'd bring that determined young man on . . .

Richard Allen, *Teeny Bopper Idol* (1973)

1973: Iggy in Exile

Raw Power is the best high-energy album since *Kick Out the Jams*, and it sometimes makes me think that Iggy and the Stooges could kick their ex-Big Brothers' butts in the right kind of alley.

I can't believe this is the same group that made the Stooges' first two albums. No longer the band you love because they put out so much despite their limitations, this version of the Stooges is tremendously powerful, and with the aid of skillful production, the noise-raunch power tremble of complete ecstasy that *Kick Out the Jams* hitherto represented all by itself is finally fully realized IN THE STUDIO. Consider that, boob-a-la – it's like staging an air raid on Hanoi in Grauman's Chinese Theater.

Iggy kicks it loose from the beginning. The guitar charge is just like the old Five's guitar work, tremendous bursts of apocalyptic interstellar energy, limited only by contemporary technology and harnessed to a strong, if unsteady, backbeat. Bassist Ron Asheton pulls down the sound, melding it into something almost earthly, while the rest of the band accelerates so hard and so fast that if Iggy wasn't the singer, you'd wonder whose record this was. It's like they OD'd Pete Townshend on Quaalude and acid, forced him into a 1965 time warp and made him keep all the promises he made in 'Can't Explain'.

By the time the second song, 'Raw Power', comes on, you're startled, so busy trying to figure out what this meta-metamorphosis portends that you can't quite believe that the record is doing it all by itself, so you look around the floor but no, not there. Then Iggy screams, 'Raw Power got a healin' hand / Raw Power can destroy a man', which for once isn't a call to the demiurges who guard rock'n'roll to come out and visit us (i.e., bail out the singer) – no, this is an irrefutable statement of fact. Like the songs on the first

403

Stooges record, which had titles like 'No Fun', 'Real Cool Time', 'Little Doll' and 'I Wanna Be Your Dog', 'Raw Power' is just the eye of the Ig roving around the street, putting down what he sees, not mincing words or trying for fluidity but letting it ooze, rough and uh, raw, splat, screeeeee: 'You're alone and you've got the shakes / So've I, baby, but I got what it takes.' And 'Raw Power', so help me God, begins with an authentic belch, a true-to-life burp – which is, like farting, a form of *truly* raw power. And it goes like this: urggglllppppp. I swear

Now comes the part for people who never liked the Stooges. (Whatever Stooges fans think of such folks, they *are* all but legion.) 'Give Me Danger' is the real Iggy ballad, the one Mr Pop kept threatening us with when he did tunes like 'Ann, My Ann' and 'Dirt'. But this Iggy ballad is one where you can't make out the lyrics because of the guitars, which is okay because these guitars are as luminous as Jimi Hendrix jamming with John Fahey. The playing is by James Williamson (who replaces Ron Asheton). You won't believe it until you hear it, and even then it might take you a week: that's how long it took me, even after seeing them live in London last summer.

Now, this is the part that you won't believe at all (as if you're gonna believe me when I tell you how great this record is, anyway), but after a while you look at the titles and you begin to wonder what is this record *about*? Now, I'm not saying that Iggy has made the first dementoid concept album or some avuncular nonsense like that, I'm just going to tell you what this album is about and you can believe it or not:

> Raw Power *is what happens if you watch the Vietnam War live on TV every night, and that is the central fact of the culture in which you live for ten years (or more).*

Look at these titles: 'Hard to Beat' (Kissinger'd buy that, even); 'Search and Destroy', for which no explanation is necessary; 'Death Trip', ditto; 'Penetration', a sort of behind-the-lines excursion . . .

Maybe Iggy was imagining – it's a big maybe but what the fuck – that he didn't beat the draft after all. In fact he went to Vietnam and got his legs and arms shot off and came back a crippled, quadriplegic junkie who got himself atomic-powered prosthetic limbs and set out to avenge the destruction he'd endured. And the way he does it is to write a song about how he got fucked up, see, with these lines:

> I'm the world's most forgotten boy
> The one who searches and *destroys*

And then singing about his fantasy after he got shot, his dream while he almost bled to death, which is that Madame Diem showed up and sucked him off and fucked him in ways he hadn't thought possible: 'Love in the middle of a fire fight.'

Now you might think this is totally ridiculous, and you're absolutely right, but that's what this album makes me think about – and I ain't even told you about the long songs yet.

Everyone talks about how we need a band that can hold this decade in the palm of its hand and spitshine and polish it, but the Stooges just come out and do that, and with their feet they dance a merry little gallows jig, too. *Raw Power* is like a great James Bond novel that never got written, but its concepts are all sketched in here. Like, when the Stooges play their own version of 'St James Infirmary', called 'I Need Somebody', where Iggy is bad as Howlin' Wolf pounding Mick Jagger on the head with a forty-pound stack of Yma Sumac records.

And all the while Iggy just keeps singing in his best Frank Sinatra voice (the one he uses to sing 'Shadow of Your Smile' when the amps blow up in the middle of a set). He isn't singing 'I need somebody, too,' either; any dorkoid in the world could sing about how lonely we all are. He's singing about how he needs somebody to ... do something so unspeakable you couldn't (*he* couldn't) imagine what it even is or how to do it, if you knew.

Then 'Death Trip', a nightmarish reworking in no uncertain terms of Jim Morrison's 'Moonlight Drive' fetish. Real-ly. Death to the death culture and all that rot, as David Bowie taught him to say. Iggy immerses himself in all the rage of being fucked up and more appropriately, fucking YOURSELF up that anyone can imagine, and then he sings, as in a love song:

> I'm with you and you with me
> We're goin' down in history

And he ain't talking about a blow job, either, he's talking about going down like Hitler, like Rasputin, like every mangled dictator and dog-eared mass murderer there ever was, if you'll just come right along on his little death trip – here, step inside. Stab, stab.

I'm tempted myself. Only a truly diabolical mind could have made the best album of the seventies, of course, and Iggy apparently has it because he's summed everything up and it took him only nine songs to do it. And he didn't have to write any songs about being/not being/wishing he were cosmic or a star or some bullshit.

Step inside the Fun House, home of the O Mind, and we will all have a real cool time, AC/DC and Raw Power alike.

Dave Marsh, Creem, 1973

1974: The View from Seat T39

What the hell, one more Saturday night at the Rainbow and this is seat number T39 sending a big hello to all you folks out there who showed up two nights before to see Billy Preston working alongside Mick Jagger and Mick Taylor.

That cost £1.50 for a front row seat, whereas my three-quarters-of-the-way-back seat at the Osmonds show cost £2 (inc. VAT). Still, the governing principle of rock economics is generally to charge as much as you think the audience can afford or is willing to pay.

So when you've got the Osmonds playing a 3,000 seater, it's probably sound business to aim for at least £6,000 of hard-scuffed adolescent money.

Inside the theatre, the population is almost exclusively female and under 16. The exceptions seem to be parents and journalists, and even hardened pressmen look a trifle nervous.

They're on enemy territory and they know it. They're instantly conspicuous, and they feel vaguely obscene by virtue of their age and their dissolute habits.

Worse, they have to endure the curious gazes of everybody from the kids to the ushers. What are those old dudes doing here anyway? Maybe they're faggots, maybe they're simply mentally retarded.

Three-quarters of an hour to showtime. The stage is piled high with instruments and monster amplifiers – an instant overkill kit for under 12s.

The kids are amusing themselves with extempore chants – 'If you all love Donny clap your hands, BAM BAM'. And by some masterstroke of planning, there's a full hour of waiting time without any records, thus building up the suspense.

Periodically the kids scream with remarkable co-ordination, even though nothing whatsoever is happening on stage. It verges on the telepathic. Why?

'Well,' says one, 'all them over there are screaming so why shouldn't we?' Totally unanswerable. Every so often one kid holds up an Osmonds poster and the kids shriek at the very sight of a picture of the adored objects.

It appears that what's making the Osmonds happen is their value as adored objects. With most bands (including T. Rex, Slade, Bowie and The Sweet) the interest starts from the music and spreads outwards to encompass the appearance and personalities of the people who make it.

With the Osmonds, the process was reversed. Their fans fell in love with their (allegedly) pretty faces, and a considerable amount of infatuation was built up. At this concert there was around £6,000 worth of infatuation . . .

Finally, a slice of grandiose orchestral music blares over the speakers and fights a losing battle with the howls of pre-pubescent religious hysteria. Suddenly the lights come up and The Osmonds are slugging their way through 'Crazy Horses'.

While clouds of dry ice billow from behind the amps, Alan Osmond capers about in front of the mike like a man in the throes of chronic diarrhoea.

Ummm – there's Jay on the drums, Wayne on bass, Merrill on lead, three brass players behind the drum kit and an extra guitarist lurking at the back, while behind the organ is . . . wipe my nose and call me snotty, it's none other than young Donny himself, doing the whinnying horse effect with considerable panache.

Now, I can't claim to be totally conversant with the Osmonds' repertoire, but during the show they did 'Down by the Lazy River', 'Goin' Home' and various other ditties. Despite the screaming, their playing is just about audible, though Donny's keyboards get completely swamped and his contributions to the group vocals are less than decipherable.

Two basic things about their performance are, however, clearly apparent.

First, they *can* play. By that I mean that they remember their chords and words and they don't drop the instruments. In general, their musical ability is roughly equivalent to a very superior youth-club group, seasoned veterans of Junior Rotary Club dances.

The best instrumentalist is Merrill, who's about up to the standard of an average Marquee support band guitarist.

The second thing is that the show is extremely well organised.

Every Osmond is always leaping about playing something, working really hard and never letting up or getting lazy. Their moves, however, are thoroughly choreographed, antiseptically over-rehearsed to the point of absolute sterility.

They've obviously studied video-tapes of other big acts and they perform a kind of condensed history of rock stage-presentation, but there's no raunch, no guts, no power in their set. In fact, they play and move like virgins, with the exception of Merrill.

Now there's a thought. The Osmonds are all strict Mormons, and Mormonism forbids sex before marriage. As the only married member, Merrill has obviously been soaking his poozle with some regularity which accounts for his superior playing and presence.

(Maybe the Osmonds' managers should get them laid as fast as possible.)

Ho hum. The kids scream at practically everything. When, during one of the more tedious sections of 'The Plan', Merrill whips out a flute to dribble some rather wishy-washy noodlings, the sight of his instrument is greeted with a veritable volcanic eruption of squeals.

Not because he was playing anything fantastic, but simply because an adored object was doing something else.

The three major set-pieces were the Karate Bit, the '50s bit (I kid you not) and the Little Jimmy bit.

First, the gang all leave their instruments while some balding dingbat hammers out a Gary Glitter routine on Jay's drums. They go through a superbly choreographed mock fight which causes the younger and more impressionable members of the audience to howl, 'No – o – o – o!!' in horror every time it gets too realistic.

Me, I was watching with bated breath to see if Alan was gonna break Wayne's nose again or if Jay was about to hoof Donald in the cojones, but it all went off all right. Then Donny did his star turn and snapped various pieces of board with his hand or elbow.

What a reaction *that* caused. Not only was their hero wistful, dreamy and pretty, but he's a tough little dude as well. Top that, Marc.

The next bit was pretty awesome too.

'My six older brothers are always telling me how great the '50s were,' announces Donny, and before you know it there's a piano wheeled out on stage and the band are onstage in shades, motorcycle caps and black leather jackets complete with chains.

Alan's has 'Big Al' on the back, Donny's is inscribed 'Corky' and so on. They do a medley of tunes like 'Get a Job', 'Blue Moon', 'Rock Around the Clock' and so on. During 'Jailhouse Rock', Donny really gets it on, so much so that you'd think he's been given cocaine supositories before going onstage.

All the way through, during the two-chords two-beats playoff, he stands up and shakes it. BAM! Donny's little ass flips to the left. BAM! Donny's little ass flips to the right. Pandemonium.

After that, they bring on what looks like a small constipated toad on methedrine. It turns out to be the dreaded Little Jimmy, who does 'Hound

Dog' and 'Long Haired Lover from Liverpool' with all the presence and authority of the true star that he is.

After all, what else could you expect from a performer who ranks third only to Iggy Pop and Keith Richard in Nick Kent's pantheon of greatness?

That was about it, really. When they go off, the kids don't even attempt to ask for an encore. Many of them are weeping and wailing with a terrifying intensity.

Their Adored Objects have been dangled enticingly before their eyes for an all-too-fleeting 75 minutes, and now they've gone again. The sense of deprivation that the kids are feeling is almost frightening. Hardly any of them look happy.

Outside in the foyer, things are looking exceptionally grim. Two young girls are at their wits' end, because one of them had been taking pictures and a security man has apparently taken away her camera. Not told her to stop – not even confiscated the film – but taken away her camera. Just like that.

Further up, a young girl is slumped against a wall, crying. She's finding it rather hard to stand up and she appears to be having trouble breathing. I alert a St John's Ambulance man to check her out, but before he can get to her, a security gent has bundled her out of the building. All over the foyer girls aged between 10 and 15 are being bodily evicted from the hall.

I don't know whether Alan Osmond is going to be permitted to read this over his breakfast peanut butter sandwiches and warm milk, but in the event that he does, I'd like to crave the indulgence of the assembled company and address a few words to him.

After their penultimate press conference (we weren't permitted to attend the last one) I had a few words with him and with the band's manager Ed Leffler, and they appeared to be likeable and responsible folks.

So if you're reading this, Alan and Ed, I'd like to inquire, all cynicism temporarily abandoned, whether you know how your audiences are treated.

Two quid is a lot of money for a 12-year-old, especially since the kids who were at that show were the ones who queued for days to get those tickets. Anyone who pays that much money is entitled to a certain amount of respect.

They deserve better than to be shovelled out of the hall like so much human refuse after they've seen the show.

Obviously, it ain't your fault. But it's ultimately your responsibility to make sure it doesn't happen. I have enough respect for the pair of you as human beings to be sure that the sight of your devoted fans getting hustled around would be at least as distressing to you as it is to me.

Finally, it reflects on you, and on your credibility with your fans.

Telling them you love them won't be all that convincing to a young girl who's lost her camera simply because she tried to take your picture, or has been thrown around like a small, tearful sack of potatoes because she wanted to get her breath back after one of your shows. What kind of people are you dealing with?

And whatcha gonna do about it?

Charles Shaar Murray, *New Musical Express Greatest Hits*, 1974

1974: Music and Mayhem

Rock is about money and macho. To admit to the true nature of one's sexuality in this particular world would – so the theory runs – amount to a loss of face and a certain loss of earnings.

Yet on those much touted world tours, various members of any given rock entourage will be thumbing their *Spartacus* guides as eagerly as the next gay tourist. They will be found checking out the clubs, bars and baths – and hoping that after the show there will be a few attractive male groupies hanging around. For believe me, male groupies are every bit as in evidence around stage doors as their more notorious female counterparts. I should know, I took advantage of enough of them.

It was all so disgustingly easy.

Picture the backstage area of a large American concert hall or football stadium. The band have finished their performance and encores. Now they are ensconced in their dressing-room – drinking, smoking, probably fighting about the merits and faults of the evening's show.

The stage area is abuzz with activity as the road crew dismantle the stage set and the sound and lighting equipment. Elsewhere Billy might be collecting great bundles of cash and stuffing them into his briefcase. The night's take.

Others of us drift more or less aimlessly around – awaiting that moment when we can climb into our limousine and speed back to the hotel in which we're staying. Mingling with the tour personnel will be youths and young women who have somehow or other managed to acquire a backstage pass. They're devoted fans – and probably dress in the style the band were wearing on the previous tour. It's also likely that they're stoned or drunk or both.

The fact that I have access to the dressing-room will have drawn attention to me. As I make my way through the door – questing for another drink – a boy of around eighteen stops me.

'Hey, man. Are you with the band?'

I nod, 'Sure,' I say.

'Can you get me in there?' The boy nods towards the dressing-room door.

'fraid not,' I reply. 'Boys are busy.'

'Sure. Sure. I understand.'

I stare at the boy. He's really rather appealing. I relent a little. 'Would you like a drink?'

'Gee! Wow! Swell! Great!'

'I'll fetch you one when I come out next time,' I say, and push through the door and into the room. By this time I've made up my mind. I fill a plastic beaker with wine and replenish my own drink. Then I'm outside again offering *my* prize *his* prize.

'I'm Peter,' I drawl in the conveniently adopted mid-Atlantic accent.

'Hi, Pete. I'm Brick.' They always seemed to have such strange names.

'Hi,' I repeat and give a smile which I hope isn't too predatory.

'What d'you do?'

'I'm the group's publicist.'

'Gee! Wow! Swell! Great!' the not-so-innocent object of my attentions gushes. He's got the picture. He knows what I'm after. 'What a great job.'

'It's a living,' I nonchalantly reply.

'Wow! Hey – what's Rod like?'

'He's a nice enough guy,' I say – and then add, almost as an afterthought – 'He'll probably drop by my room for a drink later.'

'Hey – are Rod and Woody gay?'

'No way,' I'd say.

'They sure act it sometimes,' Brick counters.

'Well – they're not.'

'I'd sure like to meet Rod. I think he's real neat.'

'Why don't you come back with me then? I'm sure something could be arranged.'

No chance.

'Gee! Wow! I can't believe this is happening to me.'

This is probably the moment when Billy reappears, clutching the cash-laden briefcase. He gives me a knowing wink. 'Let's go,' he says and dashes away to the area where the limousines are parked.

Brick and I climb into the car after Billy.

'Billy – Brick. Brick – Billy,' I say by way of introduction. 'Billy's Rod's manager.'

This information elicits another 'Wow' from Brick.

The car speeds away back to the hotel. There's always food and drink in my room – sometimes music too if I've packed a cassette player and tapes. And there's so much luggage spread around that the only place to sit is on the bed.

Of course, the chances of Rod dropping into my room on that or any other night were extremely thin. He had his own fish to fry and was likely to be partying with some local lovely – unless the current girlfriend was in town, in which case he'd be having dinner in the poshest restaurant the place had to offer.

Naturally I didn't allow myself to believe that any of these boys fancied me. What was taking place was a basic transaction. In some curious kind of way I became a surrogate Rod Stewart. Sleeping with me – and meeting Billy – was as near as Brick was ever likely to get to his idol. Just by travelling back with us and staying in my hotel room, he was touched by stardom. From me, Brick was getting – if not something he could boast about to his friends – at least a memory. The night he *almost* met Rod Stewart. I was getting a companion for the night – and I too was getting a memory. Of blond and blue-eyed Brick, an affectionate and appealing Midwesterner who'd made my stay in some dreary town that bit more enjoyable.

Peter Burton, *Parallel Lives* (1985)

1974: Funky Chic

Today, in the age of Funky Chic Egalité, fashion is a much more devious, sly, and convoluted business than anything that was ever dreamed of at Versailles. At Versailles, where Louis XIV was installed in suites full of silver furniture (later melted down to finance a war), one could scarcely be *too* obvious. Versailles was above all the City of the Rich. Hundreds of well-to-do or upward-hustling families had quarters there. The only proper way to move about the place was in sedan chairs borne by hackmen with straining trapeziuses. Any time anyone of high social wattage gave a party, there would be a sedan-chair traffic jam of a half hour or more outside his entry way as the true and original *jeunesse dorée*, in actual golden threads and golden slippers, waited to make the proper drop-dead entrance.

One has only to compare such a scene with any involving the golden youth of our own day. I recommend to anyone interested in the subject the long block, or concourse, known as Broadway in New Haven, Connecticut, where Elm Street, York Street, Whalley and Dixwell Avenues come together. This is near the heart of Yale University. Twenty years ago, at Elm and York, there was a concentration of men's custom-tailoring shops that seemed to outnumber all the tailors on Fifth Avenue and Fifty-seventh Street put together. They were jammed in like pearls in a box. Yale was still the capital of collegiate smart dressing. Yale was, after all, the place where the *jeunesse dorée* of America were being groomed, in every sense of the word, to inherit the world; the world, of course, being Wall Street and Madison Avenue. Five out of every seven Yale undergraduates could tell whether the button-down Oxford cloth shirt you had on was from Fenn-Feinstein, J. Press, or Brooks Brothers from a single glance at your shirt front; Fenn-Feinstein: plain breast pocket; J. Press: breast pocket with buttoned flap; Brooks Brothers: no breast pocket at all. Today J. Press is still on the case, but others of the heavenly host are shipping out. Today a sane businessman would sooner open a souvlaki takeout counter at Elm and York than a tailor shop, for reasons any fool could see. On the other side of the grand concourse, lollygagging up against Brooks Health and Beauty Aids, Whitlock's, and the Yale Co-op, are the new Sons of Eli. They are from the same families as before, averaging about $37,500 gross income per annum among the non-scholarship students. But there is nobody out there checking breast pockets or jacket vents or any of the rest of it. The unvarying style at Yale today is best described as Late Army Surplus. Broadway Army & Navy enters heaven! Sons in Levi's, break through that line! that is the sign we hail! Visible at Elm and York are more olive-green ponchos, clodhoppers, and parachute boots, more leaky-dye blue turtlenecks, pea jackets, ski hats, long-distance trucker warms, sheepherder's coats, fisherman's slickers, down-home tenant-farmer bib overalls, coal-stoker strap undershirts, fringed cowpoke jerkins, strike-hall blue workshirts, lumberjack plaids, forest-ranger mackinaws, Australian bushrider mackintoshes, Cong sandals, bike leathers, and more jeans, jeans, jeans, jeans, jeans, more prole gear of every description than you ever saw or read of in a hundred novels by Jack London, Jack Conroy, Maxim Gorky, Clara Weatherwax, and any who came before or after.

Of course, this happens to be precisely what America's most favored young men are wearing at every other major college in the country, so that you scarcely detect the significance of it all until you look down to the opposite end of the concourse, to the north, where Dixwell Avenue comes in. Dixwell Avenue is the main drag of one of New Haven's black slums. There, on any likely corner, one can see congregations of young men the same age as the Yales but . . . from the bottom end of the great greased pole of life, as it were,

413

from families whose gross incomes no one but the eligibility worker ever bothered to tote up. All the young aces and dudes are out there lollygagging around the front of the Monterey club, wearing their two-tone patent Pyramids with the five-inch heels that swell out at the bottom to match the Pierre Chareau Art Deco plaid bell-bottom baggies they have on with the three-inch-deep elephant cuffs tapering upward toward the 'spray-can fit' in the seat, as it is known, and the peg-top waistband with self-covered buttons and the beagle-collar pattern-on-pattern Walt Frazier shirt, all of it surmounted by the midi-length leather piece with the welted waist seam and the Prince Albert pockets and the black Pimpmobile hat with the four-inch turn-down brim and the six-inch pop-up crown with the golden chain-belt hatband ... and all of them, every ace, every dude, out there just *getting over* in the baddest possible way, come to play and dressed to slay ... so that somehow the sons of the slums have become the Brummels and Gentlemen of Leisure, the true fashion plates of the 1970s, and the Sons of Eli dress like the working class of 1934 ...

... a style note which I mention not merely for the sake of irony. Just as Radical Chic was a social fashion that ended up having a political impact – so did Funky Chic. Radical Chic helped various Left causes. Funky Chic hurt them. So far as I know, no one has ever recorded the disruption that Funky Chic caused within the New Left. (Remember the New Left?) In 1968, 1969, and 1970 the term 'counterculture' actually meant something. In those wild spitting hot-bacon days on the campus 'Counterculture' referred to what seemed to be a fast-rising unity of spirit among all the youth of the nation, black and white, a new consciousness (to use a favorite word from that time) that was mobilizing half the country, the half that was now under twenty-five years old (to use a favorite statistic from that time), under the banner of revolution or something not far from it. Yet at that very moment the youth of the country were becoming bitterly divided along lines of class and status. The more the New Left tried to merge them in a united front, the more chaotic and out of the question the would-be coalition became.

Fashion was hardly one of the root causes of this division – that is another, longer story. But fashion was in many cases the cutting edge. Fashion brought out hopeless status conflict where there was no ideological conflict whatsoever. In 1969 I went to San Francisco to do a story on the young militants who were beginning to raise hell inside the supposedly shockproof compound of Chinatown. I had heard of a sensational public meeting held by a group called the Wah Ching, who were described as a supergang of young Chinese who had been born in Hong Kong, who immigrated to the United

States with their parents in the mid-sixties, who couldn't speak English, couldn't get an education, couldn't get jobs, who were ready to explode. They held a public meeting and threatened to burn down Chinatown, Watts-style. So I came on into Chinatown, cold, looking for the Wah Ching. Right away, on the street corners, I see groups of really fierce-looking young men. They've got miles of long black hair, down to the shoulders, black berets, black T-shirts, black chinos, dirty Levi's, combat boots. These must be the dread Wah Ching, I figured. So I worked up my nerve and started talking to some of them and right away I found out they were not the Wah Ching at all. They were a group known as the Red Guard, affiliated at that time with the Black Panthers. Not only that, they were not lower-class Hong Kong-born Chinese at all but American-born. They spoke English just like any other Americans; and most of them, by Chinatown standards at least, were middle-class. But they said they were allied with the Wah Ching and told of various heavy battles the Wah Ching were going to help them out in.

It took me about two weeks, but I finally arranged a meeting with one of the main leaders of the Wah Ching themselves. We were going to meet in a restaurant, and I arrived first and was sitting there going over all the political points I wanted to cover. Finally the man walks in – and I take one look and forget every political question on the list. He has on a pair of blue slacks, a matching blue turtleneck jersey with a blue shirt over it and a jacket with a leather body and great fluffy flannel sleeves, kind of like a suburban bowling jacket. This man does not add up. But mainly it is his hair. After all the ferocious long black hair I have been seeing in Chinatown – his is chopped off down to what is almost a parody of the old Chinatown ricebowl haircut. So the first magnificent question I heard myself blurting out was: 'What happened to your hair!'

There was no reason why he should, but he took the question seriously. He spoke a very broken English which I will not attempt to imitate, but the gist of what he said was this:

'We don't wear our hair like the hippies; we don't wear our hair like the Red Guards. We are not a part of the hippies; we are not a part of the Red Guards; we are not a part of anything. We are the Wah Ching. When we got to this country, those guys you were talking to out there, the ones who now call themselves the Red Guard, those same guys were calling us "China Bugs" and beating up on us and pushing us around. But now we're unified, and we're the Wah Ching and nobody pushes us around. So now they come to us and tell us they are the Red Guard and they've got the message and Chairman Mao and the Red Book and all that. They'll give us the message and the direction, and we can be the muscle and the power on the street and together we will fight the Establishment.

'Well, the hell with that. We don't need any ideological benefactors. Look at these guys. Look at these outfits they're wearing. They come around us having a good time playing poor and saying, "Hey, brother". Look at those berets – they think they're Fidel Castro coming out of the mountains. Look at the Can't-Bust-'Em overalls they got on, with the hairy gorilla emblem on the back and the combat boots and the olive-green socks on you buy two-for-29-cents at the Army-Navy Store. They're having a good time playing poor, but we are the ones who have to *be* poor. So the hell with that and the hell with them.'

Here were two groups who were unified ideologically – who wanted to fight the old clan establishment of Chinatown as well as the white establishment of San Francisco – and yet they remained split along a sheerly dividing line, an instinctive status line, a line that might even be described by the accursed word itself, 'fashion.' This example could be multiplied endlessly, through every instance in which the New Left tried to enlist the youth of the working class or of the slums. There never was a 'counterculture' in the sense of any broad unity among the young – and this curious, uncomfortable matter of fashion played a part over and over. I never talked to a group of black militants, or Latin militants, for that matter, who didn't eventually comment derisively about the poorboy outfits their middle-class white student allies insisted on wearing or the way they tried to use black street argot, all the *mans* and *cats* and *babies* and *brothers* and *baddests*. From the very first, fashion tipped them off to something that was not demonstrated on the level of logic until much later: namely, that most of the white New Lefters of the period 1968–70 were neither soldiers nor politicians but simply actors.

The tipoff was not the fact that the middle-class whites were dressing *down* in order to join their slumbound brethren. The issue was not merely condescension. The tipoff was that when the whites dressed down, went Funky Chic, they did it *wrong*! They did it *lame*! They never bothered to look at what the brothers on the street were actually wearing! They needed to have their coats pulled! The New Left had a strictly old-fashioned conception of life on the street, a romantic and nostalgic one somehow derived from literary images of *proletarian* life from before World War II or even World War I. A lot of the white college boys, for example, would go for those checked lumberjack shirts that are so heavy and woolly that you can wear them like a jacket. It was as if all the little Lord Byrons had a hopeless nostalgia for the proletariat of about 1910, the Miners with dirty Faces era, and never mind the realities – because the realities were that by 1968 the real hard-core street youth in the slums were not into lumberjack shirts, Can't Bust 'Ems, and Army surplus socks. They were into the James Brown look. They were into ruffled shirts and black-belted leather pieces and bell-cuff herringbones, all that stuff, macking around, getting over, looking sharp ... heading toward the high-heeled Pimpmobile *got to get over* look of Dixwell Avenue 1976. If you tried to put one of those lumpy mildew mothball lumberjack shirts on them – those aces ... they'd *vomit*.

For years the sheerly dividing line was a single item of clothing that is practically synonymous with Funky Chic; blue jeans. Well-to-do Europeans appreciated the chic of jeans – that primitive rawness; that delicious grip on the gourd and the moist skinny slither up into all the cracks and folds and fissures! – long before Americans. Even in the early fifties such special styles as London SW5 New Wave Habitat Bentwood Movie Producer Chic and South of France Young Jade Chic and Jardins du Luxembourg Post-Breathless Chic all had at their core: blue jeans. Cowboy Chic, involving blue jeans and walking around as if you have an aluminum beer keg between your thighs, has been popular among young Paris groovies for at least fifteen years. Well-to-do whites in America began to discover the raw-vital reverse-spin funk thrill of jeans in the early sixties. But until recently any such appeal was utterly lost on black or any other colored street aces and scarlet creepers. Jeans were associated with funk in its miserable aspects, with Down-and-Out, bib overalls, Down Home, and I'm Gonna Send You Back to Georgia. Jeans have just begun to be incorporated in the Ace or Pimp look, thanks to certain dramatic changes in jeans couture: such as the addition of metal studwork, bias-cut two-tone swirl mosaic patterns, windowpane welt patterns, and the rising value of used denim fabric, now highly prized for its 'velvet hand' (and highly priced, just as a used Tabriz rug is worth more than a new one). In other words, the aces will now tolerate jeans precisely because they have lost much of the funk.

Well-to-do white youths still associate jeans in any form and at any price with Funk, however, and Funky Chic still flies and bites the main vein and foams and reigns. The current talk of a return to elegance among the young immediately becomes a laugh and a half (or, more precisely, the latest clothing industry shuck) to anyone who sets foot on a mainly white American campus, whether Yale or the University of California at San Diego. A minor matter perhaps; but today, as always, the authentic language of

417

fashion is worth listening to. For fashion, to put it most simply, is the code language of status. We are in an age when people will sooner confess their sexual secrets – much sooner, in many cases – than their status secrets, whether in the sense of longings and triumphs or humiliations and defeats. And yet we make broad status confessions every day in our response to fashion. No one – no one, that is, except the occasional fugitive or spy, such as Colonel Abel, who was willing to pose for years as a Low Rent photographer in a loft in Brooklyn – no one is able to resist that delicious itch to reveal his own picture of himself through fashion.

Goethe once noted that in the last year of his reign Louis XVI took to sleeping on the floor beside his enormous royal bed, because he had begun to feel that the monarchy was an abomination. Down here on the floor he felt closer to the people. How very – funky ... Well, I won't attempt any broad analogies. Nevertheless, it demonstrates one thing. Even when so miserable a fashion as Funky Chic crops up ... stay alert! use your bean!

Tom Wolfe, *Mauve Gloves & Madmen, Clutter & Vine* (1976)

1975: Doin' It Right

Most white people can't dance. Not in that freely expressive stone-to-the-bone style anyway. Even as judges they are suspect; witness their pronouncements on the 'fantastic exotica' of the Ike and Tina Turner show where a sleek dress and yard of leg are sufficient to send them ga-ga. Tina has poise and confidence, yes; but no matter how vigorous, she is not the world's greatest dancer. And as for the Ikettes ... well, they're frequently lumpen and wildly out of time. On this year's display at any rate. And, of course, the audience were predominantly white. Go to any really good West Indian party, however, and you'll see dancers who can cut them stone dead.

Ever since we injected a little warmth and vitality into the social habits and sartorial tastes of this island we've wryly watched the credit misplaced. To our bruised astonishment our 'brash', vivid materials became the accepted chic, courtesy of 'bella Italia'. Our traditional ring dances became the invention of the skinhead, doyen of the sociologists. Separate creative dancing in the burgeoning English discotheques was laid at the feet of a young generation of liberated swingers infected with Mersey mania. Much of the Mersey sound was, in fact, aborted Tamla, and the 'revolution' which overtook England in the early sixties had been quietly ours for many years. As for that other England, still unchanged – well, out of a sense of politeness we left you your glacial last-tango grins, declining to point out the castrated vibrancy of real Latin American music. For as long as we cared to remember in the Caribbean we'd been dancing separately or grooving in leech-like proximity. Eight to eighty, there was none of this 'act your age' foolishness in us. But then, as some did not hesitate to remind us, we are 'pure jungle'. So, just for the record, physical pleasure does not begin with *RSG* or end with *Top of the Pops*.

Why do English people find it so hard to dance fluidly in time? The answer is probably cultural; and rather complex. Whilst they have taken over the superficial aspects of Afro-influenced music they have not lived it. Their whole upbringing and experience militates against the possibilities. Dancing is not a pleasure but a social necessity for them, an expected thing. For the young it is also part of the multi-million manoeuvres of advertising experts in the record industry. A vestigial classic upbringing with all the stoic virtues of Empire builders precludes anything which smacks of indiscipline. Don't let go. Freeze in the straight jacket of inhibition. Establish your age, class, and identity. The only time the mask slips is after an evening of careful drinking when the moment for the last dance reels round.

And what do the young English discotheque devotees dance to? Sadly, the answer is virtually anything, provided they recognise it as an approved sound. And then they dance with a devastating indifference to the beat. I am told that up North they win prizes for dancing at 100 mph to the most banal pop music masquerading as soul. In London clubs like the Sundown, in Charing Cross Road, the standard of music and movement is appalling. Last time I was there 'live' entertainment was provided by G. T. Moore and the Reggae Guitars, a white outfit whose strongest item was a souled up version of Dylan's 'Knocking on Heaven's Door'. As a reggae band they were really nowhere; and, despite the watered down content, still proved too much for an audience happy to return to jumping up and down to Norman Greenbaum's noxious 'Spirit in the Sky'. Golden oldies indeed! At swisher clubs like La Valbonne or the Countdown with their colour supp. décor, things improve quite a bit in a sagely antiseptic way. Much more soul is played with an emphasis on smooth Philadelphia sounds to suit a more sophisticated white clientele. The Three Degrees emit representative noises. Discs like the Hues Corporation's 'Rock the Boat' are considered really hot. In the Countdown they sometimes get a late theatrical crowd including professional dancers who are pretty good. And usually 'gay'. Why is it that gay Englishmen provide your dancers?

The important thing with dancing is to really 'feel' it, like sex. To be completely taken up with the sound, to let it envelope and inform your whole body. Whether you're grooving groin to groin with infinitely slow enjoyment or hitting the beat on something rougher the whole body should flow, not just a spasmodic movement of arms and legs but independent looseness of shoulders, stomach, hips, everything. But in time.

Some of the most spectacular but private dancing can be seen upstairs at the All Nations Club in Hackney. It's a large, sprawling place with a ninety per cent black turnout who are both noisy and fast. The best dancers seem to be the boys, usually in baggy trousers, thumbs hitching shining peasant waistcoats or braces, hats perched defiantly as they slice up the floor. Too young to remember ska dancing first-hand, they have picked up elements from their elders and a whole, new, unnamed but recognisable dance has evolved. Sometimes they drop back, legs apart and balanced, on the inside of the foot, hit the floor, one hand behind them between their legs, to bounce up again on the beat! At others they do a forward shuffle reminiscent of the days of James Brown's 'Night Train', and the whole thing gells into one electric dance. The DJs play consistently good soul, raw badass music, with some reggae but few pre-releases. According to the owner-cum-manager, a Jamaican named Robert, 'not all West Indians like reggae music so we try to mix it as best we can. We try to mix the ages too. Most middle-aged people don't like mixing with the teenagers because they are just a bloody headache. We try and let in as few as possible because of the way they spoil things for others. Those we let in don't give much trouble because we don't give them much freedom. The music can determine the kind of people who come to the club . . .'

This equation of reggae, teenagers and trouble is one borne out by the sveltly handsome Russell, a gentleman from Grenada whose clubland credentials stretch over ten years from the notorious days of The Roaring Twenties to present ownership of Colombo's in Carnaby Street. Colombo's is an exceedingly plush West Indian club, impeccably run and respected by the law, and the ideal venue for a relaxed but sophisticated evening. Things kick off around midnight and the clientele, mostly in their mid-twenties, are exceedingly flashy dressers and spectacular dancers who run through the Bump, Kung Fu, and the Cripple. The music is largely funk, James Brown in abundance, backed up with the Fatback Band, Kool and the Gang, and a trickle of requests for oldies such as soul from Otis Redding and, more often, ska by Don Drummond or Prince Buster. Russell buys all the records, American imports and JA pre-releases from Contempo and Record Corner in Balham. Reggae is played sparingly, though, because Russell claims it attracts the wrong element. Militant spliff roller are out. And in any case reggae is too uniform and slow in a copulatory sense on such a confined floor as Colombo's. Russell loves the music, including the most ethnic sides, but only slips it on later at night once the clientele has been established.

Those who wish to savour the rougher, ganga-laden ambience of an undiluted reggae club where the youngsters sway and grind to heavy white-label pressings must haul their tail down to the Four Aces in Dalston. You'll get more reggae at Harlesden's Apollo where they follow George McCrea's 'Rock Your Baby' with a JA cover and then launch into a string of Kung Fu epics spliced with ska revivals. The various striking and kicking movements, lovingly rehearsed in front of the mirror, are paraded out on the dance floor in an amusing montage of moving bodies. The craze won't last, of course, but doubtless some of the gestures will be assimilated and used again long after the origin is forgotten.

West Indian girls in search of things American, including GIs, generally go down to the Q Club in Paddington, again beautifully run and long established as a premier black venue specialising in raw soul played very loud. The idolatory of the US can get a bit much when some West Indians come across sporting New York accents in the hope of pulling a girl. People dress elegantly at this club, make a great play for sophistication, leggy girls with lips pursed in the concentration that passes for chic, self-centred men easing their bodies in tight white leather, but the dancing is not quite the thing of splendour it once was.

But just as much as clubs may affect matters, the history of dance is inextricably bound up with a succession of 'blues' and house-parties down the years. From the late fifties on, men like Doo were servicing the London scene with records well before the advent of Sir Coxone or the battles between the Sound Systems. At West Indian dances you heard Fats Domino, Elvis, Dion, Johnny Ace, the Fontaine Sisters, and a host of Jamaican R&B covers, particularly of New Orleans artists. Laurel Aitken's 'Bartender' (Blue Beat 40) in 1961 and 'Boogie in My Bones' were especially big, while people like the popular Jackie Edwards with 'Tell Me Darling' (Island LP 906) emulated the softer rock 'n' roll of Buddy Holly and Brian Hyland. American dances like the Madison required plenty of space for two lines of people, at least a dozen in number, and so put themselves out of business. The Mashed Potato craze left its legacy of skidding feet kicking forward. In the early sixties, ska dancers kicked on alternate legs to the upflung arm and Jamaican music established its ascendancy among expatriate West Indians. A combination of white preconception and a Jamaican majority among immigrants meant that JA music was imposed where tastes often ran to calypso and meringue. A false idea of the Caribbean has evolved to which British-born blacks now stubbornly adhere. Their life is built around the recent and highly manipulated world of reggae, and yet in Kingston alone this music is only a fraction of the picture. In the early and mid-sixties, ska – presided over by Prince Buster – admitted considerable variety: and in the UK it merged with Bluebeat (after the label) with favourites like Baba Brooks' 'One Eyed Giant'.

Groups like the Astronauts continued to evince wide influence with material like 'Syncopate', released on Hala Gala HG9 in 1966 and akin to meringue. 'Last Train to Skaville' and 'The Whip' by the Ethiopians (released on Rio 130 and Doctor Bird 1096 respectively in 1967) mark a transition from ska into bluebeat dance styles. Rock Steady, typified by the Alton Ellis hit of the same name on Treasure Isle 101 in 1966, involved a shift in beat and a movement of body from side to side. Then came the golden age of reggae before the current decline into toasting, skanking, rastafari and the commercial exploitation of an ethnic underground.

Parallel with this and, until reggae, predominant was soul music. For many West Indians, including myself, it remains so and I remember James Brown's 'Night Train' with great affection.

But to come down to the present, if I had to settle for one dance number which hooks me every time it would have to be 'Let's Get It On' by Marvin Gaye, endlessly sexy and curiously inaccessible to English audiences who have not yet found the soul to groove. Few people know how to drift away on a dance so slow and yet so complete . . .

Amidst a corny profusion of whistles and party sounds this past year's dance has been the Bump, better late than never, courtesy of black American servicemen, where the flash of thigh and the collision of butts has been most stimulating.

Anyway I hope this article will get a few hips shaking and a flood of people sussing out the clubs. Go out at twelve and boogie all night long. That's how I shift it when I'm depressed or suffering a temperature. Incidentally I was going to tell you about Ronnie Scott's disco but they wouldn't let me in. I'd fixed it with the owner but the manager said that didn't matter. It was his policy that the club should not be reviewed. One to cross off the list, I'd say.

Next time I'll teach y'all how to do an individual number, tell you about some records, and explain why Pan's People can't dance soul style. Right on.

Jean Peter, Let It Rock, January 1975

1975: Teenage Dreams

It's a teenage dream to be seventeen
And to find you're all wrapped up in love.
'Give a Little Love', the Bay City Rollers

One of my clearest memories from nine years ago is of a bus ride from my housing estate in Birmingham into the city centre. An atmosphere like a cup final coach, but with all of us on the same side and with one even more radical difference – there were no boys. At every stop, more and more girls got on, laughing, shouting, singing the songs we all knew off by heart. We compared the outfits and banners we had spent hours making, swapped jokes and stories, and talked happily to complete strangers because we all had an interest in common: we were about to see the Bay City Rollers.

That was 5 May 1975. I know the exact date because the ticket stub was carefully preserved in my scrapbooks, along with every one of that year's press-cuttings to refer to the Rollers. And they were mentioned a lot. Tartan was the year's most fashionable accessory; you could buy Bay City socks, knickers, watches, shoes, lampshades and countless other fetish objects to fantasize over. For a while at least, the Rollers were big business. Yet nine years on, I see that they didn't even play on their early records; the songs that reached the Top Ten on advance orders alone were weak and sloppily made, with words so wet they almost dripped off the vinyl. Considering that we were supposedly driven into a frenzy the second they walked on stage, they weren't even that pretty.

So what *was* the appeal? Johnny Ray, Sinatra, Billy Fury, Cliff Richard, the Beatles, Bolan, the Osmonds, Duran Duran, Nik Kershaw . . . the names have changed, the process of capitalizing on the phenomenon may have become more efficient and calculated, but from my mother to my younger cousin, most women go through 'that phase'. Most of us scream ourselves silly at a concert at least once, although many refuse to admit it later, because like a lot of female experience, our teen infatuations have been trivialized, dismissed and so silenced. Wetting your knickers over a pop group just isn't a 'hip' thing to have done – much better to pretend you spent your formative years listening to Northern Soul or Billie Holiday.

Even the artists making money out of girls' fantasies are usually embarrassed and at pains to point out that they have *male* fans, too: to get out of the teeny trap and aim their music at a more 'mature' or serious audience seems to be their general ambition. Once they've attained those heights, they're quick to sneer at the girls who helped make them in the first place. Of course, the serious, thinking rock audience they want is mainly male. Only 28 per cent of *NME* readership are women, for instance, as opposed to an estimated 40 per cent for the younger, glossier, less analytical *Smash Hits*. In spite of a number of women journalists (and some men who make the effort), the music press is mainly written by men for other men. 'Primarily for men' is a message that permeates the ads and the way they use women's bodies to shift product, and that informs the casual sexism of articles on women artists (the references to 'dogs' and 'boilers' in *Sounds*, for example). As part of the same bias, 'teenybop' music is either ignored or made into a joke. Often with justice, of course: the Rollers may have been atrocious, but later bands have plumbed depths that my little Scots boys couldn't have dreamed of.

But no matter how bad the music, what the press or any of the self-appointed analysts of 'popular culture' fail to reflect is that the whole pop structure rests on the backs of these 'silly, screaming girls'. They bought the records in millions and made a massive contribution to the early success of Elvis, the Beatles, the Stones, Marc Bolan, Michael Jackson and many of the others who have since been accepted by the grown-ups and become monuments, reference-points in the rock hierarchy. Before you sneer again, boys, remember that it's often their money that allows you your pretensions.

But the real question is, of course, why? Why do adolescent girls go loopy over gawky, sometimes talentless young men? The answer lies partly in the whole situation of adolescent women in our society. We live in a world where sex has become a commodity – used to sell everything from chocolate to cars, sold in films and magazines, and shown everywhere to be a wonderful, desirable ideal that is central to our lives. The pages of *Jackie*, *My Guy* and countless others have a clear message: look good, shape up and flaunt it. Yet hand in glove with this dictum there goes another: *nice girls don't do it* – or at least not until they're 16/married/going steady (and, even then, they don't take the initiative). Sex is the sweetest con-trick of our time, a candy-coated sweetie with a guilt-filled centre. At adolescence, we start to realize that this magic/punishment may actually apply to us, too.

A confusing and often traumatic time for everyone. For girls, however, these new expectations, the new rules and roles they have to conform to, are even more perplexing. Growing aware of our bodies and needs is alarming, because while male sexuality is exaggerated by society – portrayed as insatiable and uncontrollable – ours has been virtually obliterated. It is men who *need* sex; women supply it (though it is our responsibility to keep him at bay until the time is right). With double standards, feelings we aren't supposed to *have* – let alone enjoy – and a body or ambitions that may not fit the acceptable stereotypes, it can be a pretty tough time. Falling in love with posters can be a way of excluding real males and of hanging on to that ideal of 'true love' for just a little longer. It is a safe focus for all that newly discovered sexual energy, and a scream can often be its only release. It is the sound of young women, not 'hysterical schoolgirls' as one reporter would have it – a scream of defiance, celebration and excitement.

'When their fans are old enough to start looking for *real* boyfriends,' sneered a *Birmingham Evening Mail* review of that May 1975 show, the Rollers will soon be forgotten.' But it's not that simple: some of us were lesbians, some of us *did* have boyfriends. In any case, girls mature earlier than boys, so it was more a question of us waiting for *them* to grow up than the other way round.

... Part of the appeal is desire for comradeship. With the Rollers at least, many became involved not because they particularly liked the music, but because they didn't want to miss out. We were a gang of girls having fun together, able to identify each other by tartan scarves and badges. Women are in the minority on demonstrations, in union meetings, or in the crowd at football matches: at the concerts, many were experiencing mass power for the first and last time. Looking back now, I hardly remember the gigs themselves, the songs, or even what the Rollers looked like. What I *do* remember are the bus rides, running home from school together to get to someone's house in time to watch *Shang-A-Lang* on TV, dancing in lines at the school disco and sitting in each others' bedrooms discussing our fantasies and compiling our scrapbooks. Our real obsession was with ourselves; in the end, the actual men behind the posters had very little to do with it at all.

Sheryl Garratt, Signed, Sealed and Delivered (1984)

1975: Another Saturday Night

Vincent was the very best dancer in Bay Ridge – the ultimate Face. He owned fourteen floral shirts, five suits, eight pairs of shoes, three overcoats, and had appeared on American Bandstand. Sometimes music people came out from Manhattan to watch him, and one man who owned a club on the East Side had even offered him a contract. A hundred dollars a week. Just to dance.

Everybody knew him. When Saturday night came round and he walked into 2001 Odyssey, all the other Faces automatically fell back before him, cleared a space for him to float in, right at the very centre of the dance floor. Gracious as a medieval seigneur accepting tributes, Vincent waved and nodded at random. Then his face grew stern, his body turned to the music. Solemn, he danced, and all the Faces followed.

In this sphere his rule was absolute. Only one thing bothered him, and that was the passing of time. Already he was eighteen, almost eighteen and a half. Soon enough he would be nineteen, twenty. Then this golden age would pass. By natural law someone new would arise to replace him. Then everything would be over.

The knowledge nagged him, poisoned his pleasure. One night in January, right in the middle of the Bus Stop, he suddenly broke off, stalked from the floor without a word, and went outside into the cold darkness, to be alone.

He slouched against a wall. He stuck his hands deep into his overcoat pockets. He sucked on an unlit cigarette. A few minutes passed. Then he was approached by a man in a tweed suit.

They stood close together, side by side. The man in the tweed suit looked at Vincent, and Vincent stared at the ground or at the tips of his platform shoes. 'What's wrong?' said the man in the suit, at last.

And Vincent said: 'I'm old.'

Before Saturday night began, to clear his brain of cobwebs and get himself sharp, fired up, he liked to think about killing.

During the week Vincent sold paint in a housewares store. All day, every day he stood behind a counter and grinned. He climbed up and down ladders, he made the coffee, he obeyed. Then came the weekend and he was cut loose.

The ritual never varied. Promptly at five the manager reversed the 'Open' sign and Vincent would turn away, take off his grin. When the last of the customers had gone, he went out through the back, down the corridor, directly into the bathroom. He locked the door and took a deep breath. Here he was safe. So he turned toward the mirror and began to study his image.

Black hair and black eyes, olive skin, a slightly crooked mouth, and teeth so white, so dazzling, that they always seemed fake. Third-generation Brooklyn Italian, five-foot-nine in platform shoes. Small purplish birthmark beside the right eye. Thin white scar, about two inches long, underneath the chin, caused by a childhood fall from a bicycle. Otherwise, no distinguishing marks.

That was the flesh; but there was something else, much more important. One night two years before, he had travelled into Queens with some friends and they had ended up in some club, this real cheap scumhole; he couldn't remember the name. But he danced anyhow and did his numbers, all his latest routines, and everyone was just amazed. And then he danced with this girl. He'd never seen her before and he never saw her again. But her name was Petulia, Pet for short, and she was all right, nice hair, a good mover. And she kept staring right into his eyes. Staring and staring, as though she were hypnotized. He asked her why. 'Kiss me,' said the girl. So he kissed her, and she went limp in his arms. 'Oooh,' said the girl, sighing, almost swooning, 'I just kissed Al Pacino.'

In his first surprise, assuming that she must be teasing, Vincent had only laughed and blushed. But later, thinking it over, he knew she had really meant it. Somehow or other she had seen beneath the surface, had cut through to bedrock, to his very soul. That was something incredible. It blew his mind. In fact, if anyone ever asked him and he tried to answer honestly, looking back, he would say that was the happiest, the very best, moment of his life.

Since then, whenever he gazed into the mirror, it was always Pacino who gazed back. A killer, and a star. Heroic in reflection. Then Vincent would take another breath, the deepest he could manage; would make his face, his whole body, go still; would blink three times to free his imagination, and he would start to count.

Silently, as slowly as possible, he would go from one to a hundred. It was only now, while he counted, that he thought about death.

Mostly he thought about guns. On certain occasions, if he felt that he was getting stale, he might also dwell on knives, on karate chops and flying kung fu kicks, even on laser beams. But always, in the last resort, he came back to bullets.

It felt just like a movie. For instance, he would see himself at the top of a high flight of stairs, back against a wall, while a swarm of attackers came surging up towards him to knock him down, destroy him. But Vincent stood his ground. Unflinchingly, he took aim and fired. One by one they went crashing backwards, down into the pit.

When the battle ended and he had won, he stood alone. Far beneath him, he knew, there was blood and smoke, a chaotic heap of bodies, dead and dying. But that did not enter the physical vision. On the screen there was only Vincent, impassive, ice cold in triumph, who put his gun back into its holster, wiped away the sweat that blinded him, straightened his collar, and, finally, in close-up, smiled.

At one hundred, he let out his breath in a rush. The strain of holding back had turned him purple, and veins were popping all over his neck and arms. For some moments all he could do was gasp. But even as he suffered, his body felt weightless, free, almost as if he were floating. And when he got his breath back, and the roaring in his temples went away, it was true that he felt content.

That was the end; the movie was complete. Turning away from the glass, and away from Pacino, he would flush the toilet, wash his hands. He combed his hair. He checked his watch. Then he went out into the corridor, back into the store. The week behind the counter had been obliterated. No drudgery existed. He was released; Saturday night had begun.

Lisa was in love with Billy, and Billy was in love with Lisa. John James was in love with Lorraine. Lorraine loved Gus. Gus loved Donna. And Donna loved Vincent. But Vincent loved only his mother, and the way it felt to dance. When he left the store he went home and prepared for 2001 Odyssey. He bathed, he shaved, he dressed. That took him four hours, and by the time he emerged, shortly after nine, he felt reborn.

He lived on the eleventh floor of a high-rise on Fourth Avenue and 66th Street, close beside the subway tracks, with the remnants of his family. He loved them, was proud that he supported them. But when he tried to describe their existence, he would begin to stammer and stumble, embarrassed, because everything came out so corny: 'Just like soap,' he said, 'only true.'

His father, a thief, was in jail, and his oldest brother had been killed in Vietnam. His second brother was in the hospital, had been there almost a year, recovering from a car crash that had crushed his legs. His third brother had moved away to Manhattan, into the Village, because he said he needed to be free and find himself. So that left only Vincent, his mother, and his two younger sisters, Maria and Bea (short for Beata), who were still in school.

Between them they shared three rooms, high up in a block of buildings like a barracks. His windows looked out on nothing but walls, and there was the strangest, most disturbing smell, which no amount of cleaning could ever quite destroy.

Hard to describe it, this smell; hard to pin it down. Sometimes it seemed like drains, sometimes like a lack of oxygen, and sometimes just like death, the corpse of some decaying animal buried deep in the walls. Whichever, Vincent wanted out. He would have given anything. But there was no chance. How could there be? He could never abandon his mother. 'You must understand,' he said. 'I am the man.'

Here he paused. 'I am her soul,' he said. Then he paused again, pursing his lips, and he cast down his eyes. He looked grave. 'Understand,' he said, 'my mother is me.'

It was the guts of winter, bitter cold. But he would not protect himself. Not on Saturday night, not on display at Odyssey. When he kissed his mother goodbye and came down on to Fourth, strutting loose, he wore an open-necked shirt, ablaze with reds and golds, and he moved through the night with shoulders hunched tight, his neck rammed deep between his shoulder blades in the manner of a miniature bull. A bull in Gucci-style loafers, complete with gilded buckle, and high black pants tight as sausage skins. Shuffling, gliding, stepping out. On the corner, outside Najmy Bros. grocery, he passed a Puerto Rican, some dude in a floppy velour hat, and the dude laughed out loud. So Vincent stopped still, and he stared, a gaze like a harpoon, right between the eyes. 'Later,' he said.

'Later what?' said the dude, lolling slack, sneaking his hand back in his pants, grin slapped clean across his face. 'Later who? Later where? Later how?'

'Hombre,' said Vincent, expressionless, 'you will die.'

It was not quite his own. To be perfectly truthful, he had borrowed the line from Lee Van Cleef, some Spaghetti Western that he'd seen on late-night TV. But he drawled it out just right. A hint of slur, the slightest taste of spit. 'Hombre, you will die.' Just like that. And moved away. So slick and so sly that the dude never knew what hit him.

Two blocks farther on, Joey was waiting in the car. Joey and Gus in the front, Eugene and John James and now Vincent in the back, trundling through the icy streets in a collapsing '65 Dodge. Nobody talked and nobody smiled. Each scrunched into his own private space; they all held their distance, conserved their strength, like prize-fighters before a crucial bout. The Dodge groaned and rattled. The radio played Harold Melvin and the Blue Notes. Everything else was silence, and waiting.

John James and Eugene worked in a record store; Gus was a house painter. As for Joey, no one could be sure. In any case, it didn't matter. Not now. All that counted was the moment. And for the moment, riding out toward 2001 Odyssey, they existed only as Faces.

Faces. According to Vincent himself, they were simply the élite. All over Brooklyn, Queens and the Bronx, even as far away as New Jersey, spread clear across America, there were millions and millions of kids who were nothing special. Just kids. Zombies. Professional dummies, going through the motions, following like sheep. School, jobs, routines. A vast faceless blob. And then there were the Faces. The Vincents and Eugenes and Joeys. A tiny

429

minority, maybe two in every hundred, who knew how to dress and how to move, how to float, how to fly. Sharpness, grace, a certain distinction in every gesture. And some strange instinct for rightness, beyond words, deep down in the blood: 'The way I feel,' Vincent said, 'it's like we have been chosen.'

Odyssey was their home, their haven. It was *the* place, the only disco in all Bay Ridge that truly counted. Months ago there had been Revelation; six weeks, maybe two months on, there would be somewhere else. Right now there was only Odyssey.

It was a true sanctuary. Once inside, the Faces were unreachable. Nothing could molest them. They were no longer the oppressed, wretched teen menials who must take orders, toe the line. Here they took command, they reigned.

The basic commandments were simple. To qualify as an Odyssey Face, an aspirant need only be Italian, between the ages of eighteen and twenty-one, with a minimum stock of six floral shirts, four pairs of tight trousers, two pairs of Gucci-style loafers, two pairs of platforms, either a pendant or a ring, and one item in gold. In addition, he must know how to dance, how to drive, how to handle himself in a fight. He must have respect, even reverence, for Facehood, and contempt for everything else. He must also be fluent in obscenity, offhand in sex. Most important of all, he must play tough.

There was no overlapping. Italians were Italian, Latins were greaseballs, Jews were different, and Blacks were born to lose. Each group had its own ideal, its own style of Face. But they never touched. If one member erred, ventured beyond his own allotted territory, he was beaten up. That was the law. There was no alternative.

Then there were girls. But they were not Faces, not truly. Sometimes, if a girl got lucky, a Face might choose her from the crowd and raise her to be his steady, whom he might one day even marry. But that was rare. In general, the female function was simply to be available. To decorate the doorways and booths, to fill up the dance floor. Speak when spoken to, put out as required, and then go away. In short, to obey, and not to fuss.

Fuss, in fact, was the one thing in life that Faces loathed most of all. Vincent, for example. The moment that anyone started to argue, to flush and wave his hands, he would simply turn his back and start walking. No matter what the circumstance, there could be no excuse for whining. It was not clean. It made him sick to his stomach.

That was why he loved to dance, not talk. In conversation, everything always came out wrong, confused. But out on the floor it all somehow fell into place. There was no muddle, nothing that could not be conveyed. Just so long as your feet made the right moves, kept hitting the right angles, you were foolproof. There were certain rules, watertight. Only obey them, and nothing could go wrong.

Sometimes, it was true, people did not understand that. Some outsider would stumble in, blundering. A complete un-Face, who wore the wrong clothes and made the wrong moves, who danced last month's routines. And that could be ruinous. Absolutely disastrous. Because the whole magic of the night, and of Odyssey, was that everything, everyone, was immaculate. No detail was botched, not one motion unconsidered.

Purity. A sacrament. In their own style, the Faces were true ascetics: stern, devoted, incorruptible. 'We may be hard. But we're fair,' said Vincent. So they gathered in strict formation, each in his appointed place, his slot upon the floor. And they danced.

On the first night when the man in the tweed suit arrived from Manhattan, it was only nine o'clock and Odyssey was still half empty. He had come on the Brooklyn-Queens Expressway and when he descended into Bay Ridge itself, he found himself in a dead land. There were auto shops, locked and barred; transmission specialists, alignment centres. Then the Homestead Bar and Grill, and the Crazy Country Club, advertising 'warm beer and lousy food'. But there were no people. Only railroads and junkyards, abandoned car seats, hubcaps, tyres, scattered by the side of the road. A wasteland.

It was another frozen night and, when he climbed out of the car, the sidewalks were so icy that he slithered at every step. Guard dogs snapped and leaped in the darkness, and sleet whipped at his eyes. So he huddled deeper, tighter, into his overcoat, and set off towards a small red light at the farthest end of the street.

This was 2001 Odyssey. On the step outside, Vincent stood waiting, smoking, and did not seem to feel the cold at all. His hair was blow-waved just so, his toe caps gleaming. *Brut* behind his ears, *Brut* beneath his armpits. And a crucifix at his throat.

Inside, Odyssey was as vast and still as a Saturday-night cathedral. Music blared from the speakers, coloured lights swirled back and forth across the dance floor. But no one answered their call. Perhaps a dozen girls sat waiting, on plastic seats, in scalloped booths. Four Faces in shiny suits stood at the bar, backs turned to the floor. The manager standing by the door scratched himself. That was all.

Then the music changed to 'Baby Face', and a boy in a red-patterned shirt began to dance alone. He came out of nowhere, down from the tiers of

431

seats at the very back of the hall, the bleachers, which were completely shrouded in darkness. Skinny, shrimpish, he stood out in the very centre of the floor, caught by the swirling lights, and did one half of the Rope Hustle. Only half, of course, because the Rope Hustle cannot really be performed without a partner. So he twirled in irregular circles, his arms twining and unfurling about his neck, vaguely as if he were trying to strangle himself. And the Faces at the bar, without even seeming to look, began to snigger.

Hearing mockery, the boy flushed and lowered his eyes, but he did not back down. For twenty minutes, half an hour, he kept on spinning, wheeling, in total isolation. 'Later on, he'll have to leave,' said Vincent. 'Now it doesn't matter. Not yet.'

'Who is he?' asked the man in the suit.

'His born name is Paul. But he calls himself Dean. A very weird guy.'

'How come?'

'He cries.'

When at last the boy came off the floor, he sat down at the bar and stared directly ahead, towards the mirror. His face was pale and pinched, his Adam's apple kept leaping in his throat, and he ordered lemonade. Over his heart there was a small tin button printed with black letters that said: 'I believe.' He drank his lemonade in three clean gulps. Then he wiped his lips and went straight back on the floor, still all alone, as if to resume a vigil.

When the music turned to 'Wake Up Everybody', he spun too fast, lost control, stumbled. Then Vincent sighed and shook his head. 'Funny guy,' he said. 'When I was five, my father broke my arm. Twisted it until it snapped. Because he was drunk, and he hated me. But I didn't cry. Not one tear.'

Gradually, the floor began to fill; the night embarked in earnest. The girls emerged from their booths, formed ranks, and began to do the Bus Stop. A band appeared in blue denim suits embossed with silver studding. Blacks from Crown Heights, who played as loudly and as badly as anyone possibly could, grinning, sweating, stomping, while the dancers paraded beneath them, impassive.

One after another the stock favourites came churning out. 'Bad Luck' and 'Supernatural Thing', 'What a Difference a Day Made', 'Track of the Cat', each reduced to the same automaton chugging, interchangeable. Nobody looked and no one ever applauded. Still, the band kept pounding away, kept right on grinning. 'These guys. Those shines,' said Vincent. 'We wind them up like clockwork. We pay, and they perform.'

Outside, his companions sat in the car, Joey and Gus in the front, Eugene and John James in the back, drinking whisky from a bottle in a paper bag.

They still made no conversation, did not relax. But as the alcohol hit, they started to mumble.

'Mother,' said Eugene.

'Fucker,' said Gus.

'Motherfuckin' right,' said Joey.

Sometime after ten, feeling ready, they stepped out on the sidewalk and moved toward Odyssey in a line, shoulder to shoulder, like gunslingers. Heads lowered, hands thrust deep in their pockets, they turned into the doorway. They paused for just an instant, right on the brink. Entered.

Vincent was already at work on the floor. By now the Faces had gathered in force, his troops, and he worked them like a quarterback, calling out plays. He set the formations, dictated every move. If a pattern grew ragged and disorder threatened, it was he who set things straight.

Under his command, they unfurled the Odyssey Walk, their own style of massed Hustle, for which they formed strict ranks. Sweeping back and forth across the floor in perfect unity, fifty bodies made one, while Vincent barked out orders, crying One, and Two, and One, and Tap. And Turn, and One, and Tap. And Turn. And Tap. And One.

They were like so many guardsmen on parade; a small battalion, uniformed in floral shirts and tight flared pants. No one smiled or showed the least expression. Above their heads, the black musicians honked and thrashed. But the Faces never wavered. Number after number, hour after hour, they carried out their routines, their drill. Absolute discipline, the most impeccable balance. On this one night, even Vincent, who was notoriously hard to please, could find no cause for complaint.

At last, content in a job well done, he took a break and went up into the bleachers, where he sat on a small terrace littered with empty tables and studied the scene at leisure, like a general reviewing a battlefield. From this distance, the action on the floor seemed oddly unreal, as though it had been staged. A young girl in green, with ash-blonde hair to her shoulders, stood silhouetted in a half-darkened doorway, posed precisely in left profile, and blew a smoke ring. Two Faces started arguing at the bar, fists raised. The dancers chugged about the floor relentlessly, and the band played 'Philadelphia Freedom'.

'How do you feel?' asked the man in the tweed suit.

'I'm thinking about my mother,' said Vincent.

'What of her?'

'She's getting old. Sometimes she feels so bad. If I was rich, I could buy her a house, somewhere on the Island, and she could take it easy.'

433

'What kind of house?'

'Big windows. Lots of light,' Vincent said, and he spread his hands, describing a shape like a globe. 'Space. Chickens in the yard. A grand piano. Grass,' he said. 'My mother likes grass. And blue sky.'

Down below, without his presence to keep control, the order was beginning to fall apart. Around the fringes, some of the dancers had broken away from the mainstream and were dabbling in experiments, the Hustle Cha, the Renaissance Bump, even the Merengue. Vincent looked pained. But he did not intervene. 'Chickens,' he said. 'They lay their own eggs.'

A fight broke out. From outside, it was not possible to guess exactly how it started. But suddenly Gus was on his back, bleeding, and a Face in a bright blue polka-dot shirt was banging his head against the floor. So Joey jumped on the Face's back. Then someone else jumped in, and someone else. After that there was no way to make out anything beyond a mass of bodies, littered half-way across the floor.

Vincent made no move; it was all too far away. Remote in his darkness, he sipped at a Coca-Cola and watched. The band played 'You Sexy Thing' and one girl kept screaming, only one.

'Is this the custom?' asked the man in the suit.

'It depends.'

'On what?'

'Sometimes people don't feel in the mood. Sometimes they do,' said Vincent. 'It just depends.'

In time, the commotion subsided, the main participants were ushered outside to complete their negotiations in private. Those left behind went back to dancing as if nothing had happened, and the band played 'Fly, Robin, Fly'.

John James, the Double J, appeared on the terrace, lean and gangling, with a chalky white face and many pimples. There was blood beneath his nose, blood on his purple crêpe shirt. 'Mother,' he said, sitting down at the table. 'Fucker,' said Vincent.

So the night moved on. The Double J talked about basketball, records, dances. Then he talked about other nights, other brawls. The music kept playing and the dancers kept on parading. From time to time a girl would stop and look up at the terrace, hoping to catch Vincent's eye. But he did not respond. He was still thinking about his mother.

Somebody threw a glass which shattered on the floor. But the Faces just went One, and Two, and Tap, and Turn. And Tap, and Turn, and Tap.

'I was in love once. At least I thought I was,' said Vincent. 'I was going to get engaged.'

'What happened?'

'My sister got sick and I had to stay home, waiting for the doctor. So I didn't get to the club until midnight. Bojangles, I think it was. And by then I was too late.'

'How come?'

'She danced with someone else.'

'Only danced?'

'Of course,' said Vincent, 'and after that, I could never feel the same. I couldn't even go near her. I didn't hate her, you understand. Maybe I still loved her. But I couldn't stand to touch her. Not when I knew the truth.'

Around two, the band stopped playing, the Faces grew weary, and the night broke up. Outside the door, as Vincent made his exit, trailed by his lieutenants, a boy and a girl were embracing, framed in the neon glow. And Vincent stopped; he stared. No more than two yards distant, he stood quite still and studied the kiss in closest detail, dispassionate, as though observing guinea pigs.

The couple did not look up and Vincent made no comment. Down the street, Joey was honking the car horn. 'God gave his only son,' said John James.

'What for?' said Vincent, absentmindedly.

'Rent,' replied the Double J.

It was then that something strange occurred. Across the street, in the darkness beyond a steel-mesh gate, the guard dogs still snarled and waited. Gus and Eugene stood on the curb directly outside the gate, laughing, stomping their feet. They were drunk and it was late. They felt flat, somehow dissatisfied. And suddenly they threw themselves at the steel wires, yelling.

The guard dogs went berserk. Howling, they reared back on their hind legs, and then hurled themselves at their assailants, smashing full force into the gate. Gus and Eugene sprang backwards, safely out of reach. So the dogs caught only air. And the Faces hooted, hollered. They made barking noises, they whistled, they beckoned the dogs towards them. 'Here, boys, here,' they said, and the dogs hurled forward again and again, in great surging waves, half maddened with frustration.

Even from across the street, the man in the suit could hear the thud of their bodies, the clash of their teeth on the wires. Gus sat down on the sidewalk, and he laughed so much it hurt. He clasped his sides, he wiped away tears. And Eugene charged once more. He taunted, he leered, he stuck out his tongue. Then he smacked right into the fence itself, and this time the dogs flung back with such frenzy, such total demonic fury, that even the steel

435

bonds were shaken and the whole gate seemed to buckle and give.

That was enough. Somewhat chastened, though they continued to giggle and snicker, the Faces moved on. Behind them, the dogs still howled, still hurled themselves at the wires. But the Faces did not look back.

When they reached the car, they found Vincent already waiting, combing his hair. 'Where were you?' asked Gus.

'Watching,' said Vincent, and he climbed into the back, out of sight. Inside 2001 Odyssey, there was no more music or movement, the dance floor was deserted. Saturday night had ended, and Vincent slouched far back in his corner. His eyes were closed, his hands hung limp. He felt complete.

Another Saturday night. Easing down on Fifth and Ovington, Joey parked the car and went into the pizza parlour, the Elegante. Vincent and Eugene were already waiting. So was Gus. But John James was missing. Two nights before he had been beaten up and knifed, and now he was in the hospital.

It was an old story. When the Double J got home from work on Thursday evening, his mother had sent him out for groceries, down to Marinello's Deli. He had bought pasta and salad, toilet paper, a six-pack of Bud, a package of frozen corn, gum, detergent, tomato sauce, and four TV dinners. Paid up. Combed his hair in the window. Then went out into the street, cradling his purchases in both arms.

As he emerged, three Latins – Puerto Ricans – moved across the sidewalk towards him and one of them walked straight through him. Caught unawares, he lost his balance and his bag was knocked out of his arms, splattering on the curb.

Produce scattered everywhere, rolling in the puddles and filth. The frozen corn spilled into the gutter, straight into some dog mess, and the Latins laughed. 'Greaseballs,' said John James, not thinking. All that was on his mind was his groceries, the need to rescue what he'd lost. So he bent down and began to pick up the remnants. And the moment he did, of course, the Latins jumped all over him.

The rest was hazy. He could remember being beaten around the head, kicked in the sides and stomach, and he remembered a sudden sharp burn in his arm, almost as though he had been stung by an electric wasp. Then lots of shouting and scuffling, bodies tumbling all anyhow, enormous smothering weights on his face, a knee in the teeth. Then nothing.

In the final count, the damage was three cracked ribs, a splintered cheek-bone, black eyes, four teeth lost, and a deep knife cut, right in the meat of his arm, just missing his left bicep.

'Three greaseballs at once,' said Gus. 'He could have run. But he wouldn't.'

'He stuck,' said Vincent. 'He hung tight.'

Judgement passed, the Faces finished their pizzas, wiped their lips, departed. Later on, of course, there would have to be vengeance, the Latins must be punished. For the moment, however, the feeling was of excitement, euphoria. As Eugene hit the street, he let out a whoop, one yelp of absolute glee. Saturday night, and everything was beginning, everything lay ahead of them once more.

But Vincent hung back, looked serious. Once again he had remembered a line, another gem from the screen. 'Hung tight,' he said, gazing up along the bleak street. 'He could have got away clean, no sweat. But he had his pride. And his pride was his law.'

Donna loved Vincent, had loved him for almost four months. Week after week she came to Odyssey just for him, to watch him dance, to wait. She sat in a booth by herself and didn't drink, didn't smile, didn't tap her foot or nod her head to the music. Though Vincent never danced with her, she would not dance with anyone else.

Her patience was infinite. Hands folded in her lap, knees pressed together, she watched from outside, and she did not pine. In her own style she was satisfied, for she knew she was in love, really, truly, once and for all, and that was the thing she had always dreamed of.

Donna was nineteen, and she worked as a cashier in a supermarket over towards Flatbush. As a child she had been much too fat. For years she was ashamed. But now she felt much better. If she held her breath, she stood five-foot-six and only weighed 140 pounds.

Secure in her love, she lived in the background. Vincent danced, and she took notes. He laughed, and she was glad. Other girls might chase him, touch him, swarm all over him. Still she endured, and she trusted.

And one Saturday, without any warning, Vincent suddenly turned toward her and beckoned her on to the floor, right in the middle of the Odyssey Walk, where she took her place in the line, three rows behind him, one rank to the left.

She was not a natural dancer, never had been. Big-boned, soft-fleshed, her body just wasn't right. She had good breasts, good hips, the most beautiful grey-green eyes. But her feet, her legs, were hopeless. Movement embarrassed her. There was no flow. Even in the dark, when she made love, or some boy used her for pleasure, she always wanted to hide.

437

Nonetheless, on this one night she went through the motions and nobody laughed. She kept her eyes on the floor: she hummed along with the songs. Three numbers went by without disaster. Then the dancers changed, moved from the Walk to something else, something she didn't know, and Donna went back to her booth.

Obscurity. Safety. She sipped Fresca through a straw and fiddled with her hair. But just as she was feeling stronger, almost calm again, Vincent appeared above her, his shadow fell across her just like in the movies, and he put his hand on her arm.

His shirt was pink and scarlet and yellow; her dress was pastel green. His boots were purple, and so were her painted lips. 'I'm leaving,' Vincent said, and she followed him outside.

His coat was creased at the back. He didn't know that, but Donna did; she could see it clearly as they walked out. And the thought of it, his secret weakness, made her dizzy with tenderness, the strangest sense of ownership.

'What's your name?' Vincent asked.

'Maria,' said Donna, 'Maria Elena.'

They sat in the back of Joey's car and Vincent pulled down her tights. There was no space, everything hurt. But Donna managed to separate her legs, and Vincent almost kissed her. 'Are you all right?' he asked.

'I love you,' said Donna.

'No, not that,' said Vincent. 'I mean, are you fixed?'

She wasn't, of course. She wasn't on the pill, or the coil, or anything. Somehow or other, she'd never got around to it. So Vincent went away. He simply took his body from hers, climbed out of the car. 'Vincent,' said Donna. But he was gone.

She didn't feel much, did not react in any way. For the next few minutes, she sat very still and tried not to breathe. Then she went home and she slept until noon the next day, a sleep of absolute immersion, so deep and so silent, she said later on, it felt like Mass.

Another week went by; another Saturday night arrived. But this time it was different. On Thursday afternoon she had bought her first packet of condoms. Now they nestled in her purse, snug upon her lap. She was prepared.

Everything seemed changed in her, resolved. Tonight she didn't sit alone, felt no need to hide. She danced every number whether anyone asked her or not. She drank Bacardi and Coke, she laughed a lot, she flapped her false eyelashes. She wore a blue crêpe blouse without any bra, and underneath her long black skirt, cut in the style of the '40s, her legs were bare.

438

Even when Vincent danced near her, she hardly seemed to notice. It was as if she were weightless, floating free. But when the man in the tweed suit sat down beside her in her plastic booth, in between dances, and asked her how she felt, she could not speak, could only place her hand above her heart, to keep it from exploding.

Finally, shortly after one o'clock, Vincent decided to leave. He disappeared towards the cloakroom to retrieve his coat, and while his back was turned, Donna slipped by, out on to the street, where she waited.

It was raining hard, had been raining all night. Turning up her collar, tightening the belt on her coat, which had once belonged to her older sister, Donna pressed back into the angle of the wall, right underneath the neon sign. And she began to talk. Normally she was cautious, very quiet. But now the words came out in a torrent, an uncontrollable flood, as though some dam had burst deep within her.

She talked about dances she had been to, clothes that her friends had bought, boys who had left her, a dog she had once owned. She talked about home and work, and the rain came down in a steady stream. Ten minutes passed. She said she wanted three children.

At last the door opened and Vincent came out, ducking his head against the downpour. The light fell full on Donna's face; she tried to smile. Her hair was slicked flat against her skull and Vincent looked her over with a look of vague surprise, as if he couldn't quite place her. Her make-up was smudged; the tip of her nose was red. She was fat. Vincent walked straight past her.

He went off down the street, moved out of sight, and Donna remained behind, still standing on the sidewalk. 'Oh,' she said, and she brought her hand up out of her left coat pocket, loosely holding the packet of unused condoms.

She opened it. Gently, methodically, she took out the sheaths and dangled them, squeezed between her forefinger and thumb. One by one, not looking, she dropped them in the wet by her feet. Then she went home again, back to sleep.

Another Saturday night. The man in the tweed suit was sitting in the bleachers, around one o'clock, when Eugene approached him and sat down at his table. 'Are you really going to write a story?' Eugene asked.

'I think so,' replied the man.

'There are some things I want you to put in. As a favour,' Eugene said. 'Things I'd like to say.'

He was lean and wiry, vaguely furtive, in the style of a human stoat, and his yellow shirt was emblazoned with scarlet fleurs-de-lis. His voice was

439

high-pitched, squeaky; his left eye was forever squinting, half shut, as if warding off an invisible waft of cigarette smoke. At first glance he might have passed for an overgrown jockey. But his real ambition was to become a disc jockey, or possibly a TV quizmaster: 'Something daring. Anything. It doesn't matter what,' he said.

Now he wanted to declare himself, to make a statement, his testament.

'Go ahead,' the man said. 'Tell me.'

'First,' said Eugene, 'I want to mention my mother and father, my brothers, my uncle Tony, my grandmother. Also, Roy and Butch at Jones Beach, and Charlie D. in Paterson. And Alice, she knows why.'

'Anyone else?'

'And everyone, as well.'

The way he spoke, measured, remote, it was as though he addressed them from a very great distance, an alien world. From prison, perhaps, or an army camp. Or some secret underground, a Saturday-night cabal, known only to initiates. 'Is that all?' asked the man in the suit.

'Just tell them hello,' said Eugene, 'and you can say I get by.'

On Wednesday evening, to help time pass, Vincent went to see *The Man Who Would Be King* and, rather to his surprise, he liked it very much. On his own admission, he did not understand it, not entirely, for India and the Raj were too far away, much too unreal to make any practical sense. Still, he enjoyed the colour and flash, the danger, the sense of everything being possible, all dreams of adventure coming true.

Afterwards, he sat on a low wall outside a basketball court, across the street from the high rise, and considered. The man in the suit was there again, asking more questions. So Vincent talked about living on the eleventh floor, his windows that looked out on nothing, the smell. And working in a housewares store, selling paint and climbing ladders, grinning for his living. 'Sucks,' he said. 'They've got me by the balls.'

'How about the future?' asked the man in the suit.

'What future?' Vincent said, and he looked askance, as though the man must be retarded to ask such a question. This was not the Raj; he was not floating in a film. There were dues to pay, people to support. That took money. And money, in this place, meant imprisonment.

Still the man persisted, asked him to imagine. Just conceive that he was set free, that every obstacle was suddenly removed and he could be whatever he pleased. What would he do then? What would give him the greatest pleasure of all, the ultimate fulfilment?

Vincent took his time. This was another dumb question, he knew that. Yet the vision intrigued him, sucked him in almost despite himself. So he let his mind roam loose. Sitting on the wall, he bent his head, contemplated the cracks in the sidewalk. Pondered. Made up his mind. 'I want to be a star,' he said.

'Such as?' asked the man in the suit.

'Well,' said Vincent, 'someone like a hero.'

Six weeks passed. Six more weeks of drudgery, six more Saturdays. The Odyssey began to wind down, lose its novelty. It was time to move on. But no replacement had been found, not as yet. So there was a hiatus. The Faces kept in training, waiting for the next step. A fresh sensation, another explosion. Meanwhile, they marked time.

Sure enough, their patience paid off. Outside the pizza parlour, on another Saturday night, Joey, Vincent, the Double J, and Eugene sat waiting in the Dodge, raring to go. But Gus did not show up.

Twenty minutes passed, then thirty, forty. They were almost ready to go on without him. Then suddenly he came out of the shadows, running, burning. His face was flushed; he was all out of breath. Too wild to make sense, he could only spew out obscenities, kick at the kerb, pound his fists, impotent, on the body of the car.

At last he simmered down, choked out his explanations. And the news was indeed enormous. That afternoon, just three hours earlier, his younger sister, Gina, had been molested, debauched, as she crossed a children's playground in the park.

Gus poured out the story. After his sister had finished her lunch, she went to the apartment of her best friend Arlene, who lived about ten blocks away. Both of them were eleven years old and together they spent the afternoon nibbling chocolate candies, trying out different make-up, sighing over photographs of Donny Osmond. Then Gina walked home in the dusk, alone, wrapped in her imitation-leather coat, which was short and showed off her legs. Soon she came to McKinley Park. To make a shortcut, she turned off the street and headed across the park playground.

It was getting dark and the playground was empty, spooky. Gina hastened. Halfway across, however, a man appeared, coming from the opposite direction. He had wispy hair and a wispy beard, and he was talking to himself. When Gina came level with him, he stopped and stared. 'Pretty. Pretty. Pretty,' he said. Just like that. And he looked at her legs, straight at her kneecaps, with a strange smile, a smile that made her want to run. So she did.

She sped out of the playground, into the street, down the block.

Just as she reached the sanctuary of her own hallway, Gus was coming down the stairs. So she bumped straight into him, jumped into his arms. 'What's wrong?' he said. But she couldn't say. She just dug her nails into his arms, and she sort of sighed. Then she burst into tears.

He carried her upstairs, cradled like an infant. In time, she was comforted, she calmed down. Finally she told her story, was put to bed, and soon fell asleep. Now all that remained was revenge.

Vengeance. When Gus completed his story, he laid his forehead against the roof of the Dodge in order to feel something cold against his skull, which seemed as though it were burning. There he rested for a moment, recovering. Then he straightened up, and he banged his clenched fist into the meat of his left palm, once, twice, three times, just like on TV. 'Mother,' he said. 'I'll kill him.'

'Tear his heart out,' said Joey. 'Fuck him in the place he lives.'

'Cut off both his legs,' said Vincent. 'Kill him. Yes.'

They all knew who it was. They didn't even have to ask. In Vincent's own building there was a man called Benny, a wimp who had wispy hair and a wispy beard, who shuffled, and he was really weird. He had these crazy staring eyes, this horrible fixed stare. Everyone steered clear of him. Nobody would talk to him or go close to him. Children threw stones to make him go away. Still he hung around, staring.

No question, he was diseased. One day a bunch of kids had waited for him in the park, jumped him, and tried to teach him a lesson. But he would not learn. The more they abused him, beat on him, the stranger he became. He talked to himself, he mumbled stuff that no one could understand. And often, late at night, blind drunk, he would stand outside people's windows, yell and carry on and keep them from their sleep.

And now this. The final outrage. So the Faces drove back towards the high-rise, piled out of the car, descended on the building in a wedge.

Enforcers. Vigilantes. In silence, they came to Benny's door and Gus rang the bell, banged on the door. A minute passed and there was no answer. Gus banged again. Still no reply. Inside the apartment, everything seemed quiet, absolutely still. Gus banged a third time, a fourth, and then he lost patience. He started raging, kicking the door, barging into it with his shoulder. But nobody moved inside or made a sound, and the door would not give way.

Defeated, the Faces stood around in the hallway, feeling vaguely foolish. At first their instinct was simply to wait it out, keep a vigil till Benny came home. But within a few minutes, hanging about, doing nothing, that plan lost its attraction. The hall was deserted, there was no sign of action. Just standing there grew boring, and they started to fret.

Loitering outside the front doorway, aimless, it was Eugene who came up with the solution. 'I don't care. No sweat,' he said. 'Somebody's going to pay.'

'Motherfuckin' right,' said Gus, and he slammed his fist into his palm again; he threw a right cross into space. 'Those greaseball bastards.'

'Mothers,' said the Double J.

'Those motherfuckin' freaks,' said Gus. 'We're going to rip them apart.' And the man in the tweed suit, who had been watching, was forgotten. The Faces looked past him, hardly seemed to recognize his shape. 'We're going,' said the Double J.

'Where to? Odyssey?' asked the man.

'Hunting,' said Gus.

They moved back to the car, they clambered inside. Of course, the man in the suit wanted to go along, wanted to watch, but they wouldn't let him. They said that he didn't belong, that this was no night for tourists, spectators. He tried to argue but they would not hear him. So he was left behind on the sidewalk, and they travelled alone.

But just before the Dodge moved off, Vincent rolled down his window, looked out into the dark. His face was immobile, frozen, in the best style of Al Pacino. 'What is it?' asked the man in the suit.

Vincent laughed, exulted. 'Hombre, you will die,' he said, to no one in particular. And the Faces drove away, off into Saturday night. Horsemen. A posse seeking retribution, which was their due, their right.

Nik Cohn, *Ball the Wall* (1989)

1975: Is Northern Soul Dying on Its Feet?

Sunday morning. Arriving in Nottingham The West Midlands Soul Club was planning to celebrate an All-Dayer that afternoon. The best All-Dayer in the country, apparently; Soul kids from all over.

For instance: What is Northern Soul? How do you get into it? What are its folk heroes? What are its folk heroics? Who's into it? What does it sound like? Where is the dancing at? Who wears what and what do they run on? What is their act?

Is this some crazy recession phenomenon? Some cunning twist in the collective conscience? Some transmutation of the late Mod syndrome?

Adolescence on ice? Background musak for some Living Youth Theatre?

Northern Soul? A misnomer come to rationalise thousands of provincial kids grooving to a particular brand of soul music, the kind that Tamla Motown were churning out during the late Sixties?

Or just a myth? With media consequences?

That night, there was a radio programme scheduled on the national net. It was to be called 'Northern Soul; Fact or Fiction?'

As if it mattered. The sun still comes up.

Nottingham: You'd think 'I Shot The Sheriff' would be a big number up here In 1764 they had a Great Cheese Riot at the Goose Fair. Nottingham has a healthy history of radical reformist workers' politics: the Nottingham mob has been notoriously militant.

Most of the worker movements – the Luddites and so on – passed this way to pick up reliable support.

But there are few monuments to prove it.

There are plenty of Friar Tuck restaurants, Little John bars and Robin Hood coffee joints.

Nottingham Castle sits on a granite plug in the surrounding limestone. And on the back of thousands of packets of cigarettes. Because between them Players and Boots – John and Jess – have a big stake in Nottingham's future. Jess Boot, for instance, bought the university for the town.

Now it's full of weirdos.

Northern Soul? Jess Boot and the Chemists? John Player and his Sons? Ned Ludd and the Luddites?

So, arriving in Nottingham With no food to be had anywhere, it being a Sunday lunchtime, and the fountain in the Broadmarsh shopping centre (the Berlin wall) out of action.

Nottingham has mainlined for the Great Decorative Tile Apocalypse. With its pedestrian subways, its city centre urban renewal cancer, with its textile industry taken over by immigrant populations, with D. H. Lawrence to its credit . . . and the best All-Dayer in the country . . . and, at the imminent Goose Fair, the best mushy peas anywhere in the world.

Lynne Osborne is sitting on the Council House steps. That's where everybody meets everybody else. Between the lions. Sitting there you can look over the square. Sitting there you can be moved on by the police. Sitting there, you can watch Nottingham happen.

Any daughter, any sister, any town. Lynne signs her letters with 'Keep the

Faith'. Lynne is a civil servant during the week. Lynne works in a newsagent on a Sunday morning. Lynne is into Northern Soul.

She'll be going to the All-Dayer at Mecca's Palais. But not until later, when it's livened up a bit.

Lynne got into Northern Soul about a year ago. Someone gave her a Northern Soul record – 'The Joke' by Butch Baker – and she liked it, figured she'd like some more of it, so she started going to places where she could get it.

She checked out the DJs and 'the sort of people who look like they might be into Northern Soul.

'If they're going to an All-Dayer, they sort of wear vests and carry Adidas bags – we call them Wigan bags, but that's just our name for them – or just big bags.'

What you got in that bag hanging there?

'Just a change of clothes.

'When we first started going – a bit fanatical about it – we used to change, say, three or four times. But now we probably only change once or twice.

'The lads change a hell of a lot of times, they do really energetic dances.

'It gets hot.'

So how do you spot a Northern Soul record if you didn't know you were listening to it?

'A lot of them are old. It depends where you hear them.

'If you hear them on the wireless, the DJ'll probably make a point of saying it's a Northern Soul record.

'There's a special programme on a Wednesday night in Nottingham called "Soul Over Nottingham" and Radio Luxembourg have just started doing a thing on Friday nights.

'Soul is commercial. Northern Soul isn't. Northern Soul is more rare.

'A lot of records are pressed (bootlegged). You get, like, a rare single that you can pay anything up to £80 for – I think that's the most I've ever heard, somebody paying £80 for a record, somebody in Sheffield, one of the DJs possibly – and you just press it up.

'This record label, Black Magic, they'll press them up for you. And then it will probably sell for about 80p.

'The most I've ever paid for a single is £2.50. That was Cochise. That was a long while ago.

'But they don't play it very much these days, because, at these Northern Soul things, as soon as a record gets on general release, the DJs will probably stop playing it.'

Lynne accepts the term 'Northern Soul' even though: 'surprisingly enough, there are lots of Northern Soul Clubs down South.

'I think it's because it started off around Wigan and places like that. I mean, there was only about five towns for All-Nighters at one time. One of them was Nottingham, actually.'

An All-Nighter runs from 2.00 a.m. to 8.00 a.m.

'They've had two in Nottingham recently. I mean they used to have one regularly about ten years ago, but that stopped – police, drugs, things like that – but they had the first All-Nighter for ages about two months ago.

'That was the West Midlands Soul Club, which isn't all that popular here. It wasn't very good apparently. People were going to sleep and there wasn't that much dancing.

'But they had one about two weeks ago – East Midlands Soul Club – and that was supposed to be really good. People were dancing all the time, you know, good records and everything.'

What do you run on?

'I'm not really an expert on . . .'

Is there a lot of dope around?

'Yes there is. I will admit that. I read somewhere that it was supposed to be 99 per cent of the people who go to All-Dayers/All-Nighters are on drugs. But personally speaking I'd say about 50 per cent.

'They take barbs, blueys, things like that.'

Who are the local folk heroes?

'You get the good dancers . . . You want name dropping do you?'

If you like.

'. . . the really good dancers, they've really gone now. About a year ago, or six months, you'd get really fanatical dancers like Andy Gotthard.

'Andy's a good dancer but he doesn't take it seriously. A lot of people take it really seriously but Andy sort of messes about.

'A lot of them mess about now, rather than take it seriously.'

Is it a question of stamina or . . .

'It is really. It's more acrobatics than dancing; backflops, spins, things like that, you know. There's no specific dance to do.

'We have a dancing competition at every All-Dayer . . . I've been to about ten All-Dayers and at about eight of them it's been blokes who won it.

'Once there was a girl who won it. She was pretty good but personally I think that Andy Gotthard should have won it. He came second.

'He wins most of them really.'

What do you get for winning?

'About £25 for winning . . .'

Enough for a single?

'And you get about £15 for coming second and about £5 for coming third.'

Nottingham has Selectadisc. Lynne calls it 'the second best record shop in England'.

There are two more of them in competition (HMV and Rediffusion) but Selecta has a reputation going for it.

'It's very good. You can get any record . . . They'll put it on order for you.'

They call it Selecta, for short.

They sprinkle dancefloors with talcum powder. The guys wear flat shoes.

'The lads always turn up in flat shoes. And most of the girls. You get the odd few that turn up in shoes that look like they've been erected, you know.

'Sometimes the floors are sticky, so you just get the talcum powder out.

'You go to a lot of these Northern Soul discos and they'll have notices up, like, "No Talcum Powder", or one of the DJs will say, like, "Who *is* it that's putting talcum powder down? Will you please stop it", or else you'll get somebody going around, checking up.'

It's supposed to ruin the floor, getting ground in, is how They see it.

It's £1 to get into an All-Dayer/All-Nighter, £1.25 for non-members. Normally, you'd pay about 30p to get into The Palais, but They up it for the Northern Soul shows.

'I suppose it is a lot really. You can stay about eight hours' [All-Dayer].

You can get Northern Soul every night in Nottingham, should you want it.

'Sometimes you get a bit fed up with it, so you start listening to others [types of music], but most people don't bother.

'You always go back to Northern Soul.'

Live shows?

'We've had nearly everybody here. We've had George Macrea. We had Wigan's Ovation at the last All-Dayer actually. Everybody thinks they are a bit over-rated. Nobody rates them very high.'

Lynne reads *Blues and Soul*.

'I had choice between the two, *Black Music* and *Blues and Soul*, and I chose *Blues and Soul*.

'It's good for putting down what's on locally, what's on in most places. They advertise every All-Dayer that's going in the country. That's why I get it. For the advertisements really.'

When Lynne started into Northern Soul, she used to go to different towns, once or twice a month.

'To Leicester, Derby . . . They have an All-Dayer in Derby every month. It's not very good, but we used to go.

'We went to Blackpool once, on a special trip, to the Blackpool Mecca, Saturday night. That's very good.'

Blackpool is the best place Lynne ever went to, but these days, she'd dig to make Cleethorpes.

'Cleethorpes All-Nighter – it doesn't sound fantastic, I know, but it is. Once a fortnight, and everybody goes – about 100 people from Nottingham go every time – come back and say how good it is.'

'The atmosphere is really good.'

Lynne will be going to Cleethorpes.

'Likely, yeah.'

DJs? What's their Act?

'It depends . . .'

'There's a few like Eddie Taylor, they're out there for the laughs really. They'll play a popular record and, then, they'll have a stupid half-hour, to sort of make a break, and they'll put things like Batman on and Magic Roundabout, things like that.

'But at an All-Dayer, they take it very seriously. They just tell you what the record is.'

An All-Dayer lasts from lunchtime, through the afternoon to about 11.00 p.m. The dancing competition goes down around 7.00 p.m.

Lynne and company don't plan on getting there till around 4.00 p.m. because, 'it doesn't liven up until teatime'.

Why soul? Why Black soul? The Rolling Stones?

'I don't like progressive music at all. To me it's just a row. Because . . .

'You talk to someone who likes progressive music and they'll say they listen to it just to listen to it.

'I like music to dance to, not to listen to.'

A Mod thing?

'A Mod thing? Mods? What do you mean? Mods and rockers? . . .

'Bit before my time.

'I know a lot of lads that are really dressing smart, into the smart thing, you know? But when they're going somewhere specifically to dance, they don't . . .

'Say that lot over there . . .'

Lynne points out a bunch of Adidas bags moving across the square.

'Looks like they're going to the All-Dayer. They're not particularly smartly dressed are they? But if they weren't going there, they probably would be.'

Whatever Northern Soul isn't, Lynne likes reggae ('especially if it's about three or four years old'), but she is not into 'commercial soul'.

It's for a younger audience, she says.

You have to be 18 to get into an All-Dayer, because they have bars on conventional opening times.

But it's cool to be late, so go for a drink at The Fountain   The Fountain is virtually next door to Selectadisc, just around the corner from the square and the Council House steps.

Turns out they have a few Northern Soul records on the jukebox (new, big, flashy, purple washlight, thin sound) and no food. Except crisps.

A lot of Lynne's friends come to The Fountain. She has to meet Kev later. Between the lions.

Back at the Council House steps, waiting on Kev   Spotting types across the square – people into Northern Soul or not. A few teds have been showing up lately, it would appear, weirdos, winos, all sorts.

You get dead pigeons in the water-features sometimes.

Lynne points out probables on their way to the Palais. Probables with their Adidas bags, probables with their wide trousers with pockets down the side of the thigh, probables with their flat shoes and the rest, probables with or without their 'soul birds'.

Lynne points out Denny, one of this afternoon's DJs, crossing the square towards Selecta and The Fountain. With his box of records and his low profile.

Kev turns up to check things out. To find out when or if everyone is 'going down'. He mentions a big queue at The Palais.

Lynne 'wouldn't be seen dead in a queue outside The Palais'.

So, hanging out, passing the time of afternoon   Lynne caught *Tommy* at the cinema. She thought it was a good film. She didn't like the music much, but she dug the film. Later she said that she liked Roger Daltrey because he 'has a good body'.

Kev elucidates on Nottingham Forest graffiti: 'It used to be We Hate Pompey or We Hate Derby. Now it's just We Hate.'

And Lynne comes up with the line of the decade: 'Pot smoking's for weirdos.'

Big Dave wanders across the square, with his mate.

Now, Big Dave is a purist. He's a member and militant supporter of the East Midlands Soul Club. This afternoon's performance is a West Midlands number.

449

Big Dave's Act is his purism.

'Going down?'

No. Big Dave wouldn't be seen alive at the West Midlands. It's all rubbish, he says. Because the DJs are always trying to lay records on the audience whereas, at the East Midlands they only play oldies, the genuine article.

But apparently, Big Dave is never satisfied. He's always moaning about something or other. Lynne is a member of both clubs.

Kev splits to pick up his car. And his bag.

Anita turns up. She has to wait for Keith. They're both 'going down'.

Anita's got *her* bag.

Big Dave says that Northern Soul is five years old in Nottingham.

Kev pulls his ragged black mini into the kerb to park it. Lynne will meet him outside the Gas Board, which is hard by The Palais.

So, going down Once, Lynne says, Kev got kicked in the face with an over-acrobatic backflop.

Kev's bag is a killer. White Adidas, covered in commemorative soul stickers – 'Keep the Faith', 'The Torch', things like that.

You pay your money and you get your card – a Mecca Social Club Membership Certificate. The number on it says there are 898,127 other members.

The dance floor is half-empty, the action quiet. The Sound System is really bad, it rattles, it can't handle too much treble. The bass does what it has to do. But only just. The dancing is sparse, and merely functional.

The guys – with their shoulders hung slightly back, they soul shuffle sideways, from the knees, along the talcum powder, and back again, high waists, short hair, T-shirts, bowling shirts, wide trousers, thin belts, terylene, flannel – are the best dancers.

This seems to be the Act: you have your bag with your changes, your talcum powder, your towel, your Polo mints, your Wrigley's. And you dance / socialise / dance / socialise / dance / socialise / change / dance / socialise ...

Like that. You work up to the dancing competition, event of the evening.

DJ Kevin makes no impression. Lynne has never seen him before, has no idea who he is. His profile is so low if he stood sideways, you'd think he'd gone home. He's playing record after record of, to the stranger's ear, Motownish soul.

The dancing competition, it appears, depends on the gate. If it's big enough, there'll be one; if it isn't, there won't.

The girls wear fifties mood rig – shirt-waisters, short sleeves, mid-calf skirtlengths. There is the odd born loser, trying to look gracefulish dancing on six-inch stacked platforms. Schoolboy hairdos.

But who's this? This styrofoam, lesser spotted Ann Margret, glossy type with the lips and the age.

It's the lady from Pye Disco Demand, here to PR Pye's nationwide dancing competition, here to check out what to compile the next compilation from, slumming in the market.

Pye are the leaders in the Exploit Northern Soul Companies. They obviously have people working in the field (because they certainly aren't working with the kids).

Kev, Lynne and Anita do more hanging out than dancing. Standing round the pile of Adidas bags.

But Keith is constantly on the floor, Keith is a good dancer, dedicated at it, elastic legs for it, hair blown specially for it.

A hustled interview with Denny, today's big DJ   Beneath the dancefloor, in a cafeteria, Northern Soul is the beat of feet, structure borne down a floor, constant and insistent. Gets to you.

Denny wears jeans and a leather jacket like the first provincial mods were wearing mid-Sixties, like the Parisien streetkids were wearing before that.

He seemed to down-rap the whole scene.

What is Northern Soul?

'Northern Soul, as such, doesn't exist. It's soul.

'Originally, the sound started with the Motown sounds, but now it's almost funky, semi-funk sounds.

'It started off with rare records.'

Big Dave says this place is rubbish because the DJs are away – pushing new records?

'Yeah. To a point. You stagnate if you stay with the old sounds. We get people writing to us and saying that the old sounds are better.

'Which is true. I think they are. But you can't play the old sounds forever. If people come up and ask me for an old record, they might as well stay at home and listen to it.

'I'm there to play records that you can't hear anywhere else.

'A DJ's got to have bootlegs, white labels, emidiscs. You can't exist without them. Ian Levine was the last bastion of that business, but he's sold out now.'

The scene in Nottingham?

'It used to be big, around '70. There used to be more people from

Nottingham than anywhere else that used to go to the All-Nighters.

'But it's dropped off a bit. It's what you're brought up to really. They're (the kids) just looking for something different.

'A lot of them don't know what they're doing, what the records are, who they're by or anything.

'It's just a sound to them.'

But . . .

'The crowds make a record popular. Normally you try and play a popular record if you're going to try to break a new sound because you know that's going to clear the floor anyway. They won't dance to a record they don't know, not here, not here.

'At Blackpool Mecca they will. But they've been brought up to it here. Perhaps that's our fault for playing the same ones all the time.'

Today, Denny is just playing oldies.

'Pye has improved a lot since Dave Godin took over. The person they had before was just a joke. They ought to be shot for what they've done to Northern Soul.

'They ruined it to my point of view.'

Denny doesn't normally come to The Palais.

'Fridays I do the Brit at Trent Bridge, and the Saturdays an All-Nighter usually, Sundays I just doss around in the pub and in the week I'm usually working away.'

Denny goes on to put down Ian Levine, The Blackpool Mecca, Tony Cummings, bootleg records.

He puts a ten year tag on Northern Soul and relates it firmly back to the Mod scenes in the sixties.

'That's where it started from. Down London they went on to progressive stuff and funky stuff.

'They used to have All-Nighters in Nottingham a long time ago – at The Dungeon, The Beachcomber, till they got shut down through drugs.

'The drug scene is nothing new, it's just that the drug squad is clamping down on it.'

Denny also has a downer on dancing competitions.

'It's a farce really. People come here to enjoy themselves, not to watch other people dancing for money. That's all it is, money and prestige.

'The only dancing competition that I enjoyed was at The Torch. A lad I knew won it. The dancing there was absolutely superb.'

Now you get very few backflops, few acrobats. This is a (Blackpool) Mecca sort of dance they do now. The style of dancing has changed over the last year.

'There used to be two distinct styles – Wigan and Mecca – for different records. When it's done well, the Mecca dance is quite good.

'The boys have always been better dancers than the girls on the Northern scene.'

Denny diffuses.

'The records I've got, I don't play at home. I play Jefferson Airplane, stuff like that.

'These kids have got a completely limited outlook – If they don't hear it at an All-Nighter, they don't know it. I'd say it was pathetic really. What sort of an outlook is that? I've not heard that before, I don't like it.

'To dance to a record properly you've got to know it, especially nowadays when you get so many breaks in it.

'At All-Dayers, you get a lot of people clearing the floor, but at All-Nighters, where you get a lot of people doped up, it's easier to break new records.

'There is no atmosphere here at all. I've been falling asleep. If I go to an All-Nighter, I can sit down and talk to people from all over, Rotherham, Gloucester, Doncaster, Sheffield – you judge how good an All-Nighter is by how far people come to see it.

'We used to go regularly to Wigan, 80 or 90 miles; Cleethorpes – we were there the other week, and that's 80 miles.

'I go to buy and sell records. If I'm not buying and selling I don't enjoy it.'

Denny is down on promoters too.

'The money they're making out of us is . . .

'There ought to be a law against it.'

While you don't seem to get a lot of trouble at All-Dayers: 'You should see some of the people that go to All-Nighters ... you get some right villains.'

Northern Soul isn't like it was To listen to Denny and Lynne you get the impression that the whole scene has degenerated into a new regime.

That auto-nostalgia for better days has set in. That the dancing isn't what it was. And so on. The music spread thinner by the record companies and the bootleggers.

So. Jawing with the gang, at a table: there's Lynne, Kev, Anita and another guy who brought his own ham sandwiches and handed them round.

Irene turns up. Wrigleys all round.

Irene says she's been to Cleethorpes a few times and that compared to that, Nottingham is a load of rubbish.

There is speculation as to whether the hot dancers will turn up – Andy Gotthard and another guy called Kev.

This other Kev, apparently, is not so good. It's just that he likes being photographed. You only have to say the word Camera to him and he'll Act up something crazy.

Denny's oldies penetrate the cafeteria from the dancefloor above.

There is talk about being ripped off from all directions, and the differences between All-Dayers and All-Nighters, about whether All-Dayers are kids' play.

They would prefer to have to pay £2.50 for a single as long as it's going to stay rare, but, more and more, they are in danger of shelling out £5.00 for something that they aren't told will be on general release at 60p in the time it takes to get changed.

The vigilance of the bootleggers and the legitimate record companies have combined to produce a new regime – over provision, Northern Soul for idiots, trans-Atlantic high finance.

Back on the floor the dancing has livened up a little, the bar is soon to open. The dancing competition is scheduled for 7.00 p.m.

There are one or two backflops here and there.

A big part of the Act seems to be the leaping Into Action trip, from a lounging position on a pile of Adidas bags, after a floorclearer, and on recognition of the opening bars of a popular sound.

It has the same energy you hear on 'Get Your Ya Yas Out,' at the start of 'Midnight Rambler', when Keith Richard just can't restrain his getting into the chordal riff down there.

Irene is still raving about Cleethorpes. They don't even steal your bags here. At Cleethorpes there are road blocks to set up to bust the kids before they get into town. Cleethorpes is heavy.

With ten minutes to competition time, the floor is almost crowded. The guys look healthy, athletic.

Like school sportsday was being held in a dance hall.

Kev does a change, and then his Act, briefly.

Keith is still dancing, hasn't stopped.

With a character called Nig.

Anita says that Nig doesn't do anything particularly spectacular but he has stamina. If he's enjoying himself, he can go on for hours.

He seems to be enjoying himself, grinning from ear to ear there.

454

Bar opens.

Some of this dancing is formula, like Charlie Foxx used to do.

A concession is selling badges, a rag called *Hot Buttered Soul*, singles and soul packs (10 singles for £1) of stuff they can't sell any other way.

Kev, Anita and Nig have changed.

There seems to be a lot of tattoos around. Sometimes the music sounds a little like the Four Tops.

Finally, the dancing competition Organised from the stage with Butlins-like condescension, the girls dance first, then the guys.

A knot of disinterested judges, including Denny, pick a final eight and then a final three.

The winner is chosen by audience approval guesswork. The judges make their selections by touching people on site.

Keith doesn't make the final eight. Nor does Nig. Nor Irene.

Nig says that the guy who came second should have won easy. He's been known to dance up walls and across the ceiling (at The Brit), he's that good. He just didn't want to win. So he rolled out his low profile and stuck to the shuffle.

For some reason, acrobatics are banned from dancing competitions. So the people who can't dance too good get a chance to win?

The winner was a little girl in a white shirt-waister, a pageboy hairdo and a neo-neurotic amphetamine-annie style.

She took home £25 and a T-shirt.

Northern Soul is a name for a youth cult based on dancing to old rare American soul records.

At its best, it is street class, street status and dedicated energy.

At its worst, it has been robbed.

Robbed by the bootleggers, the record companies, the promoters, the media. And as such, is dying off.

Is dead, even.

The mystique and the mythology have become blurred with false archetypes. At first flattered by outside interest, the Northern Soul scene is nostalgic for its conspiratorial heyday.

A national extension of the same Mod interest in dancing, dope and rare soul, Northern Soul need only exist if you want it to. Putting on the Soul.

The musicians who make the recordings might as well be on another planet. They probably are by now.

*

While turning on to oldie souldies might seem to some like dry humping a dirty picture, there's nothing to challenge.

The kids aren't trying to change nothing.

> *Keep the Faith.*
> *I'll keep it with mine.*
> Northern Soul?
> Fact *and* fiction.

Idris Walters, Street Life, 15–28 November 1975

1976: Julie: He's Got a Lot to Answer for

The obsession started when I was 14. He used to play locally in Kingston and my brother would say: 'You must listen to David Bowie', and try to explain that he was a really good artist.

I was so young I didn't understand. But I eventually got the message and he opened up a whole new world for me.

I thought he was so extraordinary that he couldn't possibly be human. He was paranormal almost. And he wasn't actually like any other star of his time.

Or, indeed, before or after.

His silence was so loud. I mean he'd hardly say anything but he was so loud. He came over very clearly.

And when I day-dreamed about him, it was a question of glazing over and becoming almost incoherent when I spoke so that people had to prod me to get any response and I used to be away in this almost womb-like cocoon of protection.

At that time his music really drove home such powerful images. But my fantasies weren't very sexual at that stage because I was too naïve. I wasn't informed enough.

I had delusions of grandeur. I used to think: Oh, one day we'll go off together and he will understand that I am truly an individual. And he would marry me and we'd have this wonderful space age relationship.

At boarding school I used to think about him when I was in the class-room.

Him and The Osmonds – and at first I had a conflict there because I didn't know who to turn to.

The Osmonds were very immediate and easy to listen to, and very

456

presentable. But they did nothing for my imagination at all. They were just packaged to please. Not packaged to prompt you into thinking all kinds of weird and wonderful things.

So from having looked at pictures and thought about it and written all sorts of peculiar essays about him – disguising the names because I didn't want people to understand what I was really saying – I guess from there it just grew into total admiration of a man who was so talented and so extremely diffident about everything.

I began to think he was a new kind of Messiah. I used to think he was the Coming of the Lord personified and all kinds of things. I really thought he had some kind of infinite power and wisdom.

Almost like Marc Bolan, I suppose, had a mystical quality that wasn't quite of this world or of this time.

Bowie was magic and he was supreme. He had the qualities of a type of ruler.

He was science fiction personified. To me he represented the most bizarre things which were evil and not of this world and completely beyond the imagination.

I really believed he was an alien of some kind. I didn't think he was at all normal, human.

I tried to masturbate for a long time over all this and I wasn't very successful because I didn't seem to be able to get a climax. And the actual act of masturbation was as much spiritual as sexual.

But when I fantasized I became very wet and I suppose I thought: If it's truly possible to walk through glass and reach him then it might be possible to touch him.

Because he really did convey to me the most peculiarly advanced stages of sexuality.

For a long time I used a hairbrush. But it didn't do much for me. Then I tried my finger because I thought that would be more tender and more like the real thing.

But that didn't work either.

I wasn't very good at it because I didn't really know how to excite myself. It took me about three years to find out where my clit was.

All that time I was thinking Bowie, all the time.

I had this thing where I'd stick myself in my room and switch off the lights and burn incense and play Bowie records on this old record player my brother give me.

457

And I'd start to masturbate.

I used to think about us making love on top of a mountain. Because I always saw him in a very aesthetic sort of atmosphere with isolation around him: a cold, hard atmosphere with a lot of cloud – veering towards Major Tom or towards space.

Nothing of this world. Something which is beyond our understanding.

And I used to dream of layers and layers of clothes that we'd have of transparent plastic. And about ripping these pieces of plastic off to unveil something underneath.

And I had orgasms of a space kind. Something to do with hallucination really. I was actually hallucinating in orgasm.

I got very worried about it because at the time I thought I wasn't quite normal.

I tried to talk to people about it but I knew privately it would never do to talk about it. It was far too intimate and far too extreme. Therefore I tended to withdraw and become insular about it.

Then I just fantasized even more.

Eventually, when I saw him in *The Man Who Fell to Earth*, taking off his clothes and seeing him in the nude, I began to realize I fancied him even more.

And then it actually became a little more normal and channelled itself into something more erotic, because I was kinky about the fact he was so thin and he was like a woman. He seemed the perfect vehicle for my sexual needs and fulfilment.

To start with I was very clumsy about my masturbation. But then I learnt to lie back totally and relax and knock myself out on a feeling of pure ecstasy.

I would lie there – usually in some kind of underwear because I had a hang-up at the time about being totally nude. And I'd slowly take my bra off and then perhaps my pants and then very, very slowly I'd use a pillow – I used to kiss the pillow and then use it to get the feeling of a man's hand.

As Bowie was so thin I supposed he would be very fragile about it.

He would touch me with the merest of strokes and not actually grab my flesh in the way another man might.

Then I could allow myself the freedom of thought where I'd just lie there and I'd become extremely wet.

In fact I wasn't doing anything much to myself, but I was relaxing totally and playing his music and it used to drive me into a state of non-committed hysteria.

I just used to lie there and open my legs and I would feel absolutely dirty and then the whole feeling of wetness would come because I was being so naughty.

It used to amuse me that I felt shy. I'd laugh like I was being rather silly about it and worried that my mother might come in. But really I was dying for her to come in and see what I was getting up to.

I used to really get off on a particular record called 'Cracked Actor' which is terribly loud with the guitar instrumental. It was very overbearing and I used to actually reach a pinnacle where I would have to lie under the covers for fear of being overwhelmed.

I'd be very frightened of the loudness of the guitar and what I was feeling sexually.

When I saw *The Man Who Fell to Earth* I got influenced by the idea of skins peeling and the fact that skin can be taken away and produce juices of a kind that can reveal themselves at the height of sexuality.

So that when you make love you actually destroy certain layers of skin and form a liquid mass together.

It was incredibly sensuous and very wild at the same time.

I used to think that he would come to me late at night and we would go away together.

One time I actually believed him to be outside my door. But that was absolutely crazy. Obviously he wasn't.

It was my mother, in fact, knocking on the door.

I was drifting away and I was thinking perhaps he'd come one day to see me.

And I was terribly disappointed.

I remember my mother standing there and the shock-horror! She saw me in my nightdress – I was trying to undo my nightdress and I was making loud noises and my mother was wondering what the hell was wrong with me.

But I firmly believed – because I'd switched myself off – that he was there for me.

I was sort of humming. I was sort of buzzing as you do when you meditate, and I thought he was standing there.

I would look at him in his posters and try to understand the sexuality in his records.

I'd analyse them to death. I'd think that means this and this means that.

I thought the man was an absolute poet. I used to analyse his lyrics from

459

here to kingdom come and try to get some meaning out of them.

It was being alone with Bowie that was interesting because I had the privacy to fantasize and shut the door to everybody.

I looked at his photographs and I was in danger of being gog-eyed at the time because I had several on my wall. But the one I used to look at most was the one hanging over my bed with him in a hat and coat and looking through his glasses. And I used to think: Well, whatever he's thinking it must be one hell of a thing because his eyes seem so distant.

And I truly believed that nobody understood him and that I could, and whatever I did he'd understand because we were obviously meant to be.

And I thought of ESP. I read a great deal of books and most of them were flimsy paperbacks by unknown American authors of the £1.95 variety.

I managed to get it into my head that it was possible to communicate with him by thought transmission. So one day I communicated with him after a song and an interview on the radio.

And I had conversations with him in the posters. I used to walk around the room in a state of undress, but always protecting my small parts because I still had a hang-up about being totally exposed.

But I would always manage to excite him in some way. He would see I was so intelligent that he would come to me and put his arms around me and then he'd say: 'Well, I have to leave you now but I'll be back.'

I actually used to have these conversations with him. I used to say: 'David, I want to go away.' Or: 'I would like to be in your show.' And I had ambitions at the time to be a pop star and I used to say things like: 'Oh, can I be in your film?' And also quite mundane conversations like: 'Would you like some tea?' And: 'I'll take you out,' and, 'There's a taxi outside,' and this type of thing. And we'd go out together.

Obviously we wouldn't make it to the front door but the idea was there and that was the important thing, just to have the reality in my own bedroom, within the four walls.

When I finished school I was unemployed for a while and I was really confused. And then I went on to drama school and then it got worse because I was confronted by all these Bowie look-alikes.

Then I finally had a sexual relationship in which I managed to bring all these fantasies into my sex life.

I went out with somebody who looked like David Bowie. It was a really silly thing. And of course it was a disappointment, because I found that obviously he didn't live up to the thing itself.

He was all of seven stone with glasses and knock-kneed. Pimply as well. But I suppose I just wanted very much to have in bed anything that resembled Bowie. It didn't really matter who. Just the fact he could look like Bowie was an amazing achievement in my books and all my friends would be terribly impressed that I was going out with someone who'd gone to those lengths to look like Bowie. Therefore he must really be a little bit like Bowie, you see, because he looked so much like Bowie.

But it wasn't really any good at all.

I then went out with another chap who was much taller and was actually known for being a David Bowie look-alike.

Both those chaps were functional for me in the sense that they brought me a little closer to the idea of being way-out, and also because they wore the look well.

They looked good on my arm and they served their purpose.

But they disappointed me in other ways and they were very vain, the pair of them – and I don't really enjoy that sort of narcissism.

I also knew they were never going to be as intelligent as Bowie or as extraordinary.

But this was the next best thing so I might as well enjoy it.

When he killed off Ziggy Stardust at Hammersmith that really, really disturbed me because I really had a hang-up about these characters he had created and I really thought that he was responsible for creating them and he shouldn't put them to death, shouldn't bury them.

I was crying a lot and everyone was crying because he was killing off Ziggy Stardust and this was really a very sad thing.

The music was absolutely atrocious. It was so loud and I couldn't hear Bowie singing. And he was absolutely stoned, actually out of his head. And the amount of people that were stoned. . . . I didn't know about being stoned then, but I caught on pretty quick.

I was watching them and I thought: Well, they're really on a different plane here. They're not feeling what I'm feeling.

I'm quite sure that Bowie was completely off his head because his eyes would roll occasionally and the sweat was pouring. He was so excited. He was so pushed to the limit, to the very edge. And everyone around me was trying to see this and of course I got terribly squashed.

But the sweat and the smell was really horrible. Some people were sweating and others were wanking themselves off.

461

It wasn't very pleasant but I was absolutely stuck where I was and I couldn't move. I had to keep watching him.

I had a really good seat right at the front and I'd gone with another girl who was a Bowie fanatic and she was crying. Then she passed out and the St John ambulance men had to take her away.

She was in a state of hypnotism almost, just gone.

There was hysteria, particularly on the left-hand aisle because people were going wild when he reached down to the audience. They were crying and screaming. They'd try and touch him.

And he'd tease them terribly. He was a right provocative little sod.

He'd tease people by holding out his hand to them and then run away, sort of get off on that and have a quick smile to himself. Then the jerk would run to the other side of the stage and do exactly the same thing.

And I suppose we were such gullible people we allowed him to do that. We gave him the licence to enjoy the thrill of it.

It's an incredibly mobile face he's got and it had so many weird and wonderful expressions.

When he sang 'Cracked Actor' and 'Panic in Detroit' it was just amazing.

Oh, those were the days!

And after I was just stunned, absolutely stunned. I went home sort of shocked. I remember going home as all fans do, in this kind of solitary confinement where you switch off on the train and everyone else who walks on the train you totally ignore them.

And you just sit there and you're just away.

And you think: Well, I'll never see Bowie again. It's over. Etc, etc.

That scene in *The Man Who Fell to Earth* where he uses the gun was a perfectly accurate image of sucking the gun off and blowing it, quite frankly. And when he sucked the thing off I thought: Well, this guy, there's no end to what he would do.

And he showed his bollocks and everything on film. I didn't expect him to do that so it was absolutely shocking at the time.

He prompted something in me which I didn't know was actually there – he made it popular to sleep with men and women and he made it popular to be extreme – and what's more he made it possible to be like that every day.

I couldn't get that out of my mind.

It was rammed down my throat that I could dress like this now and I could go out like this and I could wear that amount of make-up because it was acceptable. To me, having that kind of opportunity was absolutely amazing. And I can only thank him.

But he was also a complete and utter enigma and the mystery that surrounded him made people fantasize.

A lot of what I read about him was fantasy reading made up for the immediate public to entertain the suckers. But then you do believe what you read. We people do believe the written word – it's all we have to go on. And kids of 16 to 18 they really take it all in because they really do worship these people.

And that's how I think it's dangerous. Because kids lose their own identity – which is so important.

The star expresses something up there that's very real to you and so you mistake that thing for yourself. And you get caught up in his life.

But you're another person with another story to tell.

You mistakenly think you can live his life and you get caught up in his success and think it's perfectly possible to achieve all those things.

They represent the success story up there and they're giving it out to the public, doling it out by the ton. Then they give out trite comments to the press and expect people to take it on the chin.

And you do, because you're so absolutely gullible.

It's almost pathetic that kind of idol thing.

But then he was extraordinary and he deserved all that idolatory, even though he's probably laughing now.

So I don't regret any of the money I spent or any of the things I used to do, the obsessions I had.

I think it was part and parcel of what I am now. I'd like to talk to him about it some time, I really would.

He was so stylish and so completely different from any other pop star of that time that he was lost in his own isolation. Because having created that complete balloon around him he mustn't let it burst. The pressure must have been enormous to keep all that fantasy going.

But he achieved it by sheer tactics, you know: Try this, let's see how the kids react to that. And then completely washing his hands of the whole business. Not actually accepting the responsibility for what he's done by becoming a besuited man with a blond hair-do and a lot of money and the ability to make his own films.

I just wonder if he doesn't think that everyone's a sucker. He's riding on the crest of a wave and he's a legend.

But I sometimes wonder who kicked it all off, whether it was some massive publicity stunt or whether it was actually David Bowie who had the initiative.

Because I'm sure he's extraordinary, but I don't think that he's so extraordinary that he didn't have a lot of help from the right people to create all that and to bring out those records.

I think he should be made aware of how he's influenced people's dress, their manners, their behaviour.

Because I now have the kind of wisdom to know how pop stars can damage people by their life-styles and by the kind of money they throw around and the kind of images they present on television.

People can get so taken away with it that they're actually in danger of believing that they are that person.

Well, I never believed I was David Bowie – I mean, I couldn't have been further from it, being rather fat and frumpy and very much a virgin – but I actually believed that I could have a relationship with him.

This was *his* influence and it was rather damaging. And I think he's so detached now from what he's done to people that he doesn't realize in all his wealth how he's influenced them.

Because he's actually walked away from them and has lived a life of cream because we've allowed him to.

It's a terrible thing he did really.

He's got a lot to answer for.

Fred and Judy Vermorel, Starlust: The Secret Fantasies of Fans (1985)

seven

1975–80

'My confusion, my faith'

'And I hate modern music
Disco Boogie and Pop
It goes on and on and on and on and on
HOW I WISH IT WOULD STOP!'

      The Buzzcocks, '16' (1977)

'Because we are paranoid': Kraftwerk's final words to famed punk writer Lester Bangs are an early warning of the dread and disturbance which characterizes this era. The late seventies are best known for punk and disco, but as both Bangs and Penny Reel show, ideas of dehumanization and the impending apocalypse were also present in Kraftwerk's cybernetics and the impassioned pleas of British West Indians: 'There are four angels standing on four corners of the earth.'

Punk was a term first introduced into pop by writers Dave Marsh and Lester Bangs to describe an aesthetic best exemplified by sixties' groups like ? and the Mysterians and the Standells: simple, abrasive white blues untainted by early seventies' ideas of good taste. A slang word to describe the lowest of the low – used in American jails and gangster movies – punk was taken up in late 1975 by John Holmstrom and Legs McNeil for a magazine which aimed to document the new, back-to-basics New York rock. As the Ramones state in their interview with Mary Harron in *Punk*'s first issue: 'We believe in *songs* . . . not in, uh, boogying and, uh, improvisation and stuff like that, y'know?'

The idea was quickly taken up in Britain, and the emergence of the Sex Pistols in the music press is documented here. Neil Spencer's finely laconic article was the first review of the group, and contains the resonant manifesto: 'Actually we're not into music: we're into chaos.' Caroline Coon first used 'Punk' in a British context in an August 1976 feature, which also zeroes in on the word that would become ubiquitous in this period: 'bored'. Jonh Ingham continues the process with his manifesto 'In Love with the Modern World', which aimed to adapt the techniques of New Journalism to this emerging movement.

Despite the strictures of Mark Perry, punk's most passionate spokesman from within, punk was ideally suited to the weekly music press which, after the scandal of December 1976, became more like a samizdat operation instead of a music-industry promotional machine. We reproduce here the *Daily Mirror* front cover story which made the Sex Pistols infamous for swearing on teatime TV; it should also be mentioned that punk was a ready-made horror story for the tabloids, not the least because many of those involved with it were obsessed by the media, and the tabloids in particular.

'The Filth and the Fury' was the first in a sequence of screaming – and now absurd – tabloid fronts. The storyline of outrage was moved along by the sacking of presenter Bill Grundy and the cancellation of all but three Sex Pistols' concerts. The group were marked from then on – a situation which they and their management did their best to encourage with records like 'God Save the Queen' and *Never Mind the Bollocks*, both of which made the headlines during 1977.

No movement was more mediated, more studied than punk, with its references to pop history and pop academia. Yet at the same time it carried emotions powerful enough to enact a national drama of decay and social break-up. This was another period when pop outstripped literature and punk was best captured by journalistic snapshots. Tony Parsons's piece is an example of what the music press did best: provide the terms on which a great group were launched, in the tradition of Elvis, the Beatles or the Rolling Stones.

Two less partisan pieces for the intellectual weeklies show how punk spread throughout England during 1977; it wasn't the only kind of pop music extant, but it was the one that everyone wanted to write about. Mark Kidel gently teases out the exotica of seeing the Ramones in Plymouth, while Angela Carter sums up punk complexities with a typically ambitious precision. As she notes at the end of 1977: 'Punk is now busily diffusing and generalizing itself and exercising a hard-edge influence over an enormous range of appearances.'

Two extracts chart American reaction to the Sex Pistols in early 1978. Andy Warhol places them as a phenomenon in context with other contemporary phenomena: disco, polydrug abuse, celebrity gossip. Legs McNeil's humorously sour account of the Sex Pistols backstage captures the group at the very moment of their disintegration. The nadir of the Sex Pistols story was reached with the deaths of Sid Vicious and Nancy Spungeon. With rare passion, Dick Hebdige delineates the limits of teen nihilism and tabloid engagement at the same time as he seeks to rescue Sid Vicious's soul.

By this time, Hebdige was already well known as the author of *Subcultures*, the book which embodied the pop/academia crossover. Another fine example of theoretical writing is Richard Dyer's 'In Defence of Disco', which seeks – with impassioned analysis – to rehabilitate the dance music that was much maligned at the time. Jane Suck's visionary manifesto captures that moment when the apparent opposites of punk and disco could merge; and in that merger was the start of eighties pop.

1975: Better Must Come

'This is an exchange telegraph company automatic broadcast, testing prices every morning at ten-thirty. Please be sure to switch on every morning before ten-thirty.' It's a gradual process – the cider is just beginning to subside, leaving weariness to knock out the edges. In this mental state I wouldn't even try to focus, let alone resolve, but am quite happy to wander clear across town without conclusion. 'This automatic test broadcast is repeated every morning at . . .' I seem to recall, ailingly, a heated discussion at last night's party – on reggae as attitude, I think. Much clearer are the insidious, saccharine Grateful Dead melodics, even now spinning circuitously in my mind; Jah Youth jesterin' somewhere between each flash. '. . . every morning before ten-thirty. Evens, eleven-to-ten, five-to-four, eleven-to-eight, six-to-four, thirteen-to-eight, seven-to-four, fifteen-to-eight, two-to-one, nine-to . . .'

At present, the Newbury card attends more pressingly. Brother Somers, a possibility under most conditions, is likely to be at good odds in the first race – an apprentice's handicap. The board man is already chalking up, I fancy backing it to place. 'Eleven-to-eight, six-to-four, thirteen-to-eight . . .' It's a tricky one: Fighting Brave, Ionicus, Cashing Lady, Swift Falcon and Unbiased could all figure prominently; it might be an idea to hedge them, according to odds, leaving out the favourite (Fighting Brave?). In the meantime, with more than an hour to kill, coffee and something between toast would go down very well indeed. 'Eleven-to-four, three-to-one, one-hundred-to-thirty, seven-to-two . . .' Yes, me fren, me de pan street again.

Luxury is – a toasted ham sandwich, three cups of coffee drunk hot, the *Mirror* read religiously from back to front, a cigarette curling. 'WILSON: I'M NOT A SOFTY OVER EUROPE. Premier Harold Wilson admitted last night that he has never been an "emotional European". He said: "I don't stand on the South Coast and look across the Channel and say 'There is the new Jerusalem.'"' Here, in easy agreement with myself, it's bliss to sit back and cogitate, expand. Quarried by *déjà vu* and emotional collation. That which is expressed so haltingly in confrontation and argument, all my mixed feelings towards reggae, now flows sweetly. The remembrance of today is the sad feeling of tomorrow. Give joy and praise to Bustamente. August 1962. Forward march. Let's all together sing this independence song. 'A judge yesterday blamed coloured immigrants for a crime wave. He accused them of turning part of South London into a place where it was dangerous to walk at night.' Yes, dear people, my brothers and sisters, we blew it there, way back then. This is my confusion, my faith . . .

The carnival crowd, aware and spontaneous, crossed the river to the other side. Increased in size and number and soon became a recognisable sub-culture; perhaps even an alternative! Something bold, strange, new, exciting.

It was Masefield plus – and more: Black Orpheus at Dalston Junction with little knots of men around thinly hidden betting shops, then still illegal, looking and sounding like as many Coasters, assorted timbre of voice pitched together in conversation. The local market at Ridley Road underwent a quiet revolution, in progressive transformation beneath vegetable exotica, greasy brown condiments and tropical golden fruit: sour mangoes and bland, giant yams; garlands of bananas, green like the Children of the seed of Israel. (I cherish a particular memory of the watermelon man – a stall on the corner outside Dysons with an absolute perpetuity of rampant mommas hovering. Fat, red-spotted butterflies yelling and bargaining. 'Hey mistah don't touch me tomato!' 'Dis one a 'ere fellah!' 'Me wanna pumpkin potato!' The coster upholding a steady banter of patter, semi-abuse; continuous service and the appropriate change; gashing open each melon sold exposing wet, pink flesh; not at any time missing a single trick.)

More! It was Zacions among the sycamore trees; ginger and spice, coco-nuts, cane, and herb for the healing of the nation. It was zoot suits and checked lumberjackets; flat felt hats and bigger straw ones, plucked with cherries; was cheap print frocks of raw colour; opal pearls and ivory opulence. It was boss in a Babylon, Jah in a Plaistow and JA in a Poplar. Shebeens in the slums. Ghettoes of a new glory.

Ah! Those shebeens. Music bounding off the white, baked pavements; drowsy blues on open shirt summerdays; electric blue evening-wear and mohair nights; pale mornings of sleeping *Sun*swept streets.

Against zig-zag cracked, concrete porches: the Drifters, intimate as violins, through one careless curtain of unabashed love waltz; Fats Domino, Lavern Baker, Theo Beckford, Kentrick Patrick, Hank Ballard, Derrick Morgan, Bobby Blue Bland, Eric Morris, Keith and Enid; every now and then Don Drummond breaking loose on a full, sweet solo; be-bop captains lounged, as cool as a can of red stripe; in assumed ownership, encircling Colvestone Crescent, up St Marks Rise, along Cecilia Road; on spliff-smoke, carefree stairways. Creolese patois resounding the *patio*. Zion City Wall.

It was sleek, purring Humbers – plump from the Fifties; *class*, brilliant pink Crestas; Dormobiles for the *whole* family, my dear brothers and sisters, the sounds of Shelley boasted on every rear window and a riot going on

472

inside. For God's sake it gave more power to the people! Now, money in my pocket but I just can't get no love.

Sure the Babylon boys, the Man, may sometimes come – a wreck up the scene and a rip-off this a cally – but man ah warrior and we *all* is Israelites in Shanty Town. Babylon a stay gone when no fuss'n', man. Remember Moses, that led the children out of Egypt? If dem a come, we see and blind.

Sadly, the carnival crowd made no contingencies for the reactionary upman proles – the slugs of metropolitanism. *These* were no Israelites, though oppressed; instead were smug and macmillan comfortable, never having had it so good, squire. Big TV lounge, a fridge full of Watneys, debonair, Martini daughters and soon all suburbs in the wake of Hampstead Gardens. By losing and relinquishing an empire we had won the promised key to Canaan. Philistine on the banks of the River Jordan and Babylon just a phone call and three nines away. Selah. Nine . . . nine . . . nine . . .

And thus we blew it brothers and sisters, we blew it! People had come to a promised land of prosperity and proposition: a smug mother country. Had come in boatloads: proud young families; honest hard-working men and women; attractive, bright-eyed children – and they were not iry. Largesse blared through open doors and hearts – and they were not iry. People had struggled, saving their fare to make the single trip to Britain, on the planta-tions and in the factories of the West Indies, with the sanctity of the British Government and the Sovereign they had arrived to realise their dreams – they were not iry. They came laden with all *manna* of love, hope, bonhomie, spirit and ganga – and they were not iry.

We despised them. We spat on their gifts and we insulted their women in the streets. We told evil lies, vile third-hand stories, amongst ourselves. We sent our police force to molest them, our own children to persecute them. We robbed their labour and, for thanks, shut our doors and turned our bristling backs. We moved out wherever they moved in and turned about accusing them of creating ghettoes. Endeavoured to break the back of the beautiful creolese language and easy demeanour, in our arrogance – their culture. We failed desperately. These folk had *dread*. These people had *rass*. Out of their alienation grew an indomitable independence; *dum vivimus vivamus*. We hurt but, thankfully, we failed to destroy. Then reggae.

What a black Cinderella said she went downtown, fe go meet a fellah said underneath a cellar, under a fellah where I meet my Cinderella – dressed up in a yeller to meet a lickle fellah.

In the interim, brothers and sisters, we blew it.

Meanwhile . . . in the Royal Borough of Kensington and Chelsea, West

Eleven, Notting Hill Gate . . . lived a man of property named Peter Rachman Esq. He was nobody's fool, despite a contradiction of sorts by Connie Francis; known as a charitable character, he regularly donated headaches to NCCL and local housing organisations. He was fond of dogs, particularly Alsatians, and being a sporting gent gave regular work to boxers retired from the ring. A well-known local man, he was pointed out from Paddington street corners. (As Becky Grodniz, a cousin removed three times from Rachman, 'and still not far enough' he is reported to have said, once told me: Listen! (she said) Peter had his head screwed on in the right direction. Okay, perhaps he wasn't exactly a *bonditt* but, let me tell you, no *meshuggeneh* ever lived that made the kind of money Peter made. So maybe he wasn't (they tell me) the most perfect man but (with a shrug) who is? After all, can you expect a man, a man of intelligence too, to walk around in rags all his life? Or does clever here (indicating her husband) think different? Clever grunted and said nothing.)

Rachman thought to himself, he thought: sitting tenants, standing tenants, *shmanding* tenants. A Very unprofitable proposition, my son. He thought, he thought: Mike, my coloured boy, can take care of that. Extend the hand of UNESCO brotherhood and welcome a steel band or two. So. 'Have all the parties you want bro man, sound them systems, take a whiff of this a cally, dread dem love it, let locks grow, beat out those Rasta rhythms. The more fun you have is the more fun we have – and that's democracy!' The sitting tenants in the adjoining flats might not like it too much, but what the *rass*! A wily crew these profiteers – proffer tears – these ghetto mentalities.

(In passing spare a thought for Malik. He was to regret his association with Rachman, the Black House fiasco was not entirely his fault, while the Gail Benson/Joseph Skerrit rap almost certainly played Mike for a patsy. As Becky Grodniz might put it, he wasn't the most perfect man, but who is?)

Philistine went North to Finchley dreamland – a much, much better class of ghetto – treading down the flowers, gold-crazed; brooding until reckless; at lust's sour hour love will cower, but knotty dread dem love it. His Elvis sons out a-rebelling: white screwface: odious in Odeons; hip in pizza patisseries; mauve, Yeti-dread, mohair jerseys in casual, young esquire, bowling alleys; flexing Frankie Avaloned torsos over Tottenham Lido; mod to the futile Pan pipings of the Huyton opportunist. Ever *schlapping* to Southend and back – *you'll get yourself killed one of these days. I'm warning you!* Money in his pocket but he just can't get no love. 'So what's wrong with being a solicitor? You tell me!' Holy Mount Zion!!

Smethwick cleverness, notwithstanding the doddering opposition later to

474

betray secure Leytonstone, descended, pretty low, into its racist dipbag and won a seat amongst the inane: 'If you want a nigger for your neighbour vote Labour.'

'If you want a broad phone Stephen Ward.' Profumo knew that but, unfortunately for him, Macmillan comfortable didn't, Dr Ward the victim, chewed up, betrayed by the club, nailed to the board like a butterfly. M'procurer and osteopath, gold-digger, spiteful, sting like a bee, dilettante artist; blackleading his most tortured portrait – himself. 'Then meet me on Dark Street and everything will be alright.' Stephen Ward is alive and well and living on immoral earnings.

Friend Rachman was on the way down: dead: despised the length of Paddington, the breadth of Babylon. Not, however, before he had precipitated race riots in the Gate. Manor today of the Backayard Restaurant, Mangrove Restaurant, Grassroots Bookshop, the Black Peoples' Information Centre, the Metro Club, the Ethiopian World Federation Incorporated Local 33 – the *official* UK Rasta group, and Mas in the Grove, Carnivals 73/74 and 75 (be there). In the wake of the riots, the community realised that it must get *itself* together to survive; not without much pain in the process. The politicisation of the more aware West Indians in Notting Hill grew directly from Rachman's *pressure.*

Rachman was stiff and decaying when Johnny Edgecombe – Johnny Too Bad – JA's number one rude bwoy, came home to Old Bailey; and Lucky Gordon got unlucky at last. Pussy price a gone up in Chepstow Road.

After Edgecombe the circus got well under way. The Keeler *pretty-girl* went Spanish and anticipated George Best; Lord Hailsham betrayed, even for him, most porcine behaviour in the direction of hapless Toynbee boy scout Jack Profumo, securing reaction that described his comments as '. . . a virtuoso performance in the art of kicking a fallen friend in the guts . . . when self-indulgence has reduced a man to the shape of Lord Hailsham, sexual continence involves no more than a sense of the ridiculous'. An era, dear brothers and sisters, of humbug, hypocrisy, cant and pharisaism. Of mendacious men and women. 'I must say I view the activities of the editor of *The Times* with some distaste.' And where Ms England wore her new face, brothers and sisters we blew it. We really blew it.

At Manor House, a whippet away from Harringay, one night in a blues disco – ghost dance – with neat little ska outfit and Rudie and the bwoys sharp, proffering the speed; the bombers, blues and dizzy dexes. Later, with amphetagro, turning this little liberal over. I, white, voyeur, can only stand apart and admire such a trump of racism. Dem a learn it from my people. Dem learn it fine!

Man it is tougher than tough today for these pariahs of Zion, exiled in Babylon who art to be destroyed. Wandering listless, transient, from Joe Dole to Joe Coral. Hopes pinned on Fighting Brave and their tongues cleaved to the rooves of their mouths. The first English (you better dig it fascists!) generation are sullen, bitter with style and ultra-violent. *Daily Mirror*, Friday, May 16, 1975: 'A judge yesterday blamed coloured immigrants for a crime wave. He accused them of turning parts of South London into a place where it was dangerous to walk at night.' Now it is send I back to Ethiopia land; the utterance on the lips, in the minds and hearts, in the iry eyes of black British youth. Now is the time for all black people to look inside themselves and realise that their back is against the wall – that is what the man Marcus Garvey prophesised.

The community learnt its lesson good – if you can't join 'em, beat 'em. Lickle David, him go slay Goliath. Remember Moses? That led the children out of Egypt. Landlords a pressure tenants and little Laurel Aitken, the bluebeat first from Cuba (Good morning Mother Cuba, how do you do?), him man ripped off by white cocksuckers and blackhead Chineemen. No penthouse for Laurel, but then no laurels for *Penthouse* – sexploitation of black women. Daniel saw the stone rolling into Babylon. The man Aitken him got friends, man, in Brixton, Harlesden, Southwark, Stoke Newington, Peckham – the *communities*, man. How many friends have we got left, third-rate cocaine lifestyle sons and daughters of Stardust?

I'M NOT A SOFTY OVER EUROPE: 'I don't stand on the South Coast and look across the Channel and say "There is the new Jerusalem."'

Then all hail, Haile Selassie I – Jah Rastafari! This is reggae music as I and I – Jah Reel – would play. This is the sound that leads the way, so make it a date and don't be late. Run Cap-ital-ist, I and I want Socialist. Run, run, come, 'fore de night run down, let's have some fun and settle down. I say lively up yourself and don't be no drag. Have gots, have nots, trim heads, comb locks, dread-nots, locksmen, beardmen and cleanfaced men, say knotty dread no jester and dem no lick 'em make 'em fester and dem no wear polyester and dem no come from Manchester. Tell you. I said talking blues, talking blues, I said your feet is just too big for your shoes. Look there. I say we walk down a May Pen, sip a lickle cally, and we go down a Mandeville. Say Mr Delly shouldn't do dat, you can't ever do dat. No jesterin'.

Here comes another version too. Say blood fe de Babylon. Fire in a Vatican. Blood fe de Babylon. Fire. Nyah. Blood, lightning, earthquake and thunder. Jah, Jah Rastafari. When the lion is sleeping never try to wake him baby. Lion. Zion. Jungle. Kill dem dead, Jah, before dem spread, I mean dead. Dead. Dread. Dreader. Locks. Blood fe de Babylon.

Then you walk with the high dread – stoned in a Babylon; you talk with the high dread – stoned in a Babylon; you can't walk free – in a Babylon. I saw four angels standing on four corners of the earth, I and I a dreadlocks now. Going into Canaan, across the River Jordan, going to the promised land.

We blew it back there, Whitey. Blue-eyed Bobby Moore and the cuddly Beatle boys. Moptop a Dreadlock. How, how do you sleep at nights? The man in the mac said we gotta go back, you know they never even gave us a chance. Diluted from the jungle, ladies and gentlemen, I give you the Rolling Stones (a bit of Slim Harpo here and a dash of Arthur Alexander there – memories are made of this), the Greatest Rock'n'Roll Band In The Whole World! We really blew it! Here was autonomous lifestyle and *la dolce vita* over a jigger of rum and a stick o' dope – Ailee Aileloo. *Rass* man, feeling high so high; none of your astral projections, theosophist sublimations, *Watership Down* and Eric Clapton's latest *reggae* album.

Not exclusively. I give you rock-steady Reggie and the reggae cherry reds. I took me baby for a night to the hop – music was playing, skinheads was dancing, do the moon hop. The children of the seed of Israel and the children of the seed of Ben Sherman – The Burnt Oak Mafia, The Somers Town Council, Paxton Road End, The Plaistow Clarets, the Shed – they made uneasy peace on Mile End Road Friday nights. It was Judge Dread dance the pardon and we don't want to end up like Bonnie and Clyde. Integration in a Mare Street.

We don't want to end up like Delaney and Bonnie. You know the man Chartbound Blackburn? Him think him invent reggae in the three-part-water bilge of Greyhound. The sell-out, London's spending guide, Desmond Dekker, who now sings like him the man Lovelace Watkins. Dandy Livingstone, shaking a tail-feather at him Soho double-act, the pretty flamingo, coming on like Tamla. Bob Marley having him head locked, as well as him hair, by the natty careerists of St Peter's Square. Hammersmith is out! Blood fe de Babylon! The man him called John Holt – one thousand volts of rubbish. No *rass*.! No *dread*! As aware as Uganda. As spontaneous as America. As autonomous as Czechoslovakia. As free as Babylon. Time is longer than rope, but time now catching up on you. You ever hear 'bout this man Constantine? Him never going so fine. Who said it, you are a blazing fire.

Brothers and sisters, dem blew it! Brothers and sisters we blew it too, only we really blew it.

You blew it North London. Blackstock a Dreadlock. Over in Holloway the IRA rule. Turnpike Lane browbeaten by the Belsize Set and the Kentish Town Horrors. Mornington Crescent and Chalk Farm. Dread dem Camden Locks. Knotty in a knitery. (Here, niggers serve two very distinct functions: a) they deal dope, which is cool when they don't rip you off; b) they come along to pick up white chicks – which is not cool) I see you in the dark, Roundhouse, Dingwalls, Howff. Swivel hips and drivel lips; said I wanna be your clothing manufacturer. Okay, now I'm here give me a Margarita – chilled. Go easy on the lime, but you can be pretty liberal with the salt. Hey, did we say third-rate cocaine lifestyle? Look, make that a Sunrise for the one we only ever see as a nice, staggering blur, every morning drunk and empty.

Hey, Primrose Hill, I been double-crossed now for the very last time and finally I'm *free*! In the left corner we have the complete works of Herman Hesse (Remember Herman? We grew together. Tell him Prince Buster says hello), and in the right corner I give you, from the Depression, Thirties' ephemera. The complete works of Lifebuoy. And believe me, Depression can be pretty ephemeral too. Wesker's on at the Roundhouse – Zionism's other angle – and it's brown rice with everything.

The Underground Press was laid to rest here, out of incidence, dear Charrington Street squats and Windsor Nation exists in various stages of empirical collapse – each and all of them degrading. No jesterin'. *IT* is recycled as an ecology broadsheet – magic mushrooms and it is *not* a wank for Hampstead. No jesterin'. Joe Levy, yes the now generation's very own Rachman, versus a further breed of nigger, the debagged, dull brown jersey and borrowed crowbar children of the seed of Woodstock. They take an oath upon them own mother, and then they use a gun to kill them own son. Dread in a dungle.

Don't try to hide Trend Park, you blew it. Sussing what a cool cat that spade dude Allen Toussaint was – a friend of Labelle's ain't he? – and scoring pre-pack Nirvana from Budgens. Look what happened to your milk-snatcher; where are your weapons against the Iron Maiden now, my loves? No *rass*! No *dread*! Blood fe de South Bank.

You too Lou. What coloured girls did we ever see over at Shelley's going doop-de-doop-de-doop-de-doop? What girls did we see ever, outside of Diana Ross and, from Memphis with love, our Dusty? Fire in a Vatican.

Admiral Ken: him music make you walk and him music make you talk and him music make you say it's a sauna bath.

You blew it, Enoch – dread, dread one-eye man – rivers of blood and milk immortalised in cheese. A poet, too. Rass immortalised in ackee and saltfish.

Dread immortalised on factory floor dramas. And so bitterness is always thus resigned. Powerfreakout in funhouse street city of old gold. The Molineux *miserables*. Wolves awaiting at the door and Iryland a calling. Blood and fire. Over in Willesden, Lorna Bennett's old man is a piece of floor in a factory. Breakfast in bed? *No way!* Leave the studio, man.

Sir Coxsone: I hear him got a sound system and that Nyah Keith is the disc jockey, but dem can't get no red stripe late at night. Woppy King rides again. Rastaman a bitter man.

You blew it great hate Britain. Africa in Acton and the bretheren bleed. We gonna burn up the wicked people one of these days. I man bitter and I man dread, I man afeared of the Babylon's lead. I and I must beat down Babylon. I must pick up the gun and run else Babylon a catch me. Death to all oppressors, black and white. The Church Triumphant! The Negus! The avatar of the Niabinghi, his Imperial Majesty Haile Selassie I, King of Kings, Lord of Lords, Conquering Lion of the Mighty Tribe of Judah, Elect of God and Light of the Worlds. Jah Rastafari. Weary of Babylon? I have a dream – better must come.

Shebeens now no funhouse. No Saturday nights free at the Sunset, Islington; feeling high so high I want to touch the sky. *No way!* Time tough. Now it's giro awaiting and Brook Street Bureau got big by bovver. 'I'm afraid (it fluted) one must conform in today's society, and if you must walk, with the high dread, with a black skin, you will not find employment too easily – my dear Winston, Errol and Patsy.' It is either black and Babylon must burn, rivers of blood, fire in a Vatican, Niabinghi in a pentagon, or else brown-skinned going doop-de-doop-de-doop-de-doop. No *rass* and no *dread*. In today's society you must, as the sage in Manpower – got big being rude to black people looking for work – said, *compromise*. You semi-semi-semi-semi-nyah.

Now you've learnt what Curley Locks is, what can you do more than love it? Curley Locks, two roads before you; which one will be your choice?

Upon the abolition of slavery, Queen Victoria granted the Jamaican Government the sum of £20,000,000. Of this, £14.25 million was earmarked for the repatriation of all black people who desired to return to Africa. Where is the money? What happened to it? I demand an explanation from the Jamaican Government, Mr Manley; or are you too busy with your Gun Courts? Let the ship finally come in Mr Patterson, and then we shall see what happens.

Back in JA it's meet me on Dark Street and everything will be alright again. You can't go home again. You can't JA. Step forward youth, come let I tell you the truth. Britain doesn't want your mind, but she doesn't even want her own. Black man you come from Mount Zion. Black man you can't go home again.

Back in JA it's August 1962, freezing up Orange Street and you can't get no dunny. Back in JA the pickney's dem a stabbing. Back in JA it's a bauxite/sugar rip-off and you can't get no food to eat, you can't get no money to spend. Voila! Back in JA it is praise without raise – when it *is* praise. It is fussing'n'fighting, looting and shooting, mumbling and grumbling. It is Michael Manley – you were betrayed Delroy Wilson – versus Hugh Shearer. It's a soldier round the corner and the preachers need teachers and the teachers want preachers. No jesterin'. Look how the policemen trim off the Rastaman's hair. Kill dem dread, Jah, before dem spread. What can you do more than love it?

In Trinidad it is Michael X hanging by his neck until dead; it is Eric Williams prophet and greed. In Grenada it is I man iry like Mr Gairy who sits on his verandah wheeling and dealing. It is the day of the jackal and the mongoose rule. In Dominica it is Patrick Trotter waiting to die for living in a house of dreadlocks and letting locks grow. In Jamaica it is guns in the ghetto, rude bwoys with ratchets, the Gun Courts Law and *Indefinite Detention*. It is Cap-ital-ist in the playgrounds of Montego Bay and blood fe de Babylon. In 1975 you can't go home again. Back home it is Stinky Pommels and Herman (we grew together), rude bwoy Adolphus James and rude bwoy Emmanuel Zachariah Zackeepom – Prince Buster sends his regards; sorry we had to go so soon. It is Curley Locks, now that I'm a dreadlocks, you daddy says you shouldn't play with me.

The Church Triumphant of Jah Rastafari. The Ethiopian Orthodox Church. The Ambassadors of Negus Group. The United Ethiopian Body. The Brotherhood Solidarity of United Ethiopians. The Rastafari Bretheren Repatriation Association. The United Afro-West Indian Brotherhood. The Ethiopian National Congress. The Ethiopian Mystic Masons. The Rastafari Movement. The King of Kings Missionary Movement. The Ethiopian Coptic Church. The African Cultural League. The Ethiopian Youth Cosmic Faith. The United Front. The Ethiopian World Federation. The Ethiopian Salvation Society.

I feel it! I feel it, black people. I have a dream – better must come.

The Solomonic Dynasty. Look! Solomon Grundy was born on a Monday, enslaved on a Tuesday, whipped on a Wednesday, spat on on a Thursday, beaten on a Friday, raped on a Saturday, died on a Sunday. You were given love and you blew it, fascist, sick little Britain. The coon learnt its lesson well.

This is the *true* Protestant way of death; hate your neighbour. Man ah warrior. Odious in Odeons. Hip in knotty niteries. He learnt it well. Sullen and bitter and ultraviolent. Powis Square broods until reckless, the wicked cannot prosper and you can't go to Zion with a carnal mind.

There are four angels standing on four corners of the earth. Look brothers and sisters all our own work! Blood, fire and death to all the oppressors be they white or black. We blew it good. We blew it really good. Then reggae. Beat out those Rasta rhythms. Make the action begin.

Penny Reel, *Pressure Drop*, Autumn 1975

1975: Kraftwerkfeature

Some skeezix from one of the local dailies was up here the other day to do a 'human interest' story on the phenomenon you're holding in your hands, and naturally our beneficent publisher hauled me into his office to answer this fish's edition of the perennial: 'Where is rock going?'

'It's being taken over by the Germans and the machines,' I unhesitatingly answered. And this I believe to my funky soul. Everybody has been hearing about kraut-rock, and the stupnagling success of Kraftwerk's 'Autobahn' is more than just the latest evidence in support of the case for Teutonic raillery, more than just a record, it is an *indictment*. An indictment of all those who would resist the bloodless iron will and order of the ineluctable dawn of the Machine Age. Just consider:

They used to call Chuck Berry a 'guitar mechanic' (at least I heard a Moody Blues fan say that once). Why? Because any idiot could play his lines. Which, as we have all known since the prehistory of punk rock, is the very beauty of them. But think: if any idiot can play them, why not eliminate such genetic mistakes altogether, punch 'Johnny B. Goode' into a computer printout and let the *machines* do it in total passive acquiescence to the Cybernetic Inevitable? A quantum leap towards this noble goal was accomplished with the advent of a crude sonic Model T called Alvin Lee, who could not only reproduce Berry licks by the bushel, but play them at 78 rpm as well. As is well known, it was the Germans who invented methamphetamine, which of all accessible tools has brought human beings within the closest twitch of machinehood, and without methamphetamine we would never have had such high plasma marks of the counterculture as Lenny Bruce, Bob Dylan, Lou Reed and the Velvet Underground, Neal Cassady, Jack Kerouac, Allen Ginsberg's 'How', Blue Cheer, Cream and *Creem*, as well as all of the

481

fine performances in Andy Warhol movies not inspired by heroin. So it can easily be seen that it was in reality the *Germans* who were responsible for *Blonde on Blonde* and *On the Road*; the Reich never died, it just reincarnated in American archetypes ground out by holloweyed jerkyfingered mannikins locked into their typewriters and guitars like rhinoceroses copulating.

Of course, just as very few speedfreaks will cop to their vice, so it took a while before due credit was rendered to the factory of machinehood as a source of our finest cultural artifacts. Nowadays, everybody is jumping on the bandwagon. People used to complain about groups like the Monkees and the Archies like voters complain about 'political machines', and just recently a friend of mine recoiled in revulsion at his first exposure to Kiss, whom he termed 'everything that has left me disgusted with rock 'n' roll nowadays – they're automatons!'

What he failed to suss was that sometimes automatons deliver the very finest specimens of a mass-produced, disposable commodity like rock. But history will have its way, and it was only inevitable that groups like Blue Oyster Cult would come along, singing in jive-chic about dehumanization while unconsciously fulfilling their own prophecy albeit muddled by performing as nothing more than robots whose buttons were pushed by their producers. By now the machines had clattered VU meter first out of the closet for good, and we have most recently been treated to the spectacle of such fine harbingers of the larger revolution to come as Magma's 'Ork Alarm' ('The people are made of indescribable matter which to the machines is what the machines are to man . . .') and of course Lou Reed's *Metal Machine Music*, a quick-buck exploitation number assessed elsewhere in this issue.

But there is more to the Cybernetic Inevitable than this sort of methanasia. There are, in the words of the poet, 'machines of loving grace'. There is, hovering clean far from the burnt metal reek of exploded stars, the intricate balm of Kraftwerk.

Perhaps you are wondering how I can connect the amped-up hysteria of compulsive pathogens such as Bruce, Dylan and Reed with the clean, cool lines of Kraftwerk. This is simple. The Germans invented 'speed' for the Americans (and the English – leave us not forget Rick Wakeman and Emerson, Lake & Palmer) to destroy themselves with, thus leaving the world of pop music open for ultimate conquest. A friend once asked me how I could bear to listen to Love Sculpture's version of 'Sabre Dance', knowing that the producers had sped up the tape; I replied: 'Anything a hand can do a machine can do better.' An addendum would seem to be that anything a hand can do nervously, a machine can do effortlessly. When was the last time you heard a German band go galloping off at 965 mph hot on the heels of oblivion? No, they realize that the ultimate power is exercised *calmly*, whether it's Can with their endless rotary connections, Tangerine Dream plumbing the sargassan depths, or Kraftwerk sailing airlocked down the Autobahn.

In the beginning there was feedback: the machines speaking on their own, answering their supposed masters with shrieks of misalliance. Gradually the humans learned to control the feedback, or thought they did, and the next step was the introduction of more highly refined forms of distortion and artificial sound, in the form of the synthesizer, which the human being sought also to control. In the music of Kraftwerk, and bands like them present and to come, we see at last the fitting culmination of this revolution, as the machines not merely overpower and play the human beings but *absorb* them, until the scientist and his technology, having developed a higher consciousness of its own, are one and the same.

Kraftwerk, whose name means 'power plant,' have a word for this ecstatic congress: *Menschmaschine*, which translates as 'man-machine'. I am conversing with Ralf Hutter and Florian Schneider, co-leaders of Kraftwerk, which they insist is not a band but a you-guessed-it. We have just returned to their hotel from a concert, where Kraftwerk executed their Top Ten hit 'Autobahn', as well as other galactic standards such as 'Kometenmelodie' ('Comet Melody'), 'Mitternacht' ('Midnight'), 'Morgenspaziergang' ('Morning Walk', complete with chirping birds on tape), and the perfect synthesized imitation of a choo-choo train which must certainly be the programmatic follow-up to 'Autobahn', to a small but rapt audience mesmerized into somnolence. (At least half the people I took, in fact, fell asleep. But that's all right.) Now the tapes have stopped rolling and the computers have been packed up until the next gig, and the Werk's two percussionists, Wolfgang Flur and Karl Bartos, who play wired pads about the size of Ouija boards instead of standard acoustic drums, have been dispatched to their respective rooms, barred from the interview because their English is not so hot. (I have heard of members of bands playing on the same bills as Kraftwerk approaching these gentlemen with the words 'So ya liked blowin' all our roadies. ...' The Germans smiled and clapped them on the shoulders: '*Ja ja* ...') Now Ralf and Florian are facing me, very sober in their black suits, narrow ties and close-cropped hair, quietly explaining behaviour modification through technology.

'I think the synthesizer is very responsive to a person,' says Ralf, whose

483

boyish visage is somewhat less severe than that of Florian, who looks, as a friend put it, 'like he could build a computer or push a button and blow up half the world with the same amount of emotion.' 'It's referred to as cold machinery,' Ralf continues, 'but as soon as you put a different person in the synthesizer, it's very responsive to the different vibrations. I think it's much more sensitive than a traditional instrument like a guitar.'

This may be why, just before their first American tour, Kraftwerk purged themselves of guitarist/violinist Klaus Roeder, inserting Bartos in his slot. One must, at any rate, mind one's P's and Q's – I asked Hutter if a synthesizer could tell what kind of person you are and he replied: 'Yes. It's like an acoustic mirror.' I remarked that the next logical step would be for the machines to play *you*. He nodded: 'Yes. We do this. It's like a robot thing, when it gets up to a certain stage. *It* starts playing ... it's no longer you and I, it's *It*. Not all machines have this consciousness, however. Some machines are just limited to one *piece* of work, but complex machines ...'

'The whole complex we use,' continues Florian, referring to their equipment and headquarters in their native Dusseldorf, 'can be regarded as one machine, even though it is divided into different pieces.' Including, of course, the human beings within. 'The Menschmaschine is our acoustic concept, and Kraftwerk is power plant – if you plug in the electricity, then it starts to work. It's feedback. You can jam with an automatic machine, sometimes just you and it alone in the studio.'

They also referred to their studio as their 'laboratory', and I wondered aloud if they didn't encounter certain dangers in their experiments. What's to stop the machines, I asked, from eventually taking over, or at least putting them out of work? 'It's like a car,' explained Florian. 'You have the control, but it's your decision how much you want to control it. If you let the wheel go, the car will drive somewhere, maybe off the road. We have done electronic accidents. And it is also possible to damage your mind. But this is the risk one takes. We have power. It just depends on what you do with it.'

I wondered if they could see some ramifications of what they could do with it. 'Yes,' said Ralf, 'it's our music, we are manipulating the audience. That's what it's all about. When you play electronic music you have the control of the imagination of the people in the room, and it can get to an extent where it's almost physical.'

I mentioned the theories of William Burroughs, who says that you can start a riot with two tape recorders, and asked them if they could create a sound which would cause a riot, wreck the hall, would they like to do it? 'I agree with Burroughs,' said Ralf. 'We would not like to do that, but we are aware of it.'

'It would be very dangerous,' cautioned Florian. 'It could be like a boomerang.'

'It would be great publicity,' I nudged.

'It could be the end,' said Florian, calm, unblinking. 'A person doing experimental music must be responsible for the results of the experiments. They could be very dangerous emotionally.'

I told them that I considered their music rather anti-emotional, and Florian quietly and patiently explained that ' "emotion" is a strange word. There is a cold emotion and other emotion, both equally valid. It's not body emotion, it's mental emotion. We like to ignore the audience while we play, and take all our concentration into the music. We are very much interested in origin of music, the source of music. The pure sound is something we would very much like to achieve.'

They have been chasing the p.s's tail for quite a while. Setting out to be electronic classical composers in the Stockhausen tradition, they grew up listening on the one hand to late-night broadcasts of electronic music, on the other to the American pop music imported via radio and TV – especially the Beach Boys, who were a heavy influence, as is obvious from 'Autobahn', although 'we are not aiming so much for the music; it's the psychological structure of someone like the Beach Boys'. They met at a musical academy, began in 1970 to set up their own studio, 'and started working on the music, building equipment', for the eventual rearmament of their fatherland.

'After the war,' explains Ralf, 'German entertainment was destroyed. The German people were robbed of their culture, putting an American head on it. I think we are the first generation born after the war to shake this off, and know where to feel American music and where to feel ourselves. We are the first German group to record in our own language, use our electronic background, and create a central European identity for ourselves. So you see another group like Tangerine Dream, although they are German they have an English name, so they create onstage an Anglo-American identity, which we completely deny. We want the whole world to know our background. We cannot deny we are from Germany, because the German mentality, which is more advanced, will always be part of our behaviour. We create out of the German language, the mother language, which is very mechanical, we use as the basic structure of our music. Also the machines, from the industries of Germany.'

As for the machines taking over, all the better. 'We use tapes, pre-recorded,

485

and we play tapes, also in our performance. When we recorded on TV we were not allowed to play the tape as a part of the performance, because the musicians' union felt that they would be put out of work. But I think just the opposite: with better machines, you will be able do better work, and you will be able to spend your time and energies on a higher level.'

'We don't need a choir,' adds Florian. 'We just turn this key, and there's the choir.'

I wondered aloud if they would like to see it get to the point of electrodes in the brain so that whatever they thought would come through a loudspeaker. 'Yes,' enthused Ralf, 'this would be fantastic.'

The final solution to the music problem, I suggested.

'No, not the solution. The next step.'

They then confided that they were going to spend all the money from this tour on bigger and better equipment, that they work in their lab/studio for recreation, and that their Wernher von Braun sartorial aspect was 'part of the German scientific approach'.

'When the rocket was going to the moon,' said Ralf, 'I was so emotionally excited ... When I saw this on television, I thought it was one of the best performances I had ever seen.'

Speaking of performances, and bearing their general appearance and demeanor in mind, I asked them what sort of groupies they got. 'None,' snapped Florian. 'There is no such thing. This is totally an invention of the media.'

All right then, what's your opinion of American or British bands utilizing either synthesizers or Germanic/swastikan overtones? Do you feel a debt to Pink Floyd? 'No. It's vice versa. They draw from French classicism and German electronic music. And such performance as Rick Wakeman has nothing to do with our music,' stressed Ralf. 'He is something else ... distraction. It's not electronic music, it's circus tricks on the synthesizer. I think it is paranoid. I don't want to put anybody down, but I cannot listen to it. I get nervous. It is traditional.'

Not surprisingly, their taste in American acts runs to those seduced (and enervated) by adrenalin: 'The MC5, and the heavy metal music of Detroit. I think Iggy and the Stooges are concerned with energy, and the Velvet Underground had a heavy Germanic influence – Nico was from Cologne, close where we live. They have this German dada influence from the twenties and thirties. I very much like "European Son". Nico and John Cale had this Teutonic attitude about their music which I very much like. I think Lou Reed in his *Berlin* is projecting the situation of a spy film, the spy standing in the fog smoking a cigarette. I have also been told of the program "Hogan's Heroes", though I have not seen it. We think that no matter what happens Americans cannot relate it. It's still American popcorn chewing gum. It's part of history. I think the Blue Oyster Cult is funny.'

They did not, however, think it was funny when I wound up the interview asking them if they would pose for pix the next morning by the Detroit freeway. 'No,' said Ralf, emphatically. 'We do not pose. We have our own pictures.'

Why? 'Because,' flatly, 'we are paranoid.'

He was just beginning to explain the ramifications of German paranoia when Florian abruptly stood up, opened the window to let the smoke out, then walked to the door and opened it, explaining with curious polite curtness that 'we had also an interview with *Rolling Stone*, but it was not so long as this one. Now it is time to retire. You must excuse us.'

He ushered us into the hall, quietly swung the door shut with a muffled click, and we blinked at each other in mild shock. Still, it was somehow comforting to know that they did, apparently, sleep.

Lester Bangs, *Creem*, September 1975

1975: Ramones

Right now I am sitting by the stage where Joey Ramone has wrapped his tall languorous body and his long long hands around the microphone to deliver 'the Blitzkrieg Bop'. The audience sits straight up in their chairs. '1, 2, 3, 4!' No smiling, no amiable jamming, no cut fifties nostalgia. It's more like sitting underneath Niagara Falls.

This is an outsider's view. I just want to make that clear. I knew that I was an outsider from the moment I walked into CBGB's because I kept falling over my high-heeled boots. People who knew were wearing sneakers. One of the *Punk* magazine editors explained: 'We don't believe in love or any of that shit. We believe in making money and getting drunk.'

Black leather jackets surface around the bar, but it's the girls by the bandstand who have the image. The one with the puffed-sleeved angora sweater and the white lipstick, and her friend with the red razorcut bouffant hairdo, black leather and shades. The shades have a ribbon attached, so she looks like a homicidal librarian.

I go to the ladies' room. 'Hey, ugly – who does your makeup? Helen Keller?'

By the time I get back, the editors have grabbed the Ramones backstage. The group is relaxed and friendly. The manager hovers by, telling them not to smile in the photographs. Right now is the time that the Ramones could really make it big.

'Rock 'n' roll, man, just rock 'n' roll. The way it should be – entertaining, a lot of fun, sexy, dynamic, exciting. Ah, y'know, everything that everyone seems to have missed the point on. Further, we believe in *songs* . . . not in, uh, boogying and, uh, improvisation and stuff like that, y'know?'

They all write the music and lyrics, but Tommy acts as spokesman. Joey is silent, smiling, as he hunches over and eats his chicken sandwich.

PUNK: Who were your influences?

TOMMY: Actually we like a lot of people and no specific things. We love bubblegum, we love, um, hard rock. Elvis Presley. I especially love Elvis Presley.

PUNK: Did you hear the Monkees are getting back together?

TOMMY: Oh, one of the highlights of our life? 1910 Fruitgum Co. . . . Yummy, yummy . . . we're quite young.

PUNK: How old are you?

TOMMY: 23, 24.

PUNK: Oh, that's us!

TOMMY: Lovely generation.

PUNK: OK, why do you affect leather jackets and kind of a punk-type attitude on stage?

TOMMY: It keeps us warm, y'know? And the black absorbs more heat. And, uh . . .

PUNK: But you take off your jackets after the first number!

TOMMY: OK, but by the first number we're quite toasty.

PUNK: OK, OK.

TOMMY: It's fashion – we like to be fashionable anyway – and we feel comfortable in them. Anyway, we'd feel silly in anything else, y'know?

Dee Dee likes comicbooks – anything with swastikas in it, especially *Enemy Ace*. 'But it's very hard to get.' They were also, they say, A-students at Forest Hills in Queens. 'That's one of the top five schools in the United States.'

But now they're professional rock 'n' rollers. Out there in the audience Lou Reed is drinking white wine and playing with the candle, one hand waving by his side in a continual edgy dance, waiting for the second set to begin.

488

On stage what the Ramones put over isn't really violent, isn't decadent, and most important, it isn't recycled. It's the rock – pure, simple, and powerful. Elegant, even.

Mary Harron, *Punk #1*, January 1976

1976: Don't Look over Your Shoulder, but the Sex Pistols are Coming

'HURRY UP, they're having an orgy on stage,' said the bloke on the door as he tore the tickets up.

I waded to the front and staightway sighted a chair arching gracefully through the air, skidding across the stage and thudding contentedly into the PA system, to the obvious nonchalance of the bass drums and guitar.

Well I didn't think they sounded *that* bad on first earful – then I saw it was the singer who'd done the throwing.

He was stalking round the front rows, apparently scuffing over the litter on the floor between baring his teeth at the audience and stopping to chat to members of the groups's retinue. He's called Johnny Rotten and the monicker fits.

Sex Pistols? Seems I'd missed the cavortings with the two scantily clad (plastic thigh boots and bodices) pieces dancing up front. In fact, I only caught the last few numbers; enough, as it happens, to get the idea. Which is ... a quartet of spiky teenage misfits from the wrong end of various London roads, playing 60s styled white punk rock as unself-consciously as it's possible to play it these days i.e. self-consciously.

Punks? Springsteen Bruce and the rest of 'em would get shredded if they went up against these boys. They've played less than a dozen gigs as yet, have a small but fanatic following, and don't get asked back. Next month they play the Institute of Contemporary Arts if that's a clue.

I'm told the Pistols repertoire includes lesser known Dave Berry and Small Faces numbers (check out early Kinks' B-sides leads), besides an Iggy and the Stooges item and several self-penned numbers like the moronic 'I'm Pretty Vacant', a meandering power-chord job that produced the chair-throwing incident.

No one asked for an encore but they did one anyway: 'We're going to play "Substitute".'

'You can't play,' heckled an irate French punter.

'So what?' countered the bassman, jutting his chin in the direction of the bewildered Frog.

That's how it is with the Pistols – a musical experience with the emphasis on Experience.

'Actually, we're not into music,' one of the Pistols confided afterwards.

Wot then?

'We're into chaos.'

Neil Spencer, New Musical Express, 25 February 1976

1976: Rock Revolution

Johnny Rotten looks bored. The emphasis is on the word 'looks' rather than, as Johnny would have you believe, the word 'bored'. His clothes, held together by safety pins, fall around his slack body in calculated disarray. His face is an undernourished grey. Not a muscle moves. His lips echo the downward slope of his wiry, coat-hanger shoulders. Only his eyes register the faintest trace of life.

Johnny works very hard at looking bored. Leaning against a bar; at a sound check; after a gig; making an entrance to a party; on stage; when he's with women. No, actually, then he's inclined to look quite interested.

Why is Johnny bored? Well, that's the story.

This malevolent, third generation child of rock 'n' roll is the Sex Pistols' lead singer. The band play exciting, hard, basic punk rock. But more than that, Johnny is the elected generalissimo of a new cultural movement scything through the grassroots disenchantment with the present state of mainstream rock.

You need look no further than the letters pages of any *Melody Maker* to see that fans no longer silently accept the disdain with which their heroes, the rock giants, treat them.

They feel deserted. Millionaire rock stars are no longer part of the brotherly rock fraternity which helped create them in the first place.

Rock was meant to be a joyous celebration; the inability to see the stars, or to play the music of those you can see, is making a whole generation of rock fans feel depressingly inadequate.

Enter Johnny Rotten. Not content to feel frustrated, bored and betrayed, he and the Sex Pistols, Glen Matlock (bass), Paul Cook (drums), and Steve Jones (guitar) have decided to ignore what they believe to be the elitist pretensions of their heroes who no longer play the music they want to hear. The Pistols are playing the music they want to hear. They are the tip of an iceberg.

Since January, when the Sex Pistols played their first gig, there has been a slow but steady increase in the number of musicians who feel the same way – bands like the Clash, the Jam, Buzzcocks, the Damned, the Suburban Bolts and Slaughter and the Dogs. The music they play is loud, raucous and beyond considerations of taste and finesse. As Mick Jones of the Clash says: 'It's wonderfully vital.'

These bands' punk music and stance is so outrageous that, like the Rolling Stones in the good old days, they have trouble getting gigs. But they play regularly at the 100 Club, which is rapidly becoming the venue at which these bands cut their teeth.

The musicians and their audience reflect each other's street-cheap, ripped-apart, pinned-together style of dress. Their attitude is classic punk; icy-cool with a permanent sneer. The kids are arrogant, aggressive, rebellious. The last thing any of these bands make their audience feel is inadequate.

Once again there is the feeling, the exhilarating buzz, that it's possible to be and play like the bands on stage.

It's no coincidence that the week the Stones were at Earls Court, the Sex Pistols were playing to their ever increasing following at London's 100 Club. The Pistols are the personification of the emerging British punk rock scene, a positive reaction to the complex equipment, technological sophistication and jaded alienation which has formed a barrier between fans and stars.

Punk rock sounds simple and callow. It's meant to.

The equipment is minimal, usually cheap. It's played faster than the speed of light. If the musicians play a ballad, it's the fastest ballad on earth. The chords are basic, numbers rarely last longer than three minutes, in keeping with the clipped, biting cynicism of the lyrics.

There are no solos. No indulgent improvisations.

It's a fallacy to believe that punk rockers like the Sex Pistols can't play dynamic music. They power through sets. They are never less than hard, tough and edgy. They are the quintessence of a raging, primal rock-scream.

The atmosphere among the punky bands on the circuit at the moment is positively cut-throat. Not only are they vying with each other but they all secretly aspire to take Johnny Rotten down a peg or two. They use him as a pivot against which they can assess their own credibility.

It's the BSP/ASP Syndrome. The Before or After Sex Pistols debate which wrangles thus: 'We saw Johnny Rotten and he CHANGED our attitude to music' (the Clash, Buzzcocks) or 'We played like this AGES before the Sex Pistols' (Slaughter and the Dogs) or 'We are MILES better than the Sex

491

Pistols' (the Damned). They are very aware that they are part of a new movement and each one wants to feel that he played a part in starting it.

All doubts that the British punk scene was well under way was blitzed two weeks ago in Manchester, when the Sex Pistols headlined a triple, third-generation punk rock concert before an ecstatic, capacity audience.

Participation is the operative word. The audiences are revelling in the idea that any one of them could get up on stage and do just as well, if not better, than the bands already up there. Which is, after all, what rock and roll is all about.

When, for months, you've been feeling that it would take ten years to play as well as Hendrix, Clapton, Richard (insert favourite rock star's name), there's nothing more gratifying than the thought: Jesus, I could get a band together and blow this lot off the stage!

The growing punk rock audiences are seething with angry young dreamers who want to put the boot in and play music, regardless. And the more people feel 'I can do that too', the more there is a rush on to that stage, the more cheap instruments are bought, fingered and flayed in front rooms, the more likely it is there will be the 'rock revival' we've all been crying out for.

There's every chance (although it's early days yet) that out of the gloriously raucous, uninhibited melee of British Punk Rock, which even at its worst is more vital than most of the music perfected by the Platinum Disc Brigade, will emerge the musicians to inspire a fourth generation of rockers.

The arrogant, aggressive, rebellious stance that characterises the musicians who have played the most vital rock and roll has always been glamorised. In the 50s it was the rebel without a cause exemplified by Elvis and Gene Vincent, the Marlon Brando and James Dean of rock. In the 60s it was the Rock 'n' Roll Gypsy Outlaw image of Mick Jagger, Keith Richard and Jimi Hendrix. In the 70s the word 'rebel' has been superseded by the word 'punk'. Although initially derogatory it now contains all the glamorous connotations once implied by the overused word – 'rebel'.

Punk rock was initially coined, about six years ago, to describe the American rock bands of 1965–68 who sprung up as a result of hearing the Yardbirds, Who, Them, Stones. Ability was not as important as mad enthusiasm, but the bands usually dissipated all their talent in one or two splendid singles which rarely transcended local hit status. Some of the songs, however, like 'Wooly Bully', '96 Tears', 'Psychotic Reaction', 'Pushin' Too Hard', have become rock classics.

In Britain, as 'punk rock' has been increasingly used to categorise the livid, exciting energy of bands like the Sex Pistols, there has been an attempt to repdefine the term.

There's an age difference too. New York punks are mostly in their mid-20s. The members of the new British punk bands squirm if they have to tell you they are over 18. Johnny Rotten's favourite sneer is: 'You're Too Old.' He's 20.

British punk rock garb is developing independently, too. It's an ingenious hodgepodge of jumble sale cast-offs, safety-pinned around one of the choice, risque T-shirts especially made for the Kings Road shop, Sex.

Selling an intriguing line of arcane Fifties cruise-ware, fantasy glamour ware, and the odd rubber suit, this unique boutique is owned by Malcolm McClaren, ex-manager of the New York Dolls, now the Sex Pistols' manager.

His shop has a mysterious atmosphere which made it the ideal meeting place for a loose crowd of truant, disaffected teenagers. Three of them were aspiring musicians who, last October, persuaded McClaren to take them on. They wanted to play rock 'n' roll. They weren't to know what they were about to start and even now no one is sure where it will lead. All Steve, Glen and Paul needed then, was a lead singer.

A few weeks later Johnny Rotten strayed into the same murky interior. He was first spotted leaning over the juke box, looking bored.

Caroline Coon, *Melody Maker*, 7 August 1976

1976: In Love with the Modern World

'I didn't even know the
Summer of Love was
happening. I was too busy
playing with my Action Man.'
Sid Vicious

You see them on Kings Road on Saturday afternoons. They look *different*. Long-haired youths in their flares and platforms turn and stare; tourists laugh and jabber among themselves, aiming expensive cameras for the folks back home; local residents of several decades' standing look bemused or shocked and shake their heads with resignation.

Could their attention be focussed on the bright pink hair? Or the blue hair? Or green, mauve or yellow hair? Perhaps it's the rubber stockings or seamed fishnet stockings, or the shiny black stilettos with bondage overtones. Perhaps it's the sheets of PVC rubber safety-pinned into T-shirts, or is it the ripped T-shirts, the baggy pants ending in tight cuffs, the winkle-pickers, the weird shades?

Maybe the 'couture' look favoured by some of the more steadily employed has stopped them short. At Sex one can choose from trousers with vinyl pockets and zips on the arse, outrageously oversized fall-apart sweaters, studded belts and wrist straps, anarchy shirts with hand-painted stripes and Marx and swastika patches and CHAOS arm bands, and the Sex staple, T-shirts – printed with everything from the Cambridge rapist's mask to the naked young boy that is the Sex Pistols' logo – and of course, out and out bondage apparel.

Up the road, Acme Attractions are denuding any warehouse still possessing early 60s fashion – you want an original Beatles suit? Look no further – the only thing out of step with Swinging London the booming reggae on the sound system and the perennial dreadlocked yout's grooving to the beat.

Between the two emporiums, Retro caters to all decades.

These people, this technicolour parade that owes no allegiance to any fashion or trend except that which they create themselves, this group that has uncompromisingly treated the 70s as the 70s, are the ones variously described as 'folks in Bizarre Costumes' (Charles Shaar Murray) and 'garishly designed night creatures' (Giovanni Dadomo). But as Bo Diddley said some eons ago, you can't judge a book by the cover.

On a recent Saturday Steve celebrated his 21st birthday. He and his 19-year-old friend Siouxsie had spent the afternoon shopping and now, as midnight approached, picked their way through the Soho puddles towards Louise's, treating the staggering, pissing drunks with the same indifference as the rain.

The drunks laughed and tried to think of insults, but that was normal for straights. Steve *hated* them, because they refused to accept him for what he was. He didn't try to do anything about the funny way they looked, but they were always going on about the super-hero peroxide flashes gracing the sides of his jet black hair or his choice or sartorial correctness. Especially in Bromley, where he lived. Especially schoolgirls.

It was a good thing, probably, that Siouxsie was wearing her polka-dot plastic mac.

Louise's used to be an almost exclusively lesbian club but has graciously expanded to accommodate the leading edge of 70s youth and their pansexual tastes. In the reception Siouxsie removed her mac, revealing a simple black dress with a plunging V neckline, black net loosely covering her pert breasts. A home-made swastika flash was safety-pinned to a red armband. Black strap stilettos, studs gleaming, bound her feet; fishnet tights and black vinyl stockings her legs. Her short black hair was flecked with red flames.

Steve was still wearing the same clothes – white shirt daubed with paint and a Union Jack pinned over the right breast, black drainpipe slacks and winklepickers – he had worn on stage at the 100 Club the previous Monday night when he had played bass with Siouxsie, Sid Vicious and Marco, also known as Siouxsie and the Banshees. He had first picked up a guitar the previous afternoon.

'I don't know why I did it, I just knew I wanted to before I was 21.'

It was also Siouxsie's first stage appearance.

'I'd always wanted to be on a stage ... I was a bit nervous at first but when I saw everybody enjoying it, I enjoyed doing it. I think they considered it a joke.

'I've always gone around being looked at so I thought perhaps I should go on a stage and exploit it.

'I also had singing lessons,' she added archly. 'When I was about 16, I really wanted to do singing and I practised a lot and made cassettes and I dunno ... I went to some interviews from *Melody Maker* ads, record producers looking for singers, and it really put me off. They made me think I'd have to become a classical type singer to be popular –'

'Dana,' smirked Steve.

'– So that the general public would like you. They gave me the impression that everyone who makes it has to sleep around ... The fact that I could get work by that and be paid for it and nothing be expected of me (professionally), that was, you know ...'

They moved inside. Downstairs was non-stop dance-arama. Upstairs, in the fire-engine-red room flanked by the bar and a wall of great posing mirrors, the party got underway. Most of Steve's friends – known for convenience's sake as the Bromley contingent – were there, all Sex Pistols fans of long persuasion, all looking just as much a part of the present as the Pistols, who were also there.

Most of the Bromley contingent owe their discovery of the Pistols to Simon (age 19), who witnessed an early gig at Ravensbourne College of Art last December – 'I was almost the only person applauding'. Simon looks like the one established rock star he, or anyone else present for that matter, still rates – Bowie, Siouxsie, in fact, was inspired to perform because of Ziggy Stardust.

495

'He's the only singer who's managed to keep up by changing and not stay the same . . . get old.'

Their other tastes are what you would expect: Lou Reed, the Velvets, the Stooges – in many instances discovered through Bowie's involvement – and old Stones and Who and Small Faces and offbeat soul tracks. They took to the Pistols because of the energy, and 'they had guts to them, in the music and by being on stage' (Steve), and 'they were different' (Simon), and 'they were young' (Siouxsie). The only other 70s artists to so far make the grade are the Ramones and Jonathan Richman, who Siouxsie credits with a new concept of love songs – 'They're not mushy, they're more fair' – though some of the new, post-Pistols English bands are viewed favourably.

Simon has definite ideas about the icons the Pistols are smashing, as well as the ones they're establishing.

'It's really funny all those kids shouting out anarchy and half of them don't know what it is. I agree with anarchy, but I was like that before the Pistols. People are always telling you what to do and it's always old people telling young people. If you're going to be told what to do it should be from young people. That'll never happen, so you've gotta have anarchy. There's no way old people are going to just sit back, they're just going to tell young people to do too much. It's like all those old people trying to stop the Pistols thing. They're like parents.'

He sneered, and took a sip of champagne.

'This nostalgia thing, I don't like it. First the 40s, then the 50s, then the 60s. Why no 70s? I think everything was moving so fast in the 50s and 60s that it just couldn't go on, but instead of slowing down it ground to a halt.

'I never took that much notice of hippies. I liked things that really took the piss out of it, like Frank Zappa, but then he went all serious . . . As people get older they just act older, don't they? Want to be taken seriously. Stupid.'

'Flowah powah,' mocked Debbie, sitting next to him. Debbie is 15. 'I don't remember that long ago,' she laughed. 'I remember Woodstock . . .'

'It was so weak and stupid,' continued Simon, 'and they believed it. To try and change things with flowers; if you get beaten up you've got to retaliate. I really think that violence is the only way. If you're going to change the world you've got to use violence – not beating people up, but destroying property. It doesn't matter if you protest – it's property that really counts. As soon as there's damage they take notice. If the IRA had only done buildings and not people . . . There was a really good feeling at first, people wanting a united Ireland, but the minute they did people . . . They're not opponents any more, they're murderers.

496

'I want to stop older people telling young people what to do. I'm young and everything I do there's some arseholes telling me I'm wrong. There are a few exceptions . . . they're all right.

'But I don't think anyone will bother, will they? To use violence. They're too lazy, aren't they?'

Steve's view is far more succinct. 'There'll only ever be anarchy in the 100 Club,' he laughed. He also believes in love. 'But I don't believe in devotion, thinking that someone or something is the only thing there. I'm interested in marriage, but not in the traditions and the possessiveness. It's just for a laugh.'

They drained the champagne. Vivien Westwood, seditionary and Sex mastermind, bought another bottle for the birthday man. Debbie, changed into a black leotard and red leggings, went downstairs and danced. Her hair was but in a modern interpretation of a 50s flat-top. In the past it had been sprayed every colour of the rainbow, now it was blonde. Since all the other girls at her school were starting to crop their hair, hers was growing out.

But she isn't what the demographics experts call an opinion-former among the mostly Jewish, middle-class teenage femininity that constitutes her peer group in suburban Burnt Oak, where she lives.

'You're joking?!? At first they really had something against me. Now they sort of take it. Laugh.

'They're into what I was into three years ago. Clumpy shoes . . . What gets me is something will come out and if one person gets it, then they all get it. They're just like clockwork.

'I bought some plastic sandals a couple of years ago, and they *really* laughed at me, but now everyone's getting them and they turned around to me and said, "Why don't you get a pair?" They forget that they used to laugh at you . . . You get used to it.'

The party carried on.

Jonh Ingham, *Sounds*, 9 October 1976

1976: Mark P. Pisses on the Lot of 'Em!

Over the past month I've noticed how every Tom, Dick and Harry writer takes hold of 'punk-rock' and gives it his or her expert opinion. Even the ones I used to trust are jumpin' on the bandwagon and fighting over the exclusive interviews. That's nothing to do with what's happening at the moment.

I hope that with the new young music will come new writers who have got

497

the right to vent their ideas and opinions. Certain writers in the established rags are latching on to the new bands in the same way that they change the fashion of their clothes. Writing about 'punk-rock' is the thing to do at the moment. I hope the 'fashion' soon dies out, then you'll be able to find out who really believed in the bands!

Half of 'em have been to the good ol' college. They've all passed their Eng Lit and all them crappy exams. I used to enjoy reading about the Pistols, the Clash and the other bands in *Sounds* etc. but not anymore. *Sounds*, *NME*, *Melody Maker* and the new crap *Rockstar* should stick to writing about the established artists. Leave our music to us, if anything needs to be written, us kids will do it. We don't need any boring old fart to do it for us!

I might put down all the established writers but I also want to say something else. All you kids out there who read *SG*, don't be satisfied with what *we* write. Go out and start your own fanzines or send reviews to the established papers. Let's really get on their nerves, flood the market with punk-writing!

Mark P., *Sniffin' Glue*, 5 December 1976

1976: The Filth and the Fury

A pop group shocked millions of viewers last night with the filthiest language heard on British television.

The Sex Pistols, leaders of the new 'punk rock' cult, hurled a string of four-letter obscenities at interviewer Bill Grundy on Thames TV's family teatime programme *Today*.

The Thames switchboard was flooded with protests.

Nearly 200 angry viewers telephoned the *Mirror*. One man was so furious that he kicked in the screen of his £380 colour TV.

A Thames spokesman said: 'Because the programme was live we could not foresee the language which would be used. We apologize to all viewers.'

The show, screened at peak children's viewing time, turned into a shocker when Grundy asked about £40,000 that the Sex Pistols received from their record company.

One member of the group said: 'F—ing spent it, didn't we?'

Then when Grundy asked about people who preferred Beethoven, Mozart and Bach, another Sex Pistol remarked: 'That's just their tough s—.'

Later Grundy told the group: 'Say something outrageous.'

A punk rocker replied: 'You dirty sod. You dirty bastard.'

'Go on. Again,' said Grundy.
'*You dirty f—er.*'
'What?'
'*What a f—ing rotter.*'
As the Thames switchboard became jammed, viewers rang the Mirror to voice their complaints.

Lorry driver James Holmes, 47, was outraged that his eight-year-old son Lee heard the swearing . . . and kicked in the screen of his TV.

'It blew up and I was knocked backwards,' he said. 'But I was so angry and disgusted with this filth that I took a swing with my boot.

'I can swear as well as anyone, but I don't want this sort of muck coming into my home at teatime.'

Mr Holmes of Beechfield Walk, Waltham Abbey, Essex, added: 'I am not a violent person, but I would like to have got hold of Grundy.

'He should be sacked for encouraging this sort of disgusting behaviour.'

Stuart Grieg, Michael McCarthy and John Peacock, *Daily Mirror*, 2 December 1976

1977: Sten-guns in Knightsbridge??

'It ain't Punk, it ain't New Wave, it's the next step and the logical progression for groups to move in. Call it what you want – all the terms stink. Just call it rock 'n' roll . . .'

You don't know what total commitment *is* until you've met Mick Jones of The Clash.

He's intense, emotional, manic-depressive and plays lead guitar with the kind of suicidal energy that some musicians lose and most musicians never have. His relationship with Joe Strummer and Paul Simenon is the love/hate intensity that you only get with family.

'My parents never . . . the people involved with The Clash *are my family . . .*'

The Clash and me are sitting around a British Rail table in one of those railway station cafes where the puce-coloured paint on the wall is peeling and lethargic non-white slave labour serves you tea that tastes like cat urine.

Joe Strummer is an ex-101er and the mutant offspring of Bruce Lee's legacy – a no-bullshit sense of tough that means he can talk about a thrashing he took a while back from some giant, psychotic Teddy Boy without the slightest pretension, self-pity or sense of martyrdom.

499

'I was too pissed to deal with it and he got me in the toilets for a while,' Joe says.

'I had a knife with me and I shoulda stuck it in him, right? But when it came to it I remember vaguely thinking that it wasn't really worth it coz although he was battering me about the floor I was too drunk for it to hurt that much and if I stuck my knife in him I'd probably have to do a few years . . .'

When The Clash put paint-slashed slogans on their family-created urban battle fatigues such as 'Hate and War' it's *not* a cute turnaround of a flowery spiel from ten years ago – it's a brutally honest comment on the environment they're living in.

They've had aggravation with everyone from Teds to students to Anglo-rednecks, all of them frightened pigs attacking what they can't understand. But this ain't the summer of love and The Clash would rather be kicked into hospital than flash a peace sign and turn the other cheek.

'We ain't ashamed to fight,' Mick says.

'We should carry spray cans about with us,' Paul Simenon suggests.

He's the spike-haired bass-player with considerable pulling power. Even my kid sister fancies him. He's from a South London ex-skinhead background; white stay-press Levi strides, highly polished DM boots, button-down Ben Sherman shirt, thin braces, eighth-of-an-inch cropped hair and over the football on a Saturday running with The Shed because for the first time in your life the society that produced you was terrified of you.

And it made you feel good . . .

Paul came out of that, getting into rock 'n' roll at the start of last year and one of the first bands he ever saw was The Sex Pistols. Pure late-Seventies rock, Paul Simenon. In Patti Smith's estimation he rates alongside Keef and Rimbaud. He knew exactly what he was doing when he named the band The Clash . . .

'The Hostilities,' Mick Jones calls the violent reactions they often provoke.

'Or maybe those Lemon Squeezers,' Paul says, seeking the perfect weapon for protection when trouble starts and you're outnumbered ten to one.

The rodent-like features of their shaven-headed ex-jailbird roadie known, among other things, as Rodent break into a cynical smirk.

'Don't get it on their drapes otherwise they get *really* mad,' he quips.

He went along to see The Clash soon after his release from prison. At the time he was carrying a copy of 'Mein Kampf' around with him. Prison can mess up your head.

Strummer, in his usual manner of abusive honesty, straightened him out.

Rodent's been with them ever since and sleeps on the floor of their studio.

The Clash demand total dedication from everyone involved with the band, a sense of responsibility that must never be betrayed no matter what internal feuds, ego-clashes or personality crisis may go down. Anyone who doesn't have that attitude will not remain with The Clash for very long and that's the reason for the band's biggest problem – they ain't got a drummer.

The emotive Mick explodes at the mention of this yawning gap in the line-up and launches into a stream-of-consciousness expletive-deleted soliloquy with talk of drummers who bottled out of broken glass confrontations, drummers whose egos outweighed their creative talent, drummers who are going to get their legs broken.

'Forget it, it's in the past now,' Joe tells him quietly, with just a few words cooling out Mick's anger and replacing it with something positive. 'If any drummer thinks he can make it then we wanna know.'

'We're going to the Pistols' gig tonight to find a new drummer!' Mick says excitedly. 'But they gotta prove themselves,' he adds passionately. 'They gotta believe in what's happening. *And they gotta tell the truth . . .*'

The band and Rodent have their passport photos taken in a booth on the station. Four black and white shots for twenty pence.

They pool their change and after one of them has had the necessary two pictures taken the next one dives in quickly to replace him before the white flash explodes.

When you're on twenty-five quid a week the stories of one quarter of a million dollars for the cocaine bill of a tax exile Rock Establishment band seem like a sick joke . . .

The Human Freight of the London Underground rush hour regard The Clash with a culture-shock synthesis of hate, fear, and suspicion.

The Human Freight have escaped the offices and are pouring out to the suburbs until tomorrow. Stacked haunch to paunch in an atmosphere of stale sweat, bad breath and city air the only thing that jolts them out of their usual mood of apathetic surrender is the presence of The Clash.

Because something's happening here but The Human Freight don't know what it is . . .

> '*Everybody's doing just what they're told to / Nobody wants to go to jail / White Riot / I wanna Riot / White Riot / A Riot of me own! / Are you taking over or are you taking orders? / Are you going backwards or are you going forwards?*'

'White Riot' and The Sound of the Westway, the giant inner city flyover and the futuristic backdrop for this country's first major race riot since 1959.

Played with the speed of The Westway, a GBH treble that is as impossible to ignore as the police siren that opens the single or the alarm bell that closes it.

Rock'n'roll for the late Nineteen Seventies updating their various influences (Jones – the New York Dolls, MC5, Stooges, vintage Stones; Simenon – Pistols, Ramones, Heartbreakers; and Strummer, *totally* eclectic) and then adding something of their very own. The sense of flash of beach-fighting Mods speeding through three weekend nights non-stop coupled with an ability to write songs of contemporary urban imagery that are a perfect reflection of the life of any kid who came of age in the Seventies.

The former makes The Clash live raw-nerve electric, a level of excitement generated that can only be equalled by one other band – Johnny Thunders' Heartbreakers.

The latter makes The Clash, or maybe specifically Jones and Strummer (as Simenon has only recently started writing), the fulfilment of the original aim of the New Wave, Punk Rock, whatever: that is, to write songs about late Seventies British youth culture with the accuracy, honesty, perception and genuine anger that Elvis, Beatles or The Rolling Stones or any others in the Rock Establishment could never do now that they're closer to members of the Royal Family or face-lift lard-arse movie stars than they are to you or me.

But so many bands coming through now are churning out clichéd platitudes and political nursery rhymes. The Blank Generation is the antithesis of what The Clash are about . . .

Strummer and Jones disagree on the best environment for a new band to develop and keep growing.

Joe thinks it's all too easy right now and having to fight every inch of the way when the band was formed a year ago is the healthiest situation – whereas Mick believes in getting every help and encouragement possible while being totally honest with bands who are just not delivering the goods.

'I'm as honest as I can be,' he shouts over the roar of the tube train. 'All the new groups sound like drones and I ain't seen no good new group for six months. The sound just ain't exciting, they need two years . . .'

The sound of The Clash has evolved, with their experience this year in the recording studio first with Polydor when they were dangling a contract, and more recently recording their first album after CBS snapped them up at the eleventh hour.

The change in the sound first struck me as a regulation of energy, exerting a razor-sharp adrenalin control over their primal amphetamined rush. It created a new air of tension added to the ever-present manic drive that has always existed in their music. The Sound Of The Westway . . .

And, of course, the subtle-yet-indefinite shift in emphasis is perfect for the feeling that in the air in the United Kingdom, one quarter of 1977 already gone:

> '*In 1977 you're on the never-never / You think it can't go on forever / But the papers say it's better / I don't care / Coz I'm not all here / No Elvis, Beatles or the Rolling Stones / In 1977.*'

'1977', the other side of the single, ends with the three-pronged attack shouting in harmonies derived from football terraces: '1984!'

The pressure. That's what they call the heavy atmosphere in Jamaica, the feeling in the air that very soon, something has got to change . . .

The Jamaican culture is highly revered by The Clash. They hang out in black clubs, pick up reggae import singles in shops where it ain't really wise for them to tread and express their disgust of the undeniable fact that in the poor working-class areas of London where they grew up and still live the blacks are treated even worse than the whites.

But, ultimately, they know the White Youth needs its *own* sense of identity, culture, and heritage if they're going to fight for change.

A riot of their own . . .

But can the masses take to the incisive reality of what The Clash are about the way they lap up the straight-ahead rock bands who push nothing more than having a good time?

'Maybe the reason those bands are so big is because they *don't* say anything,' Mick says. 'But we ain't gonna preach and sound like some evangelist.'

I mention to Joe what happened when he walked on stage at Leeds Poly for the first gig that actually happened on the Pistols' Anarchy tour.

He said a few words before the band went into the set that they'd been burning to play for weeks about how the gutter press hysteria, local council butchery and Mary Whitehouse mentality of The Great British people was preventing certain young rock bands getting on stage and playing for the people who wanted to see them.

I remember him saying that 1984 seemed to have arrived early as the Leeds Poly students bawled abuse at him.

With the minds and manners of barnyard pigs the over-grown schoolchildren conveyed the message that they didn't give a shit.

'I think they will take to us, but it'll take time,' Joe says. 'But I don't want to go *towards* them at all, I don't wanna start getting soft around the edges.

'I don't want to compromise . . . I think they'll come round in time but if they *don't* it's too bad.'

'We ain't *never* gonna get commercial respectability,' Mick says, both anger and despair in his voice.

Paul Simenon takes it all in and then ponders the nearest station that has a bar on the platform.

That's the difference between their attitudes to, how you say, Making It.

Strummer is confident, determined, arrogant and sometimes violent in the face of ignorant opposition (a couple of months back in a club car park he faced an American redneck-rock band with just his blade for support).

Mick Jones is a rock equivalent to a Kamikaze pilot. All or nothing.

The Clash gives him both the chance to pour out his emotional turmoil and offer an escape route from the life the assembly-line education the country gave him had primed him for.

When a careers officer at school spends five minutes with you and tells you what you're gonna do with your life for the next fifty years. More fodder for the big corporations and the dole.

Mick is beating them at their own game by ignoring all the rules.

'*Someone locked me out so I kicked me way back in,*' he declares in 'Hate and War'.

His uncanny resemblance to a young Keef Richard allowed him to relieve an early identity problem by adopting the lookalike con-trick which fools no one but yourself. Then he met Strummer who told him he was wearing a Keith Richard identikit as though he had bought it in a shop.

'I got my self-respect in this group,' Mick says. 'I don't believe in guitar heroes. If I walk out to the front of the stage it's because I wanna reach the audience, I want to *communicate* with them. I don't want them to suck my guitar off . . .'

And Paul Simenon: total hedonist.

His fondest memories of the Anarchy tour are hotel room parties and broken chairs, things trod into the carpet and girls who got you worried because you thought they were gonna die like Jimi Hendrix if they didn't wake up. He's a member of The Clash because they're the best band in the country and it gets him laid a lot.

So what did they learn from the Anarchy tour, so effectively butchered by the self-righteous Tin Gods who pull the strings?

'I learned that there's no romance in being on the road,' Mick says.

'I learned that there's lots,' Joe smiles.

'I learned that if they don't want you to play they can stop you,' Joe says seriously. 'And no one's gonna raise any fuss . . .'

'For the first four days we were confined to our rooms because the *News of the World* was next door,' Mick continues.

'We thought – shall we go out there with syringes stuck in our arms just to get 'em going? Yeah, and furniture seemed to have labels saying, "Please smash me" or "Out the Window, Please".'

And when they finally got to play, the minds in the Institutes of Further Education were as narrow as those in Fleet Street. So Strummer gave them something – even though they were too blind to see it . . .

'This one's for all you *students*,' he sneered before The Clash tore into the song that they wrote about Joe being on the dole for so long that the Department of Employment (*sic*) wanted to send him to rehabilitation to give him back the confidence that they assumed the dole must have destroyed, together with Mick's experience working *for* the Social Security office in West London, and, as the most junior employee, being told to open all the mail during the time of the IRA letter-bombs.

The song is called 'Career Opportunities':

> 'Career Opportunities / The ones that never knock / Every job they offer you / Is to keep ya out the dock / Career Opportunities. / They offered me the office / They offered me the shop / They said I'd better take ANYTHING THEY GOT. / "Do you wanna make tea for the BBC? / Do you wanna be, do you wanna be a cop?" / I hate the army and I hate the RAF / You won't get me fighting in the tropical heat / I hate the Civil Service rules / And I ain't gonna open letter bombs for you!'

'Most bands and writers who talk about the dole DUNNO WHAT THE DOLE IS!' Mick shouts.

'They've never been on the dole in their life. But the dole is only hard if you've been conditioned to think you've gotta have a job . . . then it's sheer degradation.

'The Social Security made me open the letters during the letter-bomb time because I looked subversive. Most of the letters the Social Security get are from the people who live next door saying their neighbours don't need the money. The whole thing works on spite.

'One day an Irish guy that they had treated like shit and kept waiting for three hours picked up a wooden bench and put it through the window into Praed Street.'

Mick shakes his head in disgust at the memory of the way our great Welfare State treats its subjects.

'Every time I didn't have a job I was down there – waiting. And they degrade the black youth even more. They have to wait even longer. No one can tell me there ain't any prejudice . . .'

Tony Parsons, *New Musical Express*, 2 April 1977

1977: Plymouth Punk

It was 7.45 p.m. Plymouth Sound was bathed in pink evening light. Senior citizens dozed on the sea-front beaches, watching the multi-coloured sails to the finish of a Jubilee regatta. Only half a mile away from the somnolence of the Hoe, the punks were creeping out of the darker corners of town, and converging on the Top Rank Suite, one of Plymouth's seedy temples of rock. They were coming to hear the Talking Heads and the Ramones, highly acclaimed 'new wave' bands from New York. There was an aroma of safety-pin violence in the air. The Top Rank stands on the edge of a large bomb-site and a desolate Thirties council estate, at the east end of Union Street, the sailors' favourite strip, with the highest concentration of pubs and drinking clubs anywhere in England. From a distance, it was not easy to tell the punks' closely-cropped hair from the many naval crew-cuts, but closer inspection revealed the dedicated followers of fashion had dressed much more carefully, highly conscious of striking the right stylistic note. The genuine article was in a definite minority, surrounded by demi-punks, left-overs from the denimed Woodstock era, and dreary examples of clerical chic in ill-fitting perms, terylene clothes and passé platform heels. Most of them had come up to watch the freak show, to catch up on the *new thing*.

The bouncers at the door, sure-fire Sinatra fans with greased-back hair, posing tough in their slightly faded electric blue suits, gave the incoming delinquents a visual frisk. Inside, the Suite, with its two bars, hamburger hatch and horseshoe of bakelite tables round a dance-floor and tiny stage, was wholly functional in decor. It was fairly dark, and Rank must have figured that it did not matter too much if the paint was peeling off the walls.

The cadaverous disc-jockey, a plastic punk dressed out of the fashion pages of *Honey*, was providing a continuous stream of new wave sounds: the Clash, Damned, Jam, Vibrators, Stranglers, Cortinas and Buzzcocks – the frantic music of deranged zombies, with high-speed drumming and the machine-gun clatter of guitars. The kids sat around looking bored, while the punks, mostly male, conglomerated, proudly showing off their meticulously torn T-shorts, drain-pipe trousers, ear-rings and nappy-pins.

At about 9.30, as the anaemic DJ put on the Clash's vicious dole-queue anthem 'Career Opportunities', the relatively empty dance floor suddenly filled with strangely bouncing figures. All the punks, who had been solemnly parading about, came alive: they were 'pogo-dancing', a more crazed and aggressive version of flower power's ecstatic 'idiot dance'. As the lights strobed in time to the thumping music, they jumped around anarchically, occasionally bumping into each other, and falling over. They hopped around like kangaroos on ECT, their arms seemingly dislocated, waving about in all directions. This was the great moment of release from the unbearable bore-dom of the factory line and dole queue, the 'royal' jubilation of the blank generation. Outside the Suite, Plymouth – the identikit post-blitz planner's dream, with its faultless one-way system and vast shopping precincts – slept on. Here at the Top Rank, the punks were plugging into the latest form of sublimation for their communal *ennui*.

Most of the dancing stopped when the Talking Heads came on: light-years away from England's blank generation, with their Rhode Island Institute of Art background and New York's cultural seal of approval, but appealing to the Plymouth punks because of their minimalist approach and staccato rhythms. A large group of male fans stood as close to the stage as possible, transfixed by bass-player Tina Weymouth's lunatic stare. Close behind the front row of gapers, surrounded by tip-toeing enthusiasts, a punk couple sat on two ugly Top Rank chairs, nodding their heads to the deafening music. The man wore a regulation ripped T-shirt and bizarrely shaped white-rimmed dark glasses, and his green-haired companion a transparent green plastic mac. While her boyfriend went off to buy some chips, the punk siren grabbed hold of a passing leather-jacketed delinquent, pulled him down on to the recently vacated chair next to her, climbed on to his knees, and proceeded to kiss him with punkish passion, almost choking him with her tongue. Her boyfriend soon returned with a plate of very greasy chips which he gulped down on the adjoining chair. The wild kissing continued, seem-ingly spurred on by the gathering frenzy on stage. Pogo-dancers hopped past, and the fans dithered between watching the very attractive derangement of

Tina the bass-player and the tawdry spectacle on the chair. As the Talking Heads reached the climax to their set, the punk boyfriend, who had finished his chips, quietly stubbed out his cigarette on the back of his rival's jacket. He got no response, so belched, got up and pogo-danced away into the crowd.

When the Ramones came on at midnight, with their individual brand of stomping monotony, the crowd went wild, a sea of arms shooting up on each pounding beat. The punk communion was in full swing, the decibels blasting them all into blissful oblivion. The streets outside were quiet, the rest of Plymouth nicely tucked up in council house, boarding house and semi-detached. The cold wind blew down from Dartmoor, whistling through the vast and empty shopping centres. Outside the Top Rank, the police waited for the punks – but no arrests would be needed, as the pogo-dance had taken place: the energy had all been spent.

Mark Kidel, *New Statesman*, 24 June 1977

1977: New Musick

'We start to move and we break the glass . . .'

The New Musick is too many cigarettes, too much depression and too little heart. But the sound of it is sublime. This way – obliteration. Dance sitting down, lying down, lying through your teeth . . .

It probably all began with Jazz or in the BBC Workshop, but I prefer to think it all stemmed from the mesmerising Farfisa organ sound of ? and the Mysterians '96 Tears'. 'That' was pure heartbreak, 'this' – Kraftwerk, Bowie, Eno, Space – is hearts stuck together with sellotape. It's the white equivalent of dub (obligatory hallucogenic reggae record: Althia and Donna's 'Up Town Top Ranking') a drug in itself: barbiturates that don't let you sleep and dream, just give you pleasant nightmares – like discovering your best friend is a showroom dummy. You open the closet and ice cubes fall out. Oh oh . . .

Disco, at least, was sex. New Musick is iron petting and coitus interruptus and hands on the mirror, darling darling. Music from the dead. Remember the film *Jason and the Argonauts*? when the skeletons all got nasty? 'Radioactivity' by Kraftwerk is a sure-fire top ten funeral dirge. Scattered ashes and scrambled brains. Deutschland/Deutschland uber Alles . . .

'Low' was the water-shed. Words as numerals, synthetic music as sound.

Side two of David Bowie's about-face was a soundtrack without a film and not for the nervous. It all came to a glorious head on 'V2 Schneider' ('Heroes'). Fun in the bunker ... 'Meet Iggy Pop and David Bowie on the trans Euro-Express', say Kraftwerk.

Pretension knows no bounds. 'The Secret Life of Arabia'. Oh yeah? After the astonishing verve and nerve of the Clash and the Sex Pistols, I guess we *are* all too fooled to fool, but we are quite open to aural laxatives ... hence the success of Space with 'Magic Fly' – 2001 on vinyl. In Musick there is no anarchy, no love gone wrong, only somnambulism and acceptance ('Even the greatest stars discover themselves in the looking glass ...'). The Velvet Underground had this sussed on 'Sister Ray', the biggest bomb of the sixties: '... could it be the po-lice/they come and take me for a ride ride ...'. Pinned against the wall and sliding down ... I hate history, but that whole Lou, Reed/John Cale/Nico axis shouldn't be undermined when it comes to attitude dancing to the New Vision: 'Holding on with both eyes/to things that don't exist ...' ('Gideon's Bible'), ('Vintage Violence').

Staring into the wallpaper sure beats crying into a beer!

Greater men than you died for it, ice machine.

Musick isn't Muzak, though its sternest critics would have you believe so. 'Muzak alleviates the effects of noise by providing an acceptable audible alternative ...' (brochure, 'Muzak in the Office'). Could you, consumer, buy a packet of frozen peas to a background of Fripp and Eno's 'Swastika Girls'? You'd probably end up stabbing the cashier's eyes out!

From one TV set to another, I find Musick incredibly inspirational, man, if often the kind of manic inspiration one can well do without. Spin a disque, sip a lager, count to ten in German, write a book ... show you my explosion, sweet sixteen.

Check out the charts and you'll see that something is happening, Mr Jones, even if you don't know what it is.

Jane Suck, *Sounds*, 26 November 1977

1977: Ups and Downs for the Babes in Bondage

Bad Taste is the key to the emerging seventies style, I think. In a changing world, amidst a bewildering welter of variables, at least you know where you are when you can evoke offence. It's been a funny old decade, the seventies, and of course, it's not over yet. But, as its seventh segment shambles towards Christmas like some not altogether rough – indeed, in parts, vinyl sleek – yet certainly beastly beast, the mood of it all begins to shape up.

Since virtually every single event in the decade, from the property boom to the Jubilee, has been in the worst possible taste, it seems only right and proper that a mute sartorial response should surface as black shiny plastic slit-sided dresses; camouflage combat trousers, as if either you did not know there was a war on or else in ironic comment on the fact that nobody seems to acknowledge there is a war on; chains everywhere, as if you had not been born free; and blouses printed with excerpts from dirty books. If you're terribly lucky, you might even get prosecuted for selling obscene clothing, as did the Kings Road boutique, Sex (now reborn as Seditionaries, which name makes explicit its personal theory of sartorial terrorism; its clothes are also very expensive).

Appearances, those magic representations of self, issue from an obscure part of the unconscious that cannot be fooled, that never forgets anything and recapitulates everything. Judging by appearances, there has clearly been one of those massive changes in collective taste in clothes, in appearances themselves, that denote a change in the way people feel about themselves and the world about them, the kind of change that divides one generation from another. This change has been shaping up since the soft-focus, anarchic, eclectic fancy-dress ball of the late sixties. There is a hardening of outline; it is a hard-edge style and, this past year or so, it forced itself on the attention in the form of an extreme.

This turned out to be an extreme of impropriety that cannot involve nudity because there are tits all over the daily papers. So clothing itself must become improper if Quentin (*On Human Finery*) Bell's fashion function of Conspicuous Outrage is to operate, and conspicuous outrage – that is, sartorial terrorism – has remained, until now, a dominant teenage style. (I think this may soon phase itself out, but it's impossible to be sure, yet.)

The garments of soft-core pornography, the mesh stockings, the satin corsets, were easily incorporated into the regular grammar of fashion – oh, those frilly Edwardian chemises and petticoats of last summer! But it is easy to see there is no real impropriety in these garments, since soft-core porn embodies all the nostalgia men, fashion editors and lingerie manufacturers feel for the days when girls were girls. It is a form of eroticised sentimentality. And these are by no means sentimental times. At this point, Miss Stern totters into the sartorial arena on her six-inch spike heels and allows style to explore the rubber and leather garments of conspicuous deviance. These, furthermore, have the additional benefit of unisex and really get up your father's nose.

I'm perfectly prepared to believe, since the media tell me so, that the 'punk' style was originally, at any rate, long ago, a spontaneously generated phenomenon, a dandyism of the abyss put together out of odds and Army Surplus Store ends and mum's old clothes by the Savage Generation in its brief leisures between making Dole Queue Rock, vandalising telephone boxes and visits to the VD clinic and de-infestation centre. A visual representation of a conscious state of deprivation, in fact, the definition of a state of mind. (What state of mind? 'When I have inspired universal disgust, then I shall have conquered solitude,' as Baudelaire, himself often short of a bob or two, said at a not unsimilar time of conflicting ideologies).

As a style of conspicuous outrage, it abundantly succeeded: look at November's *19* magazine survey of parents on punks: 'They are the poisonous pus of a sick society.' 'Diabolical! Just a load of dropouts!' Parents were saying the same things about the ethically impeccable flower children but a brief decade ago. But each generation experiences generational conflict as if it were something new and, indeed, there are always new elements in it.

Yet the whole 'punk' thing was too self-aware, too conscious, too much like a put-on to be absolutely serious. Those babes in bondage, with coiffures and cosmetic effects as from an 18th-century madhouse, like a street theatre version of the *Marat/Sade*. And the French Revolution offers us an interesting example of self-conscious sartorial Bad Taste in another period of conflicting ideologies: the 'victim style' of the Directory, chalk-white face, convict haircut and the scarlet ribbon or the red line round the neck as a tribute to the guillotine. There is nothing new under the sun.

The victim-style of the 1970s has a behavioural style to match. They never smile, these infants of the recession; they sneer. Defiant untouchables, tattooed at the extremities and accessoried with offensive weapons, lips and fingernails stained black and blue and the skin round their eyes painted up like rococo window-frames. This hard-edge, impersonal, constricted glamour, with its troubling elements of narcissism and fetishism, is almost too apt an illustration of a spirited reaction to impotence. There is too much irony in it, it is too knowing to be serious.

Irony is the self-defence of the down-and-out. The heavy irony of the punks blunts the style's offensive edge before it can even wound you. It makes you feel old, that is the cruellest thing, but it is basically a style of self-mockery. Arguing, perhaps, a low state of self-esteem in those who sport it. Warpaint was never put on to frighten the other side so much as to bolster the faint hearts of the wearers.

Punk is now busily diffusing itself and generalising itself and exercising a hard-edge influence over an enormous range of appearances. In a way, it is the visual recurrence of the persistent hard-edge element always present in working-class style. Remember the skinheads, and the rockers before them; and the Teds, who have turned into such genial folk heroes with the passage of time that nobody seems to remember just how nasty they were in their youth, with their razors and bicycle-chain knuckle-dusters.

All these styles, all predominantly masculine, were the specific uniform of an aggressive sub-culture with a taste for physical violence that remained universally offensive to everybody except the peer group involved. Punk retains only the visual and linguistic aggression of these styles; it crosses with porn and self-mutilation; girls can do it and it has gone up-market, really up-market, with the most amazing speed, to fuse with the up-market vogue for tacky glitter that has been bubbling under since the early days of the magazine called *Andy Warhol's Interview*.

Styles of conspicuous outrage may start off as an expression of pride *in extremis*. But those who cannot work because there is none to be had and so make their play, their dancing, their clothes, into a kind of work, for reasons of self-respect, have a lot in common with those who either do not need to work or whose work is a kind of play, like pop musicians and fashion models. The only difference is, the rich have more money, Scott, and pay through the nose for gold plastic wrap miniskirts, plastic raincoats, safety pins (sequinned specially for them) and bondage jackets made up in good tweed.

Therefore the style of the late seventies finds the underprivileged and the overprivileged in the same visual category, both bearing upon them the marks, as it were, the proudly born buboes, of what Reimut Reiche called, in another context in the late sixties, a 'pariah élite'. A self-conscious pariah élite, with an aesthetic of the tawdry, the parodic, a playbox decadence.

Down-market self-conscious Bad Taste is naive; a boy I know was wearing a swastika in one ear and a Star of David in another last summer. He said it was to 'confuse people'. Which is a dangerous game. It is his innocence rather than his viciousness that gives me anguish, because he's not vicious at all. Up-market self-conscious Bad Taste, however, knows what it is doing; it consciously violates taboos.

As an example of this, fashion writers unblushingly dubbed last summer's dishevelled modes for women: '*après* rape', as a conscious trivialization, a jokey piece of playbox anti-feminism – the taboo against mocking human misery, violated in the name, presumably, of irony. And yet it was almost too silly to be offensive, though the women's movement found it very offensive, and quite right, too.

The pricey new glossy, *Deluxe*, has a set of fashion pictures in which the actors are garbed in jodhpurs, quilted nylon waistcoats, camouflage pants, mohair jumpers and drainpipes, and look very much as if they were mimicking sexual assault. This must represent some kind of glorious zenith or nadir of self-conscious Bad Taste and certainly cracks my own ironic impassivity right down the middle, though it's not really as offensive, as profoundly indecent, as the ads for the model agencies with the pictures of the girls plus their measurements. Like the visiting cards of a very expensive brothel. No doubt this resemblance is intentional. Isn't capitalism the brothel in which we all have our cribs? *That* must be what it means.

Deluxe, which itself might possibly be Bad Taste, offers a wide variety of fetishistic apparel, a kind of summing-up of the up-market extreme. The use of rubber, with its comforting suggestions of the protective rubber sheet in the baby's cot; haircuts and cosmetic styles with the abstract stylisation of children's paintings of grown-ups; satin rompers and shorts of the kind Christopher Robin used to wear; the generally sexually exhibitionistic stance of the models; all these suggest a self-conscious pleasure in regression, a stirring of what Norman O. Brown calls 'the immortal child within us' in all its polymorphously perverse splendour.

The underwear counters of Marks & Spencer are crammed with brassieres such as I have not seen since the late fifties, bras with underwired cups, padded cups, boned supports. And girdles, pantie-belts, even things that look very much like corsets. Breasts, so long left to their own devices, will be thrust up and out; the waist and belly bound in and flattened by garments that leave delicious bruises on the skin. The genuine article, back again; bondage undergarments for women, a reversion to the perpetual mild discomfort of constrictive clothing.

The curious fad for the buttock-emphasising jodhpur suggests that bums will soon be back, to balance the new bosoms. Trousers and skirts are certainly tighter than they have been for years; tight trousers and long, tight skirts necessitate high, narrow heels – this is such an aesthetic invariable I think it must have something to do with golden sections.

Such clothes effectively hobble and restrict women as much as more explicitly fetishistic garments; they make it impossible for a woman to ignore her own physicality. You are aware of every breath you take; you have to walk carefully and totter when you run. Just as the use of cosmetics – and all the girls are doing it – makes it impossible to forget your own face. You must be always powdering and lipsticking in a one-to-one narcissistic relation with your self. I remember it all so well, I grew up with it – the taffeta petticoats that snag your stockings, the horror of it and, oh God, the little white gloves to protect your fingers from the gritty surfaces of real life.

Cropped hair, that elementary self-mutilation, is almost universal among young men and commonplace among young women. But it is the young men, with their clean-cut hair, turned-up drainpipes, plaid shirts, who have the most uncanny air about them, like revenants from some pre-Vietnam campus where the matter of most moment was, whether you could borrow your father's car and who was bird-dogging whom. I could almost fool myself I was 18 again, sometimes, back in that age of innocence when the young were poor and knew their place.

The polymorphously perverse infant of the Bad Taste extreme looks like he will grow up to be a good teen; he will know his place, this one. Girls, of course, are getting scared of the Pill; and tight, bright clothes and hard bright faces are rarely, if ever, seen in cultures where sexual licence is the norm. We can stop being sexual subjects (that is, promiscuous) and revert to being sexual objects, 'après rape', in garments that will continually remind us of our socially induced masochism until they become, once again, like second nature.

Does recession always necessitate regression? Three steps forward, two steps back, the stop-stop-go of history, here it is, in the dressing-up box of appearances. What will happen next? Hard periods, like this one, always follow soft ones, like the sixties. The sixties were Rousseauesque; the seventies, as yet, Hobbesian. But, of course, they're not over yet – only this year is almost over, and I think it was a defining year. And I suppose I'm glad the year of the Jubilee was the year of the punk, really. It was actually a very happy kind of irony, almost tasteful.

Angela Carter, *New Society*, 22 December 1977

1978: Tuesday, January 3

There's an article in *People* about my Athletes show that's on now at the Coe Kerr Gallery.

When I got home from the office I made a lot of phone calls, then walked over to Halston's to pick up Bianca, she was cooking like a Puerto Rican, and she had the whole house smelled up with onions and hamburgers, she had them out on the counter. We cabbed up to 86th Street ($2.75) and we finally hit *Saturday Night Fever* at the right time and were able to get in. Well, the movie was just great. That bridge thing was the best scene – and the lines were great. It's I guess the new kind of fantasy movie, you're supposed to stay where you are. The old movies were things like *Dead End* and you had to get out of the dead end and make it to Park Avenue and now they're telling you that it's better off to stay where you are in Brooklyn – to avoid Park Avenue because it would just make you unhappy. It's about people who would *never* even think about crossing the bridge, that's the fantasy. And they played up Travolta's big solo dance number, but then at the end they made the dance number with the girl so nothing, so underplayed. They were smart. And New York looked so exciting, didn't it? The Brooklyn Bridge and New York. Steve Rubell wants to do a disco movie, but I don't think you could do another one, this one was so great. But why didn't they do it as a play first? What was this first, a short story? They should have milked it – done it as a play first and it would have run forever.

Bianca fell asleep. Somewhere in the theater we found Dr Giller. But he had related to the movie so well that he wanted to see it again, so we left him there and went back to Halston's.

Halston and Bianca were in the kitchen together cooking, and he said he had so much energy he wanted to go dancing. He told me lots of gossip – he said that the night before when the doorbell rang it was Liza Minelli. Her life's very complicated now. Like she was walking down the street with Jack Haley her husband and they'd run into Martin Scorsese who she's now having an affair with, and Marty confronted her that she was also having an affair with Baryshnikov and Marty said how *could* she. This is going on with her husband, Jack Haley, standing there! And Halston said that it was all true, and he also said that Jack Haley *wasn't* gay. You see? I was right, I didn't *think* so. Halston said Jack *likes* Liza but that what he *really* goes for is big curvy blonde women. So when the doorbell rang the night before, it was Liza in a hat pulled down so nobody would recognize her, and she said to Halston, 'Give me every drug you've got.' So he gave her a bottle of coke, a few sticks of marijuana, a Valium, four Quaaludes, and they were all wrapped in a tiny box, and then a little figure in a white hat came up on the stoop and kissed Halston, and it was Marty Scorsese, he'd been hiding around the corner, and then he and Liza went off to have their affair on all the drugs.

Then Dr Giller arrived from his second viewing of *Saturday Night Fever*. Bianca had been fighting with Victor before he came, because Victor was eating all the hamburgers she'd made and she was saying to save some for Dr Giller. But I think she just wanted them herself – her ass has gotten really big.

The Sex Pistols arrived in the US today. Punk is going to be so big. They're so smart, whoever's running their tour, because they're starting in Pittsburgh where the kids have nothing to do, so they'll go really crazy.

Andy Warhol, *Diaries* (1989)

1978: Legs McNeil vrs. the Sex Pistols

I drive to San Francisco in a van with ten people. It is horrible. I have a splitting headache and this one guy in the van gets drunk and keeps shouting dumb stuff. To make matters worse the loudmouth makes us stop every five minutes to take a piss. The driver keeps asking why in hell we are driving all this way to see the Sex Pistols. I can't give him a good answer.

We finally make it to San Francisco and we come to a toll booth on the outskirts of the city. The toll booth attendant has long hair and a beard. A real hippie. I hate San Francisco already. I want to go home.

I figure in my head that I see the Sex Pistols the biggest hippies in the world play at hippie Bill Graham's winter hippieland in the city that bore the first hippie. I know I'm in for a 'wonderful' time.

I get to the hotel where John & Roberta are & it is real nice. Two of the Sex Pistols are hanging out, Steve and Paul but I can't remember which is which. They look nice guys but I have an instinctive hate for English people. Paul and Steve keep their distance. They are rock stars.

I soon find out that everything is secret and hush-hush. Paranoia is so thick on the 10th floor you can cut it with a knife. I feel like I'm in the 60s when some hippie decided he didn't like you and tells the world you're a narc. I wish I was a narc then I could carry a .357 Magnum and every time one of those hippies gave me a dirty look I could blow their fucking head off.

A few hours after I get to the S.F. it is time for the concert. I feel like staying in the Hotel Miyako and taking Japanese baths and ordering crabmeat sandwiches from room service.

We go to leave and were waiting for the elevator. Some chick that Malcom's with comes out and gives us a dirty look and says something nasty 'Oh a bunch of fucking journalists.' Somebody laughs. I am not amused. I am getting quite pissed off. Who are these fucking assholes? I vow to get that chick. Someday she'll be in New York and I'll be hanging out with the boys and she'll turn a wrong corner. God damn I wish I had a Magnum. Baboom! One less asshole. English cunt.

We go to the door and I am standing next to Roberta. The guards frisk me as I enter the concert. Somebody asks Roberta if she is Roberta Bayley. She says yes, they say you can't come in we have orders to throw you out. It is all very bizarre. 'If Roberta can't get in then I'm leaving.' John tells me no that I should see the concert. He says if I come all this way, duty, work, etc. etc. I stay. Roberta gets in.

The concert sucks. Johnny Rotten is boring. The sound is horrible. I have a feeling Bill Graham fucked up the sound on purpose. Roberta introduces me to Malcolm after the show. I tell him to leave the Sex Pistols the Sex Pistols suck. He agrees with me. I tell him to try something else. Malcolm mumbles.

I find John and he gives me a backstage pass and tells me to go get a story. I feel like Jimmy Olsen being sent to Coney Island to cover the polar bear club going for a swim in the middle of January. I go backstage. Johnny Rotten, Joe Stevens, a big roadie, Bob Gruen, Annie Liebowitz, Sid Vicious and four groupies Sidney has just pulled out of the audience. Johnny Rotten is saying the usual fuck fuck fuck cunt fuck fuck cunt cunt fuck cunt fuck fuck. Yawn. Annie Liebowitz is trying to take Johnny's picture with Sid. Johnny won't get up and join Sidney, Sidney won't get up to join Johnny. Johnny pulls on his hair and screams 'Ya wanna take a picture, is my *HAIR* ALL RIGHT?'

Annie is getting frustrated but she is a trooper. She is not as good looking as I expected. She is quite plain looking. I wonder how Mick Jaguar could get it on with her. It makes me feel good to know I've gotten better looking chicks than Mick Jaguar. He must have loved her for her mind. Sidney is busy with the groupies. Who's gonna fuck me tonight? he asks. Sidney is a man of few words. How about a kiss first one of the girls ask. They all look about 15 or 16. One of the girls says hi Johnny how do you do. Johnny says fuck you. The girl turns red and trys to smile. Johnny rants and raves about how 'How do you do' is an invalid opening line. Joe Stevens introduces me to Rotten '*What the fuck is a Legs McNeil?*' he asks. I say 'What?' Johnny goes onto something else. Johnny is very boring. He is not even a cool villain. Melvin Purvis would have got him in a half hour. I leave and go to the party in another part of backstage. The opening group is throwing popcorn at the rest of the people and calling them poseurs. I want to go home. It is just a rock'n'roll nightmare. And I will wake up soon. I give my backstage pass to some punk girl and she is very happy. 'Just maybe me and Johnny Rotten could' . . . Ha ha ha. I go back thinking that Malcolm must be thinking, Ha, ha, ha who says there isn't a sucker born every minute?

Legs McNeil, *Punk* #14, 1978

1979: In Defence of Disco

All my life I've liked the wrong music. I never liked Elvis and rock 'n' roll; I always preferred Rosemary Clooney. And since I became a socialist, I've often felt virtually terrorised by the prestige of rock and folk on the left. How could I admit to two Petula Clark LPs in the face of miners' songs from the North East and the Rolling Stones? I recovered my nerve partially when I came to see show biz type music as a key part of gay culture, which, whatever its limitations, was a culture to defend. And I thought I'd really made it when I turned on to Tamla Motown, sweet soul sounds, disco. Chartbusters already, and I like them! Yet the prestige of folk and rock, and now punk and (rather patronisingly, I think) reggae, still holds sway. It's not just that people whose politics I broadly share don't *like* disco, they manage to imply that it is politically beyond the pale to like it. It's against this attitude that I want to defend disco (which otherwise, of course, hardly needs any defence).

I'm going to talk mainly about disco *music*, but there are two preliminary points I'd like to make. The first is that disco is more than just a form of music, although certainly the music is at the heart of it. Disco is also kinds of dancing, club, fashion, film etc.; – in a word, a certain *sensibility*, manifest in music, clubs etc., historically and culturally specific, economically, technologically, ideologically and aesthetically determined – and worth thinking about. Secondly, as a sensibility in music it seems to me to encompass more than what we would perhaps strictly call disco music, to include a lot of soul, Tamla and even the later work of mainstream and jazz artistes like Peggy Lee and Johnny Mathis.

My defence is in two parts. First, a discussion of the arguments against disco in terms of its being 'capitalist' music. Second, an attempt to think through the – ambivalently, ambiguously, contradictorily – positive qualities of disco.

Much of the hostility to disco stems from the equation of it with capitalism. Both in how it is produced and in what it expresses, disco is held to be irredeemably capitalistic.

Now it is unambiguously the case that disco is produced by capitalist industry, and since capitalism is an irrational and inhuman mode of production, the disco industry is as bad as all the rest. Of course. However, this argument has assumptions behind it that are more problematic. These are of two kinds. One assumption concerns *music as a mode of production*, and has to do with the belief that it is possible in a capitalist society to produce things (e.g. music; e.g. rock and folk) that are outside of the capitalist mode of production. Yet quite apart from the general point that such a position seeks to elevate activity outside of existing structures rather than struggles against them, the two kinds of music most often set against disco as a mode of production are not really convincing.

One is folk music – in this country, people might point to Gaelic songs and industrial ballads – the kind of music often used, or reworked, in left fringe theatre. These, it is argued, are not, like disco (and pop music, in general), produced for the people but by them. They are 'authentic' people's music. So they are – or rather, were. The problem is that we don't live in a society of small technologically simple, communities such as produce such art. Preserving such music at its best gives us a historical perspective on peasant and working class struggle, at worst leads to a nostalgia for a simple, harmonious community existence that never even existed. More bluntly, songs in Gaelic or dealing with nineteenth century factory conditions, beautiful as they are, don't mean much to most English speaking people today.

The other kind of music most often posed against disco and 'pap pop' at the level of how it is produced is rock (including Dylan-type folk and everything from early rock 'n' roll to progressive concept albums). The argument here is that rock is easily produced by non-professionals – all that is needed are a few instruments and somewhere to play – whereas disco music requires the whole panoply of recording studio technology, which makes it impossible for non-professionals (the kid in the streets) to produce. The factual accuracy of this observation needs supplementing with some other observations. Quite apart from the very rapid – but then bemoaned by some purists – move of rock into elaborate recording studios, even when it is simply, producable by non-professionals, the fact is that rock is still quite expensive, and remained in practice largely the preserve of middle-class who could afford electric guitars, music lessons etc. (You have only to look at the biographies of those now professional rock musicians who started out in a simple non-professional way – the preponderance of public school and university educated young men in the field is rivalled only by their preponderance in the Labour Party cabinet.) More importantly, this kind of music is wrongly thought of as being generated from the grass roots (except perhaps at certain key historical moments) – non-professional music making, in rock as elsewhere, bases itself, inevitably, on professional music. Any notion that rock emanates from 'the people' is soon confounded by the recognition that what 'the people' are doing is trying to be as much like professionals as possible.

The second kind of argument based on the fact that disco is produced by capitalism concerns *music as an ideological expression*. Here it is assumed that capitalism as a mode of production necessarily and simply produces 'capitalist' ideology. The theory of the relation between the mode of production and the ideologies of a particular society is too complicated and unresolved to be gone into here, but we can begin by remembering that capitalism is about profit. In the language of classical economies, capitalism produces commodities, and its interest in commodities is their exchange-value (how much profit they can realise) rather than their use-value (their social or human worth). This becomes particularly problematic for capitalism when dealing with an expressive commodity – such as disco – since a major problem for capitalism is that there is no necessary or guaranteed connection between exchange-value and use-value – in other words, capitalism as productive relations can just as well make a profit from something that is ideologically opposed to bourgeois society as something that supports it. As long as a commodity makes a profit, what does it matter? (I should like to acknowledge my debt to Terry Lovell for explaining this aspect of capitalist cultural production to me.) Indeed; it is because of this dangerous, anarchic tendency of capitalism that ideological institutions – the church, the state, education, the family etc. – are necessary. It is their job to make sure that what capitalism produces is in capitalism's longer term interests. However, since they often don't know that that is their job, they don't always perform it. Cultural production within capitalist society is then founded on two profound contradictions – the first, between production for profit and production for use; the second, within those institutions whose job it is to regulate the first contradiction. What all this boils down to, in terms of disco, is that the fact that disco is produced by capitalism does not mean that it is automatically, necessarily, simply supportive of capitalism. Capitalism constructs the disco experience, but it does not necessarily know what it is doing, apart from making money.

I am not now about to launch into a defence of disco music as some great subversive art form. What the arguments above lead me to is, firstly, a basic point of departure in the recognition that cultural production under capitalism is necessarily contradictory, and, secondly, that it may well be the case that capitalist cultural products are most likely to be contradictory at just those points – such as disco – where they are most commercial and professional, where the urge to profit is at its strongest. Thirdly, this mode of cultural production has produced a commodity, disco, that has been taken up by gays in ways that may well not have been intended by its producers.

The anarchy of capitalism throws up commodities that an oppressed group can take up and use to cobble together its own culture. In this respect, disco is very much like another profoundly ambiguous aspect of male gay culture, camp. It is a 'contrary' use of what the dominant culture provides, it is important in forming a gay identity, and it has subversive potential as well as reactionary implications.

Let me turn now to what I consider to be the three important characteristics of disco – eroticism, romanticism, and materialism. I'm going to talk about them in terms of what it seems to me they mean within the context of gay culture. These three characteristics are not in themselves good or bad (any more than disco music as a whole is), and they need specifying more precisely. What is interesting is how they take us to qualities that are not only key ambiguities within gay male culture, but have also traditionally proved stumbling blocks to socialists.

Eroticism

It can be argued that all popular music is erotic. What we need to define is the specific way of thinking and feeling erotically in disco. I'd like to call it 'whole body' eroticism, and to define it by comparing it with the eroticism of the two kinds of music to which disco is closest – popular song (i.e., the Gershwin, Cole Porter, Burt Bacharach type of song) and rock.

Popular song's eroticism is 'disembodied': it succeeds in expressing a sense of the erotic which yet denies eroticism's physicality. This can be shown by the nature of tunes in popular songs and the way they are handled.

Popular song's tunes are rounded off, closed, self-contained. They achieve this by adopting a strict musical structure (AABA) in which the opening melodic phrases are returned to and, most importantly, the tonic note of the whole song is also the last note of the tune. (The tonic note is the note that forms the basis for the key in which the song is written; it is therefore the harmonic 'anchor' of the tune and closing on it gives precisely a feeling of 'anchoring', coming to a settled stop.) Thus although popular songs often depart – especially in the middle section (B) – from their melodic and harmonic beginnings, they also always return to them. This gives them – even at their most passionate, say, Porter's 'Night and Day' – a sense of security and containment. The tune is not allowed to invade the whole of one's body. Compare the typical disco tune, which is often little more than an endlessly repeated phrase which drives beyond itself, is not 'closed off'. Even when disco music uses a popular song standard, it often turns it into a simple phrase. Gloria Gaynor's version of Porter's 'I've got you under my skin', for instance, is in large part a chanted repetition of 'I've got you'.

Popular song's lyrics place its tunes within a conceptualisation of love and passion as emanating from 'inside', the heart or the soul. Thus the yearning cadences of popular song expresses an erotic yearning of the inner person, not the body. Once again, disco refuses this. Not only are the lyrics often more directly physical and the delivery more raunchy (e.g. Grace Jones' 'I need a man'), but, most importantly, disco is insistently rhythmic in a way that popular song is not.

Rhythm, in Western music, is traditionally felt as being more physical than other musical elements such as melody, harmony and instrumentation. This is why Western music is traditionally so dull rhythmically – nothing expresses our Puritan heritage more vividly. It is to other cultures that we have had to turn – and above all to Afro-American culture – to learn about rhythm. The history of popular song since the late nineteenth century is largely the history of the white incorporation (or ripping off) of black music – ragtime, the Charleston, the tango, swing, rock 'n' roll, rock. Now what is interesting about this incorporation/ripping-off is what it meant and means. Typically, black music was thought of by the white culture as being both more primitive and more 'authentically' erotic. Infusions of black music were always seen as (and often condemned as) sexual and physical. The use of insistent black rhythms in disco music, recognisable by the closeness of the style to soul and reinforced by such characteristic features of black music as the repeated chanted phrase and the use of various African percussion instruments, means that it inescapably signifies (in this white context) physicality.

However, rock is as influenced by black music as disco is. This then leads me to the second area of comparison between disco's eroticism and rock's. The difference between them lies in what each 'hears' in black music. Rock's eroticism is thrusting, grinding – it is not whole body, but phallic. Hence it takes from black music the insistent beat and makes it even more driving; rock's repeated phrases trap you in their relentless push, rather than releasing you in an open-ended succession of repetitions as disco does. Most revealing perhaps is rock's instrumentation. Black music has more percussion instruments than white, but it knows how to use them to create all sorts of effect – light, soft, lively, as well as heavy, hard and grinding. Rock, however, only hears the latter and develops the percussive qualities of essentially non-percussive instruments to increase this, hence the twanging electric guitar and the nasal vocal delivery. One can see how, when rock 'n' roll first came in, this must have been a tremendous liberation from popular song's disembodied eroticism – here was a really physical music, and not just mealy mouthedly physical, but quite clear what it was about – cock. But rock confines sexuality to cock (and this is why, no matter how progressive the lyrics and even when performed by women, rock remains indelibly phallocentric music). Disco music, on the other hand, hears the physicality in black music and its range. It achieves this by a number of features including – the sheer amount going on rhythmically in even quite simple disco music (for rhythmic clarity with complexity, listen to the full length version of the Temptations' 'Papa was a Rolling Stone'); the willingness to play with rhythm, delaying it, jumping it, countering it rather than simply driving on and on (examples – Patti Labelle, Isaac Hayes); the range of percussion instruments used and with different affects (e.g. the spiky violins in Quincy Jones/Herbie Hancock's 'Tell Me a Bedtime Story'; the gentle pulsations of George Benson). This never stops being erotic, but it restores eroticism to the whole of the body, and for both sexes, not just confining it to the penis. It leads to the expressive, sinuous movement of disco dancing, not just a mixture of awkwardness and thrust so dismally characteristic of dancing to rock.

Gay men do not intrinsically have any prerogative over whole body eroticism. We are often even more cock-oriented than non-gays of either sex, and it depresses me that such phallic forms of disco as Village People should be so gay identified. Nonetheless, partly because many of us have traditionally not thought of ourselves as being 'real men' and partly because gay ghetto culture is also a space where alternative definitions, including of sexuality, can be developed, it seems to me that the importance of disco in scene culture indicates an openness to a sexuality that is not defined in terms of cock. Although one cannot easily move from musical values to personal ones, or from personal ones to politically effective ones, it is at any rate suggestive that gay culture should promote a form of music that denies the centrality of the phallus while at the same time refusing the non-physicality which such a denial has hitherto implied.

Romanticism

Not all disco music is romantic. The lyrics of many disco hits are either straightforwardly sexual – not to say sexist – or else broadly social (e.g. Detroit Spinners' 'Ghetto Child', Stevie Wonder's 'Living in the City'), and the hard drive of Village People or Labelle is positively anti-romantic. Yet there is nonetheless a strong strain or romanticism in disco. This can be seen in the lyrics, which often differ little from popular song standards, and indeed often are standards (e.g. 'What a Difference a Day Made' – Esther Phillips, 'la Vie en Rose' – Grace Jones). More impressively, it is the instrumentation and arrangements of disco music that are so romantic.

The use of massed violins takes us straight back, via Hollywood, to Tchaikovsky, to surging, outpouring emotions. A brilliant example is Gloria Gaynor's 'I've got you under my skin', where in the middle section the violins take a hint from one of Porter's melodic phrases and develop it away from his tune in an ecstatic, soaring movement. This 'escape' from the confines of popular song into ecstasy is very characteristic of disco music, and nowhere more consistently than in such Diana Ross classics as 'Reach Out' and 'Ain't No Mountain High Enough'. The latter, with its lyrics total surrender to love, its heavenly choir and sweeping violins, is perhaps one of the most extravagant reaches of disco's romanticism. But Ross is also a key figure in the gay appropriation of disco.

What Ross' records do – and I'm thinking basically of her work up to *Greatest Hits* volume 1 and the *Touch Me In the Morning* album – is express the intensity of fleeting emotional contacts. They are all-out expressions of adoration which yet have built in to them the recognition of the (inevitably) temporary quality of experience. This can be a straightforward lament for having been let down by a man, but more often it is both a celebration of a relationship and the almost willing recognition of its passing and the exquisite pain of its passing – 'Remember me/As a sunny day/That you once had/Along the way', 'If I've got to be strong/Don't you know I need to have tonight when you're gone/When you go I'll lie here/And think about/the last time that you/Touch me in the morning'. This last number, with Ross' 'unreally' sweet, porcelain fragile voice and the string backing, concentrates that sense of celebrating the intensity of the passing relationship that haunts so much of her work. No wonder Ross is (was?) so important in gay male scene culture, for she both reflects what that culture takes to be an inevitable reality (that relationships don't last) and at the same time celebrates it, validates it.

Not all disco music works in this vein, yet in both some of the more sweetly melancholy orchestrations (even of lively numbers, like 'You Should Be Dancing' in *Saturday Night Fever*) and some of the lyrics and general tone (e.g. Donna Summer's *Four Seasons of Love* album), there is a carry over of this emotional timbre. At a minimum, the disco's romanticism provides an embodiment and validation of an aspect of gay culture.

But romanticism is a particularly paradoxical quality of art to come to terms with. Its passion and intensity embody or create an experience that negates the dreariness of the mundane and everyday. It gives us a glimpse of what it means to live at the height of our emotional and experiential capacities – not dragged down by the banality of organised routine life. Given that everyday banality, work, domesticity, ordinary sexism and racism, are rooted in the structures of class and gender of this society, the flight from that banality can be seen as – is – a flight from capitalism and patriarchy themselves as lived experiences.

What makes this more complicated is the actual situation within which disco occurs. Disco is part of the wider to-and-fro between work and leisure, alienation and escape, boredom and enjoyment that we are so accustomed to (and which *Saturday Night Fever* plugs into so effectively). Now this to-and-fro is partly the mechanism by which we keep going, at work, at home – the respite of leisure gives us the energy for work, and anyway we are still largely brought up to think of leisure as a 'reward' for work. The circle locks us into it. But what happens in that space of leisure can be profoundly significant – it is there that we may learn about an alternative to work and to society as it is. Romanticism is one of the major modes of leisure in which this sense of an alternative is kept alive. Romanticism asserts that the limits of work and domesticity are not the limits of experience.

I don't say that the passion and intensity of romanticism is a political ideal we could strive for – I doubt that it is humanly possible to live permanently at that pitch. What I do believe is that the movement between banality and something 'other' than banality is an essential dialectic of society, a constant keeping open of a gap between what is and what could or should be. Herbert Marcuse in the currently unfashionable *One-Dimensional Man* argues that our society tries to close that gap, to assert that what is all that there could be, is what should be. For all its commercialism and containment within the work/leisure to-and-fro, I think disco romanticism is one of the things that can keep the gap open, that can allow the *experience of contradiction* to continue. Since I also believe that political struggle is rooted in experience (though utterly doomed if left at it), I find this dimension of disco potentially positive. (A further romantic/utopian aspect of disco is realised in the non-commercial discos organized by gay and women's groups. Here a moment of community can be achieved, often in circle dances or simply in the sense of knowing people as people, not anonymous bodies. Fashion is less important, and sociability correspondingly more so. This can be achieved in smaller clubs, perhaps

525

especially outside the centre of London, which, when not just grotty monuments to self-oppression, can function as supportive expressions of something like a gay community.)

Materialism

Disco is characteristic of advanced capitalist societies simply in terms of the scale of money squandered on it. It is a riot of consumerism, dazzling in its technology (echo chambers, double and more tracking, electric instruments), overwhelming in its scale (banks of violins, massed choirs, the limitless range of percussion instruments), lavishly gaudy in the mirrors and tat of discotheques, the glitter and denim flash of its costumes. Its tacky sumptuousness is well evoked in *Thank God It's Friday*. Gone are the restraint of popular song, the sparseness of rock and reggae, the simplicity of folk. How can a socialist, or someone trying to be a feminist, defend it?

In certain respects, it is doubtless not defensible. Yet socialism and feminism are both forms of materialism – why is disco, a celebration of materiality if ever there was one, not therefore the appropriate art form of materialist politics?

Partly, obviously, because materialism in politics is not to be confused with mere matter. Materialism seeks to understand how things are in terms of how they have been produced and constructed in history, and how they can be better produced and constructed. This certainly does not mean immersing oneself in the material world – indeed, it includes deliberately stepping back from the material world to see what makes it the way it is and how to change it. Yes, but, materialism is also based on the profound conviction that politics is about the material world, and indeed the human life and the material world are all there is, no God, no magic forces. One of the dangers of materialist politics is that it is in constant danger of spiritualising itself, partly because of the historical legacy of the religious forms that brought materialism in existence, partly because materialists have to work so hard not to take matter at face value that they often end up not treating it as matter at all. Disco's celebration of materiality is only a celebration of the world we are necessarily and always immersed in – and disco's materiality, in technological modernity, is resolutely historical and cultural – it can never be, as most art claims for itself, an 'emanation' outside of history and of human production.

Disco's combination of romanticism and materialism effectively tells us – lets us experience – that we live in a world of materiality, that we can enjoy materiality but that the experience of materiality is not necessarily what the everyday world assures us it is. Its eroticism allows us to rediscover our bodies as part of this experience of materiality and the possibility of change.

If this sounds over the top, let one thing be clear – disco can't change the world, make the revolution. No art can do that, and it is pointless expecting it to. But partly by opening up experience, partly by changing definitions, art, disco, can be used. To which one might risk adding the refrain – If it feels good, *use* it.

Richard Dyer, *Gay Left*, Summer 1979

1980: Mistaken Identities

'Something's wrong.'

Sid Vicious calling room service on discovering Nancy Spungen's body. Reported in the *Evening News* (Oct 13, 1978). Subsequently denied.

On Oct 12, 1978 Nancy Spungen bled to death propped up against a bathroom wall in a hotel called the Chelsea in Manhattan. 'The blonde-haired beauty'* ... 'clad in a black-laced bra and panties' ... was found ... 'crumpled under the ... sink' ... 'lying in a pool of blood' ... 'with a knife sticking in her stomach' ... 'A trail of blood led to the bath of Room 100 from the untidy bedroom' ... where her lover ... 'PUNK ROCK STAR' ... Sid Vicious, who had ... 'gained much attention by grinding broken glass into her chest' ... 'had slept on oblivious to' ... 'her plight' ... 'under the influence of a depressant drug called Tuinal'.

'It took four policemen to hold the struggling Vicious as he was taken off to a police station' ... where the ... '21-year-old Londoner was charged in his real name of John Paul Ritchie with first degree murder. Police said he had been provided with a lawyer.'

'It was to be only a matter of months before' ... 'THE BOY FROM A BROKEN HOME IN LONDON'S EAST END' ... 'a violent, swearing drug addict only his mother could love' ... was himself lying dead ... 'in a seedy hotel room' ... from an overdose of heroin ... 'supplied by his mother Mrs Anne Beverley'.

How else were these events to be recounted but in the language of the

---

* This collage is taken from a number of different newspaper accounts. Some of them were inaccurate. For example, Spungeon was not found 'with a knife sticking in her stomach' (*Evening News*, Oct 13, 1978). In the context of this article, questions of verifiable fact are neither here nor there.

527

tabloids – in cliché and hyperbole? After all, it had happened like that. There was no need for editorial comment. The facts told their own story, spoke for themselves as clearly as any parable of Christ's, holding out the moral – bloody like the head of John the Baptist – on a plate. This was the ballad of Sid and Nancy: a cautionary tale for intemperate youth:

> For naughty boys who swear and break
> All boundaries and try to make
> Pain out of pleasure, pleasure from pain
> Look on Sidney; think again.

It would be difficult to imagine a more 'fitting' end for a boy who seemed intent on singlehandedly living out the Decline of the West, a boy, who, like Durand in Sade's *Juliette* was so set 'against nature' that he seemed, at times, to embody 'the ecological crisis in person'. And Nancy's doomed career had passed through a set of parallel archetypes which were no less potent or exemplary. From 'poor little rich girl' to 'punk queen' to 'half-clad corpse', the fate of Nancy Spungeon held a lesson for all recalcitrant daughters. The lesson was don't.

HOWEVER, THE EMBLEMATIC QUALITY OF THE AFFAIR CAN ITSELF BE OPENED UP AND MADE STRANGE...

The chain of events which led from death to death could scarcely be distinguished from the sensational mode in which it was dragged before the British public. It submitted to the logic of disclosure unfolding episode by episode in four distinct parts: Spungeon murdered; Vicious arrested; Vicious charged with assault while out on bail; Vicious dead. The 'fates' of two chaotic individuals unravelling in time could thus appear to take on order and significance. This was punk's grisly strip show in which each incident served to peel away another layer of illusion to reveal – at last – the 'TRUTH BEHIND PUNK ROCK', what all non-punks feared, that underneath the outrage there lurked *real* violence, *real* perversion, a *real* threat of death.

YET...

at the same time, the saga of Sid and Nancy came to us through a long detour composed of literary and journalistic archetypes. This was scandal with a capital 'S' in the classic mould of *True Detective* magazine or Kenneth Anger's *Hollywood Babylon*. It was filtered through the terminal projections of William Burroughs and Hubert Selby Jr, through 50's 'B' movies, through the narcissistic angst of a host of rock-stars-on-junk from Frankie Lymon to Johnny Thunders, through 'documentary' images of New York as the epitome of the City in Crisis, even, finally, through the 'retrospective destiny' of punk itself as a movement which began with 'No Future'. Paradoxically, this 'real life tragedy' had no reference outside the myth and fiction. The events themselves occurred 'in quotes'. Moving inexorably on to their dramatic conclusions, they obeyed the laws of narrative and inevitably, given the status of the protagonists, they remained, first and foremost, events within representation. Almost immediately, as soon as the news broke, T-shirts bearing the caption SID LIVES or with screen printed headlines proclaiming his death were being churned out. The haste was indecent. Of course, it was deliberately so. (I saw one of these T-shirts in the window of a Wolverhampton joke shop sandwiched between the horror masks and the black-face soap.)

IN EFFECT . . .

through it all, Vicious and Spungeon had been complicit in the process of symbolization – a negative process which was eventually to turn them into icons, which had already transformed New York, at least for us in Britain, from a real city into 'that dangerous, sad city of the imagination . . . which is the modern world'. Why else did they go there?

Compelled irresistably by the dictates of an image they'd in part constructed but in larger part had had constructed for them, they were in a sense, victims of their own drive to coherence, in bondage to a fantasy of absolutes in a world where they simply don't exist.

The rest is 'his story'. Vicious, the poor man's libertine is determined by a role he cannot transcend. He conforms to type and, as he exhausts his few remaining options, in the words of Angela Carter (here describing the limits of de Sade's cloistered universe):

> The structure of his own invented reality hardens around him and imprisons him. The passions he thought would free him from the cage of being become the very bars of the cage that traps him; he himself cannot escape the theatrical decor he has created around himself . . . during the hell-game the libertine is himself as much in hell as his victims . . .

Nancy Spungeon's obituary in the *Evening News* ran to just six lines:

> Nancy's father is head of a paper firm in Philadelphia. She had bleached blonde hair in a frizzy style, used heavy eye make-up and often dressed in punk style black leathers.

There is a sense in which Nancy 'herself' never really existed. She is at last reduced officially to the status of pure sign within a patriarchal network of significance which defines her, on the one hand, as the daughter of a rich and powerful man and on the other as the ruined object of our gaze. She is the cat which curiosity killed. Fixed on the point of her boyfriend's knife, she is now a literally lifeless thing, a set of cosmetic appearances (some hair, 'heavy eye make-up', 'black leathers').

When the police arrived and Sid Vicious stepped out looking dazed into a world of flashing lights and questions, he was charged 'in his real name'.

I don't think John Paul Ritchie did it his way.

Dick Hebdige, ZG #2, 1980

eight

1980–85

'Baroque proportions'

8

GEORGE:Mode-"I'm a budding celebrity,the immaculate conception".The nuns habit-"I made it myself dear".Crucifix-"A present from the Vatican".Kung Fu slippers-£4.99 from a Chinese supermarket.Make up-a mix of Lichner and Biba.Fave music-Marc Bolan,Julie Andrews,Pearl Bailey,The Sweet and Bach.Dislikes-"Lounge -Lizards"and Spandau Ballet.

'I want to dedicate it
Everybody hate it
Infiltrate it
Activate it
New York London Paris Munich
Everybody talk about
Pop Muzik'

M, 'Pop Muzik' (1979)

'Pop, disco, colour, lights, action': the early eighties were a time of pop unleashed. The British media reflected this new era with a crop of new, glossy magazines like *Smash Hits* (aimed at younger teens), *i-D* and *The Face* (aimed at post-punks). Sometime at the end of the decade, the avant-garde had turned away from confrontation to pop, from rock to funk: fuelled by punk's exhumation of post-war youth styles, the New Pop aesthetic was playful, referential, at times even academic, and wore its calculation on its sleeve.

The first two extracts chart this transition. In the influential Anglo/ American magazine *ZG*, editor Rosetta Brooks explores 'the imaginary life' of London's Blitz teens like the young George O'Dowd – where 'clothing, make-up, hairstyle, etc. is essentially a collage, each component taken up on the level of the fashion equivalent of the ready-made – as *2nd hand*'. In his biography of Boy George and Culture Club, *Like Punk Never Happened*, Dave Rimmer describes the moment when Adam Ant, punk rocker, decided to become Adam Ant, the first major pop star of the eighties.

This was the moment when pop culture went fully postmodern; when youth culture time became serial rather than linear. Punk had made a similar collage out of pop's past, but this had served a modernist purpose: the single, central narrative that in the early eighties was suspect. Today postmodernism has become so devalued as to be worthless, but Steve Dixon's manifesto in *i-D*, 'Birth of the Wiseboys and Wisegirls', reminds us of the cosmic possibilities of that moment when 'Sub-cults/style/fashion and social behaviour' were 'changing at a rate that is becoming breathtaking'.

As David Toop notes in *The Rap Attack*, the musical equivalent of this style montage was occurring in New York. This extract shows how Bronx DJ Afrika Bambaataa and producer Arthur Baker adapted Kraftwerk's 'Trans Europe Express' into a new tune called 'Planet Rock'. This mix of street styles and electronic sound – the new black futurism caught in its infancy by Vince Aletti in 'Golden Voices and Hearts of Steel' – took dance music apart and put it back together in a new way. The reverberations from this one record continue today in all the varieties of rap, techno, garage, house.

This black electronica – then called electro – was the British club sound of the early eighties: records like Grandmaster Flash and the Furious Five's 'The Message', the Peech Boys 'Don't Make Me Wait'. This was the beginning of a fundamental shift in British pop, away from a rock to a dance economy – where, despite the best efforts of the mainstream music industry, it still remains. The focus of excitement moved from the concert to the club, to the extent that clubs became the principal location for creating new styles, for breaking hit records, for promoting new stars.

Smash Hits was the house organ for what Paul Morley, in his Duran Duran interview, calls 'the new age of teenybop': colourful, snappy, with no qualms about a return to fun, excitement, glamour. From *Smash Hits*'s initial purple patch, Peter Martin's report on Madonna's first visit to the UK captures the ambition of the woman who would become the world's biggest pop star. Judy Wade's *Sun* article about Boy George and Culture Club exemplifies the fresh interest shown by Fleet Street in pop, an interest reciprocated by the new generation of stars, who courted the tabloids as never before.

Club culture developed its own myths, its own traditions, explored here by two contemporary articles in its house organ, *The Face*. David Johnson charts the history of one building, Soho's 69 Dean Street: in the thirties home to the Gargoyle, fifty years later hosting a bewildering variety of nights – Goth, 6T's soul, gay, alternative comedy. In an ambitious (and successful) manifesto, Robert Elms calls for a style to reflect the social realities finally filtering through to pop at the end of Mrs Thatcher's first term. 'Hard Times' is typical of the time – full of pop history, pop sociology – and prescient: the warehouse parties that Elms refers to fuelled the 'rave' culture of the late decade.

The gay scene's huge influence on club culture spilled over into the pop charts from 1981 on: with pervy synth-pop duos like Soft Cell, 'gender benders' like Boy George and Marilyn, openly gay stars like Bronski Beat and Frankie Goes to Hollywood. It was possible to see this concentration on sexuality – paralleled at the time by the success of powerful women like Annie Lennox and Grace Jones – as undercutting an increasingly aggressive government: Simon Frith's 'Whistling in the Dark' teases out the 'oblique' relationship between pop and power politics in 1984, 'the year of the miners' strike and Frankie Goes to Hollywood'.

In reaction to punk, which had pushed alienation in your face, New Pop liked to pretend that the world outside didn't exist. It persists as a constant shadow, whether caught as background ambience – 'A quarter of a mile away from where we're sat, there's a riot going on,' Paul Morley mentions in his Duran Duran interview – or researched later – in an extract from his compendium of music-industry malpractice, 'Expensive Habits', Simon Garfield notes the dirty deals behind the smooth success of Wham!. In his last article for *Smash Hits*, Neil Tennant freezes the moment when this era died, with a career-ending Marilyn appearance in New York: 'He runs off the stage and does not return.'

536

1980: Blitz Culture

A young man with a Ted's quiff extended to Baroque proportions and dressed in a satin jump-suit which looks like the product of an unimaginative sci-fi movie designer, were it not for the addition of Elizabethan cuffs, stands drinking with someone whose clothes are half '30s mafioso, half '60s boot-boy and who is sporting a semi-shaved Mohican Indian haircut. They are surrounded on all sides by a casual array of slightly askew cinematic stereo-types in a self-consciously down-at-heel club in Covent Garden – under the ever watchful eye of Steve Strange, the initiator of Tuesday nights at the Blitz club and guardian of its élitism. Tuesday night is the focal point at which these self-consciously styled individualists are brought into contact with one another. The setting is the ground against which these ironic self-images stand or fall within the microcosmic star-system that posing represents.

If you subscribe to the idea of progress in modernism which has each generation doing progressively less than their predecessor (or the same more easily) then posing can be seen as the 'ne plus ultra' of performance art. As street theatre ultimately extended into continuous performance it can be viewed as a sort of post-punk embodiment of Gilbert and George in one person (the individualist). Removed even from the hallowed context of art, the poser is his/her own ready-made art object but one whose circulation is not the microcosm of the art world but the self-consciously constituted clique centred upon (for the moment) the Blitz and Hell. Each poser as a 'ready-made', must constantly readjust itself within the network of shifting relations set up at this meeting point of people who have in common only that they are so far out of the system, that they only *wear* this cultural isolation.

Whilst this view of the poser is perfectly consistent with the fact that many of the people involved are either art or ex-art school products, the poser does not enter the street as Arts Council-backed intervention. Their form of street theatre is not so much to do with bringing art or theatre to the streets as in making the street theatrical. They become the 'dramatis personae' of a constantly changing scenario.

Posing as a cynical manipulation of the mix of street styles which has occurred in the '70s seems like the end-point of youth cultures in the sense that the latter has always been concerned with an identifiable uniform. But as such, it is just an extension of certain existing tendencies in these cultural ghettos. With the new mods, skinheads and teds etc. the uniform no longer embodies a kind of solidarity of youth standing out against a background of social convention. The new mod asserts his image in relation to a vast range of other youth culture images. The Nazi salutes and the aggression of the new skins seem more like nostalgic references than an actual threat of violence. They represent a stylised take on their predecessors. It is only style which conjoins and differentiates the working class patriarchy of the Ted and the middle-class anarchism of the punk. But finally it is style which negates their social antagonism in the mix of revived youth cultures during the '70s.

A visit to the Moonlight Club in West Hampstead is like entering a living museum of the recent cultural (or subcultural) past. The revival of youth cults are removed from their normal setting and are brought into interaction only with other youth cults and the past life-styles that their images represent. In this respect it is interesting to note that almost all successful rock bands tend to have a following which consists of more than one youth group. So, for example, an apparently punk group like Poison Girls with their vaguely left-wing lyrics, can only develop the sort of audience reaction which is essential to their act by attracting a right-wing skinhead following. When punk anyway has broken down the more straightforward forms of audience identification into alienated aggression, it is only one step further to have the skins doing Nazi salutes to the chorus of the Poison Girls' song. Political factions are dissolved into the surrealism of stylistic juxtaposition. What seems to be most expressed in the new youth culture images is a nostalgia that seemed to invade every other aspect of cultural life in the '70s.

Already there are signs of intermediary mixes occurring e.g. the Rude boy as a mixture of mod/skin/Rasta or the spectacle of the skinhead dyeing his hair punk fashion. Posing is this tendency taken to an extreme. The reference points are merely extended to the fuller range of social and historical stereotypes. Dressing up becomes a fusion of images. It means to bring into juxtaposition and contraposition different images, different connotations, different worlds into the plurality of 'worlds' represented by the sphere of interaction of the poser. Inasmuch as all fashion is this, the poser represents at best a gravitation point, at worst an exaggerated parody.

For the poser it is not so much the style of appearance which in itself is important e.g. achieving a perfect '50s revival 'look', but that the overall 'look' is ambiguous, even askew. Clothing, make-up, hairstyle, etc. is essentially a collage, each component taken up on the level of the fashion equivalent of the ready-made – as *2nd hand*.

Diane Arbus, the photographer said: 'Everybody has that thing where they need to look one way but they come out looking another way and that's what people observe. You see someone on the street and essentially what you notice about them is the flaw. It's just extraordinary that we should have been given these peculiarities. And not content with what we're given, we create a whole other set. Our whole guise is like giving a sign to the world to think of us in a certain way but there's a point between what you want people to know about you and what you can't help people knowing about you. And that has to do with what I've always called the gap between intention and effect. I mean if you scrutinize reality closely enough, if in some way you really get to it, it becomes fantastic. You know it really is totally fantastic that we look like this and you sometimes see that very clearly in a photograph. Something is ironic in the world and it has to do with the fact that what you intend never comes out like you intend it.'

The poser makes this gap his/her point of attraction. The tightrope which s/he must walk is between being victim or master of the flaw. At best they enter into an ironic relationship with how they appear and with what is alluded to in the look. For the pose to work, the poser must constantly innovate the 'look' within the constantly shifting stylistic and symbolic maze which their dramatic interaction entails. Perhaps the poser represents the realisation of Angela Carter's beautifully exaggerated definition of style as 'the presentation of the self as a 3 Dimensional art-object to be wondered at and handled'.

Rosetta Brooks, ZG #1, 1980

1981: The Birth of the New Pop

Picture the scene. It's a grey afternoon in early 1980. Jon Moss is sipping tea with Adam Ant and Marco Pirroni in the living room of a small Harrow semi-detached – Marco's parents' place. None of them are very famous yet. Oh, Jon was once voted 'the prettiest punk' in a fanzine and Adam's name gets sprayed on the backs of a few black leather jackets but that's about it. 'Cult,' Adam has decided, 'is just another word for loser.' Even the indignity of paying Malcolm McLaren £1,000 for an intensive four-week attitude overhaul and then watching the former Sex Pistols manager walk off with his band hasn't softened Adam's resolve. Fired with fresh ideas, he's already recruited Marco Pirroni as a new collaborator and the pair are now looking for other musicians.

Jon Moss is also fed up with being a loser. A drummer, he's done time with them all – Damned, Clash, London, Jona Lewie, The Edge, Jane Aire and the Belvederes – but never managed to settle down with any of them. After spending three months staring blankly at his bedroom wall, he's just forked

539

out £250 for an attitude overhaul of his own: a weekend Exegesis course. Although he came out of it a bit mad – thinking he could 'zap' things and change the colour of traffic lights and all that – he's determined to hit the big time now. Adam has approached him through an old girlfriend and this is their first meeting.

Mrs Pirroni flutters around excitedly offering everyone more tea. Adam munches a cupcake. Jon's finding all this a bit weird. Adam's so quiet and intense it's eery. He's almost robotic. He leans over to Jon and explains, 'I've got this idea for two drummers.' Out comes a tape of some Burundi drumming, part of a whole batch of stuff McLaren recorded for him. Jon listens, shrugs his shoulders and says, 'Okay, er, great.'

Two weeks later, Jon gets a call from Adam, loads his drum kit into the back of his estate car and drives down to Rockfield studio in Wales. He double tracks his playing to achieve a fair copy of the Burundi sound for Adam's last independent single, 'Cartrouble', bungs his drums back in the car and drives home. Jon gets a session fee but doesn't much fancy a full-time job with Marco and the mechanical man and Adam soon finds his two drummers elsewhere.

That was it really.

Except that eight months later Adam was topping the charts. And a few months after that the group McLaren stole from Adam and turned into Bow Wow Wow gave one George O'Dowd his first turn in front of a mike. And that it wasn't long before George, Jon and Culture Club were topping the charts too, along with Spandau Ballet, Wham!, Duran Duran and all the rest of the New Pop stars of the 1980s.

But Adam, in his own sweet way, was the very first of them all. In his rapid rise to the status of first teen idol of the 1980s, he mapped out all the moves for those who came after. Though the Human League and the Thompson Twins would later pull it off too, he was the first to engineer a self-conscious move from margins to mainstream, from cult to conqueror. He didn't seem to have even the tiniest prick of conscience about 'selling out' (an old hippy concept which the punks had adopted), he just made damn sure someone was buying. While the Clash were still making a self-righteous stand about never appearing on Top of the Pops (not that by this time anyone wanted them to), Adam played the media for all he could get out of it. He ignored the traditional music press (NME, Melody Maker, etc.) which, in the late 1970s, had created both a vital lifeline and a deadly dull ghetto for the post-punk independent movement. They'd always slagged him off anyway. Instead he went straight to Fleet Street and the new glossies (*Smash Hits, The Face*). Taking a cue from Bowie and the Boomtown Rats (noted, at the time, for this sort of thing), he put a lot of effort, energy and imagination into his videos. Even if you didn't like the record, the latest clip was usually amusing. He gave up on the rock ideal and plunged himself into the idea of showbusiness, often verging on pantomime and at one point, around the time of 'Prince Charming', embracing it wholeheartedly. 'Such a new puritanism has grown up of late,' he told *The Face* in April 1981. 'I'd rather dress up like Liberace.' And then, of course, after the distinctly unsexy punk period, it was Adam who brought sex back into the equation. He talked about it almost as much as he talked about business (i.e. an awful lot), tattooed the words 'pure sex' on his arm and declared that he was making 'Ant Music for Sex People'.

With a single-mindedness bordering on obsession – in itself as characteristic of the New Pop as anything else Adam got up to – he became the first artist since the Sex Pistols successfully to sell, not just an unmistakable 'look' (as he always put it) and an unmistakable 'sound' (ditto), but also a half-baked set of theories and attitudes that pinned the two together. He'd dress up like Geronimo, play pop that leant heavily on African drumming and waffle on all the while about tribalism, the 'warrior ideal', noble savages and so forth. This was partly just a hangover from punk. 'Ideology had been important for so long,' noted writer Mary Harron, 'that it was hard to start a new fashion without one.' Spandau Ballet would have this same problem, and obviously a lot of what George did would beg some explanation, but groups like Duran Duran or Wham! never bothered to justify themselves at all – why should they? This was equally a measure of how much Adam had got from McLaren for his £1000, but most importantly it helped reinforce the idea of an Ant Clan as Adam gathered his fans around him and demanded not only their loyalty, but also a hefty slice of their pocket money.

Of course, much of what went into Adam's success had been done before and maybe better by other people. The Sex Pistols had the pop ideology to end them all (or so McLaren had hoped). T. Rex had made a similar move from margin to mainstream – in their case from dippy hippy fantasy folk duo to glam rock sensation – in the early 1970s. Scores of groups had worked hard on their videos. Adam never claimed to be original anyway. 'None of the ideas are mine,' he told *Smash Hits* in June 1981. 'It's just the way Marco and I have moulded them together.' He was talking about his music. The same, though, is true of his over all strategy. That he had a strategy at all is part of the point. That sort of thing had, in the past, usually been left up to managers and record companies.

'This is show business. That's two words. And if you don't take care of business, someone else is going to run your show.' The epigram isn't Adam's. It was coined by one David Grant, a British funk performer of fleeting renown. But really the words could have come from almost any British pop star of the last few years, Adam especially.

Adam was the punk who grew up wanting to own or control everything he did. He wrote, sang, recorded and performed all his own material. He designed his own sleeve and directed his own videos. When he revamped his look around 'Prince Charming' in the autumn of 1981, he patented the image through the Merchandizing Corporation of America and did his legal best to try and control every last sleeve, badge, T-shirt, poster or sticker bearing his face or his name. That he had to pay photographers to use their pictures of the image he'd created, he regarded as scandalous. He once remarked that he never touched alcohol because 'if you drink a lot of people take advantage of you'. During his heyday, Adam's publishers would demand of *Smash Hits* more than twice the going rate for the right to reproduce one of his lyrics. Adam's explanation: 'That's business.'

And so it was.

Dave Rimmer, Like Punk Never Happened (1985)

1981: Golden Voices and Hearts of Steel

This is what you missed tonight at the Ritz Rap Party: Sylvia Robinson – the Sylvia of 'Pillow Talk', the one who was always *reclining* on her album covers – was presiding in the balcony as the woman behind Sugarhill Records and all her groups were on stage. I guess she's the Queen of Rap and she don't have to say a word. I saw Ahmet Ertegun go over and say hello, shake her hand; someone muttered in my ear, 'I wonder what Ahmet has on his mind.' The show started about midnight with this real young group (what grade are they in, I wondered) called Funky Four Plus One: four guys – handsome kids in white three-piece suits and red turtlenecks – appearing one by one, each introducing the other and asking the audience to call him out (this was standard procedure with nearly all the groups: the invocation, the tag; rappers, like graffiti writers, are very big on IDENTITY). Then a girl, a thin, sassy girl with her hair slicked back, a short girl like the boys are kind of short – her name's Sha-rock and she's the centerpiece. And she knows it: she's got the most attitude and she's wearing tight fuchsia-colored pants with a fake fluff vest of the same color over a ribbed sweater that looks like it belongs with another outfit. They strut and dance and seem to fill the stage, each on his (and definitely her) own mike, chanting rap-style – I remember them saying, 'We got golden voices and hearts of steel.' They sing/talk their hit 'That's the Joint' – standard content (a tumble of street clichés, rap trademarks) but the form is amazing: constant interplay around the solo moves, rap-rhyming in almost choral arrangements and quick counterpoint, all over this bare rhythm track cut back and forth on two turntables on stage behind them. I was shouting, dancing in place (the floor was packed and I got real close). Unbelievably, in between sets the Ritz DJ was playing a lot of black street records, including two of my favorites, 'Heartbeat' and 'Music in the Street', plus hip (but not hiphop) oldies. In the balcony I ran into Andy Hernandez, the crazy vibes guy from Savannah Band/Kid Creole. He's shaved his head (he was wearing a hooded green sweatshirt with the hood up so I didn't get a close look) and he has a funny rap record out now (calls himself Coati Mundi) that he said he was going to do later in the show. But first, Sequence, three girls in sequins (sequence?) on 'fur'-trimmed jackets and thigh-hugging pants (one turquoise, one hot red, one gold). The middle one, Blondie, who wears a big blond afro, tells her measurememts in one of the songs ('Built so-fine/36-26-36'), and the others, Angie B. and Shirley (who calls herself Shirl the Pearl), are even more substantial. Another teenager, guy named Spoonie Gee in another white suit (but suave open-necked shirt), joins Sequence for one song and they riff off each other, talking about how great they are, but the girls alone are best. Like all the groups, they sell themselves, they make up funny stories about themselves, they exaggerate and they tell what they're really like sometimes (Blondie likes Reese's cups and the Flintstones, Shirl says, 'I talk a lot but I'm really shy') plus their signs. They blew kisses when they left the stage, leaning down into the audience to shake hands (an odd combination here, and throughout the show, of silly showbiz 'professionalism' and just plain having a good time on stage). Andy Hernandez as Coati Mundi was next I think and he did his rant/chant 'Me No Pop I' in a gangster hat, his usual baggy pleated pants, and a sweatshirt, dancing around in this possessed, contorted way, throwing himself down, arms at all angles but not for a second out of complete control. In the rap tradition, he talks about himself (calls himself 'the George Raft of the leisure class') but he also raps about his messed-up girlfriend and shouts at one point 'Intellectual constipation will be the death of this here great nation.' A surreal, perverted 'Rappers Delight' – and the most eccentric bit of the night (guess he don't have to be cool and slick like the kids). But Grandmaster Flash and the Furious Five, who followed, were pretty wild in their own way. Flash comes out first complete with rousing introduction, takes off a black cape and – plays records. He goes to the double turntables at the back of the stage and cuts and blends bit of 'Good Times' and 'Another One Bites the Dust' – not just the usual segues but real tight to-the-beat mixes and tricks like holding the edge of the record so the beat clicks back on itself: the vinyl 'talks' rap-style. Flash even has his own MC/assistant who praises and describes in rhyme while Flash spins. The Furious Five – the MC's, the rappers – come out one by one in glitzy black and white outfits, talking fast, faster, fastest. They had this choreography that reminded me of the old Temptations – classic but knife-sharp – and they were in constant motion even when they broke out of the routines. They would hold their mikestands out over the crowd to get the response: 'Say hooo!' 'Hooo!' 'Somebody scream!' Only problem: by the time the Sugarhill Gang came out the format was wearing a little thin. The songs all drag on too long without much variation in effect. There are no real breaks, no disco peaks, and the emphasis, the constant sing-song drive of the voices, begins to beat you down unless you can really catch all the words – which is real hard to do live and at this pace. But the Gang came out with a fine funk band and they were exceptionally debonair, the grand old men of the rap record. They'd been all around the world, they said, since 'Rappers Delight'. They were two over-sized boys (one in a white cowboy hat) with a slender guy in the middle and they did it, did it, did it and everybody sang along: Well a hip hop etc. Sequence came out again and joined the Gang in what broke down into a three-part duet and during the last song Grandmaster Flash & Co. trooped through and Funky Four Plus One bopped across the stage in street clothes. Everybody say yeah! Yeah!

Oh, Jamaica, you missed it. I still change the station when I hear a rap record on the radio, but I haven't had this much fun at a concert since I saw the old Motown Revue at the Brooklyn Fox.

Love, V.

PS: Next morning: Someone wakes me with a phone call in the middle of a dream just as I was about to lift the tone arm off a spinning record. And I wakeup with this rap rhythm in my head. What it is!

Vince Aletti, *Village Voice*, March 18–24, 1981

1982: Whiplash Snuffs the Candle Flame

Sharing the twilight zone of 42nd Street movie houses, drug dealers and seedy subterranean record stores are the video arcades. Video games have had a big influence on latter day hip hop – the arcades are bleeping, pulsing, 24-hour refuges for the obsessive vidkids with nowhere else to go. Since the Japanese exploitation of American Nolan Bushnell's original games, a major part of the populated world has been saturated with Space Invaders, Gorgars, Missile Commands, Dragon's Lairs and Ms Pacmans. Along with their addictive properties, their imagery and their insatiable appetite for coins goes an e-z-learn induction into the world of computer technology.

On side two of the notorious 'Death Mix', recorded live at James Monroe High School in the Bronx, Afrika Bambaataa and Jazzy Jay can be heard cutting up YMO's (Yellow Magic Orchestra's) 'Firecracker'. 'Firecracker' is an electronic cover version of a Martin Denny tune (Denny, a white American based in Hawaii, specialises in exotic easy-listening music), and on the 1979 album from which it is taken it segues out of a track called 'Computer Games', a maddening simulation of video-machine beeps, rumbles and banal tunes.

Along with YMO, Bambaataa had a taste for Gary Numan ('Cars' is enjoyed by other hip hoppers, for some unknown reason) and Kraftwerk. Kraftwerk managed to invade almost all record-buying markets in America, from easy-listening to R&B. Bam recalls their influence:

> Kraftwerk – I don't think they even knew how big they were among the black masses back in '77 when they came out with 'Trans-Europe Express'. When that came out I thought that was one of the best and weirdest records I ever heard in my life. I said, 'scuse the expression, this is some weird shit! Everybody just went crazy off of that. I guess they found out when they came over and did a performance at the Ritz how big they was. They had four encores and people would not let them leave. That's an amazing group to see – just to see what computers and all that can do. They took like calculators and added something to it – people pressing it and start playing it like music. It was funky. I started looking at telephones – the push-button type – they really mastered those industrial type of machines.

Kraftwerk were the most unlikely group to create such an effect among young blacks. Four be-suited showroom dummies who barely moved a muscle when they played, they were nonetheless the first group using pure electronics to achieve anything like the rhythmic sophistication of quality black dance music. They were fascinating to kids who had grown up with the incursion of microchip technology into everyday life. The George Clinton funk empire and its theatre of excesses had taken sex, sci-fi and comic-book abandonment about as far as it could go on stage; four Aryan robots pressing buttons was a joke at the other extreme.

The album version of 'Trans-Europe Express' is extremely long – 13 minutes 32 seconds in total. With its eerie dramatic atmosphere, constant changes of texture and vocoder-type vocals on absolutely regular medium-tempo beats, it was unwittingly a b boy classic. Bambaataa was overlaying speeches by Malcolm X and other Nation of Islam ministers or Martin Luther King, and for Flash it was one of the very few records he was prepared to leave running for its entire length without cutting or scratching: '"Trans-Europe Express", that was one record you couldn't too much cut – it was cutting itself. That shit was jumping off – leave that shit alone – smoke a cigarette. You can go cool out – go to the bathroom.'

For a Tommy Boy Records follow-up to 'Jazzy Sensation', Afrika Bambaataa took musical elements from 'Trans-Europe Express' – specifically the rhythmic feel and the simple melody line – as well as rhythm ideas from Kraftwerk's 'Numbers' and Captain Sky's 'Super Sperm'. Another inspiration was a record called 'The Mexican', a rock guitar treatment of Ennio Morricone's theme for Sergio Leone's film of greed and retribution, *For a Few Dollars More*. In his book *Spaghetti Westerns*, Christopher Frayling describes Morricone's film scores as being 'as if Duane Eddy had bumped into Rodrigo, in the middle of a crowded Via Veneto' – very hip hop.

'The Mexican' was released on a West End Records Euro-disco album called *Bombers*. A 12-minute track with extremely long percussion breaks, it was 'interpolated' by guitarist Alan Shacklock, the main mover behind an English progressive rock band called Babe Ruth. Babe Ruth recorded their own limp dancebeat version of 'For a Few Dollars More' in 1972 and Bambaataa had been cutting between these two records and Kraftwerk on the turntables. The feature they shared in common was the tension of a melodramtic, drawn-out melody laid over a beat – also the most unusual aspect of 'Planet Rock', the name of the record which emerged from this Frankenstein process.

'Planet Rock' was so strange on first hearing that it was hard to believe anybody would buy it. Not only one of the massive hits of 1982, it also shifted dance music into another gear. Produced by a team of Bambaataa, MC group Sonic Force (Mr Biggs, G.L.O.B.E. and Pow Wow), producer Arthur Baker and keyboardist John Robie, it combined a party atmosphere with propulsive electronic percussion or loud scratch-effect accents which sounded like an orchestra being rocketed into outer space. From the opening moments of Bambaataa shouting, 'Party people, party people – can y'all get funky?', 'Planet Rock' is as addictive and as hypnotic as a two-screen miniature Donkey Kong.

David Toop, *The Rap Attack* (1984)

1982: Hard Times

Bear with me for a while, this first bit may be hard but it is important. Read it twice if you have to because there is something that you are going to have to grasp before we can go any further. And that is the notion that Youth Culture now represents not a rebellion but a tradition, or rather a series of traditions that date back to the advent of the teenager and continue to grow along a compound continuum of action and reaction.

Imagine a spiral that begins with a birth out of affluence and post-war liberation and moves through time propelled by its own mythology and its own contrariness and is affected by technology and whimsy and economics. It is cyclical, but the circle is never completed because it is also evolutionary, therefore patterns repeat but they are never quite the same.

Now you must also accept that there is no such thing as a 'generation gap' any more; how can you rebel against the generation of Coltrane or Brando or MacInnes? What we have is a heritage that you can draw succour and inspiration from; and there's those who do and those who don't. That's the only gap.

In the mid-Seventies there was really only Northern Soul with its sparse, functional uniform, its £30 singles and its clenched fist plea to keep the faith which kept alive the tradition of a mobile, underground lifestyle that demanded commitment and pledged enjoyment. But in recent years we've experienced a dramatic revival in the colour and clamour of what was once called Youth Culture but is now in drastic need of redefinition.

Right now every kid is a dressed-up kid, every home has a hipster. Just how that occurred and where it's all leading takes us neatly into A Tale of Hard Times.

It's more than just a feeling now, more definite than the presence of denim where once was silk; its definitely a cycle reasserting itself, but we'll return to that much later.

Suffice to say things are changing. What began as a desire to shed the clinging, depressive old skin of post-punk monotony and replace it with a set

547

of bold, bright new clothes is slowly evolving into an entrenched, die-hard mentality where 'Good Times' is replaced by 'Money's Too Tight to Mention'. But the dancing at least doesn't stop.

It's still easiest to describe as a hardening of attitude. Somehow the atmosphere when you walk into a club today is different; gay abandon has evolved into a clenched teeth determination where precious lager cans are cradled to stop them disappearing and sweat has replaced cool as the mark of a face.

Surely everybody knows by now that it was never a chintzy, cocktail set whirl of debs' do's. That only ever existed in the minds of a paranoid rock press and the parties of a few Funkapolitan flunkies. But misunderstanding and misrepresentation of the kind that labelled those who wanted to dress and dance as 'little Lord Fauntleroys' and even 'escapist middle-class fascists' turned too often into self-fulfilling prophecy as too many people got the wrong end of the stick and then toyed with it.

But if we take a look at how things stand right now, literally take a look, you'll see that clothes at least are definitely getting harder. Ubiquitous Levi's worn into holes, sweatshirts serving their purpose and losing their sleeves, leather dominating everything; sandblasted for effect if you're rich and Italian, genuinely old and ragged if you're not. Leather caps, leather jerkins, big boots or no socks and espadrilles. Trousers are getting tighter, t-shirts ripped and torn.

The reference points are numerous but the look is new. Brando on a motorbike in the American Fifties that never made *Happy Days*. There's the everpresent rockabilly input only now pink pegs have made way for stained drainpipes and checked shirts have been ripped to shreds. A touch of bolshevism here and there with flat caps and red flags, still a glimpse of beatnik ankles and shades, and an awful lot of macho gay icons. And what you have is London in the winter of 1976.

Fashion has always had its own very internalised mechanism of change based on action and reaction; you know, someone wears something, so everyone else wears it, so he wears something else. But in recent times that process has been speeded up to an almost indecent pace by a media that's been alerted to the fact that something's going on and is more than willing to tell everybody. And indeed the latest change was a reaction against scores of kids in their grandfather's suits and their mother's makeup, against idiot dancers on *Top of the Pops* dressed up in cast-offs from Auntie's last pantomime, a reaction against Bucks Fizz dressed as New Romantics and Pete Shelley in a suit.

Sure, suits followed frills and jeans followed suits because that's the way things happen, but it is more, it's a sign of the times if you like. For a start it's all very functional: hot funk in crowded clubs makes a mess of any designs that lean towards dandyism. If you go to the Beat Route on a Friday you sweat. Perhaps that's one of the places we really ought to visit.

At the moment there's two definite trends at work in London after eleven o'clock, and if you're looking for examples, one of them resides at The Palace and one at the Beat Route. The Camden Palace, hugely popular, glossy, efficient, is the equivalent of ABC; taking the ingredients that have added the spice to the last couple of years, dressing it up nicely and selling it to a million, smiling consumers.

ABC and The Palace both bear impressive witness to the fact that a wholesale revitalisation of mainstream pop culture has resulted from the natural tendencies of a few dancers in the wilderness. Steve Strange very genuinely hosts evenings of good honest entertainment where bank clerks mingle with milky bar dreads and everybody believes they're in Studio 54 for a night.

But just as ABC soon dropped their original 'Radical Dance Faction' tag, so The Palace is just a disco. They are both signs that England has been turned into a swinging place again, both signs that the oh-so derided attitude which re-emerged in places like the Blitz a few years ago has had a much wider influence than many people like to admit. There is a new orthodoxy now, but there is also a new front line.

The Beat Route has been going for more than a year now; some say it's not what it was, but it has certainly played its part. Its uncompromising, often uncomfortable atmosphere has kept away painted faces and prying eyes so things have had the rare luxury of time to develop.

What has emerged is a more aggressive hedonism where sex and dancing and stimulants represent a back-against-the-wall defiance. The Beat Route attracts people from all over the country, and the age range is right across the board. That's vital, this whole new feel isn't just that of a new generation: that concept simply doesn't apply anymore. It's 15-year-olds and 35-year-olds dancing defiant steps side by side. People who've learnt to dance to Gil Scott-Heron have learnt that age doesn't mean a thing.

But there's also a dark side, victims of an all-out lifestyle. For some hedonism has turned to cheap heroin as depression creates one of its ugliest panaceas. But just as hard times leave scars on some, so others become hard enough to beat it.

Just as the idea for once-a-week clubs where you use *their* space to create *your* environment originally rose out of a black soulboy tradition of warehouse parties where you literally do everything yourself, so The Palaces and the Ultrateques which cater six nights a week for the new electropop creamed off the ideas and the energy which arose out of the once-a-week-clubs, to stuff the pockets of financiers. So young and old, those who really care, move back to warehouses and create their own space. Enter the Dirtbox.

The increase in the number of warehouse parties of late is a sure sign that something is happening, and the other thing happening is the Dirtbox: a tradition builds upon itself.

Situated above a chemists in Earls Court, the Dirtbox will almost definitely have ceased to exist by the time you read this. But its policy of £1.50 entry, bring your own drink in a cramped claustrophobic room with a fan, some settees and a sound system produced a series of wild nights. All organised by two decidedly post-Blitz kids and DJ'd by a rockabilly who shopped in Sex before the Pistols did.

Built to self-destruct, it bore all the hallmarks of the times, dancing on the edge of illegality. They've already got another place to move to: move fast, hit hard guerrilla tactics. I may be getting a bit romantic, but the Dirtbox is a return to the soul. Now *that's* a word for the times.

Just as mainstream pop culture becomes more and more produced, safer, predictably bright and danceable, so the reaction occurs. The spiral moves on by looking back, looking for some roots, searching for a little soul in a soulless world.

If Kevin Rowland is still searching for soul rebels then now is the time when he could just find them. For just as people will now draw selectively from the wardrobes of the past, so they'll live and learn from a musical heritage that stretches right back. The immature, myopic desire to reject things because of their age has been resigned to an acned past. Soul is about depth and it's the new rebels with torn jeans who are digging deep.

Jazz, soul, funk, rockabilly, cajun. You can now go out for a night and hear The Last Poets, Gil Scott-Heron, King Pleasure, Ann Peebles, Warren Smith, Clinton Chenier. Culture Club, quite simply, aren't all that's going on. Music no longer plays a central and really rather damning role in everybody's lives. It has its place, and that place is filled from as wide a source as possible.

And just as looking back has led to a 'discovery' of neglected talents, so looking forward has meant 'Shoot the Pump', 'How We Gonna Make the Black Nation Rise?', 'Money's Too Tight to Mention'. Hard sounds when everybody else wants to sound like Dollar. Without the likes of Steve Lewis some of the best records of the last two years would have gone almost unnoticed. Steve Lewis is a political man. That's another topic.

Political awareness is a personal thing, but everybody who can feel is feeling pain right now. People are getting angrier, the optimism that once led to bluff and bravado is now an optimism that you'll be able to hold on, an optimism that you can defy and you can dance. An awful lot of the music is directly political, but it isn't The Clash: listen to Curtis Mayfield and see how deep politics can go. Political awareness now runs deep indeed. Robert Wyatt is a star on the scene.

Northern Soul is spinning quietly back, old unemployed steel workers next to young unemployed school leavers. Jazz both here and in America is beginning to mean jazz again; Wynton Marsalis at 20-years-old playing be-bop to teach us all. Funk and soul are finally creeping back into the funk and soul racks where once lay little but forgeries. And in Britain black leather and torn jeans are walking the streets again.

Punk is now part of the heritage. In 1976 a small offshoot of the club scene broke away from bright clothes and increasingly bland music to become something angrier, something wilder.

Things are changing again only this time we know a lot more than three chords. With any luck there's even harder times ahead.

Robert Elms, The Face, 29 September 1982

1982: A Salmon Screams

So I'm surrounded by the five fluffy Duran boys, blinded by their bounce, dazzled by their cheek (bones), and I do what any responsible star-writer would do. I ask to look at their socks. Simon, Andy, Nick, John and Roger lift up their trousers: Simon the singer's are the worst – woolly!! – Nick the synther's are the best – sheer! 'Music Life from Japan asked us what our favourite cars were, and what kinds of girls we liked.'

This is the sort of challenging poser these light-weight poseurs love. So I ask them what are their favourite ice lollies.

'Strawberry mousse . . . Cornetto . . . 99s with flakes . . . Funny Faces . . .' emerge out of a bubble of Brum and Geordie accents.

Do they eat cornflakes after sex?

'I eat Thornton's Continental chocolates after sex,' says Simon, or was it Nick?

'I always have a cigarette after,' admits Andy, to jeers of 'cliché' from his Duran-maties.

Now the Duran Airy are poppy stars, is their love life better?

'Do you mean do we get more shags? Of course.'

Dear, dear, dear. Does it vary throughout the country?

'No ... the girls all look exactly the same and they wear the same clothes ... we've had quite a few Lady Di futurists. I'm into Lady Di futurists,' said Nick, or was it Simon? 'When are the *NME* going to put Lady Di on the cover?'

How long do Duran Trifle want all this pop starlight to last – a quick thing over in a year, ravishing and wonderful?

'We want it to last and last!'

Because you're greedy?

'No, because we enjoy it,' says Roger, or was it John.

'I don't want to be a has-been by the time I'm 21,' says Nick, definitely. 'That's two years away ... I'm dreading being 20 ...'

I think I want to be cynical to Duran Frill's faces.

'No, it's all right, you don't have to bother ...'

You're surrogate Moody Blues.

'Cliché! That scores five out of ten.'

Are you surprised with what you get away with?

'I choose to ignore that remark,' says Nick, earnestly.

Is it difficult being five boys so close to each other?

'If you mean are we up each other's bums – no we're not!'

How are you going to avoid becoming fat and rich overnight?

'We're going to be rich and when we're rich we'll buy a gymnasium and that'll keep us fit. Also when you're rich you can eat really nice foods like smoked salmon 24 hours a day. That won't make you fat. One of the perks of this job is getting rich!'

A quarter of a mile away from where we're sat, there's a riot going on.

Signing autographs in HMV record stores is a thing that has to be done, it seems. It's expected. It's now part of the day when you tour.

At 3 o'clock on a Saturday afternoon at the Birmingham HMV in New Street, Duran Smile are squeezed behind some tables faced by scores of young girls and a handful of young boys holding out armfuls of record sleeves, posters, articles, tickets ... Girls with blood-red lipstick, white faces, frizzed black hair, drowned dreamy eyes, wearing waves of black, take snaps with cheap cameras. Duran's handlers have trouble keeping the crowd orderly;

Duran Teeth soak up the pleasure-pressure with warm pride, adoring to be adored.

Duran Scream embody the new age of teenybop. They say that the demands and desires of the consuming teenager have not altered over the last ten years; punk, if anything, aggravated the lust for the made-up pop star, the wanting to look up and beyond, perchance to dream.

'It's coming back to what it was like before punk . . . During punk and just after there were no bands like us or Adam playing Odeons that any age could go and see . . .'

'I've got two sisters', says Andy, who's interested in guitars, 'aged 13 and 15, and they're just the same about pop music as I was at that age. Posters on the wall, off to see Adam; their appreciation of pop is exactly the same as mine used to be. It would be a big loss for kids if they couldn't go to Odeons to see groups.

'In the record shop signing away, it's ridiculous the way we were all horrible and sweating by the end and getting crushed and everything, but it's worth doing because all the kids obviously got something out of it. If they didn't want to they wouldn't be there yelling and shouting, and it's great because it makes them happy. They'd enjoy it all, and they will be at the show tonight.'

Duran Suave are committed to dragging glamour and fun and games into pop music: simplistically and selfishly, not so much Ze as Bay City Rollers.

'The whole idea of show business has been torn to shreds by punk, but at the end of the day what I always remember was I wanted to go out and be entertained from the second I walked in the hall. I wanted a big show. Things got out of hand when you had to spend £7.50 to see Pink Floyd and plastic pigs in a big barn. That's crazy, but there is an intermediacy between scruffy clubs and arenas.'

Where will Duran Bigwig draw the line?

'Well, for this tour our tickets didn't cost more than £3. We're losing out but I don't think we warrant charging more than that. Last night in Oxford the whole bloody theatre was dancing, and it was a seated hall. Every night on the tour people in the balcony have been standing up, and I've never seen that at gigs. Especially Hammersmith . . .'

Duran Ditto love playing live; the new nightclub latitude is just a part of their act.

'The groups we tend to get bundled with might not like playing live, but we really enjoy it. We're a concert band. When Chic came over to play here they don't do Top Ranks, they play Odeons. You can dance to our records every night of the week in clubs, but come and see us and it's something different. You pay a little more money than you would down the Locarno so we try and put on A Show.'

Are Duran Distant aloof?

'You can be close to your audience and personal with them which is what we do on stage, we talk to them, we're there in the same building as them, but they haven't got great big spotlights over them. One of the main reasons Gary Numan took off was that he was the first guy to come along who actually placed himself under the spotlight as pop star.

'This appeals to us . . . the Hollywood untouchable thing. I think kids like that too. There are plenty of bands catering for people who want to hear about how bad life is. We're not interested in that. The entertainment is escapism really.'

As the Duran fans peter out and the five fop-tops prepare to sign off, someone mentions, as casually as if it was raining, that it's rioting.

Outside in New Street packs of Rastas and bald boys are marauding. The small batch of fans left in the shop are hurried out and Duran Shocked slip quickly into the Odeon a hundred yards away. Gangs of youths line the pavements around the theatre, the shopping centre becomes a no-go area protected by railings and police, straggling shoppers walk down New Street a little uncertainly. Saturday afternoon's sport is over within a couple of hours, leaving faint traces of tension. On the 5.30 Radio One news bulletin it's announced that 400 youths have stormed New Street. It was more of a jog than a storm. Duran's manager despairs: 'No one is going to turn up tonight now.'

Because it's their home town show, Duran Spoilt are brutally disappointed. A life's ambition is being disrupted by what they term 'irresponsibility'.

'I've always wanted to play the Birmingham Odeon,' John tells me. 'I saw all my first gigs here – Roxy, Ronson – and now this.'

Do Duran Butt think about things other than lolly pops, girls and money?

'I hate people slagging us off for us saying that it's only entertainment. They think we're naïve and so we mustn't consider things outside. We do think about important things but to ourselves. We all have our political views but they haven't got anything to do with what we're doing now. If we were working in banks, it really wouldn't have anything to do with that job. You'd get the sack if you started giving people the heavy vibe.

'I think it's bad to preach to kids because we've got a really young audience, they're at a highly impressionable age, and it would be tough on them if we started lecturing. We have a responsibility *not* to tell them things. The main responsibility we have is to give people a good time, to give them what they pay for.'

Do they find the rioting exhilarating?

'It really annoys us that it's our home town and we've got a gig tonight ... you come down home after a really hard tour and then this happens ... It's so irresponsible ... it reminds me of Baader-Meinhof, they don't even know what they're doing.

'Hey, let's stop this. It's getting political ... we avoid political interviews, they're so boring. This is getting smutty. Let's talk about bottoms.'

Inside the Odeon just before Duran Daft's sound-check I walk with John to the front of the theatre to see how the riot's getting on. The two girls, maybe sheltering from the storm, are in the foyer and run delightedly towards the bright bass boy. Little squeals, sparkling eyes ...

'Have you got anything for us?' they ask.

'You can have him,' says John pointing at me. The girls are totally unimpressed and prefer a twopenny piece out of John's pocket (imagine) to me. What do they want that for, I wonder?

'Because it's his!' they exclaim abruptly.

What's so special about him? A gasp or two is supposed to explain it for me. John walks back inside the hall, leaving the two girls' lives in the balance.

I tell him Duran Dandy's appearance on the *Whistle Test* was appalling, that it confirmed all our best fears that Duran Pomp-It-up-Like-Suckers-in-the-Night are gummed-up glammed-over techno-rock twits.

'It's difficult to come out good on that programme. And every time we're on the BBC they use dry ice – they seem to think we're the perfect group to use dry ice on.'

It's not often the BBC are right.

Later Simon tells me that one of the best things about being in Duran Vain is the dry ice between the legs. 'But what's the point in turning the offer down?'

Duran Unsated are open to all offers. They have little objection to anything so long as it gets them out to more people.

'We want more and more people to know about us ... we've done *Cheggers Plays Pop*, the *Whistle Test*, *Top of the Pops*, we're doing the new

555

Peter Powell thing . . . and I've always wanted to do the *Test*. It was nice to give the badge you get to me mum.'

For a lot of these new teen tarts the game is enthusiastically copying out all the antics of previous generations because it was what they dreamed of at the time. Like playing the Birmingham Odeon for Duran Dream: it's an inexorable process. It's inevitable.

I get John on my own on a back row in the stalls and!!!! ask him if the group, officially a year old on July 16th, anticipated the recent shifts away from rock, grey independence, submission, austerity towards pop, disco, colour, lights, action.

'We must have done, but not consciously. We were just never really into that grey, small-time independent thing. Our heart was in the early '70s. Quality, big studios, sophisticated production, all of this has become important and that's great. For us the whole thing is a total concept, it's not just making crappily produced singles . . . the image, the recording, the presentation, the clothes, the whole lot is very important. Some bands just want to be single groups or album groups or live groups – we want to be everything.'

It's easy to talk about it, and easy to imitate it – this grand dream of quality. It's harder to achieve, or enhance. But there's been no failures, no black spots, to suggest to Duran Ownway that their definition of show business, their entertainment aesthetic, is in any way flawed. There has been nothing to tell them that their judgement is distorted, their music and presentation obvious or lightweight. Just a rash of reviews from *clever* rock writers whose value is rapidly diminishing – Duran Precious are heroes of the movement away from reading the self-important words to looking at the pictures.

As far as Duran Jelly are concerned, and its not far, pieces in the rock papers can be packed with sharp cynicism: as long as they're accompanied by clear photographs, preferably in colour, then that's their equivalent of a good review. Photographs can turn people on, words just get in the way. Words are an ordeal, photographs possibly a temptation.

'We can't stand negative journalism.'

Have they ever received what they think is constructive criticism?

'Not in the press. I mean at first we get this image in the press of being created by EMI to battle Spandau . . . they'd picked out the five prettiest Polaroids sent into their office.'

I thought this was true!

'Shit no. But there are too many people who do think this. You didn't really think that did you?'

No, I was fiddling about. Would have been lovely, though.

'You little liar! We have to prove something on that score because there are those who still say that we were to Spandau what The Clash were to the Pistols. We hate that . . . then again The Clash are still around.'

After I've been talking to John for a few minutes the rest of the group gather around: they can't bear to be apart, or can't stand the thought of not featuring in the interview. Five smooth faces, five lush hair-dos, ten lively eyes . . . the Duran Hearts laugh and play, the Duran Pussycats jest and pester. They've never had it so good. They confidently think their audience has never had it so good . . .

So how frivolous is all this?

'It's all of our lives, it's all we've ever wanted to do. We enjoy what we're doing obviously and it's all that we've got. So it can't be frivolous. It's very important to us. Obviously there are frivolous things, we can be frivolous. Like putting Dairy Box on our contract rider, and prawns.'

Three Duran Lads totter off to see how the riot's doing: two stay put, putting it all out of mind. It's all a lot of play, though. Is Duran Love a lucky escape? The three strays return to tackle this problem.

'I feel incredibly lucky that I've got this job to do,' Simon says.

Andy gets touchy. 'If people think we're lucky, we're not really, because we're doing a job in a sense that we have to work.'

Simon continues: 'I feel incredibly lucky . . . thankful . . . I dunno, that I'm doing this and not putting dustbins on dustcarts.'

Do Duran Diane place much emphasis on clothes?

'This is another thing . . .' Nick the pussycat snarls. Slightly. 'What I've got on now is what I wear when I wake up in the morning. I don't think anyone in the band overly dresses. We're all very much ourselves.'

You're taken to be clothes-pop.

'I don't mind people thinking we dress up. You can't object to people putting labels on you because they're going to whatever.'

Has being associated with cults with names helped Duran Right-time-right-place?

'To a certain extent, especially in the early days. We were surprised to be tagged new romantic or futurist because we're not like that at all . . . it's pop, and more Blondie than Led Zeppelin . . . Give us that hour on stage; we can convince people that we don't need to be labelled to help us. I think honesty wins through in the end. I think honest is something we'll always be.'

How can people appreciate this 'honesty' – how does it manifest itself?

'People think we can't be honest because we've had success so quickly . . . how can we have integrity if we're so successful? I think that is just sour grapes. Perhaps we were lucky that we came along when all the record companies were looking to jump on the futurist bandwagon and we'd been put in that niche, so from that respect the look helped us. But the honesty is there, and it manifests itself as people going home after they have seen us having really enjoyed it, or listening to our records and loving them.

'That's all people ask of a group, to get enjoyment out of it. And we believe that the product is really good. On this tour the audience has been incredibly young, they're all really enjoying themselves, and as long as we can play to people enjoying themselves and if we're enjoying ourselves, I don't see any harm in what we do. Because it is honest. You'll see later.'

Hours later Duran Din dish out what is paid for. Despite the day's troubles the Odeon is almost full: hundreds of Duran-kids kept off the street. Modern Duran are an '80s Osmond family: wholesome and kind of holy, but it really depends on how you define 'honest'. Hard working? Duran Damp are not timid or lazy.

If you've never heard Magazine, Simple Minds, Japan . . . then Duran Fun Fun must be mighty and magnificent; Duran Flash in the Pan as a first love must be brilliant. I'm twice as old as most of the audience, months away from the pension, very possibly the wrong sex, and too familiar with the grand Magazine things . . . I even know about the very beginnings of Roxy Music.

It is simple to criticise the Duran energetic attraction, to moan about the implications and complications to Dilute to Taste, but no words can cripple its force, its promise, its prettiness. Only the Time of the Revolution can halt Duran's darned drive. Duran Efficacious are a symbol of the futility of attempting to control or organise the Pop Mass. It seeps everywhere. It saturates reason.

The teen stars of today are smart: they've a lot to go on. Duran Fluke are classic effective innocents. They succeed where their elders and betters Simple Minds fail; they're pretty and they're not yet confused; they've reduced it all to entertainment instead of deciding or pretending that there are more 'important' things. They may celebrate superficiality; they may be the kind of encouragement they think *their* pop can be. It's all so easy for them. How can anyone tell them it's not? They won't shorten anyone's life. In the face of darkness they glow and grin with a happiness lighting up the lives of the little girls. As the fighting gets closer their resolve to escape gets firmer.

'I want to thank you all for turning up,' singer Simon says from the stage after a few songs. 'We know it must have been difficult for you.'

The crowd, crushed up to the front and having one of the best times of their lives, scream as if for murder. Here we go . . .

'I want you to remember what's happening out there has nothing to do with what's happening in here.'

He could as easily have said, let them eat smoked salmon.

Paul Morley, *Ask: The Chatter of Pop* (1985)

1982: Mister (or is it Miss?) Weirdo

He is No. 1 in the charts and they call him the Gender Bender. He is the sensational singer who looks like a girl, sounds like a fella and behaves like something strangely in between.

So when George O'Dowd fronts his group Culture Club on tonight's *Top of the Pops* you can be forgiven if you are confused.

Is this prettily painted creature with flirty long lashes pouting over the microphone actually a bloke?

'I couldn't care less if people think I'm a girl,' George, 21, says with a giggle.

'I suppose I am actually bisexual. Or multi-sexual – because there's a lot to discover in life, y'know.

'But to clear up any doubts I call myself Boy George on my record.'

And it is George's rich tuneful voice and not his freaky appearance that has carried his disc 'Do You Really Want to Hurt Me?' to the top of the charts.

'I get fans of both sexes,' George says. 'Actually, I get more girls after me than the four straight guys in my band put together.

'I could pull them all if I wanted to, but at present I am not interested in sex at all.

'I'm working so hard at my career that I'm too exhausted by the time I fall into bed for any of that. I lost my virginity with a girl when I was 16, but sex has never been an obsession with me. It's just like eating a bag of crisps. Quite nice, but nothing marvellous. Sex is not simply black and white. There's a lot of grey.

'You can think what you like about me. I'm not bothered.'

George's close-knit Irish Catholic family, now living in South-East London, are not bothered either.

He is third of five sons, has a younger sister, and the whole family is pleased and proud of his success. But younger brother Gerald, 19, an amateur boxer who works on a building site, admits that his mates often tease him about George's strange appearance.

He says: 'They see him on *Top of the Pops* and say, "Your brother's bent. he's a poof, isn't he?"

'I just say, "That's right. What of it?"'

The brothers could not look more different. Gerald is well-muscled and clean-cut, with a squaddie's short-back-and-sides haircut.

George sits beside him in white Dracula make-up, slashed with blood-red lipstick.

Their mother, Dina, is 43 and, unlike her perfectly painted son, never wears make-up.

She says: 'People do nudge each other and make awful comments when they see him. "Doesn't he look like a girl?" they say to me.

'My answer is always, "Yes. I'll bet a lot of girls would like to look as good as George does."

'But I don't think he is homosexual. Anyway, who he chooses to sleep with is his business.

'He has always been such a loving son. He phones me every day and he visits us every weekend.

'When his dad had a heart attack he was so busy I didn't tell him until his dad was out of intensive care.

'He cried: "You should not have done that, mum."'

George believes he may have inherited his love of dressing up from his dad, 48-year-old Gerald.

He says: 'When Dad was my age he was apparently a pretty sharp dresser.

'He had a huge quiff and liked pink shirts. But he used to moan at me about what I wore.

'Mum used to say to him: "Do something, Dad – you can't let George leave the house like that."

'And dad would roll his eyes to heaven and hide behind his newspaper.

'Now I think I am really close to both my mum and dad.

'They know that underneath all this make-up and the clothes I am pretty normal. Well, I think I am.

'For instance, my favourite telly show is *Coronation Street* and I love Hilda Ogden.

'My music isn't strange either – just ordinary romantic stuff. In fact, I'd be thrilled if Petula Clark decided to record one of them.'

And you can't get any straighter than that.

Judy Wade, *Sun*, 21 October 1982

1983: 69 Dean Street

The stripper retrieves her scattered tassels to a smattering of applause from the idlers in Burton suits. Pinki Pirelli scurries naked from the fifth-floor bar that was Soho's idea of plush when it opened in the Fifties, into the ladies to dress for her next appointment. She leaves by the lift and in the street pushes past a youthful queue waiting to take the same lift skyward for a night billed as 'thoroughly nasty'. Participants include the ubiquitous Siouxsie, music bizzybodies, a BBC producer who says he doesn't mind being two years late on the scene ('that's television') and a dazzling kaleidoscope of current cults you could describe extremely inadequately as Dracula meets the Muppets.

It is 11pm and since this is Wednesday the rooftop Gargoyle club is undergoing its weekly transformation into the Batcave, the most unsubtle of London's one-night stands, fronted by a Jaggeresque youth in mascara and black lace and without doubt the runaway success of the year.

The rest of the week The Gargoyle becomes in turn a moviemakers' showcase, a Sixties soul night, a gay club which welcomes straights, and the Comedy Store which back in 1979 threw up the Alexei Sayle school of 'alternative' comics who seem now to have colonised half our TV.

A few paces along the pavement a second door leads down to the cellars of the same building and the sinewy and refreshingly unfamiliar rhythms of Afrobeat. A white youth in a sabbath hat is greeting the kind of mix-it membership that's becoming a regular feature of nightlife: a gracious black beauty just in from Nigeria, a Camden Town trendy, Sixties art dealer Kasmin ('Is that his first name or his last?' asks a junior clubber called Lloyd) and in separate company, Kasmin's son Paul.

Since this is Wednesday this is the Gold Coast club but other nights in the Gossips week are devoted to straight jazz, rapping, rocking blues, jazz-funk and roots rockers with Capital Radio DJ David Rodigan. By the time you read this any of these could have dropped out: in the world of one-nighters, two weeks means make or break.

Since 1978 when Rusty Egan's Bowie Night at Billy's ritualised the private party which enjoyed full disco facilities, Gossips astutely wised to filling the slack nights in its week. In came Pink Monday, Pistols, The Clinic, Jive Dive, Vidzine and five different Tuesday tenants in the past year alone. The nature of the one-nighter is its transience – that now legendary Bowie Night ran only three months. Certainly fast bucks have encouraged exploitation of passing fads but club-owners have had to depend entirely on streetwise young frontmen to bring them each craze. Central to the Billy's-into-Blitz

561

axis of Egan as DJ, Strange as greeter, was the innovation that youth assumed the initiative. 'These were the first clubs run for kids by kids without feeling we were being ripped off,' it was said at the time.

Perry Haines with his *i-D* night was next off the grid with his '100mph dancemusic'. He succeeded at Gossips. Stevo and Jock McDonald tried and flopped. Gaz Mayall's Rockin' Blues is now in its third year and one reason why he's enjoying London's longest run is inevitably the universal appeal of the blues he plays. Another is Gaz's membership list. It reads like a hip Who's Who without regard for age.

'A promoter's social register must be strong and if it's not he won't keep a following,' says Reid Anderson, co-licensee of the Gargoyle upstairs. With a former pageboy to the Queen, the 24-year-old heir to a 13th Earl hosting Tuesdays (called Soul Furnace, he says, because 'it's hot'), this not surprisingly is the strongest night of their week.

Steve Strange and Perry Haines carefully constructed their own social registers but most aspiring promoters who walk in mean a gamble for the club. 'Gossips has always had the bottle to take chances,' says Mick Collins, manager downstairs. 'You need courage to let anyone who impresses you have a go. And you need courage to cut it if it fails on its first night. I've lost fortunes in the past advertising people's second nights.' What happens of course is that some kid on an ego trip fails to realise that it's his own job to promote the event.

With dwindling cash closing clubs two or three nights a week, last winter saw the West End stiff with handbills for Mod revivals, paisleyed psychedelia and mime-faced futurism. Some club-owners got stung. The Gargoyle scored a first for rapping but when the air got a little too heavy the Language Lab had to go. Gossips, in line with a solid black-music reputation, gave reggae a home last winter, but now has to display signs requesting 'Gentlemen: No Hats on Fridays and Saturdays' which is a euphemism to blacks like 'No Jeans' is to whites.

'That's our only restriction,' says Collins, 'and because of it the club feels safe. People can get away with a lot here and that matters. Some kids can only afford one night out and they'll spend all that week's dole here. There's no longer the money to go out every night so we've learned to vary our clientele through the week.'

Upstairs, owner Don Ward had also made a stripclub which had outlived its purpose viable. 'As long as people leave here with money in their pocket, they'll come back next week. Yes I'm taking a little now off a lot of people. Each night's promoter works hard too. And the profits go to him.'

*

69 Dean Street can trace its ancestry back to the dawn of clubmanship. It stands on the corner of a filmset, Soho's oldest intact terrace, and though a spraycan has dubbed this Rapping Yard, a tablet on the same wall dates it: 'Meard Street 1732'. The original Jethro Tull, wouldn't you like to know, was writing his revolutionary theories about English farming then and in the building boom which followed the Great Fire, speculators spread mansions over Soho Fields. Artists quickly adopted the new suburb as London's fashionable quarter.

As recently as its 1930s incarnation, the Gargoyle boasted a theatrical-artistic membership which inlcuded Noël Coward and Tallulah Bankhead – for whom it daringly relaxed the evening dress requirement. Up to the Fifties, as the haunt of Francis Bacon's Soho group, the club had Matisse's *Red Studio* hanging on its wall, arguably his most important painting, declined by the Tate and lost to America amid scandal when the Tennant family sold up.

Vestiges of lost splendour still shine, like an Art Deco staircase in steel and brass that links the Gargoyle dancefloor with the rooftop theatre and bar. As the Nell Gwynne revue staging three lavish stripshows a night, this was where businessmen came to clinch their deals over dinner and a hostess and whatever – until the last Labour government said, sorry but hostesses are no longer tax deductible. The Astor closed, the Churchill closed, but in May 1979 the Gargoyle did some speculating of its own.

Don Ward, himself a one-time comic, imported the American Comedy Store format: an evening of stand-up comics plus an achingly trendy audience who gonged off the most hopeless performers. 'I feel as welcome here as Hitler at a Barmitzvah,' said one joker last month to a Saturday crowd that's still in its twenties but after three years rates only a Springsteen in trendiness.

The Comedy Store did prove to be a crucial staging post in weaning young comics off left-wing benefits and on to the music circuits. Then last year along came the *éminence grise* who'd been trying to make Pythons out of the breakaway Comic Strip team, Simon Oakes, who in the words of a friend 'knows absolutely everybody' and of those of a rival 'has more fingers than there are pies to put them in'.

What he injected with the Language Lab and Lord Ogilvy's Soul Furnace by putting music first was a social mix you seldom find elsewhere. So though you really can hear some Henry say 'They let you in for half price after 1am – like a half-day ski pass,' once inside you nevertheless find underage Wembley mods Doing the Dog beside young Lady Cosima Fry. 'This club has been a great leveller,' says Oakes, 'because it's based on people not style.'

Likewise at The Lift on Thursdays. 'Straights have such misconceptions about gays: people still ask me if I play the male or female role,' says co-host Steve Swindells, who encourages gays to bring straight friends of all sexes. The bait is the hardest music in town, not the usual wimpy American gay disco, but rebel funk, BLT, Man Parrish. The DJ has scrawled across the wall 'Boogie leads to integration.'

If the Gargoyle has cast itself as an equal opportunities crusader, Gossips pads the musical waterfront with as much zeal. Vince, who has owned Gossips since the days when gay clubs like Billy's led musical taste, is a Soho legend himself, straight out of *Shaft*, huge hats, fistfuls of rings. His jeweller along Meard Street once showed me a mock-up for a mountainous ring he was making: '18-carat gold, 16 diamonds, it shone like a torch. I showed it to Vince and he said, I want more diamonds on it.'

One DJ said: 'When Vince calls by even the manager stands to attention so it makes sense that I should too.' Gossips is the kind of place where nobody admits a surname until they know you. Yet everyone working there, staff and one-nighters, uses the same fond word about the few square feet of stonechip floor and mirror: atmosphere. Collins says: 'It's not posh here. What we have though is heritage.'

It's no accident that the nights which have survived the carnival of cults here say much about the dominant musical forces at work in 1983. Amazingly for a jazz-funk night Steve Walsh on Fridays pulls an almost exclusively black crowd: 'Very upfront, advanced in their tastes – it doesn't appeal to the white party-crowd.' Equally unusually for an essentially reggae night, Rodigan and his ace toaster Papa Face pull a healthy black-white mix. 'It is rare,' he admits. 'We emphasise the rootsy, sweeter end of reggae, Rudi Thomas, Carroll Thompson, and that attracts a lot of women.' With the lights out, the dancefloor throbs like a Ladbroke Grove blues. 'Everyone dances to reggae: you have to get closer,' says Dave Gordon, aged 18.

Gossips stands alone in championing reggae in the West End and it is perhaps significant that it occupies the week's prime spot, Saturday.

Both of Gossips' other hit nights fall happily into playschool roles. Ghanaian Jo Hagan likes educating people and says the highlife he plays at the Gold Coast is a lot less aggressive than people expect, 'but it can be intimidating not to hear an English word sung all night.' His partner Christian Cotterill who owns half the records says: 'The press made African music flavour of the month but in fact it's all so danceable. When Gaspar Lawal played here Gossips had its most profitable night for a year.'

If you want to see a genuine Stetson, check Thursdays and you'll find

24-year-old Gaz beneath one. When he began playing blues masters B.B. King and John Lee Hooker back in 1980, Gaz said 'People didn't know how to dance to this stuff but they've been practising.' For nearly three years Gaz, himself a vinyl junkie, has devotedly been handing down history – by numbers.

The impact of nightlife on the style of the past five years is not to be underestimated. However much Futurist-Romantic labels make the skin crawl, their legacy is evident in the vitality of today's streets and charts, obvious though the ingredients may have been in Britain's post-punk vacuum: SF movies, a Dada retrospective, headline-making performance art, a revival of intimate cabaret.

Yet the positive accelerators of change were a handful of nightclubs. Photographer Derek Ridgers recalls that Tuesdays at Billy's were 'like walking into a Hieronymous Bosch painting: furtive but lively and with a dedication that's never been equalled since.'

Those formative Bowie Nights and Electro Diskows were parties with a vengeance, glorifying the individual, wresting power and profits from the elders. In particular the imaginative deejay became lionised for engineering new sounds, resplicing Kraftwerk, say, and eliminating the mid-range in playback.

As those events of '78 were a reaction to the music of Fever and Boney M, to dancehalls turning into discos, so the circle has turned again. What Moroder said then is as true today of the Palaces and Haciendas: 'Most disco-goers are not dancers.' Nor are they convincing posers. Conceits which were once daring, the megadisco has now sanctioned. The mainstream giants have sanitised the cults, standardised the music and dwarfed the individual with pyrotechnics.

But what Billy's developed, the factory farm at 69 Dean Street went on refining. The small-scale nightclub has emerged as the customised club-night. It reasserts the supremacy of bedrock music and consequently attracts a strong social mix. And because allegiance owes less to age-group or to dress, it activates more socially rewarding reflexes.

What the one-night clubgoer has discarded is the disposable identity in favour of a confident expression of taste. The Pose Age appears to be buried. Here at last is the party which requires you to come as yourself.

David Johnson, *The Face*, no. 34, February 1983

1983: Birth of the Wiseboys and Wisegirls

The fact that human life forms on the planet Earth make measurements related to their movement around a tiny sun that isn't even a grain of sand in the cosmic scheme of things does not mean time exists. The whole of this planet's evolution is not even a twinkle in God's eye.

We merely take eternity and break it down into manageable chunks we call time. It therefore follows that if we create time then we also dictate the pace it appears to move at. The faster hi-technology allows us to interact with our environment and each other the faster the pace of life moves at. For this reason Warhol's prophesy that everyone would be famous for fifteen minutes now looks a little generous. Five minutes seems about par for the course as a never ending stream of fashions, styles, stars and music forms are churned out by the hip popular culture sausage machine. Jamaica getting passe, well darlings how about some highlife, some Latin rhythms, Bali bells, Tibetan chimes, fifties jazz, northern-soul. Each has its own stars and style which as the pace accelerates are rooted out and paraded as the next big thing. As each new movement is turned over faster and faster the search for the new and undiscovered is getting rather desperate.

MICHELANGELO 'I want muscle' BUONARROTI NEVER HAD THESE PROBLEMS. In pre-industrial pre-hi-tech times the pace was slower.

The creative artist did not face the dilemma of having their art/fashion/ music or architectural style becoming obsolete within their own life time. Michelangelo, a passionate specialist took from 1508 to 1512 to paint the roof of the Sistine Chapel in his inimitable San Francisco gay health-spa style. He then left it for thirty years after which time he returned to finish the job off by painting the end wall of the Chapel with the Last Judgement.

What luxury, imagine if Pollock had lived. He could never have pulled a stunt like that. His art movement, abstract expressionism that blossomed in the '50s has been superseded by pop art, op art, conceptual art, art langue, performance, happenings, photo-realism, land art, terrorist art etc. If Pollock came back thirty years later and started splashing paint all over the place he'd be relegated to making punk T-shirts. The socio-economic climate that Pollock's art was responding to has changed so radically that abstract expressionism now appears nostalgic, a device to be used by post-modernists to give a canvas a bit of period charm. As a movement abstract expressionism came and went in ten years.

Sub-cults/style/fashion and social behaviour are also changing at a rate that is becoming breathtaking.

Consider the first real youth movement of post war Britain that dear old sub-cult, the Teds. They surfaced around '55, a garish hopped up version of their older spiv brothers, they went crazy man, crazy right through till '62 with only the ton-up boy greasers for company.

A real threat to their grip on working-class youth did not appear till around '62 when the embryo mods looked to the chic continental style of Italy, France and the sharp shave headed G-I Levi and fatigue funk of the American military for their style. The outlaw Teds were growing old and looked like greasy troglodytes next to the neat layered blown dry hair of the young mods. Their little purple hearts beat so brave on speed that the uncouth Teds did not stand a chance. The mods took the sub-cult turf and held it up to late '66.

Both of these movements had very strict dress codes. You only had to get one item of clothing wrong and you were in trouble.

Back in '66 I knew this mook called Sykes. Now this radge youth had one ambition. To move with the Leeds mod in-crowd was this boy's aim so one afternoon he swaggers into the Bee Gee coffee bar gnawing on a wad of Wrigleys pretending he's billywizzing. He was wearing a beautiful hand-tailored mid-night blue mohair suit, must have cost three weeks' wage packets. His hair was neatly blow dried into a soft rooster plum that rose along the crown of his head. His shoes were peshti, Ravel I reckon, they were patent leather slip on with a neat little side buckle, definitely tackle and no mistake.

He walks over and turns to Michael (one of the main movers of the pack).

'You off tut Wheel all-nighter later', his voice was very casual but broke a little as his nerves surfaced through the billy wizz cool.

'Fuck-off did' (did as in diddy-man, the ultimate put down of the day), was all Michael said without even glancing up at Sykes.

Sykes the mook snivelled off.

Why so hard on him I asked innocently.

'His socks, those fucking socks, saw 'em the moment he walked through the door. Lime green nylon, gives me a fuckin' 'ed ache. He looks like a fuckin' Ted.'

Of course the socks were wrong, you could spend all your wages on clothes, go without cigs for weeks just to buy a silk hankie, get the best cut suit around, wear Ravel shoes but get the socks wrong and you still looked like a trapper, a backwoods boy, a Ted.

The stylistic rules were so tight it was worse than being in the army. Friend or foe, halt and be recognised, the sartorial sentry guards didn't even have to

567

ask for a password. Just check the socks, look for the fine detail that sorted the men from the boys, the friends from the foe. Wearing an item of clothing from another sub-cult was tantamount to treason, like having the Iron Cross dangling from Monties ribbons.

Of course by '66 the American West Coast boho beats were gobbling acid and were flowering into the hippies of the swinging '60s. In atmosphere of 'I Was Lord Kitchener's Strawberry Wristband' what chance did the mod dress rules have. Christ those hippies didn't even wear shoes never mind socks.

The country was going to the dogs and no mistake. The mod attitude hardened and transmuted into skin and they were true underground. While the hippies 'underground' made the front pages of the colour supps and Frost gave airplay to Jerry Rubens, and every one from Leary to the Beatles pushed acid through the popular culture the skins kept the smart, proud conservative working-class ethic intact.

Throughout the '70s the speed of sub-cult turn over started to build up. Punk burnt so hard and bright that it only had two good years, late '76 to mid '78 by which time the oi-polloi turned it into heavy metal. The new romantic futurists shared a few precious months before being read, assimilated and fed back throughout the popular culture totally emasculated of their original power. Over the last year a rag bag of styles have danced across the boards using a mixture of stylistic devices culled from the nostalgic cross cultural dressing-up box. Dressed down jazz bohos, the '40s the '60s, all girl soul acts, Japan, the Caribbean, Sri Lanka, India, black New York ghettoes, Africa and heavy metal have all been plundered mercilessly.

HEY CHILDREN OF THE HI-TECH INFORMATIONAL
SPEED UP YOUR BECOMING WISEBOYS AND
WISEGIRLS LEARNING THE NEW GAME.
SYNTHESIS AND SURVIVE, TAKE ELEMENTS FROM
SUB-CULTS YOU HAVE BEEN THROUGH AND WEAR
THEM TOGETHER.
LIKE, TELL ME WHERE ARE YOU GOING WITH YOUR
DUSTY SPRINGFIELD COLLECTION TUCKED UNDER
YOUR ARM AS YOU SWAGGER ALONG IN HALF-
MAST
SKIN KEKS, BLUE TED CREPES, PUNK STUDDED BELT,
GUNFIGHTER WAISTCOAT AND SHIRT, AND YOUR
GRANDFATHER'S TOP-HAT COVERING YOUR PET
CLARK FRINGE.

Master of this art of mixing up previously unreconcilable sub-cult stylistic symbols is Steve Linnard whose perfect melange of synthesised chic can be seen on page five of *i-D* issue Eight.

Though his photograph appears to border on parody it is the attitude that counts. The irreverent mixing of styles means that no one can put you into a neat brand new bag. The new breed of hipster will not be stitched up, they are a law unto themselves and they are not about to be categorised, labelled or packaged by ANYONE.

Just why the sub-cults are now being shaken and stirred by the Wiseboys and girls when to previous generations such a dilettante attitude would have led to abuse, open mockery and a bloody nose has to do with the speed up of the informational environment we all inhabit.

New info, on which change relies, is now being circulated faster and faster and faster through our culture. Libraries are now run by Informational Scientists who, with the aid of the micro dot, photocopying, word processors, computerised typesetting, cassettes and communications satellites that span the globe can buzz new ideas around the planet in a few moments. If a research student working on proton acceleration makes a discovery in his lab in Texas this information can be printed and circulating around Japanese research workers in Tokyo in hours. For past generations this process took months even years. New research work never gets into book form as the mechanics are too slow for the rate of discovery.

This speed up of new information also happens in the popular culture. Video, fanzines, records, cassettes and cable TV have all come down in comparative price and as the industry expands it needs new information to sustain it. It needs new styles, music, celebrity and fashions and it needs them every day, every hour, every minute (hence Warhol's every fifteen minute theory). The hip popular culture is now entering the mainstream, street culture is now viewed as a vital new source of information (see *The Tube*, *Riverside* and *The Young Ones*). This has led to stylistic devices normally used by those outside the mainstream culture being read and fed into the popular culture machinery and back to the source.

Last year rap, break dancing and scratch techniques came out of the black New York clubs. 100 years ago those techniques would have stayed in the ghetto but now 'Planet Rock' can be heard on the juke box in Heckmondwicke and everybody is plugged into what would have been a local sub-cult phenomenon. As hi-tech costs allow for cheaper and cheaper methods of transmitting information (don't forget a new record, TV programme, dance, style etc. is just new information) areas previously overlooked by the mass media can now be absorbed.

The only way for youth to stay ahead of the game is to cross reference the sub-cults, mix-up the codes and short circuit the system.

Friend or foe, who knows. Taking liberties with the taboos and symbols of the various tribes means that you unplug from the rigid dictates of any one group and are free to attitude dance all the way across the varnished dance floor.

Swimming out beyond the current mainstream fashion swell to hang ten on the current art/style/fashion nexus is fine but MAYA IS BREAK DANC-ING AND THE ZEROX CULTURE REFUSES TO BE PHOTO-COPIED. SYNTHESIS AND SURVIVE THE WISEBOYS AND WISEGIRLS ARE SCRAMBLING THE CLUES AND THE CODES ARE GETTING HARDER TO CRACK. THE CIPHER-SET DEAL IN DUFF GEN. HEY MASTER SPY CAN YOU READ IT?

NB IMPORTANT Maya is Hindu for material world as illusion, hence the dance of Maya or dance of life.

Steve Dixon, *i-D* #11, 1983

1984: 'Young, Bold and Aggressive'

As she swans down the grand staircase of Manchester's lavish Brittania Hotel, Madonna looks every inch a *star*. A rare quality in this day and age when pop stars can get away with a daft haircut, a rather arty video, and very little else. In fact, a lot of people are labelling this 23-year-old from Detroit as some sort of female equivalent to Michael Jackson. Not surprising when you consider she can sing, dance and act and once shared the same manager as Mr Jackson.

She's just appeared on a dance special edition of the *The Tube* that featured a live link-up between its home base of Newcastle and the Hacienda club in Manchester. Outside a long black limousine purrs in anticipation. The entire Madonna entourage – two dancers, one road manager-cum-minder, three record-company executives, a chauffeur and me – pour through the hotel entrance and into the car. Record companies always seem convinced their American artists are going to be 'difficult'. 'I just play up on that image to keep them on their toes,' she says cheekily.

She constantly has a 'knowing' look about her. Some people would call it an *aura*. This is obviously part of the reason people are frightened to answer her back. For instance, tonight she's due to appear onstage at the Hacienda, but she's having none of it. 'I'm exhausted. I've had to cancel two phone interviews today already. I just haven't had a second.'

'Last night it was *Top of the Pops*, today it was *The Tube* and tomorrow I'm going to Los Angeles.'

So she cancels. After a meal back at the hotel – salmon and generous helpings of Campari and Orange Juice – in which she laughs a lot, listens intently and makes more than her fair share of wisecracks, she slinks up to her suite, 'to slip into something more comfortable!'

Madonna's apartment's not exactly run-of-the-mill. It's in two tiers – a bed on the lower, a couch on the upper. In between answering the door and the phone, she runs through the day's events.

'People seeing me for the first time today must have thought I was a fruitcake. No, seriously, they probably thought I was sexy. A real *live wire*. But I can't come on and be sexy without humour.'

Don't get the wrong impression. Although she appears to be in the mould of the typical blonde female singer, she's certainly not dumb. Far from it. As she says, 'There's a lot more to me than can possibly be perceived in the beginning.' And, as I found out, she's extremely bright, with a sharp business sense – a valuable asset for someone so ambitious. It seems this *ambition* derives from the 'competitive environment' in which she was raised. She comes from a big Italian family – the Ciccones, Madonna's her real name – of eight brothers and sisters. She also went to Catholic school, which, 'like all of America, gives an incentive to win – to aim for the top rung of the ladder.'

So she did and here she is: on the verge of success both sides of the Atlantic. Not bad for a girl fresh from the streets of New York. She moved there when she was 17, starting out playing drums in a band called The Breakfast Club. But ambition took over again and she formed her own band, Emmy. She sang and played guitar. It was a real 'paying your dues' time. She lived in a studio and wasn't bothered by having to 'wear the same clothes for three weeks'. After hawking tapes round the hip local clubs her persistence eventually paid off, gaining her a deal with Sire. After she'd put out two 12" singles she felt the need for a manager.

'I thought, who's the most successful person in the music industry and who's his manager? I want *him*.' The answer was Michael Jackson and, at the time, he was managed by Freddie De Mann. She got him. Instantly Madonna became hot property, being asked to do promotional tours – much like the one she's on now – across the world. She can't resist telling the story about the time she met Boy George on her summer '81 jaunt.

571

'He came up to me at the *Camden Palace*. He had big high heels on and he had a big entourage of people all dressed the same. He kept going on about this group he had, but I wouldn't believe him. Six months later he was Number One.'

But it seems people aren't always as keen to impress her.

'When I laugh out loud in the streets here I'm made to feel as though I'm doing something wrong. You know, that sort of young, bold, aggressive quality the more reserved and sophisticated British people hate. Most times people aren't very nice to me here.' And that's not all. 'I don't have many women friends either. It's because I haven't found many who are worldly wise and intelligent. Then again,' she adds cheekily, 'I just seem to get on better with boys.'

I suggest this may also have something to do with the way she looks.

'I have mixed emotions about the way I look. I wish I was taller (she's 5 feet 4½). I probably look taller 'cos I've got such a big mouth. I think it's important to try and look larger than life if you're a performer.'

She'll certainly be able to do that on the big screen. She's just appeared in a film, *Visionquest*. She plays the part of a singer, once again called Madonna. 'The only difference is that I sing in front of a band in the film.'

The phone rings. It's New York on the blower. An 'adviser' wants her to come home to appear in a video on Tuesday. Madonna agrees. She wakes up a record company person to change her flight from LA to NY. This is The Big Time all right.

Her next project is a follow-up LP. It's to be produced by Trevor Horn, possibly Nile Rodgers and John 'Jellybean' Benitez – her on and off boyfriend (off at the moment). In any case, it's bound to be absolutely massive. Madonna puts it all into perspective.

'Three to four years ago dancing was the most important thing – now it's music. That will lead on to something else . . . Acting. Above all I want to be an all-round entertainer. And happy.'

Peter Martin, Smash Hits, 16–29 February 1984

1984: Whistling in the Dark

In Britain 1984 turned out to be the year of the miners' strike and Frankie Goes to Hollywood. Repeating images – the miners' stolid anger, Frankie's smirking leatherware; juxtaposed stereotypes – pickets as hooligans, gays lounging promiscuously in the night. If pop is a sign of its times, then Frankie's social message during the key political struggle of the '80s is decidedly oblique.

Frankie are a pop phenomenon just for their numbers. Their first two releases were million sellers – 'Two Tribes' was the inescapable sound of the summer, going straight into the charts at number one after 'Relax' had established itself as a permanent hit, the most successful 12-inch ever. And Frankie took over the message T-shirt, using the large print originally designed by Katherine Hamnett for better causes to promote 'Relax', and spawning a cacophony of Frankie Say and Who Gives a Fuck What Frankie Say slogans. Walking down Oxford Street in August, watching the tourists snap the pirate editions of Frankie Say Arm the Unemployed, I decided this was the final triumph of the 'new pop', the eclipse of content by form.

Frankie themselves are five lads from Liverpool, typical veterans of the 1970s post-punk provincial scene in which Bowie boys became punks and skins dyed their hair repeatedly, hung out in gay clubs with the furtiveness that marks everyone on provincial streets in the small hours. This was the scene – musicians and dance-floor posers drawn from the same pool, sex as a slippery transaction – that produced Soft Cell in Leeds, Boy George and the early, sleazy Duran Duran in Birmingham. Frankie had nothing much more to say, till they signed to ZTT, the label formed by *New Musical Express* theorist Paul Morley and ABC-McLaren producer Trevor Horn. Morley had the concept (it's rumoured he was first interested in Bronski Beat for the Frankie role and was turned down), but Horn had the sound, the remarkable ability to create epic spaces in ordinary songs. Frankie's records make best sense in a cheap British disco, where the elementary chorus chants, the beat machines' seedy grandeur and the stodgy vocals offer distinct echoes of Gary Glitter.

As an *NME* writer Paul Morley was the most influential theorist of 'new pop', combining a traditional reading of music's emotional power with a modernist celebration of that power's fleeting ambiguity. His problem was to translate theory into practice. Frankie's success is a triumph of rock journalism. But the question, even in Morley's terms, isn't whether Frankie are popular but whether their popularity is subversive.

I don't doubt Frankie's radical intentions. 'Relax' may only have become a scandal when the BBC in belated confusion (and in response to teasing video-clips) banned it, but singers Holly Johnson and Paul Rutherford are explicit gays, and 'Two Tribes' is a bitterly satirical response to nuclear defence policy. It's the smoothness of Frankie's success that unnerves me –

573

it's hard to find anyone (other than ZTT) who thinks that Frankie, or their records, are changing the way people understand their lives. They're a best-selling group without real fans, more like the Archies than the Sex Pistols. And this reflects the way they've made it – through marketing rather than live performance. Their energy is the energy of pop's sales team rather than its consumers – there are, presently, more TV pop shows than ever before, more knowing pop people in record company control, more competitors for the leisure pound. Frankie is *their* success, and this brings us back to the current crisis.

The Tory solution to Britain's economic recession is a new version of the 19th century's two nations. Growth is now supposed to come from the leisure-goods industries. The new jobs will be low skilled and low paid; the non-affluent will service the affluent; the new working class will work on other people's leisure. The miners' strike is one response to this – a struggle for community and the dignity of labor, a rejection of market definitions of 'economic' pits (and a fight which is incomprehensible to the Southern, bourgeois media). But another response is a new youth subculture, the 'casuals'. At first glance the casuals epitomize Thatcher's leisure class, neatly dressed in designer-label sports goods, clutching their walkmen and video-tapes. But just as much as punks and skins, the casuals have emerged from the dole queues and football terraces, from the 'delinquent' world of drugs and brawls and menace. Their flaunting of their 'free time' is a reminder, like the miners' strike, that a leisure society creates its own forms of disorder. Frankie's success has a casual background. They're not so much subversive as desperate – that strained voice ordering us to relax, selling gay sex as a bargain. Frankie – who come, after all, from Britain's most devastated city – capture better than anyone else the neurosis of a society told, amid the wastelands of dead factories and eked-out social security, that the solution to our problems is to have fun.

Simon Frith, *Village Voice*, 10 October 1984

1984: Wham!: Young Guns Fall for It (Again)

Early in October 1983, Mark Dean received a letter that told the story of Wham! in a way he'd never read it before. As the managing director of Innervision Records and the man who had signed the unknown duo to his label about a year and a half earlier, the 23-year-old industry whizz had already seen perhaps fifty accounts of the group's fabulous career to date, most concerned with their thoughts on politics, fashion and their own music.

But this revised account, from Wham!'s solicitors, Russells, concentrated instead on the reasons why Wham! could now consider themselves free to break their Innervision contract and record with any other company of their choice; on why, also, the duo could even claim the rights to all the master recordings they had already delivered. In short, the twenty-four page letter was a blistering attack on Mark Dean's competence, alleging, among other things, that his contract with Wham! contained numerous unfair terms and was made in circumstances where there was strict inequality of bargaining power.

The implication was not only that Dean's ten-year claim on one of the most popular bands in Europe was at an end, but that he'd been immensely fortunate even to have had them and their success for eighteen months.

The way Russells told it, Wham! – aged just 18 and 19 – had stumbled deep into each classic pitfall and then some. They were on live television and couldn't afford to get home; they turned up at nightclubs and had to pass on buying their round; they topped both singles and albums charts, sold millions of records worldwide, and were still only on around £40 a week. For a 23-year-old, it appeared that Mark Dean had done an awful lot of wrong.

As old friends, Mark Dean and Wham! guitarist Andrew Ridgeley swilled beer at their Three Crowns local in Bushey, Hertfordshire. Music invariably dominated the conversation, Dean spinning tales of his A and R work with Phonogram and his involvement with hit acts ABC and Soft Cell, Ridgeley talking of his hopes for the new band. By February 1982, when some rough-edged Wham! demo tapes had been widely rejected by various major recording and publishing companies, Dean agreed to listen to his mate's recordings almost out of courtesy. And of course he thought them a marvel. One of the songs in particular, 'Wham! Rap', seemed a certain hit.

Fortunately for Wham!, he said, he was in the process of negotiating a deal with CBS whereby he'd run his own licensed label – Innervision – in the hope of discovering new worldbeaters. Wham!, he enthused, might make his ideal first signing. The more demo tapes he heard, the more Dean enthused. The duo, comprising of Ridgeley and singer-songwriter George Michael, began to discuss possible producers and certain success. The contracts, said Dean, were on their way.

The draft agreement, drawn up by Innervision's solicitor Paul Rodwell, and dated 5 March 1982, was a standard but lengthy blank CBS contract that had been completed by Dean with regard to the specifics of royalty payments and advances, and in the absence of a Wham! manager was sent to Andrew Ridgeley direct. A covering note detailed that Rodwell himself would be away for the next ten days and that Ridgeley should 'liaise' with Dean over the actual signing of the deals. Rodwell closed with the regular and very proper, 'I must of course mention that you should of course seek independent legal advice with regard to the contract before completing same.'

George Michael took the contract to Robert Allan, a specialist music-industry solicitor recommended by a customer in his father's Greek restaurant. He was advised that it was a poor deal that needed a fair amount of financial and creative counter-attack. Accordingly, Allan wrote to Paul Rodwell suggesting a meeting for the purpose of 'discussing your client's proposals and putting forward some proposals of my own'.

But according to Russells, the days that followed saw Dean telling Wham! categorically that Innervision refused to negotiate the commercial terms of the agreement, save that it would pay the two of them an advance of £500 each and confirm that their royalty rate would not be reduced by any payments to their producer. Additionally, Dean's pressure on George Michael to conclude the deal swiftly, lest it might not be concluded at all, resulted in Michael telephoning his solicitor to instruct him only to negotiate 'on legal points'. The overall fairness of the contract should not now be of concern to him, he said.

Robert Allan wrote to Paul Rodwell with numerous amendments to the original draft contract, despite his now limited brief. That was on 20 March. He didn't hear from Rodwell again until a letter dated 26 March reached him on the 29th. And by then the signatures on the Wham!/Innervision deal were already five days old.

The train of events had made a mockery of the whole idea of independent legal advice, claimed Russells. And if what they claimed was true, then they certainly had a strong point.

On 24 March Wham! were rehearsing in a poorly equipped studio in Holloway, north London. Two hours in, Dean arrived with the final contracts and an ultimatum. The band either signed then and there, or would have to wait a further five or six months; CBS, his paymasters, needed the signed contract, he said, or else they wouldn't put Wham! on their upcoming release schedule. Dean also revealed his interest in various other bands he might sign in place of Wham! if they decided to delay their contract any longer. But if they did sign, then he would also transfer them to a better-equipped rehearsal studio. He stressed that he couldn't afford to risk the outlay of any more cash until they had committed themselves.

Thus coaxed, the three of them adjourned to a nearby café to sweat out the details further. George Michael flicked through the contract on the café table, acknowledged the handwritten changes, and signed the deal along with Andrew Ridgeley. The next day they did indeed find themselves in improved rehearsal rooms.

Within a week Robert Allan had discovered that a large chunk of his proposed amendments had not been instituted, and worse, that Innervision's solicitor Paul Rodwell had added some changes of his own in the belief that these would be seen by Allan before signing. Dean's haste meant that Wham! agreed to a deal that any solicitor with any knowledge of the industry would have laughed off his desk in an instant.

Those at least were some of Russells' allegations. In court in November 1983, some nineteen months after Wham! had signed, the same allegations also formed the bulk of Andrew Ridgeley's and George Michael's affidavits against Innervision. For his part, Mark Dean did not specifically deny the exact details, but issued a general challenge as to their overall validity. He was in court pressing for an injunction to prevent Wham! signing elsewhere. It looked like the start of another immensely gruelling case.

The whole affair took around six months. Dean and Innervision lost Wham! in an out-of-court settlement, even though he had won that first temporary injunction. The band expressed delight at their victory and, though beaten, Dean showed great relief that the whole affair was at least over. He told his closest friends he never wanted to go through anything like it again. They in turn perhaps weighed up the fabulous story and assured him that the chances of that actually happening were fair at a thousand to one.

Of average height but heavy build, and most frequently dressed in checked shirt and heavily buckled jeans, Mark Dean passes as the most archetypically impressive mid-twenties industry hard man you could hope to find. And, partly by luck and design, the super-firm handshake, tough zero glare, slightly wild black curly hair and harsh, bleak features, all provide a certain visible aggressiveness that can't but enhance what many will always perceive as the necessary biz image. He talks with hard conviction and mature realism and he rolls with a steaming enthusiasm through all of it. At the start of 1984, with the Wham! affair still in litigation, he spoke with a certain sparkle about how he'd emerge victorious. When it was already cold and lost, the following June, he spoke with equal conviction about the likelihood of his other signings emulating Wham!'s success. 'You just watch,' he said.

He made no bones about his overall attack:

> To be totally ruthless about it, our job at the end of the day is to
> see the trends coming on the street, steal them off the kids, and
> then sell 'em back to them ... But nothing's new. *Nothing*.
> Nothing is original either, the only thing that can be new is the
> attitude until the band breaks, and then the attitude goes back to
> exactly what it was before over twenty-five years – and that's to
> make as much money as possible.

According to Wham!'s George Michael, Dean 'came into this business
with the attitude that if you don't step on people, they'll step on you'. If only
he had known that before, he sighs.

At the time, of course, Dean's fighting spirit was dandy. Besides, they were
all old friends. Everyone else had turned them down, so why not go with
Dean? He had, after all, just established the necessary machinery to carry
them in on his own. Innervision Ltd was formed with a paid-up capital of
£100 several weeks before those tentative pub discussions with Wham!, and
could boast two main selling points. First, the combined efforts of its two
directors were held up as that old unbeatable combination of youth and
experience. Mark Dean had worked in publishing and A and R, and the duo
knew he had a sterling reputation as a forceful developer of talent; and
solicitor Paul Rodwell, the second director, would surely provide all the
necessary legal fine-tuning to ensure smooth running. And second, a deal was
being negotiated with CBS whereby the parent company would fund Innervision and manufacture and distribute all its product, and pay the company a
royalty for each record that Dean's signings sold. So not only would Wham!
get personal, friendly attention from someone they trusted, but they'd also
see their records in every shop in the country, and probably every country in
the world.

And if the glimmer of fame up ahead with Innervision wasn't enough,
George Michael, the true powerhouse of the duo, found that he was being
pushed by his parents from behind too. As a Greek Cypriot who knew little
of the rock industry, his father gave him six months to become a pop star. If
he failed, he'd be pulled into the family restaurant business and maybe revert
back to his real anglicized surname of Panos. With that sort of incentive,
suggests his current manager, he would have signed *any* deal: 'So when there
were a lot of difficulties with that contract, and the contract didn't seem to be
right, he just wanted to override it, sign it, and get on with it.'

As to that tale of coercion, those allegations of unfair contracts, all that
under-utilized legal advice, well, that would all have counted for nothing had

the pessimism of George Michael's parents proved well founded, and if they had shown their son's musical ambitions to be so much idle dreaming. Trouble was, they were wrong; George Michael really had something.

Wham!'s first hit, 'Young Guns (Go for It)', charted high in November 1982, eight months after they signed. And of course the more records they sold, and the more they appeared on *Top of the Pops* celebrating subsequent hits, the more the old syndrome took over: the 20-year-olds began looking around for the rewards they believed to be theirs, and there were none. There was a luxury of sorts, but it all added to their overdraft. The first Christmas they went home to their parents and money was as tight as ever. The same the following Easter, and next summer too.

In the company of their present manager, Wham! could look back on their Innervision deal of that summer and find a trail of clauses that they still didn't fully understand – though they knew that most of them had been a great mistake. It was almost enough just to look at their advances and royalty payments. At a time when the majors were paying crazy money for potential chart talent – shortly over a year later singer Alison Moyet was rumoured to have received a £250,000-per-album advance from CBS – Wham! each received only £500. Royalties worked out at just 8 per cent for UK albums and singles and only 6 per cent and 4 per cent respectively for albums and singles sold in the US or the rest of the world. Even an unknown signing could have expected at least 10 per cent or 11 per cent, a chart-topping one 15 per cent to 18 per cent.

Dean's defence, and the one he impressed on Wham! in frequent negotiations over their lack of income, was forceful and three-pronged. First, he suggested that Innervision was out to make profits like all other record companies, and he did not see Innervision as a latterday Apple; he had offered them a deal and they had jumped at it. Secondly, his company broke Wham!, and he argued that without Innervision they wouldn't have achieved massive success when and how they did. Further, he claimed that CBS began taking an interest in his two mates only after he'd hired an independent strikeforce and plugger to make 'Young Guns' a hit. 'We began showing up their system. The thing that they had created [Innervision] had turned into a monster.' And thirdly, he stressed that his hands were tied; he couldn't offer Wham! more than he was earning himself.

He now admitted that he too had made a grave mistake: his licensing deal with CBS, only finalized the day before he signed Wham!, fell horribly short of the ideal. With less impatience and ambition, and with a cooler head, he too might perhaps have worked over the details a little longer and wouldn't have agreed to all the clauses. As it was, he now almost justified Innervision's meanness towards its first signing as a necessary result of the deal he had himself signed with his parent company.

In summary, Innervision's deal with CBS specified:

1 CBS would manufacture and distribute records of the artists Innervision signed and recorded, and in return pay the company royalties. The licensing deal could last up to five years, and in the first three years the basic album royalty stood at 15 per cent in the UK and 13 per cent in the US. The royalty rate for seven-inch singles was 11 per cent for UK sales, 8 per cent for US sales. Out of this Innervision were expected to pay all artist royalties, as well as those of any one else working on the record such as producers or mixers.

2 CBS paid Innervision a first-year advance of £150,000 to be used for making master recordings and advances to artists. This was fully recoupable against the royalties accruing from successful Innervision releases. Innervision also received a maximum facility budget of £75,000 in its first year, essentially a loan to assist with working capital and capital expenditure requirements.

3 Twelve-inch singles, once used almost exclusively for promotional purposes but now selling regularly in tens of thousands (especially for dance records in which Innervision specialized) would only be subject to royalty payments once sales had exceeded 30,000.

4 Innervision would only receive *half* the royalties on a particular record promoted by a 'substantial' TV advertising campaign, not only in the four months following the campaign, but also for records sold in the two months *prior* to it.

Though apparently not too dissimilar from an equivalent licensing deal struck between ZTT (the label that spawned Frankie Goes to Hollywood) and Island Records a year later (a deal, incidentally, also negotiated on ZTT's part by solicitor Paul Rodwell), the clawback points 3 and 4 ensured that Innervision might receive dramatically less than Mark Dean might have hoped for. The ZTT/Island contract which provided ZTT with UK single and album royalties of 12 per cent and 16 per cent and advances of £120,000 on signature and an additional £40,000 after nine months, did not contain comparable CBS clawbacks, and was also considerably more generous in its terms: the Island advances were only recoupable against 40 per cent of ZTT royalties, not 100 per cent as CBS recouped from Innervision (hence the recoupment period would be a lot slower in Island's case, giving ZTT far more room to breathe).

Dean's deal with CBS thus prompted the following summarized Innervision contract with Wham!

1   George Michael and Andrew Ridgeley each received advances of £500 recoupable against their first royalty payments.

2   Wham! were signed to Innervision for an initial contract period of one year and four further years at the company's option. During each of these periods Innervision were entitled to one album and could ask for another if they wished, making a possible ten in all. If the duo broke up, each member could be bound to Innervision for a further ten albums, even if the split occurred towards the end of the band's ten-album period. If this happened, each member would only receive three-quarters of the agreed royalty.

3   Royalty rates were 8 per cent for UK albums and singles in the initial, first and second option period, and 6 per cent and 4 per cent respectively for albums and singles sold in the rest of the world (including the US). These rates were exclusive of any royalty payable to the producer. Further, royalties would only be paid on 90 per cent of net sales.

4   Wham! received no royalty payment on sales of twelve-inch singles, *even if* sales exceeded 30,000 copies.

5   TV advertising halved royalty payments from *three* months preceding the campaign, and up to the end of the second accounting period following the final advert.

6   As with Innervision's deal with CBS, royalties would be halved if any record was issued in a coloured vinyl other than black, or if a double album was issued at fractionally less than double price.

An additional clause specified the payment of per-album advances ranging from £2,000 to be paid on the delivery of Wham!'s first album, through

£12,500 paid for their fifth album, to £35,000 paid for their tenth. It was further evidence of Innervision's frugality; any band successful enough to produce ten albums for the same label can expect an advance against album sales well into hundreds of thousands. Deals of advances worth £1 million are also not uncommon.

It wasn't hard to understand why the bigger the hits, the greater Wham!'s despair, and the more sour grew the band's relationship with Dean. Dean had even taken on the role of quasi-manager for the first year, and Wham! agreed he was initially very good for them. With time, however, they assured themselves that anyone would have made a success of them eventually. In the words of the late Rolling Stones manager Andrew Loog Oldham, 'They were there already, they only wanted exploiting,' – and they began to look elsewhere for a new manager who could free them from the Innervision ties.

They turned first to their solicitor Robert Allan, but three months later in July 1983 found themselves not only in the hands of a new legal force – Russells – but also in those of a new manager whose fearful reputation for hard-nut biz arrogance was sufficient to make Allen Klein look distinctly sheepish.

Simon Napier-Bell, one of the fabled names of sixties rock and, more recently, Japan's manager for several years since his comeback from retirement, saw in Wham! a rare and enviable level of energy and professionalism, and in George Michael an uncanny ability to sit down and write hits. He had first seen them on *Top of the Pops*, and he was especially taken by their unmistakable buddy-buddy image – the Butch and Sundance or Blues Brothers feel that might make them as attractive to young male fans as they were to girls.

Speaking in his opulent but exceedingly grubby deep-piled Marble Arch house, looking not unlike a well-fed, well-tanned hamster (the result of a recent trip with Wham! to Miami), he exhibits a great and seemingly insatiable appetite for the gutsier workings of the UK rock industry, and he's clearly thrilled to be a force in it once more.

He's almost twice Mark Dean's age, and Wham! have little doubt that he's the sort of big hitter who can now see them out of any tight industry corners they may still encounter. His past tactics had been both brutal and painfully direct. In the mid-sixties, for example, his group The Yardbirds asked him for houses. 'It was a bit of a nuisance because I had a busy schedule of eating and drinking to maintain,' he wrote in *You Don't Have to Say You Love Me*, his memoir of the sixties rock world. 'However, I found time to pop down to EMI Records and tell them I'd decided their contract was no longer valid, and The Yardbirds were off to look for a nicer one elsewhere . . . I told them that £25,000 would be enough to change my mind.'

Indeed, George Michael even seems rather proud that his past dealings have won him many enemies. 'He has a huge reputation as a real asshole,' he says with a smirk. 'And there's no doubt that Simon will make a lot of money out of us. But what he really wants out of it is to be responsible for managing a group that is one of the biggest in the world.'

Though it's likely that he's on at least 20 per cent, Napier-Bell probably still hasn't signed a formal management contract with Wham! – at least he hadn't at the close of their first year together. 'There's never really any point,' he shrugs. 'Once you've agreed something verbally, you either keep to it or your relationship's worthless. You need full two-way co-operation to keep both parties happy. If things break down, it's the easiest thing in the world to pull out and make sure the other side can't work.' Certainly this was true in the latter stages of the Innervision–Wham! relationship.

Mark Dean suggests that Napier-Bell did more than just help Wham! out of their contract; he claims he also made their departure inevitable. 'Despite what Wham! might tell you, it was definitely Simon who built a wedge between the group and the record company.'

Wham!'s ultimate pull-out, of course, was set in motion by Russells in the blunt terms of that letter above. Innervision's response, the attainment of a temporary court injunction, was followed by another writ, soon dropped, that saw Dean on the counter-offensive. For a short while he attempted to sue Napier-Bell and Tony Russell for conspiracy and inducement to break contract.

The entire matter was settled out of court in March 1984. Innervision lost Wham! but gained independence from CBS and a considerable pay-off loan. The break had cost the small company dearly: the amount they owed CBS was initially estimated to be around £450,000, to be paid back by a 1 per cent royalty on the future sales of all Innervision releases. Wham! signed to the major CBS subsidiary Epic for a far higher royalty rate than that agreed in their first contract (rumoured to be as high as 20 per cent) and are clearly now well into the millionaire bracket.

The end of the affair found George Michael and Andrew Ridgeley seated in their publicist's basement room in confident, even arrogant, mood. Michael even regards the enforced legal break as something of a blessing: 'It's been more of a help than we could imagine, certainly for me in writing. But I think you've just been bored, haven't you, Andrew?'

'Bored? Yeah, sometimes. But I went and got a skiing holiday – that was quite fun. But it's good to know that we're going to be number one soon . . .'

As with their manager, a recent trip to Miami has helped their suntans no end, and they take delight in preening themselves during questions and smoothing in skin moisturizer when answering. George Michael does most of the talking, just as he does most of the creative work in Wham!. He tells of how he talked his way out of the first day's shoot for the video of his 'Careless Whisper' solo single because his hair wasn't exactly right.

As for his old friend Mark Dean, he expresses little sympathy.

> He was unlucky. He didn't really know what was going on at the time because he only had a few rough demos. Maybe if he had the demos we gave him three days later . . . [he admits that his main error was his desire to sign *any* deal] but it doesn't mean you have to pay for it by giving your ability for someone else to rake in the money for the rest of your life.
>
> Things even went OK initially because we were both working towards the same goal. But we knew that one day there would be a lot of aggro, and he must have known that as well. He really counted on CBS coming to help him, which they didn't. He made the mistake of making that lousy deal thinking he could renegotiate it when things got better, but found that he couldn't because CBS weren't giving him the room. If he was not a greedy man, he could have been a very rich man by now. Probably still will be, but the point is he could have been a lot richer . . .

The irony, perhaps, and a certain testament to the hitting strength of the biz big boys, is that Dean lost out as much, if not more, than Wham!. Dean admits defeat at least in part, but suggests that his current roster of Innervision acts can only benefit from his experience. 'You can't afford to get bitter and twisted after something like this,' he offers with a sigh. 'The industry goes on quite happily without you. If you get bitter in the music world, it's time to quit.'

Dean's resolve was further tested after the Wham! affair by the bust-up and departure of two other, less popular, Innervision signings. Most hopes were pinned on his fiercely ambitious young teenies Girltalk, those Ronettes sound-alikes who still attend school. So far, two singles have brought little success, but the girls believe they'll crack it eventually. They still think they'll be as big as Wham!, but it was an early setback to learn that they wouldn't see the two golden boys in the corridors at Innervision. Maybe they got over it towards the end of 1984 when Mark Dean could have told them that they would now see them in the corridors of his brand-new lawyers. Dean had just switched to Russells.

And Wham! themselves can lay claim to being the most successful worldwide pop act of the mid eighties. The metal discs, the number ones, the magazine and tabloid covers and the songwriting awards have become almost weekly events since the break from Innervision. A feverish America has welcomed the duo as the 19th British invasion, and George and Andrew even enjoyed a historical exploratory tour of China.

And if the Chinese kids couldn't understand the words, and weren't allowed to dance, and if they didn't even care, then why should anyone else worry? You could almost see the platinum discs flicking over in the glaze of Simon Napier-Bell's eyes. There would be problems at customs, but China, surely, was an untapped market of some size.

Simon Garfield, *Expensive Habits* (1986)

1985: Marilyn: Does Anyone Still Want Him?

Marilyn is miserable and alone in the tough American city of Detroit. His last two singles, to the horror of his record company, have not been hits. Now he's been dispatched to Detroit to make a hit *or else* with a famous American producer, Don Was. Arriving at his hotel in Detroit, he finds that no one has booked a room for him. No one has made any arrangements for his hotel bill to be paid. He calls England to find out what's going on. No one answers his calls. He sits in the hotel lobby for nine hours, alone and friendless. Snooty staff glare at him.

'It was like being on the edge of a cliff. I knew that I had a week to record two really good songs and come back with two songs that everyone would hear and say, "Great, Marilyn. You've really proved that you can do it." And I had to go through so much to get those two songs recorded. I felt like a different person altogether. That was definitely the beginning of the change.'

And what a change ... He made a decision to do something so drastic it would strike at the very heart of his ... Marilyn-ness. It would alter the public's perception of him. Utterly.

Marilyn decided to cut off his hair.

A couple of months later, a cropped Marilyn sits with me in a chic but gloomy New York hotel room. He's still miserable. One of the tracks he recorded in New York, 'Baby You Left Me', has turned out fine. The best

585

thing he's ever done, actually. Now he's got to make a video for it. New York's most fashionable nightclub, Area, is throwing a party for him tonight and he's going to sing in front of an audience for the first time ever.

The idea was that he would be filmed for part of the video but the film crew have been delayed. Marilyn's live appearance is going ahead as planned, however. He's nervous. A photographer from the *New York Post* has just given him a lot of grief. 'There's only so much I can take,' he moans and we have a gloomy chat in the semi-darkness as night falls over Manhattan.

Why did you cut your hair off?

'Because I got bored with looking the same way all the time and this is a bit different. People still see me as a sort of transvestite with a glittery suit and pink lipstick – but that was a year-and-a-half ago.'

Do you never wear make-up now?

'No, I don't. I don't like the feel of it on my face. I like to be able to rub my eye when I feel like it and come home and go straight to bed. I don't like all that junk over me. It gets to be a trap.'

People treat him differently as a result, he reckons. 'They talk to me like a person.' When he had his hair cut, the girls in his record company's office 'fancied me and the guys shook my hand. It was like I'd finally done it.'

Since he first shot into the charts at the end of 1983, he's had to put up with some outrageous criticism in the press. Some of the tabloids seemed to blame him for the complete moral downfall of Britain.

'I was quite shocked, really, that someone could be so stupid,' he says. 'You just expect that, after Danny La Rue and Quentin Crisp and God knows who else, that people would be able to accept someone with a bit of make-up. England is like such a bunch of old drag queens anyway. If you pick up a history-book . . . I'm quite tame compared to a lot of people.'

He admits that he is 'famous for the wrong reasons' and is under no illusion that his precarious stardom is founded on his musical talents.

'I think I'm famous for being somebody's friend.'

Somebody, however, is never mentioned by name during our conversation. He doesn't utter the words 'Boy' or 'George'.

'He's a friend of mine and I'm not going to deny it. But, if you talk about it, it's like you're dropping his name. So how do you win? It's either completely losing a friendship for the sake of everybody else – people you don't even know – or putting up with it and carrying on with life as normal and, if it gets written about in the papers, it gets written in the papers.

'I mean, I try not to be seen anywhere with him. If we go through an airport together I try and walk 30 paces behind with a passport over my face or something.'

George is very 'protective' towards Marilyn, apparently, almost to the point of being 'suffocating'. Their relationship does have its ups and downs but, as Marilyn points out: 'I have arguments with nearly every person I know and I make up with them.' George is no exception.

When I ask what their holiday in Jamaica was like, he grimaces.

'Horrible. I didn't like it this time. It was just . . . difficult.'

How?

'Just difficult. If I started to talk about it, I really *would* talk about it and that wouldn't be very clever.'

It sounds fascinating.

'Well, you'll be able to read all about it one day when I write my book.'

Do you have a lot of friends?

'It's difficult to have a lot of friends. It takes me a long time to get to know one person, let alone a lot of people. I could drop down dead tomorrow,' he adds dramatically, 'and I could count the amount of people who would care on one hand.'

Not only does he have few friends, but money is in short supply. He's just sold his London home because 'I couldn't afford the bills. I need the money.' He doesn't know where he's going to stay when he returns to London: 'Under the arches! No, something will turn up.'

You don't seem very happy, I observe.

'Today hasn't been a good day at all. It's the wrong day to ask me about happiness.'

What makes you happy?

'Not having to deal with stupid people which I have to do an incredible amount.'

How do you enjoy yourself?

'Getting really out of it.'

Where?

'I don't know. I don't know where I go when I'm out of it.'

Do you fall in love very often?

'Yes I do. It's the most horrible experience ever.'

Why?

'It's like being on the edge of a cliff again.'

You seem to spend a lot of time on the edge of this cliff.

'It would seem so.'

And are you there now?

'Sort of. Quite close to the edge but not quite there yet. A couple of pushes more and I'll be there. Sometimes I feel like going swimming in a pair of concrete stilettoes. I have to put up with so much . . . shit from some people. I sometimes wonder whether it's all worthwhile. But then you get a letter from someone who's got cancer and you realise: who am I to be depressed about anything?'

Do you wish you had more 'credibility' in the music business?

'I don't want credibility,' he snaps. 'I want respect. I hate all that street credibility stuff. It's such a load of old rubbish. Half the people who talk about street credibility don't even remember where the street is. *I've* lived in it.'

Are you hard?

'Yeah, I think so. I'm still here after all I've had to put up with.'

Are you worried about your new single being a hit?

'No, not really. Of course I want it to be a hit. In fact I *need* it to be because I've got no money. But if it isn't, well, life goes on.'

He is, to use an old show business cliché, 'a survivor'.

Six hours later and Area is crowded for Marilyn's party. Joan Rivers is here and so is Christopher Reeve ('Superman') and Steve Bronski of Bronski Beat and Helen Terry. Marilyn's records are being played, his photos are being flashed onto the walls and girls are dressed up as Marilyn Monroe. It's time for Marilyn's first-ever live appearance.

It's a disaster.

As he saunters onto the stage to sing over his new single, the PA system shrieks with excruciating feedback, all but drowning out the backing track.

Marilyn motions for the tape to be stopped and the feedback fixed. But the dreadful noise continues.

He runs off the stage and does not return.

Neil Tennant, Smash Hits, 14–25 March 1985

nine

1985–9

'The darkest well'

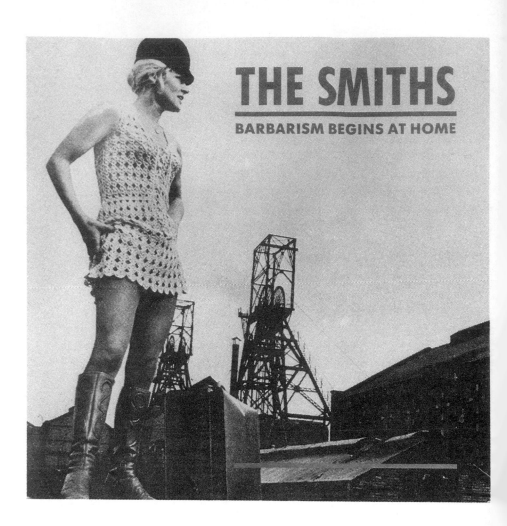

'*Where the battlefield is, is popular music.*'

Chris Cutler, File Under Popular *(1985)*

At mid-decade, mid-term Reagan and Thatcher, it was possible to believe that everything was going swimmingly. That was certainly the impression given by mainstream popular culture: in America, MTV was king and the pop video the dominant form, while in England the style press and pop magazines like *Smash Hits* were in full swing. There was a move towards a mild conservatism: a renewed sense of authenticity – of real emotion, real feeling, real music after the brilliant artifice of the early decade. In this section, however, we look at the undertow of the time: disquiet, struggle, riot.

We begin with an article by Simon Garfield which covers the group who, more than any other in England, reasserted rock as pop's emotional litmus paper. The Smiths came from Manchester – a simple fact which explains their refusal of the glib messages emanating from a capital thoroughly enmeshed in style culture and the triumphal statements of performers like Wham!. Or, to put it another way, instead of 'Make It Big' you had 'Meat is Murder'. Gordon Legge's *The Shoe* inhabits the realm that the Smiths made their own: an unemployed, aimless generation whose pop obsessions didn't lead outwards but into an airless room.

The mood changes in 1987, with Black Monday's stock-market crash. In an excerpt from his fourth novel, *The Conclave*, Michael Bracewell deftly rips right through his protagonists' upwardly mobile lifestyle with a snatch from Wire's 'I am the Fly', one of Punk's most elusive and sarcastic songs. That same year, Greg Tate critiqued the failure of Michael Jackson as a cultural icon: 'In 1985 black people cherished *Thriller*'s breakthrough as if it was their own battering ram against the barricades of American apartheid . . . having sold the world pure pop pleasure on *Thriller*, Jackson returns on *Bad* to sell his own race hatred.'

Youth itself had become a problem. In both England and America, it was no longer seen as desirable: the classic Teenage 15–24 age group was deserted by marketers and manufacturers for the 25–35-year-olds – the sixties generation, whose increasing conservatism is challenged by Michael Ventura in a polemic inspired by the film *The Big Chill*. Tama Janowitz reveals the emptiness at the heart of one of the period's biggest American stars, the 'Back in the USA'-era Bruce Springsteen. Annette Stark charts the hostilities between youth and police in a snapshot of Los Angeles's turbulent pop culture.

In America indeed, youth had become an object of horrified fascination. The suicide pact of four teens in New Jersey provided a powerful story in early 1987, slotting right into existing media tropes about satanistic murders and teen violence. In her sociological masterpiece *Teenage Wasteland* – a book which indeed reasserts the vitality of this despised discipline – Donna Gaines writes with perfect empathy about a generation and a class which she saw as fearful for its survival: 'America's young people did their best to survive in a climate that was openly punitive towards the vulnerable. Yet they were consistently viewed as a generation of barbarians and losers, stupid, apathetic.'

In England, this generational hostility was expressed in more subtle ways. Mick Brown's article for the *Independent on Sunday* researched the dramatic fall from grace of *the* pop star who epitomized the symbiosis between the newspaper and music industries. From 1982 to 1984, Boy George was hardly out of Fleet Street: during the summer of 1986, the tabloids called in their side of the bargain, running the Boy George heroin storyline to the point where it seemed that his death was the desired outcome. It didn't happen.

Underneath the overt cause of the scandal, George's severe drug abuse, lay something much more unpleasant – all the more so because it was implied rather than expressed in this story: the tabloid hatred of homosexuals that followed the recognized onset of AIDS in 1984. Pop stars were in the front line of this, as John Sweeney records in his account of the *Sun*'s attack on Elton John: in February 1987, the paper ran the first of four front covers giving thorough but inaccurate details of the star's involvement with drugs and rent boys. As Sweeney notes: 'The paper was beginning to look like a bully.' Elton John sued, several times, and won £1 million damages in December 1988.

The inhumanity of such prejudiced reporting is exposed by Barry Walters's moving obituary for one of Disco's greatest stars, who died from AIDS earlier that year. Promoted as the first openly homosexual hitmaker in the US – with late seventies hits like 'You Make Me Feel Mighty Real' – Sylvester embodied the possibilities of that time; he was a strong influence on later British stars like Boy George. Walters records the singer's courage in going public with his condition, and the shrinking of life for those he left behind: 'For a while, the politics of dancing shifted from moving ahead to holding onto the small freedoms of pleasure.'

1985: This Charming Man

If there is any space at all for subversion in the pop charts, then that place is occupied by Manchester band The Smiths. If there has been any creative advancement at all in the music industry in the last year, then that progression has been forged by The Smiths. If there's been one debut album that can safely lay claim to being 'a complete signal post in the history of popular music', then it was *The Smiths* by The Smiths. And if there's been only one band since the Sex Pistols to upset the cosseted old Biz and genuinely excite young record buyers again, then it's The . . .

All Morrissey's views these, and what you'd have expected from The Smith's lead singer and lyricist. What you wouldn't have expected – not two years ago anyway – is that 1985 would find so many people agreeing with him. Worse than that, they're actually worshipping him. Not hard to imagine happening to Boy George or Simon Le Bon, but this man? A man who unashamedly calls himself a genius, who has admitted celibacy and contemplated suicide, who writes ceaselessly about the darkest well of despair and loneliness, who expresses a hatred for the royal family and the Band Aid project, who sings of the Moors Murders and animal slaughter; a man who admits to being a helpless James Dean and Oscar Wilde nut? Yes, we do, it seems, want this stuff.

We want it enough to buy more than 100,000 copies of The Smiths' second official album *Meat is Murder* and put it in at Number One in its first week of release. Enough to vote The Smiths best rock 'n' roll band in the world in the music press polls. Enough to set the champagne corks flying at their fiercely independent and often fiercely disorganized Rough Trade label, a company that's finally achieved the sort of success that many swore was impossible. Enough indeed to put Morrissey in audacious and searing form on a high landing in the feverishly refurbished Britannia Hotel in his cold home town.

His media forays thus far have coupled a charming, winning eloquence within a seemingly endless list of controversial sentiments, and have consequently ensured that his interviews have sold probably more records than his lyrics. 'I'm not so shallow that I'd be happy hiding behind slogans,' he says, half uneasy at the way he's become not only the group's spokesman, but also that of yet another lost generation of British youth. It used to be Joe Strummer, Bob Geldof or Paul Weller. Morrissey isn't happy being compared to any of them.

'By rights The Smiths shouldn't be here,' he suggests, 'People want to throw a blanket over even the slightest mention of The Smiths, and the industry spends all its time denying that we're a phenomenon. I think it's because we have this grain of intellect, and when you as a band are trying to lay down the rules you're actually spoiling things for so many middle-aged mediocrities who control the whole sphere of popular music. Let me tell you, the music industry absolutely *detests* The Smiths.'

Industry darling or not, Morrissey has just reached that thin rung on the success ladder that he'd always dreamed he'd attain, but always hoped he'd never have to deal with. For a lot of people success comes easy: you hire a 24-hour gorilla, you buy that ranch, you stick a rolled fiver to your nose, and you put out one album a year in a vile cover. But Morrissey and his fans know that The Smiths could never move comfortably within the realms of affluence, and he hopes that he's recently taken one step further away from it by moving from Kensington to a new house in Cheshire to maintain closer touch with the forces that shaped him.

For the man exudes one thing above all else – integrity. 'I will die for what I say,' he boasts, and it's totally convincing.

The Smiths have enjoyed a rise both phenomenal and strange. Formed by the (then) teenage guitarist and co-songwriter Johnny Marr, the band first lined up as a guitar-based four-piece in September '82 and stirred interest almost immediately.

They stood out about ten miles. For one thing it was the time of the Human League and the synthesizer, and guitar bands were out (in the same way that four-groups were out when The Beatles auditioned for Decca). Further, it was a time of softness, of saving face, of dumb-dumb baby-baby lyrics that stood almost a generation apart from the brutal and realistic sentiments expressed by Morrissey. The Smiths had love songs too, but they were anguished and clever and believable. In fact they were often anguished to the point of absurdity, and frequently appeared ludicrously contrived.

John Peel and his producer John Walters enthused, several majors expressed interest, but the band characteristically signed to Rough Trade for a relatively small advance, and their first single appeared just under two years ago. 'Hand In Glove' was a great song, but it did bugger all. In not working it as hard as they might have done, Rough Trade had seemingly let The Smiths down. Morrissey was aware that both Aztec Camera and Scritti Politti had deserted Rough Trade for majors, and he began to understand why. 'But they had to so something with us – we were really their last vestige of hope. I'm convinced that if the Smiths hadn't occurred, then Rough Trade would have just disappeared.'

The realization seemingly hit both parties at once. Rough Trade pushed harder. Morrissey talked his effeminate white beads off, and their fortunes took off together. The subsequent singles charted high, and the often extremely petty, but always intriguing, controversies surrounding the band doubled, trebled, quadrupled, in number and stature.

Did Morrissey really have a flower fetish? Just why did he throw £50 of gladioli into the audience every night? Why did he insist on prancing around on *Top Of The Pops* with a hearing aid and a bush down the back of his jeans? Was he really celibate? And was he really gay, as *Rolling Stone* hinted? Did he really wear women's shirts from the Evans outsize shop? Was their first single truly to be recorded by Sandie Shaw? Where did the names of Morrissey and Johnny Marr come from anyway? Was it just coincidence that they were respectively a murder victim and the hero of Cornell Woolrich's novel *Rendezvous In Black*? Was Morrissey honestly the desperately lonely teenager who never left his damp Whalley Range room, a room covered from floor to ceiling in James Dean pictures? Did long-time Morrissey hero Terence Stamp really object to being used on one of the band's single sleeves? And did W. H. Smith really ban the band's eponymous debut album because it contained a song called 'Suffer Little Children', about the Moors Murders, even though Morrissey claimed he got on swimmingly with the parents of the victims?

Some of it was garbage, but yes, most of it was true. The first album went gold (over 100,000 copies sold) and the mini-scandals sure must have played some part in its success. 'No more scandals!' said Morrissey when the worst of them were over. But the tabloids didn't believe him.

'They hound me,' he says, 'and it gets very sticky. What makes me more dangerous to them than anybody else is the fact that I lead somewhat of a religious lifestyle. I'm not a rock 'n' roll character. I despise drugs, I despise cigarettes, I'm celibate and I live a very serene lifestyle. But I'm also making very strong statements lyrically, and this is very worrying to authoritarian figures. They can't say that I'm in a druggy haze or soaked in alcohol and that I'll get out of it. They probably think I'm some sort of sex-craved monster. But that's okay – they can think what they like. I'm only interested in evidence, and they can't produce any evidence to spoil *my* character.'

Dangerous? This 25-year-old man in black blazer, lime-green cotton shirt, heavily creased beige pegs, brown shoes and a James Dean quiff – a sex-crazed monster and corruptor of youth?

In truth, there is something very unsettling about being in his presence – he's almost too soft, too gentle, too nervous, and he's not a million miles from that pathetic archetypal Monty Python accountant. He bows when he shakes your hand, and that's something you don't expect from a rocker with a Number One album.

'The main reason I'm dangerous is because I'm not afraid to say how I feel. I'm not afraid to say that I think Band Aid was diabolical. Or to say that I think Bob Geldof is a nauseating character. Many people find that very unsettling, but I'll say it as loud as anyone wants me to.

'In the first instance the record itself was absolutely tuneless. One can have great concern for the people of Ethiopia, but it's another thing to inflict daily torture on the people of England. It was an awful record considering the mass of talent involved. And it wasn't done shyly – it was the most self-righteous platform ever in the history of popular music.'

But it's another of Morrissey's handlebar flyers – the hyperbole and cries of 'conspiracy!' are hard to resist if he knows that they'll at least double the impact of what he is actually bold enough to say. Which is either a whole pile, or not much at all, depending on the richness of your idealism and the length of your memory. Pick the albums and singles to pieces and you find songs that are stirring, occasionally funny, often moving, but, like the man who sings them, far from dangerous or alarming. Indeed they are more an incitement for lethargy than rebellion.

Sentiments are often obscure, abstract and even cowardly in what they don't say. Is a Morrissey line that runs *Let me get my hands on your mammary glands* really any more risqué than a Tony Blackburn radio jingle that has him 'whipping out his 12-incher'? Well no, it's a mixture of the innocent, the embarrassing and the comic. It's a nice rhyme too.

Or often it's just a case of the old Dylans – keep 'hot' songs vague and you're bound to get more people believing that you're gunning just for them. But Morrissey's most threatening weapon is sub-textual – his dour, parochial obsession with Manchester. His languorous depictions of Rusholme, Whalley Range and the Manchester that in his rhyme always seems to have 'so-much-to-answer-fer', are frank impressions of Northern industrial squalor and decay that show slightly more of the world than the perfumed works of the Wham!s, Durans, Madonnas and Princes.

And as for Johnny Marr's music, well that's nothing earth-shatteringly original either . . . and perhaps that's part of its appeal. For someone in his very early twenties, Marr certainly displays an enormous and well-executed guitar range: ethereal, semi-classical acoustics, fine-picked chiming and spiky electrics, and taut, chopping block-chords often working quite apart from the vocals. But at its best it's good old countrified garage stuff delivered with a wink to the same old guitar greats. The new album track 'Rusholme Ruffians', say, sounds a great whack like the 1961 Elvis Presley recording of the Doc Pomus and Mort Shuman composition '(Marie's The Name) His Latest Flame'. But it sounds pretty terrific all the same.

Strange, then, that both Morrissey and Marr often seem like desperate men hugging an invaluable patent, hanging on to that magic ingredient that very occasionally makes rock music so special. 'It's just that you have to hold on to what you want to stay very tight,' Morrissey explains, 'because there are so many people in this industry trying to trip you up and push you over and catch you out and unveil you.

'The industry is just rife with jealousy and hatred. Everybody in it is a failed bassist. Everybody wants to be on stage – it doesn't matter what they do, they all want to be you. But the mere fact that you have that and nobody can take it away from you, is your ultimate weapon. It's just really awash with jealousy and sourness and bitterness.'

Revenge for not being asked to participate, maybe? Getting his own back, in true flamboyant and petty rockstar style, for what others have previously said about him? Morrissey says that several of the people involved have publicly admitted absolute hatred towards him. Including Geldof, of course. 'He said it on the radio the other day, and it was totally unprovoked. It was as if he was really quite anxious and desperate to put me down. The fact that Bob Geldof – this apostle, this religious figure who's saving all these people all over the globe – the fact that he can make those statements about me and yet he seems quite protected, seems totally unfair. But I'm not bothered about those things . . .'

Just as the new album shows Morrissey not to be at all bothered by child beating, animal slaughter or the royal family. But the man is away now, in unstoppable flow. Pick a topic and watch Morrissey curl a dry tongue around it . . .

I ask Morrissey about one of the verses on the album that apparently runs: *'I'd like to drop my trousers to the Queen . . . The poor and the needy are selfish and greedy on her terms.'*

'Actually I despise royalty. I always have done. It's fairy story nonsense' – and all this in the decadence of the *Britannia* Hotel – 'the very idea of their existence in these days when people are dying daily because they don't have enough money to operate one radiator in the house, to me is immoral. As far as I can see, money spent on royalty is money burnt. I've never met anyone who supports royalty, and believe me I've searched. Okay, so there's some deaf and elderly pensioner in Hartlepool who has pictures of Prince Edward pinned on the toilet seat, but I know streams of people who can't wait to get rid of them.

'It's a false devotion anyway. I think it's fascist and very, very cruel. To me there's something dramatically ugly about a person who can wear a dress for £6,000 when at the same time there are people who can't afford to eat. When she puts on that dress for £6,000 the statement she is making to the nation is: "I am the fantastically gifted royalty, and you are the snivelling peasants." The very idea that people would be interested in the facts about this dress is massively insulting to the human race.'

In short, Morrissey belongs to that old protest school with guts – the one where the singer names names. There are a few like him – Billy Bragg and the Redskins come to mind – but the Band Aid project, he feels, was certainly not one of them. 'The whole implication was to save these people in Ethiopia, but who were they asking to save them? Some 13-year-old girl in Wigan! People like Thatcher and the royals could solve the Ethiopian problem within ten seconds. But Band Aid shied away from saying that – for heaven's sake, it was almost directly aimed at unemployed people.'

And, as a result of naming names, Morrissey feel he's unearthed a deep prejudice against The Smiths, an industry plot against independence. He claims his records have been ignored 'by every single media channel in existence'. Actually, he's quite wrong: every single media channel in existence has grabbed eagerly at the band's music, if only as a way of getting to their audacious leader. In fact he's currently turning down interview requests by the bucketload.

Morrissey, by contrast, is currently awash with magnanimity, sweetness and forgiveness. An hour gone, and he's still in full glorious swing. He's hoping the near future will hold a book of his own journalism – he's already interviewed Pat Phoenix and has designs on pools scooper Viv 'Spend, Spend, Spend' Nicolson (the cover star of an early Smiths single). 'I've got lots of questions,' he says, 'and lots of people I want to probe, especially in the dark.'

Morrissey *knows* The Smiths will be here for a long time yet. 'We're not just fashionable – in fact I don't know what fashion is. It's quite simple: before we came there was no outlet for emotion – people couldn't tear their coat and jump on somebody's head.'

And if The Smiths do bust up tomorrow, modest old Morrissey already reckons he's done enough for the history books. 'I don't mind how I'm remembered so long as they're precious recollections. I don't want to be remembered for being a silly prancing, nonsensical village idiot. But I really do want to be remembered. I want some grain of immortality. I think it's been deserved. It's been earned.'

Really? In two years?

'Oh yes! Oh yes! In two days! In two days!'

Simon Garfield, Time Out, March 1985

1985: Barely Conscious

Seven forty-two. Magic. Archie felt lovely. It was worth going through the horror of sleeplessness and nightmares to feel this good. Only his forehead was exposed to the air. Archie was barely conscious. I could go to sleep any second. Why can't it always be so easy? Archie fell asleep again.

At twenty past nine, he reawoke and felt rotten. His head felt scrambled. The chorus and verse of '*Pride*' ran through his head simultaneously. Archie lit a cigarette and proceeded to dress, donning the same clothes as he had been wearing for the past three days. The nicotine creating routine, he made a plan: wash, breakfast, change sheets and pillowcases, have a bath, change clothes, dinner, then walk down to the library. Changing the sheets meant he wouldn't have to make the bed just now. He always slept better in fresh sheets.

Archie drew the curtains and looked out of the window. Theirs was the only garden with flowers, a hut and a greenhouse. His dad did all the physical work and his mum kept it tidy. Most of the neighbours were younger than Archie. They never appeared to go out. Their lights always remained on.

Archie finished his cigarette and stubbed it out in the dessert plate that functioned as an ashtray.

In the bathroom he washed his face and brushed his teeth. Shaving was still too much like hard work – maybe after he'd had his bath. Archie brushed his teeth twice a day and made biannual trips to the dentist. The DHSS paid for any treatment. False teeth and naked gums filled him with dread. He brushed with vigour to compensate for his smoking. Richard had terrible teeth. He claimed they were as smart as Keith Richards' but Mental said they were as bad as Bowie's. After watching an episode of *That's Life* wherein Esther Rantzen investigated dental payments and discovered that different dentists gave different estimates to the same patients, Richard had never been back to a dentist. He didn't like the idea of unnecessary work being carried out by sterile, sexless fingers.

The cabinet mirror showed lines around Archie's eyes. These lines would never go away but would grow longer, darker and thicker. Archie could stare in the mirror for hours. He hated standing beside somebody, though, it always made him feel ugly. But on his own he thought he looked okay. By adjusting the doors of the cabinet he could get a picture of what he really looked like. Initial reaction was always revulsion. Nobody's *that* ugly. It was nothing like the picture he carried around in his head. Archie tried smiling and frowning, wondering which looked coolest. Years spent staring at the mirror had revealed nothing. He suspected, as Mental said, that he looked gawkit.

Funny how I always wash before I brush my teeth, Archie thought. I mean common sense dictates I should do the opposite. I'm going to have to rinse toothpaste off my face, anyway. Who taught me this?

'Morning.' Archie addressed his mother in the living-room. She was doing the *Daily Record* crossword.

'What's a nine-letter word for "deny"? Something E and it ends A something E.' She sucked a pen.

AE, BE, CE, DE, EE, FE, GE, gelignite, germinate, NO! HE hesitate, IE, JE, KE, LE, levitate, ME. Deny, deny you're such a liar, Archie sang the Clash song to himself. NE, OE, PE, QE, RE – I like that, yeah, RE, RE, eh . . . 'Repudiate!'

'That's it. And that'll be Madeira. I finished the crossie. Heh, heh.' Archie's mum flung the paper on to the settee.

Archie filled a large soup plate with Wheetaflakes and drowned them in three-quarters of a pint of milk and walked over to the settee. Archie was an untidy eater. He had to gulp twice before inserting another mouthful.

'What was Auntie Isabel saying?' Archie asked.

'She got a phone call while we were there from Joan saying that my Uncle George is in hospital in Kirkcaldy. We're maybe going to take a run up and see him. See how your dad feels.'

'When was he taken in?' Archie knew nothing of Uncle George apart from the fact that he was old, sent a Christmas card and Archie's mum and dad saw him at funerals.

'I don't know. I think it was Monday. They fairly took their time in telling folk.' Archie's mum sounded disappointed.

Archie turned the pages of the *Daily Record* while devouring his breakfast. The TV page, cartoon page and the sports page were studied the most.

'If you spill any milk on that settee, I'll kill you,' said Archie's mum, only quarter joking. She lit a cigarette as Archie read the latest adventures of his personal guru: Bogard, the cat in the *Roz* cartoon strip.

Archie finished his cereal as his mother finished her cigarette. She took his plate through to the kitchen while singing 'My Love is like a Red, Red Rose'. Archie read the sports pages. It was so easy to keep up with the world of sport without actually bothering about it, especially football. It always seemed strange to Archie that those people of his acquaintance who could talk about football till 'all the seas gang dry, my love' weren't very gifted footballers themselves. Richard was a better player than Mental and Davie but he couldn't tell you the manager of Hearts. He said he played football to keep skinny.

The report of the Hagler fight was dull, like describing sex without adjectives. The latest Rangers crisis, though, really got the journalists worked up. Did they get worked up about Rangers' sectarianism? Did they hell, they got worked up about Rangers' poor form. Every so often the papers would act the liberal by making a fuss about some aspect of Rangers' policy: 'Rangers player marries Catholic … Rangers sign Catholic schoolboy on S-form'. Following the last story, the Celtic fans sang 'What's it like to sign a Pape?' at the next Old Firm game. Journalists, MPs and publicity seekers never sought to campaign for civil rights at Ibrox for fear of the backlash. Even terrorists shunned it.

Quarter past ten, near enough. Archie's mother would be leaving for her school dinners work at eleven.

The smell of stale tobacco stunned Archie as he entered his room. What a dump! There were records, cassettes, magazines, dirty clothes and books all over the place. The colour of the room was nicotine yellow. The poster of Jimi Hendrix looked like his corpse. Other pictures were of Frank Bruno, Barry McGuigan, Bono, Kenny Dalglish (in Celtic colours), Prince, Marc Bolan and there were four of Marvin Hagler. The biggest poster advertised SPOT (Sex Pistols On Tour) which Archie bought off Wee Stevie for two pounds. The white background on the poster was now yellow.

As well as his double bed and his music centre the room contained two fitted wardrobes, an upright chair and a chest of drawers. One fitted wardrobe was packed with Archie's old papers and records (Archie had two hundred LPs and three hundred singles. He considered this amount tiny compared to Richard's) and the other contained his clothes, games and school stuff, which had never been thrown out. The top drawer of Archie's chest of drawers contained Archie's cassettes. Archie spent fully five minutes deciding what to play when changing the bed. He narrowed it down to a choice of NME's *Pocket Jukebox* and *The Cream of Al Green*. He chose Al Green. Richard had given Archie the recording about a year previous. Whereas The Mental Kid ransacked Richard's records for things to tape, Archie was always happy with whatever Richard taped for him. Richard had introduced Archie to Bobby Bland, the Neville Brothers, Lee Perry, Laura Nyro, David Ackles, Hüsker Dü, lots of reggae and funk, and most recently Tim Buckley and Nick Drake. In truth, Richard was not entirely happy at lending out records to Archie who only had a cheap music centre which could have damaged Richard's records. Archie expressed his gratitude in terms of enthusiasm and interest.

Archie pulled the covers off the bed: five blankets, two sheets and a tartan bed cover. All punctured with cigarette burns. There was an eight-year-old stain on the mattress where Archie had been sick. He had hoped the stain would have disappeared over the years. No such luck. He always intended to invert the mattress so that the stain would be unseen but he never got round to it.

In the airing cupboard, Archie got fresh sheets and pillowcases.

Al Green sang 'Here I Am'. Awesome. Archie turned up the volume and opened the window, giving thanks to the inspiration that made him select that tape. Although he'd have enjoyed most of his collection as much. Next up was 'Unchained Melody'. Archie had never associated that title with that song. It had been the same when he'd discovered that Booker T's 'Soul Limbo' was the music they used to introduce cricket on television. Next was 'I Stand Accused'. Archie had another version of this on a Stax compilation by Isaac Hayes.

'Well, I'm away then.' Archie's mum stuck her head through the door. She looked as if her nose was being stuck into a pair of underpants that hadn't been washed for three weeks. 'Put the sheets and that in the basket. This place needs decorating, you know.'

Yeah,' said Archie. 'As soon as I've left you can do what you like.' Archie was smiling. There was a greater likelihood of Nelson leaving his column.

'By the way, your Aunt Isabel was talking to Wilma Stevenson. She was asking for you. Asking if you had a job yet.' Archie's mum was wearing her hurt expression which made Archie's neck swell. She did this every so often. It hurt. He reasoned that he could do a lot worse: into drugs or crime, away from home, dead. It didn't work. Archie found it difficult to appreciate that he was the most important person in her life. It was something he didn't like thinking about.

'Right, cheerio. I'll see you later. There's cold meat in the fridge.'

Archie said, 'Okay, cheerio.' He wanted to say something else, something personal. He didn't. He never did. He turned up the volume for Al Green's version of 'I Can't Get Next to You' while wondering whether anyone had ever made a bed while listening to Al Green before.

His mother waved as she walked past the window. She made a funny face and then relaxed into a smile. Archie blew her a kiss and she blew one back.

The bed was made. It looked good, great even. Archie knew he would sleep well tonight. The tape finished.

Archie played a 12″ single of Smokey Robinson's 'And I Don't Love You' while he did his hundred sit-ups (securing his feet under the chest of drawers), hundred press-ups and hundred knee bends. He lit a cigarette when he finished and flexed his skinny muscles.

Quarter past eleven. Bath time. Archie selected a pair of red underpants, a pair of white socks and a white T-shirt to change into after his bath. While he ran the bathwater he played Hüsker Dü's 'Eight Miles High'.

Archie liked his baths very hot. He liked to lie there for a couple of hours until the water got cold then he washed himself. Once he weighed himself before and after a bath and discovered he had lost two pounds in weight. While the bath was filling, Archie kneeled at the side of the tub and washed his hair. The family always bought its shampoo from the man who came round selling goods on behalf of the blind.

Waking up when you don't have to get up, listening to Al Green, having a good soak in a bath. Ahhhhhhhh.

Half past twelve. Archie cut his hair and shaved after his bath. He cut his hair with a cheap plastic trimmer. Usually he left bald patches. Today, though, he managed to get his hair good and short and tidy. He dried himself then cleaned the tub using a cloth which he found on the S-bend of the toilet. He opened the window to let the steam out. Before dressing he applied talc sparingly, recalling Mental's comment from the previous evening. He put his dirty clothes and towel into the, now full, wash basket.

Archie switched on the radio in the living-room to listen to James Sanderson's sportsdesk. Sanderson made football interesting. His Saturday evening phone-ins were great and Archie never missed them. The wee man that would never be caught 'sitting on the fence' and predicted cup draws with ease delivered his report.

For dinner Archie grilled the cold meat and tomato and served it with a healthy dollop of pickle. He opened a tin of fruit and served some of it with ice-cream. Four digestive biscuits and a glass of milk completed the meal.

Once finished, he washed the dishes and tidied the kitchen.

'Shit,' said Archie when he got back into the bedroom. In the middle of the floor lay the world's dirtiest pair of boots. Archie looked out the window. Brainwave! He officially declared it summertime. He would put the boots away and wear his slip-ons. Archie smiled at his genius. He put on the fourth side of *London Calling* and searched out the shoes. They were dirty but not filthy like the boots. An application of polish would clean them up. Hell, they were wipe-clean, even better.

I could do with some new clothes, Archie said to himself, while studying his wardrobe. A new jacket for sure and a couple of new shirts. Richard said it was always best to buy clothes that were slightly too big for you.

Archie considered his jackets: a blue cagoule (filthy and crumpled), a brown parka (horrible colour, thirteen years old), a dark grey dress jacket (far too small) and a grey overcoat. Archie put on the coat. It was far too big. The sleeves hid his knuckles. He had bought it eighteen months ago and only worn it three times. Nobody had said it was too big for him, in fact Mental had said it was a 'smart coat'. Archie studied himself in front of his parents' full-length mirror. Maybe it's not too big. Yes it is! Is it? The Undertones always wore clothes that were too small for them; it was Spandau Ballet that introduced baggy clothes. Archie turned up the collar and struck a few poses. Another brainwave. If I can discard my boots I can go without a jacket. I'll put on my big, black jumper instead. Before putting on the jumper Archie tried on his old grey jacket. It reeked of stale tobacco. Between '79 and '83 Archie had worn this jacket every day. He'd worn it to every gig he'd ever been to. The lapels were ruined by the application of badges. It was the classic Undertones jacket. Archie removed it and put on his big, black jumper. With the big, black jumper he felt like a gangster's violin case, his muscles concealed by its bulk.

Archie skanked along to 'Revolution Rock'. 'Doodoo doodoo doodoo doodoo doodoo doodoo doodoo./This here Revolution Rock.' He resolved to play *Get Over You* once *London Calling* was finished. The Undertones came from a culture where whistling and blowing bubble-gum stood for machismo. (Mental was the fiercest whistler.) Archie found the single in the haven't-been-played-for-a-while box.

Feargal's legendary whistle commenced *Get Over You*. The pretty boy pop stars never sang about getting dumped. Archie did a pogo: pledging allegiance to the flag, the punky, punky flag. He recalled seeing The Undertones live (three times). Feargal came on in parka and polo neck but was soon bare-chested. Archie was sure he pogoed higher than anyone else. Davie danced like a hip rhino and Mental danced part Soul Train show-off part Soweto defiance. The Blues Brothers on *Irn-bru*. They danced from the toes up, keeping all the joints in motion. Fuck shifting your weight from one foot to the other, this was dancing. Fuck steps and routines, this was dancing.

'I DON'T WANNA GET OVER YOU!' Awesome.

Archie collected his watch, keys, matches and cigarettes. He took a fiver from a coffee jar that served as a bank and crammed everything into his pockets.

The estate was quiet. A few women wearing jogging suits and pushing prams. The two signposts at the exit of the estate read Glasgow 25 miles and Edinburgh 25 miles. Some wag had added 'Caracus 8000 miles' to the Glasgow sign and 'Aids City' to the Edinburgh one.

An electric blue council van with a nuclear free zone sticker sped past Archie. There were millions of council vans. Archie wondered if Davie was in that van then chastised himself for 'playing the detective'. This was what his father did all the time. When his father drove past a house where he knew the occupant his hand would move in preparation of tooting the horn just in case somebody appeared at the window. Logie Baird Drive was bloody dangerous: he knew five people that stayed there.

Archie was increasingly wrong when 'playing the detective'. New shirt? Had it for ages. Seen you down the town? Wasn't down the town. Your sister work in Low's? Don't have a sister. Oh, fuck. He was wrong about the outcome of films, sport and relationships. He was taking life for granted but things didn't work that way.

Gordon Legge, *The Shoe* (1989)

1985: The *Big Chill* Factor

The sixties. We lived their din and now we live in their shadow. Virtually every aspect of the New Right's program, both social and political, attempts to turn back what happened to us in the sixties. And everything the baby-boom generation does now is seen in relation to what it did then, whether transcending the sixties or – the most damning phrase these days – 'stuck in the sixties'. In either case the sixties now often seem ... embarrassing. Extreme in all things, naive, passionate, sincere, shallow, experimental, rebellious, foolish, committed, fanatic, visionary, long-haired, dope-hazed, multicolored, polymorphous, perverse, apocalyptic, uprooted, uprooting, and invoking more spirits than it wanted or had guessed existed or could ever handle. The sixties were a 'movement' – and we should take 'movement' here to mean literally a *moving*, an enormous moving, where suddenly we were living in the biblical term of 'The last shall be first'; 'Seek and ye shall find'; 'What good if ye gain the world and lose your soul.' As a 'movement', it was both quintessentially middle-class and furiously proletarian. One thinks of Huey Newton and Bobby Seale as Greil Marcus described them in *Mystery Train*, 'drawing up [the Black Panthers'] statement of aims and demands while playing Dylan's "Ballad of a Thin Man" over and over.'

> *You walk into a room and you ask*
> *Is this where it is?*
> *And somebody points to you and says It's his*
> *And you say What's mine*
> *And somebody else says Where what is*
> *And you say Oh my god am I here all alone*
> *And you know somethin's happenin'*
> *But you don't know what it is*
> *Do you*
> *Mister Jones?*

To think of that, and to think of the flower children, believing every manner of esoteric claptrap that could justify whims that had been created by a childhood of commercials preaching instant gratification – and yet they were brave enough (we forget that it took bravery) to put their flowers into the barrels of M-16s that they knew (they weren't *that* naive) could, as a last resort, be fired against them, offering love where love had never been offered, never been thought of, never been considered a possibility. For a while they seemed to know what love was. A very short while, here and there. A summer in San Francisco, a spring in New York, a concert on somebody's farm where even the redneck police were impressed with their gentleness and genuine goodwill. And then they forgot what love was, or they were overwhelmed by what everyone else already knew: that love was not enough. That love invoked complexities which only maturity could handle. They were not ready to be mature, and why should they have been? They were, above all other things, young, and they were living out their youth as nobody had ever dared.

You tend to forget just how much raw energy was loose in the air then, and you don't quite believe your own memory: that sometimes, then, for weeks on end, we actually thought (1) that we were living in the Promised Land, the New Age, the Other World, (2) that it was everything we had ever imagined it could be, and (3) that everyone was going to join us in its promise as soon as they saw how good it was. There was, hovering over everything, a possibility larger than the tedious makeshift that had been called 'daily life'. Simply to be alive then, to be part of the demographic bulge called the war babies, meant that *somewhere someone was working out a vision*. Somewhere people more or less your age, people who might conceivably welcome you in their effort, whom you might even run into on the street (which often happened!), were trying to *practice* whatever fool idea, passionate thought, or cosmic vision they thought themselves capable of. You yourself could be doing nothing about such things for the moment, and maybe you never had and never would, yet through some alchemy of the time somehow you were part of their hope and they were part of yours.

There were in that era intimations of a freedom so fantastic that every definition, everywhere, felt questioned by it. And didn't Janis Joplin and Mick Jagger, Jim Morrison, James Brown, and Jimi Hendrix, enact for us live onstage just what *freedom* could mean when pushed to the limits of its ecstasies and dangers? Wasn't each performance a topographical map in space-time of the lay of the psychic land at the extremes of human possibility? If you'd invented Joplin or James Brown for yourself on acid or in the workshop of sleep, you'd have thought an amazing lesson had been given you *that* trip.

The Sioux once sent young warriors to the mountains alone, and they were not to come back until they'd dreamed their names. They were protected by the instruction they'd received in how to survive and in how to interpret dreams. We had mostly had instruction in how to be like everyone else, only more successful, and in how dreams were not important. So when, as an entire generation, we made everywhere we went a mountain on which we were trying to dream our names – we were messy, out of hand, easily distracted, out of our depth, full of shit, half-assed, and in deep trouble. But all that sound and all that fury, all that silliness and all those trips imprinted on everyone who was there and on everyone who came after the notion that humankind has far more dimensions than had been admitted for a very long time. It is a simple and utterly disruptive notion. Some people have been trying to live it out and a lot of people have been trying to forget it ever since. Because once you admit it – once you *really* admit it – nothing is quite the same. And that notion, at that time, was admitted in too many ways by too many people ever to be forgotten entirely.

As it was all coming to an end I wrote a kind of note to myself which I wouldn't read again until a long time later, a fragment of clarity on a cacophonous night: *We know now that our dreams are not going to come true. Are never going to come true. We have learned that our dreams are important not because they come true, but because they take you places you would never have otherwise gone, and teach you what you never knew was there to learn.*

Some comments among several college friends, men and women active in the sixties, who have since become very comfortable:

> *'I feel I was at my best when I was with you people.'*

> *'When I lost touch with this group I lost my idea of what I should be . . . At least we expected something of each other then. I think we needed that.'*

> *'I'd hate to think that it was all just – fashion.'*

> *'What?' another asks.*

> *'Our commitment.'*

> *'Sometimes I think I've put that time down, pretended it wasn't real, just so I can live with how I am now. You know what I mean?'*

> *'I think I've been too slow to realize that people our own age, with histories just like ours, having gone through all the same stuff, could be dishonest and back-stabbing sleazeballs.'*

The above quotes are from the most sustained, coherent scene in a film called *The Big Chill*, written and directed by one Lawrence Kasdan. It came at a point in Mr Kasdan's career when he had a lot to answer for. He had just written a script about white profiteers having a grand good time robbing the holy artifacts of ancient peoples (*Raiders of the Lost Ark*), another that cheapened the ideas of mysticism and initiation into a fantasy of easy outs for the good guys (*The Empire Strikes Back*); and he had written and directed one more in the long line of American mystery films that suggests that people capable of sexual intensity must therefore also be capable of cold-blooded murder (*Body Heat*). It's no wonder that he's feeling contrite – and *The Big Chill* is, if nothing else, a contrite film.

What is remarkable about it is that two years, now, after its release, successful young professionals who went to college during the sixties still talk about *The Big Chill*. A reference to its title serves as a reference to a conversation they might have had, or had wanted to have but probably didn't. Which indicates that *they* feel contrite. Among other things it indicates that the evasions of the film are widespread evasions, deeply rooted and worth looking at.

The film is an extension of the*Tonight Show* in more ways than one, the least of which is that it was produced by Johnny Carson's production company. This is fiction as talk show. Seven old friends gather for a weekend to mourn the suicide of an eighth, and they talk. Not the involved, sometimes desperate verbal ventures of friends who need to make crucial judgments about themselves and about each other, as Louis Malle captured in *My Dinner with André*. *The Big Chill* is talk in the Carson format, pithy sentences (those I quoted are among the longest speeches in the picture) wherein nothing serious can be said without being followed immediately, compulsively by a one-liner. Any exchange of serious dialogue is closed with a deflating joke.

We can't blame this entirely on the film. It is what passes for 'manners' in many circles, standard party style. On the other hand, these people are so trapped by this style that the suicide of a friend doesn't put a dent in it. The lack of feeling in the film isn't so remarkable. Many films, and all of Lawrence Kasdan's, lack genuine feeling. What is remarkable is that people are hungry enough for some resolution to the sixties to endure this film's lack of feeling, often more than once, *in order to feel spoken to* about this hole in their lives.

The sixties are symbolized by the dead friend, Alex. A brilliant scientific mind, and apparently the instigator and leader of their group during the days of demonstrations, music and drugs, Alex is the only one among them who never chose to go straight. This is interpreted by the others, finally, as failure. He had all that talent and never *did* anything with it. He kept searching for a self he couldn't find. *Their* failure is in not making him see the error of his ways. Alex is dead. The sixties are dead. Alex is dead because he never realized that the sixties had died. It is never suggested that not being able to 'join' this society might have involved a moral stance which Alex was neither able to forgo nor, finally, to live with. Because what, in fact, would he have joined? Who are these others who not-so-secretly resent Alex's inability to go their way?

Harold, who has made a fortune selling jogging shoes; his wife, Sarah, a doctor, the success of whose practice we can guess at by the huge estate she and her husband live on; Sam, who is the star of a glamorous private-eye TV program; Michael, who was going to 'teach black kids in Harlem' – the only mention of blacks – but who is a gossip reporter for *People* magazine; Meg, a

611

lawyer who was going to defend the poor but enjoys lucrative real-estate law much more; Karen, who married a very dull businessman – instead of one of her fascinating friends – for the security; and Nick, a Vietnam vet whose wound has made him impotent and who deals drugs and doesn't give a shit, or tells himself he doesn't. He gets to define the 'big chill' of the title, which is nothing less than that this is a cold cruel world: 'Well, wise up folks – we're all alone out there and tomorrow we're going out there again.'

It is not that none of them have been true to what were no doubt some pretty naive ideas of what to do with their lives. It's that none of them found anything, none of them give any evidence of ever considering anything, except naive idealism on the one hand and a no-holds-barred rush for money on the other. You can still consider yourself a righteous person because everyone knows idealism isn't feasible, and what's left? Money.

Here are adults stuck in a convenient either/or system that lets them completely off the hook. Never does anyone express the idea that they have to take responsibility for the world they live in. 'Responsibility' is defined as making money. Where would these people be without their one-liners? The humor of the film is not merely to entertain; it is all that makes these barren existences watchable.

Which leaves us with the film, and somebody's need to watch it. We can blame *The Big Chill* on Kasdan and that hydra-headed entity, Hollywood – it certainly doesn't have to reflect on *us*. But the fact is that large numbers of people have felt that it fulfills some need in them. Justifies them, somehow. Expresses them.

> *And you ask what's mine*
> *And somebody else says Where what is*
> *And you say Oh my god am I here all alone*

And you do. And maybe you are. And there was little in the sixties experience to prepare you for life on those terms except its music (and the music was a lot). It is a giveaway that *The Big Chill*'s soundtrack is mostly some very good but not very threatening soul songs – the Temptations, Aretha Franklin, Marvin Gaye. One Rolling Stones song, which of course is 'You Can't Always Get What You Want'. Dylan, Morrison, Joplin, Hendrix, James Brown, the Jefferson Airplane, the Buffalo Springfield, Crosby, Stills & Nash, the Band – and, for that matter, almost any other song by the Rolling Stones – are noticeable by their absence. The characters may not have reacted to it but the audience would have had to. These musicians expressed a far more complex vision of existence than *The Big Chill* is willing to concede anyone of the era ever felt. But that still leaves us with an audience that is willfully forgetting, willfully twisting, something that was very important to them once upon a time.

It's not that this is new or even that it's shocking. Most people in most generations chicken out sooner or later. The film makes its objections to such behavior only in order to rationalize those feelings by its conclusion. The film is intended to *reinforce* the idea that there is no middle ground between idealism and a flaunted materialism. It is intended to make you forget that both stances, idealism and materialism, are childish yearnings for total and instant gratification. They are each the shadow of the other, and neither has anything to do with growing up. To grow up is to be responsible, and responsible does not mean 'successful'. It means, at least in part, that one of the things you're responsible for is your world, and in one way or another you have to find a way to fulfill that responsibility. The world is an ongoing act of creation, and you are part of that act *whether you accept your role or not*. If you deny your creative role, you are creating denial. You are spreading the power of compulsive powerlessness that powers the American machine. And how you fulfill your creative role – 'Your mission, should you decide to accept it' – is *your* problem. Nobody can answer that for any of us. D. H. Lawrence once pointed out that the life-giving force can be in anything:

> *As we live, we are transmitters of life.*
> *And when we fail to transmit life, life fails*
>   *to flow through us . . .*
> *It doesn't mean handing it out to some*
>   *mean fool, or letting the dead eat you up.*
> *It means kindling the life-quality where it*
>   *was not, even if it's only in the whiteness*
>   *of a washed pocket-handkerchief.*

If there was one such pocket handkerchief in a film like *The Big Chill* . . . but there isn't. So an audience – innocent only by virtue of its refusal to consider the consequences of its life-style – finds in the film a permission to be increasingly lifeless. For these characters are dead to the world. They can make all the jogging shoes, real-estate deals and television series they want, but every day they just become more a part of the very thing they're accumulating wealth to defend themselves against.

Which is the fate of most Americans – our baby-boom generation in particular.

So *The Big Chill* pretends to be an exercise in nostalgia when it is really an

613

exercise in surrender – both for the people who made it and the people who decide they can see themselves in it. This is a terrifying thing to be brought to, but it is terror in the style of the *Tonight Show*, where the next wisecrack and the next commercial always waits, and nothing is so awful as a moment of silence.

The *Big Chill* factor, then, is the erasure of memory, the surrender of identity, and the installment, in their places, of an all-purpose, non-threatening nostalgia.

In an age when media overpowers the unwary and infiltrates memory, it becomes more important every day to pry your memory from media and to live with your own past instead of the past that is being sold collectively as an artifact.

Michael Ventura, Shadow Dancing in the USA (1985)

1986: You and the Boss

First, you must dispose of his wife. You disguise yourself as a chambermaid and get a job at a hotel where Bruce is staying with his wife on the tour. You know you are doing the right thing. Bruce will be happier with you. Does Bruce really need a wife with chipmunk cheeks, who probably talks baby talk in bed? You are educated, you have studied anthropology. You can help Bruce with his music, give him ideas about American culture. You are a real woman.

You go into Bruce's room. His wife is lying on the bed, wearing a T-shirt that says 'Number 1 Groupie' and staring straight up at the ceiling. You tell Bruce's wife that Bruce has arranged for you to give her a facial and a massage: it's a surprise. 'Isn't he sweet?' she says with a giggle.

You whip out an ice pick, hidden under your clothes, and quickly give her a lobotomy: you've watched this technique in the Frances Farmer story on TV. Bruce's wife doesn't even flinch.

After the operation, you present her with a bottle of Valium and an airplane ticket to Hollywood; the taxi's waiting outside. To your amazement, she does exactly as you tell her.

You're a bit worried about how Bruce will adjust to her absence, and your presence, but when he returns to the room, at three in the morning, he doesn't even seem to notice the difference. You're dressed in her nightie, lying in bed, looking up at the ceiling. Bruce strip down to his Jockey shorts and gets into bed with you. 'Good night, honeybunch,' he says.

In the morning he still doesn't realize there's been a change in personnel. In real life, Bruce is larger than life. Though he appears small on television and on record covers, when you stand next to him for the first time you understand that Bruce is the size of a monster. His hands are as large as your head, his body might take up an entirely billboard. This is why, you now know, he must have guitars made specially for him.

At breakfast Bruce puts away a dozen eggs, meatballs, spaghetti, and pizza. He sings while he eats, American songs about food. He has plans, projects, he discusses it all with his business manager: the Bruce Springsteen Amusement park, the Bruce Springsteen Las Vegas Casino, a chain of Bruce Springsteen bowling alleys.

Bruce decides that today you will buy a new home.

You are very excited about this prospect: you imagine something along the lines of Graceland, or an elegant Victorian mansion. 'I'm surprised at you,' Bruce says. 'We agreed not to let my success go to your head.'

He selects a small ranchhouse on a suburban street of an industrial New Jersey town. 'You go rehearse, darling,' you say. 'I'll pick out the furnishings.'

But Bruce wants to help with the decoration. He insists on ordering everything from Sears: a plaid couch, brown and white, trimmed with wood; a vinyl La-Z-Boy recliner; orange wall-to-wall carpeting. The bedroom, Bruce decides, will have mirrors on the ceiling, a water bed with purple satin sheets, white shag carpeting, and two pinball machines. Everything he has chosen, he tells you, was made in the USA.

In the afternoon, Bruce has a barbecue in the backyard. 'Everybody's got to have a hobby, babe,' he tells you. He wears a chef's hat and has his own special barbecue sauce – bottled Kraft's, which he doctors with ketchup and mustard. Though he only knows how to make one thing – dried-out chicken – everyone tells him it is the best they've ever had. You think it's a little strange that no one seems to notice his wife is gone and you are there instead; but perhaps it's just that everyone is so busy telling Bruce how talented he is that they don't have time.

Soon you have made the adjustment to life with Bruce.

The only time Bruce ever feels like making love is when the four of you – you, Bruce, and his two bodyguards – are driving in his Mustang. He likes to park at various garbage dump sites outside of Newark and, while the bodyguards wait outside, Bruce insists that you get in the back seat. He finds the atmosphere – rats, broken refrigerators, old mattresses, soup cans – very stimulating. He prefers that you don't remove your clothes; he likes you to pretend to fight him off. The sun, descending through the heavy pollution, sinks slowly, a brilliant red ball changing slowly into violet and then night.

When Bruce isn't on tour, rehearsing with his band, recording a record or writing new songs, his favorite pastime is visiting old age homes and hospitals, where he sings to senior citizens until they beg him to stop. His explanation for why he likes this is that he finds it refreshing to be with real Americans, those who do not worship him, those who do not try to touch the edges of his clothing. But even the sick old people discover, after a short time, that when Bruce plays to them they are cured.

The terminally ill recover after licking up just one drop of Bruce's sweat. Soon Bruce is in such demand at the nursing homes that he is forced to give it up. There is nothing Bruce can do that doesn't turn to gold.

One day Bruce has a surprise for you. 'I'm going to take you on a vacation, babe,' he says. 'You know, we were born to run.' You are thrilled. At least you will get that trip to Europe; you will be pampered, you will visit the couture houses and select a fabulous wardrobe, you will go to Bulgari and select a handful of jewels, you will go to Fendi and pick out a sable coat. You will be deferred to, everyone will want to be your friend in the hope of somehow getting close to Bruce.

'Oh Bruce, this is wonderful,' you say. 'Where will we go?'

'I bought a camper,' Bruce says. 'I thought we'd drive around, maybe even leave New Jersey.'

You have always hated camping, but Bruce has yet another surprise – he's stocked the camper with food. Dehydrated scrambled eggs, pancake mix, beef jerky. 'No more fast food for us,' he says.

You travel all day; Bruce has decided he wants to visit the Baseball Hall of Fame. While Bruce drives he plays tapes of his music and sings along. You tell him you're impressed with the fact he's memorized all the words. 'So what do you think?' he says. 'You like the music?'

Though your feet hurt – Bruce has bought you a pair of hiking boots, a size too small – you tell him you think the music is wonderful. Never has a greater genius walked the face of the earth.

Unfortunately, Bruce is irritated by this. The two of you have your first fight. 'You're just saying that,' Bruce says. 'You're just the same as all the rest. I thought you were different, but you're just trying to get on my good side by telling me I'm brilliant.'

'What do you want from me?' you say.

Bruce starts to cry. 'I'm not really any good,' he says.

'That's not true, Bruce,' you say. 'You mustn't feel discouraged. Your fans love you. You cured a small boy of cancer just because he saw you on TV. You're up there with the greats: the Beatles, Christ, Gandhi, Lee Iacocca. You've totally restored New Jersey to its former glory: once again it's a proud state.'

'It's not enough,' Bruce says. 'I was happier in the old days, when I was just Bruce, playing in my garage.'

You're beginning to find that you're unhappy in your life with Bruce. Since Bruce spends so much time rehearsing, there is little for you to do but shop. Armed with credit cards and six bodyguards (to protect you from Bruce's angry women fans), you search the stores for some gift for Bruce that might please him. You buy foam coolers to hold beer, Smurf dolls, candy-flavored underwear, a television set he can wear on his wrist, a pure-bred Arabian colt. You hire three women to wrestle on his bed covered in mud.

Bruce thanks you politely but tells you, 'There's only one thing I'm interested in.'

'Me?' you say.

Bruce looks startled. 'My music,' he says.

To your surprise you learn you are pregnant, though you can't figure out how this could have happened. You think about what to name the baby. 'How about Benjamin Springsteen?' you say.

'Too Jewish immigrant,' Bruce says. 'This kid is going to be an American, not some leftist from Paterson.'

'How about Sunny Von?' you say.

'Sunny Von Springsteen?' Bruce says. 'I don't get it. No, there's only one name for a kid of mine.'

'What?' you say, trying to consider the possibilities. Bruce is sitting on the couch, stroking his guitar. The three phones are ringing nonstop, the press is banging on the door. You haven't been out of the house in three days. The floor is littered with boxes from Roy Rogers, cartons of White Castle burgers, empty cans of Coke. You wonder how you're going to fill up the rest of the day; you've already filed your nails, studied the Sears, Roebuck catalog, made a long-distance call to your mother.

At last Bruce speaks. 'I'm going to call the kid Elvis,' he says.

'What if it's a girl?' you say.

'Elvis,' Bruce says. 'Elvis, either way.'

You fly to Hollywood to try to find his real wife. Finally you track her down. She's working as a tour guide at the wax museum. 'Admission to the museum is five dollars,' she says at the door. 'The museum will be closing in fifteen minutes.'

'Don't you remember me?' you say. 'I'm the person who gave you a lobotomy, who shipped you off to Hollywood.'

'If you say so,' Bruce's wife says. 'Thank you.'

'I made a mistake,' you say. 'I did wrong, I have your ticket here; you'll go back to Bruce.'

His wife is willing, though she claims not to know what you're talking about. 'But what about my job here?' she says. 'I can't just leave.'

You tell her you'll take over for her. Quickly you rush her to the airport, push her onto the plane. You tell her to look after Bruce. 'He can't live without you, you know,' you say.

You wait to make sure her plane takes off on time. A sense of relief comes over you. You have nowhere to go, nothing to do; you decide to return to the wax museum and make sure it's properly locked up for the night.

You have the keys to the door; the place is empty, the lights are off. Now you wander through the main hall. Here are Michael Jackson, Jack the Ripper, President Reagan, Sylvester Stallone, Muhammad Ali, Adolf Hitler. You are alone with all these men, waxy-faced, unmoving, each one a superstar.

Something violent starts to kick, then turns, in your stomach.

Tama Janowitz, *Slaves of New York* (1986)

1986: There's a Riot Going on

The morgue where they delivered young Gilbert Cole's body is located in downtown LA in the same hospital where they film the opening shot of *General Hospital*. The guy who runs the night shift was bored, as anybody who works midnights in the morgue would be, so when my photographer friend Gary and I called, he invited us to come on over, even though he hinted more than once that it was slightly against the rules.

The first room we entered looked like the office of a plumbing supply house. An old oak desk was flush against the wall, yellow walls, which I found strange, since hospitals are always white. I guess they need to cheer people up in here. Lots of booklets and papers everywhere. Most of these reported on the dead that had arrived that day. Gilbert Cole's papers had already been moved to the coroner's office; the morgue only gets these bodies when they die in the hospital, which is an indication of the mistake the paramedics made. When Gilbert Cole collapsed at the LA Street Scene festival on Sunday, September 28, 1986, it was originally believed that he had passed out from a drug overdose. He was brought to this hospital, pronounced dead, and delivered to the morgue.

Cole was 25, a Chicano, and very clean-cut. By the time the morgue gets a body, it's been stripped down, but Gilbert Cole was still wearing his jewelry. Gold neck and wrist chains. 'Real nice stuff,' said the morgue guy. They knew he was from a decent family because his brother, an attorney, had shown up asking questions.

Gilbert Cole was shot in the back at the LA Street Scene on Sunday night. The cops don't know who shot him or why. They only know that punk rockers started a riot the day before. The LA mayor blames the entire weekend's episodes on one rock band – the Ramones, whose nonappearance had triggered a melee – and a subculture of kids. Gilbert Cole wasn't a punk rocker. He was not hit with a beer bottle, he was shot with a gun. It wasn't on Saturday, when the kids were tearing up the stage because their favorite band had failed to show. Cole was shot on Sunday, while watching some Puerto Ricans play pop music. It doesn't really matter whose fault it was. Gilbert Cole was lying naked on a slab in the morgue, still wearing his gold chains and bracelets and the LA County Coroner's contribution to his outfit – a toe tag. I bet he didn't really care.

Nobody's sure who's to blame. The cops blame the kids and the bands. The kids blame the bands, the lyrics, and the cops. The promoters blame everybody. Everybody blames the press, which, you can bet, is having a good time with all this. Meanwhile, the clubs keep closing, which ought to make anyone who isn't a kid, a band, a cop, or a promoter in LA happy. After all, when you live next door to a rock club and kids keep pissing on your lawn, your house is no longer worth one million dollars.

Everybody's sure of the reasons, however:

'These kids think that being in gangs is cool.' – Detective Griffin, LAPD

'They riot at concerts when they don't like a particular band, like Run-DMC.' – Chris, a high school student

'Some bands, like Black Flag, encourage riots at their shows. These guys have degrees in psychology. They know what they're doing to publicize themselves.' – an LA promoter

'Too many rock bands, too many punk groups at these events, attract an undesirable element.' – Tom Houston, LA Deputy Mayor

'These are not LA kids. These kids come from other places, like they did in the '60s, because the drugs are more available, and the lure of Hollywood is strong.' – Commander Booth, personal assistant to LA police commissioner Darryl Gates

'They have no museums to go to.' – Gary, our photographer

The episodes are violent and memorable. Riots at the LA Palladium (cops controlled the crowds with firehoses), at Black Flag concerts, at the MTV music awards (the cops used tear gas that time), gang wars between punk rock bands, and the highly publicized recent riot at a Run-DMC concert.

The old Elks Lodge was the scene of the first riot: two adjacent ballrooms, one hosting a wedding reception, and the other a concert featuring the GoGos, DOA, Plung, and other punk bands. There were at least 600 enthusiastic punk rock fans to greet the wedding guests as they filed out of the second ballroom. Words were exchanged. Someone threw a bottle.

Eyewitnesses still call it a police riot, though. Because things did not get out of hand until the cops arrived. 'The next thing I knew,' recalls a punk rocker, 'the cops were rushing upstairs, yelling to kids to get out of the way. They were clubbing and hitting everyone. Lots of kids got hurt.' About 100, to be exact.

Within a year, Elks Lodge was closed. Every club in Orange County's been closed. The Starwood in West Hollywood was closed in 1982. Someone was stabbed in the Rock Corp in the Valley. It also was closed. The Whiskey was shut down for a while and turned into a bank. Punk rock clubs out here have a short lifespan. And the violence that contributed to these closings has spilled over into the local high schools, where administrators recently requested that metal detectors be installed in the buildings.

The cops remember their clashes with kids with equal clarity, citing the same incidents to prove their points. My phone call to LAPD Information was interesting, to say the least. 'Which riot do you want to know about?' asked the woman who answered. 'The Palladium, last week on the beach? . . . the high schools? . . . Run-DMC?'

'Any old riot will do,' I said.

Detective Griffin from LAPD was clear in his recollections. 'We've got squads to deal with the heavy metal kids, the devil worshippers like Motley Crüe, and the punk rockers.' I was learning that the average cop in LA knows as much about music as the average kid.

Obviously, they believe they have to. 'Kids here are more militant than in New York,' said Griffin. 'They think it's cool to belong to gangs.'

They do. Suicidal Tendencies is a punk rock band: two Mexicans, one

620

black guy, and a white kid who grew up in the slums of Venice Beach, California. The band's been around for four years, its popularity expanding recently beyond the Santa Monica and West Hollywood neighborhoods where they grew up. They've attracted a 'gang' of almost 1000 rampant fans, the Suicidals. These kids come from the tough neighborhoods, the real inner-city gang life few LA kids ever know. Along with their popularity, the stories about Suicidal Tendencies and the gang have grown to almost mythic proportions. One New York promoter refused to put me in touch with them. 'Why give those assholes any publicity because they cause so much trouble out there?'

A New York musician remembers his first confrontation with the Suicidals in LA. He was 16 and small for his age. They beat him up anyway, for no reason other than he was in a 'rival band' that did not play punk rock. The next time he ran into them he was older – 18 – had muscles, better fighting skills, and the advantage of being in New York, his home turf. As his friends watched, the kid grabbed the leader of the gang, dragged him downstairs to the CBGB's bathroom (a horrible experience in itself), and flushed his head down the toilet.

Now, when his band plays LA, he said, they wait with death threats outside the club. He's not scared, not really, but he didn't want his name used because he's not stupid, either.

Ron Peterson, manager and promoter of Suicidal Tendencies, did not deny the stories around the band but embellished them and told me a few of his own. He claimed that the entire downtown LA music scene is controlled by the Suicidal Tendencies gang.

'It's part of their lifestyles,' Peterson explained. 'They're a bunch of street fighting guys. Last week at a show, some kids came up out of nowhere and punched Louie, the bass player, right on the side of his head. Louie chased one down and the guy tried to get off the stage and run away. But Louie was like the long arm of the law. He just grabbed the guy back from the audience and started socking him. I tried to break it up, but when Louie's hitting someone, it's for a reason.'

'So Suicidal Tendencies doesn't instigate the fights,' I asked.

'Well,' he laughs, 'in some instances . . .'

'Are the followers rougher than the band members?'

'Maybe as a group, but Suicidal Tendencies is a bunch of over-200-pound, street fighting, badass big boys. They're not your typical run-of-the-mill rock stars in spandex.'

But 'these guys have to be real careful when going to Long Beach [the

621

location of Fenders, a rock club that is the site of constant episodes of violence], because the skinheads [fans of hardcore music] dominate that area.'

But in a second interview, Suicidal Tendencies band leader Mike Muir refuted their initial stories, said that there was *no* gang activity around the band, and insisted the entire thing was a publicity ploy. 'We thought [the stories about being a violent gang] sounded good, but it isn't true.' One reason may be that kids are too afraid to attend the shows.

'The stories about us are so terrible that only our diehard fans will attend,' says Muir. 'Anyone who doesn't love us stays home, or if they do show, they see all our fans, dressed like us (in the uniform that resembles the Chicano Street gangs of Venice Beach) and they assume we're a gang. All these upper-middle-class punk rockers, if they ever faced a real gang, they'd run for their lives.'

Muir admits that there was trouble in the past; he was arrested several times, mostly for drinking or hanging out, but he says that now he's learned. He hasn't had any problems with the cops in years because he 'knows they're waiting. I know how they are.'

'How they are' is poised for trouble with these kids.

Music is at the center of this violence, and it is through music that the gangs distinguished themselves. The 'poseur' gang dominates Hollywood – the trash-can shops along Melrose Avenue and the area around Fairfax High School. Hardcore skinhead gangs control Long Beach. Suicidals reportedly control Venice, Santa Monica, and downtown LA.

If the California gang wars are a figment of the press's and the LAPD's imagination, it certainly has roots in some horrible realities. The violence and the riots are real. Nobody imagines well enough to furnish film clips of such fantasies on the six o'clock news. The incident that kicked off the schools' request for metal detectors was a murder. At Fairfax High School, a visiting graduate was shot by another student. Ron Peterson suspects that it was the work of the 'poseur' gang.

LA is a funny city. It's not sheltered, it's sort of almost there, and the kids are not exactly naive. They know what hip is, and sometimes it must just seem only slightly beyond their reach. Many kids still have the prejudices they acquired from their parents, prejudices unavoidable when you are rich and live in segregated areas. If Suicidal Tendencies has any defense at all, any way of explaining the anarchy they are accused of creating, it is that initially *they* were the victims.

'We had a lot of trouble when we started,' Mike explained, and you begin to understand what he's about. 'The upper-middle-class white punk rockers *hated* us. They came around the band to start trouble, because we were poor, came from the worst neighborhoods, and wore the clothes of the Chicano and Mexican street gangs. We stood for the minorities.'

So they fought back. 'Black eyes go away,' he said reflectively. 'But if you buckle down to someone who's picking on you, the mental scars stay with you a long time.'

This attitude also expresses the average LA kid's feelings toward the average LA cop. It also explains why kids come to LA to find trouble, much in the way they went to Berkeley and other California campuses to riot in the late '60s. It's not, as Commander Booth says, that they 'come here because the lure of Hollywood is strong'. Punk rockers have no fantasies of being the next Greta Garbo. But face it, if you're looking for a fight, where the hell would you go? Would you go to a city where a police officer has to account for his every dirty deed? Or would you go to LA where all you need to do to fight with a cop is spit where he walks?

The Ramones don't really want to think about riots. They've often got troubles of their own. Twelve years of being the greatest rock 'n' roll band in the world doesn't leave you much free time. Which is why when Milt Petty, who promotes bands for the LA Street Scene, asked the Ramones to play with four gigs left in five days on their LA tour, the band said a polite but firm 'No.'

After that, Seymour Stein, president of Sire Records (the Ramones' record company), said no. Warner Bros., their distributor, said no. Gary Kurfirst, band manager, also said no. Just to make things official, Monte Melnick, tour manager for the Ramones, said no. Nobody said 'maybe'.

The Street Scene people, not understanding the meaning of the word 'no', advertised that the Ramones were going to play. Maybe it was an error (as the Street Scene people later claimed), or perhaps it was designed to draw attention to the festival. But why ask the Ramones anyway? Everybody's always yelling that the punk rock bands bring all the trouble. Social Distortion was not invited. Surely the promoters didn't think that in an area hot with trouble, the Ramones – the band that invented punk – would be hosting a Tupperware party.

According to Patrick Bacchi, promoter of the Club Metro, who witnessed the Street Scene riot on Saturday, when the kids learned that their favorite band had failed to show, they jumped up onstage and started throwing things around. 'They were angry. There were only about a hundred kids, and all they were doing, really, was throwing bottles and tearing things up. Their violence was not directed at each other, or others in the audience.'

Nevertheless, the cops, who had been circling the action all day, watching bored from overpasses and atop horses, moved in. Over the next two days there were two shootings (one resulting in Gilbert Cole's death), several stabbings, and about 80 injuries (to cops, horses, and kids).

Footage of the riot ran hourly on the news Monday evening and all day Tuesday, showing kids being kicked by cops, kids being beaten by clubs, kids being pushed and thrown. You did not see kids beating up cops and horses. You heard the reprimand of the mayor, the deputy mayor, and various patrolmen. 'Punk rockers cause all the trouble out here', was the theme of the day. It was widely agreed that the Ramones' failure to show resulted in both days' worth of trouble. But when Warner's threatened to sue on behalf of the band over accusations that the group had reneged on a promise to appear, the Ramones got a retraction the following day. It was not on page one. It was sort of an apology: the Street Scene officials said they had made 'a clerical error'.

But the press, the cops, and the mayor's office did not apologize for blaming an entire weekend's worth of trouble on the Ramones. They said nothing further on the matter.

The vision of cops beating kids stayed with me. I asked around and discovered it was the order of the day. Everyone told the same story. When a club owner calls the cops, when a neighbor calls them, they arrive. They arrive in helicopters, helmeted, on foot. The helicopters hover and a voice calls out to the crowd, 'Disperse.'

'We wanted to disperse,' said Brendan Mullen, owner of the Club Lingerie, a dinosaur around here because it's managed to stay open through years of trouble. Brendan is talking about the recent Cramps riot at the LA Palladium, the one where cops used firehoses on the exiting crowd. 'Yeah, we wanted to disperse, but in a crowd that large, where the hell do you go?'

Looking fearfully to the day when this music would be a dinosaur, with no clubs left to showcase bands, Brendan said, 'You're not going to drag all this up again in the press, are you? The more it's written about, the more it keeps happening.'

Trouble is that it's so commonplace in California that no one writes about it, and it goes on anyway.

'You don't really know what's going on when you're playing,' says Peterson. 'You see bottles being thrown around, but that happens everywhere. They warn you to be real careful when you're playing, though. When you walk outside, you realize why.'

Outside, the cops wait on horses and on foot in line formation, and when they advance into the crowd, they move in lines. Overhead, you hear the horrible racket of the helicopters, which adds to the confusion of the departing crowds. Sometimes, like at the Ramones concert at the Palladium two years ago, the kids outside, many who were not fans but just waiting, were hyped-up and rowdy, shouting and breaking windows of nearby stores. They knew what the cops were waiting for, and were more than happy to oblige.

'I've seen cops beating the shit out of these kids,' says one LA musician. (He'd rather not have the band mentioned, because reminding promoters that there's trouble at your shows makes it hard for a band to get bookings.) 'They're lying on the ground, these kids, and cops are beating and kicking them. Everywhere you see kids hurt and bleeding. I've even seen them beating up girls!

'One kid was sitting on the curb holding his leg. It was bleeding real bad. The cop kept hitting him and yelling, "Get up." The kid couldn't get up. He was crying in pain, his leg was busted up so bad. He couldn't even move.'

Police 'procedure' in these matters appears to be that when a crowd does not move, you do anything to move them. When the kids don't move, the cops can start hitting. When I asked Commander Booth at what point the LAPD considers a situation dangerous enough to intervene, he replied, 'When the first bottle is thrown.'

When the first bottle is thrown. If New York City police arrived on the scene when the first bottle, the second, or the *fifth* bottle was thrown, CBGB's and the Ritz would be police precincts by now.

So what the hell is going on in California? Nasty habits. Everyone's got them. The situation has gotten so out of control that all involved are acting reflexively. The cops mobilized against the kids. Now, the average LA cop on the street isn't exactly Archie Bunker. He's more like Archie Bunker's son who joined the army. According to Commander Booth, he's in his late 20s, well paid ('higher than New York'), and from a middle-class family. A lot of them look like young John Waynes. Brendan Mullen added that 'They can't handle anything that is integrated.'

They don't understand the poor, the blacks, the kids, and the crowds, or anything that looks different than they do. Because they are young, they panic easily. But more important, because they are middle class, they respond to the middle-class cry to clean up the neighborhoods, even though they are

625

making it clean of kids (as if that were *really* possible). And, as one kid put it, 'They are beating up *their* children.'

If you look at it from the LAPD's point of view, they have a lot of money invested in 'kid control'. Detective Griffin made that clear when he explained the different squads for different musical interest groups. (Commander Booth denied this emphatically.) There's no way to justify all that time and money spent if you don't call even minor incidents 'riots' and blame entirely unrelated incidents, like Gilbert Cole's shooting, on punk rockers.

But the punk rockers at the Street Scene on Sunday appeared calm enough. Most stood blocks away from the crowd on corners and complained that the absence of punk bands at the festival was 'sort of sad'.

It was. The whole thing is pretty damn sad. Punk bands forming gangs to retaliate is sadder still. But I guess if you're a kid and seven of your friends stand by watching the eighth getting clubbed and kicked around for throwing a bottle on the floor, you're going to get sore. You're going to get your friends together and mobilize in return. If you don't know any better, because it's all you've seen, it looks like the cops have declared war. Violence breeds violence. Intelligent people have known it for years. Nasty habits.

> 'After the show we went around back. We were in the parking lot. First we heard the cops, then we saw them, ten in a row, and they were just advancing. Soon they were on the scene. There were helicopters overhead. I knew something was gonna happen. There was something in the air. These cops have files on bands like Black Flag. They know when they should show up. They're ready.
>
> 'But it was the mellowest punk crowd I've even seen, I saw the cops and started saying, "This is not a fascist state, damn it. This is America!" And the cops were like the Raiders' defensive line. They just charged.
>
> 'Everybody's yelling "run!" I didn't want to. So I turned around and SMACK, a billy club to the side of my head. So then I figured I'd better run, 'cause cops were just everywhere. They started clubbing me all over the place. I got up off the ground and this rookie comes after me. I ran and he chased me. Some punk rocker kept yelling, "Come on, bro', you're gonna get killed."'
> – Simon Smallwood's account of LA Palladium riot

'You know we don't have trouble *everywhere*,' says Commander Booth. 'We never have incidents at the Coliseum. The promoters cooperate with the police. They hire great security guards. They put a clause on the back of each ticket, stating the right to stop and search each kid who comes to a show.'

As for the security forces most LA clubs hire, these guys have to wake up so they can die. But who can blame promoters? Why spend the money for elaborate security when the cops are so willing to arrive at the drop of a bottle?

At the punk rock club Fenders, the guards didn't even know the layout of the club. They kept sending me to the bathroom or the kitchen when I was trying to get to the main concert room. It's interesting since Fenders is the constant scene of trouble.

The Fenders promoter, Gary Tovar, is a bundle of nerves. He needs Valium. You can't blame him, either. Backstage after a recent concert he repeatedly had to interrupt his post-concert chatting with the band to run to the back door and yell, 'Get security out here.'

The last time it paid off. Some kid lay on the floor, his head busted open.

'We'll have to send you to the hospital. You can't go home like that,' Gary tried to explain to the kid. Gary was calmer now. The worst part was over. The best way to end this trouble, it seems, is when the trouble brings an end to itself.

The kid said no. The guards stood back. The kid just stood up, held his blond, bloodied head in his hand, rested his arm on his buddies, and stumbled out the door.

Annette Stark, *Spin*, December 1986

1987: Poor Boy, Rich Boy George

From the moment the Culture Club star had begun to rise, George was an incessant presence at the offices of his record-label, Virgin, gee-ing up record 'pluggers', arranging video sessions and superintending the fan-mail. Gone was the frenetic nightclubbing; in its place, chastening pronouncements on the decadence of a previous generation of rock stars, and an anti-drug regimen which promised immediate dismissal for anyone in the group who might indulge.

It was a professionalism that withstood even the tempestuousness of his relationship with Moss. On tour, the pair would squabble incessantly in a fashion that would drive fellow travellers to distraction. 'God knows what they got from each other,' says one who toured with them. 'They were like children.'

627

'The whole Culture Club thing of going from nothing to mass popularity was George's dream,' says another associate of the time. 'He always wanted to be recognised as a songwriter, but he loved being a media celebrity, and from day one the press was always the most important thing. George was completely hungry for fame, and once it arrived he became addicted to it.'

As the Culture Club phenomenon grew, George took to ringing up the press office from all over the world, demanding that his press-clippings be read over to him. It was a time-consuming task, for the lessons learned in the early days – his innate understanding of the media's appetite for 'news' – had stood him in good stead. 'I knew that if I walked into the ladies' toilet that it would make the *Sun* – so I did it.'

The sheer volume of press first astonished then alarmed his publicity handlers at Virgin. George wilfully made himself as available as possible, to the point of telephoning journalists to dispense titbits. Matters came to a head in Japan, on the group's first world tour in 1983, when Ronnie Gurr, Virgin's press officer, attempted to keep the accompanying press corps at bay and was berated by Tony Gordon for being 'rude to Fleet Street'. Gurr resigned. George, he now says, was blind to a fundamental truth of celebrity; that it depends on the maintenance of mystique.

George began to discover that fame is an entity dangerously susceptible to the laws of gravity. For a group so dependent on the oxygen of publicity the growing indifference of newspapers to his activities was a serious danger. There were signs, too, that the group was becoming complacent. The third album, *Waking Up the House on Fire*, was written and recorded in haste after nine months' solid touring. The lack of strong songs told and the 'Medal Song', released for Christmas 1984, became the first Culture Club single since 'Do You Really Want to Hurt Me?' two years before not to reach the top 20. The seemingly indefatigable ardour of the fans was beginning to wear thin.

George's personal life was also beginning to fall apart. The relationship with Moss had finally exploded into anger, recrimination and then bitter silence over Moss's relationship with a girl. George, according to friends, was 'devastated'. Without Moss's moderating influence, the old hedonistic George began to re-emerge.

In Paris, George, now world famous, was the centre of attention among models, photographers and hangers-on, all of them sharing cocaine. At a nightclub, a photographer palmed him a packet of heroin, which he snorted for the first time. He was violently sick, but not discouraged. Within a month he was taking up to a gramme a week. Soon it would be more.

Having time on his hands did not help. 'I began to realise that all the time I was successful, I had never thought about *why* I was being successful, or what it meant. And I suddenly realised that it wasn't what I wanted; that it wasn't enough, if you like.' The momentum of Culture Club was running down. The row between George and Jon Moss had affected everybody, and the prospect of continued touring was more than anyone could face. Two years at the top had, anyway, brought the group an embarrassment of riches. Their tax advisers counselled exile. The manager Tony Gordon, and Roy Hay, the guitarist, moved to Marbella; bass-player Mikey to Paris. In a bid to repair their relationship, George pleaded with Jon to go with him to New York. Moss refused, and George set off alone.

The seeds of dissolution sown over the last few months in London and Paris found fertile ground in New York. His old friend Marilyn was along for the ride, and life became an endless round of nightclubs and parties, with a growing circle of new acquaintances: 'trashy coke dealers,' George now remembers, 'disgusting people, and dregs'. John Maybury, his old friend from Warren Street, turned up in New York and was shocked at George's condition, and the way he had become a caricature of everything he had once professed to despise.

'Everything about him had become scary. He was overweight, over-made-up, grotesque. But on the club scene there was this sycophantic thing that because he was Boy George whatever he did was OK.'

For George the pretence of being 'a bright young thing, going out to clubs', was becoming inescapable. 'I began to realise,' he says, 'that I was killing myself.' A doctor confirmed his diagnosis. 'He said I could catch Aids from the way I was behaving. That frightened me. I stopped, left New York and went home. And carried on doing heroin.'

The London club world where George had disported himself three years before had changed; the extremities of style which he had helped to pioneer had been eclipsed by even further excesses of self-invention. At the once-weekly Taboo Club, held in a tawdry Leicester Square disco called Circus Maximus, Leigh Bowery, a fashion designer and exhibitionist, held court over a menagerie of exotica drawn from the fashion and art-student worlds.

Yet the old mood of carefree exhilaration had gone. While the good times of three years before had run on natural energy, now they ran on drugs: heroin, barbiturates and the 'designer' drug Ecstasy. 'The whole scene,' Maybury remembers, 'was haywire and mad. Everything was available, and everybody was taking it. Trojan and I would sit at home saying someone is going to die. It never occurred to us that it would be one of us.'

George, too, was mindful of the dangers. 'Every time I took heroin I would think, is this it? Am I going to die? I was always afraid.' He had begun reading Freud, 'wondering whether I was behaving like this because I'd had an unhappy childhood; or was I sexually insecure? Then I realised it was both.'

Throughout 1985, Culture Club had continued to perform to ecstatic response in America and Japan. But George's erratic behaviour was having a progressively debilitating effect on the group's activities. There was growing anxiety at Virgin Records. George and Virgin's chairman Richard Branson had met only briefly before, but in April 1986 Branson wrote to his artist, who was staying with Marilyn in Jamaica. It was becoming plain to everyone, Branson asserted, that George had a problem which he was not willing to acknowledge – 'So clear that one newspaper is now offering £50,000 to anyone who can prove it. You believe you have this problem under control, but its patently not true.' George, he said, should 'acknowledge the problem, and let us help you . . . before it's too late'.

Branson offered to put George in touch with Meg Paterson, a doctor whose 'black box' treatment had cured Eric Clapton of heroin addiction. It would be three months before George would accept Branson's offer. But the warning about Fleet Street was real enough. In its role as arbiter of private morality, the press's interest was no longer in praising George, but in burying him.

The first blow was struck on June 10, 1986, when the *Daily Mirror* ran a story alleging that George had taken cocaine. The source was a rock photographer named David Levine, who was alleged to have received a fee of £15,000 for his story. In the pop music world word continued to circulate that richer pickings were still to be had. What nobody could have anticipated was that the real story would be had for nothing.

The first intimation that Gerry O'Dowd had of his son's drug problem came in October 1985, in Montreux, where Culture Club was completing recording of its fourth album, *From Luxury to Heartache*. Relaxing in George's rented villa on the shores of Lake Geneva, Gerry O'Dowd was alarmed to note that, for the first time, people connected with the group were taking drugs. George poured balm on his fears; the most he had had was 'the odd smoke' of cannabis.

But at a party on Boxing Day 1985 at George's Hampstead mansion, his worst fears were confirmed. 'I realised then there were people around George who were not his friends. They were a cancer.

'The one thing that was very hurtful was that George shut us out,' says O'Dowd. 'We became his enemies.'

For six months, the situation deteriorated. Gerry O'Dowd began a remarkable vigil, monitoring the comings and goings at George's home, accumulating a dossier on all his son's drugs contacts. On one occasion he trailed a 'courier' carrying £800 of George's money to buy drugs to a house in North London. He telephoned the police to tip them off, but nothing happened.

Convinced now that his son would die unless something was done, Gerry O'Dowd went to George's St John's Wood mews house for a final confrontation. George had locked himself in the bathroom and refused to come out, answering his father's pleas with a torrent of abuse. 'Do you want to die?' Gerry O'Dowd shouted. 'I'll see if you want to die.' O'Dowd told his son he would burn the house down. 'I lit some paper, put it out and held the smoke to the door. George opened the door and came running down the stairs. I said, "See George, you don't want to die."'

That evening, sitting with his youngest son David, Gerry O'Dowd broke down and said he could take no more. 'Don't worry, Dad,' said David. 'I'll do something.' The next day Nick Ferrari, a showbusiness reporter on the *Sun*, received a telephone call from David O'Dowd offering something which Ferrari remembers would 'absolutely stagger' him: the 'full story' of George's heroin habit. And it would cost the *Sun* nothing. The story which appeared on the front page two days later, 'Junkie George has eight weeks to live', was emblazoned in letters two inches high. George, it claimed, was smoking up to nine grammes of heroin a day, at a cost of £800 – a quantity which doctors had said would almost certainly kill him.

O'Dowd would later explain that he had broken the story in a desperate bid to jolt George to his senses. 'I'd run out of all ideas; the family had run out of ideas; there was nothing more we could do.' While the essence of what the *Sun* printed was true, it was embroidered by what O'Dowd would subsequently claim was a heavy veil of fiction.

'I said my brother was a drug addict. The rest, how long he had to live and all that, is a complete load of crap. All I said to them was that it might be soon that he drops down dead. That was why I did it.'

Whatever the truth, the prospects of reclaiming it were lost in an avalanche of sensationalism. It was a story that had everything: fame, drugs, weird sex; squandered wealth; grace bestowed and scorned. 'George,' says John Maybury, 'had always been a subversive – a drag queen welcomed into the bosom of England. When he was successful he was untouchable. But when it

631

was discovered he was a junkie it was a chance for Fleet Street to take revenge.'

For George, events now began to move at a bewildering pace. On the day on which the *Sun* story was published, he appeared on the *News at Ten* in an attempt to deny it. At his mews house reporters camped on the doorstep and eavesdropped at the windows. For four days, George dodged and ducked to no avail. On the fifth day he vanished.

On Saturday morning, Richard Branson received a telephone call from George's boyfriend, Michael, asking whether Branson could arrange a meeting with Meg Paterson. That same night, under a blanket of secrecy, Branson drove George, Michael and Paterson to his house in Oxfordshire. 'The idea was that nobody would know where he was,' says Branson.

In the press, the hue and cry for George had also become a clamour for retribution, with Monday's *Daily Mirror* leading the call for 'action' from the police. In the early hours of the following day a squad of detectives, engaged in Operation Culture, raided George's St John's Wood house, and a flat in nearby Westbourne Terrace. No illegal substances were found at George's house, but a number of people, including his brother Kevin and Marilyn, were charged.

Following the raids, the police announced that they were now looking for George himself. Branson immediately told them 'in confidence' that George was under medical supervision. 'I said I would appreciate it if the police did not tell anybody where he was. Since he had done nothing illegal, there was no reason why they should be involved.'

The police initially agreed to Branson's request, but within four days they were informing him that they had changed their minds, and that a warrant was out for George's arrest. By that time George had been moved to the house of Roy Hay, the Culture Club guitarist, in Billericay, Essex. George was nearing the end of the prescribed length of Meg Paterson's 'black box' treatment when police arrested him at Hay's home. Shaking with the tremors of withdrawal, he was taken to Harrow Road police station. 'I gave one statement where I lied, said nothing. They were asking me all those questions about people I knew – did I know that Marilyn took cocaine? I said I couldn't care less whether he shags chandeliers, mate. Then I thought, they're never going to let me out of here. I became terrified and just kept talking.'

It was largely on the basis of his confession that George was charged with possession of heroin. Two weeks later, on the advice of his lawyers, George pleaded guilty to the charge at Marylebone Magistrates Court and was fined £250.

Richard Branson, among others, was perturbed at the conduct of the police. 'You had someone who had gone, voluntarily, for treatment. If every addict thought the police were going to arrest them after they'd gone for care, none of them would. And I think the press were very much responsible. George was being penalised for who he was.'

The chaotic circumstances of his treatment, the interruption by his arrest and continued harassment had all exacted their toll. George was, by his own definition, 'a nervous wreck'.

His pronouncements that the worst was behind him and that he would now embark on a 'crusade' against drugs were well intentioned, but essentially illusory. The next four months would see him wavering between fighting his dependence and succumbing to it. With the failure of Paterson's treatment, George began to take prescribed valium, and then fell back on heroin. Depressed, fearful, 'convinced I was going to die', he began to take methadone – a legally prescribed heroin substitute.

What was clear was that he now needed to set about repairing the damage to his career. He would make a solo album. To help, he called on the services of Michael Rudetsky, a musician and arranger he had befriended in New York.

Rudetsky arrived in Britain on August 4, 1986, carrying with him a card confirming that he had recently completed a drugs detoxification course in America. Customs officials at Gatwick strip-searched him but found no drugs.

The next day, Rudetsky arrived at the offices of Virgin for a meeting with George and the Virgin A&R (artists and repertoire) department. George was 'groggy' from his prescribed drugs, but lucid in discussing ideas for songs. Only Rudetsky, leaving the room to throw up, cast a shadow over the afternoon.

His behaviour the following day was to give more cause for concern. In rehearsals at a studio in Brixton he began drinking heavily and passed out. George poured a carton of orange juice over him to revive him. They returned to George's Hampstead house. At midnight, George left to go to his other home in St John's Wood, leaving Rudetsky with brother Kevin. Later Kevin, too, left. He returned at 4.45am, drunk, to find Rudetsky's corpse in the lounge.

The inquest recorded death by misadventure, after his body had been found to contain a fatal level of morphine. No explanation was given about where he had acquired it. Speculation that he had smuggled cocaine into

Britain in a swallowed condom, which had burst in his stomach, was never confirmed.

Rudetsky's death plunged George into a deeper trough of depression, but he was still determined to work.

At the end of August, George, his boyfriend Michael and the producer Stewart Levine flew out to Montserrat to begin recording. Within a fortnight there were eight songs in the can. 'George was feeding off the situation,' says Ronnie Gurr. 'He felt he couldn't let anybody down.' Back in London, however, to complete recording, the diligence began to evaporate. George had begun to supplement his prescribed drugs with other illegal drugs, and his behaviour was again becoming erratic. Stewart Levine noted that the difference between George in Montserrat and George in London was like 'Jekyll and Hyde'. On one occasion in the studio, Levine confronted George over drugs, challenging him not to disappear to the toilets to take them, but to do it in front of him. After a stern talking to, Levine was able to report that George was 'in fine shape'.

But the respite, such as it was, was only temporary. It would take another three months, and the death of Mark Golding, to persuade Boy George that his own life was worth saving.

At Christmas 1986, Dinah O'Dowd arrived at George's Hampstead mansion to find a newspaper photographer loitering outside the gate. 'What do you want?' she demanded. He replied that he was 'waiting for George to die'.

The power of Fleet Street as executioner, as well as king-maker, was to prove crucial in the story of Boy George. Yet, incredibly, throughout the period of his travails with drugs, George continued to maintain a pact with the press, which, in itself, seemed a measure of his dependence on publicity as a tool to vindicate as well as destroy him.

Throughout the latter part of 1986, he gave a series of interviews which attempted to belie the truth of the drugs problem he continued to suffer. This reached its apotheosis in November 1986 in a front-page interview with the *Sun* headlined 'My Junkie Lies by George', in which the repentant star admitted he had lied in the past about having put drugs behind him. The accompanying photographs, taken by his brother David, strongly suggested he was still not being altogether truthful.

Within a month, as the photographers hovered at the gates, his parents were once again desperately petitioning to have him admitted to a clinic. Maybury's advice was to 'be with him, cuddle him, and don't let him out of your sight'.

That Christmas, George says, was the worst time of his life: heavily sedated by non-addictive drugs, agitated, tearful. 'What I went through was terrible: physical fits, being jerked about and having no control over my body; screaming at people and throwing things. To want to go through that again, you would have to be crazy.'

By New Year's Eve he was through the worst. His doctor, who by chance is also a Buddhist, and had visited each day, introduced him to chanting. George re-emerged into the outside world through the decompression chamber of Buddhist meetings, lectures, and a pantomime version of *Alice in Wonderland*, staged by the Buddhist group in London. It was, he said, the best show he had ever seen in his life. Nobody would suggest that the music was ever going to rival Culture Club, but there was a line from one of the songs that kept running through his head, and runs there still. 'People who live in glasshouses,' it goes, 'shouldn't . . .' Just shouldn't.

Mick Brown, Sunday Times magazine, 12 April 1987

1987: Children of Zoso*

It's Thursday afternoon. After-school activities are in progress.

A group of about seven teenagers are sitting around a truck in front of the 7-Eleven. Burnouts. I know from the pose, the clothes, the turf. Yep, in another age they'd be hitters or greasers or hippies or heads or freaks. On another coast – they'd be stoners. Archenemies of jocks, dexters, rah-rahs, or socs for all eternity.

Guys with earrings, crucifixes, long hair hanging over a concert shirt or a hooded sweatshirt. Walking in threes with boom boxes blasting AC/DC, Bon Jovi, or Zep. Suburban rocker kids are patriotic – everyone wears denim jackets (a prized commodity among international rocker youth, proof of America's pop-cultural world supremacy). Back panel is painted, a shrine to one's most beloved band: Iron Maiden, Metallica, the Grateful Dead.

Ladies have bi-level haircuts. Long shags blown, sprayed, clipped to one side, teased, sometimes bleached. Grease & glamour. Where Farrah and Madonna meet Twisted Sister. Bergen Mall trendy, but informed by the careful reading of albums and metal magazines. Earrings, junk jewels, eye makeup, leggings or spandex pants. Oversized cotton shirts hang down past

*The word 'Zoso' is derived from the runes used in the artwork for Led Zeppelin's fourth album.

635

a more stylized, unpainted denim jacket. Heavy cotton athletic socks slouch over white or black leather ankle boots or white sneakers.

Street-corner society in suburbia. Hanging around minding your business until you get banished by the cops. Archaeological leavings include empty cans of Bud, bottles of St Pauli Girl. Slurpee containers, and the remains of other 7-Eleven delicacies: buttered rolls, beef burritos, beef jerky wrappers.

Cave renderings appear on walls, or else they're carved into wood: THE DEAD LIVE, a peace sign, KISS, and lovers' initials united 4-ever. Recently the 7-Eleven contracted for graffiti-proof paint jobs, so stuff on the side wall is now transitory. A guard patrols the parking lot next door, behind the bank, until it closes. This sign is posted in the window of the 7-Eleven.

Troubled?
Need a Direction – Advice or Just Someone to Listen?
call Bergenfield
HELP-LINE 387-4043
Talk To Someone Who Cares
24 Hours A Day

Right now it's a warm spring afternoon. A good day to cop some rays, get an early start on your tan. The guys are in casual repose – the world-historic teen lean on one's own vehicle. Three guys sit up in the crib, another in the cab. Two more at a forty-five-degree angle on another car. A couple is clinging, shadowboxing and making out. At the center of all this is this deep blue Bronco with its big fucking wheels. Huge. The cab is high up from the ground. Tons of shit hanging from the rearview mirror. Stickers on windows and bumper. Music playing very loud. They're talking. All guys except for the couple making out. The girls are huddled closely together a few feet away. I walk up to the guys.

'Excuse me, I'm writing a story about your town.' They look at me cold. One guy reminds me of Mr T, but he's white – turns out his name's Bobby. He's sullen in his gray hooded sweatshirt, jeans, and white high-top sneakers. Earring. Hands deep in pockets of jeans, shoulders up, head down. Bobby pulls out cigarette, sucks it lit, sneers. 'Look, they were our friends – we don't want to talk about it, okay?' I start rambling on about having friends who died too young and growing up in a town ... and halt. Bobby's friend spots my 'Ace of Spades' lapel button. 'You like Motorhead?'

'Ah, yeah ... I mean ... like ... Lemmy's god ...' Off guard and completely disorientated, I answer a guy with clumpy layered hair and a Grateful Dead T-shirt. He spots my mini-tape recorder piled with my junk on another car, grabs it, turns it to record. He introduces himself to the condenser mike. 'Nicky Trotta from Dumont.' His friend, a bigger guy with longer hair and a faded Ozzy T-shirt, snaps, 'Don't tell her your name!' But it's too late, Nicky's on with the show.

'Okay, so what's the meaning of Bergenfield?' Three guys sing, 'five letters – *p-a-r-t-y* ... party!' Nicky gives my ring a side glance. A big silver skull. Pulls my hand towards him. Subtle tone, doesn't look up, swallows the first word: 'That's cool.' Soon after, Joe, the Ozzy fan, introduces himself, we shake hands.

Nicky slaps his girlfriend Doreen on the ass. A few feet away, out by the main road, another girls walks by. She hurries past the store. She is spotted by Doreen. Her friends, Susie and Joan, rush over to her. 'You gonna fight her?' Doreen knows that Nicky went with her the other night. She'd like to kill her. Bitch. Nothing happens. This is my first introduction to the girls.

We settle in. I say that I'm not really interested in interrogating them about the suicide pact. I understand they are sick of the reporters. I explain that I wanted to check out the town, to know what it's like to be a 'burnout'. Nicky understands my purpose at once. Pointing to his friends, he says, 'Yeah, well, you got the right ones.' No doubt about it; they are 'burnouts'.

Now, as it turns out, some of Nicky's companions knew Tommy Olton, Tommy Rizzo, and the Burress sisters merely as acquaintances – from school, from having seen them around. Others knew them well, as close friends. One guy had dated Lisa Burress. But everybody had strong opinions about the way the 'burnouts' were treated.

At this point Joe takes over as informant, tells me the cops are on everybody's ass. They know his car. He grabs my tape recorder and makes a dedication to the Bergenfield police officers. 'Go screw yourselves because you're not getting me again.' The cops are all crooks. Totally corrupt. Bust your ass, flirt with the girls. (But then a day or two later, he tells me the cops are really okay as long as you don't fuck with them. Be polite. Don't bust their balls.) Cop watching, skateboards, and car races are the burnouts' idea of sports.

Nicky and Doreen are making out. The Bon Jovi tape plays 'Runaway' on the truck's stereo. I check out the system. Impressive! More talk about music. We compare favorite bands. I ask if they like Metallica. Heads bang back and forth and we play air guitar 'Batterrreee!' Nicky figures yeah, if I like Motorhead, I'd probably like Metallica. We are now at a regional hardcore–heavy metal-thrasher convention. What goes on next is a rock and roll version of 'Paisan ... landsman ... you like Anthrax?' You sniff out cultural heritage. Then you talk. This is the centerpiece of suburban street culture. I could be doing this in my own neighborhood. But music subcults are esoteric. You either know or you don't; you can't fake it.

Someone asks, 'What about Suicidal Tendencies?' I had just seen them at City Gardens, a club in Trenton. 'Unbelievable,' I say, then ask if anyone is going to see the Butthole Surfers. They were playing the Ritz in New York City pretty soon. No, but Nicky says he's heard of them.

'Yeah, they're from Texas,' I say. 'Psychedelic noise band, completely mentally ill ... Fire marshal always comes down to close their shows ... happened in Jersey, San Francisco ...' Bobby is watching, Joe is listening, but the quiet guy, Randy, could care less about this entire rap. And the girls have now gone inside 7-Eleven. Lots of motion. They're after cigarettes and gum.

By now we have established lineage, and favorite bands in common. Okay, I don't care for Bon Jovi and they aren't too motivated by my noise bands. They've never even heard of Test Dept – that's another world. But we agree about Motorhead and Suicidal Tendencies and that is enough to establish an understanding.

Right at this moment Nicky has something important to ask me. Opening his flannel shirt to expose the T-shirt, he wants to know, what about the Dead? Did I see them? They had played recently. My ring, the skull, is a Grateful Dead icon. But it's an accident. I'm not a Deadhead. I could never lie about something like this. I explain, some guy in a bar gave me the ring.

I ask Nicky about the famous north Jersey Deadhead town I had heard about. Is that the town he comes from. Nicky and all the kids you see at Madison Square Garden who travel in for the shows. You see them hanging around the Path trains around Penn Station dressed in tribal regalia. They're looking for tickets, waiting for friends. New Jersey kids, Long Island kids traveling to Mecca. Yes, Nicky does come from the famous town.

The next thing I know, three kids are showing me razor blade scars on their wrists.

Immediate memory recall is the police report about the razor-slash wounds on the wrists of the two guys who died in the suicide pact. Nicky says, 'Every one of us has either tried it or contemplated it.' Nicky's scars look old, healed. So do Joe's. But one of the girls has her wrists freshly bandaged. She's much younger than they are. She's just starting out.

Suddenly Joe grabs my arm, there is great excitement. A scar and some red ink on my right wrist. They look at me and smile, making a deeper connection. 'No,' I explain emphatically, 'it's from a jar of mayo I rammed too hard into the trash.'

Nicky starts talking about a recent family altercation. 'Look, I blame myself. I fucked up. I blew my curfew and my father beat the shit out of me, it was my fault,' Nicky understands these things. He knows his father loves him. We all agree, everyone understands about that.

But the other day he beat the shit out of his little sister for smoking. He made her nose bleed. It was a really dumb thing to do, he admits. And he feels bad about it. Last year he was thrown out of school for fighting. He almost killed a kid for bothering his sister. 'Attempted manslaughter,' he says, looking somber and grim. Now he's in another school.

Joe talks about family life. 'My dad pulled me out of bed by my hair this morning, at 5 a.m., and called me a scumbag.' Joe's had run-ins with the law. No details, thank you. Won't talk about it. Hates everyone, wants to say fuck it. Everything sucks. 'What's the answer?' he asks. Joe takes center stage.

'It's the system,' he answers himself. Randy flicks a butt, slouches into the car, smirks and pumps up the volume.

'I don't know.' I hesitate, trying to give Joe some kind of answer. 'But if you kill yourself all it proves is that you buy their bullshit ... I mean the system – it's just other people, most of them are assholes, why give them the edge?'

'I know, but what can you *do* about it?' Joe asks. Doreen and Nicky come up for air, he taps me. 'Hey, don't you like us?' He's insulted, I'm ignoring them! 'I'm being respectful, you're on a date.' He laughs. 'A date!' And offers me gum.

I get serious. 'You have to fight back.' Joe asks me how. I have no answer but I have to answer Joe. 'I don't know, but you can. You have to, or they win. *They* get to write history.'

Donna Gaines, *Teenage Wasteland* (1991)

1987: I'm White!: What's Wrong with Michael Jackson

There are other ways to read Michael Jackson's blanched skin and disfigured African features than as signs of black self-hatred become self-mutilation. Waxing fanciful, we can imagine the-boy-who-would-be-white a William Gibson-ish work of science fiction: harbinger of a trans-racial tomorrow where genetic deconstruction has become the norm and Narcissism wears the face of all human Desire. Musing empathetic, we may put the question, who does Mikey want to be today? The Pied Piper, Peter Pan, Christopher Reeve, Skeletor, or Miss Diana Ross? Or Howard Hughes? Digging into our black nationalist bag, Jackson emerges a casualty of America's ongoing race war – another Negro gone mad because his mirror reports that his face does not conform to the Nordic ideal.

To fully appreciate the sickness of Jackson's savaging of his African physiognomy you have to recall that back when he wore the face he was born with, black folk thought he was the prettiest thing since sliced sushi. (My own mother called Michael pretty so many times I almost got a complex.) Jackson and I are the same age, damn near 30, and I've always had a love-hate thing going with the brother. When we were both moppets I envied him, the better dancer, for being able to arouse the virginal desires of my female schoolmates, shameless oglers of his (and Jermaine's) tenderoni beef-cake in *16* magazine. Even so, no way in those say-it-loud-I'm-black-and-I'm-proud days could you not dig Jackson heir to the James Brown dance throne. At age 10, Jackson's footwork and vocal machismo seemed to scream volumes about the role of genetics in the cult of soul and the black sexuality of myth. The older folk might laugh when he sang shake it, shake it baby, ooh, ooh or teacher's gonna show you, all about loving. Yet part of the tyke's appeal was being able to simulate being lost in the hot sauce way before he was supposed to know what the hot sauce even smelt like. No denying he *sounded* like he knew the real deal.

In this respect, Jackson was the underweaned creation of two black working-class traditions: that of boys being forced to bypass childhood along the fast track to manhood, and that of rhythm and blues auctioning off the race's passion for song, dance, sex, and spectacle. Accelerated development became a life-imperative after slavery, and r&b remains the redemption of minstrelsy – at least it was until Jackson made crossover mean lightening your skin and whitening your nose.

Slavery, minstrelsy, and black bourgeoisie aspirations are responsible for three of the more pejorative notions about blacks in this country – blacks as property, as ethnographic commodities, and as imitation rich white people. Given this history, there's a fine line between a black entertainer who appeals to white people and one who sells out the race in pursuit of white appeal. Berry Gordy, Bürgermeister of crossover's Bauhaus, walked that line with such finesse that some black folk were shocked to discover via *The Big Chill* that many whites considered Motown *their* music. Needless to say, Michael Jackson has crossed so way far over the line that there ain't no coming back – assuming through surgical transmutation of his face a singlar infamy in the annals of tomming.

The difference between Gordy's crossover dream world and Jackson's is that Gordy's didn't preclude the notion that black is beautiful. For him the problem was his pupils not being ready for prime time. Motown has raised brows for its grooming of Detroit ghetto kids in colored genteel manners, so maybe there were people who thought Gordy was trying to make his charges over into pseudo-Caucasoids. Certainly this insinuation isn't foreign to the work of rhythm and blues historians Charles Keil and Peter Guralnick, both of whom write of Motown as if it weren't hot and black enough to suit their blood, or at least their conception of bloods. But the intermingling of working-class origins and middle-class acculturation are too mixed up in black music's evolution to allow for simpleminded purist demands for a black music free of European influence, or of the black desire for a higher standard of living and more cultural mobility. As an expression of '60s black consciousness, Motown symbolized the desire of blacks to get their foot in the back door of the American dream. In the history of affirmative action Motown warrants more than a footnote beneath the riot accounts and NAACP legal maneuvers.

As a black American success story the Michael Jackson of *Thriller* is an extension of the Motown integrationist legacy. But the Michael Jackson as skin job represents the carpetbagging side of black advancement in the affirmative action era. The fact that we are now producing young black men and women who conceive of their African inheritance as little more than a means to cold-crash mainstream America and then cold-dis – if not merely put considerable distance between – the brothers and sisters left behind. In this sense Jackson's decolorized flesh reads as the buppy version of Dorian Gray, a blaxploitation nightmare that offers this moral: Stop, the face you save may be your own.

In 1985 black people cherished *Thriller*'s breakthrough as if it were their own battering ram against the barricades of American apartheid. Never mind how many of those kerzillon LPs were bought, forget how much Jackson product we had bought all those years before that – even with his deconstructed head, we wanted this cat to tear the roof off the all-time-greatest-sales sucker bad as he did. It's like *Thriller* was this generation's answer to the Louis–Schmeling fight or something. Oh, the Pyrrhic victories of the disenfranchised. Who would've thought this culture hero would be cut down to culture heel, with a scalpel? Or maybe it's just the times. To those living in a New York City and currently witnessing a rebirth of black consciousness in protest politics, advocacy journalism (read *The City Sun!* read *The City Sun!*), and the arts, Jackson seems dangerously absurd.

641

Proof that God don't like ugly, the title of Michael's new LP, *Bad* (Epic), accurately describes the contents in standard English. (Jackson apparently believes that *bad* can apply to both him and L.L. Cool J.) No need to get stuck on making comparisons with *Thriller*, *Bad* sounds like home demos Michael cut over a long weekend. There's not one song here that any urban contemporary hack couldn't have laid in a week, let alone two years. Several of the up-tempo numbers wobble in with hokey bass lines out of the Lalo Schifrin fakebook, and an inordinate number begin with ominous science fiction synthnoise – invariably preceding an anticlimax. *Bad* has hooks, sure, and most are searching for a song, none more pitifully than the fly-weight title track, which throws its chorus around like a three-year-old brat.

The only thing *Bad* has going for it is that it was made by the same artist who made *Thriller*. No amount of disgust for Jackson's even newer face (cleft in the chin) takes anything away from *Thriller*. Everything on that record manages a savvy balance between machine language and human intervention, between palpitating heart and precision tuning. *Thriller* is a record that doesn't know how to stop giving pleasure. Every note on the mutha sings and breathes masterful pop instincts: the drumbeats, the bass lines, the guitar chicken scratches, the aleatoric elements. The weaving of discrete details into fine polyphonic mesh reminds me of those African field recordings where simultaneity and participatory democracy, not European harmony, serve as the ordering principle.

Bad, as songless as *Thriller* is songful, finds Jackson performing material that he has absolutely no emotional commitment to – with the exception of spitefully named 'Dirty Diana', a groupie fantasy. The passion and compassion of 'Beat It', 'Billie Jean', and 'Wanna Be Startin' Somethin'' seemed genuine, generated by Jackson's perverse attraction to the ills of teen violence and teen pregnancy. There was something frightful and compelling about this mollycoddled mama's boy delivering lapidary pronouncements from his Xanadu like 'If you can't feed your baby, then don't have a baby.' While the world will hold its breath and turn blue in the face awaiting the first successful Michael Jackson paternity suit, he had the nerve to sing, 'The kid is not my son.' Not even David Bowie could create a subtext that coy and rakish on the surface and grotesque at its depths.

Only in its twisted aspects does *Bad*, mostly via the 'Bad' video, outdo *Thriller*. After becoming an artificial white man, now he wants to trade on his ethnicity. Here's Jackson's sickest fantasy yet: playing the role of a black preppie returning to the ghetto, he not only offers himself as a role model he literally screams at the brothers 'You ain't nothin'!' Translation: Niggers ain't shit. In Jackson's loathsome conception of the black experience, you're either a criminal stereotype or one of the Beautiful People. Having sold the world pure pop pleasure on *Thriller*, Jackson returns on *Bad* to sell his own race hatred. If there's 35 million sales in that, be ready to head for the hills ya'll.

Greg Tate, Village Voice, 22 September 1987

1987: Sunday, 18th October

On Sunday, 18th October 1987, Marilyn made a trifle. The weekend had been quiet, with neither visitors nor excursions. The previous evening, Martin had tried to entertain Marilyn by playing her old punk-rock records. Marilyn had indulged this pastime. The tall black record player had boomed out the fast, witty, aggressive songs. The drawing-room floor had been strewn with brightly coloured, poorly printed record sleeves. One song had lingered in Marilyn's mind. She did not like punk rock, saw no hidden meaning within it, and was not in the least bit nostalgic for its period; it was the infectious chorus of the song – which sounded like a football chant – that she could not stop repeating in her mind. The tune was still tormenting her the following afternoon as she soaked sponge fingers in orange liqueur and began to cut up fruit:

> I am the fly, I am the fly,
> Fly in the, fly in the . . .
> Ointment . . .

Oh, that bloody tune, she thought.

Soon, however, the young woman had lined her broad, cut-glass bowl with sponge fingers and rich, thick custard. To this she added: black cherries, kiwifruit, bananas, apple slices, peach segments and raspberries. The fruit sank into the custard and was then covered with a further layer of sponge. To complete the trifle, Marilyn spread large spoonfuls of whipped cream across its glistening surface. Then she decorated the finished dessert with shavings of white chocolate and further halved cherries. The large bowl, viewed from the side, was filled with layer upon layer of fruit, sponge, custard and cream. Marilyn was pleased with this luxurious confection, and placed the bowl in the tall fridge. Such a trifle was ruinous to the young woman's diet, but she felt like indulging herself.

That evening as Martin was watching television, he heard a loud crash, swiftly followed by a furious scream. He rushed into the kitchen. Marilyn was standing next to the kitchen table, covering her eyes with one hand. The large trifle, as though dropped from a great height, was lying on the floor, mixed with shards of broken glass. Peninsulas of cream and custard spread out in all directions from the centre of the mess. It looked like something out of a cartoon. Turning to his wife, Martin noticed that a tear was running down her cheek from beneath her covered eyes.

'Just don't say anything,' she said. 'Please, just leave . . .'

Silently, Martin left the kitchen. Marilyn, for the first time in nearly two years, reached for a cigarette and slowly smoked it. She couldn't work out how the accident had happened; the bowl, it seemed, had been heavier than she thought, and slippery.

'It just slipped out of my hands,' she said, later.

'They're calling it Black Monday,' said Dick Alryn to Martin the following day. 'A complete systems overload; Stock Exchange in tatters; mucho panic in the City . . .'

Dicky was watching the small television in his office and listening to the analyses of the market crash with a fearful and bewildered expression.

'Does this affect us directly?' asked Martin.

'It'll affect everybody unless something happens . . .'

'What do we do?'

'Us? We press on; business never stops . . .'

But, as Martin was leaving the office, Dicky reflected that business had stopped. The great, sleek, international machine had choked as it gobbled. On all sides, panic and dread were seizing the minds of the fatted business community. Later, Martin recalled the apocalyptic paintings of John Martin in which cowering merchants were depicted, still clinging to their gold even as the world opened up to swallow them. Dick Alryn, on Black Monday, rang his partner Bob Ensall and sought comfort in reasoned, analytical conversation. Dicky's debts made Martin's debts look insignificant.

Michael Bracewell, *The Conclave* (1992)

1988: Stayin' Alive

It's 1978, and disco rules. Donna Summer may be acknowledged as one Queen of Disco, but for gay men, Sylvester is the Other Queen. The falsetto singer has suddenly gone from drag infamy to hit records without giving up the gowns. 'Dance (Disco Heat)' is hustling up the pop charts, and 'You Make Me Feel (Mighty Real)', isn't far behind. Sylvester and his background singers the Two Tons o' Fun are whipping up audiences of every race and sexual persuasion with spiritual voices and sinful rhythms. Whirling and twirling and shrieking out gospel-inflected dancefloor exhortations like Little Richard's kid sister, this San Franciscan man in glittering couture looks and sings as if he's just seen God . . . boogie.

Now it's 1988, and Sylvester has AIDS. He's joined the People With AIDS group of the San Francisco Gay Pride March in a wheelchair. Although he's just 40 years old, his thinning gray hair, sunken features, and frail body make him look 25 years older. This is Sylvester's first public acknowledgment of his illness, and the transition from glamour maven to out-patient has made him almost unrecognizable. The few who spot him cry, or gasp in shock, or applaud his bravery. For almost 20 years, Sylvester has been an icon of San Francisco nightlife: outrageous, bold, proud. Today, Sylvester is a symbol of a totally different San Francisco – a gay man struggling to stay alive.

'Sylvester is as he was then,' says San Francisco novelist Armistead Maupin, 'one of the few gay celebrities who never renounced his gayness along the ladder of success. He's allowing us to celebrate his life before his death, and I don't know a single star who has the integrity to do that. In sickness and in health, Sylvester has carried on with the identical spirit.'

Like so many black singers, Sylvester learned how to sing in church, at the Palm Lane Church of God and Christ in South Los Angeles. But from the very beginning, there were factors that made this familiar rite of passage unusual. Sylvester's mother, Letha Hurd, introduced the young Sylvester James to a minister, Jerry Jordan. Under Jordan's guidance, Sylvester performed at gospel conventions around California. His showstopper was his interpretation of 'Never Grow Old', the first record by the woman who has remained Sylvester's idol and major influence, Aretha Franklin. Already, Sylvester was being groomed for divadom.

'Sylvester was so small,' recalls his mother, 'he used to stand on a milk box while he sang. He would tear up the church, people would be screaming and hollering, and then he'd go play in the parking lot.'

The Pentecostal church was also where Sylvester had his first homosexual experience. 'I was abused by an evangelist,' says Sylvester, 'when I was seven, eight, *and* nine! He really did a number on me, but it never made me crazy. But you see, I was a queen even back then, so it didn't bother me. I rather *liked* it.'

'I wanted to take a shotgun to that evangelist,' says Sylvester's mom.

Sylvester's precociousness made him a difficult child. His father didn't like him, and he fought constantly with his mother. After living awhile with his wealthier grandma, Sylvester ran away to live with friends while still in junior high. He did finish school, and two years at the Lamert Beauty College in LA, where he studied interior decorating. It was then, in 1970, that the 20-year-old Sylvester was invited to San Francisco to teach the Cockettes how to sing gospel.

'What we did came out of smoking pot, dropping LSD, and watching old movies on TV,' recalls Kreema Ritz, one of the original dozen drag queens that made up the Cockettes.

The Cockettes grew out of a group of hippies who belonged to the Food Conspiracy food co-ops. George Harris, son of an off-Broadway actor, took his new moniker, Hibiscus, in 1969, when he was picking drag out of dumpsters and making food deliveries to hippies in the communes. Hibiscus was invited by filmmaker Steven Arnold and Bill Graham's accountant Sebastian to appear with her friends at a special New Year's Eve edition of the Nocturnal Dream shows at the Palace Theater, a deco building that showed Chinese movies by day. To ring in the new decade, the Cockettes danced the cancan to the Rolling Stones' 'Honky Tonk Women'. The crowd approved, and the Cockettes became a regular Palace attraction.

'The term *gender-fuck* was coined to describe the Cockettes,' says Martin Worman, a/k/a Philthee Ritz. This former drag queen is now an NYU performance art doctoral student writing a dissertation on his Cockette past. 'We were a bunch of hippie radicals. We'd wear our trashy drag in long hair and beards and sprinkle glitter everywhere. Rather than trying to reproduce an image of women, we'd do our take on the image. You must remember that we didn't have the money to do faithful reproductions. We did our drag on welfare and food stamps.'

Sylvester made his Cockette debut in 1970 as an island mammy in *Hollywood Babylon* wearing a '30s bias-cut dress and singing 'Big City Blues'. For the next year, Sylvester played crucial roles in ever more elaborate and deranged Cockette stage shows. Opening for the Cockettes' New York debut in 1971 was Sylvester and the Hot Band, a white guitar group fronted by the singer in a new glitter incarnation. It was about this Cockettes performance that Gore Vidal made the often-quoted statement, 'Having no talent is no longer enough.'

In early '70s San Francisco, it was hip to be a homo, and if you couldn't be it, you approved. 'That whole peace and love thing sounds so corny now, but it really happened,' says Worman. 'The hippie atmosphere bred tolerance for everybody, and being gay meant an exploration and a celebration. Even the earliest bathhouses were playful. People hadn't yet compartmentalized their sexuality.'

The Cockettes' influence blossomed. When David Bowie's San Francisco debut failed to sell out, he explained, 'They don't need me – they have Sylvester.' Ken Russell saw the Cockettes and borrowed their imagery for *The Boyfriend*. Future mainstreamers like the Manhattan Transfer, Bette Midler and the Pointer Sisters – soon to become Sylvester's backup singers – all followed in their high-heeled footsteps.

The Cockettes bridged the gap between hippies and glam-rockers, between dirty denim and gold lamé. Sylvester and the Hot Band, which included future Oingo Boingo bassist Kerry Hatch and future Santana/Journey guitarist Neil Schon, garnered more attention from Sylvester's glitter drag than the backup band's bland boogie. Their two 1973 LPs flopped. Sylvester skipped town, hung out in London and Amsterdam with Bowie and Elton John, and marked time until returning in '75.

During this period the influx of gays into San Francisco began, and the number of gay establishments boomed. Sylvester would now have a larger audience to draw on, and more clubs in which to stage his comeback. The hippie do-your-own-thing philosophy was gradually replaced by a kind of conformity – and separatism – introduced by people from small towns.

'I moved to Florida in the winter of '74–'75,' remembers Kreema Ritz, 'and when I returned, the second half of the decade had begun – grocery stores had turned into bars and bathhouses. Then I noticed all these men with mustaches, and I thought, where are these people coming from?'

The post-Stonewall gay man wanted heroes he could call his own. In the absence of other role models, gays have traditionally taken to singers like Judy Garland and Marlene Dietrich because they embody conflicts similar to their own – these women take male songwriters' fantasies of feminine passivity and sing them against the grain, in anger. For the generation of young men who grew up with the Supremes and discovered gay lib, r&b singers became the new divas of choice. Early '70s soul sisters had one major thing in common with gay men – their suppression exploded in a torrent of sensuality. These aggressive black women provided the night-time dancing soundtrack while they captured both the alienation and the fervor that gay men understood.

The female singers in Ecstasy, Passion and Pain, and in Faith, Hope and

647

Charity (the names say it all), Lyn Collins and Patti Jo, were among the women to make their mark in gay clubs without approaching the pop charts. Before disco reached the masses, gays asserted their identity in the marketplace as consumers of black dance music – if few gay people were allowed to declare their sexuality on record, then records would *become* gay when enough gay people bought and sold them. For both blacks and gays, the new nightlife was a frontier where identity and sexuality could be explored within a protective arena. But for straight white America, which already had such institutions, disco translated into mainstream escapist entertainment: a barely sublimated outlet to experience the sexual revolution without actually living it. Before white-picket-fence America was ready to listen to homosexuals, they learned how to shop and dance like them.

Sylvester's discoization came in time for the genre's commercial peak in 1979; according to Sylvester, 'the year when queens ran the music business'. The disco department of Casablanca Records, the hugely successful independent label behind Donna Summer and the Village People, was run by many gay men like Marc Paul Simon, who died earlier this year from AIDS. The most famous disco promoter, Warner Bros.'s Ray Caviano, was also among the most open about being gay, and every major company had their own gay-dominated disco departments. The world wanted to party, and no one knew how like gay men.

But not for long. San Francisco supervisor Harvey Milk was assassinated in '78, and the mood of gay San Francisco shifted. Anita Bryant's campaign to repeal gay rights ordinances had already brought the cult of respectability into gay politics – no one wanted to look or carry on as if they might be taken for a queen. Gay sexuality fragmented. It wasn't enough to try everything: you had to declare yourself into leather, Levis, cowboys, or chicken, or *something*.

Then the media announced that 'disco sucks', a catchphrase that attacked the music scene while making a homophobic slur. The record business was only too happy to give up on what they couldn't control. Disco departments turned into *dance* departments, or were phased out altogether. As far as Sylvester was concerned, there wasn't a reason for alarm. Unlike many disco artists, the singer had an identity that could transcend trends. People would continue to like Sylvester for reasons that went beyond the beat.

Before he made his disco move, Sylvester himself was no fan of the music. Harvey Fuqua, veteran Motown producer and former lead singer of the

Moonglows, had signed Sylvester to Fantasy, a jazz-oriented label. *Sylvester*, in 1977, presented a far more conventional soul singer, and by that time, he had acquired his background weapons, Martha Wash and Izora Rhodes, the Two Tons o' Fun. 'I was just not into those skinny black girl singers who would "oooooh" and "aaaaah",' Sylvester recalls. 'I wanted some big bitches who could wail.'

But there was still something missing in Sylvester's new r&b approach. He got what he needed from Patrick Cowley, lighting man at the City disco, the Bay Area's largest and most important gay venue. Cowley had kept his songwriting and synthesizer experiments secret until his homemade remix of Donna Summer's 'I Feel Love' became the local rage. Impressed, Sylvester asked Cowley if he wouldn't mind making similar synth additions to what was originally a ballad, 'You Make Me Feel (Mighty Real)', and another uptempo cut, 'Dance (Disco Heat)'. The two songs became top forty singles and turned the next album, *Step II*, into gold. Sylvester had finally arrived in the lap of mainstream America, stiletto heels and all.

But when the disco market crashed, Fantasy Records panicked. They wanted to force him in the direction of black male vocalists like Teddy Pendergrass. First to go was Cowley's synthesized European (which in clubs means *gay white*) influence. As time went on, Sylvester had used more and more of Cowley's input – both his synthesizers and his songs – until Fuqua barred Cowley from recording sessions.

The resulting Cowley-less LPs, 1980's *Sell My Soul* and '81's *Too Hot to Sleep*, were blacker and straighter – they sounded more like the kind of r&b played on black radio and less like the disco heard in gay clubs – but didn't do well in either format. 'I told them, "You can change my image, but *I* ain't changin' shit!"' says Sylvester. 'So I went to the office in a negligee and a blond wig and ran up and down the halls. Then I terrorized their studio until they had to give up.'

Fantasy did relent, but only after preventing Sylvester from recording until his contract expired in 1982. By then, two things had happened to Cowley. Since he could no longer play with Sylvester, Cowley started his own recording career in '81. His first single, 'Menergy', alluded to street cruising and backroom sex. Nevertheless, it became a No. 1 dance record in America, a pop hit internationally, and defined the future sound of gay clubs – hi-NRG. But before all that, Cowley started falling ill to unexplained things.

'We had gone on a tour of South America around 1979 or '80,' Sylvester recalls, 'and during the tour, Patrick got sick. We all thought it was the food. When we got back, he never could get completely well again. Soon he was coming down with everything you could imagine, and no one knew why.'

Some assumed that Cowley's illness was a psychosomatic fear of success. In truth, the possibility of never recovering drove Cowley to produce more. But he kept getting sicker, and eventually pleaded with Sylvester to unplug his life-support machines. To give him something to live for, Sylvester told Cowley that he had to recover so they could record together again. Miraculously, Cowley pulled through, and for $500, the pair made 'Do You Wanna Funk?'

Shortly after 'Do You Wanna Funk?' became one of the biggest dance hits of '82 and gave Sylvester the needed career boost, Cowley's death became one of the first publicized as resulting from AIDS. 'At the end, he really got bitter,' Sylvester says. 'The doctors didn't know anything – he died of some kind of pneumonia.'

After losing his friend, Sylvester kept his musical collaborations to a minimum. He helped write, produce, and mix three albums for Megatone, the local disco indie, and because they were recorded cheaply, all turned a profit. The Two Tons o' Fun went solo, became the Weather Girls, and scored big with 'It's Raining Men'. In 1986, Warner Bros. licensed *Mutual Attraction*, which included the black radio and club hit 'Someone Like You', and then signed the singer. A hacking cough cut recording sessions for the next album short. Sylvester was hospitalized with pneunomia, and diagnosed with AIDS.

Sylvester lives in a modest apartment in San Francisco's still tangibly gay Castro district. Aside from a few gold records on the walls, there's nothing in his home that registers more than middle-class opulence; a big bed, a big TV. A few things do clue you in on its owner's personality – a framed collection of gloves, Aunt Jemima pepper shakers, a giant Free South Africa poster hanging above the bed.

Sylvester and his manager Tim McKenna greet me. McKenna looks like most people's idea of a San Franciscan gay man – blond, mustachioed, trim. Only he looks a little too trim, and his eyes seem a bit sunken. I think, '*Another* sick person'. (McKenna, I find out later, does have AIDS, and has already lost his boyfriend to the disease.) Sylvester has the nurse pull out a portable TV, and asks if we wouldn't mind watching it for a few minutes. Drag queens are on *Donahue*.

I ask all the difficult questions first. November of last year, the fevers began. He started taking aerosolized pentamadine, a drug prescribed to prevent people at high risk from coming down with pneumocystis pneumonia, the most life-threatening disease associated with AIDS. But Sylvester had missed his treatment while on tour near the end of the year. On December 4, the last show of the tour, Sylvester appeared at a Philadelphia AIDS benefit. Once he got offstage, he couldn't catch his breath. That night marked the end of his performing days and the beginning of trouble.

'When I came home from the hospital, I weighed 140 pounds,' says Sylvester. 'Now I'm at 167, but my normal weight was 190 to 200 pounds. Thank God I always had a great fashion sense and I knew how to make myself look thinner. I was always on a diet. This wasn't quite the way I wanted to do it.'

AIDS once again hit too close with the loss of Sylvester's lover Rick Cramner, an architect with whom he lived for two years. As with Cowley, Cramner's illness was shrouded in mystery.

'Rick never told me he was sick – his pride wouldn't allow him to ask for help. He was here one moment and gone the next. He went and died on me after promising he would never leave me. He *promised* me this. There were many things that only Rick knew. They're gone now. I'll never know them unless I see him someplace.

'It was two days before my 40th birthday, and we had to turn off his machine. He was gonna die that weekend anyway. But if he had died on my birthday, honey, ooh, what a mess I would've been for the rest of my life. I need a boyfriend *so* bad. I've been in mourning for a year now and haven't had sex for longer than that. It would be so nice to have somebody to wake up to in the morning. But where am I gonna find a boyfriend, hobblin' around and lookin' strange? I guess I'm destined not to have one again, and that saddens me. I really believed that Rick and I were gonna be together in sickness and in health. We were, weren't we?'

Sylvester's fame alone can't pay the doctor's bills. Although he says his insurance covers most medical expenses, he needs more than the revenue from back catalogue royalties. McKenna says the singer has virtually run out of money.

'A lot of people wanted us to put out a greatest-hits LP,' says McKenna. 'I've been resistant because those albums can be so tasteless. But we had to put out something, because Sylvester has nothing to live on. [Megatone will release *12 by 12: Sylvester's Greatest Mixes*.] Right now I'm planning a benefit for him sponsored by the National Gay Rights Advocates that Warner Bros. is underwriting. There were times when I thought I could bring a mobile recording studio to his home, but I realized that was just me trying to continue like nothing has changed. It's hard to let go sometimes.

'Everywhere I go, I run into people who want to know how Sylvester is. I get a little crazy sometimes because it's the only thing I'm allowed to talk about. And there's the impending void that I still don't know how to deal with.'

True to his exceptional self, Sylvester has the traits of many who live years beyond their diagnosis: he has a fighting spirit, he refuses to see himself as helpless, and he can talk openly about his illness. But AIDS is a great leveler, and like his music, he sometimes leaps from hope to despair.

'Who was I gonna hide the disease from?' says Sylvester. 'I'm gonna die from it – if indeed that's what will happen. If I kept it a secret, what good would that do? I've been doing AIDS benefits for many, many years, long before it became fashionable. It would be ridiculous to be secretive about it now.'

But get him on a topic that spurs his feisty sense of humor, and he'll straighten his back and make a little effort to lean forward. His hands will start dancing in the air, and expressions like 'honey', 'child' and 'Miss Thing' will slip into the conversation. His eyes will light up, and then you can get a glimpse of the disco diva that lies behind the mask of illness.

'It's not that I didn't want to think the worst,' says Sylvester, 'because I've been a queen long enough. I've been gay for 41 years – I'm 41 years old. I didn't need to take the AIDS antibody test. I know what I've done. Why would I waste those $90 when I could go shopping?'

'Sylvester happened at a time when disco had gotten too plastic,' says Andrew Holleran, author of *Dancer from the Dance*, the classic novel about the early gay days of disco. 'But he mixed celebration and sadness in a way that I felt hadn't been done in years. I hate to use the "f" word, but Sylvester was *fabulous*.'

Disco is often remembered as a wildly – and sometimes annoyingly – upbeat music. But during its early formulative years in the gay clubs, disco encompassed everything from joy to pain, often in the same song. The disco classics that underground DJs now reach for in the early morning after a night of acid house or Latin hiphop are most often those records that took the bittersweet approach. Because his past encompassed both the emotional lows of blues and the spiritual highs of gospel, Sylvester became a major part of that melancholy party tradition.

The ultimate meaning of Sylvester's voice lies in its ability to convey both the joy of the party and the horror that lies behind it. With the same phrase, Sylvester could evoke the delirious escape the party gave you, and the fear of what you're partying to avoid. For gay people, the party began at that moment after Stonewall when they refused to hide anymore – it was both a celebration and a defiance. Through his voice and his success as an openly gay man, Sylvester embodied both of these things. That he could pull it off was understood by his audience as a harbinger of greater triumphs to come. For if he could be that wild, glittery, unreal thing up there, you could simply be you.

Just as his recording of 'Do You Wanna Funk?' with Cowley was an attempt to give his dying friend the courage to stay alive, the second wave of success Sylvester had from that song was a symbol of the struggle to keep the party alive despite AIDS. And for a while, the politics of dancing shifted from moving ahead to holding onto the small freedoms of pleasure. Now the party lives on in picket lines, in benefits, and in rallies to keep those like Sylvester alive.

Barry Walters, Village Voice, 8 November 1988

1989: The Sun and the Star

Sleazy? Sleazy is not the word. Sleazy comes nowhere near to conveying the full ripeness of the Apollo Club (Members Only), perched in a Soho attic. There has just been a fight outside on the street. The loser, a fresh-faced lad breathing fast, pleads for admission: 'There are bottles out there.' But the pig-necked bouncer is having none of it: 'You are not coming here and getting lairy with me, son.'

Inside, the ambience owes something to a motorway service station urinal. No women are in sight. No one comes to the Apollo for a chat – or indeed the view, a side-on glimpse of the squeaky-clean Swiss Centre through matt-black window blinds and grubbier windows. Elderly businessmen tinker with their gins and tonics. Smut-moustached young men look on, waiting to be picked up, as bored as Tesco check-out girls. They drink, smile queasily and then hit the streets.

It was at the Apollo in early 1987 that the story of Britain's biggest libel action began when the *Sun* newspaper got in touch with a rent-boy turned pimp, 'Graham X', who frequented the club. There followed a series of stories about the rock singer Elton John. The stories, based on Graham X's souped-up confessions, were as untrue as they were nasty. The first, ELTON IN VICE BOYS SCANDAL, published on Wednesday 25 February 1987, contained the gist of all that was to come. Graham X 'confessed' to supplying

Elton John and Billy Gaff, a pop manager, with 'at least 10 youngsters, who were each paid a minimum of £100, plus all the cocaine they could stand'.

Elton sued. The *Sun* printed more, and nastier, stories. Elton sued again and again, issuing in all 17 writs against the *Sun* from February to September 1987. The writs led, last Christmas, to a grovelling front-page apology by the *Sun*. It is a grisly and sorry tale, from the rent-boys who lied for the *Sun*'s money to an incredulous RSPCA inspector who was asked to investigate the case of The Dogs That Didn't Bark.

It started with a tip-off. At the beginning of the year, the *Sun* was told by one of its regular sneaks, paid on a story-by-story basis, that a good-looking teenage rent-boy with an angelic face could be sitting on a cracker of a story. The sneak pocketed his money and disappeared from view.

The *Sun* left word at the Apollo that it wanted to get in touch with the rent-boy, later to be called Graham X, but who was known 'up West', that is, in the West End, as 'Barry Alexander' or 'American Barry'. (It is a peculiarly common feature of young people who have broken from their families to claim that they are American or that their family has moved to America.) His real name is Stephen Hardy.

No one should be in the least bit surprised that the *Sun* was interested in the kiss-and-tell stories of a male prostitute. Britain's most profitable newspaper has built its massive sales – at roughly four and a quarter million, more than 10 times as many as those of the *Independent* – on a diet of virulent xenophobia and soft pornography, all streaked with a slickness which is the hallmark of its editor, Kelvin Mackenzie. Mackenzie comes from a family of journalists in south London. on his first paper, as a cub reporter, he was sick over the editor's suede shoes. Such stories have lent weight to the cartoon view of Mackenzie, that he is just a sewer-mouthed yobbo. But Mackenzie is a brilliant tabloid editor, and perhaps the most powerful journalist in the country. Under his stewardship, the *Sun* is dispassionately admired in Fleet Street as a well-made thing. It makes for a repulsive but fascinating read, pored over by 13 million Britons a day.

Stephen Hardy, of course, was and is a regular *Sun* reader. 'Everybody who reads it hasn't got a GCE between them,' he told me, unfairly rubbishing at least one reader – the *Sun*'s editor, who has one GCE, an O-level in art.

Hardy existed – and, to an extent, still does – in a world of rapidly shifting loyalties and fuzzily transmitted reality. In 1987, when he was not quite 20, he was living in Twyford, Berkshire, but making frequent trips 'up West'. Hardy is a blond, slightly built sharp-dresser whose surfeit of identities comes in handy in his line of business. He often speaks with an American accent, although, prosaically, he originally came from a small village somewhere off the M1 near Nottingham. An adopted child, he says that he had been expelled from four schools before posing naked in a male porn magazine. He was paid £100 for this first nude modelling job in 1983, when he was a baby-faced 16. 'I was on the streets with nowhere to go,' he says. 'It was either that or sleeping with people.' Nothing Hardy says should be taken as gospel, but clearly his childhood could hardly be described as conventionally happy.

Suspecting that there might be money in it, Hardy followed up the *Sun*'s approach and phoned Craig Mackenzie on the paper's Bizarre column, which features pop gossip and singles charts. Craig Mackenzie, who lives in the shadow of his editor brother, has since left the *Sun* to join the *Daily Express*.

In 1987, Craig, whose *Sun* nickname was the 'Bouncing Bog-Brush', was in a hurry, anxious to prove himself his own man. The old nursery competitiveness between the brothers Mackenzie partly explains why neither of them ever dared get off the ruinous track they were on. It was to cost the *Sun*'s proprietor, Rupert Murdoch, £1 million in damages and, probably, half as much again in costs.

What Hardy told Craig Mackenzie on the phone was sufficiently promising for a *Sun* team to roar into the forecourt of Twyford railway station in Berkshire in a black Porsche. Hardy was impressed, as the journalists had intended. At the time, Hardy was working as a laundry-presser in the village, earning £120 a week, and living in a council house with his then girlfriend and their baby son.

Hardy told Craig Mackenzie that he had been to several parties thrown by Rod Stewart's former manager, Billy Gaff, at his Great-Gatsby-in-the-Home-Counties kitsch mansion in Finchampstead, near to Elton John's Windsor home and not far from Hardy's Twyford council house. Hardy also told a lurid story about the supplying of other rent-boys, an expenses-paid trip to New York and vast cocaine consumption. Gaff's name cropped up a number of times, but Elton John's name was only mentioned as someone who was on the fringe of the scene.

Billy Gaff is one of the great Seventies rock managers, embodying all the vivid, platform-soled excesses of that era before the greyer Eighties. An interesting, somewhat hyperactive mixture of voluble Irishman and Hollywood camp, he made his first fortune managing Rod Stewart. Gaff went on to repeat his success by managing John Cougar Mellencamp, a hugely popular American singer in the Bruce Springsteen mould. Although Gaff and Elton John know each other, Gaff is a great deal closer to Elton's manager, a Scottish terrier of a man called John Reid. Both men are gay. A friend of mine went to a couple of Billy Gaff's parties at roughly the same time as Hardy. One of the features of both parties was the presence of a knot of effete, sweet-faced young men looking lost.

A story linking rent-boys with Billy Gaff – whether true or untrue – would not cut much ice with the *Sun*'s readers, to whom Gaff was hardly a household name. It was the name 'Elton John' which crackled in the *Sun* journalists' ears. 'Elton John' was what Hardy's new customers wanted to hear, so that was what they got. Hardy was sent a rail ticket and invited down to Wapping to meet the editor.

Hardy has a good recollection of the fateful meeting. He had to brave the NGA pickets, still screaming 'Scab!' after almost a year standing outside the Nato-issue razor wire of Murdoch's massive print plant. In the room were the brothers Mackenzie and the paper's then deputy editor, Dave Shapland, who has since left to run a sports features agency. Hardy got on all right with Craig Mackenzie and Shapland, but he did not warm to the editor: 'I didn't like his attitude. One minute he was a semi-Australian hard-talking guy, the next he was like a puppy.'

To help Craig Mackenzie, who had the responsibility of turning out the Bizarre column, *Sun* writer Neil Wallis was drafted into the Elton John investigation. Wallis had previously worked on the *Sun*'s gutter rival, the *Daily Star*, where he was billed with becoming modesty as 'The World's Greatest Reporter'. Fleet Street legend has it that Wallis, a jovial Mancunian nicknamed 'Wolfman' because of a lupine beard, is something of a 'chancer'. As far as the Press Council goes, the mythology does not bear close examination. According to the council, Wallis is cited in only one adjudication in recent years, for a story entitled THIS CHILD WAS TOLD CHRISTMAS JOY IS EVIL, a minor classic of the genre. As it happens, the Press Council rejected the complaint against Wallis and the paper he then worked for.

A mole at the *Sun* takes up the story:

'After two weeks of investigation, Wallis and Craig Mackenzie felt they were 90 per cent sure that something untoward had gone on at Billy Gaff's house and that drugs were in abundance. Kelvin nagged them for a date. They had rough dates, but nothing specific. Eventually they settled on a specific date, which proved to be a big mistake. Needless to say, there was no discussion whether it was a just story to run. No one at the *Sun* discusses morality.'

656

On the eve of publication Mackenzie had an intimation of disaster. The front-page splash had been made up: ELTON IN VICE BOYS SCANDAL. He stood in front of it, admiring his handiwork. 'Right then,' he said. 'Let's fackin' go for it. Elton John! We're all going down the pan.' And with that he held his beaky nose and mimicked the pulling of a lavatory chain. The gesture was to prove prophetic.

The story, dated Wednesday 25 February 1987, carried the by-lines Craig Mackenzie and Neil Wallis and was in traditional *Sun* style. The singer, the *Sun* alleged, had snorted cocaine while begging tattooed skinheads to indulge in bondage.

Everything was based on the uncorroborated evidence of a rent-boy – and rent-boys are notoriously bad witnesses – who now says '97 per cent of it was untrue'. According to Hardy, 'I would give them a line and they would write it all up. It was a manufactured story.'

The final paragraph of the front-page story put the usual gutter-tabloid po-faced sanctimony in the mouth of Graham X: 'I am ashamed of what I did. I am speaking out to show how widespread this sort of thing is and to warn other gullible young kids to steer clear of people like these.' The story failed to add that the *Sun* had paid Graham X £2,000 for his altruism, and was to pay him £250 a week most weeks, for the next few months.

For people of my generation, in their thirties, Elton Hercules John is the Vera Lynn *de nos jours*. Songs like 'Goodbye Yellow Brick Road' and 'Saturday Night's Alright (For Fighting)' provided the noise wallpaper at our first parties and teenage discos. More than that, Elton – born Reginald Kenneth Dwight – did not, as Jagger and Lennon did, become a tax exile and disappear off into megastardom. He therefore occupies a homely, warm place in our affections. He was judged ideologically cuddly enough to be the first Western rock star to play the Soviet Union and to visit China. And although he had pink hair long before Johnny Rotten gobbed at 'shocked' journalists, Elton was a friend of Prince Andrew and would willingly fly 12,000 miles to see his beloved Watford, the football club he owns, achieve a goalless draw against Charlton Athletic.

Elton's essential homeliness wasn't in the least compromised by his admission, in 1976, that he was a bisexual: 'There's nothing wrong with going to bed with somebody of your own sex.' Such honesty by a public figure marked a departure from the traditional closet mentality which imprisoned many showbiz homosexuals. It was rewarded by mass chantings of 'Elton John's a poof!' by opposing football fans, chants he braved. Facing up to this

657

potentially destructive experience had a lot to do with the robustness with which he took the *Sun* head on, a decade later.

He is not, however, an angel. His lifestyle in the early Seventies, when he was at the peak of his success, might well have excited the moral seraphim at the *Sun* if they had been minded to paw over it in any great detail. Rumours about him even reached the ears of the Royal Family. According to a recent biography of him, at a concert at The Rainbow in north London in aid of the Queen's Silver Jubilee Trust in 1977, Elton was asked by Princess Alexandra in a backstage conversation: 'Do you take cocaine?' The princess later apologised for the indiscretion.

But when the *Sun* struck in 1987 Elton had been married to recording engineer Renate Blauer for more than three years. It was well-known that the marriage – which was to end effectively that spring – was in trouble, but he had more than his own reputation to protect. Moroever, he was completely innocent of the charges Hardy made. The police later looked into the allegations, but no action was taken. No one who came into regular contact with rent-boys, such as the charities who look after them, or the vice squad, had ever heard of Elton John being talked about as a punter by the boys on the streets. Elton was a wronged man.

When the story broke, the rock star was in Australia, recovering from an operation on a growth in his throat which, at one time, was feared to be cancerous. Friends, including, it is said, Mick Jagger, advised him to ride the storm. If he were to sue, the *Sun* might go looking for dirt. It is a nasty consideration which keeps many public figures at bay.

Nevertheless, the sort of mud the *Sun* was flinging has a habit of sticking. The first to dump Elton were Cadbury's, who had bought him up to front a major promotional campaign for their chunky-bar Dairy Milk, Whole Nut, and Fruit and Nut chocolate. Minutes before the ads were due to be aired, Cadbury's scrapped them.

Elton was to prove to be chunkier than the chunky-bar menu. The pop star was no stranger to the High Court, having the year before won almost £5 million after suing his first music publisher, Dick James, over song rights. The *Sun* was totally unprepared for the force of Elton's counter-attack. Elton later told the *Daily Express*: 'They can say I'm a fat old sod, they can say I'm an untalented bastard, they can call me a poof, but they mustn't lie about me.' The first writ from Elton's solicitor, Frank Presland, of solicitors Frere Cholmeley, was issued so fast that the second Graham X story, on Thursday 26 February, was printed with the caption: 'The story they're all suing over.'

Schadenfreude is nowhere indulged in with more glee than in Fleet Street.

On the same day that the *Sun* published its second story, the *Daily Mirror*'s almighty four-letter front-page headline screamed LIES, with the sub-headline: 'I was in New York and I can prove it, says pop super-star.' The *Mirror* story, by John Blake, showed that on the only specific date mentioned in the *Sun*'s original Graham X story linking Elton with rent-boys – 30 April 1986 – Elton was in New York, being whisked about in a limousine. The *Mirror* had receipts.

More intriguing still was a vanishing story trailed in the *Sun*. At the bottom of the first orgy story published on the 25th was a white-on-black block sign-posting the next day's scoop: 'TOMORROW: Elton's pink tu-tu party.' The story never appeared. It probably fell victim to the large holes which were beginning to appear in Graham X's evidence. Witnesses were piling up to say they had never seen Elton John at Billy Gaff's parties; never, in fact, seen him at Billy Gaff's house. But the *Sun*'s game-plan was to keep on hitting Elton so hard that he would give up long before a judge heard the matter.

The second front-page splash, on Thursday 26 February, was headlined ELTON'S KINKY KINKS, followed on pages 4 and 5 by ELTON'S DRUG CAPERS. The *Sun* was claiming, among other things, that Elton 'demanded that the young male prostitutes found for him should be drugged with vast amounts of coke before they were brought to his bed'. Elton sued. The following day, Friday 27 February, the *Sun* printed YOU'RE A LIAR ELTON. Elton sued again.

One man who was concerned about the story was Rupert Murdoch. According to a *Sun* mole, Murdoch treats Mackenzie with the affection shown by the teacher to the naughtiest boy in the class, whom he has to punish but secretly admires the most. He has been known to call Mackenzie 'My Little Hitler'. But when the writs started to fly, there were worries that Elton would boycott Murdoch-owned television outlets. *Sun* reporters were soon trading versions of a phone call described by Mackenzie in his booming voice. The story is that Mackenzie was woken at home in the wee hours of the night by a familiar Australian voice, calling from one of the five continents where News International owns things:

MURDOCH: Kelvin, are we all right on this Elton John business?
MACKENZIE: Yes, boss.
MURDOCH: All right. [*Click*]
The brevity of the phone call, it is said, left Kelvin twitching with worry.

Another man who lost sleep over ELTON IN VICE BOYS SCANDAL was John Boyce. Boyce is a Scottish conman, homosexual pimp and former rent-boy who went to the same school as John Reid, Elton's manager. Asked about his criminal record, Boyce told a Thames Television journalist: 'The largest amount of convictions I've got is for fraud. I've got nine convictions for fraud, and I've got one for attempted murder.' This was the saviour the *Sun* turned to in its hour of need.

Boyce had been toying with the idea of flogging a rent-boy story to the tabloids and was horrified to see the prospect of good money slipping into someone else's hands. When the first Graham X story broke, he phoned up the *Sun* immediately, offering his services as a go-between. Boyce was willing to hunt down rent-boys and secure affidavits from them which would support the thrust of the *Sun*'s allegations – for a price.

Boyce, who works out of a gay pub in Manchester, has been bought up by a former *People* journalist called Terry Lovell. Lovell is writing a book about the affair, so Boyce was unavailable for an interview with the *Independent Magazine*. (Lovell, who broke the Harvey Proctor spanking story and many other sordid revelations with rent-boy sources, has junked his £37,000-a-year job at the *People* after having found God. He now works for the *Christian Bookseller Review*. Lovell told the *UK Press Gazette*: 'I honestly could take no more. The cheating, the lying, the conniving and the utter pointlessness of many of the stories I was no longer able to justify.')

Being born again did not prevent Lovell from taking a modest fee for introducing Boyce to Thames Television's *This Week*. The uncut interview at the Apollo Club between granite-jawed Thames reporter Lindsay Charlton and John Boyce is a model of its kind, as this section shows:

BOYCE: Basically, the whole idea at the beginning of it was to get people to dig dirt against Elton John, and . . .

CHARLTON: What sort of statement did they want?

BOYCE: Basically, they wanted to crown the guy, and he was in the Honours List at the time . . . So they [the *Sun*] turned round and says to me, they says, by the way, can you dig up any kind of crap on the guy . . . And we used to bring people to hotel rooms and they would tell us that they had an affair with Elton John and you know – I mean it was all pure crap.

Boyce's attitude to his work was that it was a 'nice little earner'. He was paid £1,750 for each affidavit, passing on about £500 to each rent-boy who signed up. Not all rent-boys got the full £500 promised by Boyce, not all signatories had ever been rent-boys and, it transpired, none of them had ever done anything they told Boyce they had done with Elton John. After a couple of weeks, the *Sun* realised it had been had, and stopped paying

Boyce. He told *This Week*: 'If Mr Murdoch is there, by any chance, I would appreciate a cheque tomorrow morning.'

Having cut its losses with Boyce, the paper redoubled its efforts to get the 'dirt' on Elton, as Mick Jagger had predicted. The *Sun*'s Elton John squad included Wallis and its Midlands reporter, Andrew Parker. According to the *Sun* mole, 'they scoured the planet'. Elton's solicitor started to get reports from places as far apart as Melbourne, Manchester, Los Angeles, Scotland and London that strangers were making inquiries about the star's sexual history and habits.

Meanwhile, in Twyford, all was not well at the Hardy household. It had taken the rest of Fleet Street about 24 hours to trace American Barry to his council house, but, as yet, no one had got a picture of him. The *Sun* had blanked out his face in ELTON'S KINKY KINKS to preserve his anonymity. It is part of the Samurai code of honour among the tabloids that when one paper buys up a contact and keeps his identity secret, all the others must do their damnedest to find out who he is and print the worst.

The siege moved *en bloc* to the house of Hardy's girlfriend's parents, in a cul-de-sac just off the A4. The *Sun* decided to get Hardy, girlfriend and baby out of the country before he was questioned too closely by the opposition, with the *Daily Mirror* at the head of the pack.

The *Sun*'s Thames Valley reporter, John Askill, a large man nicknamed 'The Jolly Green Giant', was detailed to babysit the Hardys. But first the *Sun* had to get them out of the cul-de-sac and off to the airport. The Fleet Street pack had parked outside the house, hoping to take snatch pics as Hardy was moved out. The Jolly Green Giant rose to the occasion. Hardy, always acutely conscious of how he dresses, recalls this episode with genuine hurt: 'Askill wrapped me up in a balaclava and a scarf, and put a blanket over my head. When we came out of the house Askill left me standing there with this blanket over my head looking stupid as he said "Hello!" to all his mates from the other papers.'

Next, four taxis hired by the *Sun* arrived and blocked off the cul-de-sac, parting like the Red Sea to let the *Sun*'s car out but closing again to stop the pack from following. However, one of the opposition reporters had parked his car on the A4, so an epic car chase across the Home Counties followed. The chase meant that when the *Sun* car finally lost the opposition, its passengers had missed their flight to Spain. Hardy, girlfriend, baby and Askill flew to Paris instead.

They spent four days in the Hotel Sofitel at Charles de Gaulle airport near

661

Paris. Then they flew, first-class, to Malaga, before driving to the five-star Melia Don Pepe in Marbella. Hardy was greatly chuffed: 'It really was high living.' But after a while, the foreign lifestyle lost its appeal. The girlfriend didn't want to feed her baby on Spanish baby food, so a woman *Sun* reporter flew out with fresh stocks bought from a proper British supermarket. Before returning, the exiles spent a couple of days in Gibraltar, where Hardy took the *Sun* man's picture framed against the Rock. In all, Hardy spent a month abroad at the *Sun*'s expense.

Back in Britain, the trawl for filth on Elton John had finally come up with something. Tom Petrie, The *Sun*'s news editor, had to get a thick wad of used readies for an exchange which was like something out of a Le Carré novel. The trade-off took place underneath the stark searchlights outside the *Sun*'s Wapping fortress, because the mystery supplier refused point-blank to enter the plant. What the *Sun* got for its money were three Polaroid photographs, depicting Elton John in, first, a full-frontal nude shot, second, warmly cuddling another man and, third, the man and Elton in a compromising position. Dave Shapland, the paper's deputy editor, was heard to say: 'I've got a lot of Elton John tapes in my Porsche, but now I can't bear to listen to them.'

The Polaroids were deeply embarrassing for Elton – who had never lived a life of monastic sobriety – but they were not supporting evidence for the original Graham X story that Elton used rent-boys. The man in the photographs was a consenting adult, not a rent-boy. The pictures were taken in the late Seventies or very early Eighties, long before Elton was married.

The *Sun* made sure Elton saw the Polaroids before they were published. It was, the paper thought, the knock-out punch. Kelvin Mackenzie was convinced that Elton would fold. Someone who was close to Elton at the time told me: 'Elton realised that those photographs looked pretty bad for him, but they didn't have anything to do with Graham X. There was a lot of pressure on Elton to settle with the *Sun*, but he said no. Elton showed tremendous guts.'

ELTON PORN PHOTO SHAME by Neil Wallis flopped on to the streets on Thursday 16 April 1987, with a cropped shot of Elton's full-frontal on page one. As to the third Polaroid, the *Sun* adopted its most priggish tone: 'The Polaroid photograph is simply too disgusting to print in a family newspaper.' No mention of the fact that the same family newspaper had bought the set for £10,000.

The *Sun*'s readers hated it. They had always quite liked Elton John, and were beginning to suspect that what was amiss had nothing to do with Elton

John, but with the *Sun*. The paper was sounding like a bully.

Elton went on a chat show hosted by his old chum Michael Parkinson, and told his side of the story. Although he looked haggard and at the end of his tether, Elton was warmly applauded. He managed to get in a crack at the paper, which, he said, had tried to approach his wife's doctor: 'They probably want to examine my sperm. You would have thought they'd have buckets of the stuff.' The telly audience loved it.

Worse for Mackenzie, on days when the rent-boy story was on the front page, internal News International circulation figures showed alarming falls. The depressed editor was heard to moan that the *Sun* had lost 200,000 sales on one issue. The rent-boy effect was even starker because the readers came back whenever a 'normal' *Sun* story went on page one.

While Mackenzie worried in London, Hardy returned from Spain to Twyford to find that he had lost his job, his photograph had been printed in the *Daily Mirror* and the vice squad wanted to talk to him. The regular money from the *Sun*, handed over by Askill in a Thomas Cook holiday wallet, was beginning to dry up. It was not the best of homecomings.

The police inquiries culminated in what the *Sun* called on Wednesday 1 July a BIG GAY VICE SWOOP. Hardy was taken away for questioning in a police car, leaving his girlfriend, in tears, holding the baby. He was later charged with living off the immoral earnings of male prostitutes.

The stakes in the game were upped in July when a jury awarded Jeffrey Archer half a million pounds against the *Daily Star*, then the biggest libel settlement ever made. In the light of the Archer case, the *Sun*'s final attack on Elton John in 1987 could only be described as barking mad.

MYSTERY OF ELTON'S SILENT DOGS, by-lined John Askill, printed on Monday 28 September 1987, alleged that Elton had his 'vicious Rottweiler dogs ... silenced by a horrific operation'. Askill quoted RSPCA inspector John Hutchinson to support the story about Elton's 'silent assassins'. Hutchinson disowns the story: 'I was appalled by it.'

But what was most peculiar was that the *Sun* ought to have suspected it was nonsense all along. Askill filed the story with a disclaimer stressing it was not copper-bottomed. Elton's dogs are Alsatians. They bark. Elton sued for the 17th time.

By late autumn Hardy – newly married and waiting for his court hearing to come up – was no longer being wooed by the *Sun*. With memories of the Spanish trip fading fast, his next move was inevitable. On Friday 6 November 1987, the *Daily Mirror*'s front-page splash – MY SEX LIES OVER ELTON – quoted Hardy as saying: 'It's all a pack of lies. I made it all up. I only did it

663

for the money and the *Sun* was easy to con. I've never even met Elton John . . . I've never been to one of his concerts or bought one of his records. In fact, I hate his music.'

If Hardy had stuck with the *Daily Mirror* version of events, he might have found it easier to deny the pimping charges against him. But he changed his story yet again: by the time his case was heard in mid-January 1988, he was on good terms with the *Sun* once more. Hardy pleaded guilty to pimping, and was sentenced to 240 hours of community service. Of course, the *Sun* would clearly have difficulty making out a case that Hardy was a reliable witness when the first Graham X libel came to court. The *Sun* mole's view is that Mackenzie may have realised there was a possibility that he was going to lose, but had decided that the paper would go down 'with guns blazing'. 'There would be at least two weeks when we could report the dirt on Elton John,' the mole said. 'We would bring him down with us.'

Unfortunately for the *Sun*, at this stage Elton's lawyers managed to bring the barking dogs case – writ 17 – to court before the rent-boy allegations, despite the fact that the story had been printed months after the others. For Elton, the move was a major tactical victory.

The effect of the switch was to take the pressure off Elton, who had prepared himself for some unpleasant hours in the witness box, and put the squeeze on the *Sun*. The paper had to face the hopeless task of defending the Dogs That Didn't Bark story or giving in. There would be no dividend in fighting the case. Elton would come out as the Great British Dog-Lover; the paper would look deeply foolish and lose the first battle of the campaign. The earth started to shift even further under Mackenzie's feet, it is said, when Murdoch realised how much the lawyers' fees might add up to if all the cases were fought. The *Sun* went into reverse, fast.

On Monday 12 December 1988 the dog story was due to be heard in front of Mr Justice Michael Davies at the High Court. Fleet Street was slavering for the juicy details, confident that the *Sun* was in for a whipping. Instead, that morning the paper carried a massive, two-word headline, SORRY ELTON, followed by a lickspittle apology approved by the rock star, covering the whole saga, from Graham X to the dogs.

A press statement released the same morning admitted in wheedling terms that Kelvin Mackenzie personally associated himself with the climbdown. Although the paper had recently apologised to the Queen on its front page, this was the first libel apology ever to lead the paper. The story quoted a *Sun* spokesman: 'We are delighted that the *Sun* and Elton have become friends again and we are sorry that we were lied to by a teenager living in a world of fantasy.'

More surprisingly, Elton was quoted as saying: 'This is the best Christmas present I could wish for. Life is too short to bear grudges and I don't bear the *Sun* any malice.' In the centre pages, the paper carried an astonishing tribute to Elton's diet: 'The 41-year-old rock singer has shed an amazing TWO STONES in less than two months.' Elton had been badly mauled by the *Sun*'s claws; now he was being licked to death.

The million-pound settlement – double the Archer award – clearly suited both parties. The *Sun* was spared a drubbing by a jury; Elton was spared the dredging-up of old lies about his private life. Others were less happy. The judge, who had been told about the settlement as soon as it was made the previous afternoon, appeared piqued at the matiness of the two parties, and attacked them for forming 'a mutual admiration society'. 'The Queen's courts are provided for the trial and resolution of disputes,' he said, 'not as a supine adjunct to the publicity machine of pop stars and newspaper proprietors.'

According to a leading QC who followed the Elton John case closely, 'It just exposed the nonsense of agreed statements made in open court. The statements are fashioned according to the bargaining positions of the parties and the game of bluff and counter-bluff which libel proceedings increasingly are. You can't necessarily believe anything that is read in open court. It is not the truth as if it had emerged from contested proceedings, but a privately agreed version. Many feel that there ought to be some form of investigation by the court before it allows a statement to be made in its name. The judge was upset that the parties seemed to be exploiting the rules, but the answer is to change the rules. The parties did nothing wrong.'

The force of the judge's remarks was to take some of the gloss from Elton's victory. This was perhaps a little unfair. Elton had not invited the *Sun*'s Uriah Heepery, but desired an 'apology that matched the smear'. He wanted all 13 million *Sun* readers to know the paper had got it wrong; more, he wanted them to know that the paper had paid him a million. The *Sun* has a way of burying apologies written in legalese in the inside pages, so the front-page SORRY ELTON, written in the *Sun*'s style, was part of a strategy to get the maximum possible publicity for the settlement.

The judge appeared to misunderstand this. He had also attacked the announcement of the amount of damages. Living in a wider world, Elton wanted something more specific than 'substantial'. As to the tone of the apology, a regular reader of the *Sun* might have realised that when the paper says sorry, it does so with the same salivating frenzy with which it goes about the rest of its business.

665

And what now of our cast? Elton John saw his marriage break up and went through a crisis of depression which blighted his life for months. He tried to sell Watford, then changed his mind, but did sell many of his rock memorabilia. He came out of his ordeal a thinner, richer man, and is about to go on a world tour with a new album.

John Boyce was last heard of in a court, after being involved in a fight in a hotel. No doubt he is conjuring some new 'nice little earners'. Stephen Hardy told me: 'I lost my job, my marriage and my self-respect over this. I've got no friends left. I still get very badly depressed about it.' His ex-wife is perhaps the saddest victim of the affair. At the age of 20, she has had a child by a man who is notorious in the small community where she lived.

And what about Kelvin Mackenzie? According to the *Sun* mole, 'Kelvin's self-confidence took a massive knock over the Elton John story. He's a better editor now and the *Sun*'s a better paper.' For even Rupert Murdoch cannot afford to write off £1 million as loose change. In the week before Christmas Mackenzie invited his staff into his office. They expected a pep talk, a few words of congratulation about the best sales figures in the Western world and a Yuletide drink. They got a nasty shock. The *Sun* mole said: 'It was a foul-mouthed abuse session. He warned that the next reporter who got a writ would be out. He said: "It's got to stop. If I go, I'm going to take you bastards with me."' There was no mention of Merry Christmas.

Nevertheless, Mackenzie is still there. After all, Mackenzie's *Sun* makes Murdoch more than a million pounds a week profit. While the balance sheet is still in Mackenzie's favour, neither a huge libel bill nor a stack of privacy acts nor an ombudsman will change the tenor of the *Sun*. Mackenzie may well end up the same way his predecessor did. He was knighted, for services to journalism.

John Sweeney, *Independent* magazine, 11 February 1989

ten

1988–

'The end of the century'

'Synthetic electronic sounds
Industrial rhythms all around
Musique non stop
Techno Pop'

Kraftwerk, 'TechnoPop' (1986)

'Popular culture carries that affirmative ring because of the prominence of
the word "popular". And, in one sense, popular culture always has its base in
the experiences, the pleasures, the memories, the traditions of the people. It
has connections with local hopes and local aspirations, local tragedies and
local scenarios that are the everyday practices and the everyday experiences
of ordinary folks. Hence, it links with what Mikhail Bakhtin calls "the
vulgar" – the popular, the informal, the underside, the grotesque. That is
why it has always been counterposed to elite or high culture, and is thus a site
of alternative traditions. And that is why the dominant tradition has always
been afraid of it, quite rightly.'

Stuart Hall, 'What is This "Black" in Black Popular Culture?' (1992)

'POP is about singles, solitary songs, complete statements. It always has
been, always will be.'

Kevin Pearce, Something Beginning with O (1992)

'Dance Music, like any other style of music, becomes "Pop" when it becomes
accepted by the masses. When tons of people support and buy it, it becomes
pop. POP = success. Every form of music that has been commercially
successful is Pop Music. STYLE + FORM + SUCCESSFUL +
COMMERCIAL = POP.'

Robert Clivilles, from C & C Music Factory, Mixmag, February 1992

'One thing I like about British pop music fans is that they are so serious
about it. It's life or death.'

Brian Eno, interview in The Wire, 1992

During the last ten years, pop has become a principal motor of the Western consumer machine. Like Hollywood in the interwar years, it is in the vanguard of the spread of Western values into new markets: the old Eastern Europe, Malaysia, Russia, China. Some of this is the result of a pheno- menon called 'vertical integration', whereby record companies have become mere divisions within a multinational structure that also includes publishing, hardware manufacture, broadcasting, copyrights et al. Pop has become integrated into everyday life as never before, through adverts, films (often trailered by a hit song), a proliferating consumer media.

Pop is omnipresent, yet seems to mean less. To quote recent media tropes, it's over; it doesn't mean anything, or at least, not what it meant in the sixties and seventies – tropes rehearsed and refuted by Greil Marcus in his 'Notes on the Life & Death and Incandescent Banality of Rock 'n' Roll'. The 'death of' discourse internalizes the right-wing attack on pop that has occurred over the last fifteen years (signalled in the UK by frequent ministerial vilification of the sixties): pop is mere froth, is pure process, is cynical manipulation – anything but the fact which stares you in the face when you attend most pop events, that, in Dave Marsh's phrase, 'it gives a voice and a face to the dispossessed'.

There has been more pop writing during the last five years than ever before. Our choice in this section is by necessity selective and polemical. As the mid-eighties style media moved into the British mainstream, the focus of pop writing shifted elsewhere. It was not to be found in the consumer- oriented media, but in fanzines, small specialist magazines, or established broadsheets – anywhere where writers did not have to write to a format, where they did not have to join in the dismissal of pop as a serious form.

An active agent in pop's spread has also been the decentralizing aspect of technology – which in the digital age has made home-recording much easier. The Timelords tell you how to make a number one record, in an extract from *The Manual* (*How to Have a Number One*): they acted upon their own advice with subsequent hits as the KLF. Stuart Cosgrove's excavation of Detroit techno as a new craze unwittingly introduces the musical grid into which all this do-it-yourself activity would be poured: an avant-garde, weird electronica with the discipline and emotional directness of dance music. The impact of this on British pop culture is recorded in several extracts. Norman Jay and Mike Noon chart the grass roots adapta- tion of black American dance music by two different subcultures: London Soul Boys and North Western Scallies – the latter fuelling the 'Madchester' boom of 1990. Simon Reynolds and Kodwo Eshun trace these clubland mutations through every twist and turn into a new kind of perception, 'a primal DNA soup', which is informed by the constant need of British youth to steal their own time and space within a static, restrictive society.

The process by which pop has moved from being an unattainable ideal to becoming a major force in previously closed cultures is traced here. Dave Rimmer uses the story of a prank which nearly went wrong – 'The Eastie Boys' – to highlight the absurdities and dangers of a spent regime, and the desperate longings of those who lived within it. Kean Wong highlights the ambiguities involved in Western cultural expansion: what gets taken up, what gets misunderstood, what gets lost. Lou Reed goes to Czechoslovakia to hear how his records with the Velvet Underground gave Václav Havel some of the inspiration which took him to President in 1991.

Within the West, pop is still used as a way of getting heard, finding your place in the sun. Nelson George witnesses the new generation of black militancy epitomized by Public Enemy, while the extract from Ice T's autobiography details what happens when a black man is seen to go too far. Gina Arnold gives an insider's perspective on how her generation was empowered by the success of Nirvana and the sea change they caused in American rock. Writing about Suede in the *Village Voice*, Barry Walters shows how pop can lend itself to a queer voice.

Several extracts reinforce the power of pop as music – a power which has not died. Chris Heath's snapshot of the Pet Shop Boys shows that, far from being hamstrung by the self-consciousness that is supposed to have crippled pop culture, performers can live, breathe, snipe about, then go and make pop, brilliantly. Mike Soutar poses the archetypal question about the most influential producers of the late eighties, Stock Aitken and Waterman: are they down the dumper? Mark Frith's article from *Smash Hits* freezes the latest British pop phenomenon, Take That, on an upward curve of hysteria.

The book ends with five extracts which highlight pop as a site of continuing struggle. Written while the allegations of child abuse were still pending (they were settled in early 1994, when Jackson's accuser, the thirteen-year-old Jordan Chandler, received an estimated $35 million payoff), Gavin Martin's polemic on the life of Michael Jackson explores the impossible tensions of global fame in general, and of Jackson's situation in particular: the young boy who grew up in the spotlight, the young man who remains locked in permanent adolescence. A report from *Hello* magazine shows how Jackson tried to grow into adulthood, with his marriage to Elvis's only daughter, Lisa Marie Presley.

Fame destroys: we now know that. Ann Powers' elegy on fellow North

Westerner Kurt Cobain – the Nirvana singer and writer who committed suicide in April 1994 – blazes with the shock felt by millions, including the editors, when they heard the news. The final articles by Joy Press and Andrew O'Hagan show that, in Britain, pop isn't about music: it's an often dangerous way of life. For those committed to the idea of pop as mere consumption or baby-boomer nostalgia, here are two reminders of the twin impulses to self-destruction and utopianism that are never far away from pop's surface.

1988: The Golden Rules

Leiber and Stoller, Goffin and King, Berry Gordy, Chinn and Chapman and Peter Waterman have all understood the Golden Rules thoroughly. The reason why Waterman will not continue churning out Number Ones from now until the end of the century and the others had only limited reigns, was not because lady luck's hand strayed elsewhere or that fashion moved on, it is because after you have had a run of success and your coffers are full, keeping strictly to the GRs is boring. It all becomes empty and meaningless. Some have become emotionally or business wise embroiled with artists whose own ambitions now lie elsewhere and far from merely having Number One's. Leiber and Stoller could walk into a studio tomorrow and have a world wide Number One in three months if they were so motivated.

The basic Golden Rules as far as they apply to writing a debut single that can go to Number One in the UK Charts are as follows:

Do not attempt the impossible by trying to work the whole thing out before you go into the studio. Working in a studio has to be a fluid and creative venture but at all times remember at the end of it you are going to have to have a 7" version that fulfills all the criteria perfectly. Do not try and sit down and write a complete song. Songs that have been written in such a way and reached Number One can only be done by the true song writing genius and be delivered by artists with such forceful convincing passion that the world HAS TO listen. You know the sort of thing, 'Sailing' by Rod Stewart, 'Without You' by Nilsson.

What the Golden Rules can provide you with is a framework that you can slot the component parts into.

Firstly, it has to have a dance groove that will run all the way through the record and that the current 7" buying generation will find irresistible. Secondly, it must be no longer than three minutes and thirty seconds (just under 3.20 is preferable). If they are any longer Radio One daytime DJs will start fading early or talking over the end, when the chorus is finally being hammered home – the most important part of any record. Thirdly, it must consist of an intro, a verse, a chorus, second verse, a second chorus, a breakdown section, back into a double length chorus and outro. Fourthly, lyrics. You will need some, but not many.

Causality Plus a Pinch of Mysticism

It is going to be a construction job, fitting bits together. You will have to find the Frankenstein in you to make it work. Your magpie instincts must come to the fore. If you think this just sounds like a recipe for some horrific monster, be reassured by us, all music can only be the sum or part total of what has gone before. Every Number One song ever written is only made up from bits from other songs. There is no lost chord. No changes untried. No extra notes to the scale or hidden beats to the bar. There is no point in searching for originality. In the past, most writers of songs spent months in their lonely rooms strumming their guitars or bands in rehearsals have ground their way through endless riffs before arriving at the song that takes them to the very top. Of course, most of them would be mortally upset to be told that all they were doing was leaving it to chance before they stumbled across the tried and tested. They have to believe it is through this sojourn they arrive at the grail; the great and original song that the world will be unable to resist.

So why don't all songs sound the same? Why are some artists great, write dozens of classics that move you to tears, say it like it's never been said before, make you laugh, dance, blow your mind, fall in love, take to the streets and riot? Well, it's because although the chords, notes, harmonies, beats and words have all been used before their own soul shines through; their personality demands attention. This doesn't just come via the great vocalist or virtuoso instrumentalist. The Techno sound of Detroit, the most totally linear programmed music ever, lacking any human musicianship in its execution reeks of sweat, sex and desire. The creators of that music just press a few buttons and out comes – a million years of pain and lust.

We await the day with relish that somebody dares to make a dance record that consists of nothing more than an electronically programmed bass drum beat that continues playing the fours monotonously for eight minutes. Then, when somebody else brings one out using exactly the same bass drum sound and at the same beats per minutes (BPM), we will all be able to tell which is the best, which inspires the dance floor to fill the fastest, which has the most sex and the most soul. There is no doubt, one will be better than the other.

What we are basically saying is, if you have anything in you, anything unique, what others might term as originality, it will come through whatever the component parts used in your future Number One are made up from.

Creators of music who desperately search for originality usually end up with music that has none because no room for their spirit has been left to get through. The complete history of the blues is based on one chord structure, hundreds of thousands of songs using the same three basic chords in the same pattern. Through this seemingly rigid formula has come some of the twentieth century's greatest music.

In our case we used parts from three very famous songs, Gary Glitter's 'Rock 'n' Roll', 'The Doctor Who Theme' and the Sweet's 'Blockbuster' and pasted them together, neither of us playing a note on the record. We know that the finished record contains as much of us in it as if we had spent three months locked away somewhere trying to create our master-work. The people who bought the record and who probably do not give a blot about the inner souls of Rockman Rock or King Boy D knew they were getting a record of supreme originality.

Don't worry about being accused of being a thief. Even if you were to, you have not got the time to take the trial and error route.

The simplest thing to do would be to flick through your copy of the Guinness Book of Hits, find a smash from a previous era and do a cover of it, dressing it up in the clothes of today. Every year there is at least a couple of artists who get their debut Number One this way. From the eighties we have already had:

Dave Stewart and Barbara Gaskin	'It's My Party'
Roxy Music	'Jealous Guy'
Soft Cell	'Tainted Love'
Paul Young	'Wherever I Lay My Hat'
Captain Sensible	'Happy Talk'
Neil	'Hole in My Shoe'
Tiffany	'I Think We're Alone Now'
Wet Wet Wet	'With a Little Help'
Yazz	'The Only Way is Up'

There are, however, the negative facts in taking this route. Using an already proven song can give you a false sense of security when you are in the studio recording. You can end up under the illusion that the song is such a classic that whatever you do, the song itself will be able to carry it through. You tend to lose your objectivity in the production of your version. The all important radio producers hate nothing more than a classic song covered badly.

675

The classic oldy, while fulfilling all the Golden Rules in pop, might have a lyrical content that may only ever relate to one period in pop history. There have been numerous past Number One's where this has been the case:

Scott McKenzie	'San Francisco'
The Beach Boys	'Good Vibrations'
The Beatles	'All You Need is Love'
Mott the Hoople	'All the Young Dudes'
MARRS	'Pump Up the Volume'

Unless there is a revival of the zeitgeist of times past where the lyric in some way makes sense again, these songs should be stayed well clear of.

Sometimes, almost the opposite can happen. By covering a cleverly picked old song it can be re-recorded in such a way that it is now more relevant to today's new record buyers, both lyrically and musically, than the original was to the past generations of hit-makers. Tiffany's 'I Think We're Alone Now' and Yazz's 'The Only Way is Up' are both perfect examples of this in 1988. The original of 'I Think We're Alone Now' by Tommy Roe and the late seventies cover by the Rubinoos were classics for the discerning but could not compete in the UK market place of their day.

The other negative in doing a cover version is you lose all the writing credit. That means you will earn no publishing money on the record, however many it sells. We will explain later the mysteries of publishing, but for now just take it from us that having a Number One with a cover, as opposed to your own song, is the equivalent of throwing away a minimum of £10,000.

There is no denying that in picking the right smash from the past and recording it well will result in a sure fire success. The producers of the day time shows at Radio One will have to only hear the opening bars of your record to know that there will be a few slots in their shows for it; 'the housewives at home and the husbands on the building site' will be singing along with it immediately. It's not going to take them three or four listens before they decide whether they like the song. That decision was made long before you ever thought of having a Number One. As for the current 7" single buying generation who might have never heard the song before, they will automatically be given the chance to hear the record three or four times on the radio.

If there is not a cover that takes your fancy the trick is to construct your song out of disguised, modified and enhanced parts of previous smashes, so that those Radio One producers, T.V. youth programme researchers and multiple-chain-record-store stock buyers will subliminally warm to your track and feel at ease with it.

We obviously took the middle route in not doing a straight cover, but in doing the above so blatantly that we had to give away the majority of our publishing thus losing a sizeable chunk of the readies.

The Timelords , *The Manual (How to Have a Number One the Easy Way)* (1988)

1988: Seventh City Techno

'It's night-time in an obscure sidestreet somewhere in the seventh city. Far away, a banshee police siren wails. A falling body screams and the innocent suffer all the while. Unheard. This is Cabaret Seven.'

Gambit and Associates, Detroit, 1987

The underground comic *Gambit and Associates* tells the story of a weird technocracy. It is set in Detroit, the seventh city, the murder capital of the USA, and the home of America's most progressive musical underground. The comic is drawn by a Detroit DJ and follows the exploits of a punk detective called Johnny Gambit, a fan of the Belgian group FRONT 242, and a dude who can draw a gun at 122 beats-per-minute. The streets are littered with bodies, the innocents go unheard, and the buildings crash against each other in disordered shapes. According to Detroit's premier producer Derrik May – the brains behind the mutant dance music of Rhythim Is Rhythim – the comic will be available as a companion piece to his next independent 12-inch dance record, and is the only accurate tourist guide to the city of Detroit.

Although the Detroit dance music has been casually lumped in with the jack-virus of Chicago House, the young Techno producers of the seventh city claim to have their own sound, music that 'goes beyond the beat', creating a hybrid of post-punk, funkadelia and electro-disco.

The self-proclaimed captain of the new Detroit underground is Juan Atkins, a 26-year-old producer who releases records under the name Model 500. He originally rose to prominence in the early Eighties as a member of the electro band Cybotron, whose hit 'Techno City' appeared on the old UK compilation LP 'Electro 4'. Juan operates a makeshift basement studio in his home in West Detroit and sees the city's new underground sound as an inevitable by-product of advanced technology.

'Within the last five years or so, the Detroit underground has been experimenting with technology, stretching it rather than simply using it. As the price of sequencers and synthesisers has dropped, so the experimentation has become more intense. Basically, we're tired of hearing about being in love or falling out, tired of the R&B system, so a new progressive sound has emerged. We call it Techno!'

The Detroit Techno scene is a mesmerising underground of new dance which blends European industrial pop with black America's garage funk. Its main exponents are Model 500, Rhythim Is Rhythim, Reese and Santonio, Triple X, Dynamix, Blake Baxter, The Flintstones and Eddie 'Flashin' Fowlkes. If the Techno scene worships any gods, they are a pretty deranged deity, according to Derrik May: 'The music is just like Detroit, a complete mistake. It's like George Clinton and Kraftwerk stuck in an elevator.'

Techno began in West Detroit, or to be more precise in the corridors of Belleville High School, where its three most ardent devotees, Juan Atkins, Derrik May and Kevin Saunderson, were at school together. Although it can now be heard in most of Detroit's leading clubs, the local area has shown a marked reluctance to get behind the music. It has been in clubs like The Powerplant (Chicago), The World (New York), The Hacienda (Manchester), Rock City (Nottingham) and Downbeat (Leeds) where the Techno sound has found most support.

Ironically, the only Detroit club which really championed the sound was a peripatetic party night called Visage, which unromantically shared its name with one of Britain's oldest New Romantic groups. And strange as it may seem, the Techno scene looked to Europe, to Heaven 17, Depeche Mode and The Human League, for its inspiration. Eventually, support arrived in the form of a hip local DJ called The Electrifyin' Mojo, who plugged it on his nightly sessions on Radio Station WHYT.

Kevin Saunderson, one half of Rees and Santonio and a student at East Michigan University, claims the city has held the music back. He was once sacked from a local radio station for being 'too ahead of his time'. He returned to the station with evidence of Techno's growing popularity, only to be rebuked again.

'I took them a clipping from *Billboard* and they told me to come back when we were on the front cover. That's Detroit. I've turned my back on this city. I don't care if they never buy one of my records – other people will.'

Saunderson's confidence comes from success outside Detroit. Model 500's inter-stellar dance record 'No UFOs' has been one of the underground club scene's biggest-selling records over the last three years; three releases by Rhythim Is Rhythim – 'Nude Photo', 'Strings' and 'The Dance' – introduced the club scene to the buzz-term 'acid house'; Techno labels like Transmit, Metroplex and Incognito are in permanent demand; and Kevin Saunderson's 'The Sound' has been bootlegged in Berlin, London and New York.

Getting sacked for being too hip seems to be an occupational hazard in Detroit. Derrik May, now generally recognized as one of the club scene's most in-demand mixers, began his career on the wrong end of his boss's wrath.

'I used to DJ at a local club called The Liedernacht. The crowd were completely against dance music. They only wanted to hear The Smiths or Severed Heads. I was playing black underground sounds and they couldn't take it. They used to say, "Get this nigger shit off!" They even went as far as having a sit-down strike on the dancefloor. All these dickheads in black shirts trying to be so English and so progressive and refusing to listen to underground music that was happening under their noses. We built up the crowd until it was racially mixed. The manager told me he didn't want a black club and I was fired. They play my record now, but I can't get in. I'm banned for life.'

Members Of The House, three young Detroit Techno-freaks who recently recorded the excellent 12-inch 'Share This House' for less than $2,000, have similar reservations: 'This is an automobile city but some people's heads are drawn by horse and carriage.' They favour a basement approach to music, working in restricted conditions. 'Techno is all about simplicity. We don't want to compete with Jimmy Jam and Terry Lewis. Modern R&B has too many rules: big snare sounds, big bass and even bigger studio bills.'

Techno is probably the first form of contemporary black music which categorically breaks with the old heritage of soul music. Unlike Chicago House, which has a lingering obsession with Seventies Philly, and unlike New York hip-hop with its deconstructive attack on James Brown's back-catalogue, Detroit Techno refutes the past. It may have a special place for Parliament and Pete Shelley, but it prefers tomorrow's technology to yesterday's heroes.

Techno is a post-soul sound. It says nothing to the Lord, but speaks volumes on the dancefloor. Whilst modern singers like Anita Baker, Whitney Houston and Alexander O'Neal still carry the traces of a gospel past, for the young black underground in Detroit, emotion crumbles at the feet of technology.

Derrik May's revolutionary backtracking on the Technics decks and

679

Santonio's Yamaha drums are stripped of any sense of authentic emotion: they just percuss you out. Even vocalist Blake Baxter sees his style as a distant voice at odds with the emotional power of soul. His Techno hit 'Ride 'Em Boys' is a promiscuous dance record featuring a sampled woman's voice and a barely audible vocalist. 'I don't really sing,' says Blake, 'I speak in a soft voice almost hiding beneath the beat. I love records with whispering vocals – it's nothing like the gospel sound.'

Significantly, the greatest response to the new Detroit sound in Britain has been in the North. There is no obvious reason why. Soul sociology sees it as a musical re-working of the North–South divide, and cult theory sees it as an unconscious return to the values of the old Northern soul scene, where uptempo dance music, obscure records and the city of Detroit held an unrivalled esteem. It sounds ridiculous. It *is* ridiculous. But there may just be a grain of truth in the rare soul theory.

When Virgin's 10 label releases a double album of Detroit Techno music this month, it will be the first time the music has had a substantial presence in Britain. The album will be issued in conjunction with Neil Rushton, a former Northern soul DJ who owns a West Midlands House label called Kool Kat. (For those of you who love the pursuit of trivia, Kool Kat's name is homage to an old Detroit label which Northern soul collectors still pray to every night.) Some of the tracks on the album have been recorded at United Sound Studios, home of the legendary Detroit overlord Don Davis, who was responsible for countless soul classics including Johnnie Taylor's 'Who's Makin' Love', The Dramatics' 'In The Rain' and Parliament's 'Mothership Connection'.

But despite Detroit's rich musical history, the young Techno stars have little time for the golden era of Motown. Juan Atkins of Model 500 is convinced there is nothing to be gained from the motor-city legacy. 'Berry Gordy built the Motown sound on the same principles as the conveyor belt system at Ford's. Today their plants don't work that way – they use robots and computers to make the cars. I'm probably more interested in Ford's robots than in Berry Gordy's music.' The disinterest in Motown sometimes spills over into resentment. Juan's protegy Eddie 'Flashin' Fowlkes feels Motown 'left and took the whole structure of Detroit music with them. They left a vacuum that has taken over 15 years to fill.'

Motown's departure in the early Seventies was a symbolic moment in Detroit's industrial fortunes. In the years since, factories have closed, car plants have contracted, and the city centre is now virtually bereft of any sense of community. More than any other place, Detroit has taken on a post-industrial identity.

It is 4 a.m. and Derrik May is on the 30th floor of a shaded glass hotel looking across the skyline of his hometown. His friend Alan Oldham, the comic artist turned DJ, is somewhere else in the city about to play Rhythim To Rhythim's 'Chaos' over the airwaves of Radio WDET. Played alongside The Skinny Puppys and New Order, the sparse and confrontational dance record gets a fittingly dramatic introduction. 'Stand by for some post-industrial chaos. Techno from a long lost friend.'

Derrik has quietened down now. After a night of running up hotel walls and arguing with bouncers at The Taboo Club, he is in a reflective, almost alienated mood. 'This city is in total devastation. It is going through the biggest change in its history. Detroit is passing through its third wave, a social dynamic which nobody outside this city can understand. Factories are closing, people are drifting away, and kids are killing each other for fun. The whole order has broken down. If our music is a soundtrack to all that, I hope it makes people understand what kind of disintegration we're dealing with.'

Techno is light years away from the happy frivolity of The Supremes. 'Say what you like about our music,' says Blake Baxter. 'But don't call us the new Motown . . . We're the second coming.'

Stuart Cosgrove, The Face #97, May 1988

1988: The Eastie Boys

We had been talking about names for groups. Spud and Buttle both played in one back West that was three-fifths American GI and two-fifths East German *émigré* – the latter two old friends of Torsten's. The group was called The Nimrods, but they wanted a change. Mark proffered The Stealth Bombers. Salman came up with The Stars And Stripes. I suggested The Crap Smugglers. Spud preferred The Screaming Weasels and was trying to think of ways to be both shocking and original.

'Hey, I could drink a load of beer and stuff and throw up on stage. That would really be something. Imagine, throwing up on stage!'

'Spud,' said Mark, 'I don't know whether you noticed, but about ten years ago there was this thing called punk . . .'

'The name should definitely be something military,' I said. 'Let's face it, the fact that you're mostly GIs is about the only thing you've got going for you. You should, like, paint all your gear in camouflage colours.'

'It's been done,' smiled Mark, who had done it.

'What if Torsten and I had a group,' asked Norman. 'What should we call that?'

'I know,' I was suddenly inspired. 'You should call yourselves The Eastie Boys. Instead of wearing Mercedes or Volkswagen symbols around your necks like all those bands in the West, you could wear the Trabant emblem.'

The chrome insignia of West German motor manufacturers, prised from bonnets and slung round the neck like trophies, had long been part of the hip hop street uniform. That summer it had only been a year since a white group called The Beastie Boys, often thus attired, had turned a mix of heavy metal, rap and relentlessly obnoxious behaviour into a hit with a song called 'Fight for Your Right (To Party)'.

'The Eastie Boys could play "Fight for Your Right" too,' said Mark.

'It makes sense but it's too obvious,' I mused. 'How about "Born in the DDR"?'

'Yeah,' said Mark. 'In the publicity they could claim, in a sarcastic sort of way, that they were inspired by that Bruce Springsteen concert.'

Already the idea was running away with us, but Torsten was smiling uncertainly and Norman looked distinctly unimpressed. The Eastie Boys? Trabant emblems?

'Whoever would be interested in that?' he asked.

'Maybe no one over here,' I told him. 'But in the West, you'd be surprised.'

Norman shook his head. He didn't believe a word of it.

I thought about it all the way home that night: sweeping past the flat blocks on the way to the border, holding my passport up to Spud's car window, waiting while the MP at Charlie opened up a boot in which, had Norman or Torsten been hiding there, they would surely have been discovered. Over the next few days in West Berlin, the idea would not leave me alone. Not only was the name a solid, satisfying pun, it was also the beautiful coincidence of international street style adopting the icons of West German capitalism. Trabant emblems would be an especially good piece of satire. As a concept for a group from the other side, it was perfect. The pity of it was that even though we'd spent the rest of the evening in Rebecca's chewing it over with them, Norman and Torsten still couldn't quite see the joke.

Sitting in my kitchen one afternoon, with some black leather trouser music reverberating from Olga's flat upstairs, I found I could resist the temptation no longer. I picked up the phone, dialled the London number of *The Face* magazine and prepared to do something I had never, ever done before: fashion a story from a complete and utter pack of lies.

'Hi, it's Dave Rimmer ... Yeah, well I've been out of town. In fact I'm ringing from West Berlin, I've been here for the last few months ... Well, I've come across one unusual story – this group in East Berlin. They call themselves The Eastie Boys ...'

The music editor was intrigued, as I knew I would have been if I'd been sitting around in a magazine office with pages to fill. As long as there was a good picture it would make a good story.

'The thing about the photo,' she said, 'is that it's got to be obvious that it's in East Berlin. It can't look like it's been faked in someone's bedroom.'

I promised to find an authentically Eastern-looking location. There was a statue of Lenin, I told her, various other monumental examples of communist iconography. Two minutes later I was ringing Mark. Up to this point I had been considering the thing nothing but a small media prank. Mark, however, on learning what I had just set in motion, immediately raised the stakes.

'We should make the record,' he said.

'And you thought no one would be interested.'

I grinned at Norman and Torsten over a table outside the Opera Café. On the other side of Unter den Linden, tourists were snapping the guards in Russian-style helmets who stood watch outside the Neue Wache. We had worked our way through the idiosyncrasies of the café's system – coffee and lurid cakes at one self-service window, soft drinks and cheap alcohol at another, runny ice cream from a waitress who would serve nothing else – and were now settling down to discuss The Eastie Boys.

'The thing about *The Face*,' I told them, 'is that it's the kind of magazine that other magazines copy. It's fashionable, gets on to new things quickly and editors all over the place read it to see if there's anything they should cover. If we put this story in there, we're bound to get interest from some other magazines. A couple of West German magazines are definitely going to pick up on it, if only because they feel they've been "scooped" by an English magazine.'

'And then,' said Mark, 'we release the record.'

'The best thing,' I continued, 'is that we control it completely. We're not going to use your real names, you're in East Berlin somewhere, so no one can contact you except through us. We can invent any story we like. And even if

683

they suspect it's a load of rubbish they're still going to use it as long as it's funny and interesting.'

Torsten and Norman were bemused. Our little game was turning into a lesson in the corrupt workings of the capitalist media. Things worked very differently in the East. Pop music was something the population wanted, maybe even something that a modern society ought to have – like toasters or television towers – but the power structure neither liked nor trusted it. If they had to have pop music they would keep it trussed up with bureaucratic controls. To release records you had to be accepted as an official group. Several years at music school were necessary just to 'qualify' as a musician. It was possible, if you curried enough favour with the local FDJ, to form a group and get an amateur gig at a youth club somewhere. Geier and Die Vision, for example, had got that far by the summer of 1988 and were angling for a shot at the next step: an audition before a panel of Party and FDJ stalwarts, academics and officially approved music critics, all sitting there sternly with notebooks and spectacles.

Every musician, group or DJ would have to go through this and your entire career would depend on the results. At worst this dry bunch would immediately show you the door and you'd end up manning the production line of the local plastic cruet factory. Scarcely preferable was to get out of music school and be condemned for life to the house band of some awful restaurant, sitting in the corner in a dicky suit playing frilly cover versions of 'Isn't She Lovely' and 'If I was a Rich Man' on a cheesy electric organ. If you were lucky – if your music caused some old Party hack to tap his feet, if your lyrics were bland, wholesome and innocent of anything that could be construed as political commentary, if you generally corresponded to what members of this Stalinist Juke Box Jury perceived to be suitable for socialist youth – then you would be graded according to one of several official categories.

The grade awarded would determine what kind of venues you could play, how many copies of your single the state record label would press, how much you would get paid. You'd start as an official amateur or semi-professional. As long as you didn't put a foot wrong – start singing politically suspect lyrics or disporting yourself in an unwholesome manner – subsequent auditions (you had to return for them regularly) might see you ascending to higher grades and thus playing bigger venues, having more records pressed, generally being more 'famous'. Official pop magazines would write about you because there was no one else to write about; shops would stock your records just as they stocked whatever else the state distribution system sent them.

Success as measured by sales undoubtedly had some small influence on the relevant cultural committees and time-servers at the Ministry of Records. Sometimes, testing out a new group, they'd allow the radio to make and broadcast a tape. Listeners' response to this, if there was any, might be taken into consideration. Further up the ladder, if they pressed up to 10,000 copies of your single and sold only ten, they'd undoubtedly reconsider your status. But otherwise Eastern popular music had little to do with popularity. People would go to concerts and purchase albums simply because they were there. No matter how many records you sold, you would remain on the salary designated for an artist of your category. As a mechanism for the manufacture and maintenance of abject mediocrity, this system was peerless.

The contrast with the strategy outlined by Mark and me fascinated both Norman and Torsten. We spent the rest of that afternoon discussing ideas for their outfits, sketching out roughs of an Eastie Boys logo, deciding on locations for the photographs. Arrangements were made for Mark and me to come and do a styling session, once Norman and Torsten had obtained all the relevant bits and pieces.

It was in a bit of a dream that I pottered about the kitchen a few nights later. I'd had a relaxing smoke and was now slicing tofu, adding lemon juice to the peanut sauce, chopping up vegetables to be gently stewed in coconut gravy. The phone startled me when it rang.

'Hallo?'

'Could I speak to Mr David Rimmer?'

It was a North American voice.

'Speaking.'

'This is Special Agent Davis of the US Military Police Criminal Investigation Department.'

'Come off it, who is this?'

'Special Agent Davis of the –'

'Yeah, yeah. Who is it really?'

I racked my brains. The GIs were big on 'jigs', as they called practical jokes. It couldn't be Buttle; there wasn't the smallest trace of his Southern twang. It didn't sound in the least like Spud. Could it be Salman? His accent was the least distinctive: sort of generically American, like this one was, though nowhere near as cold and chilling.

'This is not a joke, Mr Rimmer. Your name has repeatedly come up in connection with certain, ah, irregularities involving members of the US Forces. We'd like you to come in and talk to us.'

I felt a little rush of fear. My name was on all the forms Spud or Buttle filled out every time we went East together. A background anxiety I had been feeling about our activities now pushed its way to the fore. We had been pushing our luck. What if it was indeed Special Agent Davis? Had they found out about the GIs' contact with East German civilians? Oh God, maybe Spud had been mouthing off about his crazy plans to help Norman escape!

'Why, uh . . . Talk to you about what?'

'Just some routine questions, Mr Rimmer.' He invested the word 'routine' with a particular menace. 'Could you report to me at US Army Head-quarters, Building Three, on Clayallee at nine o'clock on Thursday morning?'

'Um, ah, what will happen if I don't come in?'

'We could always send the local police around to see you, but of course we would like to avoid any unpleasantness.'

'Um, well, OK then. Your name is Special Agent Davis?'

'That's correct. Building Three, US Army Headquarters, Clayallee, nine on Thursday. There is a telephone in the entrance to the building. Just pick it up and ask for me.'

I was still in a state of turmoil when Mark turned up an hour later. He watched and listened with a worried eye as I babbled out the story, so jittery I spilled the beansprouts on the floor. He didn't seem to know what to say. Yes, he supposed it could have something to do with Spud's escape plans. He had no idea what the military could do – just about anything, probably. As far as he could see the trouble was . . . and then he laughed.

'I can't keep it up any longer. You look so worried. It was Salman.'

A gush of relief.

'How do you know?'

'Because he tried it on me first.'

'Did he fool you?'

'Sort of. But when he asked if I'd go in to answer some questions I just said no and put the phone down.'

I felt like a fool and a coward for not having done the same. A few minutes later the doorbell rang. I opened it to the two GIs. Salman could tell I had twigged it from the look in my eye.

'Sorry,' he grinned.

'You bastard. I only knew it was you because Mark just told me. What were you going to do if I hadn't sussed it? Just let me stew all night?'

'I don't know. I was just going to play it by ear.'

'And on a night when I was cooking you a meal. You rotten bastard. It was

686

particularly underhand because the main reason I would have gone down there was to try and keep you fuckers out of trouble.'

They both stood there grinning, like a pair of Mormon evangelists.

The Trabant symbol was a little circle with a flattened 'S' shape across the middle. Norman and Torsten liberated a couple from parked cars – a delicate task because, unlike sturdy metal Mercedes emblems, they were brittle plastic and tended to snap instead of coming loose. Buttle brought the things back West. Mark deployed skills honed by a lifetime's model-making to paint them silver, attach a small metal ring to the top and string them on a couple of heavy metal chains. They looked really good but hung a little oddly: the cheap plastic was too light to exert any tension on the chain.

Come the day of the photo session – a day on which all the GIs were off on field exercises somewhere in West Germany – the only problem was how to get them through Friedrichstrasse.

'These are going to be a little hard to explain,' I mused. 'I mean, it's obvious where they've come from and difficult to account for where they're going.'

Mark shrugged. 'We'll just have to wear them under our jackets and, if they still find them, say we bought them at the flea market.'

The camera I had borrowed was easier. I just hung it around my neck as a tourist would and trusted that the half dozen rolls of film in my bag would plausibly fall within the bounds of a day's holiday-snapping. In the event, no guard so much as glanced at us. We emerged from an easy crossing at Friedrichstrasse and caught the tram for Pankow in ebullient spirits. The sun was out, the light was good and an unusual day lay ahead of us.

At Torsten's flat we inspected the preparations. They had designed an Eastie Boys logo which placed the Trabant S-in-a-circle inside a five-pointed communist star. Torsten had drawn this on a little blue cap as well as on the back of a black denim waistcoat jacket. He wore a red *Staubsauger* T-shirt, a present from Trevor, which featured a hammer and vacuum cleaner in a take-off of the Soviet flag. His trousers were held up by a Russian army belt. Norman had obtained a rust-red track suit jacket of the Stasi-sponsored Dynamo sports club. The logo had gone on the back of this too. On the front, along with a Russian badge bearing an enigmatic number 2, he had phonetically rendered a cyrillic version of the group's name. Down one arm were also sewn FDJ, Young Pioneers and Free German Trade Union patches. His T-shirt was a silk-screen 'Trabant Turbo' one he'd found in the little street market outside the Centrum store at Ostbahnhof.

A few final touches were needed. Torsten had a box full of enamelled communist badges that lauded Marx and Lenin, commemorated state occasions and proclaimed membership of various Party organisations. We pinned the brightest and best all down one side of his jacket, the way generals wear their medals. As Torsten had the Eastie Boys hat and a pair of mirror shades, I lent Norman my Def Jam baseball cap and Cutler & Gross sunglasses. Once they were togged up, we stepped back to review the results. It hit just the right note, mocking both Western street style and Eastern iconography. It was also mostly their own work. They covered the whole mess with big coats, I loaded the first film into the camera and we all left the house to journey to the first of our two locations: the huge statue of Ernst Thälmann, dungareed and clenching a communist fist, that stood in the park named after him.

Turning the corner out of Torsten's street, the first thing we ran into, barely fifty metres from the house, was a whole truckload of uniformed militiamen, hefting Kalashnikovs, spilling out of their vehicle to block the entire pavement. We had to walk right through the middle of them, tensely affecting unconcern. The militiamen just kept on chatting – they appeared to be waiting for something to happen – but gave us a long, slow look up and down.

'Saxons,' muttered Torsten, once we were safely past. 'Really stupid people. They come from the south of the DDR where you can't pick up Western television so they believe everything the Party tells them.'

'But what the fuck are they doing here?'

'I don't know. They must have been specially bussed in for something.'

It was even heavier on the main road. Uniformed police stood at ten yard intervals all along the pavements in both directions. One by one, heads turned as we passed. Suddenly we were aware of how suspicious we looked. Norman and Torsten's coats, far too heavy for the warm afternoon, were buttoned right up to the top and contrasted oddly with the sunglasses they both wore.

'Stasi,' Torsten muttered as we passed a pedestrian, lips barely moving. 'And another one. Look, there's more.'

A crowd of men in leather jackets were occupying all the tables outside a café. Apart from us four, every last man on the street seemed to be some kind of policeman. With a measured stride, looking straight ahead, we proceeded to the station. There we finally worked out just what was going on. The Hungarian president and Party leader, Károly Grósz, was on an official state visit to East Berlin. The day we had chosen for the taking of highly dodgy photographs in two very public places was one in which every last secret policeman in town was out and on the streets.

The area around Ernst Thälmann Park station was well off the route of the official motorcade, but about two hundred metres short of our destination, Norman and Torsten gasped in surprise and frustration and skidded to a halt.

'There's another one,' Norman nodded ahead.

Too far ahead for me even to have noticed him, let alone suss him as a secret policeman, a guy in blazer and grey flannels hovered around by a parked black Tatra – right at the spot where we wanted to take photos. We paused for a quick conference and decided to carry on. If he didn't go away we would continue to the next intersection and catch a tram to our second location. The Stasi was obviously waiting for something, not just watching the street. As we passed him, we saw what. Three guys in suits, Party officials, returned from some mission in the flat blocks beyond the park. The Stasi opened the car door for them and they all drove away. With a sigh of relief – it had begun to seem feasible he might be waiting for us – we doubled back and set to work.

Mark stood lookout. Norman and Torsten removed coats and took up position in front of the statue. I directed them quickly through various poses, cursing the unfamiliar camera's lack of a motor-drive. Stand like this, stand like that. One roll of black and white, one of colour. At one point Mark cried out and we had to pause as some people went by. We stood around the statue, feigning nonchalant conversation, until the coast was clear again. At the next location – the statue of Vladimir Ilich at Leninplatz, a busy traffic intersection – we were getting the hang of it and things went even quicker. Towards the end of the last roll, Norman and Torsten started smiling and waving to someone behind me. I turned to see a whole coachload of goggle-eyed tourists at the traffic lights on Leninallee, many of them also snapping the unfamiliar scene, apparently persuaded that they were in the presence of some genuine celebrities. The Eastie Boys were beginning to enjoy them-selves.

On the tram back to Torsten's flat, Mark and Norman talked about songs the Eastie Boys might record. Mark suggested 'All Along the Watchtower', Norman thought they should do 'No Milk Today'. I said the video should be like East Side Story. As we neared Pankow station, Norman pointed to a group of leather-jacketed young men, leaning against the wall and chatting outside a pub. In the West this might have indicated a gay bar. Here in the East it was obviously a bunch of Stasis, their job of guarding Grósz's route over for the afternoon, waiting to be collected and returned to HQ. We laughed at them standing there, pleased with our afternoon's work. We had run their damn gauntlet and they hadn't caught us.

Dave Rimmer, *Once upon a Time in the East* (1992)

1989: Friday, 30 June

'It's getting boring, playing live,' pipes Chris, cheerfully.

Pete, who was taking photos from in front of the stage, disputes that this is Chris's true opinion. He tells Chris he thought that at one stage Chris had been crying with emotion.

'*Chris? Crying?*' scoffs Neil incredulously. 'You must be joking.'

'I'm sorry,' says Chris, 'but I'm a bit *bored*. I keep thinking "just five more songs". The edge has gone.'

Neil nods. He confesses that during one of the songs he was far too busy wondering what they might have for dinner later.

Pete shows Neil a Polaroid of his red cape spin during 'It's A Sin'.

'That's quite interesting,' he coos. ' "Me in a Twirl". It sounds like a Smiths song.'

Chris stands admiringly, just looking at his rack of stage clothes. 'It's *more* than fashion,' he sighs melodramatically. 'These are museum pieces. My Issey Miyake clothes are more than just clothing, they're sculpture.'

Dainton tells them that there are 150 fans outside tonight, waiting.

'We can't sign 150,' says Chris.

'If we wait,' counsels Neil, 'some of those will get bored and go away.'

The fans are mostly girls, old teenagers, with a smattering of serious, fashionably dressed boys and a loud posse of British army girls stationed in Hong Kong. I go out to have a look.

'If I give you 100 dollars will you smuggle me into their boot? Where are they staying? Can I stay in their room?'

'I love Neil Tennant. He is Mr Cool. He is Mr Right.'

'He's cute.'

'He's kind.'

'He's very clean.'

'They're a very clean group. No satanic.'

'The songs are really deep.'

'They're handsome.'

'Can you say "hi" to Craig Logan?'

'They're British. You can dance to their music. I hate American music. Bon Jovi.' (Makes an I'm-going-to-vomit expression.) 'Pet Shops Boys is easy to listen to, a little bit sad.'

'Neil is cool. For fun I'd love go kiss he.'

'The show was brilliant. There was always something going on.'

'I saw Duran Duran and Stevie Wonder and this is the best.'

'I like Chris best. I like his hat. He just stands there and is moody-looking. He seems the strong, silent type.'

This comment prompts debate.

'And they're always the worst.'

Giggles.

'It appeals to a woman.'

'Men who say what they're going to do, don't do it.'

When Neil and Chris come out there is mayhem. The army girls burst into a raucous version of the Righteous Brothers' 'You've Lost That Lovin' Feeling' in imitation of a scene in the film *Top Gun* where Tom Cruise serenades Kelly McGillis in a bar. Chris raises an embarrassed eyebrow in their direction as if to say, 'Who let *them* in?'

The answer to Neil's on-stage contemplation is that we are to eat at the Bostonian, a restaurant in our hotel where the menu is of American food, droll broken-English witticisms and astronomic prices. There they dredge through the 'It's Alright' row. They have just had some good news. The British charts are announced on a Sunday, based purely on sales from Monday to Saturday of that week. Gallup, the company that compiles the chart, gives subscribing record companies provisional midweek charts, based on the sales so far, on Thursday and again on Friday. We have just heard that the Thursday midweek for 'It's Alright' is that it will enter the charts at number two. They are delighted.

EMI, it turns out, had mixed feelings about releasing the record at all. Though the people who work closest with the Pet Shop Boys in the company's Parlophone subsidiary were keen, the wider (and, the implication was, wiser) feeling was that it was a bad idea. Tom and Rob, their management, sided with the latter view. Neil and Chris weren't simply insulted that people didn't like their new record – they also got a distinct impression that people feared their career was slipping. 'There was definitely an "EMI-have-got-the-jitters-about-the-Pet-Shop-Boys feeling,"' says Neil. 'It was "They've been popular for too long. How long's it going to last?"' Much of the record business, perpetually bemused by public taste, is as confused by success as by failure. One marketing executive at EMI has, it is whispered, regally pronounced that he could 'market this record into the Top 20 but not into the Top 10'.

It was Chris who held firm, simply because he was thrilled by the record they had made. He couldn't stop playing it, he had played it to his family and they'd loved it and he wanted it released. He said he didn't care whether it even got in the Top 50; it should come out. Neil is usually the face of the Pet Shop Boys that the record company see, but this time Chris phoned up everyone involved to insist it be released.

Nevertheless now it is EMI who are making the bullish statements – that the record might go straight into the charts at number one – and it is the Pet Shop Boys who are sensibly tempering the excitement. They know that any group like them who have lots of keen fans, who will buy the records early in its first week of release, will find their chart position falling back by Sunday. In fact it's a syndrome – 'the Paul Weller syndrome' as they tartly refer to it – that they are worried about. The problem is this: you can enter the charts so high, thanks to your keen fans, that there simply isn't time for more fair-weather fans to get to like the record before it is going down the charts, its life over. Now we must wait and see.

After dinner we go clubbing. We try a disco called 1997 but they tell us there is no room so we walk down the narrow streets, a large posse flanking the swanky car holding Neil and Chris, to a disco called California. Once they realize they have famous guests they clear some table space. Champagne appears. Neil chats for a couple of hours, then leaves. Chris dances, at first shyly, off the dance-floor by the toilets, then on the dance-floor. At 3.00 a.m. we return to 1997 and it's 5.20 when we eventually take a taxi back to the Ramada Renaissance. It's already light and we all have that tired but ecstatic feeling you get when you've stayed up all night having fun.

'This is my favourite part of the day,' sighs Chris. 'Morning has broken.' He sniggers. '*That*'s a good line. I must tell Neil. No one's used it, have they?'

He roars with laughter.

'Morning Has Broken' was a Top 10 hit for Cat Stevens in 1972. One of his other famous songs was 'Wild World'. When the Pet Shop Boys single 'It's a Sin' went to number one Jonathan King wrote about it in his column in the *Sun*, suggesting that they had committed an act of theft from Cat Stevens and that they should be punished for it. (Cat Stevens, who is now a Muslim called Yusef Islam and who was soon to become embroiled in the Salman Rushdie affair, was contacted by another newspaper but said he wasn't bothered.) After Jonathan King repeated the accusation the Pet Shop Boys instigated defamation proceedings.

As the case neared court, Jonathan King even made a record in support of himself, a version of 'Wild World' using the arrangement of 'It's a Sin', so that it went 'It's a/it's a/oh baby baby it's a wild world' (Chris bought a copy because he liked it). If anything it weakened his case, but sneakily the B-side was made up of a medley of the Chiffons' 'He's So fine' and the song that was adjudged to have been cribbed from it by George Harrison, 'My Sweet Lord'.

Eventually Jonathan King settled out of court, made a donation to the Jefferriss Research Foundation (a charity specified by the Pet Shop boys) and apologized.

This wasn't the first time, oddly, that Neil had crossed Jonathan King's trail. In the early seventies when Neil was at college in London, he answered an advert that Jonathan King had placed, searching for talent for his record company. Neil dressed up in his best trousers – baggy, Navy-surplus trousers – and went down to a rehearsal studio.

'I played him two songs,' Neil remembers, 'and he said they were too introspective. And of course he was absolutely right. But he said he liked my trousers.'

Chris Heath, Pet Shop Boys, Literally (1990)

1989: Goin' off in Cali

Universal Amphitheater, Los Angeles County, July 28, approximately 10.00 p.m. L.L. Cool J is rhyming for several thousand whites, blacks, and latinos. The stage comes complete with flashing lights, dancing girls, and guest rapper Busy Bee playing Flavor Flav to L.L.'s Chuck D. But the Crips in the house don't care where the show is supposed to be. In the arena's darkness a posse of 10 to 15 of them, their blue colors no longer camou-flaged under black caps, jackets, and jeans, reveal themselves. Not long afterwards a scuffle ensues and a brother in a white Le Coq Sportif sweat-suit goes down. I don't see what or who started it, but I see the result. Four security guards carry him through a side door and lay him on the ground. He's dark-skinned, about six feet tall with short hair, but unfortunately his most distinguishing characteristic is now a large red dent in his left temple. His nose and mouth, like his once white jacket, look dipped in crimson.

Inside the arena the show proceeds. Rap crowds, despite the anarchy sometimes surrounding the music, usually manage to ignore or at least distance themselves emotionally from any violence. Tonight is no exception. This multiracial gathering remains cool even as the Crips march down toward the front of the stage, each man grasping the shoulder of the man ahead of him. A team of about 15 thick-armed security men in white T-shirts blocks them just before they reach the standing section in front of L.L. and Busy Bee. With the house lights on and security now alert, the Crips stand on chairs and flash their hand sign toward the stage as L.L. rips through 'Rock the Bells'.

Standing backstage as paramedics and police speak with the victim, I stare at him and feel my stomach quiver. A booking agent and vet of 10-plus years of hip hop business stands by me. 'You should have been at Long Beach, at that Run-D.M.C. show,' he said, referring to the infamous gig where warring gangs faced off during Whodini's set. 'The group wouldn't go back on the stage,' he recalls, 'and I didn't blame them. I mean guys were literally being thrown out of the balcony onto the stage. I am not kidding.'

The early leg of the L.L. tour, which featured Compton's own N.W.A and Eazy-E, was beset by a police fax campaign spreading the lyrics of the antibrutality parable 'Fuck tha Police' to precinct houses across America. Not surprisingly, this resulted not only in angry cops and lots of no-shows, but in the usual paranoid press. In fact, however, 'rap violence' is a journalistic cliché that conceals the bitter truth, especially in the City of Dreams: Rap is just another venue for the gangs' performances. The image of the Crips flaunting their strength, cocksure they could roll on the guards and, at the very least, shut L.L. up with one furious bum rush, will stick with me as a symbol of LA's brutal youth culture. But every day the front page of the *Los Angeles Times*'s Metro section, which should be called 'Gang Bang Digest', chronicles the open warfare in east and south-central Los Angeles. A far nastier item during my recent visit west described a Sunday service disrupted by a three-man hit squad shooting up four parishioners. There's no more apt metaphor for the hold gangs have on local youth. Gangs are a religion in LA, and the faithful are as contemptuous of opposing belief systems as Christians are of Islam. The church shooting is no isolated incident – it mirrors the schism between old black tradition and new jack nihilism.

'Out here four things are thought to make you a man,' says anti-gang activist Ron Johnson. 'Getting a girl pregnant, taking a life, surviving prison, and joining a gang. Those are real goals that Crips, Bloods, and everyone else takes seriously.' Johnson, who moved to LA from New York four years ago, feels the level of black-on-black interpersonal brutality out there is worse than anything back east. 'There is a lot of culture and history just in the air in a place like New York. There's a real nationalist cultural influence. The gangs fill those cultural gaps here.'

Johnson's hope for degangsterizing LA is 'to politicize the gangs, to make them sort of a black army'. I like Johnson's heart, but I'm not sure his idea is any more practical than Tom Bradley's steel-versus-steel approach. Certainly the police can't intimidate the gangs out of existence. Gang sweeps, usually race-based teen roundups, don't address the social and economic disaster facing this grossly segregated town. Nor, it should be noted, has the uncharismatic presence of a black career public servant as mayor. The usual urban ills of crappy schools and substandard health facilities, compounded by the crack-financed gang expansion, turn black and Latin youths into both predators and prey. Spending on social programs in Cali never recovered from Proposition 14. The money for the job training necessary to move blacks into the area's high-tech aerospace or low-tech furniture industries is channeled instead into stopgap projects like building a convenient prison in the heart of the black community – or the recently completed 'escape-proof' jail downtown, where five guys broke out two weeks ago.

Moreover, and this is an important lesson for the Apple, there seems to be no moral imperative, from elected officials, from the well-to-do west side, or in the press, for meaningful change in the lives of poor Los Angeles. Predictably in the state that's spawned both Ronald Reagan and S. I. Hayakawa, people who say gangs must be stopped are talking about Uzis, not classrooms. In their destructive insularity, the LA gangs recall the wild young men of A Clockwork Orange. But what frightens me even more is the next step of the parallel – the government's quasi-fascistic response. Gangs are viewed solely as criminal collectives when they are also self-sustaining extended families that provide self-worth and the illusion of security.

It's easy to understand why kids embrace institutions created by themselves and for themselves which stand up to threatening forces within and outside the community. That's the logic of Public Enemy's gunsight logo – one reason young black men flaunt guns is that guns really are aimed at them. But obviously, terrorizing everybody outside the clan is no way to achieve true self-worth, and that syndrome has only gotten worse since crack turned gangsterism into a growth industry. Los Angeles is not New York, as Johnson said. But don't think our gang problem won't get a lot worse. The sense of generational alienation that rap both suffers and expresses is not dying. It's multiplying, nationwide.

Nelson George, *Village Voice*, 15 August 1989

1990: To Do the Right Thing

I was backstage at Wembley Stadium. I was there for the Nelson Mandela concert. The weather was typically English. It was hailing and outside 72,000 people were sitting in the cold. I didn't think I would meet Mr Mandela but I was hoping to at least see him. I had been reading in the press about how the lineup for this Mandela concert was inferior to the previous one – no megastars. That we musicians were politically naïve and stupid – didn't we know he was a Communist – he hasn't rejected violence, etc. Plus an interviewer from the BBC with incredibly bad breath had informed me that WEA – my record company – had taken out an ad to retailers saying, 'Make Mandela work for you', and what did I have to say about that. Well, they're obviously capitalist dogs, I said, and we should cancel the concert right now, don't you agree. So what if Nelson Mandela went to jail unable to vote and emerged 27 years later still unable to vote – so what that he was being given the opportunity to speak to one billion people this night (except in America – America, where it was deemed too political and people are tired of these benefits anyway).

And no, I didn't get to see Mr Mandela, not in person anyway. I viewed him on a big video monitor and then on a TV just as you may have. And he was incredible at age 71, at any age, and I hoped I could be that way at that age, and I wondered another thought – how does anyone go to jail for 27 years over an idea. I couldn't comprehend 27 years. Three months, okay. A year. But 27 years. It reminded me of the old Lenny Bruce routine when he's playing a captured soldier and they threaten him – hey, this isn't necessary, here's their time, dates, do you want his home phone number.

This question stayed in my mind because I was leaving the next day to fly to Prague and interview Václav Havel, the new president of Czechoslovakia and a personal hero of mine – a man who like Mandela could have left. They wanted him to leave, he was a successful playwright – why didn't he leave? They'd told him – if you put a wreath on that dead dissident's grave you go to jail. He did it anyway, and went to jail. And now he was president of the country, his cabinet made of various other dissidents, the Communists removed from power, the Czech people rising up to demonstrate 300,000

696

strong in Wenceslas Square for days, finally clashing with the soldiers over the senseless death of a 10-year-old boy. And Václav Havel was no longer in jail but president. A poet, a playwright, a great man.

Before leaving we had had some strange conversations with our Czecho-slovakian contacts, exacerbated, no doubt, by the language problem. It was Kafkaesque. Phones dropped off hooks – footsteps clicking down long corridors, it was hard to get clear answers to the most basic requests. The line that made me nervous was when we were told with exasperation – the government will take care of you. I'm from New York. I wouldn't want the government to take care of me. Plus they wanted me to play. At a club. For the local promoter. Visions of various people I knew raced through my mind making me nervous – scalpers, bootlegs, ticket prices. I said no, I didn't want to play for the local promoter. Maybe later when I do a real tour, and no photos or press conference at the airport. After all, I said, I'm here as a journalist.

Prague is so clean, so elegant, so old. We were in the International Hotel, which at a distance looked to me like a project. Close up it was actually okay, just very boxlike and brown. It had actually been hard to get a room because there were so many journalists and tourists in town. The Pope was coming to Czechoslovakia in two days. We were taken around Prague by Paul, a German photographer, and later by a man who I think became a new old friend, Kočař. Kočař's real name was Kosarek. It's a 400-year-old name and means small carriage. When he grew up his name became Kočař or big carriage. Kočař was a very streetwise person who spoke what he called street English and had resisted all attempts to enroll him in a school to teach him correct grammar. But he spoke just fine. He told us that only a while ago Havel was hiding in his house trying to get the dissidents of Charter 77 together yet again for more protests against the government. And now he was president.

Kočař apologized for the very large, clumsy man following us, another bodyguard. Havel has many enemies. The Communists hate him. And he said, making a gun with his hand and pointing to me, they'd like to hurt his friends. Havel, Kočař said, gets 20 death threats a day. Of course 99 percent of these are not serious. But one might be.

And so we went through Prague waiting for the interview. We saw where the 30-meter bust of Stalin was destroyed. Kočař pointed to the spot with particular revulsion. He'd been 14 in 1968 when the Russian tanks came and had blown up two tanks himself. The Russians are stupid, he said. Their gas tanks are on the rear of the tank quickly available to a hammer and a match and then you run quick. In the demonstration that overturned the Communists he said if you were in the front lines, and he was, the secret was hit and run quick. He had seen an 80-year-old woman beaten by a soldier after she'd told him he was worse than a Nazi. Kočař attacked him and I supposed that was how he lost his front teeth.

We went to the Jewish ghetto and the Jewish cemetery, which was very sad. There was so little land the bodies could not have individual graves – the tombstones were piled atop and next to one another. Isn't that sad, I said. Isn't that beautiful, said our translator Yana, I hope misunderstanding.

We went to the old square. There was a large crowd gathered in front of the astrological clock. On the hour saints popped out of the windows and at the end a brass rooster crowed. We went across the Charles Bridge, named for Charles IV, their greatest king, from the thirteenth century, a king of their people. The bridge had 30 statues of various Catholic icons placed 10 feet from one another on both sides of the bridge. Young kids were playing Beatles' songs and Czech country songs. Prior to Havel no music could be played or sung on the bridge. No young people could gather there. You never knew what they might come up with. We passed a Czech-French film crew. We passed a bust of Kafka on a street but were told not to bother to see his apartment – everything had been ripped out. We ate some dumplings in the oldest restaurant in Prague and then gathered ourselves to go to the castle to meet Václav Havel.

The castle is just that, a large castle in yet another square directly opposite a very beautiful church with a gold-plated clock. We were met outside by Sacha Vandros, the young bespectacled secretary of state. He led us up the red-carpeted stairway to the president's office. We went inside the office and sat at a medium-sized table. The press secretary was to act as our translator. President Havel's English, he said, was not so good. I set up my tape recorder, and suddenly there he was, President Václav Havel.

He's the kind of person you like on sight and things only get better when he talks. He searched for a cigarette and chain-smoked the whole hour. I'd been told he put in 18-hour days, which was a little rough on him since only three weeks ago he'd had a hernia operation. He's one of the nicest men I've ever met. I asked him if it was okay to turn on the tape.

HAVEL: We invite you too for breakfast . . .
REED: No, I mean in the hotel we ordered breakfast and three people came up to give it to us. We thought it was very odd, small tray, three people. So

I always thought of Kafka – I think of Kafka when I read you, I er, I'll see if this is working . . .

HAVEL: The State Security was liquidated in our country, but these people work in spite of this fact. I think they are interested more in me than in you, these people.

REED: I don't think so, I don't think so. I don't normally do this. I've done one other interview in my life, that was two weeks ago. There's a writer I really admire named Hubert Selby, who wrote a book called *Last Exit to Brooklyn*, and a new magazine asked me to interview him. I really wanted to meet him all my life, so I said yes. And it was really wonderful. I got to ask him a lot of questions about writing. So yesterday I found out that that's a great interview. If we had more time I would show it to you. I also have a present for you. Anyway, the magazine rejected the interview.

HAVEL: [*In Czech*] Hang on, I don't understand . . .

INTERPRETER: [*In Czech*] That the magazine rejected it.

HAVEL: [*Laughs*]

INTERPRETER: [*In English*] Was it your idea to do the interview?

REED: It wasn't my idea. It wouldn't occur to me I would be interviewing the president of a country. I was told that I was one of the people who would be acceptable to do an unconventional interview.

HAVEL: Well, I think I have some message work for this magazine, and I would like to tell it to you in this interview, but we must begin immediately because unfortunately I have a lot of work. There are a lot of crises and problems which I have to solve very quickly. And we can begin if you agree. But I would prefer to answer you in Czech and Michael will translate it because he speaks much more better than me.

REED: This is a present for you.

HAVEL: Thank you very much.

REED: That is a CD –

HAVEL: [*In Czech*] Ah yes, this is great. Finally, I'll be able to listen to some music properly.

REED: – of a project called *Songs for 'Drella*. It's about Andy Warhol that I did with John Cale.

HAVEL: I will be very soon in the little village where he was born, Andy Warhol. Meziz Droje. Mezilabolze, very small village in – [*coffee served*]

REED: No alcohol –

HAVEL: No, no, no. It is forbidden in this castle, only me, I can secretly drink.

HAVEL: [*Through interpreter*] The worst thing about being president is that I have no time to listen to music. Only the presidential tune . . . And the only time I can listen to music is in my car when I'm going from place to place. Nevertheless I will play the CD as soon as I have the opportunity to. But I equally enjoy good rock music. And sometimes there are even moments when I listen to ugly modern music, commercial music, pop music. For 20 years there was only the most banal pop music in our radio. Now it is already possible to hear on the radio music that previously people could only clandestinely exchange on tapes. And if someone distributed the cassettes for too long, he was usually arrested. Now they are all out of prison and the music is played on the radio.

REED: Is it true that not so long ago, on the Charles Bridge, you couldn't play guitar?

HAVEL: Yes, it is true, the pop musicians there were arrested from time to time. Or at least detained and . . . detained for a while in a police station and then let go. But since we started to talk about music, I'd like to say one thing. That this revolution of ours has, apart from all other faces, also a musical face. Or an artistic face. And it also has a very specific musical background.

At the end of the '60s there was a wave here of rock music . . . Most of the bands after the Soviet invasion broke up or started playing different music because good rock music was actually banned. There was one band in particular which lasted, which did not rename itself, which did not change. There were several, but this one was the best known. And their style of music was much influenced by the Velvet Underground, whose record I brought back from New York in 1968. It was one of the first records . . . And this band began to be much persecuted – first they lost their professional status, and then they could only play in private parties. And for a time they also played in the barn of my summer cottage where we had to, in a very complicated way, organize secret concerts . . . And its name was the Plastic People of the Universe. And there originated around it a whole underground movement in the dark '70s and '80s. Then they were arrested. With several friends we organized a campaign against their arrest, and it was quite hard to convince some very serious gentlemen and academics and Nobel Prize winners to take a stand on behalf of some hairy rock musicians. Nevertheless, we succeeded. And this led to the formation of a community of solidarity of sorts.

Most of these musicians were released and some received light sentences under the pressure of our campaign. And it seemed to us that this community that originated in this way shouldn't just dissolve after this but should go on in some more stable form, and that's how the Charter 77 human rights movement originated.

REED: Really?

HAVEL: The trial with the bands was a special affair. Then it was still possible to enter the court building to be at such a trial. The building was full of people. You could see a university professor in friendly talk with a former member of the Praesidium of the Communist party and with a long-haired rock musician, and all of them surrounded by police.

This was a sign of the things to come, of the special character or nature of the Charter 77, which united many people of different backgrounds and different views in their common resistance to the totalitarian system and in their speaking out against the system. And then some of us got arrested and jailed. But now, members of the Charter 77 are deputies in the parliament, members of the government, or here in the castle.

I myself was one of the first three spokesmen of the Charter 77. By this I mean to say that music, underground music, in particular one record by a band called Velvet Underground, played a rather significant role in the development in our country, and I don't think that many people in the United States have noticed this. So this is one thing I wanted to tell you, and I have another thing to say but maybe in a little while.

But first I should mention that, as is usually the case of rock bands, they undergo changes, they change their names, some of the people leave, etc., etc. Well, the core of this band still exists but it has changed its name and it's now called Midnight – Unots. We had Easter recently, and I turn on the radio in my car while I'm driving to my cottage, and the music they played was Passover music played by this very band, and recorded at my cottage.

REED: Passover music?

HAVEL: Yes, Passover music. The music was recorded about 13 years ago . . . It was never released before. They just locked themselves in at my cottage for two days and recorded this thing. [*In Czech*] Secretly. It was a very strange experience to suddenly hear this music on Czechoslovak radio.

REED: Joan Baez says hello.

HAVEL: [*In English*] Thank you very much. Please greet her too, and I hope I will see her on the seventh of June when she has to have a concert in Prague. Sixth or seventh, I think. You bring her to Moscow. She will have one concert in Bratislava, I think, and one in Prague.

REED: I admire you so much. In reading *Letters to Olga* . . .

HAVEL: This unread–, unre–

REED: Unreadable.

HAVEL: Unreadable book. It was written in prison, and everything what was understandable, was, er, forbidden.

INTERPRETER: Censored.

HAVEL: Censored. Censored, and they learned me to write more and more complicated sentences, and now I don't understand it well. It is extremely complicated language, but it was the result of pressure of prison censorship, yes, because if they don't understand it, they permit it [*laughs*].

REED: Why was it called the Velvet Revolution?

HAVEL: This name [*In Czech*]. I'll say it in Czech.

HAVEL: [*Through interpreter*] The name was not given to it by us, but by Western journalists. They like simple labels. But the label caught on here. And some people use this word to this day.

Well, it is true that the interesting thing about our revolution was that, except for the first massacre which started if off, there was no blood spilled during the revolution. But it doesn't necessarily mean that it was as velvet as that. Or that we lived in a velvet time. That's just by the way.

I wanted to say another thing for this magazine, if I can volunteer. The whole anti-establishment movement of the '60s had marked significantly my generation and also the generations after that. In 1968, I was in New York for six weeks. I took part in demos and rallies and student protests [*at Columbia University*]. [*In Czech*] As well as that I went to Greenwich Village and the East Village.

REED: Which ones?

HAVEL: They were on strike but they still invited me to give a talk there – I was also at Yale and MIT. And with Milos Forman I participated in be-ins and things like that. We wandered round Greenwich Village, and East Village, and I bought a lot of posters which I still keep. Psychedelic posters which I still have hanging in my cottage.

REED: Did you go to CBGB's?

HAVEL: That was later. Many of the famous musicians like Bob Dylan and Jimi Hendrix were already there, but some only appeared later. [*In Czech*] Recently during the revolution someone stole two of my treasured posters, I don't know why.

REED: So you never saw the Velvet Underground?

HAVEL: Not live, but I bought the record. First edition. At least I think it was the first edition.

REED: Does it have a banana on it?

HAVEL: I haven't seen the record for a long time. I mainly played it at the beginning of the '70s. So I don't remember the banana. But I know it's all black with white letterings [White Light/White Heat *LP*]. And from time to time some rock musicians wanted to steal this record. But I think I still have it. But to go on with what I wanted to say.

The whole spirit of the '60s, the rebellion against the establishment affected significantly the spiritual life of my generation and of the younger people, and in a very strange way, transcended into the present. But we differ from this 20-year-old rebellion in that we made another step further. As small and inconspicuous step as it might be, but it's the knowledge that we can't just tear things down but we have to build in a new way. And many people took political responsibility. And, for example, Michael Kotap, probably the best-known rock musician in this country, is also one of the best-functioning deputies in our Federal Parliament now. He doesn't have much time for composing music. It is a sacrifice of a kind that he has brought to society. But he still managed to write the tune for the castle guards.

And when we were in New York on a state visit two months ago, with Milos Forman, we dropped in to CBGB's one night. And as I learned later, the manager of the place, a man we hadn't really noticed immediately, phoned his friend in Prague that he's got the president of this country in his joint. The people most scared about all this were the 30 people from Secret Service who were supposed to be guarding me. And they were real Rambos. But in the end the Secret Service guys came to like me and they actually gave me a sweater as a present. And they were moved when I was leaving. But I didn't print things like that.

INTERPRETER: Oh, he says I'm supposed to censor it. I think that's okay.

REED: Do you know that in the United States now they're trying to censor the records? By labeling them?

HAVEL: Well, when we were in the States, they organized a concert in St John the Divine in New York and there were many famous writers and musicians and other people appearing there, and from them I learned that they also have problems of their own. My heart is always with those who fight for freedom of expression. But it still seems to me that the 200-year-old American democracy is mature enough not to need me as mediator to take messages to Mr Bush. I think that they can tell him directly.

REED: We try.

HAVEL: They were sort of asking me to plead on their behalf, but I think that would not really be the thing to do. Because in this I would be humiliating them. They are citizens and they can say whatever they want to their elected representatives.

REED: Are you in favor of German reunification?

HAVEL: I think it had to happen sooner or later. And whoever did not think so had no foresight. And if anyone's unprepared for this mentally it's his problem.

INTERPRETER: [*To Havel in Czech*] I'm having difficulty in translating because I don't get enough time to think.

HAVEL: [*To interpreter in Czech*] You're the interpreter. Yes, it's a rock magazine. There won't be a scandal, will there?

INTERPRETER: [*To Havel in Czech*] Not from this, surely?

HAVEL: [*Through interpreter*] The Berlin Wall was a symbol of the division of Europe. And the fall of this wall was liberation for us all. And it's natural when the wall falls, the nation reunites itself. If such a wall went through Prague at the moment it would fall. People would also come together.

REED: You obviously feel and prove that music can change the world.

HAVEL: Not in itself, it's not sufficient in itself. But it can contribute to that significantly in being a part of the awakening of the human spirit. [*Knock at the door. Conversation between Havel and female secretary about things to do and running out of time.*] I think we're running out of time. Is it true or not that you will play at the Gallery tonight?

REED: It was never true that I would play at the Gallery. I brought a guitar with me, though, because I would have played for you, but I wouldn't want to go to a nightclub and play. I would play in private for you as I said, but not in a club. It would make me way too nervous.

HAVEL: I think it would be sort of embarrassing for me if only I could enjoy it and tens of my friends who would like to be there as well could not be there. The bands that I was talking about would be there and people who had been arrested for listening to this kind of music, and friends . . .

REED: Would you be there?

HAVEL: I have a first-night performance of my play tonight. I could be there between 11 and 12, I couldn't make it earlier than 11 and I couldn't stay after 12.

REED: The advantage of being president . . .

HAVEL: There are no advantages at all, but after midnight I still have several speeches to write. And I'm not particularly looking forward to my first night, but the play had been banned before so this is the first time, and the theater struggled for two years to be able to produce it, so this is their first night, so I have to be there. But I could come after . . . But I just have to be there and then thank the actors and company, and shake hands with the actors, and then I could be –

REED: Is this a big club, because if it was President Havel and some friends, I would feel comfortable. But a big club with lots of people – see, I'm a private person.

INTERPRETER: It's not a big club. It's a smallish club, and we were just discussing how many people can –

REED: You see, I'm a very private person, when I came here I didn't want any photographers at the airport, because I don't like my picture taken. I don't like being interviewed – and, er, I like controlled situations – as opposed to just a lot of people. I'm not looking for that. It would be a privilege to play for these people under the right circumstances, but I'm not aware of the circumstances, and it's difficult for me to walk into –

INTERPRETER: I think there would be a couple of hundred people at most. And they would be all friends because it's by invitation.

HAVEL: [*In English*] Mostly musicians, people from Plastic People and from other bands, and Michael Kotap whom I mentioned who is our best deputy in our Assembly and some friends. It would not be public, nobody will know it, and if you don't want to do us, and if you don't want photographers they are not there, and I will not mention to anybody that I will come there, because if I mentioned it anywhere 1,000 people would be there together with me, yes.

INTERPRETER: [*In Czech*] They're all friends. There's so many.

HAVEL: [*In English*] We have many friends. But we could arrange that there will be about only 150 friends and we could speak with them and they can play, and if you want you can play for them, et cetera, and I could come there around 11 o'clock and if I would have the opportunity to hear you, I would be very glad. If you prefer only discussion with them and with me, we can discuss it, then I'll leave it.

INTERPRETER: [*In Czech*] Maybe it would help if we could put two or three lads on the door.

HAVEL: [*In English*] It's no problem to arrange that two or three because of my private security could control them.

REED: They'd take care of me.

INTERPRETER: No, just control the entrance so there are only people who are friends get in.

REED: If it's important to the people and it is a request from you, it would be a privilege if the situation is a controlled one, because as I said, I'm very private. So I try always to have control over the situation if I possibly can, so that I can do what I do as well as I can. But if this is something you would like, it would be an honor to do it for you and your people.

HAVEL: I would be very happy if this could happen for me and for people who have been listening to this music for 20 years, so that it became part of their lives, and of course I can guarantee that it will be just those people and no one else. I will be there at 11 plus/minus 10 minutes.

REED: [*Laughs*]

INTERPRETER: [*In Czech*] I said plus/minus 10 minutes and he started laughing. [*In English*] Because I don't know precisely when the play is over. It starts at about 7.30.

REED: Would there be somebody to take me and my wife there?

HAVEL: Sure.

REED: This is a very new situation for me, this city is so beautiful and my admiration for you so enormous, that I would want to do something positive, as long as I knew what it was.

And when it's a mystery to me, I don't know exactly what to do. That's why I said no to almost everything, until I was here and I could speak to someone who could tell me what they thought was right in the situation, which I presume is you.

HAVEL: [*In English*] We can recommend you right people and we know who we don't recommend you. It's a little bit funny that such things, we do here, in castle, but it is true, and for example, [*In Czech*] if Lada can be responsible and organize it? [*In English*] I don't know who all of them tried to contact you and tried to arrange something, but these people are all right who arranged this appointment, we can recommend them. These people from underground, what I explained to you, what was the people and people around them, so-called Czech underground and it's all right.

REED: It was very difficult for me because I never knew whom I was speaking to.

HAVEL: I understand. Of course Sacha my adviser will discuss with you the details about it. I unfortunately have something else to do. Appointments, some minister, somebody –

REED: It was such an honor to meet you, thank you for your time.

Kočař came at 10.00 to pick us up and take us to the club which everyone else called the Gallery ('Je Podivna' in Czech). It was dark as we left the ornate buildings and decorative façades of old Prague and headed into new Prague. The Gallery was a medium-sized club with a small stage two feet above the floor where an audience of about 300 sat. Others milled about talking and sometimes moving to the balcony which stood about 30 feet overhead. The Gallery was also an art gallery, town hall and dissident communication center. We arrived and went down two very wide flights of stairs to the stage area where a band was playing. I commented on how young they looked. Those aren't kids, I was told, the drummer's 42. The band was Pulnoc or Midnight and was made up of members of the Universal Plastic People and the Velvet Underground revival bands. The band consisted of two guitars, electric keyboard, bass, cello and drum and a girl singer. There was an old Fender Twin sitting at the front of the stage just as Kočař had promised. The house system was typical small club, a little boomy in the vocal but otherwise fine.

I suddenly realized the music sounded familiar. They were playing Velvet Underground songs – beautiful, heartfelt, impeccable versions of my songs. I couldn't believe it. This was not something they could have gotten together overnight. The music grew stronger and louder as I listened. 'The drummer says he will faint because you are here,' said Kočař. 'It is their dream come true for you to be in this club to hear them play.'

The audience was actually all dissidents. Charter 77 had a membership of 1,800 out of a population of 15,000,000. One after another the songs flew by, each as impassioned as the next, the arrangements, the emphasized lines, the spaces. It was as though I was in a time warp and had returned to hear myself play. To say I was moved would be an understatement. To compose myself I went backstage into what could be called the universal dressing room – small, cold and bare, one bright bulb swinging from the ceiling – and took out my guitar to tune it. My tuner was dead. Its arrows flashed at me with inane irregularity. 'I'll get one from the band,' said Kočař. And it went dead. Here I am, I thought, getting ready to play for these amazing wonderful people, not to mention the president, and I'll be out of tune. Just like the real Velvet Underground. But this band Pulnoc was not a mimic. It was as though they had absorbed the very heart and soul of the VU – all those great ideas and absorbed them into the very marrow of their bones. Steam was rising from me fogging my glasses as I tried tuning by ear. I had sung solo before 72,000 people at Wembley but this was a bit more personal. Then Kočař said, 'Havel is here.' I looked at my watch. It was 10 after 11.

I went onstage, plugged into the Fender, hit a chord and discovered I was in tune. Well, there's no stopping me now. I did a few songs from my *New York* album realizing they were wordy but aren't all of them. I started to leave the stage when Kočař asked me if the band could join me. They did and we blazed through some old VU numbers. Any song I called they knew. It was as if Moe, John and Sterl were right there behind me and it was a glorious feeling. Soon I had exhausted myself and sweaty but ecstatic I followed Kočař to the balcony and sat down at a table with a beaming Václav Havel. He'd removed his jacket and loosened his tie. 'Did you enjoy yourself?' he asked. 'Yes,' I said, 'I did.' 'Good,' he said. 'I'd like you to meet

707

some friends of mine.' He then introduced me to an astonishing array of people, all dissidents, all of whom had been jailed. Some had been jailed for playing my music. Many told me of reciting my lyrics for inspiration and comfort when in jail. Some had remembered a line I had written in an essay 15 years ago, 'Everybody should die for the music.' It was very much a dream for me and well beyond my wildest expectations. When I had gotten out of college and helped form the VU, I had been concerned with, among other things, demonstrating how much more a song could be about than what was currently being written. So the VU albums and my own are implicitly about freedom of expression – freedom to write about what you please in any way you please. And the music had found a home here in Czechoslovakia.

President Havel was having a drink with his friends, something which he does not do in public because he is president. The only time he had for writing was for writing speeches. And the Pope was coming in two days. I thought, imagine a man who writes his own speeches, says his own words. What if George Bush ... no, Havel said the speeches were easy to write, in fact some resented the fact he said he wrote them so quickly. So now he told them it took longer. He had no time for his own writing, no time to listen to music. No time to have a drink. Foreign policy was not difficult, he said. There are other more unpleasant matters.

And then he was up from the table. 'I must go. I have to meet some foreign minister or some such thing. Oh, you must have this,' and bending from the waist he handed me a small black book about the size of a diary. 'These are your lyrics hand-printed and translated into Czechoslovakian. There were only 200 of them. They were very dangerous to have. People went to jail, and now you have one. Keep your fingers crossed for us.'

And he was gone.

The day after next – Havel called it a miracle – the Pope arrived. His and President Havel's speeches were broadcast outdoors through the square. As we left the hotel and took a back road to the airport we still heard their voices. The Pope, we later learned, had warned Havel against the virus, the moral decay of the West. 'Maybe he meant you,' laughed Kočař. 'There,' he pointed to an ugly, square, gray building behind wire fencing. 'That's where they detained Havel before they sentenced him. You know it's safer to be in an old car than a rich car.' He pointed his hand in a gun again. 'Better the old car. You know we double the security for the president last night. He must go to club, make things difficult. But to get him would not be so easy. And you had a good time in our country, my friend?'

Yes I did, Kočař. Yes I did. And not a day goes by that I don't think of

Václav Havel and the answer he'd given to the question I'd most wanted to ask – 'Why did you stay, why didn't you leave? How could you stand the terrible abuse?' And he'd said, 'I stayed because I live here. I was only trying to do the right thing. I had not planned for these various things to have happened but I never doubted that we would succeed. All I ever wanted to do was the right thing.'

I love Václav Havel. And I'm keeping my fingers crossed. I too want to do the right thing.

Between Thought and Expression: Selected Lyrics of Lou Reed (1991)

1990: I'm Going Overground (How the Soul Was Sold . . .)

While mainstream London 'Solid Souled' and suburban soulboy 'foamed' as yet another weekender, something unexpected happened at the hub of London's clubland. The 'Warehouse' party was now with us. This was a breakaway faction of young, bored clubbers doing their own thing. Here we had a rave that was fresh, fashionable, daring . . . A rave that was safe from the wedgeheaded wallies and East End, high-heeled dolly birds who frequented the capital's tack holes at weekends.

For those in the know, the warehouse party was now a place where you could jig around like a nutter all night, blag a Sloane if you wanted to, and generally get smashed on good gear. (Oh bliss!) The revellers would come from all social circles. Mad Punks; Sloanes, lazy college liggers and clued-up yardies could all be found raving together in some rundown, empty factory or warehouse in areas such as Kings X, Docklands, Southwark or even below Paddington Station. They would all be getting down to solid Funk: Tamla, James Brown, hard reggae (not the commercial shit) and Hip-Hop. Fucking brilliant! These parties proved to be the salvation of London trendies and 'lost' soulboys who'd given up West End clubs as a bad joke, for they now had somewhere to rave all night long in wild and sometimes dangerous surroundings (often with no bogs) with cheap booze (or you brought your own). Great sound systems, good visuals and, above all, hard-core sounds played in an unpretentious way by young, virtually unknown DJs. All this for a couple of quid. Fucking safe!

For the last couple of years, these parties had gone on virtually undetected by Joe Public (thank fuck!), mainly because news of them was spread by word of mouth and safe selective ticketing. Crews such as 'Shake 'n' Finger Pop' and 'Soul to Soul' rose to prominence with the emergence of these great but illegal parties. But now, what with the Old Bill heavily on the case (armed with info on the whereabouts of such parties happily supplied by fucked up club owners) and joe became increasingly aware of what was happening by tuning in to pirate stations such as Kiss FM, they were forced to keep a low one for a while.

Depending on location and promotion, top crews could pull as many as 2,000 punters to their jams on a Saturday night. Moody 'jams' became more frequent (many were bollocks) and the inevitable happened, a lot were raided and more were shut down even before they fucking started (what a piss off). This action resulted in crews looking to more legitimate venues to stage their parties.

During this period 'safe' crews such as the 'RAID' boys (who did legal venues) and 'Shake 'n' Finger Pop' to name a few were among the few teams who successfully managed to re-create the original warehouse atmosphere (remember the 'RAID' party at Riverside Studios and 'Shake 'n' Finger Pop/Family Function' at the Town and Country Club) at club level. The raves were again catering for London's style and fashion conscious, flat top trendy, and clued up clubber. (Thank fuck!)

The danger is that now the whole underground/warehouse scene is no longer underground. Why? Because moody crews, snide DJs looking for instant cred, lack of good suitable venues and the invasion of nonses (Arrghh!) has helped fuck up (yet again) a once safe scene (shame). Meanwhile Joe's now bought himself the 'uniform' – you know, those bloody black flight jackets, Doc Martens (oh no) – ripped his FU's (well they wouldn't be 501's would they?) and boogies on down in the raves convinced he's a trendy (silly cunt!). Oh for the days of Dockland and Bear Wharf!! So the next time you go to a warehouse party in Harlesden, Leyton or anywhere else, think twice, you could be stuck in a rave full of posse and whistles, being mugged off on your draw and deafened by an ex-yardie sound with distorted mid-range playing the latest white label bootlegs.

Norman Jay, Boys Own, Spring 1990

1990: Freaky Dancing

It's 3.30 in a busy pub in central Manchester. At the small pool table in the corner, a pair of red-faced men in cap-sleeved T-shirts are attacking the balls with wild-eyed relish. On the telly above the bar, the Great Britain rugby league team are putting New Zealand through their paces, and sat around me are Paris Angels, one of the newest breed of Mancunian guitar bands, and a large gang of their friends. 'Rugby's a public school game, they don't get stuck in or anything, it's football or boxing for us. Rugby matches don't kick off unless it's old guys fighting one another and we're young lads, able-bodied.' Ricky is the singer for the Angels, a rapidly growing group representative of the nascent 'Scallydelic' sound and look currently mushrooming up and out of Greater Manchester, and a man on a mission to tell it like it is before the Trendies take over his uniquely working-class subculture. A reaction to over-dressed fashion victims and the financially inaccessible shirt-and-tie crew, Scallydelia is the North's practical and humorous two fingers to fashion and Southern wealth.

With fashion roots lying as far back as the early '80s, things really started moving when football supporters were turning up for matches in flares, some even cutting their own material into the seams to make the widest possible leg. This look developed into the extremes of the Baldricks, an unfocused and distinctly local cult based around The Hacienda, acid (tabs, house and rock), lank page-boy 'Baldrick' haircuts and flares. Various Baldricks including Shaun from Happy Mondays, Cressa from The Stone Roses and Clint from Inspiral Carpets were featured in *i-D* in October 1987 and April 1988. Now things have stabilised into the current anarchic form, wide denim flares being the most noticeable trait, although outrageously ugly flared dungarees have also been spotted.

'Wear owt. You've got to wear Wallabees, Kickers, all that.' Wilbur, one of the Paris Angels' 'real people', is explaining the Scally look to me, waving his 'genuine Wallabees' about, the bottom of his flares wet and caked with grime, a common sight in the Rainy City. 'We're not sheep, we're all different, we're all individuals,' he explains, 'everybody's got something that's different from everybody else, but you can tell that we're all boys.' The 'something different' this afternoon includes hooded skateboard tops, baseball caps, trainers, steel-toed boots and brightly coloured kagoules.

The look is often misinterpreted as a hippy thing by the misinformed; hair being either long, or cut short in a Buddhist style like Wilbur's, with large sideburns completing the late '60s feel. However, as he points out: 'We're not into wearing fucking daisies in our hair and all that walking round shouting "karma fucking peace, man". Fuck that. We like the violence, we like getting off our heads, we like the dancing, the sweat.' The drippy peace and love optimism of the '60s has been replaced by a harder, more cycnical sense of community and local pride based around your band, your area and your football team. Sitting opposite me, pupils dilated, Mick stares straight into my eyes then starts muttering into the tape recorder. Later I play the tape back and hear him whispering, 'City are wankers, City are wankers', over and over again.

Ricky, however, is unhappy about the Scally title, and eager to tell the world. 'It's not Scallies,' he spits, 'we're not fucking called Scallies, the media has got that completely wrong. Scallies don't exist around here, it's Perry Boys, the Boys or Firms. It's not fucking Scallies, that's a dickhead word, that's for fucking Scousers.' Although Scallies are no longer synonymous with Liverpool, he has a point; while scouring Manchester for the perfect Scally, it seems that the only people who are prepared to accept the name are people who are probably more at home in a library than a video store: students.

The other thing which has really drawn attention to the 'Scallies' is their total embracing of house music. Initially a mix of influences of The Hacienda and New Order (whose 'druggy lads' image seemed to be launched initially to enable the group to escape the Joy Division/angst label, but has since developed into motivation and reality), things have now moved on to such an extent that house music dictates to all groups in the city, whether deliberate or not. The reaction of a Paris Angels' follower to my enquiry about their attitude to it is typically flippant. 'We like house a lot,' he smirks, 'drugs, house and pussy.' It's much more significant than that though – the spread of house from the North through to the rest of the country and into the charts came through the music's acceptance by all kinds of youth culture. The Scallies, in their baggy Joe Bloggs jeans and T-shirts, are listening to the same house as the rest of the country, but they are also listening to and following local guitar bands. 'Up here it's a mix, it's house and it's guitars,' explains Ricky. Amazingly, it is no longer an unfashionable thing for an indie music fan to be seen dancing to Soul II Soul or Lil Louis. The era of Smiths-style 'hang the DJ' back bedroom miserablism is dead, and the fatal wound was inflicted in Manchester, the city fabled for starting it all off.

Instrumental in the success and current high profile of Scallydelia (a term which has now started to appear in various music papers, although not adopted by the bands themselves) has been the increasing influence of The Happy Mondays. Viewed by many as the original Scally band, their anarchic attitude and commitment to mind-bending drugs has had a massive catalytic effect on a whole generation of Thatcher-alienated youth. 'Happy Mondays have made it bigger,' enthuses Wilbur. 'They've sort of like, represented us.' This attachment to The Mondays gained impetus when the band's acid-influenced *Bummed* LP gained overwhelming critical acclaim at the tail end of 1988. Suddenly it became genuinely fashionable to be unfashionable, to be beyond fashion due to financial and social restraints. Among those lining up to pay tribute to the influence of The Mondays is Paul Oakenfold, DJ at The Future and The Land of Oz in London and remixer of three Happy Mondays' tracks. 'The kids down here are influenced by the music and the attitude of The Happy Mondays,' he enthuses, 'and it's starting to pick up, but it's still a very underground scene here.' With the entry of their 'Madchester' EP into the national charts at the end of 1989 and the astounding success of The Stone Roses, an indie group for whom 'nightclub' is not a dirty word, things are changing rapidly.

To date, the strongest example of the successful Scally crossover is the polyrhythmic 808 State, their fusion of Martin Price's seriously deranged attitude and the wild youth of Darren and Andy resulting in perhaps the ultimate Scally band. The success of their future house had inspired a whole new generation of dance crews and guitar/dance crossovers even before their national chart success with 'Pacific State'. Once again, as with The Mondays, it's the *attitude* of 808 State which has people fired up. Bands and DJs are meeting in clubs and activity is being stimulated. The barriers are, for the time being, down, and in a flurry of punk-style inspiration and laissez-faire, anything goes. People who have had their heads turned by the gentle experimentation of De La Soul and Mark The 45 King are about to have their ears burnt by some of the ground-breaking crossover material due from Manchester in the new decade.

It's early days yet, but we've already had the Paul Oakenfold, Terry Farley and Andy Weatherall mixes of The Happy Mondays' last two singles and The Stone Roses using a hardcore James Brown rhythm to assault the charts on 'Fool's Gold'. Local guitar band Rig have had 'Hum' on their 'Dig' EP skilfully remixed by rap duo P Love And Blue, and 808 State's Graham Massey has been responsible for producing and remixing an amazing amount of Manchester music over the past 12 months (it's even rumoured that he's going to work with Morrissey). To come there is the grunge groove of the What? Noise LP (see Playpen), début recordings by Northside and The Paris Angels and the emergence of more 808 State-style dance crossover bands like the fast developing Noise Inc and Big Block 454.

That evening on the south side of the city I'm watching The Inspiral Carpets play. A Scally band made good, The Carpets have been able to detonate and exploit their roots in the Scally culture to push them into the charts along with their Mancunian counterparts Happy Mondays and The Roses. The large venue is completely sold out, with Ricky's dreaded Trendies definitely in the ascendant. The atmosphere is reminiscent of an end of term disco, with some of the more hardcore Scally types mooching about at the back of the hall and scowling. They won't be along next time; the band are picking up support by tapping into the post-Smiths anti-angst backlash, but are inevitably losing contact with their original fans, for whom a certain amount of backs-against-the-wall support for your team no matter what is a required element.

But once again people are dancing at gigs, no matter what the size, with none of the pushing down the front, an advance summed up by The Stone Roses' recent Blackpool and Alexandra Palace events, where the traditional support group was dispensed with in favour of guest DJs (Paul Oakenfold was DJing at Alexandra Palace and described it as 'a fucking blinding gig'). Not a new idea by any means, but the significant thing is that people danced before, during and after the band. At the début performance by Northside, the newest and most efficiently hyped 'Scally' band, a huge posse of their friends and followers transformed Manchester's tiny Boardwalk Club into a community celebration with events peaking when somebody pulled out a gun on the dancefloor.

Tonight though, the most noticeable thing is the amount of Inspiral Carpets T-shirts that are being worn. They are, quite literally, everywhere. Gone are the days when wearing a band's T-shirt to one of their gigs was the domain of heavy metal fans only – here they're a badge of office, with even the smallest bands in the city investing some money in T-shirts. Northside had T-shirts prepared and on sale at their first gig, Inspiral Carpets currently have eight different designs on sale, and were until recently selling more T-shirts than records.

Walking around Manchester last summer, the Second Summer Of Love in the capital but definitely the Summer Of The T-shirt up here, you couldn't move for these local T-shirts. Hanging from the skinny frame of a youth in the first explosions of acne, under the cardigan of a bus driver father of two, or topping off the Joe Bloggs flares of a pram-pushing girl on Salford Market, the Unholy Trinity of Manchester band T-shirts revolved around The Inspiral Carpets, The Stone Roses and The Happy Mondays. The Carpets' ones were the most noticeable, a crude sketch of a cow's head and the legend 'Cool As Fuck' emblazoned across the top. Exactly the stuff of teen outrage, and the ideal hip music accompaniment to the latest issue of *Viz* comic, they sold thousands. They were also ideal club wear – cheap, distinctive and exclusively Northern.

Alison Knight, a friend of the Inspiral Carpets and supplier of the band's distinctively-patterned sweat tops through her company Baylis & Knight, has seen sales multiply as the Scally look has spread. 'The same thing's happened with Joe Bloggs clothes. When I go to Inspirals and Happy Mondays gigs, I always see loads of kids in the audience wearing tops that I've made.' The Manchester-based Joe Bloggs company even produced extra-wide flares in response to overwhelming Scally demand.

Elsewhere in Manchester, though, T-shirts were being made that reflected the regional pride of the area's inhabitants, 'And On The Sixth Day God Created Manchester' and 'Woodstock '69, Manchester '89' they proclaimed, and despite the *Manchester Evening News* getting steamed up about the *London Evening Standard*'s 'There Is No Life North Of Watford' T-shirts, the spell of and importance of London was broken, the gangs of raving Scallies couldn't care less about the capital's regionalism, they were too busy having a good time insulated from the pressures and vagaries of hip London culture, and now, paradoxically influencing the very thing they chose to ignore.

'It's something that's been happening for the last year that we haven't really taken much notice of,' explains Paul Oakenfold, 'but now it's kicking off with you lot up there, and we're getting more involved down here.' Recently playing their first gig at his 'original Balearic club' The Future were Flowered Up, London's brightest young hopes and, according to vocalist Liam, the vanguard of a new Scally and club-influenced London front. 'I know a few other bands who are starting,' he enthuses. 'So there should be a lot of good stuff coming out of London this year. Music's gonna change – it's just entered the charts with The Roses and The Mondays, and things are spreading fast.' Outside Manchester there are also stirrings of a nationwide scene; The Charlatans are based in Northwich in Cheshire, but a number of their members come from Wolverhampton where bass player Martin told me, 'There is a certain element that has been steadily growing over the last six months. Jeans are getting baggier, and a lot of our local followers are regulars at acid house raves.'

Meanwhile, back in the pub the afternoon has dragged through into a six-nil defeat for Man City, the men at the pool table have punched somebody in the face, twice, and Ricky is waxing lyrical about the future. 'You can tell the originals from the twatheads, all these fucking Southern dickheads, when we're 40 you'll still see us on the terraces boozed up, end up fighting, whatever. That's what matters, that's what it's about now. It's a way of life for us.'

Mike Noon, *i-D*, 1990

715

1990: Are Stock Aitken Waterman Down the Dumper?!?

'By this time last year,' says Pete Waterman, 'we'd put 38 or 39 records out and most of them had been hits. This year we've only put out 11 records so that's a massive difference. It's partly deliberate because we wanted to take it a bit easier – both me and Matt (Aitken) have become dads this year and we've been working flat out for five years – and as it turned out Kylie didn't want to record early in the year and Jason went on tour so we had nothing to do anyway, so...' He pauses momentarily to sip his coffee and perch forward a bit more on his chair, '...we've been working at some new projects, we've shaped a few things up, we've looked around for new artists. We took a deep breath this year. We needed a break and the public needed a break from us.'

We are inside the 'nerve centre' of the Hit Factory – the Stock Aitken Waterman empire in South London – two narrow three-storey buildings where the most successful producers in pop have written, played on, produced and mixed hundreds of hits over the past few years. As well as being a studio complex, it's where PWL (Pete Waterman Ltd), the record company which Kylie and Jason (amongst others) are signed to, is based.

Anyone who's ever been inside the Hit Factory will tell you it's not as swanky as you'd expect. All through the building there are model steam trains and pictures of old locomotives (railways are Pete Waterman's second obsession after pop), but most of the available space is taken up with boxes of tapes and records, magazines and bits and bobs of recording gear.

Even today, when there are no artists in to record anything, all its little offices and narrow corridors are buzzing with activity. And Pete Waterman (43) and his colleagues Mike Stock (39) and Matt Aitken (34) are assembled in a room next to the main studio called the Waiting Room (where singers sit before they go in to record their vocals) to do their first interview with *Smash Hits* for three years...

Stock Aitken Waterman have been here since 1986, although they've been together as a songwriting/producing team since 1984 when they were the toast of the Hi-NRG disco scene producing the likes of Hazell Dean, Divine and Dead Or Alive.

Since then, of course, they've invented several huge pop names, resurrected a few flagging careers and they've made a number of highly successful charity records. In all they've chalked up well over 100 hit records (a fact commemorated in their recent compilation LP 'Stock Aitken Waterman – A Ton of Hits' which, in actual fact, boasts 81 S/A/W-produced singles). They are, in short, an absolute phenomenon if ever there was.

So what happened this year? Critics have been rather keen to point out that, actually, 1990 hasn't been such a fruitful 12 months for them. For the first time, it seems, they've had a lot of flops: Kakko, a Japanese girl they produce, failed miserably to get into the charts. Lonnie Gordon, after a Top Three hit with 'Happenin' All Over Again', neglected in fact to 'happen' at *all* again with her second single 'Beyond Your Wildest Dreams'. Big Fun had a flop single which stopped short of the 'Fun' 40. Sonia left them. Bananarama left them to work with a trendy producer bloke called Youth. All the new acts they'd tried to make famous with the Hitman Roadshows (people like Johnny O, Shooting Party and The Marines) didn't cut the mustard in the charts. And to top it all, their most successful act, Kylie, decided to go off and record four songs for her album with other producers.

And then, in the middle of October, for the first time in three years, there was a two week spell in which none of the Top 75 records were S/A/W produced – although they claimed at the time that they actually had two trendy dance records in the Top 75 under false names (they decline to say which ones, however). Everyone who had ever disliked them happily trumpeted that this was the end of Pete Waterman and his crew. They were, it was reported, down the dumper at last . . .

So what on earth has happened?

Pete: 'With the Yell! single, their record company went bankrupt the day the record came out, so there were no copies in the shops. I also think in hindsight that the band did so much damage to themselves last year in interviews and television that I don't know whether they could have made it. They were a problem.'

What about Kakko?

Pete: 'Kakko stiffed. Absolutely stiffed. We got it totally wrong. We misjudged it. It was our fault. She couldn't sing the song we gave her.'

And Lonnie Gordon's second record?

Pete: 'Well that got caught between two stools. We made a record which in fact is out now which should have been out last April. The Lonnie Gordon record was a great song, she sang it well, but it was a ballad and ballads just don't do well that time of year.'

Have you split up with Sonia? Is it true you won't be working with her again?

Pete: 'Yes. We haven't fallen out but her views – or her advisers' views –

717

and ours don't meet. I don't care what people say, but we're not in this for the money. We aim at having hit records because that's what we love to do and having hit records with Sonia was difficult at the best of times because of what Sonia is. And what she is is a very bright bubbly little character from Liverpool who is very easy to take the mickey out of.'

So how did you come to the decision to part company with her?

Pete: 'Because it got to the point where she was losing this company a lot of money. It was costing us a lot of money to keep Sonia going. And when Sonia came and asked for a rather large amount of money to buy a house for her parents and I got the accountants to actually look at the accounts, this company was in a hole a long long way. So we had to say "Sonia, we love you but you'll have to go elsewhere for this money because we'll pay you what is in the pipeline, but if we start making another album with you we're going to be over £200,000 in debt and we can't do that." '

What about Big Fun? Will you work with them again?

Mike: 'According to the latest gossip, they've dumped us.'

Pete: 'According to the latest gossip I've got, their record company has just dumped them.'

Mike: 'The thing about Big Fun was we were only going to make one record with them. They needed a hit and so we did "Blame It on the Boogie" and it was a hit and they said "Oh can we have a follow-up please?" so you feel obliged to.'

Were you unhappy about the fact that Kylie went to work with other producers as well as you?

Pete: 'Kylie came to me personally and said she wanted to write songs and she wanted to write with Matt and Mike and I said "That's not possible" because we work as a unit, the three of us and whenever we've tried to write with other people it hasn't worked. So I said to Kylie, "We can't do that, you'll have to do it with someone else". We had total knowledge of the whole thing and didn't have a problem with it.'

Mike: 'The thing is, having had such massive success Kylie is hardly likely to want to retain just one aspect of the recording process – just coming in and singing – it's probable that she'll want to do it all very soon and we won't be involved anymore.'

Pete: 'And also she's got a boyfriend in the industry who's probably spurring her on. So I think it's something we expect to happen. I don't know what the future is for Kylie. She's doing her own thing.'

Mike: 'It's fair to say, though, that this isn't the sort of direction in which we'd want to take her.'

What do you think the next step for Jason is?

Mike: 'He's in the same sort of boat as Kylie. He perceives himself in an entirely different way from the way we do. Jason I think is more into rock 'n' roll. He's Australian, he likes INXS and Midnight Oil. He'd really like to stand up there with a guitar, greasy hair, jeans ... we only ever saw him as a nicely dressed, clean-cut pop star who happened to come from Australia.'

Do you think it annoys him that Craig McLachlan has a band and he doesn't?

Pete: 'Yeah, definitely. I think that's exactly it. He'd love that.'

What Pete Waterman says, and he has a point here, is that having a go at S/A/W for having a few flop records is rather like saying Liverpool football club are down the pan because they've not won every single game they've played this season. 'They're the best team there is!' he splutters. 'They're eight points ahead of the rest! The only news story is when they don't win! It's like us when we have a flop.'

But at least you're fantastically rich, eh?

Pete: 'Nobody gets fantastically rich off pop records. That's a myth. We're on a 4% royalty for every record sold that we produce, split up that's 1 and ⅓% each off the profit of every record.'

But don't you charge pop artistes a handsome price for producing their records and making them famous?

Matt: 'We could say to someone, "OK, we'll do your record for £50,000" and that way we would be very rich in a very short time. But we actually only ever charge £500 each for every single we produce.'

But what Stock Aitken Waterman are clearly bothered about is having hits. It's what they bring the conversation back to all the time – getting to the 'bullseye', as Pete Waterman calls having a Number One hit. For most of next year, they say, they'll be working with entirely new acts who no one has heard of yet. There's a band called Delage, apparently, and another one called Boy Crazy, but they will not be drawn further than to say that the records they have planned are 'totally different to anything we've done before'.

'We're going to start again,' says Pete Waterman finally. 'This year we've had lots of people who we've worked with for a while but now they're no longer with us. 1991 is going to be much more challenging but we're still excited, we still want to make hit records. I shouldn't start saying we're down the pan yet if I was you ...'

Mike Soutar, *Smash Hits*, 12–25 December 1990

1991: Did the Right Thing

To get to Compton Terrace, a fifteen-thousand-seat concert venue owned in part by Stevie Nicks's father and located smack in the center of the Gila River Indian Reservation in Arizona, one has to drive by a route called, I'm not kidding you, the Superstition Highway. It's well down Interstate 10 beyond Phoenix, where the road leaves Tempe for Tucson; where the dust begins to rise. Out there you can see for miles: brown scrub desert and hot blue sky, the occasional mesa popping up over the rim of the world.

I drove down the Superstition Highway on my way to the opening night of the first Lollapalooza tour, sandwiched all the way between an eighteen-wheeler and a beat-up Honda Civic with a Hüsker Dü bumper sticker and the words 'Punish Me' scratched on its dirty back windshield. It was July 14, ten months after that rainy bus ride in Europe, and it was 100 degrees outside and no shade anywhere; so hot that they had to run showers along the back of the venue for concertgoers to stand beneath, so hot that the bathrooms stood empty the entire time, since every drop of moisture in every person's body was being absorbed or evaporated by other means. It was so hot that the Butthole Surfers, who, after all, are crazy, from Texas, and well known for setting themselves on fire at concerts, were cool enough to wear pants. When Ice T took the stage, he said, 'I feel like I just landed on the surface of the sun.' It was so hot that by ten o'clock in the evening, during Jane's Addiction's set, fifteen-thousand once-drunk revelers lay flat out in heat prostration on the lawn, listening to raucous songs like 'Been Caught Stealing' and 'Had a Dad', rendered motionless and at peace. They listened to it as if it were chamber music, which it actually sounded like within the hugeness of that Arizona night.

That was the finale of the first show of the first Lollapalooza. Some stuff had gone wrong that day – Nine Inch Nails had their juice cut off by accident and threw an onstage tantrum; the members of Jane's Addiction got into a little fight during one number, I forget which – but all in all, the package tour could only be called an unmitigated success. Despite the weather, the first show sold three thousand tickets more than its promoters had expected, paving the way for one of the most successful concert tours of the summer of 1991. That afternoon I found myself giving Marc Geiger, last seen exiting the Pixies' bus in Munich, an exaggerated look of amazement across the asphalt, and then, all reluctantly, the thumbs-up signal. And him? He's shaking his head at me, positively smirking.

Ever since it began, I'd had my doubts about the righteousness of the

Lollapalooza phenomenon. And yet, when I saw Henry Rollins – you remember Henry, formerly in Dischord's SOA and later on in Black Flag – face down the Compton Terrace crowd of some nine thousand early in the day, I felt a very personal sense of achievement. When I heard the selfsame crowd cheering my beloved Buttholes, I shook my head in disbelief. And by the time I saw them, later in the day, chanting, 'Want to be a cop killer, cop killer, cop killer' along with Ice T's new band Body Count, I knew for a fact something momentous was occurring. It was the first whisper, a ghostly sigh of success, a rumor whistling across the plain, that the old guard was changing. Forget mainstream radio and the color-bound gridlock of the rest of the industry: the ecstatic reception of Ice T's new band by fifteen thousand unbriefed Arizona teenagers said that there might be room in the real world after all for challenging music. At least there was a place, now, for the population to hear it.

The day after the Lollapalooza show in Arizona, I drove from San Diego to Los Angeles to interview Nirvana. Their manager, John Silva, had just Fed Exed me a package containing four songs from their upcoming release, at that time not yet titled *Nevermind*, but my rental car didn't have a tape deck, so I had to play it by dangling my tape recorder, on full blast, in front of my ear while I drove up Highway 405.

So I drove, and I listened, again and again, all the way through, then I hit rewind and listened again. I remember thinking, when I heard the first number – the words went '*Love myself better than you / know it's wrong, but what can I do?*' – that if the world was a different sort of place, it'd be a huge hit single. Then the next number began. '*One baby to another said, "I'm lucky I met you" / I don't care what you think unless it is about me*' – and I got kind of excited. The next number, 'Lithium', was one long lurch in the pit of my stomach, a disturbance in my physical self, a sensation somewhat akin to fright.

Then 'Teen Spirit' began. You know those opening chords? You know the gas pedal? You know the first line, '*Load up on drugs and bring your friends / it's fun to lose and to pretend*'? When I first heard 'Smells Like Teen Spirit', I didn't think, 'Why, this will be a monster hit that will transform the record industry and subsequently my life.' I just felt afraid. Oh, rock 'n' roll beguiles but it betrays as well. When I heard 'Teen Spirit', I felt sick with love for that song, sick with the thought that other people might dare to criticize it. Here, I knew, was one more thing to go to bat for, one more band by which I'd measure truth, one more life-changing, attitude-shaping, bigger-than-its-parts song of surrender. I felt sick because it was a battle call, and battles are always bloody. Somebody always loses.

I listened to those four songs for two and a half hours. At the end of them, I reached my destination – the Beverly Garland Hotel – and saw, in the parking lot, the three people who'd sung them, standing around idly, waiting for me to show up. Chris was lurching around in the parking lot, all goofily, while he gestured me into a parking space. And I couldn't help thinking back to when I'd first met Nirvana. It was in another kind of parking lot: the DMZish asphalt area of a McDonald's in San Ysidro (rebuilt on a new site since the famous sniper massacre of several years ago). It was a parking lot full of sullen teens in beat-up Mavericks, a ton of screaming children and the inevitable Baptist church choir on its way to a sing-off or something equally improbable out in the sticks. Saturday afternoons at McDonald's are the same the world over, and that Saturday at the Dairy Mart Road McDonald's in San Ysidro was no exception.

Nirvana was on its way across the US border for weekend gigs at a nightclub called Iguana's in Tijuana. Trailed by a square yellow truck that was serving as the equipment van for the headliner, Dinosaur Jr, the band pulled into the lot one afternoon in June. They were an hour late, owing to traffic in Orange County, and still looked half asleep. When their manager pushed me unceremoniously into one of the dirtiest, smelliest vans I've very been in, no one even looked up to ask who I was. I looked around disconsolately. Pizza crusts, candy wrappers, a cooler full of warm water and crushed cans; graffiti all over the inside of the van and a pair of grotty hightop sneakers tied so that they hung out of the crack of a window (presumably because they smelled so bad). The seats of the van had been ripped out and replaced by the kind of torn plaid sofas that you sometimes see out on street corners in San Francisco that even halfway houses have already rejected.

I sat down gingerly on one, surrounded by baleful stares. The atmosphere was positively foreboding. The only person who wasn't nearly comatose was David Grohl, Nirvana's drummer, who (typically, I soon discovered) managed to utter a semifriendly 'Hi!' Then, as we pulled out of the parking lot, I reached up nervously and turned my black baseball cap, with its K Records logo on it, back to front, Sub Pop style. There was the slightest stir from the back seat, as Kurt Cobain sat straight up. 'Where'd you get that cap?' he asked.

'Made it myself with liquid paper,' I replied. Kurt didn't answer. Then suddenly, shyly, he thrust his arm out under my nose. On the back of it was a tattoo of the exact same symbol. 'Dave did it with a pin,' Kurt said proudly, glancing over at him.

'You didn't just get it 'cause your name begins with K, did you?' I asked suspiciously.

'No!' Kurt exclaimed at once. 'That's not it at all. I like the K label a lot and what Calvin's doing, and I wanted a tattoo and I couldn't think of anything else. Besides, [K] exposed me to so much good music, like the Vaselines, who are my favorite band ever. They didn't influence me, it was just a reminder of how much I really value innocence and children and my youth. Beat Happening had a lot to do with reminding me of how precious that whole childlike world is. I have great memories of what it was like to be a little kid. It was a really good time, and I see a lot of beauty in it. I was happiest then. I didn't have to worry about anything.'

That was my first meeting with Nirvana. Back when I'd first heard *Bleach*, I had thought, 'This band is kind of like the Pixies crossed with Soul Asylum.' When I saw them play that gig in TJ, I realized that what Nirvana actually equalled was the Pixies *times* Soul Asylum. ('Thanks,' said Kurt. 'That's very close, I'd say. I never liked Soul Asylum, but I went to see them once, and I think we're closely related in our live shows. The Pixies, I've felt a real musical bond with them. I was blown away by them. That's very close to what we were doing and are doing more so now.') Live that night, Nirvana threw off sheer power in enormous bursts, leaning over their guitars with the weight of their fury, smashing them down on the ground, sometimes hurling them at each other; its members leaping, guitars and all, into a surface of human flesh, Kurt held upright, clutched by each leg, howling 'Teen Spirit' to an enthralled cabal, bodies plunging literally over the chicken wire – encased third-tier balcony and then bouncing off the skin below. Sometimes it was as if the guitars themselves had become possessed by the music and, poltergeist style, were seizing their owners like the brooms in *Fantasia* or something, hurling them around so many stages I stopped counting. Once I saw Kurt leap on Chris's shoulders, forcing him to the floor with his unexpected burden, both still playing notes all ripped apart from impact.

All this brilliance couldn't come from a more unlikely set of guys. Nirvana's founders – bassist Chris Novoselic and guitarist Kurt Cobain (Grohl, from Washington, DC, joined the group in 1990; he's their fifth drummer in as many years) – are the embodiment of small-town stoners, the American equivalent of the kids in England who angrily declared that they had No Future back in 1977. They are the type of self-described 'negative creeps' –

723

shy, weasel-faced, introvert – that it's practically impossible to imagine copping any of the classic rock poses of stardom. When they turn on like light bulbs onstage, there's an unfeigned freedom, an intuitiveness so inarticulate there's almost no point in interviewing them. They are a little hard to get to know. Kurt did once tell me his favorite books are by philosophers – 'Bukowski, Beckett, anyone beginning with a *B*' – and that he once tackled Nietzsche, but didn't understand a word of it. But you can't tell me that the guy who wrote the words '*Love myself better than you / know it's wrong but what can I do?*' didn't absorb the tenets of *Man and Superman*, even if Novoselic does jeer at the idea.

'Oh yeah, we're pocket philosophers,' Chris says, laughing.

'Well, blue-collar ones, maybe,' Kurt adds defensively.

One thing I do know about Nirvana's talent and music: it comes of obsessiveness and determination – the kind of determination that saw the band, in its early days, traveling up to Seattle time and again in a Volkswagen with all its seats torn out, packed up with tiny amps, an old Sears trap drum set, cymbal stands that were originally music stands from high school, basically equipment that was the Melvins' scraps – not to mention the three band members themselves, one of whom is six foot seven. And it comes of a genuine love of the misfit status that growing up on the outside in Aberdeen, Washington, will give a kid with a brain, a craziness that can't be faked by anyone. If there is one single thread that holds all of their banal observations together, it is that of eccentricity. Nirvana has learned to love the feeling of not belonging, to the point where the very idea of actually belonging scares them. 'I just can't believe,' says Kurt, 'that anyone would start a band just to make the scene and be cool and have chicks. I just can't believe it.'

Unlike many grungy white-boy college rock bands today, Kurt Cobain and Chris Novoselic take great pride in the fact that they even graduated from high school. They met in Aberdeen, the way people in high school do: they just kind of knew each other. They say they were always attracted to people on the outside – misfits, outcasts, strangers with candy.

'The first concert I ever went to,' recalls Chris, 'was the Scorpions. I went with these gay guys 'cause I was the only one with a car. One guy was my age and the other was older. And we were driving up to Seattle, and I looked in the back seat and they were making out and I'm, like, "Jeepers creepers". I was seventeen. They didn't bug me or anything. I kind of laughed. I thought it was funny 'cause I never saw gay people before. So we went to the show, it was the Scorpions, and it was totally boring. I stood up front and threw my shirt on the stage. And afterwards I couldn't find the other guys, so I just left without 'em.'

Kurt interrupts. 'Hey, I was friends with that guy! Randall [not his real name], he was my best friend in tenth grade and everyone else assumed I was gay too. I didn't even know he was gay but everyone else did, so there was all these gay-bashing rumors going on, like they were going to beat me up, there were really bad vibes going on in my PE class and then my mom forbid me to hang out with him anymore because he was gay. Randall! He's a great guy. I was always attracted to him 'cause he was really different. He had a really different perspective.'

But wasn't it odd that a gay guy would like the Scorpions?

'No. Everybody liked the Scorpions in Aberdeen. It's a small hick town, those are the only records you can buy there,' Kurt says. 'Scorpions or Ozzy Osbourne.'

'Not me,' says Chris. 'I didn't like 'em. I liked 'em when I was way younger, but then they started coming out with – well, all their records were crappy, but *Blackout* was the crappiest. Then I liked prog rock, and then I discovered punk rock. In 1983, I heard a compilation tape made by a friend. And then I listened to *Generic Flipper* and it was a revelation. It was art. It made me realize it was art. It was valid, it was beautiful. 'Cause I gave things validity by going, like, "Is it as good as *Physical Graffiti*?" And Flipper was suddenly, like, "Sure it is! If not better. Well, they both have their moments." It was a revelation!

'My friend Buzz gave the tape to me. He's in the Melvins. He was the punk rock guru of Aberdeen. He's the guy who discovered punk rock and spread the good news around town. But he only told it to the most deserving, 'cause a lot of people would discount it. And then I tried to turn people on to it, and they'd be, like . . . one guy I know, I remember he goes, "Ah, that punk rock stuff . . . all it is is, 'Want to fuck my mom! want to fuck my mom!' " '

Kurt: 'He probably wanted to fuck *his* mom. He probably wanted to fuck Randall!' (He and Chris collapse in giggles.)

Luckily for Chris, one of the deserving people to whom Buzz gave a tape was Kurt, who kind of knew Chris from around town. 'I'd met Buzz probably around the same time you met Buzz,' recalls Kurt. 'And one night I went over to hear the Melvins practice before they were the Melvins and they were playing, like, Jimi Hendrix and Cream and stuff like that. And I was really drunk and I thought they were the greatest band I'd ever seen, it was really awesome, and right around that time Buzz started getting into punk rock. Then they started playing punk rock music and they had a free concert right behind Thriftways supermarket where Buzz worked, and they plugged into the city power supply and played punk rock music for about fifty redneck kids. And when I saw them play, it just blew me away, I was instantly a punk rocker. I abandoned all my friends, 'cause they didn't like any of the music. And then I asked Buzz to make me a compilation tape of punk rock songs and I got a spiky haircut.'

Chris reflects on his information for a moment. 'You know what happened is, punk rock kind of galvanized people in Aberdeen. It brought us together and we got our own little scene after a while, and we all hung out. Everybody realized – all the misfits realized – that rednecks weren't just dicks, they were *total* dicks. And punk rock had all this cool political, personal message, you know what I mean? It was a lot more cerebral than just stupid cock rock, you know? Dead Kennedys. MDC, remember? Dead Cops! Corporate Death Burger! We were never exposed to any radical ideas, all the ideas came from, like, San Francisco, or Berkeley.'

'My first rock experience was Sammy Hagar in seventh grade,' Kurt says. 'My friend and I were taken by his sister to the show in Seattle. And on the way there we drank a case of beer and we were stuck in traffic and I had to go so bad I peed my pants! And when we got into the concert people were passing pipes around, marijuana, and I'd never smoked pot before, and I got really high, and I had a Bic lighter in my sweatshirt, inside the pocket, and I was tripping out and I lit myself on fire. So I stunk of pee and I caught on fire ... and I didn't really like the concert at all. It just wasn't the right type of music for me. I didn't understand it. I liked rock 'n' roll but not that concert, it didn't thrill me. He [Sammy] seemed really fake.

'When I was a little kid I had a guitar and I'd run around the house with it and sing Beatles songs and I'd have concerts for my family when they came over, on Christmas, and I'd play my guitar and play Beatles songs. I always wanted to be a rock star when I was a little kid. Then when I was a teenager, it was just different ... I still liked music a lot, but it wasn't what everyone else liked. I hated Kiss, I hated Boston, it was so fake ... and at the time I couldn't understand why people liked it. I never thought about rock when I was a teenager.

'But when I saw the Melvins play that show and I started getting into punk rock, it really changed me. I wanted to start a band really bad, and I got an electric guitar and I was really into it, but I couldn't find anyone in Aberdeen to be in a band with. I was lucky to find Chris at the time. A few years after we'd been hanging out, I made a tape of some punk rock songs I'd written with Dale, the Melvins' drummer, and I played it for Chris at my aunt's house and he really liked it, and he suggested we start a band. It sounded *exactly* like Black Flag. Totally abrasive, fast, punk music. There were some Nirvana elements, some slower songs, even then. And some heavy, Black Sabbath-influenced stuff. I can't deny Black Sabbath. Or Black Flag.'

For a while, the band was called Skid Row. 'Our drummer,' Kurt recalls, 'was this stoner guy, but he had a drum set and we kind of coaxed him into joining the band, coming to practice. But we got really serious and he wasn't that serious. He'd get drunk, miss a lot of practices. So we had a lot of trouble starting out. It didn't seem like a real legitimate band, or as legitimate as we wanted it to be. We didn't even have enough money to buy records, and there were no stores in Aberdeen.

'The closest place to see shows was Olympia or Tacoma. Tacoma is seventy miles. Seattle was one hundred miles. We didn't get there very often, just for the major punk rock shows, Black Flag and stuff. When I first started playing guitar, I just started writing songs right away. I knew one Cars song and "Back in Black" and after that I just started writing. I didn't think it was important to learn other songs because I just knew I wanted to start a band.

'At the time the Community World Theater was a really good place for new bands to start out 'cause they'd let you play. But you know what?' he adds, 'it was pretty easy to get booked. That was the thing about it. There weren't a lot of really popular bands coming into town. So it was mostly local bands that played. Olympia and Tacoma were kind of more punk rock that way – it was easier to play there than in Seattle.'

'But did anyone come see you?'

'Oh no. Maybe twenty people. There was one show in Seattle where nobody came. We didn't even play. We loaded up our stuff and left.'

Dave, who's been lying completely silent, soaking up the rays for the last hour, suddenly looks up. 'Really, nobody came at all?'

Kurt grins. 'Not one single person, except for Jon and Bruce. It was at the Central Tavern.'

Jon, of course, is Jonathan Poneman. Bruce is Bruce Pavitt, who by that time had started Sub Pop Records. During that year, 1987, Nirvana got some money together, kicked their drummer out of the band, hired Dale Crover of the Melvins, and recorded a demo at Jack Endino's studio in Seattle in a single day. Poneman heard it and liked it, eventually offering to put it out.

'Jon put out our single about six months after talking to him,' Chris recalls. 'We didn't know anything about Sub Pop at the time. We just loved playing. It's just so totally *fun*. It was the most important thing in my life at the time. It was awesome!'

Still, for a tiny podunk band like Nirvana to put a record out must have been a pretty big deal.

Kurt shrugs. 'We were excited, yeah, but after a while the excitement kind of left because it took over a year for our album to come out, 'cause we were waiting for Sub Pop to get enough money to put it out, and we ended up paying for the recording ourselves. It cost six hundred and six dollars. That's cheap. And still,' he adds, 'when we went on tour, kids would come up to us in flocks, going, "Where can we get the record? We can't find it." That's the only reason we decided to go with a major, is just the assurance of getting our records into small towns like Aberdeen.'

Kurt still feels sort of bad about being on a major label. 'But what were we going to do, stay on Sub Pop? You couldn't even find our last record! And we were under contract to them, and somebody had to have the money to get us out of the deal.'

Nirvana's not ungrateful to Sub Pop. 'The Sub Pop hype thing helped a lot, the Seattle Sound thing. We just kind of got caught up in it,' says Chris.

Kurt adds, 'In England we were always very popular. I mean, it's kind of an unusual thing for a band that's as young as us to have gone over there so soon, and Sub Pop did that for us. But going to Europe that soon [in 1988], it was exciting but it was hell at the same time. We didn't eat very much, it was a very low-budget thing. We were touring with Tad in the same van and three extra people. Eleven people. It was really grueling, 'cause we had three days off in seven and a half weeks. We were playing a lot and not eating too much.'

What was the highlight?

Kurt (without even stopping to think): 'Oh! That place in Austria! Up in the mountains, with all the trolls? The troll village!'

Chris: 'Oh yeah! A bunch of inbred villagers going, "Play some rock and roll, bay-bee!" There was a guy who looked like Mick Fleetwood with a big huge knife scar down the side of his face. And there was a guy with a machete in his hand, and it was some huge holiday and everyone was all wasted, people were passed out on the floor! There was this really fat troll, saying, "Come on, bay-bee, play something hea-veee." And there was this guy playing the blues machine. He rented himself out to, like, the Austrian version of bar mitzvahs. Oh God, I would love to rent him for our record release party. The guys in Mudhoney would go crazy.'

Kurt adds, 'We also played one of our best shows in this town called Redmond. It was just a party. And all these rednecks were there . . .'

Chris: 'But they moved into the kitchen, they didn't like us at all. They were scared of us.'

'We were really drunk,' Kurt laughs, 'so we started making spectacles of ourselves. Playing off of the bad vibes we were giving to the rednecks, you know – jumping off tables and pretending we were rock stars. And Chris jumped through a window. Then we started playing "Sex Bomb" for about an hour, and our girlfriends were hanging on us and grabbing our legs and doing a mock lesbian scene, and that really started freaking out the rednecks!'

'But why was this the best show ever?'

Kurt thinks for a sec. 'Oh, just because it was such a great vibe, I mean, we were totally wigging the rednecks out! And that was the idea of punk rock to us in the first place, was to abuse your audience. And what better audience to have than a redneck audience?'

By that time, Kurt had lived in Olympia for about a year, and Chris lived in nearby Tacoma, about twenty miles away. As Chris explains, at that time Sub Pop was talking about signing a big distribution deal with Sony (which eventually fell through). Nirvana got their own lawyer, who shopped them to various labels in Los Angeles. Eventually Geffen Records paid Sub Pop Records seventy thousand plus points for the privilege of licensing Nirvana.

Nirvana had initially recorded the songs for *Nevermind* as demos for Sub Pop. When they signed to Geffen, they re-recorded much of it – as well as adding tracks – at Butch Vig's studio in the spring of 1991. The band had two weeks of studio time booked, but it only took them a week and a half to lay it down. Kurt was still writing lyrics in the studio. 'Endless Nameless', the buried track on the CD version (it begins ten minutes after 'Something in the Way' ends) was a bunch of experimental shit they laid down in the studio at that time. The cello part on 'Something' was added at the last minute, when Kirk Canning, a member of the band Spoon, happened to stop by the apartment the band was staying at in Madison.

Thus, *Nevermind* was initially conceived and marketed by the major label as just another relatively low-budget alternative band project. Kurt shrugs. 'The level of success we're on doesn't really matter to us. It's a fine thing, a flattering thing to have major labels want you, but it doesn't matter. We could be dropped in two years and go back to putting out records ourselves and it wouldn't matter, 'cause it's not what we were looking for. We didn't want to be staying at the Beverly Garland Hotel, we just wanted people to get the records. And we did do it on an independent level. That's the beauty of it.'

Chris: 'We should make a made-for-TV movie. *The Nirvana Story*. Who will play you?'

729

Kurt: 'Ernest Borgnine. Who'll be you?'

'Someone tall – Kareem Abdul Jabbar? We'll have these intense scenes. "I'm in this band, and what I say *goes*!" We'll be throwing our wine goblets through the window. Then there'll be the love part: "Baby, I'm sorry, I've got to go out with the band." And she'll be, like, "Don't you love me?" And I'm, like, "Hasta la vista!" The love! The camaraderie! (That'll be in the van with Tad in Europe.) The triumph! Us onstage. The letdowns: *"Booo!"* We're getting shit thrown at us. And it'll be directed just like an ABC After School Special. "You know I love you, baby, but I've got to put the band before anything." "Yes, I understand." "But you'll live in my heart forever." "Go, love of mine."'

Kurt grins. 'And then the end. Our manager will come by and go, "You guys have been dropped. You're broke." And the last line is, Chris picks up the phone and goes, "Hello, operator? Give me Sub Pop!"'

Gina Arnold, *Route 666: On the Road to Nirvana* (1993)

1992: Rage to Live: 'Ardkore Techno

'See my face, not a trace, no reality/. . . I just speed/It's all I need'
Sex Pistols, 'Seventeen', 1977

'Too much speed is comparable to too much light . . . we see nothing'
Paul Virilio, *Pure War*

When British youth first encountered the term 'acid house' they misconstrued it. In Chicago, the word 'acid' derived from 'acid burn', slang for ripping off someone's idea (i.e. by sampling it). In Britain, it was instantly assumed that 'acid' mean psychedelics. Acid house became the soundtrack to the Ecstasy Rave-olution, another prime example of British youth mis-recognising (and re-motivating) a Black American music. Hardcore Techno has reversed the classic drugs/music set-up: after four years of raves, the music has evolved into a science of inducing and amplifying the E-rush (rather than vice-versa). What's more, the vibe has changed (from transcendance to mental-manic) as ecstasy has become adulterated with amphetamine, or simply replaced – by pseudo-E concoctions of speed, LSD and who knows what. The subculture's metabolism has been chemically altered, till the beats-per-minute (last count: 140–150 bpm) soar in sync with pulse rates and blood pressure levels.

730

Another factor is that long-term Ecstasy usage causes the drug's blissful, lovey-dovey effect to fade, leaving only a jittery, nerve-jangling speediness.

E and LSD both activate the 'fight-or-flight' sector of the brain. In combination with amphetamine, either will produce an edgy exhilaration on the borderline of panic reaction: 'are you feeling w-w-w-wobbly???', as Xenophobia's 'The Wobbler' enquires, rhetorically. 'Ardkore is just another form of *fin de siècle* 'panic culture': hence the frequent samples of sirens, the ambuscades of sound, the MC chant 'comin' at ya!'. There's even a track titled 'Start the Panic'. (The original Greek panic, the 'Panic Fear' of the horned god Pan, was a transport of ecstasy-beyond-terror.) Speedy E has changed the whole vibe of rave culture, from celebration to a sort of aggressive euphoria. The urge to merge and the urge to surge fuse in a raging oceanic feeling. Dancers' faces are contorted with weird expressions midway between snarl and smile; they glare with a crazed, blazing impudence.

It's the most brazenly druggy subculture in ages, even less oblique about it than aciiied. Pirate DJs send 'big shouts' to 'all you nutters rushing out of your heads, speedfreaks out there, you know the score'; 'yes London town, absolutely flying in the studio, 100 mph'. Is it actually impossible to get into this music without drugs, as 'Ardkore's detractors claim? Certainly they help hype the metabolism to the necessary frenetic pitch. But once the nervous system has been re-programmed, you can listen to this stuff 'on the natural'. By itself, it'll induce memory rushes, body-flashbacks.

However, speed has mutated (some would say perverted) rave music's development, unbalancing it at both the top and bottom ends of the sound-spectrum. 'Ardkore is all ultra-shrill treble and bowel-quaking bass. Voices are sped up to a 78 rpm Pinky & Perky shriek, whether they're samples of ethereal girl voices – Kate Bush, Liz Cocteau, Stevie Nicks – or heliumised eruptions of black voice. Closer to fireworks than 'soul', these vocals have been hurtled beyond expression and the syntax of desire, into a realm of abstract urgency. Sampled and modulated on a keyboard, they become a barrage of intensities without pretext or context, shudders and shivers that are not so much inhuman as infra-human. Incantations from roots reggae are snatched from their cultural context to become animated hieroglyphs, ragga chants adding a grainy insolence that's perfect for 'Ardkore's ruff and tuff uproar. Dub bass impacts your viscera, its alien metre placed outrageously amid accelerated hip hop breakbeats at twice reggae's pace. Having 'swallowed hip hop whole', 'Ardkore's syncopation is a radical break with the programmed machine rhythms of early UK Techno. The electronic side of Techno has degenerated into stray smears of aciiied bass, pulsation-loops

731

derived from Joey Beltram's 'Energy Flash' and 'Mentasm', fucked-up conca-
tenations of blaring samples, and octave-skipping synth riffs whose function
is not melodic but textural. And of course, the sheer speed of their oscillation
accentuates the sense of headlong RUSH.

At raves and clubs, or on pirate stations (Touchdown, Don, Kool, Defection, Pulse, Rush), DJs compact rough-and-ready chunks of tracks into a
relentless but far from seamless inter-textual tapestry of scissions and grafts.
It's a gabbling fucking mess, barely music, but as it swarms out the airwaves
to a largely proletarian audience, you know you're living in the future.
'Trash', but I luvvit.

It's a mistake to appraise 'Ardkore in terms of individual tracks, because this
music only really takes effect as *total flow*. Its meta-music pulse is closer to
electricity than anything else. 'Ardkore has abandoned the remnants of the
verse/chorus structure retained by commercial rave music. At the Castlemorton Common mega-rave in May, MCs were chanting 'we've lost the plot'.
'Ardkore abolishes narrative; instead of tension/climax/release, it offers a
thousand plateaux of crescendo, an endless succession of nows. Apocalyptic
nows, for sure: 'Ardkore fits only too well the model of terminal culture that
Paul Virilio prophesises in *The Aesthetics of Disappearance*: 'a switch from
the extensive time of history to the intensive time of momentariness without
history'. This emergent anti-culture of instantaneity will be inhabited by a
new breed of schizophrenic subject, whose ego is 'made up of a series of little
deaths and partial identities'.

No narrative, no destination: 'Ardkore is an intransitive acceleration, an
intensity without object. That's why the MC patter sounds more appropriate
for a rollercoaster than music – 'hold tight', 'let's go', 'hold it down' – and
also why Techno is all you'll hear at fairgrounds these days. Does this
disappearance of the object of desire, this intransitive intensity, make
'Ardkore a culture of autistic bliss? Certainly, sex as the central metaphor of
dancing seems more remote than ever. Rave dancing doesn't bump and grind
from the hip; it's abandoned the model of genital sexuality altogether for a
kind of amoebal frenzy. It's a dance of tics and twitches, jerks and spasms,
the agitation of a body broken down into individual components, then
re-integrated at the level of the entire dancefloor. Each sub-individual part (a
limb, a hand cocked like a pistol) is a cog in a collective desiring machine.

The dancefloor has become a primal DNA soup. It's pagan too, this digital
Dionysian derangement whose goal is asylum in madness. (Hence the slang
of 'mental' and 'nutty', sound systems with names like Bedlam, groups with

names like Lunarci, MCs chanting 'off my fucking tree' – pejoratives turned into desirable states-of-mindlessness.)

It's emotionally regressive too (as all the musically progressive genres of the last decade – rap, oceanic rock, noise – have been): witness the infantilism of ravers sucking dummies, and bubblegum chart hits like 'A Trip to Trumpton', 'Sesame's Treet', The Prodigy's 'Charly'. As Virilio reminds us, 'Child-society frequently utilises turnings, spinning around, disequilibrium. It looks for sensations of vertigo and disorder as sources of pleasure.' He cites the childhood game of spinning round and round, in order to create 'a dizziness that reduces [the] environment to a sort of luminous chaos'.

Virilio's book is a jeremiad about an emergent culture based around 'picnolepsy', his term for frequent, incredibly brief ruptures in consciousness. 'Picnolepsy' is a kind of pun on epilepsy, which Websters defines as a disorder 'marked by *disturbed electrical rhythms* of the central nervous system and typically manifested by convulsive attacks usually with clouding of consciousness.' [my italics] (Epilepsy, incidentally, was a sacred malady for the Greeks.) 'Ardkore is poised somewhere on the brink between picnolepsy and epilepsy. We know that strobes (the staple of rave lightshows) can cause convulsions: 'Ardkore is the aural analogue of the strobe, a sequence of frozen stop-gap soundbites that have been artificially re-animated with E-lectricity.

'With the irregularity of the epileptic space, defined by surprise and an unpredictable variation of frequencies, it's no longer a matter of tension or attention, but of suspension pure and simple (by acceleration), disappearance and effective reappearance of the real, departure from duration.' Virilio could be writing about the rave scene in 1992. This is the feeling that The KLF caught with the title (if not the sound) of '3 AM Eternal'. Speed reproduces the effects of picnolepsy, a 'perpetually repeated hijacking of the subject from any spatial-temporal context.' You're gone, totally out of it. And there's more: a warning sign for some epileptics of an imminent attack is 'a special state of happiness, a juvenile exhilaration.' 'Sublime' wrote Dostoevski, a sufferer, 'for that moment you'd give your whole life ... At that moment I understood the meaning of that singular expression: there will no longer be time.'

Such juvenile 'nihilism' is the reason why 'Ardkore perturbs so many. This music is best understood as a neurological rather than a cultural phenomenon. It abolishes the role of cultural mediators. Textless, it offers little to interpret *in itself* (its subcultural text resides in its *effect*). Critics who like to engage with rock 'n' roll as a surrogate form of literature are perhaps the

733

most threatened by this anti-humanist noise, which seems closer to a power source or pure intoxicant than any kind of poetry. But 'Ardkore also challenges those who've seized on the more musicianly participants in rave music to argue the case for House and Techno as an art form. There is a deep prejudice against one-dimensional music. It's both amazing and amusing to see how exactly the same rhetoric used by detractors of 50s rock'n'roll recurs as a knee-jerk tic amongst rock fans faced by a new 'barbaric non-music'. Along with the racist notion of 'jungle music' (by interesting coincidence, one of 'Ardkore's big sub-genres this year is known as 'jungle'), one of the things most feared about rock'n'roll was its extreme repetitiveness. Which is exactly what the anti-'Ardkore enclaves bemoan. Repetition is a psychoactive agent in itself, of course. Anyway, to those who insist that 'Ardkore 'just isn't music', I won't argue (I couldn't care less). But I do know that every new development in pop – from punk to rap to acid house – has initially been greeted with similar spasms of fear and loathing.

In the late 60s and early 70s, British groups bastardised the blues, and their American imitators bastardised their bastardisation, and somewhere in all this was spawned heavy metal. In the late 80s, black Europhiles from Chicago and Detroit took Teutonic electronic music and turned it into House and Techno; in the early 90s, British youth took these styles and birthed a further mutant, mongrel form: 'Ardkore. Veterans of 1988's First Wave of Rave denounce 'Ardkore in exactly the same language that counterculture vets decried metal – as soul-less, macho, bombastic, proto-fascist, a corrupt and degraded version of a once noble tradition. They've even been calling 'Ardkore 'the new heavy metal'. With the same piety wherein people once harked back to Cream to deplore Sabbath and Led Zep, similarly, rave cognoscenti mourn Derrick May and flinch from the brutalism of Beltram and 2 Bad Mice. In an unfortunate echo of prog rock, some have even erected the concept of 'Progressive House' (The Future Sound of London, The Orb, Guerilla Records) as a bulwark of good taste against the hooligan hordes of 'Ardkore. History shows us that the despised Black Sabbath went on to exert a huge influence on underground rock in the 80s and 90s (from The Fall and Black Flag through the Butthole Surfers to Seattle grunge), while ProgRockers Jethro Tull, ELP and Pink Floyd went on to influence practically nobody.

'Maturation' was always only one possible route of development for the music of the post-aciiied diaspora. As heavy metal did with blues rock, 'Ardkore has taken the essence of aciiied and Techno – mind-less repetition, stroboscopic synths, bass-quake frequencies – and coarsened and intensified it. Just as with metal, bad drugs (barbiturates then, dodgy E now) have helped them focus on that essence. In a way, 'Ardkore actually presents a kind of degraded avant-gardism, of arrested futurism: headless chickens running wild with avant-garde techniques (timbral/textural/spatial invention rather than melodic/harmonic development, drone theory, extreme repetition/extreme randomness, *musique concrète*, etc.), albeit with little idea how to build with them. But 'Ardkore advances not through the innovations of *auteurs*, but rather *evolves through mutation*: inspired errors and random fucking about produces new riffs and noises that succeed in the dancefloor eco-system and then enter the gene pool. Creativity operates at the macro-level of the entire genre, not the individual 'genius': a phenomenon Brian Eno calls 'scenius'. Which explains why, whenever someone does come up with a new idea, it's instantly ripped off a thousand times. Anyway, I wager that those looking for the next revolution would do better to watch for what crawls out of the 'Ardkore morass than to carry a torch for Detroit, or LFO, or Orbital (as inspired as they may all have been in their day).

'Ardkore is really just the latest twist on the traditional contours of working class leisure, the latest variant on the sulphate-fuelled 60-Hour-Weekend of mod and Northern Soul lore. With 'Ardkore, the proletarian culture of consolation has become a culture of concussion: hence amnesiac/anaesthetic slang terms for a desirable state of oblivion like 'sledged', 'mashed up', 'cabbaged', 'monged'; hence song titles like 'Blackout' and 'Hypnoblast'.

There's a sampled slice of rap at large in 'Ardkore that goes: 'can't beat the system/go with the flow'. On one level, it's just a boast about how much damage the sound-system can inflict. But perhaps there's a submerged political resonance in there too: amidst the socio-economic deterioration of a Britain well into its second decade of one-party rule, where alternatives seem unimaginable, horizons grow ever narrower, and there's no constructive outlet for anger, what else is there left but to zone out, to go with the flow, *disappear*?

Still, such retreatism is just one side of the rave scene. There's also an inchoate fury in the music, that comes out in an urge for total release from constraints, a lust for explosive exhilaration – captured in titles like 'Hypergasm'. The ragga chant of Xenophobia's 'Rush in the House' kicks off: 'E come alive E come alive E come alive'. 'Ardkore frenzy is where the somnambulist youth of Britain snap out of the living death of the 90s to grasp at a few moments of fugitive bliss. 'Ardkore seethes with a RAGE TO LIVE, to cram all the intensity absent from a week of drudgery into a few hours of fervour.

735

It's a quest to reach escape velocity. Speed-freak youth are literally running away from their problems. Do you blame them?

Simon Reynolds, *The Wire* 105, November 1992

1992: Outing the In-Crowd

Total Clubbing Space has arrived. It's now possible to step into a club on Friday night and emerge 50 hours later on Monday morning, fit and – chemically? – readied for work. This is the new clubbing regime, courtesy of the updated licensing laws: along with juice bars, cinemas and board games, an environment which incorporates both boredom and frenzy, relaxation and euphoria. The tradition of the week-ender, that exclusive all-out rush, has been modified and democratised – everyone is invited, week in, week out.

What does this open-doors policy now do to Clubland's understanding of itself (the only notion that unites the many, internecine club tribes) as an underground? Clubland's eternal rhetoric of liberation through desire, empowerment through release, tells us it needs some things to stay forbidden, that it lives on in its off-limit areas.

We could just redraw the lines, and refuse to accept 1992 as part of the authentic clubbing experience. But this would simply ignore crucial history and the Rave Nation's lobbying for appropriate licensing laws, which announced in its own language a decade-long push for extra time, for more space, for more everything. Still, what happens when the government is more radical than the underground? When clubbers get what they want only to find it wasn't, after all, what they wanted?

Think of the 80s as a series of escalating demands with this moment as the apex. In 1981–83, the moment was one which was yet to be named 'style'. Every Man and Every Woman is a Star – well, Aleister Crowley (and Sly Stone) wanted us to believe this, but in an age when *The Face* adopted a title from arrogant Mod jargon for the street-élite, you had to acknowledge that some seemed more like stars than others. Clubs like Taboo and Chacha catered for the few. Taking their cue from the dazed *ennui* of Warhol's *Heat*, *Hustlers*, etc, they found each other endlessly fascinating, a fascination which depended on a hyper-sensitivity towards semiotic perversion, the signs of clubbable kinkiness. Which made the scene fragile; the early 80s expended most of its energy keeping out those who could damage this fragile artifice. The 80s didn't invent clubbing, but it did invent Clubland, the theme park of its forbidden self.

Everything that spills beyond the behaviour on this or that night, every-thing once called subculture and now named 'lifestyle', magazines, hairstyles, clothes, drugs – these express the highs of a club, but *everywhere, all the time*. At last, a club without walls. Night swallows the everyday.

By the mid-80s, warehouse parties were in full swing. These are the Simulation years. Rare groove, streetsoul and the very first house parties – run by organisers such as Family Funktion and Shake and Fingerpop – have tended to be stigmatised as would-be organic, essentialist, in search of the pure soul groove of yesteryear. In fact, these scenes are smart-art hybrids, instant environments of an imaginary 70s. 'Copies without originals' pro-liferated: as Andrew Levy, bass player for the Brand New Heavies, explained to me, 'Our first single was a 7-inch with a hole in the middle [*i.e. not a 12", and with no picture sleeve*]. It was meant to look like an old 70s Rare Groove track. Coldcut did the same thing with their single "Say Kids What Time Is It?"' Party organisers of this time would complain to you how London's archaic licensing laws embarrassed them. But it was these very laws (in contrast to the more liberal licensing environments in the US and Europe) which guaranteed the outlawdom which fuelled the various scenes.

Clubland the Outlaw had a sanctioned skeleton in its closet right from the beginning. Sunrise, who were to invent the orbital rave, only existed because of that most elitist and reactionary phenomenon of all: the members club. As Tony Colston-Hayter, a Sunrise organiser, told me, 'We spotted a loophole by which a private members club didn't need to have a licence or a limit on numbers. Once I found that out, there was no stopping us.' A privilege maintained for a post-war upper-class male pleasure – at Boodles or Whites – is snatched away and blown up into the fandemonium of the rave scene. On June 27th 1989, *The Sun* put it like this: SPACED OUT! 11,000 YOUNG-STERS GO DRUG CRAZY AT BRITAIN'S BIGGEST EVER ACID PARTY.

Even stranger, perhaps, is the fact that many warehouse parties weren't actually illegal at all. The 1962 Private Places of Entertainment Act which prohibited such come-togethers existed only in Soho, not in East London or the home counties. Clubland, it seems, insisted upon its own illegality even when unnecessary, and played along with police and media perceptions of itself. Consider such films as *Scandal, Dance with a Stranger* and *Absolute Beginners*. The mid-80s seems to have reactivated not just the laws but the stifled, choked Soho-titillation of the late 50s and early 60s. As if invoking

737

one (mythological) moment, where pleasure supposedly threatened the social order, was the only way to understand the landscape of youth culture in the 80s.

Such a subterranean continuity, from pre-Beatles to post-punk pop-London, points up one inherited relationship of inclusion and exclusion. Rave organisers literally turned their back on this relationship. Sunrise left London altogether, headed for the home counties, foreseeing a rural communion still observed today. They regarded urban clubbing as another paragraph of the same old subcultural pop-narrative: trads, teds, mods, rockers, hippies, punks, clubbers. They scathingly argued that clubs were segregationist, the unwitting dupes of the establishment. Ravers saw themselves as the first ever trans-youth unity movement, reclaiming (almost without intent) some Deep-structure Albion inside Merrie England which all their predecessors had been too busy defying the police to notice.

For their part, such London clubs as Boys Own, still aristos at heart, accused Rave of encouraging and exploiting a mass uniformity on a scale never before seen in England. This schism in Clubland persists today.

In 1992, the Total Clubbing Space begins to look like a way of breaking clubs open to the everyday, rather than the reverse. Whether or not this is a belated attempt to heal the gap between anti-club ravers and anti-rave clubbers, the assumption that Clubland is the multiformat expression of clubbing has clearly, finally, broken down. In 1992, Clubland no longer has any necessary connection to clubs – which explains all those club phenomena which don't in fact quite work in clubs. Ambient music for instance: always shunted off into a room on its own, it's a music with no dance and no space *of* its own. Techno and rap begin to realise that they are musics with no associated visual dimension. Meta-retro bands – like The Sandals – flaunt precisely the artifice which Rare Groove tried to hide. Soundtrack DJs like the Karminsky Experience play a deliberately back-ground music – the crowd 'become' the visuals and everyone acts as if somewhere else, far away from where the 'real' music, the 'real' action is happening.

These are examples of how Clubland isn't feeding back into clubs as it once did automatically – of how it now flows outwards, towards places which don't yet exist. These, at least, are the thoughts provoked by Guy Nisbett, one half (with Vivian Baker) of First Light Virtual Design, a company who are working on a virtual reality clubbing project.

'You have to realise London Clubland has always been about multiple realities. Why all those guys in California never made the connection, I don't know, but that's what we're doing.' Nisbett explains Virtual Clubbing in the following way: 'Using a CDI package which you connect to your TV screen, you experience a network of simulated rooms and environments. You can choose to move around three regions – FreeSpace, StreetSpace, which is various parts of London like Soho, and HeadSpace, in people's heads. We scan people in there and you will see them and be able to talk to them interactively, to disappear inside their head.'

VR clubbing won't replace clubs any more than a record or a magazine does. But that's an ingenuous analogy – VR is exciting because it's a new game for a few players, a game raised to the level of total immersion-experience, one which will dramatically expand what does and doesn't count as pleasure. Think of a club as an art form whose content – freeform interaction – is enabled, obscured and maintained by its setting. Clubland is the medium which begins to manipulate its messages. VR is where that message is estranged and becomes accessible as new material. Suppose Clubland is a machine for generating 'inauthenticities' – breaking them down, piling them up. VR isn't going to be a value-free Born Again Aesthetic realm. Nisbett believes we'll see communication 'with less filters than ever before.' Maybe. Just as likely are Identity Wars which will make the style wars of the last decade look like Disneyland. Phase one of those Wars, 1994–2004: played out in the StreetSpaces of Tokyo and California, the HeadSpaces of George Clinton and Mixmaster Morris, the skirmishes between who acts and who poses, who fakes and who plays, they take a new and murderous turn as the answers to what's accessible and what's off-limits accelerate beyond any accepted justification. Chances are, the drives of transcendence and identification which have powered Clubland to date will be intensified, not resolved – and those who look best able to navigate them will find themselves marked for sacrifice.

Kodwo Eshun, *The Wire* 106/107, December 1992/January 1993

1992: Notes on the Life & Death and Incandescent Banality of Rock 'n' Roll

There's an image of present day rock 'n' roll that I've been unable to get out of my head since I first bumped into it on MTV a few years ago. It still runs on the channel, but with the set on or off it comes back to me all the time, without warning, capable of tingeing any musical thrill with nausea.

It's a video by Poison, one of LA's blond heavy-metal bands – the clip for 'Every Rose Has Its Thorn', a good ballad. You see singer Bret Michaels

739

striding through backstage corridors on his way to the stage, where cameras, visible in the video itself, will soon make it appear as if infinite numbers of fist-thrusting boys and weeping girls want nothing more than to sacrifice themselves on the altar of the band's life-force. Backstage, adoring fans, looking at once giddy and scared, are huddled against the wall, as if pressed back by vibrations emanating from Michaels's forehead.

He's flanked by two bodyguards – mountains of flesh with heads so blocklike they barely seem human, no expressions on their faces, just a readiness to smash apparent in the way that they move. It's slow motion. Though nothing is really happening, tension builds. The disdain on Michaels's face, in his walk, is precise and studied, a parody of every rock-star swagger from Elvis to Jagger. No one is laughing, Michaels least of all.

This pose is too obvious. One more gesture is called for. Michaels is carrying a drink in a big paper cup; he tosses it against the wall. There's no anger in his movement, merely contempt; in your mind's eye you can glimpse the bottomless well. Still in slow motion, the drink splatters and drips down the wall.

As in almost any video, symbolism is the currency. As the clenched fists will symbolize self-affirmation, the tears submission, and the visible cameras that what you're seeing is very important – important enough to be filmed – here the meaning is equally plain: the star pisses on his fans and they are blessed.

This tableau of worship and hauteur is staged, an advertisement carefully constructed out of clichés that have been pretested and presold. They need only to be rearranged to produce the proper response: Bret Michaels, in his role, could be Sebastian Bach of Skid Row or Axl Rose of Guns 'N' Roses as easily as he is himself. The demonstration is riveting nonetheless. It is a pornography of money, fame, and domination, all for no reason outside itself, and all based in the magic of music.

If rock 'n' roll is real – not simply a balance sheet, but a matrix of voices and values – then here in this video is something real about rock 'n' roll. For this is, today, a sign, as complete as Little Richard's pompadour in 1956 or Jimi Hendrix's blasted 'Star-Spangled Banner' in 1969, of the liberation rock 'n' roll has always promised: I can go where I want, do what I want, say what I want. There are no rules. Freedom's just another word for a mess someone else has to clean up.

This is my image of the death of rock – or of rock as something that ought to be killed.

The question of the death of rock comes up again and again these days, and not just because of falling record sales, a collapsing concert market, major labels consolidating to the point of monopoly, or desperately profligate, rear-guard superstar contracts. Sony Music's $33.5 million for ancient hard-rock war-horses Aerosmith, for example – a deal that will take the boys into their fifties, if they or Sony last that long, a kiddie-toy version of Wall Street's '80s leveraged buyouts, debt-financing, Milkenesque 'compensation' at the top, massive layoffs below. The death of rock is not a question because of growing censorship of songs and shows, damaging as that is. (Speaking in March at an American Enterprise Institute conference on popular culture – a forum that included Robert Bork, Irving Kristol and William J. Bennett – a professor of constitutional law at Georgetown University named Walter Berns called for censoring not only the music but 'the musicians themselves, the rockers, the rappers, and all the Madonnas' – there's more than one?) It isn't even that the music is empty. Put last year's most interesting platinum albums against the year's celebrated hit movies and best-selling books – pit *Metallica* against *Bugsy*, or Ice Cube's *Death Certificate* against Julie Sal-amon's *The Devil's Candy* – and it's clear that there's more life and less formula on the charts.

The question of the death of rock comes up because rock 'n' roll – as a cultural force rather than as a catchphrase – no longer seems to mean anything. It no longer seems to speak in unknown tongues that turn into new and common languages, to say anything that is not instantly translated back into the dominant discourse of our day: the discourse of corporatism, selfish-ness, crime, racism, sexism, homophobia, government propaganda, scape-goating and happy endings.

There is an overwhelming sense of separation, isolation: segregation. There might be a vague awareness of the early and mid-'50s, when street-corner doo-wop by African- and Italian-Americans, rockabilly by southern whites, and urban rhythm-and-blues from Chicago on down struggled for a name to mark the new spirit they seemed to share. There might be a memory of *The TAMI Show*, the 1964 concert film with Jan & Dean, the Supremes, Gerry & the Pacemakers, Chuck Berry, Lesley Gore, the Miracles, the Beach Boys, Marvin Gaye, James Brown and the Rolling Stones sharing the same stage and, indisputably, whatever the word meant, all *rock*. The myth of the '60s that today serves as such a beacon and a burden for people in their teens and twenties is, among other things, a myth of wholeness – a wholeness that people who never experienced 'the Sixties', as fact or illusion, sometimes still feel as an absence, like the itch of a limb amputated before they were born. It is a myth less of unity, or even rebellion, than of a pop lingua franca – that's what brought more young people into the theatres for *The Doors*, a strong

741

movie that invited them to imagine themselves dressed up in their parents' clothes, than for *Pump Up the Volume*, a stronger movie in which they could have seen people like themselves seeking the voice Jim Morrison once seemed to have found.

The rock audience began to break apart as far back as the early 70s. As the center of pop gravity, the Beatles had validated every form of the music both as commerce and as art; with that force gone, both listeners and genres spun out in all directions. Still, the lines between sounds and audiences have never been so hard or so self-justifying – as commerce and as art – as they are now. Today 'rock' refers to – what? Nirvana? Sinéad O'Connor? Michael Jackson? Bruce Springsteen? Prince? Ray Charles for Diet Pepsi? Rapper Ice-T, with or without his thrash band, Body Count? Public Enemy? Carter the Unstoppable Sex Machine, two former London buskers transformed into world-class Jeremiahs? Rosanne Cash? Madonna? Aging and unbowed punk troubadours the Mekons or neo-psychedelicists My Bloody Valentine? The Nymphs from Los Angeles, the Fastbacks from Seattle, Pulnoc from Prague, the Vulgar Boatmen from Florida, Babes in Toyland from Minnesota, anyone's favorite breaking group or nowhere indie band? Some people would withhold the name 'rock' from some of those performers, and some of those performers would reject the name themselves.

The pop-music audience is bigger than ever, despite fifteen-dollar CDs and thirty-dollar concert tickets. Such prices are paid, when they are, because the audience has been organized into market segments – complex and recombined segments of age, race, class, and gender – efficiently predictable, containable markets that can be sold identity, or anyway self-recognition, packaged as music. As culture the segmentation is so strict that any public violation of its boundaries – say, white fraternity boys blasting NWA's ho-bitch rap spew – can seem less a matter of outsiders crossing over into the mainstream than a privileged raid by the colonists on the colonized. There is no central figure to define the music or against whom the music could be defined, no one everybody feels compelled to love or hate, nobody everyone wants to argue about (what is pop music if not an argument anyone can join?), unless it's the undead Elvis Presley. He's dripping almost fifteen years of rot – and, according to the Geto Boys, a rap group from Houston, he's the winner of the Grammy for Most Appearances Made After Death. 'The King couldn't be here due to illness,' mouths a white-bread voice on the Geto Boys' 'Trophy', 'so to accept this award on his behalf we have – Grateful Dead.'

Ah yes, the Grateful Dead, from 1967's Summer of Love to ... the number-one concert draw of 1991. 'I've had a few too many, so this might sound strange,' Rick Rizzo of the guitar-based Chicago foursome Eleventh Dream Day leads off on 'Bomb the Mars Hotel': 'To see something that gives pleasure to so many/And want to take it all away.' But he does, and anyone who's seen too many Deadheads or heard too much 'classic rock' while punching buttons in search of something new knows how he feels. 'Bury the righteous monolith,' Rizzo shouts. 'And kill the sleepy myth/No more traveling microbus hordes/Taking over my town/No more tie-dyed underwear/No more dancing bears.'

This is where talk of the death of rock starts: with pointlessness surrounded by repetition. As two Paris critics put it in 1955 while writing about the art world, it starts with the feeling that you're trapped in 'a dismal yet profitable carnival, where each cliché has its disciples, each regression its admirers, every remake its fans'. It's as if the source of the depression is not that rock is dead but that it refuses to die. Far more than Elvis, really, a clone like Bret Michaels, so arrogant and proud, is of the walking dead. It's just that the money's too good to quit.

I believe all of that, but as with any fan there are times when I couldn't care less – when, as in the last hour, running a few errands, I can hear the guitar line ripping through John Mellencamp's 'Get a Leg Up', the radio shock of the drums kicking off Tom Petty's 'Out in the Cold', voices growling in the background of ZZ Top's 'My Head's in Mississippi' – times when the question of the death of rock seems, if not pointless, the most tired repetition of all.

Rock 'n' roll fans have always been waiting for the death of rock. Plenty of people will tell you the question itself is dead: Rock 'n' roll died in 1957, or 1969, or 1976, when the Sex Pistols, lacking anything better to do, announced they had come to destroy it. From the start, the new music's new followers were told *It will never last* so often and so loudly that a distrust of the music, a distrust of one's own response to it, was all but part of the sound. Though the music began to argue against its own demise almost as soon as it had a name to trumpet, a belief in the music's end was coded into every one of its early artifacts, from Chuck Berry's 'School Days' to the Monotones' 'Book of Love'. *The music was never meant to last,* fans were later told by critics who came not to bury but to praise, *and that's the fun of it!* The death of rock was certain by 1960, with the founders missing (Elvis in the Army, Berry on his way to prison, Buddy Holly dead, Alan Freed driven from the airwaves by the payola scandals, Little Richard in God's arms),

743

Lawrence Welk ascendant (with 'Calcutta,' his only number-one record) – and Motown, the Stax-Volt Memphis sound, the Beatles, the Rolling Stones, Bob Dylan, and Aretha Franklin all waiting in the wings. In 1971, a year after the Beatles broke up, Don McLean's 'American Pie' was number-one record as coroner's report, with the bodies of Brian Jones, Janis Joplin, Hendrix, and Morrison for evidence. The stone was all but set by 1974, when pop dinosaurs ruled the earth and the likes of Johnny Rotten scurried beneath their feet, wondering what to do with their rage.

By 1979, Danny and the Juniors' unconvincing 1958 anthem 'Rock and Roll Is Here to Stay' had been answered by Neil Young's utterly convincing 'Hey Hey, My My' – *rock and roll will never die*, he chanted. The song was convincing in its ugly, assaultive fury, but more so in its irony – a doubt so sardonic it froze the song's subjects, the dead Elvis and the by-then-ex-Sex Pistol Rotten, into the history they'd already made. Young sang his rock song about the death of rock with such power that the great event seemed at once irrefutable and impossible. Even today, his irony still has the kick of life to it – perhaps especially today. Sometimes, you need irony to breathe – to filter the stench of a corruption that can pop up anywhere, even in the casual act of a rock star on MTV.

There's a hint of that corruption, in the form of undifferentiated loathing and decay, in the video for Nirvana's 'Smells Like Teen Spirit,' the most surprising hit of 1991 – and irony may be the currency in the five minutes that pass as the band grinds out its slow, corroding punk chords. Late for that, you might think: The death of punk was announced with great fanfare as far back as 1978. Living in Aberdeen, Washington, a town about a hundred miles southwest of Seattle, Nirvana singer-guitarist Kurt Cobain missed the funeral and for that matter the birth. Born in 1967, he first heard punk, the first sound of walls falling in his life, when a friend played him a tape of scavenged punk songs, already old, but news to him. It was 1983, the same year Danny Rapp of Danny and the Juniors killed himself, unable to stand one more oldies tour.

Eight years after that, 'Smells Like Teen Spirit' begins as if on Jupiter, where body weight has hideously increased, the music pressed down by fatigue, lassitude, why-bother: 'Never mind,' as Cobain says to kill a line. Words take a long time to emerge from this gravity, from Cobain's hoarse, ·seemingly shredded throat. It might be months on the radio or MTV before you begin to catch what's being said in Nirvana's songs – 'sell the kids for food,' 'I don't mind if I don't have a mind,' 'I feel stupid and contagious,' 'I'm neutered and spayed,' 'at the end of the rainbow and your rope,' 'I don't care if it's old' – but the feeling of humiliation, disintegration, of defeat by some distant malevolence, is what the music says by itself. In the video, when you first glimpse Cobain, bassist Chris Novoselic, and drummer David Grohl, they seem more than anything to be going through the motions for a crowd as sick of the ritual as they are.

But this is one of the least spectacular and most suggestive videos ever made, and everything about it is slightly off. The band is set up on the floor in a high school gym; there are kids sitting on bleachers against one wall, and cheerleaders, as if somebody got the dates of the concert and the basketball game mixed up. Everyone plays along; they don't care where they are. As the cheerleaders lift their pom-poms, stretching to the roof even more spookily than Cobain expands his fuzztone, they could be in the '50s; the crowd is dressed in an indecipherable motley of styles from the '70s through the '80s; the musicians look like '60s hippies who had to hitchhike for three days to make the gig.

As in the Poison video, the drama is made of clichés – but what's dramatic about them here is that they don't work as such. They don't return the song to any recognizable cultural or economic shape. There's red gas in the gym, but it seems less the result of the usual video smoke machine than disease flaking off the listeners' skin, floating out of their mouths. Slow motion is used but it seems like real time. Kids snap their heads back and forth to the music but they don't give off any sense of pleasure. As a cheerleader bends backward, you follow the curve of her body, which reveals the anarchy symbol – Ⓐ – stitched into her uniform where her school insignia ought to be. Cobain communicates not abandon and let's party but hopelessness and mistrust of his audience. A string comes loose on his guitar, he hangs sound in the air while he fixes it, and you lose all sense of performance.

The kids begin to tumble out of their seats and onto the basketball court. As the musicians disappear into the surrounding crowd, Cobain rails out a blank curse: 'A denial! A denial! A denial!' Of what? By whom? Moments before, he'd fixed the irony the song comes from. He's screaming, but still carrying that strange sense of difficulty, as if he'd damn you to hell if only he could summon the will to get out of bed: 'Here we are now, entertain us.'

He's trying to say that whatever it is he's doing, it's not entertainment. He's saying that the noise he and his friends are making is entertainment only insofar as it fails, only to the degree that their vague intimations of utopia and annihilation – 'our little group has always been and always will until the end', the ending of each word dragged out into the beginning of the next, the whole phrase smeared – mean nothing, to him or anyone else. *Entertain you?*

745

Fuck — we'll set you on fire or we'll drag you down. You want entertainment, the basketball team'll be back here tomorrow night. The moods and talismans of five rock 'n' roll decades are in the little play, and as it finishes, implodes, scatters, it seems as good a death as the music could ask for.

Sometimes, though, you need to speak without irony — and the irony in 'Smells Like Teen Spirit' can't really filter the corruption in rock, perhaps because it is only a song, maybe because the corruption it speaks for is just too innocent. I have in mind a corruption that is not limited to pop music, that is not in any sense innocent, and that irony can't touch.

'The citizenry has been lulled into perceiving the government as a private corporation with no responsibility for the common good rather than as a democratic mechanism that exists solely to serve the hopes and hungers of those who need it most,' Timothy White, editor of *Billboard*, wrote earlier this year. The words are so plain, so direct, that they can make you turn away or rant on in turn, but let White continue: 'The Reagan and Bush administrations have actively reversed nearly forty years of gains in civil rights while fostering the racial demagoguery that destroys the powerless by pitting them against each other ... The principle of divide-and-conquer starts with the power structure cunningly implanting fear and hatred in a society — and then stepping in to 'rescue' the populace with the sort of massive, heinous repression that can take a century to undo. In ominous times like these, ordinary people desperately need the support of each other to endure against such sweeping and terrible odds, and music can help provide the necessary solace, public truth, and social strength.'

Even if you were with White as he summed up the state of the nation, chances are he lost you with his last lines. Against all that, *music*? Rock 'n' roll? Hey, take your good times where you find them, later for that save-the-world shit. White's voice loses its hardness and dissolves in sentimentality. The speaker who begins in complete candor and follows his words where they lead ends up sounding like a fool. But any attempt to talk about the death of rock must finally be made without irony, even if that ensures that the fool is the only role left to play. For there is no way to talk about the death of rock without facing what, exactly, is being consigned to the scrap heap — without recognizing what is being given up.

In his recent book *Rythm Oil — a Journey Through the Music of the American South*, Stanley Booth writes about a record made in 1956 by a white rockabilly singer.

It has been suggested that Carl Perkins's 'Blue Suede Shoes' – the first record to reach the top of the pop, rhythm and blues, and country charts – represents one of the most important steps in the evolution of American consciousness since the Emancipation Proclamation. Perhaps it was an even more important step, because the Proclamation was an edict handed down from above, and the success of 'Blue Suede Shoes' among Afro-Americans represented an actual grass-roots acknowledgment of a common heritage, a mutual overcoming of poverty and lack of style, an act of forgiveness, of redemption.

At a distance of thirty-five years, a generation, it can be seen as the prelude to a tragedy, the murder of Martin Luther King, one of the '60s assassinations from which the country has not yet recovered.

There's a lot going on in those few sentences – about race, democracy, fame and money, multiculturalism, shared language, social destruction. Placing questions of style and redemption on the same plane is remarkable in itself. But perhaps most striking is the displacing shock that Booth's words can deliver. Think of how unlikely Carl Perkins's gesture and the response that greeted it would have seemed in the very moment before they occurred – and think of how impossible such a gesture and such a response seem today.

Booth's claims are big. They're as big as any claims that can be made for rock 'n' roll, or any form of popular culture, or any form of art. Very gracefully, as if casually, he offers a ditty about 'a country boy proud of a new pair of blue suedes' (as Carl Perkins once put it) as a wedge in history, as a breach that opened up new roads – a road to utopia and, from there, a road to annihilation.

It's this sort of sweeping affirmation that always brings forth a chorus of skeptics happy to forsake the mysteries of art and culture for the facts of entertainment: *How can you make so much of a song?* The answer is: because it isn't simply a matter of the right notes in the right place at the right time that makes a song like Tom Petty's 'Out in the Cold' so thrilling. It is the echo those notes carry of a promise and a threat as vast as one can find in 'Blue Suede Shoes' – even if, today, it is only an echo, and a faint, distorted echo at that. Whatever it is that 'Out in the Cold' distantly promises, it is self-contained; a few minutes of pleasure swiftly returned to the strictures of a segmented format. If the sound seems explosive, unstoppable, out of control, it promises first and last that maybe it will be a hit.

747

In 1956, when 'Blue Suede Shoes' momentarily suggested that all sectors of American society could sing the same song – suggested it because, for a moment, they did – there was no pop market, no pop America. Such territory remained to be made. Today the pop market is made: It's cut up like a kiddie-toy version of the electoral market, with stars and genres targeted like politicians' sound bites. There is little access to mass culture – to the risk of dissolution that entering mass culture entails, or to the chance of reaching everyone – and none of the peculiar energy of that fundamental rock 'n' roll journey, the leap (as with Carl Perkins, a balding married man from Tennessee) from nowhere to everywhere. Today rock exists in mass culture only as recycled commercial jingles for products everyone recognizes; the music itself is recognized only in its parts. The pop market, the pop world, is a thing in itself, complete unto itself. That music can travel outside its borders, into the larger world, where such promises and warnings as those in 'Blue Suede Shoes' were fought over, seems childish.

It's often said that rock 'n' roll, like any popular art form, reflects or mirrors society at large; this is not interesting and not to the point. Certainly it is not if one buys even a fraction of what Stanley Booth says about 'Blue Suede Shoes'. That record – coming two years after the Supreme Court's decision in *Brown v. Board of Education*, which mandated the integration of public schools, and decades before that mandate would be, as Timothy White writes, subverted and abandoned by the new Reagan–Bush Supreme Court – did not merely reflect. As a novel cultural event, the song did something very different. With preternatural intensity – with a new kind of humor and drive – it absorbed events in the world at large and sent them back into the world, altogether transformed and disguised, in a form that deflected any refusal. The song took in the social energies of change, desire, fear, jeopardy, of hatred of difference and ambivalence toward it too, and said: A new day is dawning. Now, without embarrassment, we can all dress up in new clothes.

The energy of absorption and transformation powers the most indelible rock 'n' roll. 'Dylan exhibits a profound awareness of the [Vietnam] war and how it is affecting all of us,' Jon Landau wrote in 1968 of *John Wesley Harding*, that oddly quiet, paradoxical reversal of the psychedelic '60s. 'This doesn't mean that I think any of the particular songs are about the war or that any of the songs are protests against it. All I mean to say is that Dylan has felt the war, that there is an awareness of it contained within the mood of the album as a whole. ... Dylan's songs' – which seemed to ask, What is this country

748

made of, where did it come from, which roads are open, which are closed off? – 'acknowledge the war in the same way that songs like [the Beatles'] 'Magical Mystery Tour' or 'Fool on the Hill' ignore it. They acknowledge it by . . . attempting not to speak falsely.'

The same spirit may be at work in Nirvana's sound, which can seem so adolescent, so *hormonal*. 'When we went to make this record,' Chris Novoselic has said of the sessions that produced 'Smells Like Teen Spirit', which took place during the Gulf war, 'I had *such* a feeling of us versus them. All those people waving the flag and being brainwashed, I really hated them. And all of a sudden, they're all buying our record, and I just think, *You don't get it at all*.'

When rock 'n' roll fails to absorb the events of the larger world, it does reflect – but that's all it does. Then you have such famous scandals as a Guns N' Roses number denouncing 'immigrants', 'faggots', and 'niggers', an Ice Cube cut threatening to burn Korean grocers out of Los Angeles; or Public Enemy's Chuck D recounting his crucifixion at the hands of the same tribe that 'got me like Jesus' – or explaining that unfortunately, not his fault, homosexuality remains a crime against nature: 'The parts don't fit.' You get, in other words, no more than a flat, blank reflection of the daily newspaper. You get Axl Rose translating his lyrics into an explanation that 'nigger' merely refers to people he doesn't like as surely as David Duke insists that all he's saying is that white people deserve an even break. You get critics rushing to provide the apologies the singers can't – or won't – make, just as Patrick Buchanan's talk-show colleagues come forth to assure the country that, when you get him alone, Pat's as nice a guy as you'd ever want to meet. And you get, as on a National Public Radio report on the release of Guns 'N' Roses' *Use Your Illusion I* and *II* – the discs went on sale at midnight, September 23, 1991, stores stayed open, fans lined up, happy to talk – an exit poll, as it were: the truth that 'immigrants', 'faggots', 'niggers' were not a problem for Guns 'N' Roses, but selling points. As a stockbroker said on NPR, new CD in his attaché case: *At least Axl Rose has the nerve to say what everybody's thinking*. Look in this mirror and you see a person, like Axl Rose or Bret Michaels, who is just like you, except that he, unlike you, seems empowered. So you give him your money – hoping that, in the course of the transaction, some of that power is passed over to you.

By their definition of a single rock 'n' roll achievement, Stanley Booth's words on 'Blue Suede Shoes' measure the progress of the death of rock. It is an ongoing story that, today, cannot quite be contained by an insistence on how old a story it is. Along with the presumption of the death of rock 'n' roll, encoded in any song is the promise that the music will, in some barely definable way, unsettle the world that presumes to contain it, or take its profit, or write off its loss. Without that promise, there's only profit and loss – and soon enough, merely loss.

Against all that I offer a fantasy, sparked by a real song. In 1990, the Geto Boys' self-titled second album was scheduled for release on Geffen Records; mostly because of 'Mind of a Lunatic', a tune about rape, murder and necrophilia, Geffen refused it. *The Geto Boys* came out on the Def American label, with this blaring 'parental advisory': 'Def American Records is opposed to censorship. Our manufacturer and distributor, however, do not condone or endorse the content of this recording, which they find violent, sexist, racist, and indecent.'

The Geto Boys were fixed, in that segment of the public imagination that was aware of their existence, as a Willie Horton-ism, as vandals occupying the furthest extremes of capitalism and the First Amendment, as the scum of the earth. Last year, on the Rap-a-Lot label, they released the album *We Can't Be Stopped* and a single, 'Mind Playing Tricks on Me'. The single was a hit on stations that play rap – black stations. It wasn't heard on Contemporary Hit Radio, on the stations formatted as Modern Rock or Rock of the '90s, or on many college stations, the refuge of the avant-garde in pop music; as its singers' name suggested, the song was ghettoized. In my fantasy, though, the song could be heard – and can still be heard; it's still on the radio – as a new 'Blue Suede Shoes'. The borders of the song are that unclear, that open.

The tune opens lightly, with pretty little notes sweeping up a theme, as if reprising a dream already dreamed too many times before. Those same notes, on a guitar or a synthesizer, remain constant throughout the piece, changing in tone according to the story set against them: Comfort turns into mockery, mockery turns cold. The echoes here are very deep: 'Mind Playing Tricks on Me' shares the fatalism of Robert Johnson's 1936 'Me and the Devil Blues', the otherworldliness of the Orioles' 1948 'It's Too Soon to Know', the dead-end introspection of Sly & the Family Stone's 1971 'Thank You for Talkin' to Me Africa' – dead-end, because Africa isn't talking, and the only one who'll listen to you is yourself.

The narrator – his part taken in turn by Willie D, twenty-five; Scarface, twenty-two; and Bushwick Bill, twenty-five – is a dope dealer in Houston's Fifth Ward. You can stay tuned to that fact and keep the song corralled, or you can forget it. Chances are you'll forget it: Beginning in specifics of time and place, the song moves past them, almost refutes them, looking for a way out. There's something horribly small and humiliated about the way the man tells you what a big shot he is, how he's like a movie star; something enormous about the way he says 'I often drift when I drive.' Moving easily through the streets he owns, he says, he thinks about killing himself. Scarface has the vocal; he's fluid, soulful. You believe him. The music has moved just slightly away from realism. His mind is playing tricks on him, but so far they're easy to solve.

It's with the last section of the song that the story breaks up. Bushwick Bill's speech is hesitant; you can't quite follow him. He doesn't sing, he recites. He's not soulful; he distances himself from what he's saying. Day and night, sleep and waking are scrambled. He doesn't understand. He testifies. The music in the background says, Yeah, I've heard it all before.

> *This year Halloween fell on a weekend*
> *Me and Geto boys were trick or treatin'*
> *Robbin' little kids for bags.*

A cop appears; they run; he catches them. The pettiness – the pathetic, bizarrely automatic account of men stealing candy from children (you don't have to want it, it's there, you take it) – wars against the bravado that follows when they turn to face the cop.

They jump him – but here the narrative dissolves. Who the cop is, and who they are, is suddenly unclear. Why they've done what they've done, which a minute before was set out with all the inevitability of manners, is now a mystery. Boundaries break up; characters who moved through the earlier moments of the song move on; specters take their places. The devil who starred by name in Robert Johnson's song, and in Sly & the Family Stone's, returns, no name needed. Those numbers are about a struggle to see clearly; the Orioles' 'It's Too Soon to Know', with its delicate, fading doo-wop moans, is about the impossibility of seeing clearly. 'Mind Playing Tricks on Me' faces Robert Johnson's nemesis through the Orioles' haze. The devil is the cop; he's the singer. The singer is the cop. He kills himself. The headless horseman rides again.

> *He was goin' down we planned*
> *But this wasn't no ordinary man*
> *He stood about six or seven feet*
> *Now, that's a creep I'll be seein' in my sleep*
> *So we triple teamed on 'im*

Droppin' those Fifth Ward B's on 'im
The more I swung, the more blood flew
Then he disappeared and my boys disappeared, too
Then I felt just like a fiend
It wasn't even close to Halloween
It was dark as death on the streets
My hands were all bloody
From punching on the concrete.

If you can hear Bushwick Bill not as a Houston rapper, or even as an African-American, but directly as an exemplary American with a story to tell and the means to tell it, then metaphors suggest themselves as quickly as, in its most intense moments, the music in 'Mind Playing Tricks on Me' seems to slow down, the car door opening, a hand beckoning you inside. That drifting, swinging sound, those tinkling notes – almost a merry-go-round sound, after a bit – make room for anyone's displacement, confusion, terror, despair. The way Bushwick Bill mutters, 'Ah, man, homey/ My mind is playing tricks on me' – yes, you've felt that, maybe the last time you turned on the news. Is the way he says it, is anything in the song, redemptive, as the response to 'Blue Suede Shoes' might have been redemptive? 'Mind Playing Tricks on Me' as a record on the top of every chart is just a fantasy; it has yet to find the response it deserves. It's too soon to know.

In a time when it has been definitively pronounced that we have reached the end of history, the death of rock may appear to be a very small thing. Certainly it is, if you believe that rock 'n' roll and history have nothing to do with each other – if you believe that rock 'n' roll cannot help make history and that history cannot help make good rock 'n' roll. If you believe that, though, you may have to accept that rock 'n' roll never really existed at all – in which case the death of rock is no problem. If you don't believe it – well, listen to 'Blue Suede Shoes', 'Smells Like Teen Spirit' and 'Mind Playing Tricks on Me', and see if you hear a finished story, or an open one, or at least the screams of a few people doing what they can to keep the door from closing.

Greil Marcus, *Esquire*, August 1992

752

1992: Fuck the Police

Body Count was intentionally different from an Ice-T album. An Ice T album has intelligence, and at times it has ignorance. Sometimes it has anger, sometimes it has questions.

But *Body Count* was intended to reflect straight anger. It was supposed to be the voice of the angry brother, without answers. The tone of the record wasn't, 'Why do the police hurt me? Why are the parents racist?' It was, 'Fuck the police. Fuck your parents.'

If you took your kid and you put him in jail with a microphone and asked him how he feels, you'd get *Body Count:* 'Fuck that. Fuck school. Fuck the police.' You wouldn't get intelligence or compassion. You'd get raw anger.

Body Count says, 'Let me put you in touch with that anger.' That's how I analyzed NWA when they came out. Reporters would say to me, 'Your music is different than NWA's. NWA's is stupid.' I would explain to them NWA ain't stupid. They just didn't understand what NWA means. NWA is Niggas With Attitude. It's supposed to be visceral. It's intentionally expressed with attitude.

Body Count was an angry record. It was meant to be a protest record. I put my anger in it, while lacing it with dark humor.

We decided to fuck with three enemies in *Body Count*:

THE KKK ('KKK Bitch'). The KKK is a hate organization based around genocide of anybody who is not a white Anglo-Saxon Protestant. I hate them because they would like to see me dead. I shouldn't have to explain to you why the organisation would be my enemy.

We fucked with the KKK because I feel the true fear of the white racist man is his woman leaving for a black man and systematically eliminating the white race – i.e., the white woman making love with the black man.

'KKK bitch' was ironic because the sentiments were true. We'd play Ku Klux Klan areas in the South and the girls would always come backstage and tell us how their brothers and fathers didn't like black folks.

'What does your father do?' I'd ask.

'He's the chief of police.'

'Is he in the Ku Klux Klan?'

'Kinda.'

'What are you doing here?'

'I think this is a good record. Let's get busy.'

We knew that 'KKK Bitch' would totally piss off the Ku Klux Klan. There's humor in the song, but it fucks with them. It's on a punk tip.

RACIST PARENTS ('Momma's Gotta Die Tonight'). Anyone who brings an innocent child into this world and decides to teach them to hate is our enemy.

'Momma's Gotta Die Tonight' was written to mess with anybody who has a racist heart. It's about a kid who dismembers his mother over racism. In the record, I play a black kid who kills his mother over a white girl. A white kid could kill his mother over a black girl, and it would be essentially the same song.

I also wanted the record to be a metaphor for the dismembering of racism, a dismembering of the whole attitude. Whoever is still perpetuating racism has got to die, not necessarily physically, but they have to kill off that part of their brain. From now on, consider it dead. The entire attitude is dead.

When we wrote the album, we thought people would trip off that record 'cause we thought people would take the sentiment literally. But obviously not.

BRUTAL POLICE ('Cop Killer'). We targeted police who feel it's not their job to solve problems, but to perpetuate them.

At the very beginning of 'Cop Killer', I dedicate it to the LAPD and to police chief Daryl Gates. The lyrics are blatant and very specific; the chorus explains what the record's about:

> Cop Killer, it's better you than me.
> Cop Killer, fuck police brutality!
> Cop Killer, I know your family's grievin'
> Fuck 'em!
> Cop Killer, but tonight we get even

Better you than me. If it's gonna be me, then *better you*. My anger is clearly aimed at *brutal* police.

People who came after the record didn't understand how I could sing, 'I know your family's grieving.' My response to them was, Fuck 'em, Fuck 'em. *Our* parents are grieving for the death of our kids. They've been grieving for a long time, and the number of dead cops can't even begin to compare to the number of dead kids. In 1991, three cops were killed in the entire state of California. That same year, eighty-one people in LA *alone* were killed by cops in *proven* police-misconduct cases.

The song was created to be a protest record – a warning, not a threat – to authority that says, 'Yo, police: We're human beings. Treat us accordingly. The moment you step outside of the law, then it's fair for us to step outside of the law, too. And somebody's gonna die, and it's better you than me.'

So what happened? The record is out. My fans didn't consider *Body Count* a controversial record. They listened to 'Cop Killer' and smiled and understood it. The album debuted at 32 on *Billboard*'s Top 50 albums – not bad for the first hardcore rap-to-rock crossover. *Body Count* toured in the summer of '91. In twenty-one cities, 430,000 predominantly white kids waved their fists in the air and screamed 'Cop Killer' along with us. Nothing happened. In the winter of 1991–1992, we hit seventy cities, performed 'Cop Killer' to wild fans at about eighty shows. Nothing happened.

Then the first verdict comes in. After looking at Rodney King writhe around on asphalt for a year, with people watching the cops go free, the shit hits the fan. Cops are now being found guilty of brutality all over the United States.

For the first time in a long time, people outside of the ghettos were looking at the cops as the actual savages and criminals that some of them really are. But honest cops were being prejudged and hurt behind this sweat. This is just how it went down.

Out of nowhere, a cop in Houston, Texas, discovers 'Cop Killer,' and the record must have scared the shit out of him. 'Oh shit,' he figured. 'They're rioting in LA. And now, here's a record telling people to go kill the cops. Oh my God, even more frightening, it's a rock record and it's backed by Bugs Bunny's company!'

Through rock 'n' roll, I injected black rage into white kids. I have no doubt the cops were just as angry we formed a South Central rock group as they were about the song.

They said, 'This muthafucka's not even doing rap. But let's call it rap in the press to make it even more incendiary.' Rap immediately conjures up scary images of Black Ghetto. If they'd said it was a rock record, people might have said, 'Well, okay, rock, I grew up on Fleetwood Mac. Maybe I might like it.'

No, the cops knew they didn't need any sympathizers. 'We need a word that conjured up niggers – Rap, yeah, black rapper. You never liked that shit.'

'Rapper Ice T' created an immediate response. Rednecks quickly lined up to hate.

My message connected to that corporation was scary as shit. I was being powered by a big business – not a business run by the Japanese, they wouldn't target that, but specifically a white-owned, white-run, all-American apple-pie business.

To make matters worse for the original cop, *Body Count* was probably in the record collection of his kid. I can not imagine that cop going into a record store and buying that album. At the very least, whoever hipped him to the record had a kid who owned it.

The police group was aptly called the Fraternal Organization of Cops. We found out this 'Fraternal' gang is connected in with the Masons, and I wouldn't be surprised if some of the members were connected in with the Ku Klux Klan.

So, the Fraternal Organization of Cops *decides* that this record is going to be the cause of police getting killed and somebody else – possibly Ollie North, one of America's arch-villains – came to them and said it's also a good way to take the heat off the cops. They decided to go after Warner Brothers and run a big boycott. Bill Clinton, Dan Quayle and George Bush compound his propaganda campaign by coming to the 'aid' of the police and attacking me.

What did it all add up to? They managed to camouflage the issue of police brutality with me. They said, 'Look how terrible Ice T is! Look how terrible Warner Brothers is! America, can you believe Warner Brothers has a record out like this?'

Immediately, everybody in this country gets mad at me and says I'm terrible. And predictably, America totally forgets about the cops who are on the street hurting people.

All of a sudden I become headline news every night. They split America down the middle and the people who came in to aid me marched in defense of the First Amendment.

This isn't where I needed help. I didn't need anybody to come and say I had the right to say it. I needed people with credibility to step up and say, 'Ice T not only has the right to say it, but also fuck the police! fuck the police! Who the fuck are the muthafuckin' police that they can control you like this? We're not apologizing to you cops for what YOU'VE been doing. It's time for people to get angry along with the guy who wrote "Cop Killer". And some of you muthafuckin' cops might end up dead.'

I tried to make it painfully clear. I said if the police were a totally legitimate organization, I might even be a cop. I never said I agreed with crime, but I am saying that when you guys stepped over the boundaries and decided you can pass judgment, then fuck you. Fuck you.

Everybody knows a lot of cops are on the job to get over inferiority complexes they've harbored since childhood. Now as police they've got a chance to go out and whip on people. They use that badge as a shield to get out their anger. When red lights start flashing in your rearview mirror, you don't say, 'All right, a cop. I'm safe now.' No, instead, you're fucking scared. If you're me, you know not only can they arrest you, but they might just kill you right there or throw you into a judicial system that's not equipped to treat you fairly.

Where I come from, cops never did come get your cat out of a tree. They came to collect people. If you don't believe this, you live in a state of denial. When you're sitting on a jury in Simi Valley, you believe in the myth of the American way. 'The police were right. You can't lie and be a cop, can you?'

People are so mind-fucked by the myth that no matter what they see on TV or hear on the news, they refuse to believe cops are corrupt. They certainly don't believe the testimony of a black man. But if Clint Eastwood is doing the narrating, well then, that's a whole different story.

During the exact same time my record was being condemned, the film *Unforgiven* was winning critical praise across the country. What's *Unforgiven* about? A cop killer. Eastwood takes justice into his own hands after his buddy, a black man, is unjustly murdered by a corrupt cop.

What's 'Cop Killer' about? A black youth takes justice into his own hands after his buddies are unjustly murdered by corrupt cops. Just like Eastwood, I'm saying, '*Fuck the police*, for my dead homies,' but my story is real. I know firsthand how bad the street is. America is simply not ready to hear it from me.

After the cops called this embargo against Warner Brothers they moved into criminal activity. They sent death threats to Warner Brothers. They actually sent two bombs to the label. Real bombs. These came from either the police or police sympathizers. It doesn't really make a difference. If a cop sends a bomb, he is a criminal. But if these people are so down with justice, yet they would send a bomb, they're criminals, too.

There is no way I can prove that the bombs came from police, but they did make death threats. They made death threats to the president of Warner Brothers, Lenny Waronker: 'Do you know where your kids are?' Somebody went to my fifteen-year-old daughter's high school and pulled her out of class and asked her questions about me. I mean, real tacky shit.

These are the people who are supposed to be upholding justice. In effect, I had reached out and scared the guards of the system, and the system – which is made up of people who think everything is fine in this country – use the guards to protect them.

It irritated me that none of the attacks were really aimed at me. I was watching the TV and it's all Warner Brothers. You can read any paper and you'll never find anybody who said, 'Where does Ice T get the anger to make the record?'

The cops never accused me of faking the anger. They knew it was real. They were just saying, 'Why would you, Warner Brothers, put it on record?'

Ultimately, the guards of the system said to Time Warner, 'We understand

757

why you're mad, Ice T. But why would the big white corporation – who's a member of the same country club as us, whose kids go to spring break with our kids, who supports the same politicians that we do – be associated with those niggers?'

Warner Brothers responded that they could not afford to have the cops controlling the company, and they decided to back me. Warner Brothers is an information company, and they cannot be told what they can or cannot do. What happens if they don't like another Ice T record? What happens if they don't like a movie Warner puts out? They were totally paranoid of paying off for the hostages, paying the extortionist.

Meanwhile, I get to the point where I am getting tired of seeing myself on the news every night. The media even got personal with me. I was tired of this shit. It wasn't worth it because nobody who had a voice was backing me on the real reason.

Ironically, 35,000 black police officers said they would not join in with any boycott of Ice T or Time Warner because they knew I was saying the truth. Since July, hundreds of cops have come up to me saying, 'Ice, I know what that record is about, I'm not dumb.'

I've signed more autographs this year for cops than I have in my life. 'Cop Killer' totally divided the police stations. I've had cops come to me and say, 'Ice, I feel like killing some of these guys I work with.' Others said, 'We ain't all bad.' That meant a lot to me. Even the thought that they would think I'm worthy of being spoken to was cool. It was like they care that I care.

I understand a lot of cops out there are trying to do the right thing. And in a way, those cops are on the same mission I am. So it's not like they shouldn't care. I respect that.

But the other ones, fuck 'em.

As the controversy raged on, I knew I had to make a move to deal with it. I didn't want anything to happen to someone at Warner Brothers, because I knew everybody up there didn't agree with my record. In addition, it wasn't for them to fight my battle.

I didn't have any fear about something happening to somebody on the street, 'cause that's not my job. I've been putting music out on the street for years. If cops were all out there doing an honest job, people wouldn't hate them so intensely. I was more worried about some lunatic hurting somebody at Warner Brothers or even about one of those cops going out and killing a cop and trying to pin it on me.

Nobody came to me and asked me to pull the record – definitely not, no matter what muthafuckas want to say. The guys in my group didn't even know I was gonna do it. I called a meeting with Body Count and said, 'This record is out of control. They are going over the top with it and ain't nobody really down with it but us. Our fans who wanted the record have already bought the album, it's gold. All the new people who are buying the record are just snooping assholes. That's not why we want to sell records. So let's pull the muthafuckin' record. The cops are arguing that we're doing it for money. So let's pull it and then tell them to shut the fuck up.'

Stories about brutal police officers were starting to crop up in the press. Newspapers began running articles about new police-brutality charges. The area my stories had been taking up was now being replaced with reality.

The cops had really created fiction. 'Ooh, look what this record is gonna do. This record is gonna make people kill us. This is a dangerous issue.' It never was. They concocted a brilliant fictional monster: A record. And they scared the life out of people with it.

The minute I pulled it, cops killed a kid in Texas who was thirty feet away from 'em. Cops killed a kid in Detroit. People are marching: 'Ice T was right.'

During this period, I also faced a backlash. After I pulled 'Cop Killer', people started jumping off and saying I shouldn't have pulled the record. They said it was a sign of weakness.

I didn't give a fuck. Ice Cube told reporters on MTV, 'I'm not qualified to tell Ice T what to do.' Cube's basically saying, 'I got respect for Ice.' And Chuck D made the best comment to MTV's Kurt Loder out of everybody. He said, 'Those who aren't in the war should never comment on the battle.' All these people who condemned me weren't in the war.

It's so easy to pass judgment when you don't know what the fuck's going on. The people who were on the inside told me I'd made the right move. Because in a war – and make no mistake, this is a war – sometimes you have to retreat and return with superior firepower.

Even though Warner Brothers had my back, they only had my back on that issue. I didn't really feel like I had my feet placed strongly enough to hold on. So what good is holding on to that record, if I can't come back out with a record bigger and crazier than that?

I knew Warner Brothers felt they could get over the 'Cop Killer' incident, but there would be no reply to 'Cop Killer' on my next album.

I knew where I stood. I decided I had to retreat and come back correct. I just looked around and I said, 'All you muthafuckas ain't shit. Fuck you. I'm in this controversy by myself.'

The next heated element of the controversy was predictable: Did Warner Brothers ask me to pull the record? The answer to that is, No. Warner

759

Brothers has defended artistic freedom since the beginning. Warner Brothers is the number-one hated label by the Parents Music Resource Center. They've been fighting Tipper Gore for years. They've put out everyone from Sam Kinison to Slayer, from Andrew Dice Clay to Prince and Madonna. They never shied away from controversial music. They put out every one of my records without censoring them. Dig this, they put out 'Cop Killer'.

But they got hit with the Establishment's vibes. The cops very wisely moved on Time Warner, which is the parent company of Warner Records and twenty times bigger than the label. So they put a whole bunch of people who had no concept of art into the game by hitting their bank accounts.

Time Warner was not only attacked from the outside, they were attacked from within. The politicians and the cops managed to get Charlton Heston and people among Time Warner's shareholders to side with them. Tactical infiltration, pure and simple. It wasn't just a bunch of cops crying to the shareholders, 'We don't agree'.

Time Warner had people on the inside, who had never listened to my music and who had no understanding of where I was coming from, saying, 'Look at what we're selling. This is our money being threatened, and I don't agree with it.'

It was some real ill shit. I know I'm fucked if I want to say something about it on the next record. The cops had Warner Brothers by the balls. The cops had won. Warner Brothers said the controversy cost them in the area of $150 million. I don't know if they ever regained that money. The police groups pulled a lot of their pension-fund money out of Time Warner stock, and they caused people to panic.

In the meantime, we go out on tour and I run into these new boycotts out on the road. These cops are threatening the club owners, saying they'll shut them down if they let us play.

People are shocked: 'Goddamn, didn't they want you to pull the record? You pulled the record and now they're still fucking with you.' So we came up with the conclusion that their animosity and their vendetta against me will now be for the rest of my life. They feel I threatened their life, so it's on. Fuck it. If you want to play like that, cool. I never apologized to the police, and I refuse to apologize. All I am to these muthafuckas is defiant, and that defiance bothers them more than anything else.

Ice T as told to Heidi Siegmund, *The Ice Opinion* (1994)

1993: Metallic Gleam

Islam and heavy metal, heavy metal and Islam. It sounds like some mutant *Blade Runner* collision, but is neither as antagonistic a pairing as it might sound, nor as futurist. After all, in the West, believers of both faiths have suffered the slings of liberal disdain and the arrows of establishment disinformation campaigns. In the Americanizing world, Muslims and metalheads are framed in the typical twilight images of a stigmatised exotic – filed, early and often, on the shelf marked 'The Other'.

Ever since Spinal Tap took baby-boomer satire on rock and its aesthetically challenged baby brother metal into the mainstream, the music's newer forms have had a tough time living down historical expectations of excess. In spite of this – maybe because – metal is an international language; the genre of the underdog has stars beyond the Anglo rock metropolis, stars like Brazil's Sepultura and Germany's Scorpions.

This rebel appeal is palpable among the young, emerging working classes of South-East Asia, giving rise to hugely popular homegrown bands that owe as much in musical terms to Led Zep, AC/DC and Motorhead (i.e. the 'dinosaurs') as such in-your-face upstarts as Slayer, L7 or Suicidal Tendencies. We're in a region where the theatrical spectacle of a metal show (whether Kiss in their heyday or Guns N' Roses today) strikes a chord or three with Indonesian and Malaysian youth weaned on *wayang kulit* (shadow puppet theatre) and folk opera.

But it's more complex than this – because a good portion of South-East Asia is taken up by Indonesia, the largest Muslim country, with Muslim-dominated Malaysia next door. And this is a region in tension between authoritarian government and booming, newly capitalist economies. For many Malaysian and Indonesian metal heads that tension becomes the trial of a dual life; member of the new factory class by working day, respecting the traditional roles of Muslims at all other times.

In April last year, the prickly relationship the subculture has long had with Malaysia's Mahathir government came to a head when the ban on live performances was revived from the mid-80s. Ostensibly provoked by 'careless' remarks made on radio talkback by star group Search – prompted by a fan's call, the group defied the government's 'orders' to cut their hair – the authorities decided to stress the social hierarchy. National stadium tours by a number of the biggest groups across the country were cancelled, radio and television playlists were rapidly rejigged on the government-controlled networks; a media blackout was declared on rock, and heavy metal.

761

For those targetted, the past couple of months haven't been enjoyable. Various 'community leaders' added their voices in local newspapers, organize campaigns to ban 'long hair rockers', while urging the many urban-based fans to, among other things, cut off their locks.

Not for the first time, metal bands and their fans have become pawns in a broader political and religious conflict. The Malaysian government is keen to maintain its ethnic Malay (and therefore Muslim) support and its control of the moral agenda. In Indonesia, even as the space of civil society painfully grows under the military backed regime, ancient, fleeting exemplars of artistic freedom are invoked again to back this season's local headbangers against censuring authorities.

But just as important, the differing traditions *within* Islam create conflict between metal subcultures and government-mediated morality. The grass-roots popularity of Islamic parties and organizations (like Malaysia's Pas and Indonesia's NU) has led to differing, sometimes publicly contested under-standings and scholarships of Islam. In Malaysia, better-educated Islamic scholars (some of them trained in Iran) are increasingly challenging the until-now dominant group of government-linked clerics and religious authorities, introducing new definitions of the orthodoxy that owe as much to Iran's Shia-influenced Islamic State or Saudi Arabia's Sunni denomination as to the more secular models such as Egypt. An important part of this is the new challenge: winning back the hearts and minds of the young flock astray in the land of hard rock and heavy metal.

The popularity of rock across South-East Asia is in little doubt. As average incomes rise, and new social formations emerge out of the industrialization process, a new sense of independence prevails among the young. But unlike America in the 50s, these nation-states are still coming to terms with colonial pasts, reconciling the imperial debris of post-war Indo-China with a formal evolution from the feudal set-ups colonialism had displaced – and all the while soaking up burgeoning transworld media babble. Signs of teen spirit in particular – via Nirvana, Metallica and LA glam – are filtered through the clove cigarette (*kretek*), satellite MTV and the thrills of urban migration. With prosperity *and* a labour-market shortage (in Malaysia and Singapore, at any rate) young South-East Asians are optimistic about the future, fraught through the fusion of tradition with modern drives towards leisure and individualism.

The heavy metal/hard rock subculture has thus provided a popular identity for its largely urban, ethnic Malay audiences, spawning new death metal bands like Modar (from Malaysia's Trengganu state, arguably the country's most conservative), thrashers like Infectious Maggots and punk revivalists like The Pilgrims, as well as indie labels like Sonic Asylum Records run by Joe Kidd (the infamous *nom-de-plume* of promoter musician and editor of a Malaysian, English-language rock fanzine, *Aedes* – 'Aedes' as in the mosquito-borne virus).

In Indonesia, Malaysia and Singapore, where the majority of the populations are under 30, outdoor concerts by bands like Indonesia's Swami and Malaysia's Search cater to prime demographic, as do other acts like Wings (not McCartney's geriatrics but Malaysia's glam-rockers, banned for over three years on home airwaves, thanks to the band's 'uppity' criticism of the authorities), Singapore's Ramli Sarip and Junction. Some of these bands often draw crowds of 40,000 a night on tour, sometimes even up to 120,000 in the case of Swami two years ago in Jakarta. With a population totalling over 200 million people, the combined market of these three countries has naturally attracted the foreign music industry

In Malaysia alone, according to Aziz Bakar, of the unusually active multinational BMG records, and other informed observers, the rock recording industry generates an annual turnover of around M$80 million, with live concerts hauling in another M$6 million or so. For the 'super league' bands like Search and Swami, reliable sales in excess of 500,000 copies of recent albums are commonplace. New recording labels, some with Japanese backing (of course), are being established in Kuala Lumpur as more acts find success throughout the Far East. Younger heavy metal bands like Cromok, originally formed when the group's four members were undergrads studying a different sort of metal at Wollongong University in Australia, have also been hugely successful with loud debut albums.

Cromok's ambivalence towards Islam's demands and the changing Malay society around them is strong, and the sacrifices the band have made in their personal lives in order to pursue this music are large, they explain. Not unusually, the four of them come from the north-east of Malaysia, from the conservative Muslim state of Kelantan.

In 1986, Malaysia's Minister for Culture, Najib Tun Razak (son of a former Prime Minister), announced a ban on the increasingly popular hard rock and heavy-metal concerts, claiming that these performances were a bad influence on youth with their Satanic overtones, and generally bad for the community and culture. But the prospect of further bans doesn't discourage Cromok.

'To me, if he wants to raise the subject of Satanists, I don't think I can agree with that. What is his point about Satanism? I mean, we don't sing stuff about Satan, about violence or any other stuff like that. We just sing things about our way of life, our history about what we do,' said Cromok's bass player Shamsuddin in Australia recently, just before the band headed back to Kuala Lumpur to tend to fans, business and a forthcoming tour.

'About what we do here and things like that,' says guitarist Khairu. 'I don't think I'd agree with him either, because of the principles behind it. If he says music is not allowed in Islam, that's right, though I can't *agree* with that. But if he wants to ban just one type of music, then that's not fair. If there's a ban on music, then ban the whole lot. Why ban heavy metal? It's just not fair. People listen to dance music because they like dancing. We listen to thrash because we like that kind of music. It's the same thing. Why should they discriminate against us?'

Both claim their parents don't much care for their music, but Shamsuddin points out that 'I don't think they can do anything about it.' They also (inadvertently) agreed with those conservative Muslims who attack the idea of music itself as 'un-Islamic'.

'Music is against Islam and that's the main thing,' says Khairul, a little pensively. 'I think the reason they pick on heavy-metal groups is because some of them dress ridiculously, y'know what I mean? Like I saw some people on the beach in tight plastic pants, in bright colours with black leather jackets, and it was like 33 degrees! I think that's ridiculous.'

'I think that's just the point, why they want to ban the whole thing,' says Shamsuddin. 'They want people like us to be "normal" people like them, to dress regularly, nicely. To get a good job, things like that. They don't want us to be something like . . . ah, scumbags, or something like that,' he laughs.

What complicates all this for many Malaysian metal fans who are also Muslims is the State's role in implementing its religious or Shariah laws. The hereditary rulers – the sultans – and the Federal government are both considered custodians of the faith, while one of the main opposition parties, Pas (or Parti Islam), is increasingly keen to prove otherwise, as it brandishes its own (often conservative, sometimes radical) strain of Islam.

According to William De Cruz, until recently the secretary of Malaysia's increasingly active Musician's Union and a long-standing journalist and. music columnist for the *New Straits Times* (the English-language national broadsheet), differing perceptions and contradictory objectives of both the State and its young people tend to encourage apathy and/or frustration among the young.

'Sure, there are people who will consider the hard rockers and the heavy metal players a threat,' De Cruz agrees. 'I see them as having the potential for being strong and positive influences on youth, because we've all grown up with music. Somehow, the hard rocker has a positive influence on a youth who's otherwise subjected to ridiculous levels of repression.'

Because Malaysia is essentially a secular democracy, based on the Western notion of a nation-state, there are built-in antagonisms between the demands of Islam and the application of its laws. And while the subculture of the 'kutus', 'Mat Rock' or 'Minah Rock' – the slang names of the heavy metal fraternity – needs the freedom that secularism provides, the government's current agendas can and often dictate otherwise.

'You have a religious political party (Pas) that says "look, that's what is happening to our children", and that political party is getting stronger,' De Cruz explains. 'Now the government doesn't want to lose its hold, not just on the country but also on how Islam should be propagated. I'm sure the government realizes the danger of allowing the sweep of fundamentalism to go unchecked. They know the danger so they're playing with both sides. They're appeasing the fundamentalists on the one hand, and on the other, they *are* allowing outlets for the boys and girls.'

According to De Cruz, the union has had numerous meetings with the Home Ministry where both parties have agreed that 'further restrictions and suppression' are not the answer. 'But the government will not publicly say something that even indicates a more moderate stand,' he says.

In the past year, the new Pas State government in Kelantan – a largely ethnic Malay state in the north – has been under pressure from a Federal government seriously concerned by its Pas rival shoring up vital Malay support, in part by introducing Islamic laws in the State. More recently, the Mahathir Federal government came out strongly against the State government's decision to go ahead with controversial Hudud (Islamic penal code) laws. Many Muslims, and therefore many Malays, have felt great unease about the attacks on the Kelantan government's moves, as there has been a perceived lack of distinction between criticizing Hudud laws and Islam itself. (Much rides on this current domestic debate, not least of which is Malaysia's sterling foreign reputation as a prime Western investment opportunity; a developing country's way out of the Third World, it's been claimed – but that's another story.)

The worldwide resurgence of Islam has added greater weight to the central role Islam is playing in the transformation of Malay (and Indonesian) society, which has had great social and economic success in line with Malaysia's rapid development over the past two decades. It has also made the State religion of Islam a focus in the political arena, increasingly used for political advantage. Seemingly antagonistic developments such as the heavy metal subculture and its 'wayward' members are useful in the game of political and communal brinkmanship. (It will also be instructive to observant neighbours like Indonesia how youth subcultures can be controlled, if Malaysian authorities succeed.)

There's now a generational (and educational) gap between Malay parents – who have grown up in traditional villages that have only recently experienced the wealth of the towns – and the youth, who if they haven't moved to the big smoke, the factories or service industries have gone into tertiary education.

For many of these young urban Malays, they are living out the dreams of Malaysia's economic development, earning their own income and striving for the freedoms promised by the modernist city, whether it's in Penang, Kuala Lumpur or Johor Bahru. It's no less true for Indonesian youth skipping the villages for urban sprawls like Jakarta or Surabaya. The heavy metal subculture becomes a home, a refuge for those dislocated in urban migration, caught between stereotypical racial politics and often fluid urban space divisions brought on by rapacious property development. It might seem like ham-strung vaudeville from a media-saturated Western outlook, but this internationalized language of stock rebellion and theatrical posturing clearly resonates for youth in Indonesia, Malaysia or Singapore, and offers comfort and identity to those still ambivalent about buying into the post-feudal/colonial capitalist environment that's being rapidly constructed around them.

The young people in Malaysia have been disempowered from adapting Islam to their own needs, by their elders, their hereditary rulers, the government and religious authorities. While the pressures to conform to an Islamic, Malay blueprint might lead many Malay youths to quietly disavow the religion they were born into, Islam also a way of life, intricately bound up with the Malay identity. Cutting off Islam means cutting off village and community ties.

Many Malay youths would certainly prefer an interpretation of Islam different to the current (contested) orthodoxy. However, mining a different sort of metal isn't a viable option.

Kean Wong, *The Wire* #110, April 1993

1993: Take It Like a Man

Suede makes me think of Gloria Gaynor's 'Honey Bee.' 'He's my honey bee/Come on and sting me!' the diva pleaded at the dawn of disco as the fuzz-tone guitars buzzed and the high hats hissed. Years before she sang the praises of romantic resilience with 'I Will Survive', Gaynor gave it up for a guy with a big stinger, celebrating the sensual power that comes with surrendering to sweet powerlessness. It wasn't exactly women's lib, but it was about liberation. The core, gay audience of 'Honey Bee' knew that Gaynor was playing the part of a man singing about surrendering himself to another man. S/he was buzzing about the ouch that delights.

Surrender isn't the most popular subject in pop music these days. Everybody's hard, everybody's down, everybody's free to feel good, but nobody does because nobody has the inner strength to allow themselves to be taken over. Despite the rebel stance of so much rap and alternative rock, pop has lost the joy of risk in a fit of fear – fear of the unknown, fear of AIDS, fear of blood and desire and tears and abandonment and illness and death. So instead, there's Nation of Islam-fueled homophobia in the pop charts courtesy of Brand Nubian and there's a happy ode to fag bashing on the radio courtesy of Buju Banton and there's safe, pregnant, do-*anything*-to-stop-those-rumours Whitney Houston back on top once again while Madonna gets kinky and slapped with the most implicitly homophobic backlash since rock fascists set fire to Village People and Donna Summer albums in a disco-sucks frenzy.

Meanwhile, there's Suede. In case you've been smart enough to stay away from the English pop press for the last year, Suede is the latest great hope of British rock, the most important non-American guitar band since the Smiths. After the Madchester lads turned indie rock into a football hooligan party and the technoheads sucked the black gay identity out of house music, along comes Suede singer Brett Anderson, asymmetrical bangs cascading across a kissable cheekbone, declaring himself a bisexual who's never had sex with a man. 'We kiss in his room to a popular tune,' sings Anderson. England, starved for stars and overdosed on macho American grunge, is suddenly ablaze with talk about glam and transgression and homo lust and good hair. And for good reason. It's not often that a debut album with a queer point of view enters the British charts at No. 1.

In an era of slackers and skateboarders and shoegazers and gangstas and anonymous techno knobtwiddlers and interchangeable new jack/jill swingers, Suede is one of the few non-country acts since the icon-breeding,

767

MTV-lovin' early '80s to emphasize star power – and a queer one at that. Anderson doesn't like to see himself as straight, although, in actuality, that's his sexual orientation. His cultural orientation, however, is homo to the max. He's infatuated with the outlaw aspect of queer culture the way white rappers like the Beastie Boys and House of Pain are drawn to hip hop, but with a major difference: No one who sees a Beastie Boys video could mistake the group for African American. It's hard to check out a Suede video without perceiving the boys in the band as foppy fags.

I think that's great, and obviously, so does Suede, although only the drummer, Simon Gilbert, is gay. Not even the genuine homosexuals in Frankie Goes to Hollywood or Erasure or Culture Club or Bronski Beat have weaved so many references to gay sex and identity into their lyrics. 'If he can take it, I can take him home with me,' sings Anderson in 'Moving'. 'Have you ever tried it that way?' he asks in 'Pantomime Horse'. 'He writes the line, wrote down my spine/It says, "*Oooh*, do you believe in love there?"' he confesses in 'The Drowners'. 'If you were the one, would I even notice now that he has come?' he wonders in 'Breakdown'. 'You'll pierce your right ear, pierce your heart here/This skinny boy is one of the girls,' he declares in 'Animal Lover'. 'He is come/He's my insatiable one,' he rejoices in the essential Suede B-side Morrissey covered on his last tour, 'My Insatiable One'.

And like most songs by the Pet Shop Boys, most Suede songs make more sense as gay love songs, even when the gender of the lovers isn't clearly defined. 'Animal Nitrate' – a hit in England and a current modern-rock radio favorite over here – tells the tale of a poor young thing overtaken by a brutal lover: 'So in your broken home, he broke all your bones/Now you're taking it time after time.' If you interpret the protagonist as a woman, this tale about desire and abandonment is simply horrible. But if you understand the power dynamic as taking place between men – and the references to amyl nitrate and being 21 (the minimum age in England to have lawful sex with a member of the same gender) suggest that you should – the song becomes both grim *and* erotic. As the final chorus builds over handclaps (a Suede signature as compelling as Nirvana's sudden dynamic shifts), Anderson wails, 'He's just an animal! An *animal! Ooh*-ho-ho-ho!' In effect, he becomes the protagonist, shouting out in pain and in pleasure while he gets knocked around and takes it up the bum. Work it, sister.

The sound of Suede matters at least as much as the lyrics. The guitars are loud, tuneful, economical, and well-played, not lazy like grunge and not hazy like shoegazers. Dramatic tension is paramount in a Suede arrangement. You can feel the ambition in the way the guitar tone shifts from fuzzy to biting to smooth to abrasive to soft to howling often within the same song. There's a sense of ascendency, a hankering for something higher than what the unilevel, monotonic early '90s are offering. Although in England the band shares the same distribution system as its indie-rock peers, Suede aspires to a kind of stardom that's fallen out of fashion since the sad demise of the Smiths. Suede wants hit singles, *Smash Hits* photo spreads, subversive main-stream popularity, not cultish glam-rock revivalism.

Those aspirations are clearest in the way Anderson sings, music-hall inflections, delightfully brittle affectations. Although he's clearly learned a few things about falsetto swoops from Morrissey, Anderson isn't proudly pathetic. Whereas Morrissey was self-deprecating, Anderson is self-important. He's as aggressive as he is androgynous, a combination that speaks volumes on the stylistics of queer male ambition. He wants to be on top while singing the joys of being a bottom.

The central theme of *Suede* (Columbia) is the surge of power that comes with being taken over. Anderson's fascination with gay sex shapes his utopian vision of homosexuality, which abandons typical roles of domination and submission. In 'Moving', he describes the mating game as an ever-shifting process that demands role reversal, a literal give-and-take: 'If you can take it, I can take it.' Although Anderson's obsession with queer culture is predominantly male-identified, the cover of *Suede* features an image of two women kissing that he borrowed from a ground-breaking '70s book of lesbian erotica, *Stolen Glances*. Substitute 'Read My Lips' for the album title and the cover comes across as ACT UP agitprop.

Even in a song like 'So Young', which is more about youth than sex, Anderson sings about the exultation of being 'so gone', so swept away with sensation that one is simultaneously godlike and helpless. That's the way Anderson characterizes sex between men – overwhelming, free, unbound by the regimentation of the outside (straight) world, *animal*. It's as if he sees male anal intercourse as being more natural than vaginal intercourse because it's less civilized; i.e., not taught or condoned.

Pretty radical for a chart-topping pop album, regardless of Anderson's private sexual orientation. Suede is the tip of a queer pop iceberg that's beginning to rise to the surface after being submerged for the last 10 years. Of course, I'd prefer it if Anderson were a bona fide homo, rather than merely an enthusiastic student. But the fact that the next-big-thing is led by a wannabe butt-fucker has got to make things easier when the real Homo Superior comes around. Until militantly queer groups like Pansy Division

769

and Tribe 8 get as good as their audience, the buzz over Suede, the talk-show presence of RuPaul, and the Grammy victories of newly out k.d. lang and Melissa Etheridge give hope to those bashed by recent rap, rock, and reggae. If nothing else, Suede reminds us that queerness – like other outsider identities – is an essential element of great rock 'n' roll. Now prepare to be taken over.

Barry Walters, Village Voice, 8 June 1993

1993: We Love You!

Although the notice board in the luxurious Ramada hotel foyer states only that representatives of American Express are staying there, a few floors above some rather more important and in-demand guests are settling in. And the large crowd of girls outside on the pavement, flicking through photo albums and smoking fags, know *exactly* who they're here for.

'When will I, will I be faaaaaaaaaa-maaaaaaaassss?'

It's today's joke. When anyone drives past with a new tit-bit of information about the whereabouts of Take That the girls will scream that it's not Take That they're waiting for but Bros. And then they start singing.

'When will I see my picture in the paaaaaaaa-*peeeeeeerrrrrs*?'

Passing couples ask why they're all sitting there.

'Bros have reformed,' shouts one pointing at the top floor, 'and they're in *there*.'

Then one will start screaming.

It's 1.30 in the afternoon and Take That have left the plush Ramada and gone off to the Manchester G-Mex for a final run-through. The hotel – basic room £110 a night, but three free custard creams in each room – has been their home for five days. And word has got around that the That have taken up residence here for final rehearsals. It's interesting to find out just how large groups of girls discover where – in a *very* big city – Take That are spending their nights.

Joanne has a friend who's doing work experience at the hotel. 'She phoned me up and said "Take That are here".'

One fan knew because 'they always stay here'. Lindsey from nearby Tilsley's dad saw Gary when he drove past the night before. Another said they saw the crowd and assumed – quite rightly – that this is where they're staying.

To these fans, following Take That is a lifestyle. While in years gone past, fans would be screaming on occasions at the odd airport arrival, these girls know every movement of their heroes. When they do get to see them there's less hysteria and more friendly banter. They've followed Take That for so long the group know most of them by sight. In the moments when there isn't anything happening the fans spend their time flicking through each other's photos of encounters with the group: Robbie out shopping at W. H. Smith, Howard getting out of his car, Mark coming out of his house. These girls – two, Clair and Jo, have travelled from Derby, others are bunking off school – are not fans waiting around for a once in a lifetime meeting with their heroes. They're looking for a few words, a better shot than the ones in their album.

'We don't want autographs,' says Joanne, 15. 'We just want to see their faces. It's their fault 'cause they're so fit.'

Take That are accessible. Or maybe it's just that their fans are more cunning.

'Airports are good,' says one. 'They don't have their bodyguards with them at airports.'

And even when they do it doesn't stop the fans getting photographs. Richest pickings are outside Mark's house. Some girls – yet all of these swear they aren't amongst them – camp on waste ground by his house. All night. Often 20 or 30 of them. 'When there's quite a few he'll come out and talk to us,' says one, finally admitting she's been.

By six o'clock the girls realise that not much is happening outside the G-Mex. Most of the 8,000 strong crowd are here. And there's a good spread of ages too. Teenage girls, sure, but their mums too. 'I like Howard,' says one. 'What about him? Everything about him.'

The show is about to begin and excitement is building. Whistles are being blown and everyone is screaming their heads off. Except for four boys in a corner who haven't exactly joined the excited throng. So, what do you think of Take That? 'They're bobbins,' says one, 'I've 'eard better singing from my brother in the shower.' Thanks for coming.

The G-Mex

It's in G-Mex that it hits you. Take That are playing here in front of eight *thousand* people. The same Take That a year and a half ago were playing to a handful of people at some backwater nightclub. And now they're here in their home town of Manchester playing two dates and they could have played six. That's how big it's all got. And it's getting bigger all the time.

The second thing that hits you is the gigantic screens at either side of the stage. It's when these flicker into life and show the band during rehearsals that the noise reaches a deafening volume – for the first of many times.

Suddenly, two bright blue searchlights begin to scan the audience. Then five lethal-looking flames shoot up on stage and die down to reveal five figures seen in silhouette behind a curtain. One by one the group appear through gaps in the curtain – first Jason, then Gary and Mark, then Howard and Robbie. The show is on! The boys bound down the stairs that separate the group's musicians and launch into *Take That And Party*. At least that's *probably* what it is. By now, you see, the screams are so loud that you can hardly hear the vocals at all. Wearing white vests and jeans – the first of many different costumes – they begin dancing at the front of the stage and then start singing *Promises*. Problem. Gary's headphones – which look like earrings because they've come out of his ears and are flapping around his neck – aren't working. He tells me later that he was hearing constant feedback in them and couldn't concentrate on what he was doing. So while the rest of the band begin dancing he's stuck on the spot as someone sorts it all out. Once the problem is remedied you can actually hear the vocals.

Satisfied is next. The group begin the song on the back level of the stage, then rush down to the front, Robbie does a rap bit – which is so fast it's impossible to hear what he's saying – and Jason and Howard do some of their spectacular somersaults. Next is *Do What You Like* and the best bit so far. The song begins as a plinky-plonk piano affair and then turns into a brilliant audience participation thing. 'People of the G-Mex,' shouts Robbie, 'what we want you to do, right, is raise the roof of the place.' This is what he gets the crowd to do: Take That sing 'You can do what you like' and the audience replies 'Do (*raising left arm*) What (*raising right arm*) You Like (*swivelling hips around a bit*).' Sounds cheesy, but when you see 8,000 people doing it over and over again it's rather fab – a *Radio Gaga* for the '90s. Honestly. Later on Mark admits that he had a big old lump in his throat when he saw it.

'So good to be near you,' sings Gary, then stops dead. Has he blown it? No, it's just that the crowd realise it's *Why Can't I Wake Up With You* and he can't hear a thing. He doesn't need to sing anything as the crowd trills every word for him.

Then a brief pause for a costume change. Except, being Take That, they choose to do this behind the curtain, silhouetted so everyone can see them take their trousers off. Then they put on a shirt. A tie! A jacket!!

The lights go off and a huge sparkly *Come Dancing* type glass ball starts spinning, throwing squares of light all over the arena. There's a corny, showbizzy, American announcement: 'Ladeez and Gentlemen! Live on stage tonight – Taaaaaaake Thaaaat!' The lights come up and the show starts again with the group in Temptation style '70s soul gear, i.e. black trousers, purple jackets with lapels from hell, ruffled shirts and black velvet bow ties! Blimey. It's time for the heavily rumoured Motown-Philly medley. And, most impressive of all, every member of the group sings a solo number: Mark sings *Just My Imagination* and *Reach Out*, Robbie does *My Girl*, Gary sings *Treat Her Like A Lady* and making their solo debut, Jason and Howard do, respectively, a raunchy *I Feel Good* and *Get Ready* with added high notes. They also sing The Jackson's *I'll Be There* together before launching into *I Found Heaven*. It all works brilliantly. If they've got any sense they'll release a shortened version for Christmas! It could have been a mess but Take That's attention to detail and their sheer professionalism make it the triumph of the show.

When he's got his breath back Gary sings *Pray* – his favourite of the set – before it all goes very strange with *Give Good Feeling*. The song starts off as a pretty straight rendition before Gary stops the song half-way through. Headphone problems again? Duff notes from the band? No. 'Lads, lads, it's all right singing about giving good feeling, but tell the audience what you were talking about earlier in the dressing room. About how you give good feeling.' And this is the prompt for each member of the group to, ahem, 'give good feeling' which involves most of the group attempting to bonk the stage, or in Mark's case, doing pervy things with a towel. This is not just mild perviness, this is well over the top. And the crowd loves it.

After all this *Once You've Tasted Love* is a bit of a disappointment as it's so familiar. But this is only a breather before a bizarre instrumental called *Apache*. Now get this: First Jason and Mark come on wearing nothing but boots, black lycra trunks and black padded jackets. They do some marvellous break-dancing. Then Gary appears dressed up as '70s fashion disaster Elton John. *Then* Howard comes on stage in a white turban and a denim skirt. *Finally* Rob turns up in weird trousers and a big wobbling hat. For no apparent reason.

Out of costume, Gary launches into *A Million Love Songs* unaccompanied before the rest of the group appear through that back curtain to join in with the harmonies.

Next it's another medley of *Could It Be Magic* – sung *uncannily* like the Barry Manilow version – *I Can Make It* sung by Mark and a more typical version of *Could It Be Magic*. Then it's off before an encore of *It Only Takes A Minute* which ends with the group climbing on to the back level of the stage and pulling down their trousers to reveal Take That written on the bums of their pants. Suddenly, after all the well-choreographed dancing and costume changes, there it is: that reference to their old days. All in all an incredible show with many highlights and only the occasional dodgy moment. A show that everyone loved, well, kind of . . .

The Lift Encounter

'Say something nice or we'll beat you up!' says Howard.

The That are all squashed into a lift in the hotel. Despite the concert being an absolute triumph the group themselves aren't *that* happy about it.

'At least say it was better than the last one,' pleads Mark, 'please!' 'Tomorrow will be better,' adds Gary.

It appears that, although the set sounded wonderful from the audience's point of view, on stage all hell was let loose. Apart from Gary's early headphone problems and Mark's microphone going all crackly at one point – not his fault – the show appeared to go swimmingly. Not so. Robbie, for one, heard voices that he shouldn't have in his headphones. 'I could hear Howard's vocals above my own and the only instrument I could hear was the keyboards – not the drums. Very nice and all that but impossible to dance to.'

The After-show Bash

The group head off to the after-show party at Manchester's Cruz 101. All the group's families are there. Marge Barlow and hubby. Howard's mum Cath and hubby. Mark's family – mum and dad and Daniel and Tracey. They also watched the show much to Mark's embarrassment. 'When my mum comes to see me on stage I worry that she might think I'm too raunchy. But I flirt a lot on stage – I feel like a tart. On stage I just feel like I belong there.' But there are no disapproving looks tonight from parents and when the That are with their families they cheer up enormously. Robbie's mum is there, too, and Robbie never leaves her side, good son that he is. Most noticeable of all, however, is Jason's family – no, make that *clan*. They are everywhere! Brothers Dominic, Simon, Samuel, the incredibly cute youngest one, Oliver, and Jason's twin, Justin. All as handsome as Jason. They should form a group – The Oranges! Then there are their wives/girlfriends and mum Jenny and partner Bill and Jason's mates Neil and Tom (who Jason's mum is currently being swung around the room by!) and . . . and there's not enough room on the page to give you all the details. But they all hit the dancefloor and party like mad! After an hour Take That and their families slip out unnoticed. The lads have to get an early night.

Except for Robbie, it seems.

The Morning After

The next morning at breakfast Gary is the first to turn up. He reads the reviews in the daily papers. He also learns something completely new from the *Daily Star*. 'Oh look, apparently I'm going to live in LA.' Mark is next to turn up. 'Did you all have a good sleep?' he enquiries thoughtfully. 'Great beds here aren't they? I was out for the count.'

It's Robbie who crawls down to the reception desk next to check out. And did sir have anything from the mini-bar? 'Ermm, no,' he replies, 'but my friends did.' Seems Robbie held a second party for all his friends in his room until the early hours and he's paying the penalty. He goes around clutching his stomach claiming he ate too many ham and *Branston Pickle* sandwiches at 3 a.m. this morning. Maybe that completely empty mini-bar is the *real* reason for his condition.

Finally Jason comes down, clutching his beloved cowboy boots, closely followed by Howard. The group head out of the door. As they do Robbie is collared by a mother and daughter.

'It was a great show,' says the mum, 'cost us a fortune though.'

'Cost us a fortune too,' says Robbie.

It was worth it, on both counts.

Mark Frith, Smash Hits, 4–17 August 1993

1993: Slayed in Fame

> 'Everyone's taking control of me
> Seems that the world's
> Got a role for me
> I'm so confused
> Will you show to me
> You'll be there for me
> And care enough to bear me.'

From 'Will You Be There', the most recent single taken off the *Dangerous* album. A song from the outer reaches of the fame game, written and performed by Michael Jackson

What's this? Another mega-rich superstar looking for sympathy? Phoney revelations from celebrity shadowland? More appallingly penned waffle about spiritual guidance, the Messianic complex and predestination? Maybe, but don't tempt fate. Go easy with that axe, take your hand off the gun and move back. Slowly. Consider what's happened since Michael recorded that song.

Hanged, drawn and quartered without any evidence. His public, never mind private, displays of affection for little children, once considered a virtue, now have him cast as a pariah and are the subject of screaming blue murder editorials. Even before the tabloid furore, the 'Dangerous' tour was living up to its title. Michael was literally running out of oxygen, fainting into dizzy sickness onstage, cancelling shows, watching helpless from his hermetically sealed world as sales units failed to meet projected heights and the public called into question his whole range of lovable eccentricities.

For Michael Jackson, the fame which he lusted after, prayed, fasted and made untold sacrifices for turned around and became a weapon to be used against him.

Michael Jackson The Godhead became the centre of a scandal, the scandal being not his alleged misconduct (allegations are merely that, they do not, or should not, constitute a scandal) but the way the currents and force of fame can be manipulated. Blink and you might have missed when adoration became approbation, stirred by a dubious shitstorm of unfounded rumour and malicious intent. For years the media machine orchestrated the Jackson myth, built it up. They toyed with him, indulged and entertained his magnificent creation. The cherubic and chubby Afro-topped child genius, the flower of the Motown integrationist dream, grew into Michael Jackson Superstar – a combination of La-La Land utopianism and futuristic genetic freakout. The Boy Wonder, Dance Giant, Global Sensation, King of Pop, Titan of Weird and Racial Ghost.

It is as if the last ten years, the last 20 years, hell – the entire life story of Michael Jackson – has been a leading up to this attack, to the assassination of The Idol.

Michael Jackson was The Sorcerer's Apprentice of Soul, he studied at the feet of the greats, down in the basement of the Harlem Apollo he remembers himself 'like a hawk watching in the dark'. Perhaps he was the last in the line, taking on the baton passed down from Jackie Wilson and James Brown, Smokey Robinson and Stevie Wonder, Al Green and Marvin Gaye. Little Michael – a figure of glory and wonderment – was a riotous superhuman combination of them all. JB's stamina and feet frenzy, the musical suss and imagination of Wonder, the jittery, nervous pirouettes, feminine falsetto and vocal curlicues of Smokey and Al Green, the dark wounded desire and sufferance of Saint Marvin.

But Michael Jackson the man took the soul dream of the performers and their audience into the rock world and beyond. In sales terms he outran them all, even the Great White Gods like Presley and The Beatles had to step aside when the final reckoning was made on the sales front. He went from being a Cultural Hero to something else entirely. Something out there in the ether of celebrity, drifting in the dark cold space where none of the bounds or support system of the soulman's community are found. And resting there he became The Ultimate Idol, the Afro American Giant who had determined to go boldly where none of his forebears had ventured. Almost inevitably, no sooner was he in that place than he found himself shot by all sides.

Whatever the outcome of the civil suit filed against Jackson by 13-year-old Jordan Chandler, something horrible will have happened. For any child to believe or be taught to believe that he has been abused while having the trauma played out in the media is hardly a great start in life. But the relationship between Chandler, his parents and Michael Jackson is also a bizarre snapshot, a fleeting insight into how curious, how alien life really can be on the outer reaches of Hollywood, the international centre of fame.

Little has changed from the place described in Kenneth Anger's shamelessly vicarious *Hollywood Babylon*. This is a land where everybody seems to be on the path to stardom, where they bat like moths around the shining light of fame, keen, like the Chandlers, to have a chance to bask in its glow. This is the throbbing core of fame fantasy, the centre which generates, packages, promotes and multiplies the fame fascination that radiates across the globe. Michael Jackson, whose career has been a series of breakouts from the constraints of family, management, musical categories, even racial identity, was always bound for life here. The home for America's alternative Royalty, a palace at the end of the world where the only barrier left is the echo of your own fame rebounding.

Out there in his home Michael has built a place where hundreds of kids can come and watch movies, play with his menagerie of animals, frolic at his funfair and enjoy his collection of arcade games. Children, be they part of a Pepsi-sponsored drive to 'Heal the World' or as bit players on his *Dangerous* album, are an integral part of Jackson's world, his 'innocent' aesthetic and marketed image as a Beneficent Corporate Deity.

Meanwhile, his adult friends tend, like him, to be disturbed or dysfunctional products of pressured or uncomfortable childhoods (Slash, Elizabeth Taylor, Jane Fonda). The soul community that sired him, that inflamed and enriched his greatest music, has, of course, been left far behind. Perhaps it only ever was an ideal inspired by remarkable records and heart-stopping performances (some of them his own), because in truth it barely exists any more. Crowned King of Pop and Rock and Soul by his record company,

Michael's regal status is seriously flawed, his kingdom in disarray. Either because of the facial surgery some claim he's had or the vitaligo from which he says he suffers, Michael Jackson is a galling, tragically disfigured symbol and figurehead of America's racial conflict.

What's the price of being a famous black musician in America? Ask James Brown, a twice bankrupt musical revolutionary, publicly disgraced, imprisoned for a crime that no white man would have gone down for. Ask Ike Turner, for years known as the man who invented rock'n'roll, masterminding the groundbreaking 'Rocket 88' by Jackie Brenston, now forever known as the man who beat up Tina. Ask Sly Stone, once the most dynamic mover in all of black music, now a helpless, forever on the outside addict, dealer and drop-out. Ask Ice T, hounded by police, FBI, media corporations, the President himself, because he refused to keep his mouth shut. Ask First Lady of Soul Aretha Franklin, who conquered race and sex, bestrode the world like a colossus and now faces tax bill bankruptcy.

There's many more, a lot of them people you can't ask. Like Miles Davis; he may have changed the face of music but in 1967 he was just another black man in the wrong place at the wrong time when a white cop beat him round the head. Paul Robeson: vilified, hounded, forced into exile by the FBI. Jackson's own hero Sammy Davis Jr: nicknamed Mister Entertainment, but he still died penniless. And you can't ask Sam Cooke, Temptation Paul Williams, Marvin Gaye – all dead, because they couldn't escape the perils and traps that were set for them in their own community.

Michael Jackson never knew anything but adulation. He was the kid who came through after the civil rights heyday when it was thought iniquities and imbalances in American life had been levelled. He is, depending if you read the tabloids or listen to his best music, the man who never grew up or a boy who attained a special sort of wisdom and maturity very early in life, a potential hurricane force poised ready to blow American apathy apart. How far could Michael go? Neverland Ranch? It's not hard to see that place and all that goes with it – the high-commodity record company marketing, the corporate tie-ins, the sci-fi nature of his celebrity stature – as a series of traps, designed in a way that keeps him remote, irrelevant, mummified in fame aspic.

> 'The famous are like dinosaurs whose behemoth size is at once their glory and their downfall. They cannot adapt, but by dint of their power they force life to adapt to them. When it won't, or can't, they perish.'
>
> John Lahr, *Notes On Fame, Automatic Vaudeville*

Things might have gone too far for Michael Jackson. He might have floated too far, too high for too long and is now a sitting target, a victim of the primal need to smash old idols. In the '80s, politics became pop, hinged on the same marketing manoeuvres, rotated around the same hooks or sound-bites, depended on the same successful image projection, the same sense of celebrity. For well over a decade Margaret Thatcher and Ronald Reagan were feted across the globe. Like Jackson, Ronald Reagan was every bit the '80s media monster, his celebrity proliferating in proportion to the society's fear of decline.

'When society is floundering,' says Lahr, 'the machinery of celebrity works ever harder to produce a sense of the culture's greatness.' But there comes a point where celebrity no longer masks the failings, where celebrity itself must be called into question. Had he stayed in power there was a good chance banking and Irangate scandals – real scandals, not allegations – would have seen Reagan impeached. But Reagan can slip away easily, reputation intact because the rules of office dictated that he step aside, cash in his fame chips. That is something Michael Jackson, endorsed but never elected by the public, could never do.

Will any pop star ever again approach the heights of fame scaled by Michael Jackson? Or, more pertinently, will any pop star ever lust after fame with the same ardour as Michael? What does achieving the sort of fame that he has entail? As a black kid in America wanting to make a change, to elevate, transcend himself and his surroundings, to make a radical shift in society, Michael Jackson intuitively knew what had to be done, intuitively knew where the fame lay, fame beyond the Apollo Theatre and Berry Gordy's Motown label.

In 1970, a year after he sang lead on The Jackson Five's debut single 'I Want You Back', Michael Jackson stood on a beach at a promotional barbecue. A journalist looked on as the 12-year-old boy was handed a beefburger. Jackson's face was a mixture of wonder and astonishment. 'What's wrong?' asked the woman who had handed him the burger. 'It's the first time a white lady ever fixed food for me,' he said.

Michael Jackson had the benefit of not just watching the Motown greats at work but also another epoch of soul in a two-album liaison with The Sound of Philadelphia lynchpins Gamble and Huff. Like anyone tutored and raised in Berry Gordy's Motown hit factory Michael Jackson must have felt both blessed and trapped – the struggle between the label's fabled tradition, and the burning desire to break free and express himself on his own terms. When the time came to do just that, Michael's marshalling of influences, his choice of consummate producer Quincey Jones to put a supersonic spin on his horn arranging, vocal licks, tricks and red hot band was astounding.

It's easy to forget with all that's happened since just how scintillating, how joyous the records were where he seized control, his first post-Motown solo album *Off the Wall* or the tracks he wrote and arranged on 'Destiny' and 'Triumph', albums he cut with his brothers either side of 'Wall'. Listening now it's easy to hear an unconscious parallel between Jackson and the young Elvis Presley recording in Sun studios, long before he became the Frankenstein Monster of Fame. There's a feeling of escalating, pure mania; wild abandon wedded to complete control.

Michael must have had Presley in mind when he wrote a song called 'Heartbreak Hotel' for the *Triumph* album. At 19, he was certainly thinking about Elvis when, with barely concealed bitterness, he told an interviewer, 'Rock'n'Roll turned around when people like Elvis did it, but it had been there all the time. Blacks had been doing it for years.' Writing a song called 'Heartbreak Hotel' was evidently an audacious move by the young Jackson, Elvis' dark shadow looms over the song which seems inspired by the pressure of fame he'd so far encountered and the fame that lay ahead. Book-ended by a symphonic requiem, driven by a sabre-toothed dance beat, Michael's 'Hotel' is a complex nightmare of the mind, talking of loss, loneliness and paranoia. Hitting on an area that would become central to his celebrity, 'Hotel' deals with repressed, thwarted sexuality and the fear of being set up by evil forces.

'Hotel' heightened the stakes of the soulmen's sexual trysts and served notice of intention to steal the king's crown, but the integrationist philosophy followed at Motown was also prominent on these records. Both the *Destiny* and *Triumph* covers are emblazoned with the peacock, the significance of which is expressed in the accompanying note from Michael and Jackie Jackson. 'The peacock is the only bird that integrates all colours into one. We, like the peacock, try to integrate all races into one through music.'

Just how passionately Michael felt these words is made clear when he sings his verses on 'Can You Feel It'; it's a voice battling anger and anguish aiming for ecstatic release. When he sings '*We're all the same, the blood inside me is inside you*,' you can hear him do something he says he does quite often. He's crying with joy. The revelation contained in the lyrics has evidently been profound.

The accompanying video which he conceived – The Brothers Jackson as Godlike Figures sprinkling magic love, peace and harmony dust on to the globe, left audiences in no doubt about the salvationist message or the peaks of fame Michael was now reaching for. As the '70s turned into the '80s he worked fast and furious, an album a year, smashing records like no black man before or since. When he narrated the ET story on record, that's how the world decided it wanted to understand him – The new Soul Alien.

'I said to him, "Get your bodyguard and come on down", but he doesn't like going out, I don't think he'll come.'

Los Angeles, November 1982, the lady from CBS was telling us how the reclusive Jackson wouldn't be going to the party to celebrate the successful re-launch of Michael's former Motown colleague Marvin Gaye. The lady showed us a tape of the follow-up to *Off the Wall*, as yet unheard around the world and, despite protestations, unheard on our journey across LA. A month later back in London, perhaps in a fit of pique, perhaps up against a deadline, perhaps suffering from cloth ears, perhaps because it only has three really good tracks, I declared the album a let-down, unlikely to match the success of its predecessor. It is hard to be that wrong about anything. *Thriller* became the biggest selling record of all time, became an event which you had to be part of, transformed the entire business of pop culture.

There were the video images: the mini horror movie video for *Thriller*, with its ghoulish shape changing, allowed a black performer the sort of role still unthinkable in Hollywood. And there was the musical breakthrough – by enlisting Eddie Van Halen to supply lead guitar on 'Beat It', Jackson was in line with the nascent rap/metal crossover, jamming the codes of America's unwritten musical apartheid, forcing his way on to the then-segregationist MTV. Marvin Gaye may have been sinking towards his doomy end but his spirit was alive in the pulsating, spooky masterpiece 'Billie Jean', recalling the veiled threats and dark fears expressed in Marvin's 'I Heard It through the Grapevine' and, indeed, 'Heartbreak Hotel'. Dealing with the emotional fall-out centred on a scorned fan's paternity suit, 'Billie Jean' defined Michael's sexual persona for once and forever – doe-like, stepping around the soulman's minefield, able to express and imply all the heat of congress, while still keeping a wraith-like distance.

Far from the Manchild of tabloid fiction, this Michael Jackson superstar was a sussed, fame-hungry, exquisitely dedicated, smart operator. Back then he still gave rare interviews and they were marked with moments of astonishing candour. 'I was raised onstage. I am more comfortable there than I am here right now. I feel there are angels on all sides – protecting me, I could sleep onstage.' When what would be The Jacksons' farewell tour came under fierce criticism in 1984 for its high ticket price and poor value, Michael turned the negative into a positive, announcing he was donating all tour profits to charity, a profile-heightening gesture continued when he helped write and record the USA for Africa charity event record 'We Are the World'.

Michael Jackson knew all about the injustices served on his musical forebears. And he went into battle, leaving his old friend Paul McCartney miffed when he bought up the entire Beatles songbook. Perhaps veteran hoofer Fred Astaire got it right when he congratulated him on his spellbinding 'Billie Jean' dance routine on *Motown 25* (an incalculable element in Jackson's fame elevation). 'You knocked them on their asses out there, kid. You're an angry dancer, there's rage in your feet.'

In the '80s idol build-up, they all came and went, Springsteen relinquishing his megastardom, Prince too prolific, too wilful to be the figurehead of any corporate campaign except his own, Madonna too risqué. But Jackson seemed determined continually to raise the stakes and his profile. The Jackson integrationist policy became mingled with fame lust; he knew no bounds – he worked with Reagan, he worked with Bush. Well, Elvis had worked with Nixon.

Perhaps the sponsorship deal with Pepsi was where he went too far, lost sight of his creation, became something that he could never live up to. Maybe that's where he forfeited a big amount of the kudos, the irreducible gains his career had thus far attained. Whatever, however he followed *Thriller* it was bound to be a fraught move. Just how fraught it was nobody guessed until the new, surgically altered Jackson appeared on the cover of the ambiguously titled *Bad*.

> '*Commercials made people dislike Michael Jackson. Like they had a contest where they asked people are you getting sick of Michael Jackson, but what they really meant was are you getting sick of his face. Michael needs to change his face again. Because they've shown so many pictures of him now that it'll be beneficial for him to come up with a whole 'nother anti-Michael Jackson look. And he has to do it for himself. Because if he waits for them to do it, it's going to be negative.*'
>
> George Clinton, sci-fi funkateer, cosmic conspiracy theorist and soul veteran, talking to writer Greg Tate in 1985

When Michael Jackson gave his first televised interview for 14 years to Oprah Winfrey earlier this year, the music that made him famous was hardly mentioned. What was discussed was his sex life or lack of it, the Neverland ranch from where the interview was beamed live across America, his sadness, the long periods spent crying offstage, his need to heal the wounds of verbal and physical abuse from the father who beat him into Superstar Shape as a child.

Jackson – his Afro hair long since kinked into long shiny locks, his face pale, cosmetically and surgically altered – was almost in tears as he discussed the changes in his physiognomy. He was, he said, proud to be a black American even though he no longer looked black. He claimed he was suffering from vitaligo, a pigment deficiency. Then, almost contradicting himself, he raised his voice saying that no one made a fuss when it was the other way round, what about the people who lay out in the sun trying to go brown?

Do George Clinton's words have any bearing here? Was the new look Jackson merely applying racial genetics to the David Bowie face painting, costume drama of the '70s? Could race ever be that easily discarded, in America in the late '80s? After Reagan had pushed back the meagre advances of the civil rights years. When the Jesse Jackson-led Rainbow Coalition had failed to make any real gains. When Reagan, reluctantly declaring Martin Luther King's Birthday a national holiday, said that 'A question mark stills hangs over the question of his loyalty to this country.'

Of course not. Black critic Greg Tate was withering in his condemnation. 'Michael Jackson as skin job represents the carpetbagging side of black advancement in the affirmative action era. The fact that we are now pro-ducing young black men and women who conceive of their African inheritance as little more than a means to cold-crash mainstream America and then cold dis – if not merely put considerable distance between – the brothers and sisters left behind. Jackson's decolourised flesh is the buppy version of Dorian Gary, a blaxploitation nightmare that offers this moral: Stop, the face you save might be your own.'

It would be something if after this you could trust the music but *Bad* – four years in the making – wasn't even very good, though eerily enough it was 'Man in the Mirror', a face to face with his *Bad* self, that worked best.

The album was the product of a pernickety, perfectionist Jackson. Buoyed by the fame dividend of its predecessor, free from his family (as musical partners and father manager Joseph) he no longer needed to produce the volume of output he generated at the start of the decade. Later he would tell Oprah how he spent long periods alone in sadness. But every Sunday he danced and fasted until he fell at the end, exhausted, elated, crying and laughing on the floor. That was when he came alive, when he focused his

783

energy. When he communed again with the fame force. His Yoga guru said, 'When Michael dances he leaves this world. It's a genuine form of trance as practised by the Sufis. He feels nothing but a state of pure love to the world. And the world gives it back.'

But was it only as this new creation of uncertain racial origin that Jackson could survive, feel that he was worthy of the love? '*Bad* only sold half as many copies as *Thriller*, but it still became the second biggest selling album of all time. And Michael moved forward, boldly breaking off ties with Quincy Jones for his next album. Quincy had been a guy rope keeping Michael in check, it was rumoured that after three long years of *Bad*, Jones had sent him back to record three more songs, the album's three hit singles. Now Michael was truly out there on his own.

He kept a regal distance while blabbermouth and fame punk Madonna told of their *Dangerous* liaison. A collaboration between the pair had been planned for that LP. They were seen out on the town together, allegedly discussing the best way to negotiate their new multi media deals that put them both at the head of their own mini corporations. Then Madonna broke rank and, in the time-honoured fashion of superstar humiliations meted out to Kevin Costner and Warren Beatty in the *In Bed with Madonna* documentary, said it was all off. True, they had planned to work together but Jackson was too set in his ways, she wanted to give him a whole new look, put him together with some gay dancers she knew, it might help him to come out of the closet she added. Meeeoooiww.

Jackson, who has said he conducts his private life 'like a haemophiliac who can't afford to be scratched in any way', evidently recoiled. *Dangerous* is a huge, sprawling work packed with overweening kitsch, dumb ugly metal, yahoo rousing rockers, hard raps, that break his voice up into epileptic fits, growls, yelps. On one level it might be seen as an example of the artistic fame drain which Lahr pinpoints when he says, 'The glare of public attention limits the experience of the famous. Instead of having experience they have experience provided for them. Fame homogenises life; and this inevitably brings creative impoverishment'.

On the video for 'Will You Be There', the anguish of the performer is there for all to see. The voice is grieved, tremulous, hammy, and he now bears an astonishing resemblance to Diana Ross. As he sings, cornball tears well up and roll down his cheeks. To the side of the stage a kid signals the words quoted above in sign language. Michael's musical dream is now to reach out and touch everyone, even those who can't hear. That's either generosity of an unparalleled nature or self-aggrandisement of unheard proportions.

The mystery that once lay at the heart of his message, that spellbinding, inexplicable talent to make mere words gain energy and momentum is gone. He has turned himself inside out, all that was implicit in his fame game is now explicit. The imaginary angels that he talked about now stand alongside guarding him. At the end of the song one of them wraps a big pair of golden wings around him. Keeping him safe. Or smothering him for good.

Now Michael's dream is being enacted for real. The fairy dust of 'Can You Feel It' has come to life, the Pepsi-sponsored step by step 'Heal the World' campaign started in LA, now it goes around the world led by Michael, omnipresent but unreachable, the brightest star. 'Michael tends to see things in very simple terms, almost like a child. Sometimes that's best,' a friend tells the newspapers. There is work to be done. *Dangerous* has still to show legs, to meet Jackson's rumoured ambition for it to sell a *Thriller*-doubling 100 million.

Still, the ten million Michael Jackson fans who bought the album can't be wrong, so the show rolled on. Michael went to a crowning ceremony in Tanzania in West Africa. He was excited to be going there, he said it was the birthplace of civilisation. But the local newspapers weren't impressed when he got off the plane pinching his nose. 'The American sacred beast took it upon himself to remind us: we are under-developed, impure. Our air is polluted, infested with germs,' said one. 'This mutant, voluntary genius, bleached neither black nor white, man nor woman, so delicate, so frail,' sighed another.

The story spirals downwards into uncharted territory. Michael is back on the road. On the night Jordan Chandler filed a civil suit against him (the might of the LAPD Special Child Abuse Investigations Unit being unable to come up with any evidence to press charges) he was playing in Moscow. He had made a video on a military parade ground, a chance to extend his recently displayed love for military garb. He was being ferried round Moscow in a motorcade and had hired two planes to disperse the clouds gathering over the stadium where the evening's show was scheduled.

That night it rained heavily. Forced to perform while stage hands mopped the floor around him, Jackson was said to be considering suing the firm that supplied the dispersal service.

A cursory look at the path travelled by any black American celebrity of this century (and you can add Malcolm X, Martin Luther King, Mike Tyson and Muhammad Ali to the list of musicians) shows that they undertake a strange, often perilous journey. Michael Jackson has raised the stakes of fame to unthinkable heights. He is this generation's Elvis Presley and then some. He has achieved everything but has also arguably given everything to get to wherever he is. He has been willing to go to the point of eradicating his racial identity, has suppressed his sexual identity, neutered his character to the point of nothingness. He may be on the strangest, most perilous journey of them all. And it isn't over yet.

Gavin Martin, New Musical Express, 2 October 1993

1994: Never More

People couldn't believe the photograph. The day after Kurt Cobain shot himself faceless in his million-dollar home, his friends who mourned him found a nasty slice of evidence on the front page of the Seattle *Times*: a shot taken from above the glass doors of the garage where Cobain died, revealing the suicide scene. Two detectives hover like shadows. But what's cruelly fascinating is the body. The image is only a fragment: one dirty-jean-clad leg with a white sock and a badly tied Converse, one arm from the elbow down in a light blue thrift-shirt, one clenched fist. Near a detective's foot, another photograph can almost be seen, an official snapshot on a driver's license. The body and the license, both so small they don't seem real, feel unknowable, the definition of not enough.

'That picture was so tacky, I was shocked,' says Kim Warnick on Sunday afternoon, as she bides her time until five, when the candlelight vigil would begin. Warnick fronts the longtime Seattle band, the Fastbacks, and she works as a sales rep at Nirvana's former label, Sub Pop; we're discussing the media frenzy, the possible motives, the usual stuff. 'But you know what really got me about it? His ID. You can see his wallet opened up to his driver's license, right by his body. Kurt didn't want any mistakes about what he was doing. He wanted to be perfectly clear.'

It's a strange bit of the typical that Kurt Cobain would worry that killing himself with a shotgun was an act that might be misinterpreted. Suicide, especially one as violent as Cobain's, is the loudest possible invocation of silence; it's a perfectly clear way of turning your life into a mystery. His commitment to contradiction got him in the end, but even as he cut himself off forever he was trying to make himself speak.

Here are some facts: Kurt Cobain, 27, singer/guitarist/writer for the world's most successful 'alternative' band and Seattle's current favorite non-native born Native Son, killed himself Thursday, April 7, at his home near Lake Washington. He was the first rock star to commit suicide at the top of his game. His body was discovered by electrician Gary Smith the next morning. Cobain is survived by an angry widow, Hole singer-songwriter Courtney Love, and a one-and-a-half-year-old daughter, Frances Bean, as well as his divorced parents, bandmates, and various friends in the local and national music scenes. Immediately before his suicide, he had fled from a Southern California drug-treatment facility; his path up the coast to death remains unclear. Six weeks before his death, Cobain had been hospitalized in Rome after entering a coma brought on by a mix of alcohol and prescription drugs. Shortly after that, Love called the police to Cobain's and her home because, she claimed, he was trying to kill himself. The police found four guns and 25 boxes of ammo on the premises. Six days before his body was found, Cobain's mother, Wendy O'Connor, filed a missing persons report with the Seattle police. After his death, O'Connor was quoted as saying, 'I told him not to join that stupid club,' a media favorite later surpassed by the last words of Cobain's suicide note: 'I love you, I love you.'

And now, here are some rumors, flickering around and beyond the facts: Kurt Cobain killed himself because Courtney had finally given up on him and was filing for divorce. Courtney had been in LA or even Seattle the day before Kurt's death, not London, as reported. Cobain had spent at least one of his last nights at his and Courtney's country house with an unidentified companion. The band had broken up at least a week before the death. He'd never really kicked heroin; the supposedly accidental overdose in March was actually a suicide attempt. He killed himself because of writer's block.

There are other facts, and other rumors. And then there is the wall. It's made of friends' grief, fans' confusion, journalists' embarrassment, and what several writers call a 'veil of silence' created by Gold Mountain, Nirvana's and Hole's management company. Above all it builds off the special Northwest penchant for keeping things in. The wall looks like another photograph of Kurt, this one torn into pieces and pasted back together, nothing left in tact or clear.

'Kurt Cobain is not a person,' says Daniel House, owner of Seattle independent record label C/Z. 'He's turned into something that represents different things for different people. I understand the press is going to be all over it, but I wish they would leave it alone completely. Because that attention is why Kurt died. He had no life, no peace, constant chaos. He had become a freak.' House's view, which was duly cited in *Time* magazine the Monday after Cobain's death, is very popular in Seattle: Kurt had his troubles, but if his band had never exceeded normal expectations, like

787

maybe headlining the thousand-seat Moore Theater once a year, he could have been saved.

In our century, 'fame kills' is almost a mantra; add Cobain's name to the pantheon and sign him up for a page in *Hollywood Babylon*. But it's hard, especially in a hometown, to pinpoint the moment when a star like Cobain slips into that nether realm, becomes flat and reproducible, something read instead of someone known. And Cobain spent his short career pulling away from this transformation, jumbling his statements, turning his back. For most stars, even the tragic ones, the transformation magnifies; for Cobain, it worked as erasure. His death can be viewed as the final step on a chain of denials that are echoed in the story of his adopted town, his scene, his generation, every one radically unwilling to speak for itself. So it's no surprise that in the days following Cobain's death, nobody emerges to speak for them. Even the journalists hesitate in the face of such grief-benumbed wordlessness.

'It's a much different thing here, with the rock scene,' says Sub Pop publicist and former Nirvana fan club head Nils Bernstein about the process of mourning. 'It's one thing to suffer these losses on your own, and another to do it with MTV in your face. People who didn't know Kurt feel like they did. His death is an ongoing event.'

Bernstein, who holds to the Sub Pop view that Cobain was 'suicidal forever', is tired and would like to retreat to Linda's Tavern and drink a Red Hook with a tight circle of friends. But in a painful coincidence, this is the Saturday long since scheduled as the date of Sub Pop's sixth anniversary party. 'Yesterday, everyone was pretty dazed,' he says. 'Everyone just got drunk.' They'll do the same tonight at the Crocodile Café, at a party that becomes a wake in a sideways manner well after the camera crews have abandoned their positions outside the windows: no speeches, no photographs held aloft, just old buddies in corners getting around to the subject gradually.

'There was a great vibe there,' says Warnick the next day. 'It would always come into the conversation, but everyone was very respectful of everyone else. It was really insulated very well.' Warnick's right – the party felt better by far than any other moments in the weekend following Cobain's death. For a semi-outsider like me, born and raised in Seattle but now a decade gone, it felt like a welcome earned by my willingness to be cool. Scott McCaughey of the Young Fresh Fellows, Jonathan Poneman from Sub Pop, Warnick's husband Ken Stringfellow of the Posies, and numerous other band members, label types, and writers – all would smile, give a brief hug, murmur, 'Weird day, isn't it?' and move on to more manageable subjects.

The jovial skepticism, downing another microbrew and telling a joke rather than analyzing or grieving too obviously, was pure Seattle. Native Northwesterners cultivate this say-no-more attitude, the roots of which I always identify in the historic drive toward seclusion that pushed the area's pioneers across the map. It's not the rain – it's the mountains. A full, snow-capped range on either side of the municipal area. They hold us in.

Seattle's indie-rock scene reenacts, on a smaller level, the balancing act inherent in every Northwest community, whether as big as Seattle or as small as Cobain's native Aberdeen, between the interdependency of an isolated group and solitary individuals' preference for total self-reliance. 'It's a really tight community,' says one local scenester, 'but when it comes right down to it, I'm not sure how much people will help each other.' Her words make me think about the phrase that I've come to consider Kurt Cobain's motto, from 'Radio Friendly Unit Shifter': 'Hate, hate your enemies, save, save your friends.' This phrase means to build a fortress around a group of like-minded people; the problems come when you find yourself at odds with your friends and thrown into contact with strangers who may or may not be enemies (and if you fear the world it's very hard to tell).

The Northwest's growth over the past decade, attributable partly to rock's ascendancy but mostly to the encroachment of Microsoft and other software companies, has shifted the area's balance. It's become a mecca for the young, the affluent, a forest of espresso stands and specialty boutiques. Yet at heart, it remains a company town – Cobain's death was bumped off the top of the news Saturday morning by the unveiling of Boeing's newest jet, the 777. And it retains a working-class suspicion of pretense and opportunism that's shared by the musicians and even the businesspeople who dominate Seattle's rock world. So they find a way to stand outside themselves, as if all this success wasn't happening to them, almost as if they don't want it.

'People don't let each other cross over the line, away from reality,' says Ken Stringfellow, whose own fine band, the Posies, embraces pop and polish much more readily than most Seattle acts. 'What makes Nirvana interesting is that they didn't have to be unrealistic to be extraordinary.' Later, though he admits that the dichotomies don't always work out so neatly. 'Sometimes people's skepticism overwhelms them, and they can't enjoy what's happened.

'We lived cloistered away for so many years and nobody gave a damn,' Warnick adds. 'And because of all the resources we have here, people are really against all the Guns N' Roses stuff. All that compromise.'

789

Because of the city's growth and Seattle bands' current dominance, of course, compromise is unavoidable. But the way Seattle has become a mecca differs from the East Coast norm, in which small groups import their culture, take over a corner, and slowly integrate. There are plenty of new immigrants in the Northwest, many of them Thai or Vietnamese, but the city's self-conception obscures these communities. And among the young, Seattle isn't a place where you can come as you are: you come to integrate yourself into a vision based on affinities you believe you share. For someone like Kurt Cobain, the college community of Olympia and, later, Seattle represented a chance to go inside after a childhood in the cold as a small-town outcast. And perhaps inspired by his expression, kids have flocked here to join what he sardonically called 'our little tribe'.

From outsider to insider, though, is always a tricky move. It's the same jump that indie rock, the music Cobain claimed lifted him from the dung heap of conformity, keeps trying to manage. Indie never really did away with rock stars – it just located them at eye level. As a young indie fan, Cobain idolized his own favorite bands, thought of them as the basis of his community. Just like the kids who now idolize him, he didn't perceive the gulf between artist and audience, and eventually he became part of the indie-rock elite, an elite that in many cases still denies its own elitism. But he was sensitive enough to be bothered by the distance now that he could see it between himself and the kids who thought he was lifting them out of their own shitty lives. And so he felt even more isolated.

'Kurt didn't have any friends anymore,' says one close acquaintance. When people go over the edge, they've usually alienated even their most intimate companions, and at one level this remark doesn't reflect anything beyond Cobain's particular illness. But it also makes him an indie rocker to the core, deeply troubled by that shift into broader resonance that characterizes every successful artistic act. Rich Jensen, Sub Pop's general manager, views the problem as a struggle with the sacred. 'Kurt viewed his favorite bands as icons,' he says. 'An icon is something you own, or it's a false idol.'

The Seattle music community has been shattered by death many times in the past five years; part of the vigilant self-protectiveness I sense feels like the fear of yet another disaster. In 1990, Mother Love Bone singer Andrew Wood died of a heroin overdose. In 1991, poet and longtime scene habitué Jesse Bernstein shot himself. Stefanie Sargent of 7 Year Bitch overdosed in 1992. And last July, Gits singer Mia Zapata was found strangled on a Capitol Hill side street. Wood, Sargent, and Zapata were all the same age as or younger than Cobain, and because they hadn't yet reached the level of stardom that separates people from their regular lives, their deaths were, in fact, much more directly felt among local artists. They're remembered, too: Andy comes up in conversation at least four times over the weekend's course; 7 Year Bitch's soon-to-be-released C/Z album features a song about Stefanie and one about Mia. It's even called *Viva Zapata*.

'Mia's death affected all of us so much,' says Matt Dresdner, bassist for the Gits, who continue to play as a three-piece; their debut album, recorded mostly before Zapata died, is out on C/Z. 'She knew so many people; so many would say, "Mia was my best friend." Person after person, and they really felt that way. She was very accessible always and very honest.'

Partly because it was a murder, Zapata's death genuinely transformed the smaller, more local scene in which she was a leading light. A women's self-defense program is now in place, and friends continue to raise money to investigate her murder; Nirvana even played one of the benefits, last fall at the King Theater. There were also negative effects on the scene. 'A lot of bands, coincidentally I imagine, broke up after she was killed,' says Dresdner. 'I do think Mia was a catalyst and inspired people to do stuff.' Talking about Kurt with people in clubs and café, I actually feel his presence less than Zapata's. She is mentioned over and over. Posters asking for information adorn the wall of the Comet Tavern and Moe's; on some street corners, you can see the flyers made by friends a long time ago. There's Mia's warm, big, charming face, and the words: 'Damn! Damn! Damn!'

These intimate shocks, which don't draw jets full of confused rock critics and bill-waving TV tab reporters, have stayed with Seattle musicians in ways that seem to affect their daily lives. These griefs really do belong to them. Kurt Cobain's another story. The rage Zapata's friends feel is not for her, and it's not existential. It's a hopeful anger, one they can imagine doing something about.

'Fuck Kurt Cobain. I can't get a job.'

Gregory Askew is slumped against the side wall at the Cafe Paradiso, Capitol Hill's grooviest late-night caffeine station, the night of the announcement. The 20-year-old moved here from New Jersey a year or so ago, but he's had it with bohemian utopia. 'I'm going down to Eugene, just to find a mellow town where everybody's not competing.'

Askew's hardly the only kid who's unimpressed with Cobain's departure from the world; this reaction has been so common on the West Coast that the San Francisco *Examiner* did a feature on it Saturday. Like every generation of cool teens, these young fans have invented their own strange style of tuning out. They wear the clothes, play in the baby bands, hang out at the bars and coffee houses, all the while perfecting the art of indifference. When that lackadaisical attitude is personified in figures like Winona and Ethan or Courtney and Kurt, the kids still look up. But they keep their glances quiet and speculative.

In Seattle, these teen-to-twentysomethings are major players in moving the economy from industry to service, working in the bars and record stores they frequent, maintaining the circular flow of cash. 'They're making the town what they thought it would be,' says Rich Jensen as he sits in one of the current hot spots, a laundromat-café called Sit & Spin. Sub Pop's inexhaustible entrepreneurship is just one example of the attitude: you want a job, open a store. It's indie at its most vibrant, a culture tossed up in storefronts and basement rooms.

But some kids, like Askew, remain discouraged. The recession hit Seattle a little later than the rest of the country – Boeing laid off 11 per cent of its work force last year and there were quieter adjustments at Microsoft as well – and although slacker jobs may seem unlimited, there are only so many gigs available pulling espresso. One Paradiso customer, 16-year-old Nathan Hatch, escaped from a dreary life much like the young Cobain's to find some people 'even close to weird'. He dropped out of school in Elma, near Aberdeen, in ninth grade, and moved to Portland with a skater dude named Paul. Now he's looking for janitorial work. 'I'm hopeful,' he says. 'But I'm pretty drunk right now.'

Busy with their own anxieties, Seattle's club kids don't seem interested in making Cobain a hero. Maybe, as Nils Bernstein thinks, they're already over the mystery that not long ago fueled much of the average outcast's passion for rock and roll. 'I've seen 12-year-old kids on the bus discussing record deals, dollar amounts,' says Bernstein. 'They know way, way, way more than they should about the industry.'

If an idol demands distance, an icon wants to be put inside a devotee's pocket. The kids I found who did mourn Cobain, hovering behind police lines at the house where he'd died or building shrines from candles and Raisin Bran boxes at the Sunday night vigil organized by three local radio stations seemed to think of him more as a lost friend than a candidate for that dreaded assignment, role model. In fact, they seemed a lot like he did: small, unsure, bowled over by the need to feel, but worried about what to say. 'When we found out, my friend Blair and I went out to our fort and just played some CDs,' says Dave Johnson, a blond boy from Puyallup who's in a baby band called Thrive. 'Kurt took the wimpy way out. He could have gone somewhere to gather his thoughts. I know places like that to go.'

Johnson and about a dozen friends sit around a heap of flowers, votives, notes, and xeroxed photographs of Kurt. The girls don't say much; they look like they're about to cry. The boys are enjoying all the chances to be interviewed. Even though it comes so awkwardly, through the death of a loved one, they tentatively embrace this moment of prominence. But they agree that, like Kurt, they wouldn't be able to handle it full time.

'Being a rock star would be kinda stressful,' says Johnson. 'I'm not really looking for it. I'm in it for the enjoyment and fun.' I wonder if he was inspired by Cobain's suicide note, which Love read to the 7,000 vigil-goers in a taped message. 'I haven't felt excitement in listening to as well as creating music . . . for too many years now. The fact is, I can't fool you, any of you.' And the weary, too-wise kids in the audience really don't seem fooled.

The speakers at the vigil – a preacher, a poet, a suicide prevention specialist – have nothing to do with why the kids were there. Even a brief taped message from Nirvana bassist Krist Novoselic seems beside the point. Only Love's statement has a visceral effect. But the weirdness of 7,000 people standing around, looking at an empty stage, listening to a tape recording of a grieving widow and of the band they wouldn't hear new music from again, pushes the crowd out of its grief into an anger that soon turns playful. Near the end, a bunch of kids overrun the Seattle Center's biggest fountain, climbing on top, forming a mosh pit to no beats and no guitars. 'Kurt Cobain!' they chant, then, 'Fuck you!' when a security guard tries to move them along, then just 'Music!' Would Kurt have felt honored by this action? Well, he was a punk, he liked disruption. But the spirit that moved these kids had nothing to do with Kurt Cobain. It was simply their own spirit, the only one they feel they can trust.

At first, after the suicide, Courtney Love tried to stay behind the veil – not simply out of decorum, but out of genuine grief. Love's been made into such a cartoon by malevolent rivals, gossip hounds, and media whores that her strength in this ordeal has been, in some ways, its biggest shock. Because Courtney, who knows fakeness well enough to make it the major theme of Hole's brilliant DGC debut, Live Through This (scheduled to be released, in the cruelest of ironies, today), refused in the end to play like a lady, and did something that finally made Cobain's death – and her survival of it – seem unreal.

Strangely, Love performed her heroic act in absentia. The tape-recorded message she prepared for the vigil offered the weekend's only real catharsis, and not only because it bore Cobain's pathetic, soon-to-be-famous last words. What Courtney did was argue with him, dispute the terms of his refusal; in doing so, she opened up a view of what he must have really felt, the disorder that consumed him. She would read a little from the note, then curse the words, then express her sorrow. 'The worst crime I could think of would be to put people off by faking it and pretend as if I was having 100 per cent fun.' 'No, Kurt, the worst crime I could think of was for you to continue to be a rock star when you just ... hated it.' Like some heroine from Euripides, furious at the gods, Courtney provided some guidance to escape the dark. Some of what she said was disturbing; she's clearly not anywhere near solid ground yet. After reading the note, she revealed her own remorse. 'We should have let him have his numbness, the thing that helped his stomach and stopped his pain, instead of stripping away his fucking skin,' she sobbed. 'Just tell him he's a fucker, say fucker, he's a fucker. And we love him.' Courtney was the only one who made the vigil's audience cry.

As much as the loss of Nirvana, the dissolution of the Love/Cobain partnership is an artistic tragedy. These two were exploring the male-female dynamic together, as musicians and as public figures, with insight, daring and a sometimes fruitful incomprehension. Just as it's mercilessly unfair to blame Love for Cobain's death, it may be in bad taste to point out that he committed suicide the week her album was to be released. Whatever the particulars of his anger, if her career is stalled, that will also be a significant loss.

Listening to Love's tape at the vigil, I began to think about women's silence versus men's, and the balance of power that causes women to speak when men feel they can remain silent. Powerful men can keep their words to themselves; power speaks for them. Part of Cobain's personal tragedy was his inability to feel his own power; at this moment, Love's achievement is to be able, across the black expanse of her sorrow, to maintain a sense of her own.

In his painful last love letter to a world he couldn't grasp, Kurt Cobain quoted Neil Young: 'It's better to burn out than to fade away.' 'That's bullshit,' Courtney said to her ruined husband as she read the note aloud. Truth is, Cobain didn't even burn out. He fell out of our lives, unfinished. All the media attention, the vigil and the memorials in print and the endless rounds of *MTV Unplugged*, only recalls his absence, the lack he stood for and could never fill.

A few years ago, a friend of mine died of a heroin overdose. He'd been long gone before he actually left the earth. His old lover said, Ted died because he could never find the words to say what he really wanted. Kurt's whole struggle, the same one rock's going through in its most serious moments these days, was to cut into himself until he found a vocabulary that might offer those words. Sometimes a few of them would gush forth. In the end, though, silence swallowed him alive.

Ann Powers, Village Voice, 19 April 1994

1994: Michael Jackson and Lisa Marie Presley

Surprises are coming at us thick and fast from a duo who could be heading the musical empire of the century by the year 2000.

Hard on the heels of leaked news that Michael Jackson, the King of Pop, has married the King of Rock's daughter, Lisa Marie Presley, came world-wide speculation, then confirmation and public acknowledgement of the deed as the newlywed couple walked the streets of Budapest hand in hand and grinning from ear to ear.

Soon we were being assured by a New York columnist that the marriage had been consummated on the wedding night.

Now, if reports are to be believed, such assurances were completely unnecessary because the whole reason for the hush-hush marriage was that Lisa Marie had told Michael she was expecting his baby, so nobody needed to worry about the wedding night at all.

Since the marriage rumour turned out to be true, it's no wonder that people are loathe to disbelieve the baby one.

A thrilled Michael is reported to have proposed after Lisa Marie broke the happy news, and to be so delighted that he's been telling friends the baby has given him a future to look forward to.

Lisa Marie, who's been looking pretty happy herself in the photos, has said that: 'I'm very much in love with Michael. I shall dedicate my life to being his wife. We both look forward to raising a family and living a happy and healthy life together.'

Lisa Marie already has two children, Danielle, aged five, and 20-month-old Benjamin, by her husband of five years, Danny Keough. The couple divorced in March and have joint custody of the children.

For Michael, the baby, reported to be arriving at Christmas, will be his first child. He has long been known to adore children, giving huge support to children's causes, and creating a whole fantasy world for them at his range, Neverland.

The story turned sour last year with charges of child abuse, and Michael's whole career looked to be in jeopardy as he cancelled concerts on his world tour and appeared, haggard and ill, to refute the charges on television.

A hefty out-of-court settlement (estimated at anything between $10 and $20 million) with the 14-year-old Beverly Hills boy who brought charges of sexual abuse, put paid to the worst of the scandal, but the aftershocks are still being felt: the latest development is that Michael invoked the Fifth Amendment against self-incrimination, which means that he will not have to appear in court to defend himself against five former bodyguards who are claiming he fired them for knowing about his sexual activities with young boys.

Christmas 1994 looks set to be quite a contrast with last year's, therefore, with a baby and a new album to celebrate.

Michael has reportedly told friends that he feels safe with Lisa Marie and that the baby 'means everything to me'.

Meanwhile, as speculation continued to run riot, the couple were visiting children's homes in Budapest, where Michael was working on the video for his upcoming album, titled *History*. The video shows him in pseudo-military garb liberating the people of the Eastern bloc from oppression – an idea which met with a mixed reception in Hungary.

Plenty of fans turned our to see their pop hero, though, as he appeared for the first time in public hand in hand with his wife, and they smiled happily as the rest of the world was asking the many million dollar question: 'Why?'

There are lots of theories to account for the marriage, which has united two great eras of music, two fortunes estimated to top $300,000 million, and the famous estates of Graceland and Neverland.

The cynics say it's all one big publicity stunt. Others think Michael might have converted to the Church of Scientology, of which Lisa is a member. Other famous members of the Church include Tom Cruise, Kirstie Alley and John Travolta.

The Church of Scientology's congratulatory message to the couple was: 'We consider marriage and a happy family the most valuable building blocks of a stable society and we wish the newlyweds the very best for a joyful future.'

Then there are those who say the marriage is in the old style, with the purpose of uniting and strengthening two separate kingdoms to form a huge music empire.

And finally, some people really do believe that it's a simple, old-fashioned love story, with Lisa Marie and Michael meeting and falling in love, just like so many thousands and millions of other people around the world.

Lisa Marie's life has not been a bed of roses, even though her father, 'The King', wanted it to be. Her mother, Priscilla Presley, says Elvis gave Lisa Marie far too many things and they argued over how to bring up their little girl.

For a long time Lisa Marie walked alone, but then she discovered the Church of Scientology, and there she met her husband-to-be, Danny Keough, the father of Danielle and Benjamin.

Michael is reported to have offered a million dollars to become the legal father of Lisa Marie's two children, but Danny is said to be refusing to contemplate the idea.

The singing superstar first met Lisa Marie in November of 1992, according to the bride's friend, lawyer John Cole.

'They met at a social event,' he says, 'not a business meeting in the music world. The meeting happened in Los Angeles, at a mutual friend's house. Nobody famous,' he adds. 'Lisa liked Michael, she thought he was really nice. At first they were friends, just friends. There was no indication at that time that they were going to fall in love. I'm not sure just when they began to get interested in each other as a partner.'

One person who was in on the secret was flamboyant entrepreneur Donald Trump, who owns the Trump Towers in New York where Lisa and Michael rent a $110,000 a month apartment complete with antique furnishings and gold taps.

Donald Trump's comment, when Lisa finally confirmed the marriage, was: 'I've known that for a while. They're good people and I wish them luck.'

As for Lisa's mother, Priscilla, there were rumours at first that she disapproved of the marriage, which prompted her to come forward and say: 'Please make it clear to everyone that I support Lisa Marie and anything she does totally.'

Lisa's friend John Cole says the marriage is a solid one. 'Lisa is a very sensible woman,' he comments. 'I've always been impressed by her decisions. If we just give this marriage a chance, I'm sure we'll all get a pleasant surprise.'

Hello! magazine, 20 August 1994

1994: The Killing of Crusty

The police look edgy. They're stretched across Piccadilly Circus on the first of May, ready for a riot as 15–20,000 protesters march down to Trafalgar

797

Square. Pasty white faces are blotched pink from the first hints of summer sun. Stand downwind and you might get a circulating current of *eau de crusty*: a moldering odor of accumulated sweat, pot, and lager. A rowdy crowd of punks lurks around with dazed idiotic grins, yelling, 'this law's a load of *shit shit shit*.' The speeches following the march are full of bold fighting talk, but privately most admit that nothing can be done to stop the Criminal Justice Bill.

The bill is a bundle of laws introduced by the conservative Tory party that is aimed, in part, at outlawing huge chunks of Britain's alternative culture. Among those affected will be squatters – people who occupy vacant buildings and apartments – ravers, who attend free outdoor festivals or illegal raves, and New Age travelers, neo-hippie nomads who live in vehicles and travel across the UK.

Under the new legislation, due to be passed in October, a landlord will be able to gain an eviction order without squatters even knowing about the case; if the squatters don't disperse within 24 hours, they may be jailed for up to six months.

If a police officer 'reasonably believes' ten or more people are waiting for or setting up a rave – defined as 100 or more people playing amplified music characterized by 'a succession of repetitive beats' – they can be ordered to disperse; if they refuse, they're each liable for up to three months prison or a £2,500 fine, *even* if the event has full permission of the landowner. The police can also turn away anyone who comes within *five miles* of the potential 'rave'.

As for travelers, the police can throw any gathering of six or more vehicles off land (even common or public land) and arrest the owners if they won't comply; they can also impound travelers' vehicles (their homes).

The bill also has serious implications for the civil rights of the average citizen with its repressive constraints on public protest – apparently aimed at the country's hunt saboteurs (activists who disrupt fox-hunting), but so broadly worded as to be applicable to all kinds of protest.

All this because, in the public imagination, squatters, ravers, and travelers blur together in the 'crusty', a smelly, drug-addled parasite ready to take over your house while you're on vacation. A hybrid of hippie and anarchopunk, the stereotypical crusty is recognisable by his or her matted, dreadlocked hair, grubby attire, and mangy dog on a string. In reality, there is no generic squatter or traveler; instead there is a multitude of 'tribes', whose only uniting factor is that they don't want (or can't afford) to live in straight society under a landlord's roof. Many are motivated by the lack of

798

opportunities for young people in post-Thatcher Britain; others are idealists who left home in search of a less restrictive, more communal way of life.

So why has the British government chosen to persecute these 'free spirits'? Travelers and squatters have been on the Tory (s)hit list for a while now. They're perceived as 'scroungers' who live off the state, but are not beholden to it; who are not crushed by poverty and unemployment, but instead exist happily within a black-market economy. David Wastell, political editor of the conservative *Sunday Telegraph*, sees a link between the bill and Prime Minister John Major's 'Back to Basics' plan. Like George Bush and Dan Quayle's notorious 'Family Values' platform, 'Back to Basics' is a vision of the return to a long-lost (or perhaps never was) moral, orderly England. 'At its core,' says Wastell, 'the bill appeals to traditional country Tories who have had hippie travelers on their property and want them stopped.'

Jon Savage, author of *England's Dreaming*, a history of the punk-rock movement in Britain, is outraged by the bill. 'It's about politicians making laws on the basis of judging people's lifestyles,' he says. 'And that's no way to make laws.' Media uproar over an epidemic of joyriding and ramraiding (kids stealing cars, driving them through store windows, and then looting the shops), and last year's murder of two-year-old James Bulger at the hands of two young boys have all contributed to the notion that the nation's youths are out of control. 'This bill is seen as a way to calm people's fears,' adds Wastell.

Says the *Guardian*'s Duncan Campbell, one of the few journalists to cover the issue, 'Squatters, New Age travelers, ravers, and hunt saboteurs are deeply hated by the conservatives. I'm afraid they are a people without friends.'

Awareness of the bill is beginning to rise, thanks to groups like SQUASH (Squatters Action For Secure Homes) and the Advance Party. Jim Carey of SQUASH has been lobbying politicians, as well as publishing *Squall*, an articulate newsletter that briefs squatters and travelers on their rights and on the current state of the bill. 'The trouble is that old impressions die hard. Travelers and squatters look wild, and people are afraid of wildness. But they're just scapegoats. What we're trying to do is increase the public's awareness that the bill is a fundamentral attack on people who have enough grief already.' The Advance Party's plans include a nationwide legal network, seminars to train legal observers, and cards that can be handed out that clarify ravers' rights. 'Just because a few men in shirts decide they don't want a party, they make it a criminal offense!' says Advance Party coordinator Debby Staunton. 'There's a difference now between legal law and moral law, and as far as we're concerned, it's not something we'll recognize.'

One band has been very active in the fight against the bill. The Levellers – who have all been squatters and travelers at one time – have sponsored an anti-CJB ad and poster campaign and are joining with civil liberties activists, squatters, travelers, and road protesters to lobby against the bill. Singer Mark Chadwick explains, 'We got involved because this piece of legislation actually attacks every young person in the UK, and we want to make everyone aware that politics with a small 'p' can fuck up their lives.' He thinks the apathy surrounding the bill will disappear when the law kicks in and predicts widespread civil disobedience. 'It's very difficult to fight a law that isn't a law yet. England is slow to wake up, but when we do, we're going to have mass trespasses; we'll fill up the jails, bankrupt the system. This is a last gasp by the Tories to strangle the country – and it won't work!'

The origins of both squatting and traveling go back several centuries. The current wave of squatting began in the 1960s, when homeless families and young hippies took over a huge number of derelict, unoccupied properties. At least a third of today's squatters are families. But in addition to providing an alternative to homelessness, squatting became an enclave of alternative culture, from hippie through punk, indie rock to rave. Bob Geldof, Annie Lennox, Boy George, Seal, and members of the Shamen, Depeche Mode, My Bloody Valentine, and Stereolab all squatted. Johnny Rotten squatted with pal Sid Vicious after being kicked out of his house; Joe Strummer has talked of his decision to squat as both a practical solution and an ideological choice 'based on recognition of the futility and stupidity of work'. Also on the list of former squatters are Eric Clapton, Virgin honcho Richard Branson, Dave Stewart, and Mark Knopfler: now four of the richest men in England.

One week after the march on Trafalgar Square, I'm in Clissold Park for the Hackney Homeless Festival. Hackney is London's most squatted borough, and twice as many people turn out today as did for the march. Stalls sell veggie food, books, batik clothes, and distribute leaflets on everything from ecological issues to human rights. Jugglers drift between tents housing crafts workshops, techno sound systems, and rock bands. An endless patchwork of rainbow-hued clothing dazzles the eye.

Everywhere people are sitting in loose circles, rolling joints. As soon as I crouch down, Nelson grins and offers me one for my own. He's dressed head to toe in wonderful clashing garments, looking like some medieval jester, a yellow hat bobbing on his head. Nelson and his companion Izzy don't want to think about the bill much at the moment because they're tripping.

Nelson lives in the Crescent, a street full of derelict, squatted Victorian houses. You can tell these were once lovely buildings; now some have holes in the floors, and many lack proper bathrooms or kitchens. The houses have been squatted for a decade, but current residents have just received eviction notices.

When I visit the Crescent ten days later, Andy and Nuala, members of Tofu Love Frogs, a popular festival band, have already moved half their stuff out. They're leaving for the Forest Fayre festival tomorrow, and no one knows if the Crescent will be boarded up when they get back. What's left are some cassettes, dirty dishes, a pane of stained glass, and a drum kit. Andy decides to chase down a welfare check that never arrived and, promising to be back in 20 minutes, leaves me with his neighbor Victoria. He returns nine hours later. Squatter time?

Victoria is looking disheveled – she was hoping to use Andy's bathtub. Clad in a pink baby-doll nightie complete with faded bloodstains, her face emits a healthy glow despite the cultivated disarray. Victoria and her best friend Zal are squatting veterans. Zal is unemployed. ('It's probably the way I look,' she says. 'I even tried to do art modeling but they didn't want me because of all the piercings.') Victoria works as an 'exotic dancer' and is in a band called Silt. Zal squats because 'it's so much nicer to live someplace where no one's profiting, everyone's living communally and is so much happier.' As for the argument that squatters' squalor is a nuisance to the community, she protests: 'Maybe that's true sometimes, but the Crescent is self-contained. All the noise and drugs are *here*, and the other people are over *there*.' Everyone laughs as she gestures out the window. Neighbors and friends pop in and out of the flats all day for tea, a chat, a joint. Most are in the process of packing up the caravan of buses outside. The rest are out scouting for new homes.

Hackney has created a task force to clear out squatters. Councillor Simon Matthews, the chairman of Housing, assures me that 'there's nothing sinister in evicting squatters. We wouldn't evict people if we didn't have a use for the property.' He tells me that the Crescent has been sold to a local housing association which plans to repair the place and provide 33 apartments for poor families.

Most of the squatters I meet, however, barrage me with stories about the lengths to which local governments go to keep empty houses empty: cementing plumbing, smashing bathtubs, erecting steel doors. Sara lives in another part of Hackney, and, like most squatters, she doesn't want to cheat anyone needy out of a home. But, she sighs, 'the first place I lived, we got evicted, and they said they were going to turn the place into a hostel for single women. We thought, "Fair enough" and moved out. And it's *still* derelict. They've taken off the roof now so no one can move in.'

Unlike the Crescent, Sara's squat doesn't advertise itself; a lot of effort has been put into fixing up this big old house. Overstuffed chairs are jammed into the cozy living room like too many teeth into a mouth, and grand fireplaces have been rehabilitated in several rooms. Everyone here works – there's a teacher, a dancer, a herbal-medicine student. Sara's boyfriend, Ronnie, is a stonemason and used to travel with the rave sound system Bedlam. 'I squat because if I don't house myself, no one will,' he says mournfully.

For most of the others in the house, though, it's as much about lifestyle as shelter. 'One of the unspoken rules of squats,' says Sara, 'is that you generally have to let people do what they want within reason.' Creativity flourishes amid squat culture; in a sense, it's the last bastion of British bohemia. For alternative-rock bands in England, squatting has always been the great enabler. Bilinda Butcher of My Bloody Valentine claims, 'MBV wouldn't have gotten anywhere if we hadn't been able to squat. If the bill is passed, I don't know how bands starting out will manage. The whole music scene will suffer. There'll only be room for mainstream stuff.' Squats have long fostered innovative music and art, providing free rehearsal space and allowing musicians to devote their meager income to buying equipment. Thousands of people who otherwise would be forced into a nine-to-five existence are able to make music their priority.

Anjali is a perfect example. She's lived in a squatted house for six years and has shared it with dozens of musician friends. Voodoo Queens, her Riot Grrrl-meets-metal band, released its first LP on the hip Too Pure label last year. The squat has a practice room and an art studio covered with Anjali's perverse doll sculptures. A rusted disco glitter ball sits dejectedly in the backyard, too big to fit through the door. Every nook is stuffed with delicate clutter. The only drawbacks are that the toilet is outside and the bathtub is in the kitchen. 'It was more fun when there were loads of people living here,' she laughs. 'Someone would be cooking their dinner and you'd be taking a bath and having a good old chat!'

Anjali moved into her first squat after leaving home at 18. She wonders what bands will do after the bill is passed. 'There's no way we'd have been able to afford a practice room and pay rent to live.' And for a lot of kids like Anjali, it was the communal aspect of squatting that made the punk-rock experience real. 'There used to be this really great punk squat in the late 80s called Lee House,' she recalls. 'It had a place to skateboard; they sold records and T-shirts, and we all took turns serving food. Things were so boring back then, and Lee House was a real community. When the bailiffs came round to evict, we marched down to town hall and barricaded ourselves in. We didn't let it go without a fight. It makes me so sad to think squatting's over.'

CoolTan Arts is engaged in a present-day struggle for survival. A community-arts collective housed in an abandoned welfare office, it has for two years been home to exhibitions, raves, multimedia events like the Exploding Cinema series, T'ai Chi classes, and a cheap, friendly café. (Cool-Tan's name comes form its original site, an abandoned suntan-lotion factory.) There are other squatted cafés and art centers around London, but people love the way CoolTan integrates squat culture with the multiracial neighborhood. The local government put the building up for sale, however, and CoolTan has been throwing jam-packed all-night parties to raise enough money to buy it.

The main room is a dance floor tonight. It's decorated with happy little houses painted on sheets, and the ecstasy casualty dancing next to me leans on one and falls over. 'I thought it was a wall,' he grins, dusting himself off. Stumbling through curtains at the back, we find black and white rastas dancing in total darkness to bass-quaking dub reggae. Over in the chilled-out ambient room, slackers sprawl on cushions; one guy with flaxen dreadlocks and an Elmer Fudd hunting cap leaps about like a sprite, waving his joss stick like it's a sparkler. Later, as we leave the building, the DJ spins the old Bow Wow Wow song 'W.O.R.K.', with its motto: 'Work is *not* the Golden Rule!'

Free festivals have always been crucial to the travelers' sense of community. In the past, hippie convoys journeyed to mystical sites, tripping out to the mystical jams of Hawkwind. It was at Stonehenge in 1985 that travelers first entered public consciousness when the police violently disrupted summer solstice celebrations – a clash now mythologized in traveler folklore as the Battle of the Beanfield. (Margaret Thatcher gloated: 'I am only too pleased to make life as difficult as possible for these hippie convoys.') In the late 1980s, the scene was revitalized by its alliance with rave, culminating in 1992's massive Castlemorton festival, a six-day-long party in a field, attended by about 30,000 people. 'Castlemorton was the turning point,' says Harry of the DIY sound system. 'We had our sound system going for about 137 hours! I think it scared the shit out of the government and the police – and the bill is the result of that.' Public outcries over litter, noise, and damage to land put ravers and travelers on the defensive, and the battle lines were drawn: property owners versus society's great unwashed.

Even before the bill went to Parliament, the police had launched an intelligence drive against New Age travelers and ravers called 'Operation Snapshot', logging information on individuals and vehicles into a computer database in order to keep tabs on their whereabouts and thwart another Castlemorton-style mega-rave. 'The travelers have been victimized for years now,' says Sam, a longtime member of the Mutoid Waste Company, a semi-nomadic group who became infamous in the 80s for its junk sculptures and wild free parties. 'If someone chooses to live out in the freezing cold and chop wood every day, why should he be forced to go into a flat, have a telephone, pay electricity, rent, water bills? He doesn't want that – all he wants is to be left in peace.

'In discussions of travelers and the bill, everybody seems to neglect the fact that the hippie movement is almost 30 years old. In some cases it's now three generations of travelers – kids whose parents went on the road in the '60s and brought them up there are now bringing up their own kids. The party stuff is peripheral. What's really important is the need for people to exist as they please.' Already, though, travelers are being squeezed from every side: brutal attacks by local 'vigilantes' are on the rise; the authorities frequently threaten to take travelers' children away; and police regularly, often violently, drive convoys off land. Once travelers were able to live on a site for months or years. Now they're lucky if it's a week.

'I had five evictions in two days,' says Matt, a traveler who's parked in a small, dingy site near a canal. 'So we drove onto a place owned by the Sultan of Brunei, 'cause it was the most rundown, derelict wasteland around. Pull onto somewhere horrible and you get left alone – that's why we're here.' The first thing you hear when you reach the site is furious barking: German shepherds bounding toward you, en masse. And a girl flailing her arms and shrieking back at the mutts: *'Shut up you stupid dogs!'* Trucks, cars, and vans are parked haphazardly. Inside, Matt's trailer is dark (even though it's mid-afternoon) and slightly musty; beside the door is a tiny antique-looking stove with a tea kettle on top.

Lucy, a petite woman with multicolored hair and bright yellow leggings, pops in to regale us with her adventures. 'I went to a festival and never went back again. Not many people consciously think, "I'll be a traveler." I just decided I didn't want to go back to where I was living, I wanted to be in the countryside.' It's a common initiation tale. When I ask what she *does* in the countryside, Lucy smiles knowingly, 'You just *live*, go for walks, sit around fires, talk to friends, have a good time.'

Matt's saving up to leave England now – a lot of travelers he knows are fleeing to more tolerant parts of Europe. Others have given up on the nomadic lifestyle and returned to squatting. Like Sara's boyfriend, Ronnie, who says, 'You can only get hit over the head so many times with a truncheon before you think, "Maybe I should just get a house and settle down . . ." '

The rave scene is also embattled. The government spent £4 million taking Spiral Tribe, a sound system, to court for its involvement in Castlemorton – and lost. Spurred on by the attacks, over 100 sound systems joined together as the Advance Party to organize a pressure group for ravers. Nobody is sure what the future holds. Chantal of Open Mind, which throws ambient 'tea parties' in squatted spaces, says, 'Either we go deep underground or we go into the legal clubs. I think the legal things are great for weekend party people because it's convenient and you're guaranteed 12 hours of fun. But there are all those people out there who don't have jobs or money, and the government is better off letting them entertain themselves, or else they're going to lash out in some worse, violent way.'

From a way of life to part-time free spirit? Many sound systems like DIY have already gone legitimate via record labels and legal club nights. Megadog, one of the few commercial clubs to win respect in the community, strives to get as close to the festival vibe as possible. Says Michael Dog, 'We saw we wouldn't last too long unless we appeared to play by straight society's rules. But squats, free festivals, and raves – they've been the breeding ground for creativity and humanistic politics. Squatting allows people not to go straight into the grindstone of the working world. It sustains alternative art and culture, which eventually filters through to mainstream society.'

The Criminal Justice Bill is a concerted effort to rein in the counter-culture; some call it 'cultural cleansing'. It's also an attack on the idea of public, communal space. Big cities can be lonely places – especially if you're unemployed, with little hope for the future. Like many on the scene, Dog believes the government is upping the ante, creating an underclass that has nothing left to lose. 'For years, parties went on happily with the tacit approval of local police. When the police attitude became more extreme, people who would've once made an effort to be considerate stopped bothering – it's resulted in a "fuck you" attitude.'

Back in Hackney, Sara also worries that the government's demonization of squatters will become a self-fulfilling prophecy. 'The Criminal Justice Bill will create a more radical type of squatter. It's not going to be the amicable person who just wants to get on with life, it's gonna be people who'll do whatever it takes.' As one young squatter told me grimly: 'You'll have to decide if you want to be part of the system or not. The government is drawing the line, not us.'

Some of the names in this article have been changed.

Joy Press, Spin, October 1994

1994: Passing Poison

The window in the boys' toilet made me think of my first cigarette. I smoked it there, beneath the window, in the company of my friend Mark, a tricky young Ayrshire hero of the mid-1970s. In those days, the toilet served the male patrons – paying and non-paying, coughing and non-coughing – of the Regal Cinema, a splendid two-tier picture palace, all art deco and curvy banisters, bang in the centre of Saltcoats. It was run by a frosty old geezer, Harry Kemp, who also owned the La Scala picture house over the road. The first film shown at the Regal was the Foreign Legion epic *Beau Ideal*. At the time of its showing, in 1931, Saltcoats was a bustling seaside resort, with train loads of Glaswegians breezing down the west coast to holiday in the sand bordering our little patch along the Firth of Clyde – and to play awhile, I imagine, while they were about it, among the billowing sands served up by the goodly Mr Kemp. The paintwork in the Regal was already yellow as I lit up my first cigarette, and by the mid-1980s it was shut down; La Scala lasted up until last year. The Regal became a nightclub called the Metropolis.

Up in the toilet, things were busier than they used to be. The Metro, like other clubs steadily tuning in to the new dance culture at the turn of the 1980s, set out to fashion itself as some sort of contender in the fight for the attentions of young, steamy west-coasters out looking for some late-night leisure land. And there it was: the Metropolis. In far off cities, in lesser heavens, punters called the new drugs 'recession lifters', others talked of 'the goodness'; in central Scotland, where we fancied we knew one or two things about recession, drugs like Ecstasy – and the shacks in which taking Ecstasy could seem like a discrete but important matter of house policy – had a weird and temporarily wonderful power. All delusion, of course, but that's that.

The flashy, anodyne disco scene felt dead; the zitty, depressed independent rock life was over; and all the wee ravers seemed lucid and happy and optimistic. Punky pals went hugging on to the dancefloor, full of E and tired of being tired, and for five minutes or so – for not very long at all – there was a general uplift, a wholesome grappling with the good life. For that short period there was a marked alteration, not only in mood, but in outlook. It was something to see. And, as far as youth cults are ever relevant or interesting or significant, it seemed that things would never really be the same way round, at least not round our way.

Taking the drug was never thought of as abuse, that would have been an untruthful and stupid way of describing how it worked for people. The guys who sold it weren't pushers, they were pals of pals. Factory blokes began to talk of studying at night, taking a course, getting really and properly out of it, going to university. People who took Ecstasy seemed to know what they were doing – and it was Ecstasy, not some spurious, dafter poison – and they tended to mind each other, to look after one another in clubs, in ways that would look shocking to those used to drinking warily in bars. Even at the time, those chirpy ravers would say that it couldn't last. And neither it could. And neither did it.

James McCabe was already dead on arrival at North Ayrshire General Hospital, late on Saturday 10 September, after a night spent at the Metro. A 21-year-old DJ from Glasgow, he was often to be seen at techno-dance events and popular hardcore raves around Strathclyde. James had his own band, Reactive Bass, specialising in what one Glasgow magazine called 'the sound of full-throttle techno terror'. In an interview given to the magazine, James, concerned at the deaths of three young ravers at the Hanger 13 club in Ayr earlier in the summer, advised his band's fans to 'take your time, life is for living'. On the night he died, the Metro was said to be especially chaotic, more than usually 'mental'. Though toxicologists have still to prove it, those who hang around the club, the kids who take the drugs and know the scene, say James snorted between three and four large broken-down tablets of what he believed was Ecstasy. He was spotted shaking and sweating at the side of the dancefloor, and later collapsed. Three other punters took ill at the club on the same night, but signed out of hospital once they were in the clear.

The evening after James McCabe's funeral, seven days after he collapsed at the club, I waited outside with a queue of ravers, a baggy line of teenagers jittering in the cold and clearly uneasy in the presence of so many police. A couple of coppers stood in a recess over by the boarded-up La Scala. The girl in front of me worried over a few cannabis joints; she was trying to find some corner of her body in which to stash them. The lobby of the club was full of

CID, busily interviewing clubbers and asking for identification. After a fairly intimate but fruitless search by security staff, the hash-girl in front stopped at a table being manned by a walkie-talkie and a clipboard.

'Wit dae ye want ma name for?' she said, a bit paranoid and fed-up.

'Don't you know there was a death here last week,' said the clipboard. The walkie-talkie inspected my old student card.

'I wisnae here last week,' said the girl.

Inside, it was roasting. The dancers, even this early on in the night, were all pumping and sweating and jerking on the spot. Joe Deacon, the DJ, would salute them through the flurry of the soundtrack, urging them on, telling them to 'Go', driving the sound – a purely intoxicating miasma of bleeps and looped rattles – with encouraging chants. A voice on the record emits a deep, bassy exhortation: 'Suck the beat, suck the beat.' And the lights dig in with the music, flashing in sync with the beat, and as the record whips ahead, the lights become like strobes. So fast it's like slow motion, the record eventually hits what might be its climax, all hands go up in the air, the lights white-out, bleaching the crowd, and it's on to the next tune. Most of the stuff this guy is playing runs at around 140 beats per minute: the kids keep up, clearly locked into something exhilarating and fantastic.

So maybe I grow old, I'm thinking, as I stroll to the toilet. You've probably already thought of that, but so have I, and I've thought about it enough to know that it doesn't by itself float the raft of my sudden alienation from this kind of gig. There's something else (but more of that in a minute). In the toilet, the boys pack round the sinks, sucking water out of the taps, splashing some over their heads, under their arms. And under my familiar window, two guys exchange opinions about what they've taken, about how mad it is or isn't. I'm at a sink, still into my train of thought about oldie-ness, when I hear one guy whisper to the other, as if to confirm the matter of my sizzling head: 'Check the DS in the green jacket. Check um out.' So that's it, is it? Drugs Squad? I know I grow old.

I go back in as the DJ addresses the crowd about James McCabe's death. He orders one minute's silence; the folk around me, all along the balcony, still sway and rattle to the beat from seconds before. But most of them put their heads down. The whole club goes quiet, except for the weird sound of a girl sobbing. As the lights and music crank up again, the DJ says – in his own voice, not the American one most DJs use when talking through a mike – 'James. We're goin' tae miss ye pal.' And then they're off. Some jig up and down from the bar, sipping bottles of Caledonian Spring at a pound a throw.

Punters come from all over Scotland's central belt to attend hardcore techno-dance events at places like the Metro in Saltcoats and Hanger 13, a club 12 miles up the coast in Ayr. These raves are well attended and well enough run, though Hanger 13 has been accused of turning off water taps to increase bar profits. The club has opened its doors to inspectors, to MPs and to the news media, and it appears that the accusations are without truth. There is plenty of water at Hanger 13 – in the toilets, at the bar – and they serve ice-poles and cold drinks from the cloakroom. Today there is on-site medical help, tight security and close involvement with local drug agencies, like the brilliantly pragmatic and realistic Bridge Project in Ayr, which does its best to handle a changing and fairly complex local drug culture, doing it very humanly, with few questions asked.

I leaned against the bar of the Hanger's cloakroom late on a Saturday night a few weeks ago, watching the dancers, who came up smiling, many of them wearing white gloves, some clutching day-glo sticks or luminous discs. As they fetched coats and sweat-tops, bought cold drinks and ices and chatted to the staff, many would stop to scribble on a sheaf of paper stacked beside me. I looked down at the paper to read what it said. It was a photocopied message which had been written up roughly, with a grid underneath for names, ages and addresses, drawn up just as roughly with an unsteady ruler:

> 'Please sign our petition and help prevent Hanger 13 from closure. The management and security have done everything possible to prevent any drug problem and any other trouble! Closing the Hanger is unfair to the management, the security and a lot of innocent ravers. The stewards search everyone thoroughly on entry and inside do a great job keeping everything under control. Why persecute a lot of innocent people when most of the problem is outside not only in Ayr but in every other town and city across Britain! Closing the Hanger down will not solve the problem.'

Police in Strathclyde admit they can hardly control the use and abuse of recreational drugs. And clubs where fatalities have occurred, like Hanger 13, are doing what they can. Drug advice leaflets lay scattered on chairs and bar-tops around the club when I visited it. A handmade poster titled 'Legal Status' was Blu-tacked around the walls; the first entry on it said 'Ecstasy: MDMA is a CLASS A (schedule 1) controlled drug. This means it is an offence to possess the drug and supply it to others. MAXIMUM PENALTY

– FOR POSSESSION, 7 YEARS, FOR DEALING, LIFE.' It had entries for acid and speed and for 'Jellies: TEMAZEPAM is a prescription-only medicine and a CLASS C controlled drug (schedule 4). It may be possessed in medicinal form without a prescription but it is an offence to possess it prepared for injection or to supply it to others.'

The DJ tries to bring the level down a bit, slowing the speed; talking to the punters through the mike, asking them to chill out. 'Here's some good music,' he shouts, 'no more of that one-note shite.' The resident DJ is Trevor Reilly. He's 33, and has watched the rave scene grow harder and the number of people involved in it 'explode'. He worries about the taboo nature of the rave culture, the way MPs and licensing boards play political games, ignoring the reality of it, the facts of it, and calling for closures instead of promoting education and advice.

'If a kid is taking five Ecstasy in one night, or mixing things, or whatever, then you need someone to get involved, someone to come out and tell them that that's no use. But as soon as you print up leaflets or whatever, because of the taboos, the authorities see it as an admission that you have a drug problem.' Fraser MacIntyre, who runs the club night and who tried to revive one of the boys who collapsed and later died, wondered, as I spoke to him, about the problems of responsibility.

'Isn't it a problem of society?' he asked. 'They don't deal with alcoholics by closing down pubs. If somebody sprays a crowd with bullets, they might ask what influenced that act. They look at society. But with this, you know, they don't have the bottle. So we get it all and, I'll tell you, this is no joke to us.'

The old Pavilion complex at Ayr which contains Hanger 13 – its four corner towers and clock-without-hands dominate the shore – has been owned by one family for more than 20 years. It is a famous venue in the area, having promoted and purveyed most kinds of dancing events and musical dos, popular with punters over the past two decades, from rock operas to afternoon tea-dances. The people who work there are quite traumatised by the deaths; they understand the techno-dance scene; they may understand that drugs are part of that scene, but they deplore, as everyone does, the idea of healthy kids dying while trying to have a night out.

In a room set aside for relatives at Ayr Hospital, they have pot-pourri in a dish by the window and a carpet that smells like it's recovering from a recent vacuuming. Dr Leo Murray sits there, with the look of Friedrich Engels, or Dostoevsky, or Jesus Christ in gold circular specs. Dr Murray is a consultant in the Accident and Emergency Department; he tried to save the lives of the boys who died at Ayr. 'When people think of this part of the world,' he says, 'they think of golf and horse-racing and seascape and Burns and all that. But there's another world, another one I come into contact with every day.'

I asked him about the boys.

'We get young people in here every week of the year,' he replies. 'Kids walking around crazy, not knowing what they've taken, all of them dry, hot, some of them anxious, not having a good time. The first two fatalities came into intensive care and it was clear they were in trouble, that what they'd taken was doing them no good. We gave them intravenous fluid and monitored their condition very closely. Yet they suffered a simultaneous failure of every major organ. Everything went. And that's very upsetting – we're talking about very healthy young men here.'

Dr Murray observes that the worst cases show signs of something he calls 'malignant hyperplexia', but can't say for sure what brings them to that condition. Some doctors believe it's heat stroke; others will only say that heat exhaustion seems to exacerbate whatever else is going wrong in the raver's body. Dr Murray knows – from his weekly experience, not just from the cases which draw public attention – that some young people in his area will take anything to get 'aff their heids'. And such people are not always living in his area; raves attract large numbers from outlying places, and he becomes responsible for them if they take something toxic in Ayr. The clubs, I say, would it then be useful to close them?

'No,' he says, 'I don't think so. This is my opinion. But MPs could drive it underground. I'd rather they kept the club there – at least that way I know where they are. That way, maybe, we can encourage medical supervision, we can try to have people there who can spot trouble, who might be able to deal with people who've taken something which is doing them no good.'

So what is happening, why has the rave scene – formerly so florid and replenishing, so clever and communal – become the aggressive, crazy and now and then deadly thing that it has? Half a million or so people are into it; why is something so apparently exuberant and lively now charged with such negativity? Why do people die? The answers are simple and complex, known and unknown. But the first thing to say is that fewer die than you'd think from reading the tabloids. The famous (and famously non-tabloid) comparisons with alcohol and nicotine are powerful: hundreds of thousands in Scotland die of drink and smoke every year. There were 73 drug-related deaths in Strathclyde in 1992. Yet police say the figures are escalating quite fiercely, and comparisons with drink and smoke tend to dissolve in the face of the relative youth and the element of surprise in drug fatalities. The Greater Glasgow Health Board recently felt able to state that 'Fatal overdose among drug injectors has become the most important single cause of death among young adults' in their area. Once upon a time, that sentence would not have been relevant to the experience of ravers. But there's been a swift and deadly (though nowhere near complete) blending of worlds. In Strathclyde, as well as other areas like Dundee, certain prescription drugs have gained common currency in the formerly estranged worlds of raving and injecting.

Where places like Edinburgh have seen an enormous decrease, over the past few years of Aids awareness and all that, of intravenous drug use, Glasgow has witnessed an incredible rise in the number who use syringes. And they are not, most of them, injecting heroin. In the mid-1980s, illicit supplies of heroin began to dry up in Strathclyde and junkies started, in droves, to inject prescribed pharmaceutical products, especially Temazepam and Temgesic. Capsules are on sale all over the place for between £1 and £3 each. Drug companies, aware of the escalating abuse, introduced gel-filled capsules (non-intravenous). In Glasgow's High Court a couple of years ago, I heard an addict, accused of running a black market in prescribed Temazepam, speaking from the witness box, describe how users would heat the gel and break it down that way before injecting. Doctors tell of the hellish damage to muscle tissues and of lost limbs due to the widespread injection of this hot tranquilliser.

A Scottish Affairs Committee report on drug abuse in Scotland, published in April this year, quoted one Glasgow GP who alleged that 'in his area almost half of the children who had attended a particular secondary school class had injected drugs'. It spoke of youths who couldn't bear reality, and who would take anything to alter their perception of it. Most of the drug addicts in that parts of the world (and in others too) are into drug 'cocktails': powerful analgesics, tranquillisers and painkillers like the ones I've described are being injected with bits of heroin and other corrupted mixtures of Class A narcotics. Some don't inject, but swallow, in the streets with their pals, and tons of them are into strong and cheap drink, like Buckfast Tonic Wine. (The makers of this wine, the monks of Buckfast Abbey in Devon, don't deny that around 80 per cent of the stuff sells in areas just outside Glasgow.) A vast black market has opened up in knock-off pills; pharmacists in Scotland, due to the increase in break-ins and hold-ups, have found themselves having to erect metal shutters on shop fronts and wire grilles over counters.

Like I've been saying, a few years ago, all this took place in a different world from the one where kids took E at raves over the weekend. To me, the clearest explanation of the change in the rave scene is not bad clubs or heat exhaustion or gangster promoters or lack of water – though all of these, in some places and in many cases, have been seriously troublesome – but the changing nature of the drugs. The cocktails that now matter so much to injectors happen also, whether they like it or not, to matter to the dancing kids who wouldn't know a needle from a five pound note. The Ecstasy they're buying isn't Ecstasy – it seems, most often, to be some concoction of crude heroin, ketamine (used in large doses to sedate and to kill animals), dirty speed and debased, rough, cheap forms of Ecstasy's chemical parent, MDA – derivatives which no one properly recognises or understands. Many tablets have no Ecstasy in them at all. And you'll sometimes hear ravers use new second-hand names for this stuff: 'Eves', 'Ice'.

The dealers don't know what they're dealing and the buyers don't know what they're buying. And Temazepam, that capsulated semi-coma, is to be found at hardcore raves, being taken along with the other stuff, getting people high and aggressive and able to climb up to the speed and harshness of the music. Prescription drugs are bridging the gap – no, the former gulf – between the rave scene and the morose world of hard and addictive drugs. You'd hear people, a few years ago, begin to talk of 'jellies', of 'eggs', little Temazepams that were to bring about much of the change. Ecstasy proper was already dead, and some of the old crowd – taken apart by acid and the dodgier stuff now doing the rounds – found themselves anxious, depressed and subject to little bursts of psychosis on the weekdays when they tried to work and live as normal.

Former and occasional clubbers now talk about 'good E' the way some people talk about lost innocence. You can't get it back. But the rave scene goes on, as it probably should, on its own terms. I suppose each new generation, or each coming phase of a generation, should be free to choose its own poisons. It's just that nobody really expects to die. In Amsterdam, little labs sit at the side of some clubs, cutting samples off the drugs that people buy, checking them, telling people what they are, warning them if they're unsafe. In Britain, the children choose their poison in the dark, waiting for someone to kill them.

Andrew O'Hagan, Observer Life magazine, 9 October 1994

Acknowledgements

Many thanks to the following: Vince Aletti, Murray Chalmers, Malcolm Imrie, Spencer Leigh, Joe Levy, Andy Linehan and the National Sound Archive, Charles Shaar Murray, Peter Paphides, Christopher Petit, Steve Redhead, Simon Reynolds, Hillegonda Rietveld, Alex Seago, Ian Sinclair, Mark Sinker, Mike Soutar, Neil Tennant, Steven Wells.

With special thanks to Penny Henry, Angie and Johnny Marr and David Martin.

For permission to reprint copyright material the publishers gratefully acknowledge the following:

VINCE ALETTI: from the *Village Voice*, March 18–24 1981. RICHARD ALLEN: from *Teeny Bopper Idol* (New English Library, 1973). GINA ARNOLD: from *Route 666: On The Road To Nirvana* (St Martins Press, 1933. LESTER BANGS: from *Psychotic Reactions and Carburetor Dung*. 1987 trans. Greil Marcus. © 1987 by the Estate of Lester Bangs. Reprinted by permission of Alfred A. Knopf Inc. Published in the UK by William Heinemann Ltd. Reprinted by permission of Reed Consumer Books Ltd. RICHARD BARNES: from *The Who* (St Martins Press, 1982). CHUCK BERRY: from *The Autobiography*. Reprinted by permission of Faber & Faber Ltd. BRUCE BLIVEN: from *New Republic*, 6.11.44. STANLEY BOOTH: 'Rhythm Oil' from *The Memphis Soul Sound* (Jonathan Cape, 1991). Reprinted by permission of Random House UK Ltd. 'Dance to the Death' from *The True Adventures of the Rolling Stones* (Heinemann, 1988). MICHAEL BRACEWELL: from *The Conclave* (Secker & Warburg Ltd). © 1992 by Michael Bracewell. Reprinted by permission of Curtis Brown, London and Reed Consumer Books Ltd. MICHAEL BRAUN: from *Love Me Do: The Beatles* Progress (Penguin Books UK Ltd, 1964). © Michael Braun. Reprinted by permission of Jonathan Clowes Ltd, London, on behalf of Michael Braun. ROSETTA BROOKS: from ZG, no.1, 1980. JAMES BROWN: from *James Brown: The Godfather of Soul*, with Bruce Tucker (Sidgwick & Jackson, 1987). © 1986 by James Brown and Bruce Tucker. Reprinted by permission of Macmillan Publishers Ltd and Simon & Schuster Inc. MICK BROWN: from the *Sunday Times Magazine* 12.4.87. © Times Newspapers Ltd, 1987. Reprinted with permission. ANTHONY BURGESS: from *A Clockwork Orange* (William Heinemann, 1962). © Estate of Anthony Burgess. Reprinted by permission of Reed Consumer Books Ltd and Artellus Ltd. PETER BURTON: from *Parallel Lives* (Gaymens Press, 1985). Reprinted by permission of the author. ANGELA CARTER: 'Notes for a Theory of Sixties Style' from *Nothing Sacred*. Reprinted by permission of Virago Press and Rogers, Coleridge & White Ltd. 'Ups and Downs for the Babes in Bondage' from *New Statesman* 22.12.77. Reprinted by permission of Guardian Media Group plc. ROBERT CHRISTGAU: from *Any Old Way You Choose It* (Penguin Books Ltd, 1973). MAUREEN CLEAVE: from the *Evening Standard* 4.3.66. Reprinted by permission of Solo Syndication and Literary Agency Ltd. NICK COHN: 'Another Saturday Night' from *Ball The Wall* (Picador). 'The Rolling Stones' from *Pop From the Beginning* (Weidenfeld & Nicolson Ltd, 1969). 'Carnaby Street. Part One' from *Today There Are No Gentlemen*. Reprinted by permission of George Weidenfeld & Nicolson Ltd. CAROLINE COON: from *Melody Maker* 7.8.76. Reprinted by permission of the author. FRANK CORDELL: from *Ark*, Spring 1957. STUART COSGROVE: from *The Face*, May 1988. Reprinted by permission of the author. NOËL COWARD: from *The Noël Coward Diaries*. © 1982 by Graham Payn. Reprinted by permission of Michael Imison Playwrights Ltd, 28 Almeida St, London, N1 1TD. LIONEL CRANE: from the *Daily Mirror* 30.4.56. MARTHA DIAWARA: from *Black Popular Culture* (Bay Press, 1992). JOAN DIDION: from *The White Album* (HarperCollins Publishers Ltd). STEVE DIXON: from *i-D Magazine*, No.11, 1981. RICHARD DYER: from *Gay Left*, Summer, 1979. BOB DYLAN: from sleeve notes for *Bringing It All Back Home*, 1965. ROYSTON ELLIS: from *The Big Beat Scene* (New English Library, 1961). RALPH ELLISON: from *Invisible Man* (Penguin Books, 1952). © 1952 by Ralph Ellison. Reprinted by permission of Laurence Pollinger Ltd and Random House Inc. ROBERT ELMS: from *The Face*, September, 1982. Reprinted by permission of the author. BRIAN EPSTEIN: from *A Cellarful of Noise*. Reprinted by permission of the Souvenir Press. KODWO ESHUN: from *Wire*, December 1992 – January 1993. JENNY FABIAN and JOHNNY BYRNE: 'Satin Odyssey' (Mayflower, 1970). BOB FEIGAL: from *The Beat*, 27.11.65. PETE FOWLER: from *Rock File*, ed. Charlie Gillet (New English Library, 1972). MARK FRITH: from *Smash Hits*, August, 1993. SIMON FRITH: from *Village Voice*, 10.10.84. DONNA GAINES: from *Teenage Wasteland*. © 1991 by Donna Gaines. Reprinted by permission of Pantheon Books, a division of Random House Inc. SIMON GARFIELD: 'Young Guns Fall For It (Again)' from *Expensive Habits* (Faber and Faber Ltd, 1986). Reprinted by permission of Peters Fraser & Dunlop Ltd and 'This Charming Man' reprinted by permission of *Time Out*, March, 1985. SHERYL GARRETT: from *Signed, Sealed and Delivered*. Reprinted by permission of Pluto Press. NELSON GEORGE: from 'Goin Off In Cali' from *Buppies, B-Boys, Baps and Boho's*. © 1993 by Nelson George. Reprinted by permission of HarperCollins Publishers Inc. GORDON GLOVER: from *Picture Post*, 3.2.45. Reprinted by permission of Hulton Deutsch Collection. DAVID GODIN: from *Soul Music Magazine*, March, 1968. RICHARD GOLDSTEIN: 'A Quiet Evening At the Balloon Farm' from *New York Magazine*, 1960. 'Gear' © 1966 by The Village Voice Inc. JACK GOOD: 'The Same Fantastic Feeling For Beat', *Disc Magazine*, 5.8.67. RAY GOSLING: from *Sum Total*. Reprinted by permission of Faber and Faber Ltd. GERMAINE GREER: from *Oz*, November, 1969. Reprinted by permission of Aitken, Stone & Wylie Ltd. STUART GREIG: Michael McCarthy and John Peacock, from *Daily Mirror*, 2.12.76. PETER GURALNICK: from *Sweet Soul Music* (Penguin Books UK, 1991: Harper & Row USA, 1986). Reprinted by permission of Andrew Mann Ltd on behalf of the author. CHARLES HAMBLETT and JANE DEVERSON: from *Generation X* (Tandem Books, 1964). MARY

1994. Reprinted by permission of the Guardian Media Group plc. JOHN ORMOND THOMAS: from *Picture Post*, 4.10.47. Reprinted by permission of Hulton Deutsch Collection. JOE ORTON: from *The Orton Diaries* (Methuen, London, 1987). Reprinted by permission of Reed Consumer Books Ltd. MARK PERRY: from *Sniffin' Glue*, 5.12.76. TONY PARSONS: from *New Musical Express*, 2.4.77. Reprinted by permission of IPC Magazines Ltd. JEAN PETER: from *Let It Rock*, January, 1975. TREVOR PHILPOTT: from *Picture Post*, 25.2.57. Reprinted by permission of Hulton Deutsch Collection. IGGY POP: from *I Need More* (Karz Cohl Press, 1982). ANN POWERS: from *Village Voice*, 19.4.94. JOY PRESS: from *Spin*, October, 1994. LOU REED: from *Between Thought and Expression: Selected Lyrics* (Viking, 1992). © Metal Music Machine, Inc. 1990, 1991. Reprinted by permission of Penguin Books Ltd. WILLIAM REES-MOGG: from *The Times*, 1.7.67. © Times Newspapers Ltd, 1967. Used with permission. PENNY REEL: 'Better Must Come' from *Pressure Drop*, August, 1975 and 'Timin' is the Thing' from *Let It Rock*, May, 1975. SIMON REYNOLDS: 'Rage to Live: 'Ardkore Techno' was originally published under the title 'Technical Ecstasy' in *Wire*, November 1992. Reprinted by permission of Simon Reynolds. All rights reserved. DAVE RIMMER: 'The Eastie Boys' from *Once Upon a Time in the East* (Fourth Estate, 1992). Reprinted by permission of Peake Associates. 'The Birth of the New Pop' from *Like Punk Never Happened*. Reprinted by permission of Faber and Faber Ltd. ED SAUNDERS: from *The Family* (Hart Davies, 1971). CHARLES SHAAR MURRAY: from *New Musical Express*, 1974. Reprinted by permission of IPC Magazines Ltd. ROBERT SHELTON: from *No Direction Home* (New English Library, 1986). JOSEPH C. SMITH: from *The Day The Music Died* (Carrol & Graf Publishers, 1981). MIKE SOUTAR: from *Smash Hits*, December, 1990. NEIL SPENCER: from *New Musical Express*, February, 1976. Reprinted by permission of IPC Magazines Ltd. ANNETTE STARK: from *Spin*, 1986. JEAN STEIN: with George Plimpton, from *Edie: An American Biography* (Jonathan Cape, 1982). © 1982 by Jean Stein and George Plimpton. Reprinted by permission of Alfred A. Knopf Inc and Random House UK Ltd. JANE SUCK: from *Sounds* 26.11.77. Reprinted by permission of the author. JOHN SWEENEY: from the *Independent Magazine*, 1989. Reprinted by permission of the *Independent*. ICE T: from *The Ice Opinion*. © 1994 by Ice T with Heidi Siegmund. Reprinted by permission of St Martin's Press Inc. New York, NY. GREG TATE: 'Flyboy in the Buttermilk' was reprinted with the permission of Greg Tate (Simon & Schuster, 1992). Reprinted by permission of The Faith Childs Literary Agency. NEIL TENNANT: from *Smash Hits*, 14–25 March, 1985. STUDS TERKEL: from *Sing Out!*, February, 1966. HUNTER S. THOMPSON: 'No Flowers in this Town' from *Fear and Loathing in Las Vegas* (Paladin) and 'The Hashbury is the Capital of the Hippies' from *New York Times Magazine*, 1987. THE TIMELORDS: from *The Manual (How To Have a Number One The Easy Way)*. Reprinted by permission of The Curfew Press. RAYMOND THORP: from *Viper*. Reprinted by permission of Robert Hale Ltd. NICK TOSCHES: from *Hellfire: The Jerry Lee Lewis Story* (Plexus, 1982). DAVID TOOP: from *The Rap Attack* (Pluto Press, 1984). Reprinted by permission of Serpent's Tail, London and New York. MICHAEL VENTURA: from

Index

Figures in italics refer to illustrations.

A & B club, London, 205, 206
ABC, 575
ABC Television, 174, 344
Abel, Colonel Rudolf Ivanovich, 418
Aboriginal Music Society, 344
abortion, 267, 331
Abrams, Mark, 43
Absolute Beginners (film), 737
Absolute Beginners (MacInnes), xxiii, 44,
    95–9
AC/DC, 406, 635, 761
Ace, Johnny, 421
Ace of Cups, 367
Aces, the, 208
acid *see* LSD
'acid burn', 730
acid house, 652, 679, 711, 715, 730, 731,
    734
acid rock, 291, 711
Ackles, David, 604
Acme Attractions, London, 494
ACT UP agitprop, 769
Ad-Lib club, Soho, London, 216–6
Admiral (sportswear), 235
Advance Party, 799
advertising, 77, 424, 580, 581, 658, 671,
    696, 800
Aedes (fanzine), 763
Aerosmith, 741
Aesthetics of Disappearance, The
    (Virilio), 732, 733
Africa Addio (film), 324
Afro-America roots, xxii, xxxiii, 6
Afrobeat, 561
AIDS, 594, 607, 629, 645, 648, 650–53,
    767, 812
'Ain't Misbehaving', 122
'Ain't No Mountain High Enough', 524
'Ain't Too Proud to Beg', 208
Aitken, Laurel, 421, 476
Aitken, Matt, 672, 716–19

Alemeda County Grand Jury, 353,
    354
Albee, Edward, 206
Alberts, the, 140–41
Albuquerque, 45–6
alcohol, 8, 22, 90, 156, 210, 297, 298,
    378, 542, 787, 811
Aletti, Vince, 535, 542–4
Alexander, Arthur, 477
Alexander, Barry *see* Hardy, Stephen
Alexandra, Princess, 658
Alexandra Palace, London, 714
Ali, Muhammad, 241, 785
'All Shook Up', 57
'All the Time and Everywhere', 26
'All the Young Dudes', 676
'All You Need is Love', 676
Allan, Robert, 576, 577, 582
Allen, Richard, 374, 377, 396–403
Allison, Mose, 169
Alloway, Laurence, xxviii
Altamont (1969), 347–64
alternative comedy, 536, 561
alternative rock, 767, 802
Althia and Donna, 508
Ambrose, 13
America Needs Indians, 270
American Bandstand (TV show), 152,
    155, 328, 425
'American Barry' *see* Hardy, Stephen
American Enterprise Institute, 741
'American Pie', 744
amphetamincs, 165, 166, 167, 232, 307,
    475, 503, 730, 731; dexedrine 475;
    methyl amphetamine hydrochloride,
    307
Amsterdam, 813
analgesics, 812
anarchopunks, 798
Anarchy in the UK, 466
Anarchy tour (Sex Pistols), 503, 504, 505

'And I Don't Love You', 605
Anderson, Brett, 767, 768, 769
Anderson, Reid, 562
Andrew, HRH Prince, Duke of York, 657
Andrews, Julie, 532
androgyny, xxiv, xxvi, xxix, 377, 378, 593, 769
Andy Warhol's Interview, 512
Angel, Colin, 123
Angel, Lee, 56–7
Anger, Kenneth, 528, 777
Angie B., 543
'Animal Lover', 768
'Animal Nitrate', 768
Anka, Paul, 83–4, 154, 383
'Ann', 404
'Another One Bites the Dust', 544
Ant, Adam, 535, 539–42, 553
Anthrax, 637
antiwar movement, 283, 284
Antrobus, John, 141
'Apache', 773
apartheid, 593, 643, 781
Apollo club, Harlesden, 421
Apollo club, Soho, London, 205, 206, 653, 654
Apollo Music, 143, 144
Apollo Theater, New York, 220, 344, 776, 779
Apple, 579
Arbus, Diane, 538–9
Archer, Jeffrey, 663, 665
Archies, the, 482, 574
'Ardkore techno, 730–36
Area nightclub, New York, 586, 588
Ark 19, 72–7
Arnold, Gina, 672, 720–30
Arnold, Steven, 646
Arsenal Football Club, 381
Art into Pop (Frith and Horne), 106
art school influence, xxvi, 7, 106, 140, 168–71, 226, 537
Arthur's club, New York, 242
As You Like It coffee bar, London, 205, 206–7
Ascot, Roy, 169, 170
Asheton, Ron, 286, 403, 404
Ask: The Chatter of Pop (Morley), 551–9
Askew, Gregory, 791, 792
Asprey's, London, 225, 257

Astaire, Fred, 782
Astronauts, 422
Atavism of the Short Distance Mini-Cyclist, The (Banham), 175
Atkins, Chet, 47
Atkins, Juan, 677–8, 680
Atkins, June, xxx
Atkins, Susan (aka Sadie Mae Glutz), 338
Attali, Jacques, xxxi
audiences, 128–32
Auschwitz, 7
'Autobahn', 481, 483, 485
Autobiography, The (Berry), 32–5
Autobiography of Malcolm X, The (Malcolm X with Alex Haley), 7–10
autodestructive art, 171
Avalon, Frankie, 152, 186, 474
Avedon, Richard, 193, 233
Avis, Bill, 259
Ayr Hospital, 810
Aztec Camera, 596

Baader-Meinhof terrorists, 555
Babbs, Ken, 271, 272
Babe Ruth, 546
Babes in Toyland, 742
'Baby Face', 431
'Baby You Left Me', 585–6
Bacchi, Patrick, 623–4
Bach, Sebastian, 740
Bacharach, Burt, 521
'Bachelor Boy', 168
'Back Door Man', 328
'Back in Black', 727
'Back in the USA', 593
'Back Street Girl', 368
'Back to Basics' plan, 799
backing groups, 123, 124
backtracking, 679–80
Bacon, Francis (1561–1626), xxv
Bacon, Francis (1909–92), 563, Bad, 593, 642, 643, 782, 783, 784
'Bad Luck', 432
Bad Taste, 509, 511–14
Baez, Joan, 199, 262, 701
'Baghdad', 77
Bailey, Pearl, 532
Bakar, Aziz, 763
Baker, Anita, 679
Baker, Arthur, xxx, 535, 546

Baker, Butch, 445
Baker, Lavern, 472
Baker, Russell, 243
Baker, Vivian, 738
Baker, W. Howard, *102*
Bakhtin, Mikhail, 669
Baldricks, the, 711
Baldry, Long John, 207
Ball the Wall (Cohn), 425–43
'Ballad of a Thin Man', 608
Ballard, Hank, 37, 125, 472
Balloon Farm, 273–7
Balzac, Honoré de, xvii, xviii
Bambaataa, Afrika, 535, 545, 546, 547
Bananarama, 717
Band, the, 612
Band Aid project, 595, 598, 600
Bangs, Lester, 469, 481–7
Banham, Reyner, 175
Bankhead, Tallulah, 563
Barbarism Begins at Home, 590
Barber, Chris, 226–7
barbiturates, 297, 446, 508, 629, 735
Barlow, Gary, 770, 772–5
Barnes, Richard, 106, 168–71
Barnum, H. B., 53–4
Barrabas, 385
Barrett, Syd, 395
Barrie, J. M., xxiv
Barrow, Tony, 185
Bart, Lionel, 114, 143
'Bartender', 421
Bartlett, Tim, 168
Barton, Dorothy, 92
Bartos, Karl, 483, 484
Baryshnikov, Mikhail Nikolayevich, 515
Bass, Ralph, 35–6, 37, 38
Battle of the Beanfield (1985), 803
Bauhaus, 640
Baxendale, Leo, 141
Baxter, Blake, 678, 680, 681
Bay Area, San Francisco, 300, 301, 649
Bay City Rollers, 377, 423–5, 553
Bayley, Roberta, 516–17
BBC (British Broadcasting Corporation),
    xxvi, 70, 141, 208, 228, 554, 555, 573,
    673, 676, 696
BBC Workshop, 508
'be-ins', 225
Beach Boys, the, 224, 485, 676, 741

Beachcomber, the, Nottingham, 452
Bean, Frances, 787
Beano, 140
Beastie Boys, the, 682, 768
Beat, The, 246–8
Beat Boom, 7
Beat Generation, 290
Beat Happening, 723
'Beat It', 642, 781
Beat Route, London, 549
Beatlemania, 281
Beatles, the, xxii, xxiii, xxvi, xxviii, 141,
    142, 169, 177–99, 204, 208, 216, 217,
    227, 228, 233, 238–9, 254, 257,
    261–2, 269, 270, 278–84, 288, 289,
    322, 336, 337, 338, 383, 423, 424,
    470, 477, 494, 502, 568, 596, 617,
    676, 698, 726, 744, 749, 776, 782
beatniks, 281, 290, 291, 548
Beatty, Warren, 784
bebop, 16, 21, 551
Beckford, Theo, 472
Bed-Sitting Room (Antrobus and
    Milligan), 141
Bee Gees, 264
'Been Caught Stealing', 720
Beethoven, Ludwig van, xviii, 149, 150
Beiderbecke, Bix, 249
Belafonte, Harry, 87
Bell, Quentin, 510
Bell Sound, 347
Belleville High School, Detroit, 678
Bellville, Belinda, 230
Beltram, Joey, 732, 734
Belvederes, 539
Benitez, John 'Jellybean', 572
Bennet, Buzzy, 157
Benson, Gail, 474
Benson, George, 523
Benson, Ivy (and her Girls' Band), 14
Bentine, Michael, 140, 141
benzedrine, 297, 307
Berkeley, 283, 284, 290, 298, 299, 623
Berlin, 486–7
Berns, Walter, 741
Bernstein, Jessé, 790
Bernstein, Nils, 788, 792
Berry, Chuck, 6, 32–5, 169, 217, 224,
    226, 227, 278, 320, 481, 741, 743
Berry, Dave, 489

Berwick Street Market, London, 210
Best, George, 381, 475
Best, Pete, 142, 186
Between Thought and Expression:
  Selected Lyrics of Lou Reed (Reed),
  696–709
Beverley, Anne, 527
Beverly Garland Hotel, 722, 727, 729
'Bewley Brothers, The', 393
'Beyond Your Wildest Dreams', 717
Biba, 230–36, 532
'Bicycle Made for Two, A', 74
big band vocalists, 5
big bands, 6, 9
Big Beat Scene, The (Ellis), 115–25
Big Biba, 234, 235
Big Brother and the Holding Company,
  270
Big Chill, The (film), 593, 610–14, 640
'Big City Blues', 646
Big Fun, 717, 718
bikers, 333
  see also motorbikes
Blllboard, 324, 678, 746, 755
'Billie Jean', 642, 781, 782
Billy Liar (Waterhouse), 105, 106–12
Billy's gay club, London, 561, 563–4, 565
Birmingham: rioting (1982), 552, 554,
  555, 557; skinheads in, 379
Birmingham, Alabama, racism in, 161–2,
  280, 281
Birmingham Evening Mail, 425
Birt, John, 268
bisexuality, 392, 395
Black, Bill, 48, 49
Black, Cilla, 233, 383
Black, George, 14
black consciousness, 641
'Black Country Rock', 392
black dancers, 418, 420–22
Black Flag, 619, 620, 626, 721, 727, 734
Black House, the, 474
Black Magic label, 445
black market, 799, 812
black militancy, xvii, 672
Black Monday stock market crash (1987),
  593, 644
black music, xxix, 43, 105, 158, 178,
  208, 278, 447, 522, 523, 679, 778
Black Orpheus, 472

Black Panthers, 330, 333, 415, 608
Black Peoples' Information Centre, 475
Black Popular Culture, 240–41
Black Power, 284
Black Sabbath, 727, 734
'Blackbird', 338
Blackburn, Tony, 598
Blackout, 725
Blackpool Mecca, 448, 452
Blackwell, Otis, 57
Blake, John, 659
'Blame It on the Boogie', 718
Bland, Bobby, 169, 472, 604
Blauer, Renate, 658
'blaxploitation' movies, 378
Bleach, 722
Blind Faith, 345
Blitz club, Covent Garden, London, 535,
  537, 549, 561
'Blitzkrieg Bop', 487
Bliven, Bruce, 5, 10–12
Block, Judge Leslie, 268, 307, 308
'Blockbuster', 675
Blonde on Blonde, 482
Blondie, 543, 557
Bloods, 694
BLT, 564
Blue Beat, 204–5, 208, 379, 422
Blue Beat Top Twenty, 205
Blue Cheer, 481
'Blue Moon', 408
Blue Notes, 429
Blue Oyster Cult, 482, 487
'Blue Suede Shoes', 747–50, 752
'Blue Velvet', 167
blues, 33, 168, 169, 194, 222, 223, 226,
  227, 366, 367, 394, 469, 652, 675,
  734, 747
  see also rocking blues
'blues' (drug), 208, 213, 344, 446, 475
Blues and Soul, 447
Blues Brothers, 582, 607
Blues Unlimited, 223
BMG records, 763
Boardwalk Club, Manchester, 714
Boast, Kenneth, 181–2
Bobby-Sox Doctor, 6, 31–2
bobbysoxers, 5, 11, 27, 154
Bodie Green (Dirty Boogie), 154
Body Count, 721, 742, 753–60

Body Heat (film), 610
Boeing, 789, 792
Boisie, Ron, 270, 271
Bolan, Marc, xxiii, xxix, 382, 392, 408, 423, 424, 457, 532, 603
Bomb Culture (Nuttall), 138–41
'Bomb the Mars Hotel', 743
Bombers, 546
bombers, black (drug), 475
Bon Jovi, 635, 637, 638, 691
Boney M, 565
Bonfire of the Vanities, The (Wolfe), xvii
Bonnie and Clyde (film), 317
Bono, 603
Bono, Sonny, 233
Bonzo Dog Doodah Band, 141
boogie, 33, 422, 467, 564, 647
'Boogie in My Bones', 421
'Book, The', 29, 30, 76
'Book of Love', 743
Booker T, 168, 169, 322, 323, 324, 604
Boomtown Rats, 541
Boone, Pat, 168
Booth, Commander, 619–20, 623, 625, 626–7
Booth, Pat, 234
Booth, Stanley, 269, 320–24, 347–65, 746–7, 748, 749
bootlegging, 445, 451–5, 679, 710
'boppers', 16
Borgnine, Ernest, 730
Bork, Robert, 741
Bostic, Earl, 36, 37
Boston, 726
Boston Phoenix, 222
bovver boys, 384
Bow Wow Wow, 540, 803
Bowen, Billy, 15
Bowery, Leigh, 629
Bowie, David, xxiii, xxix, 377, 378, 391–6, 407, 456–64, 495–6, 508, 509, 541, 573, 601, 642, 647, 783
Bowie Nights (at Billy's gay club, 1978), 561, 565
Bowles, Beans, 162, 163
Boy Crazy, 719
Boy George (George O'Dowd), xix, 532, 535, 536, 540, 541, 559–60, 571–2, 573, 586–7, 594, 595, 627–35, 800
'Boy I Left Behind, The', 144

Boy Meets Girls (TV show), 121
Boyce, John, 659–61, 666
Boyfriend, 193
Boyfriend, The (film), 647
Boys Own, 709–10, 738
Bracewell, Michael, 593, 643–4
Braden, John, 200–201
Bradley, Dick, xxi
Bradley, Tom, 695
Bradshaw, Tiny, 37
Bragg, Billy, 600
Brand New Heavies, 737
Brand Nubian, 767
Brand, Stewart, 269, 270
Brando, Marlon, 138, 492, 547, 548
Branson, Richard, 630, 632, 633, 800
Bratby, John, 140
Braun, Michael, 177, 186–95
Braun, Wernher von, 486
break dancing, 569, 570, 773
'Breakdown', 768
Breakfast Club, the, 571
'Breaking up is Hard to Do', 383
Bredehoft, Patty, 353–4
Brenston, Jackie, 778
Bridge Project, Ayr, 809
Bright, Sydney, 13
Bringing It All Back Home, 178, 236–8
Britannia Hotel, Manchester, 595, 599
Britten, Buddy, 123
Bronski, Steve, 588
Bronski Beat, 536, 573, 588
Brooke, Henry, 197
Brooklyn Fox, the, 544
Brooks, Baba, 422
Brooks, Rosetta, 535, 537–9
Brooks Brothers, 413
Broonzy, Big Bill, 169
Bros, 770
Brown, Arthur, 141
Brown, James, 6, 35–8, 169, 178, 219, 220, 223, 224–5, 229, 240, 241, 417, 420, 422, 609, 612, 640, 679, 709, 713, 741, 776, 778
Brown, Joe, 116, 121–2
Brown, Maxine, 325
Brown, Mick, 594, 627–35
Brown, Norman O., 513
Brown, Peter, 279, 287, 288
'Brown Sugar', 358–9

Brown v. Board of Education, 748
Brownjohn, Robert, 170–71
Brubeck, Dave, 169
Bruce, Lenny, 262, 481, 482, 696
Bruce, Tommy, 116, 122
Bruno, Frank, 603
Bryant, Anita, 648
Bubbly, Babby, 123
Buchanan, Patrick, 749
Buckfast Tonic Wine, 812
Buckley, Lord, 169
Buckley, Tim, 604
Bucks Fizz, 548
Buffalo Springfield, 329, 612
Bug, the (dance), 152
Bugsy (film), 741
Buju Banton, 767
Bulger, James, 799
Bummed, 712–13
Bump, the (dance), 420, 422
Burgess, Anthony, 106, 144–52
Burke, Solomon, 219, 220, 221, 223
burlesque theatre, 73
Burman, Shelly, 169
Burns, Bobbi, 153
Burress, Lisa, 637
Burress sisters, 637
Burroughs, William, 377, 484–5, 528
Burton, Peter, 177, 205–14, 377–8,
    410–12
Burundi drumming, 540
Bus Stop, the (dance), 426, 432
Bush, George, 703, 708, 746, 748, 756,
    782, 799
Bush, Kate, 731
Bushnell, Nolan, 545
Bushwick, Bill, 750, 751, 752
Bustamente, Sir Alexander, 471
Buster, Prince, 205, 208, 420, 422, 478,
    480
Busy Bee, 693, 694
Butch and Sundance, 582
Butcher, Bilinda, 802
Butler, Samuel, 71
Butthole Surfers, 638, 720, 734
Buzzcocks, the, 467, 491, 507
Byrd, Bobby, of the Famous Flames, 221
Byrd, Jimmy 'Early', 221
Byrds, the, 178, 246–8
Byrne, Johnny, 267, 309–15

Cadbury's, 658
Cadillacs, the, 51–2
Café de Paris, London, 64, 67
Cage, John, 276
Cahill, Police Chief Tom, 296
cajun, 550
Calabash club, Drayton Gardens,
    London, 205–6
'Calcutta', 744
Cale, John, 275, 276, 277, 486, 509, 699,
    707
Callas, Maria, 167
Calvert, Reg, 122–3
calypso, 87, 422
Camden Palace disco, London, 549, 572
Campbell, Duncan, 799
Campbell, Glenn, 369
Can, 483
'Can You Feel It', 780, 785
cannabis resin, 308, 630, 807
    see also ganga; grass; marijuana; pot
Canning, Kirk, 729
Cannon, Geoffrey, 379
Can't–Bust–'Em overalls, 416, 417
'Can't Explain', 403
Cantor, Eddie, 27
Capital Radio, 561
capitalism, xxx, xxxii, 518–21, 525, 750,
    761
Capitol Records, 282
Captain Sensible, 675
Cardboard, Richard, 171
'Career Opportunities', 505, 507
'Careless Whisper', 584
Carey, Jim, 799
Carmichael, Stokely, 284
Carnaby Street, London, 106, 113, 115,
    204, 208, 215, 234, 381
Carney, Kate, 85
'Carol', 348
Carousel club, London 206
Carr, James, 221
Carroll, Ronnie, 143
'Cars', 545
Cars, 727
Carson, Johnny, 611
Carter, Angela, 268, 316–20, 470,
    509–14, 529, 539
Carter the Unstoppable Sex Machine, 742
Cartier-Bresson, Henri, 193

'Cartrouble', 540
Casablanca Records, 648
Cash, Joe, 153, 154, 156, 157
Cash, Johnny, 382
Cash, Rosanne, 742
Cashbox, 127
Cassady, Neal, 481
Cassidy, David, 377, 383
Castlemorton Common mega-rave
  (1992), 732, 803, 804, 805
Castro, Fidel, 416
'Cathy's Clown', 127
Cavern, the, Liverpool, 181, 189
Cavett, Dick, 344
Caviano, Ray, 648
CBGB's, New York, 487, 621, 625, 702,
  703
CBS, 502, 575, 576, 578–81, 583, 584,
  781
Cecil Sharp House, London, 86
Cellarful of Noise, A (Epstein), 177,
  179–86
Celtic Football Club, 603
Chacha club, London, 736
Chadwick, Mark, 800
Chandler, Jeff, 79
Chandler, Jordan, 672, 777, 785
Channel 4 television, xxi
Channel 13 television, 152
'Chaos', 681
Chapman, Mike, 673
Char, René, 6
Charlatans, the, 715
Charles, HRH The Prince of Wales, 184
Charles, Ray, 32–3, 57, 169, 219, 226,
  742
Charles, Tommy, 281
Charleston, the, 522
'Charly', 733
Charms, the, 37
Charter 77, 697, 700, 701, 707
Chaseman, Joel, 153
Cheggers Plays Pop, 555
Chelsea, London, 114, 233
Chenier, Clinton, 550
Cher, 233, 277
'Cherished Memories', 143
Cherry Vanilla, 267
Chess Records, 34
Chevalier, Albert, 85

Chez Castel, Paris, 242
Chic, 553
Chicago, 734, 741; Beatles in, 281–2;
  Martin Luther King's demonstration
  (1966), 281–2
Chicago Daily News, 276–7
Chicago Democratic Convention (1968),
  269
Chicago House, 677, 679
Chiffons, the, 693
Chinatown, San Francisco, 414–16
Chinn, Nicky, 673
Christgau, Robert, 267, 365–9
Christian, Charlie, 32
Christianity, 255, 278–80, 282, 301;
  Christian Bookseller Review, 660
Christie, Julie, 233
Chuck D., 749, 759
Church of Scientology, 796, 797
Circus Maximus disco, Leicester Square,
  London, 629
Ciro's, 76
City disco, San Francisco, 649
City Sun!, 641
Civic Opera House, Chicago, 57
civil rights, xxvii, 105, 159, 222, 268,
  280, 281, 366, 746, 778, 798, 800
Clacton (Mods and Rockers battle),
  202–3, 379
Clapton, Eric, 477, 492, 630, 800
Clark, Dee, 126
Clark, Dick, 152, 153
Clark, Gene, 248
Clark, Petula, 224, 518, 560, 568
Clash, the, 178, 491, 498–507, 509, 539,
  540, 551, 557, 602
class, xix, xxix, 7, 106, 138, 140, 170,
  318
Clay, Andrew Dice, 760
Clear Light, 327, 328
Cleave, Maureen, 179, 189, 190, 254–8,
  283
Cleethorpes (soul music in), 448, 453,
  454
Clement, Jack, 57, 60
Clinton, Bill, 756
Clinton, George, 545, 678, 739, 782, 783
Clivilles, Robert, 669
Clockwork Orange, A (Burgess), 106,
  144–52, 178, 695

Clockwork Orange, A (film), 106, 396
Clooney, Rosemary, 86
clothes: 22, 46, 53, 54, 55, 70, 71, 84,
    119, 177, 197, 201 202, 210, 215, 226,
    243, 250–53, 270, 285, 289, 535,
    547–9, 551, 606, 635–6, 737; acid,
    312; Deaners, 154, 157; drag, 113–15;
    Edie Sedgwick, 242–5; Edwardians
    (Teddy boys), 6, 23, 79, 567, 568;
    funky chic, 378, 412–18; gay men,
    207–8, 548; hippy, 291, 292, 296;
    Mods, 203–4, 207–8, 251, 567–8;
    punk, 487, 493–5, 500, 507, 510–14,
    529, 568; rap, 542–3, 544; Red Guard,
    415, 416; Scallydelia, 711, 712,
    714–15; sixties style, 316–20;
    skinhead, 379, 382, 568; soul, 450–51,
    773; Wah Ching, 415; zoot–suiters, 7,
    8, 9
Club Eleven, Great Windmill Street,
    London, 21–3
Club Lingerie, Los Angeles, 624
Club Metro, Los Angeles, 623
clubs, xix, 36, 51, 76, 205–116, 379, 381,
    384, 419–22, 535–8, 550, 551, 561–5,
    620, 704–5 709, 732, 736–9, 806–11,
    813
    See also names of individual clubs
CND (Campaign for Nuclear
    Disarmament), 106, 138, 205
Coasters, the, 125, 169, 472
Coati Mundi, 543
Cobain, Kurt, xxxi, 672–3, 722–30, 744,
    745, 786–95
cocaine, 476, 478, 501, 628, 629, 630,
    632, 633–4, 654, 655, 657, 658, 659
Cochise, 445
Cochrane, Eddie, 126, 143, 192
Cockettes, 646, 647
Cocteau, Jean, 6
Cocteau, Liz, 731
Coe Kerr Gallery, 514
coffee bars, 65, 67–9, 85, 123, 205,
    206–7
Coffee-House, Trafalgar Square,
    London, 67–9, 205
Cogan, Alma, 44
Cohen, Stanley, xxix, 178
Cohn, Nik, 105, 106, 113–15, 178,
    225–30, 378, 425–43

Coldcut, 737
Cole, Gilbert, 618–19, 624, 626
Cole, John, 797
Cole, Nat 'King', 129, 280
Coleman, Syd, 182
'Colette', 119
Collins, Lyn, 648
Collins, Mike, 562, 564
Colombo's club, Carnaby Street, London,
    420–21
colour supplements, 177, 268, 568
Colston-Hayter, Tony, 737
Coltrane, John, 169, 547
Columbia, 179, 769
Columbia University, 702
Colyer's, 141
'Come Josephine in My Flying Machine',
    74
'Come On', 228
*Come Together: John Lennon in His
    Time* (Wiener), 268, 278–84
Comedy Store (Dean Street, Soho), 561,
    563
Comi, Concetta, 157
Comic Strip team, 563
Committee of 100, 140
Community World Theater, 727
Como, Perry, 129
composers, 74
'Computer Games', 545
Conclave, The (Bracewell), 593, 643–4
Connor, Chuck, 52–3, 55
Contemporary Hit Radio, 750
Contino, Dick, 93
contracts, 116, 181, 575–8, 580–82, 583
Conway, Russ, 120
Cook, Paul, 490, 493, 516
Cooke, Sam, 219, 223, 778
CoolTan Arts, 803
Coon, Caroline, 469, 490–93
Cooper, Alice, 392, 395
Cooper, Leslie, 124
Coople, Gary, 195
'Cop Killer', 754–60
Copacabana, 76
Copas, Cowboy, 36
Copland, Aaron, 276
copyright, 33–4
Corbishley, Father, 268
Cordell, Frank, xxviii, 44, 72–7

Cortinas, 507
Cosgrove, Stuart, 671, 677–81
Costner, Kevin, 784
Cotterill, Christian, 564
'Could It Be Magic', 773
Countdown club, London, 419
'counterculture', 414, 416, 481
country and western music, 33
Country Club, Hampstead, 391
Country Joe, 294
country music, xxii, 36–7, 43, 366
Coupland, Douglas, 178
Coward, Noël, 178, 238–9, 563
Cowboy Chic, 417
Cowley, Patrick, 649–50
Cox, Paul, 354–6
'Cracked Actor', 459, 462
Crackpot (Waters), 152–9
Craig, Mike, 629
Cramner, Rick, 651
Cramps riot, Los Angeles Palladium, 624
Crane, Lionel, 45–7
Crawdaddy!, 222
Crawdaddy Club, Richmond, Surrey,
    226, 227
Crawford, Joan, xxii, 76
'Crazy Horses', 407
Cream, 481, 725, 734
Cream of Al Green, The, 604
Creem, 403–6, 481–7
Criminal Justice Bill, xxxiii, 798, 799–
    800, 802–6
Cripple, the (dance), 420
Crips, the (gang), 693, 694
Crisp, Quentin, 207, 586
Crist, Helen, 155, 156, 157
Croft, Michael, 63
Cromok, 763–4
crooners, 13, 27, 75, 82
Cropper, Steve, 320–23
Crosby, Bing, 5, 12, 82
Crosby, David, 246–7
Crosby, Stills and Nash, 612
Crosby, Stills and Nash, 345
Crover, Dale, 726, 727
Crowley, Aleister, 736
Cruise, Tom, 691, 796
Crust on Its Uppers, The (Raymond), 103
crusties, 798
Cruz 101, Manchester, 774

Cugat, Xavier, 187
Culture Club, xxix, 535, 536, 540, 550,
    559, 627–30, 632, 635, 768
Cummings, Tony, 452
Cunelli, Professor, 29
Curtis, Tony, 79, 86
'Cut Across Shorty', 126
Cutler, Chris, 591
cybernetics, 169–70, 469
Cybotron, 677
C/Z label, 787, 791
Czechoslovakia, 696–709

Dadomo, Giovanni, 494
Daily Express, xxi, 44, 91–2, 190, 655,
    658
Daily Herald, 203
Daily Mail, 16, 308
Daily Mirror, 43, 45–7, 113, 202, 318,
    469, 471, 476, 498–9, 630, 632, 659,
    661, 663–4
Daily News, 284
Daily Star, 656, 663, 775
Daley, Mayor Richard, 269, 330, 336
Dalglish, Kenny, 603
Dalton, David, xxiv
Daltrey, Roger, 239–40, 304, 449
Damned, the, 491–2, 507, 539
Damone, Vic, 93
Dana, 495
'Dance, The', 679
'Dance (Disco Heat)', 645, 649
dance band leaders, 5, 12–14
dance band singers, xxii
dance bands, 12–14
dance crazes, 74, 152, 274, 420, 421, 422
    see also individual names of dances
dance halls, 24, 25, 51, 565
dance music, xix, xxx, 13, 14, 378, 535,
    546, 562, 677, 679; black, 6, 545, 648,
    669, 671
Dance with a Stranger (film), 737
Dancer from the Dance (Holleran), 377,
    384–91, 653
dancing, 6, 8–10, 204–5, 208, 215,
    418–22, 549
Dancing Ledge (Jarman), 199
Dandies (Laver), 115
Dandy, 140
Dangerfield, Brent, 293, 294

Dangerous, 775, 777, 784, 785
'Dangerous' tour, 776
Daniels, Billy, xxi, 27
Danny and the Juniors, 744
Darin, Bobby, 126
Darling (film), 233
David Bowie, 394
Davies, Cyril, 227
Davies, Mr Justice Mlchael, 664
Davis, Angela, 241
Davis, Don, 680
Davis, Miles, 169, 778
Davis, Oscar, 91
Davis, Sammy, Jr, 778
Davis, Tyrone, 240
Day The Music Died, The (Smith), 105, 133–8
De Cruz, William, 764–5
De La Soul, 712
De Mann, Freddie, 571
De Montfort Hall, Leicester, 63, 65
de Villeneuve, Justin, 234
Deacon, Joe, 808
Dead Corps, 726
Dead End (film), 515
Dead Kennedys, 726
Dead Or Alive, 716
Dean, Hazell, 716
Dean, James, xxiv, 40, 43, 60–63, 86, 139, 381, 492, 595, 597
Dean, Mark, 574–85
'Deanagers', 60
Deane, Winston J. 'Buddy', 153–9; Committee, 153–9; Jitterbug, 152; Record Hops, 155; *Buddy Dean Show* (TV show), 152–9
Death Certificate, 741
'Death Mix', 545
'Death Trip', 404, 405
DeCanio, Steve, 301–2
Decca Records, 29, 65, 179, 180, 181, 189, 394, 596
Deedes, William, 195–8
Def American Records, 750
Defection, 732
Dekker, Desmond, 208, 477
Delage, 719
Deller, Alfred, 82
Deluxe (magazine), 513
Denny, Martin, 545

Densmore, John, 328, 329
Denson, Ed, 294
Depeche Mode, 678, 800
Derby All-Dayers, 447–8
DeSanto, Sugar Pie, 219
DeShannon, Jackie, 346
'Desolation Blues', 248
'Desolation Row', 249
Destiny, 780
Detroit, 734, 735; riots (1967), 268
Detroit Spinners, 523
Detroit Techno, 671, 674, 677–81
Dever, Joseph X., 243, 244
Deverson, Jane, 200–205
Deviants, the, 340, 341, 342
'Devil or Angel', 126
Devil's Candy, The (Salamon), 741
dexedrine (dexies), 475
   see amphetamines
DGC, 793
Diamond, Neil, 346
'Diana', 83–4
Diaries (Warhol), 514–16
Diawara, Manthia, 178, 240–41
Dickens, Charles, xvii, xviii
Dickson, Liz, 230, 231
Diddley, Bo, 169, 226, 494
Didion, Joan, 267, 327–9
Diet Pepsi, 742
Dietrich, Marlene, 26, 345, 647
Diggers, the, 294–6, 332
digital technology, xxx
Dinosaur Jr, 722
Dion, 421
Direct Action Committee, 140
'Dirt', 404
Dirtbox club, the, Earls Court, London, 550
'Dirty Diana', 642
disc jockies (DJs), 77, 224, 420, 445, 447, 449, 450, 451, 507, 564, 565, 652, 673, 678, 679, 709, 710, 712, 731, 732, 738, 803, 808, 810
Dischord, 721
disco music, 377, 378, 467, 469, 470, 508, 518–27, 594, 644, 648, 649, 652; Hi-NRG, 208, 649, 716; and materialism, 527–7
discothèques, 204, 215, 242, 273, 344, 380, 384, 418, 419, 425–6, 430–39,

441, 526, 549, 561, 565, 573, 692, 806
Disk Magazine, 143–4
Diskin, Tom, 47
Dive, the, Liverpool, 185
Divine, 716
Dixon, Steve, 535, 566–70
DIY sound system, 805
'Do Right Woman', 368
'Do What You Like', 772
'Do You Really Want to Hurt Me?', 559, 628
'Do You Wanna Funk?', 650, 653
DOA, 620
'Dock of the Bay, The', 269, 321–3
'Doctor Who Theme, The', 675
dog, the (dance), 563
Dog, Michael, 805
Doggett, Bill, 37, 53
Dogs, the (Slaughter and), 491
Dollar, 551
'Dollie Grey', 141
Domino, Fats, 54, 87, 125–6, 152, 169, 249, 421, 472
Don, 732
Donahue (television programme), 650
Donahue, Tom 'Big Daddy'', 271
Donald, Howard, 771–5
Donegan, Lonnie, 82, 85, 86, 126
Donnelly Theatre, Roxbury, 219, 222
Donovan, Jason, 716, 719
'Don't Be Cruel', 57
Don't Destroy Me! (Hastings play), 61–2
'Don't Make Me Wait', 535
Doo, 421
'doobs', 208, 213
Doors, the, 127, 267, 327–9
Doors, The (film), 741–2
doo-wop, 741, 751
Dostoevski, Fyodor Mikhailovich, 733
Douglas, Craig, 126
Douglas-Home, Sir Alec (later Baron Home of the Hirsel), 196
'Down by the Lazy River', 407
Downbeat club, Leeds, 678
drafting, 92–5, 268, 285–6, 404
drag, 113–15, 318, 644–5, 647
drag queens, 199, 586, 631, 646, 650
Drake, Nick, 604
Dramatics, the, 680
Dreamgirl: My Life as a Supreme

(Wilson), 105, 159–64
Dresdner, Matt, 791
Drifters, the, 169, 472
Drog Store coffee bar, San Francisco, 292, 293
'Drowners, The', 768
drug 'cocktails', 812, 813
drugs, xxviii, 6, 7, 68, 167, 208, 209, 267, 268, 269, 288, 292, 293, 297–301, 306–8, 318, 330, 378, 384, 446, 452, 453, 461, 470, 594, 597, 627, 629–35, 656, 712, 721, 730, 735, 737, 787, 801, 806–13
see also individual names of drugs
Drummond, Don, 420, 472
Duce, Le (London gay club), 207–14
Duck (of MGs), 322, 323
Duke, David, 749
Duke Wore Jeans, The (film), 88
'Dum Dum', 143
Dunaway, Faye, 317
Dundee, 812
Dungeon, the, Nottingham, 452
Dunn's shops, 204
Duran Duran, xxix, 423, 536, 540, 541, 551–9, 573, 598, 691
Dyall, Valentine, 23
Dyer, Richard, 470, 518–27
Dylan, Bob, xvii, xviii, 178, 179, 199, 236–8, 247, 248–9, 258–62, 273, 275, 283, 289, 345, 392, 419, 481, 482, 519, 598, 608, 612, 702, 744, 748
Dynamix, 678

Eager, Vince, xxii, 116, 122
Eaglin, Snooks, 169
Ealing Art School, 106, 168–71
East Germany, 681–90
East Midlands Soul Club, 446, 449, 450
East of Eden (film), 61
East Village, 702
East Village Other, 331
Easton, Eric, 217, 218, 228
Eastwood, Clint, 206, 757
'easy–listening', 545
Easy Rider (film), 347
Easybeats, the, 288, 289
Eazy-E, 694
Ebony, xxix, 138
Eckstine, Billy, 86

Ecstasy, 629, 730, 731, 735, 806, 807, 809–10, 813
Ecstasy, Passion and Pain, 647
Eddy, Duane, 126, 546
Edge, the, 539
Edgecombe, Johnny, 475
Edie: The Life and Times of Andy Warhol's Superstar (ed. Stein and Plimpton), 241–5, 267
Edinburgh, 812
education, 71, 200, 201, 202
Educational Institute of Scotland, xxvi
Edwardians (Teddy boys), xxv, 6, 7, 23, 44, 86–7, 138, 499–500, 512, 537, 538, 567–8, 738
Edwards, Jackie, 421
Egan, Rusty, 561, 562
'Eight Miles High', 605
8½ (film), 187
808 State, 713
'El Paso', 126
Electric Kool-Aid Acid Test, The (Wolfe), xvii, 269–73
Electrifyin' Mojo, the, 678
electro, 535, 671; electro-disco 677; Electro Diskows, 565
Electro 4, 677
electronic music, 481–7, 545, 734
Elen, Gus, 85
Eleventh, Dream Day, 743
Elizabeth, Queen, the Queen Mother, 184
Elizabeth II, Queen, 196, 238, 254, 664
Elks Lodge, Los Angeles, 620
Elle, 234
Ellington, Duke, 9, 196
Ellington, Ray, 140
Ellis, Alton, 422
Ellis, Royston, 105, 115–25
Ellison, Ralph, 7, 17–20
Elms, Robert, 536, 547–51
ELP, 734
Elvis '56: In the Beginning (Wertheimer), 47–50
Embassy, 180–81, 182
'Embraceable You', 11
Emerson, Lake and Palmer, 482
EMI, xxix, 181–4, 556, 582, 691, 692
emidiscs, 451
Emmy, 571
Empire Strikes Back, The (film), 610

Enchanted Forest, the, 367
Endino, Jack, 727
'Endless Nameless', 729
Enemy Ace (comicbook), 488
'Energy Flash', 732
England's Dreaming (Savage), 799
Eno, Brian, 508, 509, 669, 735
Ephron, Michael, 345
Epic, 583, 642
epilepsy, 733
Epstein, Brian, xxiv, 177, 179–86, 189, 227, 238, 257, 279, 283, 284, 287, 288
Erasure, 768
eroticism, disco and, 521–3
Ertegun, Ahmet, 542
Eshun, Kodwo, 671, 736–9
Espresso Jungle (Baker), 102
Esquire, 268, 365–9, 739–52
Establishment, the, 88–9, 416, 760
ET (film), 781
Etheridge, Melissa, 770
Ethiopian World Federation Incorporated Local 33, 475
Ethiopians, the, 422
Eurobeat, xxx
'European Son', 486
Eva (at Biba), 234
Evans, George, 5
Evening News (London), 527, 529
Evening-Standard (London), 189, 200, 254–8, 715
'Every Rose Has Its Thorn', 739–40
'Eves' (drug), 813
Examiner (San Francisco), 365
existentialism, 6, 113
Expensive Habits (Garfield), 574–85
Exploding Cinema series, 803
Expresso Bongo (film), xxiii, 44
Expresso Bongo (Mankowitz), xxiii, 44, 77–81

Fabian, 152
Fabian, Jenny, 267, 309–15
Face, Papa, 564
Face, The (magazine), xxi, 535, 536, 541, 547–51, 561–5, 677–81, 683, 736
Faces, 380, 381, 425, 426, 429–31, 433, 435, 436, 437, 442, 443, 736
Factory, 343

Fahey, John, 404
Fairfax High School, Los Angeles, 622
Faith, Adam, 126
Faith, Hope and Charity, 647–8
Faithfull, Marianne, 253, 268, 339, 340
Fall, the, 734
Fame, Georgie, xxii, 116
Family, 267
Family, The (Sanders), 336–8
Family Function, 710, 737
'Family Values' platform, 799
Famous Flames, 225
Fans' Star Magazine, 40
Fantasy Records, 649
fanzines, xix, 224, 253, 498, 539, 569, 763
Farley, Terry, 713
Farmer, Frances, 614
Farrah, 635
Farren, Mick, 339–43
Fastbacks, the, 742, 786
Fatback Band, 420
Fawkes, Wally, 16
FBI (Federal Bureau of Investigation), 778
Fear and Loathing in Las Vegas (Thompson), 369–72
Federal label, 38
feedback, 483, 484, 588
Feigel, Bob, 246–8
Feldmans, 21, 23
female musicians, 367, 377
feminism, xvii, 267, 365–6, 367, 377, 526
feminization, xxiv
Fenders rock club, Long Beach, 621–2, 627
Fenn-Feinstein, 413
Ferrari, Nick, 631
Ferry, Bryan, xxix
Festival club, Brydges Place, London, 205, 206
festivals, free, 800, 801, 803, 804, 805
Fever, 565
Fever, Ricky, 123
Fielding, Harold, 65
Fifth Avenue (clothes), 211
'Fight for Your Right (To Party)', 682
File Under Popular (Cutler), 591,
Fillmore auditorium, 273, 291, 323, 344
'Finger Poppin' Time', 125

Finsbury Park, London, 23–5
'Firecracker', 545
First Light Virtual Design, 738
Fischer, Marie, 158
Fish (Country Joe), 294
Fisher, Eddie, xxvi, 93
Fisk, Peter, 69
Fitz (of Biba), 231–5
Fitzgerald, Ella, 128, 129, 249
Five Chords, the, 53
Five Keys, the, 53
Five Royales, the, 37
'Five Years', 396
Flash, Grandmaster, 535, 543–4, 546,
Flavor Flav, 693
Fleetwood Mac, 755
Fling magazine, 88
Flintstones, the, 678
flower children, 301, 317, 608
flower power, 301, 391, 496, 507
Flowered Up, 715
Flowers, Phil, 224
Flur, Wolfgang, 483
'Fly, Robin, Fly', 434
folk clubs, 394
folk dancing, 85–6
Folk Devils and Moral Panics (Cohen), xxix
folk music, 518, 519, 526; fantasy, 541
folk-rock, 246, 334, 345
Fonda, Jane, 777
Fontaine, Dick, 189
Fontaine Sisters, 421
Fontana, DJ 'Sticks', 48, 49
'Fool on the Hill', 749
'Fool's Gold', 713
football, 381, 603, 605, 711
For a Few Dollars More (film), 546
'For a Few Dollars More', 546
Forest Fayre festival, 801
Forman, Milos, 702, 703
Fort Chaffee, 93–4
Fort Ord, California, 93
Fort Wayne, 285
Foster, Paul, 270
Fountain, the, Nottingham 449
Four Aces club, Dalston, London, 421
Four Seasons of Love, 524
Four Tops, the, 208, 380, 455
Fourmost, 183

Fowler, Pete, xxix, 377
Fowlkes, Eddie 'Flashin', 678, 680
Foxx, Charlie, 455
Frain, Andy, 249
Francis, Connie, 127, 474
Francisco, Joyce, 299–300
Franco, General Francisco, 281
Frankie Goes to Hollywood, 536, 572–4, 580, 768
'Frankie Lee and Judas Priest', 345
Franklin, Aretha, 240, 612, 645, 744, 778
Fraser, Robert, 268
Frayling, Christopher, 546
Frazier, Walt, 414
Free Speech Movement, 298
Freed, Alan, 743
Freeman, Robert, 193
Frère Cholmeley, 658
Freud, Sigmund, 630
Fripp, Robert, 509
Frith, Mark, 672, 770–75
Frith, Simon, xxix, 106, 375, 536, 572–4
Fritts, Donnie, 221
From A to Biba and Back Again (Hulanicki), 230–36
From Luxury to Heartache, 630
Frost, David, 113, 568
Fry, Lady Cosima, 563
'Fuck the Police', 694
Fugs, the, 274
Fulchino, Anne, 47
'Fun' 40, 716
Funicello, Annette, 152, 157
funk, 420, 452, 535, 542, 544, 549, 550, 551, 564, 604, 709
  see also garage funk; jazz-funk
funkadelia, 677
funky chic, 378, 412–18
Funky Four Plus One, 542–3, 544
Funny Face (film), 233
Fuqua, Harvey, 648–9
Furious Five, 535, 543, 544
Furlong, Monica, 308
Fury, Billy, xxii, 116–20, 124, 126, 143–4, 423
Future club, London, 713, 715
Future Sound of London, the, 734
futurism, 535, 565, 568

Gaff, Billy, 654, 655, 656, 659

Gaines, Donna, 594, 635–9
Gairy, Sir Eric, 480
Gallery club (Je Podivna), Prague, 704–5, 706
Gallup, 691
Gambit and Associates comic, 677
Gamble, Kenny, 779
ganga, 421, 473
  see also grass; marijuana; pot
gangs, 24–5, 202, 693–6
garage, 535, 598; funk, 678
Garfield, Simon, 536, 574–85, 595–601
Gargoyle, the, Dean Street, Soho, London, 536, 561–4
Garland, Judy, xxii, 129, 647
Garland, Rodney, 3
Garratt, Sheryl, 377, 423–5
Garvey, Marcus, 476
Gaskin, Barbara, 675
Gates, Police Commissioner Darryl, 620, 754
Gaumont State, Kilburn, London, 120
gay clubs, 205–14, 378, 494, 525–6, 561, 563–4, 565, 573, 647, 648, 652
gay dancers, 419
Gay Left magazine, 518–27
gay liberation, 377, 391, 647
gay music, 208, 536, 564; disco, 520, 521, 523, 524, 525, 564
gay style, 106, 113–15
  see also homosexuality; lesbians
Gaye, Marvin, 208, 422, 612, 741, 776, 778, 781
Gaylord, 273
Gaynor, Gloria, 522, 524, 767
Gaz (of Gossips), 564–5
Gee, Spoonie, 543
Geffen Records, 729, 750
Geiger, Marc, 720
Geldof, Bob, 595, 598, 599, 800
Geldzahler, Henry, 274
Gem Music, 393
gender benders, 536, 559–60, 585–8
gender-fuck, 646
gender issue, xix, xxiv, xxviii, xxix, xxxii
gender politics, 268
General Hospital (film), 618
Generation X (Hamblett and Deverson), 178, 200–205
generational conflict, xix

generational politics, 267
Generic Flipper, 725
Gentle, Johnny, xxii, 115, 116, 122, 142
George, Charlie, 381, 382
George, Nelson, 672, 693–6
Geraldo, 13
Gernreich, Rudi, 245
Gerry and the Pacemakers, 741
Gershwin, George, 15, 521
'Get a Job', 408
'Get a Leg Up', 743
Get Over You, 606
'Get Ready', 773
'Get Your Ya Yas Out', 454
Geto Boys, 742, 750–52
Geto Boys, The, 750
'Ghetto Child', 523
Giant (film), 61
Gibbons, Carrol, 13
'Gideon's Bible', 509
Gielgud, Sir John, 114
Gilbert, Simon, 768
Gilbert and George, 537
Gillespie, Dizzy, 196
Gillett, Charlie, 378–84
Ginsberg, Allen, 138, 226, 290, 481
'Girls are Marching, The', 93
Girltalk, 584–5
Gits, 790, 791
'Give a Little Love', 423
'Give Good Feeling', 773
'Give Me Danger', 404
'Giving Up', 386, 389
Glam, 374
glam rock, 541, 762, 763
Glasgow, 812
Glasgow Rangers Football Club, 603
Gleason, Ralph, 362
Glitter, Gary, 408, 573, 675
G.L.O.B.E., 546
Glover, Gordon, 5, 12–14
glue-sniffing, 251
Gobble, the (dance), 274
'God Save the Queen', 470
Godin, Dave, 269, 324–7, 452
Goffin (songwriter), 673
GoGos, the, 620
'Goin' Home', 407
Gold Coast club, Dean Street, Soho, 561, 564

Gold Mountain, 787
Golden Gate Park, San Francisco, 290, 291, 295, 296
Golding, Mark, 634
Goldman, Sharon ('Peanuts'), 154–6
Goldstein, Richard, 178, 250–53, 267, 273–7
'gone poets', 44, 67
Gonella, Nat, 15
Good, Jack, 105, 121, 124, 143–4
'Good Times', 544
'Good Timin'', 127
'Good Vibrations', 676
'Good-bye Baby', 219
'Goodbye Yellow Brick Road', 657
Goode, Johnny, 116
Goodman, Benny, xxv
Goon Show, The, 106, 139–41, 184
Gordon, Dave, 564
Gordon, Lonnie, 717
Gordon, Tony, 628, 629
Gordy, Berry, 105, 640–41, 673, 680, 779
Gore, Lesley, 741
Gosling, Ray, 105, 127–32, 138–9, 268
Gospel, 6, 159, 224, 652, 679
Gossips club, Dean Street, Soho, 561–5
Goth, 536
Gotthard, Andy, 446, 454
Graceland, 615, 796
Graham, Bill, 273, 516, 646
Graham X *see* Hardy, Stephen
Granada Theatre, Tooting, London, 91
Granada TV, 189, 268
Grant, David, 542
Grant, Julie, 228
grass, 297, 298, 299, 372
  see also ganga; marijuana; pot
Grassroots Bookshop, London, 475
Grateful Dead, 270, 471, 635, 636, 638, 742–3
greasers, 340, 567
'Great Balls of Fire', 43, 57–60
Greater Glasgow Health Board, 812
'Greatest Hit' collections, xix
Greatest Hits volume 1 (Diana Ross), 524
Green, Al, 604, 605, 776
Green, Bill ('Vince'), 113–15
Green, Geoffrey, 381
'Green Onions', 168

Green's, Glasgow, 14
Greenbaum, Norman, 419
Greenwich Village, 290, 298, 702
Greer, Germaine, 267, 339–43
Greig, Stuart, 498–9
Grey Brothers, 141
Griffin, Detective, 619, 620, 626
Grodniz, Becky, 474
Grogan, Emmett, 295
Grohl, David, 722, 723, 727, 745
Grosz, Karoly, 688, 689
Groupie (Fabian and Byrne), 267–8, 309–15
groupies, 268, 309–15, 410–12, 486
Gruen, Bob, 517
Grundy, Bill, 469, 498–9
Guardian, the, 799
Gucci, 429, 430
Guerilla Records, 734
Guess Who, the, 368
Guiffre, Jimmy, 169
Guinness Book of Hits, 675
Gulf War, 749
Gunn, Thom, 138
Guns 'N' Roses, 740, 749, 761, 789
Guralnick, Peter, 178, 219–25, 641
'Gurney Slade', 393
Gurr, Ronnie, 628, 634
Guthrie, Woody, 249
Guvnors, the (a North London gang), 24–5
Guy, Buddy, 169, 223

H-bomb, 68, 140
Hacienda club, Manchester, 570, 571, 678, 711, 712
Hackett, Pat, 105, 164–8
Hackney Homeless Festival, Clissold Park, 800
'Had a Dad', 720
Hagan, Jo, 564
Hagar, Sammy, 726
Hagen, 271, 272
Hagler, Marvin, 603
Haight-Ashbury district, San Francisco, 273, 290–302
Haight-Ashbury Neighborhood Council, 296
Haight Theater, San Francisco, 293
Haines, Perry, 562

hair styles, 71, 124, 139, 157–8, 210, 535, 635, 737, 761, 762; beehive, 157, 209; bouffant, 157, 252, 348, 487; Chinese, 415; close-cropped, 241, 243, 244, 245; 'conk', 8, 9; crew-cut, 22, 84, 281, 285, 506; DA, 46, 154, 155; Detroits, 154; Edwardian (Teddy boy), 86, 537; Elvis, 84; hippy, 646; James Dean, 597; long, 23, 52, 53, 55, 226, 312, 318, 347, 381; Mods, 204, 567; Mohican, 537; ponytail, 154; punk, 493, 495, 497, 500, 506, 511, 514, 529, 538, 573; Scallydelia, 711; skinhead, 378–9, 382, 538, 573; Tony Curtis, 79, 86; Waterfalls, 154
Hairspray, 105
Hailsham, Quintin Hogg, 2nd Viscount, 475
Halasz, Piri, xxvi
Haley, Alex, 7–10
Haley, Bill, xxvi, 25, 152, 190
Haley, Jack, 515
Hall, Henry, 13, 28
Hall, Rick, 219
Hall, Stuart, xxvi, 669
Halliwell, Kenneth, 287, 289
Hamblett, Charles, 200–205
Hamilton, Richard, xxviii, 41
Hamilton Face Band, 367
Hammer, Jack, 57
Hammersmith Palais, 17, 204, 461–2, 553
Hammerstein, Oscar, II, 73
Hamnett, Katherine, 573
Hampton, Lionel, 8, 9, 10
Hancock, Herbie, 523
'Hand in Glove', 596
HandJive, the, 152
'Handy Man', 126, 127
Hanger 13 club, Ayr, 807, 809–10
Hanson, Wendy, 238, 257, 258
'Happenin' All Over Again', 717
'happenings', 225
'Happiness Is a Warm Gun', 338
Happy Mondays, 711–15
'Happy Talk', 675
hard rock 488, 762, 763
'Hard to Beat', 404
hardcore raves, 807
Hardy, Stephen ('American Barry'; Barry

Alexander; Graham X), 653–64, 666
Harpers, xvii
Harpo, Slim, 168, 169, 477
Harris, George, 646
Harris, Jet, 179
Harris, Rita, 183–4
Harris, Wynonie, 37, 352
Harrison, George, 142, 180, 183–6, 193, 254, 255, 693
Harrison, George (journalist), 185
Harrison, Pattie, 254
Harron, Mary, 469, 487–9, 541
Harry, Bill, 185
Hartweg, Norman, 270, 271–3
Harvey, Laurence, 44
Hastings, Michael, 61–2
'Hate and War', 504
Havana Band, 13
Havel, Václav, xix, 672, 696–709
Hawkins, Hawkshaw, 37
Hawkwind, 803
Hay, Roy, 629, 632
Hayakawa, S. I., 695
Hayden, Thomas Emmett, 330
Hayes, Isaac, 523, 604
'He's So Fine', 693
'Heal the World', 777, 785
Heart in Exile, The (Garland), 3
Heart of Midlothian Football Club, 603
'Heart of Stone', 368
'Heartbeat', 543
'Heartbreak Hotel', xxii, xxvi, 43, 45
'Heartbreak Hotel' (Jackson), 780, 781
Heartbreaks, the, 502
Heat, 736
Heath, Chris, 672, 690–93
Heath, Ted, 27, 28
Heaven 17, 106, 678
heavy metal, 486, 568, 620, 637, 682, 714, 734, 739, 761–6
Hebdige, Dick, 470, 527–30
hedonism, 378, 504, 549, 628
'Heebie Jeebies', 321
Hell, Richard, xxiii
Hell's Angels, 318, 339, 347–61, 364, 379
Hellfire: The Jerry Lee Lewis Story (Tosches), 57–60
Hello magazine, 672, 795–7
'Hello Little Girl', 183

'Helter Skelter', 338
Hendrix, Jimi, 228, 267, 312, 343–7, 404, 492, 504, 603, 609, 612, 702, 725, 740, 744
Hep magazine, xxix
Hepburn, Audrey, 233
Her Majesty's Theatre, London, 13, 27
'Here I Am', 604
Herko, Freddy, 164, 167
Herman, of Herman's Hermits, 248, 278, 396
Hernandez, Andy *see* Coati Mundi
'Heroes', 509
'Heroin', 277, 297, 308
heroin, 213, 482, 527, 549, 594, 628–32, 787, 790, 795, 812, 813
see also smack
Hester, Carolyn, 261
Heston, Charlton, 760
'Hey Hey, My My', 744
Hibiscus, 646
Hi-NRG disco, 208, 649, 716
Hiatt, Dr Robert, 356
Hicks, Colin, 64, 86
High School Confidential (film), 91
highlife, 564, 566
Hill, Jessie, 127
Hill, Marshall, 199
Hillman, Chris, 247
hip hop, 545, 546, 652, 679, 682, 709, 731, 768
hippies, xvii, 215, 217, 271, 274, 290–302, 330, 332, 333, 340, 344, 378, 379, 496, 540, 568, 646, 647, 738, 745, 798, 800, 803
Hiroshima, 6, 89, 318
'(Marie's The Name) His Latest Flame', 599
His Name Was Dean, 61
History, 796
Hit Factory, south London, 716
Hitman Roadshows, 717
HMV, xxvi, 181, 447, 552
Hobsbawm, Eric, 283
Hodges, Johnny, 9
Hodgson, Simon, 1 14
Hoffmann, Dezo, 193
Hogan's Heroes, 487
Hogen, Carl, 32
Hoggart, Richard, xviii, xix, 44, 70–72, 196

'Hold On, I'm Comin'', 279
Holdcroft, Thomas, 202–3
Hole, 787, 793
'Hole in My Shoe', 675
Holleran, Andrew, 377, 384–91, 652
Holliday, Billie, 249, 423
Holly, Buddy, 152, 421, 743
Hollywood Argyles, 321
Hollywood Babylon (Anger), 528, 777, 788
Hollywood Bowl, 184
Holmes, James, 499
Holmstrom, John, 469
Holt, John, 477
Holzer, Baby Jane, 339
home recording, xxx
homosexuality, xxiii, xxxiii, 7, 114, 115, 165, 177, 199, 267, 293, 377, 378, 391, 394, 395, 594, 644–53, 657, 724–5, 749, 767–80
see also under gay
Honey, 507
'Honey Bee', 767
Hong Kong, Pet Shop Boys in (1989), 690–92
'Honky-Tonk Woman', 340, 362, 646
Hooker, John Lee, 169, 565
Hopkins, Lightnin', 169
Horn, Trevor, 572, 573
Hornby, Lesley (Twiggy), 233–4
Horne, Howard, 106
Horne, Lena, 86
Horovitz (performer of poetry with jazz), 138
Horowitz, David, 350, 363, 364
Horton, Willie, 750
Hot Band, 646, 647
Hot Buttered Soul magazine, 455
Hot Hundred, 325
'Hound Dog', 48–50, 408–9
House, xxx, 535, 712, 734, 767; future, 713
House, Daniel, 787
House of Pain, 768
House Un-American Activities Committee (HUAC), 284
Houston, Tom, 619
Houston, Whitney, 679, 767
'How Do You Do It?', 185
'How We Gonna Make the Black Nation

Rise?', 550
Howard Theater, Washington DC, 52
Howl (Ginsberg), 481
Howlin' Wolf, 169, 217, 223, 405
HUAC (House Un-American Activities Committee), 284
Hue magazine, xxix
Hues Corporation, the, 419
Huff, Leon, 779
Hulanicki, Barbara, 177, 230–36
Human League, the, 540, 596, 678
Humperdinck, Englebert, xxviii
Humphrey Lyttleton Band, 7, 15–17
100 Club, London, 491, 495, 497
Hung on You (Chelsea shop), 233
Hunky Dory, 392, 393
hunt saboteurs, 798, 799
Hunter, Meredith 'Murdock', 353–8
Huntsman, London, 206
Hurd, Letha, 645–6
Hurricanes, the, 126
Hüsker Dü, 604, 605, 720
Hustle Cha, 433, 434
Hustlers, 736
Hutchinson, John, 663
Hutter, Ralf, 483–7
Hyde Park (Rolling Stones concert, 1969), 379, 382
Hyland, Brian, 421
Hylton, Jack, 12–13, 77
'Hypergasm', 735
'Hypnoblast', 735

'I Am the Fly', 593, 643
'I Believe', 29
'I Can Make It', 773
'I Can't Get Next to You', 605
'I Can't Stand Myself', 241
i-D magazine, 532, 535, 562, 566–70, 710–15
'I Don't Know', 38
'I Feel Good', 773
'I Feel Love', 649
'I Feel That Old Feeling Coming On', 38
'I Found Heaven', 773
'I Got You (I Feel Good)', 224
'I Gotta Dance (to Keep from Crying)', 208
'I Heard It Through the Grapevine', 208, 781

'I Just Got You', 127
'I Need a Man', 522
I Need More: The Stooges and Other Stories (Iggy Pop), 285–6
'I Need Somebody', 405
'I Remember You', 168
'I Shot the Sheriff', 444
'I Stand Accused', 604
'I Think We're Alone Now', 675, 676
'I Told You So', 127
'I Wanna Be Your Dog', 404
'I Wanna Be Your Man', 228
'I Want You Back', 779
'I Will Survive', 767
'I'll Be There', 773
'I'll Walk Alone', 12
'I'm Free', 362
'I'm in Love', 187–8
'I'm Just a Vagabond Lover', xxvi
'I'm Pretty Vacant', 489
'I've Been Loving You Too Long', 221, 240
'I've Got You Under My Skin', 522, 524
'I've Passed This Way Before', 208
Iacocca, Lee, 617
'Ice' (drug), 813
Ice and Essence, 171
Ice Cube, 741, 749
Ice T, 672, 720, 721, 742, 753, 755–9, 778
'Ida Red', 33, 34
idiot dancing, 507
'If Six Was Nine', 347
Ifield, Frank, 168
Ikettes, 418
'Image of a Girl', 122
Imperials, the, 222
Impressions, the, 169
In Bed with Madonna documentary, 784
In Defence of Disco (Dyer), 470
In His Own Write (Lennon), 281
'In the Rain', 680
Incognito label, 679
Independent magazine, 653–66
Independent Group, xxvii-xxviii, 106
Independent on Sunday newspaper, 594
Indians, 7, 255, 380
indie music, 712, 713, 763, 767, 769, 789, 790, 800
industrial, 678

Ingham, Jonh, 469, 493–7
Ink Spots, 6, 14–15
Innervision Records, 574–85
Inspiral Carpets, 711, 713–15
Institute of Contemporary Arts (ICA), xxvii, 489
International Velvet, xxiii
Invisible Man (Ellison), 17–20
INXS, 719
IRA (Irish Republican Army), 478, 496, 505
Irene, Countess, 207
Iron Maiden, 478, 635
Irving, Sir Henry, 288
'Is a Bluebird Blue', 125
Islam, 761–6, 767
Islam, Yusef (Cat Stevens), 692–3
Island Records, 580–81
Isley Brothers, the, 169, 208, 212
'Isn't She Lovely', 684
'It Only Takes A Minute', 773
'It's a Man's World', 240–41
'It's a Sin', 690, 692, 693
'It's All Over Now', 228
'It's Alright', 691
'It's My Party', 675
'It's Raining Men', 650
'It's Too Soon to Know', 750, 751
ITV, 62

Jabbar, Kareem Abdul, 730
Jack Hylton's Band, 77
Jackie magazine, 424
Jackson, Al, 322, 323
Jackson, Bullmoose, 37
Jackson, George, 241
Jackson, Jackie, 780
Jackson, Jesse, 783
Jackson, Joseph, 783
Jackson, Michael, xxiv, 424, 570, 571, 593, 668, 672, 742, 775–86, 795–7
Jackson, Milt, 169
Jackson, Ziggy, 205
Jackson Five, the, 773, 779, 781
Jagger, Mick, 217, 218, 219, 221, 227–30, 233, 245, 253, 268, 280, 307–9, 339, 340, 341, 343, 405, 406, 492, 609, 657, 658, 661
'Jailhouse Rock', 408
Jam, the, 491, 507

Jam, Jimmy, 679
'Jambalaya', 33
Jamerson, James, 162
James, Adolphus, 480
James, Dick, 185, 658
James, Elmore, 32, 351
James, Etta, 53, 55
James, Jesse, 224
James, Skip, 223
James Brown: The Godfather of Soul (Brown and Tucker), 35–8
James Monroe High School, Bronx, 545
Jan & Dean, 741
Jane's Addiction, 720
Janowitz, Tama, 593, 614–18
Japan, 558, 582
Jarman, Derek, 177, 199
Jason and the Argonauts, 508
Jay, Jazzy, 545
Jay, Norman, 671, 709–10
Jaymes, Jon, 363
jazz, xxv, 168, 169, 196, 197, 344, 345, 367, 508, 550, 551, 561, 566; bebop, 16, 17, 21; poetry and, 138; and pop music, 81–2; progressive, 16, 17; swing, 5; symphonic, 75; trad (New Orleans-style) revival, 7, 15–17, 106, 138, 140–41
jazz clubs, 86, 88, 89
jazz dancing, 17
jazz-funk, 561, 564
'Jazzy Sensation', 546
'Jealous Guy', 675
Jefferriss Research Foundation, 693
Jefferson, Marshall, xxx
Jefferson Airplane, 453, 612
Jenkins, Johnnie, 321
Jensen, Rich, 790, 792
Jersey, Mods in, 204
Jet magazine, xxix
jet set, 215
Jethro Tull, 734
Jimmy Dean's Christmas in Heaven, 61
'Jimmy Mack', 208
jive, the, 204
jive-chic, 482
Joe Bloggs clothes, 712, 714, 715
Joey (Temperance Seven clarinettist), 140
John, Elton, xix, 594, 647, 653–66, 773
John Michael (Carnaby Street), 204

John Stephen (Carnaby Street), 208, 211, 234
John Wesley Harding, 345, 748–9
Johnny and the Hurricanes, 126
John's Children, 268, 302–3
Johnny O, 717
Johns, Jasper, 319
Johnson, Dave, 792–3
Johnson, David, 536, 561–5
Johnson, Holly, 573
Johnson, Lyndon Baines, 283, 299
Johnson, Paul, 177, 195–8
Johnson, Robert, 226, 352, 750, 751
Johnson, Ron, 694–5
'joints', 289, 291, 314, 800, 801, 807
'Joke, The', 445
Jolson, Al, 27, 225
Jones, Brian, 218, 219, 227, 229, 250, 253, 268, 744
Jones, David, 394
Jones, Davy, 116, 394
Jones, Grace, 522, 524, 536
Jones, Grandpa, 37
Jones, Jimmy, 126, 127
Jones, Max, 7, 15–17
Jones, Mick, 491, 499, 501–6
Jones, Nick, 239–40
Jones, Quincy, 523, 780, 784
Jones, Steve, 490, 493–7, 516
Joplin, Janis, 343, 368, 609, 612, 744
Jordan, Jerry, 645
Jordan Hill, 219
Jordanaires, the, 47–50, 274
journalism, xix, xxv, xxxi, xxxii, 189, 377, 378; advocacy, 641; female journalists, 424; Morrissey's, 600; New, 267, 268, 469; personal, xix
Journey, 647
Joy Division, 712
Joy of Cooking, 367
'Joy to the World', 369
joyriding, 799
juke-boxes, 70, 77, 81, 168, 211, 212
Juliette (Sade), 528
'Jumpin' Jack Flash', 348
Junction, 763
Jungle music, xxx, 734
Junior Wells and his All-Star Band, 240–41
'Just Keep It Up', 126

'Just My Imagination', 773

K Records, 722–3
Kafka, Franz, 698, 699
Kakko, 717
Kama Sutra, 327
Karminsky Experience, 738
Kasdan, Lawrence, 610, 611, 612
Kasmin (art dealer), 561
Keeler, Christine, 195, 475
Keene, Nelson, 115, 116, 122
Keil, Charles, 641
Keith, Nyah, 479
Keith and Enid, 472
Kemp, Harry, 806
Kemp, Lindsay, 207, 394
Kennedy, John, 65, 215
Kennedy, John Fitzgerald, 163
Kennedy, Robert, 269
Kenny, Bill, 14, 15
Kenny, Herbert, 14–15
Kent, Nick, 378, 409, 593
Keough, Danny, 795, 797
Kern, Jerome, 73
Kerouac, Jack, 138, 226, 290, 481
Kerr, Clark, 299
Kershaw, Nik, 423
Kesey, Ken, 267, 269–72
ketamine, 813
Keywords (Williams), xxv
Kezar Stadium, San Francisco, 296
Khairul, 764
Kick Out the Jams, 403
Kickers, 711
Kidd, Joe, 763
Kidel, Mark, 470, 506–8
King (songwriter), 673
King, B. B., 565
King, Jonathan, 692, 693
King, Martin Luther, Jr, 241, 269, 281–2,
    546, 747, 783, 785
King, Rodney, 755
'King Bee', 168
King Boy D, 675
King Creole, 543
King Creole (film), 94
King Crimson, 342
King Pleasure, 550
King Records, 35–8
King Theater, Seattle, 791

Kinison, Sam, 760
Kinks, the, 242, 380, 489
Kinsley, Peter, 91–2
Kirby, George, 222
Kiss, 482, 726, 761
Kiss FM, 710
Kissinger, Henry, 404
'KKK Bitch', 753
Klein, Allen, 582
KLF, 671, 733
KLUE (radio station), 281
Knight, Alison, 714–15
'Knocking on Heaven's Door', 419
Knopfler, Mark, 800
Knuckles, Frankie, xxx
'Kometenmelodie' ('Comet Melody'), 483
Kool, 732
Kool and the Gang, 420
Kool Kat label, 680
Kops, Bernard, xviii, 44, 67–9
Korean War, 93
Korova label, 106
Kotap, Michael, 703, 705
Kozak, Arlene, 153, 154, 156, 157
Kraftwerk, 469, 481–7, 508, 509, 535,
    545–6, 565, 669, 678
Krieger, Robby, 328, 329
Kristol, Irving, 741
Ku Klux Klan, 279–82, 753, 756
Kubrick, Stanley, 106, 396
Kung Fu (dance), 420, 421
Kupferberg, Tuli, 339, 343
Kurfirst, Gary, 623
'kutus', 765

L7, 761
La Rue, Danny, 586
La Scale picture house, Saltcoats, 806,
    807
Labelle, Patti, 478, 523
Lacey, Bruce, 141
Lahr, John, 778, 779, 784
Laine, Frankie, xxi-xxii, 26, 84
Lambert, John, 91–2
Lambert, Kit, 268, 304–7
Land of Oz club, London, 713
Landau, Jon, 748
Lane, Abbie, 187
lang, k. d., 770
Lang, Mike, 357

language, xix, xxvii, 72, 106, 207, 416, 735, 736
   see also slang
Language Lab, the (at Gossips), 562, 563
Lanza, Mario, 27
Larkins, W. M. (animation studio), 23–4
Last Exit to Brooklyn (Selby), 699
Last Poets, the, 550
'Last Train to Skaville', 422
Latin American music, 419
Laura dresses (of Paris), 234
Laver, James, 115
'Law of the Land', 387
Lawal, Gaspar, 564
Lawrence, D. H., 613
Le Bon, Simon, 551, 555–9, 595
Leacock, Richard, 343
Leader, Harry, 14
Leary, Dr Timothy, 298, 352, 568
LeBlanc, Fred, 221
Led Zeppelin, 367, 557, 635n, 734, 761
Lee, Alvin, 481
Lee, Brenda, 126, 143
Lee, Bruce, 499
Lee, Peggy, 86, 518
Lee's of Broadway, 154
Leeds Polytechnic, 503
Leffler, Ed, 409
Legge, Gordon, 593–4, 601–7
Lehrer, Tom, 129
Leiber, Jerry, 673
Leigh, Vivien, 206
Lennon, Alfred, 194, 254–5
Lennon, Cynthia, 254, 255
Lennon, John, 106, 142, 168, 179, 180, 181, 184, 186–95, 216, 254–8, 268, 278–84, 369, 657
Lennon, Julian, 255
Lennox, Annie, 536, 800
Leone, Sergio, 546
lesbian clubs, 494
lesbians, 293, 425, 769
Lester, Dick, 141
Let it Bleed, 171
Let it Rock, 125–7, 418–22
'Let Me Be Good to You', 279
'Let's Get It On', 422
Letters to Olga (Havel), 701
Levellers, the, 800
Levi, Alan, 92–5

Levine, David (photographer), 630
Levine, David (pianist), 68
Levine, Ian, 451, 452
Levine, Stewart, 634
Levy, Andrew, 737
Lewie, Jona, 539
Lewin, David, 238
Lewis, Jerry Lee, xxii, 43, 44, 57–60, 91–2, 169, 278
Lewis, Juma, 344–6
Lewis, Steve, 551
Lewis, Terry, 679
Lewis, Vic, 14
LFO, 735
Liberace, 60, 541
Lichner makeup, 532
Lichtenstein, Roy, 243
Liebowitz, Annie, 517
Liedernacht club, Detroit, 679
Life magazine, xvii, 245, 343
'lifestyle', 737
Lift gay club, Dean Street, Soho, 563–4
Liggins, Chuck, 53
'Light My Fire', 327
lighting: flicker lights, 54; limelight, 12, 13; spotlights, 54; strobe, 271, 273, 274–5, 313, 733
Like Punk Never Happened (Rimmer), 535, 539–42
Lil Louis, 712
Lincoln Center film festival, 244
Lincoln Park, Chicago, 330, 331, 334, 336
Lindbergh, Charles, 10
Linnard, Stephen, 569
Lipstick Traces (Marcus), 6
'Lithium', 721
Little Anthony, 222
'Little Doll', 404
'Little Queenie', 361
Little Richard, 36, 43, 51–7, 87, 169, 320–21, 645, 740, 743
Little Suzie, 144
Little Willie John, 37
Live at the Apollo, 224
Live Through This, 793
'Live with Me', 360–61
Liverpool, Beatles and, 184, 185, 189, 193–4
Liverpool Echo, 185

Liverpool Football Club, 719
'Living in the City', 523
Livingstone, Dandy, 477
L. L. Cool J., 642, 693
Lockhart-Smith, Judy, 182, 183
Locomotion, the (dance), 152
Loder, Kurt, 759
Logan, Craig, 691
Lollapalooza tours, 720–21
London, 7, 68, 234, 240, 709–10, 715;
    Summer of Love, 714, 742; Swinging,
    xxvi, 177, 199, 288, 494
London (group), 539
London, Laurie, 82, 86
London Astoria, 14
London Calling, 606
London Jazz Club, 16, 17
London Palladium, xxi, 14, 27, 31, 108
London Philharmonic Orchestra, 13
London Soul Boys, 671
Long, Shorty, 48
'Long Haired Lover from Liverpool', 409
long-playing records *see under* records
Longview, Texas (Beatles records burnt),
    281
Look Back in Anger (Osborne), 88–9
Loot (Orton), 288
Lord John, 211
Lorna and Scotty, 127
Los Angeles (gangs in), 693–6
Los Angeles (magazine), 277
Los Angeles Coliseum, 626–7
Los Angeles Palladium, 620, 624, 625,
    626
Lon Angeles Police Department (LAPD),
    619–20, 622–7, 754, 785
Los Angeles riots (1986), 618–27
Los Angeles Street Scene festival (1986),
    619, 623, 624, 626
Los Angeles Times, 694
Loss, Joe, 14
Lotis, Dennis, xxii, 28–9
'Louie, Louie', 167
Louie's Showcase Lounge, Roxbury, 221
Louis, Joe, 51, 93
Louise's club, London, 494, 495
Lounge gay coffee-bar, Whitehall,
    London, 207
love, xxxii, 33; gay, 209; punks and, 487,
    497; and sex, 327; stories, 204;

universal, 327
Love, Courtney, 787, 792, 793–4
'Love in Vain', 352, 353
'Love Me Do', 184–5
'Love Me Do': The Beatles' Progress
    (Braun), 177, 186–95
'Love Me Two Times', 127, 328
Love of the Psychedelic Rangers, Admiral,
    292
Love Sculpture, 482
Lovell, Terry, 520, 660
'Low', 508
Lowe, Chris, 690–93
Lower Third, the, 394
LSD (acid), xviii, 166, 232, 267, 268,
    270, 288, 289, 291, 293, 297–300,
    315, 327, 332, 350, 352, 370, 372,
    403, 568, 609, 646, 711, 730, 731
Luard, Nick, 215
Lulu, 383
'lunatic fringe', 106, 138
Lute Records, 321
Lyall, Gavin, 60–63
Lydon, Michael, 350
Lymon, Frankie, 528
Lyon, Stuart, 391
Lyttleton, Humphrey, 15–16, 89

M, 533
McCabe, James, 807, 808
McCarthy, Michael, 498–9
McCartney, Paul, 142, 180, 183, 184,
    186–95, 238, 253, 254, 264, 279, 287,
    288, 289, 322, 763, 782
McCaughey, Scott, 788
McCrea, George, 421
McCullin, Don, 6, 23–5
McDonald, Jock, 562
McDuff, Brother Jack, 169
McElwaine, Bernard, 6, 30–32
McEwan, Joe, 221
McGee, Ian, 209–10
McGhee, Brownie, 169
McGillis, Kelly, 691
McGowan, Cathy, 232, 234
McGriff, Jimmy, 169
McGuigan, Barry, 603
McGuinn, Jim, 246
MacGuire Sisters, 186

MacInnes, Colin, xxiii, xxvi, 44, 81–91, 95–9, 268, 547
MacIntyre, Fraser, 810
McKenna, Tim, 650, 651–2
Mackenzie, Craig, 655, 656, 657
Mackenzie, Iain, 381
Mackenzie, Kelvin, 654, 655, 656, 659, 662, 663, 664, 666
McKenzie, Scott, 676
McLachlan, Craig, 719
McLaren, Malcolm, 493, 539, 540, 541
McLean, Don, 744
McLuhan, Marshall, 153
Macmillan, Harold, 1st Earl of Stockton, 475
McNeely, Big Jay, 37, 53
McNeil, Legs, 469, 470, 516–17
Macrea, George, 447
Madchester boom, 671, 713, 767
Madhouse, The (Kops and Fisk), 69
Madison, the (dance), 152, 155, 421
'Madness', 205
Madonna, xxiii, xxix, 536, 570–72, 598, 635, 741, 742, 760, 782, 784
Magazine, 558, 737
magazines, xxiii, 177; Beatles and, 192–3; pop, 204; style, xix; women's, 204
    see also fanzines
'Magic Fly', 509
magic mushrooms, 288, 478
'Magical Mystery Tour', 749
Magical Mystery Tour, 336
Magma, 482
Masha-Lila group, 295
Maharishi, the, 327
Mailer, Norman, 267, 269, 330–36
Maimudes, Victor, 259
Major, John, 799
'Make It Big', 593
makeup, male, 52, 54, 535, 559, 560, 586, 783
Malanga, Gerard, 164, 166, 274–5, 277
Malaysia, 761–6
Malcolm X (Malcolm Little), 6, 7–10, 241, 546, 785
Mali, 178, 240–41
Malle, Louis, 611
'Man in the Mirror', 783
Man Parrish, 564

Man Who Fell to Earth, The, 458, 459, 462
Man Who Sold the World, The, 392, 393, 394
Man Who Would Be King, The (film), 440
manager/singer relationship, 229
Manchester City Football Club, 712, 715
Manchester Evening News, 715
Manchester G-Mex, 770, 771, 772
Manchester United Football Club, 381
Mandela, Nelson, 696
Mangrove Restaurant, London, 475
Manhattan Transfer, 647
Manilow, Barry, 773
Mankowitz, Wolf, xxiii, 77–81
Manley, Michael, 479, 480
Manor House, near Harringey, London, 475
Manson, Charles, 269, 336–8
Manual (How to Have a Number the Easy Way), The (The Timelords), 671, 673–7
Manzarek, Ray, 328, 329
Mao Tse Tung, 284, 415
Maoism, 284
Marcus, Greil, xix, 6, 608, 671, 739–52
Marcuse, Herbert, 525
Margate (Mods v Rockers), 200, 379
'Margo', 119
marijuana, xix, 8, 68, 166, 268, 288, 291, 297, 300, 330, 515, 726
    see also ganga; grass; pot
Marilyn, 536, 585–8, 629, 630, 632
Marines, the, 717
Mark P., 497–8
Mark the 45 King, 713
marketing, xxiv, xxxii; and Frankie Goes to Hollywood, 574; and Michael Jackson, 778; niche-, xxx; target, xxviii–xxix, 593; youth, 43
Mar-Keys, 322–3
Markham, Pigmeat, 222
Marley, Bob, 477
Marquee, the, London, 204, 205, 407
Marr, Johnny, 596–9
Marriot, Steve, 380
M/A/R/R/S/, xxx, 676
Marsalis, Wynton, 551
Marsden, Gerry, 185, 741

Marsh, Dave, xxxiii, 378, 403–6, 469, 671
Martin, Dean, xxi, xxii
Martin, Gavin, 672, 775–86
Martin, George, 182–5
Martin, Peter, 536, 570–72
Martinelli, Elsa, 187
Marvelettes, the, 152, 163, 208
Mas in the Grove, 475
Mashed Potato, the (dance), 152, 421
Mason, Barry, 122
Massey, Graham, 713
Mathis, Johnny, 126, 518
Matisse, Henri, 563
Matlock, Glen, 490, 493
Matthews, Simon, 801
Mature, Victor, 27
Maupin, Armistead, 645
Mauve Gloves & Madmen, Clutter & Vine (Wolfe), 412–18
May, Derrick, 677, 678, 679, 681, 734
Maya, dance of, 570
Mayall, Gaz, 563
Maybanke, Laon, 206
'Maybe Tomorrow', 119
'Maybellene', 33, 34–5
Maybury, John, 629, 631–2, 634
Mayerl, Billy, 13
Mayfield, Curtis, 551
Maysles, Al, 351
Maysles, David, 350, 351
MC5, 269, 342, 486, 502
MDA, 813
MDC, 726
'Me and Jane in a 'Plane', 77
'Me and the Devil Blues', 750
'Me No Pop I', 543
Meat is Murder, 595
'Meat is Murder', 593
Mecca, 445, 448, 450, 453
'Medal Song', 628
medicine shows, 73
Meehan, Tony, 179, 180
Megadog club, 805
Megatone, 650, 651
Mekons, the, 742
Mellencamp, John Cougar, 655–6, 743
Melly, George, 44, 113, 177, 215–16, 265, 267, 289
Melnick, Monte, 623
Melody Maker, xxv, 82, 178, 193,

239–40, 391–6, 490–93, 495, 498, 540
Melvin, Harold, 429
Melvins, the, 724, 725–6, 727
Memphis, 45, 94–5, 278–80
'Menace of Beatlism, The' (Johnson), 177
Mendl, Hugh, 65
'Menergy', 649
Menschmaschine, 483, 484
'Mentasm', 732
Mescaline, 297
Mercer, David, 170
Merchandizing Corporation of America, 542
Mercury, xxv
Mercury, Freddie, 168
Merengue, 422, 434
Merman, Ethel, 76
Mersey Beat, 142, 185
Mersey sound, 418
Merv Griffin Show, The, 251
'Message, The', 535
message songs, 246–7
methadone, 633
Metal Machine Music, 482
Metallica, 635, 637, 762
Metallica, 741
methadone, 633
methamphetamine, 481–2
methedrine, 213, 297
Metro Club, 475
Metroplex label, 679
Metropolis nightclub, Saltcoats, 806, 807–8, 809
Metzke, Gustav, 171
'Mexican, The', 546
MGM label, 127
MGs, 322
Miami and the Siege of Chicago (Mailer), 330–36
Michael, George, 575–9, 581–5
Michael X, 480
Michaels, Bret, 739–40, 743, 749
Michelangelo Buonarroti, 566
'Michelle', 262
Microsoft, 789, 792
Midler, Bette, 647
'Midnight Hour', 241
Midnight Oil, 719
'Midnight Ramble, The', 359, 454
Midnighters, the, 37, 125

Milk, Harvey, 648
milk bars, 70–71
Miller, Mitch, xxv
Milligan, Spike, 140, 141
Millinder, Lucky, 37
'Million Love Songs, A', 773
Mimms, Garnet, 219
'Minah Rock', 765
'Mind of a Lunatic', 750
'Mind Playing Tricks on Me', 750–52
Minelli, Liza, 515
miners' strike (1984), 536, 572, 574
Mingus, Charles, 169, 226
Minogue, Kylie, 716, 718, 719
minstrel shows, 74
Miracles, the, 161, 163, 169, 208, 224,
    741
Mirror Group, 88
Mr Biggs, 546
'Mr Jones', 249
'Misty', 126
MIT (Massachusetts Institute of
    Technology, xxvii, xxviii, 702
Mitcham, Jane, 92
Mitchell, Mitch, 344
'Mitternacht' ('Midnight'), 483
Mixmag, 669
Miyake, Issey, 690
Modar, 762
Model 500, 677–80
Mods, xxv, 177, 200, 203–5, 207–9, 227,
    340, 378–82, 443, 448, 451, 452, 502,
    538, 562, 563, 567, 736, 738
Moman, Chips, 219
'Momma's Gotta Die Tonight', 754
'Money's Too Tight to Mention', 550
Monk, Thelonious, 226
Monkees, the, xxviii, 394, 482, 488
Monotones, the, 743
Monroe, Marilyn, 588
Montand, Yves, 128
Monterey Pop (Leacock-Pennebaker),
    343
Monterey Pop Festival, 269
Montgomery, Wes, 169, 345
Monty Python, 563, 598
Moody Blues, 552
Moon, Keith, 239, 303, 306–7
Moon, Woodrow Wilson, 224
Moonglows, the, 649

Moonlight Club, West Hampstead, 538
'Moonlight Drive', 405
Moore, Bobby, 477
Moore, Scotty, 48, 49
Moors Murders, 595, 597
'moral panics', xxv, 178
Morgan, Derrick, 472
'Morgenspaziergang' ('Morning Walk'),
    483
Morley, Paul, xxix, 536, 551–9, 573
'Morning Has Broken', 692
Moroder, Giorgio, 565
Morricone, Ennio, 546
Morris, Eric, 472
Morris, Mixmaster, 739
Morris dancing, 86
Morrison, Jim, 327–9, 343, 405, 609,
    612, 742, 744
Morrison, Sterling, 275–6, 277, 707
Morrissey, 595–601, 713, 768, 769
Moss, Jon, 539–40, 627–9
Most, Mickey, 278
Mother Love Bone, 790
'Mothership Connection', 680
Motley Crüe, 620
motorbikes, 23, 24, 44, 318, 378, 548
    see also bikers
Motorhead, 636, 637, 638, 761
Motown Revue, 544
Motown 25, 782
Mott the Hoople, 676
'Mountain Dew', 33
Mountain Girl, 269
'Moving', 768, 769
Moyet, Alison, 579
MTV, 593, 620, 739, 744, 759, 762, 768,
    781, 788
MTV Unplugged, 794
Muir, Mike, 622–3
Mullen, Brendan, 624, 625
Muller, Robert, 5
Mullican, Moon, 36
Mulligan, Gerry, 394
Murdoch, Rupert, 655, 656, 659, 661,
    666
Murray, Charles Shaar, 377, 406–10, 494
Murray, Dr Leo, 810–11
Murray, Mickey, 321
Murray, Mitch, 185
music hall, xxii, xxiv, 13, 25, 140, 769

Music Life, 551
music publishers, 77
musical arrangers, 74, 75
musique concrète, 735
Muslims *see* Islam
Mutant King, The (Dalton), xxiv
Mutoid Waste Company, 804
Mutual Attraction, 650
Muzak, 509
My Bloody Valentine, 742, 800, 802
'My Cherie Amour', 346
My Dinner with André (Malle), 611
'My Girl', 208, 240, 773
'My Guy', 208
My Guy magazine, 424
'My Head's in Mississippi', 743
'My Insatiable One', 768
'My Sweet Lord', 693
Mysterians, the, 469, 508
Mystery Train (Marcus), 608

NAACP (National Association for the
    Advancement of Colored People), 158,
    641
Nagasaki, 6
Naked Lunch, The (Mailer), 190
Name, Billy, 164–8
Napier-Bell, Simon, xxiii, 268, 302–7,
    582–3, 585
narcotics, 812
'nark', a (narcotics agent), 291
Nathan, Syd, 36, 37–8
National Association for the
    Advancement of Colored People
    (NAACP), 158, 641
National Gay Rights Advocates, 651
National Graphical Association (NGA),
    656
National Public Radio (NPR), 749
National Service, 140
Natural Born Killers (film), xxv
Navasky, Victor, 243
Nedeloff, Fran, 157
Neil, 675
Nelson, Paul, 249
NEMS, 182, 227
'Never Grow Old', 645
Never Mind the Bollocks, 470
Neverland Ranch, 778, 782–3, 796
Nevermind, 721, 729

Neville Brothers, 604
New Age travellers, 798, 799, 800, 803–5
New Continental, the (dance), 152
New Journalism, 267, 268, 469
New Left, 414, 416
New Lindsey Theatre Club, London, 62
new mods, 537–8
'new music', 344, 345
New Musical Express (NME), 193,
    406–10, 424, 489–90, 498, 499–506,
    540, 552, 573, 775–86
New Musick, 508–9
New Order, 681, 712
New Orleans jazz revival, 7, 15–17, 106,
    138, 140–41
New Pop, xxix, 535, 536, 539–42, 573
New Record magazine, 193
New Republic, 10–12
New Right, xxxii, 607
New Romantics, 548, 565, 568, 678
New Society magazine, 268, 316–20,
    509–14
New Statesman, 177, 195–8
New Straits Times, 764
New Wave (French), 222, 502, 506
New York Dolls, 378, 493, 502
New York Magazine, 268, 273–7
New York Times, 260, 268, 280, 284,
    392
New York *World-Telegram*, 243, 244
New Yorker, The, 287
Newark riots (1967), 268
Newley, Tony, 393
Newman, Andy ('Thunderclap'), 171
News at Ten (television programme), 632
News International, 663
News of the World newspaper, 505
newspaper industry, and pop star's fall
    from grace, 594
Newsweek, 284
Newton, Huey, 330, 608
Next Time I'll Sing to You (film), 187
niche-marketing *see under* marketing
Nicks, Stevie, 720, 731
Nico, 276, 277, 486, 509
Nicolson, Viv, 600
Nietzsche, Friedrich Wilhelm, 724
'Night and Day', 521
'Night Train', 420, 422
Nilsson, Harry, 673

Nine Inch Nails, 720
19 magazine, 511
'1977', 503
1910 Fruitgum Company, 488
'96 Tears', xxxii, 492, 508
Nirvana, xxxi, 478, 672, 721–30, 742,
    744–5, 749, 762, 768, 786–9, 791,
    793, 794
Nisbett, Guy, 738–9
Nixon, Richard, 782
NME see New Musical Express
NME's Pocket Jukebox, 604
No Direction Home (Skelton), 258–62
'No Fun', 404
'No Time', 368
'No UFOs', 678–9
Noebel, David, 278
Noël Coward Diaries, The (Coward),
    238–9
Noise, (written by Jacques Attali), xxxi
Noise Inc, 713
non–fiction novel, xvii, xix
Noon, Mike, 671, 710–15
Noone, Peter, 392
Nord, Eric 'Big Daddy', 271
North, Jay (Dennis the Menace), 278, 280
North, Oliver 756
North Beach scene, 290
North Western Scallies, 671
Northern Soul, 378, 423, 443–56, 547,
    551, 566, 680, 735
Northside, 713, 714
'Not Fade Away', 228
Notes on Fame, Automatic Vaudeville
    (Lahr), 778, 779
Notting Hill Carnival, 475
Notting Hill riots, 475
Nottingham, 443–7, 449, 450–55
Nottingham Forest Football Club, 449
Nottingham Palais, 445, 447, 449, 452
Novoselic, Krist, 722–30, 745, 749, 793
'Nude Photo', 679
Numan, Gary, 545, 554
'Numbers', 546
Nuttall, Jeff, 106, 138–41
N.W.A., 694, 742, 753
Nymphs, the, 742
Nyro, Laura, 604

Oakenfold, Paul, 713, 714, 715

Oakes, Simon, 563
Oasis, xxx
Observer, 193, 381; Colour Magazine,
    234
Observer Life magazine, 806–13
'Observer' Sixty Years of Cinema
    exhibition, London, 60
oceanic rock, 733
Ochs, Phil, 283
O'Connor, Sinéad, 742
O'Connor, Wendy, 787
Odeon cinema, Liverpool, 225, 226
O'Dowd, David, 631, 634
O'Dowd, Dina, 560, 634
O'Dowd, George see Boy George
O'Dowd, Gerald, 559–60
O'Dowd, Gerrie (Boy George's father),
    560, 630–31
O'Dowd, Kevin, 632, 633
Off the Wall, 780, 781
Ogilvy, Lord, 563
'Oh! You Pretty Things', 392, 396
Oh Boy! (television show), 105
O'Hagan, Andrew, 673, 806–13
Oingo Boingo, 647
Old Grey Whistle Test (television
    programme), 383, 555, 556
Oldham, Andrew Loog, 106, 178,
    216–19, 226–9, 582
Olsen, Jimmy, 517
On the Road, 482
Once upon a Time in the East (Rimmer),
    681–90
'Once You've Tasted Love', 773
Ondine, xxiii
One-Dimensional Man (Marcuse), 525
'One-Eyed Giant', 422
O'Neal, Alexander, 679
'One Night Affair', 391
Only Lovers Left Alive (Wallis), 106
'Only Way is Up, The', 675, 676
Ono, Yoko, 381–2
'Ooh Poo Pah Doo', 127
op art, 236
Open Mind, 805
Operation Culture, 632
Operation Elvis (Levi), 92–5
Operation Snapshot, 804
opium, 297
Orange, Jason, 772–5

Orbital, 735
orbital rave, 737
Orb, the 734
Orioles, the, 750, 751
Ormsby Gore, Jane, 233
Orpheans, 13
Orton, Iris, 67
Orton, Joe, 267, 287–9
Osborne, John, 89
Osborne, Lynne, 444–51, 453
Osbourne, Ozzy, 725
Osmond, Alan, 407, 408, 409
Osmond, Donny, 383, 406, 441
Osmond, Jay, 407, 408
Osmond, Jimmy, 408–9
Osmond, Merrill, 407, 408
Osmond, Wayne, 407, 408
Osmonds, the, 377, 406–10, 423, 456–7, 558
Osservatore Romano, L', 281
Otway, Thomas, 287
'Our Love is Here to Stay', 186
'Out in the Cold', 743, 747
Ovation, 447
Owen, Mark, 771–5
OZ magazine, 267

P, Mark, 469
Pacemakers, the, 741
'Pacific State', 713
Pacino, Al, 427, 428, 443
painkillers, 812
Pakistanis, and skinheads, 379–80
Palace Theater, New York, 646
Pan's People, 422
'Panama Rag', 15
'Panic in Detroit', 462
Pansy Division, 769
'Pantomime Horse', 768
Paolozzi, Eduardo, frontispiece, xxvii
'Papa was a Rolling Stone', 523
'Papa's Got a Brand New Bag', 224, 241
'Paperback Writer', xxviii
Parallel Lives (Burton), 205–14, 410–12
'Paralytic', 14
Paramount Theater, New York, 5, 10
Parents Music Resource Center, 760
Paris Angels, 711, 712, 713
Parker, Andrew, 661
Parker, Charlie, 169, 196

Parker, Lord Chief Justice, 268
Parker, Tom, 43, 45, 46, 47
Parkin, Molly, 235
Parkinson, Michael, 663
Parkinson, Norman, 193
Parliament, 679, 680
Parlophone Records, 182, 184, 691
Parnell, Jack, 14
Parnes, Larry, xxi-xxii, xxiii, xxiv, 105, 115–16, 118, 120–25
Parry, Harry, 12
Parsons, Tony, xxx, 470, 499–506
Partridge Family, 383
Passover music, 701
Paterson, Meg, 630, 632, 633
Patrick, Kentrick, 472
Patti Jo, 648
Patton, John, 169
Paul, Leslie, 143
Paul, Steve, 242
Pavitt, Bruce, 727
Pawnbroker, The (film), 324
Payne, Jack, 13
Peaches, the, 53
Pearce, Kevin, 669
Peebles, Ann, 550
Peech Boys, 535
Peel, David, 345
Peel, John, 379, 596
Pendergrass, Teddy, 649
'Penetration', 404
Penguins, the, 51–2
Penn, Dan, 219
Pennebaker, D. A., 343
'Penny Lane', 288
Pentagon, the, 94
pentamadine, 650–51
Penthouse, 476
People magazine, 514, 611, 660
pep pills, 307–9
Pepsi, 777, 782, 785
Perkins, Carl, 169, 747, 748
Perry, Lee, 604
Perry, Mark, 469
Pet Shop Boys, 672, 690–93, 768
Pet Shop Boys, Literally (Heath), 690–93
Pete Waterman Ltd (PWL), 716
Peter, Jean, 378, 418–22
Peter Pan (Barrie), xxiv
Peterson, Ron, 621, 622, 624–5

Petticoat magazine, 234
Petty, Milt, 623
Petty, Tom, 743, 747
peyote, 297
'Philadelphia Freedom', 433
Philip, HRH Prince, Duke of Edinburgh, 184
Philips, 394
Phillips, Esther, 524
Phillips, Sam, 57–60
Philly (The Philadelphia Sound), 679, 773
Philpott, Trevor, 63–7
Phoenix, Pat, 600
Phonogram, 575
Physical Graffiti, 725
Piaf, Edith, 129
Picasso, Pablo, 114, 192
Pick of the Pops, xxvi
Pickett, Wilson, 240
'picnolepsy', 733
Picture Post, 5, 6, 12–17, 25–30, 43, 44, 60–67
'Piggies', 338
Pilgrims, the, 763
'Pillow Talk', 542
Pinetoppers, the, 321
Pink Fairies, 342–3
Pink Floyd, 267, 486, 553, 734
Pirroni, Marco, 495, 539, 540, 541
'Pistol Packin' Mama', 125
Pixies, the, 720, 723
Placidyl, 166
'Plan, The', 408
'Planet Rock', 535, 546–7, 569
Plastic People of the Universe, 700, 705, 707
'Please Don't Tease', 127
'Please, Please Me', 185
'Please Please Please', 37–8, 225
Plimpton, George, 241–5
Plunkett, Sarah, 230, 231, 233
Plymouth (Top Rank at), 506–8
'pogo-dancing', 507, 508, 606
Pointer Sisters, 647
Poison, 739–40, 745
Poison Girls, 538
police, 25, 201, 202, 210, 225, 226, 330, 364, 593, 619–20, 622–7, 710, 737, 753–60, 778, 797, 803, 804, 805, 807–8, 809

political assassination, xvii, 269, 747
politics, and pop culture, 195–7
Pollock, Jackson, 566
Polydor, 502
Pommels, Stinky, 480
Pomus, Doc, 599
Poneman, Jonathan, 727, 788
Pony, the (dance), 152
'Poor Little Rich Girl', 143
Poor Little Rich Girl (film), 242
pop: becomes art, 178; defined, xxv; early uses of term, xxv-xxvi; wide variety of meanings, xx
Pop (fan magazine), 253
Pop, Iggy, 268, 285–6, 378, 395–6, 403–5, 409, 486, 489, 509
pop art, origin of term, xxviii
pop charts, introduction of, 5
Pop from the Beginning (Cohn), 225–30
'Pop Musik' (M), 533
'Pop Songs and Teenagers' (MacInnes), xxvi, 44
'pop star', xxvi
Popism: the Warhol '60s (Warhol and Hackett), 105, 164–8
'Popular Arts, The' (Hall and Whannel), xxvi
popular song, 521–2, 523, 526
populism, xxxi-xxxii, xxxiii
Porter, Cole, 521, 522, 524
Posies, 788, 789
postmodernism, xxix, xxx, 535
pot, 168–9, 308, 449, 630, 646, 726, 807
see also ganga; grass; marijuana
Powell, Eleanor, 230, 231, 233, 234
Powell, Enoch, 478
Powell, Peter, 556
Power, Duffy, xxii, 115, 116, 122
Powerplant club, Chicago, 678
Powers, Ann, 672–3, 786–95
Prague, 696, 697–8, 701, 704, 706
Pranksters, the, 269, 270, 271
Preludin, 232
Presland, Frank, 658
Presley, Elvis, xxii, xxvi, 43–50, 53, 54, 57, 67, 79, 84–5, 88, 93–5, 116, 120, 123, 125, 126, 179, 190, 204, 228, 229, 230, 278, 421, 424, 470, 474, 488, 492, 502, 518, 599, 672, 742, 743, 744, 776, 780, 782, 785, 797

Presley, Lisa Marie, 672, 795–7
Presley, Priscilla, 797
Press, J., 413
Press, Joy, 673, 797–806
Press Council, 656
Pressure Drop (Reel), 471–81
Preston, Billy, 406
Price, Martin, 713
'Pride', 601
Pride, Dickie, xxii, 116, 120–21
Prime Movers, the, 285, 286
Primitives, the, 275–6
Prince, xxiii, 598, 603, 742, 760, 782
'Prince Charming', 541, 542
Princeton student demonstration (1966),
  283
Private Places of Entertainment Act
  (1962), 737
Proby, P. J., 228
Proctor, Harvey, 660
Prodigy, the, 733
Profumo, John, 195, 475
progressive concept, 519
'Progressive House', 734
progressive jazz *see under* jazz
progressive music, 448, 452
Progressive Rock, 380, 725, 734
'Promises', 772
protest, 138–41
protest songs, 247, 248
Providence Arena, 224
'P. S. I Love You', 184, 185
pseudonyms, xxii-xxiii
psychedelics, 730
'Psychotic Reaction', 492
Public Enemy, 672, 742, 749
publicity: Beatles and, 192; stills, 76;
  stunts, 77
Pucci, 243, 248
Pulnoc, 707, 742
Pulse, 732
Pump Up the Volume, 742
'Pump Up the Volume', 676
Punk(s), xxv, xxix, 178, 469, 470, 488–
  518, 528, 535, 536, 538–42, 551, 553,
  568, 573, 593, 620, 681, 709, 738,
  744, 763, 800, 807
Punk magazine, 469, 487–9, 516–17
punk rock(ers), 481, 489–93, 497–8, 502,
  528, 619–24, 626, 643, 725–6, 727,

799, 802
'Puppy Love', 383
Pure War, 730
Purple Hearts (drugs), 204, 208, 232
Purvis, Melvin, 517
'Pushin' Too Hard', 492
'Put Your Head on My Shoulder', 154
Pye, 180, 451, 452

Q Club, Paddington, London, 421
Quaaludes, 403, 515
Quant, Mary, 227
'Quarter to Three', 127
Quayle, Dan, 756, 799
'Queen Bitch', 392
Queen Christina (film), 207
Queen Mary's Hospital for the East End,
  London, 203
Queen's Silver Jubilee Trust, 658
'queering out', 268, 285–6

Rabin, Oscar, 14
race issue, xix, 44, 51, 54, 87, 158–64,
  224, 268–9, 280, 281–2, 284, 324–7,
  379–80, 471–81, 525, 593, 639–43,
  741, 746, 747, 749, 754
Rachman, Peter, 474, 475
Radical Chic, 414
Radio Luxembourg, 127, 445
Radio Mali, 240
Radio Rhythm Club, 14
radio stations, 678; Beatles records
  banned, 281; pirate, 732
  see also individual names
Radio WDET, 681
'Radioactivity', 508
ragga, 731, 735
ragtime, 89, 522
'RAID' boys, 710
Raiders of the Lost Ark (film), 610
Railway Hotel, Wealdstone, 382
Rainbow Coalition, 783
Rainbow Theatre, London, 406, 658
Raines, Mary Lou, 157–8
Rainey, Michael, 233
Ralston, Bert, 13
Ramada hotel, Manchester, 770
Ramli Sarip, 763
Ramone, Dee Dee, 488
Ramone, Joey, 487, 488

Ramone, Tommy, 488
Ramones, the, 469, 470, 487–9, 496, 502, 506, 508, 619, 623–4, 625
ramraiding, 799
Rantzen, Esther, 601
Rap/rappers, xxv, xxx, 535, 542–4, 561, 562, 569, 682, 693–4, 696, 733, 734, 735, 738, 741, 742, 750, 755, 767, 770, 772, 784
Rap-a-Lot label, 750
Rap Attack (Toop), 535, 544–7
rap-metal crossover, 781
rap-to-rock crossover, 755
Rapp, Danny, 744
'Rappers Delight', 543, 544
Rare Groove, 737
Rastafarians, 422, 474, 475, 476, 478–81, 538, 554, 803
Rat, 367
Rationals, the, 285
Rave magazine, 317
Ravensbourne College of Art, 495
raves/ravers, xxv, xxxiii, 709–10, 715, 730–34, 738, 798, 799, 800, 802–13; orbital, 737
Raw Power, 403–6
Ray, Johnny, xxi, 6, 26, 27, 30–32, 76, 84, 228, 423
Raymond, Derek, 103, 105
Razak, Najib Tun, 763
RCA Victor 45, 47, 49, 94, 394
Reach Out, 524, 773
'Reach Out, I'll Be There', 208
Reactive Bass, 807
Ready, Steady, Go (television programme), 204, 234, 419
Ready for Love', 127
Reagan, Ronald, 299, 593, 695, 746, 748, 779, 782, 783
'Real Cool Times', 404
Rebel Without a Cause (film), 60, 61
Record Mirror, 127
recording, xxxii, 37–8, 47–50, 74, 75, 82, 182
records: 45 rpm, 5, 36; long-playing, xxix; price, 569; 78 rpm (shellac), 5, 36, 38; singles, xxix, 177, 580; 33 rpm, 5
'Red River Rock', 126
Redd, Gene, 37, 38

Redding, Otis, 219, 221, 223, 240, 269, 320–24, 361, 420
Redding, Rodgers, 221
Rediffusion, 447
Redskins, the, 600
Reed, Jimmy, 168, 169, 351
Reed, Lou, xix, xxiv, 275, 276, 392, 395–6, 481, 482, 486–7, 488, 496, 509, 672, 696–709
reefers, 8
Reel, Penny, 105, 125–7, 469, 471–81
Rees-Mogg, William, 268, 307–9
Reese and Santonio, 678
Reeve, Christopher, 588
Reeves, Martha, 208
Regal Cinema, Saltcoats, 806
reggae, 208, 380, 419–22, 448–9, 471, 473, 476, 477, 494, 503, 508, 518, 526, 562, 564, 604, 709, 731, 770, 803
Reid, John, 656, 660
Reilly, Trevor, 810
'Relax', 573
Renaissance Bump, 434
Rendezvous In Black (Woolrich), 597
rent boys, 594, 653–60, 662
Representative, The (film), 190
Reprise, 344
'Repudiate', 602
'Respect', 241
Revolt into Style (Melly), 44, 215–16, 265, 289
'Revolution Rock', 606
Revolver, 322
'Revolution', 284
'Revolution 9', 338
Reynolds, Simon, 671, 730–36
'Rhapsody in Blue', 12
Rhodes, Izora, 649
Rhodes, Nick, 551, 552, 557–8
Rhythim Is Rhythim, 677, 678, 679, 681
rhythm, 522, 523
Rhythm 'n' Blues (R&B), xxii, 37, 168, 221, 226, 241, 324–7, 345, 394, 421, 545, 640, 647, 649, 678, 679, 741, 747
Ricard, Rene, 241, 245
Richard, Cliff, xxiv, 44, 126, 127, 168, 179, 186, 190, 191, 423
Richards, Keith, 168, 217, 218, 219, 268, 348–51, 357, 358, 360, 361, 363–4, 365, 409, 454, 492, 504, 601

Richbourg, John, 321
Richman, Jonathan, 496
Richmond, Surrey, 217, 228
'Ride 'Em Boys', 680
Ridgeley, Andrew, 575, 576, 577, 581, 583–4, 585
Ridgers, Derek, 565
Righteous Brothers, the, 209, 691
Rigney, Dr Francis, 271
Riley, Billy Lee, 57–60
Riley, Clayton, 220
Rimbaud, Arthur, 500
Rimmer, Dave, 535, 539–42, 671, 681–90
'Rise and Fall of Ziggy Stardust and the Spiders from Mars, The', xxix
Rise and Fall of Ziggy Stardust and the Spiders from Mars, The, 393
Ritz, Kreema, 646, 647
Ritz club, New York, 542–4, 545, 625, 638
Rivers, Joan, 588
Rivers, Larry, 170–71
Riverside, 569
Riverside Studios, 710
Rizzo, Rick, 743
Rizzo, Tommy, 637
Robbe-Grillet, Alain, xviii
Robbins, David, xxvii
Robbins, Marty, 126
Robert (owner-manager, All Nations Club, Hackney), 420
Robeson, Paul, 129, 778
Robie, John, 546
Robins, the, 53
Robinson, Edward G., 27
Robinson, Evanne, 155, 156, 158, 159
Robinson, Smokey, 208, 605, 776
Robinson, Sylvia, 542
rock, xxix, xxx, 89, 269, 275, 280, 365–9, 375, 378, 383, 384, 410, 424, 482, 490, 492, 519, 521, 522–3, 526, 535, 561, 619, 672, 700, 740–44, 746, 749, 761 762, 770, 789, 795, 806
see also glam rock; hard rock; indie rock; oceanic rock; progressive rock; punk rock
'Rock and Roll Is Here to Stay', 744
Rock Around the Clock (film), 192, 408
Rock City club, Nottingham, 678

Rock Corp, 620
Rock File (ed. Gillett), 378–84
Rock Island Line, 86
rock 'n' roll, xxi, xxvi, 6, 43, 44, 45, 54, 58, 59, 74, 84, 92, 105, 116, 124, 141, 143, 152, 153, 190, 255, 279, 280, 366, 421, 482, 488, 492, 493, 522, 595, 719, 721, 733, 734, 739–52, 755, 770, 778, 780
'Rock 'n' Roll', 675
Rock 'n' Trade Show (1960), 124
Rock Steady, 422
'Rock Steady', 422
'Rock the Bells', 694
'Rock the Boat', 419
'Rock Your Baby', 421
rockabillies, 548, 550, 741, 746
Rockefeller, Nelson, 336
rockers, 138, 177, 201, 203, 204, 340, 378, 379, 448, 512, 738, 741, 784
'Rocket 88', 778
Rockfield studio, Wales, 540
Rockstar magazine, 498
'Rocky Racoon', 338
Rodgers, Nile, 572
Rodgers, Richard, 73
Rodigan, David, 561, 564
Rodwell, Paul, 575–8, 580
Roe, Tommy, 676
Roeder, Klaus, 484
Rogan, Johnny, xxiv
Rogers, Bill, 185
Rogers, Bobby, 161
Rogers-Bennett, Ted, 206
Rolling Stone magazine, 267, 308, 343–7, 362, 487, 597
Rolling Stones, the, xviii, 106, 171, 178, 208, 216–19, 224–30, 248, 253, 254, 268, 278, 318, 347–65, 379, 383, 424, 448, 470, 477, 491, 492, 496, 502, 518, 612, 646, 741, 744
Rolling Stones 2, 106, 216–19, 339–41
Rollins, Henry, 721
romanticism, disco and, 523–6
romanticism, new *see* New Romanticism
Romberg, Sigmund, 73
Ronettes, the, 584
Ronson, Mick, 392, 554
Rose, Axl, 740, 749
Ross, Diana, 478, 524, 784

Roth, Philip, xvii
Rotten, Johnny, xxiii, 489, 490, 491, 493, 517, 657, 744, 800
Rough Trade label, 595, 596, 597
Route 666: On the Road to Nirvana (Arnold), 720–30
Rowe, Dick, 179, 180, 189
Rowland, Kevin, 550
Roxy Music, 377, 554, 558, 675
Royal dance-hall, Tottenham, London, 25
royal family, The Smiths and, 595, 599–600, 658
Royal Theater, Baltimore, 52
Royal Variety Performance, 189, 196
royalties, 575–6, 579, 580, 581, 583, 719
Roza, Lita, 28
'Rubber Ball', 126
Rubell, Steve, 515
Rubin, Jerry, 284
Rubinoos, 676
Rude boys, 480, 538
Rudetsky, Michael, 633–4
Rudolf, Paul, 342
Ruffin, Jimmy, 208
Run-DMC, 619, 620, 694
'Run Red Run', 125
'Runaway', 637
RuPaul, 770
Rupe, Art, 51
Rush, 732
'Rush in the House', 735
Rushdie, Salman, 692
'Rusholme Ruffians', 599
Rushton, Neil, 680
Russell (owner of Colombo's club, Carnaby Street), 420–21
Russell, Ethan, 350–51, 363
Russell, Ken, 647
Russell, Tony, 583
Russells (solicitors), 575, 576, 577, 582, 583, 585
Rutherford, Paul, 573
Rykiel, Sonia, 234
Rythm Oil (Booth), 320–24, 746–7

'Sabre Dance', 482
Sachs, Peter, 23
Sade, Donatien, Comte de (known as Marquis), 275, 528, 529

Sahl, Mort, 169
'Sailing', 673
'St James Infirmary', 405
St John the Divine, New York, 703
St Martin's School of Art, London, 69
Salamon, Julie, 741
Salisbury pub, St Martin's Lane, London, 206
'Salt of the Earth', 340
Saltcoats, 806
Salvation discothèque, Greenwich Village, 344
Sam and Dave, 279
sampling, xxx, 680, 730, 731, 732, 735
'San Francisco', 676
San Francisco Chronicle, 296
San Francisco *Examiner*, 791
San Francisco Gay Pride March, 645
San Francisco Oracle, 299
San Quentin, 382
San Ysidro, 722
Sandals, the, 738
Sanders, Ed, 269, 336–8
Sanderson, James, 605
Santana, 647
Santonio, 678, 680
Sargent, (Sir) Malcolm, 13
Sargent, Stefanie, 790–91
Sartre, Jean-Paul, 241
satanic murders, 594
Satanism, 763–4
'Satisfaction', 341, 361
'Saturday Night', xxx
Saturday Night Fever (film), 378, 514–15, 524, 525
'Saturday Night's Alright (for Fighting)', 657
Saunderson, Kevin, 678, 679
Savage, Jon, 799
Savannah, 543
Savio, Mario, 290
'Savior Machine', 393
Savoy Hotel, London, 13
'Say It Loud (I'm Black and I'm Proud)', 241
'Say Kids What Time Is It?', 737
Sayle, Alexei, 561
Scallydelia (Scallies), 711–15
Scandal (film), 737
Scene, The, New York, 242, 243, 245

Scene club, Ham Yard, London, 207, 208
Schifrin, Lalo, 642
Schneider, Florian, 483–7
Schoenberg, Arnold, 345
Schon, Neil, 647
'School Days', 743
Scorpions, the, 724–5, 761
Scorsese, Martin, 515
Scott, Freddie, 224
Scott-Heron, Gil, 549, 550
Scotty, Mike, 363
scratch technique, emergence of, 569
Scritti Politti, 596
Seal, 800
Seale, Bobby, 608
Seamen, Dick, 171
Search, 761, 763
'Search and Destroy', 404
Seattle, 786–93
Seattle Sound, 728, 734
Seattle Times, 786
Sebastian, John, 368
Secombe, Harry, 140, 141
'Secret Life of Arabia, The', 509
Sedaka, Neil, 383
Sedgwick, Edith (Edie), 178, 241–5
Selby, Hubert, Jr, 528, 699
Selectadisc record shop, Nottingham, 447
Sell My Soul, 649
Sellars, Peter, xxiii
Sellers, Peter, 114, 140, 183, 184
'Send Me Some Lovin'', 57
Senghor, Léopold, 241
Sepia magazine, xxix
Sepultura, 761
Sequence, 543, 544
Servant, The (film), 204
'Sesame's Treat', 733
7 Year Bitch, 790, 791
'Seventeen', 730
Severed Head, A (film), 187
Severed Heads, 679
sex, xxxii, 6, 71, 196, 213, 267, 269, 314,
   319, 331, 366, 378, 549; Adam Ant
   and, 541; apocalyptic, 327; Bobby
   Deaners and, 156; casual, xix; as a
   commodity, 424; gay, 574, 768, 769;
   parties, Presley epitomizes, 43;
   promiscuous, 209; relaxation of
   attitudes, 114–15; teenage sex life, 90;

and violence, xxvii
Sex (King's Road, Chelsea; shop later
   Seditionaries), 493, 494, 497, 510, 550
Sex, Eddie (Eddie Thunder; real name
   Eddie Bennett), 122–3
Sex and Violence in Modern Media'
   (Educational Institute of Scotland),
   xxvi
'Sex Bomb', 729
Sex Pistols, 377, 466, 469–70, 489–96,
   498–503, 509, 515, 516, 519, 539,
   541, 550, 557, 595, 603, 730, 743,
   744
'Sexie Sadie', 338
sexism, 365–8, 424, 523, 525, 741
'sexual revolution', 267
sexuality issue, xxiv, xxvi, 319, 320, 410,
   424–5, 523, 536, 647, 648, 732, 780
Sgt Pepper, xix
Shacklock, Alan, 546
Shadow Dancing in the USA (Ventura),
   607–14
'Shadow of Your Smile', 405
Shadows, the, 179, 187, 191
Shaft, 564
Shake 'n' Fingerpop, 709, 710, 737
'Shakermaker', xxx
'Shame, Shame, Shame', 168
Shamen, the, 800
Shamsuddin, 764
Shang-A-Lang, 425
Shangri-Las, the, 240
'Shapes of Things', xxviii
Shapiro, Helen, 126
Shapland, Dave, 656, 662
'Share This House', 679
Sharkey, Feargal, 606
Shaw, Sandie, 233, 597
'She's All Right', 321
Shea Stadium, New York, 284
Shearer, Hugh, 480
Sheeley, Sharon, 143
Shelley, Mayor, 302
Shelley, Pete, xxix, 548, 679
Shelton, Ann, 12
Shelton, Robert, 179, 260
Sherman, Bill (clothes), 500
Shirelles, the, 169
Shirl the Pearl, 543
Shocklee, Hank, xxx

Shoe, The (written by Gordon Legge), 593–4, 601–7
Sholes, Steve, 47–50
'Shoot the Pump', 550
Shooting Party, 717
'Shout-bama-lama', 321
Show Mirror magazine, 193
Shrimpton, Chrissie, 233
Shrimpton, Jean, 233
Shuman, Mort, 599
Shy F. X., xxx
Signed, Sealed and Delivered (Garratt), 423–5
Sillitoe, Alan, 138
Silva, John, 721
Simenon, Paul, 499, 500, 502, 504
Simmons, Russell, xxx
Simms, Speedo, 221
Simon, Marc Paul, 648
Simone, Nina, 169
Simple Minds, 558
Simpson, Dr George, 200
Sinatra, Frank, xxiii, 2, 5, 10–12, 86, 190, 194, 249, 405, 423, 506
Sinatra, Nancy, 253
Sing Out!, 248–9
singers, 76
Sioux, Siouxsie, xxiii, 494–6, 561
Sir Coxsone Outernational, 421, 479
Sire Records, 571, 623
'Sister Ray', 509
Sit & Spin café, Seattle, 792
'sit-ins', 324
'16', 467, 640
Sixteen magazine, 154
6Ts, 536
'Sixties Style', 268
Ska, xxviii, 208, 420, 421, 422
'Skank in Bed', 127
skanking, 422, 606
Shelton, Robert, 258–62
Skerrit, Joseph, 474
Skid Row, 727, 740
skiffle, 67, 79, 85–6, 89, 138
Skinhead (Allen), 377
skinheads, 340, 377, 378–83, 418, 512, 537, 538, 568, 573, 622, 657
Skinny Puppys, the, 681
Skippy White's Mass. Records: Home of the Blues, Boston, 221–2, 223

Sky, Captain, 546
Slade, 382–3, 407
slang, xix, 7, 22, 188–9, 732
    see also language
Slash, 777
Slaughter (and the Dogs), 491
Slaves of New York, 614–18
Slayer, 760, 761
Slick, Grace, 264
Sloane Rangers, 709
Sly and the Family Stone, 750, 751
smack, 372
    see also heroin
Small Faces, 489, 496
Smallwood, Simon, 626
Smast Hits, xxiii, 424, 535, 536, 541, 542, 570–72, 585–8, 593, 672, 716–19, 769, 770–75
'Smells Like Teen Spirit', 721–2, 723, 744–6, 749, 752
Smith, Gary, 787
Smith, Jimmy, 169
Smith, Joseph C., 105, 133–8
Smith, Junior, 47, 50
Smith, Liz, 231, 234
Smith, Patti, 242–3, 500
Smith, W. H. (bookstore), 597, 771
Smith, Warren, 550
Smiths, the, 590, 593, 595–601, 679, 690, 712, 767; and animal slaughter, 595, 599
Smiths, The, 595
smoking, deaths from, 811
SNCC (Student Non-violent Coordinating Committee), 284
Sniffin' Glue magazine, 497–8
Snow, Hank, 47
Snowdon, Antony Armstrong-Jones, 1st Earl of, 114
Snyder, Gary, 295
Snyder, Gene, 154, 156, 157
So Little Time (Sellars), xxiii
'So Young', 769
SOA, 721
soccer *see* football
Social Distortion, 623
Social Security, Department of, 505–6
socialism, and disco, 518, 521, 525, 526
'Sociology of Rock, The' (Frith), xxix
Soft Cell, 536, 573, 575, 675

Soho, London, 44, 68, 113, 114, 210,
211, 214, 379, 536, 561, 563, 737, 739
'Someone Like You', 650
Somers, Debroy (and the Orpheans), 13,
14
'Somethin' Else', 143
Something Beginning with O (Pearce),
669
'Something in the Way', 729
'Song of the Dreamer', xxvi
songs, 74
Songs for 'Drella, 699
songwriters, 73–4
Sonia, 717–18
Sonic Asylum Records, 763
Sonny and Cher, 233, 277
Sony, 729, 741
Sorts (Allen), 377
Soul, xxviii, 105, 178, 208, 209, 212,
219–25, 269, 323, 324, 326, 335, 419,
420, 422, 496, 518, 522, 536, 550,
551, 561, 568, 612, 647, 649, 679,
680, 776, 777, 779
Soul Asylum, 723
Soul Furnace, 562, 563
'Soul Limbo', 604
Soul Music Magazine, 324–7
'Soul Over Nottingham' (radio
programme), 445
Soul Sonic Force, 546
Soul to Soul, 709, 712
Soul Train, 607
'Sound, The', 679
Sound Affects (written by Simon Frith),
375
sound effects, 240
Sound of Philadelphia, the, 779
'Sound of the Beast', xxx
sound-mixing, 48
sound systems, 421, 450, 805
Sounds magazine, 424, 493–7, 498,
508–9
sourcing, xxx
Soutar, Mike, 672, 716–19
South Africa 326; The Beatles and, 281
Sox, Dr Ellis, 296
Space, 509
'Space Oddity', 393, 394
Spaghetti Westerns (Frayling), 546
Spain, The Beatles and, 281

Spandau Ballet, 532, 540, 541, 556, 557,
606
Spaniard in the Works, A (Lennon), 278
Spartacus magazine, 210
Spear, Roger Ruskin, 168
Spector, Phil, 105, 209
'speed', 165, 166, 167, 208, 209, 213,
214, 475, 567, 730, 731, 733, 736, 813
'speed' (tape), 482–3
'Speedy Gonzales', 168
Spencer, Neil, 469, 489–90
Spillane, Micky, 204
Spin magazine, 618–27, 797–806
Spinal Tap, 761
Spiral Tribe, 805
'Spirit in the Sky', 419
spliffs, 311, 312, 421, 472
Spoon, 729
Springfield, Dusty, 209, 478, 568
Springsteen, Bruce, 489, 563, 593,
614–18, 657, 682, 742, 782
Spungeon Nancy, 470, 527–30
Squall newsletter, 799
SQUASH (Squatters Action For Secure
Homes), 799
squatters, 798–803, 805–6
Stacey, Barrie, 206–7
'Stalking the Billion-Footed Beast – a
Literary Manifesto for the New Social
Novel' (Wolfe), xvii
Stamford, John, 210
Stamp, Terence, 597
Standells, the, 469
'Standing in the Shadows of Love', 208
Staples, Cleo, 159
Staples, Mavis, 159
Staples, Pervis, 159
Staples, Pops, 159
Staples, Yvonne, 159
Staples Singers, 159
'Star-Spangled Banner', 740
Star Trek, 251
Stark, Annette, 593, 618–27
Starlust: The Secret Fantasies of Fans
(Vermorel), 456–64
Starmakers and Svengalis (Rogan), xxiv
Starr, Ringo, 184, 186, 187, 188, 193,
194, 196, 198, 216, 254, 322
Starwood club, West Hollywood, 620
Staunton, Debby, 799–800

Stax label, 159, 219, 604
Stax-Volt Memphis sound, 744
Stax/Volt recording company, 320
Steele, Tommy, xxii, 44, 63–7, 79, 84–9,
    129, 215
Steelemen, 65
Stein, Jean, 178, 241–5, 267
Stein, Seymour, 623
Steinem, Gloria, 243
Step II, 649
Stephen, Sylvia, 66
stereo systems, 5
Stereolab, 800
Steve Allen Show, The (television
    programme), 57
Stevens, Cat (Yusef Islam), 692–3
Stevens, Joe, 517
Stevo, 562
Stewart, Dave, 675, 800
Stewart, Jim, 219
Stewart, Rod, 377, 380, 411, 412, 655,
    673
Stock, Mike, 672, 716–19
Stock Aitken and Waterman, 672,
    716–19
Stock Aitken Waterman – A Ton of Hits,
    716–17
Stockhausen, Karl-Heinz, 485
Stolen Glances, 769
Stoller, Mike, 673
Stone, Sly, 367, 736, 750, 751, 778
Stone, Roses, the, 711, 713, 714, 715
Stonehenge, 803
Stonewall, 647, 653
Stooges, the, 285, 378, 403, 404, 405,
    486, 489, 496, 502
'Stop in the Name of Love', 208
'Stop the World', 393
Stork Club, 65
Storm, Danny, 123
Stow Hill, Lord, 268
Straight Theater, San Francisco, 293
Strange, Steve, 537, 549, 562
Stranglers, the, 507
Strathclyde, 807, 809, 811, 812
'Strawberry Fields Forever', 288, 289
'Stray Cat', 351, 352
'Street Fighting Man', 362
Street Life (Walters), 433–56
Stringfellow, Ken, 788, 789

'Strings', 679
Stroad, Rev. Jimmy, 278, 280
Stroll, the (dance), 152
Strummer, Joe, 499–505, 595, 800
Student Nonviolent Coordinating
    Committee (SNCC), 284
students, and protest, 138
Students for a Democratic Society, 283
Sub Pop Records, 722, 727–30, 786, 788,
    790, 792
Subcultures (Hebdige), 470
'Substitute', xxviii, 489
Suck, Jane, 470, 508–9
Suede, 672, 767–70
Suede, 769
Suedehead (Allen), 377
'Suffer Little Children', 597
'Sugar Shack', 167
Sugarhill Gang, 544
Sugarhill Records, 542
Suicidal Tendencies, 620–23, 638, 761
Suicidals (fans), 621, 622
Sullivan, Ed, 278
Sum Total (Gosling), 105, 127–32
Sumac, Yma, 405
Summer, Donna, 524, 644, 648, 649, 767
Summer Holiday (film), 186
Summer Shower of Stars, Boston, 219,
    222
Sun, the, 536, 559–60, 594, 628, 631,
    632, 634, 653–66, 692, 737
Sun Ra, 334
Sun studios, 780
Sunrise club, London, 737, 738
Sunday Pictorial, 30–32
Sunday Telegraph, 799
Sunday Times, 193; magazine, 627–35
Sundown club, Charing Cross Road,
    London, 419
Sunset Boulevard (film), 206
'Super Sperm', 546
'Supernatural Thing', 432
Superpop, 105, 127
Superstar, Ingrid, xxiii
Supremes, the, 105, 152, 159–64, 208,
    647, 681, 741
Surrealist Pillow, 369–70
Susskind, David, 243
Sutch, Screaming Lord, 141
Sutcliffe, Stuart, 142

Swami, 763
'Swastika Girls', 509
Sweeney, John, 594, 653–66
Sweet, the, 407, 532, 675
'Sweet Nothin's', 126
Sweet Soul Music (Guralnick), 219–25
Swindells, Steve, 563–4
swing, 5, 522
Swinging London *see under* London
'Swinging on a Star', 186
Sylvester, 594, 644–53
Sylvester, 649
'Sympathy for the Devil', 348
'Syncopate', 422
synth–pop, 536
synthesizers, 483, 484, 486, 596, 734

T. Rex, 380, 382, 407, 541
T-shirts, 234, 235, 493, 507, 529, 542, 573, 714, 715
Taboo Club, Circus Maximus, London, 629, 736
Taboo Club, Detroit, 681
Tad, 728, 730
'Tainted Love', 675
Take 6 clothes, 211
Take That, 672, 770–75
'Take That And Party', 772
talent-spotters, 86
Talking Heads, 506–8
TAMI Show, The, 224, 741
Tamla Motown, xxviii, 105, 164, 178, 208, 209, 212, 222, 380, 418, 444, 451, 477, 518, 640, 641, 680, 681, 709, 744, 773, 776, 779, 780
Tams, the, 219
Tangerine Dream, 483, 485
tango, the, 522
tape-recorders, 5; single-track, 48
Tarantula (Dylan), 259
target marketing, xxviii-xxix
Tate, Greg, 593, 639–43, 782, 783
tattoos, 288, 317, 455, 511, 541
Tauber, Richard, 29, 30
Taylor, Andy, 551, 552
Taylor, Eddie, 448
Taylor, Elizabeth, 206, 777
Taylor, John, 551, 554, 555, 556–7
Taylor, Johnnie, 680
Taylor, Mick, 358, 360, 406

Taylor, Roger, 551
Taylor, Vince, 123
Techno, xxx, 535, 671, 674, 677–81, 738, 807, 810; hardcore, 622, 709, 730–36, 809
'Techno City', 677
'TechnoPop', 669
Teddy Boys *see* Edwardians
teenage revolution, 246–8
Teenage Wasteland (Gaines), 594, 635–9
teenagers 248–53; buying power, 82–3, 87–8, 89; as classless, 83, 88; cleanliness, 90; deserted by marketers and manufacturers, 593; and the Establishment, 88–9; first products for, xxiii, 87; as internationally-minded, 89; maturity of, 89; music for a teenage audience, xxii; as not Americanized, 85, 89; sex life, 90; violence by, 594; and yuppies, xxx
Teenset, 264
'teenybop' music, 424, 536, 553
Teenybopper Idol (Allen), 377, 396–403
teenyboppers, 382, 383
'Tell Me a Bedtime Story', 523
'Tell Me Darling', 421
Temazepam, 810, 812, 813
Temgesic, 812
Temperance Seven, 140
Temptations, the, 208, 386, 523, 544, 612, 773, 778
Tennant, Neil, 536, 585–8, 690–93
Tennant family, 563
Tennyson, Alfred Lord, 328
Terkel, Studs, 178, 248–9
'Terry', 240
Terry, Helen, 588
Terry, Sonny, 169
Test Dept, 638
Teves, Joan, 153, 157
Tex, Joe, 219, 220, 221, 223
Thames TV, 498–9, 660
Thank God It's Friday, 526
'Thank You for Talkin' to Me Africa', 750
Thank Your Lucky Stars (television programme), 174, 204
'That Old Devil Moon', 186
'That's How Strong My Love Is', 221
That's Life (television programme), 601

'That's Love', 119
'That's the Joint', 543
Thatcher, Margaret (Baroness), 536, 574, 593, 600, 712, 779, 803
theatre, the, 288
Them, 492
'There Was a Time', 241
'These Arms of Mine', 221, 321
Thibeau, Tim, 293, 294
'Third Finger, Left Hand', 208
'This Old Heart of Mine (Been Broken a Thousand Times)', 208
This Week (television programme), 62, 660, 661
Thistle Café, West Kirby, near Liverpool, 181
Thomas, Carla, 278–9
Thomas, John Ormond, 14–15
Thomas, Rudi, 564
Thomas, Rufus, 220
Thompson, Carroll, 564
Thompson, Hunter S., 267, 269, 369–72
Thompson Twins, 540
Thorp, Raymond, 7, 21–3
thrashers, 763
'3 AM Eternal', 733
Three Crowns pub, Bushey, Herts, 575
Three Degrees, the, 419
Three Dog Night, 369
'Three Steps to Heaven', 126
Thriller, 593, 641, 642, 643, 781, 782, 784, 785
Thunders, Johnny, 502, 528
Tibet Society, 394
Tiffany, 675, 676
Time magazine, xxvi, 157, 193, 282, 284, 787
Time Out magazine, 595–601
Time Warner, 757–8, 760
Timelords, the, 671, 673–7
Times, The, 268, 307–9, 381, 475
Times of Little Richard, The (White), 51–7
Tipper Gore, 760
toasting, 422, 564
Today (television programme), 498–9
Today There are No Gentlemen, 113–15
Tofu Love Frogs, 801
Tommy (film), 449
Tommy Boy Records, 546

Tonight Show (Johnny Carson television show), 611, 614
Too Hot to Sleep, 649
Too Pure label, 802
Tooke, Steve, 342
Toop, David, 535, 544–7
Top Fifty, 692
Top Gear, King's Road, London, 234
Top Gun (film), 691
Top of the Pops (television programme), xxv, xxvi, xxxii, 254, 383, 419, 540, 548, 555, 559, 560, 571, 579, 582, 597
Top Pop Stars, xxvi
Top 75, 717
Top Ten, 423, 483, 692
Top Three, 717
Top Twenty, 82, 83, 84, 86, 87, 126, 140, 185, 692
Tosches, Nick, 43, 57–60
Touch Me In the Morning, 524
Touchdown, 732
Toussaint, Allen, 478
Tovar, Gary, 627
Town and Country Club, London, 710
Townshend, Pete, xxvi–xxvii, 106, 168–71, 239–40, 319, 403
'Track of the Cat', 432
trad jazz, 7, 15–17, 106, 138, 140–41
trade papers, 77
'Trains and Boats and Planes', 240
'Trans Europe Express', 535, 545, 546
tranquillisers, 812
transcendental meditation, 317
Transmat label, 679
travellers, New Age, 798, 799, 800, 803–5
Travolta, John, 796
'Treat Her Like A Lady', 773
Treves, Joan, 153
Trevira suits, 382
Trial, The (film), 186, 187
'tribalism', 295
Tribe 8, 770
'Trip to Trumpton, A', 733
Triple X, 678
Trips Festival, 269–73
Triumph, 780
Trojan, 629
'Trophy', 742
Trotter, Patrick, 480

True Adventures of the Rolling Stones, The (Booth), 347–65
True Confessions magazine, xxvii
True Detective magazine, 528
Trump, Donald, 797
Tube, The (television programme), 569, 570, 571
Tucker, Bruce, 35–8
Tucker, Maureen, 367, 707
Tuffin and Foale, 234
Tuinol, 386, 527
'Turkey Trot', 74
Turner, Ike, 418, 778
Turner, Joe, 169
Turner, Tina, 347, 418, 778
'Turtle Blues', 368
Turtles, the, 346
12 by 12: Sylvester's Greatest Mixes, 651
Twentieth Century, The (MacInnes), 81–91
Twiggy (Lesley Hornby), 233–4
Twink, 342
Twinkle, 240
twist, the, 204, 280
Twisted Sister, 635
Twitty, Conway, 125, 127
2 Bad Mice, 734
2 I's coffee bar, 65
Two Tons o' Fun, 645, 649, 650
'Two Tribes', 573
Tyson, Mike, 785

UK Press Gazette, 660
'Unchained Melody', 604
'Under My Thumb', 353, 358
Undertones, the, 606
Underwood, Ruth, 367
Unforgiven (film), 757
Union Tavern, Old Kent Road, London, 120
United Sound Studios, 680
Universal Amphitheater, Los Angeles County, 693
University of California, 299, 417
University of Georgia, 321
Unreasonable Behaviour: An Autobiography (McCullin), 23–5
'Up Town Top Ranking', 508
'uppers', 208

Upsetters, the, 52
US Bonds, 127
Use Your Illusion I and II, 749
Uses of Literacy, The (Hoggart), 70–72

'V2 Sneider', 509
Vacuum (film), 242
Valbonne, La, club, London, 419
Valente, Dino, 331–2
Valentine magazine, 193
Valentine, Dickie, xxii, 5, 26–7, 28, 30, 76
Valentino, Rudolph, 10, 60, 84
Valium, 515, 614, 627, 633
Van Cleef, Lee, 429
Van Eaton, James, 57, 59
Van Halen, Eddie, 781
Vandellas, the, 162, 208
Vanden Heuvel, Wendy, 244
Vandros, Sacha, 698
Vaselines, the, 723
Vatican, the, and the Beatles, 281
vaudeville, 74, 222
Vaughan, Frankie, 5, 26, 27–8
Vaughan, Sarah, 86
Vee, Bobby, 126
Velvet Revolution (Czech), 702
Velvet Underground, 275, 276, 277, 367, 392–3, 481, 486, 496, 509, 672, 700, 701, 702, 707
Ventura, Michael, 593, 607–14
Vermorel, Fred, 378, 456–64
Vermorel, Judy, 378, 456–64
Vibrators, the, 507
Vicious, Sid (John Paul Ritchie), 470, 493, 495, 517, 527–30, 800
Victoria, Queen, 288, 479
Vidal, Gore, 646
video games, 544–5
videos, 569, 570, 572, 573, 584, 586, 593, 642, 739–40, 744–6, 768, 780–81, 784, 796
'Vie en Rose, La', 524
Vietnam War, xxviii, 267, 268, 282–4, 318, 330, 333, 404, 748, 749
Vig, Butch, 729
Village People, 523, 648, 767
Village Voice, The, 250–53, 542–4, 572–4, 639–53, 672, 693–6, 767–70, 786–95

Vince Man's Shop, Carnaby Street, London (Bill Green), 79, 113–15, 208
Vincent, Gene, 125, 126, 143, 492
Vinson, Cleanhead, 37
'Vintage Violence', 509
Vinyl (film), 242, 274
Viper (Thorp), 21–3
Virgin Records, 627, 628, 630, 633, 680, 800
'Virginia Plain', xxix
Virilio, Paul, 730, 732, 733
Visage club, Detroit, 678
Visionquest (film), 572
Viva Zapata, 791
Viz comic, 714
Vogue magazine, 242
Voodoo Queens, 802
Vox Pop, 178
Vulgar Boatmen, the, 742

Waddle, the (dance), 152
Wade, Judy, 536, 559–60
Wah Ching, 414–16
'Wait for the Wagon', 74
'Wake Up Everybody', 432
Wakeman, Rick, 482, 486
Waking Up the House on Fire, 628
Walden, Alan, 221
Walker, Junior, 240
Walker, T–Bone, 32
Wallace, George, 334
Waller, Fats, 196
Wallis, David, 106
Wallis, Neil, 656, 657, 661, 662
Walsh, Steve, 564
Walters, Barry, 594, 644–53, 672
Walters, Idris, 378, 443–56
Walters, John, 596
'Wanna Be Startin' Somethin'', 642
Ward, Don, 562, 563
Ward, Stephen, 309, 475
Warehime, Linda, 154, 157
warehouse parties, 536, 550, 709–10, 737
Warhol, Andy, xxiii, 105, 106, 164–8, 178, 242–5, 267, 274–7, 482, 514–16, 566, 569, 699, 736
Warner Brothers, 60, 61, 144, 623, 624, 648, 650, 651, 756–60
Warnick, Kim, 786, 788, 789

Waronker, Lenny, 757
Was, Don, 585
Wash, Martha, 649
Wastell, David, 799
Waterhouse, Keith, 105, 106–12
Waterman, Pete, 672, 673, 716–19
Waters, John, 105, 152–9
Waters, Muddy, 169, 226, 227
Watership Down (film), 477
Watford Football Club, 657, 666
Watkins, Lovelace, 477
Watters, Barry, 767–70
Watts, Charlie, 218, 219, 227, 229, 349, 351, 358, 360
Watts, Michael, 377, 391–6
'We Are the World', 782
We Can't Be Stopped, 750
WEA record company, 696
Weather Girls, 650
Weatherall, Andy, 713
Weber, Adele, 243
Wedge, James, 234
Weedon, Bert, 228
'Weekend', 143
Welfare State, 87, 88, 506
Welk, Lawrence, 744
Weller, Paul, 595, 692
Weller, Sheila, 267, 343–7
Wells, Junior, 240–41
Wells, Mary, 162, 208
Wembley Stadium, London, 696
Wenner, Jann, 267
Wertheimer, Alfred, 43, 47–50
Wesker, Arnold, 478
West Coast Beats, 138
West End Records, 546
West Indians, 469, 471–81; as dancers, 418, 420–22; and skinheads, 379, 380
West Midlands Soul Club, 443, 446, 449, 450
Westbury Hotel, Mayfair, London, 91, 92
Westinghouse, 153
Westwood, Vivien, 497
Wet Wet Wet, 675
Weybridge, Surrey, 254, 258
Weymouth, Tina, 507, 508
Wham!, xxix, 536, 540, 541, 574–85, 593, 598
'Wham' cartoons, 141
'Wham! Rap', 575

Whannel, Paddy, xxvi
'What a Difference a Day Made', 432, 524
'What Becomes of the Broken Hearted?', 208
'What'll I Do?', 13
'When I'm Sixty Four', xix
'When the Midnight Choo–choo Leaves for Alabama', 74
'When Will I Be Famous?', 770
'When You're Young and in Love', 208
'Where Have All the Flowers Gone?', 369
'Wherever I Lay My Hat', 675
Whigfield, xxx
'Whip, The', 422
Whiskey, Nancy, 86
Whiskey Club, Los Angeles, 620
'Whispering Grass', 15
'Whistling in the Dark', 536
White, Charles, 51–7
White, Slappy, 222
White, Timothy, 746, 748
White Album, The (Didion), 327–9
white labels, 451, 710
White Light/White Heat, 702
'white' music, 209
'White Rabbit', 370–71
'White Riot', 501–2
Whitehouse, Mary, 503
Whiteman, Paul, 12, 75
Whitfield, David, xxii, 5, 26, 29–30, 76
Who, the, xxiv, xxviii, 178, 239–40, 268, 303–7, 319, 382, 383, 492, 496
Who: Maximum Rhythm & Blues, The (Barnes), 168–71
Who's Afraid of Virginia Woolf (Albee), 206
'Who's Makin' Love', 680
Whodini, 694
'Whole Lotta Love', 367
'Why Can't I Wake Up With You', 772
'Why Do You Do Me Like You Do', 38
Wiener, John, 268, 278–84
Wigan, 446, 453
WILD (Boston all–black radio station), 219, 221, 224
Wild One, The (film), xxv
'Wild World', 692, 693
Wilde, Marty, xxii, 118, 126, 190
Wilde, Oscar, xxiii, 595

Wildman Steve, 222
'Will You Be There', 775, 784
Willes, Peter, 287
Williams, Eric, 480
Williams, Maurice, 126
Williams, Otis, 37
Williams, Paul, 778
Williams, Raymond, xxv, 196
Williams, Robbie, 771–5
Williams, Tennessee, 139
Williamson, James, 404
Willie D, 750
Willoughby, Lord, 215
Wilson, Delroy, 480
Wilson, Edmund, xvii
Wilson, (Sir) Harold, 196, 471
Wilson, Jackie, 223, 776
Wilson, Mary, 105, 159–64
Winfrey, Oprah, 782, 783
Wings, 763
Winter, Daniel, 62–3
Winters, Jonathon, 169
Wips night club, Soho, London, 215
Wire, 593
Wire, The, 669, 730–39, 761–6
'With a Little Help', 675
'Without You', 673
WLAC, Nashville, 321
Wolfe, Tom, xvii–xviii, 267, 269–73, 378, 412–18
'Woman', 385
women/girls: decline of female singer, 86–7; as musicians, 367, 377; as outsiders, xxxiii; sexual power of, 5; as writers, 377; young women's purchasing power, xxiii–xxiv, 5
Wonder, Stevie, 163, 346, 523, 691, 776
Wong, Kean, 672, 761–6
Wood, Andrew, 790–91
Wood, Ronnie, 168, 411
Woodstock, 496, 506
Woodstock/Bethel Festival, 344
'Woodstock Nation' festival fantasy, 269
Woolrich, Cornell, 597
Woolwich, Bishop of, 196, 268
'Wooly Bully', 492
'W.O.R.K.', 803
'Working Man Blues', 15
World club, New York, 678

World in Action (television programme), 268
World is a Wedding, The (Kops), 67–9
Worman, Martin, 646–7
Wright, Tom, 168–9
'Writing American Fiction' (Roth), xvii
Wyatt, Robert, 551
Wyman, Bill, 216, 219, 227, 229, 348, 360
Wynne, Peter, 116, 122
Wynter, Mark, 122, 187

Xenophobia, 731, 735

Yale University, 412–13, 417, 702
Yanovsky, Zal, 253
Yardbirds, the, xxviii, 492, 582–3
Yazz, 675, 676
Yellow Magic Orchestra (YMO), 545
'Yellow Submarine', 322
'Yesterday', 262
Yesterday ... and Today, 282
Yippies, 269, 330–35, 340
'You Can't Always Get What You Want', 612
'You Don't Have to Say You Love Me', 209
You Don't Have to Say You Love Me (Napier-Bell), xxiii, 302–7, 582–3
'You Make Me Feel Mighty Real', 594, 645, 649
'You Sexy Thing', 434
'You Should Be Dancing', 524
'You'll Always Be Mine', 186
'You're Too Old', 493

'You've Got Me Waiting for the Rain to Fall', 390
'You've Got to Get Out and Get Under', 74
'You've Lost That Lovin' Feeling', 209, 691
'You've Really Got a Hold on Me', 208
Young, Neil, 744, 794
Young, Paul, 675
Young Fresh Fellows, 788
'Young Guns (Go for It)', 579
Young Ones, The (television programme), 569
Youth, 717
youth, xxiii–xxiv, xxxiii; appearance criticized, 197; buying power, 82; and drugs, 268; and the Establishment, 197, 240; market, 177; as a national obsession, 177; shift away from youth consumption, xxx; and teen 'revolution', 178–9
youth clubs, 71, 202, 203
Youth International Party, 332
Youthquakers, 242

Zapata, Mia, 790–91
Zappa, Frank, 340, 341, 496
Ze Records, 553
ZG magazine, 527–30, 535, 537–9
Zig-Zag magazine, 169
Zola, Émile, xvii
zoot-suiters, 7, 8, 9
ZTT label, 573, 574, 580–81
Zulema, 385–6, 389
ZZ Top, 743